Goldmine

PRICE GUIDE

to

· COLLECTIBLE ·

· RECORD ·

ALBUMS

FIFTH EDITION

Neal Umphred

Published by

**krause
publications**

700 E. State Street • Iola, WI 54990-0001
Telephone: 715/445-2214

Please call or write for our free catalog of music publications.
Our toll-free number to place an order or obtain a free catalog is 800-258-0929
or please use our regular business telephone 715-445-2214
for editorial comment and further information.

Library of Congress Catalog Number: 89-83584
ISBN: 0-87341-374-1
Printed in the United States of America

TABLE OF CONTENTS

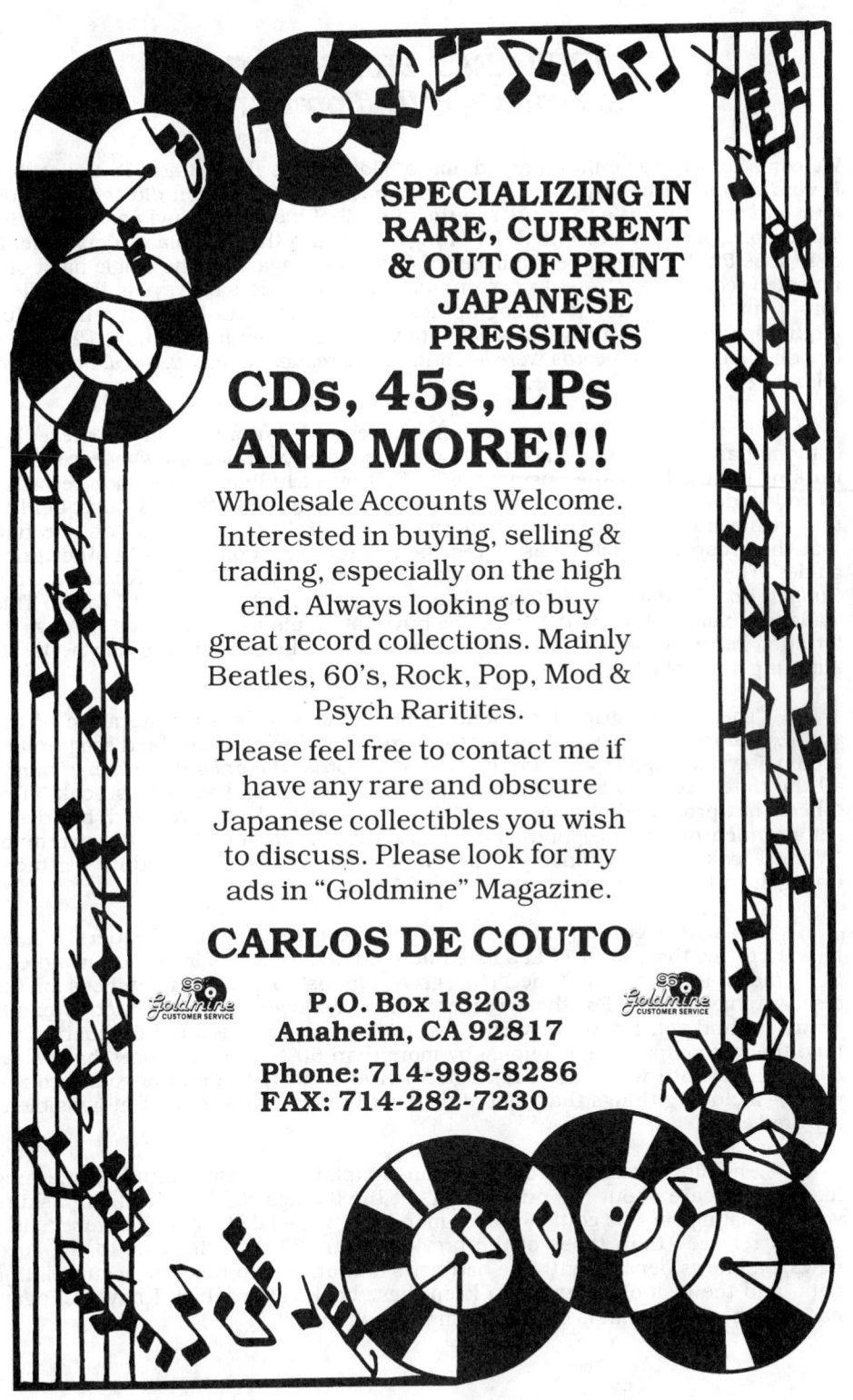

HEY! READ THIS FIRST!
A Frankly Fifth Foreword

Welcome to another enkindling edition of *Goldmine's Price Guide To Collectible Record Albums*. I hope you enjoy this fifth one as much as you did the previous four *and* that it helps each reader in the pursuit of his or her vinyl passions. With salutations properly presented, I'll plunge right into the "complaint department" of Krause Publications, the publisher of *Goldmine* magazine. The single most oft-repeated request in letters, in person, and in their readers surveys is that collectors want more complete discographies in this book. As the minimum value required to make these pages escalated (it was $10 in the third edition, $25 in the fourth), many, many records were left out. . . *But readers want the $4 albums listed with the $40 and $400 albums.*

The fact that "lesser" collectibles have not been present in the preceding editions has led to some unfortunate occurrences: Even dealers who have a fine working knowledge of the business gripe that by excluding the common records I leave the determination of those values in the hands of others. Consequently, they relate horror stories of their attempts to purchase collections only to find that the prospective seller has priced the records based on values in other price guides. There, used record store staples like *Voulez-Vous, Thriller, Rumours, Low Budget, Double Vision,* and *Moody Blue,* are often valued in the $8-12 range. This leads to consternation as the would-be buyer attempts to explain that he pays $1 for such records to be able to sell them for $4 without sounding like he is attempting a rip-off!

The biggest gripe I *personally* hear, more or less a reiteration of the above, is along the lines of "I only collect rock'n roll albums so the discographies are terribly incomplete and the not-so-rare records, the ones that change hands all the time, aren't to be found here so I [shudder] gotta use Jerry's book!" Two others that prompted changes were "There ain't enough pictures and, besides, I get as much out of the photo captions as I do the listings!" and the perennial "When I look up a reference you list under one artist there's nothin' pertinent under the artist to whom I was referenced!"

This fifth edition addresses each of these problems. Readers will be pleased to see thousands of LPs listed here, many not seen since the second edition, many for the first time. This greatly adds to the completeness of the discographies within. For those readers who actually enjoy my strained attempts at insight and wit, I have increased the number of pages devoted to illustrations (and their accompanying captions) by more than 50%. The references *have been checked out* both ways and back again twice! But, by the end of each project, gaffes— including things that should be there but are not— are all but invisible to my tired eyes.

The single most oft-repeated non-complaint I receive sounds something like "I don't care about the prices; just get the listings right." And, I can assure you, the listings in this edition are far more accurate— label, catalog number, title, year of release— than those of the previous four. Which brings us to the good news/bad news department: The bad news is that, due to the ever-accumulating data, and the lack of pages (gotta keep these books affordable), I have yet again had to jettison thousands of titles from this edition!

That's right, thousands of LPs that were in the last edition are missing from this one (good reason to hang onto your fourth edition). The good news, if you're a collector of rhythm'n blues, rock'n roll, or soul, is that the deleted listings have been replaced with even more listings from those fields! (For more on where the deleted data has gone, refer to *Umphred On-Line* in this foreward.)

Now, let's take a look at the records that are here: The values in this book attempt to document what records are worth on the current collectors market. What that means to you, the average reader, is that *these prices reflect more or less what you should expect to pay an established dealer to acquire a record that you desire*. Should you, a collector, choose to sell your records, *the chances are good that you will not see these prices being paid for your records*. Which brings us, willy-nilly, to:

Umphred's Three-Tiered System For Pricing Records; or, How To Avoid Abuse With The Use Of This Book

For the learn-by-experience-impaired, here is the way that I recommend my book be used: Think of the buying and selling of collectible records as pyramidical with [at least] three definable levels. Those dealers with the best reputations and the most smarts tend to be at the apex, the smallest part of the pyramid. While they make up only a small portion of the field, they are the ones on the leading edge. Like it or not, they set the tone for the rest of the field. Almost without exception, these are dealers that ply their trade through the mail, offering their wares to the broadest possible number of potential buyers. *So, unless you are among the elite, breathing the rarified air at the top, you should not expect to see these prices paid to you on a regular basis.*

The next level down in the rare record hierarchy are the smaller [usually part-time] mail-order sellers and those shop-owners, generally in good-sized urban areas, that specialize to some degree in collectibles. That is, they are not just "used-record stores" but attempt to cater to a collector-oriented clientele with at least a modicum of expertise. Store owners tend to have a much larger overhead than mail-order dealers but have a dramatically reduced customer base and are limited to selling to local collectors. These sellers make up a greater portion of the market than those at the top but are not usually among those leading the way. For the most part, I would suggest that such dealers seek 60% to 90% of the listed values.

The lowest organized level on the pyramid, and the one that applies to the greatest number of wheeler-dealers, is the "record convention." Sellers at such events have ridiculously lower expenses than either of the two top tiers yet often take great umbrage at buyers balking at the asking of big bucks for their records. While it really *shouldn't* make a difference to the would-be buyer where, or from whom, he makes his purchase, it nonetheless does. And this applies to *every* show I have ever attended or heard about.

So, with the hope of easing the transfer of merchandise and the flow of cash, those of you selling at shows who take your role as a dealer of rare records somewhat seriously, consider asking approximately 50% to 75% of the values in this book. Of course, in most instances this suggestion is unnecessary, as it would appear that the majority of record conventions in this country either are or are fast becoming, bargain-basements for dealers and collectors alike. *This is the opposite of what should be occurring:* Based on the most simple maxims of

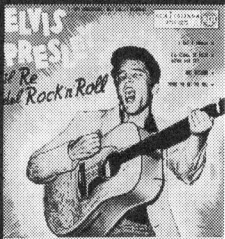

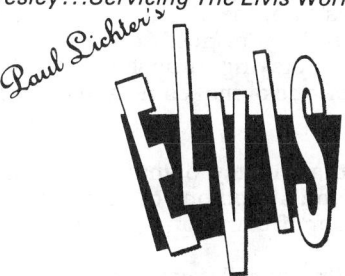
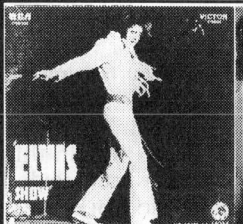
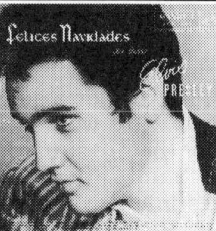

supply & demand, as the supply of truly collectible records dwindles (which they are) and the demand remains somewhat constant (which it is), the prices should be going up (which they ain't). Instead, an inexplicable fire-sale mentality permeates seller after seller, show after show.

While this draws no complaints from the buyers, it all too often leads to the show being reduced to a junk strewn flea market. The amount of virtually unsalable product that the sellers bring to these shows only lowers the expectations of both the buyers and the sellers. As much fun as it is to search the tables and make a great find (i.e., a good record in collectible condition for a pittance), it is often a fruitless, and time consuming, search through endless copies of VG-second pressings overpriced at a buck

This leads indirectly to the fact that clean rock' roll and rhythm'n blues LPs from the '50s have vanished, an observation that has escaped few dealers or collectors. That quality albums from the '60s are also rapidly drying up is, finally, becoming a matter of concern. Buyers need to know that replenishing stock is imperative for dealers intent on staying in business. Selling Near Mint '60s rock or soul albums for a couple of bucks makes no sense (unless, of course, they're Herman's Hermits albums).

I will also mention that, in my opinion, general swap meets and flea markets do not count. When you attend one of these and the seller has *any* price guide, you're probably in for more frustration than the record you want is worth.

For those of you wanting to sell your records but not wanting to open up a store (expensive and requires a bit of a commitment), auction through the pages of *Goldmine* or *DISCoveries* (time consuming and rather more work intensive than a neophyte might guess), or set up at a show (the most practical method although not always possible and, for those not prepared, all too often a Herculean test of one's bonhomie), consider selling "wholesale" to a dealer. Remember that even the most honest and reputable of dealers are only going to pay a fraction of the record's value. (According to *Webster's II*, a fraction is "a small part.") So go back and scan the three tiers above and keep in mind that the fraction involved in the transaction is based on what *the dealer* believes he can get for the item, not what you believe that it is worth! For more information and advice, refer to Perry Cox's "Selling Your Albums," in the appendices of this book.

As for actually referring to this book for values: For most used records, the reader, whether established dealer or novice collector, should start with the first, lower price and work his way up to a reasonable estimate. *Most used records are not Near Mint and the reader is advised not to delude himself that the high price applies to each and every record he has in hand.*

With the values assigned in this book (this where the litany begins for long-time readers familiar with my rants), I strive for a sense of internal consistency with the pricing so that the book as a whole works as a guideline for each region of the country to use as on outline for their own market. Every item in this book has been scrutinized by several contributors. The values that were decided upon represent a ball park value that takes into account each of the prices submitted by those contributors.

Now, the price that anyone will buy (or sell) an item for is often linked closely with the geographic and economic environment he or she is living in. A collector who is a regular patron of a shop in Greenwich Village should expect to

pay more for a given item than a collector from Wilkes-Barre, PA. After all, the Manhattan collector pays more for rent, a slice of pizza, a restaurant dinner, or tickets to the Mets and Yankees, because a New York City resident will be paid commensurately more for his job. Similarly, just as a dealer takes for granted that he or she will pay less for records when stocking his or her shop in Wilkes-Barre, the dealer should also expect to sell them for less in the same market.

Oh so important: The prices in this book are for Near Mint *albums*. An "album" is "A set of phonograph records stored together under one binding." (*Webster's II* again.) This is terminology from the old 78 RPMs that was carried over to the 33 1/3, long-playing medium. The prices in this book are for the album, the record and the jacket, not just the record. . . I stress this because far too many folks out there selling used records haven't the foggiest notion of what the grades are meant to indicate. Please turn to that portion of the introduction dealing with "Grading Records."

Our Cover Story

That collectors and dealers often browse through stacks of used records without taking the time to check each and every item is a given, if only for the sake of sanity. But, there are some records that beg to be scrutinized with the wariest of eyes. The front cover features a quartet of relatively "common" albums, any one of which you, the reader, might own. But what you see is not always what you get. . . Each of these albums was manufactured with the intention of reaching the consumer (i.e., there is a commercial pressing). While the overwhelming majority of copies that exist, then and now, are of the aforementioned common version, each has at least one variation on the "released" cover or record that places it among the rarest of the rare!

Released in 1963, *The Freewheelin' Bob Dylan* (Columbia CL-1986, mono, and CS-8993, stereo) has several permutations that should be memorized by the avid collector. The jacket on the cover could hold any one of *at least* a half-dozen pressings, one of which has fetched five figures while the rest usually sell for $5-25. While the listings in the body of the book identify the variations, the story behind this record can be found in the front text as "The World's Most Valuable Album(s)."

Yesterday And Today (Capitol T-2553 and ST-2553) from the summer of 1966 is arguably the "world's most collectible album." The jacket on the cover may be exactly what it appears to be and, depending on the record inside, worth $10-50. Or, it may be a "second state butcher cover" hiding a collectible jacket worth thousands of dollars! (Refer to the listings for this album for more info on the terms used here.) While the supply of butcher covers is relatively plentiful, the demand seems never-ending. This is the one record that even non-collectors know about—and are willing to spend good money for! In fact, the demand is such that "peeled" ones that appear utterly ravaged will *still* sell to someone *if the price is right* .

Also from '66 is *Jefferson Airplane Takes Off* (RCA Victor LPM-3584 and LSP-3584). Original pressings of this album with twelve songs have taken off in the past few years. The jacket pictured needs to be examined: It could be a first pressing cover listing the twelve songs or a reissue, listing eleven. And, more important, it could hold an original twelve track record (worth more than $4,000), an eleven-track second pressing ($1,000+), or a later pressing with negligible value.

(Note that first pressing covers may contain second or third pressing records.) The first stereo pressing is the rarest variation of this under-appreciated gem, making the "Top 50 Most Valuable Albums" in this edition for the first time.

David Bowie's popularity with the public and the value of his records with collectors often seem as chameleon-like as his artistic persona. While both peaked several years ago, the original *Diamond Dogs* (RCA Victor CPL1-0576) remains a hot item among rare record collectors. The jacket artwork shown is the front part of a gatefold, or fold-open, cover that depicts the "bowiedog" in a relaxed position. Turning the jacket over, or unfolding it, will usually show a shadowed area around the critter's loins. But some covers have a clearly illustrated set of genitalia. While this cover was pulled prior to general release, original "dog dick" covers do turn up and NM copies have sold for as much as $5,000!

Here's the big plug for you casual browsers who are standing in a book store somewhere reading this without having purchased it: Needless to say, without this book in your hands on a daily basis, you may not only miss out on the chance to purchase these oddities, but hundreds of other rarities that escape the attention of other price guide editors!

Acknowledgments

While I receive a good deal of input from collectors and dealers from many countries—through phone calls, at record shows or shops, mostly through the mail—much of it consists of a single addition, correction or a bit of advice. I simply can't acknowledge each and every one in these pages, but I do like to reserve space for those who contribute more than a little, some quite a bit more.

So thanks to George Bigelow in Everett, WA; Gregg Biggs of CVC Collectables in Celina, OH; Jim Blatt in Vancouver, WA; Cory Carrier in Salt Lake City, UT; Christopher Chatman of Beyond Records in Los Angeles, CA; John Christensen in Renton, WA; John DeBlaiso in Renton, WA; David Edwards in Eaton, OH; Mark Erbach in Whittier, CA; Charlie Essmeier of Retro Records in Salt Lake City, UT; Norman Feinberg of Blue Chip Records in South Salem, NY; Joe Goldmark in San Francisco, CA; Tom Grosh of Very English & Rolling Stone in Lancaster, PA; David Holder in Indianapolis, IN; Ernest A. Huber, Jr. in Clifton, NJ; Ashley Johnson in Corpus Christi, TX; John C. Knapp in Rockville Centre, NY; Joseph Kusbel in Hammond, IN; Viktor Lindner in Salzburg, Austria; Jef Michael Piehler in Burbank, CA; Richie Ranno in River Edge, NJ; Rich Rockford in Vancouver, BC, Canada; Neal Skok in Redmond, WA; Rod Sweetland in Sacramento, CA; Kate Turney in Newport News, VA; Tom Ventris in Long Beach, CA; and Barry Wickham in Terra Linda, CA.

Special thanks to Stephen Braitman in San Francisco, CA, for his continuing interest in seeing my job is done correctly. Also to the three psycheteers, Scott Davis in Bellevue, WA, Craig Green in Olympia, WA, and Rick Haney of Calendula Records in Seattle, WA, for spending the time it took to update anything vaguely of interest to '60s psych collectors.

And, most importantly, to Gary Johnson of Rockaway Records in Los Angeles, CA, without whom this edition, like each of the previous, would be a different, and lesser, source book indeed.

The majority of the photos were taken by John Christensen (who provided the negatives to KP for processing). Should the reader be interested in submitting photos of albums for consideration, please follow this advice: Use a 35 MM camera with 400 ASA (or 27° ISO) black & white film (Tri-X appears to work best) at 1/125th-of-a-second shutter speed (or faster) to prevent blurring. Shoot the covers from directly above— not at an angle— on a pure white backdrop allowing as much of the cover to fill the frame as possible without cutting off the edges of the album. Set at least two table lamps with non-glare bulbs on either side of the cover and, holding the camera with a masterful hand or using a tripod, making sure that there is as little glare as possible on the cover. Any and all photos should be addressed to me, Box 40116, Bellevue, WA, 98015 USA.

Umphred On-Line

For those wishing to contribute corrections, additions or suggestions for future editions, please don't hesitate to write me at the same address. While I can't promise that each and every letter will get a personal response, I do assure you that every bit of data is entered into the computer and given consideration. For those who can't get off-line to put pen to paper, I have established a WebSite page for record collectors. The address for my WebSite page is:

---

http://www.aa./~umphred

Like so many such on-line projects, the site is under constant construction but the intention for this page is multi-fold: One section will be devoted to making available articles, essays and opinions on the music and the collectibles it has left behind, primarily by yours truly. A second will be set up as a "Question & Answer" board where you can send record related queries and I will, given time and opportunity, post both your question and my answer. I am considering a section that will offer collectible records for sale. The most important for serious collectors will contain news and updates on projects I am working on, such as new price guides due in the near future.

For the past six years I have been working on a book exposing the secrets of the buying and selling of "the world's rarest records." Tentatively titled *Rhythm & Blues Records Of The '50s— A 45 RPM Discography & Price Guide*, it will be co-authored by one of the field's biggest and most trusted dealers, John Tefteller. This long-awaited book will cover black, blues-based 45s and EPs from 1948-1963, including blues, rhythm'n blues, rock'n roll, and R&B vocal groups. *The information in this book is going to send sticker-shock throughout the record collecting community!* Collectors who have been referring to other books for guidance will, at long last, know why a record that is "only" valued at a few hundred bucks in other guides is impossible to find at thrice the price.

This 45 RPM R&B book will be at the printer as you read this! It will be followed by a companion volume, *Rhythm & Blues Records Of The '50s— A 78 RPM Discography & Price Guide*. I will again be assisted by Mr Tefteller, as he is recognized as the leading figure in the buying and selling of this format in the hobby. Aside from the thousands of titles that were issued at both speeds, this second volume will include hundreds of desirable records that were never issued as 45s.

Books on the drawing board of special interest to LP collectors include: A country & western album book; a movie and TV soundtrack book; an easy-listening instrumental book, which will focus on the "space age, bachelor pad, cocktail music" phenomena; and a "pop & personality" vocal book. Price guides of a more specialized interest will include one on "private pressing" albums of the '60s and '70s, focusing on garage, punk, psychedelic, progressive, and Christian rock. Another book will be devoted exclusively to audiophile albums, including current values for Mint and "still-sealed" copies of half-speed mastered titles from Mobile Fidelity, Nautilus, etc.

For Elvis fans, the second edition of *A Touch Of Gold* is in the works. It will address the state of the confusing Presley market, which can be summed up thus: The really rare stuff in truly Near Mint condition is climbing; everything else is falling. *ATOG Volume 2* will also have expanded coverage of the CD scene, both legitimate and not. More importantly, it will include new chapters with, for the first time, accurate values on movie related collectibles and '50s memorabilia manufactured with the blessing of Elvis Presley Enterprises.

Caveat Emptor

While I continue to hear that "so & so" *always* over-grades the records he sells, I also continue to hear that so & so continues to sell to the same people who are doing the complaining! Hint: Over-grading one or two records could be the sign of fatigue on behalf of the seller. *Always* over-grading indicates a must to avoid. . .

I said this last time and I'll say it every time hence: Will every dealer and collector-who-occasionally-sells please Please PLEASE me by putting a stop to the practice of affixing price stickers to the front covers of albums! I know this is stretching things a wee bit, but every time I walk into a store or browse through a show and witness this willful assault upon the integrity of the artifact for sale I wonder if, when selling a used car, this person paints the asking price on the hood. If you can't put the records in protective plastic bags with stickers, why not try removeable labels on the back cover.

Neal "The Tullamore Dude" Umphred
March 17, 1996

PS: Thanks for the many nice words from readers who followed my recommended listenings found in the photo captions of previous editions. I'm especially glad that readers discovered the joys to be found within the grooves of such over-looked '60s faves as *Of Cabbages And Kings*, *Song Cycle*, and *Triangle*. Here are a few photo-less recommendations of under-appreciated, quintessentially '60s titles, from the era when a new album meant something: *After Bathing At Baxter's*, *Anthem Of The Sun*, *Arthur*, *Children Of The Future*, *Happy Trails*, *More*, *Smiley Smile*, and *Sunshine Superman*.

INTRO REDUNDO
A Revised Text To Correctly Using This Book

Before you go running off to your dictionary, "redundo" is just a coined take on "redundancy." This is a [hopefully] clever way of alerting those [few] readers who have read my intros in the past editions that they can safely skip this one. (Unless, of course, they are enamored of my really rather arid approach to communicating in what is, after all, a "technical" book). For the familiar, the ways and means of this edition are the same as that of its predecessors.

"Yo! Just because one person paid 'X' for a record doesn't mean that's what the record's *really* worth!" This is the remark I hear most often concerning the [presumed] excessively high values assigned to some records in one of my books. And I agree with the sentiments in this observation. . . most of the time. Not only do I generally *not* consider an extreme price paid for a fairly common record, but the knowledgeable reader will note that I tend to take a rather conservative tack when navigating the values of the more recent "collectibles" or artists. In most cases, it takes time for an artifact to establish itself as a true collectible, although certain items, genres, or artists may seem, during their Warholian fifteen minutes of fame, to have arrived.

In the early '80s, Blondie was hot and anything bearing Debbie Harry's likeness was an instant sale (including bootlegs featuring Ms. Harry's lovely face superimposed upon some rather raunchily posed figures). And who can forget the great Police vogue that followed? Springsteen collectors have long paid excessive prices for new promos that have gained little in value since their release. Recently we have Tori Amos: Following her reincarnation as a singer/songwriter, an obscure album with the daunting title of *Why Kant Tori Read* (Atlantic 81845-1 from 1988) featuring the then Tori Bullard as a leatherish rock vixen, went from the dollar bins to the top of the heap. At its peak, it was selling for $200+, even though more and more copies kept turning up. Now that Tori-mania has died down, the album is settling into a more comfortable price zone (although I believe the [drastically reduced] values assigned in this edition will prove to be a bit too high, too soon).

But, when the *only* copy of a record that has been offered for sale or auction on the open market for several years sells above and beyond anyone's wildest imaginations, when that sale is the *only documented sale of that item in recent memory* (and likely to be the only one for some time), then that sale, by definition, *must* have a bearing on the value assigned that record. For example, a mint copy of one of two known stereo pressings of *Jefferson Airplane Takes Off* (RCA Victor LSP-3584 from 1966), with twelve tracks instead of the more common eleven, sold for more than $8,000 in 1995 with a single phone call! That sale, my friends, more or less defines the value of that record (although readers will note that I hedge my bets on the listing within these pages).

There *are* going to be instances where the information in this book is incomplete or wrong, and not just the values. It is almost unimaginable for any book listing tens of thousands of records not to make some errors. These may range in nature from common typographical errors, to transferring erroneous data from a flawed source, to incomplete research.

Page Breakdown

Artists are listed alphabetically using a single artist's last name while the first important word in a group's name is the basis for their listing. When an artist used two names professionally, the less common one follows the listed one in brackets. For instance, "MILLER, STEVE [THE STEVE MILLER BAND]" tells the reader that albums listed under either of those two names can be found under that one listing. In this case, while the second, bracketed name is the group's original name, the first is the one with which virtually every one refers to this artist's career.

When two different artists' names appear in a heading, such as "MILLER, STEVE / QUICKSILVER MESSENGER SERVICE / THE BAND," the reader needs to understand that the album(s) listed there is a compilation of tracks by the different artists. In the case of this particular example, it refers to a boxed set with one entire record by each of the three groups.

References are kept to a minimum although they are far more inclusive than those of previous editions. Listing references for artists who appeared on other artist's recordings is a book in itself. Should the reader desire one, Terry Hounsome and Tim Chambre's *Rock Record* (Blandford Press, 1987) is recommended, with thousands of listings of who played on what, when, and where!

The records are listed chronologically by label. I have used fairly standard alphabetization; there should be no real surprises for anyone familiar with an encyclopedia. Necessary notes are usually listed in italics in parentheses below the appropriate section or selections. Following is an example, again using Mr. Miller:

MILLER, STEVE [THE STEVE MILLER BAND]

Capitol SKAO-2920	(S)	**Children Of The Future**	1968	10.00	25.00
Capitol STBB-177	(S)	**Children Of The Future/Sailor** *(2 LPs)*	1969	10.00	25.00
		— Capitol albums above have black rainbow labels.—			
Capitol SKAO-2920	(S)	**Children Of The Future**	1970	3.20	8.00
Capitol STBB-177	(S)	**Children Of The Future/Sailor** *(2 LPs)*	1970	3.20	8.00
		— Capitol albums above have green labels.—			
Capitol SOO-11872	(DJ)	**Greatest Hits 1974-78** *(Blue vinyl)*	1978	12.00	30.00
Capitol SOO-11872	(S)	**Greatest Hits 1974-78**	1978	.80	4.00

The first column indicates the label and catalog number. The second describes the record's sound: An "M" denotes a monaural recording, while "S" means the record is [at least] two-channel stereo. An "E" indicates that the stereo effect of the album has been electronically created from a monophonic source. "P" indicates a partially stereo record: While some of the tracks *are* stereo, one or more are either mono or electronic stereo. A "Q" indicates a four-channel, quadraphonic recording. Finally, the term "DJ" means that the record was issued exclusively for promotional reasons. This would generally indicate in-store samplers to arouse consumer interest, and radio station specials, such as interviews, live performances or samplers. Promos in the '50s and '60s should be assumed to be mono; those from the '70s on, stereo.

The record's title is the middle column; specific notes short enough to place on the same line follow. In this case, the existence of a colored vinyl version of Capitol SOO-11872 is noted. This is followed by the regular first pressing on black vinyl. This is followed by the year of release. The final two columns, the prices, are for records in the two most "collectible" conditions, very-good-plus (VG+) and near-mint (NM), and are dealt with at length below.

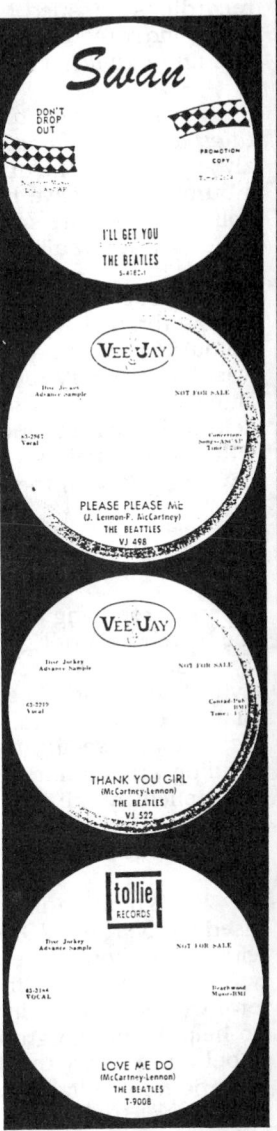

For those artists who achieved a long lasting popularity that saw their recordings reissued I have attempted to list notations about particular records. *Notes indented beneath an album and enclosed in parentheses refer only to the title under which it is listed* (unless, of course, the note says otherwise).

Notes that are centered and lacking parentheses refer to two or more titles and are almost exclusively dealing with label specifications. These notes always include the qualifier "above" in their statements! In the example: "Capitol albums above have black rainbow labels" applies to all of the albums above it. Following that are second and later pressings, as with the green label reissues of Miller's first few albums.

There are several other parenthetical notes that are used on the same line as the title (space allowing): "No cover" indicates a record issued in a plain, unmarked cardboard sleeve (usually privately printed albums). Similarly, while it was unnecessary to denote titles by specialist labels (Mobile Fidelity, Nautilus, Direct Disk) as half-speed masters, major labels that dipped into the audiophile field with such product are noted as "Half-speed master" (or simply "Half-speed"). Other peculiarities (colored vinyl, white label promos, etc.) are also noted in parentheses with the title.

Grading the Records

When purchasing a record at a show or through the mail (or even many stores), the buyer does not get to listen to it. For that reason, records are usually graded by visual standards, not aural. Unfortunately, this method relies on the subjectivity of the grader's eyes— or viewpoint— and the fact that records do not always play as good, or bad, as they look. For this reason *records almost always look better when selling than when buying.* Of course, the arguments against play-grading are similar: The subjectivity of the listener is also a factor, one that is multiplied by the type of equipment the grader is playing the record on to form his or her judgement. So, for the sake of convenience and necessity, visual grading is the standard by which almost all dealers and collectors work.

When grading a disc, *grade the overall wear of the vinyl.* A record advertised as "NM" or "VG" should tell the prospective buyer the shape of the playable vinyl. Common sense should be used. (For example, un-played records that are warped cannot be Mint.) When defining the grades, it is difficult to describe several without discussing defects and/or the way the disc plays; these are included to help define the grade, not to cause confusion. Such defects as stickers on the label or tape on the jacket should be addressed separately with abbreviated notations. A reliable set of these notations have been developed over the years covering virtually every type of defect that can occur to a record or its cover; a list of most of the more common abbreviations and their meanings follow the grading definitions below.

Visual grading is most important in mail-order transactions where a buyer doesn't see his purchase until his check has cleared the bank. The aim of grading is to make the buyer visualize the record and not be disappointed when that record arrives! A record that is accurately graded should play the same (or better) than the grading. In-person deals do not require a grade of any sort; if you are holding a record that has obviously been played a hundred times, you don't need a grade to determine whether or not you are going to purchase that disc.

Always grade records under a good, steady light. A 100 watt light bulb in a common desk-lamp will do an adequate job; most major defects will jump out and allow you to make a reasonably accurate assessment. Grading a record using light from the ceiling or from deflected sunlight entering the window will often "hide" paper scuffs, discoloration, groove wear and even some fingerprints. Remember, mistakes in grading are a problem all dealers and collectors are prone to make. Do not condemn a dealer for one mistake; but, when the mistake is the norm, find someone else to buy your records from. . .

Mint. A Mint (M) record should appear to have just left the manufacturer without any handling; that is, it should appear perfect! No scuffs or scratches, blotches or stains, labels or writing, tears or splits; nothing. And age has nothing to do with it; *the same standards for Mint apply to a 10" soundtrack from 1954 as they do to a "grunge" album from 1994!*

A Mint album cover should appear to have never had a record in it; no ring-wear (defined here as *any* imprint on the cover from the record that it formerly held), dog-eared corners, writing, seam-splits. Uh-uh. Mint means perfect and nothing else.

Near Mint. A record that is otherwise Mint but has one or two tiny, inconsequential flaws that do not affect the play is Near Mint (NM) and should command 80-90% of the Mint price. For many, NM and Mint-Minus mean the same thing; for the sake of this book, they are interchangeable. When dealing with a seller that discriminates between the two, inquire as to what the dealer means when he calls one record M- and another NM. Many dealers and collectors take the position that any used (opened) record cannot be verified as Mint so they use M- to describe what appears to be a perfect record that has been opened.

Covers should still be close to perfect with minor signs of wear or age just becoming evident: slight ring-wear, minor denting to a corner, or writing on the cover should all be noted properly.

Many records *are available* in NM/M condition, although these are generally more recent and the prices are nominal. That is, most dealers set a minimum price on the records they sell in their store, usually $3.99-4.99, just for normal, everyday, readily-available records. Whether they are un-played or "merely" NM, the price will be the same. It wouldn't be worth the dealer's time to stock the record unless that minimum price was met.

Sometimes referred to as "Excellent," a **Very Good Plus** (VG+) record has been handled and played either infrequently or very carefully. That is, an item obviously not perfect, but not *too* far from it. On a disc, this could mean that there are light paper scuffs from sliding in and out of a sleeve or the vinyl may have lost some— *not all*— of its original luster. A slight scratch that did not affect play in an otherwise NM disc would be acceptably VG+ for most collectors. A scratch of any sort that audibly clicked throughout the music would not be acceptable. Always list the flaws in a VG+ record or cover.

As a rule of thumb, a VG+ item is worth 40-60%, of the NM value, the ratio varies with the rarity of the item. That is, a record that is fairly common in NM/M condition has little real value in VG+ to most collectors; consequently 25-35% may be more appropriate. On the other hand, truly rare records will fetch 75% in VG+. On covers, some wear from storage is acceptable, especially light wear that does not affect the beauty of the artwork. Listing the flaws when selling is safest.

Very Good (VG) records will display visible signs of handling and playing, such as loss of vinyl luster, light surface scratches, groove wear, and spindle trails from countless spins on the turntable. A VG record looks like it will have some audible surface noise when it is played, although any such noise should not overwhelm the musical experience. VG records should appear to have been well-played although well-loved by a responsible owner. Gouges in the plating from slapping the disc down onto the spindle, rips in the label from pulling stickers formerly affixed, etc., are all unacceptable.

As more and more collectors spend more and more money on their acquisitions, the lower limits of acceptability for an item to be admitted into their collection rises. That is, to many collectors, a record in VG condition is not acceptable unless the item is truly rare and virtually unavailable in any other condition! And then, only if the price is scaled appropriately to match the condition. Used but not abused might sum up this grade. A VG record should command approximately 20-30% of the NM price.

This is a difficult grade when discussing paper goods. Like a disc, usually a cover is VG when a variety of problems are evident: ring wear, seam splits, bent corners, loss of gloss, stains, etc. An aggravated combination of two of these problems— never all of them— would likely cause a sleeve to be graded VG.

Good ("G") in record collecting parlance all too often means a beat, trashed, take-it-to-the-flea-market frisbee. Good should mean that the record is well-played with any number of defects that collectors normally shy away from, such as an almost complete loss of surface sheen, aggravating surface noise, etc. Still, the purchaser, knowing full well that he or she is buying a Good record, should be able to take it home, slap it onto the turntable and have a good time listening to it. Records that do not provide this most fundamental requirement are just no good. A Good record should command 10-15% of the NM price.

A Good cover has seen considerable handling over a course of years and displays the obvious signs: ring-wear on the cover; some seam-splitting, particularly along the bottom, which would receive the brunt of the record's sliding in and out; corners may be dog-eared to a light degree; an infatuated owner may have written his or her name somewhere; etc. If a record or cover is beneath your contempt, it is not in "G" condition; look below for the appropriate grade.

Any record or cover that does not qualify for the above "Good" grading should be seen as *Poor* and command 0-5% of the Mint price. Make a friend and give any "P" record away as a freebee to anyone who expresses interest in it. . .

Finally, it should always be borne in mind that visual evidence can be deceiving. A record properly manufactured with a high quality plating may look VG+ and play NM. This is particularly true of records from the '50s through the mid '60s, when print runs were dramatically smaller, vinyl was fresher and more care was paid to the entire procedure. Records from this period are a better investment in VG+ condition than the more recent American product.

In fact, many LPs from the '50s can be purchased in VG condition at reasonable prices and will play far better than the price paid would indicate. A record manufactured from recycled vinyl with poor plating may look Mint and play VG. Still, most dealers do not have the time to listen to each item in their inventory, so visual standards remain.

Record Collecting Abbreviations

Listed here are common abbreviations used in advertising to describe flaws and their locations on a record or cover. Dealers have different ways of using these abbreviations; some capitalize them ("DJ"), some use periods after each letter ("n.a.p.") and some use a slash ("c/o"). Those marked with an asterisk (*) should always be listed when advertising an item for sale or auction.

cc	cut corner*
co	cut out*
coh	cut-out hole*
c-33	compact-33 1/3 rpm single or EP
cvr	cover
dj	disc jockey, or promotional, copy
imp	import
ips	inches per second
lbl	label
lp	12" 33 1/3 rpm long playing album
mo	mono
nap	(does) not affect play
ol	on label
org	original
pln cvr	plain paper jacket (no picture or titles)
promo	promotional copy
q	quadraphonic
re	reissue
reel	reel to reel tape
repro	reproduction, or counterfeit
2nd pr	second pressing
slt wrp	slight warp*
sm	saw mark (a cut-out mark)*
sm splt	seam split*
sol	sticker on the label*
sr	slight ring-wear on the front cover*
st	stereo
ss	still sealed
stkr	sticker
10"	10" 33 1/3 rpm album
t&ts	(disc jockey) title & timing strip
toc	tape on the cover*
tol	tape on the label*
ts	taped seams*
wlp	white label promo
wol	writing on the label*

Those abbreviations not listed here but that assist the buyer in visualizing the record for sale should be just as scrupulously applied by the seller. . .

Pricing the Records

If you, as a collector, have spent years hunting for a key item for your collection, all the while assuming that *you will find it in nice shape at an affordable price* (the goal—and, too often, the delusion—of every collector of anything), at some point the realization that such a goal may not be as attainable as first surmised will probably occur. Which brings me to a bit of sagely advice: *When you are offered a record for which you have been actively searching for more than five years, do not argue with the price. . . pay it.* The corollary to this bit of wisdom would be: If you don't, you may not see it again for another five years, *and* it will cost even more.

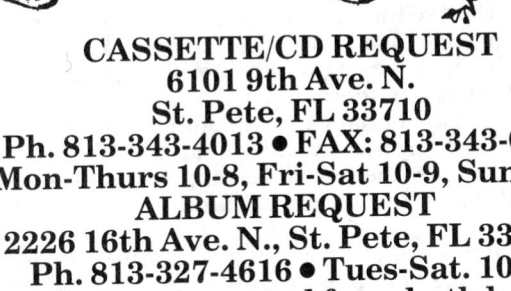

As for the fluctuations in the market, well, for those readers who expect values to rise automatically, the collectibles market is not all that different from the commodities market or the stock exchange, and *everyone* knows the wild fluctuations that occur there. So, while most prices do remain stable, or rise gradually, some rise dramatically while others actually go down. Value is established almost solely by supply and demand: Prices go up when the current demand is greater than the available supply; prices go down when the available supply is greater than the current demand.

Any number of factors can cause prices to rise or decline. The factors that cause the value of a rare, desirable record to rise are obvious. The most dramatic leveller is probably the quantity find, where boxes of a supposedly rare record turn up in sufficient quantities to meet the immediate demand, driving its value down for the near future. One of the most sought-after of privately-pressed psych albums, *The Music Emporium*, saw its value plummet when someone related to the band dumped over 130 sealed copies in a sale to a local shop. The store noted the value in the last edition of this book ($3,000 in NM), and promptly offered them for sale at $750 apiece, with substantial discounts for purchases of several copies.

On the most mundane of levels, the value of a fairly common, out of print album can decline when that album is released as a compact disc, although the drop is usually temporary. When the supply dropped on the market in the wake of the record's digitalized debut is exhausted, the record will often return to its earlier value.

So, the dealer should use this guide as just that. . . a guide. Basically, if you only find that this book helps point out the relatively rare pieces from the more common items, *even if you don't believe that you can get those prices in your market,* then the book is of value. Of course, for the collector, what may be of paramount importance is not the prices but the discographies themselves.

I believe that the more accurate, encompassing and detailed this book is the better it serves everyone involved. For the dealer who is concerned that he or she may no longer be able to pick up good records for a [pitiful] fraction of their value—and as precarious an existence as wheeling and dealing in collectibles can be, that is certainly a justifiable fear—I maintain that while you will almost certainly find the instances of buying $100 records for a buck are diminished by the existence of this book, that the verification of the true market value of collectible vinyl *by this book* encourages more and more people to spend their hard-earned money on otherwise dubious investments. That is, the advantage you lose in those buys are more than compensated for by being able to service a broader market, a more educated clientele.

Should this sound like a snow job, bear in mind that in virtually every other field of collecting the price guide(s) recognized by the collectors in that field have helped the dealers enormously. One has only to turn his or her attention to what comic books and sports cards have become. Both were once regarded as "lowly" as records—lower, really—and both have left records far behind as a volatile, fluid place of business and, yes, fun.

This book is not billed as the bible for record collectors nor as the blue book of vinyl junkies. *And* it is certainly not the "official" price guide for anything. Nor does this book reflect *my opinions* of what *your records* are worth. The prices here are an attempt *to document what collectible records are worth on the open*

collectors' market, primarily that market that is reached both nationally and internationally by dealers and collectors through the mail, either through such collectors' publications as *Goldmine* or through individual mailing lists that have been assembled over a period of time. That is, that market which is the largest and most eager to purchase really rare records.

This book does not reflect my opinions of what your records are worth. Instead, I solicited the assistance of many collectors and dealers whom I have known for several years, both personally and professionally. Each dealer and collector was requested to provide *current values based on recent sales or purchases*, not transactions from years ago.

The prices quoted reflect the market during the period in which this book was assembled; *I cannot guarantee that they will remain the same for any length of time following the publication of this book*. In fact, price guides tend to have a direct—and often immediate—effect on the very market they attempt to chronicle.

Okay—We've arrived at a point where my opinion of what your records are worth *does* come into play. There are some records that can be found in lesser conditions but are apparently impossible to find in NM. In those cases no figure was assigned to the NM price column but a suggested range was noted parenthetically beneath the title. This is not to imply that the record is worth either the highest or the lowest value but rather that this range is a reasonable assessment of the transactions over the past. Using The Beatles as an example:

BEATLES, THE

Vee Jay LP-1062	(M)	**Introducing The Beatles** *("Ad back")*	1963	*See below*
Vee Jay SR-1062	(P)	**Introducing The Beatles** *("Ad back")*	1963	*See below*

(Includes "Love Me Do" and "P.S. I Love You." The back cover has ads for 25 other Vee Jay albums. Mono copies have a suggested NM value of $3,000-5,000. Stereo copies, $10,000-15,000.)

As noted in the price column, the reader's attention is referred to the note, which gives an estimated NM value for the mono version of the album of $3,000-5,000 and $10,000-15,000 for the stereo pressing. What this means for a seller with a NM stereo copy is that he/she might consider asking $15,000 for the album but should not be upset if "forced" to accept a mere $10,000.

Conversely, while a buyer might win this record for as "little" as $10,000, he/she should not be surprised to find the bidding escalate to the $15,000 range. The same title in lesser condition should cut the estimated value dramatically, as I use the minimum value in the spread as the base for the calculations. So, a VG+ stereo copy would have a range of approximately $6,000-10,000; a VG copy, $2,500-5,000.

Bear in mind that these are my suggestions, not dictates. They also apply to records that meet the standards of grading espoused by this book, sold on the open, competitive market, and, generally, by dealers or collectors with some reputation for accuracy and honesty. Instances where these records sell for less (or more) will occur—do occur. The *average* dealer or collector is often months (or a few years) behind the reality of the market when it comes to the specialized knowledge of truly rare records. They are so rare that few, if anyone, ever sees them for sale at any price.

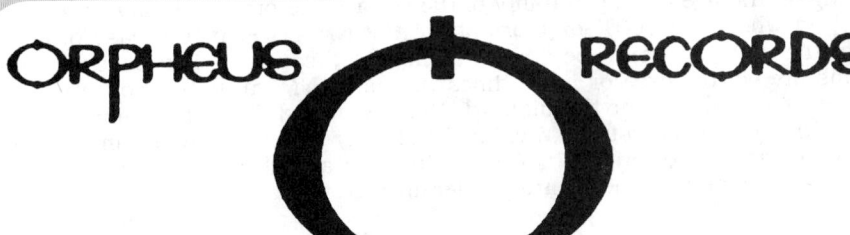

The more knowledgeable you are, the more useful and informative this book will be, if only that the informed reader will be better able to assimilate the information and make use of it regularly.

Many collectors have expressed concern over the effects the overseas buyer has had on American records. The continued slump in the economy makes it difficult for the average working-class American to match the bids of a rabid European or Japanese. But to ignore this situation in establishing values would be both futile and counter productive. Thus, a reasonably common item that goes for a bigger dollar overseas is not unduly affected because the foreign collectors only purchase a fraction of the copies put up for sale each year!

But what of a record that turns up infrequently and invariably leaves the country? If the overseas collector regularly bids two or three times what American collectors believe the record is "really" worth, then the domestic collectors had better learn to adjust their sights. Those prices *must* determine the value of those records! I would, in effect, be doing you, the user of this book, a disservice were I to choose any other option.

The average American collector needs to know what he or she should expect to have to bid to win a truly rare and desirable record in an open auction on the open market. Please bear in mind that many of the records listed here, especially those with three figure values, will sell for considerably more overseas.

On Still-Sealed Albums

In many cases collectors are willing to pay a premium for still-sealed copies. Depending on the age and desirability of the record, the premium may be a modest 10% to a whopping 100% or more above the NM price. In the case of certain items, the increase would be greater: Still-sealed copies of The Beatles' Capitol albums are worth three or more times the listed NM value but collecting them represents a real test for the diehard. Factory sealed Capitol albums are easily worth three times the listed NM value. While any sealed mono album is an original (mono was discontinued by Capitol in 1968 and thus saw none of the later label changes), stereo albums are a different matter.

The easiest way to identify an original Capitol stereo album in a sealed jacket is to tap the album till the inner sleeve is flush against the plastic wrap along the edge. As Capitol issued all their LPs in different colored paper sleeves advertising other LPs, the appearance of such a sleeve would almost certainly assure an original record within. Of course, all of the above applies to albums by other Capitol artists from this period.

But beware: Shrink-wrapping albums at the factory was not a common practice until the early to mid-'60s. A label as large as Capitol was using the fact that their albums were "poly-wrapped in the factory" as late as January 1964 as a selling point to the consumer. Should you be offered an album from the '50s or early '60s still sealed in shrink-wrap, think twice.

Generally, a dealer cannot be held responsible for what is inside a sealed jacket. When purchasing a valuable sealed collectible at a shop or show, pay for the record *with the mutual understanding* that you will open it *immediately after purchase, in front of the dealer,* and if the record inside is not what it should be, *you may return it on the spot.* Do not purchase a sealed record, leave, and return

later claiming that you got the wrong record or a damaged copy. Naturally, very few dealers will offer a refund in such a case. On a less savory note, there are more than a few dealers and shops that do their own shrink-wrapping.

On Bonus Photos & Cover Stickers

Companies often included a "bonus photo" to special albums or deluxe packagings. These bonuses are noted when known throughout the listings. Should the reader have an album with such a bonus that is not listed, he or she should certainly consider the photo to be a desirable acquisition worth more than the album without such a photo.

Also, most albums that included a bonus called the potential purchaser's attention to the extra with a sticker on the cover or shrinkwrap. Albums with a sticker on the shrink-wrap advertising an enclosed bonus or calling attention to a hit single generally command a premium above and beyond what plain shrink-wrap would generate. Even more important is the practice of applying stickers directly to the cover. While either of these practices could lead to a modest premium paid for common albums or less collectible artists, it can double the price of a rare record or desirable name.

On Printed Extras On The Cover

In the mid '60s, record companies began printing on the covers of select albums a black circular notification of the title's being awarded a "Gold Record Award Audited And Certified By RIAA." This was, no doubt, meant to impress upon prospective purchasers the fact that since so many others had already bought the album that perhaps he or she should also add this to his or her collection. These stickers were added to the album *after it had sold the required amount.* So, excepting those albums that were certified Gold based on advance orders, it must be assumed that copies of an album bearing this seal are, in fact, technically second pressings and that first pressings exist without the seal.

Which brings us to stock copies that are stamped promo, which are starting to receive attention from starved collectors who have everything else by a favorite artist. Albums designated promotionally by being stamped or having stickers affixed to the cover, etc., are escalating in value, a trend that should continue. One thing I will not be a part of is placing premium values on albums with holes punched out of them, ridiculously referred to as "promo-holes." It's simply too easy for anyone with a hole-punch to make up all the promos for which he/she can find unsuspecting buyers. So, in my guides, these are simply cut-outs. This does not include covers where "PROMO" or "FREE" are perforated into the corner. At this point, these aforementioned promos remain, for the most part, uncatalogued.

On Foreign Releases

Although the scope of this book is wide-ranging in terms of domestic releases, it does not begin to detail the staggering variety of collectible records from around the world. In most countries, an album need sell only 100,000 copies to qualify for gold status, one-fifth the minimum for an American release. In effect this means that hit records in many countries are "rare" by American standards. The likeli-

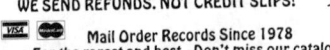

hood of their turning up here years later is remote. While those Americans who actively collect foreign records are relatively few, the even smaller amount of the truly rare pieces makes competition intense. A rare and desirable rock 'n roll album from the '50s from such major markets as Canada, England or France in VG condition will regularly sell for hundreds of dollars, as NM ones may not exist at this point in time! Imports since 1970 are more common and command reasonable prices.

The attraction of these records are self-evident upon examination: In terms of the variety of releases and the quality of both the pressing and the appearance, the United States takes a back seat to many other countries. It is difficult to view a collection of foreign records and not feel the desire to plunge right into a whole new field of collecting, one that is as rewarding and far more aesthetic than merely collecting domestic releases. Some dealers make a point of keeping large inventories of the more desirable recent releases. At the time, there is no reliable source for pricing and comparative shopping is nearly impossible. If the reader chooses to get into this aspect of the hobby, he or she will have to contact other fans and collectors and learn from scratch.

Caveat Emptor. . .

The counterfeiting of records has existed almost since the first record was manufactured. In the collectibles market of the past thirty or so years, most unauthorized reproductions of rare records have been done on a small scale *by* collectors *for* collectors. That is, the repros have rarely been presented as anything but repros. This is not the case with the current mania for RIAA Gold and Platinum Record Awards, where duplicity appears to be as ingrained in many of the suppliers as the desire to hang a cherished Award on the wall is with the buyer. This sorry state of affairs cannot be dealt with at length in this volume, but readers should always be cautious of buys that are "too good to be true" from otherwise apparently knowledgeable sellers.

There is also the practice of re-sealing albums. This was done over the years by the record companies and by firms specializing in remainders (I don't remember anyone calling them cut-outs in the '60s). Prior to the sales boom of the mid '70s, the industry had a very loose policy regarding returns; many of us over "thirtysomething" grew up able to test a purchase out on the store's turntable before taking it home. (*And* were often able to return records that we just plain didn't like. Of course, those were pre-corporate days when retail operations were independently owned and operated, and the proprietor knew most of his customers and catered to their needs).

Without trying to sound *too* alarmist: The Reader should be aware that there are dealers out there *right now* practicing this very act of deception on a regular basis and laughing their way to the bank 'cause they know that most collectors ain't gonna read this bit of advice and most of the ones who do. . . *ain't gonna give it no credence!*

THE WORLD'S MOST VALUABLE ALBUM(S)

The observant reader will note that the title of this article is a wee bit different from the last few editions of this book. An 's' has been added to the final word in the title. Yup, where once a lone album held the position of the "world's most valuable album," with this book two records now vie for the top spot. I say vie ("To strive for. . . superiority." *Webster's* again) because both records have identical "suggested Near Mint values" and, should a NM copy of each appear after the publication of this book and sell at auction, one might fetch more than the other and establish itself as the field's sole leader. . .

Talkin' Freewheelin' Mispressin' Blues

On May 12, 1963, Bob Dylan was scheduled to appear on Ed Sullivan's Show, guaranteeing him his largest audience outside of the circumscribed world of folk music. Dylan was planning to perform "Talkin' John Birch Blues," a farcical romp from his upcoming album, *The Freewheelin' Bob Dylan*. He had auditioned the song for Sullivan and the show's producer, and both were enthusiastic. Needless to say, Dylan's manager, Albert Grossman, was ebullient at the possibilities such exposure meant. On the eve of the show during a dress rehearsal the editor in charge of CBS-TV programming decided there were problems with the lyrics, which lampooned the absurdities of racism in general and Birchers in particular.

CBS decided that the risk of offending viewers below the Mason-Dixon was too great and Dylan was informed that he would not be singing that particular song. It was suggested he opt for something less topical, perhaps something the audience might already be familiar with, "like a Clancy Brothers tune." Dylan walked out. The stories that circulated in the folk world riled up everybody, all of whom were righteously on the singer's side.

The song had already been recorded and the album, widely anticipated by retailers as a big seller, was ready for shipping. Suddenly, the album was pulled and taken back into the studio. There are two versions of this story: One has Columbia, the recording branch of CBS, taking the logical conclusion (at least, based on the Sullivan decision) that the song was potentially libelous and should not be on the album, thus dictating the change. Another has the vindictive singer claiming that what wasn't good enough for TV couldn't be fit for disc and, at Columbia's expense, he had the record remastered.

Along with the Birch track, also pulled were "Gamblin' Willie's Dead Man's Hand," "Rocks And Gravel," and "Let Me Die In My Footsteps," a powerful condemnation of the bunker mentality then permeating much of America when citizens were being scared into spending a fortune constructing [ultimately useless] underground shelters in case of nuclear war. The three additional tracks, requiring both sides to be remastered, stand as some proof that the album's callback was at least partially instigated by Dylan.

During the pressing of the new version of the album, at least one run using the original stampers was made, although the new labels listing the replacement songs were pressed onto the vinyl, and they were slipped into the second version cover. Mono copies of this album with the matrix number in the trail-off vinyl that end with a dash and a numeral one ("—1") followed by a letter indicate the original stamper. Copies with a "2" or above are the later, remastered stampers. It was long assumed that only mono pressings existed, as that was all that had been found. In fact, in the entry for this album in the first two editions of this book, I noted that "all known copies are mono" and did not even list the possibility of a stereo version!

Then, in April 1992 a collector in New York found a stereo copy at a church thrift shop! While the record was well-played, the labels correctly listed the deleted tracks, something none of the monos had done. It was offered for sale through Strider Records in New York's Greenwich Village. A second stereo copy in VG was found and sold by Christopher K. Chatman, a dealer in California. Both copies fetched five figures when sold. Therefore, I felt comfortable in assigning a suggested Near Mint value of $20,000-30,000 for a record that has twice sold for $12,000 in VG condition.

Finally, while the John Birch song has been a staple of bootlegs since the early '70s where it is generally listed as "Talkin' John Birch Society Blues," on Columbia's three CD boxed set of rare Dylan material, *the bootleg series, volumes 1-3*, it is listed as "Talkin' John Birch Paranoid Blues." It should be noted that the label on the 1963 stereo album lists the song as "Talkin' John Birch Blues."

Introducing The The Stereo Title-Backs

In 1963, EMI/Parlophone offered Capitol Records, their American representative, the rights to represent their hottest new act, The Beatles. But the decision-makers in Hollywood knew better than to think that a British beat group could score in the States and politely declined. EMI then offered the group around, finding a reception in the more humble offices of Vee Jay Records, a Chicago-based indie specializing in rhythm 'n blues. As America's most successful black-owned and operated label prior to Berry Gordy's Tamla/Motown empire, Vee Jay had scored nationally with several quality artists, notably Jerry Butler, although by 1963 it was a white group, The Four Seasons, which kept their cash flowing and their logo afloat.

Taking a chance on the Liverpool foursome, the label issued a couple of singles and an album, *Introducing The Beatles* (Vee Jay 1062) in the summer of '63 to an unresponsive public. The first pressings of the LP featured both sides of the group's initial chart UK hit, "Love Me Do" and "P.S. I Love You." While the cover art remained the same, three different versions of the album jacket's back cover are known to exist. One variation, the most common, lists the song titles in two columns. A second sports a series of reproductions of twenty-five other albums from the Vee Jay catalog. A third is completely blank, devoid of any printing whatsoever.

The stereo covers for the latter two variations are among the hobby's rarest and most expensive collectibles. And, while the mono covers for these two are much rarer than the mono title back cover, there are no known stereo covers with the titles on the back! Or, there weren't prior to a sale in January 1995. East Coast dealer Gary Hein auctioned off a set of 1062s that included the first known stereo title back. Graded VG+, the purchaser later admitted that approximately one-half, or nearly $15,000-20,000 of the price he paid was for the privilege of being the sole owner of this sole copy.

I felt comfortable in assigning a suggested Near Mint value of $20,000-30,000 for a record that has sold for approximately $17,500 in VG+ condition. Most collectors and dealers were openly skeptical of the record's authenticity prior to the sale. Had there been more willingness to believe, there might have been heavier bidding and an even higher price reached.

Back to the album's history: When Capitol, no longer able to ignore the unprecedented overseas success of the Fab Four, opted to pick up the rights to the group starting in January 1964, Beatlemania unfolded and a new definition of "youth culture" was born. By the second quarter of '64, The Beatles were in the enviable position of having six companies pushing their product in the States: Swan, MGM and Atco each had rights to early sessions for Polydor in Germany while United Artists had the enormously profitable soundtrack, *A Hard Day's Night*. Vee Jay issued a slightly revamped version of the first album, replacing "Love Me Do" and "P.S. I Love You" with both sides of the hit "Please Please Me" and "Ask Me Why." From January through the rest of 1964, millions of copies of Vee Jay albums flooded the market as the label repackaged the same sixteen tracks into four differently titled albums.

Exactly when the counterfeiting of The Beatles' first American long-player began is a moot point. That they were readily available and plentiful "way back when" is not. The steady demand for the album left the door open for any entrepreneur with the willingness to circumvent the more traditional avenues of business in record manufacturing. There are many different counterfeits of this album, fortunately most being so obvious that it is often amazing to realize that anyone who collects records could be fooled. But there are also counterfeits of surpassing excellence.

As cash came in from the album's sales, Vee Jay hired several pressing plants to make the record, resulting in a plethora of variations on the pressings, adding immensely to the confusion. Legitimate covers *always* have a glossy sheen. The photo of the group should always be crisp and clear with an obvious shadow cast by the lads against the photographer's backdrop. The covers were made from grey or tan poster board with 1/4" flaps over the top and bottom.

Both *Introducing The Beatles* and "The Beatles" are printed above the spindle hole on a glossy label. On those labels using the rainbow border, the shift in the color-band is smooth and lovely. The trail-off vinyl is between 7/8" and 1" wide. Finally, should your copy have the word "Stereo" printed on the label, or "Audio Matrix," "MR" or "ARP" machine-stamped in the trail-off vinyl, you have an original although not *all* originals have these identifying scores.

Counterfeit covers have a flatter finish with the clarity of the photo's details compromised. On the really bad fakes, the shadow is more of an indecipherable blur. These fakes are made from white cardboard (check the inside of the jacket) and the flaps may vary in size. Fakes may have the title above the hole and the group's name below; the label may be flat or *slightly* finished; or the color gradation in the rainbow may be abrupt. The trail-off varies and often visibly exceeds the one inch mark.

ROCKIN' RARITIES
THE 50 MOST VALUABLE ALBUMS

Below are the albums with the highest assigned current market values as of 1996 listed in this edition. The item must be a domestically manufactured vinyl album, either commercial or promotional. Acetates, incomplete cover slicks and Compact Discs are ineligible. Titles are listed in descending order of value (naturally). Those with the same value are listed alphabetically by artist; two or more titles by the same artist with the same value are listed chronologically. An average value was taken from the suggested range of Near Mint values in the main listings of the book. That is, a near mint copy of that record could sell for quite a bit less or considerably more than the value listed below.

---

1. **BOB DYLAN**
   Columbia CS-8786   *(S)*   **The Freewheelin' Bob Dylan**   *1963*   **25,000.00**
   (Original pressings contain four songs— "Talking John Birch Blues," "Let Me Die In My Footsteps," "Rocks And Gravel" and "Gamblin' Willie's Dead Man's Hand"—deleted from all subsequent pressings. For more information refer to the article "The World's Most Valuable Album" above.)

   THE BEATLES
   Vee Jay SR-1062   *(S)*   **Introducing The Beatles** *(Title back cover)*   *1963*   **25,000.00**
   (First pressing with "Love Me Do." The back cover has the song titles in two columns." For more information refer to the article "The World's Most Valuable Album" above.)

3. **BILLY WARD & THE DOMINOES**
   Federal 295-94   *(10")* **Billy Ward & His Dominoes**   *1955*   **20,000.00**

4. **BOB DYLAN**
   Columbia CL-1986   *(M)*   **The Freewheelin' Bob Dylan**   *1963*   **15,000.00**
   (Original pressings contain four songs— "Talking John Birch Blues," "Let Me Die In My Footsteps," "Rocks And Gravel" and "Gamblin' Willie's Dead Man's Hand"—deleted from all subsequent pressings. For more information refer to the article "The World's Most Valuable Album" above.)

   THE MIDNIGHTERS
   Federal 295-90   *(10")* **The Midnighters: Their Greatest Hits**   *1955*   **15,000.00**

6. **IKE & TINA TURNER**
   Philles PHLPS-4011   *(S)*   **River Deep-Mountain High**   *1966*   **13,000.00**
   (No covers are known to have been completed. This was eventually issued by A&M in 1969.)

7. **THE BEATLES**
   Vee Jay SR-1062   *(S)*   **Introducing The Beatles** *(Ad back)*   *1963*   **12,500.00**
   (First stereo pressing with "Love Me Do" and "P.S. I Love You." The back cover features ads for 25 other Vee Jay albums)

   THE BEATLES / FRANK IFIELD
   Vee Jay LPS-1085   *(S)*   **On Stage** *(Portrait cover)*   *1964*   **12,500.00**
   (This second pressing cover features a full-color painting of the Fab Four in place of the cartoon of an eccentric British chap on the original.)

   THE BEATLES
   Vee Jay PRO-202   *(DJ)* **Hear The Beatles Tell All** *(White label promo)*   *1964*   **12,500.00**

10. **ELVIS PRESLEY**
    RCA Victor LOC-1035 *(M)* **Elvis' Christmas Album** *(Red vinyl)*   *1957*   **10,000.00**
    (Apparently another one-of-a-kind collectible pressed after hours by an employee.)

THE BEATLES
United Arts. UAS-6366 *(S)* **A Hard Day's Night** *(Black label on pink vinyl)* *1964* **10,000.00**

12. **THE BEATLES**
Capitol ST-2553 *(S)* **Yesterday And Today** *(First state butcher cover)* 1966 **9,000.00**
(Refer to the listings under THE BEATLES for a more detailed account of its origins.)

THE BEATLES
Apple SO-385 *(S)* **The Beatles Again** *(Alternate cover)* *1970* **9,000.00**
(Several alternate cover prototypes were designed for this album when it bore the working title of "The Beatles Again." Several graphic variations— including one design that had the front and back cover photos reversed— are known to exist. The suggested value in this edition refers to any of the possible variations.)

THE ROLLING STONES
London LL-3402 *(M)* **12 X 5** *(Blue vinyl)* *1966* **9,000.00**

15. **JOHNNY BURNETTE & THE ROCK 'N' ROLL TRIO**
Coral CRL-57080 *(M)* **Johnny Burnette & The Rock 'N' Roll Trio** *1956* **6,500.00**

16. **CHARLES BROWN**
Aladdin 702 *(10")* **Mood Music** *(Red vinyl)* *1952* **6,000.00**

JEFFERSON AIRPLANE
RCA Victor LSP-3584 *(S)* **Jefferson Airplane Takes Off!** *1966* **6,000.00**
(Original pressings contain "Runnin' 'Round This World" and alternate takes of both "Go To Her" and "Let Me In")

AMOS MILBURN
Aladdin 704 *(10")* **Rockin' The Boogie** *(Red vinyl)* *1954* **6,000.00**

AMOS MILBURN / WYNONIE HARRIS / CROWN PRINCE WATERFORD
Aladdin 703 *(10")* **Party After Hours** *(Red vinyl)* *1954* **6,000.00**

PRINCE
Warner Bros. 25677 *(DJ)* **The Black Album** *(2 LP promo)* *1987* **6,000.00**
(This promotional version of Prince's withdrawn album is actually two 12" records that play at 45 RPM and contains the entirety of the regular album.)

THE ROLLING STONES
London NPS-3 *(DJ)* **Through The Past, Darkly** *(Picture disc)* *1969* **6,000.00**
(Prototypes for a rejected picture disc back in '69. Two variations are known: one has the cover from "High Tide & Green Grass" on both sides the other has "High Tide" backed with Ten Years After's "Sssh.")

22. **FRANK BALLARD**
Phillips Inter.1985 *(M)* **Rhythm-Blues Party** *1962* **5,000.00**

THE BEATLES
Vee Jay SR-1062 *(S)* **Introducing The Beatles** *(Blank back)* *1963* **5,000.00**
(First pressing with "Love Me Do" and "P.S. I Love You." The back cover is completely blank, devoid of any printing.)

THE BEATLES / FRANK IFIELD
Vee Jay LP-1085 *(M)* **On Stage** *(Portrait cover)* *1964* **5,000.00**
(This second pressing cover features a full-color painting of the Fab Four in place of the cartoon of an eccentric British chap on the original.)

THE BEATLES
Apple KAL-1004 *(DJ)* **Yellow Submarine** *(Radio spots)* *1968* **5,000.00**

BOB DYLAN
Columbia PC-33235 *(DJ)* **Blood On The Tracks** *(Original test pressing)* *1975* **5,000.00**
(Original test pressings— issued in plain cardboard jackets— feature alternate takes of five songs of "Tangled Up In Blue," "If You See Her Say Hello," "You're A Big Girl Now," "Idiot Wind" and "Lily, Rosemary And The Jack Of Hearts.")

THE FIVE ROYALES
Apollo LP-488   *(M)*   **The Rockin' Five Royales** *(Purple & silver label)*   *1956*   **5,000.00**

28. **BOYD BENNETT**
King 395-594   *(M)*   **Boyd Bennett**   *1956*   **4,500.00**

THE FIVE KEYS
Aladdin 806   *(M)*   **The Best Of The Five Keys** *(Maroon label)*   *1956*   **4,500.00**

BIG JAY McNEELY
Federal 295-96   *(10")*   **Big Jay McNeely**   *1954*   **4,500.00**

SMILEY LEWIS
Imperial LP-9141   *(M)*   **I Hear You Knocking** *(Green vinyl)*   *1961*   **4,500.00**

PAUL McCARTNEY
Apple MAS-3375   *(DJ)*   **Ram** *(Mono promo)*   *1971*   **4,500.00**
(The label does not identify this as a promotional release but it clearly states that the album in "Monaural." In most cases it was was shipped to radio stations in the same cover as the regular stereo version, sometimes the two LPs were side by side in the same jacket.)

PRINCE
Warner Bros. 25677   *(S)*   **The Black Album**   *1987*   **4,500.00**
(This is the version prepared for commercial release in 1987 but pulled by Prince.)

THE ROLLING STONES
London NP-1   *(DJ)*   **High Tide & Green Grass** *(Alternate cover)*   *1966*   **4,500.00**
(This cover prototype has the same graphics as the released version except title on the front is on two lines [the released version has the title on three lines] and in radically different type.)

VARIOUS ARTISTS
Philles PHLP-100   *(M)*   **The Phil Spector Spectacular**   *1966*   **4,500.00**

36. **THE BEATLES**
Vee Jay LP-1062   *(M)*   **Introducing The Beatles** *(Ad back)*   *1963*   **4,000.00**
(First mono pressing with "Love Me Do" and "P.S. I Love You." The back cover features ads for 25 other Vee Jay albums.)

THE BEATLES
United Arts. UAL-3366 *(DJ)*   **A Hard Day's Night** *(White label promo)*   *1964*   **4,000.00**

THE BEATLES
United Arts. Help-Show *(DJ)*   **Help!** *(One-sided, open-end interview)*   *1965*   **4,000.00**

THE BEATLES
Capitol T-2553   *(M)*   **Yesterday And Today** *(First state butcher cover)* *1966*   **4,000.00**
(Refer to the listings under THE BEATLES for a more detailed account of its origins.)

THE CRICKETS
Brunswick BL-54038   *(M)*   **The Chirping Crickets** *(Yellow label promo)*   *1957*   **4,000.00**

BOB DYLAN
Columbia CL-1986   *(DJ)*   **The Freewheelin' Bob Dylan** *(White label promo)* *1963*   **4,000.00**
(For the story on this title, refer to the first listing of this list. This white label promo plays the second version with "Masters Of War," etc., but the front cover has a DJ title & timing strip listing the deleted tracks, including "Talkin' John Birch Blues.")

THE FENDERMEN
Soma MG-1240   *(M)*   **Mule Skinner Blues** *(Blue vinyl)*   *1960*   **4,000.00**

FRANK FROST & THE NIGHTHAWKS
Phillips Inter.1975   *(M)*   **Hey Boss Man!**   *1961*   **4,000.00**

THE MIDNIGHTERS
Federal 541   *(M)*   **The Midnighters: Their Greatest Hits** *(Red cover)* *1955*   **4,000.00**

GATEMOUTH MOORE
King 684   *(M)*   **Gatemouth Moore Sings The Blues**   *1960*   **4,000.00**

SOUNDTRACK
DCA Productions   *(DJ)* **Rock, Rock, Rock** *(With cover)*   *1956*   **4,000.00**
(Publisher's demo disc intended for inclusion in the soundtrack for the movie of the same name. The price here is for the rare version with a printed cover. The album was issued to most stations in a plain jacket.)

SOUNDTRACK
Universal Unlimited   *(10")* **Rock, Pretty Baby** *(Red vinyl)*   *1956*   **4,000.00**
(Promotional radio transcription from the film. Commercially issued by Decca.)

48. **JOHNNY ACE**
Duke DLP-71   *(M)* **Memorial Album For Johnny Ace** *(Red vinyl)*   *1961*   **3,500.00**

LLOYD GLENN
Swing Time 1901   *(10")* **Lloyd Glenn**   *1952*   **3,500.00**

ELVIS PRESLEY
RCA Victor   *(S)* **International Hotel Presents Elvis, 1969**   *1969*   **3,500.00**
(Complimentary boxed set presented to the hotel's dinner guests for Elvis' first show of the year. The box contains a letter of introduction and thanks from Elvis, Colonel Parker and RCA, which is essential for completeness and a variety of souvenirs and records generally available elsewhere. More than 95% of the value is for the box alone.)

ELVIS PRESLEY
RCA Victor   *(S)* **International Hotel Presents Elvis, 1970**   *1970*   **3,500.00**
(Complimentary boxed set presented to the hotel's dinner guests for Elvis' first show of the year. The box contains a letter of introduction and thanks from Elvis, Colonel Parker and RCA, which is essential for completeness and a variety of souvenirs and records generally available elsewhere. More than 95% of the value is for the box alone.)

HANG ON TO YOUR EGO!
The Many Lives Of The Rock's Greatest Album

In 1993, Capitol Records released *Good Vibrations—Thirty Years Of The Beach Boys,* a boxed set of five compact discs compiled by Mark Linnett, Andy Paley and David Leaf. This excellent overview of the group's career was warmly received by fans and reviewers alike, comfortably outselling the company's admittedly modest expectations. The set included a 60-page photo booklet annotated by Leaf, including the following astute observation: "In the 1960s, the Beach Boys created a body of work so commercially and artistically valuable that their records would simultaneously solidify rock's importance in the marketplace, confirm its validity as an art form, and challenge and overturn the conventions that governed artists in the music business."

That a claque of, ahem, aging observers continues to champion an album entering its fourth decade should surprise few. These include writers as well-known as Paul Williams, founder of *Crawdaddy,* the first magazine to take the "new music" seriously, and Timothy White, current editor of *Billboard,* along with such lesser luminaries as the author of *Goldmine's Rock'n Roll 45RPM Record Price Guide.* In a rather amazing tribute, the staff of writers and reviewers from England's *Mojo* magazine, many of them born years after its initial release, voted *Pet Sounds* as the #1 Rock album of all time in a 1995 survey!

Still, Leaf's statement expresses an opinion that should, at this point in time, be unimpeachable. But, in the less than formal atmosphere of rock'n roll historians, it is taken to represent the type of sentiments that one expects from the egoistic fanboys that seem to dominate the field's debates. Perhaps only The Grateful Dead cause the peevish polarizing of what should be levelheaded opinions as do The Beach Boys. And the gist of the argument for both sides generally lies in the recording and release of one album. . .

Brian Wilson's *Pet Sounds*

It was thirty years ago today, in May of 1966, that Capitol released *Pet Sounds,* the eleventh album from California's Beach Boys. The album carried a catalog number of T-2458 for its monaural pressing. Ths stereo version was designated DT-2458, indicating that a two-track master was not provided and the company was required to use its "Duophonic" method of electronically rechanneling the mono master into odious ersatz stereo. While the multi-tracks have always existed, Brian never made them available, even to trustworthy Chuck Britz, the Capitol engineer responsible for previous stereo mixes of Brian's material.

From the completion of the sessions, those involved in creating the music realized that this album represented a very different approach to record-making from a group with a very established sound. And, needless to say, for the bewildered folk in Capitol's promo department, it called for a new approach to record-selling. The core of the album was a cycle of ten interrelated songs that dealt with the transition from the innocence of young love ("wouldn't it be nice to live together in the kind of world where we'd belong") to the self-conscious reflection of experience ("it's so sad to watch a sweet thing die").

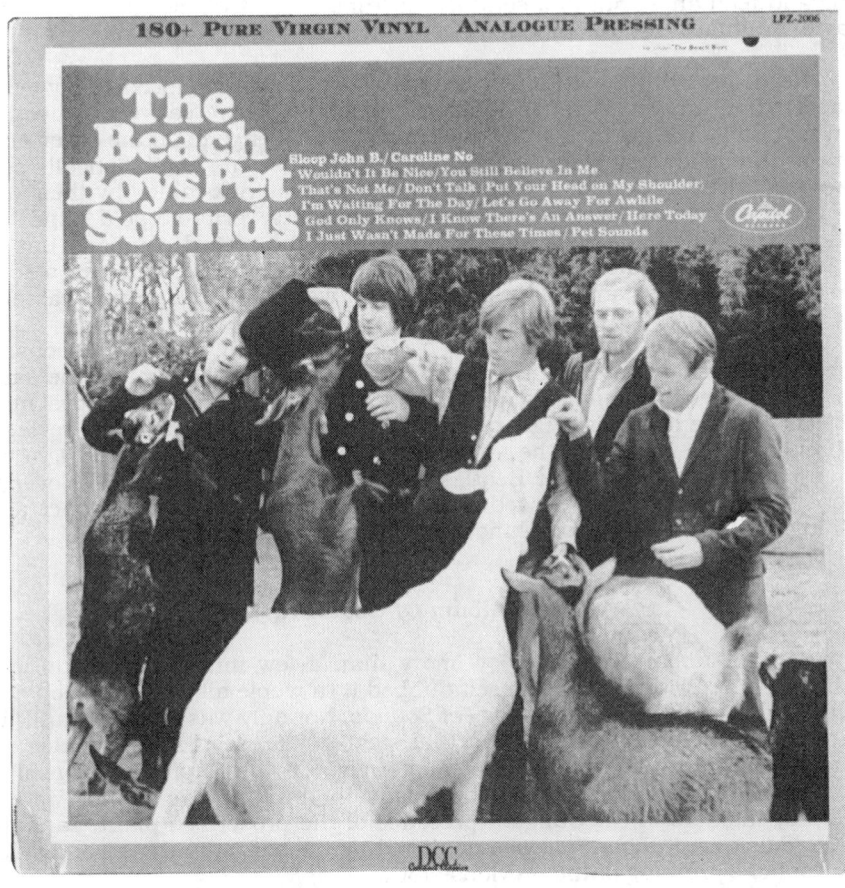

Pictured here is DCC's Compact Classic numbered, limited edition of Pet Sounds. I always believed that "audiophile" pressings should represent the best music on the best possible pressings. Instead, when the half-speed craze took off in the early '80s, the independent labels all went for the best sounding music, regardless of quality. And it had to be stereo. Thus, an album such as Pet Sounds, despite being admired as the greatest mono Rock album of its era (it recently was selected #1 by the writers of Mojo magazine in England), despite having quotable admirers such as The Beatles, despite being a precedent-shattering and precedent-setting recording achievement, despite this and more, such an album was not acceptable by the self-imposed standards of the these otherwise excellent companies. Finally, DCC has rectified the situation. (Refer to the text of "Hang On To Your Ego" for more information.) Now, if this caption reads a bit too much like a paid advertisement, remember, the best possible endorsement is a satisfied customer. And this customer intends to wear out several copies of this record. . .

Pet Sounds was the vision of one man, Brian Wilson. He wrote the music and worked closely with lyricist Tony Asher, honing each song to perfection. He arranged and produced every session, using Los Angeles' finest musicians in lieu of the five touring Beach Boys, who were busy conquering Japan. To the astonishment of those who participated in the sessions, he even taught the older, more experienced musicians their parts. More accurately, he showed them how to "unlearn" their musical predispositions so that the parts they played fit the aural schemata that filled his head. The young Wilson also sang all of the vocals, the dense, choir-like backing parts along with the complex lead lines. The result was an album of wondrous music that dealt with such secular topics as sexual longing and teen angst but in a soulful, spiritual, tone. And, despite the bravura display of multifaceted virtuosity, it still sounded like fun!

Regardless of its merits, Pet Sounds was problematic for virtually everyone involved on any level, professional and personal. The creatively competitive Wilson justifiably viewed it as ground-breaking, a challenge to all the other major movers in the heady pop music scene of the mid-'60s. The capitalistically competitive executives at Capitol just as correctly saw it as risk-taking by their West Coast clients, a group that had proven themselves a veritable gold mine. The direction of this new music intimidated not only the record company but the band itself, especially the more fractious members, setting the stage for a series of personal and professional confrontations that would last the group's career.

As for the precedents shattered by Pet Sounds and Capitol's response, it has been recited so often that the company had no problem accepting the daring do's of The Beatles but fought the progressive elements of The Beach Boys' music that it has become litany among fans and historians. Actually, a careful review of the chronology of events and the inferences gleaned from a bit of hindsight render this point moot. While The Beatles' music had grown appreciably over the previous three years, it had evolved gradually, record by record. And, once again benefiting by the obviousness of hindsight, the music evolved logically.

A Whole Album Of Good Stuff

It is true that Rubber Soul did blow more than a few minds during the early months of 1966. Brian Wilson himself dubbed it "a whole album with good stuff" and credited it as the inspiration for Pet Sounds. Not only was it "good stuff," but there was an ambience to the album that, gestalt-like, seemed far greater than the sum of its parts (of which there were twelve on the Capitol version of the album, fourteen on Parlophone's). The mystically introspective sounds were attributed by insiders to the pungent presence of the proscribed plant, cannabis. Still, the music on Rubber Soul was predicted by the songs on the second side of the Parlophone pressing of the previous album, Help!

Of course, we Yanks did not get to hear many of these: To the rest of the world, Parlophone issued Help! as the group's new album, their fifth, with the seven songs from the film on the first side and seven new, more ambitious, tracks on the second. In the States, Capitol issued it as a "soundtrack," combining the seven film songs with incidental music by George Martin's studio orchestra. This made the transition from Help! to Rubber Soul appear far more dramatic for Stateside fans than for the rest of the Beatlized world. This contributed mightily to the perception, and the enduring memories, of astonishing stylistic leaps in The Beatles' albums.

The first truly "far-out" sounds from the Fab Four were the psychedelic excursions of John Lennon and the overtly Indian influences on George Harrison's compositions being prepared for *Revolver,* an album that would follow in *Pet Sounds'* wake four months later in September. Even the threatening edge of experimentalism on *Revolver* was softened by the release of *Yesterday & Today* in July. This US-only compilation previewed three of the aforementioned Lennon tracks (against his will, an indication that the company's arrogance was not reserved for specific clients) alongside the first American appearance of leftovers from the Parlophone versions of *Help!* and *Rubber Soul.*

Thus, with *Pet Sounds'* release in the early summer of 1966, there was in fact precious little precedent for Capitol to be anything *but* uncomfortable with the plainly progressive sounds from a group they associated with deuce coupes, girls on the beach, and the warmth of the sun. Which, while not exonerating the company for its lack of foresight, nonetheless does explain their apparent lack of desire to, as they say in the biz, "get behind" the strange new album.

While it is evident that Capitol was taken aback by *Pet Sounds*, Brian *had* provided warning signals with a trio of singles. "The Little Girl I Once Knew" was issued during the latter weeks of '65 and, according to legend, failed to reach the top of the charts because of the reluctance of jocks and programmers to play a single with several moments of "dead space" in its decidedly daring arrangement and production. While the sound of this single and its lyrical content perfectly fit *Pet Sounds'* thematic and musical concept, it was not included on the album. David Leaf has aptly noted that "In retrospect, 'The Little Girl I Once Knew' was to *Pet Sounds* what 'Penny Lane' / 'Strawberry Fields' would be to *Sgt. Pepper.*"

"Caroline, No" was released in March '66. . . but not as the new Beach Boys' single. Instead, the label bore only the name of Brian Wilson, who was all but unknown to the majority of radio station personnel and listeners alike. Still, this brief, plaintive farewell to a love lost enjoyed modest movement on the national charts. There has been long running speculation that had this single been a hit, he may have opted to release the album as a solo project, the necessity of the group's voices voided by Brian's increasing mastery of overdubbing and his confidence in his abilities to sing all the parts.

This was followed in a matter of weeks by Brian's arrangement of "Sloop John B." It was the first release to showcase The Beach Boys' new "mature" sound, which jumped out at listeners in 1966. With the lead sung by Brian in a relaxed register, the harmonies, while still full, seemed positively subdued compared to former singles. The cause was the reigning in of the more adenoidal tendencies in the group's harmonizing, taming such instantly identifiable trademarks as Mike Love's nasal voicings and Brian's ethereally swooping falsetto. The fact that the song was an accepted folk standard instead of another of their patented teen fantasies also lent a degree of now necessary credibility to a group that was being dubbed the "ball-less wonders" by members of the increasingly hip circles dominating the international pop scene.

Poo-Pooed By The Big Boys

While "Caroline, No" played an essential part on the album, Capitol insisted on the inclusion of "Sloop John B" as a sales vehicle, even though the song played no part in the album's concept. Brian obliged and found a spot for it as the last song on the first side, neatly reversing the then common practice of kicking off an album with the big hit as the first song on the first side. To add further distance, it was further segregated, at least lyrically, from the rest of the album's songs by an instrumental. Although these three 45s had reached the Top 20, Top 40 and Top 5, respectively, still Capitol did not see any commercial potential in selecting a single from the similar sounding tracks on the album.

There *were* potential hits in the new material. Brian argued for the issuance of "God Only Knows," only to be poo-pooed by those who believed they knew better than the man who had already provided the company with eighteen Top 40 hits. After EMI called the label's hand by releasing the single in Great Britain, where it soared to the top of the charts. Capitol acquiesced and issued it domestically, but as the B-side to the more upbeat "Wouldn't It Be Nice." The group found their "new" single uncharacteristically (for the '60s) released months after the album. The fact that the single was a double-sided hit certainly vindicated Brian's projections and subsequently garnered enough attention to push *Pet Sounds* into the Top 10 on the LP charts.

July also saw the big boys at Capitol release the previously unannounced *Best Of The Beach Boys*, a compilation of singles and LP sides whose selection was without rhyme or reason, assembled without the cooperation of the group. When Capitol started meeting reorders for *Pet Sounds* by substituting copies of the hits package, retailers found themselves in the position of being unable to stock a Top 10 album at the height of its demand! While *Best Of The Beach Boys* received heavy promotion, *Pet Sounds*, with more than 250,000 copies sold, was placed in the commercially awkward but historically interesting position of achieving collectible, cult-like status at the very time it should have been a well-stocked item in every store in the country!

In 1969, The Beach Boys broke free of their contractual obligations to Capitol Records. The group dropped a lawsuit in which they claimed the label owed them in excess of $1,000,000, back royalties that had been kept from them through an archaic "breakage" clause in their contract. This also put a halt to the series of conflicts with the label that had hampered them since '66 (although it did not end the internecine differences). The Beach Boys accepted their release and acquired the masters and rights to six albums: *Pet Sounds, Smiley Smile, Wild Honey, Friends, 20/20,* and the now mythically unreleased *Smile.*

Broken Records & Broken Promises

The group signed with the artist-oriented Warner Bros/Reprise conglomerate. At the very least, Brian would certainly feel comfortable alongside such idiosyncratic, commercially irrelevant artists as Capt. Beefheart, Ray Davies, Randy Newman, Van Dyke Parks, Neil Young and Frank Zappa. Aside from their desperately needed hit-making abilities, The Beach Boys brought their new company a veritable treasure trove of a catalog with them. Their first album was the glorious *Sunflower*, the group's shining moment as a group. *Sunflower* was seen by some as the natural, if four years too late, follow-up to *Pet Sounds*. In Great Britain it was loudly hailed as "the Beach Boys' *Sgt. Pepper*" before becoming their poorest selling album to date.

Pet Sounds finally re-entered the market six years after its initial release as the first in a planned series of special double-albums that sold for a buck more than a single. Reprise paired the now recognized monophonic classic with the group's latest stereo recordings, the most musically anemic effort of their career. On the sixth anniversary of *Pet Sounds'* original release, the album was released as 2MS-2083 with the unwieldy title of *Carl & The Passions—So Tough / Pet Sounds*. Unfortunately, by coupling the group's weakest album with its best, Reprise and the band all but dared critics and consumers to compare the two and *not* find the current work inferior to their previous achievements. The series was unceremoniously cancelled.

1974 saw the phenomenal, and completely unexpected, multi-platinum success of Capitol's *Endless Summer*. This two-record compilation of '60s hits and misses spent more weeks on the charts than their previous ten albums combined! Reprise countered with a pair of two-fers, coupling *Friends* with *Smiley Smile* and *Wild Honey* with *20/20*, and reissuing *Pet Sounds* as a single album, again in mono, despite its stereo catalog number, MS-2197. Sales of the three packages were negligible and Reprise let it quietly go out of print. (And, of course, *Smile*, for which the group had accepted a $50,000 advance, was never handed over, despite several announcements in the '70s of its imminent release.)

With nary a word of advance publicity, Capitol leased the masters of the late '60s titles *back* from the group. The five titles were included in a line of budget reissues in 1980 as a part of a revamping of the company's entire catalog. *Pet Sounds* was once again available in a reasonable replication of the original green bordered cover as a "Capitol Re-Issue Monophonic" (SN-16156). Shortly after this release, the American record industry recognized the dawning of the digital age and negotiations with The Beach Boys for digital reissue rights were arduous. *Pet Sounds* again reentered vinyl twilight zone. . .

Still Not Quite Gold. . .

Pet Sounds first appeared as a compact disc in 1987 on Toshiba-EMI's Green Line series (CP28-1003). The Japanese manufacturer included a pair of bonus tracks, primarily "Hang On To Your Ego," a song that had undergone major lyric changes (reputedly to assuage the sensibilities of one of the other Beach Boys) to appear on the original album as "I Know There's An Answer." Also included was a snippet which featured Brian creating a wordless chorale as part of one of the album's vocal backing tracks. While this CD has not attracted the attention of many American fans, it is quite collectible in Japan.

Capitol followed a year later with a US pressing (CDP 48421 2) which topped the Japanese original by including a third bonus track, "Trombone Dixie," a New Orleans jazz-flavored instrumental. By this time, the album's reputation as a '60s classic was sufficient to send domestic sales of the CD into six figures. The compact disc's modest success pushed *Pet Sounds'* total sales past the 400,000 mark, gradually closing in on the half-million unit level and a coveted RIAA Gold Record Award.

Several other previously unreleased outtakes from *Pet Sounds*, graced the previously mentioned boxed set, *Good Vibrations* (CDP 0777 7 81294 2 8), notably the original version of "God Only Knows." While structurally similar to the released version, it features a lead vocal by Brian with an ending that featured a popishly baroque arrangement that would be used to outstanding effect on the group's final single of 1966! Also included were several more takes of "Hang On To Your Ego" that provided insight into Brian's working methods circa 1966.

In 1993, DCC Compact Classics issued a 24-karat gold-plated compact disc version of *Pet Sounds* for digitally seduced audiophiles. The CD was "prepared with the original unequalized monophonic master mixes" and remastered by Steve Hoffman in April of that year. More important for record collectors is DCC's numbered, limited edition LP on "180+ Pure Virgin Vinyl." Again mastered by Hoffman (in June 1995) utilizing an "all vacuum-tube cutting system," this is the finest sounding presentation of this music that we are likely to hear and a must-own for the discriminating listener. The DCC analog LP, catalog number LPZ-2006, and gold-coated compact disc, GZS-1035, both carry a list price of $29.95 but can be difficult to locate. To order direct from the company, call 800-301-MUSIC (and tell 'em Neal sent you).

Good Vibrations & Excitations

Scheduled by Capitol for release later in '96 is *The Pet Sounds Sessions: A 30th Anniversary Collection.* This boxed set of four CDs is being assembled by Leaf and Linnett with Brian Wilson and addresses several perceived "problems," including those of the stereophiles: Disc #1 contains the entire album from start to finish in its first "true stereo" mix! The rest of the first disc and all of the second contain, in Leaf's words, "a chronological audio documentary, in which we present highlights from each tracking session, in stereo, followed by a completed track without vocals." The third disc contains a "stack 'o vocals" section that features the album's vocal tracks sans backing instrumentals. It also showcases a dozen alternate mixes by Brian from 1966 rescued from the vaults, plus "a few surprises along the way." The fourth, or "bonus disc," contains the complete album in mono remastered in 1996 using a 24-bit HDCD process.

The 6" x 12" box includes a 42-page booklet similar to the one included in *Good Vibrations* that includes detailed session notes. Also included in this package is the 124-page "The Making Of Pet Sounds" which documents the album's genesis, completion, and the headaches involved in its release. Interviewed for this book were musicians and engineers who took part in the original sessions; both Brian and primary lyricist Tony Asher; Beatles producer George Martin; and former Fab Paul McCartney. In a neat quid pro quo, Paul, once perceived by Brian as his chief rival, cites *Pet Sounds* as the influence for *Sgt. Pepper:* "I played it for John so much that it would be impossible for him to escape the influence."

Another song was written by Brian and Mike at this time and recording began during the completion of the album's sessions. It was set aside and continuously reworked, eventually finding its way onto AM radio waves in the fall of '66 as the group's final single before the debacle that would be *Smile.* "Good Vibrations" topped the charts, turning the pop music world upside down, establishing The Beach Boys as a world-class Rock-With-A-Capital-R group and earning Brian Wilson a reputation as a genius. Appropriately, it is often cited as the #1 Rock single of all time.

For a brief while, "Good Vibrations" was considered for *Pet Sounds.* Heard as the album's coda, it would have brought the songs' primary theme, that of love found and lost and wisdom achieved through pain, around full circle. Its presence would have given the album a cyclical motif, replacing the yearning resignation of "Caroline, No" with renewed expectancy. It would have left the listener aware that, when one is receptive, good vibrations and excitations *(sic)* are available everywhere, "on the wind that lifts her perfume through the air," and anytime, especially "in the morning when the day is new."

RECORD COMPANY LABEL DIRECTORY

This section outlines the many graphic changes record companies' labels have undergone through the years and will assist the reader in identifying original albums from later pressings. I have kept the explanations as brief and to the point as possible. The dates and catalog numbers during the label transitions are approximate; you may find that you have pressings of an album on an earlier label than I have listed. I would certainly appreciate having any such errors of this type called to my attention so that future editions can be corrected.

One area that needs a little exposition is that of promotional releases. The most common method of printing promotional records has been to press them with white labels with plain black print, hence the term "white label promo." As these white labels are obvious manifestations of the company's special attention, they are the most popular with collectors. Some labels used their regular label, or a slightly modified version, and had "Audition Copy" or "Promotional Copy" incorporated into the label's typesetting; these are also promos. In this book records with such notices stamped on or with a sticker affixed to the label or cover are not considered promos (although this will change).

Promotional records are usually pressed in small runs on quality vinyl—often at plants that specialize in small print runs—making it a better pressing than the stock copies. Needless to say, they are quite collectible and generally command a premium above the normal value of the record, although the premium may be minimal. To list each and every promo version of the albums in this book would practically double the size of the book. Instead, the reader should assume that a promo of most records exist and, in pricing, that such a promo is worth no less than the value listed for the stock copy and, generally, no more than twice the listed value. Listed exceptions are those albums that are more common than the stock version or those promos that are worth considerably more than the stock or, in a very few cases, where the promo is different or noteworthy.

In a money saving move, many companies dropped the practice of printing special promo records and simply took to designating stock copies as intended for promotional purposes by affixing a disclaimer to the cover usually reading "For Promotional Use Only-Not Intended For Sale." This took the most common form of stamping the disclaimer in [black] ink or embossing it with gold print. For a while in the mid-'60s Columbia affixed a gold "promo" sticker to the cover. Generally, these do not command a great deal of attention from collectors. Certainly a slight premium may be attached to a record so designated, but these disclaimers do not, for the most part, set the hearts of collectors afire.

One exception is Capitol Records, who, during the '60s, often added the word "PROMO" or "FREE" in perforated lettering in the upper right corner. While this is a blatant damage to the artwork, albums so marked do draw collectors' attention and regularly fetch a reasonable premium. Capitol also took to the practice of punching a hole in the corner of the cover and handing these out as promos. *These so-called "promo-holes" are not recognized by this book as worth attention.* Anyone with a hole-punch can construct all of such promos he or she might need to soak gullible collectors.

When large amounts of records were deleted in the mid-'60s, many of which were monos, most companies simply "cut out" the number from their catalogs and sold the remaining copies to wholesalers, where they ended up in "5 & 10s" around the country for 99¢. By the '80s, companies began clipping the corners of deleted titles; this was originally a small clip but grew to the point where huge portions of covers were left lying on the floor after the record was sent out to the distributors. Almost without exception cut-out marks on albums reduce any record's value. The sole exception being Warner Bros. and Reprise, who had the novel idea of placing a small brass rivet in the upper left corner of their cut-outs during the waning '60s. These tend to attract some collectors, who will pay a regular price for such a cut-out.

And then, of course, there are the budget labels. . . Many labels sprang up over the years that specialized in leasing masters of previously released material, usually of artists who were no longer hot, and all too often issuing albums in the cheapest possible manner: poor mastering, poor pressings on low grade vinyl, etc. These labels include Crown, Diplomat, Grand Prix, Guest Star, Spin-o-rama, Wyncote, and the undisputed king of low budget labels in America, Pickwick. While some of these *did* collect important material (Crown began by issuing great R&B) most of them issued albums of less than collectible consequence. Springboard seemed to flood the department stores of America with a slew of new titles in the first few years of the '70s, many compiling sides that had not previously appeared on albums and which have become modestly collectible. Needless to say, most of the albums have little value and are almost impossible to sell, even sealed, for more than a few bucks.

<u>A&M</u>   From 1963 through mid-'73, A&M used a brown label. From then until 1985 the label was a silver gray with a large brown "AM" fading into the background.

<u>ABC-Paramount</u>   From 1956 through 1961 (#101-400) a black label was issued with ABC-Paramount on top and "A Product of Am-Par Record Corp" on the bottom. From 1962 through 1966 (#400-560s) the black label reads "A Product of ABC-Paramount Records Inc." During 1966-67, the logo was changed to "abc records" in a box at the top. Throughout these years, mono albums bore an "ABC" prefix; stereo had an "ABCS" prefix. White label promos were issued.

From 1968 to 1974, the label was black with "abc" on top and "New York, NY" on the bottom. Other labels include black with the logo in children's blocks in and purple on gold from 1973 to 1978. In 1979 ABC came under MCA's control.

<u>Ace</u>   From inception through the early '60s a black label was issued with "Ace" in silver print on top. This was replaced by a black label with "ACE" in an oval. The final releases on this label carried a predominantly blue label with "ACE" in white letters in a blue oval.

<u>Aladdin</u>   Early 10" LPs had blue (on the bottom) and silver (on top) label with a blue print "Aladdin" in an arc across the top. Later 10" albums have a solid blue label with silver print, "Aladdin" arcing across the top, and four stars on each side "Long Playing Microgroove" on the bottom. 12" LPs have dark red labels with silver print. Some 12" LPs have the blue label used on the latter 10" albums.

Apple   From November 1968 through early 1970 the Apple label read "A subsidiary of Capitol Industries, Inc" on the bottom. This was replaced with "Mfd. by Apple Records, Inc" from 1970 until 1974. The final run of albums from 1974-75 included an "All Rights Reserved" disclaimer.

Arista   From 1972 through 1976 (#4000-4105) the label was light blue with "Arista Records" beneath the logo on top. For a few months in late 1976 and early 1977 the blue label read "Arista" beneath the logo on top. This was replaced with a black label (#4110-4205). From 1978 until 1984 the company returned to a blue label with "Arista" on the left side of the logo on top. Beginning in 1985 a black & blue label was used with "Arista" floating above a mountain skyline.

Asylum   For the first few releases (#5051-5066) the label was white with the company's logo in a circle on top. In 1973 the label used a sky with clouds motif (#5067-5099, 1000-1040s). This label was modified slightly in 1975 to include the Warner Bros. logo in the lower right; this label ran through 1984. Note: A solid blue label was used briefly in 1976. In 1985 the label turned black & orange.

Atco   A subsidiary of Atlantic, initial pressings from 1958 through the latter part of 1961 (#101-138) were on a solid yellow label with a harp in the upper left. From 1961 through 1968, mono albums had a gold & gray label with a white stripe through the center with "ATCO" in large print (#139-226). Stereo albums were purple & brown with the white stripe (#139-256).

In 1969, after the demise of mono, all albums returned to a solid yellow with an 1841 Broadway, NYC address printed on the bottom. When Atlantic was sold to the Warner conglomerate, the address was changed to 75 Rockefeller Plaza, NYC. From 1978 through 1984 the company used a solid gray label; since then Atlantic has used a gray label made up of countless tiny "Atco" logos.

Atlantic   10" LPs have a yellow label with black print. The early 1200s (through at least #1211) have the same yellow label. From 1950 through mid 1960, mono albums were issued on a black label with silver print (1212-1332 and 8000-8040). In 1958 select titles were mixed into stereo and issued on a green label, all of which are difficult to find.

A transition label, referred to as the "bullseye label," was in use briefly from approximately 8026-8036: Mono albums had an orange, purple & black fan around the spindle hole with "Atlantic" in an orange & purple band on top. For stereo albums there is a green & blue border around the label; the fan around the hole is also green & blue. There may have been no new titles released on this bullseye label, only reissues of previously issued titles.

From 1960 through late '61 (#8032-8059 and 1333-1378) Atlantic mono LPs were orange & purple while stereo albums were green & blue. Each label had a white band through the center with a white pinwheel— or "fan"— logo in a black box on the right side. From the end of 1961 through '66 (#8060-8125 and 1379-1463) the fan switched to black on white with "Atlantic" running vertically alongside it. From 1966 through 1968 (#8126-8178 and 1464-1499) "Atlantic" ran horizontally beneath the fan. After 1968 the label, now stereo only, switched to a green & orange with the company's 1841 Broadway, NYC address on the bottom.

From 1973 through 1975 a Rockefeller Plaza address appeared at the bottom, and from 1975 through the late '80s "A Warner Communications Company" appeared on the bottom. White label promos were issued from the mid-'60s on.

Bang   From inception through the mid-'70s Bang used a red & white label with a derringer on top. This was replaced in the early '70s with a yellow label. From 1973 through 1977 a sky with clouds design was employed. This was followed by a light brown label with a red logo on top.

Bearsville   Initial releases had a light brown label with "Distributed by Ampex" on the bottom. From 1971 through the mid-'70s the label read "Distributed by Warner Bros." on the bottom. 1977 until 1981 saw no distribution motto; however, in 1981 a "3300 Warner Blvd" address was added.

Bell   From inception through 1969 a blue label was issued with silver print. The label was silver from 1970 through 1975.

Big Tree   In 1970 the label was red with "Product of Big Tree Enterprises Limited" on the bottom. This was replaced by "Distributed by Ampex" in 1971-72; "Distributed by Bell" in 1972-73; and "Distributed by Atlantic" from 1974-76.

Blue Thumb   The first four LPs had a black label. From the fifth release through approximately the mid-60s the off-white label had a thumb print on top. This was finally replaced with a purple label with the "abc" logo on top in 1974.

Bluesville   Originals on this subsidiary of Prestige have bright blue labels with the logo in block print on top. Second pressings had flat blue labels with the Prestige trident logo on the right side.

BluesWay   During the first year, 1967-68, the label was blue. This was replaced by a black label with a blue perimeter.

Brother   The Beach Boys' label saw one LP issued in 1967, *Smiley Smile*, manufactured by Capitol. The label was resurrected in 1970 under the Warner /Reprise umbrella. During 1970-76 the pale yellow label read "A Subsidiary and Licensee of Warner Bros., Inc" on the bottom. From mid-'76 through 1979 the label read "A Division of Warner Bros. Records, Inc" on the bottom.

Brunswick   From 1950 through at least 1963, Brunswick used a black label with silver print. Yellow label promos were issued. From late '63 or early '64 through 1972, the company switched to a black label with a rainbow through the center and "A Division of Decca Records" along the perimeter.

Throughout these years mono albums bore a "BL" prefix, while stereo LPs carried a "BL-7" prefix. Since 1972 a black label was used with the rainbow and "Manufactured by Brunswick Record Corp" along the perimeter.

Buddah   From 1968 until 1973 the multi-color label had a silhouette of a Buddah on the bottom. From 1973 through 1978 an orange label was used with a smiling Buddah on the bottom. This was replaced by a black label with the Arista logo on the bottom.

Cadence From inception through 1962 a maroon label was used with a silver top. During the company's final year the label was red with a black border.

Cadet   From 1965, when Cadet took over Argo, through 1968, the company used a blue label. In 1969 a blue label fading into white was issued. A pink & yellow label was in effect in the early '70s, replaced briefly by a pink & orange label.

Calendar   During 1967-68 the label was orange with Zodiac figures around the perimeter. During late 1968-69 it was orange with a "K" on top. The label then became Kirshner Records.

Camden This budget subsidiary of RCA Victor repackaged material from the parent label's catalog, sometimes using obscure 45 and EP tracks. Camden's original label was a pink/purple. From 1958 through 1964, a blue label was used with a purple perimeter. From 1964 until 1968, a blue label was used with a dark blue perimeter fading into light blue.

Throughout this time mono albums bore a "CAL" prefix; stereo titles had a "CAS" prefix. Stereo numbers ending with an "e" denoted reprocessed stereo. From 1969 until 1975 a dark blue label was in effect. In 1976 the entire line was turned over to Pickwick.

Cameo From 1959-61 the label was orange with a cameo logo on top. From 1961 through the rest of the decade it was a red & black label with the cameo on the right. In the late '60s a purple label was used with the cameo on top.

Capitol   From 1949 through 1953 (#100-344), they basically issued a green label with "Long Playing Microgroove" on the bottom. Ten-inch albums bore an "H" prefix. From 1953 through 1958 (#345-1050s) a turquoise label with "Long Playing" on the bottom was in effect, with a gray or flat black label also used during this time. The twelve-inch albums generally carried a "T" prefix although certain titles carried a "W." Yellow label promos were issued.

In 1958 Capitol introduced its first stereo titles on its new label: Glossy black with a rainbow perimeter and the Capitol dome logo on the left side. For a brief period, new releases had the mono on the turquoise label and its stereo counterpart on the black "rainbow" label.

In 1958-59 (#1021-1225) Capitol switched the mono over to the new glossy black "rainbow" label with "Long Playing High-Fidelity" printed on the left side. From 1959 until 1962 (#1225-1660s), the black/rainbow label had the logo and a silver line on the left. Black label promos were issued with "Not For Sale" on the bottom. The "T" and "W" prefixes were used for monos, an "ST" or "SW" was for stereos.

A "DT" or "DW" indicates that the album was electronically rechanneled stereo using Capitol's patented "duo-phonic stereo" process method of altering the mono signal beyond recognition. Special releases with gatefold covers received "KAO" or "MAS" prefixes with either an "S" or "D" added for stereo.

From 1962 through 1969 (#1658-2999 and the new series beginning with 100 through the early 200s), Capitol continued the glossy black label with the logo on top, using the "T"/"ST" prefix. Note: On each of these black rainbow labels the copyright data is along the lower perimeter in white print on the black label and reads "Mfd. by Capitol Records, Inc., U.S.A." A later variation of this label used briefly in 1969 reads "Mfd. by Capitol Records, Inc. A Subsidiary of Capitol Industries, Inc., U.S.A." In 1984 Capitol returned to the classic black rainbow label of the '60s except this time the copyright data was on top in black print in the rainbow.

After 1969 the situation is rather confusing: A [lime] green label was used from mid-'69 through mid-'72 (#208-11105). A red label with a purple target-like logo on top was used from mid-'72 through mid-'75. Simultaneously, an orange label was used with "Capitol" on the bottom from late 1972 through late 1975. In late 1975 an "Unauthorized duplication" disclaimer was added to the perimeter print on top of the orange label from late 1975 through early 1978. From mid-'78 through 1983 the label was purple. During this time a variety of prefixes were used, although "ST" remained the primary designation.

Capricorn   In 1970 the label was a yellow Atco label with "Capricorn Records Series" on the bottom. In 1971 it was pink. From 1972 through 1974 the label was a plain tan. From 1975 until 1978 it was light brown with a large goat facing right. This was replaced by a light brown label with a [different] goat facing left.

Casablanca   In 1974 the label was blue with "Manufactured and Distributed by Warner Bros. Records, Inc." on the bottom. In 1975 and early 1976 the blue label read "Manufactured and Distributed by Casablanca Records" on the bottom. From 1976 through 1977 (#7026-7050) the label featured a desert scene with three camels in the foreground. 1976 until 1981 (#7050s-7250s) saw the camels replaced with a film crew and "Manufactured and Distributed by Casablanca Records" on the bottom. Since 1981 the label has read "Manufactured and Distributed by Polygram Records" on the bottom.

Challenge   Through the mid-'60s the label was blue with "Challenge" in an oval on top. During the '60s the label carried a plain "CHALLENGE" logo on top.

Chancellor   Initial releases in 1958-59 had pink labels; after that, black.

Checker   From inception through 1966 (the 1400 series and 2900-2996) the label was black with silver print although some were maroon with silver. In 1966 (#2997-3001) a light blue label was used with checkers on top. From 1967 through the early '70s a blue label that fades into white at the bottom was in effect. Finally, a blue label was used with a purple band through the center.

Chess   Through 1966 (#1400-1490s), Chess used a black label with silver print although some were blue with silver. White label promos from these years are rare. During 1966 they used a black label with a chess piece on top. From 1967 through the early '70s a blue label that fades into white at the bottom was used.

From 1972 until 1977 the label was orange with a blue band through the center. The 50000 and 60000 series used then was under the direction of the GRT Corporation. Later issues were owned by the All Platinum Record Group. The '80s had a blue label with a checker-like effect along the lower perimeter.

Chrysalis   From 1972-76 (#1000-1130s) the label was green. In 1977 a blue label fading up into white was used with an "All Rights Reserved" disclaimer added in 1982.

Clarion   This was a budget subsidiary of Atlantic that repackaged old material.

Colgems   The red & white label in 1966-67 read "TM of Colgems Records" beneath the logo on top. This motto was dropped in 1968.

Colpix   From inception through the early '60s the company used a gold label with "Colpix" in large red letters on top. In 1963 a strip of movie film was added. Later pressings were on a blue label. Stereo numbers are decidedly rarer than their mono counterparts.

Columbia   From 1949 through 1955 Columbia used a red label with gold print and "Long Playing" on the bottom (#500-650). A variety of prefixes, "CL," "GL" and "ML," were used before the company settled on "CL." From 1955 through 1962 (#650 through the early 1800s) mono albums had red labels with six white-on-black, highly stylized camera "eye"-on-a-tripod logos on each side of the label.

From 1962 through 1965 (#1780-2379) the white-on-black eye logos were replaced with two white eye logos, one on each side of the spindle hole, and read "Guaranteed High Fidelity" on the bottom. From 1965 through 1968 (#2380-2811) the red mono label read "360 Sound Mono" in white on the bottom. Note: Some later pressings from 1967-68 read "Mono" only.

Columbia apparently began manufacturing stereo albums (the 8000 series) in early 1959; the initial 8000 numbers were assigned randomly as mono albums were mixed into stereo and released. By 1960 designating stereo was simple: CS-6800 was added to the mono catalog number to denote stereo. Thus, Columbia CL-2372, The Byrds' *Mr. Tambourine Man*, would be CS-9172!

8000-8579 featured the red label with the six eye logos. From 1962 through 1965 (#8630-9128) stereo labels featured the two white eye logos with "360 Sound Stereo" in black on the bottom. Two arrows, one on each side pointing up, were added to the "360 Sound Stereo" in the last 1/3 of 1963. From 1965 through 1970 (#9130-9999, 1-30, and 30000-30050), stereo labels read "360 Sound Stereo" with the arrows in white at the bottom.

After 1970 the red label reads "Columbia" in gold letters a half-dozen times around the perimeter. The only way to note a first pressing is by the prefix in the catalog number, which have included, but are not limited to, "CS," "C," "G," "KC," and "PC," although some of these prefixes have been used on reissues of earlier titles. Columbia subsidiaries include Epic and Harmony.

Coral   From inception through at least late 1963, Coral albums were issued on a maroon label; blue label promos were issued. From late '63 through '68 a black label was used with a rainbow center and read "A Subsidiary of Decca Records." From 1968 through 1970 "A Subsidiary of MCA" replaced the Decca motto. Throughout these years, mono albums bore a "CRL" prefix; stereo albums, a "CRL-7." Refer to MCA.

The illustrations above may help to clarify certain differences in Columbia labels: The design used throughout the '50s and into 1962 (illustrated here by Adventures Of The Heart) is often referred to as the "eyes logo" label as it carried three highly stylized, white-on-black camera logos on each side of the spindle hole (a total of six per label). This was modified and the trio of eyes were replaced by a single white-on-red eye logo. During this period, stereo labels were first issued with the "360 Sound" motto in black print on the bottom without an arrow on each side (Bob Dylan), then black with arrows (Another Side Of Bob Dylan), and finally, in white with the arrows (Johnny's Newest Hits). In 1970, the label was altered again, this time with a series of six tiny eye logos interspersed around the label with a half-dozen "Columbias," all in gold print.

Cotillion From 1969 till late 1972 this Atlantic subsidiary used a grey label with an "1841 Broadway" address on the bottom. The address was changed to "75 Rockefeller Plaza" in the mid-'70s. Finally, Cotillion switched to a purple label.

Crown Arising from the ashes of Modern Records, Crown used a black label with silver print through 1960, often reissuing the earlier label's titles. By 1960, Crown specialized in low budget reissues, pressed on the cheapest vinyl available and often with completely misleading credits. Second labels were gray, followed by another black label with the Crown logo in color. When Crown began issuing albums in rechanneled stereo, the sound was among the worse ever developed. Consequently, the fake stereo titles are avoided by all but completists.

Curtom From 1968 until 1972 the plain yellow label had a Broadway address on the bottom; 1973 until 1975 saw the address changed to 7th Ave. After the mid-'70s the yellow label sported a psychedelic multi-color top.

Decca From 1949 through 1954 Decca had a black label with gold print (the early 8000s). From 1954 through 1963 (through approximately 4450) they had a black label with silver print. Pink label promos were issued for both.

From late '63 through '66 (#4500s-4830s), the label was black with a rainbow stripe and reads "Mfrd. by Decca Records." From 1967 through 1971 "A Division of MCA" was printed beneath the rainbow. White label promos were issued.

For approximately one year, 1971-72, "Mfd. by MCA" was added. After that, reissues appeared on the MCA label. Mono albums bore a "DL" prefix; stereo albums with a "DL-7." By 1973 MCA had entirely eaten up the label and its product.

Del-Fi Original label (1201) was blue with a black border containing blue circles. The next label (1202-1246) was basically black with blue/gold diamonds around the border. Reissues from the '80s have a gold label.

DeLuxe A King subsidiary, early pressings have a black label with silver print. The catalog numbers were issued as part of the King line. That is, DeLuxe 570, was preceded by King 569 and followed by King 571.

Deram From inception through the early '70s the label was basically white with "London" beneath the Deram logo on top. During the '70s the white label had a brown top. The '80s versions read "Manufactured by Phonogram, Inc" on top.

Dolton From 1959 until 1962 the mono 2000 series and the stereo 8000s had a light blue label with a Sunset Blvd. address on the bottom. From late 1962 through late 1965 Dolton used a dark blue label with a fish logo on the left. This was replaced in 1966 by a black label with a "D" logo on the left. By 1967 Dolton was owned by Liberty.

Dore Initial releases in the early '60s were on a light blue label with a feather on top. The '70s version was a dark blue with a larger feather on top. The late '70s saw a black label with a still larger feather.

Dot During 1955-56 (the 3000 series), Dot issued a maroon label with "Gallatin, Tennessee" on the bottom. During late 1956 or early '57 the address was "Hollywood, California." From 1957 through 1967 (#3030-3830s), a black label was used with "Long Play" and "Dot" in script on the top. In 1968 "A Division of Paramount" appeared on the bottom. Throughout these years, mono albums bore a "DLP" prefix with a 3000 number; stereo albums bore the same "DLP" but were a 25000 series; i.e., the last three digits of the mono and stereos were identical.

From 1968 through 1970 the Paramount mountain logo appeared in a box with the Dot logo at the top of the label. From 1970 through 1974, the Dot logo appeared in a box on top with "A Division of Famous Music Corp" on the bottom. During 1974 until 1978, a purple & yellow label was in effect. After 1978 select Dot titles were reissued on ABC.

<u>Duke</u> From inception through 1961 the label was purple & yellow. During the remainder of the decade the label was orange.

<u>Dunhill</u> From 1965 through 1968 (#50000-50020s) the label was black with "Dunhill" on top with "Distributed by ABC Records" on the bottom. From 50020s - 50031 the label read "A Subsidiary of ABC Records." From 1968 through 1974 (#50032-50170s) both "Dunhill" and the "abc" logo were in a box on top. In 1973 a black label was used that featured children's blocks on top. During its final year, 1974-75, the label was purple. By 1975 Dunhill was a part of ABC.

<u>Elektra</u> During the '50s a white label was used with an electron logo on top. This was replaced with a grey label with a small guitar player on top. From 1961 until 1966 a gold label was used with a large guitar player on top. The gold label was replaced from 1966 until 1969 (the early 4000s through the early 5000s) with a flat brownish label. During 1969-70 the label was red. Throughout the rest of the decade the label was multi-colored with a butterfly in the upper right. This was replaced by a red label with a Warner Bros. logo on the bottom. After 1983 the label was black.

<u>End</u> The label was originally gray with a dog on top that read "Product of End Music, Inc" at the bottom. This was replaced with a gray "dog" label that read "A Division of Roulette Records, Inc" on the bottom. This was replaced in the early '60s with a label that had "End" on end on either side.

<u>Enjoy</u> A subsidiary of Fire, Enjoy has gold labels with black print.

<u>Epic</u> As Columbia's primary subsidiary, from inception through 1962 Epic carried a yellow label with black lines radiating out along the perimeter; stereo issues read "Stereorama" across the top. During 1962-63, a yellow label was used with "Epic" appearing eight times around the perimeter for mono albums; stereos read "Stereo" and "Epic" three times each around the perimeter.

From 1963 through 1965 (#24/26040s-24/26150s) a yellow label was used with "A Product of CBS" on the bottom. From 1965 through 1972 (#24/26150s-31992) the same yellow label deleting the CBS motto was in print. From 1973 until 1978 Epic issued an orange label and replaced that with a black label in 1978.

Initially, mono albums bore an "LG" or "LN" prefix. When titles from the 3000 series were issued in stereo they carried a "BN" prefix and were part of the 500 series. By the '60s, the bulk of the releases were either in the LN-24000 mono series or the BN-26000 stereo series.

<u>Etiquette</u>   Original labels were red with a Tacoma, WA address on the bottom. Reissues have a purplish red label but bear a Seattle, WA address and the copyright date along with a 1984 on the bottom.

<u>Everlast</u>   A subsidiary of Fire, Everlast has orange labels with black print.

<u>Excello</u>   The company's original orange label was replaced in the latter '60s with a white label with a colored arrow on top.

<u>Fantasy</u>   From inception through the 1960s, mono albums had a red/maroon label. 10" albums bore a number "3" prefix. 12" albums began with 200 and also bore the "3" prefix. When the label added stereo in the early 1960s, they used an 8000 series number; these originals had a blue label with silver print and were pressed on stiff, non-flexible vinyl. White label promos were issued.

Fantasy began pressing its albums on colored vinyl with their 10" series; copies of these albums have been seen on red, blue, green & purple vinyl; some were on rainbow-like pressings of different colors; these are rather rare. With the inception of their 12" line in 1955, all new albums were pressed on red vinyl. This book assumes that *all* of the original mono releases from 1955 through 1957 were pressed on thick, dark red vinyl, often with a mottling effect of the red dye in the vinyl. For a brief period, approximately twelve months during 1957-58, new releases were pressed on black vinyl. By '58 red wax was back. . . Pressings from this point on were still on the thick vinyl but were a lovely, translucent red. In-print titles were pressed on this wax before reverting to black in the early '60s.

When Fantasy began issuing stereo in 1962, these were pressed on the same thick vinyl as the mono only using a translucent blue. These would then revert to modern black vinyl for the duration of the decade.

A popular title could have been pressed first on thick, dark red vinyl then on the thick black vinyl of the '50s with little or no "grooveguard" around the disc's perimeter to keep the stylus from sliding off. Third pressings would be on the thick translucent red vinyl while final mono pressings from the early '60s would have been on thinner, more modern black vinyl with the now familiar grooveguard. Then a blue stereo pressing in 1962 followed by a black vinyl stereo reissue through the rest of the decade.

From 1972 through 1978, Fantasy used a brown label on both their new original releases and their various reissues, including the jazz label, Milestone. Eventually, Fantasy absorbed a number of labels and *their* subsidiaries, including Prestige, New Jazz, Bluesville, Moodsville, Swingville, Riverside, Debut, Milestone, Pablo and Galaxy. Much of this music was reissued as new titles on Milestone in the '70s (often as annotated two-fers) or as part of their Original Jazz Classic series ("OJC" prefix) of reissues in the '80s.

<u>Federal</u>   A King subsidiary, Federal albums have black labels with silver print. The catalog numbers were issued as part of the King line. That is, DeLuxe 530, *Big Jay McNeely In 3-D*, was preceded by King 529 and followed by King 531.

<u>Fire</u>   Original labels were white with red print (100-102). Later pressings have red labels with black print. Refer to Enjoy; Everlast; Fury.

Flip   Flip used a blue label with silver print.

Folkways   Original Folkways 12" albums were issued in thick, cardboard jackets with a textured finish, usually black. The front cover sheet was affixed to the jacket and wrapped around the spine with approximately 3" of the cover sheet overlapping onto the back. This bit usually contained the album's contents and related data. Later pressings have full front and back cover slicks affixed to a white cardboard jacket with liner notes on the back.

Forum   Subsidiary of Roulette used to reissue previous albums. While Forum had its own numbering system, the reissues kept the same titles, contents and covers.

Fury   A subsidiary of Fire, Fury LPs have yellow labels, black print, and a logo that looks like a horse emerging from a tornado.

Gee   In the '50s the label was red label; they switched to a gray label in the '60s.

Geffen   In the early '80s the cream label had technical information printed around the perimeter. In 1984 the print was not used and in 1985 the label was changed to black.

Gordy   A purple label with "Gordy" in yellow script on top was used from 1962 through 1967. After 1967 the purple label had a yellow slash through the middle with the logo on the left side.

Harmony   This budget subsidiary of Columbia repackaged material from the parent label's catalog. Harmony used a maroon label from 1957 through 1959 (#7000-7150). For the next twelve years they issued a black label.

Harvest   A yellow & green label was used from 1969 until 1976. From 1977 until 1985 the label had an EMI Records Ltd. copyright notice on the bottom.

Hi   Hi's first release (12001) had a black label with "Hi" in red print outlined in silver. They then switched to an orange & white label through 1976 (12/32002 through stereo 32089). This was replaced by a plain gray/silver label with "Hi" on the left. A few titles in 1972-73 were issued with a white label with the "Hi" logo on top with the "London" logo beneath it. After 1976 the label was black.

Hickory   Through the early '60s a black label was used with "Hickory" in silver print on top. From 1964 until 1972 a black label with colored stripes on top was in effect, and from 1973 until 1975 the label was brown with the MGM logo on the right. The rest of the '70s saw a purple & yellow label with the "abc" logo on top.

I.R.S.   From the late '70s through the first years of the '80s the label was white. It was replaced in 1981 by a silver label and, again in 1985 by a goldish label.

Imperial   From 1950 through 1958 (#9000-9040s) Imperial featured a maroon label. From 1958 through 1964 (#9045-9267) they used a black label with stars and colored rays on top. White label promos were issued. A black & pink label was in effect from 1964 through 1966 (#9268-9320s). From 1966 through 1969, a black & green label was used with "Product Of Liberty Records" on the bottom.

Mono albums bore an "LP" prefix and were part of the 9000 series. When stereo was added in the late '50s, these albums carried the same "LP" prefix but were part of the 12000 series. For the first one hundred and seventy-four releases (12000-12173), stereo albums were mixed and released according to perceived need. That is, the stereo release numbers do not correspond with the catalog numbers of the original mono albums.

With 12174 on, the mono and stereo catalog numbers coincided (for example, the mono was LP-9174 while the stereo was LP-12174, etc.) Original stereo albums featured a black label with silver print; later pressings had the black label with the stars. After Liberty was purchased by United Artists in 1970, "Liberty/UA, Inc" was added to the label.

International Artists Each of this company's original '60s albums were reissued in 1979 with identical covers and labels. The originals are on thick vinyl; reissues are on the thinner vinyl and have "Masterfonics" stamped in the trail-off vinyl.

Island In 1972-73 the label had a sunray motif with the logo. In 1974 the label featured a stylized figure on water skis. From 1975 until 1978 the label was black. From 1978 until 1981 it was orange & blue. In 1982-83 the label had a purple top with a skyscraper on the left. After 1983 the blue or black label noted the Warner Communication Corporation along the bottom.

Jamie In 1958 the label was yellow. From 1959 until 1967 it was white & gold and from 1967 through 1970, brown & orange.

Janus From 1970 until 1976 (the 3000 series and the early 7000s) the label was light brownish gold. In 1977-78 the label was a reddish orange.

Josie From inception through the early '60s the label was a cream color with blue print. Through the latter '60s and into the '70s the label was light brown.

Jubilee From inception through 1958 Jubilee used a blue label. From 1958 through 1960, a black label was used with "jubilee" in a silver "sunburst" oval on top. Throughout the '60s, a black label was used with "jubilee" in a multicolored "sunburst." Mono albums carried a "JGL" prefix; stereos had a "JGS."

Judd Label owned and operated by Judd Philips, brother to ol' Sam. Labels are purple with silver print. Labels also had an "NRC" on them, indicating distribution by National Recording Corporation.

Kama Sutra From 1965 until 1969 (#8000-8070s) the label was yellow. From 1969 until 1972 (#2000-2050s) the label was pink. After 1972 the label had a forest scene on top.

Kapp From 1956 through 1959 Kapp used a maroon or blue label. A black & blue label with a "K" logo was in effect from 1959 through 1962. A black & blue label with a red major's hat was used from 1962 through 1964. From 1964 through 1971, the label was black with the major's hat on top.

Throughout these years, mono albums bore a "KL" prefix and were part of the 1000 series; white label promos were issued. Stereo albums were designated with a "KS" and a 5000 number. An orange & purple label was used during 1971-73.

King 10" LPs have dark red labels with silver print. 10" albums bore a "295" prefix for the suggested retail price of $2.95.

12" albums through most of the 600 series have black labels with silver lettering and, most importantly, the "KING" logo on top was 2" wide from "K" to "G" in thin print. White label promos from these years are very rare. The first 12" albums carried a "395" prefix through 1960.

Covers: Original covers (#500 through approximately 610) have the logo in a box in the upper right with "King" in script and "HiFi" in block print. From 1958-60 (#610-690), the logo was an ellipse with "KING" in block letters. For the last few titles in the 600 series and the first few 700s 1960 through 1962, the logo read "High Fidelity" with "KING" in open block letters.

From late 1960 or early '61 (the early 700s) through 1966, the black crownless label remained except the "KING" logo on top was noticeably larger, with thicker print that made it 3" wide. The few stereo albums from this time had blue labels. White label promos from these years are rare. Covers: From 1960 through 1962 (early 700s-810), the logo read "High Fidelity" with "KING" in open block letters. From 1963-66, the logo had a crown atop the "KING" in open block letters.

From 1966 through the mid-'70s a blue or black label was used with a crown on top. Covers: From 1966-68 (through the 1040s), the logo had a crown atop "KING" in open block letters. After 1969, the logo was a stylized "K" with "KING" in capital letters as the K's leg. Throughout the rest of the label's run a brownish gold or black label with a "K" logo on top was in service.

Kirshner From 1969 until 1973 the label was the same as the latter Calendar label: Orange with a "K" logo on top. After 1974 it was white with a multi-color top.

Laurie The original label (1002) was gold with black lettering, "Laurie" in a semi-circle on top and "Mastersound" around the bottom. After that it gets confusing: The labels of originals and reissues are essentially the same except on the original pressings the dots in the five points of the star are large with plenty of white space. On later pressings the dots are noticeably smaller with considerably less white space.

LeGrand The original '60s releases have a red & gold label without a crown on top. Reissues from the '80s have a crown on top and a white band in the middle.

Liberty From inception through 1960 (#3000-3130s) Liberty boasted an aqua blue, or turquoise, label with silver print. When stereo albums, many of which were reprocessed, were issued on the 7000 series in the late '50s, a black label was used with silver print. Throughout these years, mono albums bore an "LRP" prefix; white label promos were issued. Some titles were issued as part of the 6000 series with an "LRS" prefix. Stereo albums were designated with "LST."

For the first one hundred releases (7000-7099), stereo albums were mixed and released according to perceived need. That is, the stereo release numbers do not correspond with the catalog numbers of the original mono albums. With 7100 on, the mono and stereo catalog numbers coincided (for example, the mono was LRP-3100 while the stereo was LST-7100, etc.)

A black label with a rainbow and a gold logo was used from 1960 through 1966 (#3150-3440 and 13/14000s). From 1966 through 1969 (#3440-7620s and 13/14000s) "Liberty Records, Inc" was added beneath a blue logo. Off-white or cream label promos were issued. After Liberty was sold in 1970, "Liberty/UA, Inc" was added beneath the blue logo. In the '80s a gray label was in use.

London   From inception through 1964, mono albums had maroon labels with silver print and featured an "London/ffrr" (the latter an abbreviation for Full Frequency Range Recording) logo in a box on top. (Note: The ffrr was followed by a drawing of an ear in the logo box.) White label promos were issued. During 1964-65, mono albums dropped the "ffrr" from the logo on the maroon label. From late 1965 through their deletion in 1967, mono labels were red. Throughout these years, mono albums bore an "LL" prefix and carried a four digit number.

When stereo was added in the late '50s and early '60s, a rich, deep blue "ffrr" label was used. From 1963 through 1965, stereo LPs had a deep blue label with "London" in silver print on top. From 1965 into the early '70s, the label was still deep blue but "London" appeared in blue print in a silver box on top. During the '70s, the label was a noticeably lighter shade of blue and, for reissues, the vinyl was comparably thinner. Throughout these years, stereo releases had a "PS" prefix and a three digit number, usually dropping the first number from the mono designation.

Mainstream   Original albums in 1965-66 bore a light, silvery-blue label. White label promos were issued. Later pressings had a "Red Lion Production" in the upper right.

MCA   From 1973 through 1978 (#2000-2300s) a black label was used with a rainbow. A light brown label with a darker perimeter was used from 1977 until 1979 (the 3000 series and the early 5000s). After 1980 the label showed a blue sky & clouds motif. Note: A blue label with rainbow was used on the MCA reissues.

Mercury   Original albums in 1949 on the 1000 series had a black label with gold print. From the mid-'50s through 1963 (#20000-20700) mono albums had a black label with silver print and a plain logo on top. Mono albums carried an "MG" prefix; yellow label promos were issued. The first stereo albums (the SR-60000 series) appeared in 1957 with a black label with silver print. From 1961-64 (#20600-20900) the label for mono and stereo was black with an oval logo on top.

From 1964 through 1968 (#20900-61190) a red label was used with Mercury's head on top. White label promos were issued. A red label with twelve oval logos around perimeter was used from 1969 through 1973 (#61200-61300s and 600-670s). During 1973-74 (#680-on) Mercury issued a red label with seven oval logos around perimeter. A colored label with a skyscraper was in print from 1974 through 1982 (the 1000 series). After 1982 the label was black with "Marketed by Polygram" on the bottom.

Mercury's budget label was Wing and they distributed several others, primarily the Norman Granz labels, Clef, Down Home, Norgran and Verve through 1960, along with Savoy and Regent.

MGM   Original MGM albums of the '50s (#3000-3770s) have a yellow & black label. From 1960 through 1968 (#3770s-4515) MGM used a black label with a multicolor logo. Yellow & white label promos were issued. Throughout these years, mono albums bore an "E" prefix; stereo albums carried an "SE." From 1968 through 1976 the label was a blue & gold swirl label with "A Division of Metro-Goldwyn-Mayer" on the bottom. From 1976 on the blue & gold swirl label had a street address on the bottom. Yellow label promos were issued.

MGM's subsidiaries include Metrojazz and later the budget label, Metro. In 1961 they purchased Verve from Norman Granz, altering that label's cataloging system. For more information refer to Verve below.

Minit   Through most of the '60s the label was orange. This was replaced by a black label in the late '60s and early '70s.

Modern   10" LPs have black labels with silver print. The 12" albums have black labels with silver print. "Modern Record" appears in block print on two lines on top with "Telesonic Sound / Ultra High Frequency / Made In Hollywood U.S.A." on the bottom. Refer to RPM.

Monument   1961-62 releases had a copper & white swirl label. This was replaced in 1962-63 with a white & rainbow swirl label. From 1963 until 1976 a light green label was used with a gold perimeter and a Henderson, Tennessee, address on the bottom. From 1966 until 1971 the Tenn. location was dropped. A brownish orange label was used from 1971 until 1976. This was replaced in 1976 with a black label. Finally, a silver label was used in the early '80s.

Motown   Some original labels were white. From 1962 on Motown used a blue label with a map pinpointing Detroit at the top of the label. On original pressings during 1962-63 the map extended from the East Coast to Kansas; there was a W. Grand Blvd. address beneath the map. Original pressings on this label (600-62?) did not have any yellow in the logo!

These were reissued with yellow added to the logo. From 1963 until 1969 the map was scaled down to extend from Pennsylvania to Indiana, and the W. Grand Blvd. address was printed at the bottom. From 1969 until 1983 "A Product of Motown" appeared on the bottom in lieu of the Detroit address. After 1983 the label notes MCA as the distributor.

Musicor   Initial pressings in 1962 were on a brown label. A black label with "Distributed by United Artists" on the bottom was used from 1962 into 1964. The United Artists reference was dropped from mid-'64 through 1969. During the first half of the '70s the label was orange; later, the label was green & yellow.

Ode   From 1968 until 1970 the label was yellow. During 1970-71 it was white & silver with "Ode 70" in the upper right. From 1971 until 1975 the white & silver label specified "Ode Records Inc." Finally, a light brown label with the Epic logo was in effect from 1975 until 1978.

Paramount   In 1969 the label was gray with "A Division of Paramount Pictures" on the bottom. In the early '70s the gray label read "A Division of Famous Music." A few titles in 1971-72 featured a blue label. Note: This company is not affiliated with ABC-Paramount.

Parkway In 1960-61 the label was orange with a "harp, horns & score" logo on each side. From 1961 until 1966 the label was orange & yellow with two harps on top. During 1967-68 the label was gold.

Parrot From 1965 until 1971 the label was black with "Distributed by London Records, Inc" on the bottom. From 1972 until 1974 the black label read "A Product of London Records."

Philips From inception through 1963 (#001-120s) Philips used a black label with "Chicago 1, Illinois" on the bottom. From 1964 until 1966, the black label had "Vendor: Mercury" on the bottom. From 1966 until 1970, the black label was used with no disclaimers on the bottom. Throughout this time, mono albums bore a "PHM" prefix and were part of the 200-000 series; stereo titles had a "PHS" prefix and were part of the 600-000 series. Gold or white label promos were issued. From 1970 until 1974 a black label was used with "Manufactured and Distributed by Mercury" on the bottom.

Polydor From 1969 until 1978 the label was red with no street address. From 1978 until 1982 the red label carried a Seventh Ave. address on the bottom.

RCA Victor From 1950 through 1954, RCA Victor albums had a green label. For one year, 1954-55, the company switched to a glossy black label with Nipper the dog on top in outline only. The 10" albums bore an "LPT" or "LPM" prefix and were issued with a 3000 number.

From 1955 through 1963 (LPM 2000-2700s) the classic shiny black label with the full-bodied Nipper on top appeared with "Long 33 1/3 Play" on the bottom. During 1963-64, (LPM 2700s-2999), "Mono" was printed on the bottom, which was ultimately replaced by "Monaural" from 1964 until 1968 (LPM 3000-3900s). Note: Some albums issued in 1966-67 read "Mono Dynagroove."

Stereo albums from 1958 through 1963 (LSP 2000-700s) had a shiny black label with the full-bodied Nipper on top with "Living Stereo" on the bottom. From 1964 through 1968 (LSP 3000-4000s) only "Stereo" appeared on the bottom. Note: Some albums issued in 1966-67 read "Stereo Dynagroove."

From late 1968 through 1971 (LSP 4000-4460s) an orange label was issued on stiff, non-flexible vinyl. Many, if not most, of these were reissued with identical labels on RCA's ridiculously flimsy "dynaflex" vinyl. From 1971 through 1976 (LSP 4460s-1039) the same orange label was in effect but with "dynaflex" printed on the bottom. During 1975-76 the label was a light brown label. In 1976, the label was again black except Nipper was now located in the upper right at approximately 1 or 2 o'clock.

Reprise Initially Frank Sinatra's pet project, Reprise was incorporated into Warner Bros. within a few years. From inception through 1968, Reprise used a pink, gold, & green label with a large steamboat in the upper left (#6000-6280s). Note: Reprise had a jazz series that was yellow, red, & green with an angel in the upper left in print during the early '60s. From 1968 through 1970, a brown & orange label was used with a smaller steamboat and the "W7" logo on top (#6280s-6400s and 2000-2025). White label promos were issued.

Throughout this time, mono titles on the 6000 series had an "R" prefix; stereo titles were originally issued with an "R6" and then an "RS" prefix. This applied to the 1000 series, basically reserved for Sinatra. Eventually, the mono 1000s had an "F" prefix while the stereos had an "FS." During 1970-76 a brown label was used without the "W7" logo (the early 6400s on). White label promos were issued.

Roulette Original issues in 1957-58 (#25000-25050) had black labels. From 1959 through 1962 (#25050-25180 and 52000-52050) a white label was issued with crisscrossed color bars. For a brief period in 1962-63, an orange & pink label was used. After 1963 Roulette used an orange & yellow label with a roulette wheel design. Throughout this time, mono albums bore a "R" prefix; white label promos were issued. Stereo titles had a "SR" prefix. Since 1977, the orange & yellow roulette wheel label shows "Made in USA by Roulette Inc" at the bottom.

RPM A subsidiary of Modern, LPs have black labels with silver print. "RPM" appears in block print on two lines on top with "Telesonic Sound / Ultra High Frequency / Made In Hollywood U.S.A." on the bottom.

RSO From 1973 until 1981 a light brown label was used with a red cow logo on top. This was replaced by a silver label with a red cow in 1981.

Scepter The original label (501) was red with "Scepter" in black script outlined in silver. From 1962 until 1971 the label was orange with an oval-like center, although a few titles had solid white or red labels. In 1972-73 a multicolor label was in use on general releases with the special "Citation Series" carrying a yellow label. From 1974 until 1976 the label was blue.

Score A subsidiary of Aladdin, LPs have a dark red label. At the top is "Score" in an oval with "Full Range Fidelity" beneath it.

Shelter The first dozen titles in 1971-72 (#8900-8910) had a red label with a Superman-like logo on the left. From 1972 through the latter part of 1973 the red label had a blacked out Superman logo on top. In 1974-75 a gold label was used with "Distributed by MCA Records, Inc" on the bottom. In 1976 a yellowish gold label had "Distributed by ABC Records" on the bottom. From 1977 until 1979 the label had a crescent moon along the left side.

Sire From 1968 through 1970 a white label was used with both the Sire and London logos on top. Since then, a yellow label was used with a blue or purple stylized "S" on top. During 1970-71 the label read "Distributed by Polydor Records" on the bottom.

From 1972 until 1974 the label read "Distributed by Famous Music Corp." From 1974 until 1976 it read "Distributed by ABC Records." During the rest of the '70s the label read "Marketed by Warner Bros." In the '80s the Warner motto was joined by a "3300 Warner Blvd" address.

Smash From 1961 through 1968 a flat red label was used with black print. From 1968 until 1971 the red label carried a Mercury logo in an oval on top.

Soul This Motown subsidiary's first releases (701-702) had a white & red label. This was immediately changed to a purple label in late 1965.

Specialty   From 1957 through the early '70s the label was gold with a black top. The '80s reissues had a white label with a black top.

Stax   From 1962 through 1968 the label on mono albums was blue with a stack of records on top; stereo albums were yellow with the stack. From 1968 until 1971 the yellow label had a finger-snapping logo in a blue box on the left and then in a brown box. Since the mid-'70s the label was purple fading into white.

Sue   From 1961 through the mid-'60s the label was orange; later titles and reissues are black.

Sunset This budget subsidiary of Liberty repackaged material from the parent label's catalog. Original releases through 1969 had a black & blue label that read "A Division of Liberty Records" on the bottom. After 1970 the same label read "Liberty/U.A." on the bottom.

Tamla   Original labels (220-231?) were white with a black & purple record overlapping the purple globe. There was a brief transition label, similar to the original, except tan & yellow, that may have only been used on a couple of [first?] pressings. These are rarer than their white label counterparts.

During 1961-63 the label was yellow with the overlapping record/globe on top. From 1963 until 1968 the yellow label showed two discs on top, one a record and one with the company imprint. After 1968 the yellow label had a brown top.

Tampa: Original labels through 1957 were black with colored vinyl pressings. As I have not been able to identify all of these, the reader will find one listing for these titles. Later black vinyl pressings have pink labels. Stereo pressings apparently also exist, although, again, information at this time is sketchy.

Threshold From 1970 until 1973 the label was white. This was replaced with a blue label in 1973.

Tower   This subsidiary of Capitol used a dull orange label from 1965 until 1968. Several titles were reissued in 1968 on a striped label. Mono albums carried a "T" prefix while stereo LPs were "ST" and rechanneled stereo, "DT."

Track   From 1967 until 1971 the label was black; during 1972, it was silver. After 1973 the label was a dark brown.

20th Century Fox   From inception through the early '60s, the label was a light blue with "20th Fox" on top. From the early '60s through the early '70s, a black label was issued. During the '70s the label changed to aquamarine. From 1977 through the '80s, a light brown label was used with spotlights on top.

United Artists In 1958-59, U.A. used a red & black label. In 1959 mono albums had red labels, while stereos were blue. A black label with a large "UA" logo on top was briefly issued in 1960. From 1960 through 1968 (#3120-6640) the label was black with "United Artists" in a box on top.

From 1968 through 1970 (#6640-6710s) the label was purple & orange. White label promos were issued. Throughout this period, mono albums (the UAL 3000 and 4000 series) and stereos (UAS 6000s and 5000s) had a "UAS" prefix.

During 1970-71 (#6710-6700s and early 5500s and 5200s) the label was black & orange. In 1971-75 (#6780 on and 100-540) the label was a light brown. From 1975 through 1977 (#540-760) "Music & Record Group" was added to the bottom of the brown label. After 1977 a "sun burst" design was used on the label.

Valiant   During the first half of the '60s the label was blue; during the latter half it was red.

Vanguard   From inception through 1963 (the 9000 mono series) Vanguard used a maroon label with silver print and a horseman logo on top. For the first one hundred and forty-one releases (2000-2140), stereo albums were mixed and released according to perceived need. That is, the stereo release numbers do not correspond with the catalog numbers of the original mono albums. With 2141 on, the mono and stereo catalog numbers were the same with a "7" added to the stereo number For example, the mono was VRS-9141 while the stereo was VSD-79141, etc.

Stereo albums (both the 2000 and 79000 series) had a black label with silver print. From 1963 through 1970 the company issued a gold-brown or silvery-gray label with a white horseman logo on the bottom. White label promos were issued. Throughout these years, monos bore a "VRS" prefix while stereos had a "VSD." During the '70s a marble "swirl" effect label was issued.

Vee Jay   The first few albums (#1000-1012) had maroon labels with a thin silver line around the perimeter. From 1013 through 1022, the labels were maroon with a thick silver line; the few stereo releases were gray with black print. From 1960 through 1963 a glossy black label was used with a rainbow perimeter and the Vee Jay logo in an oval at the top of the label (#1010s-1070s and the 3000 series). From 1963 through 1965 (#1060-1070s) the glossy black rainbow label featured the logo in brackets. During 1965-66, a flat black label was used with silver print. Throughout these years Vee Jay's basic prefix was the common "LP." White label promos were issued.

When stereos were issued they bore either an "LPS," SR" or "VRS" prefix. Note: Stereo Vee Jay albums are very rare; while this book notes the staggering difference between some monos and stereos, the necessary data is not currently available to note all of these rarities. Thus, when happening across a stereo Vee Jay bear in mind that it may be rarer than the prices in this book indicate. . .

When Vee Jay went bankrupt in 1966, the demand for their product remained and was met illegally. Many titles remained available throughout the '70s with black labels on pressings that are dramatically inferior to the originals. In fact, they resemble barely professional counterfeits: the covers are photo-reproductions of the originals, and the pressings are abominable, with poor sound and noticeable noise from recycled vinyl. While the most common was Introducing The Beatles, poorly reproduced Jimmy Reed albums and several jazz titles proliferated.

During the '70s "VJ International" and a "Vintage Series" appeared. During the '70s and the '80s, a red label with the brackets logo was also used.

<u>Vik</u>   This RCA subsidiary had black labels with a multicolor logo on top.

<u>Virgin</u>   From 1972 until 1975 the label was a full color picture of two young women— one must suppose they are the artist's, ahem, ideal virgins— with "Dist. by Atlantic Recording Corp." on the bottom. From 1975 until 1978 it read "Distributed by CBS Records." After 1978 the label was white.

<u>Volt</u>   From 1967 until 1969 the label was yellow. From 1969 until 1973 it was blue. After 1973 the label was brown.

<u>Wand</u>   Through most of the '60s (#650-690s) the label was white with a black top. From 1970-74 the label had a marble effect. After 1974, it was a dark orange.

<u>Warner Brothers</u>   From 1958 through 1962 (#1200-1470) Warner Bros. used a gray label with a black & yellow logo on top for mono albums. From 1962 until 1965 (#1470-1620) a gray label was used with a black & white logo on top. During this period stereo albums carried a gold label.

From 1966 through 1968 (#1920-1730) both the mono and the stereo releases had a gold label. From 1968 through 1970 a green label was used with the "W7" logo on top. Throughout these years, mono albums carried a "W" prefix; stereos had a "WS" prefix. White label promos were issued. During 1970-72, the "W7" on the green label was changed to a "WB" logo. During 1973-75, the label featured a Burbank street scene. From 1978 through the '80s, a tan label was issued.

<u>White Whale</u>   From 1965 until 1970 (#7100-7120s) the label was solid blue; after 1970 it was blue with concentric white circles.

<u>Wing</u> This budget subsidiary of Mercury repackaged material from the parent label's catalog. From inception through the '50s Wing had a blue label with silver print and the "Wing" logo in an oval on top, often with "Jazz" above it. Several titles were issued simultaneously on Mercury and Wing. Throughout the '60s, when Wing was exclusively a budget label, a blue or black label was used with "Mercury" above the "Wing" logo. Mono albums were on the 12000 series with an "MGW" prefix, while stereo LPs carried an "SRW" prefix on the 16000 series. From 1970 through 1971, a blue label featured both the Wing logo and the oval Mercury logo alongside it on top.

<u>World Pacific</u>: In 1957 Pacific Jazz changed its name to World Pacific; both new titles and older catalog titles were issued on the new imprints. From 1960 until 1965, the Pacific Jazz label was back, starting all over with number "1." From 1965 until 1970, both Pacific Jazz and World Pacific ran, with the later issuing non-jazz material covering the gamut from rock to pop to international. Both companies used a black, orange, & yellow label. During the late '70s and early '80s, the company used a blue & green "waves" design for the label.

<u>"X"</u> The RCA subsidiary had white labels with a huge red "X" on top.

A. B. SKHY

MGM SE-4628	(S)	A. B. Skhy	1969	4.00	10.00
MGM SE-4676	(S)	Ramblin'	1970	4.00	10.00

AARON

Eastern	(S)	Music By Aaron	1974	14.00	35.00

ABBA

Abba is a Swedish group consisting of Agnetha Faltskog, Benny Andersson, Bjorn Ulvaeus and Anni-Frid "Frida" Lynstad. The group name is taken from the letters of the four members' first names.

Atlantic SD-18101	(S)	Waterloo	1974	1.00	5.00
Atlantic SD-18146	(S)	Abba	1975	1.00	5.00
Atlantic SD-18189	(S)	Abba's Greatest Hits	1976	.80	4.00
Atlantic SD-18207	(S)	Arrival	1977	.80	4.00
Atlantic SD-19164	(S)	The Album	1978	.80	4.00
K-Tel NU-9510	(S)	The Magic Of Abba (TV advertised sampler)	1978	4.00	10.00
Atlantic PR-300	(DJ)	Abba	1978	12.00	30.00
Atlantic SD-16000	(S)	Voulez-Vous	1979	.80	4.00
Atlantic SD-16009	(S)	Abba's Greatest Hits, Vol. 2	1979	.80	4.00
Atlantic SD-16023	(S)	Super Trouper	1980	.80	4.00
Atlantic SD-19332	(S)	The Visitors	1982	.80	4.00
Atlantic SD-80036	(S)	The Singles	1982	.80	4.00
Atlantic PR-432	(DJ)	A Collection Of Hits	1982	12.00	30.00
Atlantic PR-436	(DJ)	The Abba Special (2 LPs)	1983	20.00	50.00
Atlantic SD-80142	(S)	I Love Abba	1984	.80	4.00

ABDNOR, JOHN HOWARD [THE JOHN HOWARD ABDNOR INVOLVEMENT]

Abnak ABST-2072	(S)	Intro To Change	1968	6.00	15.00

ABRAHAMS, MICK

A&M SP-4312	(S)	The Mick Abrahams Band	1971	4.00	10.00

ABSTRACTS, THE

Pompeii SD-6002	(S)	The Abstracts	1968	6.00	15.00

AC/DC

AC/DC is an Australian group fronted by brothers Angus and Malcolm Young.

Atco SD-36-142	(S)	High Voltage	1976	1.00	5.00
Atco SD-36-151	(S)	Let There Be Rock	1977	1.00	5.00
Atlantic LAAS-001	(DJ)	Live At The Atlantic Studios (Counterfeits exist)	1977	24.00	60.00
Atlantic SD-19180	(S)	Powerage	1978	1.00	5.00
Atlantic SD-19212	(S)	If You Want Blood You've Got It	1978	1.00	5.00
Atlantic SD-19244	(S)	Highway To Hell	1979	1.00	5.00
Atlantic SD-16018	(S)	Back In Black	1980	1.00	5.00
Atlantic SD-16033	(S)	Dirty Deeds Done Dirt Cheap	1981	1.00	5.00
Atlantic SD-11111	(S)	For Those About To Rock We Salute You	1981	1.00	5.00
Atlantic SD-80100	(S)	Flick Of The Switch	1983	1.00	5.00
Atlantic PR-562	(DJ)	Flick Of The Switch Interview Album	1983	16.00	40.00
Atlantic SD-80178	(S)	'74 Jailbreak	1984	1.00	5.00

ACCENTS, THE

RCA Victor LSP-4251	(S)	Yesterday, Today And A Touch Of Tomorrow	1970	4.00	10.00

ACCOLADE

Capitol ST-597	(S)	Accolade	1970	6.00	15.00

ACE

Anchor 2001	(S)	Five-A-Side	1975	1.00	5.00
Anchor 2013	(S)	Time For Another	1975	1.00	5.00
Anchor 2020	(S)	No Strings	1977	1.00	5.00

ACE, JOHNNY

Duke DLP-70	(10")	Memorial Album For Johnny Ace	1955	750.00	1,500.00
Duke DLP-71	(M)	Memorial Album For Johnny Ace	1956	250.00	500.00

(Original covers are orange & black without a playing card on the front.)
— Duke albums above have purple & yellow/orange labels.—

Sweden's ABBA was Agnetha Faltskog, Benny Andersson, Bjorn Ulvaeus, and Anni-Frid Lynstad. The group was one of the major success stories of the '70s in terms of sales. That the records were a marvel of a type of white pop music that sacrifices passion for technical perfection seemed utterly irrelevant to their fans. While the astronomical sales of their LPs mean that today, nearly twenty years after the fact, the supply greatly outstrips the demand for the more mundane artifacts of their career, items such as this eponymously titled promotional sampler are much more difficult to find than the value assigned would indicate.

Label & Catalog #		Title	Year	VG+	NM
Duke DLP-71	(M)	**Memorial Album For Johnny Ace** (Red vinyl)	1961	See note below	
		(Red vinyl pressings have a suggested NM value of $2,500-4,500.)			
Duke DLP-71	(M)	**Memorial Album For Johnny Ace**	1961	80.00	200.00
		(Later covers are red & black and have a playing card on the front.)			
		—Duke albums above have orange labels.—			
Duke DLPX-71	(E)	**Memorial Album**	1974	8.00	20.00

ACE SPECTRUM

| Atlantic SD-18143 | (S) | **Low Rent Rendezvous** | 1975 | 1.00 | 5.00 |

ACKLES, DAVID

Elektra EKS-74060	(S)	**Subway To The Country**	1969	3.20	8.00
Elektra EKS-75032	(S)	**American Gothic**	1972	3.20	8.00
Columbia KC-32466	(S)	**David Ackles' Five & Dime**	1973	3.20	8.00

ACKLIN, BARBARA

Brunswick BL-754129	(S)	**Great Soul Hits**	1968	10.00	25.00
Brunswick BL-754137	(S)	**Love Makes A Woman**	1968	8.00	20.00
Brunswick BL-754148	(S)	**Seven Days Of Night**	1969	8.00	20.00
Brunswick BL-754156	(S)	**Someone Else's Arms**	1970	8.00	20.00
Brunswick BL-754166	(S)	**I Did It**	1971	8.00	20.00
Brunswick BL-754187	(S)	**I Call It Trouble**	1972	8.00	20.00
Capitol ST-11377	(S)	**A Place In The Sun**	1975	4.00	10.00

ACROBAT

| T.M.I. 1004 | (S) | **Acrobat** | 1972 | 5.00 | 12.00 |

ADAMS, FAYE

Warwick W-2031	(M)	**Shake A Hand**	1961	600.00	900.00
Zion 2104	(M)	**Faye Adams Sings The Lord's Prayer**	196?	20.00	50.00
Savoy 14398	(S)	**Faye Adams**	1976	4.00	10.00

ADAMS, J. T.

Bluesville BVLP-1077	(M)	**Indiana Avenue Blues**	1964	30.00	75.00
		—Bluesville albums above have bright blue labels with silver print.—			
Bluesville BVLP-1077	(M)	**Indiana Avenue Blues**	196?	12.00	30.00
		—Bluesville albums above have blue labels with a trident logo on the right side.—			

ADAMS, MIKE, & THE RED JACKETS

Crown CLP-5255	(M)	**Twist Contest**	1962	10.00	25.00
Crown CST-255	(S)	**Twist Contest**	1962	12.00	30.00
Crown CLP-5312	(M)	**Surfer's Beat**	1963	10.00	25.00
Crown CST-312	(S)	**Surfer's Beat** (Colored vinyl)	1963	40.00	100.00
Crown CST-312	(S)	**Surfer's Beat**	1963	12.00	30.00
		—Crown albums above have gray labels.—			

ADDRISSI BROTHERS, THE

The brothers Addrissi are Richard and Donald.

| Columbia KC-31296 | (S) | **We've Got To Get It On Again** | 1972 | 4.00 | 10.00 |
| Buddah BDS-5694 | (S) | **Addrissi Brothers** | 1977 | 3.20 | 8.00 |

ADRIAN & THE SUNSETS

Sunset 63-601	(M)	**Breakthrough** (Multi-colored vinyl)	1963	80.00	200.00
Sunset 63-601	(M)	**Breakthrough**	1963	40.00	100.00
Sunset SE-63-601	(S)	**Breakthrough** (Multi-colored vinyl)	1963	200.00	400.00
Sunset SE-63-601	(S)	**Breakthrough**	1963	80.00	200.00

ADVANCE

| Han-O-Disk | (DJ) | **American Excello** (Picture disc) | 1981 | 6.00 | 15.00 |

ADVANCEMENT, THE

| Philips PHS-600-328 | (S) | **The Advancement** | 1969 | 8.00 | 20.00 |

ADVENTURERS, THE

| Columbia CL-2147 | (M) | **Can't Stop Twistin'** | 1961 | 30.00 | 75.00 |
| Columbia CS-8547 | (S) | **Can't Stop Twistin'** | 1961 | 40.00 | 100.00 |

AEROSMITH

Aerosmith features vocalist Steve Tyler and guitargod Joe Perry.

Columbia KC-32005	(S)	**Aerosmith** ("Walking The Dig" cover)	1973	6.00	15.00
Columbia KC-32005	(S)	**Aerosmith** ("Walking The Dog" cover)	1973	1.00	5.00
Columbia KC-32847	(S)	**Get Your Wings**	1974	1.00	5.00
Columbia KCQ-32847	(Q)	**Get Your Wings**	1974	10.00	25.00
Columbia JC-33479	(S)	**Toys In The Attic**	1975	1.00	5.00
Columbia JCQ-33479	(Q)	**Toys In The Attic**	1975	10.00	25.00
Columbia PC-34165	(S)	**Rocks**	1976	1.00	5.00
Columbia PCQ-34165	(Q)	**Rocks**	1976	10.00	25.00
Columbia A3S-187	(DJ)	**Pure Gold From Rock 'n' Roll's Golden Boys**	1976	20.00	50.00
		(Columbia 187 is a boxed set of the group's first three albums.)			

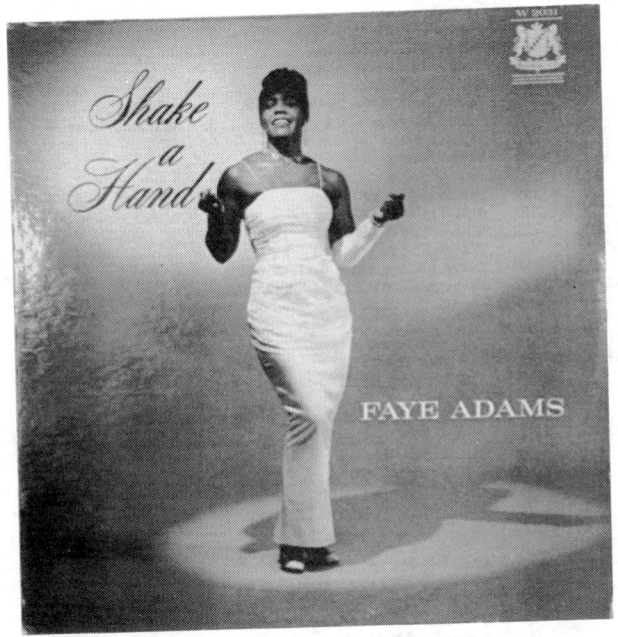

Faye Adams' claim to fame is her transcendent rhythm'n blues hit, "Shake A Hand," also the title of her highly collectible first album for Warwick. While Warwick was manu-facturing stereo albums at this time, there are only mono copies of this title known to exist.

Label & Catalog #		Title	Year	VG+	NM
Columbia *(No number)*	*(DJ)*	**The First Decade** *(8 LP box)*	1982	**50.00**	125.00
		("The First Decade" is a boxed set of the group's first eight albums.)			
Columbia PC-34856	*(S)*	**Draw The Line**	1977	.80	4.00
Columbia PC2-35564	*(S)*	**Live! Bootleg** *(2 LPs)*	1978	1.20	6.00
Columbia PC-36050	*(S)*	**Night In The Ruts**	1979	.80	4.00
Columbia PC-36865	*(S)*	**Aerosmith's Greatest Hits**	1980	.80	4.00
Columbia 38061	*(S)*	**Rock In A Hard Place**	1982	.80	4.00
AESOPS FABLE					
Cadet Concept LPS-323	*(S)*	**In Due Time**	1969	8.00	20.00
AFFECTION COLLECTION, THE					
Evolution 2007	*(S)*	**The Affection Collection**	196?	6.00	15.00
AFFINITY					
Paramount PAS-5027	*(S)*	**Affinity**	1970	10.00	25.00
AGGREGATION					
L.H.I. 12008	*(S)*	**Mind Odyssey**	1967	80.00	200.00
AKKERMAN, JAN					
Jan Akkerman originally recorded with Focus.					
Sire SASD-7407	*(S)*	**Profile**	1973	1.20	6.00
Atco SD-7032	*(S)*	**Tabernakel**	1974	1.00	5.00
Atlantic SD-19159	*(S)*	**Jan Akkerman**	1978	1.00	5.00
ALAIMO, STEVE					
Mr Alaimo also recorded with The Falconaires.					
Checker LP-2981	*(M)*	**Twist With Steve Alaimo**	1961	80.00	200.00
Checker LP-2983	*(M)*	**Mashed Potatoes**	1962	80.00	200.00
Checker LP-2986	*(M)*	**Every Day I Have To Cry**	1963	80.00	200.00
		—Checker albums above have black or maroon labels with silver print.—			
Crown CLP-5382	*(M)*	**Steve Alaimo**	1963	12.00	30.00
Crown CST-382	*(E)*	**Steve Alaimo**	1963	6.00	15.00
		—Crown albums above have gray labels.—			
ABC-Paramount ABC-501	*(M)*	**Starring Steve Alaimo**	1965	18.00	45.00
ABC-Paramount ABCS-501	*(S)*	**Starring Steve Alaimo**	1965	24.00	60.00
ABC-Paramount ABC-531	*(M)*	**Where The Action Is**	1965	18.00	45.00
ABC-Paramount ABCS-531	*(S)*	**Where The Action Is**	1965	24.00	60.00
ABC-Paramount ABC-551	*(M)*	**Steve Alaimo Sings And Swings**	1966	18.00	45.00
ABC-Paramount ABCS-551	*(S)*	**Steve Alaimo Sings And Swings**	1966	24.00	60.00
ALAN BOWN, THE					
Music Factory MFS-12000	*(S)*	**The Alan Bown**	1968	6.00	15.00
Verve/Forecast FTS-3062	*(S)*	**The Alan Bown**	1969	4.00	10.00
Deram DES-18032	*(S)*	**The Alan Bown**	1969	4.00	10.00
Island SW-9308	*(S)*	**Listen**	1971	4.00	10.00
ALBATROSS					
Harvest SMAS-671	*(S)*	**The Going's Easy**	1970	4.00	10.00
ALBERT, THE					
Perception 9	*(S)*	**The Albert**	1971	8.00	20.00
ALEONG, AKI, & THE NOBLES					
Reprise R-6020	*(M)*	**C'mon Baby, Let's Dance**	1962	10.00	25.00
Reprise R-96020	*(S)*	**C'mon Baby, Let's Dance**	1962	12.00	30.00
Reprise R-6011	*(M)*	**Twistin' The Hits**	1962	10.00	25.00
Reprise R-96011	*(S)*	**Twistin' The Hits**	1962	12.00	30.00
Vee Jay LP-1060	*(M)*	**Come Surf With Me**	1963	18.00	45.00
Vee Jay SR-1060	*(S)*	**Come Surf With Me**	1963	24.00	60.00
		—Vee Jay albums above have black rainbow labels.—			
ALEXANDER, ARTHUR					
Dot DLP-3434	*(M)*	**You Better Move On**	1962	60.00	150.00
Dot DLP-25434	*(S)*	**You Better Move On**	1962	150.00	300.00
Warner Bros. B-2592	*(S)*	**Arthur Alexander**	1972	8.00	20.00
ALEXANDER, GORDON					
Columbia CS-9693	*(S)*	**Gordon's Buster**	1968	5.00	12.00
ALEXANDER RABBIT					
Mercury SR-61291	*(S)*	**Alexander Rabbit**	1970	5.00	12.00
ALEXANDER'S TIMELESS BLOOZBAND					
Smack 1001	*(M)*	**Alexander's Timeless Bloozband**	1967	60.00	150.00
Uni 73021	*(S)*	**For Sale**	1968	12.00	30.00

Lee Allen was part of the honkin' sax players in the early years of rock'n roll and can be heard on many rhythm'n blues hits of the time, including those of Fats Domino and Little Richard. He scored a modest pop hit in 1958 with "Walkin' With Mr. Lee," after which this album was titled. Tony Allen had led a number of vocal groups in the '50s, including The Champs, The Chimes, The Wonders, The Originals, and The Wanderers. He finally saw an album with his name released on Crown. This stereo version is one of only a few real stereo records commissioned by Crown in the early '60s.

Label & Catalog #		Title	Year	VG+	NM

ALEXIS

MCA	(S)	Alexis	1977	1.00	5.00

ALIOTTA-HAYNES [ALIOTTA-HAYNES-JEREMIAH]

Ampex 10108	(S)	Aliotta-Haynes Music	1970	6.00	15.00
Ampex 10119	(S)	Aliotta-Haynes-Jeremiah	1970	6.00	15.00
Little Foot 711	(S)	Slippin' Away	1977	6.00	15.00
Big Foot 714	(S)	Lakeshore Drive	1978	10.00	20.00

ALIVE 'N KICKIN'
A&K were produced by Tommy James.

Roulette SR-42052	(S)	Alive 'N Kickin'	1969	6.00	15.00

ALL STARS, THE

Gramophone 20192	(M)	Boogie Woogie	196?	20.00	50.00

ALLAN, CHAD, & THE EXPRESSIONS: *Refer to* THE GUESS WHO

ALLAN, DAVIE [DAVIE ALLAN & THE ARROWS]
Mr Allan's fuzzed guitar can be found on such Tower and Sidewalk soundtracks as "Devil's Angels," "Hellcats," "Wild Racers," "Mondo Hollywood," and both volumes of "The Wild Angels."

Tower T-5002	(M)	Apache '65	1965	16.00	40.00
Tower DT-5002	(E)	Apache '65	1965	12.00	30.00
Tower T-5078	(M)	Blues Theme	1967	20.00	50.00
Tower DT-5078	(E)	Blues Theme	1967	16.00	40.00
Tower T-5094	(M)	Cycledelic Sounds	1968	30.00	75.00
Tower DT-5094	(E)	Cycledelic Sounds	1968	20.00	50.00

ALLEN, DAVE

International Art. 11	(S)	Color Blind	1969	20.00	50.00
International Art. 11	(S)	Color Blind	1979	6.00	15.00
		(Reissues of I.A. 11 have "Masterfonics" in the trail-off vinyl.)			

ALLEN, LEE

Ember ELP-200	(M)	Walkin' With Mr. Lee	1958	300.00	600.00
		—Ember albums above have red labels.—			
Ember ELP-200	(M)	Walkin' With Mr. Lee	196?	100.00	250.00
		—Ember albums above have "logs" labels.—			
Ember ELP-200	(M)	Walkin' With Mr. Lee	196?	60.00	150.00
		—Ember albums above have black labels.—			
Savoy MG-2234	(S)	Honkers And Screamers	196?	6.00	15.00

ALLEN, RAY, & THE UPBEATS

Blast BLP-6804	(M)	Tribute To The Six	196?	50.00	150.00
Camay 3011	(M)	Tribute To The Six	196?	20.00	50.00

ALLEN, RICHIE

Imperial LP-9212	(M)	Stranger From Durango	1963	16.00	40.00
Imperial LP-12212	(S)	Stranger From Durango	1963	20.00	50.00
Imperial LP-9229	(M)	The Rising Surf	1963	20.00	50.00
Imperial LP-12229	(S)	The Rising Surf	1963	30.00	75.00
Imperial LP-9243	(M)	Surfer's Slide	1963	20.00	50.00
Imperial LP-12243	(S)	Surfer's Slide	1963	30.00	75.00

ALLEN, TONY, & THE NIGHT OWLS

Crown CLP-5231	(M)	Rock & Roll With Tony Allen	1960	60.00	150.00
		—Crown albums above have black labels with a silver "Crown" on top.—			
Crown CLP-5231	(M)	Rock & Roll With Tony Allen	1961	30.00	75.00
Crown CST-240	(S)	Rock & Roll With Tony Allen	1961	60.00	150.00
		—Crown albums above have gray labels.—			

ALLISON, GENE

Vee Jay LP-1009	(M)	Gene Allison	1959	150.00	300.00
		—Vee Jay albums above have maroon labels.—			
Vee Jay LP-1009	(M)	Gene Allison	196?	40.00	100.00
Vee Jay SLP-1009	(E)	Gene Allison	196?	30.00	75.00
		—Vee Jay albums above have black rainbow labels.—			

ALLISON, KEITH
Produced by Gary Usher. Refer to The Falconaires;

Columbia CL-2641	(M)	Keith Allison In Action	1967	8.00	20.00
Columbia CS-9441	(S)	Keith Allison In Action	1967	10.00	25.00

ALLISON, LUTHER

Delmark DS-625	(S)	Love Me Mama	1969	10.00	25.00
Gordy G6-964	(S)	Bad News Is Coming	1973	4.00	10.00
Gordy G6-967	(S)	Luther's Blues	1974	4.00	10.00
Gordy G6-974	(S)	Night Life	1976	4.00	10.00

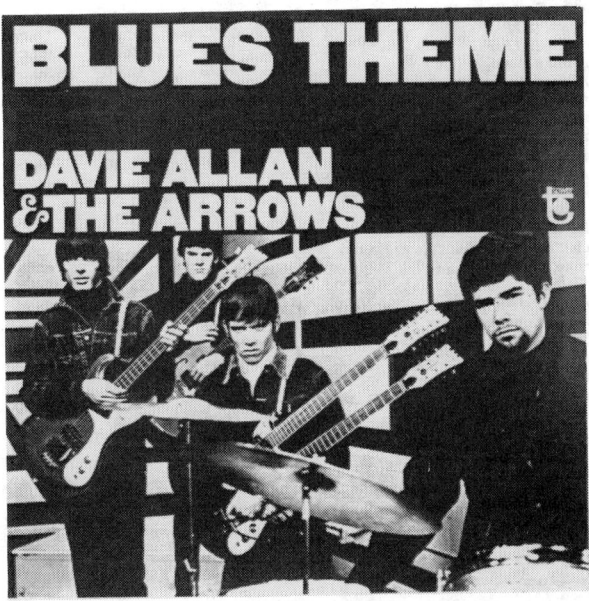

Originally scoring as The Arrows for Tower with the proto-psych "Apache '65" (a revved up remake of the 1961 hit by Jorgen Ingmann). This was followed by a trio of albums, of which Apache '65, credited to The Arrows, and Blues Theme are pictured here. Davie Allan and band quickly developed into the most sought-after musicians in Hollywood when it came to filling soundtracks for grade-B youth exploitation films with biker themes!

Label & Catalog #		Title	Year	VG+	NM

ALLMAN, DUANE
Duane Allman is one-half of The Allman Brothers, at least in the group's name.

Capricorn 2CP-0108	(S)	Anthology (2 LPs)	1972	4.00	10.00
Capricorn 2CP-0139	(S)	Anthology, Vol. II (2 LPs)	1974	4.00	10.00

ALLMAN, DUANE & GREGG
The brothers Allman originally recorded with Hour Glass.

Bold 33-301	(S)	Duane And Gregg Allman	1972	8.00	20.00
Bold 33-302	(S)	Duane And Gregg Allman	1973	4.00	10.00
		(Bold 302 is a reissue of 301.)			
Dial DL-6005	(S)	Early Allman	1973	6.00	15.00
		(Dial 6005 is a collection of pre-Allman Brothers material.)			
K-Tel NU-471	(S)	Fantastic Allman Brothers Original Hits	1974	4.00	10.00
		(K-Tel 471 reissues the Bold material.)			

ALLMAN, GREGG
Gregg Allman is the other half of The Allman Brothers group-name-wise.

Capricorn CP-0116	(S)	Laid Back	1974	1.20	6.00
Capricorn CLLP-237	(S)	Laid Back (4 track EP)	1974	4.00	10.00
Capricorn 2C-0141	(S)	The Gregg Allman Tour	1975	1.20	6.00
Capricorn CP-0181	(S)	Playin' Up A Storm	1977	1.20	6.00
Epic FE-0531	(S)	I'm No Angel	1987	.80	4.00
Epic OE-44033	(S)	Just Before The Bullets Fly	1988	.80	4.00

ALLMAN & WOMAN
Gregg Allman and Cher.

Warner Bros. BSK-3120	(S)	Two The Hard Way	1977	.80	4.00

ALLMAN BROTHERS BAND, THE
The Allman Brothers feature Duane and Gregg Allman, Dickie Betts and Butch Trucks. Refer to The 31st Of February.

Atco SD-33-308	(S)	The Allman Brothers Band	1969	4.00	10.00
Atco SD-33-342	(S)	Idlewild South	1970	4.00	10.00
Atco SD-2-805	(S)	Beginnings (2 LPs)	1973	4.00	10.00
		(Atco 805 repackages 308 and 342.)			
Capricorn SD-2-802	(S)	At Fillmore East (2 LPs)	1971	3.00	15.00
Capricorn 2CP-0102	(S)	Eat A Peach (2 LPs)	1972	4.00	10.00
Capricorn CX4-0102	(Q)	Eat A Peach (2 LPs)	1974	12.00	30.00
Capricorn PRO-545	(DJ)	Duane Allman Dialogs	1972	12.00	30.00
Capricorn 2CP-0108	(S)	Duane Allman Anthology (2 LPs)	1972	3.00	15.00
Capricorn CP-0111	(S)	Brothers And Sisters	1972	3.20	8.00
Capricorn 2CP-0131	(S)	At Fillmore East (2 LPs)	1974	4.00	10.00
Capricorn CX4-0131	(Q)	At Fillmore East (2 LPs)	1974	12.00	30.00
Capricorn 2CX-0132	(S)	Beginnings (2 LPs)	1974	3.20	8.00
		(Capricorn 0132 is a reissue of Atco 805.)			
Capricorn CP-0156	(S)	Win, Lose Or Draw	1975	1.00	5.00
Capricorn 2CX-0164	(S)	The Road Goes On Forever (2 LPs)	1975	1.20	6.00
Capricorn 2CX-0177	(S)	Wipe The Window, Check The Oil, Dollar Gas (2 LPs)	1976	1.20	6.00
Capricorn CPN-0196	(S)	The Allman Brothers Band	1978	1.00	5.00
Capricorn CPN-0197	(S)	Idlewild South	1978	1.00	5.00
		(Capricorn 0196 and 97 are reissues of Atco 308 and 342.)			
Capricorn CPN-0218	(S)	Enlightened Rogues	1979	1.00	5.00
Arista AL-9535	(S)	Reach For The Sky	1980	1.00	5.00
Arista AL-9564	(S)	Brothers Of The Road	1981	1.00	5.00
Polydor PD-1-6338	(S)	The Best Of Duane Allman	1981	.80	4.00
Polydor PD-1-6339	(S)	The Best Of The Allman Brothers Band	1981	.80	4.00
Polydor 834917	(S)	Dreams	1989	.80	4.00

ALLSUP, TOMMY
Mr Allsup was Buddy Holly's post-Crickets lead guitar player.

Reprise R-6182	(M)	Tommy Allsup Plays The Buddy Holly Songbook	1965	20.00	50.00
Reprise RS-6182	(S)	Tommy Allsup Plays The Buddy Holly Songbook	1965	30.00	75.00

ALMOND, JOHNNY
Johnny Almond was part of Mark-Almond.

Deram DES-18037	(S)	Hollywood Blues	1970	3.20	8.00

AMBASSADORS, THE

Arctic ALPS-1005	(S)	Soul Summit	1969	10.00	25.00

AMBERGRIS

Paramount PAS-5014	(S)	Ambergris	1970	4.00	10.00

AMBOY DUKES, THE
The Amboy Dukes feature the carniverously-motivated, guitar-slinging Theodore "Ted" Nugent. For additional listings refer to Godfrey Daniel (who is a group).

Mainstream 56104	(M)	The Amboy Dukes	1968	40.00	100.00
Mainstream S-6104	(S)	The Amboy Dukes	1968	20.00	50.00
Mainstream S-6112	(S)	Journey To The Center Of The Mind	1968	20.00	50.00

Label & Catalog #		Title	Year	VG+	NM
Mainstream S-6118	(S)	**Migration**	1968	20.00	50.00
Mainstream S-6125	(S)	**The Best Of The Original Amboy Dukes**	1969	12.00	30.00
Mainstream S-421	(S)	**Ted Nugent & The Amboy Dukes**	197?	12.00	30.00
Mainstream S-2-801	(S)	**Journeys And Migrations** *(2 LPs)*	1974	8.00	20.00
		(Mainstream 801 repackages 6112 and 6118.)			
Polydor 24-4012	(S)	**Marriage On The Rocks**	1970	10.00	25.00
Polydor 24-4035	(S)	**Survival Of The Fittest**	1970	10.00	25.00
DiscReet 2181	(S)	**Call Of The Wild**	1974	4.00	10.00
DiscReet 2203	(S)	**Tooth, Fang And Claw**	1974	4.00	10.00
Mainstream 414	(S)	**Dr. Slingshot**	1974	4.00	10.00

AMBROSE, AMANDA

Label & Catalog #		Title	Year	VG+	NM
Dunwich 668	(M)	**Amanda**	1966	6.00	15.00
Dunwich S-668	(S)	**Amanda**	1966	8.00	20.00

AMBROSE SLADE: *Refer to* SLADE

AMBROSIA

Label & Catalog #		Title	Year	VG+	NM
20th Century T-434	(S)	**Ambrosia** *(Black border cover)*	1975	2.00	10.00
20th Century T-434	(S)	**Ambrosia**	1975	1.00	5.00
20th Century T-510	(S)	**Somewhere Live Never Traveled**	1976	2.00	10.00
		(Fold-open pyramid cover)			
20th Century T-510	(S)	**Somewhere Live Never Traveled**	1976	1.00	5.00
Warner Bros 3135	(S)	**Life Beyond L.A.**	1978	1.00	5.00
Warner Bros 3368	(S)	**One Eighty**	1980	1.00	5.00
Warner Bros 3638	(S)	**Road Island**	1982	1.00	5.00

AMERICA
America was Gerry Beckley, Dewey Bunnell and Don Peek, through "Harbor," after which Peek fled.

Label & Catalog #		Title	Year	VG+	NM
Warner Bros. BS-2576	(S)	**America** *(Without "Horse With No Name")*	1971	3.20	8.00
Warner Bros. BS-2576	(S)	**America** *(With "Horse With No Name")*	1972	.80	4.00
Warner Bros. BS-2655	(S)	**Homecoming**	1972	.80	4.00
Warner Bros. BS-2728	(S)	**Hat Trick**	1973	.80	4.00
Warner Bros. BS-2808	(S)	**Holiday**	1974	.80	4.00
Warner Bros. BS4-2808	(Q)	**Holiday**	1974	4.00	10.00
Warner Bros. BS-2852	(S)	**Hearts**	1975	.80	4.00
Warner Bros. BS4-2852	(Q)	**Hearts**	1975	4.00	10.00
Warner Bros. BS-2894	(S)	**History/America's Greatest Hits**	1975	.80	4.00
Warner Bros. BS-2932	(S)	**Hideaway**	1976	.80	4.00
Warner Bros. BS-3017	(S)	**Harbor**	1977	.80	4.00
Warner Bros. BS-3136	(S)	**America/Live**	1977	.80	4.00
Capitol ST-11950	(S)	**Silent Letter**	1979	.80	4.00
Capitol ST-12098	(S)	**Alibi**	1980	.80	4.00
Capitol ST-12209	(S)	**View From The Ground**	1982	.80	4.00
Capitol ST-12277	(S)	**Your Move**	1983	.80	4.00
Capitol ST-12370	(S)	**Perspective**	1984	.80	4.00

AMERICAN BLUES
American Blues features Dusty Hill and Frank Beard, later of ZZ Top. Their first album was privately pressed.

Label & Catalog #		Title	Year	VG+	NM
Uni 73044	(S)	**American Blues Do Their Thing**	1969	30.00	75.00

AMERICAN BREED, THE
The AB includes Kevin Murphy, later of Rufus.

Label & Catalog #		Title	Year	VG+	NM
Acta 8002	(M)	**The American Breed**	1967	6.00	15.00
Acta 38002	(S)	**The American Breed**	1967	8.00	20.00
Acta 8003	(M)	**Bend Me, Shape Me**	1968	6.00	15.00
Acta 38003	(S)	**Bend Me, Shape Me**	1968	8.00	20.00
Acta 8006	(M)	**Pumpkin, Powder, Scarlet & Green**	1968	5.00	12.00
Acta 38006	(S)	**Pumpkin, Powder, Scarlet & Green**	1968	6.00	15.00
Acta 8008	(M)	**Lonely Side Of The City**	1968	5.00	12.00
Acta 38008	(S)	**Lonely Side Of The City**	1968	6.00	15.00

AMERICAN DREAM, THE
The AD was produced by Todd Rundgren.

Label & Catalog #		Title	Year	VG+	NM
Ampex A-10101	(S)	**The American Dream**	1970	6.00	15.00

AMERICAN EAGLE

Label & Catalog #		Title	Year	VG+	NM
Decca DL-75258	(S)	**American Eagle**	1971	8.00	20.00

AMERICAN FLYER
AF included Craig Fuller (formerly of The Pure Prairie League), Eric Kaz (The Blues Magoos), Steve Katz (Blood, Sweat & Tears), and Doug Yule (Velvet Underground).

Label & Catalog #		Title	Year	VG+	NM
United Arts. LA-650	(S)	**American Flyer**	1976	1.00	5.00
United Arts. LA-720	(S)	**Spirit Of A Woman**	1977	1.00	5.00

AMERICAN REVOLUTION

Label & Catalog #		Title	Year	VG+	NM
Flick Disc FLS-54002	(S)	**American Revolution**	1968	10.00	25.00

Label & Catalog #		Title	Year	VG+	NM

AMON DUUL
Prophesy PRS-1003	(S)	Amon Duul	1970	10.00	25.00

AMON DUUL II
United Arts. UAS-9954	(S)	Dance Of The Lemmings (2 LPs)	1971	6.00	15.00
United Arts. UAS-5586	(S)	Carnival In Babylon	1972	4.00	10.00
United Arts. LA-017	(S)	Wolf City	1973	4.00	10.00
United Arts. LA-198	(S)	Vive La Trance	1973	4.00	10.00
Atco SD-36-108	(S)	Hijack	1975	1.00	5.00
Atco SD-36-119	(S)	Made In Germany	1976	1.00	5.00

AMOS, TORI: *Refer to* Y KANT TORI READ

ANCIENT GREASE
Mercury SR-61305	(S)	Women And Children First	1970	10.00	25.00

ANDERS & PONCIA
Pete Anders and Vinnie Poncia also recorded as The Innocence; The Tradewinds.
Warner Bros. WS-1778	(S)	The Anders & Poncia Album	1969	12.00	30.00

ANDERSON, AL
Anderson originally recorded with Wildweeds and later with NRBQ.
Vanguard VSD-79324	(S)	Al Anderson	1972	8.00	20.00
Vanguard VSQ-79324	(Q)	Al Anderson	1973	12.00	30.00

ANDERSON, CASEY
Elektra EKL-192	(M)	Goin' Places	1960	8.00	20.00
Elektra EKS-7192	(S)	Goin' Places	1960	10.00	25.00
Atco 33-149	(M)	The Bag I'm In	1962	8.00	20.00
Atco SD-33-149	(S)	The Bag I'm In	1962	10.00	25.00
Atco 33-166	(M)	More Pretty Girls Than One	1964	8.00	20.00
Atco SD-33-166	(S)	More Pretty Girls Than One	1964	10.00	25.00
Atco 33-172	(M)	Live At The Ice House	1965	8.00	20.00
Atco SD-33-172	(S)	Live At The Ice House	1965	10.00	25.00
Atco 33-176	(M)	Blues Is A Woman Gone	1965	8.00	20.00
Atco SD-33-176	(S)	Blues Is A Woman Gone	1965	10.00	25.00

ANDERSON, JON
Jon Anderson is a member of Yes.
Atlantic SD-18180	(S)	Olias Of Sunhillow	1976	.80	4.00
Atlantic SD-16021	(S)	Song Of Seven	1980	.80	4.00
Atlantic SD-19355	(S)	Animation	1982	.80	4.00

ANDERSON, MARGIE
Parade P-364	(M)	The Blues	196?	12.00	30.00
Parade SP-364	(S)	The Blues	196?	16.00	40.00

ANDERSON, MILDRED
Bluesville BVLP-1004	(M)	Person To Person	1960	24.00	60.00
Bluesville BVLP-1017	(M)	No More In Life	1961	24.00	60.00
		—Bluesville albums above have bright blue labels with silver print.—			
Bluesville BVLP-1004	(M)	Person To Person	1964	10.00	25.00
Bluesville BVLP-1017	(M)	No More In Life	1964	10.00	25.00
		—Bluesville albums above have blue labels with a trident logo on the right side.—			

ANDREWS, LEE, & THE HEARTS
Lost-Nite LP-101	(M)	Biggest Hits (Yellow vinyl)	1964	50.00	125.00
Lost-Nite LP-101	(M)	Biggest Hits	1964	20.00	50.00
Lost-Nite LP-113	(M)	Lee Andrews & The Hearts Live	1965	20.00	50.00
Lost-Nite LLP-1	(10")	Lee Andrews & The Hearts (Red vinyl)	1981	4.00	10.00
Lost-Nite LLP-2	(10")	Lee Andrews & The Hearts (Red vinyl)	1981	4.00	10.00
Collectables 5003	(M)	Gotham Recording Sessions (Picture disc)	1982	4.00	10.00

ANDWELLA
Dunhill DS-50095	(S)	World's End	1970	4.00	10.00
Dunhill DS-50105	(S)	People's People	1971	4.00	10.00

ANGEL
Casablanca NBLP-7021	(S)	Angel	1975	1.00	5.00
Casablanca NBLP-7028	(S)	Helluva Band	1976	1.00	5.00
Casablanca NBLP-7043	(S)	On Earth As It Is In Heaven	1977	1.00	5.00
Casablanca NBLP-7085	(S)	White Hot	1978	1.00	5.00
Casablanca NBLP-7·127	(S)	Sinful	1979	1.00	5.00
Casablanca NBLP-7203	(S)	Life Without A Net (2 LPs)	1980	1.20	6.00

ANGELS, THE
Caprice LP-1001	(M)	And The Angels Sing	1962	40.00	100.00
Caprice SLP-1001	(S)	And The Angels Sing	1962	80.00	200.00

Label & Catalog #		Title	Year	VG+	NM
Smash MGS-27039	(M)	My Boyfriend's Back	1963	14.00	35.00
Smash SRS-67039	(S)	My Boyfriend's Back	1963	20.00	50.00
		("Til" is rechanneled on this album.)			
Smash MGS-27048	(M)	A Halo To You	1964	14.00	35.00
Smash SRS-67048	(S)	A Halo To You	1964	20.00	50.00
Ascot AM-13009	(M)	Twelve Of Their Greatest Hits	1964	10.00	25.00
Ascot ALS-6009	(S)	Twelve Of Their Greatest Hits	1964	12.00	30.00
		(The Ascot album is a repackage of Caprice 1001.)			

ANIMALS, THE [ERIC BURDON & THE ANIMALS]

The original Animals were Eric Burdon, Chas Chandler, Alan Price, John Steel and Hilton Valentine. By early 1966 Price and Steel had been replaced by Dave Rowberry and Barry Jenkins. By the end of '66, the group had split with Burdon and Jenkins forming Eric Burdon & The Animals (MGM 4433 on).

MGM E-4264	(M)	The Animals (Yellow label promo)	1964	40.00	100.00
MGM E-4264	(M)	The Animals	1964	16.00	40.00
MGM SE-4264	(E)	The Animals	1964	12.00	30.00
MGM T-90687	(M)	The Animals (Capitol Record Club)	1965	20.00	50.00
MGM E-4281	(M)	The Animals On Tour (Yellow label promo)	1965	40.00	100.00
MGM E-4281	(M)	The Animals On Tour	1965	16.00	40.00
MGM SE-4281	(E)	The Animals On Tour	1965	12.00	30.00
MGM E-4305	(M)	Animal Tracks (Yellow label promo)	1965	60.00	150.00
MGM E-4305	(M)	Animal Tracks	1965	20.00	50.00
MGM SE-4305	(E)	Animal Tracks	1965	16.00	40.00
MGM T-90571	(M)	Animal Tracks (Capitol Record Club)	1965	20.00	50.00
MGM E-4324	(M)	The Best Of The Animals (Yellow label)	1966	30.00	75.00
MGM E-4324	(M)	The Best Of The Animals	1966	8.00	20.00
MGM SE-4324	(E)	The Best Of The Animals	1966	10.00	25.00
MGM KAO-90622	(M)	The Best Of The Animals (Capitol Rec. Club)	1969	14.00	35.00
MGM SKAO-90622	(E)	The Best Of The Animals (Capitol Rec. Club)	1969	14.00	35.00
MGM E-4384	(M)	Animalization (Yellow label promo)	1966	40.00	100.00
MGM E-4384	(M)	Animalization	1966	10.00	25.00
MGM SE-4384	(S)	Animalization	1966	12.00	30.00
		("Inside Looking Out" is rechanneled.)			
MGM T-90923	(M)	Animalization (Capitol Record Club)	1966	20.00	50.00
MGM ST-90923	(S)	Animalization (Capitol Record Club)	1966	20.00	50.00
MGM E-4414	(M)	Animalism (Yellow label promo)	1966	40.00	100.00
MGM E-4414	(M)	Animalism	1966	10.00	25.00
MGM SE-4414	(S)	Animalism	1966	12.00	30.00
MGM E-4433	(M)	Eric Is Here	1967	6.00	15.00
MGM SE-4433	(S)	Eric Is Here	1967	8.00	20.00
MGM E-4454	(M)	Best Of Eric Burdon & The Animals, Vol. 2	1967	8.00	20.00
MGM SE-4454	(P)	Best Of Eric Burdon & The Animals, Vol. 2	1967	8.00	20.00
MGM E-4484	(M)	Winds Of Change	1967	8.00	20.00
MGM SE-4484	(S)	Winds Of Change	1967	10.00	25.00
MGM E-4537	(M)	The Twain Shall Meet	1968	8.00	20.00
MGM SE-4537	(S)	The Twain Shall Meet	1968	10.00	25.00
MGM SE-4553	(S)	Every One Of Us	1968	10.00	25.00
MGM SE-4591	(S)	Love Is (2 LPs)	1968	20.00	50.00
MGM SE-4602	(S)	Greatest Hits Of Eric Burdon & The Animals	1969	6.00	15.00
Wand WDS-690	(S)	In The Beginning	1970	3.20	8.00
Pickwick SPC-3330	(E)	The Early Animals With Eric Burdon	1971	3.20	8.00
Springboard SPB-4025	(E)	The Best Of The Animals	1972	3.20	8.00
Springboard SPB-4065	(E)	The Night Time Is The Right Time	1973	3.20	8.00
Abkco AB-4226	(S)	Best Of The Animals (2 LPs)	1973	3.20	8.00
Scepter/Citation 18026	(S)	The Best Of The Animals	1976	3.20	8.00
United Arts. LA790-H	(S)	Before We Were So Rudely Interrupted	1977	3.20	8.00
Accord SN-7235	(S)	The Animals With Eric Burdon	1982	1.00	5.00
I.R.S. 70037	(S)	Ark	1983	1.00	5.00
I.R.S. 70043	(S)	Rip It To Shreds	1984	1.00	5.00

ANIMATED EGG

Somerset SF-32700	(M)	Animated Egg	1967	12.00	30.00
Alshire SF-5104	(S)	Animated Egg	1967	16.00	50.00

ANKA, PAUL

Riviera 0047	(M)	Paul Anka & Others	1959	60.00	150.00
		(Riviera 0047 is a various artists album containing Anka's pre-ABC sides.)			
ABC-Paramount ABC-240	(M)	Paul Anka	1958	20.00	50.00
ABC-Paramount ABC-296	(M)	My Heart Sings	1959	12.00	30.00
ABC-Paramount ABCS-296	(S)	My Heart Sings	1959	20.00	50.00
ABC-Paramount ABC-323	(M)	Paul Anka Sings His Big 15	1960	20.00	50.00
ABC-Paramount ABCS-323	(E)	Paul Anka Sings His Big 15	196?	10.00	25.00
ABC-Paramount ABC-347	(M)	Paul Anka Swings For Young Lovers	1960	12.00	30.00
ABC-Paramount ABCS-347	(S)	Paul Anka Swings For Young Lovers	1960	16.00	40.00
ABC-Paramount ABC-353	(M)	Anka At The Copa	1960	12.00	30.00
ABC-Paramount ABCS-353	(S)	Anka At The Copa	1960	16.00	40.00
ABC-Paramount ABC-360	(M)	It's Christmas Everywhere	1960	12.00	30.00
ABC-Paramount ABCS-360	(S)	It's Christmas Everywhere	1960	16.00	40.00

Label & Catalog #		Title	Year	VG+	NM
ABC-Paramount ABC-371	(M)	Strictly Instrumental	1961	12.00	30.00
ABC-Paramount ABCS-371	(S)	Strictly Instrumental	1961	16.00	40.00
ABC-Paramount ABC-390	(M)	Paul Anka Sings His Big 15, Volume 2	1961	10.00	25.00
ABC-Paramount ABCS-390	(S)	Paul Anka Sings His Big 15, Volume 2	1961	12.00	30.00
ABC-Paramount ABC-409	(M)	Paul Anka Sings His Big 15, Volume 3	1962	10.00	25.00
ABC-Paramount ABCS-409	(S)	Paul Anka Sings His Big 15, Volume 3	1962	12.00	30.00
ABC-Paramount ABC-420	(M)	Diana	1962	10.00	25.00
ABC-Paramount ABCS-420	(S)	Diana	1962	12.00	30.00
RCA Victor LPM-2502	(M)	Young, Alive And In Love!	1962	10.00	25.00
RCA Victor LSP-2502	(S)	Young, Alive And In Love!	1962	12.00	30.00
		(Original covers for RCA 2502 has a portrait of Anka on the front.)			
RCA Victor LPM-2502	(M)	Young, Alive And In Love!	1963	6.00	15.00
RCA Victor LSP-2502	(S)	Young, Alive And In Love!	1963	8.00	20.00
		(Later covers have the portrait on the back with a new front.)			
RCA Victor LPM-2575	(M)	Let's Sit This One Out!	1962	6.00	15.00
RCA Victor LSP-2575	(S)	Let's Sit This One Out!	1962	8.00	20.00
RCA Victor LPM-2614	(M)	Our Man Around The World	1963	6.00	15.00
RCA Victor LSP-2614	(S)	Our Man Around The World	1963	8.00	20.00
RCA Victor LPM-2691	(M)	Paul Anka's 21 Golden Hits	1963	6.00	15.00
RCA Victor LSP-2691	(S)	Paul Anka's 21 Golden Hits	1963	8.00	20.00
		—RCA mono albums above have "Long Play" on the bottom of the label; stereo albums have "Living Stereo" on the bottom.—			
RCA Victor LPM-2744	(M)	Songs I Wish I'd Written	1963	5.00	12.00
RCA Victor LSP-2744	(S)	Songs I Wish I'd Written	1963	6.00	15.00
RCA Victor LPM-2996	(M)	Excitement On Park Avenue	1964	5.00	12.00
RCA Victor LSP-2996	(S)	Excitement On Park Avenue	1964	6.00	15.00
RCA Victor LPM-3580	(M)	Strictly Nashville	1966	5.00	12.00
RCA Victor LSP-3580	(S)	Strictly Nashville	1966	6.00	15.00
RCA Victor LPM-3875	(M)	Paul Anka Live	1967	5.00	12.00
RCA Victor LSP-3875	(S)	Paul Anka Live	1967	6.00	15.00
		—RCA albums above have black labels.—			
RCA Victor LSP-4142	(S)	Goodnight My Love	1969	4.00	10.00
RCA Victor LSP-4203	(S)	Sincerely - Recorded Live At The Copa	1969	4.00	10.00
RCA Victor LSP-4250	(S)	Life Goes On	1969	4.00	10.00
RCA Victor LSP-4300	(S)	Paul Anka 70's	1970	4.00	10.00
		—RCA albums above have orange labels on non-flexible vinyl.—			
RCA Victor ANL1-0086	(S)	Remember Diane	1975	3.20	8.00
RCA Victor ANL1-1054	(S)	She's A Lady	1975	3.20	8.00
RCA Victor ANL1-1584	(S)	Paul Anka Sings His Favorites	1976	3.20	8.00
RCA Victor ANL1-2482	(S)	Songs I Wish I'd Written	1977	1.20	6.00
RCA Victor AFL1-2892	(S)	Listen To Your Heart	1978	1.20	6.00
RCA Victor AFL1-3382	(S)	Headlines	1979	1.20	6.00
RCA Victor ANL1-3838	(S)	21 Golden Hits	1981	1.20	6.00
RCA Victor ANL1-3926	(S)	Both Sides Of Love	1981	1.20	6.00
Buddah BDS-5093	(S)	Paul Anka	1971	4.00	10.00
Buddah BDS-5114	(S)	Jubilation	1972	4.00	10.00
Buddah BDS-5622	(S)	This Is Anka (2 LPs)	1974	4.00	10.00
Buddah BDS-5667	(S)	The Essential Paul Anka (2 LPs)	1974	4.00	10.00
Camden ACL1-0616	(S)	My Way	1974	1.00	5.00
United Arts. LA-314G	(S)	Anka	1974	1.20	6.00
United Arts. LA-569G	(S)	The Times Of Your Life	1975	1.20	6.00
United Arts LA-653G	(S)	The Painter	1976	1.20	6.00
United Arts. LA-746H	(S)	Music Man	1977	1.20	6.00
United Arts. LA-922H	(S)	Paul Anka: His Best	1978	1.20	6.00
Sire H-3704	(P)	Gold/28 Original Hit Recordings (2 LPs)	1974	8.00	20.00
Sire K-6043	(P)	Vintage Years 1957-1961 (2 LPs)	1978	6.00	15.00
Barnaby 6103	(S)	Paul Anka Live	1975	3.20	8.00
Barnaby 4008	(S)	Paul Anka Live	1978	1.20	6.00
Pickwick SPC-3508	(S)	Puppy Love	1975	1.00	5.00
Pickwick SPC-3523	(S)	Lonely Boy	1975	1.00	5.00
Accord SN-7117	(S)	She's A Lady	1981	1.00	5.00
Liberty LN-10000	(S)	Paul Anka: His Best	1981	1.00	5.00
Liberty LN-10001	(S)	The Times Of Your Life	1981	1.00	5.00
Ranwood 8203	(S)	The Very Best Of Paul Anka	1981	1.00	5.00

ANKA, PAUL / SAM COOKE / NEIL SEDAKA

Label & Catalog #		Title	Year	VG+	NM
RCA Victor LPM-2720	(M)	Three Great Guys	1963	8.00	20.00
RCA Victor LSP-2720	(S)	Three Great Guys	1963	10.00	25.00

ANTHEM

Label & Catalog #		Title	Year	VG+	NM
Buddah BDS-5071	(S)	Anthem	1971	5.00	12.00

AORTA

Label & Catalog #		Title	Year	VG+	NM
Columbia CS-9785	(S)	Aorta	1968	12.00	30.00
Happy Tiger HT-1010	(S)	Aorta 2	1970	16.00	40.00

APHRODITE'S CHILD

Label & Catalog #		Title	Year	VG+	NM
Vertigo 2-500	(S)	666 (2 LPs with Vangelis)	196?	8.00	20.00

Label & Catalog #		Title	Year	VG+	NM
APOCALYPSE					
Colossus CS-1004	(S)	Apocalypse	1970	4.00	10.00
APOLLO 100					
Mega 1010	(S)	Joy	1972	1.00	5.00
APPALOOSA					
Columbia CS-9819	(S)	Appaloosa	1969	4.00	10.00
APPEL, DAVE					
Cameo C-1004	(M)	Alone Together	1959	12.00	30.00
APPICE, CARMINE					
Carmine Appice was a member of Vanilla Fudge. Refer to Beck, Bogert & Appice.					
Pasha	(S)	Carmine Appice	1981	1.00	5.00
Pasha AS-1368	(DJ)	The Carmine Appice Story	1982	4.00	10.00
APPLE PIE MOTHERHOOD BAND, THE					
Atlantic SD-8189	(S)	The Apple Pie Motherhood Band	1968	8.00	20.00
Atlantic SD-8233	(S)	Apple Pie	1969	8.00	20.00
APPLETREE THEATRE					
Appletree Theatre features a guest appearance by Rick Nelson.					
Verve/Forecast FT-3042	(M)	Playback	1968	10.00	25.00
Verve/Forecast FTS-3042	(S)	Playback	1968	12.00	30.00
AQUARIAN DREAM					
Buddah BDS-5672	(S)	Norman Connors Presents Aquarian Dream	1976	1.00	5.00
AQUATONES, THE					
Fargo 3001	(M)	The Aquatones Sing	1964	250.00	500.00
AREA CODE 615					
Polydor 24-4002	(S)	Area Code 615	1969	8.00	20.00
Polydor 24-4025	(S)	A Trip in the Country	1970	8.00	20.00
ARGENT					
Argent features Rod Argent; Russ Ballard.					
Epic BN-26525	(S)	Argent	1969	4.00	10.00
Epic KE-30128	(S)	Ring of Hands	1971	4.00	10.00
		— *Epic albums above have yellow labels.* —			
Epic BN-26525	(S)	Argent	197?	1.00	5.00
Epic KE-30128	(S)	Ring of Hands	197?	1.00	5.00
Epic E-32195	(S)	In Deep	1973	1.00	5.00
Epic EQ-32195	(Q)	In Deep	1974	6.00	15.00
Epic E-32573	(S)	Nexus	1974	1.00	5.00
Epic E-33079	(S)	Encore/Live In Concert (2 LPs)	1975	1.20	6.00
Epic E-33422	(S)	Circus	1975	1.00	5.00
ARISTOCATS, THE					
Hifi R-610	(M)	Boogie And Blues	1959	16.00	40.00
Hifi SR-610	(S)	Boogie And Blues	1959	24.00	60.00
ARMAGEDDON					
Amos 73075	(S)	Armageddon	1969	10.00	25.00
ARMAGEDDON					
Armageddon features Keith Relf, formerly of The Yardbirds.					
A&M SP-4513	(S)	Armageddon	1975	8.00	20.00
ARNOLD, BILLY BOY					
Prestige PRLP-7389	(M)	Blues On The South Side	1965	10.00	25.00
Prestige PRST-7389	(S)	Blues On The South Side	1965	12.00	30.00
		— *Prestige albums above have blue labels with a trident logo on the right side.* —			
ARPEGGIO					
Polydor 6180	(S)	Let The Music Play	1979	1.00	5.00
ARRIVAL					
London PS-576	(S)	I Will Survive	1970	1.00	5.00
ARROWS, THE: *Refer to* DAVIE ALLAN					
ARS NOVA					
Elektra EKS-74020	(S)	Ars Nova	1968	6.00	15.00
Atlantic SD-8221	(S)	Sunshine And Shadows	1969	6.00	15.00
ART BEARS, THE					
Ralph RR-7905	(S)	Winter Songs	1980	4.00	10.00

Label & Catalog #		Title	Year	VG+	NM
ART OF LOVIN'					
Mainstream S-6113	(S)	Art Of Lovin'	1968	80.00	200.00
ARTHUR					
Arthur Lee Harper.					
L.H.I. 12000	(S)	Dreams And Images	1968	16.00	40.00
ARTISTICS, THE					
OKeh OKL-4119	(M)	Get My Hands On Some Lovin'	1967	30.00	75.00
OKeh OKS-14119	(S)	Get My Hands On Some Lovin'	1967	40.00	100.00
Brunswick BL-54123	(M)	I'm Gonna Miss You	1967	10.00	25.00
Brunswick BL-754123	(S)	I'm Gonna Miss You	1967	10.00	25.00
Brunswick BL-754139	(S)	The Articulate Artistics	1968	10.00	25.00
Brunswick BL-754153	(S)	What Happened	1969	10.00	25.00
Brunswick BL-754168	(S)	I Want You To Make My Life Over	1970	10.00	25.00
ARZACHEL					
Arzachel features Steve Hillage.					
Roulette SR-42036	(S)	Arzachel	1969	50.00	125.00
ASGAERD					
Threshold THS-6	(S)	In The Realm Of Asgaerd	1972	6.00	15.00
ASHER, JANE					
Ms Asher is the sister of Peter Asher, then of Peter & Gordon fame. She received her recording contract due to her romantic alliance with Paul McCartney, then a Beatle o some renown.					
London OSA-1206	(M)	Alice In Wonderland	1965	20.00	50.00
ASHES					
Vault 125	(S)	Ashes	1968	10.00	25.00
ASHFORD, NICHOLAS, & VALERIE SIMPSON					
Warner Bros. BS-2739	(S)	Gimme Something Real	1973	1.20	6.00
Warner Bros. BS-2789	(S)	I Wanna Be Selfish	1974	1.20	6.00
Warner Bros. BS-2858	(S)	Come As You Are	1976	1.20	6.00
Warner Bros. BS-2992	(S)	So, So Satisfied	1977	1.20	6.00
Warner Bros. BS-3088	(S)	Send It	1978	1.20	6.00
Warner Bros. BS-3219	(S)	Is It Still Good To Ya?	1978	1.20	6.00
Warner Bros. BS-3357	(S)	Stay Free	1979	1.20	6.00
Warner Bros. BS-3458	(S)	A Musical Affair	1980	1.20	6.00
Warner Bros. 2BS-3524	(S)	Performance (2 LPs)	1981	3.20	8.00
Capitol ST-12207	(S)	Street Opera	1982	1.20	5.00
ASIA					
Geffen GHS-2008	(S)	Asia (Quiex II vinyl promo)	1982	6.00	15.00
Geffen GHS-2008	(S)	Asia	1982	.80	4.00
Geffen GHS-4008	(S)	Alpha (Quiex II vinyl promo)	1983	6.00	15.00
Geffen GHS-4008	(S)	Alpha	1983	.80	4.00
ASHKAN					
Sire SES-97017	(S)	In From The Cold	1970	12.00	30.00
ASHTON, GARDNER & DYKE					
Capitol ST-563	(S)	Resurrection Shuffle	1971	1.00	5.00
ASSAGI					
Vertigo 1004	(S)	Assagi	1971	4.00	10.00
ASSEMBLAGE					
Westbound 2004	(S)	The Assemblage Album	1972	6.00	15.00
ASSEMBLED MULTITUDE, THE					
Atlantic SD-8262	(S)	The Assembled Multitude	1970	4.00	10.00
ASSOCIATION, THE					
The Association was Gary Alexander, Ted Bluechel Jr, Brian Cole, Russ Giguere, Terry Kirkman, and Jim Yester. Alexander left after the first album and was replaced by Larry Ramos Jr. Alexander returned in late '68.					
Valiant VLM-5002	(M)	And Then... Along Comes The Association	1966	8.00	20.00
Valiant VLS-25002	(S)	And Then... Along Comes The Association	1966	10.00	25.00
Valiant VLM-5004	(M)	Renaissance	1966	6.00	15.00
Valiant VLS-25004	(S)	Renaissance	1966	8.00	20.00
		(First pressing covers do not mention "No Fair At All.")			
Valiant VLM-5004	(M)	Renaissance	1967	4.00	10.00
Valiant VLS-25004	(S)	Renaissance	1967	5.00	12.00
		(Second pressing covers have a blurb for "No Fair At All.")			
Warner Bros. W-1696	(M)	Insight Out	1967	6.00	15.00
Warner Bros. WS-1696	(S)	Insight Out	1967	8.00	20.00
		—Warner Bros. albums above have gold labels.—			

Label & Catalog #		Title	Year	VG+	NM
Warner Bros. WS-1696	(S)	Insight Out	1969	3.20	8.00
Warner Bros. WS-1702	(S)	And Then... Along Comes The Association	1969	3.20	8.00
Warner Bros. WS-1704	(S)	Renaissance	1969	3.20	8.00
Warner Bros. WS-1733	(S)	Birthday	1969	3.20	8.00
Warner Bros. WS-1767	(S)	The Association's Greatest Hits	1969	3.20	8.00
Warner Bros. WS-1786	(S)	Goodbye Columbus	1969	3.20	8.00
Warner Bros. WS-1800	(S)	The Association	1969	3.20	8.00

— Warner Bros. albums above have green labels with a "W7" logo on top. —

Warner Bros. WS-1868	(S)	The Association Live (2 LPs)	1970	3.20	8.00
Warner Bros. WS-1927	(S)	Stop Your Motor	1971	3.20	8.00
Columbia KC-31348	(S)	Waterbeds In Trinidad	1972	3.20	8.00

ASTRONAUTS, THE
The Astronauts can also be found on the RCA soundtrack "Wild On The Beach." Refer to Hardwater.

RCA Victor LPM-2760	(M)	Surfin' With The Astronauts	1963	30.00	75.00
RCA Victor LSP-2760	(S)	Surfin' With The Astronauts	1963	40.00	100.00
RCA Victor LPM-2782	(M)	Everything Is A-OK	1964	20.00	50.00
RCA Victor LSP-2782	(S)	Everything Is A-OK	1964	24.00	60.00
RCA Victor LPM-2858	(M)	Competition Coupe	1964	30.00	75.00
RCA Victor LSP-2858	(S)	Competition Coupe	1964	40.00	100.00
RCA Victor LPM-2903	(M)	The Astronauts Orbit Campus	1964	16.00	40.00
RCA Victor LSP-2903	(S)	The Astronauts Orbit Campus	1964	20.00	50.00

— RCA albums above have black labels with "Mono" or "Stereo" at the bottom. —

RCA Victor PRM-183	(DJ)	Rockin' With The Astronauts	1964	12.00	30.00
RCA Victor LPM-3307	(M)	The Astronauts Go Go Go	1965	12.00	30.00
RCA Victor LSP-3307	(S)	The Astronauts Go Go Go	1965	16.00	40.00
RCA Victor LPM-3359	(M)	Favorites For You From Us	1965	12.00	30.00
RCA Victor LSP-3359	(S)	Favorites For You From Us	1965	16.00	40.00
RCA Victor LPM-3454	(M)	Down The Line	1966	12.00	30.00
RCA Victor LSP-3454	(S)	Down The Line	1966	16.00	40.00
RCA Victor LPM-3733	(M)	Travelin' Men	1967	24.00	60.00
RCA Victor LSP-3733	(S)	Travelin' Men	1967	16.00	40.00

— RCA albums above have black labels with "Monaural" or "Stereo" at the bottom. —

ASTRONAUTS, THE / THE LIVERPOOL FIVE

RCA Victor PRS-251	(DJ)	Stereo Festival (Sampler)	1967	40.00	100.00

ASYLUM CHOIR
The Asylum Choir is Leon Russell and Mark Benno.

Smash SRS-67107	(S)	Look Inside (Toilet paper cover)	1968	16.00	40.00
Smash SRS-67107	(S)	Look Inside (Group photo cover)	1971	6.00	15.00
Shelter SW-8910	(S)	Asylum Choir 2	1971	6.00	15.00
Shelter 2120	(S)	Asylum Choir 2	1974	.80	4.00
Shelter 52010	(S)	Asylum Choir 2	1976	.80	4.00
MCA 684	(S)	Asylum Choir 2	1979	.80	4.00

ATLANTA

MCA 5463	(S)	Pictures	1984	1.00	5.00

ATLANTA DISCO BAND, THE

Ariola 50004	(S)	Bad Luck	1976	1.00	5.00

ATLANTA RHYTHM SECTION

Decca DL-75265	(S)	Atlanta Rhythm Section	1972	10.00	25.00
Decca DL-75390	(S)	Back Up Against The Wall	1974	10.00	25.00
MCA 4114	(S)	Atlanta Rhythm Section (2 LPs)	1977	3.20	8.00
		(MCA 4114 collects Decca 75265 and 75390.)			
Polydor PD-6027	(S)	Third Annual Pipe Dream	1974	1.00	5.00
Polydor PD-6041	(S)	Dog Days	1975	1.00	5.00
Polydor PD-6060	(S)	Red Tape	1976	1.00	5.00
Polydor PD-6080	(S)	A Rock And Roll Alternative	1977	1.00	5.00
Polydor PD-6134	(S)	Champagne Jam	1978	1.00	5.00
Polydor PD-6200	(S)	Underdog	1979	1.00	5.00
Polydor PD-6236	(S)	Are You Ready! (2 LPs)	1979	3.20	8.00
Polydor PD-6285	(S)	The Boys From Doraville	1980	1.00	5.00
Columbia 37550	(S)	Quinella	1981	1.00	5.00

ATLANTIS

Vertigo VEL-1016	(S)	Atlantis	1973	5.00	12.00
Vertigo VEL-1018	(S)	It's Getting Better	1974	5.00	12.00
Polydor PD-6513	(S)	Atlantis	1975	4.00	10.00

ATLEE: *Refer to* **ATLEE YEAGER**

ATOMIC ROOSTER

Elektra EKS-74094	(S)	Death Walks Behind You	1971	6.00	15.00
Elektra EKS-74109	(S)	In Hearing Of	1971	6.00	15.00
Elektra EKS-75039	(S)	Made In England	1972	5.00	12.00
Elektra EKS-75074	(S)	Atomic Rooster IV	1973	5.00	12.00

Label & Catalog #		Title	Year	VG+	NM

ATTILA

Attila features Billy Joel.

Epic E-30030	(S)	Attila	1970	10.00	25.00

AU-GO-GO SINGERS, THE

The Au-Go-Gos feature Steve Stills and Rich Furay, later of The Buffalo Springfield.

Roulette R-25280	(M)	They Call Us The Au Go-Go Singers	1964	20.00	50.00
Roulette SR-25280	(S)	They Call Us The Au Go-Go Singers	1964	30.00	75.00

AUDIENCE

Elektra EKS-75026	(S)	Lunch	1972	1.00	5.00

AUGER, BRIAN

Brian Auger's groups were The Trinity through 1970, Oblivion Express thereafter. Vocalist Julie "Jools" Driscoll is featured on Atco 258 and 701, Capitol 136, Warner Bros. 5153, and Polydor 6505.

Atco SD-33-258	(S)	Open	1968	4.00	10.00
Atco SD-33-273	(S)	Definitely What!	1969	4.00	10.00
Atco SD-2-701	(S)	Streetnoise (2 LPs)	1969	6.00	15.00
Capitol ST-136	(E)	Jools & Brian	1969	4.00	10.00
RCA Victor LSP-4372	(S)	Befour	1970	4.00	10.00
RCA Victor LSP-4462	(S)	Brian Auger's Oblivion Express	1971	4.00	10.00
RCA Victor LSP-4540	(S)	A Better Land	1971	4.00	10.00
RCA Victor LSP-4703	(S)	Second Wind	1972	4.00	10.00
RCA Victor APL1-0140	(S)	Closer To It	1973	3.20	8.00
RCA Victor APL1-0454	(S)	Straight Ahead	1974	3.20	8.00
RCA Victor APL1-1210	(S)	Reinforcements	1974	3.20	8.00
RCA Victor APL1-1230	(S)	Live Oblivion	1974	3.20	8.00
RCA Victor AFL1-2249	(S)	Best Of Brian Auger	1974	3.20	8.00
RCA Victor AFL1-2481	(S)	Live Oblivion, Volume 2	1974	3.20	8.00
Polydor PD-6505	(S)	Genesis (Trinity)	1975	3.20	8.00
Warner Bros. BS-2981	(S)	Happiness Heartaches	1977	3.20	8.00
Warner Bros. BSK-3153	(S)	Encore	1977	3.20	8.00
Springboard SPB-4044	(S)	Brian Auger	197?	3.20	8.00
Headfirst 9702	(S)	Search Party	1981	6.00	15.00

AUM

Sire SES-97007	(S)	Bluesvibes	1969	10.00	25.00
Fillmore F-30002	(S)	Resurrection	1969	12.00	30.00

AUSTIN, DONALD

Eastbound EB-9005	(S)	Crazy Legs	1973	16.00	40.00

AUSTIN, SIL

Refer to Red Prysock & Sil Austin.

Mercury MG-20237	(M)	Slow Walk Rock	1957	30.00	75.00
Mercury MG-20320	(M)	Everything Is Shakin'	1958	30.00	75.00
Mercury MG-20424	(M)	Sil Austin Plays Pretty For The People	1959	18.00	45.00
Mercury SR-60096	(S)	Sil Austin Plays Pretty For The People	1959	24.00	60.00
Mercury MG-20576	(M)	Soft, Plaintive And Moody	1960	18.00	45.00
Mercury SR-60236	(S)	Soft, Plaintive And Moody	1960	24.00	60.00
Mercury MG-20663	(M)	Golden Saxophone Hits	1961	10.00	25.00
Mercury SR-60663	(S)	Golden Saxophone Hits	1961	12.00	30.00
Wing MGW-12168	(M)	Slow Walk Rock	196?	6.00	15.00
Wing SRW-16168	(E)	Slow Walk Rock	196?	4.00	10.00
Wing MGW-12227	(M)	Everything Is Shakin'	196?	6.00	15.00
Wing SRW-16227	(E)	Everything Is Shakin'	196?	4.00	10.00
SSS International 4	(S)	Honey Sax	197?	1.00	5.00
SSS International 8	(S)	Sil And The Silver Screen	197?	1.00	5.00
SSS International 14	(S)	Honey Sax	197?	1.00	5.00
SSS International 23	(S)	Songs Of Gold	197?	1.00	5.00

AUTOMATIC MAN

Island ILS-9397	(S)	Automatic Man	1976	1.00	5.00
Island ILS-9429	(S)	Visitors	1977	1.00	5.00

AUTOSALVAGE

RCA Victor LPM-3940	(M)	Autosalvage	1968	16.00	40.00
RCA Victor LSP-3940	(S)	Autosalvage	1968	16.00	40.00

AVALANCHES, THE

Warner Bros. W-1525	(M)	Ski Surfin'	1963	20.00	50.00
Warner Bros. WS-1525	(S)	Ski Surfin'	1963	30.00	75.00

AVALON, FRANKIE

Refer to Fabian / Frankie Avalon.

Chancellor CHL-5001	(M)	Frankie Avalon	1958	20.00	50.00
Chancellor CHL-5002	(M)	The Young Frankie Avalon	1959	20.00	50.00
Chancellor CHLS-5002	(S)	The Young Frankie Avalon	1959	30.00	75.00

—Chancellor albums above have pink labels.—

Label & Catalog #		Title	Year	VG+	NM
Chancellor CHL-5001	(M)	Frankie Avalon	1960	16.00	40.00
Chancellor CHL-5002	(M)	The Young Frankie Avalon	1960	16.00	40.00
Chancellor CHLS-5002	(S)	The Young Frankie Avalon	1960	20.00	50.00
Chancellor CHLX-5004	(M)	Swingin' On A Rainbow	1960	16.00	40.00
Chancellor CHLXS-5004	(S)	Swingin' On A Rainbow	1960	20.00	50.00
Chancellor CHL-69801	(M)	Young And In Love	1960	30.00	75.00
		(Boxed set with photos and a 3-D portrait.)			
Chancellor CHL-5011	(M)	Summer Scene	1960	12.00	30.00
Chancellor CHLS-5011	(S)	Summer Scene	1960	20.00	50.00
Chancellor CHL-5018	(M)	A Whole Lotta Frankie	1961	12.00	30.00
Chancellor CHL-5022	(M)	And Now About Mr. Avalon	1961	12.00	30.00
Chancellor CHLS-5022	(S)	And Now About Mr. Avalon	1961	20.00	60.00
Chancellor CHL-5025	(M)	Italiano	1962	12.00	30.00
Chancellor CHLS-5025	(S)	Italiano	1962	16.00	40.00
Chancellor CHL-5027	(M)	You're Mine	1962	12.00	30.00
Chancellor CHLS-5027	(S)	You're Mine	1962	16.00	40.00
Chancellor CHL-5031	(M)	Frankie Avalon's Christmas Album	1962	12.00	30.00
Chancellor CHLS-5031	(S)	Frankie Avalon's Christmas Album	1962	16.00	40.00
Chancellor CHL-5032	(M)	Cleopatra Plus 13 Other Great Hits	1963	12.00	30.00
Chancellor CHLS-5032	(S)	Cleopatra Plus 13 Other Great Hits	1963	16.00	40.00
		—Chancellor albums above have black labels.—			
United Arts. UAL-3371	(M)	Songs From Muscle Beach Party	1964	10.00	25.00
United Arts. UAS-6371	(S)	Songs From Muscle Beach Party	1964	12.00	30.00
United Arts. UAL-3382	(M)	Frankie Avalon's 15 Greatest Hits	1964	8.00	20.00
United Arts. UAS-6382	(P)	Frankie Avalon's 15 Greatest Hits	1964	10.00	25.00
		(A collection of hits originally issued on Chancellor.)			
Sunset SUS-5244	(S)	Frankie Avalon	1969	6.00	15.00
Metromedia 1034	(S)	I Want You Near Me	1970	6.00	15.00
ABC X-805	(S)	16 Greatest Hits	1973	3.20	8.00
United Arts. LA-450	(S)	The Very Best Of Frankie Avalon	1975	.80	4.00
De-Lite 2020	(S)	Venus	1976	4.00	10.00
De-Lite 9504	(S)	You're My Life	1977	4.00	10.00
Trip TOP-1621	(S)	16 Greatest Hits Of Frankie Avalon	1977	.80	4.00
Koala HW-14130	(S)	Venus	1979	.80	4.00
Liberty LN-10193	(S)	Songs From Muscle Beach Party	1981	1.00	5.00
Woorell LV20-2002	(S)	Greatest Hits, Vol. 1	1982	.80	4.00
Woorell LV20-2003	(S)	Greatest Hits, Vol. 2	1982	.80	4.00
Everest 4187	(S)	Greatest Hits	1982	.80	4.00
AVERAGE WHITE BAND, THE [AWB]					
MCA 345	(S)	Show Your Hands	1973	10.00	25.00
MCA 475	(S)	Put It Where You Want It	1975	1.00	5.00
		(MCA 475 is a reissue of 345.)			
Atlantic SD-7308	(S)	AWB	1974	1.00	5.00
Atlantic QD-7308	(Q)	AWB	1975	6.00	15.00
Atlantic SD-18140	(S)	Cut The Cake	1975	1.00	5.00
Atlantic SD-18179	(S)	Soul Searching	1976	1.00	5.00
Atlantic SD-1002	(S)	Person To Person (2 LPs)	1977	1.20	6.00
Atlantic SD-19105	(S)	Benny And Us (With Ben E. King)	1977	1.00	5.00
Atlantic SD-19162	(S)	Warmer Communications	1978	1.00	5.00
Atlantic SD-19207	(S)	Feel No Fret	1979	1.00	5.00
Atlantic SD-19266	(S)	AWB/Volume VIII	1980	1.00	5.00
Arista 9523	(S)	Shine	1980	1.00	5.00
AVONS, THE					
Hull HLP-1000	(M)	The Avons (Counterfeits exist)	1960	300.00	600.00
		—Hull albums above have red labels.—			
AXEL MARS BLUES BAND, THE					
Dill Pickle 3462	(S)	Live Mars	1971	4.00	10.00
AXELROD, DAVID					
Capitol ST-2982	(S)	Songs Of Experience	1969	6.00	15.00
AYERS, KEVIN					
Sire SAS-7406	(S)	Bananamour	1973	4.00	10.00
Island ILPS-9263	(S)	Confessions Of Dr. Dream	1974	4.00	10.00
ABC 1021	(S)	Yes, We Have No Mananas	1977	4.00	10.00
AZTECA					
Columbia KC-31776	(S)	Azteca	1972	1.00	5.00
Columbia CQ-31776	(Q)	Azteca	1974	4.00	10.00
AZTECS, THE					
World Artists WAM-2001	(M)	Live At The Ad-Lib Club Of London	1964	20.00	50.00

BABE RUTH

Harvest ST-11151	(S)	First Base	1973	1.00	5.00
Harvest ST-11367	(S)	Babe Ruth	1975	1.00	5.00
Harvest ST-11451	(S)	Stealin' Home	1975	1.00	5.00

BABY

Lone Starr 9782	(S)	Baby	1974	8.00	20.00

BABY RAY

Baby Ray is a pseudonym for Ray Stevens.

Imperial LP-9335	(M)	Where Soul Lives	1967	10.00	25.00
Imperial LP-12335	(S)	Where Soul Lives	1967	12.00	30.00

BABYS, THE

Chrysalis CHS-1129	(S)	The Babys	1977	1.00	5.00
Chrysalis CHS-1150	(S)	Broken Heart	1977	1.00	5.00
Chrysalis CHS-1195	(S)	Head First	1979	1.00	5.00
Chrysalis CHS-1267	(S)	Union Jacks	1980	1.00	5.00
Chrysalis CHS-1305	(S)	On The Edge	1980	1.00	5.00
Chrysalis CHS-1351	(S)	Anthology	1981	1.00	5.00

BACHMAN, RANDY

Randy also recorded with The Guess Who and Bachman-Turner Overdrive.

RCA Victor LSP-4348	(S)	Axe	1970	4.00	10.00

— RCA albums above have orange labels on non-flexible vinyl.—

BACHMAN-TURNER OVERDRIVE [BTO]

BTO features Randy Bachman and C.F. Turner.

Mercury SRM-673	(S)	Bachman-Turner Overdrive	1973	1.00	5.00
Mercury SRM-696	(S)	Bachman-Turner Overdrive II	1973	1.00	5.00
Mercury SRM-1004	(S)	Not Fragile	1974	1.00	5.00
Mercury SRM-1027	(S)	Four Wheel Drive	1975	1.00	5.00
Mercury SRM-1067	(S)	Head On	1976	1.00	5.00
Mercury SRM-1101	(S)	Best Of B.T.O. (So Far)	1976	1.00	5.00
Mercury SRM-3700	(S)	Freeways	1977	1.00	5.00
Mercury SRM-3713	(S)	Street Action	1978	1.00	5.00
Mercury SRM-3748	(S)	Rock N' Roll Nights	1979	1.00	5.00
Compleat 101	(S)	Bachman Turner Overdrive	1984	.80	4.00

BACK STREET CRAWLER [CRAWLER]

Atco SD-136-125	(S)	The Band Plays On	1975	1.00	5.00
Atco SD-136-138	(S)	2nd Street	1976	1.00	5.00
Epic E-34900	(S)	Crawler	1977	1.00	5.00

BACON FAT

Blue Horizon BH-4807	(S)	Grease One For Me	1970	4.00	10.00

BAD COMPANY

BC consists of Paul Rodgers backed by Boz Burrell, Simon Kirke and Mick Ralphs.

Swan Song 8410	(S)	Bad Company	1974	1.00	5.00
Swan Song 8413	(S)	Straight Shooter	1975	1.00	5.00
Swan Song 8415	(S)	Run With The Pack	1976	1.00	5.00
Swan Song 8500	(S)	Burnin' Sky	1977	1.00	5.00
Swan Song 8506	(S)	Desolation Angels	1979	1.00	5.00
Swan Song 90001	(S)	Rough Diamonds	1982	1.00	5.00

BADFINGER

Tom Evans, Mike Gibbons, Pete Ham and Joey Molland originally recorded as The Iveys. They can also be found on the Commonwealth soundtrack "The Magic Christian." Refer to George Harrison & Friends.

Apple ST-3364	(S)	Magic Christian Music	1970	12.00	30.00

—Apple albums above have "A Subsidiary of Capitol" on the label.—

Apple ST-3364	(S)	Magic Christian Music	1970	8.00	20.00
Apple SKAO-3367	(S)	No Dice	1970	12.00	30.00
Apple SW-3387	(S)	Straight Up	1971	20.00	50.00
Apple SW-3411	(S)	Ass	1973	6.00	15.00

—Apple albums above have "Manufactured by Apple" on the label.—

Badfinger originally recorded as The Ivies, releasing an album on The Beatles' Apple Records in Europe and Japan, although it was never distributed in the States. Changing their name, apparently at John Beatle's inspiration, and recording Paul Beatle's "Come And Get It" for inclusion in Ringo Beatle's first feature film, "The Magic Christian," they were a worldwide smash for a couple of years. Their third album, Straight Up, was originally to be produced in its entirety by George Beatle, who was repaying them for their services as the backing band for the concert to aid Bangla Desh. Due to extenuating circumstances, it was completed under the direction of Todd Rundgren. Although the album sold well, copies flooded the nation's cut-out bins for years. Then, they were gone. This album eventually found a second life in the wake of power-pop mania, with prices for sealed copies fetching three figures, although it has since settled into a more modest place in the collectors market. Oh, and it's a good album, too. . .

Label & Catalog #		Title	Year	VG+	NM
Warner Bros. BS-2762	(S)	Badfinger	1974	5.00	12.00
Warner Bros. BS-2827	(S)	Wish You Were Here	1974	6.00	15.00
Elektra 6E-175	(S)	Airwaves	1979	4.00	10.00
Radio Records RR-16030	(S)	Say No More	1981	3.20	8.00

BADGER

Atco SD-7022	(S)	One Live Badger	1973	1.00	5.00

BAG, THE

Decca DL-75057	(S)	Real	1968	6.00	15.00

BAIN, BOB

Mr Bain's other recordings are in a non-rocking vein and not included in this edition.

Capitol T-965	(M)	Rockin,' Rollin' And Strollin'	1958	40.00	100.00
		— Capitol albums above have turquoise labels.—			

BAKER, GEORGE

The George Baker Selection is a Dutch group fronted by Hans Bouwens.

Colossus CS-1002	(S)	Little Green Bag	1970	6.00	15.00
		("Little Green Bag" is rechanneled.)			
Warner Bros BS-2905	(S)	Paloma Blanca	1975	1.00	5.00

BAKER, GINGER

Drummer extraordinaire Baker also recorded with Cream and Blind Faith.

Atco SD-2-703	(S)	Ginger Baker's Air Force (2 LPs)	1970	6.00	15.00
Atco SD-33-343	(S)	Ginger Baker's Air Force 2	1970	4.00	10.00
Atco SD-7012	(S)	Stratavarious	1972	4.00	10.00
Polydor 24-3504	(S)	Ginger Baker At His Best	1972	1.00	5.00
Polydor 26-6201	(S)	Ginger Baker's Air Force 2	1972	1.00	5.00
Sire SASD-7532	(S)	Eleven Sides Of Baker	1977	1.00	5.00

BAKER, LAVERN

Atlantic 8002	(M)	LaVern	1956	100.00	250.00
Atlantic 8007	(M)	LaVern Baker	1957	100.00	250.00
Atlantic 1281	(M)	LaVern Baker Sings Bessie Smith	1958	50.00	125.00
Atlantic SD-1281	(S)	LaVern Baker Sings Bessie Smith	1959	60.00	150.00
Atlantic 8030	(M)	Blues Ballads	1959	80.00	200.00
Atlantic 8036	(M)	Precious Memories	1959	80.00	200.00
Atlantic SD-8036	(S)	Precious Memories	1959	150.00	300.00
		— Atlantic mono albums above have black labels; stereo albums have green labels.—			
Atlantic 8030	(M)	Blues Ballads	1960	60.00	150.00
Atlantic 8036	(M)	Precious Memories	1960	60.00	150.00
Atlantic SD-8036	(S)	Precious Memories	1960	80.00	200.00
		— Atlantic mono albums above have white "bullseye" labels.—			
Atlantic 8002	(M)	LaVern	1960	12.00	30.00
Atlantic 1281	(M)	LaVern Baker Sings Bessie Smith	1960	12.00	30.00
Atlantic SD-1281	(S)	LaVern Baker Sings Bessie Smith	1960	16.00	40.00
Atlantic 8030	(M)	Blues Ballads	1960	12.00	30.00
Atlantic 8036	(M)	Precious Memories	1960	12.00	30.00
Atlantic SD-8036	(S)	Precious Memories	1960	16.00	40.00
Atlantic 8050	(M)	Saved	1961	40.00	100.00
Atlantic SD-8050	(S)	Saved	1961	60.00	150.00
Atlantic 8071	(M)	See See Rider	1962	40.00	100.00
Atlantic SD-8071	(S)	See See Rider	1962	60.00	150.00
		— Atlantic albums above have multi-colored labels with a white "fan" logo on the right side.—			
Atlantic 8002	(M)	LaVern	1962	6.00	15.00
Atlantic 1281	(M)	LaVern Baker Sings Bessie Smith	1962	6.00	15.00
Atlantic SD-1281	(S)	LaVern Baker Sings Bessie Smith	1962	8.00	20.00
Atlantic 8030	(M)	Blues Ballads	1962	6.00	15.00
Atlantic 8036	(M)	Precious Memories	1962	6.00	15.00
Atlantic SD-8036	(S)	Precious Memories	1962	8.00	20.00
Atlantic 8050	(M)	Saved	1962	6.00	15.00
Atlantic SD-8050	(S)	Saved	1962	8.00	20.00
Atlantic 8071	(M)	See See Rider	1963	10.00	25.00
Atlantic SD-8071	(S)	See See Rider	1963	12.00	30.00
Atlantic 8080	(DJ)	The Best Of LaVern Baker (White label)	1963	150.00	300.00
Atlantic 8080	(M)	The Best Of LaVern Baker	1963	60.00	150.00
		— Atlantic albums above have multi-colored labels with a black "fan" logo on the right side.—			
Brunswick BL-754160	(S)	Let Me Belong To You	1970	8.00	20.00
Atco SD-33-372	(P)	Her Greatest Recordings	1971	4.00	10.00

BAKER, MICKEY

Formerly one half of Mickey & Sylvia. Refer to Champion Jack Dupree; Brother John Sellers.

Atlantic 8035	(M)	Wildest Guitar	1959	80.00	200.00
Atlantic SD-8035	(S)	Wildest Guitar	1959	150.00	300.00
		— Atlantic mono albums above have black labels; stereo albums have green labels.—			
Atlantic 8035	(M)	Wildest Guitar	1961	20.00	50.00
Atlantic SD-8035	(S)	Wildest Guitar	1961	30.00	75.00
		— Atlantic mono albums above have multi-colored labels with a white "fan" logo on the right side.—			

Mickey Baker was a stalwart in the rhythm'n blues scene of the '50s and '60s, providing guitar for literally hundreds of records. He was also teamed with young protege Sylvia Vanderpool, recording as one of the '50s' more interesting duets, Mickey & Sylvia, scoring the ever-popular "Love Is Strange." After their break-up, Mr. Baker recorded this excellent album, to negligible sales.

Label & Catalog #		Title	Year	VG+	NM
King 839	(M)	But Wild	1963	200.00	400.00
		—King albums above have crownless black labels.—			
King 839	(M)	But Wild	196?	30.00	75.00
King KS-839	(E)	But Wild	196?	20.00	50.00
		—King albums above have blue labels with a crown on top.—			
Kicking Mule 142	(S)	The Blues And Jazz Guitar Of Mickey Baker	1978	4.00	10.00

BAKER-GURVITZ ARMY, THE
The BGA features Ginger Baker and Adrian and Paul Gurvitz of Three Man Army.

Janus JXS-7015	(S)	The Baker-Gurvitz Army	1975	4.00	10.00
Atco SD-36-123	(S)	Elysian Encounter	1975	4.00	10.00
Atco SD-36-137	(S)	Hearts On Fire	1976	4.00	10.00

BAKER, RONNIE

Warner Bros. W-1212	(M)	Oh, Johnny!	1958	14.00	35.00
Warner Bros. WS-1212	(S)	Oh, Johnny!	1958	20.00	50.00

BALDERDASH

Uni 73138	(S)	Ballad Of Shirley Goodness And Mercy	1972	4.00	10.00

BALDRY, LONG JOHN

Ascot ALM-13022	(M)	Long John's Blues	1965	20.00	50.00
Ascot ALS-16022	(E)	Long John's Blues	1965	14.00	35.00
United Arts. UAS-5543	(M)	Long John's Blues	1971	4.00	10.00
		(United Arts. 5543 is a reissue of Ascot 13022.)			
Warner Bros. WS-1921	(S)	It Ain't Easy	1971	6.00	15.00
Warner Bros. BS-2614	(S)	Everything Stops For Tea	1972	4.00	10.00
EMI SW-17015	(S)	Baldry's Out	1979	1.00	5.00
Casablanca NBLP-7012	(S)	Good To Be Alive	1975	1.00	5.00
Casablanca NBLP-7035	(S)	Welcome To The Club Casablanca	1976	1.00	5.00

BALIN, MARTY
Marty Balin founded Jefferson Airplane. Refer to Bodacious D.F.; Grootna; Jefferson Starship.

EMI SPRO-9673	(DJ)	Balin (Red vinyl)	1981	6.00	15.00
EMI SPRO-17054	(S)	Balin	1981	.80	4.00
EMI SPRO-17088	(S)	Lucky	1983	.80	4.00

BALLARD, FRANK

Phillips Int. 1985	(M)	Rhythm-Blues Party	1962	See note below	
		(Philips Int. 1985 has a suggested NM value of $4,000-6,000.)			

BALLARD, HANK
Hank Ballard was the lead singer for the legendary rhythm'n blues vocal group The Midnighters. By the late '50s management had rearranged the group and they recorded their singles as Hank Ballard & The Midnighters. As the titles below indicate, he was more or less sold to the album market as a solo, which is why the classic, early group material is listed under The Midnighters while the later recordings with and without The Midnighters is listed here.

King 618	(M)	Singin And Swingin'	1959	200.00	400.00
King 674	(M)	The One And Only Hank Ballard (Brown cover)	1969	200.00	400.00
		—King albums above have crownless black labels with the small, 2" wide "KING" logo on top.—			
King 618	(M)	Singin And Swingin'	196?	80.00	200.00
King 674	(M)	The One And Only Hank Ballard (Green cover)	1960	80.00	200.00
King 700	(M)	Mr. Rhythm And Blues	1960	80.00	200.00
King 740	(M)	Spotlight On Hank Ballard	1961	80.00	200.00
King KS-740	(S)	Spotlight On Hank Ballard	1961	150.00	300.00
King 748	(M)	Let's Go Again	1961	60.00	150.00
King 759	(M)	Dance Along	1961	60.00	150.00
King 781	(M)	The Twistin' Fools	1962	60.00	150.00
King 793	(M)	Jumpin' Hank Ballard	1962	60.00	150.00
King 815	(M)	The 1963 Sound Of Hank Ballard	1963	60.00	150.00
King 867	(M)	Biggest Hits	1963	60.00	150.00
King 896	(M)	A Star In Your Eyes	1964	60.00	150.00
		—King albums above have crownless black labels with the large, 3" "KING" logo on top.—			
King 913	(M)	Those Lazy, Lazy Days	1965	30.00	75.00
King 927	(M)	Glad Songs, Sad Songs	1966	30.00	75.00
King 950	(M)	24 Hit Tunes	1966	24.00	60.00
King 981	(M)	24 Great Songs	1968	16.00	40.00
King KSD-1052	(S)	You Can't Keep A Good Man Down	1969	20.00	50.00
		(Produced by James Brown)			
Power Pak PO-276	(E)	Mr. Rhythm & Blues	197?	1.00	5.00

BALLARD, RUSS
Russ Ballard recorded with Argent.

Epic 33252	(S)	Russ Ballard	1974	1.00	5.00
Epic 34093	(S)	Winning	1976	1.00	5.00
Epic 35035	(S)	At The Third Stroke	1978	1.00	5.00
Epic 36186	(S)	Russ Ballard & The Barnet Dogs	1980	1.00	5.00
Epic 36933	(S)	Into The Fire	1981	1.00	5.00
EMI SPRO-9404/5	(DJ)	The Fire Still Burns (2 LPs)	1985	8.00	20.00

Hank Ballard originally joined The Royals as the group's lead singer in 1953, after which they changed their name to The Midnighters and preceded to blaze up and down the rhythm'n blues charts. While The Midnighters produced several classics from this period, none found their way onto the white sales charts. (Shown here is the rare 12" version of the even rarer 10" Federal album, Their Greatest Hits.) As Hank Ballard & The Midnighters, they placed a baker's dozen's worth of sides on the pop charts between 1959 and 1962. The flip-side to their first pop hit, "Teardrops On Your Letter," was a jivey little dance number called "The Twist." It was picked up by Chubby Checker, covered in an arrangement that duplicated the original, and, of course, became a part of '60s pop cultural history. In the wake of Chubby's success, King reissued the single with "The Twist" as the A-side and Hank and the group had a Top 30 hit in 1960. By 1964, when A Star In Your Eyes was released, Ballard was recording as a solo with no real success in the pop market.

Label & Catalog #		Title	Year	VG+	NM
BALLIN' JACK					
Columbia KC-30344	(S)	**Ballin' Jack**	1971	1.00	5.00
BANANA & THE BUNCH					
Banana is Lowell Levinger of The Youngbloods.					
Raccoon/Warners BS-2626	(S)	**Mid Mountain Ranch**	1972	1.00	5.00
BANCHEE					
Atlantic SD-8240	(S)	**Banchee**	1969	6.00	15.00
Polydor 24-2066	(S)	**Thinkin'**	1971	16.00	40.00
BAND, THE					
The Band is Rick Danko, Levon Helm, Garth Hudson, Richard Manuel and Robbie Robertson. Refer to Bob Dylan; John Hammond; Ronnie Hawkins; Steve Miller / Quicksilver / The Band.					
Capitol SKAO-2955	(S)	**Music From Big Pink**	1968	10.00	25.00
		—Capitol albums above have black rainbow labels.—			
Capitol SKAO-2955	(S)	**Music From Big Pink**	1969	4.00	10.00
Capitol ST-132	(S)	**The Band**	1969	6.00	15.00
Capitol SW-425	(S)	**Stage Fright** *(With insert cover)*	1970	6.00	15.00
Capitol SW-425	(S)	**Stage Fright** *(Without insert)*	1970	4.00	10.00
		(SW-425 was originally issued with a fold-open "false" cover with a sepia-toned photo of the group seated in an old room.)			
Capitol ST-651	(S)	**Cahoots**	1971	4.00	10.00
		—Capitol albums above have green labels.—			
Capitol SKAO-2955	(S)	**Music From Big Pink**	1972	1.00	5.00
Capitol ST-132	(S)	**The Band**	1972	1.00	5.00
Capitol SW-425	(S)	**Stage Fright**	1972	1.00	5.00
Capitol ST-651	(S)	**Cahoots**	1972	1.00	5.00
Capitol SABB-11045	(S)	**Rock Of Ages** *(2 LPs.)*	1972	10.00	25.00
		—Capitol albums above have red labels with a purple "C" logo.—			
Capitol SKAO-2955	(S)	**Music From Big Pink**	197?	.80	4.00
Capitol ST-132	(S)	**The Band**	197?	.80	4.00
Capitol SW-425	(S)	**Stage Fright**	197?	.80	4.00
Capitol ST-651	(S)	**Cahoots**	197?	.80	4.00
Capitol SABB-11045	(S)	**Rock Of Ages** *(2 LPs)*	1972	6.00	15.00
Capitol SW-11214	(S)	**Moondog Matinee** *(With insert cover)*	1973	6.00	15.00
Capitol SW-11214	(S)	**Moondog Matinee** *(Without insert)*	1973	1.20	6.00
		(SW-11214 was originally issued with a fold-open "false" cover with a painting of the group in a bar scene.)			
Capitol SW-11214	(S)	**Moondog Matinee** *(Without painting)*	1973	1.20	6.00
Capitol ST-11440	(S)	**Northern Lights, Southern Cross**	1975	1.20	6.00
Capitol ST-11553	(S)	**The Best Of The Band**	1976	1.20	6.00
Capitol SO-11602	(S)	**Islands**	1977	1.20	6.00
Capitol SKBO-11856	(S)	**The Band/Anthology** *(2 LPs)*	1978	3.20	8.00
		—Capitol albums above have orange labels.—			
Warner Bros. PRO-737	(DJ)	**The Last Waltz** *(Sampler)*	1978	6.00	15.00
Warner Bros. 3WS-3146	(S)	**The Last Waltz** *(3 LPs)*	1978	5.00	12.00
		("The Last Waltz" was The Band's going-out-of-business salute that featured Eric Clapton, Neil Diamond, Bob Dylan, Emmylou Harris, Ronnie Hawkins, Van Morrison, Muddy Waters, and Ringo.)			
Capitol SN-16003	(S)	**Cahoots**	1980	.80	4.00
Capitol SN-16004	(S)	**Moondog Matinee**	1980	.80	4.00
Capitol SN-16005	(S)	**Northern Lights, Southern Cross**	1980	.80	4.00
Capitol SN-16006	(S)	**Stage Fright**	1980	.80	4.00
Capitol SN-16007	(S)	**Islands**	1980	.80	4.00
Capitol SN-16008	(S)	**Rock Of Ages, Volume 1**	1980	.80	4.00
Capitol SN-16009	(S)	**Rock Of Ages, Volume 2**	1980	.80	4.00
Capitol SN-16010	(S)	**The Band/Anthology, Volume 1**	1982	.80	4.00
Capitol SN-16011	(S)	**The Band/Anthology, Volume 2**	1982	.80	4.00
BAND OF GYPSYS: *Refer to* JIMI HENDRIX					
BANDITS, THE					
The Bandits feature Glen Campbell.					
World Pacific T-1833	(M)	**The Electric 12 String**	1964	8.00	20.00
World Pacific ST-1833	(S)	**The Electric 12 String**	1964	10.00	25.00
BANG					
Capitol ST-11015	(S)	**Bang**	1972	4.00	10.00
Capitol SMAS-11110	(S)	**Mother/Bow To The King**	1972	4.00	10.00
Capitol ST-11970	(S)	**Bang Music** *(Backing vocals by The Raspberries)*	1973	6.00	15.00
BANGLES, THE					
Faulty 1302	(S)	**The Bangles** *(5 tracks)*	1982	8.00	20.00
Columbia CAS-2270	(DJ)	**Interchords** *(Interview)*	1986	8.00	20.00
BANGOR FLYING CIRCUS, THE					
Dunhill DS-50069	(S)	**The Bangor Flying Circus**	1969	6.00	15.00

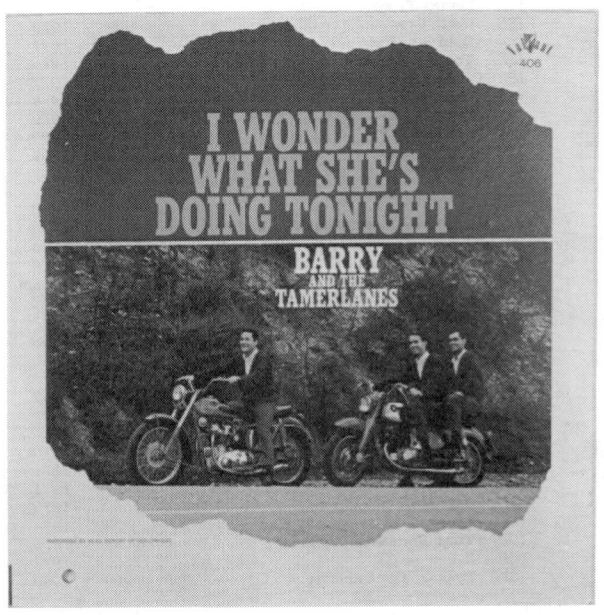

Barry & The Tamerlanes, featuring Barry DeVorzon, had a decent hit in 1963 with the title tune of their sole LP (written by Tommy Boyce and Bobby Hart, who had an even bigger hit with it four years later). Like many albums on smaller labels, the stereo pressing of this album is so rare that, until a few years ago, many collectors doubted its very existence. (And, while it is not pictured here, it does, indeed, exist.)

Label & Catalog #		Title	Year	VG+	NM
BANKS, DARRELL					
Atco 33-216	(M)	Darrell Banks Is Here	1967	10.00	25.00
Atco SD-33-216	(S)	Darrell Banks Is Here	1967	12.00	30.00
		("Open The Door To Your Heart" is rechanneled.)			
Volt VOS-6002	(S)	Here To Stay	1969	10.00	25.00
BANKS, PETER					
Peter Banks also recorded with Yes and Flash.					
Sovereign 11217	(S)	Two Sides Of Peter Banks	1973	1.00	5.00
BANKS, TONY					
Tony Banks is a member of Genesis.					
Charisma CHS-2207	(S)	A Curious Feeling	1979	1.00	5.00
BANTAMS, THE					
Warner Bros. W-1625	(M)	Beware The Bantams	1966	8.00	20.00
Warner Bros. WS-1625	(S)	Beware The Bantams	1966	10.00	25.00
BAR-KAYS, THE					
Volt 417	(M)	Soul Finger	1967	12.00	30.00
Volt S-417	(S)	Soul Finger	1967	16.00	40.00
Volt S-6004	(S)	Gotta Groove	1969	12.00	30.00
Volt S-6011	(S)	Black Rock	1971	10.00	25.00
Volt S-8001	(S)	Do You See What I See?	1972	10.00	25.00
Volt S-6023	(S)	Cold Blooded	1974	10.00	25.00
Stax 4106	(S)	Money Talks	1978	4.00	10.00
Stax 4130	(S)	Gotta Groove	1979	4.00	10.00
Stax 8510	(S)	Cold Blooded	1981	4.00	10.00
Mercury SRM-1-1099	(S)	Too Hot Too Stop	1976	4.00	10.00
Mercury SRM-1-1181	(S)	Flying High On Your Love	1977	4.00	10.00
Mercury SRM-1-3732	(S)	Light Of Life	1978	4.00	10.00
Mercury SRM-1-3781	(S)	Injoy	1979	4.00	10.00
Mercury SRM-1-3844	(S)	As One	1980	4.00	10.00
Mercury SRM-1-4028	(S)	Nightcruisin'	1981	4.00	10.00
Mercury SRM-1-4065	(S)	Propositions	1982	4.00	10.00
BARBARIANS, THE					
Laurie LLP-2033	(M)	Are You A Boy Or Are You A Girl?	1966	60.00	150.00
Laurie SLP-2033	(S)	Are You A Boy Or Are You A Girl?	1966	80.00	200.00
Rhino RNLP-008	(P)	The Barbarians	1979	4.00	10.00
		(The Rhino album is a reissue of the Laurie album plus "Moultie.")			
BARBARY, RICHARD					
A&M SP-3010	(S)	Soul Machine	1968	6.00	15.00
BARBOUR, KEITH					
Epic BN-26485	(S)	Echo Park	1969	4.00	10.00
BARCLAY JAMES HARVEST					
Sire/London SES-97026	(S)	Barclay James Harvest	1970	6.00	15.00
Sire ST-5904	(S)	Barclay James Harvest	1971	4.00	10.00
Sire ST-4904	(S)	Once Again	1971	4.00	10.00
Harvest SW-11145	(S)	Barclay James Harvest	1973	1.00	5.00
Polydor PD-6508	(S)	Everyone Is Everybody Else	1974	1.00	5.00
Polydor PD-6517	(S)	Time Honoured Ghosts	1975	1.00	5.00
Polydor PD-6173	(S)	XII	1978	1.00	5.00
Polydor PD-6267	(S)	Eyes Of The Universe	1980	1.00	5.00
BARDENS, PETER					
Peter Bardens also recorded with Camel.					
Verve/Forecast FTS-3088	(S)	The Answer	1971	4.00	10.00
Verve/Forecast FTS-3091	(S)	Write My Name In Dust	1971	4.00	10.00
BARGE, GENE					
Checker LP-2994	(M)	Dance With Daddy G	1965	20.00	50.00
BARNES, J. J., & STEVE MANCHA					
Volt VOS-6001	(S)	Rare Stamps	1969	12.00	30.00
BARNES & BARNES					
Barnes & Barnes are Billy Mumy and Robert Haines.					
Rhino RNLP-013	(S)	Voobaha	1980	1.20	6.00
Rhino RNLP-802	(S)	Spazchow	1981	1.20	6.00
Rhino RNLP-814	(S)	Amazing Adult Fantasy	1982	1.20	6.00
Rhino RNDF-282	(S)	Greatest Hits (Fish shaped EP)	1982	1.20	6.00
Boulevard B5Z-38928	(S)	Soak It Up	1982	1.20	6.00

Label & Catalog #		Title	Year	VG+	NM
BAROQUES, THE					
Chess LP-1516	(M)	The Baroques	1967	30.00	75.00
Chess LPS-1516	(S)	The Baroques	1967	40.00	100.00
BARRABAS					
Atco SD-136-118	(S)	Heart Of The City	1975	1.00	5.00
BARRETT, SYD					
Syd Barrett was the founder of Pink Floyd.					
Harvest SABB-11314	(S)	The Madcap Laughs *(2 LPs)*	1974	4.00	10.00
BARRI, STEVE: *Refer to* P. F. SLOAN					
BARRY, JEFF					
Renowned Brill Building songwriter Jeff Barry was a member of The Raindrops.					
A&M SP-4393	(S)	Walkin' In The Sun	1973	6.00	15.00
BARRY, LEN					
Len Barry was a member of The Dovells.					
Decca DL-4720	(M)	1-2-3	1965	12.00	30.00
Decca DL-74720	(S)	1-2-3 *("Lip Sync" is rechanneled)*	1965	16.00	40.00
RCA Victor LPM-3823	(M)	My Kind Of Soul	1967	10.00	25.00
RCA Victor LSP-3823	(S)	My Kind Of Soul	1967	8.00	20.00
Buddah BDS-5105	(S)	Ups & Downs	1972	6.00	15.00
BARRY & BARRY					
Barry McGuire and Barry Kane, both of The New Christy Minstrels.					
Horizon WP-1608	(M)	Here And Now!	1962	10.00	25.00
Horizon ST-1608	(S)	Here And Now!	1962	12.00	30.00
BARRY & THE TAMERLANES					
Valiant LP-406	(M)	I Wonder What She's Doing Tonight	1963	100.00	250.00
Valiant LPS-406	(S)	I Wonder What She's Doing Tonight	1963	360.00	600.00
BARTHOLOMEW, DAVE					
Imperial LP-9162	(M)	Fats Domino Presents David Bartholomew	1961	60.00	150.00
Imperial LP-12076	(S)	Fats Domino Presents David Bartholomew	1961	80.00	200.00
Imperial LP-9217	(M)	New Orleans House Party	1963	60.00	150.00
Imperial LP-12217	(S)	New Orleans House Party	1963	80.00	200.00
BARTLEY, CHRIS					
Vando VA-60000	(M)	The Sweetest Thing This Side Of Heaven	196?	20.00	50.00
Vando VAS-60000	(S)	The Sweetest Thing This Side Of Heaven	196?	30.00	75.00
BASKERVILLE HOUNDS, THE					
Dot DLP-3823	(M)	The Baskerville Hounds	1967	20.00	50.00
Dot DLP-25823	(S)	The Baskerville Hounds	1967	30.00	75.00
BASS, FONTELLA					
Checker LP-2997	(M)	The New Look	1966	30.00	75.00
Checker LPS-2997	(S)	The New Look	1966	40.00	100.00
		—Checker albums above have blue labels with red & black checkers on top.—			
Checker LP-2997	(M)	The New Look	1967	14.00	35.00
Checker LPS-2997	(S)	The New Look	1967	20.00	50.00
		—Checker albums above have blue & white labels.—			
Paula LPS-2203	(S)	Free	1972	4.00	10.00
BATDORF & RODNEY					
Asylum 6E-5056	(S)	Batdorf & Rodney	1972	1.00	5.00
Arista AL-4041	(S)	Life Is You	1975	1.00	5.00
BATTERED ORNAMENTS					
Harvest SKAO-422	(S)	Mantle-Piece	1970	16.00	40.00
BATTIN, SKIP					
Skip Battin was a member of the later Byrds					
Signpost ST-8408	(S)	Skip Battin	1972	4.00	10.00
BAXTER					
Paramount PAS-6050	(S)	Baxter	1973	8.00	20.00
BAY CITY ROLLERS					
Arista AL-4049	(S)	Bay City Rollers	1975	1.00	5.00
Arista AL-4071	(S)	Rock 'N' Roll Love Letter	1976	1.00	5.00
Arista AL-4093	(S)	Dedication	1976	1.00	5.00
Arista AL-7004	(S)	It's A Game	1977	1.00	5.00
Arista AL-4158	(S)	Greatest Hits	1977	1.00	5.00
Arista AL-4194	(S)	Strangers In The Wind	1978	1.00	5.00

Label & Catalog #		Title	Year	VG+	NM

BAYSIDERS, THE

Label & Catalog #		Title	Year	VG+	NM
Everest LPBR-5124	(M)	Over The Rainbow	1961	80.00	200.00
Everest BRST-5124	(S)	Over The Rainbow	1961	150.00	300.00

BE-BOP DELUXE

Label & Catalog #		Title	Year	VG+	NM
Harvest ST-11432	(S)	Futurama	1976	3.20	8.00
Harvest ST-11478	(S)	Sunburst Finish	1976	3.20	8.00
Harvest SPRO-???	(DJ)	Live! In The Air Age (EP)	1977	12.00	30.00
Harvest SKBB-11666	(S)	Live! In The Air Age (2 LPs)	1977	6.00	15.00
Harvest SPRO-???	(DJ)	Live Kicks (EP)	1977	12.00	30.00
Harvest ST-11575	(S)	Modern Music	1977	3.20	8.00
Harvest ST-11689	(S)	Axe Victim	1977	3.20	8.00
Harvest SW-11750	(S)	Drastic Plastic	1978	3.20	8.00
Harvest SPRO-8531	(DJ)	Be-Bop's Biggest (EP)	1978	12.00	30.00
Harvest SKBO-11870	(S)	The Best Of & The Rest Of (2 LPs)	1978	3.20	8.00

BEACH BOYS, THE

The original BBs were brothers Brian, Carl and Dennis Wilson, cousin Mike Love, and neighbor Al Jardine. The group initially laid down a set of tracks in the tiny studios of Hite Morgan before signing with Capitol in '62. Jardine left in 1963 and returned in '64, replaced during that time by David Marks. Bruce Johnston officially became the sixth member in 1966 but left in 1971. He was replaced by Rickie Fataar and Blondie Chaplin, who both left in 1973. Bruce returned in 1978.

Section 1 below lists albums that feature the Hite Morgan sides. Section 2 covers the Capitol years, 1962-69. Through 1968, Brian Wilson wrote, arranged and produced most of the group's material and mixed it all in mono. Stereo mixes that exist during this time were done by engineer Chuck Britz. Capitol 1890, 1981, 2164 and 2198 were issued completely in stereo; 1998, 2027 and 2110 are partially stereo. Section 3. collects their Brother Records imprint under the wing of Warner/Reprise and their stay with CBS' Caribou subsidiary.

For more listings refer to The Flame; Jan & Dean; Mike Love & Dean Torrence; The Moon; Brian Wilson; Carl Wilson; Dennis Wilson; and Murray Wilson. The interested reader can peruse the Capitol listings in the Various Artists section and safely assume that any surf or hot rod compilation features The Beach Boys. Of particular note are 1918, 1995, and 2024 along with PRO 2396 and 2480. These albums could easily function as Beach Boys titles.

1. Hite Morgan Recordings 1961

Label & Catalog #		Title	Year	VG+	NM
Era HTE-805	(M)	The Beach Boys' Biggest Beach Hits	1969	6.00	15.00
Orbit OR-688	(M)	The Beach Boys' Greatest Hits 1961-63	1972	4.00	10.00
Wand WDS-688	(M)	The Beach Boys' Greatest Hits 1961-63	1972	4.00	10.00
Scepter CTN-18004	(M)	The Best Of Beach Boys	1972	4.00	10.00
Springboard SPB-4021	(M)	The Beach Boys 1961	1977	1.20	6.00
Gateway GSLP-10104	(M)	Surfing With The Beach Boys, The Marketts And Frogmen	1979	1.20	6.00
Everest 4108	(M)	Rare Early Recordings	1981	1.20	6.00

2. The Capitol Years, 1962-69

Label & Catalog #		Title	Year	VG+	NM
Capitol T-1808	(M)	Surfin' Safari	1962	20.00	50.00
Capitol DT-1808	(E)	Surfin' Safari	1962	40.00	100.00
		(Original covers for DT-1808 erroneously state "Full Dimensional Stereo" across the top.)			
Capitol DT-1808	(E)	Surfin' Safari	1962	16.00	40.00
		Later covers correctly claim "Duophonic Stereo".")			
Capitol T-1890	(M)	Surfin' U.S.A.	1963	20.00	50.00
Capitol ST-1890	(S)	Surfin' U.S.A.	1963	20.00	50.00
Capitol T-1981	(M)	Surfer Girl	1963	20.00	50.00
Capitol ST-1981	(S)	Surfer Girl	1963	20.00	50.00
		(Original covers mention the influence of The Four Freshmen style on "Your Summer Dreams" in the liner notes on the back.)			
Capitol T-1981	(M)	Surfer Girl	1963	24.00	60.00
Capitol ST-1981	(S)	Surfer Girl	1963	24.00	60.00
		(Later pressings make mention of "Their other new single-record hit Little Deuce Coupe" in the liner notes on the back.)			
Capitol T-1998	(M)	Little Deuce Coupe	1963	16.00	40.00
Capitol ST-1998	(S)	Little Deuce Coupe	1963	16.00	40.00
Capitol ST-1998	(S)	Little Deuce Coupe (Yellow label)	197?	1.00	5.00
Capitol ST-1998	(S)	Little Deuce Coupe (Red label)	197?	6.00	15.00
Capitol T-2027	(M)	Shut Down, Volume 2	1964	16.00	40.00
Capitol ST-2027	(P)	Shut Down, Volume 2	1964	16.00	40.00
		("Fun, Fun, Fun" is a shorter, different mix on the stereo album.)			
Capitol T-2110	(M)	All Summer Long	1964	20.00	50.00
Capitol ST-2110	(S)	All Summer Long	1964	20.00	50.00
		(Original covers for 2110 erroneously list the last song on the album as "Don't Break Down.")			
Capitol T-2110	(M)	All Summer Long	1964	16.00	40.00
Capitol ST-2110	(P)	All Summer Long	1964	16.00	40.00
		(Later covers correctly lists the last song on the album as "Don't Back Down.")			

The electronically rechanneled stereo copy of Surfin' Safari shown here is an example of a printing error that can turn an album into a collectible: In this case, the machine that applied the front and back cover slicks goofed and the "Full Dimensional Stereo" banner that should be covered by the "Duophonic" banner ended up beneath it!

Label & Catalog #		Title	Year	VG+	NM
Capitol T-2164	(M)	The Beach Boys' Christmas Album	1964	16.00	40.00
Capitol ST-2164	(S)	The Beach Boys' Christmas Album	1964	16.00	40.00
		("Merry Christmas Baby" is 28 seconds longer on the stereo album than on the mono.)			
Capitol SM-502164	(S)	The Beach Boys' Christmas Album	197?	6.00	15.00
		(Columbia Record Club also known as 2P-6508.)			
Capitol R-133854	(S)	The Beach Boys' Christmas Album	197?	6.00	15.00
		(RCA Record Club)			
Capitol PRO-3133	(DJ)	The Beach Boys Christmas Special	1964	200.00	400.00
		(Promotional radio show built around the group's new LP.)			
Capitol TAO-2198	(M)	Beach Boys Concert	1964	16.00	40.00
Capitol STAO-2198	(S)	Beach Boys Concert	1964	16.00	40.00
Capitol STAO-8-2198	(S)	Beach Boys Concert (Record Club)	1964	30.00	75.00
Capitol T-2269	(M)	The Beach Boys Today!	1965	16.00	40.00
Capitol DT-2269	(E)	The Beach Boys Today!	1965	12.00	30.00
Capitol DT-8-2269	(E)	The Beach Boys Today! (Record Club)	1965	30.00	75.00
Capitol T-2354	(M)	Summer Days (And Summer Nights!!)	1965	16.00	40.00
Capitol DT-2354	(E)	Summer Days (And Summer Nights!!)	1965	20.00	50.00
		(DT-2354 was originally issued with an erroneous "Full Dimensional Stereo" banner across the top of the cover.)			
Capitol DT-2354	(E)	Summer Days (And Summer Nights!!)	1965	12.00	30.00
		(Later pressings have the correct "Duophonic Stereo" banner across the top of the cover.)			
Capitol MAS-2398	(M)	Beach Boys Party!	1965	16.00	40.00
Capitol DMAS-2398	(E)	Beach Boys Party!	1965	12.00	30.00
		(Issued with a sheet of perforated wallet photos.)			
Capitol MAS-2398	(M)	Beach Boys Party!	1965	12.00	30.00
Capitol DMAS-2398	(E)	Beach Boys Party!	1965	10.00	25.00
		(The prices above are for the albums without the photos.)			
Capitol T-2458	(M)	Pet Sounds	1966	16.00	40.00
Capitol DT-2458	(E)	Pet Sounds	1966	12.00	30.00
Capitol T-2545	(M)	Best Of The Beach Boys (Black rainbow label)	1966	8.00	20.00
Capitol DT-2545	(E)	Best Of The Beach Boys (Black rainbow label)	1966	6.00	15.00
Capitol T-2545	(M)	Best Of The Beach Boys (Black Starline label)	1966	10.00	25.00
Capitol DT-2545	(E)	Best Of The Beach Boys (Black Starline label)	1966	8.00	20.00
Capitol T-2545	(M)	Best Of The Beach Boys	1967	12.00	30.00
Capitol DT-2545	(E)	Best Of The Beach Boys	1967	6.00	15.00
		(Red & white "bullseye" Starline label.)			
Capitol DT-2545	(E)	Best Of The Beach Boys	1969	8.00	20.00
		(Red & white "star" Starline label.)			
Capitol DT-2545	(E)	Best Of The Beach Boys (Green Starline label)	1970	4.00	10.00
Capitol DT-502545	(E)	Best Of The Beach Boys (Columbia Record Club)	197?	4.00	10.00
Capitol R-123946	(E)	Best Of The Beach Boys (RCA Record Club)	197?	4.00	10.00
Capitol DT-602524	(E)	Best Of The Beach Boys (Record Club of America)	197?	4.00	10.00
Capitol T/DT-2580		Smile	1966	See note below	
		("Smile" remains Brian Wilson's legendary unreleased masterpiece. For Christmas 1966 Capitol printed 400,000 front and back cover slicks and a similar number of booklets with graphics and lyrics. Both the cover slicks and the booklets are priced separately below.)			
Capitol T/DT-2580		Smile Cover Sleck (Counterfeits exist)	1966	500.00	1,000.00
Capitol T/DT-2580		Smile Bonus Book (Counterfeits exist)	1966	150.00	300.00
Capitol T-2706	(M)	Best Of The Beach Boys, Volume 2	1967	10.00	25.00
Capitol DT-2706	(E)	Best Of The Beach Boys, Volume 2	1967	6.00	15.00
		(Red & white "bullseye" Starline label.)			
Capitol DT-2706	(E)	Best Of The Beach Boys, Volume 2	1969	6.00	15.00
		(Red & white "star" Starline label)			
Capitol DT-502706	(E)	Best Of The Beach Boys, Volume 2	1970	6.00	15.00
		(Green Starline label)			
Capitol DT-502706	(E)	Best Of The Beach Boys, Volume 2	197?	10.00	25.00
		(Columbia Record Club)			
Brother T-9001	(M)	Smiley Smile	1967	16.00	40.00
Brother ST-9001	(E)	Smiley Smile	1967	8.00	20.00
		(Original covers do not credit Barry Turnbull on the back.)			
Brother T-9001	(M)	Smiley Smile	1967	12.00	30.00
Brother ST-9001	(E)	Smiley Smile	1967	6.00	15.00
		(Later covers read "Title for this album by Barry Turnbull" on the back.)			
Capitol TCL-2813	(M)	The Beach Boys Deluxe Set (3 LP box)	1967	100.00	250.00
		(The mono box has a black border and contains standard copies of the albums with a "T" prefix.)			
Capitol DTCL-2813	(E)	The Beach Boys Deluxe Set (3 LP box)	1967	20.00	50.00
		(The stereo box has a maroon border and contains custom copies of the albums with a "DTCL" prefix.)			
Capitol DTCL-8-2813	(E)	The Beach Boys Deluxe Set (Record Club)	1967	60.00	150.00
		(The stereo box has a blue border and contains custom copies of the albums with a "DTCL" prefix.)			
Capitol T-2859	(M)	Wild Honey	1967	16.00	40.00
Capitol ST-2859	(E)	Wild Honey	1967	8.00	20.00
Capitol ST-8-2891	(E)	Smiley Smile (Record Club)	1968	150.00	300.00

These two copies of All Summer Long illustrate a more interesting gaffe: The song "Don't Back Down" was erroneously listed on original covers as "Don't Break Down" in a butterscotch-colored print, shown here on the stereo copy under the larger "Wendy." The mono copy has the print in black and correctly lists the title. Prophetically, the song's writer, Brian Wilson, was to suffer a nervous breakdown shortly after the release of this album.

Label & Catalog #		Title	Year	VG+	NM
Capitol DKAO-2893	(E)	Stack O' Tracks (With booklet)	1968	40.00	100.00
Capitol DKAO-2893	(E)	Stack O' Tracks (Without booklet)	1968	20.00	50.00
Capitol DKAO-8-2893	(E)	Stack O' Tracks (Record Club with booklet)	1968	80.00	200.00
Capitol ST-2895	(S)	Friends	1968	10.00	25.00
Capitol DKAO-2945	(P)	Best Of The Beach Boys, Volume 3 (Black rainbow label.)	1969	6.00	15.00
Capitol DKAO-2945	(P)	Best Of The Beach Boys, Volume 3 (Red & white "star" Starline label.)	1969	8.00	20.00
Capitol SKAO-133	(S)	20/20 (Black rainbow label)	1969	8.00	20.00
Capitol SKAO-133	(S)	20/20 (Red & white "star" Starline label)	1969	6.00	15.00
Capitol SKAO-8-0133	(S)	20/20 (Record Club. Black label)	1969	12.00	30.00
Capitol SKAO-8-0133	(S)	20/20 (Record Club. Green label) ("Do It Again" and "Time To Get Alone" are rechanneled.)	197?	16.00	40.00
Capitol SWBB-253	(E)	Close-Up (2 LPs. Black rainbow label)	1969	6.00	15.00
Capitol SWBB-253	(E)	Close-Up (2 LPs. Green label)	197?	12.00	30.00
— Capitol albums above have black rainbow labels. —					
Capitol ST-442	(P)	Good Vibrations (Green label)	1970	6.00	15.00
Capitol DT-8-442	(P)	Good Vibrations (Record Club)	1970	10.00	25.00
Capitol ST-442	(P)	Good Vibrations (Orange label)	1972	8.00	20.00
Capitol STBB-500	(E)	All Summer Long / California Girls (Lime label. Two single albums, edited versions of 2110 and 2354, bound together with a Special Double Play sticker.	1970	6.00	15.00
Capitol STBB-500	(E)	All Summer Long / California Girls (2 LPs) (Orange label with a purple "C" on top. This is two single albums bound together with a Special Double Play sticker.)	1971	8.00	20.00
Capitol SF-8-0501	(E)	All Summer Long (Capitol Record Club)	1971	4.00	10.00
Capitol SF-500501	(E)	All Summer Long (Columbia Record Club)	1971	4.00	10.00
Capitol DF-8-0502	(E)	California Girls (Capitol Record Club)	1971	4.00	10.00
Capitol ST-500502	(E)	California Girls (Columbia Record Club)	1971	4.00	10.00
Capitol STBB-701	(P)	Fun, Fun, Fun / Dance, Dance, Dance (Lime label. Two single albums, edited versions of 2027 and 2269, bound together with a Special Double Play sticker.)	1970	6.00	15.00
Capitol SF-702/DF-703	(P)	Fun, Fun, Fun / Dance, Dance, Dance (2 LPs.) (Orange label with a purple "C" on top. This is two single albums bound together with a Special Double Play sticker.)	1971	8.00	20.00
Capitol ST-8-0702	(P)	Fun, Fun, Fun (Record Club)	1971	4.00	10.00
Capitol DF-8-0703	(E)	Dance, Dance, Dance (Record Club)	1971	4.00	10.00
Capitol R-233593	(P)	American Summer (RCA Record Club)	1975	4.00	10.00
Capitol SVBB-511307	(P)	Endless Summer (Columbia Record Club)	1974	6.00	15.00
Capitol R-223559	(P)	Endless Summer (RCA Record Club)	1974	6.00	15.00
Capitol SVBB-11384	(P)	Spirit Of America (Red label)	1975	1.20	6.00
Capitol SVBB-511384	(P)	Spirit Of America (Columbia Record Club)	1975	6.00	15.00
Capitol SLB-6994	(P)	Golden Years Of The Beach Boys (2 LPs)	1975	6.00	15.00
Capitol ST-11584	(S)	Beach Boys '69—Live In London	1976	4.00	10.00
Capitol SL-8114	(P)	Beach Boys Super Hits	1978	.80	4.00
Capitol ST-12293	(P)	Beach Boys Rarities	1983	4.00	10.00
Capitol CZ-92639	(P)	Still Cruisin'	1989	.80	4.00
Capitol SY-4572	(E)	Surfin' Safari	197?	.80	4.00
Capitol SM-1890	(S)	Surfin' U.S.A.	197?	.80	4.00
Capitol SM-1981	(S)	Surfer Girl	197?	.80	4.00
Capitol SM-1998	(S)	Little Deuce Coupe	197?	.80	4.00
Capitol SM-2164	(S)	The Beach Boys' Christmas Album	197?	.80	4.00
Capitol SM-2198	(E)	Beach Boys Concert	197?	.80	4.00
Capitol SN-12011	(S)	Beach Boys '69—Live In London	1980	.80	4.00
Capitol N-16012	(M)	Surfin' Safari	1980	.80	4.00
Capitol SN-16013	(S)	Little Deuce Coupe	1980	.80	4.00
Capitol SN-16014	(S)	Surfer Girl	1980	.80	4.00
Capitol SN-16015	(S)	Surfin' U.S.A.	1980	.80	4.00
Capitol SN-16016	(S)	All Summer Long	1980	.80	4.00
Capitol DN-16017	(E)	California Girls	1980	.80	4.00
Capitol SN-16018	(E)	Fun, Fun, Fun	1980	.80	4.00
Capitol DN-16019	(E)	Dance, Dance, Dance	1980	.80	4.00
Capitol SN-16???	(P)	Be True To Your School	1982	1.00	5.00
Capitol SN-16134	(S)	Beach Boys '69—Live In London	198?	.80	4.00
Capitol SN-16155	(P)	20/20	1980	.80	4.00
Capitol SN-16156	(M)	Pet Sounds	1980	.80	4.00
Capitol SN-16157	(S)	Friends	1980	.80	4.00
Capitol SN-16158	(M)	Smiley Smile	1980	.80	4.00
Capitol SN-16272	(M)	The Beach Boys Party	1980	.80	4.00
Sears SPS-609	(E)	Summertime Blues (Sears 608 reissues material from the first two Capitol albums.)	1970	20.00	50.00
Pickwick SPC-3221	(E)	Summertime Blues	1970	1.20	6.00
Pickwick SPC-3269	(P)	Good Vibrations	1971	.80	4.00
Pickwick SPC-3309	(S)	Wow! Great Concert!	1972	.80	4.00
Pickwick PTP-2059	(E)	High Water	1973	3.20	8.00
Pickwick SPC-3351	(S)	Surfer Girl	1973	.80	4.00
Pickwick SPC-3562	(P)	Little Deuce Coupe	1976	.80	4.00
Candlelite SLB-6994	(P)	Golden Years Of The Beach Boys (2 LPs)	1975	6.00	15.00

Label & Catalog #		Title	Year	VG+	NM
Ronco R-2230	(P)	Beach Boys Super Hits	1978	4.00	10.00
Sessions SLB-8134	(P)	The Beach Boys (2 LPs)	1980	6.00	15.00

3. Brother/Reprise And Caribou

Reprise RS-6382	(S)	Sunflower (White label promo)	1970	20.00	50.00
Reprise RS-6382	(S)	Sunflower	1970	30.00	75.00
		—Reprise albums above have orange labels.—			
Reprise RS-6382	(S)	Sunflower	1970	6.00	15.00
Capitol SKAO-93352	(S)	Sunflower (Capitol Record Club)	1970	80.00	200.00
Reprise RS-6453	(S)	Surf's Up (White label promo)	1971	16.00	40.00
Reprise RS-6453	(S)	Surf's Up (With lyric sheet)	1971	4.00	10.00
Reprise R-113793	(S)	Surf's Up (RCA Record Club)	1971	8.00	20.00
Asylum R-113793	(S)	Surf's Up (RCA Record Club)	1971	60.00	150.00
		(RCA Record Club erroneously pressed copies with an Asylum label.)			
Reprise 2MS-2083	(P)	Carl & The Passion-So Tough /			
		Pet Sounds (2 LPs. White label promo)	1972	20.00	50.00
Reprise 2MS-2083	(P)	Carl & The Passion-So Tough /			
		Pet Sounds (2 LPs)	1972	10.00	25.00
		(While "So Tough" is in stereo, "Pet Sounds" is mono.)			
Reprise MS-2118	(S)	Holland (Test pressing with "We Got Love")	1973	300.00	500.00
Reprise MS-2118	(S)	Holland (White label promo)	1973	16.00	40.00
		(Issued with a white label EP, "Mt. Vernon & Fairway," with a PS.)			
Reprise MS-2118	(S)	Holland	1973	6.00	15.00
		(Issued with an EP, "Mt. Vernon & Fairway," in a PS, taped to			
		the back cover; small tape tears in the EP sleeve are common)			
Reprise 2MS-6484	(S)	The Beach Boys In Concert (2 LPs. White label)	1973	16.00	40.00
Reprise 2MS-6484	(S)	The Beach Boys In Concert (2 LPs)	1973	6.00	15.00
Reprise R-223569	(S)	The Beach Boys In Concert (2 LPs)	1973	8.00	20.00
		(RCA Record Club)			
Reprise 2MS-2166	(P)	Wild Honey / 20/20 (2 LPs. Promo label.)	1974	12.00	30.00
Reprise 2MS-2166	(P)	Wild Honey / 20/20 (2 LPs)	1974	6.00	15.00
		(For 2MS-2166, most of "20/20" is in stereo.)			
Reprise 2MS-2167	(P)	Friends / Smiley Smile (2 LPs. Promo label)	1974	12.00	30.00
Reprise 2MS-2167	(P)	Friends / Smiley Smile (2 LPs)	1974	6.00	15.00
		(For 2MS-2167, "Smiley Smile" is rechanneled.)			
Reprise MS-2197	(M)	Pet Sounds	1974	6.00	15.00
Reprise MS-2223	(S)	Good Vibrations-Best Of The Beach Boys	1975	4.00	10.00
		—Reprise albums above have yellow labels without the Warner Communication logo.—			
Reprise (No number)	(DJ)	The Beach Boys Radio Special Promo Spot	1976	20.00	50.00
Reprise RS-6382	(S)	Sunflower	197?	1.00	5.00
Reprise MS-2118	(S)	Holland	197?	1.00	5.00
Reprise MS-2223	(P)	Good Vibrations-Best Of The Beach Boys	197?	1.00	5.00
Reprise MS-2251	(S)	15 Big Ones	1976	.80	4.00
Reprise R-130223	(S)	15 Big Ones (RCA Record Club)	1976	4.00	10.00
Reprise MS-2258	(S)	The Beach Boys Love You	1977	3.20	8.00
Reprise MSK-2268	(S)	M. I. U. Album	1977	3.20	8.00
		—Reprise albums above have yellow labels with the Warner Communication logo on the bottom.—			
Reprise 2MS-6484	(S)	The Beach Boys In Concert (2 LPs)	197?	6.00	15.00
Reprise MSK-2268	(S)	M. I. U. Album	197?	4.00	10.00
Reprise MSK-2280	(P)	Good Vibrations-Best Of The Beach Boys	1978	1.00	5.00
		—Reprise albums above have brown labels.—			
Caribou JZ-35752	(S)	L. A. (Light Album) (White label promo)	1979	6.00	15.00
Caribou JZ-35752	(S)	L. A. (Light Album)	1979	3.20	8.00
Caribou JZ-36293	(S)	Keepin' The Summer Alive (White label promo)	1980	6.00	15.00
Caribou JZ-36293	(S)	Keepin' The Summer Alive	1980	3.20	8.00
Caribou Z2X-2744	(S)	Ten Years Of Harmony	1981	1.00	6.00
Caribou ZX-39946	(S)	The Beach Boys	1985	.80	4.00
Love Foundation	(S)	Fourth Of July—A Rockin' Celebration Of America	1986	8.00	20.00

BEACON STREET UNION
The Beacon Street Union later recorded as Eagle.

MGM E-4517	(M)	The Eyes Of The Beacon Street Union	1968	10.00	25.00
MGM SE-4517	(S)	The Eyes Of The Beacon Street Union	1968	12.00	30.00
MGM SE-4568	(S)	The Clown Died In Marvin Gardens	1968	12.00	30.00

BEAD GAME, THE

Avco Embassy AVE-33009	(S)	Welcome	1970	8.00	20.00

BEAGLES, THE, & THE FOUR LIVERPOOL WHIGS

Sutton SU-329	(M)	I Want To Hold Your Hand & Other Favorites	1964	6.00	15.00
Sutton SSU-329	(S)	I Want To Hold Your Hand & Other Favorites	1964	8.00	20.00

BEAGLES, THE

Harmony HL-14561	(M)	Here Come The Beagles	1967	5.00	12.00
Harmony HS-14561	(S)	Here Come The Beagles	1967	6.00	15.00

BEANS

Avalanche 9200	(S)	Beans	1971	8.00	20.00

Label & Catalog #		Title	Year	VG+	NM
BEAR					
Verve/Forecast FTS-3059	(S)	Greetings	1969	6.00	15.00
BEARCUTS, THE					
Somerset P-20800	(M)	Beatlemania	1964	6.00	15.00
Somerset SP-20800	(S)	Beatlemania	1964	8.00	20.00
BEASLEY, JIMMY					
Modern LMP-1214	(M)	The Fabulous Jimmy Beasley	1956	300.00	600.00
Crown CLP-5014	(M)	The Fabulous Jimmy Beasley	1957	60.00	150.00
		—Crown albums above have black labels with a silver "Crown" on top.—			
Crown CLP-5247	(M)	Twist With Jimmy Beasley	1961	20.00	50.00
Crown CST-247	(E)	Twist With Jimmy Beasley	1961	10.00	25.00
		(Crown 5014 and 5247 are reissues of Modern 1214.)			
		—Crown albums above have gray labels.—			
BEAST					
Cotillion SD-9012	(S)	Prelude For Today	1969	5.00	12.00
Evolution 2017	(S)	Beast	1970	4.00	10.00
BEAT-A-MANIA					
Spectrum 172	(M)	Beat-A-Mania	1964	6.00	15.00
BEATLE BUDDIES, THE					
Diplomat D-2313	(M)	The Beatle Buddies	1964	6.00	15.00
Diplomat DS-2313	(S)	The Beatle Buddies	1964	8.00	20.00

BEATLES, THE

Prior to international stardom, John Lennon, Paul McCartney and George Harrison with drummer Pete Best backed up singer Tony Sheridan on a number of sides recorded in Hamburg in 1961 (they were billed as "The Beat Brothers"). Records featuring these sessions are listed below in Section 1. Section 2 contains albums with live recordings made during their stay in Germany. By 1962, Best was history and Ringo Starr was about to make history as The Beatles' drummer. Their now legendary audition for Decca Records (who saw no commercial potential in a beat group) made the rounds of various labels after a copyright lapse in 1982. These recordings make up Section 3.

The group signed with Parlophone, an EMI subsidiary, and placed under the talented and sympathetic wing of staff producer George Martin. After taking most of the civilized world by storm in 1963, EMI offered them to their American licensee, Capitol (who saw no commercial potential in a British beat group). Consequently, their first recordings ended up on a variety of smaller, independent U.S. labels, the most significant being Vee Jay, who acquired the rights to the fourteen tracks from their first EMI album.

Section 4 lists the many attempts of Vee Jay to package those tracks. As the company often issued mono albums with stereo labels, check for an "S" suffix on the master number in the trail-off vinyl. Also, many counterfeits of the Vee Jay albums exist. Vee Jay 1062, Introducing The Beatles, is probably the most counterfeited album in recorded music's history! Fortunately most are so obvious that it is often amazing to realize that anyone who collects records could be fooled. But there are also counterfeits of surpassing excellence. Legitimate covers always have a glossy sheen. The photo of the group should always be crisp and clear with an obvious shadow cast by the lads against the photographer's backdrop. The covers were made from grey or tan poster board with 1/4" flaps over the top and bottom.

On the labels, both "Introducing The Beatles" and "The Beatles" are printed above the spindle hole on an invariably glossy label. On those labels using the rainbow border, the shift in the color-band is smooth and lovely. The trail-off vinyl is between 7/8" and 1" wide. Finally, should your copy have the word "Stereo" printed on the label, or "Audio Matrix," "MR" or "ARP" machine-stamped in the trail-off vinyl, you have an original although not all originals have these identifying scores.

While both versions of the cover for 1085, Jolly What! The Beatles & Frank Ifield On Stage!, have been reproduced, they are easily identified as neither have any printing on the spine. Also, the printing in the trail-off of the fake records is almost illegible. Finally, the cover for another Vee Jay repackage, Songs Picture And Stories Of The Fabulous Beatles, 1092, had a book-like flap, joined at the spine, covering 2/3 of the jacket. Counterfeits dispensed with this obvious luxury.

Section 5 covers the main period of the group's history in this country when all of the group's new recordings were issued on Capitol (except the songs prepared for the film A Hard Day's Night, to which United Artists had the rights). With the formation of their own Apple Records in 1968, things become complicated: Aside from new titles (listed in Section 6), the earlier catalog titles were kept in print on Capitol and reissued on Apple with the same covers and catalog numbers but with label graphics of a green apple, whole on side, cut in half on the other. "First pressings" of these Apple reissues from 1968-70 have "A Subsidiary of Capitol" on the bottom of the label; these are worth $40-50 each. Second pressings from 1971-74 have "Mfd. by Apple" on the bottom of the label; these are worth $15-25 each. Third pressings from 1975 are similar to the second but have an "All rights reserved" disclaimer on the label; these are worth $20-30 each. (And, please note that later copies of Meet The Beatles, The Beatles' Second Album, Beatles '65, Beatles VI and "Yesterday" ...And Today can be found with and without the RIAA Gold Record seal on the cover.)

After the collapse of Apple, the material reverted to Capitol (Section 7) and has remained in print since. From 1976-78 the entire catalog of previously released albums were reissued with an orange label; these are worth $10-20 each. These were followed in 1978-82 by a purple label with "Mfd. by Capitol" on the bottom. This was followed by the "new" black rainbow label. (It was during this time that Capitol issued the Parlophone versions for the first time.) This was followed by a "new" purple label with "Manufactured by Capitol" on the bottom. The LPs on each of these variations are worth $10-20 a piece. Finally, Section 8 collects a few odds 'n' ends.

Label & Catalog #		Title	Year	VG+	NM

Factory-sealed albums: *Factory sealed Capitol albums are easily worth three times the listed NM value. While any sealed mono album is an original, stereo albums are a different matter. The easiest way to identify an original stereo album in a sealed jacket is to tap the album till the inner sleeve is flush against the plastic wrap along the edge. As Capitol invariably issued all their albums in different colored paper sleeves (advertising other LPs), the appearance of such a colored sleeve would almost certainly assure an original stereo album within. Aside from the solo careers of the individual members, including original drummer Pete Best, refer to Louise Harrison Caldwell (George's sister tells all); Elvis Presley / The Silver Beatles; Sing Along With The Beatles. Finally, for more information, I recommend The Beatles Price Guide For American Records, contact Perry Cox Ent., P.O. Box 14945, Scottsdale, AZ 85267.*

1. The Tony Sheridan Sessions

Label & Catalog #		Title	Year	VG+	NM
Savage BM-69	(M)	The Savage Young Beatles	1964	80.00	200.00
		(This album of dubious legality collects Tony Sheridan material with and without The Beat Brothers. Orange label and a yellow cover. Counterfeits have "Stereo" in the upper right corner of the cover.)			
Savage BM-69	(M)	The Savage Young Beatles	1964	See note below	
		(Some copies have a yellow label and a glossy orange cover. Rare with a suggested Near Mint value of $1,500-2,500.)			
Atco 33-169	(DJ)	Ain't She Sweet	1964	600.00	1,200.00
Atco 33-169	(M)	Ain't She Sweet	1964	80.00	200.00
Atco SD-33-169	(S)	Ain't She Sweet	1964	200.00	400.00
		(Original stereo pressings have purple & brown labels.)			
Atco SD-33-169	(S)	Ain't She Sweet	1969	250.00	500.00
		(Later pressings have yellow labels with a white border on the cover.)			
MGM E-4215	(M)	The Beatles With Tony Sheridan & Their Guests & Others	1964	100.00	250.00
MGM SE-4215	(S)	The Beatles With Tony Sheridan & Their Guests & Others	1964	360.00	600.00
MGM E-4215	(M)	The Beatles With Tony Sheridan & Their Guests	1964	80.00	200.00
MGM SE-4215	(S)	The Beatles With Tony Sheridan & Their Guests	1964	500.00	750.00
		(Later pressings drop "& Others" from the cover title.)			
Metro M-563	(M)	This Is Where It Started	1966	40.00	100.00
Metro MS-563	(S)	This Is Where It Started	1966	60.00	150.00
		(Metro 563 is a reissue of MGM 4215.)			
Clarion 601	(M)	The Amazing Beatles & Other Great English Group Sounds	1966	40.00	100.00
Clarion SD-601	(S)	The Amazing Beatles & Other Great English Group Sounds	1966	70.00	175.00
		(Clarion 601 is a reissue of Atco 169.)			
Polydor 24-2504	(S)	The Beatles Circa 1960: In The Beginning Featuring Tony Sheridan *(Red label. Gatefold cover)*	1970	10.00	25.00
Polydor 24-2504	(S)	The Beatles Circa 1960: In The Beginning Featuring Tony Sheridan *(Standard cover)*	1981	6.00	15.00
Polydor SKAO-93199	(S)	The Beatles Circa 1960: In The Beginning Featuring Tony Sheridan *(Capitol Record Club)*	1970	16.00	40.00
Polydor PD-4504	(S)	In The Beginning: The Beatles	197?	16.00	40.00
		(This rare reissue alters the LP's title.)			
Polydor 422-825-073-1Y1	(S)	The Beatles Circa 1960: In The Beginning Featuring Tony Sheridan	1988	6.00	15.00

2. Live In Germany

Label & Catalog #		Title	Year	VG+	NM
Lingasong LS-2-7001	(DJ)	Live! At The Star-Club In Hamburg, Germany; 1962 *(2 LPs. Black vinyl)*	1977	100.00	250.00
		(Test pressing with different running order for the tracks.)			
Lingasong LS-2-7001	(DJ)	Live! At The Star-Club In Hamburg, Germany; 1962 *(2 LPs. Blue vinyl)*	1977	175.00	350.00
Lingasong LS-2-7001	(DJ)	Live! At The Star-Club In Hamburg, Germany; 1962 *(2 LPs. Red vinyl)*	1977	100.00	250.00
Lingasong LS-2-7001	(DJ)	Live! At The Star-Club In Hamburg, Germany; 1962 *(2 LPs. Black vinyl)*	1977	16.00	40.00
Lingasong LS-2-7001	(E)	Live! At The Star-Club In Hamburg, Germany; 1962 *(2 LPs)*	1977	6.00	15.00
Pickwick BAN-90051	(M)	Recorded Live In Hamburg, Volume 1	1978	14.00	35.00
Pickwick BAN-90051	(M)	Recorded Live In Hamburg, Volume 2	1978	14.00	35.00
Pickwick BAN-90071	(M)	Recorded Live In Hamburg, Volume 3	1978	20.00	50.00
Pickwick SPC-3661	(M)	First Live Recordings, Volume 1	1979	4.00	10.00
Pickwick SPC-3662	(M)	First Live Recordings, Volume 2	1979	4.00	10.00
Hall Of Music HM1-2200	(M)	Live 1962 Hamburg, Germany	1981	20.00	50.00

3. The Decca Audition Sessions

Label & Catalog #		Title	Year	VG+	NM
Backstage BSR-1111	(M)	Like Dreamers Do *(Gray vinyl promo)*	1982	20.00	50.00
Backstage BSR-1111	(M)	Like Dreamers Do *(White vinyl promo)*	1982	20.00	50.00
Backstage BSR-1111	(M)	Like Dreamers Do *(3 LPs)*	1982	50.00	125.00
		(Two picture discs, one an interview and one from the Decca sessions with a white gray LP that duplicates the Decca disc. Contains ten of the fifteen Decca audition tracks.)			

Label & Catalog #		Title	Year	VG+	NM
Backstage BSR-1111	(M)	**Like Dreamers Do** (3 LPs)	1982	**30.00**	**75.00**
		(Two picture discs, one an interview and one from the Decca *sessions with a white vinyl LP that duplicates the Decca disc.* *Contains ten of the fifteen Decca audition tracks.)*			
Backstage 2-201	(M)	**Like Dreamers Do** (2 LPs)	1982	**14.00**	**35.00**
		(Double album of the above with one picture disc and the white LP. *Contains ten of the fifteen Decca audition tracks.)*			
Pac UDL-2333	(M)	**Dawn Of The Silver Beatles**	1981	**30.00**	**75.00**
		(First pressings were hand numbered on the label and back cover. *Contains ten of the fifteen Decca audition tracks.)*			
Pac UDL-2333	(M)	**Dawn Of The Silver Beatles** (With the card)	1981	**24.00**	**60.00**
Pac UDL-2333	(M)	**Dawn Of The Silver Beatles** (Without card)	1981	**20.00**	**50.00**
		(Second pressings included numbered registration cards. *Contains ten of the fifteen Decca audition tracks.)*			
Audio Fidelity PD-339	(M)	**First Movement** (Picture disc)	1982	**16.00**	**40.00**
Audio Fidelity PHX-339	(M)	**First Movement**	1982	**5.00**	**12.00**
Audio Rarities AR-2452	(M)	**The Complete Silver Beatles**	1982	**6.00**	**15.00**
		(Contains twelve of the fifteen Decca audition tracks.)			
Orange ORC-12280	(M)	**The Silver Beatles** (Half-speed master)	1985	**200.00**	**400.00**
		(Test pressing in a plain jacket with a full-color cover-slick insert. *Contains all fifteen of the Decca audition tracks.)*			
Orange ORC-12280	(M)	**The Silver Beatles** (Half-speed master)	1985	**150.00**	**300.00**
		(Test pressing in a plain cardboard jacket with a title sticker. *Contains all fifteen of the Decca audition tracks.)*			

4. Vee Jay Records

Label & Catalog #		Title	Year	VG+	NM
Vee Jay LP-1062	(M)	**Introducing The Beatles** ("Ad back")	1963	See note below	
Vee Jay SR-1062	(P)	**Introducing The Beatles** ("Ad back")	1963	See note below	
		(Includes "Love Me Do" and "P.S. I Love You." The back cover has ads *for 25 other Vee Jay albums. Mono copies have a suggested NM* *value of $3,000-5,000. Stereo copies, $10,000-15,000.)*			
Vee Jay LP-1062	(M)	**Introducing The Beatles** ("Blank back")	1963	See note below	
Vee Jay SR-1062	(P)	**Introducing The Beatles** ("Blank back")	1963	See note below	
		(Includes "Love Me Do" and "P.S. I Love You." The back cover *is completely blank. Mono copies have a suggested NM value* *of $1,500-2,500.. Stereo copies, $4,000-6,000.)*			
Vee Jay LP-1062	(M)	**Introducing The Beatles**	1963	**500.00**	**750.00**
		(Includes "Love Me Do" and "P.S. I Love You." Black rainbow label *with an oval logo. The back cover lists the song titles.)*			
Vee Jay SR-1062	(S)	**Introducing The Beatles**	1963	See note below	
		(Includes "Love Me Do" and "P.S. I Love You." Black rainbow label with *an oval logo. The back cover lists the song titles. Prior to this edition,* *the existence of this record was universally doubted. . . A single copy* *in VG+ condition sold in 1995 as part of a package. Based on this sale,* *the suggested NM value for this record is $20,000-30,000.)*			
Vee Jay LP-1062	(M)	**Introducing The Beatles**	1963	**800.00**	**1,200.00**
		(Includes "Love Me Do" and "P.S. I Love You." Black rainbow label *with a brackets logo. The back cover lists the song titles.)*			
Vee Jay LP-1062	(M)	**Introducing The Beatles**	1964	**200.00**	**400.00**
Vee Jay SR-1062	(S)	**Introducing The Beatles**	1964	**1,000.00**	**2,000.00**
		(Includes "Please Please Me" and "Ask Me Why." *Black rainbow label with a "Vee Jay" logo in an oval.)*			
Vee Jay LP-1062	(M)	**Introducing The Beatles**	1964	**200.00**	**400.00**
Vee Jay SR-1062	(S)	**Introducing The Beatles**	1964	**1,000.00**	**2,000.00**
		(Includes "Please Please Me" and "Ask Me Why." *Black rainbow label a "Vee Jay" logo in brackets.)*			
Vee Jay LP-1062	(M)	**Introducing The Beatles**	1964	**200.00**	**400.00**
Vee Jay SR-1062	(S)	**Introducing The Beatles**	1964	**1,000.00**	**2,000.00**
		(Includes "Please Please Me" and "Ask Me Why." *Solid black label with plain "VJ" logo.)*			
Vee Jay LP-1062	(M)	**Introducing The Beatles**	1964	**200.00**	**400.00**
		(Includes "Please Please Me" and "Ask Me Why." *Solid black label with the "VJ" logo in an oval.)*			
Vee Jay LP-1062	(M)	**Introducing The Beatles**	1964	**660.00**	**1,000.00**
		(Includes "Please Please Me" and "Ask Me Why." *Solid black label with "VJ" logo in brackets.)*			
Vee Jay LP-1085	(M)	**The Beatles And Frank Ifield On Stage**	1964	**100.00**	**250.00**
Vee Jay LPS-1085	(P)	**The Beatles And Frank Ifield On Stage**	1964	**300.00**	**500.00**
		("Cartoon cover." The cover has a drawing of a Victorian gentleman with *a Beatles haircut. Original covers have printing along the spine.)*			
Vee Jay LP-1085	(M)	**The Beatles And Frank Ifield On Stage**	1964	See note below	
Vee Jay LPS-1085	(P)	**The Beatles And Frank Ifield On Stage**	1964	See note below	
		("Portrait cover." The cover has a full-color, painted portrait of The Beatles. *This was issued with three labels—black rainbow with oval or brackets logo* *and plain black—with most of the value in the cover. Mono copies have a* *suggested NM value of $4,000-6,000. Stereo copies, $10,000-15,000.* *Counterfeits have slightly blurred covers, no printing on the spine, and* *the markings in the disc's trail-off area are almost illegible.)*			

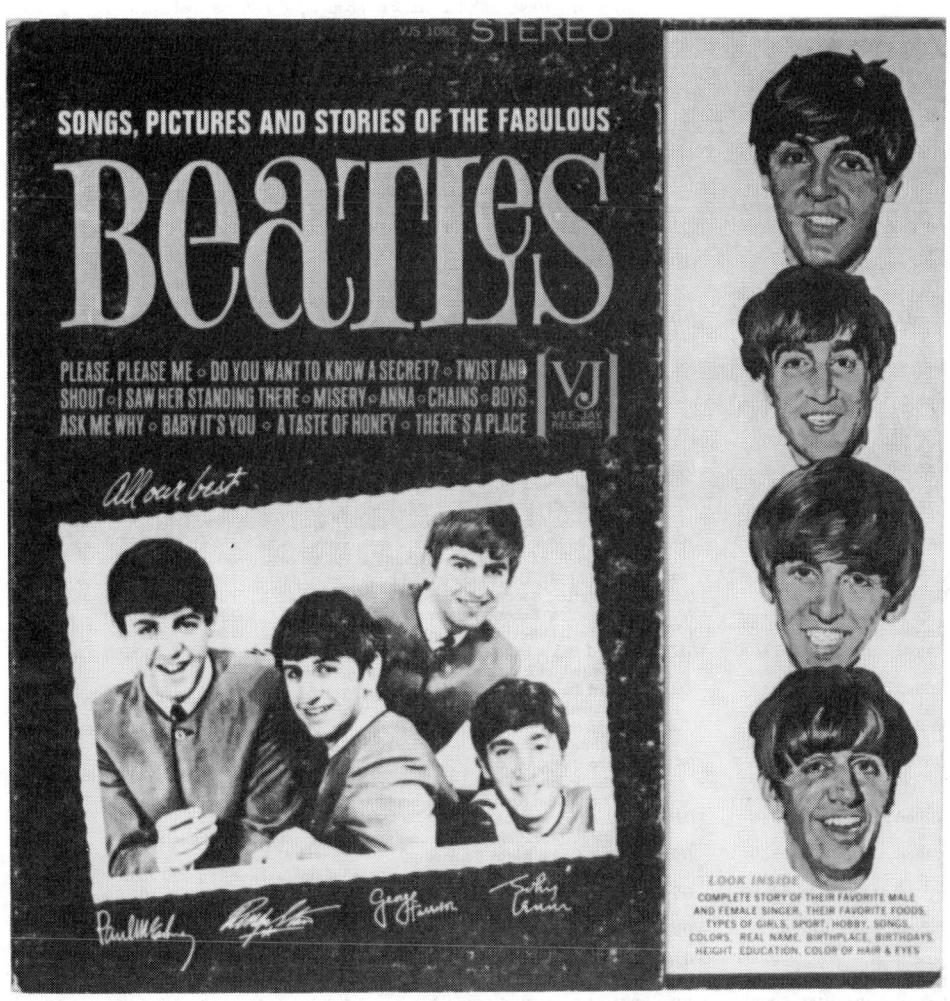

After Capitol turned down the option to pick up The Beatles' first album, Please Please Me, Vee Jay contracted for the distribution rights to the album's fourteen tracks in 1963. When The Beatles broke loose in the first weeks of '64, the little label from Chicago flooded the market with a veritable potpourri of singles and albums, all using the same fourteen tracks in one configuration after another. Songs, Pictures And Stories Of The Fabulous Beatles with its gatefold half-cover was among the more successful of these endeavors. Actual sales are impossible to estimate due to the plethora of unauthorized pressings—probably from Vee Jay after they lost their rights to the material—and out-and-out counterfeits, all of which found their way onto the retail racks of America. So, if you are not experienced, beware, as there are more phonies (all lacking the gatefold) than originals on the collectors market.

Label & Catalog #		Title	Year	VG+	NM
Vee Jay DX-30	(M)	**The Beatles Vs. The Four Seasons** (2 LPs)	1964	**660.00**	**1,000.00**
Vee Jay DXS-30	(S)	**The Beatles Vs. The Four Seasons** (2 LPs)	1964	See note below	
		(Vee Jay 30 repackages 1065, "Golden Hits Of The Four Seasons," with the second version of Vee Jay 1062, "Introducing The Beatles." Stereo copies have a suggested Near Mint value of $2,500-3,500. Original covers read "Free Bonus 8" x 15" Full Color Beatle Picture Suitable For Framing." This poster is priced separately below.)			
Vee Jay DXS-30		**The Beatles Vs. The Four Seasons Poster**	1964	150.00	300.00
Vee Jay VJ-1092	(M)	**Songs, Pictures And Stories**	1964	200.00	400.00
Vee Jay VJS-1092	(S)	**Songs, Pictures And Stories**	1964	1,000.00	2,000.00
		(Gatefold cover. Vee Jay 1092 repackages the second version of Vee Jay 1062, with the black rainbow label with the oval logo.)			
Vee Jay VJ-1092	(M)	**Songs, Pictures And Stories**	1964	200.00	400.00
Vee Jay VJS-1092	(S)	**Songs, Pictures And Stories**	1964	1,000.00	2,000.00
		(Gatefold cover. Vee Jay 1092 repackages the second version of Vee Jay 1062, with the black rainbow label with the brackets logo.)			
Vee Jay VJ-1092	(M)	**Songs, Pictures And Stories**	1964	200.00	400.00
Vee Jay VJS-1092	(S)	**Songs, Pictures And Stories**	1964	1,000.00	2,000.00
		(Gatefold cover. Vee Jay 1092 repackages the second version of Vee Jay 1062, with the solid black label with block letter logo.)			
Vee Jay VJ-1092	(M)	**Songs, Pictures And Stories**	1964	200.00	400.00
		(Gatefold cover. Vee Jay 1092 repackages the second version of Vee Jay 1062, with the solid black label with oval logo.)			
Vee Jay PRO-202	(DJ)	**Hear The Beatles Tell All** (White label)	1964	See note below	
		(White label promos have a suggested NM value of $10,000-15,000.)			
Vee Jay PRO-202	(M)	**Hear The Beatles Tell All**	1964	100.00	250.00
		(Original pressings have black rainbow labels. Counterfeits have plain black labels and no print on the spine of the cover.)			
Vee Jay 202	(M)	**Hear The Beatles Tell All**	1964	150.00	300.00
		(Later pressings have black rainbow labels but drop the "PRO" prefix from the catalog number.)			

5. The Capitol Years

Label & Catalog #		Title	Year	VG+	NM
Capitol T-2047	(M)	**Meet The Beatles**	1964	80.00	200.00
		(Original front covers have "Beatles!" in a brown print.)			
Capitol T-2047	(M)	**Meet The Beatles**	1964	40.00	100.00
		(Later front covers have "Beatles!" in an olive green print.)			
Capitol ST-2047	(P)	**Meet The Beatles**	1964	60.00	150.00
		(Original front covers have "Beatles!" in a brown print.)			
Capitol ST-2047	(P)	**Meet The Beatles**	1964	30.00	75.00
		(Later front covers have "Beatles!" in an olive green print.)			
Capitol ST-8-2047	(P)	**Meet The Beatles** (Record Club)	1964	300.00	500.00
Capitol T-2080	(M)	**The Beatles' Second Album**	1964	80.00	200.00
Capitol ST-2080	(P)	**The Beatles' Second Album**	1964	40.00	100.00
Capitol ST-8-2080	(P)	**The Beatles' Second Album** (Record Club)	1964	360.00	600.00
United Artists SP-2359/60	(DJ)	**A Hard Day's Night** (Open-end interview)	1964	1,400..00	2,000.00
		(Issued with a script in a plain cardboard jacket.)			
United Artists SP-2362	(DJ)	**A Hard Day's Night** (Radio Spots)	1964	1,000.00	1,500.00
		(Issued in a plain cardboard jacket.)			
United Artists UAL-3366	(DJ)	**A Hard Day's Night** (White label)	1964	See note below	
		(White label promos have a suggested NM value of $3,000-5,000.)			
United Artists UAL-3366	(M)	**A Hard Day's Night**	1964	80.00	200.00
		(Black label. The back cover correctly lists "I'll Cry Instead." This album also features background music by George Martin)			
United Artists UAL-3366	(M)	**A Hard Day's Night**	1964	80.00	200.00
		(Black label. The back cover incorrectly lists "I Cry Instead.")			
United Artists UAS-6366	(P)	**A Hard Day's Night** (Pink vinyl)	1964	See note below	
		(One-of-a-kind item with a suggested NM value of $5,000-15,000.)			
United Artists UAS-6366	(P)	**A Hard Day's Night**	1964	100.00	250.00
		(Black label. The back cover correctly lists "I'll Cry Instead.")			
United Artists UAS-6366	(P)	**A Hard Day's Night**	1964	80.00	200.00
		(Black label. The back cover incorrectly lists "I Cry Instead.")			
United Artists T-90828	(M)	**A Hard Day's Night** (Capitol Record Club)	1964	1,000.00	1,500.00
United Artists ST-90828	(P)	**A Hard Day's Night** (Capitol Record Club)	1964	500.00	750.00
United Artists UAS-6366	(P)	**A Hard Day's Night** (Pink & orange label)	1968	20.00	50.00
United Artists UAS-6366	(P)	**A Hard Day's Night** (Pink & black label)	1970	12.00	30.00
United Artists UAS-6366	(P)	**A Hard Day's Night**	1971	60.00	150.00
		(Tan label. The back cover is completely blank.)			
United Artists UAS-6366	(P)	**A Hard Day's Night** (Tan label)	1971	6.00	15.00
Capitol T-2108	(M)	**Something New**	1964	60.00	150.00
Capitol ST-2108	(S)	**Something New**	1964	30.00	75.00
Capitol ST-8-2108	(S)	**Something New** (Record Club)	1964	200.00	400.00
Capitol TBO-2222	(M)	**The Beatles' Story** (2 LPs)	1964	90.00	225.00
Capitol STBO-2222	(P)	**The Beatles' Story** (2 LPs)	1969	60.00	150.00
		(Assembled and produced by Gary Usher and Roger Christian.)			
Capitol T-2228	(M)	**Beatles '65**	1964	60.00	150.00
Capitol ST-2228	(P)	**Beatles '65**	1964	30.00	75.00

Label & Catalog #		Title	Year	VG+	NM
Capitol T-2309	(M)	**The Early Beatles**	1965	**80.00**	**200.00**
Capitol ST-2309	(P)	**The Early Beatles**	1965	**40.00**	**100.00**
Capitol T-2358	(M)	**Beatles VI**	1965	**60.00**	**150.00**
Capitol ST-2358	(P)	**Beatles VI**	1965	**30.00**	**75.00**
		(The back cover reads "See label for correct playing order.")			
Capitol T-2358	(M)	**Beatles VI**	1965	**60.00**	**150.00**
Capitol ST-2358	(P)	**Beatles VI**	1965	**30.00**	**75.00**
		(The back cover lists the tracks in correct order.)			
Capitol ST-8-2358	(P)	**Beatles VI** *(Record Club)*	1965	**360.00**	**600.00**
United Artists Help-A/B	(DJ)	**Help!** *(Radio spots)*	1965	**1,000.00**	**1,500.00**
		(Issued in a plain cardboard jacket.)			
United Artists Help-INT	(DJ)	**Help!** *(Open-end Interview)*	1965	*See note below*	
		(Help-INT was issued with a script in a plain cardboard jacket. *NM copies have a suggested value of $1,500-2,500.)*			
United Artists Help-Show	(DJ)	**Help!** *(One-sided open-end interview)*	1965	*See note below*	
		(Help-Show was issued with a script in a plain cardboard jacket. *NM copies have a suggested value of $3,000-5,000.)*			
Capitol MAS-2386	(M)	**Help!**	1965	**60.00**	**150.00**
Capitol SMAS-2386	(P)	**Help!**	1965	**30.00**	**75.00**
		(This album also features background music by George Martin)			
Capitol SMAS-8-2386	(P)	**Help!** *(Record Club)*	1965	**300.00**	**500.00**
		(The cover catalogue number is SMAS-2386.)			
Capitol SMAS-8-2386	(P)	**Help!** *(Record Club)*	1965	**500.00**	**750.00**
		(The cover catalogue number is SMAS-8-2386.)			
Capitol T-2442	(M)	**Rubber Soul**	1965	**60.00**	**150.00**
Capitol ST-2442	(S)	**Rubber Soul**	1965	**30.00**	**75.00**
Capitol ST-8-2442	(S)	**Rubber Soul** *(Record Club)*	1965	**30.00**	**500.00**

The "Beatles Butcher" Cover

The original cover for Capitol 2553, Yesterday And Today depicted the maliciously grinning Fabs dressed in butcher's smocks, covered with pieces of raw meat and baby doll parts. After pressing up hundreds of thousands of jackets, Capitol pulled the cover. A new cover with an innocuous photo of an unsmiling group posed around a steamer trunk was designed. Rather than destroy the original covers, employees simply pasted this new "trunk" cover over the "butcher cover" and sent them back out. This has created a situation where this album has a variety of terms applied to it according to the state of the cover: "First state" refers to the original cover as it was manufactured. That is, the butcher cover has never had the trunk cover pasted over it. "Second state," or "paste-overs," the trunk cover pasted over the butcher cover. Whether or not a copy of the album is a second-state is readily apparent: The black "V" of Ringo's sweater beneath the smock on the original cover can be seen through the paste-over midway up the right side of the cover, beneath the album title. "Third state" refers to the various attempts to remove the trunk cover from the butcher cover. These are also referred to as "peel jobs." Of course the success of the peel would dictate the value of the third-state; the closer to Near Mint the finished peel looks the more it would be worth to a collector seeking a first-state but unable or unwilling to pay for a first-state.

The easiest—and quickest—way to identify a first state from an excellent peel-job is to simply stand the album in question on its spine alongside any other Capitol album from the mid-'60s. As the paste-overs were all cropped along the mouth (to remove the excess paper from the trunk cover paste-over), a genuine first-state will be the same width as any other album. A second state will be approximately 3/16" shorter than a standard album jacket! Due to the fact that so many collectors are interested in owning an original butcher cover, the stock of second states are being depleted (especially in light of the contemporary means of removing the extraneous cover using chemicals that dissolve the adhesive without marring the paper). Finally—and ever so importantly—99% of the values listed below are for the cover alone!

Capitol T-2553	(M)	**Yesterday And Today** *("Butcher cover")*	1966	*See note below*	
Capitol ST-2553	(P)	**Yesterday And Today** *("Butcher cover")*	1966	*See note below*	
		(First state butcher cover. Refer to the notes immediately above. *Mono copies have a suggested NM value of $3,000-5,000 while* *stereo copies have a suggested NM value of $6,000-12,000.)*			
Capitol T-2553	(M)	**Yesterday And Today** *("Butcher cover")*	1966	*See note below*	
Capitol ST-2553	(P)	**Yesterday And Today** *("Butcher cover")*	1966	*See note below*	
		(Second state butcher cover, a.k.a. a "paste-over" butcher cover. *See above. Mono copies have a suggested NM value of $800-1,200* *while stereo copies have a suggested NM value of $2,000-4,000.* *Finally, third state butcher cover, a.k.a. a "peeled" second state:* *Perfectly peeled monos have a suggested value of $1,000-3,000 ;* *perfectly peeled stereo have a suggested value of $3,000-6,000.)*			
Capitol T-2553	(M)	**Yesterday And Today** *("Trunk cover")*	1966	**60.00**	**150.00**
Capitol ST-2553	(P)	**Yesterday And Today** *("Trunk cover")*	1966	**30.00**	**75.00**
		(This and all subsequent pressings of 2553 have the "trunk cover." *Refer to the notes above.)*			
Capitol ST-8-2553	(P)	**Yesterday And Today** *(Record Club)*	1966	**200.00**	**400.00**
Capitol T-2576	(M)	**Revolver**	1966	**60.00**	**150.00**
Capitol ST-2576	(S)	**Revolver**	1966	**30.00**	**75.00**
Capitol ST-8-2576	(S)	**Revolver** *(Record Club)*	1966	**300.00**	**500.00**
Capitol MAS-2653	(M)	**Sgt. Pepper's Lonely Heart's Club Band**	1967	**150.00**	**300.00**
Capitol SMAS-2653	(S)	**Sgt. Pepper's Lonely Heart's Club Band**	1967	**40.00**	**100.00**
		(Issued in a gatefold cover with a sheet of cutouts and a psychedelic *inner sleeve. Counterfeits were issued in a standard, single-pocket* *jacket, a plain white inner sleeve and without the cut-outs.)*			

Label & Catalog #		Title	Year	VG+	NM
Capitol MAL-2835	(M)	**Magical Mystery Tour**	1967	**200.00**	**400.00**
		(Gatefold covers; counterfeits have single-pocket covers.)			
Capitol SMAL-2835	(P)	**Magical Mystery Tour**	1967	**30.00**	**75.00**
		—Capitol albums above have black labels without "A Subsidiary of Capitol" on the bottom.—			
Capitol ST-2047	(P)	**Meet The Beatles**	1969	**16.00**	**40.00**
Capitol ST-2080	(P)	**The Beatles' Second Album**	1969	**16.00**	**40.00**
Capitol ST-2108	(S)	**Something New**	1969	**16.00**	**40.00**
Capitol STBO-2222	(P)	**The Beatles' Story**	1969	**20.00**	**50.00**
Capitol ST-2228	(P)	**Beatles '65**	1969	**16.00**	**40.00**
Capitol ST-2309	(P)	**The Early Beatles**	1969	**16.00**	**40.00**
Capitol ST-2358	(P)	**Beatles VI**	1969	**16.00**	**40.00**
Capitol SMAS-8-2386	(P)	**Help!**	1969	**16.00**	**40.00**
Capitol ST-2442	(S)	**Rubber Soul**	1969	**16.00**	**40.00**
Capitol ST-2553	(P)	**Yesterday And Today**	1969	**16.00**	**40.00**
Capitol ST-2576	(S)	**Revolver**	1969	**16.00**	**40.00**
Capitol SMAS-2653	(S)	**Sgt. Pepper's Lonely Heart's Club Band**	1969	**16.00**	**40.00**
Capitol SMAL-2835	(P)	**Magical Mystery Tour**	1969	**16.00**	**40.00**
		—Capitol albums above have black rainbow labels with "A Subsidiary of Capitol" on the bottom.—			
Capitol ST-2047	(P)	**Meet The Beatles**	1969	**16.00**	**40.00**
Capitol ST-8-2047	(P)	**Meet The Beatles** *(Record Club)*	1969	**80.00**	**200.00**
Capitol ST-2080	(P)	**The Beatles' Second Album**	1969	**16.00**	**40.00**
Capitol ST-8-2080	(P)	**The Beatles' Second Album** *(Record Club)*	1969	**100.00**	**250.00**
Capitol ST-2108	(S)	**Something New**	1969	**16.00**	**40.00**
Capitol ST-8-2108	(S)	**Something New** *(Record Club)*	1969	**80.00**	**200.00**
Capitol ST-8-2108	(S)	**Something New** *(Longines Sym. issue)*	1969	**175.00**	**350.00**
Capitol STBO-2222	(P)	**The Beatles' Story** *(2 LPs)*	1969	**20.00**	**50.00**
Capitol ST-2228	(P)	**Beatles '65**	1969	**16.00**	**40.00**
Capitol ST-2309	(P)	**The Early Beatles**	1969	**16.00**	**40.00**
Capitol ST-2358	(P)	**Beatles VI**	1969	**16.00**	**40.00**
Capitol ST-8-2358	(P)	**Beatles VI** *(Record Club)*	1969	**150.00**	**300.00**
Capitol ST-2356	(M)	**Beatles VI**	1988	**30.00**	**75.00**
		(The purple label with Manufactured by Capitol" were erroneously issued in mono instead of stereo.)			
Capitol SMAS-2386	(P)	**Help!**	1969	**16.00**	**40.00**
Capitol SMAS-8-2386	(P)	**Help!** *(Record Club)*	1969	**300.00**	**500.00**
		(The cover catalogue number is SMAS-8-2386.)			
Capitol SMAS-8-2386	(P)	**Help!** *(Record Club)*	1969	**100.00**	**250.00**
		(The cover catalogue number is SMAS-2386.)			
Capitol ST-2442	(S)	**Rubber Soul**	1969	**16.00**	**40.00**
Capitol ST-8-2442	(S)	**Rubber Soul** *(Record Club)*	1969	**80.00**	**200.00**
Capitol ST-2553	(P)	**Yesterday And Today**	1969	**16.00**	**40.00**
Capitol ST-8-2553	(P)	**Yesterday And Today** *(Record Club)*	1969	**80.00**	**200.00**
Capitol ST-2576	(S)	**Revolver**	1969	**12.00**	**30.00**
Capitol ST-8-2576	(S)	**Revolver** *(Record Club)*	1969	**60.00**	**150.00**
Capitol ST-8-2576	(S)	**Revolver** *(Record Club. Orange label)*	1976	**40.00**	**100.00**
Capitol ST-2576	(S)	**Revolver** *(Red label)*	197?	**60.00**	**150.00**
Capitol ST-2576	(S)	**Revolver** *(Red label)*	197?	**360.00**	**600.00**
Capitol ST-8-2576	(S)	**Revolver** *(Red label Record Club)*	197?	**300.00**	**500.00**
Capitol SMAS-2653	(S)	**Sgt. Pepper's Lonely Heart's Club Band**	1969	**16.00**	**40.00**
Capitol SMAL-2835	(P)	**Magical Mystery Tour**	1969	**16.00**	**40.00**
		—Capitol albums above have lime-green labels except where noted.—			

6. Apple Originals

Apple SWBO-101	(S)	**The Beatles** *(2 LPs)*	1968	**60.00**	**150.00**
		(First pressing labels read "A subsidiary of Capitol" on the bottom. First pressing covers have "The Beatles" in raised white letters and are sequentially numbered 1-3,000,000 in black. Copies with numbers under #10,000 affect the value—under #1,000, the value is raised substantially. Issued with a fold-open poster/lyric sheet and four glossy, full-color portraits of the group, included in the price. Note: Because of the lack of graphics on the front and back cover, this album is also known as "The White Album.")			
Apple SWBO-101	(S)	**The Beatles** *(2 LPs)*	1968	**500.00**	**750.00**
		(First pressing same as above with a large, fluorescent red sticker on the front cover with song titles, etc.)			
Apple SWBO-101	(S)	**The Beatles** *(2 LPs)*	1968	**300.00**	**500.00**
		(First pressing same as above with a small sticker on the back cover with song titles, etc.)			
Apple SWBO-101	(S)	**The Beatles** *(2 LPs)*	1968	**40.00**	**100.00**
		(First pressing without the poster and photos.)			
Apple SWBO-101	(S)	**The Beatles** *(2 LPs)*	1969	**32.00**	**80.00**
		(Second pressing label read "Manufactured by Apple" on the bottom. Covers are similar to the first except there is no number stamped on the cover. Issued with the poster and the four glossy photos.)			
Apple SWBO-101	(S)	**The Beatles** *(2 LPs)*	1969	**12.00**	**30.00**
		(Second pressing without the poster and photos.)			

From 1963 through '69 The Beatles recorded a whimsical Christmas message for distribution to members of their official fan-club. In 1970, after the unofficial demise of the group, The Beatles Christmas Album was issued. It consists of the Fab's seven previous messages and is far rarer than any of the individual messages. The fact that so many well-made counterfeits exist has acted as a drag on the escalation in value of this true Beatles rarity.

Label & Catalog #		Title	Year	VG+	NM
Apple SWBO-101	(S)	**The Beatles** (2 LPs) (Third pressing labels have an "All rights reserved" disclaimer. This and all subsequent pressings have the title printed in black on the cover and the photos are on thin stock with less gloss.)	1975	30.00	75.00
Apple KAL-1004	(DJ)	**Yellow Submarine** (Radio spots) (KAL-1004 has a suggested NM value of $4,000-6,000.)	1968	See note below	
Apple SW-153	(P)	**Yellow Submarine** (First pressing labels read "A subsidiary of Capitol" on the bottom. This album also features background music by George Martin)	1969	10.00	25.00
Apple SW-153	(P)	**Yellow Submarine** (Second pressing label read "Mfd. by Apple" on the bottom.)	1969	6.00	15.00
Apple SW-153	(P)	**Yellow Submarine** (Third pressing labels have an "All rights reserved" disclaimer.)	1975	8.00	20.00
Apple SO-383	(S)	**Abbey Road** (First pressing labels read "A subsidiary of Capitol" on the bottom. "Her Majesty" is listed on the cover and the label.)	1969	16.00	40.00
Apple SO-383	(S)	**Abbey Road** (First pressing labels read "A subsidiary of Capitol" on the bottom. "Her Majesty" is not listed on either the cover or the label.)	1969	30.00	75.00
Apple SO-383	(S)	**Abbey Road** (Second pressing label read "Mfd. by Apple" on the bottom. and may or may not list "Her Majesty" on the cover or label. Counterfeits exist; the print and colors tend to be fuzzy.)	1969	6.00	15.00
Apple SO-383	(S)	**Abbey Road** (Third pressing labels have an "All rights reserved" disclaimer. This and all subsequent Capitol pressings list "Her Majesty.")	1975	8.00	20.00
Apple SO-385	(S)	**Beatles Again** (Alternate covers) (At least two variations were made for this album when its title was "Beatles Again." One has the same photos but the back cover is purple while the other has the front and back photos reversed. Suggested values in collectible condition are $6,000-12,000 each.)	1970	See note below	
Apple SO-385	(S)	**Hey Jude/The Beatles Again** (First pressings read "Manufactured by Apple" on the label and have an "SO" prefix. While the title on the cover is "Hey Jude," on the label it is "The Beatles Again.")	1970	8.00	20.00
Apple SW-385	(S)	**Hey Jude/The Beatles Again** (Second pressings read "Manufactured by Apple" on the label. and have an "SW" prefix. While the title on the cover is "Hey Jude," on the label it is "The Beatles Again.")	1970	10.00	25.00
Apple SW-385	(S)	**Hey Jude** (Third pressings read "Manufactured by Capitol" on the label. Both the cover and the label on this and all subsequent Apple and Capitol pressings list the title as "Hey Jude.")	1970	30.00	75.00
Apple SW-385	(S)	**Hey Jude** (Fourth pressing label read "Mfd. by Apple" on the bottom.)	1970	6.00	15.00
Apple SW-385	(S)	**Hey Jude** (Fifth pressing labels have an "All rights reserved" disclaimer.)	1975	8.00	20.00
Apple AR-34001	(S)	**Let It Be** (Red Apple label. Originals have "Bell Sound" stamped in the trail-off vinyl; counterfeits do not.)	1970	10.00	25.00
Apple SBC-100	(M)	**The Beatles Christmas Album** (Fan club) (Convincing counterfeits exist although both the photos on the cover—especially the background details— and the print in the record's trail-off vinyl are slightly blurred.)	1970	200.00	400.00
Apple SKBO-3403	(P)	**The Beatles 1962-1966** (2 LPs) (First pressings have custom Apple labels.)	1973	12.00	30.00
Apple SKBO-3403	(P)	**The Beatles 1962-1966** (2 LPs) (Second pressing labels have an "All rights reserved" disclaimer.)	1975	20.00	50.00
Apple SKBO-3404	(P)	**The Beatles 1967-1970** (2 LPs) (First pressings have custom Apple labels.)	1973	12.00	30.00
Apple SKBO-3404	(P)	**The Beatles 1967-1970** (2 LPs) (Second pressing labels have an "All rights reserved" disclaimer.)	1975	20.00	50.00
Apple SKBO-3403	(P)	**The Beatles 1962-1966** (2 LPs. Red labels)	1975	10.00	25.00
Apple SKBO-3403	(P)	**The Beatles 1962-1966** (2 LPs. Blue labels)	1975	20.00	50.00
Apple SKBO-3404	(P)	**The Beatles 1967-1970** (2 LPs. Blue labels) (First pressings have custom Apple labels.)	1973	14.00	35.00
Apple (No number)	(P)	**The Beatles Special Limited Edition** (Boxed set of nine Apple label albums.)	1974	800.00	1,200.00

7. Capitol Repackagings

Label & Catalog #		Title	Year	VG+	NM
Capitol (No number)	(DJ)	**The Beatles 10th Anniversary Box Set** (Boxed set of seventeen Apple label albums. with a suggested NM value of $2,000-3,000.)	1974	See note below	
Capitol SKBO-11537	(S)	**Rock 'n' Roll Music** (2 LPs)	1977	8.00	20.00
Capitol SMAS-11638	(DJ)	**The Beatles At The Hollywood Bowl** (White label issued in a plain white jacket.)	1977	500.00	750.00
Capitol SMAS-11638	(S)	**The Beatles At The Hollywood Bowl** (Original covers have the title and photo embossed on the front.)	1977	4.00	10.00

*Beginning as a five man group, The Beau Brummels emulated the sound of the British Inva-
sion, achieving big chart success in 1964-65 with "Laugh Laugh," "Just A Little," and "Tell
Me Why." By 1967 the group was a studio trio. Both of these albums are astonishing; Ron
Elliot's guitar(s) and Sal Valentino's vocals are breathtaking. Triangle is a minor masterpiece of late '60s mood music while Bradley's Barn was one of the earliest forays into coun-
try-rock, recorded in Owen Bradley's Nashville studios with local pickers.*

Label & Catalog #		Title	Year	VG+	NM
Capitol SMAS-11638	(S)	The Beatles At The Hollywood Bowl	1978	8.00	20.00
		(Second covers are not embossed.)			
Capitol SMAS-11638	(S)	The Beatles At The Hollywood Bowl	198?	16.00	40.00
		(Later covers are not embossed and have a UPC bar-code.)			
Capitol SKBL-11711	(P)	Love Songs *(2 LPs with lyric booklet)*	1977	200.00	400.00
		(White label promo/test pressing with printed labels.)			
Capitol SKBL-11711	(P)	Love Songs *(2 LPs with lyric booklet)*	1977	6.00	15.00
		(Original pressings have an embossed front cover.)			
Capitol SKBL-11711	(P)	Love Songs *(2 LPs with lyric booklet)*	1078	12.00	30.00
		(Later covers are not embossed.)			
Capitol SEAX-11840	(S)	Sgt. Pepper's Lonely Heart's Club Band	1978	14.00	35.00
		(Picture disc in die cut cover.)			
Capitol SEBX-11841	(S)	The Beatles *(2 LPs on colored vinyl)*	1978	300.00	500.00
		(One record is on gray vinyl, the other on white.)			
Capitol SEBX-11841	(S)	The Beatles *(2 LPs. White vinyl)*	1978	20.00	50.00
Capitol SEBX-11842	(P)	The Beatles 1962-1966 *(2 LPs on red vinyl)*	1978	12.00	30.00
Capitol SEBX-11843	(P)	The Beatles 1967-1970 *(2 LPs on blue vinyl)*	1978	12.00	30.00
Capitol SEBX-11844	(P)	Love Songs *(2 LPs on gold vinyl)*	1978	40.00	100.00
		(Issued with a lyric booklet.)			
Capitol SEAX-11900	(S)	Abbey Road *(Picture disc)*	1978	20.00	50.00
Capitol SPRO-8969	(DJ)	Rarities	1978	20.00	50.00
Capitol SN-12009	(P)	Rarities *(Green label without cover)*	1978	150.00	300.00
		(Capitol 8969 and 12009 are reissues of the EMI/Parlophone album.)			
Capitol/EMI BC-13	(P)	The Beatles Collection *(14 LP box)*	1978	100.00	250.00
Capitol SN-16020	(S)	Rock 'n' Roll Music, Volume 1	1980	5.00	12.00
Capitol SN-16021	(S)	Rock 'n' Roll Music, Volume 2	1980	5.00	12.00
		(Capitol 16020 and 16021 are reissues of 11537.)			
Capitol SHAL-12080	(P)	Rarities *(Rainbow label)*	1980	6.00	15.00
		(This Rarities contains 15 tracks and is a different album than 12009 above. Original covers do not credit George Martin as producer.)			
Capitol SHAL-12080	(P)	Rarities *(Black label)*	1980	4.00	10.00
		(Later covers read "Produced by George Martin" on the back.)			
Capitol SV-12199	(DJ)	Reel Music *(Gold vinyl)*	1982	20.00	50.00
		(Back cover stamped with a "Limited Edition" number and included a souvenir program.)			
Capitol SV-12199	(S)	Reel Music *(Gold vinyl)*	1982	12.00	30.00
		(Without the "Limited Edition" number with program.)			
Capitol SV-12199	(S)	Reel Music *(Black vinyl)*	1982	4.00	10.00
Capitol SV-12245	(P)	20 Greatest Hits	1982	4.00	10.00
Capitol *(No number)*	(DJ)	The Platinum Collection *(18 LP box)*	1984	660.00	1,000.00
Capitol BBX1-91302	(DJ)	The Deluxe Box Set *(14 LP box)*	1984	150.00	300.00
Capitol C1-91135	(P)	Past Masters—Volumes One & Two *(2 LPs)*	1988	10.00	25.00

8. Miscellaneous Releases

INS Radio News DOC-1	(DJ)	Beatlemania Tour Coverage	1964	1,000.00	1,600.00
		(Open-end interview issued with a script in a plain cardboard jacket.)			
Radio Pulsebeat #2	(M)	American Tour With Ed Rudy *(Yellow label)*	1964	40.00	100.00
		(Counterfeits are on flexible vinyl with no writing in the trail-off area.)			
Radio Pulsebeat #2	(M)	American Tour With Ed Rudy *(Blue label)*	1980	10.00	25.00
Radio Pulsebeat	(M)	1965 Talk Album—Ed Rudy With New U.S. Tour	1965	360.00	600.00
		(The cover has "The Beatles" in red print above the photo. Counterfeits exist. Note: This was issued with two flyers worth $25 each.)			
Radio Pulsebeat	(M)	1965 Talk Album—Ed Rudy With New U.S. Tour	1965	150.00	300.00
		(The cover has "The Beatles" in black print under the photo. Note: This was issued with two flyers worth $25 each.)			
Sterling Prod. 8895-6481	(M)	I Apologize *(With bonus photo)*	1966	200.00	400.00
Sterling Prod. 8895-6481	(M)	I Apologize *(Without photo)*	1966	150.00	300.00
PBR Inter. 7005/6	(M)	The Beatles Tapes *(2 LPs. Blue vinyl)*	1978	20.00	50.00
PBR Inter. 7005/6	(M)	The Beatles Tapes *(2 LPs)*	1978	20.00	50.00
Great Northwest Music 4007	(M)	Beatle Talk	197?	4.00	10.00
Great Northwest Music 4007	(M)	Beatle Talk *(With "CRC" on spine)*	197?	16.00	40.00
Silhouette SM-10013	(DJ)	British Are Coming *(White label promo)*	1984	20.00	50.00
Silhouette SM-10013	(M)	British Are Coming	1984	6.00	15.00
Silhouette SM-10013	(M)	British Are Coming *(Red vinyl)*	1984	15.00	75.00
Silhouette SM-10015	(M)	Golden Beatles	1985	6.00	15.00
Silhouette SM-10015	(M)	Golden Beatles *(Gold vinyl)*	1985	15.00	75.00
Backstage BSR-1165	(M)	Beatles Talk With Jerry G *(Picture disc)*	198?	10.00	25.00
Backstage BSR-1175	(M)	Beatles Talk With Jerry G , Vol. 2 *(Picture disc)*	198?	10.00	25.00

BEATS, THE: *Refer to* THE LIVERPOOL BEATS

BEAU BRUMMELS, THE
The original members were Sal Valentino backed by Ron Elliot, Declan Mulligan, Ron Meagher and John Petersen. By 1967, the recording group consisted of Valentino and Elliot with studio assistance.

Autumn LP-103	(M)	Introducing The Beau Brummels	1965	14.00	35.00
Autumn SLP-103	(S)	Introducing The Beau Brummels	1965	20.00	50.00
		("I Would Be Happy" is in mono on this album.)			

Label & Catalog #		Title	Year	VG+	NM
Autumn LP-104	(M)	The Beau Brummels, Volume 2	1965	14.00	35.00
Autumn SLP-104	(S)	The Beau Brummels, Volume 2	1965	20.00	50.00
Warner Bros. WS-1644	(M)	Beau Brummels '66	1966	8.00	20.00
Warner Bros. WS-1644	(S)	Beau Brummels '66	1966	10.00	25.00
Warner Bros. W-1692	(M)	Triangle	1967	8.00	20.00
Warner Bros. WS-1692	(S)	Triangle	1967	10.00	25.00
Warner Bros. WS-1760	(S)	Bradley's Barn	1968	10.00	25.00
Vault LP-114	(M)	Best Of The Beau Brummels	1967	10.00	25.00
Vault SLP-114	(S)	Best Of The Beau Brummels	1967	10.00	25.00
Vault SLP-121	(P)	Beau Brummels, Volume 44	1968	10.00	25.00
Post 6000	(P)	The Beau Brummels Sing	196?	6.00	15.00
Warner Bros. BS-2842	(S)	The Beau Brummels	1975	3.20	8.00
JAS 5000	(S)	Original Hits Of The Beau Brummels	1976	6.00	15.00
Rhino RNLP-101	(S)	The Best Of The Beau Brummels	1981	.80	4.00
Rhino RNLP-102	(S)	Introducing The Beau Brummels	1981	.80	4.00
Rhino RNLP-104	(S)	From The Vaults	1981	.80	4.00
Accord SN-7175	(S)	Just A Little	1982	.80	4.00

BEAVER & KRAUSE
Paul Beaver and Bernie Krause.

Limelight 86069	(S)	Ragnarok	1969	12.00	30.00
Warner Bros. WS-1850	(S)	In A Wild Sanctuary	1969	6.00	15.00
Warner Bros. WS-1909	(S)	Gandharva	1971	6.00	15.00
Warner Bros. BS-2624	(S)	All Good Men	1972	6.00	15.00

BECK, JEFF [THE JEFF BECK GROUP]
On their first two LPs, Beck's group featured Rod Stewart and Ron Wood, joined by Nicky Hopkins on the second. After that, personnel changed regularly. Refer to Eric Clapton / Jeff Beck / Jimmy Page; Lord Sutch; The Yardbirds.

Epic BN-26413	(S)	Truth	1968	6.00	15.00
Epic BN-26478	(S)	Beck-Ola	1969	6.00	15.00
		—Epic albums above have yellow labels.—			
Epic BN-26413	(S)	Truth	1973	1.00	5.00
Epic BN-26478	(S)	Beck-Ola	1973	1.00	5.00
Epic Q-30973	(S)	Rough And Ready	1973	1.00	5.00
Epic EQ-30973	(Q)	Rough And Ready	1974	6.00	15.00
Epic E-31331	(S)	The Jeff Beck Group	1973	1.00	5.00
Epic EQ-31331	(Q)	The Jeff Beck Group	1974	6.00	15.00
Epic PE-33409	(S)	Blow By Blow	1975	1.00	5.00
Epic PEQ-33409	(Q)	Blow By Blow	1975	6.00	15.00
Epic HE-43409	(S)	Blow By Blow (Half-speed master)	1982	15.00	45.00
Epic PE-33849	(S)	Wired	1976	1.00	5.00
Epic PEQ-33849	(Q)	Wired	1976	6.00	15.00
Epic HE-43849	(S)	Wired (Half-speed master)	1982	15.00	45.00
Epic PE-34433	(S)	Live	1977	1.00	5.00
Epic PEQ-34433	(Q)	Live	1977	6.00	15.00
		—Epic albums above have orange labels.—			
Epic AS-151	(DJ)	Everything You Always Wanted To Hear By Jeff Beck But Was Afraid To Ask For (Sampler)	1977	6.00	15.00
Epic AS-796	(DJ)	Musical Montage (Sampler)	1979	6.00	15.00
Epic AS2-850	(DJ)	Then And Now (2 LPs. Sampler)	1981	8.00	20.00
Accord SN-7141	(S)	Early Anthology	1982	.80	4.00

BECK, BOGERT & APPICE
Jeff Beck with Tim Bogert and Carmine Appice of The Vanilla Fudge.

Epic KE-32140	(S)	Beck, Bogert, & Appice	1973	4.00	10.00
		—Epic albums above have yellow labels.—			
Epic KE-32140	(S)	Beck, Bogert, & Appice	1973	1.00	5.00
Epic EQ-32140	(Q)	Beck, Bogert, & Appice	1973	6.00	15.00

BECKIES, THE
The Beckies feature Michael Brown of The Left Banke.

Sire 7519	(S)	The Beckies	1976	4.00	10.00

BEDIENT, JACK, & THE CHESSMEN
Jack Bedient released several privately pressed LPs.

Fantasy 3365	(M)	Live At Harvey's	1965	16.00	40.00

BEDLAM

Chrysalis CHR-1048	(S)	Bedlam	1973	10.00	25.00

BEE GEES, THE
The Brothers Gibb are Barry, Maurice and Robin. They appear on the Atco soundtrack "Melody." Refer to Lulu.

Atco 33-223	(M)	The Bee Gees First	1967	12.00	30.00
Atco SD-33-223	(S)	The Bee Gees First	1967	8.00	20.00
Atco 33-233	(M)	Horizontal	1968	12.00	30.00
Atco SD-33-233	(S)	Horizontal	1968	8.00	20.00
Atco 33-253	(M)	Idea (White label promo)	1968	20.00	50.00
Atco SD-33-253	(S)	Idea	1968	8.00	20.00

Label & Catalog #		Title	Year	VG+	NM
Atco 33-264	(M)	Rare, Precious & Beautiful (White label)	1968	12.00	30.00
Atco SD-33-264	(E)	Rare, Precious & Beautiful	1968	6.00	15.00
		—Atco stereo albums above have brown & purple labels.—			
Atco SD-33-223	(S)	The Bee Gees First	1970	1.00	5.00
Atco SD-33-233	(S)	Horizontal	1970	1.00	5.00
Atco SD-33-253	(S)	Idea	1970	1.00	5.00
Atco SD-33-264	(E)	Rare, Precious & Beautiful	1970	1.00	5.00
Atco 33-292	(M)	The Best Of The Bee Gees (White label)	1969	12.00	30.00
Atco SD-33-292	(S)	The Best Of The Bee Gees	1969	4.00	10.00
Atco ST-142	(DJ)	Odessa (In-store sampler)	1969	30.00	75.00
Atco SD-2-702	(S)	Odessa (Red felt cover)	1969	16.00	40.00
Atco SD-2-702	(S)	Odessa (Record Club. Plain red cover)	1969	30.00	75.00
Atco 33-321	(M)	Rare, Precious & Beautiful, Volume 2 (White label promo)	1970	12.00	30.00
Atco SD-33-321	(E)	Rare, Precious & Beautiful, Volume 2	1970	4.00	10.00
Atco SD-33-327	(S)	Cucumber Castle	1970	4.00	10.00
Atco SD-33-353	(S)	Two Years On	1971	4.00	10.00
Atco SD-7003	(S)	Trafalgar	1971	4.00	10.00
Atco SD-7012	(S)	To Whom It May Concern	1972	4.00	10.00
		—Atco albums above have yellow labels with an 1841 Broadway address on the bottom.—			
RSO SO-870	(S)	Life In A Tin Can	1973	3.20	8.00
RSO SO-875	(S)	The Best Of The Bee Gees, Vol. 2	1873	3.20	8.00
RSO SO-4800	(S)	Mr. Natural	1974	3.20	8.00
RSO SO-4807	(S)	Main Course	1974	3.20	8.00
RSO SO-3003	(S)	Children Of The World	1976	.80	4.00
RSO SO-3006	(S)	Bee Gees' Gold, Vol. 1	1976	.80	4.00
RSO SO-3007	(S)	Odessa (2 LPs)	1976	1.00	5.00
RSO SO-3024	(S)	Main Course	1977	.80	4.00
RSO SO-3041	(S)	Spirits Having Flown	1979	.80	4.00
RSO SO-3042	(S)	Spirits Having Flown (Picture disc)	1979	4.00	10.00
RSO SO-3098	(S)	Living Eyes	1981	.80	4.00
RSO SO-3901	(S)	Here At Last—Bee Gees Live-Live (2 LPs)	1977	1.00	5.00
RSO SO-4200	(S)	The Greatest (2 LPs)	1979	1.00	5.00
RSO PRO-033	(DJ)	Saturday Night Fever Special Disco Version	1977	20.00	50.00
		(RSO 033 contains extended remixes of five tracks from the film.)			
RSO SMP-1	(DJ)	The Words And Music Of Maurice, Barry And Robin Gibb	1979	20.00	50.00
RSO PUB-1000	(DJ)	Unichapel Publisher's Sampler	1980	20.00	50.00
		(Both RSP 1 and 1000 are publishers samplers.)			

BEE GEES, THE / RAY CHARLES

Atlantic ???	(DJ)	Rare, Precious & Beautiful/The Other Ray Charles	1969	20.00	50.00
		(Sampler with each side devoted to one artist's latest album.)			

BEEFHEART, CAPTAIN: *Refer to* **CAPTAIN BEEFHEART & THE MAGIC BAND**

BEETHOVEN SOUL

Dot DLP-3821	(M)	Beethoven Soul	1967	8.00	20.00
Dot DLP-25821	(S)	Beethoven Soul	1967	10.00	25.00

BEGGAR'S OPERA

Verve V-65080	(S)	Beggar's Opera, Act One	1971	4.00	10.00

BEL-AIRE GIRLS, THE

Everest LPBR-5081	(M)	The Bel-Aire Girls Sing Along With The Teen-Agers	1960	30.00	75.00
Everest SDBR-1081	(S)	The Bel-Aire Girls Sing Along With The Teen-Agers	1960	40.00	100.00

BEL-AIRE POPS ORCHESTRA, THE
The BAPO are L.A. studio musicians conducted by Jan Berry and George Tipton. Refer to Jan & Dean.

Liberty LRP-3414	(M)	Jan & Dean's Pop Symphony No.1	1965	40.00	100.00
Liberty LST-7414	(S)	Jan & Dean's Pop Symphony No.1	1965	80.00	200.00

BELL, ARCHIE, & THE DRELLS

Atlantic 8181	(M)	Tighten Up	1968	16.00	40.00
Atlantic SD-8181	(S)	Tighten Up	1968	16.00	40.00
Atlantic SD-8204	(S)	I Can't Stop Dancing	1968	16.00	40.00
Atlantic SD-8226	(S)	There's Gonna Be A Showdown	1969	16.00	40.00
Phila. Inter. PZ-33844	(S)	Archie Bell & The Drells	1975	4.00	10.00
Phila. Inter. PZ-34855	(S)	Hard Not To Like It	1977	4.00	10.00
Phila. Inter. PZ-336096	(S)	Strategy	1979	4.00	10.00
Beckett 013	(S)	I Never Had It So Good	1981	1.00	5.00

BELL, CAREY

Delmark DS-622	(S)	Blues Harp	1969	6.00	15.00
Blues Way BLS-60790	(S)	Last Night	1974	4.00	10.00

Label & Catalog #		Title	Year	VG+	NM

BELL, FREDDIE, & THE BELL BOYS

Mercury MG-20289	(M)	Rock And Roll—All Flavors	1958	80.00	200.00
20th Century TF-4146	(M)	Bells Are Swinging	1964	10.00	25.00
20th Century TFS-4146	(S)	Bells Are Swinging	1964	12.00	30.00

BELL, MADELEINE
Ms Bell later recorded with Blue Mink.

Philips PHS-600271	(S)	I'm Gonna Make You Mine	1968	6.00	15.00

BELL, WILLIAM

Stax 719	(M)	Soul Of A Bell	1967	16.00	40.00
Stax S-719	(S)	Soul Of A Bell	1967	20.00	50.00
Stax ST-2014	(M)	Bound To Happen (Promo)	1969	20.00	50.00
Stax STS-2014	(S)	Bound To Happen	1969	14.00	35.00
Stax STS-2037	(S)	Wow...	1971	14.00	35.00
Stax STS-3005	(S)	Phases To Reality	1973	12.00	30.00
Stax STS-5502	(S)	Relating	1974	10.00	25.00
Mercury SRM-1146	(S)	Coming Back For More	1977	1.00	5.00
Mercury SRM-1193	(S)	It's Time You Took Another Listen	1977	1.00	5.00

BELL SHANNY MEN, THE

Orco 1002	(S)	The Bell Shanny Men	1967	6.00	15.00

BELLINE, DENNY, & THE RICH KIDS

RCA Victor LPM-3655	(M)	Denny Belline And The Rich Kids	1966	6.00	15.00
RCA Victor LSP-3655	(S)	Denny Belline And The Rich Kids	1966	8.00	20.00

BELLS, THE

Polydor 24-4510	(S)	Stay Away (Fly Little White Dove, Fly)	1971	1.00	5.00
Polydor 24-5503	(S)	Love, Luck 'N Lollypops	1972	1.00	5.00

BELLUS, TONY

N.R.C. LPA-8	(M)	Robbin' The Cradle	1960	150.00	300.00
		—NRC albums above have blue labels.—			
N.R.C. LPA-8	(M)	Robbin' The Cradle	196?	60.00	150.00
		—NRC albums above have black labels.—			

BELMONTS, THE
Refer to Dion & The Belmonts; Jimmy Soul & The Belmonts.

Sabina SALP-5001	(M)	The Belmonts' Carnival Of Hits	1962	60.00	150.00
Dot DLP-25949	(S)	Summer Love	1969	12.00	30.00
Buddah BDS-5123	(S)	Cigars, Acappella, Candy	1972	20.00	50.00
Strawberry 6001	(S)	Cheek To Cheek	1978	6.00	15.00

BELVIN, JESSE
Refer to Brook Benton / Jesse Belvin.

Crown CLP-5145	(M)	The Casual Jesse Belvin	1959	30.00	75.00
Crown CLP-5187	(M)	The Unforgettable Jesse Belvin	1959	30.00	75.00
		—Crown albums above have black labels with a silver "Crown" on top.—			
Crown CLP-5145	(M)	The Casual Jesse Belvin	196?	4.00	10.00
Crown CLP-5187	(M)	The Unforgettable Jesse Belvin	196?	4.00	10.00
		—Crown albums above have gray labels.—			
RCA Victor LPM-2089	(M)	Just Jesse Belvin	1959	14.00	35.00
RCA Victor LSP-2089	(S)	Just Jesse Belvin	1959	20.00	50.00
RCA Victor LPM-2105	(M)	Mr. Easy	1960	12.00	30.00
RCA Victor LSP-2105	(S)	Mr. Easy	1960	16.00	40.00
		—RCA albums above have black "Long Play" or "Living Stereo" labels.—			
Camden CAL-960	(M)	Jesse Belvin's Best	1966	5.00	12.00
Camden CAS-960	(S)	Jesse Belvin's Best	1966	6.00	15.00
United US-7220	(E)	...But Not Forgotten	1970	6.00	15.00

BENNINGHOFF'S BAD ROCK BLUES BAND

SSS International 15	(S)	Beethoven Bittersweet	1971	6.00	15.00

BENNO, MARC
Marc Benno also recorded with Asylum Choir.

A&M SP-4273	(S)	Marc Benno	1970	3.20	8.00
A&M SP-4303	(S)	Minnows	1971	3.20	8.00
A&M SP-4364	(S)	Ambush	1972	3.20	8.00

BENNETT, BOYD

King 594	(M)	Boyd Bennett	1955	See note below	
		(King 594 has a suggested NM value of $3,000-6,000.)			

BENNETT, CONNIE, & BILL SMYTH & THE HARLEM-AIRES

Hollywood LPH-30	(M)	Rhythm 'N Blues In The Night	1957	300.00	600.00
		(The cover, a generic pretty white girl common on R&B albums of the time, features a very young—and scantily clad—Julie Newmar.)			

Label & Catalog #		Title	Year	VG+	NM
BENTON, BROOK					
Epic LG-3573	(M)	**Brook Benton At His Best**	1959	20.00	50.00
Mercury MG-20421	(M)	**It's Just A Matter Of Time**	1959	20.00	50.00
Mercury SR-60077	(S)	**It's Just A Matter Of Time**	1959	20.00	50.00
Mercury MG-20464	(M)	**Endlessly**	1959	12.00	30.00
Mercury SR-60146	(S)	**Endlessly**	1959	16.00	40.00
Mercury MG-20565	(M)	**So Many Ways I Love You**	1959	12.00	30.00
Mercury SR-60225	(S)	**So Many Ways I Love You**	1959	16.00	40.00
Mercury MG-20602	(M)	**Songs I Love To Sing**	1960	8.00	20.00
Mercury SR-60602	(S)	**Songs I Love To Sing**	1960	12.00	30.00
Mercury MG-20607	(M)	**Brook Benton's Golden Hits**	1961	8.00	20.00
Mercury SR-60607	(S)	**Brook Benton's Golden Hits**	1961	10.00	25.00
Mercury MG-20619	(M)	**If You Believe**	1961	8.00	20.00
Mercury SR-60619	(S)	**If You Believe**	1961	12.00	30.00
Mercury MG-20641	(M)	**The Boll Weevil Song**	1961	8.00	20.00
Mercury SR-60641	(S)	**The Boll Weevil Song**	1961	12.00	30.00
Mercury MG-20673	(M)	**There Goes That Song Again**	1962	8.00	20.00
Mercury SR-60673	(S)	**There Goes That Song Again**	1962	12.00	30.00
Mercury MG-20740	(M)	**Singing The Blues**	1962	8.00	20.00
Mercury SR-60740	(S)	**Singing The Blues**	1962	12.00	30.00
Mercury MG-20774	(M)	**Brook Benton's Golden Hits, Volume 2**	1963	8.00	20.00
Mercury SR-60774	(S)	**Brook Benton's Golden Hits, Volume 2**	1963	10.00	25.00
—Mercury albums above have black labels with silver print.—					
Mercury MG-20830	(M)	**Best Ballads Of Broadway**	1963	8.00	20.00
Mercury SR-60830	(S)	**Best Ballads Of Broadway**	1963	10.00	25.00
Mercury MG-20886	(M)	**Born To Sing The Blues**	1964	8.00	20.00
Mercury SR-60886	(S)	**Born To Sing The Blues**	1964	10.00	25.00
Mercury MG-20918	(M)	**On The Country Side**	1964	6.00	15.00
Mercury SR-60918	(S)	**On The Country Side**	1964	8.00	20.00
Mercury MG-20934	(M)	**This Bitter Earth**	1964	6.00	15.00
Mercury SR-60934	(S)	**This Bitter Earth**	1964	8.00	20.00
Harmony HL-7346	(M)	**The Soul Of Brook Benton**	1965	5.00	12.00
Harmony HS-7346	(S)	**The Soul Of Brook Benton**	1965	6.00	15.00
RCA Victor LPM-3514	(M)	**That Old Feeling**	1966	6.00	15.00
RCA Victor LSP-3514	(S)	**That Old Feeling**	1966	8.00	20.00
RCA Victor LPM-3526	(M)	**Mother Nature, Father Time**	1966	6.00	15.00
RCA Victor LSP-3526	(S)	**Mother Nature, Father Time**	1966	8.00	20.00
RCA Victor LPM-3590	(M)	**My Country**	1966	6.00	15.00
RCA Victor LSP-3590	(S)	**My Country**	1966	8.00	20.00
Wing MGW-12314	(M)	**Brook Benton**	1966	5.00	12.00
Wing SRW-16314	(S)	**Brook Benton**	1966	6.00	15.00
Reprise R-6268	(M)	**Laura, What's He Got That I Ain't Got?**	1967	6.00	15.00
Reprise RS-6268	(S)	**Laura, What's He Got That I Ain't Got?**	1967	8.00	20.00
Camden CAS-2431	(S)	**I Wanna Be With You**	1970	5.00	12.00
Cotillion SD-9002	(S)	**Do Your Own Thing**	1969	5.00	12.00
Cotillion SD-9018	(S)	**Brook Benton Today**	1970	5.00	12.00
Cotillion SD-9028	(S)	**Home Style**	1970	5.00	12.00
Cotillion SD-9050	(S)	**Story Teller**	1971	5.00	12.00
Cotillion SD-9058	(S)	**The Gospel Truth**	1972	5.00	12.00
MGM SE-4874	(S)	**Something for Everyone**	1973	5.00	12.00
RCA Victor APL1-1044	(S)	**Sings A Love Story**	1975	3.20	8.00
All Platinum 3015	(S)	**This Is Brook Benton**	1976	5.00	12.00
Musicor X-4603	(S)	**The Best Of Brook Benton** *(2 LPs)*	1977	5.00	12.00
BENTON, BROOK / JESSE BELVIN					
Crown CLP-5350	(M)	**Brook Benton & Jesse Belvin**	1963	8.00	20.00
Crown CST-350	(E)	**Brook Benton & Jesse Belvin**	1963	4.00	10.00
Crown CLP-5402	(M)	**The Great Brook Benton & Jesse Belvin**	196?	8.00	20.00
Crown CST-402	(E)	**The Great Brook Benton & Jesse Belvin**	196?	4.00	10.00
—Crown albums above have gray labels.—					
BENTON, BROOK, & DINAH WASHINGTON					
Mercury MG-20588	(M)	**The Two Of Us**	1960	8.00	20.00
Mercury SR-60244	(S)	**The Two Of Us**	1960	10.00	25.00
BERMUDA JAM					
Dynovoice 31907	(S)	**Bermuda Jam**	1969	6.00	15.00
BERNARD, ROD					
Jin LP-4007	(M)	**Rod Bernard**	196?	20.00	50.00

BERRY, CHUCK

The debate over what was the first rock'n roll record will probably occupy several generations of fans the way the never-ending debate over who was the greatest hitter of all time has fueled baseball's hot-stove league for decades. It can be safely said that, by 1954, both Elvis Presley and Chuck Berry had developed a fully realized rock'n roll sound. While some camps refer to one as a genius and the other as an over-rated "phenom," I can't imagine a pyramid that doesn't find the two at the top. (And for you diamond lovers, it's both the Bambino and Teddy Ballgame.)

Label & Catalog #		Title	Year	VG+	NM
Chess LP-1426	(M)	**After School Session** *(White label promo)*	1958	300.00	600.00
Chess LP-1426	(M)	**After School Session**	1958	100.00	250.00

Label & Catalog #		Title	Year	VG+	NM
Chess LP-1432	(M)	One Dozen Berrys (White label promo)	1958	300.00	600.00
Chess LP-1432	(M)	One Dozen Berrys	1958	100.00	250.00
Chess LP-1435	(M)	Berry Is On Top (White label promo)	1959	250.00	500.00
Chess LP-1435	(M)	Berry Is On Top	1959	80.00	200.00
Chess LP-1448	(M)	Rockin' At The Hops (White label promo)	1960	250.00	500.00
Chess LP-1448	(M)	Rockin' At The Hops	1960	80.00	200.00
Chess LP-1456	(M)	New Juke Box Hits (White label promo)	1961	250.00	500.00
Chess LP-1456	(M)	New Juke Box Hits	1961	80.00	200.00
Chess LP-1465	(M)	Chuck Berry Twist (White label promo)	1962	200.00	400.00
Chess LP-1465	(M)	Chuck Berry Twist	1962	60.00	150.00
Chess LP-1465	(M)	More Chuck Berry (White label promo)	1963	200.00	400.00
Chess LP-1465	(M)	More Chuck Berry	1963	60.00	150.00
Chess LP-1480	(M)	Chuck Berry On Stage (White label promo)	1963	200.00	400.00
Chess LP-1480	(M)	Chuck Berry On Stage	1963	60.00	150.00
Chess LP-1485	(M)	Chuck Berry's Greatest Hits (White label promo)	1964	80.00	200.00
Chess LP-1485	(M)	Chuck Berry's Greatest Hits	1964	20.00	50.00
Chess LP-1488	(M)	St. Louis To Liverpool (White label promo)	1964	80.00	200.00
Chess LP-1488	(M)	St. Louis To Liverpool	1964	30.00	75.00
Chess LPS-1488	(S)	St. Louis To Liverpool	1964	30.00	75.00
		—Chess albums above have black labels with silver print.—			
Chess LP-1426	(M)	After School Session	196?	20.00	50.00
Chess LP-1432	(M)	One Dozen Berrys	196?	20.00	50.00
Chess LP-1435	(M)	Berry Is On Top	196?	20.00	50.00
Chess LP-1448	(M)	Rockin' At The Hops	196?	20.00	50.00
Chess LP-1456	(M)	New Juke Box Hits	196?	20.00	50.00
Chess LP-1465	(M)	Chuck Berry Twist	196?	20.00	50.00
Chess LP-1465	(M)	More Chuck Berry	196?	20.00	50.00
Chess LP-1480	(M)	Chuck Berry On Stage	196?	20.00	50.00
Chess LP-1485	(M)	Chuck Berry's Greatest Hits	196?	20.00	50.00
Chess LP-1488	(M)	St. Louis To Liverpool	196?	20.00	50.00
Chess LPS-1488	(S)	St. Louis To Liverpool	196?	20.00	50.00
		—Chess albums above have blue labels with silver print.—			
Chess LP-1426	(M)	After School Session	196?	8.00	20.00
Chess LP-1432	(M)	One Dozen Berrys	196?	8.00	20.00
Chess LP-1435	(M)	Berry Is On Top	196?	8.00	20.00
Chess LP-1448	(M)	Rockin' At The Hops	196?	8.00	20.00
Chess LP-1456	(M)	New Juke Box Hits	196?	8.00	20.00
Chess LP-1465	(M)	Chuck Berry Twist	196?	8.00	20.00
Chess LP-1465	(M)	More Chuck Berry	196?	8.00	20.00
Chess LP-1480	(M)	Chuck Berry On Stage	196?	8.00	20.00
Chess LP-1485	(M)	Chuck Berry's Greatest Hits	196?	8.00	20.00
Chess LP-1488	(M)	St. Louis To Liverpool	196?	8.00	20.00
Chess LPS-1488	(S)	St. Louis To Liverpool	196?	8.00	20.00
Chess LP-1495	(DJ)	Chuck Berry In London (White label promo)	1965	80.00	200.00
Chess LP-1495	(M)	Chuck Berry In London	1965	14.00	35.00
Chess LPS-1495	(S)	Chuck Berry In London	1965	16.00	40.00
Chess LP-1498	(DJ)	Fresh Berry's (White label promo)	1965	80.00	200.00
Chess LP-1498	(M)	Fresh Berry's	1965	14.00	35.00
Chess LPS-1498	(S)	Fresh Berry's	1965	16.00	40.00
		—Chess albums above have blue labels with a gold logo on top.—			
Chess LPS-1480	(E)	Chuck Berry On Stage	1966	12.00	30.00
Chess LPS-1485	(E)	Chuck Berry's Greatest Hits	1966	12.00	30.00
		—Chess albums above have black labels with a gold logo on top.—			
Chess LPS-1426	(E)	After School Session	1966	8.00	20.00
Chess LPS-1432	(E)	One Dozen Berrys	1966	8.00	20.00
Chess LPS-1435	(E)	Berry Is On Top	1966	8.00	20.00
Chess LPS-1448	(E)	Rockin' At The Hops	1966	8.00	20.00
Chess LPS-1456	(E)	New Juke Box Hits	1966	8.00	20.00
Chess LPS-1465	(E)	More Chuck Berry	1966	8.00	20.00
Chess LPS-1480	(E)	Chuck Berry On Stage	1966	8.00	20.00
Chess LPS-1485	(E)	Chuck Berry's Greatest Hits	1966	8.00	20.00
Chess LPS-1488	(P)	St. Louis To Liverpool	1966	8.00	20.00
Chess LPS-1495	(S)	Chuck Berry In London	1966	8.00	20.00
Chess LPS-1498	(S)	Fresh Berry's	1966	8.00	20.00
Chess LP-1514	(M)	Chuck Berry's Golden Decade	1967	10.00	25.00
Chess LPS-1514	(E)	Chuck Berry's Golden Decade	1967	6.00	15.00
Chess LPS-1550	(S)	Back Home	1970	8.00	20.00
Chess CH-50008	(S)	San Francisco Dues	1971	8.00	20.00
Chess CH-60020	(S)	The Chuck Berry London Sessions	1972	8.00	20.00
		(Gatefold cover. "My Ding-A-Ling" is rechanneled)			
		—Chess albums above have blue & white labels.—			
Chess LPS-1426	(E)	After School Session	1973	4.00	10.00
Chess LPS-1432	(E)	One Dozen Berrys	1973	4.00	10.00
Chess LPS-1435	(E)	Berry Is On Top	1973	4.00	10.00
Chess LPS-1448	(E)	Rockin' At The Hops	1973	4.00	10.00
Chess LPS-1456	(E)	New Juke Box Hits	1973	4.00	10.00
Chess LPS-1465	(E)	More Chuck Berry	1973	4.00	10.00
Chess LPS-1480	(E)	Chuck Berry On Stage	1973	4.00	10.00
Chess LPS-1485	(E)	Chuck Berry's Greatest Hits	1973	4.00	10.00

Label & Catalog #		Title	Year	VG+	NM
Chess LPS-1488	(P)	St. Louis To Liverpool	1973	4.00	10.00
Chess LPS-1495	(S)	Chuck Berry In London	1973	4.00	10.00
Chess LPS-1498	(S)	Fresh Berry's	1973	4.00	10.00
Chess LPS-1514	(E)	Chuck Berry's Golden Decade	1973	6.00	15.00
Chess LPS-1550	(S)	Back Home	1973	4.00	10.00
Chess CH-50008	(S)	San Francisco Dues	1973	4.00	10.00
Chess CH-60020	(S)	The Chuck Berry London Sessions	1973	4.00	10.00
Chess 2CH-60023	(P)	Golden Decade, Volume 2 (2 LPs)	1973	6.00	15.00
Chess CH-50043	(S)	Bio (Gatefold cover)	1973	5.00	12.00
Chess CH-50043	(S)	Bio (Standard cover)	1973	3.20	8.00
Chess 2CH-60028	(P)	Golden Decade, Volume 3 (2 LPs)	1974	6.00	15.00
Chess CH-60032	(P)	Chuck Berry	1975	4.00	10.00
		—Chess albums above have orange labels.—			
Chess CH3-80001	(M)	The Chess Box (3 LP box)	1981	10.00	25.00
Chess CH-8201	(M)	The Great Twenty-Eight (2 LPs)	1982	6.00	15.00
Chess CH-92521	(P)	Rock 'N Roll Rarities (2 LPs)	1986	6.00	15.00
Chess CH-9190	(P)	More Rock 'N Roll Rarities From The Golden Age Of Chess Records	1984	4.00	10.00
Chess CH-9318	(P)	Missing Berries— Rock 'N Roll Rarities, Vol. 3	1990	4.00	10.00
Mercury MG-21103	(M)	Chuck Berry's Golden Hits	1967	6.00	15.00
Mercury SR-61103	(S)	Chuck Berry's Golden Hits	1967	6.00	15.00
Mercury MG-21123	(M)	Chuck Berry In Memphis	1967	8.00	20.00
Mercury SR-61123	(S)	Chuck Berry In Memphis	1967	10.00	25.00
Mercury MG-21138	(M)	Live At The Fillmore Auditorium	1967	10.00	25.00
Mercury SR-61138	(S)	Live At The Fillmore Auditorium	1967	12.00	30.00
		(Mercury 21138 features backing by The Steve Miller Blues Band.)			
Mercury SR-61176	(S)	From St. Louis To Frisco	1968	8.00	20.00
Mercury SR-61223	(S)	Concerto In B. Goode	1969	8.00	20.00
Mercury SRM-2-6501	(S)	St. Louis To Frisco To Memphis (2 LPs)	1972	6.00	15.00
		(SRM-6501 is a repackage of previous Mercury material.)			
Pickwick SPC-3327	(E)	Johnny B. Goode	1972	3.20	8.00
Pickwick SPC-3345	(E)	Sweet Little Rock & Roller	1974	3.20	8.00
Pickwick SPC-3392	(E)	Wild Berrys	1974	3.20	8.00
Pickwick PTP-2061	(E)	Flashback (2 LPs)	1975	4.00	10.00
Aristocrat BR-100	(P)	Chuck Berry & His Friends (3 LPs TV advertised)	1974	6.00	15.00
Everest PS-321	(E)	Chuck Berry's Greatest Hits	1976	3.20	8.00
Gusto GT-0004	(E)	The Best Of The Best Of Chuck Berry	1978	3.20	8.00
Trip TOP-16-55	(E)	Chuck Berry's 16 Greatest Hits	1978	3.20	8.00
Magnum MR-703	(S)	Chuck Berry Live In Concert (2 LPs)	1978	6.00	15.00
Atco SD-38-118	(S)	Rock It	1979	3.20	8.00
Upfront UPF-199	(E)	Chuck Berry's All-Time Hits	1979	3.20	8.00
Stack-O-Hits AC-09019	(S)	Alive And Rockin'	1981	6.00	15.00
SSS International 36	(S)	Chuck Berry Live, Volume 1	1981	3.20	8.00
Accord SN-7171	(S)	Toronto Rock 'N' Roll Revival 1969, Vol. II	1982	3.20	8.00
Accord SN-7172	(S)	Toronto Rock 'N' Roll Revival 1969, Vol. III	1982	3.20	8.00
Aura 1020	(E)	Reelin' And Rockin'	1982	3.20	8.00
Phoenix-10 PHX-351	(M)	Chuck Berry (Picture disc)	1982	6.00	15.00
Phoenix-10 PHX-351	(M)	Chuck Berry	1982	3.20	8.00
Phoenix-10 P20-630	(M)	Chuck Berry/Twenty Hits	1983	3.20	8.00

BERRY, BROOKS, & SCRAPPER BLACKWELL

Bluesville BVLP-1074	(M)	My Heart Struck Sorrow	1963	40.00	100.00
		—Bluesville albums above have bright blue labels with silver print.—			
Bluesville BVLP-1074	(M)	My Heart Struck Sorrow	1964	10.00	25.00
		—Bluesville albums above have blue labels with a trident logo on the right side.—			

BERRY, RICHARD, & THE DREAMERS

Crown CLP-5371	(M)	Richard Berry And The Dreamers	1963	30.00	75.00
Crown CST-371	(E)	Richard Berry And The Dreamers	1963	14.00	35.00
		—Crown albums above have gray labels.—			
United US-7798	(E)	Rock 'N' Roll Hits Of The '50's	197?	3.00	15.00

BERRY, RICHARD, & THE SOUL SEARCHERS

Pam 1001	(M)	Live At The Century Club	196?	20.00	50.00
Pam 1002	(M)	Wild Berry	196?	20.00	50.00

BEST, PETE

Best was a member of the Beatles before they recorded for EMI/Parlophone.

Savage BM-71	(M)	Best Of The Beatles	1965	150.00	300.00
		(Original records have orange labels while the cover has a white circle around Best's face. Counterfeits have red labels; the cover has a blue circle around Best.)			
Phoenix-10 PHX-340	(M)	The Beatle That Time Forgot	1982	8.00	20.00

BETHLEHEM ASYLUM

Ampex A-10106	(S)	Commit Yourself	1970	6.00	15.00
Ampex A-10124	(S)	Bethlehem Asylum	1971	6.00	15.00

When Texas disc jockey J.P. Richardson, a.k.a. The Big Bopper, cut his first single, the A-side was a parody of two novelty hits titled "The Purple People Eater Meets The Witch Doctor." Released on the tiny 'D' label, the Bopper's contract was picked up by Mercury when the single's B-side, "Chantilly Lace," received a lot of unexpected air-play. Richardson's lone album, Chantilly Lace, sports one of the most outlandish covers of its time, cleverly highlighting the humor to be found between the grooves within. While never a big seller, it was popular enough for the company to have kept it in print through three label changes.

Label & Catalog #		Title	Year	VG+	NM

BETTS, DICKEY
Betts also recorded with The 31st Of February; The Allman Brothers Band.

Capricorn CP-0181	(S)	**Highway Call**	1974	1.00	5.00
Arista AL-4123	(S)	**Dickey Betts And Great Southern**	1977	1.00	5.00
Arista AL-4168	(S)	**Atlanta's Burning Down**	1978	1.00	5.00
Epic FE-44289	(S)	**Pattern Disruptive**	1988	.80	4.00

BIG BEATS, THE

Liberty LRP-3407	(M)	**The Big Beats Live**	1965	12.00	30.00
Liberty LST-7407	(S)	**The Big Beats Live**	1965	16.00	40.00

BIG BLACK

Uni 73018	(S)	**Elements Of Now**	1968	6.00	15.00
Uni 73033	(S)	**Lion Walk**	1969	6.00	15.00
Uni 73134	(S)	**Big Black And The Blues**	1972	6.00	15.00

BIG BOPPER, THE
The Big Bopper is a pseudonym for J. P. "Jape" Richardson.

Mercury MG-20402	(M)	**Chantilly Lace**	1959	250.00	500.00
		—Mercury albums above have black labels.—			
Mercury MG-20402	(M)	**Chantilly Lace**	1964	80.00	200.00
		—Mercury albums above have red labels with black & white logo on top.—			
Mercury MG-20402	(M)	**Chantilly Lace**	1971	10.00	25.00
		—Mercury albums above have red label with twelve oval logos around the perimeter.—			
Pickwick SPC-3365	(E)	**Chantilly Lace**	1973	6.00	15.00

BIG BROTHER & THE HOLDING COMPANY
BB&THC were Peter Albin, Sam Andrews, David Getz and James Gurley supporting Janis Joplin on the first two albums and Nick Gravenites on the final two.

Mainstream 56099	(M)	**Big Brother & The Holding Company**	1967	16.00	40.00
Mainstream S-6099	(S)	**Big Brother & The Holding Company**	1967	10.00	25.00
Columbia KCL-2900	(M)	**Cheap Thrills**	1968	40.00	100.00
Columbia KCS-9700	(S)	**Cheap Thrills**	1968	10.00	25.00
		—Columbia albums above have "360 Sound" labels.—			
Columbia KCS-9700	(S)	**Cheap Thrills**	197?	1.00	5.00
Columbia C-30222	(S)	**Be A Brother**	1970	10.00	25.00
Columbia P-13313	(S)	**Big Brother & The Holding Company**	1971	4.00	10.00
Columbia C-30631	(S)	**Big Brother & The Holding Company**	1971	4.00	10.00
		(Columbia 30631 and 13313 are reissues of Mainstream 6099 plus both sides of their final Mainstream single in stereo			
Columbia C-30738	(S)	**How Hard It Is**	1971	10.00	25.00

BIG DADDY

Regent MG-6106	(M)	**Twist Party**	1962	30.00	75.00

BIG FOOT

Winro 1004	(S)	**Big Foot**	1968	8.00	20.00

BIG MAYBELLE

Savoy MG-14005	(M)	**Big Maybelle Sings**	1957	150.00	300.00
Savoy MG-14011	(M)	**Blues, Candy And Big Maybelle**	1958	150.00	300.00
Brunswick BL-54107	(M)	**What More Can A Woman Do**	1962	20.00	50.00
Brunswick BL-754107	(S)	**What More Can A Woman Do**	1962	30.00	75.00
Brunswick BL-54142	(M)	**The Gospel Soul Of Big Maybelle**	1962	16.00	40.00
Brunswick BL-754142	(S)	**The Gospel Soul Of Big Maybelle**	1962	20.00	50.00
Scepter S-522	(M)	**The Soul Of Big Maybelle**	1964	16.00	40.00
Scepter SS-522	(S)	**The Soul Of Big Maybelle**	1964	20.00	50.00
Epic EE-22011	(M)	**Gabbin' Blues**	196?	12.00	30.00
Epic EE-22012	(E)	**Gabbin' Blues**	196?	6.00	15.00
		(Epic Encore Series features original 1952-55 recordings.)			
Rojac R-522	(M)	**Got A Brand New Bag**	1967	16.00	40.00
Rojac RS-522	(S)	**Got A Brand New Bag**	1967	20.00	50.00
Rojac RS-123	(S)	**Saga Of The Good Life And Hard Times**	196?	16.00	40.00
Paramount PAS-1011	(S)	**The Last Of Big Maybelle** *(2 LPs)*	1970	6.00	15.00

BIG ROSS & THE MEMPHIS SOUND

Pickwick SPC-3292	(S)	**Elvis Presley's Golden Hits**	1973	4.00	10.00

BIG STAR
Big Star features Alex Chilton, formerly of The Box Tops.

Ardent ADS-2803	(S)	**#1 Record**	1972	10.00	25.00
Ardent ADS-1501	(S)	**Radio City** *("O My Soul" is in mono)*	1974	12.00	30.00
PVC 7903	(S)	**Big Star's Third**	1978	10.00	25.00

BIG THREE, THE
The Big Three are Cass Elliot, James Hendricks and Tim Rose.

FM 307	(M)	**The Big Three**	1963	12.00	30.00
FM S-307	(S)	**The Big Three**	1963	16.00	40.00

Label & Catalog #		Title	Year	VG+	NM
FM 311	(M)	The Big Three Live At The Recording Studio	1964	12.00	30.00
FM S-311	(S)	The Big Three Live At The Recording Studio	1964	16.00	40.00
Roulette R-42000	(M)	The Big Three Featuring Cass Elliot	1967	8.00	20.00
Roulette SR-42000	(S)	The Big Three Featuring Cass Elliot	1967	10.00	25.00
		(Roulette 4200 reissues FM material.)			

BIG WHEELIE & THE HUBCAPS

Scepter SPS-5109	(S)	Solid Grease!	1973	4.00	10.00

BILLION DOLLAR BABIES, THE
The Babies were former members of Alice Cooper's band.

Polydor PRO-022	(DJ)	Battle Axe *(Sampler)*	1977	8.00	20.00
Polydor PD1-6100	(S)	Battle Axe	1977	4.00	10.00

BIRKIN, JANE, & SERGE GAINSBOURG

Fontana SRF-67610	(S)	Je T'aime	1970	8.00	20.00

BIRTH CONTROL

Prophesy PRS-1002	(S)	Birth Control—A New German Rock Group	1970	10.00	25.00

BISHOP, ELVIN
Bishop was a member of Paul Butterfield's Blues Band.

Fillmore F-30001	(S)	The Elvin Bishop Group	1969	4.00	10.00
Fillmore Z-30239	(S)	Feel It	1970	4.00	10.00
Epic KE-31563	(S)	Rock My Soul	1972	1.00	5.00
Epic PE-33693	(S)	The Best Of Elvin Bishop	1975	1.00	5.00
Capricorn CP-0134	(S)	Let It Flow	1974	1.00	5.00
Capricorn CP-0151	(S)	Juke Joint Jump	1975	1.00	5.00
Capricorn CP-0165	(S)	Struttin' My Stuff	1975	1.00	5.00
Capricorn CP-0176	(S)	Hometown Boy Makes Good	1976	1.00	5.00
Capricorn CP-0185	(S)	Live, Raisin' Hell *(2 LPs)*	1977	1.00	5.00
Capricorn CP-0215	(S)	Hog Heaven	1978	1.00	5.00

BIT-A-SWEET

ABC S-640	(S)	Hypnotic 1	1968	16.00	40.00

BLACK, BILL
Bill Black was Elvis Presley's bass player from 1954 through his first golden era with RCA, 1956-1959.

Hi HL-12001	(M)	Smokie	1960	24.00	60.00
		—Hi albums above have black labels with a red & silver logo on top.—			
Hi HL-12001	(M)	Smokie	1960	12.00	40.00
Hi SHL-32001	(E)	Smokie	1964	8.00	20.00
Hi HL-12002	(M)	Saxy Jazz	1960	12.00	40.00
Hi SHL-32002	(E)	Saxy Jazz	196?	8.00	20.00
Hi HL-12003	(M)	Solid And Raunchy	1960	12.00	40.00
Hi SHL-32003	(E)	Solid And Raunchy	1960	8.00	20.00
Hi HL-12004	(M)	That Wonderful Feeling	1961	8.00	20.00
Hi SHL-32004	(S)	That Wonderful Feeling	1961	10.00	30.00
Hi HL-12005	(M)	Movin'	1961	8.00	20.00
Hi SHL-32005	(S)	Movin'	1961	10.00	30.00
Hi HL-12006	(M)	Bill Black's Record Hop	1961	8.00	20.00
Hi SHL-32006	(S)	Bill Black's Record Hop	1961	10.00	30.00
Hi HL-12006	(M)	Let's Twist Her	1962	6.00	15.00
Hi SHL-32006	(S)	Let's Twist Her	1962	8.00	20.00
		("Let's Twist Her" is a repackage of "Bill Black's Record Hop.")			
Hi HL-12009	(M)	The Untouchable Sound Of Bill Black	1963	6.00	15.00
Hi SHL-32009	(S)	The Untouchable Sound Of Bill Black	1963	8.00	20.00
Hi SR-8689	(DJ)	Sears-Silvertone Presents Hi Records:			
		The Untouchable Sound Of Bill Black	1963	12.00	30.00
Hi HL-12012	(M)	Bill Black's Greatest Hits	1963	5.00	12.00
Hi SHL-32012	(P)	Bill Black's Greatest Hits	1963	6.00	15.00
Hi HL-12013	(M)	Bill Black's Combo Goes West	1963	5.00	12.00
Hi SHL-32013	(S)	Bill Black's Combo Goes West	1963	6.00	15.00
Hi HL-12015	(M)	Bill Black Plays The Blues	1964	6.00	15.00
Hi SHL-32015	(S)	Bill Black Plays The Blues	1964	8.00	20.00
Hi HL-12017	(M)	Bill Black Plays Tunes By Chuck Berry	1964	6.00	15.00
Hi SHL-32017	(S)	Bill Black Plays Tunes By Chuck Berry	1964	8.00	20.00
Hi HL-12020	(M)	Bill Black's Combo Goes Big Band	1964	5.00	12.00
Hi SHL-32020	(S)	Bill Black's Combo Goes Big Band	1964	6.00	15.00
Hi HL-12023	(M)	More Solid And Raunchy	1965	5.00	12.00
Hi SHL-32023	(S)	More Solid And Raunchy	1965	6.00	15.00
Hi HL-12027	(M)	Mr. Beat	1965	5.00	12.00
Hi SHL-32027	(S)	Mr. Beat	1965	6.00	15.00
Hi HL-12032	(M)	All Timers	1966	5.00	12.00
Hi SHL-32032	(S)	All Timers	1966	6.00	15.00
Hi HL-12033	(M)	Black Lace	1967	5.00	12.00
Hi SHL-32033	(S)	Black Lace	1967	6.00	15.00
Hi HL-12036	(M)	King Of The Road	1968	6.00	15.00
Hi SHL-32036	(S)	King Of The Road	1968	6.00	15.00

Label & Catalog #		Title	Year	VG+	NM
Hi HL-12041	(M)	Beat Goes On	1968	6.00	15.00
Hi SHL-32041	(S)	Beat Goes On	1968	6.00	15.00
Hi HL-12044	(M)	Turn Your Lovelight On	1968	6.00	15.00
Hi SHL-32044	(S)	Turn Your Lovelight On	1968	6.00	15.00
Hi HL-12047	(M)	Soulin' The Blues	1968	6.00	15.00
Hi SHL-32047	(S)	Soulin' The Blues	1968	6.00	15.00
Hi SHL-32052	(S)	Solid And Raunchy The 3rd	1969	6.00	15.00
Hi SHL-32061	(S)	More Bill Black Magic	1971	6.00	15.00
Hi SHL-32078	(S)	Bill Black's Greatest Hits, Vol. 2	1973	4.00	10.00
Hi SHL-32088	(S)	Solid And Country	1974	4.00	10.00
Hi SHL-32093	(S)	The World's Greatest Honky Tonk Band	1975	4.00	10.00
		—Hi albums above have gray labels.—			
Hi SHL-32104	(S)	It's Honky Tonk Time	1977	1.00	5.00
Hi SHL-9357-6005	(S)	Award Winners	1978	1.00	5.00
Columbia CS-9848	(S)	Black With Sugar	1969	4.00	10.00
Columbia CS-9857	(S)	Raindrops Keep Fallin' On My Head	1970	4.00	10.00
Columbia CS-1055	(S)	Basic Black	1970	4.00	10.00
Columbia LE-10621	(S)	Raindrops Keep Fallin' On My Head	197?	1.00	5.00
Mega M31-1008	(S)	The Memphis Scene	1971	4.00	10.00
Mega M31-1014	(S)	Juke Box Favorites	1972	4.00	10.00
Mega M51-5008	(S)	Rock-N-Roll Forever	1973	4.00	10.00
Mega MLPS-600	(S)	Bill Black Is Back	1973	4.00	10.00
Zodiac ZLP-5006	(S)	Bill Black Plays The Greatest Hits	1976	4.00	10.00
Press 4050	(S)	The Best Of The Bill Black Combo	1979	4.00	10.00

BLACK, CILLA

Capitol T-2308	(M)	Is It Love?	1965	10.00	25.00
Capitol ST-2308	(S)	Is It Love?	1965	16.00	40.00

BLACK DIAMONDS, THE

Alshire 5220	(S)	Tribute To Jimi Hendrix	1971	6.00	15.00

BLACK LIGHTNING

Tower ST-5129	(S)	Shades Of Black Lightning	1968	8.00	20.00

BLACK MAGIC

Atco SD-33-305	(S)	Where Love Is	1970	4.00	10.00

BLACK MERDA

Chess LP-1551	(S)	Black Merda	1970	20.00	50.00

BLACK OAK ARKANSAS

Atco SD-33-354	(S)	Black Oak Arkansas	1971	1.00	5.00
Atco SD-33-381	(S)	Keep The Faith	1972	1.00	5.00
Atco SD-7008	(S)	If An Angel Came To You, Would You Make Her Feel At Home	1972	1.00	5.00
Atco SD-7019	(S)	Raunch & Roll/Live	1973	1.00	5.00
Atco QD-7019	(Q)	Raunch And Roll/Live	1973	6.00	15.00
Atco SD-7035	(S)	High On The Hog	1973	1.00	5.00
Atco SD-36-101	(S)	Street Party	1974	1.00	5.00
Atco SD-36-111	(S)	Ain't Life Grand	1975	1.00	5.00
Atco SD-36-128	(S)	Live Mutha!	1975	1.00	5.00
Atco SD-36-150	(S)	The Best Of Black Oak Arkansas	1976	1.00	5.00
Capricorn CP-0191	(S)	Race With The Devil	1977	1.00	5.00
Capricorn CEP-0005	(S)	I'd Rather Be Sailing (Promo)	1978	4.00	10.00
Capricorn CP-0207	(S)	I'd Rather Be Sailing	1978	1.00	5.00
MCA 2155	(S)	X-Rated	1975	1.00	5.00
MCA 2199	(S)	Balls Of Fire	1976	1.00	5.00
MCA 2224	(S)	10 Year Overnight Success	1977	1.00	5.00

BLACK PEARL

Atlantic SD-8220	(S)	Black Pearl	1969	10.00	25.00
Prophesy PRS-1001	(S)	Black Pearl Live	1970	10.00	25.00

BLACK SABBATH

The original Sabbath featured Ozzy Osbourne, later replaced by Ronnie James Dio and Ian Gillan.

Warner Bros. WS-1871	(S)	Black Sabbath (White label promo)	1969	20.00	50.00
Warner Bros. WS-1871	(S)	Black Sabbath	1969	6.00	15.00
Warner Bros. WS-1887	(S)	Paranoid (White label promo)	1971	14.00	35.00
Warner Bros. WS-1887	(S)	Paranoid	1971	6.00	15.00
Warner Bros. WS4-1887	(Q)	Paranoid	1974	10.00	25.00
Warner Bros. BS-2562	(S)	Master Of Reality (White label promo)	1971	14.00	35.00
Warner Bros. BS-2562	(S)	Master Of Reality	1971	6.00	15.00
		(WB 2562 was issued with a poster, priced separately below.)			
Warner Bros. BS-2562	(S)	Master Of Reality Poster	1971	10.00	25.00
Warner Bros. BS-2602	(S)	Black Sabbath, Volume 4 (White label)	1972	14.00	35.00
Warner Bros. BS-2602	(S)	Black Sabbath, Volume 4	1972	6.00	15.00
		—Warner Bros. albums above have green "WB" labels.—			

"Swinging Cilla" Black started out sitting in with such notable groups as Kingsize Taylor & The Dominoes and, ahem, The Beatles, at The Cavern. She was signed by the Fab's manager, Brian Epstein, to his growing stable of Liverpool-based talent. And, like other acts under his wing, he launched her career with a new Lennon-McCartney composition, "Love Of The Loved." She followed with a string of hits, including ten in the Top 10 through the end of the decade, that placed her at the top of the UK popularity polls. While she never approached that level of success in the States, that doesn't explain why Capitol chose to ignore her two chart-toppers and title her sole long-player, Is It Love?, after a song she performed in the film Ferry Cross The Mersey. Nor the uninspired artwork gracing the cover, which makes the album look like it would be more comfortable with mom and dad than with someone who dug the groovy sounds from Liverpool!

Label & Catalog #		Title	Year	VG+	NM
Warner Bros. BS-1871	(S)	Black Sabbath	197?	1.00	5.00
Warner Bros. BS-2695	(S)	Sabbath, Bloody Sabbath	1973	1.00	5.00
Warner Bros. BS-2822	(S)	Sabotage	1975	1.00	5.00
Warner Bros. BS-2923	(S)	We Sold Our Soul For Rock 'N Roll (2 LPs)	1976	1.00	5.00
Warner Bros. BS-2969	(S)	Technical Ecstasy	1976	1.00	5.00
Warner Bros. BSK-2104	(S)	Paranoid	1977	1.00	5.00
Warner Bros. BSK-3186	(S)	Never Say Die!	1978	1.00	5.00
Warner Bros. BSK-3372	(S)	Heaven And Hell	1980	1.00	5.00
Warner Bros. BSK-3605	(S)	Mob Rules	1981	1.00	5.00
Warner Bros. 23742	(S)	Live Evil (2 LPs)	1983	1.00	5.00

BLACK SATIN
Black Satin features Fred Parris of The Five Satins.

Buddah BDS-5654	(S)	Black Satin	1976	6.00	15.00

BLACK VELVET

OKeh OKS-14130	(S)	Love City	1969	6.00	15.00

BLACK WIDOW

United Arts. UAS-6786	(S)	Sacrifice	1970	4.00	10.00

BLACKFOOT, J. D.

Mercury SRM-1-61288	(S)	The Ultimate Prophecy	1970	24.00	60.00
Bison B-44	(S)	Live In St. Louis, July 16, 1982	1982	12.00	30.00
Fantasy F-9468	(S)	Song Of Crazy Horse	1974	4.00	10.00
Fantasy F-9487	(S)	Southbound And Gone	1975	4.00	10.00

BLACKJACK
Blackjack features Michael Bolton.

Polydor PD-6215	(S)	Blackjack	1979	6.00	15.00

BLACKSTONE

Epic KE-30470	(S)	Blackstone	1971	6.00	15.00

BLACKWELL, OTIS

Davis 109	(M)	Singin' The Blues	1956	200.00	400.00
Inner City 1032	(S)	These Are My Songs	1977	8.00	20.00

BLACKWELL, SCRAPPER
Scrapper also recorded with Brooks Berry.

Bluesville BVLP-1047	(M)	Mr. Scrapper's Blues	1962	60.00	150.00
		—Bluesville albums above have bright blue labels with silver print.—			
Bluesville BVLP-1047	(M)	Mr. Scrapper's Blues	1964	10.00	25.00
		—Bluesville albums above have blue labels with a trident logo on the right side.—			

BLACKWOOD APOLOGY

Fontana SRF-67591	(S)	House Of Leather	1969	8.00	20.00

BLADES OF GRASS, THE

Jubilee JGS-8007	(S)	The Blades Of Grass Are Not For Smoking	1968	6.00	15.00

BLAINE, HAL
Refer to The Folkswingers.

RCA Victor LPM-2834	(M)	Deuces, "T's," Roadsters & Drums	1963	60.00	150.00
RCA Victor LSP-2834	(S)	Deuces, "T's," Roadsters & Drums	1963	80.00	200.00
		(RCA 2834 credits Hal Blaine & The Young Cougars.)			
Dunhill D-50002	(M)	Drums! Drums! A Go Go	1966	14.00	35.00
Dunhill DS-50002	(S)	Drums! Drums! A Go Go	1966	20.00	50.00
Dunhill D-50019	(M)	Psychedelic Percussion	1967	20.00	50.00
Dunhill DS-50019	(S)	Psychedelic Percussion	1967	30.00	75.00
Dunhill D-50035	(M)	Have Fun!!! Play Drums!!! (With booklet)	1969	18.00	45.00
Dunhill DS-50035	(S)	Have Fun!!! Play Drums!!! (With booklet)	1969	24.00	60.00
		(Originally issued with a bonus instruction book for drummers.)			
Dunhill D-50035	(M)	Have Fun!!! Play Drums!!! (Without booklet)	1969	14.00	35.00
Dunhill DS-50035	(S)	Have Fun!!! Play Drums!!! (Without booklet)	1969	20.00	50.00

BLAKLEY, RONEE

Elektra EKS-75027	(S)	Ronee Blakley	1972	4.00	10.00

BLANCHARD, EDGAR

Ric	(M)	Let's Have A Blast	196?	*Unreleased?*	

BLAND, BOBBY "BLUE" / LITTLE JUNIOR PARKER

Duke DLP-72	(S)	Blues Consolidated	1961	150.00	300.00
		—Duke albums above have purple & yellow labels.—			
Duke DLP-72	(S)	Blues Consolidated	196?	30.00	75.00
		—Duke albums above have orange labels.—			

Drummer Hal Blaine has reputedly played on more million-selling records than any other musician in recording history. As the best of a slew of notable Los Angeles-based session musicians, Mr Blaine can be heard every day on countless oldies stations around the country. His RCA Victor album, Deuces, 'Ts," Roadsters & Drums, has long been sought after for its cover, which features four beautifully Model 'T' Ford hot rods. His other stab at solo success came with Dunhill several years later, where he attempted to exploit the craze for anything associated with the Whisky A Go Go with Drums! Drums! A Go Go.

		Title	Year	VG+	NM
	(M)	Two Steps From The Blues	1961	80.00	200.00
	(M)	Here's The Man	1961	80.00	200.00
		—Duke albums above have purple & yellow labels.—			
	(M)	Two Steps From The Blues *(Red vinyl)*	1961	80.00	200.00
	(M)	Two Steps From The Blues	196?	40.00	100.00
Duke DLPS-74	(E)	Two Steps From The Blues	196?	30.00	75.00
Duke DLP-75	(M)	Here's The Man	1962	40.00	100.00
Duke DLPS-75	(S)	Here's The Man	1962	80.00	200.00
		(Original pressings of DLPS-75 include a spoken intro to "36-22-36.")			
Duke DLPS-75	(S)	Here's The Man	196?	40.00	100.00
		(Later pressings delete the spoken intro.)			
Duke DLP-77	(M)	Call On Me	1963	40.00	100.00
Duke DLPS-77	(S)	Call On Me	1963	60.00	150.00
Duke DLP-78	(M)	Ain't Nothing You Can Do	1964	40.00	100.00
Duke DLPS-78	(S)	Ain't Nothing You Can Do	1964	60.00	150.00
Duke DLP-79	(M)	The Soul Of The Man	1966	40.00	100.00
Duke DLPS-79	(S)	The Soul Of The Man	1966	60.00	150.00
Duke DLP-84	(M)	The Best Of Bobby Bland	1967	6.00	20.00
Duke DLPS-84	(P)	The Best Of Bobby Bland	1967	6.00	25.00
Ace/Duke DLPS-84	(E)	The Best Of Bobby Bland	197?	1.00	5.00
Duke DLP-86	(M)	The Best Of Bobby Bland, Volume 2	1968	10.00	25.00
Duke DLPS-86	(P)	The Best Of Bobby Bland, Volume 2	1968	8.00	20.00
Duke DLP-88	(M)	Touch Of The Blues	1967	8.00	20.00
Duke DLPS-88	(S)	Touch Of The Blues	1967	6.00	25.00
Duke DLPS-89	(S)	Spotlighting The Man	1969	10.00	25.00
Duke X-90	(S)	If Loving You Is Wrong	1970	10.00	25.00
Duke X-92	(S)	Introspective Of The Early Years *(2 LPs)*	1970	6.00	15.00
		—Duke albums above have orange labels.—			
BluesWay BLS-6065	(S)	Call On Me	1973	6.00	15.00
Dunhill DSX-50163	(S)	His California Album	1973	6.00	15.00
Dunhill DSX-50169	(S)	Dreamer	1974	6.00	15.00
ABC D-895	(S)	Get On Down	1975	1.00	5.00
ABC S-1075	(S)	Come Fly With Me	1978	1.00	5.00
MCA 3157	(S)	I Feel Good, I Feel Fine	1979	1.00	5.00
MCA 5145	(S)	Sweet Vibrations	1980	1.00	5.00
MCA 5233	(S)	Try Me, I'm Real	1981	1.00	5.00

BLAND, BOBBY "BLUE," & B.B. KING

Dunhill DS-50190	(S)	Together For The First Time... Live *(2 LPs)*	1974	6.00	15.00
Impulse AS-9317	(S)	Together Again... Live	1975	4.00	10.00
MCA 27012	(S)	Together Again... Live	1982	1.00	5.00

BLAND, BOBBY "BLUE" / JIMMY SOUL / JOHNNY "GUITAR" WATSON

Crown CLP-5358	(M)	Bobby Bland-Jimmy Soul-Johnny Watson	196?	10.00	25.00
Crown CST-358	(E)	Bobby Bland-Jimmy Soul-Johnny Watson	196?	4.00	10.00
		—Crown albums above have gray labels.—			

BLASTERS, THE

Crown CLP-5392	(M)	Sounds Of The Drags	1963	10.00	25.00
Crown CST-392	(S)	Sounds Of The Drags	1963	12.00	30.00
		—Crown albums above have gray labels.—			

BLASTERS, THE

Rollin' Rock 021	(S)	American Music	1980	20.00	50.00

BLATTNER, JULES

Buddah BDS-5080	(S)	Call Me Man	1971	6.00	15.00

BLENDELLS, THE: *Refer to* SONNY & CHER

BLIND FAITH
Blind Faith is Ginger Baker, Eric Clapton, Rick Grech and Steve Winwood.

Atco 33-304A	(M)	Blind Faith *(White label promo)*	1969	80.00	200.00
Atco SD-33-304A	(S)	Blind Faith *(Naked girl cover)*	1969	10.00	25.00
Atco SD-33-304B	(S)	Blind Faith *Group cover)*	1969	6.00	15.00
RSO SO-3016	(S)	Blind Faith	1976	1.00	5.00

BLODWYN PIG

A&M SP-4210	(S)	Ahead Rings Out	1969	8.00	20.00
A&M SP-4243	(S)	Getting To This	1970	8.00	20.00
A&M SP-3180	(S)	Ahead Rings Out	1982	1.00	5.00

BLOND

Fontana SRF-67607	(S)	Blond	1969	8.00	20.00

BLONDE ON BLONDE

Janus JLS-3003	(S)	Contrasts	1969	10.00	25.00

Label & Catalog #		Title	Year	VG+	NM

BLONDIE
Blondie features Debbie Harry, formerly of Wind In The Willows.

Private Stock PS-2035	(S)	Blondie	1975	4.00	10.00
Chrysalis CHR-1165	(S)	Blondie	1976	1.00	5.00
Chrysalis CHR-1166	(S)	Plastic Letters	1978	1.00	5.00
Chrysalis CHR-1192	(S)	Parallel Lines	1978	4.00	10.00
		(Original pressings contain a 3:54 version of "Heart Of Glass.")			
Chrysalis CHR-1192	(S)	Parallel Lines	1978	1.00	5.00
Chrysalis CHP-5001	(S)	Parallel Lines *(Picture disc)*	1978	4.00	10.00
Chrysalis CHS-24	(DJ)	At Home With Debbie Harry & Chris Stein	1981	4.00	10.00
		(Open-end interview with script.)			
Chrysalis CHE-1290	(S)	Autoamerican	1980	1.00	5.00
Chrysalis CHR-1337	(S)	The Best Of Blondie	1981	.80	4.00

BLOOD, SWEAT & TEARS
Originally the brainchild of Blues Project members Al Kooper and Steve Katz (CS-9616), by the second album BS&T was later fronted by David Clayton-Thomas.

Columbia CS-9616	(S)	Child Is Father To The Man	1968	6.00	15.00
Columbia CS-9720	(S)	Blood, Sweat And Tears	1969	4.00	10.00
		— Columbia albums above have "360 Sound" labels. —			
Columbia CS-9616	(S)	Child Is Father To The Man	197?	.80	4.00
Columbia HC-49619	(S)	Child Is Father To The Man *(Half-speed)*	1981	25.00	75.00
Columbia CS-9720	(S)	Blood, Sweat And Tears	197?	.80	4.00
Columbia CQ-30994	(Q)	Blood, Sweat And Tears	1973	6.00	15.00
Columbia KC-30090	(S)	Blood, Sweat And Tears "3"	1970	.80	4.00
Columbia KC-30590	(S)	BS&T: 4	1971	.80	4.00
Columbia KC-31170	(S)	Blood, Sweat And Tears' Greatest Hits	1972	.80	4.00
		("You Make Me So Very Happy," "Spinning Wheel," and "And When I Die" are in mono.)			
Columbia CQ-31170	(Q)	Blood, Sweat And Tears' Greatest Hits	1973	4.00	10.00
Columbia KC-31780	(S)	New Blood	1972	.80	4.00
Columbia KC-32180	(S)	No Sweat	1973	.80	4.00
Columbia PC-32929	(S)	Mirror Image	1974	.80	4.00
Columbia PCQ-32929	(Q)	Mirror Image	1974	4.00	10.00
Columbia PC-33484	(S)	New City	1975	.80	4.00
Columbia PC-34233	(S)	More Than Ever	1976	.80	4.00
ABC D-1015	(S)	Brand New Day	1977	.80	4.00
LAX L33-1865	(S)	Nuclear Blues *(Gold vinyl promo)*	1980	6.00	15.00
LAX L33-1865	(S)	Nuclear Blues	1980	.80	4.00

BLOODROCK

Capitol ST-435	(S)	Bloodrock	1969	4.00	10.00
Capitol ST-491	(S)	Bloodrock 2	1970	4.00	10.00
Capitol SMAS-645	(S)	U.S.A.	1971	4.00	10.00
Capitol ST-765	(S)	Bloodrock 3	1971	4.00	10.00
		— Capitol albums above have green labels. —			
Capitol SW-11109	(S)	Passage	1972	3.20	8.00
Capitol SVBB-11038	(S)	Bloodrock Live *(2 LPs)*	1972	4.00	10.00
Capitol SMAS-11259	(S)	Whirlwind Tongues	1974	3.20	8.00
Capitol SM-11417	(S)	Bloodrock 'N Roll	1975	3.20	8.00

BLOODY MARY

Family 2707	(S)	Bloody Mary	1972	12.00	30.00

BLOOM, BOBBY

L&R 1035	(S)	Bobby Bloom	1970	6.00	15.00
Buddah BDS-5072	(S)	Where Are We Going	1971	4.00	10.00

BLOOMFIELD, MIKE
Bloomfield was a member of Paul Butterfield's Blues Band; The Electric Flag.

Columbia CS-9883	(S)	It's Not Killing Me	1969	4.00	10.00
		— Columbia albums above have "360 Sound" labels. —			
Harmony KH-30395	(S)	It's Not Killing Me	1971	.80	4.00
Columbia PC-33173	(S)	Try It Before You Buy It	1975	1.00	5.00
Guitar Player 3002	(S)	If You Love These Blues	1976	1.00	5.00
Takoma 1059	(S)	Analine	1977	1.00	5.00
Takoma 1063	(S)	Michael Bloomfield	1978	1.00	5.00
Takoma 7070	(S)	Between A Hard Place And The Ground	1979	1.00	5.00
Takoma 7091	(S)	Crusin' For A Brusin'	1981	1.00	5.00
Waterhouse 11	(S)	Living In The Fast Lane	1981	1.00	5.00

BLOOMFIELD, MIKE, & NICK GRAVENITES

Columbia KC-9893	(S)	Live At Bill Graham's Fillmore West	1969	4.00	10.00
		— Columbia albums above have "360 Sound" labels. —			

BLOOMFIELD, MIKE, & DR. JOHN & JOHN HAMMOND

Columbia KC-32172	(S)	Triumvirate	1973	4.00	10.00

Label & Catalog #		Title	Year	VG+	NM

BLOOMFIELD, MIKE, & AL KOOPER

| Columbia KGP-6 | (S) | The Live Adventures Of Mike Bloomfield & Al Kooper (2 LPs) | 1969 | 4.00 | 10.00 |

—Columbia albums above have "360 Sound" labels.—

BLOOMFIELD, MIKE, & AL KOOPER & STEVE STILLS

| Columbia CS-9701 | (S) | Super Session | 1968 | 8.00 | 20.00 |

—Columbia albums above have "360 Sound" labels.—

| Columbia CS-9701 | (S) | Super Session | 1970 | 1.00 | 5.00 |
| Columbia PCQ-9701 | (Q) | Super Session | 1974 | 10.00 | 25.00 |

BLOOMSBURY PEOPLE

| MGM SE-4678 | (S) | Bloomsbury People | 1970 | 4.00 | 10.00 |

BLOONTZ

| Evolution 3020 | (S) | Bloontz | 1973 | 4.00 | 10.00 |

BLUE, DAVID

David Blue is a pseudonym for David Cohen.

Elektra EKL-4003	(M)	David Blue	1966	8.00	20.00
Elektra EKS-74003	(S)	David Blue	1966	10.00	25.00
Reprise RS-6296	(S)	These 23 Days In September	1968	6.00	15.00
Asylum 7E-1043	(S)	Comin' Back For More	1972	4.00	10.00
Asylum 7E-5052	(S)	Stories	1973	4.00	10.00
Asylum 7E-5066	(S)	Nice Baby And The Angels	1973	4.00	10.00
Elektra 7E-1077	(S)	Cupid's Arrow	1976	3.20	8.00

BLUE ASH

| Mercury SRM-1-666 | (S) | No More, No Less | 1973 | 4.00 | 10.00 |

BLUE BARONS, THE

| Philips PHM-200-017 | (M) | Twist To The Great Blues Hits | 1962 | 8.00 | 20.00 |
| Philips PHS-600-017 | (S) | Twist To The Great Blues Hits | 1962 | 10.00 | 25.00 |

BLUE BEATS, THE

| A.A. 133 | (M) | The Beatle Beat | 1964 | 20.00 | 50.00 |

BLUE CHEER

The original Blue Cheer was Dickie Peterson, Leigh Stevens and Paul Whaley.

Philips PHM-200-264	(M)	Vincebus Eruptum	1968	30.00	75.00
Philips PHS-600-264	(S)	Vincebus Eruptum	1968	16.00	40.00
Philips PHS-600-278	(S)	Outsideinside	1968	16.00	40.00
Philips PHS-600-305	(S)	New! Improved! Blue Cheer	1969	16.00	40.00
Philips PHS-600-333	(S)	Blue Cheer	1970	16.00	40.00

—Philips albums above have black labels with no print on the bottom perimeter.—

Philips PHS-600-264	(S)	Vincebus Eruptum	1970	6.00	15.00
Philips PHS-600-278	(S)	Outsideinside	1970	6.00	15.00
Philips PHS-600-305	(S)	New! Improved! Blue Cheer	1970	6.00	15.00
Philips PHS-600-333	(S)	Blue Cheer	1970	6.00	15.00
Philips PHS-600-347	(S)	The Original Human Being	1971	16.00	40.00
Philips PHS-600-350	(S)	Oh! Pleasant Hope	1971	16.00	40.00

—Philips albums above have black labels with "Distributed by Mercury" on the bottom.—

BLUE DIAMONDS, THE

| London LL-3235 | (M) | Ramona | 1963 | 10.00 | 25.00 |

BLUE EMOTIONS, THE

| Ambient Sound 38346 | (S) | Doo-Wop Doo-Wop | 1982 | 5.00 | 12.00 |

BLUE JAYS, THE

| Milestone MLP-1001 | (M) | The Blue Jays Meet Little Caesar | 196? | 20.00 | 50.00 |

BLUE MINK

Blue Mink features Roger Cook and Madeleine Bell.

Philips PHS-600323	(S)	Melting Pot	1969	4.00	10.00
Philips PHS-600339	(S)	Real Mink	1970	4.00	10.00
MCA 332	(S)	Blue Mink	1973	1.00	5.00

BLUE MOUNTAIN EAGLE

| Atco SD-33-324 | (S) | Blue Mountain Eagle | 1970 | 6.00 | 15.00 |
| Atco (No number) | (S) | Blue Mountain Eagle 2 | 1970 | Unreleased | |

BLUE OYSTER CULT

| Columbia AS-40 | (DJ) | The Live Bootleg | 1972 | 50.00 | 125.00 |

(AS-40 was issued in a printed paper sleeve. Counterfeits exist.)

Columbia KC-31063	(S)	Blue Oyster Cult	1973	.80	4.00
Columbia KC-32017	(S)	Tyranny And Mutation	1974	.80	4.00
Columbia PCQ-32017	(Q)	Tyranny And Mutation	1973	10.00	25.00

Label & Catalog #		Title	Year	VG+	NM
Columbia KC-32858	(S)	Secret Treaties	1974	.80	4.00
Columbia PCQ-32858	(Q)	Secret Treaties	1974	10.00	25.00
Columbia KC-33371	(S)	On Your Feet Or On Your Knees	1975	.80	4.00
Columbia PC-34164	(S)	Agents Of Fortune	1976	.80	4.00
Columbia JC-35019	(S)	Spectres	1977	.80	4.00
Columbia JC-35563	(S)	Some Enchanted Evening	1978	.80	4.00
Columbia JC-36009	(S)	Mirrors	1979	.80	4.00
Columbia JC-36550	(S)	Cultosaurus Erectus	1980	.80	4.00
Columbia FC-37389	(S)	Fire Of Unknown Origin	1981	.80	4.00
Columbia AS-986	(DJ)	Blue Oyster Cult (Sampler)	1981	6.00	15.00
Columbia AS-1441	(DJ)	Blue Oyster Cult Live (Sampler)	1982	6.00	15.00
Columbia KG-37946	(S)	Extraterrestrial Live (2 LPs)	1982	1.00	5.00

BLUE RIDGE RANGERS , THE
The Blue Ridge Rangers are John Fogerty of Creedence Clearwater.

Fantasy F-9415	(S)	The Blue Ridge Rangers	1973	6.00	15.00

BLUE SWEDE

EMI ST-11286	(S)	Hooked On A Feeling	1974	4.00	10.00
EMI ST-11346	(S)	Out Of The Blue	1975	1.00	5.00

BLUE THINGS, THE
The Blue Things feature Val Stoecklein.

RCA Victor LPM-3603	(M)	The Blue Things	1966	50.00	125.00
RCA Victor LSP-3603	(S)	The Blue Things	1966	70.00	175.00

BLUE VELVET BAND, THE

Warner Bros. WS-1802	(S)	Sweet Moments	1969	12.00	30.00

BLUES IMAGE

Atco SD-33-300	(S)	Blues Image	1969	10.00	25.00
Atco SD-33-346	(S)	Red, White And Blues Image	1970	6.00	15.00

BLUES MAGOOS, THE

Mercury MG-21096	(M)	Psychedelic Lollipop	1966	12.00	30.00
Mercury SR-61096	(S)	Psychedelic Lollipop	1966	16.00	40.00
Mercury MG-21104	(M)	Electric Comic Book (With comic book)	1967	14.00	35.00
Mercury SR-61104	(S)	Electric Comic Book (With comic book)	1967	14.00	35.00
		(Mercury 21104 was issued with a small, black & white comic book.)			
Mercury MG-21104	(M)	Electric Comic Book (Without comic book)	1967	10.00	25.00
Mercury SR-61104	(S)	Electric Comic Book (Without comic book)	1967	10.00	25.00
Mercury SR-61167	(M)	Basic Blues Magoos	1968	10.00	25.00
Mercury SR-61167	(S)	Basic Blues Magoos	1968	18.00	20.00
		—Mercury albums above have red labels with a black & white logo on top.—			
ABC S-697	(S)	Never Goin' Back To Georgia	1969	6.00	15.00
ABC S-710	(S)	Gulf Coast Bound	1970	6.00	15.00

BLUES PROJECT, THE
The Blues Project were Roy Blumenfeld, Tommy Flanders, Danny Kalb, Steve Katz, Al Kooper and Andy Kulberg. Refer to Blood, Sweat & Tears; Seatrain.

Verve/Folkways FV-9024	(M)	Live At The Cafe Au-Go-Go	1966	10.00	25.00
Verve/Folkways FVS-9024	(S)	Live At The Cafe Au-Go-Go	1966	12.00	30.00
Verve/Folkways FT-3000	(M)	Live At The Cafe Au-Go-Go	1966	6.00	15.00
Verve/Folkways FTS-3000	(S)	Live At The Cafe Au-Go-Go	1966	8.00	20.00
		(Folkways 3000 is a reissue of 9024.)			
Verve/Forecast FT-3008	(M)	Projections	1966	6.00	15.00
Verve/Forecast FTS-3008	(S)	Projections	1966	8.00	20.00
Verve/Forecast FT-3025	(M)	Live At Town Hall	1967	8.00	20.00
Verve/Forecast FTS-3025	(S)	Live At Town Hall	1967	8.00	20.00
Verve/Forecast FTS-3046	(S)	Planned Obsolescence	1968	6.00	15.00
Verve/Forecast FTS-3069	(S)	Flanders/Kalb/Katz, Etc.	1969	6.00	15.00
Verve/Forecast FTS-3077	(S)	The Best Of The Blues Project	1969	5.00	12.00
Capitol ST-782	(S)	Lazarus	1971	4.00	10.00
Capitol SMAS-11017	(S)	The Blues Project	1972	4.00	10.00
MGM GAS-118	(S)	The Blues Project	1972	4.00	10.00
MGM SE-2-8003	(S)	Reunion In Central Park	1973	4.00	10.00
MGM SE-4953	(S)	Archetypes	1974	4.00	10.00
Elektra EKS-7264	(S)	The Blues Project	1980	1.00	5.00

BLUNSTONE, COLIN
Colin Blunstone was the lead singer for The Zombies.

Epic E-30974	(S)	One Year	1972	3.20	8.00
Epic KE-31994	(S)	Ennismore	1972	3.20	8.00
Epic KE-32962	(S)	Journey	1974	3.20	8.00
Rocket 2903	(S)	Never Even Thought	1978	3.20	8.00

BO GRUMPUS

Atco 33-246	(M)	Before The War (White label promo)	1968	12.00	30.00
Atco SD-33-246	(S)	Before The War	1968	8.00	20.00

Label & Catalog #		Title	Year	VG+	NM
BO STREET RUNNERS, THE					
B.T. Puppy BTPS-1026	(S)	The Bo Street Runners	1969	660.00	1,000.00
BOB & EARL					
Bob Garrett and Earl Cosby.					
Tip TLP-1011	(M)	Harlem Shuffle	1964	14.00	35.00
Tip TLS-9011	(P)	Harlem Shuffle	1964	20.00	50.00
Crestview CRS-3055	(S)	Bob & Earl	196?	12.00	30.00
Upfront UPF-118	(S)	Bob & Earl	197?	1.00	5.00
BOBB B. SOXX & THE BLUE JEANS					
Bobby Sheen backed by Blossoms Darlene Love and Fanita James were produced by Phil Spector.					
Philles PHLP-4002	(M)	Zip-A-Dee-Doo-Dah *(White label promo)*	1963	600.00	1,200.00
Philles PHLP-4002	(M)	Zip-A-Dee-Doo-Dah	1963	250.00	500.00
BOBBY & I					
Imperial LP-12420	(S)	Bobby & I	1969	4.00	10.00
BOBBY & THE MIDNITES: *Refer to* BOB WEIR					
BODACIOUS D. F.					
Bodacious D. F. features Marty Balin, formerly of Jefferson Airplane.					
RCA Victor APL1-0206	(S)	Bodacious D. F.	1973	4.00	10.00
		—RCA albums above have orange labels.—			
RCA Victor AFL1-0206	(S)	Bodacious D. F.	1977	.80	4.00
RCA Victor AYL1-4243	(S)	Bodacious D. F.	1982	.80	4.00
BODINE					
MGM SE-4652	(S)	Bodine	1969	4.00	10.00
BODY & SOUL					
National General 2002	(S)	Body & Soul	1971	4.00	10.00
BOETCHER, CURT					
Produced by Gary Usher. Boetcher was a member of Milennium.					
Elektra EKS-75037	(DJ)	There's An Innocent Face	1972	6.00	15.00
Elektra EKS-75037	(S)	There's An Innocent Face	1972	10.00	25.00
BOFFALONGO					
United Arts. UAS-6726	(S)	Boffalongo	1969	6.00	15.00
United Arts. UAS-6770	(S)	Beyond Your Head	1970	6.00	15.00
BOHEMIAN VENDETTA					
Mainstream 56106	(M)	Bohemian Vendetta	1968	40.00	100.00
Mainstream S-6106	(S)	Bohemian Vendetta	1968	80.00	200.00
BOLD					
ABC S-705	(S)	Bold	1970	4.00	10.00
BOLIN, TOMMY					
Tommy Bolin originally recorded with Zephyr.					
Nemperor NE-436	(S)	Teaser	1975	4.00	10.00
Columbia PC-34329	(S)	Private Eyes	1976	4.00	10.00
Nemperor PZ-37534	(S)	Teaser	1981	.80	4.00
BOLOTIN, MICHAEL					
Michael Bolotin later recorded as Michael Bolton. Refer to Blackjack.					
RCA Victor APL1-0992	(S)	Michael Bolotin	1975	4.00	10.00
RCA Victor APL1-1550	(S)	Every Day Of My Life	1976	4.00	10.00
BOMBERS, THE					
West End 104	(S)	The Bombers	1979	6.00	15.00
West End 106	(S)	The Bombers 2	1979	6.00	15.00
BOND, GRAHAM [THE GRAHAM BOND ORGANIZATION]					
Pulsar 10604	(S)	Love Is The Law	1969	10.00	25.00
Pulsar 10606	(S)	Mighty Graham Bond	1969	10.00	25.00
Mercury SR-61327	(S)	Holy Magick	1970	8.00	20.00
Mercury SRM-1-612	(S)	We Put Our Magick On You	1971	8.00	20.00
Warner Bros. 2BS-2555	(S)	Solid Bond *(2 LPs)*	1971	8.00	20.00
BONES, THE					
Signpost 8402	(S)	Bones	1972	5.00	12.00
BONFIRE, MARS					
Mars Bonfire was formerly a member of Steppenwolf.					
Uni 73027	(S)	Mars Bonfire	1968	8.00	20.00
Columbia CS-9834	(S)	Faster Than The Speed Of Life	1969	6.00	15.00

Label & Catalog #		Title	Year	VG+	NM
BONNEVILLES, THE					
Drum Boy DLM-1001	(M)	**Meet The Bonnevilles**	1963	40.00	100.00
Drum Boy DLS-1001	(S)	**Meet The Bonnevilles**	1963	60.00	150.00
BONNIWELL, T. S.					
T.S. is Sean Bonniwell, formerly of The Wayfarers and The Music Machine.					
Capitol ST-277	(S)	**Close**	1969	8.00	20.00
BONNIWELL'S MUSIC MACHINE *Refer to* **THE MUSIC MACHINE**					
BONUS, JACK					
Grunt FTR-1005	(S)	**Jack Bonus**	1972	3.20	8.00
BONZO DOG BAND, THE					
Refer to Roger Ruskin-Spear; The Rutles.					
Imperial LP-9370	(M)	**Gorilla** *(With booklet)*	1968	12.00	30.00
Imperial LP-12370	(S)	**Gorilla** *(With booklet)*	1968	12.00	30.00
Imperial LP-9370	(M)	**Gorilla** *(Without booklet)*	1968	10.00	25.00
Imperial LP-12370	(S)	**Gorilla** *(Without booklet)*	1968	10.00	25.00
Imperial LP-12432	(S)	**Urban Spaceman** *(With booklet)*	1969	12.00	30.00
Imperial LP-12432	(S)	**Urban Spaceman** *(Without booklet)*	1969	10.00	25.00
Imperial LP-12445	(S)	**Tadpoles**	1969	10.00	25.00
Imperial LP-12457	(S)	**Keynsham**	1970	10.00	25.00
United Arts. UAS-5517	(S)	**Beast Of The Bonzos**	1972	6.00	15.00
United Arts. UAS-5584	(S)	**Let's Make Up And Be Friendly**	1972	8.00	20.00
		(With postcard still attached to the cover.)			
United Arts. UAS-5584	(S)	**Let's Make Up And Be Friendly**	1972	4.00	10.00
		(With the postcard removed from the cover.)			
United Arts. LA321H2	(S)	**The History Of The Bonzos** *(2 LPs)*	1974	6.00	15.00
BOOGIE KINGS, THE					
Montel LP-104	(M)	**The Boogie Kings**	1966	10.00	25.00
Montel LP-109	(M)	**Blue Eyed Soul**	1967	10.00	25.00
BOOKER T. & THE M.G.'S					
Refer to The Mar-Keys & Booker T. & The M.G.'s					
Stax ST-701	(M)	**Green Onions**	1962	30.00	75.00
Stax STS-701	(E)	**Green Onions**	1966	20.00	50.00
Stax ST-705	(M)	**Soul Dressing**	1965	30.00	75.00
Stax STS-705	(E)	**Soul Dressing**	1966	20.00	50.00
Stax ST-711	(M)	**And Now... Booker T. & The M.G.'s**	1966	20.00	50.00
Stax STS-711	(S)	**And Now... Booker T. & The M.G.'s**	1966	30.00	75.00
Stax ST-713	(M)	**In The Christmas Spirit**	1966	200.00	400.00
Stax STS-713	(S)	**In The Christmas Spirit**	1966	200.00	400.00
		(Original pressings of Stax 713 have a drawing of fingers and piano keys on the cover.)			
Stax ST-713	(M)	**In The Christmas Spirit**	1967	80.00	200.00
Stax STS-713	(S)	**In The Christmas Spirit**	1967	80.00	200.00
		(Reissues have multiple images of Santa Claus.)			
Stax ST-717	(M)	**Hip Hug-Her**	1967	14.00	35.00
Stax STS-717	(S)	**Hip Hug-Her**	1967	20.00	50.00
Stax ST-724	(M)	**Doin' Our Thing**	1968	14.00	35.00
Stax STS-724	(S)	**Doin' Our Thing**	1968	20.00	50.00
Atlantic 8202	(S)	**The Best Of Booker T. & The M.G.'s**	1968	8.00	20.00
Stax STS-2001	(S)	**Soul Limbo**	1968	10.00	25.00
Stax STS-2006	(S)	**Up Tight**	1968	10.00	25.00
Stax STS-2009	(S)	**Booker T. Set**	1969	10.00	25.00
Stax STS-2027	(S)	**McLemore Avenue**	1971	10.00	25.00
Stax ST-2033	(DJ)	**Greatest Hits** *(White label promo)*	1971	10.00	25.00
Stax STS-2033	(S)	**Greatest Hits**	1971	6.00	15.00
Stax STS-2035	(S)	**Melting Pot**	1971	4.00	10.00
Stax	(DJ)	**Funktion** *(In-store sampler)*	1972	8.00	20.00
Epic KE-33143	(S)	**Evergreen**	1974	1.00	5.00
Asylum 7E-1093	(S)	**Universal Language**	1977	1.00	5.00
Stax 8505	(S)	**Greatest Hits**	1981	1.00	5.00
BOOKER T.					
A&M SP-4351	(S)	**Home Grown**	1972	4.00	10.00
A&M SP-4413	(S)	**Chronicles**	1973	4.00	10.00
A&M SP-3504	(S)	**Booker T. & Priscilla** *(2 LPs)*	1973	5.00	12.00
A&M SP-4720	(S)	**Try And Love Again**	1978	1.00	5.00
A&M SP-4874	(S)	**I Want You**	1981	1.00	5.00
BOOMERANG					
RCA Victor LSP-4577	(S)	**Boomerang**	1971	6.00	15.00
BOOMTOWN RATS					
Mercury SRM-1-1188	(S)	**The Boomtown Rats**	1977	4.00	10.00

Label & Catalog #		Title	Year	VG+	NM
BOONE, DANIEL					
Mercury SRM-649	(S)	Daniel Boone	1972	4.00	10.00
BOONE'S FARM					
Columbia KC-31408	(S)	Boone's Farm	1972	1.00	5.00
BOP-CHORDS, THE					
Lost-Nite LLP-11	(10")	The Bop-Chords (Red vinyl)	1981	4.00	10.00
BORDERSONG					
Ann and Nancy Wilson of Heart provide backing vocals on "It's Time Again."					
Real Good 1001	(S)	Morning	1975	10.00	25.00
BOSTIC, EARL					
King 295-64	(10")	Earl Bostic & His Alto Sax, Vol. 1 (Red vinyl)	195?	250.00	500.00
King 295-64	(10")	Earl Bostic & His Alto Sax, Vol. 1	195?	100.00	250.00
King 295-65	(10")	Earl Bostic & His Alto Sax, Vol. 2 (Red vinyl)	195?	250.00	500.00
King 295-65	(10")	Earl Bostic & His Alto Sax, Vol. 2	195?	100.00	250.00
King 295-66	(10")	Earl Bostic & His Alto Sax, Vol. 3 (Red vinyl)	195?	250.00	500.00
King 295-66	(10")	Earl Bostic & His Alto Sax, Vol. 3	195?	100.00	250.00
King 295-72	(10")	Earl Bostic & His Alto Sax, Vol. 4	195?	60.00	250.00
King 295-76	(10")	Earl Bostic & His Alto Sax, Vol. 5	195?	60.00	250.00
King 295-77	(10")	Earl Bostic & His Alto Sax, Vol. 6	195?	60.00	250.00
King 295-78	(10")	Earl Bostic & His Alto Sax, Vol. 7	195?	60.00	250.00
King 295-79	(10")	Earl Bostic & His Alto Sax, Vol. 8	195?	60.00	250.00
King 295-95	(10")	Earl Bostic Plays Old Standards	195?	60.00	250.00
King 295-103	(10")	Earl Bostic & His Alto Sax	195?	60.00	250.00
King 500	(M)	The Best Of Earl Bostic	1956	40.00	100.00
King 503	(M)	Bostic For You	1956	40.00	100.00
King 515	(M)	Alto-Tude	1956	40.00	100.00
King 525	(M)	Dance Time	1956	30.00	75.00
King 529	(M)	Let's Dance With Earl Bostic	1958	30.00	75.00
King 547	(M)	Invitation To Dance	1958	30.00	75.00
King 558	(M)	C'mon And Dance With Earl Bostic	1958	30.00	75.00
King KSD-558	(S)	C'mon And Dance With Earl Bostic	1958	60.00	150.00
King 571	(M)	Bostic Rocks	1958	30.00	75.00
King 583	(M)	Showcase Of Swinging Dance Hits	1958	30.00	75.00
King 597	(M)	Alto Magic In Hi-Fi	1958	30.00	75.00
King 602	(M)	Sweet Tunes Of The Fantastic Fifties	1959	30.00	75.00
King 613	(M)	Workshop	1959	20.00	50.00
King 620	(M)	Sweet Tunes From The Roaring Twenties	1959	20.00	50.00
King 632	(M)	Sweet Tunes Of The Swinging Forties	1959	20.00	50.00
King 640	(M)	Sweet Tunes Of The Sentimental Forties	1959	20.00	50.00
King 620	(M)	Sweet Tunes From The Roaring Twenties	1959	20.00	50.00
King 662	(M)	Musical Pearls	1959	20.00	50.00
King 705	(M)	Hit Tunes Of Big Broadway Shows	1960	20.00	50.00
King 725	(M)	25 Years Of Rhythm And Blues Hits	1960	20.00	50.00
King 786	(M)	By Popular Demand	1962	20.00	50.00
King 827	(M)	Earl Bostic Plays Bossa Nova	1963	20.00	50.00
King 838	(M)	Fantastic Fifties	1963	20.00	50.00
King 846	(M)	Jazz As I Feel It	1963	20.00	50.00
King 881	(M)	The Best Of Earl Bostic	1964	20.00	50.00
King 900	(M)	New Sound	1964	20.00	50.00
King 921	(M)	The Great Hits Of 1964	1964	20.00	50.00
		—King albums above have "crownless" black labels.—			
King 500	(M)	The Best Of Earl Bostic	1966	4.00	10.00
King KSD-500	(S)	The Best Of Earl Bostic	1966	6.00	15.00
King 503	(M)	Bostic For You	1966	4.00	10.00
King KSD-503	(S)	Bostic For You	1966	6.00	15.00
King 515	(M)	Alto-Tude	1966	4.00	10.00
King KSD-515	(S)	Alto-Tude	1966	6.00	15.00
King 525	(M)	Dance Time	1966	4.00	10.00
King KSD-525	(S)	Dance Time	1966	6.00	15.00
King 529	(M)	Let's Dance With Earl Bostic	1966	4.00	10.00
King KSD-529	(S)	Let's Dance With Earl Bostic	1966	6.00	15.00
King 547	(M)	Invitation To Dance	1966	4.00	10.00
King KSD-547	(S)	Invitation To Dance	1966	6.00	15.00
King 558	(M)	C'mon And Dance With Earl Bostic	1966	4.00	10.00
King KSD-558	(S)	C'mon And Dance With Earl Bostic	1966	6.00	15.00
King 571	(M)	Bostic Rocks	1966	4.00	10.00
King KSD-571	(S)	Bostic Rocks	1966	6.00	15.00
King 583	(M)	Showcase Of Swinging Dance Hits	1966	4.00	10.00
King KSD-583	(S)	Showcase Of Swinging Dance Hits	1966	6.00	15.00
King 597	(M)	Alto Magic In Hi-Fi	1966	4.00	10.00
King KSD-597	(S)	Alto Magic In Hi-Fi	1966	6.00	15.00
King 602	(M)	Sweet Tunes Of The Fantastic Fifties	1966	4.00	10.00
King KSD-602	(S)	Sweet Tunes Of The Fantastic Fifties	1966	6.00	15.00
King 613	(M)	Workshop	1966	4.00	10.00
King KSD-613	(S)	Workshop	1966	6.00	15.00

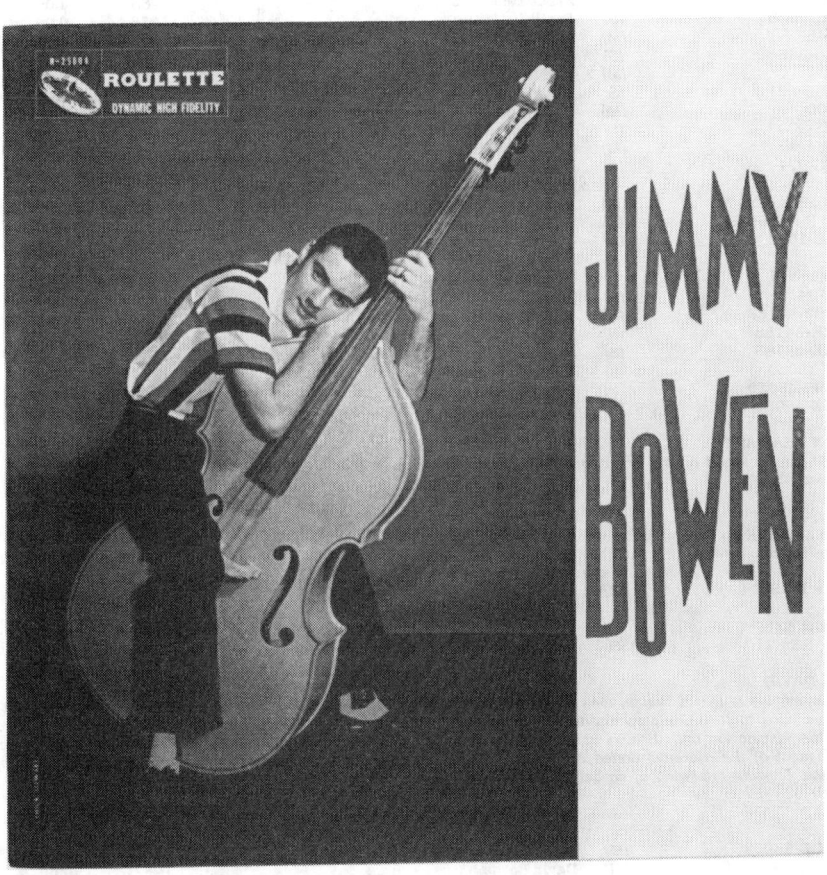

Jimmy Bowen & The Rhythm Orchids, which included Buddy Knox and Dave "Dicky Doo" Alldred, hit the Top 20 in 1957 with "I'm Stickin' With You." While he had three other charting sides, none were large hits. His self-titled first album for Roulette was his last until the mid-'60s. During that time he worked as a West Coast-based songwriter and producer, eventually landing the position of President of MCA Records.

Label & Catalog #		Title	Year	VG+	NM
King 620	(M)	**Sweet Tunes Of The Roaring Twenties**	1966	4.00	10.00
King KSD-620	(S)	**Sweet Tunes Of The Roaring Twenties**	1966	6.00	15.00
King 632	(M)	**Sweet Tunes Of The Swinging Forties**	1966	4.00	10.00
King KSD-632	(S)	**Sweet Tunes Of The Swinging Forties**	1966	6.00	15.00
King 640	(M)	**Sweet Tunes Of The Sentimental Forties**	1966	4.00	10.00
King KSD-640	(S)	**Sweet Tunes Of The Sentimental Forties**	1966	6.00	15.00
King 662	(M)	**Musical Pearls**	1966	4.00	10.00
King 705	(M)	**Hit Tunes Of Big Broadway Shows**	1966	4.00	10.00
King KSD-705	(S)	**Hit Tunes Of Big Broadway Shows**	1966	6.00	15.00
King 725	(M)	**25 Years Of Rhythm And Blues Hits**	1966	4.00	10.00
King KSD-725	(S)	**25 Years Of Rhythm And Blues Hits**	1966	6.00	15.00
King 786	(M)	**By Popular Demand**	1966	4.00	10.00
King KS-786	(S)	**By Popular Demand**	1966	6.00	15.00
King 827	(M)	**Earl Bostic Plays Bossa Nova**	1966	4.00	10.00
King KS-827	(S)	**Earl Bostic Plays Bossa Nova**	1966	6.00	15.00
King 838	(M)	**Fantastic Fifties**	1966	4.00	10.00
King KSD-838	(S)	**Fantastic Fifties**	1966	6.00	15.00
King 846	(M)	**Jazz As I Feel It**	1966	4.00	10.00
King KS-846	(S)	**Jazz As I Feel It**	1966	6.00	15.00
King 881	(M)	**The Best Of Earl Bostic**	1966	4.00	10.00
King KSD-881	(S)	**The Best Of Earl Bostic**	1966	6.00	15.00
King 900	(M)	**New Sound**	1966	4.00	10.00
King KS-900	(S)	**New Sound**	1966	6.00	15.00
King 921	(M)	**The Great Hits Of 1966**	1966	4.00	10.00
King KS-921	(S)	**The Great Hits Of 1966**	1966	6.00	15.00
		—King albums above have blue labels with a crown logo—			
Philips PHM-200-262	(M)	**The Song Is Not Ended**	1967	10.00	25.00
Philips PHS-600-262	(S)	**The Song Is Not Ended**	1967	10.00	25.00
King KS-1048	(S)	**Harlem Nocturne**	1969	10.00	25.00

BOSTON

Epic E-34188	(S)	**Boston**	1976	1.00	5.00
Epic E99-44188	(S)	**Boston** (Picture disc)	1978	6.00	15.00
Epic HE-34188	(S)	**Boston** (Half-speed master)	1981	15.00	45.00
Epic HE-44188	(S)	**Boston** (Half-speed master)	1982	12.00	35.00
Epic E-35050	(S)	**Don't Look Back**	1978	1.00	5.00
Epic E99-45050	(S)	**Don't Look Back** (Promo picture disc)	1982	10.00	25.00
Epic HE-45050	(S)	**Don't Look Back** (Half-speed master)	1982	25.00	75.00

BOSTON TEA PARTY, THE
The BTP can be found on the American International soundtrack "The Cycle Savages."

Flick Disc 45000	(S)	**The Boston Tea Party**	1968	10.00	25.00

BOWEN, JIMMY
Refer to Buddy Knox & Jimmy Bowen.

Roulette R-25004	(M)	**Jimmy Bowen**	1957	100.00	250.00
		—Roulette albums above have black & silver labels.—			
Roulette R-25004	(M)	**Jimmy Bowen**	195?	60.00	150.00
		—Roulette albums above have red labels.—			
Reprise R-6210	(M)	**Sunday Morning With The Comics**	1966	12.00	30.00
Reprise RS-6210	(S)	**Sunday Morning With The Comics**	1966	16.00	40.00

BOWIE, DAVID
David Jones, a.k.a. David Bowie, was the prime progenitor of "glam rock" in the States. His career has seen an almost obsessive need to stay one step ahead of the fans and critics with constant stylistic changes. The earliest recordings betray his fascination with British music hall and Anthony Newley (Section 1, below). His stay with RCA (Section 2) covered most of the aforementioned changes. The third section lists the few recordings he has done since splitting RCA, including the reissuing of earlier titles on the independent Rykodisc. Refer to Mott The Hoople; Iggy Pop.

1. Pre-RCA Recordings

Deram DE-16003	(M)	**David Bowie** (White label promo)	1967	80.00	200.00
Deram DE-16003	(M)	**David Bowie**	1967	40.00	100.00
Deram DES-18003	(S)	**David Bowie**	1967	60.00	150.00
Mercury SR-61246	(DJ)	**Man Of Words, Man Of Music** (White label)	1969	100.00	200.00
Mercury SR-61246	(S)	**Man Of Words, Man Of Music**	1969	40.00	100.00
Mercury SR-61325	(DJ)	**The Man Who Sold The World** (White label)	1971	60.00	150.00
Mercury SR-61325	(S)	**The Man Who Sold The World**	1971	23.00	50.00
		(The matrix number is stamped in the trail-off vinyl of originals; counterfeits have those numbers hand-etched.)			
London 628/9	(P)	**Images 1966-1967** (2 LPs)	1973	7.00	20.00
London 50007	(S)	**Starting Point**	1977	1.00	5.00
		(The London albums recycle material from Deram albums.)			

1. The RCA Years

RCA Victor LSP-4623	(S)	**Hunky Dory**	1972	6.00	15.00
RCA Victor LSP-4702	(S)	**The Rise And Fall Of Ziggy Stardust & The Spiders From Mars**	1972	6.00	15.00

Label & Catalog #		Title	Year	VG+	NM
RCA Victor LSP-4813	(S)	Space Oddity (With poster)	1972	8.00	20.00
RCA Victor LSP-4813	(S)	Space Oddity (Without poster)	1972	6.00	15.00
RCA Victor LSP-4816	(S)	Man Who Sold The World (With poster)	1972	8.00	20.00
RCA Victor LSP-4816	(S)	Man Who Sold The World (Without poster)	1972	6.00	15.00
RCA Victor LSP-4852	(S)	Aladdin Sane	1973	6.00	15.00
RCA Victor AFL1-4852	(S)	Aladdin Sane	1983	.80	4.00
RCA Victor APL1-0291	(S)	Pin Ups	1974	6.00	15.00
RCA Victor APL1-0291	(S)	Pin Ups	1977	.80	4.00
RCA Victor CPL1-0576	(S)	Diamond Dogs	1974	See note below	

(Original covers show the Bowie-dog's genitals clearly. This was withdrawn and the offending member airbrushed out for release. Rare with a suggested NM value of $2,000-4,000.)

Label & Catalog #		Title	Year	VG+	NM
RCA Victor APL1-0576	(S)	Diamond Dogs	1974	6.00	15.00
RCA Victor CPL2-0771	(S)	David Live (2 LPs.)	1974	8.00	20.00
RCA Victor APL1-0998	(S)	Young Americans	1975	6.00	15.00

— RCA albums above have orange labels.—

Label & Catalog #		Title	Year	VG+	NM
RCA Victor APL1-0998	(S)	Young Americans	1975	3.20	8.00
RCA Victor APL1-1327	(S)	Station To Station	1975	3.20	8.00

— RCA albums above have brown labels.—

Label & Catalog #		Title	Year	VG+	NM
RCA Victor APL1-0998	(S)	Young Americans	197?	.80	4.00
RCA Victor AQK1-0998	(S)	Young Americans	1984	.80	4.00
RCA Victor APL1-1327	(S)	Station To Station	197?	.80	4.00
RCA Victor AQK1-1327	(S)	Station To Station	1984	.80	4.00
RCA Victor APL1-1732	(S)	Changesonebowie	1976	1.00	5.00

(While a UK pressing of this album with an alternate take of "John I'm Only Dancing" may exist, rumors of a US pressing of this album with the alternate may be just that... rumors.)

Label & Catalog #		Title	Year	VG+	NM
RCA Victor AFL1-1732	(S)	Changesonebowie	1977	.80	4.00
RCA Victor AQL1-1732	(S)	Changesonebowie	1980	.80	4.00
RCA Victor APL1-2030	(S)	Low (With Eno)	1977	1.00	5.00
RCA Victor AFL1-2522	(S)	"Heroes" (With Eno)	1977	1.00	5.00
RCA Victor DJL1-2697	(DJ)	Bowie Now	1978	10.00	25.00
RCA Victor JD-11306	(DJ)	Peter And The Wolf (Black vinyl)	1978	8.00	25.00
RCA Victor ARL1-2743	(S)	Peter And The Wolf (Black vinyl)	1978	4.00	10.00
RCA Victor ARL1-2743	(S)	Peter And The Wolf (Green vinyl)	1978	4.00	10.00
RCA Victor CPL2-2913	(S)	Stage (2 LPs)	1978	3.20	8.00
RCA Victor DJL1-3016	(DJ)	An Evening With David Bowie	1978	20.00	50.00

(Originals have a black border along the bottom of the cover. Counterfeits do not have the border.)

Label & Catalog #		Title	Year	VG+	NM
RCA Victor AQL1-3254	(S)	Lodger (With Eno)	1980	1.00	5.00
RCA Victor DJL1-3545	(DJ)	1980 All Clear	1980	8.00	20.00
RCA Victor AQL1-3647	(S)	Scary Monsters (And Super Creeps)	1980	1.00	5.00
RCA Victor DJL1-3829	(DJ)	Special Radio Series, Volume 1: Scary Monsters Interview Album	1980	8.00	20.00
RCA Victor DJL1-3829	(DJ)	College Radio Series, Volume 1: Scary Monsters Interview Album	1980	8.00	20.00
RCA Victor DJL1-3840	(DJ)	Scary Monsters Interview Album	1980	8.00	20.00
RCA Victor AYL1-3839	(S)	Diamond Dogs	1980	.80	4.00
RCA Victor AYL1-3843	(S)	The Rise & Fall Of Ziggy Stardust & The Spiders From Mars	1980	.80	4.00
RCA Victor AYL1-3844	(S)	Hunky Dory	1980	.80	4.00
RCA Victor AYL1-3856	(S)	Low	1980	.80	4.00
RCA Victor AYL1-3857	(S)	"Heroes"	1980	.80	4.00
RCA Victor AYL1-3890	(S)	Aladdin Insane	1980	.80	4.00
RCA Victor AFL1-4202	(S)	Changestwobowie	1981	.80	4.00
RCA Victor AYL1-4234	(S)	Lodger	1981	.80	4.00
RCA Victor ABL1-4239	(S)	Christiane F.	1981	.80	4.00
RCA Victor CPL1-4346	(S)	Baal	1982	.80	4.00
RCA Victor AYL1-4653	(S)	Pin Ups	1982	.80	4.00
RCA Victor CPL2-4862	(DJ)	Ziggy Stardust, The Motion Picture (2 LPs on clear vinyl)	1983	20.00	50.00
RCA Victor CPL2-4862	(S)	Ziggy Stardust, The Motion Picture (2 LPs)	1983	1.20	6.00
RCA Victor AFL1-4792	(S)	Golden Years	1983	1.00	5.00
RCA Victor AFL1-4919	(S)	Fame And Fashion	1984	1.00	5.00

3. Post RCA Victor Releases.

Label & Catalog #		Title	Year	VG+	NM
EMI SO-17093	(S)	Let's Dance	1983	1.00	5.00
EMI SPRO-9960/1	(DJ)	Let's Talk	1983	8.00	20.00
EMI SPRO-79112/3	(DJ)	Never Let Me Down: The Interview	1987	20.00	50.00
Varese Sarabande 81184	(S)	The Hunger	1984	1.00	5.00
London Bowie 1	(S)	Love You Till Tuesday	1984	1.00	5.00
EMI SJ-17138	(S)	Tonight	1984	1.00	5.00
EMI PJ-17267	(S)	Never Let Me Down	1987	1.00	5.00
EMI E1-91990	(S)	Tin Machine	1989	1.00	5.00
Rykodisc RLP-10131*	(S)	Space Oddity	1990	4.00	10.00
Rykodisc RLP-10132*	(S)	The Man Who Sold The World	1990	4.00	10.00
Rykodisc RLP-10133*	(S)	Hunky Dory	1990	4.00	10.00

Label & Catalog #		Title	Year	VG+	NM
Rykodisc LSD-4702	(DJ)	**The Rise & Fall Of Ziggy Stardust**			
		& The Spiders From Mars	1990	40.00	100.00
		(Rykodisc 4702 contains an album and a CD.)			
Rykodisc RLP-10134*	(S)	**The Rise & Fall Of Ziggy Stardust**			
		& The Spiders From Mars	1990	4.00	10.00
Rykodisc RLP-10135	(S)	**Aladdin Insane**	1990	4.00	10.00
Rykodisc RLP-10136*	(S)	**Pin Ups**	1990	4.00	10.00
Rykodisc RCD-10137*	(S)	**Diamond Dogs**	1990	4.00	10.00
Rykodisc RCD-10138/9*	(S)	**David Live**	1990	4.00	10.00
Rykodisc RLP-20171	(S)	**Changesbowie**	1990	4.00	10.00

BOWN, ALAN: *Refer to* THE ALAN BOWN

BOX TOPS, THE
The Box Tops feature Alex Chilton. Refer to Big Star.

Bell 6011	(M)	**The Letter/Neon Rainbow**	1967	8.00	20.00
Bell S-6011	(S)	**The Letter/Neon Rainbow**	1967	10.00	25.00
Bell S-6017	(S)	**Cry Like A Baby**	1968	10.00	25.00
Bell S-6023	(S)	**Non-Stop**	1968	6.00	15.00
Bell S-6025	(S)	**Super Hits**	1968	6.00	15.00
Bell S-6032	(S)	**Dimensions**	1969	6.00	15.00
Cotillion SD-057	(S)	**A Lifetime Believing**	1971	6.00	15.00
Kory 3007	(S)	**The Best Of The Box Tops**	1977	1.00	5.00
Rhino RNLP-161	(S)	**The Box Tops' Greatest Hits**	1982	1.00	5.00

BOYCE, TOMMY

Camden CAL-2202	(M)	**A Twofold Talent**	1967	8.00	20.00
Camden CAS-2202	(S)	**A Twofold Talent**	1967	10.00	25.00

BOYCE, TOMMY, & BOBBY HART
Refer to Dillard & Boyce.; Dolenz, Jones, Boyce & Hart.

A&M LP-126	(M)	**Test Patterns**	1967	8.00	20.00
A&M SP-4126	(S)	**Test Patterns**	1967	8.00	20.00
A&M LP-143	(M)	**I Wonder What She's Doing Tonight**	1968	8.00	20.00
A&M SP-4143	(S)	**I Wonder What She's Doing Tonight**	1968	8.00	20.00
A&M SP-4162	(S)	**It's All Happening On The Inside**	1968	8.00	20.00

BOYD, BILLY

Crown CLP-5170	(M)	**Twangy Guitars**	1960	30.00	75.00
		—Crown albums above have black labels with silver print.—			
Crown CLP-5170	(M)	**Twangy Guitars**	1961	8.00	20.00
Crown CST-196	(E)	**Twangy Guitars** *(Red vinyl)*	1961	20.00	50.00
Crown CST-196	(E)	**Twangy Guitars**	1961	4.00	10.00
		—Crown albums above have gray labels.—			

BRADEN, JOHN

A&M SP-4172	(S)	**John Braden**	1969	4.00	10.00

BRADFORD, ALEX

Specialty SP-2108	(M)	**Too Close To Heaven**	1959	40.00	100.00

BRADFORD, SCOTT

Probe 4509	(S)	**Rock Slides**	1969	8.00	20.00

BRADSHAW, TINY

King 295-74	(10")	**Off And On**	1955	600.00	1,200.00
King 395-501	(M)	**Selections**	1958	500.00	750.00
King 653	(M)	**Great Composer**	1959	200.00	400.00
King 953	(M)	**24 Great Songs**	1966	20.00	50.00

BRAHMAN

Mercury SR-61348	(S)	**Brahman**	1971	6.00	15.00

BRAINBOX

Capitol ST-596	(S)	**Brainbox**	1970	6.00	15.00

BRAMLETT, BONNIE
Ms Bramlett was one-half of Delaney & Bonnie.

Columbia KC-31786	(S)	**Sweet Bonnie Bramlett**	1973	1.00	5.00
Capricorn CPN-0148	(S)	**It's Time**	1975	1.00	5.00
Capricorn CPN-0169	(S)	**Lady's Choice**	1976	1.00	5.00
Capricorn CPN-0199	(S)	**Memories**	1978	1.00	5.00

BRAMLETT, DELANEY
Mr Bramlett was the other half of Delaney & Bonnie.

Columbia KC-31631	(S)	**Some Things Coming**	1972	1.00	5.00
Columbia KC-32420	(S)	**Mobius Strip**	1973	1.00	5.00
Prodigal P6-10017S1	(S)	**Class Reunion**	197?	1.00	5.00
MGM M3G-5011	(S)	**Giving Birth To A Song**	1975	1.00	5.00

Brenda Payton led The Tabulations—Maurice Coates, Eddie Jackson and Jerry Jones—
through six chart hits in a twelve month period beginning in March 1967, all for Dionn
Records. The group's sole album, named after the first, and biggest, of the hits, followed.
Like many labels during the late '60s, when mono was being phased out, Dionn saved some
money by packaging stereo copies of her record in mono jackets and with a "Stereo" sticker
affixed to the cover, as shown here.

Label & Catalog #		Title	Year	VG+	NM
BRASS MONKEY					
Rare Earth 523	(S)	**Brass Monkey**	1971	4.00	10.00
BRAVE BELT					
Brave Belt included former Guess Who members Chad Allan and Randy Bachman.					
Reprise RS-6447	(S)	**Brave Belt**	1971	3.20	8.00
Reprise MS-2057	(S)	**Brave Belt II**	1972	3.20	8.00
Reprise MS-2210	(S)	**Bachman-Turner Overdrive As Brave Belt**	1975	.80	4.00
		(MS-2210 reissues material from 6447 and 2057.)			
BRAZELTON, AMBROSE					
Kimbo LP-8080	(M)	**And The Beatles Go On**			
		And On: Hits Of The Beatles (With book)	1971	14.00	35.00
BREAD					
Bread was David Gates and James Griffin.					
Elektra EKS-74044	(S)	**Bread**	1969	1.00	5.00
Elektra BRD-1	(S)	**Bread** (In-store sampler)	1969	4.00	10.00
Elektra EKS-74076	(S)	**On The Waters**	1970	1.00	5.00
Elektra EKS-74086	(S)	**Manna**	1971	1.00	5.00
Elektra EKS-75015	(S)	**Baby, I'm A-Want You**	1972	1.00	5.00
Elektra EQ-5015	(Q)	**Baby, I'm A-Want You**	1973	4.00	10.00
Elektra EKS-75047	(S)	**The Guitar Man**	1972	1.00	5.00
Elektra EKS-75056	(S)	**The Best Of Bread**	1973	1.00	5.00
Elektra EQ-5056	(Q)	**The Best Of Bread**	1973	4.00	10.00
Elektra 7E-1005	(S)	**The Best Of Bread, Vol. 2**	1974	.80	4.00
Elektra 7E-1094	(S)	**Lost Without Your Love**	1977	.80	4.00
Elektra 6E-108	(S)	**The Best Of Bread**	1979	.80	4.00
Elektra 6E-110	(S)	**The Best Of Bread, Vol. 2**	1979	.80	4.00
BREAD, LOVE & DREAMS					
London PS-566	(S)	**Bread, Love & Dreams**	1969	16.00	40.00
BREEDLOVE, JIM					
Camden CAL-430	(M)	**Rock 'N' Roll Hits**	1958	12.00	30.00
BREMERS, BEVERLY					
Scepter SPS-5102	(S)	**I'll Make You Music**	1972	4.00	10.00
BRENDA & THE TABULATIONS					
Dionn LPM-2000	(M)	**Dry Your Eyes**	1967	14.00	35.00
Dionn LPS-2000	(S)	**Dry Your Eyes** ("Dry Your Eyes" is rechanneled)	1967	20.00	50.00
Chocolate City 2002	(S)	**I Keep Coming Back For More**	1977	4.00	10.00
BRETHREN, THE					
Tiffany TFS-0013	(S)	**Brethren**	1970	6.00	15.00
Tiffany TFS-0015	(S)	**Moment Of Truth**	1971	6.00	15.00
BRETT, PAUL					
Janus 3026	(S)	**Paul Brett Sage**	1971	6.00	15.00
BREW					
ABC 672	(S)	**Very Strange Brew**	1969	8.00	20.00
BREWER & SHIPLEY					
A&M SP-4154	(S)	**Down In L.A.**	1968	3.20	8.00
Kama Sutra KSBS-2016	(S)	**Weeds**	1969	3.20	8.00
Kama Sutra KSBS-2024	(S)	**Tarko**	1970	3.20	8.00
Kama Sutra KSBS-2039	(S)	**Shake Off The Demon**	1971	3.20	8.00
Kama Sutra KSBS-2058	(S)	**Rural Space**	1972	3.20	8.00
Capitol ST-11261	(S)	**ST-11261**	1974	1.00	5.00
Capitol ST-11402	(S)	**Welcome To Riddle Bridge**	1975	1.00	5.00
BRIDES OF FUNKENSTEIN, THE					
The Brides are members of the Parliament/Funkadelic community.					
Atlantic 19201	(S)	**Funk Or Walk**	1978	6.00	15.00
Atlantic 19261	(S)	**Never Buy Texas From A Cowboy**	1979	6.00	15.00
BRINSLEY SCHWARZ					
Brinsley Schwarz features Nick Lowe.					
Capitol ST-589	(S)	**Brinsley Schwarz**	1970	6.00	15.00
Capitol ST-744	(S)	**Despite It All**	1971	6.00	15.00
United Arts. UAS-5566	(S)	**Silver Pistol**	1972	6.00	15.00
United Arts. UAS-5647	(S)	**Nervous On The Road**	1972	6.00	15.00
Capitol SWBC-11869	(S)	**Brinsley Schwarz** (2 LPs)	1978	1.20	6.00
		(SWBC-11869 is a reissue of 589 and 744.)			
Liberty LN-10145	(S)	**Silver Pistol**	1981	.80	4.00
Liberty LN-10146	(S)	**Nervous On The Road**	1981	.80	4.00

Label & Catalog #		Title	Year	VG+	NM

BROCK, B., & THE SULTANS
Crown CLP-5399	(M)	Do The Beetle	1964	16.00	40.00
Crown CST-399	(S)	Do The Beetle	1964	20.00	50.00
		—Crown albums above have gray labels.—			

BROCKETT, JAMIE
Capitol SKAO-601	(S)	Jaime Brockett	1970	6.00	15.00
Capitol ST-678	(S)	Remember The Wind And The Rain	1971	10.00	25.00
Adelphi 1028	(S)	North Mountain Velvet	1977	1.00	5.00

BRONSTEIN, STAN
Stan Bronstein recorded with Elephant's Memory.
| Muse 5113 | (S) | Living On The Avenue | 1976 | 4.00 | 10.00 |

BROOKLYN BRIDGE, THE
The BB features Johnny Maestro. They can be found on National General's soundtrack "Grasshopper."
Buddah BDS-5034	(S)	The Brooklyn Bridge	1969	4.00	10.00
Buddah BDS-5042	(S)	The Second Brooklyn Bridge	1969	4.00	10.00
Buddah BDS-5065	(S)	The Brooklyn Bridge	1970	4.00	10.00
Buddah BDS-5107	(S)	Bridge In Blue	1972	4.00	10.00

BROOKS, DONNIE
| Era EL-105 | (M) | The Happiest | 1961 | 60.00 | 150.00 |

BROONZY, BIG BILL
Big Bill is a guitar player, fiddler, singer and songwriter in the country blues tradition.
Dial LP-306	(10")	Blues Concert	1952	200.00	400.00
EmArcy MG-26034	(10")	Folk Blues	1954	80.00	200.00
EmArcy MG-36137	(M)	Blues By Broonzy	1958	40.00	100.00
		(EmArcy 36137 is a reissue of 26034.)			
Period SLP-1114	(M)	Big Bill Broonzy Sings (Blues)	1956	40.00	100.00
Period SLP-1209	(M)	Big Bill Broonzy Sings			
		And Josh White Comes A-Visiting	1958	30.00	75.00
Folkways FA-2315	(M)	Big Bill Broonzy	1957	20.00	50.00
Folkways FA-2326	(M)	Country Blues	1957	20.00	50.00
Folkways FG-3586	(M)	His Songs And Story (Interview)	1957	20.00	50.00
Columbia WL-111	(M)	Big Bill's Blues	1958	40.00	100.00
		—Columbia albums above have gold "Adventures in Sound" labels.—			
Verve MGV-3000-5	(M)	The Big Bill Broonzy Story (5 LP box)	1959	80.00	200.00
Verve MGV-3001	(M)	Last Session, Part 1	1959	24.00	60.00
Verve MGV-3002	(M)	Last Session, Part 2	1959	24.00	60.00
Verve MGV-3003	(M)	Last Session, Part 3	1959	24.00	60.00
		(The "Last Sessions" are taken from the boxed set above.)			
Mercury MG-20822	(M)	Big Bill Broonzy—Memorial	1963	12.00	30.00
Mercury SR-60822	(E)	Big Bill Broonzy—Memorial	1963	8.00	20.00
Mercury MG-20905	(M)	Remembering Big Bill Broonzy	1964	12.00	30.00
Mercury SR-60905	(E)	Remembering Big Bill Broonzy	1964	8.00	20.00
Epic EE-22017	(M)	Big Bill's Blues	1969	8.00	20.00
Epic EE-22018	(E)	Big Bill's Blues	1969	6.00	15.00
Archive of Folk Music 213	(E)	Big Bill Broonzy	196?	1.00	5.00
Biograph BLPC-15	(M)	Big Bill Broonzy 1932-1942	197?	4.00	10.00
Yazoo L-1011	(M)	The Young Big Bill Broonzy 1928-1935	197?	6.00	15.00
Yazoo L-1035	(M)	Do That Guitar Rag	197?	6.00	15.00
Yazoo L-1042	(M)	Uptown Blues	197?	6.00	15.00

BROONZY, BIG BILL, & SONNY TERRY & BROWNIE McGHEE
| Folkways FA-3817 | (M) | Big Bill Broonzy, | | | |
| | | Sonny Terry And Brownie McGhee | 1959 | 20.00 | 50.00 |

BROONZY, BIG BILL, & WASHBOARD SAM
Chess LP-1468	(DJ)	Big Bill Broonzy			
		And Washboard Sam (White label promo)	1962	250.00	500.00
Chess LP-1468	(M)	Big Bill Broonzy And Washboard Sam	1962	80.00	200.00

BROTH
| Mercury SR-61298 | (S) | Broth | 1970 | 8.00 | 20.00 |

BROTHER FOX & TAR BABY
BF&TB released their album privately before it was picked up by Capitol.
| Capitol ST-544 | (S) | Brother Fox & Tar Baby | 1969 | 6.00 | 15.00 |

BROTHERHOOD
Smitty, Drake and Fang of Paul Revere's Raiders, who also recorded as Friendsound.
RCA Victor LSP-4092	(S)	Brotherhood	1968	6.00	15.00
RCA Victor LSP-4228	(S)	Brotherhood, Brotherhood	1969	6.00	15.00
		—RCA albums above have orange labels on non-flexible vinyl—			

BROTHERHOOD OF MAN, THE
| Deram DES-18046 | (S) | United We Stand | 1970 | 6.00 | 15.00 |

Label & Catalog #		Title	Year	VG+	NM

BROTHERS & SISTERS OF L.A.
| Ode Z1-44018 | (S) | Dylan's Gospel | 1969 | 6.00 | 15.00 |

BROTHERS JOHNSON
The bro's are George and Louis Johnson.
A&M SP-4567	(S)	Look Out For #1	1976	1.00	5.00
A&M SP-4644	(S)	Right On Time	1977	1.00	5.00
A&M PR-4714	(DJ)	Blam!! (Picture disc)	1978	10.00	25.00
		(Promotional picture disc promotes the group's Japanese tour)			
A&M PR-4714	(S)	Blam!! (Picture disc)	1978	4.00	10.00
A&M SP-4714	(S)	Blam!!	1978	1.00	5.00
A&M SP-3716	(S)	Light Up The Night	1980	1.00	5.00
A&M SP-3724	(S)	Winners	1981	1.00	5.00
A&M SP-4927	(S)	Blast! (The Latest And The Greatest)	1983	1.00	5.00
A&M SP-4965	(S)	Out Of Control	1984	1.00	5.00

BROTHERS UNLIMITED
| Capitol ST-600 | (S) | Who's For The Young? | 1970 | 20.00 | 50.00 |

BROWN, AL, & HIS TUNE TOPPERS
Amy A-1	(M)	The Madison Dance Party	1960	16.00	40.00
Amy AS-1	(S)	The Madison Dance Party	1960	20.00	50.00
		("The Madison" is rechanneled for this album.)			
Moon LPBA-1	(M)	Al Brown Presents DynaSounds	196?	250.00	500.00
		(Various artists compilation of NY groups backed by Brown.)			

BROWN, ARTHUR
| Atlantic/Track SD-8198 | (S) | The Crazy World Of Arthur Brown | 1968 | 10.00 | 25.00 |
| Passport 98003 | (S) | Journey | 1974 | 4.00 | 10.00 |

BROWN, BUSTER
Fire FLP-101	(M)	New King Of The Blues (Purple cover)	1960	600.00	1,200.00
Fire FLP-102	(M)	New King Of The Blues (Purple cover)	1961	400.00	800.00
		— Fire albums above have white & red labels.—			
Fire FLP-102	(M)	New King Of The Blues (Purple cover)	1961	250.00	500.00
Fire FLP-102	(M)	The New King Of The Blues (White cover)	1961	200.00	400.00
		— Fire albums above have red & black labels.—			
Souffle 2014	(M)	Get Down	1973	4.00	10.00

BROWN, CHARLES
Aladdin LP-702	(10")	Mood Music (Red vinyl)	1953	See note below	
		(Red vinyl copies of Aladdin 702 with blue covers have a suggested NM value of $4,000-8,000.)			
Aladdin LP-702	(10")	Mood Music	1953	See note below	
		(Black vinyl copies have a suggested NM value of $2,000-3,000.)			
Aladdin LP-809	(M)	Mood Music	1956	Unreleased	
Score SLP-4011	(M)	Driftin' Blues	1958	500.00	750.00
Score SLP-4036	(M)	More Blues With Charles Brown	1958	Unreleased	
Imperial LP-9178	(M)	Charles Brown Sings Million Sellers	1961	300.00	500.00
King 775	(M)	Charles Brown Sings Christmas Songs	1961	80.00	200.00
King 878	(M)	The Great Charles Brown	1963	100.00	250.00
Mainstream 56007	(M)	Boss Of The Blues	1965	8.00	20.00
Mainstream S-6007	(S)	Boss Of The Blues	1965	12.00	30.00
Mainstream 56035	(M)	Ballads My Way	1965	8.00	20.00
Mainstream S-6035	(S)	Ballads My Way	1965	12.00	30.00
Mainstream SRL-368	(S)	Driftin' Blues	1972	4.00	10.00
BluesWay BLS-6039	(S)	Charles Brown—Legend	1970	10.00	25.00
Jewel 5006	(S)	Blues 'N Brown	1972	4.00	10.00
Big Town 1003	(S)	Merry Christmas Baby	1977	4.00	10.00
Big Town 1005	(S)	Music Maestro, Please	1978	4.00	10.00

BROWN, CHARLES / AMOS MILBURN
| Grand Prix K-421 | (M) | Original Blues Sounds | 196? | 8.00 | 20.00 |
| Grand Prix KS-421 | (E) | Original Blues Sounds | 196? | 4.00 | 10.00 |

BROWN, DUNCAN
| Immediate Z12-52012 | (S) | Give Me Take You | 1968 | 4.00 | 10.00 |

BROWN, JAMES
Refer to Hank Ballard; Bobby Byrd; Lynn Collins; Bill Doggett; Dee Felice; Fred & The New JB's; Martha High; The JB's; Anna King; Maceo; Sweet Charles; Fred Wesley; Marva Whitney.
King 610	(M)	Please Please Please	1958	1,000.00	2,000.00
		(Original covers features a man and a woman's legs on steps.)			
King 635	(M)	Try Me!	1959	800.00	1,600.00
		(Original covers feature a woman holding a smoking gun.)			
King 683	(M)	Think!	1960	800.00	1,600.00
		(Original covers feature a photo of a baby.)			
		— King albums above have black crownless labels with a 2" wide "KING" on top.—			

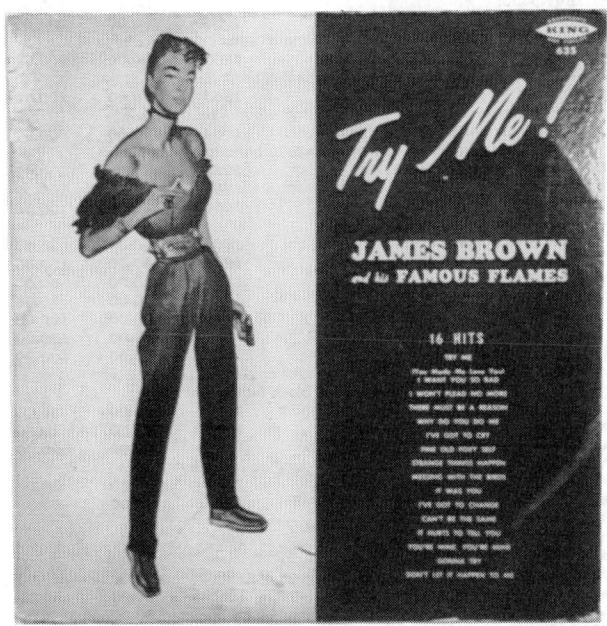

James Brown & His Famous Flames' first long-player, Please Please Please, *and his third,* Try Me!, *both had their original cover graphics changed. The original covers for both are shown here: The first has been referred to as the "stairs cover" or "legs cover" (top). The third is known as the "smoking gun" or "cigarette" cover (bottom). Later pressings for both titles featured recognizably JB covers.*

Label & Catalog #		Title	Year	VG+	NM
King 610	(M)	**Please Please Please** ("Legs" cover)	1961	600.00	1,200.00
King 635	(M)	**Try Me!** ("Smoking gun" cover)	1961	500.00	1,000.00
King 683	(M)	**Think!** (Baby cover)	1961	500.00	1,000.00
King 683	(M)	**Think!**	1963	150.00	300.00
		(Later covers have a photo of James Brown.)			
King 743	(M)	**The Amazing James Brown**	1961	300.00	600.00
		(Original covers for King 743 have JB in a fine suit.)			
King 743	(M)	**The Amazing James Brown**	1963	60.00	150.00
		(Later pressings have a white title cover.)			
King 771	(M)	**Night Train** (White label promo)	1961	650.00	1,300.00
King 771	(M)	**Night Train**	1961	150.00	300.00
King 771	(M)	**Twist Around**	1962	100.00	250.00
King 771	(M)	**Jump Around**	1963	80.00	200.00
King KS-771	(S)	**Jump Around**	1963	150.00	300.00
		(King 771 with its three different titles is a various artists album			
		featuring JB on the cover and is considered part of his oeuvre.)			
King 780	(M)	**Shout And Shimmy** (White label promo)	1962	600.00	1,200.00
King 780	(M)	**Shout And Shimmy**	1962	100.00	250.00
		(The covers and labels for King 780 read "Shout And Shimmy."			
		Original covers may contain later pressing records.)			
King 780	(M)	**Good Good Twistin'**	196?	80.00	200.00
		("Good Good Twistin'" is a repackage of "Shout And Shimmy.")			
King 780	(M)	**Excitement**	196?	60.00	150.00
		("Excitement" is a repackage of "Shout And Shimmy.")			
King 804	(M)	**James Brown & His Famous Flames**			
		Tour The U.S.A. (White label promo)	1962	600.00	1,200.00
King 804	(M)	**James Brown & His Famous Flames**			
		Tour The U.S.A.	1962	100.00	250.00
King 826	(M)	**Live At The Apollo!** (White label promo)	1963	400.00	800.00
		(White label promos of King 826 are specially banded for air-play.)			
King 826	(M)	**Live At The Apollo!**	1963	80.00	200.00
King KS-826	(S)	**Live At The Apollo!**	1963	150.00	300.00
		(Original pressings for King 826 have custom back covers.)			
King 826	(M)	**Live At The Apollo!**	1963	60.00	150.00
King KS-826	(S)	**Live At The Apollo!**	1963	80.00	200.00
		(Later covers have house ads for other King albums on the back.)			
King 851	(M)	**Prisoner Of Love**	1963	80.00	200.00
		(Original pressings for King 851 have custom back covers.)			
King 851	(M)	**Prisoner Of Love**	1963	40.00	100.00
		(Later covers have house ads for other King albums on the back.)			
King 883	(M)	**Pure Dynamite! Live At The Royal** (Promo)	1964	400.00	800.00
		(White label promos of King 883 are specially banded for air-play.)			
King 883	(M)	**Pure Dynamite! Live At The Royal**	1964	80.00	200.00
King 909	(M)	**Please Please Please**	1964	40.00	100.00
King 919	(M)	**The Unbeatable James Brown— 16 Hits**	1964	40.00	100.00
		(King 919 is a reissue of 635.)			
King 938	(M)	**Papa's Got A Brand New Bag** (Red cover)	1965	30.00	75.00
King LPS-938	(P)	**Papa's Got A Brand New Bag** (Red cover)	1965	40.00	100.00
King 938	(M)	**Papa's Got A Brand New Bag** (Green cover)	1966	20.00	50.00
King LPS-938	(P)	**Papa's Got A Brand New Bag** (Green cover)	1966	30.00	75.00
King 946	(M)	**I Got You (I Feel Good)**	1966	40.00	100.00
King KSD-946	(S)	**I Got You (I Feel Good)**	1966	60.00	150.00
King 961	(M)	**Mighty Instrumentals**	1966	40.00	100.00
		—King mono albums above have crownless black labels; stereo albums have crownless blue labels.			
		The logo on the covers have a crown with "King" in open capital block letters below.—			
King 683	(M)	**Think!** (JB cover)	1966	20.00	50.00
King KSD-683	(E)	**Think!** (JB cover)	1966	16.00	40.00
King 743	(M)	**The Amazing James Brown**	1966	250.00	500.00
		(The second press cover has "James Brown" in large letters.)			
King 780	(M)	**Excitement**	1966	20.00	50.00
King KS-780	(E)	**Excitement**	1966	20.00	50.00
King 804	(M)	**James Brown & His Famous Flames**			
		Tour The U.S.A.	1966	20.00	50.00
King KS-804	(E)	**James Brown & His Famous Flames**			
		Tour The U.S.A.	1966	16.00	40.00
King 826	(M)	**Live At The Apollo!**	1966	20.00	50.00
King KS-826	(S)	**Live At The Apollo!**	1966	30.00	75.00
King 851	(M)	**Prisoner Of Love**	1966	20.00	50.00
King KS-851	(E)	**Prisoner Of Love**	1966	16.00	40.00
King 883	(M)	**Pure Dynamite! Live At The Royal**	1966	20.00	50.00
King KS-883	(E)	**Pure Dynamite! Live At The Royal**	1966	16.00	40.00
King 909	(M)	**Please Please Please**	1966	20.00	50.00
King KS-909	(E)	**Please Please Please**	1966	16.00	40.00
King 919	(M)	**The Unbeatable James Brown— 16 Hits**	1966	20.00	50.00
King KS-919	(E)	**The Unbeatable James Brown— 16 Hits**	1966	16.00	40.00
King 938	(M)	**Papa's Got A Brand New Bag**	1966	16.00	40.00
King LPS-938	(P)	**Papa's Got A Brand New Bag**	1966	20.00	50.00
King 946	(M)	**I Got You (I Feel Good)**	1966	16.00	40.00
King KSD-946	(S)	**I Got You (I Feel Good)**	1966	20.00	50.00

Label & Catalog #		Title	Year	VG+	NM
King 985	(M)	It's A Man's Man's Man's World	1966	20.00	50.00
King KS-985	(S)	It's A Man's Man's Man's World	1966	30.00	75.00
King 1010	(M)	Christmas Songs	1966	40.00	100.00
King KS-1010	(S)	Christmas Songs	1966	60.00	150.00
		(Original pressings of King 1010 have a wreath on a gray wall on the front cover and no titles on the back cover.)			
King 1010	(M)	Christmas Songs	1967	30.00	75.00
King KS-1010	(S)	Christmas Songs	1967	40.00	100.00
		(Later pressings have a wreath on a white wall on the front cover with titles on the back cover.)			
King 1016	(M)	Raw Soul	1967	20.00	50.00
King KS-1016	(P)	Raw Soul	1967	30.00	75.00
King 1018	(M)	Live At The Garden	1967	200.00	400.00
		(Black label promo banded for air-play.)			
King 1018	(M)	Live At The Garden	1967	30.00	75.00
King KS-1018	(S)	Live At The Garden	1967	40.00	100.00
King K-1020	(M)	Cold Sweat	1967	20.00	50.00
King KS-1020	(P)	Cold Sweat	1967	30.00	75.00
King KS-1022	(S)	Live At The Apollo, Vol. 2 (2 LPs)	1968	30.00	75.00
King KS-1024	(S)	JB Presents His Show Of Tomorrow	1968	20.00	50.00
		(King 1024 is actually a various artists album.)			
King KS-1030	(S)	I Can't Stand Myself (When You Touch Me)	1968	20.00	50.00
King KS-1031	(S)	I Got The Feelin'	1968	20.00	50.00
King KS-1034	(S)	JB Plays Nothing But Soul	1968	20.00	50.00
King KS-1038	(S)	Thinking About Little Willie John And A Few Nice Things	1968	20.00	50.00
King KS-1040	(S)	A Soulful Christmas	1968	30.00	75.00
King KS-1047	(S)	Say It Loud—I'm Black And I'm Proud	1969	20.00	50.00
King KS-1051	(S)	Gettin' Down To It	1969	20.00	50.00
—King mono albums above have black labels with a crown on top; stereo albums have blue or red labels with a crown on top. The covers have a crown with "King" in open capital block letters.—					
King KSD-1055	(S)	The Popcorn	1969	16.00	40.00
King KS-1063	(S)	It's A Mother	1969	20.00	50.00
King KSD-1092	(S)	Ain't It Funky	1970	16.00	40.00
King KS-1095	(S)	It's A New Day—Let A Man Come In	1970	24.00	60.00
King KS-1100	(S)	Soul On Top	1970	16.00	40.00
King KSD-1110	(S)	Sho Is Funky Down Here	1971	16.00	40.00
King KSD-1115	(S)	Sex Machine (2 LPs)	1970	20.00	50.00
King KSD-1124	(S)	Hey, America!	1970	20.00	50.00
King KS-1127	(S)	Super Bad	1971	16.00	40.00
Smash MGS-27054	(M)	Showtime	1964	12.00	30.00
Smash SRS-67054	(S)	Showtime	1964	16.00	40.00
Smash MGS-27057	(M)	Grits And Soul	1965	12.00	30.00
Smash SRS-67057	(S)	Grits And Soul	1965	16.00	40.00
Smash MGS-27058	(S)	Out Of Sight	1965	40.00	100.00
Smash SRS-67058	(S)	Out Of Sight	1965	60.00	150.00
		(Smash 2/67058 was deleted shortly after release.)			
Smash MGS-27072	(M)	JB Plays JB Today And Yesterday	1965	12.00	30.00
Smash SRS-67072	(S)	JB Plays JB Today And Yesterday	1965	16.00	40.00
Smash MGS-27080	(M)	JB Plays New Breed—The Boo-Ga-Loo	1966	12.00	30.00
Smash MGS-67080	(S)	JB Plays New Breed—The Boo-Ga-Loo	1966	16.00	40.00
Smash MGS-27084	(M)	Handful Of Soul	1966	12.00	30.00
Smash SRS-67084	(S)	Handful Of Soul	1966	16.00	40.00
Smash MGS-27087	(M)	The James Brown Show	1967	12.00	30.00
Smash SRS-67087	(S)	The James Brown Show	1967	16.00	40.00
		("The JB Show" is a various artists album.)			
Smash MGS-27093	(M)	JB Plays The Real Thing	1967	12.00	30.00
Smash SRS-67093	(S)	JB Plays The Real Thing	1967	16.00	40.00
Smash SRS-67109	(S)	James Brown Sings Out Of Sight	1968	12.00	30.00
		(Smash 67109 is a reissue of 67058 minus one track.)			
Mercury SMX-7083	(S)	Soulful James Brown	197?	30.00	75.00
Polydor PD-4054	(S)	Hot Pants	1971	16.00	40.00
Polydor PD2-3003	(S)	Revolution Of The Mind / Live At The Apollo, Vol. III (2 LPs)	1971	30.00	75.00
Polydor PD-5028	(S)	There It Is	1972	16.00	40.00
Polydor PD-5401	(S)	Soul Classics	1972	10.00	25.00
Polydor PD2-3004	(S)	Get On The Good Foot (2 LPs)	1972	30.00	75.00
Polydor PD1-6014	(S)	Black Caesar	1973	24.00	60.00
Polydor PD1-6015	(S)	Slaughter's Big Rip Off	1973	20.00	50.00
Polydor PD-5402	(S)	Soul Classics, Volume 2	1973	10.00	25.00
Polydor PD2-3007	(S)	The Payback (2 LPs)	1974	20.00	50.00
Polydor PD2-9001	(S)	Hell (2 LPs)	1974	30.00	75.00
Polydor PD1-6039	(S)	Reality	1975	16.00	40.00
Polydor PD1-6042	(S)	Sex Machine Today	1975	16.00	40.00
Polydor PD1-6054	(S)	Everybody's Doin' The Hustle & Dead On The Double Bump	1975	16.00	40.00
Polydor PD2-6059	(S)	Hot	1976	16.00	40.00
Polydor PD2-9004	(S)	Sex Machine Live (2 LPs)	1976	20.00	50.00
Polydor PD1-6071	(S)	Get Up Offa That Thing	1976	16.00	40.00

Label & Catalog #		Title	Year	VG+	NM
Polydor PD1-6093	(S)	Bodyheat	1976	16.00	40.00
Polydor PD1-6111	(S)	Mutha's Nature	1977	16.00	40.00
Polydor PD1-6140	(S)	Jam 1980s	1973	16.00	40.00
HRB 1004	(S)	The Fabulous James Brown (2 LPs)	1978	10.00	25.00
Polydor PD1-6181	(S)	Take A Look At Those Cakes	1979	12.00	30.00
Polydor PD1-6212	(S)	The Original Disco Man	1979	10.00	25.00
Polydor PD1-6258	(S)	People	1980	12.00	30.00
Polydor PD2-6290	(S)	Live—Hot On The One (2 LPs)	1980	20.00	50.00
Polydor PD1-6318	(S)	Nonstop!	1981	12.00	30.00
Polydor PD-6340	(S)	The Best Of James Brown	1981	8.00	20.00
Polydor 422-821231	(S)	Ain't That A Groove—The JB Story 1966-69	1984	6.00	15.00
Polydor 422-821232	(S)	Doing It To Death—The JB Story 1970-73	1984	6.00	15.00
Polydor 422-827439	(S)	Dead On The Heavy Funk 1974-76	1985	6.00	15.00
Solid Smoke SS-8006	(M)	Live & Lowdown At The Apollo	1981	4.00	10.00
		(Solid Smoke 8006 is a reissue of King 826.)			
Solid Smoke SS-8013	(M)	Can Your Heart Stand It?	1981	4.00	10.00
Solid Smoke SS-8023	(M)	The Federal Years, Part 1	1984	4.00	10.00
Solid Smoke SS-8024	(M)	The Federal Years, Part 2	1984	4.00	10.00

BROWN, MAXINE
Maxine Brown also recorded with Chuck Jackson.

Wand WD-656	(M)	The Fabulous Sound Of Maxine Brown	1963	20.00	50.00
Wand WDS-656	(S)	The Fabulous Sound Of Maxine Brown	1963	24.00	60.00
Wand WD-663	(M)	Spotlight On Maxine Brown	1965	12.00	30.00
Wand WDS-663	(S)	Spotlight On Maxine Brown	1965	16.00	40.00
Wand WD-684	(M)	Maxine Brown's Greatest Hits	1967	8.00	20.00
Wand WDS-684	(P)	Maxine Brown's Greatest Hits	1967	10.00	25.00
Guest Star GS-1911	(M)	Maxine Brown	196?	4.00	10.00
Guest Star GS-1911	(E)	Maxine Brown	196?	1.00	5.00
Common. United 6001	(S)	We'll Cry Together	1969	6.00	15.00

BROWN, MAXINE / IRMA THOMAS

Grand Prix K-426	(M)	Maxine Brown And Irma Thomas	1964	4.00	10.00
Grand Prix KS-426	(E)	Maxine Brown And Irma Thomas	1964	1.00	5.00

BROWN, NAPPY

Savoy MG-14002	(M)	Nappy Brown Sings	1958	200.00	400.00
Savoy MG-14025	(M)	The Right Time	1960	100.00	250.00
Savoy 14427	(S)	Nappy Brown	1977	4.00	10.00

BROWN, ODELL

Cadet LPS-823	(S)	Odell Brown Plays Otis Redding	1969	6.00	15.00

BROWN, ROY

King 956	(M)	Roy Brown Sings 24 Hits	1966	20.00	50.00
King KS-956	(E)	Roy Brown Sings 24 Hits	1966	20.00	50.00
BluesWay BLS-6019	(S)	The Blues Are Brown	1968	10.00	25.00
BluesWay BLS-6056	(S)	Hard Times	197?	10.00	25.00
King KS-1130	(M)	Hard Luck Blues	1971	10.00	25.00
Epic BG-30473	(S)	Live At Monterey	1971	10.00	25.00
Solid Smoke 8009	(M)	San Francisco Blues Festival, Vol. 1	1984	1.00	5.00

BROWN, ROY / WYNONIE HARRIS

King 607	(M)	Battle Of The Blues, Volume 1	1958	250.00	500.00
King 627	(M)	Battle Of The Blues, Volume 2	1959	400.00	750.00

BROWN, ROY / WYNONIE HARRIS / EDDIE VINSON

King 668	(M)	Battle Of The Blues, Volume 4	1960	See note below	
		(Rare with a suggested NM value of $2,000-4,000.)			

BROWN, RUTH

Atlantic ALS-115	(10")	Ruth Brown Sings Favorites	1952	Unreleased	
Atlantic 8004	(M)	Ruth Brown	1957	150.00	300.00
Atlantic 8026	(M)	Miss Rhythm	1959	150.00	300.00
Atlantic 1308	(M)	Late Date With Ruth Brown	1959	150.00	300.00
Atlantic SD-1308	(S)	Late Date With Ruth Brown	1959	200.00	400.00
		—Atlantic mono albums above have black labels; stereo albums have green labels.—			
Atlantic 8004	(M)	Ruth Brown	1960	100.00	250.00
Atlantic 8026	(M)	Miss Rhythm	1960	100.00	250.00
		—Atlantic mono albums above have white "bullseye" labels.—			
Atlantic 8004	(M)	Ruth Brown	196?	20.00	50.00
Atlantic 8026	(M)	Miss Rhythm	196?	20.00	50.00
Atlantic 1308	(M)	Late Date With Ruth Brown	196?	20.00	50.00
Atlantic SD-1308	(S)	Late Date With Ruth Brown	196?	30.00	75.00
		—Atlantic albums above have multi-colored labels with the "fan" logo on the right side.—			
Atlantic 8080	(M)	The Best Of Ruth Brown	1963	16.00	40.00
Philips PHM-200-028	(M)	Along Comes Ruth	1962	16.00	40.00
Philips PHS-600-028	(S)	Along Comes Ruth	1962	20.00	50.00

Label & Catalog #		Title	Year	VG+	NM
Philips PH-200-055	(M)	Gospel Time	1962	12.00	30.00
Philips PHS-600-055	(S)	Gospel Time	1962	16.00	40.00
Mainstream 16034	(S)	Ruth Brown '65	1965	10.00	25.00
Mainstream S-6034	(S)	Ruth Brown '65	1965	12.00	30.00
Skye LP-13	(S)	Black Is Brown And Brown Is Beautiful	1970	6.00	15.00
Mainstream 369	(S)	Softly	1972	1.00	5.00
Dobre 1041	(S)	You Don't Know Me	1978	1.00	5.00

BROWN, TONI
Ms Brown also recorded with Joy Of Cooking.

MCA 386	(S)	Good For You Too	1974	1.20	6.00

BROWN'S HOME BREW

Vertigo 2001	(S)	Together	1974	4.00	10.00

BROWNE, JACKSON

(No label)	(DJ)	"Jackson Browne's First Album" *(2 LPs)*	1967	1,000.00	2,000.00
		(This is a publishers demo issued in a plain cardboard jacket.)			
Asylum SD-5051	(S)	Jackson Browne *(Burlap cover)*	1972	8.00	20.00
Asylum SD-5051	(S)	Jackson Browne *(Standard cover)*	1972	4.00	10.00
		—Asylum albums above have white labels with a door-in-a-circle logo.—			
Asylum SD-5051	(S)	Jackson Browne *(Standard cover)*	1974	.80	4.00
Asylum SD-5067	(S)	For Everyman	1974	.80	4.00
Asylum 7E-1017	(S)	Late For The Sky	1974	.80	4.00
Asylum EQ-1017	(Q)	Late For The Sky	1974	12.00	30.00
Reprise RS-????	(S)	Late For The Sky *(Label misprint)*	1974	12.00	30.00
Asylum 7E-1079	(S)	The Pretender	1976	.80	4.00
Asylum 6E-113	(S)	Running On Empty	1977	.80	4.00
Asylum 5E-511	(S)	Hold Out	1980	.80	4.00
Asylum 60268	(S)	Lawyers In Love	1983	.80	4.00

BROWNSVILLE STATION [BROWNSVILLE]

Palladium P-1004	(S)	Brownsville Station	1970	12.00	30.00
Warner Bros. WS-1888	(S)	No B.S.	1970	1.00	5.00
Big Tree 2010	(S)	Night On The Town	1972	1.00	5.00
Big Tree 2102	(S)	Yeah	1973	1.00	5.00
Big Tree 89500	(S)	School Punks	1974	1.00	5.00
Big Tree 89510	(S)	Motor City Connection	1974	1.00	5.00
Private Stock 2026	(S)	Brownsville Station	1977	1.00	5.00
Epic JE-35606	(S)	Air Special *(Orange vinyl promo)*	1979	6.00	15.00
Epic JE-35606	(S)	Air Special	1979	1.00	5.00

BRUCE, JACK
Jack Bruce gained fame with Cream. Refer to Manfred Mann; John Mayall; West, Bruce & Laing.

Atco SD-33-306	(S)	Songs For A Tailor	1969	6.00	15.00
Atco SD-33-349	(S)	Things We Like	1971	6.00	15.00
Atco SD-33-365	(S)	Harmony Row	1971	6.00	15.00
Polydor PD-3505	(S)	Jack Bruce At His Best	1972	1.00	5.00
RSO SO-4805	(S)	Out Of The Storm	1974	1.00	5.00
RSO SO-3021	(S)	How's Tricks	1977	1.00	5.00
Epic JE-36827	(S)	I've Always Wanted To Do This	1980	1.00	5.00
Chrysalis 1352	(S)	Truce	1982	1.00	5.00

BRUNSON, FRANKIE

Gee G-704	(M)	Big Daddy's Blues	1960	30.00	75.00
Gee SG-704	(S)	Big Daddy's Blues	1960	60.00	150.00

BRUTE FORCE

Columbia CL-2615	(M)	I, Brute Force—Confections Of Love	1967	8.00	20.00
Columbia CS-9415	(M)	I, Brute Force—Confections Of Love	1967	10.00	25.00
B.T. Puppy BTPS-1015	(S)	Extemporaneous	1971	1,000.00	2,000.00

BRUTE FORCE

Embryo 522	(S)	Brute Force	1970	6.00	15.00

BRYANT, BROWNING

Dot DLP-25968	(S)	Patches	1969	6.00	15.00
RCA Victor LSP-4356	(S)	One Time In A Million	1970	4.00	10.00
Reprise MS-2191	(S)	Browning Bryant	1974	3.20	8.00

BUBBLE GUM MACHINE, THE

Senate 1002	(M)	The Bubble Gum Machine	1967	10.00	25.00
Senate 21002	(S)	The Bubble Gum Machine	1967	12.00	30.00

BUBBLE PUPPY
Bubble Puppy later recorded as Demian and as Sirius.

International Arts. 10	(S)	A Gathering Of Promises	1969	30.00	75.00
International Arts. 10	(S)	A Gathering Of Promises	1979	10.00	25.00
		(Reissues have "Masterfonics" stamped in the trail-off vinyl.)			

Label & Catalog #		Title	Year	VG+	NM

BUCHANAN, ROY
Guitar deity Roy Buchanan's first album was privately pressed before being picked up by Polydor.

Polydor PD-5033	(S)	Buch & The Snake Stretchers	1972	8.00	20.00
Polydor PD-5046	(S)	Second Album	1973	8.00	20.00
Polydor PD-6020	(S)	That's What I Am Here For	1973	8.00	20.00
Polydor PD-6035	(S)	In The Beginning	1974	8.00	20.00
Polydor PD-6048	(S)	Live Stock	1975	8.00	20.00
Atlantic SD-18170	(S)	A Street Called Straight	1976	6.00	15.00
Atlantic SD-18219	(S)	Leading Zone	1977	6.00	15.00
Atlantic SD-19170	(S)	You're Not Alone	1977	6.00	15.00

BUCHANAN BROTHERS, THE
The Buchanan Brothers are Terry Cashman, Gene Pistilli and Tommy West.

| Event ES-101 | (S) | Medicine Man | 1969 | 10.00 | 25.00 |

BUCKINGHAM/NICKS
Lindsey Buckingham and Stevie Nicks. Refer to Fleetwood Mac.

| Polydor PD-5058 | (S) | Buckingham/Nicks (Gatefold cover) | 1973 | 12.00 | 30.00 |
| Polydor PD-5058 | (S) | Buckingham/Nicks (Standard cover) | 1975 | 4.00 | 10.00 |

BUCKINGHAMS, THE
The Buckinghams were Dennis Tufano, Carl Giammarese, Nick Fortuna, Jon Poulos, and Dennis Miccoli, who left after the group joined Columbia, replaced by Martin Grebb. Refer to Tufano & Giammarese.

U.S.A. 107	(M)	Kind Of A Drag	1967	300.00	600.00
		(Original monos contain "I'm A Man;" stereos are not known to exist.)			
U.S.A. 107	(M)	Kind Of A Drag	1967	12.00	30.00
U.S.A. 107	(S)	Kind Of A Drag	1967	16.00	40.00
Columbia CL-2669	(M)	Time And Charges	1967	6.00	15.00
Columbia CS-9469	(S)	Time And Charges	1967	6.00	15.00
Columbia CL-2798	(M)	Portraits	1968	6.00	15.00
Columbia CS-9598	(S)	Portraits	1968	6.00	15.00
Columbia CS-9703	(S)	In One Ear And Gone Tomorrow	1968	6.00	15.00
Columbia CS-9812	(S)	The Buckinghams' Greatest Hits	1969	4.00	10.00
		— Columbia albums above have "360 Sound" labels.—			

BUCKLEY, TIM

Elektra EKL-4004	(M)	Tim Buckley	1966	6.00	15.00
Elektra EKS-74004	(S)	Tim Buckley	1966	8.00	20.00
Elektra EKL-4018	(M)	Goodbye And Hello	1967	6.00	15.00
Elektra EKS-74018	(S)	Goodbye And Hello	1967	8.00	20.00
Elektra EKS-74045	(S)	Happy Sad	1969	6.00	15.00
Elektra EKS-74074	(S)	Lorca	1970	6.00	15.00
Straight STS-1060	(S)	Blue Afternoon	1970	12.00	30.00
Warner Bros. WS-1842	(S)	Blue Afternoon	1970	6.00	15.00
Warner Bros. WS-1881	(S)	Starsailor	1970	6.00	15.00
Warner Bros. B-2631	(S)	Greetings From L.A.	1972	6.00	15.00
		(B-2631 had a gatefold cover with a detachable postcard.)			
DiscReet 2157	(S)	Sefronia	1973	6.00	15.00
DiscReet 2201	(S)	Look At The Fool	1974	6.00	15.00
Rhino RNLP-112	(S)	The Best Of Tim Buckley	1985	1.00	5.00

BUDD, JULIE

| MGM SE-4545 | (S) | Child Of Plenty | 1968 | 4.00 | 10.00 |
| RCA Victor LSP-4622 | (S) | Julie Budd | 1971 | 4.00 | 10.00 |

BUDDIES, THE

Wing MGW-12293	(M)	The Buddies And The Compacts	1965	20.00	50.00
Wing SRW-16293	(S)	The Buddies And The Compacts	1965	30.00	75.00
Wing MGW-12306	(M)	Go Go With The Buddies	1965	20.00	50.00
Wing SRW-16306	(S)	Go Go With The Buddies	1965	30.00	75.00

BUDGIE

Kapp KS-3656	(S)	Budgie	1971	12.00	30.00
Kapp KS-3669	(S)	Squawk	1972	12.00	30.00
MCA 429	(S)	In For The Kill	1973	8.00	20.00
A&M SP-4593	(S)	If I Were Brittania, I'd Waive The Rules	1976	6.00	15.00
A&M SP-4618	(S)	Bandolier	1977	6.00	15.00
A&M SP-4675	(S)	Impeckable	1978	6.00	15.00

BUFFALO NICKEL JUGBAND, THE

| Happy Tiger 1018 | (S) | The Buffalo Nickel Jugband | 1971 | 10.00 | 25.00 |

BUFFALO SPRINGFIELD
Buffalo Springfield consisted of Steve Stills, Neil Young, Richie Furay, Dewey Martin, and Bruce Palmer, who left in 1968 and was replaced by Jim Messina. Refer to all the members and The Au Go-Go Singers.

Atco 33-200	(M)	Buffalo Springfield	1966	40.00	100.00
Atco SD-33-200	(S)	Buffalo Springfield	1966	60.00	150.00
		(Original pressings of Atco 200 included "Baby Don't Scold Me."			
		"Burned" is rechanneled on all stereo pressings of this album.)			

Label & Catalog #		Title	Year	VG+	NM
Atco 33-200-A	(M)	Buffalo Springfield	1967	16.00	40.00
Atco SD-33-200-A	(S)	Buffalo Springfield	1967	10.00	25.00
		(Second pressings contain "For What It's Worth.")			
Atco 33-226	(M)	Buffalo Springfield Again	1967	20.00	50.00
Atco SD-33-226	(S)	Buffalo Springfield Again	1967	10.00	25.00
Atco 33-256	(M)	Last Time Around (White label promo)	1968	40.00	100.00
Atco SD-33-256	(S)	Last Time Around	1968	10.00	25.00
		—Atco stereo albums above purple & brown labels.—			
Atco SD-33-200A	(S)	Buffalo Springfield	1969	1.00	5.00
Atco SD-33-226	(S)	Buffalo Springfield Again	1969	1.00	5.00
Atco SD-33-256	(S)	Last Time Around	1969	6.00	15.00
Atco 33-283	(M)	Retrospective (White label promo)	1969	20.00	50.00
Atco SD-33-283	(S)	Retrospective	1969	1.00	5.00
Atco SD-2-806	(S)	Buffalo Springfield (2 LPs)	1973	1.20	6.00
		—Atco albums above yellow labels with "Atlantic Recording Co." on the bottom.—			
Atco SD-33-283	(S)	Retrospective (Laminated cover)	1969	20.00	50.00
		—Atco stereo albums above gold & gray labels.—			

BUFFALO SPRINGFIELD / IRON BUTTERFLY

Atlantic SP-	(DJ)	Retrospective / Ball	1969	20.00	50.00
		(Sampler with one side devoted to each artist's latest album.)			

BUFFALO SPRINGFIELD / KING CURTIS

Atlantic SP-	(DJ)	Last Time Around / Sweet Soul	1968	20.00	50.00
		(Sampler with one side devoted to each artist's latest album.)			

BUFFETT, JIMMY

Barnaby Z-30093	(S)	Down To Earth	1970	12.00	30.00
Barnaby BR-6014	(S)	High Cumberland Jubilee	1972	12.00	30.00
Dunhill DS-50132	(S)	Living And Dying In 3/4 Time	1973	1.00	5.00
Dunhill DSX-50150	(S)	A White Sport Coat And A Pink Crustacean	1973	1.00	5.00
Dunhill DS-50183	(S)	A-I-A	1974	1.00	5.00
ABC D-914	(S)	Havana Daydreamin'	1976	1.00	5.00
ABC D-990	(S)	Changes In Latitude, Changes In Attitude	1977	1.00	5.00
ABC 2-1008	(S)	You Had To Be There (2 LPs)	1978	1.00	5.00
ABC AA-1046	(S)	Son Of A Son Of A Tailor	1978	1.00	5.00
ABC SPDJ-43	(DJ)	Special Jimmy Buffett Sampler	1978	6.00	15.00
MCA 37023	(S)	Havana Daydreamin'	1981	.80	4.00
MCA 37024	(S)	Son Of A Son Of A Tailor	1981	.80	4.00
MCA 37025	(S)	Living And Dying In 3/4 Time	1981	.80	4.00
MCA 37026	(S)	A White Sport Coat And A Pink Crustacean	1981	.80	4.00
MCA 37027	(S)	A-I-A	1981	.80	4.00
MCA 37150	(S)	Changes In Latitude, Changes In Attitude	1981	.80	4.00
MCA 6008	(S)	You Had To Be There (2 LPs)	1981	.80	4.00
MCA 5102	(S)	Volcano	1979	.80	4.00
MCA 5169	(S)	Coconut Telegraph	1981	.80	4.00
MCA 5285	(S)	Somewhere Over China	1982	.80	4.00

BUGALOOS, THE

Capitol SW-621	(S)	Bugaloos	1970	12.00	30.00

BUGGS, THE

Coronet CX-212	(M)	The Beetle Beat	1964	6.00	15.00
Coronet CXS-212	(S)	The Beetle Beat	1964	8.00	20.00

BUGSY

Dot DLP-25917	(S)	Bugsy	1969	4.00	10.00
Dot DLP-25945	(S)	Inside Bugsy	1969	4.00	10.00

BULL ANGUS

Mercury SRM-619	(S)	Bull Angus	1971	4.00	10.00
Mercury SRM-629	(S)	Free For All	1972	4.00	10.00

BULLDOG

Decca DL-75340	(S)	Bulldog	1972	4.00	10.00
Buddah BDS-5600	(S)	Smasher	1974	1.00	5.00

BUMBLE BEE SLIM

Pacific Jazz PJ-54	(M)	Back In Town (Yellow vinyl)	1962	20.00	50.00
Pacific Jazz PJ-54	(M)	Back In Town	1962	8.00	20.00
Pacific Jazz ST-54	(S)	Back In Town (Yellow vinyl)	1962	30.00	75.00
Pacific Jazz ST-54	(S)	Back In Town	1962	10.00	25.00

BUNCH, THE
Sandy Denny, Ashley Hutchings, Trevor Lucas, Dave Mattacks, and Richard Thompson, all of Fairport Convention.

A&M SP-4354	(S)	The Bunch	1973	10.00	25.00

BUNKY & JAKE

Mercury SR-61699	(S)	L.A.M.F.	1969	4.00	10.00

Label & Catalog #		Title	Year	VG+	NM

BUOYS, THE

Label & Catalog #		Title	Year	VG+	NM
Scepter SPS-593	(S)	Timothy	1971	10.00	25.00

BURDON, ERIC

Mr Burdon, former lead singer with The Animals, is backed by War on the two MGM albums.

MGM SE-4663	(S)	Eric Burdon Declares "War"	1970	6.00	15.00
MGM SAMP-4710	(DJ)	The Black Man's Burdon (Sampler)	1970	12.00	30.00
MGM SE-4710	(S)	The Black Man's Burdon (2 LPs)	1970	8.00	20.00
		(MGM 4710 was issued with a numbered, 7" x 3" war bond entitling the bearer to $1 off the admission of any War concert. This bond is worth an additional $5-10.)			
Capitol ST-11359	(S)	Sun Secrets	1974	4.00	10.00
Capitol ST-11426	(S)	Stop (Hexagonal cover)	1974	6.00	15.00
Capitol ST-11426	(S)	Stop (Square cover)	1975	4.00	10.00
ABC 988	(S)	Love Is All Around	1976	4.00	10.00
		(ABC 988 credits War Featuring Eric Burdon and was recorded in 1969-70.)			
LAX PW-37109	(S)	Spill The Wine	1981	1.00	5.00
		(LAX 37109 is a reissue of MGM 4663.)			
LAX PW-37110	(S)	Sun Secrets	1981	1.00	5.00
		(LAX 37110 is a reissue of Capitol 11359.)			

BURDON, ERIC, & JIMMY WITHERSPOON

MGM SE-4791	(S)	Guilty	1971	8.00	20.00

BURKE, SOLOMON

Mr Burke can also be found on the MGM soundtrack "Cool Breeze." Refer to Ray Charles / Solomon Burke.

Apollo ALP-498	(M)	Solomon Burke	1962	300.00	600.00
Kenwood LP-498	(M)	Solomon Burke	1964	100.00	250.00
		(Kenwood 498 is a reissue of Apollo 498.)			
Atlantic 8067	(M)	Solomon Burke's Greatest Hits	1962	20.00	50.00
Atlantic SD-8067	(S)	Solomon Burke's Greatest Hits	1962	30.00	75.00
Atlantic 8085	(M)	If You Need Me	1963	20.00	50.00
Atlantic SD-8085	(S)	If You Need Me	1963	30.00	75.00
Atlantic 8096	(M)	Rock 'N' Soul	1964	20.00	50.00
Atlantic SD-8096	(S)	Rock 'N' Soul	1964	30.00	75.00
Atlantic 8109	(M)	The Best Of Solomon Burke	1965	12.00	30.00
Atlantic SD-8109	(S)	The Best Of Solomon Burke	1965	16.00	40.00
Atlantic SD-8158	(S)	King Solomon	1968	10.00	25.00
Atlantic SD-8185	(S)	I Wish I Knew	1968	10.00	25.00
Clarion 607	(M)	I Almost Lost My Mind	1965	8.00	20.00
Clarion SD-607	(S)	I Almost Lost My Mind	1965	10.00	25.00
Bell 6033	(S)	Proud Mary	1969	6.00	15.00
MGM SE-4767	(S)	Electronic Magnetism	1971	6.00	15.00
MGM SE-4830	(S)	King Heavy	1972	6.00	15.00
Pride 0011	(S)	The History Of Solomon Burke	1972	6.00	15.00
ABC/Dunhill DSX-50161	(S)	I Have A Dream	1974	5.00	12.00
Chess CH-60042	(S)	Music To Make Love By	1975	5.00	12.00
Chess CH-19002	(S)	Back To My Roots	1976	5.00	12.00
Amherst AMX-1018	(S)	Please Don't You Say Goodbye To Me	1978	4.00	10.00
Infinity INF-9024	(S)	Sidewalks, Fences And Walls	1979	4.00	10.00
Savoy 14660	(S)	Solomon Burke	1981	3.20	8.00
Savoy 14679	(S)	Into My Life	1982	3.20	8.00
Savoy 14717	(S)	Take Me, Shake, Me	1983	3.20	8.00
Rounder 2042/3	(S)	Soul Alive (2 LPs)	1984	3.20	8.00

BURNETTE, J. HENRY: *Refer to* T-BONE BURNETTE

BURNETTE, DORSEY

Era EL-102	(M)	Tall Oak Tree	1960	80.00	200.00
Era ES-102	(S)	Tall Oak Tree	1960	200.00	400.00
Dot DLP-3456	(M)	Dorsey Burnette Sings	1963	16.00	40.00
Dot DLP-25456	(S)	Dorsey Burnette Sings	1963	20.00	50.00
Melody 501	(M)	Dorsey Burnette	196?	Unreleased?	
Era ES-800	(S)	Dorsey Burnette's Greatest Hits	1969	10.00	25.00
Capitol ST-11094	(S)	Here And Now	1972	6.00	15.00
Capitol ST-11219	(S)	Dorsey Burnette	1973	6.00	15.00
Gusto GTS-0050	(S)	The Golden Hits Of Dorsey Burnette	197?	1.20	6.00
Calliope 7006	(S)	Things I Treasure	1977	3.20	8.00

BURNETTE, JOHNNY, & THE ROCK 'N' ROLL TRIO

Coral CRL-57080	(M)	Johnny Burnette & The Rock 'N' Roll Trio	1956	See note below	
		(Originals have printing on the spine and "Made in USA" on the lower right back cover while counterfeits do not. Rare with a suggested NM value of $5,000-8,000.)			
Solid Smoke SS-8001	(M)	Tear It Up! (Blue vinyl)	1978	12.00	30.00
Solid Smoke SS-8001	(M)	Tear It Up!	1978	6.00	15.00
		("Tear It Up" repackages the Coral album with bonus tracks.)			
Solid Smoke SS-8005	(M)	Together Again	1978	6.00	15.00

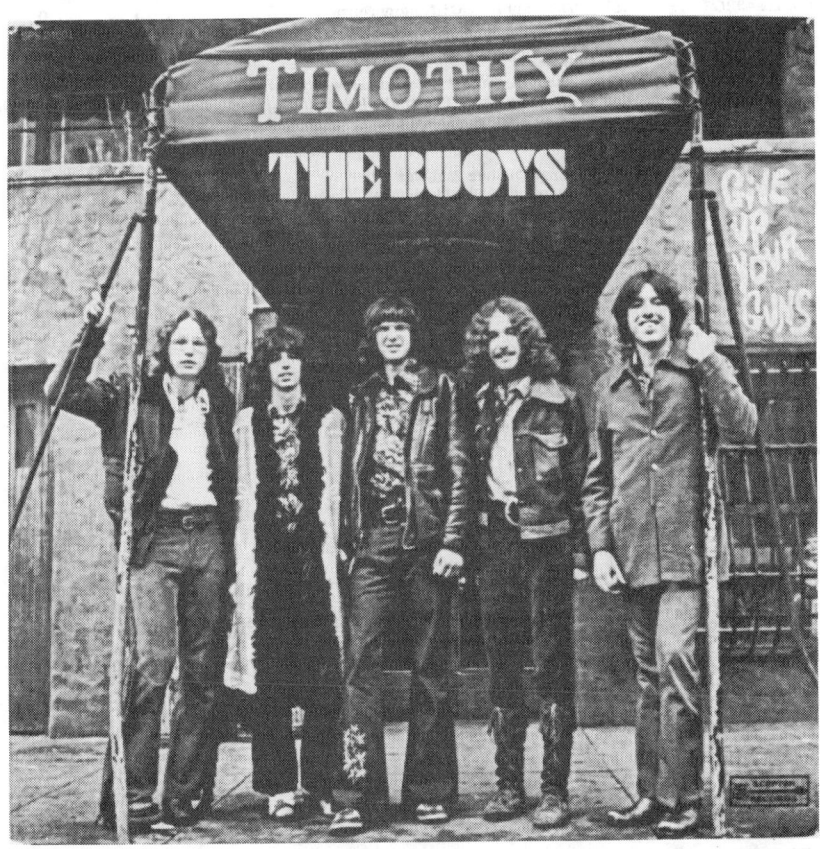

The Buoys carried the distinction of having the longest "breaking" hit single in Billboard magazine's history when "Timothy" finally scored a bullet in 1971. It then shot up to the Top 20 after months of inching its way up the nether regions of the charts. The song also enjoyed a bit of fame as the most successful song about cannibalism. The Buoys, one of the main claims to rock'n roll fame for Wilkes-Barre, PA, were unable to capitalize on the song's notoriety with succeeding releases.

Label & Catalog #		Title	Year	VG+	NM
BURNETTE, JOHNNY					
Liberty LRP-3179	(M)	Dreamin'	1960	16.00	40.00
Liberty LST-7179	(S)	Dreamin'	1960	20.00	50.00
Liberty LRP-3183	(M)	Johnny Burnette	1961	16.00	40.00
Liberty LST-7183	(S)	Johnny Burnette	1961	20.00	50.00
Liberty LRP-3190	(M)	Johnny Burnette Sings	1961	16.00	40.00
Liberty LST-7190	(S)	Johnny Burnette Sings	1961	20.00	50.00
Liberty LRP-3206	(M)	Hits And Other Favorites	1962	16.00	40.00
Liberty LST-7206	(S)	Hits And Other Favorites	1962	20.00	50.00
Liberty LRP-3255	(M)	Roses Are Red	1962	16.00	40.00
Liberty LST-7255	(S)	Roses Are Red	1962	20.00	50.00
Liberty LRP-3389	(M)	The Johnny Burnette Story	1964	16.00	40.00
Liberty LST-7389	(S)	The Johnny Burnette Story	1964	20.00	50.00
Sunset SUM-1179	(M)	Dreamin'	1967	6.00	15.00
Sunset SUS-5179	(S)	Dreamin'	1967	8.00	20.00
United Arts. LA-432G	(S)	The Very Best Of Johnny Burnette	1975	.80	4.00
BURNETTE, T-BONE					
T-Bone is a pseudonym for J. Henry Burnette.					
Uni 73125	(S)	The B-52 Band & The Fabulous Skyhawks	1972	12.00	30.00
Warner Bros. 23921	(DJ)	Proof Through The Night (Quiex II vinyl)	1983	6.00	15.00
Warner Bros. 23921	(S)	Proof Through The Night	1983	1.00	5.00
BURNS, RANDY, & THE SKY DOG BAND					
ESP-Disk' 1039S	(S)	Songs Of Love And War	1966	10.00	25.00
ESP-Disk' 1089S	(S)	Evening Of The Magician	1968	10.00	25.00
ESP-Disk' 2007	(S)	Song For An Uncertain Lady	1971	6.00	15.00
Mercury SR-61329	(S)	Randy Burns & The Skydog Band	1971	5.00	12.00
Polydor PD-5030	(S)	I'm A Lover, Not A Fool	1972	5.00	12.00
Polydor PD-5049	(S)	Still On Our Feet	1973	5.00	12.00

BURRITO BROTHERS: *Refer to FLYING BURRITO BROTHERS*

BURTON, JAMES
Guitarist Burton played with Dale Hawkins and Rick Nelson and led Elvis Presley's group from 1969 through 1977. Refer to Longbranch Pennywhistle; Ralph Mooney.

A&M SP-4293	(S)	James Burton	1971	10.00	25.00

BUSH

Dunhill DS-50086	(S)	Bush	1970	4.00	10.00

BUSH, KATE
Refer to Jimi Hendrix.

Harvest SW-11761	(S)	The Kick Inside	1978	10.00	25.00
EMI SSA-3020	(DJ)	Self Portrait/The Kate Bush Radio Special	1979	40.00	100.00
Steve Strout SSA-3020	(DJ)	Kate Bush Interview Album	1982	60.00	150.00
		(EMI issued this promo inside regular covers for "The Kick Inside." A special wrapper around the jacket identifies the contents as a special interview album. Includes a note to DJs.)			
EMI SW-17003	(S)	The Kick Inside	1982	4.00	10.00
EMI SW-17084	(S)	The Dreaming	1982	1.00	5.00
EMI ST-19004	(S)	Kate Bush	1983	1.00	5.00
EMI ST-17171	(DJ)	Hounds Of Love Folder	1986	40.00	100.00
		(Promo in 13" x 13" folder with press kit, etc.)			
EMI ST-17171	(DJ)	Hounds Of Love (Marble vinyl)	1986	12.00	30.00
EMI ST-17171	(S)	Hounds Of Love	1986	1.00	5.00

BUTLER, BILLY

OKeh OKM-12115	(M)	Right Track	1966	8.00	20.00
OKeh OKS-12115	(S)	Right Track	1966	10.00	25.00

BUTLER, FREDDY

Kapp KL-1519	(M)	With A Dab Of Soul	1968	10.00	25.00
Kapp KS-3519	(S)	With A Dab Of Soul	1968	14.00	35.00

BUTLER, JERRY
Jerry Butler was originally lead singer with The Impressions. Refer to The Ice Man's Band.

Abner R-2001	(M)	Jerry Butler Esquire	1959	250.00	500.00
Vee Jay LP-1027	(M)	Jerry Butler Esquire	1960	60.00	150.00
		(Vee Jay 1027 is a reissue of the Abner album.)			
Vee Jay LP-1029	(M)	He Will Break Your Heart	1960	40.00	100.00
Vee Jay LP-1034	(M)	Love Me	1961	20.00	50.00
		(Vee Jay 1034 is a reissue of 1027.)			
Vee Jay LP-1038	(M)	Aware Of Love	1961	14.00	35.00
Vee Jay SR-1038	(S)	Aware Of Love	1961	20.00	50.00
Vee Jay LP-1046	(M)	Moon River	1962	14.00	35.00
Vee Jay SR-1046	(S)	Moon River	1962	20.00	50.00
Vee Jay LP-1048	(M)	The Best Of Jerry Butler	1962	10.00	25.00
Vee Jay SR-1048	(P)	The Best Of Jerry Butler	1962	12.00	30.00

Ms. Bush is one of the most idiosyncratic and striking talents of the post-Beatles era. She has produced a lengthy string of hits in her native UK although her success in the States has been negligible. Her first album, The Kick Inside, was originally issued on Capitol's Harvest label (above) and then reissued on EMI-America (below), with neither having any substantial chart success.

Label & Catalog #		Title	Year	VG+	NM
Vee Jay LP-1057	(M)	Folk Songs	1963	10.00	25.00
Vee Jay SR-1057	(S)	Folk Songs	1963	12.00	30.00
Vee Jay LP-1075	(M)	For Your Precious Love	1963	10.00	25.00
Vee Jay VJS-1075	(S)	For Your Precious Love	1963	12.00	30.00
Vee Jay LP-1076	(M)	Giving Up On Love/Need To Belong	1963	10.00	25.00
Vee Jay VJS-1076	(S)	Giving Up On Love/Need To Belong	1963	12.00	30.00
Vee Jay LP-1119	(M)	More Of The Best Of Jerry Butler	1965	10.00	25.00
Vee Jay VJS-1119	(S)	More Of The Best Of Jerry Butler	1965	12.00	30.00
Vee Jay VJS-2-1003	(M)	Jerry Butler's Gold (2 LPs)	196?	6.00	15.00
Vee Jay DYS-3702	(S)	Just For You	197?	.80	4.00
Mercury MG-21005	(M)	The Soul Artistry Of Jerry Butler	1967	8.00	20.00
Mercury SR-61005	(S)	The Soul Artistry Of Jerry Butler	1967	6.00	15.00
Mercury MG-21146	(M)	Mr. Dream Merchant	1967	8.00	20.00
Mercury SR-61146	(S)	Mr. Dream Merchant	1967	6.00	15.00
Mercury SR-61151	(S)	Golden Hits Live	1968	6.00	15.00
Mercury SR-61171	(S)	The Soul Goes On	1968	6.00	15.00
Mercury SR-61198	(S)	The Ice Man Cometh	1969	6.00	15.00
Mercury SR-61234	(S)	Ice On Ice	1969	6.00	15.00
Buddah BDS-4001	(S)	The Very Best Of Jerry Butler	1969	6.00	15.00
		(Buddah 4001 repackages Vee Jay material.)			
Mercury SR-61269	(S)	You And Me	1970	5.00	12.00
Mercury SR-61281	(S)	The Best Of Jerry Butler	1970	5.00	12.00
Mercury SR-61320	(S)	Assorted Sounds	1971	4.00	10.00
Mercury SR-61347	(S)	The Sagittarius Movement	1971	4.00	10.00
Mercury SRM-7502	(S)	The Spice Of Life (2 LPs)	1972	4.00	10.00
Mercury SRM-660	(S)	Love We Have, Love We Had	1973	4.00	10.00
Mercury SRM-689	(S)	The Power Of Love	1973	4.00	10.00
Mercury SRM-006	(S)	Sweet Sixteen	1974	4.00	10.00
Kent KST-536	(S)	Just Beautiful	1968	4.00	10.00
Tradition TLP-2068	(M)	Starring Jerry Butler	196?	4.00	10.00
Sunset SUS-5216	(S)	Gift Of Love	1968	4.00	10.00
Upfront UPF-100	(S)	Souled Out	197?	8.00	4.00
Upfront UPF-107	(S)	Great Soul Hits	197?	8.00	4.00
Upfront UPF-124	(S)	All Time Hits	197?	8.00	4.00
Trip 8011	(P)	All Time Hits (2 LPs)	1971	8.00	4.00
Trip TCP-1645	(P)	16 Greatest Hits	1978	8.00	4.00
Trip X-9516	(S)	The Infinite Style Of Jerry Butler	197?	8.00	4.00
Scepter SPS-18009	(S)	The Best Of Jerry Butler	197?	8.00	4.00
Post 7000	(E)	Jerry Butler Sings	197?	4.00	10.00
Pride 0006	(S)	Melinda	197?	4.00	10.00
United Arts. LA-498E	(S)	The Very Best Of Jerry Butler	1975	8.00	4.00
Motown M6-878	(S)	Suite For The Single Girl	1977	1.00	5.00
Motown M6-887	(S)	Thelma And Jerry (With Thelma Houston)	1977	1.00	5.00
Motown M6-892	(S)	It All Comes Out In My Songs	1977	1.00	5.00
Phila. Inter. JZ-35510	(S)	Nothing Says I Love You Like I Love You	1978	1.00	5.00
Phila. Inter. JZ-36413	(S)	Best Love I Ever Had	1981	1.00	5.00
Fountain 2-82-1	(S)	Ice 'N' Hot	1982	8.00	4.00

BUTLER, JERRY, & BETTY EVERETT

Vee Jay LP-1099	(M)	Delicious Together	1964	8.00	20.00
Vee Jay VJS-1099	(S)	Delicious Together	1964	10.00	25.00
Buddah BDS-7505	(S)	Together	1969	6.00	15.00
		(Buddah 7505 is a reissue of Vee Jay 1099.)			

BUTLER, JERRY, & GENE CHANDLER

Mercury SR-61330	(S)	One & One	1971	4.00	10.00

BUTTERFIELD, PAUL [THE BUTTERFIELD BLUES BAND]
Butterfield's original band included Jerome Arnold, Elvin Bishop, Mike Bloomfield and Mark Naftalin.

Elektra EKL-294	(M)	Paul Butterfield Blues Band	1965	8.00	20.00
Elektra EKS-7294	(S)	Paul Butterfield Blues Band	1965	10.00	25.00
Elektra EKL-315	(M)	East-West	1966	8.00	20.00
Elektra EKS-7315	(S)	East-West	1966	10.00	25.00
		—Elektra albums above have gold labels.—			
Elektra EKL-294	(M)	Paul Butterfield Blues Band	1966	4.00	10.00
Elektra EKS-7294	(S)	Paul Butterfield Blues Band	1966	5.00	12.00
Elektra EKL-315	(M)	East-West	1966	4.00	10.00
Elektra EKS-7315	(S)	East-West	1966	5.00	12.00
Elektra EKL-4015	(M)	Resurrection Of Pigboy Crabshaw	1967	10.00	25.00
Elektra EKS-74015	(S)	Resurrection Of Pigboy Crabshaw	1967	6.00	15.00
Elektra EKS-74025	(S)	In My Own Dream	1968	6.00	15.00
Elektra EKS-74053	(S)	Keep On Moving	1969	6.00	15.00
		—Elektra albums above have brown labels.—			
Elektra EKS-7294	(S)	Paul Butterfield Blues Band	1970	1.00	5.00
Elektra EKS-7315	(S)	East-West	1970	1.00	5.00
Elektra EKS-74015	(S)	Resurrection Of Pigboy Crabshaw	1970	1.00	5.00
Elektra EKS-74025	(S)	In My Own Dream	1970	1.00	5.00
Elektra EKS-74053	(S)	Keep On Moving	1970	1.00	5.00
		—Elektra albums above have red labels.—			

These two lovely covers, very much a part of the psychedelic era in which they were conceived, house some truly marvelous music. The mono version of Younger Than Yesterday contains slightly different mixes, punching up the bass in particular. This is no small endorsement, as Chris Hillman's bass playing on this album ranks with the finest in rock'n roll's history, on a par with McCartney on Sgt. Pepper. And, while the hits package is just as lovely, the cover is rather unfair: Seven of the eleven tracks, including both of their #1 songs, were recorded by the five original members. Gene Clark is notably missing. . .

Label & Catalog #		Title	Year	VG+	NM
Elektra EKS-7294	(S)	**Paul Butterfield Blues Band**	197?	.80	4.00
Elektra EKS-7315	(S)	**East-West**	197?	.80	4.00
Elektra EKS-74015	(S)	**Resurrection Of Pigboy Crabshaw**	197?	.80	4.00
Elektra EKS-74025	(S)	**In My Own Dream**	197?	.80	4.00
Elektra EKS-74053	(S)	**Keep On Moving**	197?	.80	4.00
Elektra EKS-75031	(S)	**Sometimes I Just Feel Like Smilin'**	1971	3.20	8.00
Elektra 7E-2001	(S)	**Paul Butterfield Blues Band Live** (2 LPs)	1971	4.00	10.00
Elektra 7E-2005	(S)	**Golden Butter** (2 LPs)	1972	1.20	6.00
		— Elektra albums above have "butterfly" labels.—			
Red Lightnin'	(M)	**Offer You Can't Refuse**	1972	12.00	30.00
Bearsville BS-2119	(S)	**Paul Butterfield's Better Days**	1973	3.20	8.00
Bearsville BRK-6960	(S)	**Put It In Your Ear**	1975	3.20	8.00
Bearsville BRK-6995	(S)	**North-South**	1976	3.20	8.00

BUTTS BAND, THE
The BB features John Densmore and Robbie Kreiger, formerly of The Doors.

Label & Catalog #		Title	Year	VG+	NM
Blue Thumb BTS-63	(S)	**The Butts Band**	1973	4.00	10.00
Blue Thumb BTS-6018	(S)	**Hear And Now**	1975	4.00	10.00

BUX

Label & Catalog #		Title	Year	VG+	NM
Capitol ST-11459	(S)	**We Came To Play**	1976	4.00	10.00

BYRD, BOBBY
Bobby Byrd originally recorded as Bobby Day.

Label & Catalog #		Title	Year	VG+	NM
King KS-1118	(S)	**I Need Help** *(Produced by James Brown)*	1970	100.00	250.00

BYRD, JOE, & THE FIELD HIPPIES

Label & Catalog #		Title	Year	VG+	NM
Columbia MS-7317	(S)	**The American Metaphysical Circus**	1969	12.00	30.00

BYRDS, THE
The Byrds were Gene Clark, Michael Clarke, David Crosby, Chris Hillman, and Jim McGuinn, who changed his name to Roger McGuinn in '67. Clark was ousted in '66. This quartet can be found on the soundtrack for MGM's "Don't Make Waves." By the end of '67, Crosby had quit in frustration, after which Clarke left. For "Sweetheart Of The Rodeo," the members were McGuinn and Hillman with Gram Parsons and Kevin Kelly, both late of The International Submarine Band. After that, McGuinn was backed by Gene Parsons, Clarence White and John York, replaced by Skip Battin in late '69. The McGuinnbyrds can be found on the soundtracks for ABC's "Candy" and Cotillion's "Homer ." Note: "Mr. Tambourine Man," "I Knew I'd Want You," and "Turn! Turn! Turn!" are rechanneled on all stereo albums.

Label & Catalog #		Title	Year	VG+	NM
Columbia CL-2372	(M)	**Mr. Tambourine Man** *(White label promo)*	1965	80.00	200.00
Columbia CL-2372	(M)	**Mr. Tambourine Man**	1965	20.00	50.00
		— Columbia albums above have "Guaranteed High Fidelity" labels.—			
Columbia CL-2372	(M)	**Mr. Tambourine Man**	1965	12.00	30.00
Columbia CS-9172	(S)	**Mr. Tambourine Man**	1965	10.00	25.00
Columbia CL-2454	(M)	**Turn! Turn! Turn!** *(White label promo)*	1965	60.00	150.00
Columbia CL-2454	(M)	**Turn! Turn! Turn!**	1965	12.00	30.00
Columbia CS-9254	(S)	**Turn! Turn! Turn!**	1965	10.00	25.00
Columbia CL-2549	(M)	**5D (Fifth Dimension)** *(White label promo)*	1966	60.00	150.00
Columbia CL-2549	(M)	**5D (Fifth Dimension)**	1966	12.00	30.00
Columbia CS-9349	(S)	**5D (Fifth Dimension)**	1966	10.00	25.00
Columbia CL-2642	(M)	**Younger Than Yesterday** *(White label promo)*	1967	40.00	100.00
Columbia CL-2642	(M)	**Younger Than Yesterday**	1967	16.00	40.00
Columbia CS-9442	(S)	**Younger Than Yesterday**	1967	10.00	25.00
Columbia CL-2716	(M)	**The Byrds' Greatest Hits** *(White label promo)*	1967	40.00	100.00
Columbia CL-2716	(M)	**The Byrds' Greatest Hits**	1967	12.00	30.00
Columbia CS-9516	(S)	**The Byrds' Greatest Hits**	1967	8.00	20.00
Columbia CL-2775	(M)	**The Notorious Byrd Brothers** *(White label promo)*	1968	40.00	100.00
Columbia CL-2775	(M)	**The Notorious Byrd Brothers**	1968	20.00	50.00
Columbia CS-9575	(S)	**The Notorious Byrd Brothers**	1968	8.00	20.00
Columbia CS-9670	(S)	**Sweetheart Of The Rodeo** *(White label promo)*	1968	40.00	100.00
Columbia CS-9670	(S)	**Sweetheart Of The Rodeo**	1968	8.00	20.00
		(Columbia 2642, 2775 and 9670 were produced by Gary Usher.)			
Columbia CS-9755	(S)	**Dr. Byrds And Mr. Hyde** *(White label promo)*	1969	20.00	50.00
Columbia CS-9755	(S)	**Dr. Byrds And Mr. Hyde**	1969	6.00	15.00
Columbia CS-9942	(S)	**Ballad Of Easy Rider** *(White label promo)*	1969	20.00	50.00
Columbia CS-9942	(S)	**Ballad Of Easy Rider**	1969	6.00	15.00
		— Columbia albums above have "360 Sound" labels.—			
Together ST-1-1001	(S)	**Preflyte**	1969	10.00	25.00
		(Together 1001 collects the group's demo tapes from late 1964.)			
Columbia CS-9172	(S)	**Mr. Tambourine Man**	1970	1.00	5.00
Columbia PC-9172	(S)	**Mr. Tambourine Man**	197?	.80	4.00
Columbia CS-9254	(S)	**Turn! Turn! Turn!**	1970	1.00	5.00
Columbia PC-9254	(S)	**Turn! Turn! Turn!**	197?	.80	4.00
Columbia CS-9349	(S)	**5D (Fifth Dimension)**	1970	1.00	5.00
Columbia PC-9349	(S)	**5D (Fifth Dimension)**	197?	.80	4.00
Columbia CS-9442	(S)	**Younger Than Yesterday**	1970	1.00	5.00
Columbia PC-9442	(S)	**Younger Than Yesterday**	197?	.80	4.00
Columbia CS-9516	(S)	**The Byrds' Greatest Hits**	1970	1.00	5.00
Columbia PC-9516	(S)	**The Byrds' Greatest Hits**	197?	.80	4.00
Columbia CS-9575	(S)	**The Notorious Byrd Brothers**	1970	1.00	5.00
Columbia PC-9575	(S)	**The Notorious Byrd Brothers**	197?	.80	4.00

Label & Catalog #		Title	Year	VG+	NM
Columbia CS-9670	(S)	Sweetheart Of The Rodeo	1970	1.00	5.00
Columbia PC-9670	(S)	Sweetheart Of The Rodeo	197?	.80	4.00
Columbia CS-9755	(S)	Dr. Byrds And Mr. Hyde	1970	1.00	5.00
Columbia PC-9755	(S)	Dr. Byrds And Mr. Hyde	197?	.80	4.00
Columbia CS-9942	(S)	The Ballad Of Easy Rider	1970	1.00	5.00
Columbia PC-9942	(S)	The Ballad Of Easy Rider	197?	.80	4.00
Columbia G-30127	(S)	Untitled (2 LPs)	1970	6.00	15.00
		(Originals list "Kathleen" as a song on the back cover.)			
Columbia G-30127	(S)	Untitled (2 LPs)	1970	1.20	6.00
		(Later pressings correctly delete "Kathleen" from the back cover.)			
Columbia KC-30640	(S)	Byrdmaniax	1971	3.20	8.00
Columbia KC-31050	(S)	Farther Along	1971	3.20	8.00
Columbia KC-31795	(S)	The Best Of The Byrds, Volume 2	1972	1.20	6.00
Columbia KC-32183	(S)	Preflyte	1973	3.20	8.00
Columbia OC-32183	(S)	Preflyte	197?	1.00	5.00
Columbia PC-32183	(S)	Preflyte	197?	1.00	5.00
		(Columbia 32183 is a reissue of Together 1001)			
Columbia CG-33645	(S)	Mr. Tambourine Man /			
		Turn! Turn! Turn! (2 LP. White label promo)	1974	8.00	20.00
Columbia CG-33645	(S)	Mr. Tambourine Man / Turn! Turn! Turn! (2 LPs)	1974	1.20	6.00
Columbia PC-36293	(S)	The Byrds Play Dylan	1980	1.00	5.00
Columbia FC-37335	(M)	The Original Singles, Volume 1	1981	1.00	5.00
Asylum SD-5058	(S)	The Byrds (White label promo)	1973	8.00	20.00
Asylum SD-5058	(S)	The Byrds	1973	3.20	8.00
Pair PL1-7598	(S)	The Very Best Of The Byrds	197?	1.20	6.00
Re-Flyte MH-70318	(S)	Never Before	1988	1.20	6.00
Rhino R1-70244	(S)	In The Beginning	198?	1.20	6.00
		("Beginning" is a collection of alternate demos recorded in 1964 at World Pacific Studios.)			

BYZANTIUM

Label & Catalog #		Title	Year	VG+	NM
Warner Bros. B-2659	(S)	Byzantium	1973	4.00	10.00

C. C. S.

Rak KZ-30559	(S)	Whole Lotta Love	1971	12.00	30.00
Rak KZ-31569	(S)	C. C. S.	1972	12.00	30.00

C. K. STRONG

Epic BN-26473	(S)	C. K. Strong	1969	8.00	20.00

CACTUS

Cactus features Carmen Appice and Tim Bogert, both formerly of Vanilla Fudge.

Atco SD-33-340	(S)	Cactus	1970	6.00	15.00
Atco SD-33-356	(S)	One Way... Or Another	1970	6.00	15.00
Atco SD-33-337	(S)	Restrictions	1971	6.00	15.00
Atco SD-36-7011	(S)	'Ot 'N' Sweaty	1972	6.00	15.00

CADETS, THE

The Cadets also recorded as The Jacks. Refer to Aaron Collins.

Modern LPM-1215	(M)	Rockin' 'N' Reelin	1956	Unreleased	
Crown CLP-5015	(M)	Rockin' 'N' Reelin	1957	200.00	400.00
		(Crown 5015 is a reissue of the unreleased Modern 1215.)			
		—Crown albums above have black labels with a silver "Crown" on top.—			
Crown CLP-5370	(M)	The Cadets	1963	60.00	150.00
Crown CST-370	(E)	The Cadets	1963	50.00	100.00
		(Crown 5370 is a reissue of 5015.)			
		—Crown albums above have gray labels.—			
United US-7799	(E)	Rock 'N' Roll Hits Of The '50's	197?	8.00	20.00
Relic 5025	(M)	The Cadets' Greatest Hits	197?	1.00	5.00

CADILLACS, THE

Jubilee JGM-1045	(M)	The Fabulous Cadillacs	1957	250.00	500.00
		—Jubilee albums above have blue labels.—			
Jubilee JGM-1045	(M)	The Fabulous Cadillacs	1959	100.00	250.00
Jubilee JGM-1089	(M)	The Crazy Cadillacs	1959	150.00	300.00
		—Jubilee albums above have flat black labels.—			
Jubilee JGM-1045	(M)	The Fabulous Cadillacs	1960	40.00	100.00
Jubilee JGM-1089	(M)	The Crazy Cadillacs	1960	40.00	100.00
Jubilee JGM-5009	(M)	Twisting With The Cadillacs	1962	150.00	300.00
		—Jubilee albums above have glossy black labels.—			
Harlem Hit Parade 5009	(M)	Crusin' With The Cadillacs	197?	1.00	5.00

CADILLACS, THE / THE ORIOLES

Jubilee JGM-1117	(M)	The Cadillacs Meet The Orioles	1961	100.00	250.00

CAKE, THE

Decca DL-4927	(M)	The Cake	1967	8.00	20.00
Decca DL-74927	(S)	The Cake	1967	10.00	25.00
Decca DL-75039	(S)	A Slice Of The Cake	1968	10.00	25.00

CALDWELL, LOUISE HARRISON

Louise Harrison Caldwell is the sister of Beatle George.

Recar 2012	(M)	Louise Caldwell Harrison Answers Questions All About The Beatles *(With insert)*	1965	80.00	200.00
Recar 2012	(M)	Louise Caldwell Harrison Answers Questions All About The Beatles *(Without insert)*	1965	60.00	150.00

CALE, J.J.

J.J. Cale originally recorded with The Leathercoated Minds.

Shelter SW-8908	(S)	Naturally... J.J. Cale	1971	4.00	10.00
Shelter SW-8912	(S)	Really J.J. Cale	1971	4.00	10.00
Shelter SW-2107	(S)	Okie	1974	1.00	5.00
Shelter SW-2122	(S)	Naturally... J.J. Cale	1974	1.00	5.00
Shelter SW-2123	(S)	Really J.J. Cale	1974	1.00	5.00
Shelter 52002	(S)	Troubadour	1976	1.00	5.00
Shelter 52009	(S)	Naturally... J.J. Cale	1976	.80	4.00
Shelter 52102	(S)	Really J.J. Cale	1976	.80	4.00
Shelter 3163	(S)	J.J. Cale 5	1979	1.00	5.00
MCA 37102	(S)	J.J. Cale 5	1981	.80	4.00

Although she only had one real hit, "(I'm The Girl From) Wolverton Mountain," Jo Ann Campbell managed several albums in her career, including All The Hits *and* I'm Nobody's Baby. *Ms. Campbell later married Troy Seals, formerly with The Champs, and the two teamed up as Jo Ann & Troy, to little success. Later, Seals formed another duo, this time with fellow ex-Champ Dash Crofts.*

Label & Catalog #		Title	Year	VG+	NM
MCA 37103	(S)	Troubadour	1981	.80	4.00
MCA 37104	(S)	Naturally... J.J. Cale	1981	.80	4.00
MCA 37105	(S)	Really J.J. Cale	1981	.80	4.00
MCA 37106	(S)	Okie	1981	.80	4.00
MCA 5158	(S)	Shades	1981	.80	4.00
Mercury SRM-1-4038	(S)	Grasshopper	1982	.80	4.00

CALE, JOHN
Cale was a member of The Velvet Underground.

Columbia CS-1037	(P)	Vintage Violence	1970	10.00	25.00
		—Columbia albums above have "360 Sound" labels.—			
Columbia CS-1037	(P)	Vintage Violence	197?	4.00	10.00
Reprise MS-2079	(S)	The Academy In Peril	1972	6.00	15.00
Reprise MS-2131	(S)	Paris, 1919	1973	3.20	8.00
Island IXP-2	(DJ)	Hear Fear *(Interview)*	1976	20.00	50.00
Spy/IRS SP-004	(DJ)	Sabotage *(Live)*	1980	10.00	25.00

CALE, JOHN, & TERRY RILEY

Columbia CS-30131	(S)	Church Of Anthrax	1971	6.00	15.00

CALIFORNIA, RANDY
Randy California was a member of Spirit.

Epic KE-31755	(S)	Kapt. Kopter & The Fabulous Twirly Birds	1972	6.00	15.00
		—Epic albums above have yellow labels.—			
Epic KE-31755	(S)	Kapt. Kopter & The Fabulous Twirly Birds	1973	1.00	5.00
		—Epic albums above have orange labels.—			
Epic KE-31755	(S)	Kapt. Kopter & The Fabulous Twirly Birds	1975	1.00	5.00
		—Epic albums above have black labels.—			

CALIFORNIA POPPY PICKERS, THE

Alshire S-51??	(S)	Sounds Of '69	1969	14.00	35.00
Alshire S-5153	(S)	Hair-Aquarius	1969	14.00	35.00
Alshire S-51??	(S)	Today's Chart Busters	1969	14.00	35.00
Alshire S-51??	(S)	Honkey Tonk Women	1969	20.00	50.00

CALLIOPE

Buddah BDS-5023	(S)	Steamed	1968	6.00	15.00

CALLIOPE
Calliope features Danny O'Keefe.

Cotillion SD-????	(S)	Calliope	1970	4.00	10.00

CAMP, HAMILTON

Elektra EKL-278	(M)	Paths Of Victory	1965	12.00	30.00
Elektra EKS-7278	(S)	Paths Of Victory	1965	16.00	40.00
Warner Bros. W-1737	(M)	Here's To You	1967	6.00	15.00
Warner Bros. WS-1737	(S)	Here's To You	1967	6.00	15.00
Warner Bros. WS-1753	(S)	Welcome To Hamilton Camp	1969	6.00	15.00

CAMPBELL, DICK

Mercury MG-21060	(M)	Dick Campbell Sings Where It's At	1966	14.00	35.00
Mercury SR-61060	(S)	Dick Campbell Sings Where It's At	1966	20.00	50.00

CAMPBELL, JO ANN
Ms Campbell can be found on the Roulette soundtrack "Hey Let's Twist."

End LP-306	(M)	I'm Nobody's Baby	1959	60.00	150.00
ABC-Paramount ABC-393	(M)	Twistin' And Listenin'	1962	40.00	100.00
ABC-Paramount ABCS-393	(S)	Twistin' And Listenin'	1962	60.00	150.00
Cameo C-1026	(M)	All The Hits Of Jo Ann Campbell	1962	20.00	50.00
Cameo SC-1026	(S)	All The Hits Of Jo Ann Campbell	1962	40.00	100.00
Coronet CX-199	(M)	Starring Jo Ann Campbell	196?	8.00	20.00
Coronet CXS-199	(E)	Starring Jo Ann Campbell	196?	5.00	12.00

CANADIAN BEADLES, THE

Tide 2005	(M)	Three Faces North	1964	20.00	50.00

CANADIAN SWEETHEARTS, THE
The Sweethearts feature Lucille Starr.

A&M LP-106	(M)	Introducing The Canadian Sweethearts	1964	8.00	20.00
A&M SP-106	(S)	Introducing The Canadian Sweethearts	1964	12.00	30.00
Epic LN-24243	(M)	Side By Side: Pop And Country	1967	6.00	15.00
Epic BN-26243	(S)	Side By Side: Pop And Country	1967	8.00	20.00

CANARIES, THE

B.T. Puppy BTS-1007	(S)	Flying High With The Canaries	1970	40.00	100.00

CANDY STORE, THE

Decca DL-75147	(S)	Turned On Christmas	1969	10.00	25.00

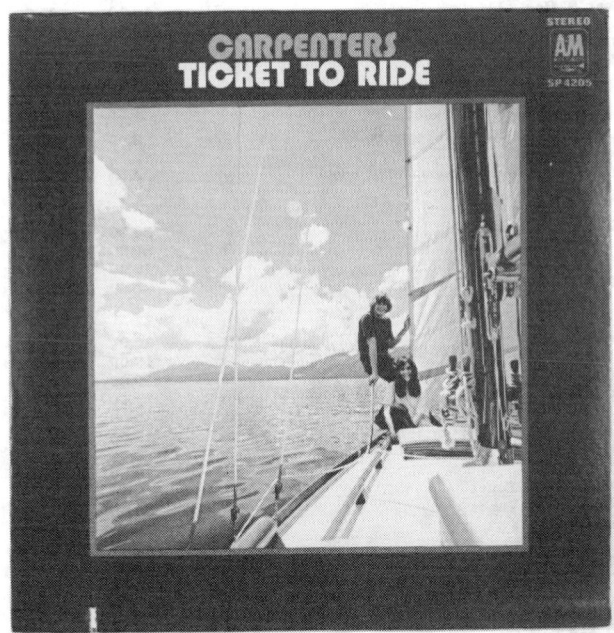

Karen and Richard Carpenter's first album, Offering, *features the siblings in '60s flower-power garb, with Ms Carpenter proffering a handful of sunflowers. After their enormous success as the purveyors of immaculately recorded pop, the album was reissued as* Ticket To Ride, *and new cover art, showing a much more relaxed, and financially secure, pair.*

Label & Catalog #		Title	Year	VG+	NM
CANDYMEN, THE					
The Candymen backed Roy Orbison on his mid-'60s recordings for Monument.					
Diplomat FM-100	(M)	The Twist	1962	5.00	12.00
Diplomat FS-100	(S)	The Twist	1962	6.00	15.00
ABC 616	(M)	The Candymen	1967	6.00	15.00
ABC S-616	(S)	The Candymen	1967	8.00	20.00
ABC S-633	(S)	The Candymen Bring You Candypower	1968	8.00	20.00
CANNED HEAT					
Liberty LRP-3526	(M)	Canned Heat	1967	8.00	20.00
Liberty LST-7526	(S)	Canned Heat	1967	10.00	25.00
Liberty LST-7541	(S)	Boogie With Canned Heat	1968	10.00	25.00
Liberty LM-1015	(S)	Boogie With Canned Heat	1980	.80	4.00
Liberty LST-7618	(S)	Hallelujah	1968	10.00	25.00
Liberty LST-27200	(S)	Living The Blues	1968	10.00	25.00
Liberty LST-11000	(S)	Cookbook (The Best Of Canned Heat)	1969	4.00	10.00
Liberty LN-10106	(S)	Cookbook (The Best Of Canned Heat)	1981	.80	4.00
Liberty LST-11002	(S)	Future Blues	1970	6.00	15.00
		("Let's Work Together" is in mono.)			
Janus JLS-3009	(S)	Vintage Heat	1969	4.00	10.00
Wand WDS-693	(S)	Live At Topanga Canyon	1970	10.00	25.00
Sunset SUS-5298	(S)	Collage	1971	4.00	10.00
Scepter CTN-18017	(S)	The Best Of Canned Heat	1971	4.00	10.00
United Arts. UAS-9955	(S)	Living The Blues (2 LPs)	1971	6.00	15.00
United Arts. UAS-5509	(S)	Live In Europe	1971	5.00	12.00
United Arts. LA-049F	(S)	New Age	1973	6.00	15.00
United Arts. LA-431E	(S)	The Very Best Of Canned Heat	1975	1.00	5.00
Atlantic SD-7239	(S)	One More River To Cross	1973	4.00	10.00
Pickwick SPS-????	(S)	Live At Topanga Canyon	197?	.80	4.00
Accord SN-7144	(S)	Captured Live	1981	.80	4.00
Rhino RNLP-71105	(S)	Infinite Boogie	1986	.80	4.00
CANNED HEAT & JOHN LEE HOOKER					
Liberty LST-35002	(S)	Hooker 'N' Heat (2 LPs)	1971	10.00	25.00
Trip TLX-3501	(S)	Boogie With Hooker And Heat	197?	1.00	5.00
		(Trip 3501 is a reissue of Liberty 35002.)			
Rhino RNLP-801	(S)	Hooker 'N' Heat (2 LPs)	1982	1.00	5.00
CANNED HEAT & LITTLE RICHARD					
United Arts. UAS-5557	(S)	Historical Figures & Ancient Heads (With comic book)	1972	6.00	15.00
United Arts. UAS-5557	(S)	Historical Figures & Ancient Heads (Without comic book)	1972	4.00	10.00
CANNIBAL & THE HEADHUNTERS					
Rampart RM-3302	(M)	Land Of 1,000 Dances	1966	20.00	50.00
Rampart RS-3302	(S)	Land Of 1,000 Dances	1966	30.00	75.00
Date TEM-3001	(M)	Land Of 1,000 Dances	1966	16.00	40.00
Date TES-3001	(S)	Land Of 1,000 Dances	1966	20.00	50.00
CANNON, ACE					
Hi HL-12007	(M)	Tuff Sax	1962	10.00	25.00
Hi SHL-32007	(S)	Tuff Sax	1962	12.00	30.00
Hi HL-12008	(M)	Looking Back	1962	10.00	25.00
Hi SHL-32008	(S)	Looking Back	1962	12.00	30.00
Hi HL-12014	(M)	The Moanin' Sax Of Ace Cannon	1963	10.00	25.00
Hi SHL-32014	(S)	The Moanin' Sax Of Ace Cannon	1963	12.00	30.00
Hi HL-12016	(M)	Aces Hi	1964	8.00	20.00
Hi SHL-32016	(S)	Aces Hi	1964	10.00	25.00
Hi HL-12019	(M)	The Great Show Tunes	1964	8.00	20.00
Hi SHL-32019	(S)	The Great Show Tunes	1964	10.00	25.00
Hi HL-12022	(M)	Christmas Cheers	1964	8.00	20.00
Hi SHL-32022	(S)	Christmas Cheers	1964	10.00	25.00
Hi HL-12025	(M)	Ace Cannon Live	1965	6.00	15.00
Hi SHL-32025	(S)	Ace Cannon Live	1965	8.00	20.00
Hi HL-12028	(M)	Nashville Hits	1965	6.00	15.00
Hi SHL-32028	(S)	Nashville Hits	1965	8.00	20.00
Hi HL-12030	(M)	Sweet And Tuff	1966	6.00	15.00
Hi SHL-32030	(S)	Sweet And Tuff	1966	8.00	20.00
Hi HL-12035	(M)	The Misty Sax Of Ace Cannon	1967	5.00	12.00
Hi SHL-32035	(S)	The Misty Sax Of Ace Cannon	1967	6.00	15.00
Hi HL-12040	(M)	Memphis' Golden Hits	1967	5.00	12.00
Hi SHL-32040	(S)	Memphis' Golden Hits	1967	6.00	15.00
Hi HL-12043	(M)	The Incomparable Sax of Ace Cannon	1968	6.00	15.00
Hi SHL-32043	(S)	The Incomparable Sax of Ace Cannon	1968	6.00	15.00
Hi HL-12046	(M)	In The Spotlight	1968	6.00	15.00
Hi SHL-32046	(S)	In The Spotlight	1968	6.00	15.00
Hi SHL-32051	(S)	The Ace Of Sax	1969	5.00	12.00
Hi SHL-32057	(S)	The Happy And Mellow Sax Of Ace Cannon	1970	4.00	10.00

Label & Catalog #		Title	Year	VG+	NM
Hi SHL-32060	(S)	Cool 'N Saxy	1971	4.00	10.00
Hi SHL-32067	(S)	Blowing Wild	1971	4.00	10.00
Hi SHL-32071	(S)	Cannon Country... Ace, That Is	1972	4.00	10.00
Hi SHL-32072/3	(S)	Aces Back To Back (2 LPs)	1972	5.00	12.00
Hi SHL-32076	(S)	Baby, Don't Get Hooked On Me	1973	4.00	10.00
Hi SHL-32080	(S)	Country Comfort	1974	4.00	10.00
Hi SHL-32086	(S)	That Music City Feeling	1974	4.00	10.00
Hi SHL-32090	(S)	Super Sax Country Style	1975	4.00	10.00
Hi SHL-32101	(S)	Peace In The Valley	1976	4.00	10.00
		—Hi albums above have silver labels.—			
Hi ACLZ-3634	(S)	The Very Best Of Ace Cannon	1975	3.20	8.00
Hi SHL-8003	(S)	Sax Man	1977	3.20	8.00
Hi SHL-8008	(S)	Cannon Country	1978	3.20	8.00
Hi SHL-6006	(S)	After Hours	1978	3.20	8.00
Gusto GTV-0061	(S)	Golden Classics	1980	3.20	8.00
Motown 5300	(S)	Memphis Gold Hits	1983	3.20	8.00

CANNON, FREDDY

Label & Catalog #		Title	Year	VG+	NM
Swan LP-502	(M)	The Explosive! Freddie Cannon	1960	80.00	200.00
Swan LPS-502	(S)	The Explosive! Freddie Cannon	1960	160.00	300.00
		("Way Down Yonder In New Orleans" and "Okefenokee" are rechanneled while "Tallahassee Lassie" was rerecorded.)			
Swan LP-504	(M)	Happy Shades Of Blue	1960	80.00	200.00
Swan LP-505	(M)	Solid Gold Hits	1961	80.00	200.00
Swan LP-507	(M)	Palisades Park	1962	80.00	200.00
Swan LP-511	(M)	Freddie Cannon Steps Out	1963	80.00	200.00
Warner Bros. W-1544	(M)	Freddie Cannon	1964	12.00	30.00
Warner Bros. WS-1544	(S)	Freddie Cannon	1964	16.00	40.00
Warner Bros. W-1612	(M)	Action!	1965	12.00	30.00
Warner Bros. WS-1612	(S)	Action!	1965	16.00	40.00
Warner Bros. W-1628	(M)	Freddie Cannon's Greatest Hits	1966	12.00	30.00
Warner Bros. WS-1628	(S)	Freddie Cannon's Greatest Hits	1966	16.00	40.00
Rhino RNLP-210	(S)	14 Blooming Hits	1982	.80	4.00

CANNON, GUS

Label & Catalog #		Title	Year	VG+	NM
Stax ST-702	(M)	Walk Right In	1962	500.00	750.00

CANYON

Label & Catalog #		Title	Year	VG+	NM
Columbia CS-1010	(S)	High Mountain	1970	4.00	10.00

CAPES & MASKS

Label & Catalog #		Title	Year	VG+	NM
Mainstream 16069	(M)	Comic Book Heroes	1966	8.00	20.00
Mainstream S-6069	(S)	Comic Book Heroes	1966	10.00	25.00

CAPITAL CITY ROCKETS

Label & Catalog #		Title	Year	VG+	NM
Elektra EKS-75059	(S)	Capital City Rockets	1973	6.00	15.00

CAPITOLS, THE

Label & Catalog #		Title	Year	VG+	NM
Atco 33-190	(M)	Dance The Cool Jerk	1966	16.00	40.00
Atco SD-33-190	(S)	Dance The Cool Jerk	1966	20.00	50.00
Atco 33-201	(M)	We Got A Thing That's In The Groove	1966	16.00	40.00
Atco SD-33-201	(S)	We Got A Thing That's In The Groove	1966	20.00	50.00
Solid Smoke 8019	(S)	The Capitols: Their Greatest Hits	1983	1.00	5.00

CAPRIS, THE

Label & Catalog #		Title	Year	VG+	NM
Ambient Sound 37714	(S)	There's A Moon Out Again	1982	5.00	12.00

CAPTAIN & TENNILLE, THE
Daryl Dragon and Toni Tenille.

Label & Catalog #		Title	Year	VG+	NM
A&M SP-3405	(S)	Love Will Keep Us Together	1975	1.00	5.00
A&M QU-54552	(Q)	Love Will Keep Us Together	1975	4.00	10.00
A&M SP-4570	(S)	Song Of Joy	1976	.80	4.00
A&M SP-4667	(S)	Greatest Hits	1977	.80	4.00
A&M SP-4700	(S)	Come In From The Rain	1977	.80	4.00
A&M SP-4707	(S)	Dream	1978	.80	4.00
Casablanca NBLP-7188	(S)	Make Your Move	1979	.80	4.00

CAPTAIN BEEFHEART & THE MAGIC BAND
Captain Beefheart is better known in the world of modern art as Don Van Vliet. The members of The Magic Band often adapted pseudonyms such as original members Jeff Cotton (also known on record as Antennae Jim Semens), Bill Harkleroad (a.k.a. Zoot Horn Rollo), and Mark Boston (a.k.a. Rockette Morton). Refer to Mallard; Frank Zappa.

Label & Catalog #		Title	Year	VG+	NM
Buddah BDM-1001	(M)	Safe As Milk (White label promo)	1967	80.00	200.00
Buddah BDM-1001	(M)	Safe As Milk	1967	24.00	60.00
Buddah BDS-5001	(S)	Safe As Milk (White label promo)	1967	80.00	200.00
Buddah BDS-5001	(S)	Safe As Milk	1967	30.00	75.00
		(Initial copies of Buddah 1/5001 were issued with a "Baby Jesus" bumper sticker, worth an additional $25.)			
Buddah BDS-5063	(S)	Safe As Milk	1969	10.00	25.00
		(BDS-5063 is a reissue of 5001.)			

Label & Catalog #		Title	Year	VG+	NM
Buddah BDS-5077	(S)	**Mirror Man** (Die-cut gatefold cover)	1971	**20.00**	**50.00**
Buddah BDS-5077	(S)	**Mirror Man** (Standard cover)	197?	**10.00**	**25.00**
Verve/Forecast FTS-3054	(S)	**Captain Beefheart & The Magic Band**	1968		Unreleased
Blue Thumb BTS-1	(S)	**Strictly Personal**	1968	**40.00**	**100.00**
		(First pressings have black labels with unbanded, continuous play tracks.)			
Blue Thumb BTS-1	(S)	**Strictly Personal**	1969	**16.00**	**40.00**
		(Second pressings have white labels with unbanded, continuous play tracks.)			
Blue Thumb BTS-1	(S)	**Strictly Personal**	197?	**10.00**	**25.00**
		(Later pressings have white labels with banded tracks.)			
Straight STS-1053	(S)	**Trout Mask Replica** (2 LPs)	1969		Unreleased?
Straight STS-2027	(S)	**Trout Mask Replica** (2 LPs white label promo)	1969	**60.00**	**150.00**
Straight STS-2027	(S)	**Trout Mask Replica** (2 LPs with lyric sheet)	1969	**30.00**	**75.00**
		(Straight 2027 was issued in a cover bearing the STS-1053 catalog number. The album was produced by Frank Zappa.)			
Reprise 2MS-2027	(S)	**Trout Mask Replica** (2 LPs)	197?	**12.00**	**30.00**
Straight RS-6420	(S)	**Lick My Decals Off, Baby** (White label)	1970	**40.00**	**100.00**
Straight RS-6420	(S)	**Lick My Decals Off, Baby**	1970	**20.00**	**50.00**
Reprise RS-6420	(S)	**Lick My Decals Off, Baby**	197?	**8.00**	**20.00**
Reprise MS-2050	(S)	**Spotlight Kid** (White label promo)	1971	**30.00**	**75.00**
Reprise MS-2050	(S)	**Spotlight Kid**	1971	**8.00**	**20.00**
Reprise MS-2115	(S)	**Clear Spot** (White label promo)	1972	**30.00**	**75.00**
Reprise MS-2115	(S)	**Clear Spot** (Issued in a clear plastic jacket)	1972	**14.00**	**35.00**
Mercury SRM-1-709	(S)	**Unconditionally Guaranteed**	1974	**4.00**	**10.00**
Mercury SRM-1-1018	(S)	**Bluejeans And Moonbeams**	1974	**8.00**	**20.00**
Warner Bros.	(DJ)	**Bat Chain Puller** (Test pressing)	1978	**200.00**	**400.00**
		(Original test pressings for "Bat Chain Puller" have different selection.)			
Warner Bros. BSK-3256	(S)	**Shiny Beast** (Bat Chain Puller)	1978	**4.00**	**10.00**
Virgin VA-13148	(S)	**Doc At The Radar Station**	1980	**4.00**	**10.00**
Virgin ARE-38274	(S)	**Ice Cream For Crow**	1982	**4.00**	**10.00**
A&M 12150	(M)	**The Legendary A&M Sessions**	1984	**1.00**	**5.00**
CAPTAIN BEEFHEART / RY COODER					
Reprise PRO-447	(DJ)	**Capt. Beefheart / Ry Cooder Interview**	1972	**200.00**	**400.00**
CAPTAIN BEYOND					
Capricorn CP-0105	(S)	**Captain Beyond** (3-D cover)	1972	**8.00**	**20.00**
Capricorn CP-0105	(S)	**Captain Beyond** (2-D cover)	1972	**4.00**	**10.00**
Capricorn CP-0115	(S)	**Sufficiently Breathless**	1973	**4.00**	**10.00**
CAPTAIN MATCHBOX WHOOPEE BAND, THE					
ESP-Disk' 3009	(S)	**Smoke Dreams**	1973	**6.00**	**15.00**
CARAVAN					
Verve/Forecast FTS-3066	(S)	**Caravan**	1969	**16.00**	**40.00**
CARAVAN, JIMMY					
Tower ST-5103	(S)	**Look Into The Flower**	1968	**8.00**	**20.00**
Vault 9007	(S)	**Hey Jude**	1969	**6.00**	**15.00**
CARAVELLES, THE					
Smash MGS-27044	(M)	**You Don't Have To Be A Baby To Cry**	1963	**30.00**	**75.00**
Smash SRS-67044	(E)	**You Don't Have To Be A Baby To Cry**	1963	**30.00**	**75.00**
CARE PACKAGE					
Liberty LST-7647	(S)	**Keep On Keepin' On**	1969	**10.00**	**25.00**
CAREFREES, THE					
London LL-3379	(M)	**From England! The Carefrees**	1964	**30.00**	**75.00**
London PS-379	(S)	**From England! The Carefrees**	1964	**40.00**	**100.00**
CARGOE					
Ardent ADS-2802	(S)	**Cargoe**	1972	**5.00**	**12.00**
CARLTON, LARRY					
Uni 73036	(S)	**With A Little Help From My Friends**	1968	**6.00**	**15.00**
CARMEN					
Epic BN-26479	(S)	**Carmen**	1969	**4.00**	**10.00**
CARMEN, ERIC					
Carmen was a member of The Raspberries.					
Arista AL-4057	(S)	**Eric Carmen** (Gold foil-like cover)	1975	**4.00**	**10.00**
Arista AL-4057	(S)	**Eric Carmen** (Plain gold cover)	1975	**1.00**	**5.00**
Arista AQ-4057	(Q)	**Eric Carmen**	1975	**6.00**	**15.00**
Arista AL-4124	(S)	**Boats Against The Current**	1977	**1.00**	**5.00**
Arista AL-4184	(S)	**Change Of Heart**	1978	**1.00**	**5.00**
Arista 9513	(S)	**Tonight You're Mine**	1980	**1.00**	**5.00**
Geffen 24042	(S)	**Eric Carmen**	1985	**1.00**	**5.00**
Arista 8547	(S)	**The Best Of Eric Carmen**	1988	**1.00**	**5.00**

Label & Catalog #		Title	Year	VG+	NM

CARNES, KIM
Refer to The Sugar Bears.

Amos 7016	(S)	Rest On Me	197?	6.00	15.00
EMI America ST-17000	(S)	Romance Dance	1980	1.00	5.00
EMI America ST-17052	(S)	Mistaken Identity	1981	1.00	5.00
EMI SPRO-9626/7	(DJ)	Kim Carnes & The Hate Boys *(Sampler)*	1981	6.00	15.00
EMI America ST-17078	(S)	Voyeur	1982	1.00	5.00
EMI America ST-17106	(S)	Cafe Racers	1983	1.00	5.00

CARNIVAL

World Pacific WPS-21894	(S)	Carnival	1969	4.00	10.00

CAROLINA SLIM

Sharp 2002	(M)	Blues From The Cotton Fields	195?	100.00	300.00

CARP
Carp features soon-to-be movie star Gary Busey.

Epic KE-30212	(S)	Carp	1970	4.00	10.00

CARPENTERS, THE
The Carpenters are siblings Karen and Richard.

A&M SP-4205	(S)	Offering	1969	16.00	40.00
A&M SP-4205	(S)	Ticket To Ride	1970	4.00	10.00
		("Ticket To Ride" is a repackage of "Offering.")			
A&M SP-4271	(S)	Close To You	1970	4.00	10.00
A&M SP-4322	(S)	Bless The Beasts And The Children	1971	4.00	10.00
A&M SP-3502	(S)	Carpenters	1971	4.00	10.00
A&M SP-3511	(S)	A Song For You	1972	4.00	10.00
A&M SP-3519	(S)	Now & Then	1973	4.00	10.00
A&M SP-3601	(S)	The Singles 1969-1973 *(Red vinyl)*	1973	250.00	500.00
A&M SP-3601	(S)	The Singles 1969-1973	1973	4.00	10.00
		—A&M albums above have brown labels.—			
A&M SP-4205	(S)	Ticket To Ride	1973	1.00	5.00
A&M SP-4271	(S)	Close To You	1973	1.00	5.00
A&M QU-54271	(Q)	Close To You	1973	6.00	15.00
A&M SP-4322	(S)	Bless The Beasts And The Children	1973	1.00	5.00
A&M SP-3502	(S)	Carpenters	1973	1.00	5.00
A&M QU-53502	(Q)	Carpenters	1973	6.00	15.00
A&M QU-53511	(S)	A Song For You	1973	1.00	5.00
A&M QU-53511	(Q)	A Song For You	1973	6.00	15.00
A&M SP-3519	(S)	Now & Then	1973	1.00	5.00
A&M QU-53519	(Q)	Now & Then	1973	6.00	15.00
A&M SP-3601	(S)	The Singles 1969-1973	1973	1.00	5.00
A&M QU-53601	(Q)	The Singles 1969-1973	1973	6.00	15.00
A&M SP-4530	(S)	Horizon	1975	1.00	5.00
A&M QU-54530	(Q)	Horizon	1975	6.00	15.00
A&M SP-4530	(S)	Horizon	1975	1.00	5.00
A&M SP-4581	(S)	A Kind Of Hush	1976	1.00	5.00
A&M SP-4703	(S)	Passage	1977	1.00	5.00
A&M SP-4726	(S)	Christmas Portrait	1978	1.00	5.00
A&M SP-3184	(S)	Close To You	198?	.80	4.00
A&M SP-3197	(S)	A Kind Of Hush	198?	.80	4.00
A&M SP-3199	(S)	Passage	198?	.80	4.00
A&M SP-3210	(S)	Christmas Portrait	198?	.80	4.00
A&M SP-3723	(S)	Made In America	1981	.80	4.00
A&M SP-4954	(S)	Voice Of The Heart	1983	.80	4.00
A&M SP-3270	(S)	An Old-Fashioned Christmas	1984	.80	4.00
Silver Eagle	(S)	Yesterday Once More *(2 LPs. TV offer)*	1984	4.00	10.00
A&M 6601	(S)	Yesterday Once More *(2 LPs)*	1985	1.00	5.00

CARR, CATHY

Fraternity 1005	(M)	Ivory Tower	1957	60.00	150.00
Dot DLP-3674	(M)	Ivory Tower	1964	10.00	25.00
Dot DLP-25674	(S)	Ivory Tower	1964	10.00	25.00

CARR, JAMES

Goldwax 3001S	(S)	You Got My Mind Messed Up	1968	80.00	200.00
Goldwax 3002S	(S)	A Man Needs A Woman	1968	80.00	200.00

CARR, LEROY

Columbia CL-1911	(M)	Blues Before Sunrise	1962	12.00	30.00
Columbia CS-8511	(E)	Blues Before Sunrise	1962	8.00	20.00
Columbia C-30496	(E)	Blues Before Sunrise	1971	1.00	5.00
Biograph C-9	(M)	Singin' The Blues	197?	4.00	10.00

CARROLL, ANDREA / BEVERLY WARREN

B.T. Puppy BP-1017	(S)	Andrea Carroll And Beverly Warren	1971	60.00	150.00

Label & Catalog #		Title	Year	VG+	NM
CARROLL BROTHERS					
Cameo C-1015	(M)	College Twist Party	1962	8.00	20.00
Cameo CS-1015	(S)	College Twist Party	1962	12.00	30.00
CARS, THE					
Elektra 6E-135	(S)	The Cars	1978	1.00	5.00
Elektra 5E-507	(S)	Candy-O	1979	1.00	5.00
Elektra 5E-514	(S)	Panorama	1980	1.00	5.00
Elektra 5E-567	(S)	Shake It Up	1981	1.00	5.00
Elektra 5E-567	(DJ)	Shake It Up (KMET FM Radio picture disc)	1981	20.00	50.00
Elektra 5E-567	(DJ)	Shake It Up (Picture disc with a blank back)	1981	16.00	40.00
Elektra 60296	(S)	Heartbeat City (Quiex II vinyl promo)	1984	6.00	15.00
Elektra 60296	(S)	Heartbeat City	1984	1.00	5.00
CARTER, CALVIN					
Vee Jay LP-1041	(M)	Twist Along With Calvin Carter	1962	40.00	100.00
Vee Jay LPS-1041	(S)	Twist Along With Calvin Carter	1962	60.00	150.00
CARTER, CLARENCE					
Atlantic SD-8192	(S)	This Is Clarence Carter	1968	16.00	40.00
Atlantic SD-8199	(S)	The Dynamic Clarence Carter	1969	16.00	40.00
Atlantic SD-8238	(S)	Testifyin'	1969	16.00	40.00
Atlantic SD-8267	(S)	Patches	1970	16.00	40.00
Atlantic SD-8282	(S)	The Best Of Clarence Carter	1971	10.00	25.00
ABC X-633	(S)	Real	1974	8.00	20.00
ABC X-943	(S)	A Heart Full Of Song	1976	8.00	20.00
Venture 1005	(S)	Let's Burn	1981	1.00	5.00
Venture 1009	(S)	Mr. Clarence Carter In Person	1981	1.00	5.00
CARTER, MEL					
Derby LPM-702	(M)	When A Boy Falls In Love	1963	250.00	500.00
CARTOONE					
Atlantic SD-8219	(S)	Cartoone	1969	6.00	15.00
CASCADES					
Valiant W-405	(M)	Rhythm Of The Rain	1963	60.00	150.00
Valiant WS-405	(S)	Rhythm Of The Rain	1963	150.00	300.00
		("Rhythm Of The Rain" is rechanneled)			
Cascade 681001	(S)	What Goes On	1968	20.00	50.00
Uni 73069	(S)	Maybe The Rain Will Fall	1969	10.00	25.00
CASEY, AL					
Stacy STM-100	(M)	Surfin' Hootenanny (Surf-colored vinyl)	1963	150.00	300.00
Stacy STMS-100	(S)	Surfin' Hootenanny (Surf-colored vinyl)	1963	200.00	400.00
CASH, ALVIN, & THE REGISTERS					
Mar-V-Lus 1827	(M)	Twine Time	196?	14.00	35.00
CASHMAN, PISTILLI & WEST					
Terry Cashman, Gene Pistilli and Tommy West, who also recorded as The Buchanan Brothers.					
ABC 629	(M)	Bound To Happen	1967	4.00	10.00
ABC S-629	(S)	Bound To Happen	1967	5.00	12.00
Capitol ST-211	(S)	Cashman, Pistilli & West	1969	4.00	10.00
Capitol ST-668	(S)	Out Of Time	1971	Released?	
CASHMAN & WEST					
Terry Cashman and Tommy West. Refer to The Chevrons.					
Dunhill SPDJ-17	(DJ)	Tale Of Two Cities—American City Suite	1972	6.00	15.00
Dunhill DS-50126	(S)	A Song Or Two	1972	3.20	8.00
Dunhill DS-50141	(S)	Moondog Serenade	1973	3.20	8.00
Dunhill DS-50179	(S)	Lifesong	1974	3.20	8.00
CASINOS, THE					
Fraternity LP-1019	(M)	Then You Can Tell Me Goodbye	1967	20.00	50.00
Fraternity LPS-1019	(S)	Then You Can Tell Me Goodbye	1967	30.00	75.00
CASSIDY, DAVID					
David was a member of The Partridge Family.					
Bell 6070	(S)	Cherish	1972	8.00	20.00
Bell 1109	(S)	Rock Me, Baby	1972	8.00	20.00
Bell 1132	(S)	Dreams Are Nothin' More Than Wishes	1973	8.00	20.00
Bell 1321	(S)	David Cassidy's Greatest Hits	1974	6.00	15.00
Bell 1312	(S)	Cassidy Live	1974	10.00	25.00
RCA Victor APL1-1066	(DJ)	The Higher They Climb... (Blue vinyl)	1975	40.00	100.00
RCA Victor APL1-1066	(S)	The Higher They Climb...	1975	6.00	15.00
RCA Victor APL1-1309	(S)	Home Is Where The Heart Is	1976	6.00	15.00
RCA Victor APL1-1852	(S)	Gettin' It In The Street	1976	16.00	40.00

Generally remembered as "soft rock" artists, Chad Stuart and Jeremy Clyde began their career recording the folk material found on their two World Artists LPs, Chad & Jeremy Sing For You and Yesterday's Gone. Because these albums were by British Invasion artists on a tiny label, it has been assumed by many dealers and at least one other price guide editor that they must be rare and, therefore, somewhat valuable. Actually, large caches of both titles, in mono and stereo, were found, once in the '70s and then again in the '80s. These finds inundated the market with factory-sealed copies, more than adequately satisfying the existing demand, which has grown little since.

Label & Catalog #		Title	Year	VG+	NM
CASTELLS, THE					
Era EL-109	(M)	**So This Is Love**	1962	60.00	150.00
Era ES-109	(S)	**So This Is Love**	1962	200.00	400.00
Collectables 5002	(S)	**Sweet Sounds**	197?	1.00	5.00
CASTOR, JIMMY					
Smash MGS-27091	(M)	**Hey Leroy!**	1967	14.00	35.00
Smash SRW-67091	(S)	**Hey Leroy!**	1967	20.00	50.00
CAT					
RCA Victor LSP-4267	(S)	**Cat**	1970	4.00	10.00
CAT MOTHER & THE ALL NIGHT NEWS BOYS					
Polydor 24-4001	(S)	**The Street Giveth And The Street Taketh Away**	1969	4.00	10.00
Polydor 24-4023	(S)	**Albion Doo-Wah**	1970	4.00	10.00
Polydor PD-5017	(S)	**Cat Mother**	1972	4.00	10.00
Polydor PD-5043	(S)	**Last Chance Dance**	1974	4.00	10.00
CATALINAS, THE					
The Catalinas feature Bruce Johnston and Terry Melcher.					
Ric M-1006	(M)	**Fun, Fun, Fun**	1964	40.00	100.00
Ric S-1006	(S)	**Fun, Fun, Fun**	1964	60.00	150.00
CATANOOGA CATS, THE					
Forward STF-1018	(S)	**The Catanooga Cats**	1969	12.00	30.00
CATAPILLA					
Vertigo 1006	(S)	**Catapilla**	1971	12.00	30.00
CATCH					
Dot DLP-25956	(S)	**Catch**	1969	4.00	10.00
CATHY JEAN & THE ROOMMATES					
Valmor 789	(M)	**At The Hop!**	1961	300.00	600.00
Valmor 78	(M)	**Great Oldies**	1962	250.00	500.00
		(Valmor 78 is a reissue of 789 with a various artists-like cover, making it difficult to identify as Cathy Jean & The Roomates.)			
CAVALIERE, FELIX					
Felix was a member of The Young Rascals/Rascals.					
Bearsville 6955	(S)	**Felix**	1974	1.00	5.00
Bearsville 6958	(S)	**Destiny**	1975	1.00	5.00
Epic 35990	(S)	**Castles In The Air**	1979	1.00	5.00
Epic AS-705	(DJ)	**Castles In The Air Sampler/Interview**	1979	8.00	20.00
CENTRAL NERVOUS SYSTEM					
Music Factory MFS-12003	(S)	**I Could Have Danced All Night**	1968	4.00	10.00
CENTURIONS, THE					
Del-Fi DFLP-1228	(M)	**Surfer's Pajama Party**	1963	40.00	100.00
Del-Fi DFST-1228	(S)	**Surfer's Pajama Party**	1963	60.00	150.00
		(This album has the same title, catalog number and cover as The Bruce Johnston Surfing Band, but plays The Centurions.)			
CESANA					
Modern M-100	(M)	**Tender Emotions**	1964	8.00	20.00
CEYLIB PEOPLE, THE					
The Ceylib People feature Ry Cooder.					
Vault LP-117	(S)	**Tanyet**	1968	16.00	40.00
CHAD & JEREMY					
Chad Stuart and Jeremy Clyde can also be found on the Sidewalk soundtrack "Three In The Attic."					
World Artists WAM-2002	(M)	**Yesterday's Gone**	1964	5.00	12.00
World Artists WAS-3002	(S)	**Yesterday's Gone**	1964	6.00	15.00
		("Yesterday's Gone" is rechanneled.)			
World Artists WAM-2005	(M)	**Chad & Jeremy Sing For You**	1965	5.00	12.00
World Artists WAS-3005	(S)	**Chad & Jeremy Sing For You**	1965	6.00	15.00
Fidu FM-101	(M)	**5 + 10 = 15 Fabulous Hits**	1966	3.20	8.00
Fidu FS-101	(P)	**5 + 10 = 15 Fabulous Hits**	1966	4.00	10.00
Capitol ST-2470	(P)	**The Best Of Chad & Jeremy**	1966	4.00	10.00
Capitol ST-2470	(P)	**The Best Of Chad & Jeremy**	1966	5.00	12.00
Capitol TT-2546	(M)	**More Chad & Jeremy**	1966	4.00	10.00
Capitol ST-2546	(P)	**More Chad & Jeremy**	1966	5.00	12.00
		(The Fidu and Capitol albums reissue World Artists material.)			
		— Capitol albums above have black rainbow labels.—			
Capitol ST-2470	(P)	**The Best Of Chad & Jeremy**	196?	3.20	8.00
Capitol ST-2470	(P)	**The Best Of Chad & Jeremy**	196?	3.20	8.00
		— Capitol albums above have red & white Starline "bullseye" labels.—			

After modest success as a sort of easy rocking, folk-type duo, Chad Stuart and Jeremy Clyde were infected with a bit of the old consciousness expansion. Their final brace of long-players in the '60s became curiouser and curiouser: Of Cabbages And Kings featured a colorful, if ludicrous, flower-power cover while The Ark featured a marvelous painting by fantasy artist Charles Bragg. Both albums are wonderful listening, far better than the self-conscious hipness of the song titles ("Painted Dayglow Smile" and "The Progress Suite, Movements 1 Thru 5") would have the discerning customer believe! Gary Usher's willingness to indulge Stuart's arrangements with expensive productions led to his dismissal as a Columbia staff producer, despite success elsewhere, notably The Byrds.

Label & Catalog #		Title	Year	VG+	NM
Capitol ST-2470	(P)	The Best Of Chad & Jeremy	197?	1.00	5.00
Capitol ST-2546	(P)	More Chad & Jeremy	197?	1.00	5.00
		— Capitol albums above have black Starline labels.—			
Columbia CL-2374	(M)	Before And After	1965	8.00	20.00
Columbia CS-9174	(S)	Before And After	1965	12.00	30.00
Columbia CL-2398	(M)	I Don't Want To Lose You Baby	1965	10.00	25.00
Columbia CS-9198	(S)	I Don't Want To Lose You Baby	1965	14.00	35.00
Columbia CL-2564	(M)	Distant Shores	1966	8.00	20.00
Columbia CS-9364	(S)	Distant Shores	1966	10.00	25.00
		("Distant Shores" is rechanneled.)			
Columbia CL-2671	(M)	Of Cabbages And Kings	1967	8.00	20.00
Columbia CS-9471	(S)	Of Cabbages And Kings	1967	10.00	25.00
Columbia CS-9699	(S)	The Arc	1968	10.00	25.00
		(Some covers for this album spell the title as "Arc.")			
Columbia CL-2899	(M)	The Ark	1968	10.00	25.00
Columbia CS-9699	(S)	The Ark	1968	10.00	25.00
		(Columbia 9457 and 9699 were produced by Gary Usher.)			
Harmony HS-11357	(S)	Chad & Jeremy	197?	1.00	5.00
Rocshire XR-22018	(S)	Chad Stuart And Jeremy Clyde	1983	1.00	5.00

CHAIRMEN OF THE BOARD

Label & Catalog #		Title	Year	VG+	NM
Invictus SKAO-7300	(S)	Chairmen Of The Board	1970	20.00	50.00
Invictus SKAO-7304	(S)	In Session	1971	20.00	50.00
Invictus ST-9801	(S)	Bittersweet	1972	20.00	50.00
Invictus KZ-32526	(S)	The Skin I'm In	1974	20.00	50.00

CHALLENGERS, THE
Refer to The Good Guys; The Surfaris.

Label & Catalog #		Title	Year	VG+	NM
Vault LP-100	(M)	Surfbeat	1963	30.00	75.00
Vault VS-100	(S)	Surfbeat	1963	40.00	100.00
Vault VS-100	(S)	Surfbeat (Orange vinyl)	1963	150.00	300.00
Vault VS-100	(S)	Surfbeat (Red vinyl)	1963	150.00	300.00
Vault VS-100	(S)	Surfbeat (Yellow vinyl)	1963	150.00	300.00
Vault LP-101	(M)	Surfing	1963	30.00	75.00
Vault VS-101	(S)	Surfing	1963	40.00	100.00
Vault VS-101	(S)	Surfing (Orange vinyl)	1963	150.00	300.00
Vault VS-101	(S)	Surfing (Red vinyl)	1963	150.00	300.00
Vault VS-101	(S)	Surfing (Yellow vinyl)	1963	150.00	300.00
Vault VS-101	(S)	Surfing (Blue vinyl)	1963	150.00	300.00
Vault LP-102	(M)	The Challengers On The Move	1963	20.00	50.00
Vault VS-102	(S)	The Challengers On The Move	1963	30.00	75.00
Vault LP-107	(M)	K-39	1964	40.00	100.00
Vault LP-109	(M)	The Surf's Up	1965	20.00	50.00
Vault VS-109	(S)	The Surf's Up	1965	30.00	75.00
Vault LP-110	(M)	The Challengers A Go Go	1966	14.00	35.00
Vault VS-110	(S)	The Challengers A Go Go	1966	20.00	50.00
Vault LP-111	(M)	The Challengers' Greatest Hits	1967	10.00	25.00
Vault VS-111	(S)	The Challengers' Greatest Hits	1967	10.00	25.00
Triumph TR-100	(M)	The Challengers Go Sidewalk Surfing	1965	8.00	20.00
Triumph TRS-100	(S)	The Challengers Go Sidewalk Surfing	1965	10.00	25.00
Crescendo GNP-2010	(M)	The Challengers At The Teenage Fair	1965	8.00	20.00
Crescendo GNPS-2010	(S)	The Challengers At The Teenage Fair	1965	10.00	25.00
Crescendo GNP-2018	(M)	The Man From U.N.C.L.E.	1965	8.00	20.00
Crescendo GNPS-2018	(S)	The Man From U.N.C.L.E.	1965	10.00	25.00
Crescendo GNP-2025	(M)	California Kicks	1966	8.00	20.00
Crescendo GNPS-2025	(S)	California Kicks	1966	10.00	25.00
Crescendo GNP-2030	(M)	Billy Strange And The Challengers	1966	8.00	20.00
Crescendo GNPS-2030	(S)	Billy Strange And The Challengers	1966	10.00	25.00
Crescendo GNP-2031	(M)	Wipe Out	1966	8.00	20.00
Crescendo GNPS-2031	(S)	Wipe Out	1966	10.00	25.00
Crescendo GNP-609	(M)	25 Great Instrumental Hits (2 LPs)	1967	8.00	20.00
Crescendo GNPS-609	(S)	25 Great Instrumental Hits (2 LPs)	1967	10.00	25.00
Crescendo GNPS-2045	(S)	Light My Fire With Classical Gas	1968	8.00	20.00
Crescendo GNPS-2056	(S)	Vanilla Funk	1970	8.00	20.00
		— GNP Crescendo albums above have red labels.—			
Crescendo GNPS-2093	(S)	Sidewalk Surfing	1975	4.00	10.00
Fantasy F-9443	(S)	Where Were You In The Summer Of '62	1970	4.00	10.00
Rhino RNLP-053	(S)	Best Of The Challengers	1982	1.00	5.00

CHAMAELEON CHURCH
Chamaeleon Church features yet-to-be would-be funnyman Chevy Chase.

Label & Catalog #		Title	Year	VG+	NM
MGM SE-4574	(S)	Chamaeleon Church	1968	6.00	15.00

CHAMBERS BROTHERS, THE
The Chambers Brothers also recorded with Barbara Dane.

Label & Catalog #		Title	Year	VG+	NM
Vault LP-9003	(M)	People Get Ready	1966	6.00	15.00
Vault LPS-9003	(S)	People Get Ready	1966	6.00	15.00
Vault LP-115	(M)	The Chambers Brothers Now	1967	6.00	15.00
Vault VS-115	(S)	The Chambers Brothers Now	1967	6.00	15.00

Label & Catalog #		Title	Year	VG+	NM
Vault VS-120	(S)	The Chambers Brothers Shout	1968	6.00	15.00
Vault VS-128	(S)	Feelin' The Blues	1969	6.00	15.00
Vault VS-135	(S)	Chambers Brothers' Greatest Hits (2 LPs)	1970	4.00	10.00
Columbia CL-2722	(M)	The Time Has Come	1967	8.00	20.00
Columbia CS-9522	(S)	The Time Has Come	1967	8.00	20.00
Columbia CS-9671	(S)	A New Time/A New Day	1968	6.00	15.00
Columbia KGP-20	(S)	Love, Peace & Happiness (2 LPs)	1969	6.00	15.00
		—Columbia albums above have "360 Sound " on the bottom of the label.—			
Columbia C-30032	(S)	New Generation	1971	1.00	5.00
Columbia C-30871	(S)	The Chambers Brothers' Greatest Hits	1971	1.00	5.00
Columbia KC-31158	(S)	Oh, My God	1972	Unreleased	
Columbia CG-33642	(S)	The Time Has Come /			
		A New Time, A New Day (2 LPs)	1975	1.00	5.00
Fantasy 24718	(S)	Best Of The Chambers Brothers (2 LPs)	1973	10.00	25.00
Avco 11013	(S)	Unbonded	1974	4.00	10.00
Avco 69003	(S)	Right Move	1975	8.00	20.00
Roxbury RLX-106	(S)	Live In Concert On Mars	1976	12.00	30.00

CHAMPS, THE

Label & Catalog #		Title	Year	VG+	NM
Challenge CHL-601	(M)	Go Champs Go (Blue vinyl)	1958	See note below	
		(CHL 601 on blue vinyl has a suggested NM value of $2,000-3,000.)			
Challenge CHL-601	(M)	Go Champs Go	1958	300.00	500.00
Challenge CHL-605	(M)	Everybody's Rockin' With The Champs	1959	100.00	250.00
Challenge CHS-2500	(S)	Everybody's Rockin' With The Champs	1959	175.00	350.00
Challenge CHL-613	(M)	Great Dance Hits	1962	60.00	150.00
Challenge CHS-2513	(S)	Great Dance Hits	1962	100.00	250.00
Challenge CHL-614	(M)	All American Music From The Champs	1962	60.00	150.00
Challenge CHS-2514	(S)	All American Music From The Champs	1962	100.00	250.00

CHAMPS, THE / THE CYCLONES

Label & Catalog #		Title	Year	VG+	NM
Design DLP-159	(M)	Spotlight On The Champs & The Cyclones	1964	8.00	20.00
Design DLPS-159	(E)	Spotlight On The Champs & The Cyclones	1964	4.00	10.00
Inter. Award AK-223	(M)	The Champs & The Fabulous Cyclones	1965	8.00	20.00
Inter. Award AKS-223	(E)	The Champs & The Fabulous Cyclones	1965	4.00	10.00

CHANDLER, GENE
Refer to Jerry Butler & Gene Chandler.

Label & Catalog #		Title	Year	VG+	NM
Vee Jay MR-1040	(M)	The Duke Of Earl	1962	60.00	150.00
Vee Jay SR-1040	(S)	The Duke Of Earl	1962	400.00	800.00
		(Original covers of SR-1040 have "Stereophonic" across the top of the front and a notation across the entire top of the back cover that begins "Important Notice. . . This is a Stereophonic Record.")			
Vee Jay SR-1040	(S)	The Duke Of Earl	1962	125.00	250.00
		(Some later copies of SR-1040 were issued in mono covers with a "STEREO" sticker on the front.)			
Vee Jay SR-1040	(S)	The Duke Of Earl	196?	30.00	75.00
		(Later pressings of SR-1040 have "Stereophonic" on the front cover but lack the notice on the back. These covers generally contain mono records and are worth $50-75. Although these are often referred to as counterfeits, they are more likely unauthorized pressings from the company's financially chaotic final years.)			
Constellation LP-1421	(M)	Greatest Hits By Gene Chandler	1964	20.00	50.00
Constellation LP-1423	(M)	Just Be True	1964	20.00	50.00
Constellation LP-1425	(M)	Gene Chandler/Live On Stage In '65	1965	20.00	50.00
Checker LP-3003	(M)	The Duke Of Soul	1967	20.00	50.00
Checker LPS-3003	(E)	The Duke Of Soul	1967	12.00	30.00
Brunswick BL-54124	(M)	The Girl Don't Care	1967	8.00	20.00
Brunswick BL-754124	(S)	The Girl Don't Care	1967	6.00	15.00
Brunswick BL-754131	(S)	There Was A Time	1968	6.00	15.00
Brunswick BL-75149	(S)	The Two Sides Of Gene Chandler	1969	6.00	15.00
Mercury SR-61304	(S)	The Gene Chandler Situation	1970	4.00	10.00
Upfront UPF-105	(E)	The Duke Of Earl	197?	4.00	10.00
20th Cent.-Fox 578	(S)	Get Down	1978	1.00	5.00
20th Cent.-Fox 598	(S)	When You're No. 1	1979	1.00	5.00
20th Cent.-Fox 605	(S)	Gene Chandler '80	1980	1.00	5.00
20th Cent.-Fox 625	(S)	Ear Candy	1980	1.00	5.00
20th Cent.-Fox 629	(S)	Here's To Love	1981	1.00	5.00

CHANNEL, BRUCE

Label & Catalog #		Title	Year	VG+	NM
Smash MGS-27008	(M)	Hey! Baby	1962	60.00	150.00
Smash SRS-67008	(E)	Hey! Baby	1962	40.00	100.00

CHANNELS, THE

Label & Catalog #		Title	Year	VG+	NM
Lost-Nite LLP-15	(10")	The Channels (Red vinyl)	1981	4.00	10.00
Lost-Nite LLP-16	(10")	The Channels (Red vinyl)	1981	4.00	10.00

CHANTAYS, THE

Label & Catalog #		Title	Year	VG+	NM
Downey DLP-1002	(M)	Pipeline	1963	80.00	200.00
Downey DLPS-1002	(S)	Pipeline	1963	150.00	300.00

Label & Catalog #		Title	Year	VG+	NM
Dot DLP-3516	(M)	Pipeline	1963	20.00	50.00
Dot DLP-25516	(S)	Pipeline	1963	30.00	75.00
		(Dot 3516 is a reissue of Downey 1002.)			
Dot DLP-3771	(M)	Two Sides Of The Chantays	1966	20.00	50.00
Dot DLP-25771	(S)	Two Sides Of The Chantays	1966	30.00	75.00

CHANTELS, THE

Label & Catalog #		Title	Year	VG+	NM
End LP-301	(M)	We're The Chantels	1958	1,000.00	1,500.00
		(Original pressings of End 301 have gray labels and a cover photo of the group dressed in Southern plantation finery that apparently brought accusations of racial stereotyping and was withdrawn.)			
End LP-301	(M)	We're The Chantels	1959	200.00	400.00
		(Second pressings have gray labels but the covers replace the group with a photo of a jukebox.)			
End LP-301	(M)	We're The Chantels	1962	80.00	200.00
		(Third pressings have gray labels with 1962 in the trail-off vinyl and were issued in the jukebox cover.)			
End LP-301	(M)	We're The Chantels	1965	20.00	50.00
		(Later pressings have a color label with 1965 in the trail-off vinyl and were issued in the jukebox cover.)			
Carlton LP-144	(M)	The Chantels On Tour	1961	80.00	200.00
Carlton STLP-144	(P)	The Chantels On Tour	1961	200.00	400.00
		(Carlton 144 contains tracks by Chris Montez, The Imperials, and Gus Backus in mono and the Chantels' tracks in stereo.)			
End LP-312	(M)	There's Our Song Again	1962	60.00	150.00
Forum F-9104	(M)	The Chantels Sing Their Favorites	196?	20.00	50.00
Forum FS-9104	(E)	The Chantels Sing Their Favorites	196?	10.00	25.00

CHARIOT
Chariot later recorded as The Knack for Capitol

Label & Catalog #		Title	Year	VG+	NM
National General NG-2003	(S)	Chariot	1969	8.00	20.00

CHARISMA

Label & Catalog #		Title	Year	VG+	NM
Roulette SR-42037	(S)	Charisma	1969	6.00	15.00

CHARITY

Label & Catalog #		Title	Year	VG+	NM
Uni 73061	(S)	Charity Now	1969	10.00	25.00

CHARLATANS, THE

Label & Catalog #		Title	Year	VG+	NM
Philips PHS-600-309	(S)	The Charlatans	1969	40.00	100.00

CHARLES, RAY
Ray Charles, "The Genius of Modern Music," started his career patterned after Nat King Cole's jazz trio. These sides have been collected on seeming countless budget label titles and are not included in this edition. Neither are his later jazz-based albums. With his signing to Atlantic he laid the foundation for the bulk of the decade's rhythm'n blues music and established the platform from which '60s soul sprang. He can also be found on soundtracks for MGM's "The Cincinnati Kid" and U.A.'s "In The Heat Of The Night." Refer to The Bee Gees / Ray Charles.

Label & Catalog #		Title	Year	VG+	NM
Atlantic 8006	(M)	Ray Charles	1957	20.00	50.00
Atlantic 8006	(M)	Hallelujah!	195?	20.00	50.00
Atlantic 1259	(M)	The Great Ray Charles	1957	20.00	50.00
Atlantic SD-1259	(S)	The Great Ray Charles	1959	20.00	50.00
Atlantic 8025	(M)	Yes, Indeed! *(Screaming girls on cover)*	1958	20.00	50.00
Atlantic 8029	(M)	What'd I Say	1959	20.00	50.00
Atlantic 8039	(M)	Ray Charles In Person	1960	16.00	40.00
		("Ray Charles In Person" is a repackage of "What'd I Say.")			
Atlantic 1312	(M)	The Genius Of Ray Charles	1960	16.00	40.00
Atlantic SD-1312	(S)	The Genius Of Ray Charles	1960	20.00	50.00
		—Atlantic mono albums above have black labels; stereo albums have green labels.—			
Atlantic 8029	(M)	What'd I Say	1960	16.00	40.00
Atlantic 1312	(M)	The Genius Of Ray Charles	1960	16.00	40.00
Atlantic SD-1312	(S)	The Genius Of Ray Charles	1960	20.00	50.00
		—Atlantic albums above have white "bullseye" labels.—			
Atlantic SD-1312	(S)	The Genius Of Ray Charles	1969	8.00	20.00
		—Atlantic albums above have brown & purple labels.—			
Atlantic 8006	(M)	Ray Charles	1960	8.00	12.00
Atlantic 1259	(M)	The Great Ray Charles	1960	8.00	12.00
Atlantic SD-1259	(S)	The Great Ray Charles	1960	6.00	15.00
Atlantic 8025	(M)	Yes, Indeed!	1960	8.00	12.00
Atlantic 8029	(M)	What'd I Say	1960	8.00	12.00
Atlantic 8039	(M)	Ray Charles In Person	1960	8.00	12.00
Atlantic 1312	(M)	The Genius Of Ray Charles	1960	8.00	12.00
Atlantic SD-1312	(S)	The Genius Of Ray Charles	1960	6.00	15.00
Atlantic 8052	(M)	The Genius Sings The Blues	1961	8.00	12.00
Atlantic 8054	(M)	The Greatest Ray Charles	1961	10.00	25.00
		—Atlantic albums above have multi-colored labels with a white "fan" logo on the right side.—			
Atlantic 8006	(M)	Hallelujah I Love Her So!	1962	8.00	20.00
		("Hallelujah I Love Her So" is a reissue of "Rock And Roll.")			
Atlantic 1259	(M)	The Great Ray Charles	1962	4.00	10.00
Atlantic SD-1259	(S)	The Great Ray Charles	1962	5.00	12.00

Label & Catalog #		Title	Year	VG+	NM
Atlantic 8025	(M)	Yes, Indeed! (With Ray on the cover)	1962	4.00	10.00
Atlantic 8029	(M)	What'd I Say	1962	4.00	10.00
Atlantic 8039	(M)	Ray Charles In Person	1962	4.00	10.00
Atlantic 1312	(M)	The Genius Of Ray Charles	1962	4.00	10.00
Atlantic SD-1312	(S)	The Genius Of Ray Charles	1962	5.00	12.00
Atlantic 8052	(M)	The Genius Sings The Blues	1962	4.00	10.00
Atlantic 8054	(M)	Do The Twist With Ray Charles!	1962	4.00	10.00
Atlantic 1369	(M)	The Genius After Hours	1962	6.00	15.00
Atlantic SD-1369	(S)	The Genius After Hours	1962	8.00	20.00
Atlantic 2-900	(M)	The Ray Charles Story (2 LPs)	1962	12.00	30.00
Atlantic 8063	(M)	The Ray Charles Story, Volume 1	1962	8.00	20.00
Atlantic 8064	(M)	The Ray Charles Story, Volume 2	1962	8.00	20.00
Atlantic 8083	(M)	The Ray Charles Story, Volume 3	1963	6.00	15.00
Atlantic 8094	(M)	The Ray Charles Story, Volume 4	1964	6.00	15.00
Atlantic SD-8094	(P)	The Ray Charles Story, Volume 4	1964	10.00	25.00
—Atlantic albums above have multi-colored labels with a black "fan" logo on the right side.—					
Atlantic SD-7101	(S)	Great Hits Recorded On 8-Track Stereo	1964	10.00	25.00
Atlantic SD-1543	(S)	The Best Of Ray Charles	1970	3.20	8.00
Atlantic SD-2-503	(S)	Ray Charles Live (2 LPs)	1973	4.00	10.00
Atlantic SD-19142	(S)	True To Love	1977	1.20	6.00
Atlantic SD-19199	(S)	Love And Peace	1978	1.20	6.00
Atlantic SD-19251	(S)	Ain't It So	1979	1.20	6.00
ABC-Paramount ABC-335	(M)	The Genius Hits The Road	1960	8.00	20.00
ABC-Paramount ABCS-335	(S)	The Genius Hits The Road	1960	12.00	30.00
ABC-Paramount ABC-355	(M)	Dedicated To You	1961	8.00	20.00
ABC-Paramount ABCS-355	(S)	Dedicated To You	1961	12.00	30.00
—ABC albums above have black labels with "ABC-PARAMOUNT" on the top and "Am-Par Record Corp." on the bottom.—					
ABC-Paramount ABC-410	(M)	Modern Sounds In Country And Western	1962	10.00	25.00
ABC-Paramount ABCS-410	(S)	Modern Sounds In Country And Western	1962	12.00	30.00
ABC-Paramount ABC-415	(M)	Ray Charles' Greatest Hits	1962	6.00	15.00
ABC-Paramount ABCS-415	(S)	Ray Charles' Greatest Hits	1962	8.00	20.00
ABC-Paramount ABC-435	(M)	Modern Sounds In Country & Western, Volume 2	1962	6.00	15.00
ABC-Paramount ABCS-435	(S)	Modern Sounds In Country & Western, Volume 2	1962	8.00	20.00
ABC-Paramount ABC-465	(M)	Ingredients In A Recipe For Soul	1963	6.00	15.00
ABC-Paramount ABCS-465	(S)	Ingredients In A Recipe For Soul	1963	8.00	20.00
ABC-Paramount ABC-480	(M)	Sweet And Sour Tears	1964	6.00	15.00
ABC-Paramount ABCS-480	(S)	Sweet And Sour Tears	1964	8.00	20.00
ABC-Paramount ABC-495	(M)	Have A Smile With Me	1964	6.00	15.00
ABC-Paramount ABCS-495	(S)	Have A Smile With Me	1964	8.00	20.00
ABC-Paramount ABC-500	(M)	Live In Concert	1965	5.00	12.00
ABC-Paramount ABCS-500	(S)	Live In Concert	1965	6.00	15.00
ABC-Paramount T-90144	(M)	Live In Concert (Capitol Record Club)	1965	6.00	15.00
ABC-Paramount ST-90144	(S)	Live In Concert (Capitol Record Club)	1965	6.00	15.00
ABC-Paramount ABC-520	(M)	Country & Western Meets Rhythm & Blues	1965	6.00	15.00
ABC-Paramount ABCS-520	(S)	Country & Western Meets Rhythm & Blues	1965	8.00	20.00
ABC-Paramount ABC-520	(M)	Together Again	1966	5.00	12.00
ABC-Paramount ABCS-520	(S)	Together Again	1966	6.00	15.00
(Repackage of "Country & Western Meets Rhythm & Blues.")					
ABC-Paramount ABC-544	(M)	Crying Time	1966	5.00	12.00
ABC-Paramount ABCS-544	(S)	Crying Time	1966	6.00	15.00
ABC-Paramount T-90625	(M)	Crying Time (Capitol Record Club)	1966	6.00	15.00
ABC-Paramount ST-90625	(S)	Crying Time (Capitol Record Club)	1966	6.00	15.00
—ABC albums above have black labels with "ABC-Paramount" on top.—					
ABC 550	(M)	Ray's Moods	1966	5.00	12.00
ABC X-550	(S)	Ray's Moods	1966	6.00	15.00
ABC 2-590	(M)	A Man And His Soul (2 LPs)	1967	8.00	20.00
ABC Y-2-590	(S)	A Man And His Soul (2 LPs)	1967	10.00	25.00
ABC SQBO-91036	(S)	The Ray Charles Story (2 LPs. Capitol Rec. Club)	196?	6.00	15.00
ABC 595	(M)	Ray Charles Invites You To Listen	1967	5.00	12.00
ABC X-595	(S)	Ray Charles Invites You To Listen	1967	6.00	15.00
ABC ST-91223	(S)	Ray Charles Invites You To Listen (Cap. Rec. Club)	1967	6.00	15.00
ABC X-625	(S)	A Portrait Of Ray	1968	4.00	10.00
ABC X-675	(S)	I'm All Yours, Baby	1969	4.00	10.00
ABC X-695	(S)	Doing His Thing	1969	4.00	10.00
ABC X-707	(S)	Love Country Style	1970	4.00	10.00
ABC X-726	(S)	Volcanic Action Of My Soul	1971	4.00	10.00
ABC H-731	(S)	25th Anniversary In Show Business (2 LPs)	1971	6.00	15.00
ABC X-755	(S)	A Message From The People	1972	4.00	10.00
ABC X-765	(S)	Through The Eyes Of Love	1972	4.00	10.00
ABC 2-781	(S)	All Time Great Country & Western Hits (2 LPs)	1973	5.00	12.00

CHARLES, RAY / SOLOMON BURKE

Grand Prix K-406	(M)	Ray Charles And Solomon Burke	196?	4.00	10.00
Grand Prix KS-406	(E)	Ray Charles And Solomon Burke	196?	1.00	5.00

CHARLES, RAY / IVORY JOE HUNTER / JIMMY RUSHING

Design DLP-909	(M)	Three Of A Kind	196?	4.00	10.00
Design DLS-909	(E)	Three Of A Kind	196?	1.00	5.00

Label & Catalog #		Title	Year	VG+	NM

CHARLES, SONNY
Refer to The Checkmates, Ltd., with whom Sonny was the lead singer.

| Highrise 102 | (S) | The Sun Still Shines | 1982 | 1.00 | 5.00 |

CHARLIE

Janus 7032	(S)	No Second Chance	1977	1.00	5.00
Janus 7036	(S)	Lines	1978	1.00	5.00
Janus JXS-7036	(DJ)	Lines *(Picture disc)*	1978	6.00	15.00
Arista 4239	(S)	Fight Dirty	1979	1.00	5.00
Mirage 90098	(S)	Charlie	1983	1.00	5.00

CHARTBUSTERS, THE: *Refer to THE MANCHESTERS*

CHARTS, THE

| Lost-Nite LLP-10 | (10") | The Charts *(Red vinyl)* | 1981 | 4.00 | 10.00 |

CHASE
Bill Chase and the rest of Chase died in an airplane crash in 1974.

Epic KE-30472	(S)	Chase	1972	4.00	10.00
Epic EQ-30472	(Q)	Chase	1974	8.00	20.00
Epic KE-32572	(S)	Pure Music	1974	4.00	10.00
Epic EQ-32572	(Q)	Pure Music	1974	8.00	20.00

CHEAP TRICK
Cheap Trick features Ben E. Carloes, Rick Nielson, Tom Peterson, and Rubin Zander. Peterson left and was replaced by Jon Brant in 1982. Refer to Fuse.

Epic 34884	(S)	In Color	1977	1.00	5.00
Epic 35312	(S)	Heaven Tonight	1978	1.00	5.00
Epic 35795	(S)	Cheap Trick At Budokan	1979	1.00	5.00
Epic AS-518	(S)	From Tokyo To You *(Promo EP)*	1978	12.00	30.00
Epic 35773	(S)	Dream Police	1979	1.00	5.00
Epic 35773	(S)	Dream Police *(Promo picture disc)*	1979	12.00	30.00
Epic 35453	(S)	Found All The Parts *(10")*	1980	4.00	10.00
Epic 36498	(S)	All Shook Up	1980	1.00	5.00
Epic 38021	(S)	One On One	1982	1.00	5.00
Epic 38794	(S)	Next Position Please	1983	1.00	5.00

CHECKER, CHUBBY
Chubby Checker is a pseudonym for Ernest Evans. It was Chubby's remake of Hank Ballard's "The Twist" that changed modern popular dancing, freeing partners from the constraints of being paired and allowing the individual to "do his or her thing." Refer to Bobby Rydell & Chubby Checker; Dee Dee Sharp & Chubby Checker.

Parkway P-7001	(M)	Twist With Chubby Checker	1960	12.00	30.00
Parkway P-7002	(M)	For Twisters Only	1960	12.00	30.00
Parkway P-7003	(M)	It's Pony Time	1961	12.00	30.00
Parkway P-7004	(M)	Let's Twist Again	1961	12.00	30.00
Parkway P-7007	(M)	Your Twist Party	1961	12.00	30.00
—Parkway albums above have plain orange labels.—					
Parkway P-7001	(M)	Twist With Chubby Checker	196?	8.00	20.00
Parkway P-7002	(M)	For Twisters Only	196?	8.00	20.00
Parkway P-7003	(M)	It's Pony Time	196?	8.00	20.00
Parkway P-7004	(M)	Let's Twist Again	196?	8.00	20.00
Parkway P-7007	(M)	Your Twist Party	196?	8.00	20.00
Parkway P-7008	(M)	Twistin' Round The World	1962	8.00	20.00
Parkway SP-7008	(P)	Twistin' Round The World	1962	12.00	30.00
Parkway P-7009	(M)	For Teen Twisters Only	1962	8.00	20.00
Parkway SP-7009	(S)	For Teen Twisters Only	1962	12.00	30.00
Parkway P-7014	(M)	All The Hits For Your Dancin' Party	1962	8.00	20.00
Parkway P-7020	(M)	Limbo Party	1962	8.00	20.00
Parkway SP-7020	(S)	Limbo Party	1962	12.00	30.00
Parkway P-7022	(M)	Chubby Checker's Biggest Hits	1962	8.00	20.00
Parkway SP-7022	(E)	Chubby Checker's Biggest Hits	1962	8.00	20.00
Parkway P-7026	(M)	Chubby Checker In Person	1963	8.00	20.00
Parkway SP-7026	(S)	Chubby Checker In Person	1963	12.00	30.00
Parkway P-7027	(M)	Let's Limbo Some More	1963	8.00	20.00
Parkway SP-7027	(S)	Let's Limbo Some More	1963	12.00	30.00
Parkway P-7030	(M)	Beach Party	1963	8.00	20.00
Parkway SP-7030	(S)	Beach Party	1963	12.00	30.00
Parkway P-7036	(M)	Chubby Checker With Sy Oliver	1964	8.00	20.00
Parkway SP-7036	(S)	Chubby Checker With Sy Oliver	1964	12.00	30.00
Parkway P-7040	(M)	Folk Album	1964	8.00	20.00
Parkway SP-7040	(S)	Folk Album	1964	12.00	30.00
Parkway P-7045	(M)	Discotheque	1965	8.00	20.00
Parkway SP-7045	(S)	Discotheque	1965	12.00	30.00
Parkway P-7048	(M)	Chubby Checker's Eighteen Golden Hits	1966	8.00	20.00
Parkway SP-7048	(P)	Chubby Checker's Eighteen Golden Hits	1966	12.00	30.00
—Parkway albums above have orange & yellow labels with the date on the bottom.—					
Parkway P-7001	(M)	Twist With Chubby Checker	196?	6.00	15.00
Parkway P-7002	(M)	For Twisters Only	196?	6.00	15.00

Label & Catalog #		Title	Year	VG+	NM
Parkway P-7003	(M)	It's Pony Time	196?	6.00	15.00
Parkway P-7004	(M)	Let's Twist Again	196?	6.00	15.00
Parkway P-7007	(M)	Your Twist Party	196?	6.00	15.00
Parkway P-7008	(M)	Twistin' Round The World	196?	6.00	15.00
Parkway SP-7008	(P)	Twistin' Round The World	196?	8.00	20.00
Parkway P-7009	(M)	For Teen Twisters Only	196?	6.00	15.00
Parkway SP-7009	(S)	For Teen Twisters Only	196?	8.00	20.00
Parkway P-7014	(M)	All The Hits For Your Dancin' Party	196?	6.00	15.00
Parkway P-7020	(M)	Limbo Party	196?	6.00	15.00
Parkway SP-7020	(S)	Limbo Party	196?	8.00	20.00
Parkway P-7022	(M)	Chubby Checker's Biggest Hits	196?	6.00	15.00
Parkway SP-7022	(E)	Chubby Checker's Biggest Hits	196?	6.00	15.00
Parkway P-7026	(M)	Chubby Checker In Person	196?	6.00	15.00
Parkway SP-7026	(S)	Chubby Checker In Person	196?	8.00	20.00
Parkway P-7027	(M)	Let's Limbo Some More	196?	6.00	15.00
Parkway SP-7027	(S)	Let's Limbo Some More	196?	8.00	20.00
Parkway P-7030	(M)	Beach Party	196?	6.00	15.00
Parkway SP-7030	(S)	Beach Party	196?	8.00	20.00
Parkway P-7036	(M)	Chubby Checker With Sy Oliver	196?	6.00	15.00
Parkway SP-7036	(S)	Chubby Checker With Sy Oliver	196?	8.00	20.00
Parkway P-7040	(M)	Folk Album	196?	6.00	15.00
Parkway SP-7040	(S)	Folk Album	196?	8.00	20.00
Parkway P-7045	(M)	Discotheque	196?	6.00	15.00
Parkway SP-7045	(S)	Discotheque	196?	8.00	20.00
Parkway P-7048	(M)	Chubby Checker's Eighteen Golden Hits	196?	6.00	15.00
Parkway SP-7048	(P)	Chubby Checker's Eighteen Golden Hits	196?	8.00	20.00

—Parkway albums above have orange & yellow labels without a date on the bottom.—

ABC 4219	(S)	Chubby Checker's Greatest Hits	1972	4.00	10.00
Everest 4111	(S)	Chubby Checker's Greatest Hits	1981	4.00	10.00
MCA 5291	(S)	The Change Has Come	1982	4.00	10.00

CHECKER, CHUBBY / GARY U.S. BONDS

Exact 236	(S)	Chubby Checker & Gary U.S. Bonds	1980	4.00	10.00

CHECKMATES LTD., THE [SONNY CHARLES & THE CHECKMATES]

The Checkmates Ltd. were an integrated soul group featuring Sonny Charles.

Ikon 122	(M)	Live At Harvey's	1965	12.00	30.00
Capitol T-2840	(M)	Live At Caesar's Palace	1966	10.00	25.00
Capitol ST-2840	(S)	Live At Caesar's Palace	1966	12.00	30.00
A&M SP-4183	(S)	Love Is All We Have To Give	1969	12.00	30.00
		(Produced by Phil Spector)			
Rustic 2001	(S)	Bobby Stevens & The Checkmates, Ltd.	1971	8.00	20.00
Fantasy 9541	(S)	We Got The Moves	1978	6.00	15.00

CHELSEA

Chelsea features Peter Criss, later of Kiss.

Decca DL-75262	(S)	The Chelsea Album	1972	50.00	125.00

CHELSEA BEIGE

Epic E-30413	(S)	Mama, Mama, Let Your Sweet Bird Sing	1971	4.00	10.00

CHER

Refer to Sonny & Cher.

Imperial LP-9292	(M)	All I Really Want To Do	1965	6.00	15.00
Imperial LP-12292	(S)	All I Really Want To Do	1965	8.00	20.00
Imperial LP-9301	(M)	The Sonny Side Of Cher	1966	6.00	15.00
Imperial LP-12301	(S)	The Sonny Side Of Cher	1966	8.00	20.00

—Imperial albums above have green & black labels.—

Imperial LP-9320	(M)	Cher	1966	5.00	12.00
Imperial LP-12320	(S)	Cher	1966	6.00	15.00
Imperial LP-9358	(M)	With Love	1967	5.00	12.00
Imperial LP-12358	(S)	With Love	1967	6.00	15.00
Imperial LP-12373	(S)	Backstage	1968	6.00	15.00
Imperial LP-12406	(S)	Cher's Golden Greats	1968	4.00	10.00
Atco SD-33-2098	(S)	3614 Jackson Highway	1969	4.00	10.00
Sunset SUS-5276	(S)	This Is Cher	1970	1.00	5.00
Kapp KRS-5514	(S)	Foxy Lady	1972	1.00	5.00
Kapp KRS-5549	(S)	Gypsies, Tramps And Thieves	1972	1.00	5.00
United Arts. UXS-88	(S)	Cher Superpak I (2 LPs)	1972	1.00	5.00
United Arts. UXS-89	(S)	Cher Superpak II (2 LPs)	1972	1.00	5.00
Springboard SPB-4028	(S)	Cher's Greatest Hits	1972	.80	4.00
Springboard SPB-4029	(S)	Cher Sings The Hits	1972	.80	4.00
MCA 2101	(S)	Bitter Sweet White Light	1973	.80	4.00
MCA 2104	(S)	Half Breed	1973	.80	4.00
MCA 2113	(S)	Dark Lady	1974	.80	4.00
MCA 2127	(S)	Cher's Greatest Hits	1974	.80	4.00
United Arts. LA-237G	(S)	The Very Best Of Cher	1974	.80	4.00
United Arts. LA-377E	(S)	The Very Best Of Cher	1975	.80	4.00
United Arts. LA-435E	(S)	The Very Best Of Cher, Vol. 2	1975	.80	4.00

Label & Catalog #		Title	Year	VG+	NM
Warner Bros. WS-2850	(S)	Stars	1975	.80	4.00
Warner Bros. WS-2898	(S)	I'd Rather Believe In You	1976	.80	4.00
Warner Bros. BS-3046	(S)	Cherished	1975	.80	4.00
Casablanca NBLT-7133	(S)	Take Me Home	1979	.80	4.00
Casablanca NBPIX-7133	(S)	Take Me Home (Picture disc)	1979	20.00	50.00
Casablanca NBLP-7184	(S)	Prisoner	1979	.80	4.00
Liberty LN-10110	(S)	The Very Best Of Cher, Vol. 1	1981	.80	4.00
Liberty LN-10111	(S)	The Very Best Of Cher, Vol. 2	1981	.80	4.00
Columbia FC-38096	(S)	I Paralyze	1982	.80	4.00
Geffen 24239	(S)	Heart Of Stone	1989	.80	4.00
Geffen 24427	(S)	Love Hurts	1991	.80	4.00

CHEROKEE

ABC S-719	(S)	Cherokee	1970	8.00	20.00

CHERRY PEOPLE, THE

Heritage HTS-35,000	(S)	The Cherry People	1968	3.20	8.00

CHESAPEAKE JUKE BOX BAND, THE

Greene Bottle 1004	(S)	The Chesapeake Juke Box Band	1972	4.00	10.00

CHESS, BUDDY, & THE TWISTERS

Acorn 677	(M)	Dance The Twister	196?	30.00	75.00
Acorn 677	(S)	Dance The Twister	196?	60.00	150.00

CHESS, TUBBY, & HIS CANDY STRIPE TWISTERS

Grand Prix K-187	(M)	Do The Twist	1961	6.00	15.00
Grand Prix KS-187	(S)	Do The Twist	1961	8.00	20.00

CHESTER, GARY

DCP DCL-3803	(M)	Yeah, Yeah, Yeah	1964	6.00	15.00
DCP DCS-6803	(S)	Yeah, Yeah, Yeah	1964	8.00	20.00

CHEVRONS, THE
The Chevrons feature Terry Cashman.

Time T-10008	(M)	Sing A Long Rock & Roll	1961	30.00	75.00

CHI-LITES, THE / THE ROMANCERS

Pickwick SPC-3319	(S)	The Chi-Lites / The Romancers	197?	6.00	15.00
		(Pickwick 3319 contains six early tracks by The Chi-Lites and three by The Romancers.)			

CHI-LITES, THE

Brunswick BL-754152	(S)	Give It Away	1969	10.00	25.00
Brunswick BL-754165	(S)	I Like Your Lovin', Do You Like Mine?	1971	10.00	25.00
Brunswick BL-754170	(S)	Give More Power To The People	1971	10.00	25.00
Brunswick BL-754179	(S)	Lonely Man	1972	10.00	25.00
Brunswick BL-754184	(S)	The Chi-Lites Greatest Hits	1972	10.00	25.00
Brunswick BL-754188	(S)	A Letter To Myself	1973	10.00	25.00
Brunswick BL-754197	(S)	The Chi-Lites	1973	10.00	25.00
Brunswick BL-754200	(S)	Toby	1974	10.00	25.00
Brunswick BL-754204	(S)	Half A Love	1974	10.00	25.00
Mercury SRM1-1118	(S)	Happy Being Lonely	1976	6.00	15.00
20th Century T-619	(S)	Heavenly Body	1980	6.00	15.00
20th Century T-635	(S)	Me And You	1981	6.00	15.00

CHICAGO [CHICAGO TRANSIT AUTHORITY]

Columbia GP-8	(S)	Chicago Transit Authority (2 LPs)	1969	10.00	25.00
Columbia KGP-24	(S)	Chicago II (2 LPs)	1970	16.00	40.00
—Columbia albums above have "360 Sound " on the bottom of the label.—					
Columbia GP-8	(S)	Chicago Transit Authority (2 LPs)	1970	3.20	8.00
Columbia GQ-33255	(Q)	Chicago Transit Authority (2 LPs)	1975	10.00	25.00
Columbia KGP-24	(S)	Chicago II (2 LPs)	1970	1.00	5.00
Columbia GQ-33258	(Q)	Chicago II (2 LPs)	1975	10.00	25.00
Columbia C2-30110	(S)	Chicago III (2 LPs)	1970	1.00	5.00
Columbia C2Q-30110	(Q)	Chicago III (2 LPs)	1974	12.00	30.00
Columbia C2X-30863	(S)	Chicago At Carnegie Hall, Vol. 1 & 2 (2 LPs)	1971	1.00	5.00
Columbia C2X-30864	(S)	Chicago At Carnegie Hall, Vol. 3 & 4 (2 LPs)	1971	1.00	5.00
Columbia C4X-30865	(S)	Chicago At Carnegie Hall (4 LP box)	1971	6.00	15.00
Columbia C4Q-30865	(Q)	Chicago At Carnegie Hall (4 LP box)	1974	20.00	50.00
		(Columbia 30865 collects 30863 and 30864.)			
Columbia KC-31102	(S)	Chicago V	1972	.80	4.00
Columbia CQ-31102	(Q)	Chicago V	1974	10.00	25.00
Columbia KC-32400	(S)	Chicago VI	1973	.80	4.00
Columbia CQ-32400	(Q)	Chicago VI	1974	10.00	25.00
Columbia C2-32810	(S)	Chicago VII (2 LPs)	1974	1.00	5.00
Columbia C2Q-32810	(Q)	Chicago VII (2 LPs)	1974	12.00	30.00
Columbia PC-33100	(S)	Chicago VIII	1975	.80	4.00
Columbia PCQ-33100	(Q)	Chicago VIII	1975	10.00	25.00

Label & Catalog #		Title	Year	VG+	NM
Columbia PC-33900	(S)	Chicago IX/Greatest Hits	1975	.80	4.00
Columbia PCQ-33900	(Q)	Chicago IX/Greatest Hits	1975	10.00	25.00
Columbia HC-43900	(S)	Chicago IX/Greatest Hits (Half-speed)	1982	12.00	30.00
Columbia PC-34200	(S)	Chicago X	1976	.80	4.00
Columbia PCQ-34200	(Q)	Chicago X	1976	10.00	25.00
Columbia HC-44200	(S)	Chicago X (Half-speed master)	1982	10.00	25.00
Columbia (No number)	(S)	Chicago (17 LP box)	1976	100.00	250.00

(Promotional boxed set of Chicago's first ten albums—a total of 17 records. The albums are stock copies stamped "Demonstration-Not For Sale." The silver box has a photo cover on one side. Complete sets include a side panel with the album embossed titles that was taped to the box to keep the albums from sliding out, and a paper wrap-around that lists the ten album titles. Approximately 60% of the listed value is for the box with the panel and the wrap-around.)

Columbia JC-34860	(S)	Chicago XI	1977	.80	4.00
Columbia FC-35512	(S)	Hot Streets	1978	.80	4.00
Columbia FC-36105	(S)	Chicago 13	1979	.80	4.00
Columbia FC-36517	(S)	Chicago XIV	1980	.80	4.00
Columbia 37862	(S)	Chicago's Greatest Hits, Volume II	1981	.80	4.00
Full Moon 23689	(S)	Chicago 16	1982	.80	4.00
Full Moon 25060	(DJ)	Chicago 17 (Quiex II vinyl)	1984	6.00	15.00
Full Moon 25060	(S)	Chicago 17	1984	.80	4.00

CHICAGO WOMEN'S LIBERATION ROCK BAND

Rounder 4001	(S)	Mountain Moving Day	1972	4.00	10.00

CHICKEN SHACK
Chicken Shack features Christine Perfect, later Christine McVie of Fleetwood Mac.

Epic LN-24414	(M)	Forty Blue Fingers, Freshly Packed And Ready To Serve	1968	40.00	100.00
Epic BN-26414	(S)	Forty Blue Fingers, Freshly Packed And Ready To Serve	1968	12.00	30.00
Blue Horizon BH-7705	(S)	O.K. Ken?	1969	10.00	25.00
Blue Horizon BH-7706	(S)	100 Ton Chicken	1969	10.00	25.00
Blue Horizon BH-4809	(S)	Accept Chicken Shack	1970	10.00	25.00
Deram DES-18063	(S)	Imagination Lady	1972	8.00	20.00

CHIFFONS, THE
Refer to The Isley Brothers / The Chiffons.

Laurie LLP-2018	(M)	He's So Fine	1963	80.00	200.00
Laurie DT-90075	(E)	He's So Fine (Capitol Record Club)	1963	150.00	300.00
Laurie LLP-2020	(M)	One Fine Day	1963	80.00	200.00
Laurie LLP-2036	(M)	Sweet Talkin' Guy	1966	40.00	100.00
Laurie SLP-2036	(S)	Sweet Talkin' Guy	1966	60.00	150.00

("Nobody Knows What's Goin' On" is rechanneled.)

B.T. Puppy S-1011	(S)	My Secret Love	1970	80.00	200.00

CHILD

Jubilee 8029	(S)	Child	197?	4.00	10.00

CHILDREN, THE
The Children's first album was pressed privately before being reissued by Atco.

Atco SD-33-271	(S)	Rebirth	1968	10.00	25.00

CHILDREN OF GOD

A&M SP-4231	(S)	This Is Our Time	1969	4.00	10.00

CHILDREN OF PRAGUE

Mercury SR-61296	(S)	Old Time Bubble Gum Music	1970	4.00	10.00

CHOCOLATE WATCH BAND, THE
The CWB can also be found on the Tower soundtrack "Riot On Sunset Strip."

Tower T-5096	(M)	No Way Out	1967	150.00	300.00
Tower ST-5096	(S)	No Way Out	1967	200.00	400.00
Tower T-5016	(M)	The Inner Mystique	1968	150.00	300.00
Tower ST-5016	(S)	The Inner Mystique	1968	200.00	400.00
Tower ST-5153	(S)	One Step Beyond	1969	150.00	300.00

(Contrary to previous editions, original covers for ST-5153 apparently do not have printing on the spine! Convincing counterfeits of both the promo and stock copies exist.)

Rhino RNLP-108	(S)	Best Of The Chocolate Watch Band	1983	1.00	5.00

CHOSEN FEW, THE

RCA Victor LSP-4242	(S)	The Chosen Few	1969	8.00	20.00

CHRISTIAN, MICHAEL

United Arts. LA963	(S)	Boy From New York City	1979	4.00	10.00

(U.A. 963 features Mark Lindsay and Drake Levin.)

Label & Catalog #		Title	Year	VG+	NM

CHRISTIE

Label & Catalog #		Title	Year	VG+	NM
Epic E-30403	(S)	Yellow River	1970	6.00	15.00

CHRISTIE, LOU [LOU CHRISTIE SACCO]
Lou Christie is a pseudonym for Lugee Sacco. Refer to The Critters & The Young Rascals & Lou Christie.

Label & Catalog #		Title	Year	VG+	NM
Roulette R-25208	(M)	Lou Christie	1963	20.00	50.00
Roulette SR-25208	(P)	Lou Christie	1963	30.00	75.00
Co&Ce LP-1231	(M)	Lou Christie Strikes Back	1966	20.00	50.00
Co&Ce LPS-1231	(P)	Lou Christie Strikes Back	1966	30.00	75.00
Colpix CP-4001	(M)	Lou Christie Strikes Again	1966	16.00	40.00
Colpix SCP-4001	(S)	Lou Christie Strikes Again	1966	20.00	50.00
Roulette R-25332	(M)	Lou Christie Strikes Again	1966	10.00	25.00
Roulette SR-25332	(S)	Lou Christie Strikes Again	1966	12.00	30.00
		(Roulette 25332 is a reissue of Colpix 4001.)			
MGM E-4360	(M)	Lightnin' Strikes	1966	6.00	15.00
MGM SE-4360	(S)	Lightnin' Strikes	1966	8.00	20.00
MGM E-4394	(M)	Painter Of Hits	1966	6.00	15.00
MGM SE-4394	(S)	Painter Of Hits	1966	8.00	20.00
		("Rhapsody In The Rain" is in mono.)			
Spin-O-Rama M-173	(M)	Starring Lou Christie & The Classics	1966	8.00	20.00
Spin-O-Rama S-173	(E)	Starring Lou Christie & The Classics	1966	4.00	10.00
Buddah BDS-5052	(S)	I'm Gonna Make You Mine	1969	4.00	10.00
		("I'm Gonna Make You Mine" is rechanneled..)			
Buddah BDS-5073	(S)	Paint America Love	1971	4.00	10.00
		(Buddah 5073 credits Lou Christie Sacco.)			
Three Brothers THB-2000	(S)	Lou Christie	1974	4.00	10.00

CHRISTOPHER

Label & Catalog #		Title	Year	VG+	NM
Metromedia 1024	(S)	Christopher *(Promo only)*	197?	150.00	300.00

CHRYSALIS

Label & Catalog #		Title	Year	VG+	NM
MGM E-4547	(M)	Definition	1968	10.00	25.00
MGM SE-4547	(S)	Definition	1968	12.00	30.00

CHURLS, THE

Label & Catalog #		Title	Year	VG+	NM
A&M SP-4169	(S)	The Churls	1969	5.00	12.00
A&M SP-4233	(S)	Send Me No Flowers	1969	5.00	12.00

CIRCUS

Label & Catalog #		Title	Year	VG+	NM
Metromedia LPS-7401	(S)	Circus	197?	12.00	30.00

CIRCUS MAXIMUS
Circus Maximus features Jerry Jeff Walker.

Label & Catalog #		Title	Year	VG+	NM
Vanguard VRS-9260	(M)	Circus Maximus	1967	8.00	20.00
Vanguard VSD-79260	(S)	Circus Maximus	1967	10.00	25.00
Vanguard VSD-79274	(S)	Never Land Revisited	1968	10.00	25.00

CITY
City features Carole King.

Label & Catalog #		Title	Year	VG+	NM
Ode Z-1244012	(S)	Now That Everything's Been Said	1969	20.00	50.00
		(Originals have color covers; counterfeits have black & white covers.)			

CITY BOY

Label & Catalog #		Title	Year	VG+	NM
Mercury SRM-1-1098	(S)	City Boy	1976	3.20	8.00
Mercury SRM-1-1121	(S)	Dinner At The Ritz	1977	3.20	8.00
Mercury SRM-1-1182	(S)	Young Men Gone West	1977	3.20	8.00
Mercury SRM-1-3737	(S)	Book Early	1978	3.20	8.00
Atlantic SD-19249	(S)	The Day The Earth Caught Fire	1979	3.20	8.00
Atlantic SD-19285	(S)	Heads Are Rolling	1980	3.20	8.00

CLANTON, JIMMY

Label & Catalog #		Title	Year	VG+	NM
Ace 1001	(M)	Just A Dream	1959	40.00	100.00
Ace 1007	(M)	Jimmy's Happy *(Red vinyl)*	1960	100.00	200.00
Ace 1007	(M)	Jimmy's Happy	1960	40.00	100.00
Ace 1008	(M)	Jimmy's Blue *(Blue vinyl)*	1960	100.00	200.00
Ace 1008	(M)	Jimmy's Blue	1960	40.00	100.00
		(The records for "Jimmy's Happy" and "Jimmy's Blue" have both the single album catalog numbers, 1007-8 and the double album catalog number, 100, on their labels.)			
Ace DLP-100	(M)	Jimmy's Happy/Jimmy' Blues *(Colored vinyl)*	1960	200.00	400.00
Ace DLP-100	(M)	Jimmy's Happy/Jimmy' Blues	1960	80.00	200.00
		(Ace 100 is a double-record set collecting 1007 and 1008 with a bonus poster, priced separately below.)			
Ace DLP-100	(M)	Jimmy's Happy/Jimmy' Blues Poster	1960	25.00	75.00
Ace 1011	(M)	My Best To You	1961	40.00	100.00
Ace 1014	(M)	Teenage Millionaire	1961	40.00	100.00
Ace 1026	(M)	Venus In Bluejeans	1962	40.00	100.00
Philips PHM-200-154	(M)	The Best Of Jimmy Clanton	1964	10.00	25.00
Philips PHS-600-154	(S)	The Best Of Jimmy Clanton	1964	14.00	35.00

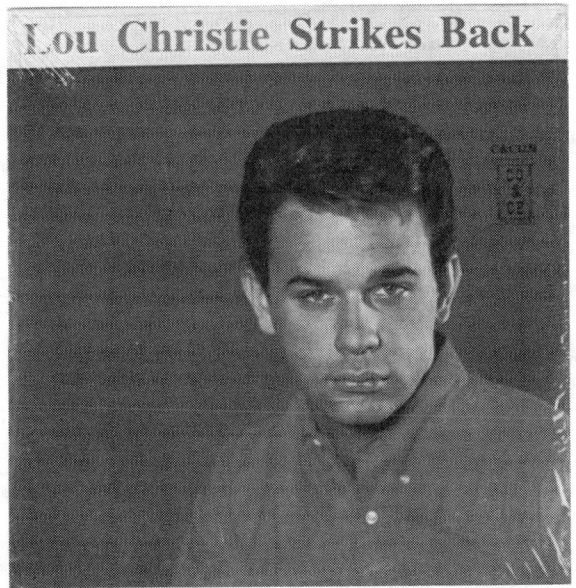

Lugee Alfredo Giovanni Sacco, a.k.a. Lou Christie, had one of the most outrageous falsettos ever waxed. He had been around the corner a few times by 1966, when he peaked with five chart entries, including the #1 smash, "Lightnin' Strikes." To capitalize on his success, no less than four different companies released LPs titled after the hit, including Lou Christie Strikes Back from CO&CE, the independent label with which he had launched his solo career in 1962.

Label & Catalog #		Title	Year	VG+	NM

CLANTON, JIMMY / BRISTOW HOOPER

| Design DLP-176 | (M) | Jimmy Clanton & Bristow Hooper | 196? | 6.00 | 15.00 |
| Design DLS-176 | (E) | Jimmy Clanton & Bristow Hooper | 196? | 4.00 | 10.00 |

CLAPTON, ERIC

Eric Clapton achieved fame with The Yardbirds and [temporary] deity status with John Mayall's Bluesbreakers and Cream. Refer to The Band; Blind Faith; Delaney & Bonnie; Derek & The Dominos.

Atco 33-329	(M)	Eric Clapton (White label promo)	1970	40.00	100.00
Atco SD-33-329	(S)	Eric Clapton	1970	4.00	10.00
Atco SD-33-329	(S)	Eric Clapton	1970	80.00	200.00
		(Some later pressings of SD-33-329 were erroneously mastered with alternate takes of "After Midnight" and "Blues Power" plus different mixes on other tracks. These can be identified by the matrix number, "STC 701879-1A CTH," in the trail-off vinyl.)			
Atco SD-2-803	(S)	The History Of Eric Clapton (2 LPs)	1972	4.00	10.00
Polydor PD-3503	(S)	Clapton At His Best (2 LPs)	1972	4.00	10.00
Polydor 24-5526	(S)	Clapton	1973	4.00	10.00
RSO 4801	(S)	461 Ocean Boulevard	1974	6.00	15.00
		(Original pressings of RSO 4801 contain "Give Me Strength.".)			
RSO 4801	(S)	461 Ocean Boulevard	1974	1.00	5.00
		(Later pressings have "Better Make It Through The Day.")			
RSO QD-4801	(Q)	461 Ocean Boulevard	1974	10.00	25.00
RSO 4806	(S)	There's One In Every Crowd	1975	.80	4.00
RSO QD-4806	(Q)	There's One In Every Crowd	1975	10.00	25.00
RSO 4809	(S)	E.C. Was Here	1975	.80	4.00
RSO 3004	(S)	No Reason To Cry	1976	.80	4.00
RSO 3008	(S)	Eric Clapton	1978	.80	4.00
RSO 3023	(S)	461 Ocean Boulevard	1978	.80	4.00
RSO 035	(S)	Slowhand (White vinyl promo)	1978	8.00	20.00
RSO 3030	(S)	Slowhand	1977	.80	4.00
RSO 1009	(S)	Backless (White vinyl promo)	1978	8.00	20.00
RSO 3039	(S)	Backless	1978	.80	4.00
RSO PRO-22-015	(S)	Classic Cuts (2 LPs. Promo comp.)	1980	8.00	20.00
RSO 4202	(S)	Just One Night (2 LPs)	1980	1.00	5.00
RSO 3095	(S)	Another Ticket	1981	.80	4.00
RSO 3099	(S)	Time Pieces	1982	.80	4.00

CLAPTON, ERIC / JEFF BECK / JIMMY PAGE

| RCA Victor LSP-4624 | (E) | Guitar Boogie | 1972 | 4.00 | 10.00 |

CLARK, CHRIS

Motown 664	(M)	Soul Sounds	1967	20.00	50.00
Motown MS-664	(S)	Soul Sounds	1967	30.00	75.00
Weed 801	(S)	C. C. Rides Again	1969	30.00	75.00

CLARK, CLAUDINE

| Chancellor CHL-5029 | (M) | Party Lights | 1962 | 150.00 | 300.00 |

CLARK, DAVE [THE DAVE CLARK FIVE]

The DC5 was drummer/manager Dave Clark with Lenny Davison, Dennis Payton, Rick Huxley and singer Mike Smith.

Crown CLP-5400	(M)	The Dave Clark Five With The Playbacks	1964	12.00	30.00
Crown CST-400	(E)	The Dave Clark Five With The Playbacks	1964	6.00	15.00
Crown CLP-5473	(M)	Chaquita/In Your Heart	1964	12.00	30.00
Crown CST-473	(E)	Chaquita/In Your Heart	1964	6.00	15.00
Cortleigh C-1073	(M)	The Dave Clark Five With Ricky Astor	1964	12.00	30.00
Cortleigh CS-1073	(E)	The Dave Clark Five With Ricky Astor	1964	6.00	15.00
		(The Crown and Cortleigh albums above are various artists albums with a cuppla early tracks by the DC5.)			
Epic LN-24093	(M)	Glad All Over	1964	30.00	75.00
Epic BN-26093	(E)	Glad All Over	1964	20.00	50.00
		(Original covers have a photo of the group sans instruments.)			
Epic LN-24093	(M)	Glad All Over	1964	16.00	40.00
Epic BN-26093	(E)	Glad All Over	1964	12.00	30.00
		(Late covers have the group with their instruments.)			
Epic LN-24104	(M)	The Dave Clark Five Return	1964	16.00	40.00
Epic BN-26104	(E)	The Dave Clark Five Return	1964	12.00	30.00
Epic LN-24117	(M)	American Tour, Volume 1	1964	16.00	40.00
Epic BN-26117	(E)	American Tour, Volume 1	1964	12.00	30.00
Epic XEM-77238	(DJ)	The Dave Clark 5 Interview	1964	300.00	600.00
Radio Pulsebeat	(M)	The Ed Rudy Interview	1964	150.00	300.00
Epic LN-24128	(M)	Coast To Coast	1965	16.00	40.00
Epic BN-26128	(E)	Coast To Coast	1965	12.00	30.00
Epic LN-24139	(M)	Weekend In London	1965	16.00	40.00
Epic BN-26139	(E)	Weekend In London	1965	12.00	30.00
Warner Bros. SP-3248	(DJ)	Having A Wild Weekend Radio Spots	1965	150.00	300.00
Warner Bros. 3296	(DJ)	Having A Wild Weekend Interview	1965	300.00	600.00
Epic LN-24162	(M)	Having A Wild Weekend	1965	16.00	40.00
Epic BN-26162	(E)	Having A Wild Weekend	1965	12.00	30.00

The Dave Clark Five, *a special, low-priced collection from the then all but defunct British Invasion hit-makers, went unnoticed by the market upon release in 1971. But it has since amassed a large collector following due to the fact that the two discs within compile twenty single and LP sides in true stereo, something that Epic had not seen fit to do for the group during its heyday in 1964-66. While the yellow label original is the one most collectors seek, the orange label reissue is much more difficult to find.*

Label & Catalog #		Title	Year	VG+	NM
Epic LN-24178	(M)	I Like It Like That	1965	16.00	40.00
Epic BN-26178	(E)	I Like It Like That	1965	12.00	30.00
Epic LN-24185	(M)	The Dave Clark Five's Greatest Hits	1966	10.00	25.00
Epic BN-26185	(E)	The Dave Clark Five's Greatest Hits	1966	8.00	20.00
Epic LN-24198	(M)	Try Too Hard	1966	12.00	30.00
Epic BN-26198	(E)	Try Too Hard	1966	10.00	25.00
Epic LN-24212	(M)	Satisfied With You	1966	12.00	30.00
Epic BN-26212	(E)	Satisfied With You	1966	10.00	25.00
Epic LN-24221	(M)	More Greatest Hits	1966	10.00	25.00
Epic BN-26221	(E)	More Greatest Hits	1966	8.00	20.00
Epic LN-24236	(M)	Five By Five	1967	12.00	30.00
Epic BN-26236	(S)	Five By Five	1967	16.00	40.00
Epic LN-24312	(M)	You Got What It Takes	1967	12.00	30.00
Epic BN-26312	(S)	You Got What It Takes	1967	16.00	40.00
Epic LN-24354	(M)	Everybody Knows	1968	12.00	30.00
Epic BN-26354	(S)	Everybody Knows	1968	16.00	40.00
Epic EG-30434	(S)	The Dave Clark Five (2 LPs)	1971	40.00	100.00

(EG-30434 is a collection of hits, etc., in honestogod stereo.)
—Epic albums above have yellow labels with a oval logo on top.—

Epic BN-26185	(E)	The Dave Clark Five's Greatest Hits	1973	16.00	40.00
Epic EG-30434	(S)	The Dave Clark Five (2 LPs)	1973	30.00	75.00
Epic KEG-33459	(M)	Glad All Over Again (2 LPs)	1975	20.00	50.00

—Epic albums above have orange labels.—

CLARK, DEE

Abner LP-2000	(M)	Dee Clark	1959	60.00	150.00
Abner SR-2000	(S)	Dee Clark	1959	150.00	300.00

(Counterfeits of Abner SR-2000 exist.)

Abner LP-2002	(M)	How About That	1960	40.00	100.00
Abner SR-2002	(S)	How About That	1960	60.00	150.00
Vee Jay LP-2000	(M)	Dee Clark	196?	60.00	150.00

(This is a Vee Jay reissue of the original Abner release with the Abner catalog number.. The copy found was in the Abner jacket.)

Vee Jay LP-1019	(M)	You're Looking Good	1960	20.00	50.00

(The existence of stereo copies of Vee Jay 1019 is in doubt.)

Vee Jay LP-1037	(M)	Hold On, It's Dee Clark	1961	20.00	50.00
Vee Jay SR-1037	(S)	Hold On, It's Dee Clark	1961	40.00	100.00
Vee Jay LP-1047	(M)	The Best Of Dee Clark	1964	20.00	50.00
Vee Jay SR-1047	(S)	The Best Of Dee Clark	1964	40.00	100.00
Sunset SUS-5217	(S)	Wondering	1968	4.00	10.00
Solid Smoke 8026	(S)	His Best Recordings	1983	1.00	5.00

CLARK, DICK: *Refer to* THE KEYMEN

CLARK, GENE
Gene Clark was a founding member of The Byrds. Refer to Dillard & Clark; McGuinn, Clark & Hillman. He can also be found on the Mediaarts soundtrack "American Dreamer."

Columbia CL-2618	(M)	Gene Clark With The Gosdin Brothers	1967	12.00	30.00
Columbia CS-9418	(S)	Gene Clark With The Gosdin Brothers	1967	20.00	50.00
A&M SD-4292	(S)	White Light	1971	6.00	15.00
Columbia KC-31123	(S)	Early L.A. Sessions	1972	6.00	15.00

(Columbia 31123 is a remixed reissue of 9418 with new vocals.)

Asylum 7E-1016	(S)	No Other (With bonus photo)	1974	6.00	15.00
RSO RS-1-3011	(S)	Two Sides To Every Story	1976	8.00	20.00
Takoma 7112	(S)	Firebyrd	1984	3.20	8.00

CLARK, PETULA
Ms Clark had been a success in her native England for two decades before teaming with producer Tony Hatch to add a little rock'n roll to her sound, after which she became the biggest white female pop singer of the '60s. She can also be found on the soundtracks for WB's "Finian's Rainbow" and MGM's "Goodbye Mr. Chips." Note: Her earlier, MOR-based LPs are not included in this edition.

Warner Bros. W-1590	(M)	Downtown	1964	6.00	15.00
Warner Bros. WS-1590	(S)	Downtown	1964	8.00	20.00
Warner Bros. W-1598	(M)	I Know A Place	1965	6.00	15.00
Warner Bros. WS-1598	(S)	I Know A Place	1965	8.00	20.00
Warner Bros. W-1608	(M)	The World's Greatest International Hits!	1965	6.00	15.00
Warner Bros. WS-1608	(S)	The World's Greatest International Hits!	1965	8.00	20.00

—Warner mono albums above have grey labels; stereo albums have gold labels.—

Coca-Cola 103	(DJ)	Petula Clark Swings The Jingle	1966	60.00	150.00
Warner Bros. W-1590	(M)	Downtown	1966	4.00	10.00
Warner Bros. WS-1590	(S)	Downtown	1966	5.00	12.00
Warner Bros. W-1598	(M)	I Know A Place	1966	4.00	10.00
Warner Bros. WS-1598	(S)	I Know A Place	1966	5.00	12.00
Warner Bros. W-1608	(M)	The World's Greatest International Hits!	1966	4.00	10.00
Warner Bros. WS-1608	(S)	The World's Greatest International Hits!	1965	5.00	12.00
Warner Bros. W-1630	(M)	My Love	1966	4.00	10.00
Warner Bros. WS-1630	(S)	My Love	1966	5.00	12.00
Warner Bros. W-1645	(M)	I Couldn't Live Without Your Love	1966	4.00	10.00
Warner Bros. WS-1645	(S)	I Couldn't Live Without Your Love	1966	5.00	12.00

Gene Clark With The Gosdin Brothers *is an essential piece in the history of one of rock'n roll's greatest groups: As the solo debut for ex-Byrd Clark it featured a rhythm section comprised of then Byrds Chris Hillman and Mike Clarke along with soon-to-be Byrds Doug Dillard (a touring member briefly in 1968) and Clarence White. Other L.A stalwarts who participated in this early country/rock masterpiece included Glen Campbell, Jerry Kole, Earl Palmer, Van Dyke Parks, and Leon Russell! And the backing vocalists, Rex and Vern Gosdin, both made careers for themselves as country singers.*

Label & Catalog #		Title	Year	VG+	NM
Warner Bros. W-1673	(M)	**Color My World/Who Am I**	1967	4.00	10.00
Warner Bros. WS-1673	(S)	**Color My World/Who Am I**	1967	5.00	12.00
Warner Bros. W-1698	(M)	**These Are My Songs**	1967	4.00	10.00
Warner Bros. WS-1698	(S)	**These Are My Songs**	1967	5.00	12.00
Warner Bros. W-1719	(M)	**The Other Man's Grass Is Always Greener**	1968	5.00	12.00
Warner Bros. WS-1719	(S)	**The Other Man's Grass Is Always Greener**	1968	5.00	12.00
		("The Other Man's Grass Is Always Greener" is rechanneled.)			
Warner Bros. W-1743	(M)	**Petula**	1968	5.00	12.00
Warner Bros. WS-1743	(S)	**Petula**	1968	5.00	12.00
		—Warner albums above have gold labels.—			
Warner Bros. WS-1765	(S)	**Greatest Hits, Vol. I**	1968	4.00	10.00
Warner Bros. ST-91598	(S)	**Greatest Hits, Vol. I** (Capitol Record Club)	1969	6.00	15.00
Warner Bros. WS-1789	(S)	**Portrait Of Petula**	1969	4.00	10.00
Warner Bros. WS-1823	(S)	**Just Pet**	1969	4.00	10.00
Warner Bros. WS-1862	(S)	**Memphis**	1970	4.00	10.00
Warner Bros. ST-93215	(S)	**Hits... My Way** (2 LPs. Capitol Record Club)	1969	10.00	25.00
		("The Other Man's Grass Is Always Greener" is rechanneled.)			
Warner Bros. WS-1865	(S)	**Warm And Tender (The Song Of My Life)**	1971	4.00	10.00
Crescendo GNPS-2069	(S)	**Live At The Royal Albert Hall**	1972	3.20	8.00
MGM SE-4859	(S)	**Pet Clark Now**	1972	4.00	10.00
Roulette 1	(S)	**Petula** (3 LPs)	1975	6.00	15.00
Crescendo GNPS-2170	(S)	**The Greatest Hits Of Petula Clark**	1984	1.00	5.00
Jango 779	(S)	**Give It A Try**	1986	1.00	5.00

CLARK-HUTCHINSON

Sire SES-97027	(S)	**A = MH Squared**	1969	10.00	25.00

CLARKE, ALLAN
Allan Clarke is the lead singer with The Hollies.

Epic KE-31757	(S)	**My Real Name Is 'Arold**	1972	6.00	15.00
Asylum 7E-1056	(S)	**I've Got Time**	1976	1.20	6.00
Atlantic SD-19175	(S)	**I Wasn't Born Yesterday**	1979	1.20	6.00
Curb 267	(S)	**Legendary Heroes**	1980	1.20	6.00

CLASH, THE

Epic JE-35543	(S)	**Give 'Em Enough Rope**	1979	6.00	15.00
		—Epic albums above have orange labels.—			
Epic JE-35543	(S)	**Give 'Em Enough Rope**	1979	1.00	5.00
Epic JE-36060	(S)	**The Clash**	1979	1.00	5.00
Epic 4E-36846	(10")	**Black Market Clash**	1980	6.00	15.00
Epic JE-36846	(S)	**Black Market Clash**	1982	1.00	5.00
Epic E3X-37037	(S)	**Sandanista Now!** (3 LPs)	1981	4.00	10.00
Epic AS-913	(S)	**Sandanista Now!** (Promo sampler)	1981	10.00	25.00
Epic AS-952	(S)	**Interchords** (Promo interview)	1981	12.00	30.00
Epic FE-37689	(S)	**Combat Rock** (Camouflage colored vinyl)	1982	6.00	30.00
Epic AS-99-1592	(S)	**Combat Rock** (Picture disc)	1982	6.00	30.00
Epic FE-37689	(S)	**Combat Rock**	1982	5.00	12.00
		(Original pressings mention "Two Thousand Flushes," a brand name product in Great Britain, in the song "Inoculated City." This reference was deleted from subsequent pressings.)			
Epic FE-37689	(S)	**Combat Rock**	1982	.80	4.00
Epic AS-1594	(S)	**The World According To The Clash** (Sampler)	1982	12.00	30.00

CLASS-AIRES, THE

Honey Bee	(M)	**Tears Start To Fall**	195?	150.00	300.00

CLASS OF '55
Class Of '55 is Johnny Cash, Jerry Lee Lewis, Roy Orbison and Carl Perkins.

American ARLP-1001	(DJ)	**Interview From The Class Of '55**	198?	20.00	50.00
American ARLP-1001	(S)	**Class Of '55**	198?	1.00	5.00

CLASSICAL HEADS

Probe CPLP-4516	(S)	**Classical Heads**	1970	6.00	15.00

CLASSICS IV, THE [DENNIS YOST & THE CLASSICS IV]

Imperial LP-12371	(S)	**Spooky**	1968	6.00	15.00
Imperial LP-12407	(S)	**Mamas & Papas/Soul Train**	1969	4.00	10.00
Imperial LP-12429	(S)	**Traces**	1969	6.00	15.00
Imperial LP-16000	(S)	**Greatest Hits**	1969	4.00	10.00
Liberty LST-11003	(S)	**Song**	1970	4.00	10.00
MGM MSH-702	(S)	**Dennis Yost & The Classics IV**	1973	4.00	10.00
United Arts. LA-4446E	(S)	**The Very Best Of The Classics IV**	1975	.80	4.00
Accord SN-7107	(S)	**Stormy**	1981	.80	4.00
Liberty LN-10182	(S)	**Spooky**	1982	.80	4.00

CLAY, JUDY, & BILLY VERA

Atlantic 8174	(M)	**Storybook Children**	1967	10.00	25.00
Atlantic 8174	(S)	**Storybook Children**	1967	12.00	30.00

Label & Catalog #		Title	Year	VG+	NM
CLAYTON, MERRY					
Ode SP-77001	(S)	Gimme Shelter	1970	6.00	15.00
Ode SP-77012	(S)	Merry Clayton	1971	4.00	10.00
Ode SP-77030	(S)	Keep Your Eyes On The Sparrow	1975	1.00	5.00
Epic PE-34948	(S)	Merry Clayton	1977	.80	4.00
Epic PE-34957	(S)	Keep Your Eyes On The Sparrow	1977	.80	4.00
CLAYTON-THOMAS, DAVID					
Mr Clayton-Thomas was the lead singer for Blood, Sweat & Tears.					
Decca DL-75146	(S)	David Clayton-Thomas	1969	8.00	20.00
Columbia KC-31000	(S)	David Clayton-Thomas	1972	1.00	5.00
Columbia KC-31700	(S)	Tequila Sunrise	1972	1.00	5.00
RCA Victor APL1-0173	(S)	David Clayton-Thomas	1974	1.00	5.00
RCA Victor APD1-0173	(Q)	David Clayton-Thomas	1974	4.00	10.00
ABC AA-1104	(S)	Clayton	1978	.80	4.00
CLEAN LIVING					
Vanguard VSD-79318	(S)	Clean Living	1972	4.00	10.00
Vanguard VSD-79334	(S)	Meadow Muffin	1973	4.00	10.00
CLEANLINESS & GODLINESS SKIFFLE BAND, THE					
Vanguard VSD-79285	(S)	Greatest Hits	1968	10.00	25.00
CLEAR LIGHT					
Elektra EKL-4011	(M)	Clear Light	1967	10.00	25.00
Elektra EKS-74011	(S)	Clear Light	1967	12.00	30.00
CLEFTONES, THE					
Gee GLP-705	(M)	Heart And Soul	1961	150.00	300.00
Gee SGLP-705	(P)	Heart And Soul	1961	250.00	500.00
Gee GLP-707	(M)	For Sentimental Reasons	1962	200.00	400.00
Gee SGLP-707	(P)	For Sentimental Reasons	1962	500.00	1,000.00
		—Gee albums above have gray labels.—			
CLIFF, JIMMY					
Jimmy Cliff became a worldwide star with his appearance in the film "The Harder They Come."					
Veep VPS-16536	(S)	Can't Get Enough Of It	1968	14.00	35.00
Reprise MS-2218	(S)	Follow My Mind	1975	3.20	8.00
CLIFFORD, BUZZ					
Columbia CL-1616	(M)	Baby Sittin' With Buzz	1961	40.00	100.00
Columbia CS-8416	(S)	Baby Sittin' With Buzz	1961	60.00	150.00
Dot DLP-25965	(S)	See Your Way Clear	1969	14.00	35.00
CLIFFORD, MIKE					
United Arts. UAL-3409	(M)	For The Love Of Mike	1965	8.00	20.00
United Arts. UAS-6409	(P)	For The Love Of Mike	1965	10.00	25.00
CLIMAX					
Rocky Road 3506	(S)	Precious And Few	1972	5.00	12.00
CLIMAX BLUES BAND					
Sire SES-97013	(S)	The Climax Chicago Blues Band	1969	4.00	10.00
Sire SES-97023	(S)	Climax Chicago Blues Band Plays On	1970	4.00	10.00
Sire SES-4901	(S)	#3	1970	1.20	6.00
Sire SES-5903	(S)	Tightly Knit	1971	1.20	6.00
Sire SES-2-7411	(S)	FM/Live (2 LPs)	1971	3.20	8.00
Sire SES-7402	(S)	Rich Man	1972	1.20	6.00
Sire SESD-7501	(S)	Sense Of Direction	1974	1.20	6.00
Sire SESD-7507	(S)	Stamp Album	1975	1.20	6.00
Sire SESD-7517	(S)	Tightly Knit	1975	1.20	6.00
Sire SESD-7523	(S)	Gold Plated	1976	.80	4.00
Sire SRK-6003	(S)	The Climax Chicago Blues Band	1978	.80	4.00
Sire SRK-6004	(S)	Lot Of Bottle	1978	.80	4.00
Sire SRK-6008	(S)	Tightly Knit	1978	.80	4.00
Sire SES-2-6013	(S)	FM/Live (2 LPs)	1978	1.20	6.00
Sire SRK-6016	(S)	Stamp Album	1978	.80	4.00
Sire SRK-6033	(S)	Climax Chicago Blues Band Plays On	1978	.80	4.00
Sire SRK-6056	(S)	Shine On	1978	.80	4.00
Warner Bros. PRO-807	(S)	Real To Reel (Promo sampler)	1979	1.20	6.00
Warner Bros. BSK-3334	(S)	Real To Reel	1979	.80	4.00
Warner Bros. BSK-3493	(S)	Flying The Flag	1980	.80	4.00
Warner Bros. BSK-3623	(S)	Lucky For Some	1981	.80	4.00
CLINIC					
Roulette SR-3010	(S)	Now We're Even	1973	4.00	10.00

CLINTON, GEORGE
George Clinton is the mastermind behind the Parliament/Funkadelic community. Refer to The Brides Of Funkenstein; William "Bootsy" Collins; Funkadelic; Eddie Hazel; The Incorporated Thang Band; Jimmy G; The P Funk All-Stars; Parlet; Parliament; The Fred Wesley Horns; Philippe Wynne.

Capitol ST-12246	(S)	Computer Games	1982	4.00	10.00
Capitol ST-12308	(S)	You Shouldn't-Nuf Bit Fish	1984	4.00	10.00
Capitol ST-12417	(S)	Some Of My Best Jokes Are Friends	1985	4.00	10.00
Capitol ST-12481	(S)	R&B Skeletons In The Closet	1986	4.00	10.00
Capitol ST-12534	(S)	The Best Of George Clinton	1986	4.00	10.00
Capitol ST-15021	(S)	The Mothership Connection Live From Houston	1986	4.00	10.00

CLIQUE, THE
White Whale WWS-7126	(S)	The Clique	1969	6.00	15.00

CLOCKWORK
Green Bottle 1013	(S)	Clockwork	1973	6.00	15.00

CLOUD, BRUCE
Capitol ST-343	(S)	California Soul	1969	4.00	10.00

CLOUDS, THE
Deram DES-18044	(S)	Up Above Our Heads	1970	6.00	15.00
Deram DES-18058	(S)	Watercolour Days	1971	6.00	15.00

CLOVER
The original line-up for Clover on Fantasy features John McFee and Alex Call, later Huey Lewis. The later line-up backed Elvis Costello on his first album.

Fantasy 8395	(S)	Clover	1969	10.00	25.00
Fantasy 8405	(S)	Forty-Niner	1969	10.00	25.00
Mercury SRM-1-1169	(S)	Clover	1977	6.00	15.00
Mercury SRM-1-3708	(S)	Love On The Wire	1977	6.00	15.00
Fantasy	(S)	Chronicle (2 LPs)	1979	3.20	8.00

CLOVER, TIMOTHY
Tower ST-5114	(S)	A Harvard Square Affair	1968	8.00	20.00

CLOVERS, THE
Atlantic LP-1248	(M)	The Clovers	1956	400.00	750.00
Atlantic LP-8009	(M)	The Clovers	1957	200.00	400.00
		(Atlantic 8009 is a reissue of 1248.)			
Atlantic LP-8034	(M)	Dance Party	1959	200.00	400.00
		—Atlantic albums above have black labels.—			
Atlantic LP-8009	(M)	The Clovers	1960	150.00	300.00
Atlantic LP-8034	(M)	Dance Party	1960	150.00	300.00
		—Atlantic albums above have white "bullseye" labels.—			
Atlantic LP-8009	(M)	The Clovers	196?	80.00	200.00
Atlantic LP-8034	(M)	Dance Party	196?	80.00	200.00
		—Atlantic albums above have purple & orange labels.—			
Poplar 1001	(M)	In Clover	1958	150.00	400.00
United Arts. UAL-3033	(M)	In Clover	1959	150.00	300.00
United Arts. UAS-6033	(E)	In Clover	1959	100.00	250.00
United Arts. UAL-3099	(M)	Love Potion Number Nine	1959	150.00	350.00
United Arts. UAS-6099	(S)	Love Potion Number Nine	1959	250.00	500.00
		("Love Potion Number Nine" and "Lovey Dovey" were rerecorded.)			
Design DLP-	(M)	Love Potion Number Nine	196?	16.00	40.00
Design DSLP-	(E)	Love Potion Number Nine	196?	8.00	20.00
Grand Prix K-428	(M)	The Original Love Potion Number Nine	1964	12.00	30.00
Grand Prix KS-428	(E)	The Original Love Potion Number Nine	1964	6.00	15.00
Atco SD-33-374	(P)	Their Greatest Recordings/The Early Years	1971	4.00	10.00

COASTERS, THE
Refer to The Drifters / The Coasters.

Atco 33-101	(M)	The Coasters	1958	200.00	400.00
Atco 33-111	(M)	The Coasters' Greatest Hits	1959	80.00	200.00
Atco 33-123	(M)	One By One	1960	80.00	200.00
Atco SD-33-123	(S)	One By One	1960	150.00	300.00
		—Atco albums above have yellow labels with a harp on top.—			
Atco 33-101	(M)	The Coasters	1960	30.00	75.00
Atco SD-33-101	(E)	The Coasters	196?	30.00	75.00
Atco 33-111	(M)	The Coasters' Greatest Hits	1960	20.00	50.00
Atco SD-33-111	(E)	The Coasters' Greatest Hits	196?	20.00	50.00
Atco 33-123	(M)	One By One	1960	30.00	75.00
Atco SD-33-123	(S)	One By One	1960	60.00	150.00
Atco 33-135	(M)	Coast Along With The Coasters	1962	40.00	100.00
Atco SD-33-135	(P)	Coast Along With The Coasters	1962	60.00	150.00
		—Atco mono albums above have gold & gray labels; stereo albums have purple & brown labels.—			
Clarion 605	(M)	That Is Rock And Roll	1964	16.00	40.00
Clarion 605	(P)	That Is Rock And Roll	1964	20.00	50.00

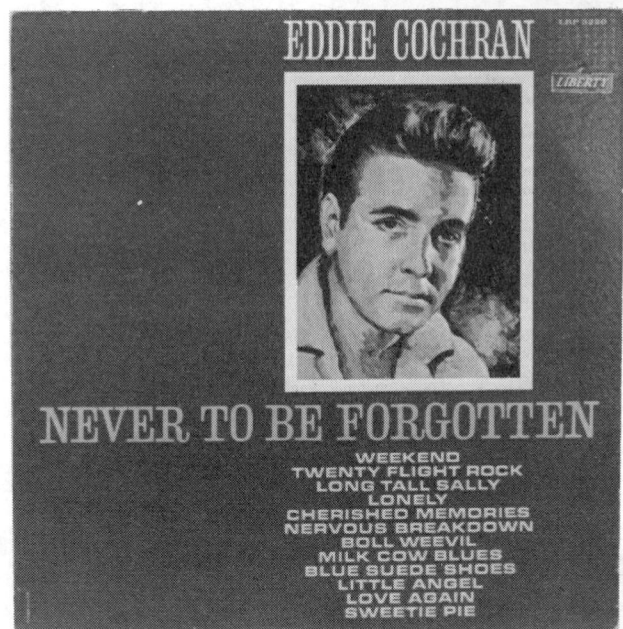

Edward Ray Cochrane began his career as half of a country 'n western duo with Hank Cochran (no relation, although they did bill themselves as the Cochran Brothers). By the time of his unfortunate demise in the same automobile accident that crippled Gene Vincent, Eddie had established himself as one of the most influential white rockers and guitar players following in the wake of Elvis. Both of these albums were released after his death; Eddie Cochran (above) is often referred to as the "Memorial Album."

Label & Catalog #		Title	Year	VG+	NM
Atco SD-33-371	(P)	Their Greatest Recordings/The Early Years	1971	4.00	10.00
King KS-1146	(M)	The Coasters On Broadway	1973	10.00	25.00
Trip TLP-8028	(E)	It Ain't Sanitary	197?	6.00	15.00
Arco 101	(E)	The Coasters	197?	4.00	10.00
Atlantic K-60163	(P)	Young Blood (2 LPs)	1982	3.20	8.00

COATS, DON, & THE PLAYBACKS: *Refer to* FRANK WOOD / DON & THE PLAYBACKS

COCHISE

United Arts. UAS-5518	(DJ)	Swallow Tales	1971	16.00	40.00
		(Promos have a fold-open cover with inserts.)			
United Arts. UAS-5518	(S)	Swallow Tales	1971	4.00	10.00

COCHRAN, EDDIE

Liberty LRP-3061	(M)	Singin' To My Baby	1957	300.00	600.00
		— *Liberty albums above have turquoise labels.* —			
Liberty LRP-3061	(M)	Singin' To My Baby	1960	150.00	300.00
Liberty LRP-3172	(DJ)	Eddie Cochran (White label)	1960	250.00	500.00
Liberty LRP-3172	(M)	Eddie Cochran	1960	80.00	200.00
Liberty LRP-3220	(M)	Never To Be Forgotten	1962	40.00	100.00
		— *Liberty albums above have black labels.* —			
Sunset SUM-1123	(M)	Summertime Blues	1966	14.00	35.00
Sunset SUS-5123	(E)	Summertime Blues	1966	10.00	25.00
United Arts. UAS-9959	(M)	Legendary Master (2 LPs)	1971	10.00	25.00
United Arts. LA428-E	(M)	The Very Best Of Eddie Cochran	1975	4.00	10.00
Liberty LN-1037	(M)	Singin' To My Baby	1981	4.00	10.00
Liberty LN-10204	(M)	Great Hits	1982	.80	4.00

COCHRAN, WAYNE [WAYNE COCHRAN & THE C.C. RIDERS]

Chess LP-1519	(M)	Wayne Cochran	1967	12.00	30.00
Chess LPS-1519	(S)	Wayne Cochran	1967	16.00	40.00
King KS-1116	(S)	Alive & Well	1970	8.00	20.00
Bethlehem 10002	(S)	High And Ridin'	1970	6.00	15.00
Epic KE-30989	(S)	Cochran	1972	5.00	12.00

COCKER, JOE
Joe broke off with his group, The Grease Band, after the first album. Leon Russell moved in as producer, arranger, and band leader during the "Mad Dogs and Englishmen" period.

A&M SP-4182	(S)	With A Little Help From My Friends	1969	4.00	10.00
A&M SP-4224	(S)	Joe Cocker!	1969	4.00	10.00
A&M SP-6002	(S)	Mad Dogs & Englishmen (2 LPs)	1970	6.00	15.00
		— *A&M albums above have brown labels.* —			
A&M SP-4182	(S)	With A Little Help From My Friends	197?	.80	4.00
A&M QU-54182	(Q)	With A Little Help From My Friends	1974	8.00	20.00
A&M SP-4224	(S)	Joe Cocker!	197?	.80	4.00
A&M QU-54224	(Q)	Joe Cocker!	1974	8.00	20.00
A&M SP-6002	(S)	Mad Dogs & Englishmen (2 LPs)	197?	1.20	6.00
A&M SP-4368	(S)	Joe Cocker	1972	.80	4.00
A&M SP-3633	(S)	I Can Stand A Little Rain	1974	.80	4.00
A&M SP-4529	(S)	Jamaica Say You Will	1975	.80	4.00
A&M SP-4574	(S)	Stingray	1976	.80	4.00
A&M SP-4670	(S)	Joe Cocker's Greatest Hits	1977	.80	4.00
		— *A&M albums above have silver labels.* —			
Asylum DP-400	(DJ)	Luxury You Can Afford (Picture disc)	1978	4.00	10.00
Asylum DP-400	(S)	Luxury You Can Afford	1978	.80	4.00

COFIELD, PETER

Coral CRL-757508	(S)	Peter Cofield	1969	4.00	10.00

COINS, THE: *Refer to* NEIL SEDAKA & THE TOKENS / THE COINS

COLD BLOOD
Cold Blood features Lydia Pense.

San Francisco 200	(S)	Cold Blood	1969	8.00	20.00
San Francisco 205	(S)	Sisyphus	1970	8.00	20.00
Reprise BS-2074	(S)	First Taste Of Sin	1972	4.00	10.00
Reprise BS-2130	(S)	Thriller	1973	4.00	10.00
Warner Bros. 2906	(S)	Lydia	1974	1.00	5.00
ABC 917	(S)	Lydia Pense And Cold Blood	1976	1.00	5.00

COLE, JERRY, & HIS SPACEMEN
Refer to Jerry Kole; Ritchie Valens / Jerry Kole.

Capitol T-2044	(M)	Outer Limits	1963	20.00	50.00
Capitol ST-2044	(S)	Outer Limits	1963	30.00	75.00
Capitol T-2061	(M)	Hot Rod Dance Party (With bonus photo)	1964	30.00	75.00
Capitol ST-2601	(S)	Hot Rod Dance Party (With bonus photo)	1964	40.00	100.00
Capitol T-2061	(M)	Hot Rod Dance Party (Without the photo)	1964	20.00	50.00
Capitol ST-2601	(S)	Hot Rod Dance Party (Without the photo)	1964	30.00	75.00

This pair of hot rod collectibles come courtesy of Jerry Cole on Capitol, Hot Rod Dance Party ("Music with a drivin' beat that'll put any party on wheels"), and Gary Usher and his ubiquitous crew, this time with The Competitors Play Little Deuce Coupe on Dot. While Cole took advantage of fads that were happening (his other albums include Outer Limits and Surf Age), Mr Usher was, along with his old songwriting partner, Brian Wilson, the chief progenitor of car-related music, also waxing eloquently about four wheels and carburetors as The Ghouls and The Knights for Capitol (among many others).

	alog #		Title	Year	VG+	NM
	112	(M)	Surf Age	1964	40.00	100.00
Capitol ST-2112		(S)	Surf Age	1964	50.00	125.00
			(Capitol 2112 includes the bonus single "Thunder Wave" / "Spanish Kiss" by Dick Dale in a special "pocket" on the cover.)			
Capitol T-2112		(M)	Surf Age (Without the single)	1964	30.00	75.00
Capitol ST-2112		(S)	Surf Age (Without the single)	1964	40.00	100.00
Liberty LRP-3362		(M)	Sounds Of The Big Irons	1964	20.00	50.00
Liberty LST-7362		(S)	Sounds Of The Big Irons	1964	30.00	75.00

COLLAGE

Smash SRS-67101	(S)		The Collage	1968	8.00	20.00
Cream 9008	(S)		Collage	1971	6.00	15.00

COLLECTORS, THE
The Collectors later recorded as Chilliwack.

Warner Bros. WS-1746	(S)	The Collectors	1968	8.00	20.00
Warner Bros. WS-1774	(S)	Grass And Wild Strawberries	1969	8.00	20.00

COLLEGIANS, THE

Winley LP-6004	(M)	Sing Along With The Collegians	195?	250.00	500.00

COLLIER, MITTY

Chess LP-1492	(M)	Shades Of Genius	1965	20.00	50.00
Chess LPS-1492	(S)	Shades Of Genius	1965	30.00	75.00

COLLINS, AARON
Aaron Collins was the lead singer for The Cadets and The Jacks.

Crown CLP-5028	(M)	Calypso U.S.A.	1958	300.00	600.00

COLLINS, ALBERT

TCF-Hall 8002	(M)	The Cool Sound Of Albert Collins	1965	150.00	300.00
Imperial LP-12428	(S)	Love Can Be Found Anywhere	1968	12.00	30.00
Imperial LP-12438	(S)	Trash Talkin'	1969	12.00	30.00
Imperial LP-12449	(S)	The Complete Albert Collins	1969	12.00	30.00
Blue Thumb BTS-8	(S)	Truckin' With Albert Collins	1969	10.00	25.00
		(Blue Thumb 8 is a reissue of TCF Hall 8002.)			
Tumbleweed TWS-103	(S)	There's Gotta Be A Change	1971	5.00	12.00
Alligator AL-4713	(S)	Ice Pickin'	1978	3.20	8.00
Alligator AL-4719	(S)	Frostbite	1980	3.20	8.00
Alligator AL-4725	(S)	Frozen Alive!	1981	3.20	8.00
Alligator AL-4730	(S)	Don't Lose Your Cool	1983	3.20	8.00
Alligator AL-4733	(S)	Live In Japan	1984	3.20	8.00
Alligator AL-4743	(S)	Showdown!	1985	3.20	8.00
Alligator AL-4752	(S)	Cold Snap	1986	3.20	8.00
Brylen BN-4520	(S)	Frosty	1982	3.20	8.00

COLLINS, LYN

People PE-5602	(S)	Think (About It)	1972	10.00	25.00
People PE-6605	(S)	Check Me Out	1975	10.00	25.00
		(Both People albums were produced by James Brown.)			

COLLINS, SHIRLEY & DOROTHY

Harvest SKAO-370	(S)	Anthems In Eden	1969	20.00	50.00

COLLINS, WILLIAM "BOOTSY" [BOOTSY'S RUBBER BAND]
Formerly of James Brown's JBs, Bootsy is a member of the Parliament/Funkadelic community. Refer to Godmoma; Mico Wave; The Sweat Band.

Warner Bros. BS-2920	(S)	Stretchin' Out	1976	8.00	20.00
Warner Bros. BS-2972	(S)	Aah... The Name Is Bootsy, Baby	1977	8.00	20.00
Warner Bros. K-3093	(S)	Bootsy? Player Of The Year	1978	8.00	20.00
Warner Bros. K-3295	(S)	This Boot Is Made For Fonk'N	1979	8.00	20.00
Warner Bros. K-3433	(S)	Ultrawave	1980	8.00	20.00
Warner Bros. K-3667	(S)	One Giveth, The Count Taketh Away	1982	8.00	20.00
Columbia 44107	(S)	What's Bootsy Doin'?	1988	4.00	10.00

COLONEL BAGSHOT

Cadet Concept 50010	(S)	Oh! What A Lovely War	1971	6.00	15.00

COLOSSEUM

Dunhill DS-50062	(S)	Those Who Are About To Die, Salute You	1969	4.00	10.00
Dunhill DS-50079	(S)	The Grass Is Greener	1970	4.00	10.00
Dunhill DS-50101	(S)	The Daughter Of Time	1970	4.00	10.00
Warner Bros. 2XS-1942	(S)	Colosseum Live (2 LPs)	1971	4.00	10.00

COLOURS

Dot DLP-25854	(S)	Colours	1968	6.00	15.00
Dot DLP-25935	(S)	Atmosphere	1969	6.00	15.00

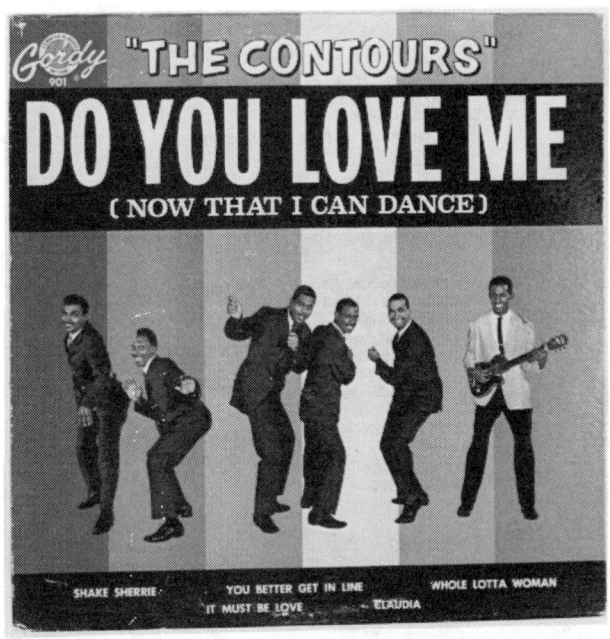

The Contours had a massive rhythm'n blues hit for the new Gordy label in 1962 with "Do You Love Me (Now That I Can Dance)." The label followed with its first LP, now one of the most collectible of all the Motown/Tamla/Gordy releases. When Motown reissued the album as part of its budget series in 1981, they replaced a number of tracks with alternate takes, making the reissue a sought-after collectible.

Label & Catalog #		Title	Year	VG+	NM
COLWELL-WINFIELD BLUES BAND, THE					
Verve/Forecast FVS-3056	(S)	Cold Wind Blues	1968	8.00	20.00
Verve/Forecast FVS-3072	(S)	Colwell-Winfield Blues Band	1969	Unreleased	
COMFORTABLE CHAIR, THE					
Ode Z12-44005	(S)	The Comfortable Chair	1968	6.00	15.00
COMMON PEOPLE, THE					
Capitol ST-266	(S)	Of The People, By The People	1969	40.00	100.00
COMPANY					
Playboy 107	(S)	Company	1972	1.00	5.00
COMPETITORS, THE					
The Competitors are a creation of Gary Usher & Co.					
Dot DLP-3542	(M)	Hits Of The Street And Strip	1963	60.00	150.00
Dot DLP-25542	(S)	Hits Of The Street And Strip	1963	80.00	200.00
COMPOST					
Columbia CS-31176	(S)	Compost	1972	5.00	12.00
COMSTOCK, BOBBY, & THE COUNTS					
Ascot ALM-13026	(M)	Out Of Sight	1966	10.00	25.00
Ascot ALS-16026	(S)	Out Of Sight	1966	14.00	35.00
CONCEPTION CORPORATION					
Cotillion SD-9031	(S)	Pause In Disaster	1970	4.00	10.00
CONDELLO [MICHAEL CONDELLO]					
Scepter SPS-542	(S)	Phase 1	1968	20.00	50.00
CONTOURS, THE					
Gordy G-901	(M)	Do You Love Me	1962	250.00	500.00
Motown M5-188V1	(M)	Do You Love Me	1981	6.00	15.00
		(Motown 188 is a reissue of Gordy 901 with alternate takes of many tracks.)			
CONTRABAND					
Epic KE-30814	(S)	Time And Space	1971	4.00	10.00
COODER, RY					
Refer to Capt. Beefheart / Ry Cooder; The Ceylib People; Longbranch Pennywhistle					
Reprise RS-6402	(S)	Ry Cooder	1970	6.00	15.00
		— Reprise albums above have brown & orange labels.—			
Reprise MS-2052	(S)	Into The Purple Valley	1972	4.00	10.00
Reprise MS-2117	(S)	Boomer's Story	1972	4.00	10.00
Reprise MS-2179	(S)	Paradise And Lunch	1974	4.00	10.00
Reprise MS-2254	(S)	Chicken Skin Music	1976	4.00	10.00
		—Reprise albums above have brown labels.—			
Reprise PRO-558	(DJ)	The Ry Cooder Radio Show	1976	40.00	100.00
Warner Bros. 3059	(S)	Show Time	1977	1.00	5.00
Warner Bros. 3358	(S)	Bop Till You Drop	1979	1.00	5.00
Warner Bros. 3489	(S)	Borderline	1981	1.00	5.00
Warner Bros. 238101	(DJ)	Borderline/Live In Europe	1981	80.00	200.00
Warner Bros. 3651	(S)	The Slide Area	1982	1.00	5.00
COOK E. JAR					
RCA Victor LSP-4159	(S)	Pledging My Love	1969	4.00	10.00
COOL, CALVIN, & THE SURF KNOBS					
Charter CLP-103	(M)	The Surfer's Beat	1963	14.00	35.00
Charter CLS-103	(S)	The Surfer's Beat	1963	20.00	50.00
COOPER, ALICE					
Originally the group's name, Alice Cooper is now pseudonymous with Vince Furnier. Refer to The Billion Dollar Babies.					
Straight STS-1051	(S)	Pretties For You (White label promo)	1969	60.00	150.00
Straight STS-1051	(S)	Pretties For You	1969	30.00	75.00
		—Straight albums above have yellow labels.—			
Straight STS-1051	(S)	Pretties For You	1970	20.00	50.00
Straight WS-1845	(S)	Easy Action (White label promo)	1970	40.00	100.00
Straight WS-1845	(S)	Easy Action	1970	20.00	50.00
		(Original covers for WS-1845 have "Alice Cooper" in black.)			
Straight WS-1845	(S)	Easy Action	1971	12.00	30.00
		(Later covers have "Alice Cooper" in white.)			
Straight WS-1883	(S)	Love It to Death (White label promo)	1971	40.00	100.00
Straight WS-1883	(S)	Love It to Death	1971	20.00	50.00
		—Straight albums above have pink labels.—			
Warner Bros. WS-1883	(S)	Love It to Death	1971	12.00	30.00
		(Cooper is gripping his cape in such a manner that his right thumb has a phallic appearance.)			

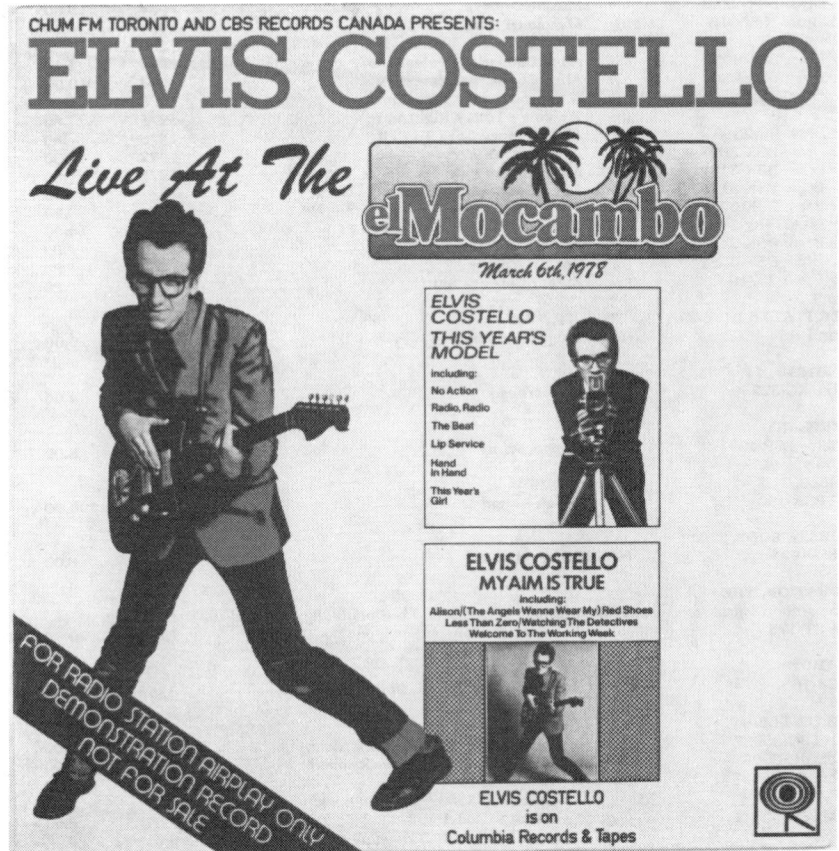

Elvis Costello's Live At The El Macambo, *recorded in March 1978, was pressed and shipped to radio stations in Canada as a promotional ploy for the singer's first two albums. While non-US releases are generally not a part of this book, the fact that this album was widely counterfeited and distributed on the collectors market gives it an in. Like the many counterfeits of* The Beatles Christmas Album, *the availability of this album as a dupe has tended to keep its value down (along with Mr C's up-and-down popularity with collectors).*

Label & Catalog #		Title	Year	VG+	NM
Warner Bros. WS-1883	(S)	Love It to Death	1971	8.00	20.00
		(The thumb remains and a white box that reads "Including Their Hit I'm Eighteen" in the corner.)			
Warner Bros. WS-1883	(S)	Love It to Death	197?	8.00	20.00
		(The cover has a broad white border at the top and bottom.)			
Warner Bros. WS-1883	(S)	Love It to Death	197?	1.00	5.00
		(Restored cover with the offending member airbrushed off.)			
Warner Bros. BS-2567	(S)	Killer (With calendar and poster)	1971	12.00	30.00
Warner Bros. BS-2567	(S)	Killer	1971	1.00	5.00
Warner Bros. BS-2623	(S)	School's Out (With panties & report card)	1972	20.00	50.00
Warner Bros. BS-2623	(S)	School's Out (With panties)	1972	12.00	30.00
Warner Bros. BS-2623	(S)	School's Out	1972	1.00	5.00
Warner Bros. BS-2685	(S)	Billion Dollar Babies	1974	1.00	5.00
Warner Bros. BS4-2685	(Q)	Billion Dollar Babies	1974	10.00	25.00
Warner Bros. BS-2748	(S)	Muscle Of Love (Box cover)	1974	4.00	10.00
Warner Bros. BS-2748	(S)	Muscle Of Love (Standard cover)	1974	.80	4.00
Warner Bros. BS4-2748	(Q)	Muscle Of Love	1974	10.00	25.00
Warner Bros. K-56018	(S)	Muscle Of Love	1974	16.00	40.00
		(W.B. 56108 was made in the U.S. for export to the U.K.)			
Warner Bros. BS-2803	(S)	Alice Cooper's Greatest Hits	1974	1.00	5.00
Warner Bros. BS4-2803	(Q)	Alice Cooper's Greatest Hits	1974	10.00	25.00
Atlantic SD-18130	(S)	Welcome To My Nightmare	1975	1.00	5.00
Atlantic SD-19157	(S)	Welcome To My Nightmare	1978	.80	4.00
Warner Bros. BS-2896	(S)	Alice Cooper Goes To Hell	1976	.80	4.00
Warner Bros. BSK-3027	(S)	Lace And Whiskey	1977	.80	4.00
Warner Bros. BSK-3107	(S)	Alice Cooper's Greatest Hits	1977	.80	4.00
Warner Bros. BSK-3138	(S)	The Alice Cooper Show	1977	.80	4.00
Warner Bros. BSK-3263	(S)	From The Inside	1978	.80	4.00
Warner Bros. PRO-789	(DJ)	The Alice Cooper Radio Show	1978	10.00	25.00
Warner Bros. BSK-3436	(S)	Flush The Fashion	1980	.80	4.00
Warner Bros. BSK-3581	(S)	Special Forces	1980	.80	4.00
Warner Bros. 23719	(S)	Zipper Catches Skin	1982	.80	4.00

COPPER PLATED INTEGRATED CIRCUIT, THE

Label & Catalog #		Title	Year	VG+	NM
Command RS-945SD	(S)	Plugged In Pop	1969	10.00	25.00

COPPERHEAD

Label & Catalog #		Title	Year	VG+	NM
Columbia KC-32250	(S)	Copperhead	1973	4.00	10.00

COPPERPENNY

Label & Catalog #		Title	Year	VG+	NM
RCA Victor LSP-4291	(S)	Copperpenny	1970	8.00	20.00

CORNELLS, THE

Label & Catalog #		Title	Year	VG+	NM
Garex LPGA-100	(M)	Beach Bound	1963	300.00	600.00

CORPORATE BODY, THE

Label & Catalog #		Title	Year	VG+	NM
MGM SE-4624	(S)	Prospectus '69	1969	6.00	15.00

CORPORATION, THE

The Corporation's first two albums were privately pressed. They originally recorded as The Skunks.

Label & Catalog #		Title	Year	VG+	NM
Capitol ST-175	(S)	The Corporation	1969	20.00	50.00

CORY, TROY

Label & Catalog #		Title	Year	VG+	NM
Assur CF-1681	(M)	Something Borrowed, Something New!	196?	14.00	35.00

COSTELLO, ELVIS

Label & Catalog #		Title	Year	VG+	NM
Columbia JC-35037	(S)	My Aim Is True (Yellow back cover)	1977	6.00	15.00
Columbia JC-35037	(S)	My Aim Is True (White back cover)	1977	1.00	5.00
Columbia PC-35037	(S)	My Aim Is True	1984	.80	4.00
		(Columbia 35037 features backing by Clover.)			
Columbia JC-35331	(S)	This Year's Model	1978	6.00	15.00
		(Red label with "Costello" around the perimeter.)			
Columbia JC-35331	(S)	This Year's Model	1978	1.00	5.00
		(Red label with "Columbia" around the perimeter.)			
Columbia PC-35331	(S)	This Year's Model	1978	.60	4.00
CBS CDN-10	(DJ)	Live At The El Mocambo	1978	150.00	300.00
		(Original copies of this Canadian promo have sharp printing on the label and the music plays clearly and cleanly. Counterfeits have a faded quality to the labels and play with excessive tape hiss.)			
Columbia (No number)	(DJ)	My Aim Is True (Picture disc)	1979	20.00	50.00
Columbia JC-35709	(S)	Armed Forces	1979	6.00	15.00
		(JC-35709 was issued with a 7" EP, "Live At Hollywood High")			
Columbia JC-35709	(S)	Armed Forces (Without EP)	1979	1.20	6.00
Columbia PC-35709	(S)	Armed Forces	1984	.80	4.00
Columbia JC-36347	(S)	Get Happy!!	1980	1.20	6.00
Columbia PC-36347	(S)	Get Happy!!	1984	.80	4.00
Costello AS-847	(DJ)	Taking Liberties (Radio sampler)	1980	10.00	25.00
Columbia JC-36839	(S)	Taking Liberties	1980	1.20	6.00
Columbia PC-36839	(S)	Taking Liberties	1984	.80	4.00

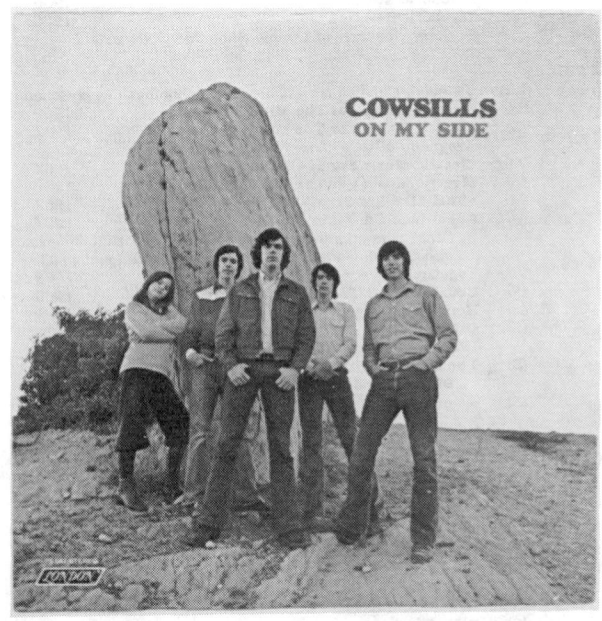

The Cowsills, a genuine family, broke big in 1967 with a whimsically wondrous single about a young lady that might best be described in the day's jargon as a "hippychick" who sold flowers in the park. "The Rain, The Park & Other Things" catapulted the siblings into fame and fortune. They followed this with a string of excellent pop singles for MGM and again reached chart-topping status in surveys around the country with their exuberant rendition of "Hair." By the time they had recorded their last album no one outside of the family was buying their records. While On My Side may not be their best LP, it is their rarest.

Label & Catalog #		Title	Year	VG+	NM
Columbia JC-37051	(S)	Trust	1981	1.20	6.00
Columbia PC-37051	(S)	Trust	1984	.80	4.00
Columbia AS-958	(DJ)	The Tom Snyder Interview (Promo)	1981	6.00	15.00
Columbia AS-1318	(DJ)	Almost Blue (Radio sampler)	1981	10.00	25.00
Columbia FC-37562	(S)	Almost Blue	1981	1.00	5.00
Columbia PC-37562	(S)	Almost Blue	1984	1.00	5.00
Columbia FC-38157	(S)	Imperial Bedroom	1982	1.20	6.00
Columbia PC-38157	(S)	Imperial Bedroom	1984	.80	4.00
Columbia HC-48157	(S)	Imperial Bedroom (Half-speed master)	1982	15.00	45.00
Columbia FC-38897	(S)	Punch The Clock	1983	1.20	6.00
Columbia PC-38897	(S)	Punch The Clock	1984	.80	4.00
Columbia FC-39429	(S)	Goodbye Cruel World	1984	.80	4.00

COSTELLO, ELVIS / NICK LOWE / MINK DeVILLE

Label & Catalog #		Title	Year	VG+	NM
Columbia/Capitol AS-443	(DJ)	Radio Radio (Orange vinyl)	1979	10.00	25.00

COTTON, GENE

Label & Catalog #		Title	Year	VG+	NM
Impact 1984	(S)	Power To Be	196?	6.00	15.00
Impact 3059	(S)	Peace	196?	6.00	15.00

COTTONWOOD

Label & Catalog #		Title	Year	VG+	NM
ABC 729	(S)	Camaraderie	1971	4.00	10.00

COUGAR, JOHN: *Refer to* JOHN COUGAR MELLENCAMP

COUNT FIVE, THE

Label & Catalog #		Title	Year	VG+	NM
Double Shot DSM-1001	(M)	Psychotic Reaction	1966	20.00	50.00
Double Shot DSS-5001	(E)	Psychotic Reaction	1966	12.00	30.00
		(Reproductions of Double Shot DSS-5001 exist.)			

COUNTRY JOE & THE FISH
Country Joe MacDonald with Fish Barry Melton, Chicken Hirsch, Bruce Barthol and David Cohen.

Label & Catalog #		Title	Year	VG+	NM
Vanguard VRS-9244	(M)	Electric Music For The Mind And Body	1967	20.00	50.00
Vanguard VSD-79244	(S)	Electric Music For The Mind And Body	1967	20.00	50.00
		—Vanguard albums above have black labels.—			
Vanguard VRS-9244	(M)	Electric Music For The Mind And Body	1967	8.00	20.00
Vanguard VSD-79244	(S)	Electric Music For The Mind And Body	1967	8.00	20.00
Vanguard VRS-9266	(M)	I-Feel-Like-I'm-Fixin'-To-Die	1967	8.00	20.00
Vanguard VSD-79266	(S)	I-Feel-Like-I'm-Fixin'-To-Die	1967	8.00	20.00
		("Die" was originally issued with a poster that folded out into a "Fish Game." This is worth an additional $10.)			
Vanguard VSD-79277	(S)	Together	1968	6.00	15.00
Vanguard VSD-6545	(S)	Country Joe & The Fish's Greatest Hits	1969	6.00	15.00
Vanguard VSD-79299	(S)	Here We Are Again	1969	6.00	15.00
Vanguard VSD-6555	(S)	C.J. Fish	1970	6.00	15.00
		—Vanguard albums above have gold labels.—			
Vanguard VSD/27/8	(S)	The Life And Times Of Country Joe & The Fish (2 LPs)	1971	4.00	10.00
Fantasy F-9530	(S)	Reunion	1977	1.00	5.00

COUNTRY JOE
"Country Joe" McDonald is the former lead singer of CJ & The Fish (above).

Label & Catalog #		Title	Year	VG+	NM
Custom Fidelity CFS-2348	(S)	Joe McDonald	1968	660.00	1,000.00
		(This was recorded in 1964 and 200 copies were pressed in 1968 in plain cardboard jackets solely for Joe's use.)			
Vanguard VSD-6546	(S)	Thinking Of Woody	1969	4.00	10.00
Vanguard VSD-6557	(S)	Tonight I'm Singing Just For You	1970	4.00	10.00
Vanguard VSD-79304	(S)	Hold On It's Coming	1971	4.00	10.00
Vanguard VSD-79315	(S)	War, War, War	1971	4.00	10.00
Vanguard VSD-79316	(S)	Incredible! Live!	1972	4.00	10.00
Vanguard VSD-79328	(S)	Paris Sessions	1973	4.00	10.00
Vanguard VSD-79348	(S)	Country Joe	1975	4.00	10.00
Fantasy F-9511	(S)	Love Is A Fire	1976	4.00	10.00
Fantasy F-9525	(S)	Goodbye Blues	1977	4.00	10.00
Fantasy F-9544	(S)	Rock & Roll Music From The Planet Earth	1978	4.00	10.00
Fantasy F-9586	(S)	Leisure Suite	1979	4.00	10.00
First American PIC-3309	(S)	The Early Years	1978	4.00	10.00
		(First American 3309 is a reissue of Custom Fidelity 2348.)			
Sweet Thunder 16	(S)	Into The Fray	198?	7.00	20.00

COUSINS, THE

Label & Catalog #		Title	Year	VG+	NM
Parkway P-7005	(M)	Music Of The Strip	1961	6.00	15.00
Parkway SP-7005	(S)	Music Of The Strip	1961	8.00	20.00

COVEN, THE

Label & Catalog #		Title	Year	VG+	NM
Mercury SR-61239	(S)	Witchcraft Destroys Minds & Reaps Souls	1969	6.00	15.00
MGM SE-4801	(S)	Coven	1971	4.00	10.00
Buddah BDS-5614	(S)	Blood On The Snow	1974	4.00	10.00

Label & Catalog #		Title	Year	VG+	NM

COVINGTON, JOEY
Joey Covington was a member of Jefferson Starship.

Grunt BFL1-0149	(S)	**Fat Fandango**	1973	1.00	5.00

COWSILL, BILL

MGM SE-4706	(S)	**Nervous Breakthrough**	1971	6.00	15.00

COWSILLS, THE

MGM E-4498	(M)	**The Cowsills**	1967	4.00	10.00
MGM SE-4498	(S)	**The Cowsills**	1967	6.00	15.00
MGM SE-4534	(S)	**We Can Fly**	1968	4.00	10.00
MGM SE-4554	(S)	**Captain Sad And His Ship Of Fools**	1968	4.00	10.00
MGM SE-4597	(S)	**The Best Of The Cowsills**	1969	4.00	10.00
MGM SE-4619	(S)	**The Cowsills In Concert**	1969	4.00	10.00
MGM SE-4639	(S)	**II By II**	1970	8.00	20.00
London 587	(S)	**On My Side**	1971	12.00	30.00

COWSILLS, THE / THE LINCOLN PARK ZOO

Wing SRW-16354	(S)	**The Cowsills Plus The Lincoln Park Zoo**	1968	4.00	10.00

COX, DANNY

Pioneer 2125	(S)	**Sunny**	1966	12.00	30.00
Together ZR-1011	(S)	**Birth Announcement** *(Prod. by Gary Usher)*	1970	12.00	30.00
Sunflower 5002	(S)	**Live At The Family Dog**	1970	6.00	15.00
Dunhill 50114	(S)	**Danny Cox**	1971	4.00	10.00

COXHILL, LOL

Ampex C-10132	(S)	**Ear Of The Beholder** *(2 LPs)*	1971	5.00	12.00

CRABBY APPLETON

Elektra EKS-74067	(S)	**Crabby Appleton**	1970	4.00	10.00
Elektra EKS-74106	(S)	**Rotten To The Core**	1971	4.00	10.00

CRAWDADDYS, THE

Voxx	(M)	**Crawdaddys Express**	1979	6.00	15.00

CRAWLER: *Refer to* BACK STREET CRAWLER

CRAYTON, PEE WEE

Crown CLP-5175	(M)	**Pee Wee Crayton**	1959	60.00	150.00
		— Crown albums above have black labels with a silver "Crown" logo.—			
Crown CLP-5175	(M)	**Pee Wee Crayton**	196?	10.00	25.00
		— Crown albums above have gray labels.—			
Vanguard VSD-6566	(S)	**The Things I Used To Do**	1971	6.00	15.00

CRAZY ELEPHANT

Bell 6034	(S)	**Crazy Elephant**	1969	8.00	20.00

CRAZY HORSE
Initially (RS-6438) Crazy Horse was Danny Whitten, Billy Talbot and Ralph Molina, all formerly of The Rockets, with Nils Lofgren and Jack Nitzsche. Refer to Neil Young.

Reprise RS-6438	(S)	**Crazy Horse**	1971	6.00	15.00
Reprise MS-2059	(S)	**Loose**	1972	4.00	10.00
Epic KE-31710	(S)	**At Crooked Lake**	1972	4.00	10.00

CREAM
Cream was Ginger Baker, Jack Bruce, and Eric Clapton with producer/silent member Felix Pappalardi.

Atco 33-206	(M)	**Fresh Cream**	1967	20.00	50.00
Atco SD-33-206	(S)	**Fresh Cream**	1967	12.00	30.00
Atco 33-232	(M)	**Disraeli Gears**	1967	20.00	50.00
Atco SD-33-232	(S)	**Disraeli Gears**	1967	10.00	25.00
Atco 2-700	(M)	**Wheels Of Fire** *(2 LPs. White label promo)*	1968	60.00	150.00
Atco SD-2-700	(S)	**Wheels Of Fire** *(2 LPs)*	1968	20.00	50.00
		(Original covers have a silver foil-like backing. Later covers are a dull grey.)			
Atco SD-7001	(S)	**Goodbye** *(With bonus poster)*	1969	12.00	30.00
Atco SD-7001	(S)	**Goodbye** *(Without poster)*	1969	8.00	20.00
		—Atco stereo albums above have purple & brown labels.—			
Atco SD-33-206	(S)	**Fresh Cream**	1969	4.00	10.00
Atco SD-33-232	(S)	**Disraeli Gears**	1969	4.00	10.00
Atco SD-2-700	(S)	**Wheels Of Fire** *(2 LPs)*	1969	6.00	15.00
Atco SD-7001	(S)	**Goodbye** *(Gatefold cover)*	1969	4.00	10.00
Atco SD-33-291	(S)	**Best Of Cream** *(White label promo)*	1969	20.00	50.00
Atco SD-33-291	(S)	**Best Of Cream**	1969	4.00	10.00
Atco SD-33-328	(S)	**Live Cream**	1970	4.00	10.00
Atco SD-7005	(S)	**Live Cream—Volume II**	1972	4.00	10.00
		—Atco albums above yellow labels with "Atlantic Recording Co." on the bottom.—			
Springboard SPB-4037	(S)	**Early Cream**	1972	4.00	10.00
Polydor 24-3502	(S)	**Heavy Cream**	1972	1.00	5.00
Polydor 24-55292	(S)	**Off The Top**	1973	1.00	5.00

Label & Catalog #		Title	Year	VG+	NM
RSO-015	(S)	**Classic Cuts** (2 LPs promo sampler)	1975	16.00	40.00
RSO RS-3009	(S)	**Fresh Cream**	1977	.80	4.00
RSO RS-3010	(S)	**Disraeli Gears**	1977	.80	4.00
RSO RS-3802	(S)	**Wheels Of Fire** (2 LPs)	1977	1.00	5.00
RSO RS-3012	(S)	**Best Of Cream**	1977	.80	4.00
RSO RS-3013	(S)	**Goodbye**	1977	.80	4.00
RSO RS-3014	(S)	**Live Cream**	1977	.80	4.00
RSO RS-3015	(S)	**Live Cream—Volume II**	1977	.80	4.00

CREAM / THE NEW YORK ROCK 'N' ROLL ENSEMBLE

Label & Catalog #		Title	Year	VG+	NM
Atco TLST-119/20	(DJ)	**Wheels Of Fire /**			
		The New York Rock 'N' Roll Ensemble	1968	20.00	50.00
		(Sampler with one side devoted to each artist's latest album.)			

CREAM / THE VANILLA FUDGE

Label & Catalog #		Title	Year	VG+	NM
Atco TLST-141	(DJ)	**Goodbye / Near The Beginning**	1969	20.00	50.00
		(Sampler with one side devoted to each artist's latest album.)			

CREATION OF SUNLIGHT

Label & Catalog #		Title	Year	VG+	NM
Windi 1001	(S)	**Creation Of Sunlight**	196?	300.00	500.00

CREEDENCE CLEARWATER REVIVAL [CREEDENCE CLEARWATER]

CCR was brothers John and Tom Fogerty with Stu Cook and Doug Clifford. They had originally recorded as The Golliwogs. Refer to Doug Sahm. Note: Several of CCR's albums were manufactured with Liberty labels for either that company's Record Club or for possible export. These are worth $50-100 each.

Label & Catalog #		Title	Year	VG+	NM
Fantasy F-8382	(DJ)	**Creedence Clearwater Revival** (White label)	1968	30.00	75.00
Fantasy F-8382	(S)	**Creedence Clearwater Revival**	1968	10.00	25.00
		(Without the blurb for "Suzie Q" on the cover.)			
Fantasy F-8382	(S)	**Creedence Clearwater Revival**	1968	6.00	15.00
		(Later pressings have a blurb for "Suzie Q" on the cover. "Porterville" is in mono on both pressings of this album.)			
Fantasy F-8387	(DJ)	**Bayou Country** (White label promo)	1969	30.00	75.00
Fantasy F-8387	(S)	**Bayou Country** ("Proud Mary" is in mono)	1969	6.00	15.00
Fantasy F-8393	(DJ)	**Green River** (White label promo)	1969	30.00	75.00
Fantasy F-8393	(S)	**Green River**	1969	6.00	15.00
Fantasy F-8397	(DJ)	**Willy And The Poor Boys** (White label)	1969	30.00	75.00
Fantasy F-8397	(S)	**Willy And The Poor Boys**	1969	6.00	15.00
Fantasy F-8402	(DJ)	**Cosmo's Factory** (White label promo)	1970	30.00	75.00
Fantasy F-8402	(S)	**Cosmo's Factory**	1970	6.00	15.00
Fantasy F-8410	(S)	**Pendulum**	1970	6.00	15.00
Fantasy F-9404	(S)	**Mardi Gras**	1972	6.00	15.00
		— Fantasy albums above have blue labels.—			
Fantasy F-8382	(S)	**Creedence Clearwater Revival**	1973	1.00	5.00
Fantasy F-8387	(S)	**Bayou Country** ("Proud Mary" is in mono)	1973	1.00	5.00
Fantasy F-8393	(S)	**Green River**	1973	1.00	5.00
Fantasy F-8397	(S)	**Willy And The Poor Boys**	1973	1.00	5.00
Fantasy F-8402	(S)	**Cosmo's Factory**	1973	1.00	5.00
Fantasy F-8410	(S)	**Pendulum**	1973	1.00	5.00
Fantasy F-9404	(S)	**Mardi Gras**	1973	1.00	5.00
Fantasy F-9418	(S)	**Creedence Gold**	1972	1.00	5.00
Fantasy ????	(Q)	**Creedence Gold**	197?	10.00	25.00
Fantasy F-9430	(S)	**More Creedence Gold**	1972	1.00	5.00
		— Fantasy albums above have brown labels.—			
Fantasy ORC-4512	(S)	**Creedence Clearwater Revival**	197?	.80	4.00
Fantasy ORC-4513	(S)	**Bayou Country** ("Proud Mary" is in mono)	197?	.80	4.00
Fantasy ORC-4514	(S)	**Green River**	197?	.80	4.00
Fantasy ORC-4515	(S)	**Willy And The Poor Boys**	197?	.80	4.00
Fantasy ORC-4516	(S)	**Cosmo's Factory**	197?	.80	4.00
Fantasy ORC-4517	(S)	**Pendulum**	197?	.80	4.00
Fantasy ORC-4518	(S)	**Mardi Gras**	197?	.80	4.00
Fantasy CCR-1	(S)	**Live In Europe** (2 LPs)	197?	1.00	5.00
K-Tel NU-9360	(S)	**20 Super Hits:**			
		The Best Of CCR ("Proud Mary" is mono)	1978	4.00	10.00
Fantasy MPF-4501	(S)	**The Royal Albert Hall Concert**	1980	1.00	5.00
Fantasy MPF-4501	(S)	**The Concert**	1981	1.00	5.00
Fantasy MPF-4509	(S)	**Creedence Country**	1981	1.00	5.00
Fantasy CCR-68	(S)	**Creedence Clearwater Revival 1968/1969**	1980	1.00	5.00
		(2 LPs. Repackage of 8382 and 8387.)			
Fantasy CCR-68	(S)	**Creedence Clearwater Revival 1969** (2 LPs)	1980	1.00	5.00
		(Repackage of 8393 and 8397.)			
Fantasy CCR-68	(S)	**Creedence Clearwater Revival 1970** (2 LPs)	1980	1.00	5.00
		(Repackage of 8402 and 8410.)			
Fantasy F-9621	(S)	**Chooglin'**	1982	1.00	5.00

CRESCENDOS, THE

Label & Catalog #		Title	Year	VG+	NM
Guest Star G-1453	(M)	**Oh Julie**	196?	24.00	60.00
Guest Star GS-1453	(E)	**Oh Julie**	196?	12.00	30.00

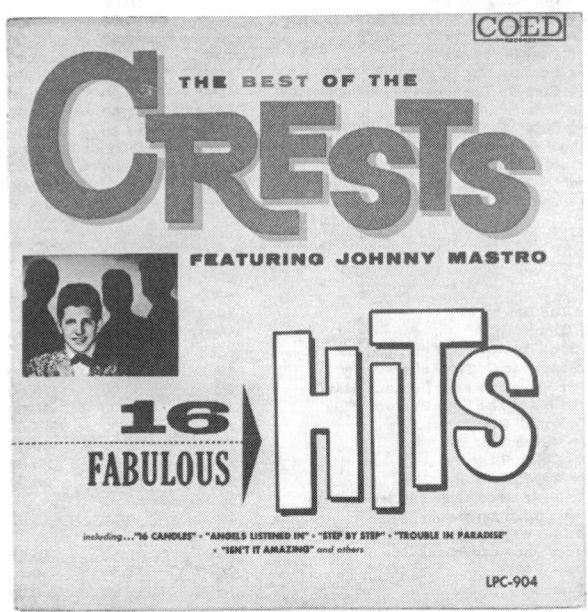

The Crests featuring Johnny Maestro are one of the few white groups that collectors of '50s rhythm'n blues group vocal records take to with great affinity, a testament to the sincerity conveyed by the young Maestro's pipes. Their two albums on Coed, The Crests Sing All The Biggies and The Best Of The Crests, are both difficult to find in collectible condition. While neither are known to have been recorded in stereo, a stereo cover for 904 was found but it contained a mono album. I would assume that the disc intended for such a jacket (and how come there's only one stereo jacket?) would be rechanneled stereo. Should a stereo record be found, it would easily fetch four figures as one of the rarest albums in the hobby.

Label & Catalog #		Title	Year	VG+	NM

CRESTS, THE
The Crests feature Johnny Maestro. Refer to The Brooklyn Bridge.

Coed LPC-901	(M)	The Crests Sing			
		All The Biggies *(Red label promo)*	1960	1,000.00	2,000.00
Coed LPC-901	(M)	The Crests Sing All The Biggies	1960	200.00	400.00
Coed LPC-904	(M)	The Best Of The Crests	1961	250.00	500.00
Coed LPS-904	(S)	The Best Of The Crests	1961	See note below	
		(A stereo cover of Coed 904 was found with a mono record inside.			
		It is doubtful at this time that a stereo record will be found. . .)			
Post 3000	(E)	The Crests Sing	196?	20.00	50.00
		(Post 3000 is a reissue of Coed 904.)			

CREW CUTS, THE
The Crew Cuts— brothers John and Ray Perkins, Pat Barrett and Rudi Maugeri— were influenced by the pop stylings of The Four Lads. The group's covers of rhythm'n blues hits remain a bone of contention among historians. To some they were the quintessence of inferior, white covers of black originals. To the more receptive, they were a major part of the popularization of black music among young whites. To their credit, they were one of the first groups to pen their own material and chart their own arrangements. And they had impeccable taste in the tunes they covered.

Mercury MG-251??	(10")	The Crew Cuts Go Longhair	1954	40.00	100.00
Mercury MG-25200	(10")	The Crew Cuts On The Campus	1954	40.00	100.00
Mercury MG-20067	(M)	The Crew Cuts Go Longhair	1954	30.00	75.00
Mercury MG-20140	(M)	The Crew Cuts On The Campus	1954	30.00	75.00
Mercury MG-20143	(M)	Crew Cut Capers	1955	30.00	75.00
Mercury MG-20144	(M)	Rock And Roll Bash	1955	30.00	75.00
Mercury MG-20199	(M)	Music Ala Carte	1956	30.00	75.00
		—*Mercury albums above have black labels.*—			
RCA Victor LPM-1933	(M)	Surprise Package	1959	14.00	35.00
RCA Victor LSP-1933	(S)	Surprise Package	1959	20.00	50.00
RCA Victor LPM-2037	(M)	The Crew Cuts Sing	1959	14.00	35.00
RCA Victor LSP-2037	(S)	The Crew Cuts Sing	1959	20.00	50.00
RCA Victor LPM-2067	(M)	You Must Have Been A Beautiful Baby	1960	14.00	35.00
RCA Victor LSP-2067	(S)	You Must Have Been A Beautiful Baby	1960	20.00	50.00
		—*RCA albums above have "Long Play" or "Living Stereo" labels.*—			
RCA Victor PR-102	(DJ)	The Crew Cuts Sing Out!	196?	10.00	25.00
RCA Victor CR-129	(DJ)	The Crew Cuts Have A Ball Plus Bowling Tips	196?	10.00	25.00
Camay CA-1002	(M)	The Crew Cuts Sing Folk	1961	8.00	20.00
Camay CA-3002	(S)	The Crew Cuts Sing Folk	1961	10.00	25.00
Wing MGW-12145	(M)	The Crew Cuts On The Campus	1962	8.00	20.00
Wing SRW-16145	(E)	The Crew Cuts On The Campus	1962	4.00	10.00
Wing MGW-12177	(M)	The Crew Cuts	1962	8.00	20.00
Wing SRW-16177	(E)	The Crew Cuts	1962	4.00	10.00
Wing MGW-12180	(M)	High School Favorites	1962	8.00	20.00
Wing SRW-16180	(E)	High School Favorites	1962	4.00	10.00
Wing MGW-12195	(M)	The Crew Cuts Sing The Masters	1962	8.00	20.00
Wing SRW-16195	(E)	The Crew Cuts Sing The Masters	1962	4.00	10.00

CREWE, BOB
Bob Crewe, as producer, writer and performer, was the "fifth" Four Season during their '60s heyday.

Warwick W-2009	(M)	Kicks	1960	10.00	25.00
Warwick WST-2009	(S)	Kicks	1960	20.00	50.00
Warwick W-2034	(M)	Crazy In The Heart	1961	10.00	25.00
Warwick WST-2034	(S)	Crazy In The Heart	1961	20.00	50.00
Philips PHM-200-150	(M)	All The Song Hits Of The Four Seasons	1964	10.00	25.00
Philips PHS-600-150	(S)	All The Song Hits Of The Four Seasons	1964	12.00	30.00
Philips PHM-200-238	(M)	Bob Crewe Plays The Four Seasons' Hits	1967	6.00	15.00
Philips PHS-600-238	(S)	Bob Crewe Plays The Four Seasons' Hits	1967	8.00	20.00
Dynovoice LP-9003	(M)	Music To Watch Girls By	1967	6.00	15.00
Dynovoice SLP-9003	(S)	Music To Watch Girls By	1967	8.00	20.00
Dynovoice DV-1902	(M)	Music To Watch Birds By	1967	8.00	20.00
Dynovoice DV-31902	(S)	Music To Watch Birds By	1967	10.00	25.00
Dynovoice DV-1906	(M)	The Bob Crewe Generation In Classic Form			
		Presents Bhen Lanzaroni	1968	6.00	15.00
Dynovoice DV-31906	(S)	The Bob Crewe Generation In Classic Form			
		Presents Bhen Lanzaroni	1968	6.00	15.00
CGC 1000	(S)	Let Me Touch You	1970	4.00	10.00
Elektra 7E-1083	(S)	Street Talk	1976	3.20	8.00

CRICKETS, THE
Original members were Buddy Holly with Jerry Allison, Niki Sullivan and Joe Mauldin; their first album is listed under Holly. After Buddy's death in 1959, this group plus Sonny Curtis recorded the Coral album. For the Liberty albums, Sullivan and Mauldin were replaced by Glen Hardin and Jerry Naylor. Refer to Bobby Vee; The Ventures.

Coral CRL-57320	(M)	In Style With The Crickets *(Blue label promo)*	1960	400.00	750.00
Coral CRL-57320	(M)	In Style With The Crickets	1960	100.00	250.00
Coral CRL-757320	(S)	In Style With The Crickets	1960	200.00	400.00
		("Deborah," "When You Ask About Love," "Time Will Tell," "I Fought			
		The Law," and "Love's Made A Fool Of You" are rechanneled.)			
Liberty LRP-3272	(M)	Something Old, Something New	1962	60.00	150.00
Liberty LST-7272	(S)	Something Old, Something New	1962	80.00	200.00

After Buddy Holly's death, the remaining Crickets continued to record, although with little success. In Style With The Crickets, *their first album sans their creative head, is a true rarity—especially in stereo (pictured here).*

Label & Catalog #		Title	Year	VG+	NM
Liberty LRP-7351	(M)	California Sun/She Loves You	1964	40.00	100.00
Liberty LST-7351	(S)	California Sun/She Loves You	1964	60.00	150.00
Barnaby Z-30268	(S)	Rockin' 50's Rock 'N' Roll	1970	8.00	20.00
Vertigo VEL-1020	(S)	Remnants	1973	8.00	20.00
Epic FE-44446	(S)	T-Shirt (With Paul McCartney)	1988	5.00	12.00

CRISS, PETER
Refer to Chelsea; Kiss.

Casablanca NBLP-7240	(S)	Out Of Control	1980	10.00	25.00

CRITTERS, THE

Kapp KL-1485	(M)	Younger Girl	1966	10.00	25.00
Kapp KS-3485	(S)	Younger Girl	1966	12.00	30.00
Project-3 PR-4001SD	(S)	Touch'n Go With The Critters	1968	12.00	30.00
Project-3 PR-4002SD	(S)	The Critters	1969	12.00	30.00

CRITTERS, THE / THE YOUNG RASCALS / LOU CHRISTIE

Boutique CA-1079	(M)	A Taste Of The Critters & The Young Rascals & Lou Christie	1966	16.00	40.00

CROCE, JIM
Jim Croce's first album was privately pressed.

Capitol SMAS-315	(S)	Jim And Ingrid Croce	1969	10.00	25.00
Pickwick SPC-3332	(S)	Another Day, Another Town	1973	1.20	6.00
		(Pickwick 3332 is a reissue of Capitol 315.)			
ABC X-756	(S)	You Don't Mess Around With Jim	1972	1.20	6.00
ABC X-769	(S)	Life And Times	1973	1.20	6.00
ABC X-797	(S)	I Got A Name	1973	1.20	6.00
ABC D-835	(S)	Photographs & Memories/His Greatest Hits	1974	1.20	6.00
Command QD-40006	(Q)	You Don't Mess Around With Jim	1974	6.00	15.00
Command QD-40007	(Q)	Life And Times	1974	6.00	15.00
Command QD-40008	(Q)	I Got A Name	1974	6.00	15.00
Command QD-40020	(Q)	Photographs & Memories/His Greatest Hits	1974	6.00	15.00
Lifesong 900	(S)	The Faces I've Been (2 LPs)	1975	1.20	6.00
Lifesong 6007	(S)	Time In A Bottle/Jim Croce's Greatest Love Songs	1977	1.00	5.00
Lifesong JZ-34993	(S)	You Don't Mess Around With Jim	1978	.80	4.00
Lifesong JZ-35000	(S)	Time In A Bottle/Jim Croce's Greatest Love Songs	1978	.80	4.00
Lifesong JZ-35008	(S)	Life And Times	1978	.80	4.00
Lifesong JZ-35009	(S)	I Got A Name	1978	.80	4.00
Lifesong JZ-35010	(S)	Photographs & Memories/His Greatest Hits	1978	.80	4.00
Lifesong JZ-35571	(S)	Jim Croce's Greatest Character	1978	.80	4.00
Cashwest TULP-77024	(S)	The Jim Croce Collection	1977	.80	4.00

CROFTERS, THE

London SW-99535	(S)	The Crofters	1971	4.00	10.00

CROME SYRCUS, THE

Command C-925SD	(S)	Love Cycle	1968	14.00	35.00

CROPPER, STEVE
Refer to Albert King & Steve Cropper.

Volt VOS-6006	(S)	With A Little Help From My Friends	1970	6.00	15.00

CROSBY, DAVID

Atlantic SD-8229	(S)	If I Could Only Remember My Name...	1971	4.00	10.00
—Atlantic albums above have green & orange labels with an 1841 Broadway address.—					
A&M SP-5232	(S)	Oh Yes I Can	1989	.80	4.00

CROSBY, DAVID, & GRAHAM NASH

Atlantic SD-7220	(S)	Graham Nash/David Crosby	1972	1.00	5.00
—Atlantic albums above have green & orange labels with an 1841 Broadway address.—					
ABC 902	(S)	Wind On The Water	1975	.80	4.00
ABC 956	(S)	Whistling Down The Wire	1976	.80	4.00
ABC 1042	(S)	Crosby/Nash—Live	1977	.80	4.00
ABC 1102	(S)	The Best Of Crosby/Nash	1978	.80	4.00

CROSBY, STILLS & NASH
David Crosby of The Byrds, Stephen Stills of Buffalo Springfield, and Graham Nash of The Hollies.

Atlantic SD-8229	(S)	Crosby, Stills & Nash	1969	4.00	10.00
—Atlantic albums above have green & orange labels with an 1841 Broadway address.—					
Atlantic SD-8229	(S)	Crosby, Stills & Nash	1973	.80	4.00
Atlantic SD-19104	(S)	CSN	1977	.80	4.00
Atlantic SD-16026	(S)	Replay	1980	.80	4.00
Atlantic SD-19360	(S)	Daylight Again	1982	.80	4.00
Atlantic 80075	(S)	Allies	1983	.80	4.00
Atlantic 82107	(S)	Live It Up	1990	.80	4.00
Atlantic 82319	(S)	CSN	1991	.80	4.00

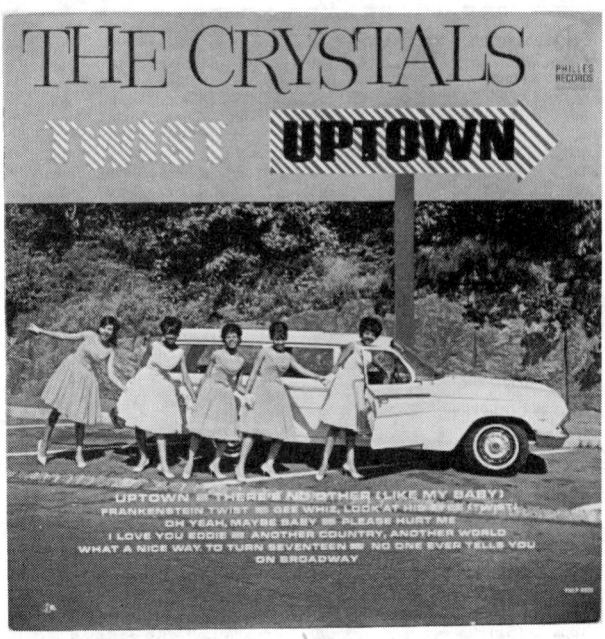

The Crystals were Barbara Alston with Lala Brooks, Dee Dee Kennibrew, Mary Thomas and Patricia Wright, all friends from the same part of Brooklyn. As part of Phil Spector's assault on the charts in the pre-Beatles '60s, their first album, The Crystals Twist Uptown, contained both of their first two hits, "There's No Other (Like My Baby)" and "Uptown." The cover art features the girls in party dresses entering a Chevy station wagon, obviously heading uptown for a little partying. Singles with the group's name reached the pop charts eight times through 1964. Unfortunately, in many cases the group on The Crystals' records wasn't The Crystals. . . For their sole #1, "He's A Rebel," the group was Los Angeles session singers, The Blossoms, fronted by the dynamic Darlene Love.

Label & Catalog #		Title	Year	VG+	NM

CROSBY, STILLS, NASH & YOUNG
The aforementioned trio plus ex-Buffalo Springfield Neil Young.

Label & Catalog #		Title	Year	VG+	NM
Atlantic 7200	(M)	Deja Vu *(White label promo)*	1970	60.00	150.00
Atlantic SD-7200	(S)	Deja Vu *(White label promo)*	1970	24.00	60.00
Atlantic SD-7200	(S)	Deja Vu	1970	1.20	6.00
		(Original covers for SD-7200 are textured with the photo pasted on.)			
Atlantic SD-7200	(S)	Deja Vu	1971	6.00	15.00
		(Later covers are textured with the photo printed on.)			
Atlantic 2-902	(M)	4 Way Street *(2 LPs. White label promo)*	1973	40.00	100.00
Atlantic SD-2-902	(S)	4 Way Street *(2 LPs. White label promo)*	1973	20.00	50.00
Atlantic SD-2-902	(S)	4 Way Street *(2 LPs)*	1971	3.20	8.00
		—Atlantic albums above have green & orange labels with an 1841 Broadway address.—			
Atlantic SD-7200	(S)	Deja Vu	1973	.80	4.00
Atlantic SD-2-902	(S)	4 Way Street *(2 LPs)*	1973	1.00	5.00
Atlantic PR-18102	(DJ)	A Rap With C, S, N & Y *(Interview)*	1973	20.00	50.00
Atlantic PR-165	(M)	Celebration/CSNY Month *(Promo sampler)*	1973	40.00	100.00
Atlantic PR-165	(S)	Celebration/CSNY Month *(Promo sampler)*	1973	20.00	50.00
Atlantic SD-18100	(S)	So Far	1974	.80	4.00
Atlantic 81888	(S)	American Dream	1988	.80	4.00

CROSS COUNTRY

Label & Catalog #		Title	Year	VG+	NM
Atco SD-7024	(S)	Cross Country	1973	4.00	10.00

CROSSFIRES, THE

Label & Catalog #		Title	Year	VG+	NM
Strand SL-1083	(M)	Limbo Rock	1963	8.00	20.00
Strand SLS-1083	(S)	Limbo Rock	1963	10.00	25.00

CROSSFIRES, THE
Members of The Crossfires later formed The Turtles.

Label & Catalog #		Title	Year	VG+	NM
Rhino RNLP-019	(S)	Out Of Control	1981	.80	4.00

CROTHERS, SCATMAN

Label & Catalog #		Title	Year	VG+	NM
Tops L-1511	(M)	Rock 'N Roll With Scatman	1956	40.00	100.00
Craftsman 8036	(M)	Gone With Scatman	1960	16.00	40.00
Motown M-777L	(S)	Big Ben Sings	1973	6.00	15.00

CROW
Crow features David Wagner.

Label & Catalog #		Title	Year	VG+	NM
Amaret ST-5002	(S)	Crow Music	1969	5.00	12.00
Amaret ST-5006	(S)	Crow By Crow	1970	5.00	12.00
Amaret ST-5009	(S)	Mosaic	1971	5.00	12.00
Amaret AST-5012	(S)	Best Of Crow	1972	4.00	10.00
Amaret ST-5013	(S)	David Wagner D/B/A Crow	1973	4.00	10.00

CROWBAR
Crowbar originally recorded with King Biscuit Boy.

Label & Catalog #		Title	Year	VG+	NM
Paramount PAS-6007	(S)	Bad Manors	1971	5.00	12.00
Epic KE-32746	(S)	KE-32746	1974	4.00	10.00

CROWELL, RODNEY

Label & Catalog #		Title	Year	VG+	NM
Warner Bros. 3228	(S)	Ain't Living Long Like This	1978	1.00	5.00
Warner Bros. 3407	(S)	But What Will The Neighbors Think	1980	1.00	5.00
Warner Bros. 3587	(S)	Rodney Crowell	1981	1.00	5.00
Columbia 40116	(S)	Street Language	1986	1.00	5.00
Columbia 44076	(S)	Diamonds & Dirt	1988	1.00	5.00
Columbia 45242	(S)	Keys To The Highway	1989	1.00	5.00
Warner Bros. 25965	(S)	The Rodney Crowell Collection	1989	1.00	5.00

CROWFOOT

Label & Catalog #		Title	Year	VG+	NM
Paramount PAS-5016	(S)	Crowfoot	1970	4.00	10.00
ABC X-745	(S)	Find The Sun	1971	4.00	10.00

CROWS, THE / THE HARPTONES

Label & Catalog #		Title	Year	VG+	NM
Roulette RE-114	(M)	The Crows & The Harptones *(2 LPs)*	1972	8.00	20.00

CRUDUP, ARTHUR "BIG BOY"

Label & Catalog #		Title	Year	VG+	NM
Fire 103	(M)	Mean Ol' Frisco	1960	800.00	1,200.00
Delmark DS-614	(S)	Look On Yonders Wall	1969	14.00	35.00
Delmark DS-621	(S)	Crudup's Mood	1969	14.00	35.00
RCA Victor LVP-573	(M)	Father Of Rock And Roll	1971	12.00	30.00
Trip BSP-7501	(E)	Mean Ol' Frisco	1975	6.00	15.00
		(Trip 7501 is a reissue of Fire 103.)			

CRUME, DILLARD

Label & Catalog #		Title	Year	VG+	NM
Alshire 5168	(S)	Soul Rockers	1970	4.00	10.00

CRY 3

Label & Catalog #		Title	Year	VG+	NM
Clear Light 102	(S)	An Odyssey Of The Spirit	1975	4.00	10.00

Label & Catalog #		Title	Year	VG+	NM

CRYAN' SHAMES, THE
The Cryan' Shames feature Isaac Guillory.

Label & Catalog #		Title	Year	VG+	NM
Columbia CL-2589	(M)	Sugar And Spice	1966	8.00	20.00
Columbia CS-9389	(S)	Sugar And Spice	1966	10.00	25.00
		("Sugar & Spice," "Ben Franklin's Almanac," "We Could Be Happy" and "I Wanna Meet You" are rechanneled on this album.)			
Columbia CL-9586	(M)	A Scratch In The Sky	1967	8.00	20.00
Columbia CS-9586	(S)	A Scratch In The Sky	1967	8.00	20.00
		— Columbia albums above have red labels with "360 Sound" on the bottom.—			
Columbia CS-9389	(S)	Sugar And Spice	1969	1.00	5.00
Columbia CS-9586	(S)	A Scratch In The Sky	1969	1.00	5.00
Columbia CS-9719	(S)	Synthesis	1969	6.00	15.00

CRYSTAL MANSION

Capitol ST-227	(S)	Crystal Mansion	1969	8.00	20.00
Rare Earth R-540L	(S)	Crystal Mansion	1972	4.00	10.00
20th Cent.-Fox 588	(S)	Crystal Mansion	1979	4.00	10.00

CRYSTALS, THE
The music of The Crystals— Barbara Alston, Lala Brooks, Dee Dee Kennibrew, Mary Thomas, and Patricia Wright— is a product of producer Phil Spector.

Philles PHLP-4000	(M)	Twist Uptown *(White label promo)*	1962	900.00	1,500.00
Philles PHLP-4000	(M)	Twist Uptown	1962	250.00	500.00
Philles T-90722	(M)	Twist Uptown *(Capitol Record Club)*	1963	300.00	600.00
Philles DT-90722	(E)	Twist Uptown *(Capitol Record Club)*	1963	900.00	1,500.00
Philles PHLP-4001	(M)	He's A Rebel *(White label promo)*	1963	900.00	1,500.00
Philles PHLP-4001	(M)	He's A Rebel	1963	200.00	400.00
Philles PHLP-4003	(M)	The Crystals Sing The Greatest Hits, Vol. 1	1963	350.00	700.00
		— Philles albums above have blue labels.—			

CUBY & THE BLIZZARDS

Philips PHS-600-307	(S)	Cuby And The Blizzards/Live	1969	8.00	20.00
Philips PHS-600-331	(S)	King Of The World	1970	8.00	20.00

CUFF LINKS, THE
The Cuff Links are the creation of Ron Dante.

Decca DL-75160	(S)	Tracy	1969	6.00	15.00

CULLY & TATE

Baton 1201	(M)	Rock 'N' Roll	195?	Unreleased?	

CULT

Starburst ST-500	(S)	The Mail Must Go Through	197?	4.00	10.00

CUMMINGS, BURTON
Cummings was a member of The Guess Who.

Portrait PR-34261	(S)	Burton Cummings	1976	1.00	5.00
Portrait PRQ-34261	(Q)	Burton Cummings	1976	6.00	15.00

CUNHA, RICK
Cunha was a member of Hearts & Flowers.

GRC GA-5004	(S)	Cunha Songs	197?	4.00	10.00
Columbia PC-33697	(S)	Moving Pictures	1975	4.00	10.00

CUPID'S INSPIRATION

Date TES-4020	(S)	Cupid's Inspiration	1970	4.00	10.00

CURB, MIKE
Before becoming one in a line of California's rabidly rightwinged Lt. Governors, Mike Curb could be found on countless '60s "B" soundtracks on Capitol/Tower/Sidewalk as producer and group leader. He normally did this under any number of nom de plumes: The Sidewalk Sounds, The Mugwump Establishment, or any of the other group names that sound sorta punk/psych but can't be traced to non-celluloid reality.

CoBurt 1002	(S)	Come Together	1970	1.00	5.00
CoBurt 1003	(S)	Sweet Gingerbread Man	1970	1.00	5.00
Forward STF-1020	(S)	The Doors Songbook	197?	6.00	15.00
Forward STF-1021	(S)	The Creedence Clearwater Songbook	197?	6.00	15.00
Forward STF-1022	(S)	The Rolling Stones Songbook	197?	6.00	15.00
Forward STF-1023	(S)	The Original Hot Wheels	197?	6.00	15.00

CURE, THE

PVC 7916	(S)	Boys Don't Cry	1980	5.00	12.00
PVC 2383-605	(S)	Faith	1981	5.00	12.00
A&M SP-06020	(S)	Happily Ever After	1981	4.00	10.00
A&M/Fiction SP-04902	(S)	Pornography	1982	4.00	10.00
Sire/Fiction 25076	(S)	Japanese Whispers	1984	4.00	10.00
Sire/Fiction 25086	(S)	The Top	1984	4.00	10.00
Elektra 60477	(S)	Standing On A Beach: The Singles	1987	1.00	5.00
Elektra 60783	(S)	Faith	1988	1.00	5.00
Elektra 60784	(S)	Seventeen Seconds	1988	1.00	5.00

Label & Catalog #		Title	Year	VG+	NM
Elektra 60785	(S)	**Pornography**	*1988*	**1.00**	**5.00**
Elektra 60786	(S)	**Boys Don't Cry**	*1988*	**1.00**	**5.00**
Elektra 60855	(S)	**Disintegration**	*1989*	**1.00**	**5.00**
Elektra 6978	(S)	**Mixed Up**	*1990*	**1.00**	**5.00**
CURFEW					
United Arts. UAS-6746	(S)	**Curfew**	*1970*	**4.00**	**10.00**
CURTIS, SONNY					
Curtis was a member of The Crickets.					
Imperial LP-9276	(M)	**Beatle Hits Flamenco Style**	*1964*	**16.00**	**40.00**
Imperial LP-12276	(S)	**Beatle Hits Flamenco Style**	*1964*	**20.00**	**50.00**
Viva V-36012	(S)	**The First Of Sonny Curtis**	*1968*	**10.00**	**25.00**
Viva V-36021	(S)	**The Sonny Curtis Style**	*1969*	**10.00**	**25.00**
Elektra 6E-227	(S)	**The Sonny Curtis Style**	*1979*	**4.00**	**10.00**
		(Elektra 227 is a reissue of Viva 36021.)			
Elektra 6E-283	(S)	**Love Is All Around**	*1980*	**4.00**	**10.00**
Elektra 6E-349	(S)	**Rollin'**	*1981*	**4.00**	**10.00**
CURTISS, DAVE, & CLIVE MALDOON					
Purple ST-880	(S)	**Curtiss/Maldoon**	*1972*	**4.00**	**10.00**
CYCLONES, THE: *Refer to* **THE CHAMPS / THE CYCLONES**					
CYMARRON					
Entrance Z-30962	(S)	**Rings**	*1971*	**4.00**	**10.00**
CYMBAL, JOHNNY					
Kapp KL-1324	(M)	**Mr. Bass Man**	*1963*	**20.00**	**50.00**
Kapp KS-3324	(S)	**Mr. Bass Man**	*1963*	**30.00**	**75.00**
CYMBALL, JOHNNY, & PEGGY CLINGER					
Chelsea 1002	(S)	**Cymbal & Clinger**	*1972*	**4.00**	**10.00**
CYNARA					
Capitol ST-547	(S)	**Cynara**	*1970*	**4.00**	**10.00**
CYRKLE, THE					
The Cyrkle can be found on the Amsterdam soundtrack "The Minx."					
Columbia CL-2544	(M)	**Red Rubber Ball**	*1966*	**8.00**	**20.00**
Columbia CS-9344	(S)	**Red Rubber Ball**	*1966*	**12.00**	**30.00**
Columbia CL-2632	(M)	**Neon**	*1967*	**4.00**	**10.00**
Columbia CS-9432	(S)	**Neon**	*1967*	**8.00**	**20.00**
CYRUS					
Elektra EKS-74105	(S)	**Cyrus**	*1971*	**4.00**	**10.00**

D' ABO, MIKE
Mike D' Abo was lead singer for Manfred Mann in the late '60s.

A&M SP-4346	(S)	Down At Rachel's Place	1972	4.00	10.00
A&M SP-3634	(S)	Broken Rainbows	1974	4.00	10.00

DADA

Atco SD-33-352	(S)	Dada	1970	6.00	15.00

DADDY COOL

Reprise RS-6471	(S)	Daddy Who? Daddy Cool!	1971	4.00	10.00
Reprise MS-2088	(S)	Teenage Heaven	1972	4.00	10.00

DADDY DEWDROP

Sunflower SNF-5006	(S)	Daddy Dewdrop	1971	8.00	20.00

DAHLSTROM, PATTI

Uni 73127	(S)	Patti Dahlstrom	1972	4.00	10.00
20th Cent.-Fox 421	(S)	Why I Am	1973	4.00	10.00
20th Cent.-Fox 461	(S)	Your Place Or Mine	1974	4.00	10.00

DAILEY, DON

Crown CLP-5314	(M)	Surf Stompin'	1963	12.00	30.00
Crown CST-314	(E)	Surf Stompin'	1963	6.00	15.00
		—*Crown albums above have gray labels.*—			

DAKILA

Epic 31756	(S)	Dakila	1972	4.00	10.00

DAKUS, WES, & THE REBELS

Kapp KL-1536	(M)	Wes Dakus' Rebels	1967	8.00	20.00
Kapp KS-3536	(S)	Wes Dakus' Rebels	1967	10.00	25.00

DALE, DICK [DICK DALE & HIS DEL-TONES]
Dick Dale was dubbed "King of the Surf Guitar." Refer to Jerry Cole.

Deltone LPM-1001	(M)	Surfer's Choice	1962	40.00	100.00
Deltone T-1886	(M)	Surfer's Choice	1962	16.00	40.00
Deltone DT-1886	(E)	Surfer's Choice	1962	12.00	30.00
		(Deltone 1886 is a Capitol reissue of LPM-1001.)			
Capitol T-1930	(M)	King Of The Surf Guitar	1963	16.00	40.00
Capitol ST-1930	(S)	King Of The Surf Guitar	1963	20.00	50.00
Capitol T-2002	(M)	Checkered Flag	1963	20.00	50.00
Capitol ST-2002	(S)	Checkered Flag	1963	30.00	75.00
Capitol T-2053	(M)	Mr. Eliminator	1964	20.00	50.00
Capitol ST-2053	(S)	Mr. Eliminator	1964	30.00	75.00
Capitol T-2111	(M)	Summer Surf *(With bonus single)*	1964	40.00	100.00
Capitol ST-2111	(S)	Summer Surf *(With bonus single)*	1964	50.00	125.00
		(Includes the bonus single "Racing Waves" / "Movin' Surf" by Jerry Cole in a special "pocket" on the cover.)			
Capitol T-2111	(M)	Summer Surf *(Without the single)*	1964	20.00	50.00
Capitol ST-2111	(S)	Summer Surf *(Without the single)*	1964	30.00	75.00
Capitol T-2293	(M)	Rock Out—Live At Ciro's	1965	40.00	100.00
Capitol ST-2293	(S)	Rock Out—Live At Ciro's	1965	60.00	150.00
Crescendo GNPS-2095	(S)	Dick Dale's Greatest Hits	1975	1.00	5.00

DALE, DICK / THE HOLLYWOOD SURFERS

Dub Tone LP-1246	(M)	The Surf Family	1964	14.00	35.00

DALE, DICK / THE STOMPERS

Cloister CLP-6301	(M)	Silver Sounds Of The Surf *(Felt cover)*	1963	80.00	200.00

DALE, DICK / BO TROY & HIS HOT RODS

Diplomat D-2304	(M)	Wild Hot Rod Wails	196?	10.00	25.00
Diplomat DS-2304	(S)	Wild Hot Rod Wails	196?	12.00	30.00

Label & Catalog #		Title	Year	VG+	NM
DALE & GRACE					
Dale Houston and Grace Broussard.					
Montel LP-100	(M)	I'm Leaving It Up To You	1964	60.00	150.00
DALLS COUNTY					
Enterprise ENS-1011	(S)	Dallas County	1970	6.00	15.00
DALTON, KATHY					
DiscReet 2168	(S)	Amazing	1973	6.00	15.00
		(Ms Dalton is backed by Little Feat.)			
DiscReet 2208	(S)	Boogie Bands And One Night Stands	1974	3.20	8.00
		(DiscReet 2208 is a reissue of 2168.)			
DALTREY, ROGER					
Mr. Daltrey is a member of The Who.					
MCA 328	(S)	Daltrey	1973	1.20	6.00
MCA 2147	(S)	Ride A Dark Horse	1975	1.20	6.00
MCA 2271	(S)	One Of The Boys	1977	1.20	6.00
MCA 37030	(S)	Ride A Dark Horse	197?	.80	4.00
MCA 37031	(S)	One Of The Boys	197?	.80	4.00
MCA 37052	(S)	Daltrey	197?	.80	4.00
MCA 5301	(S)	Best Bits	198?	.80	4.00
DAMNATION					
United Arts. UAS-6738	(S)	The Damnation Of Adam Blessing	1969	8.00	20.00
United Arts. UAS-6773	(S)	The Second Damnation	1970	8.00	20.00
United Arts. UAS-5533	(S)	Which Is The Justice, Which Is The Thief	1971	8.00	20.00
DANDO SHAFT					
Neon 5	(S)	Dando Shaft	1971	4.00	10.00
DANIEL, GODFREY: *Refer to* GODFREY DANIEL					
DANIELS, BILLY					
King KS-1113	(S)	New Black Magic	1970	6.00	15.00
DANKO, RICK					
Rick Danko was a member of The Band.					
Arista AB-4141	(S)	Rick Danko	1977	3.20	8.00
DANKS					
Colossus CS-1005	(S)	Danks	1970	6.00	15.00
DANTE, RON					
Dante was the creator of the music for The Cuff Links; The Detergents; The Archies; Mercy.					
Kirshner KES-106	(S)	Ron Dante Brings You Up (With photo)	1970	8.00	20.00
Kirshner KES-106	(S)	Ron Dante Brings You Up (Without photo)	1970	6.00	15.00
DANTE & THE EVERGREENS					
Madison MA-1002	(M)	Dante & The Evergreens	1961	250.00	500.00
DARIN, BOBBY					
Atco 33-102	(M)	Bobby Darin	1958	40.00	100.00
Atco 33-104	(M)	That's All	1959	20.00	50.00
Atco SD-33-104	(S)	That's All	1959	40.00	100.00
Atco 33-115	(M)	This Is Darin	1960	20.00	50.00
Atco SD-33-115	(S)	This Is Darin	1960	30.00	75.00
Atco 33-122	(M)	Darin At The Copa	1960	20.00	50.00
Atco SD-33-122	(S)	Darin At The Copa	1960	30.00	75.00
Atco SP-1001	(M)	For Teenagers Only	1961	80.00	200.00
		(Gatefold cover with fold-open poster includes paper insert.)	1960		
Atco SP-1001	(M)	For Teenagers Only	1960	60.00	150.00
		(Gatefold cover without the poster or insert.)			
Atco 33-124	(M)	It's You Or No One	1960	20.00	50.00
Atco SD-33-124	(S)	It's You Or No One	1960	30.00	75.00
Atco 33-125	(M)	The 25th Of December	1960	20.00	50.00
Atco SD-33-125	(S)	The 25th Of December	1960	30.00	75.00
Atco 33-126	(M)	Two Of A Kind	1961	16.00	40.00
Atco SD-33-126	(S)	Two Of A Kind	1961	20.00	50.00
Atco 33-131	(M)	The Bobby Darin Story (White cover)	1961	16.00	40.00
Atco SD-33-131	(P)	The Bobby Darin Story (White cover)	1961	20.00	50.00
Atco 33-134	(M)	Love Swings	1961	16.00	40.00
Atco SD-33-134	(S)	Love Swings	1961	20.00	50.00
Atco 33-138	(M)	Twist With Bobby Darin	1961	16.00	40.00
Atco SD-33-138	(S)	Twist With Bobby Darin	1961	20.00	50.00
		—Atco albums above have yellow labels with a harp on top.—			
Atco 33-102	(M)	Bobby Darin	196?	12.00	30.00
Atco 33-104	(M)	That's All	196?	8.00	20.00
Atco SD-33-104	(S)	That's All	196?	10.00	25.00

Summer Surf by Dick "King of the Surf Guitar" Dale was one of several surf-related albums that Capitol issued with a special bonus single tucked inside a "pocket" on the front cover promotiong another Capitol artist's latest album. For this album by Dale, "Racing Waves" / Movin' Surf" was taken from Jerry Cole's Surf Age album. Always hard to find as a complete package, these records (others include the aforementioned Cole title along with The Super Stock's Surf Route 101 and Mr Gasser & The Weirdos' Surfink!), these packages have picked up in interest and value correspondingly in recent years.

Label & Catalog #		Title	Year	VG+	NM
Atco 33-115	(M)	This Is Darin	196?	8.00	20.00
Atco SD-33-115	(S)	This Is Darin	196?	10.00	25.00
Atco 33-122	(M)	Darin At The Copa	196?	8.00	20.00
Atco 33-122	(S)	Darin At The Copa	196?	10.00	25.00
Atco 33-124	(M)	It's You Or No One	196?	8.00	20.00
Atco SD-33-124	(S)	It's You Or No One	196?	10.00	25.00
Atco 33-125	(M)	The 25th Of December	196?	8.00	20.00
Atco SD-33-125	(S)	The 25th Of December	196?	10.00	25.00
Atco 33-126	(M)	Two Of A Kind	196?	8.00	20.00
Atco SD-33-126	(S)	Two Of A Kind	196?	10.00	25.00
Atco 33-131	(M)	The Bobby Darin Story (Black cover)	196?	8.00	20.00
Atco SD-33-131	(S)	The Bobby Darin Story (Black cover)	196?	10.00	25.00
Atco 33-134	(M)	Love Swings	196?	8.00	20.00
Atco SD-33-134	(S)	Love Swings	196?	10.00	25.00
Atco 33-138	(M)	Twist With Bobby Darin	196?	8.00	20.00
Atco SD-33-138	(S)	Twist With Bobby Darin	196?	10.00	25.00
Atco 33-140	(M)	Bobby Darin Sings Ray Charles	1962	10.00	25.00
Atco SD-33-140	(S)	Bobby Darin Sings Ray Charles	1962	10.00	25.00
Atco 33-146	(M)	Things And Other Things	1962	12.00	30.00
Atco SD-33-146	(S)	Things And Other Things	1962	10.00	25.00
Atco 33-124	(M)	It's You Or No One	1962	12.00	30.00
Atco SD-33-124	(S)	It's You Or No One	1963	10.00	25.00
Atco 33-167	(M)	Winners	1963	12.00	30.00
Atco SD-33-167	(S)	Winners	1964	10.00	25.00
			1964	12.00	30.00

—*Atco mono albums above have gold & gray labels; stereo albums have purple & brown labels.—*

Label & Catalog #		Title	Year	VG+	NM
Clarion 603	(M)	Clementine	196?	8.00	20.00
Clarion SD-603	(S)	Clementine	196?	10.00	25.00
Capitol W-1791	(M)	Oh! Look At Me Now	1962	6.00	15.00
Capitol SW-1791	(S)	Oh! Look At Me Now	1962	8.00	20.00
Capitol T-1791	(M)	Oh! Look At Me Now	1962	6.00	15.00
Capitol ST-1791	(S)	Oh! Look At Me Now	1963	8.00	20.00
Capitol T-1826	(M)	Earthy	1963	6.00	15.00
Capitol ST-1826	(S)	Earthy	1963	8.00	20.00
Capitol T-1866	(M)	You're The Reason I'm Living	1963	6.00	15.00
Capitol ST-1866	(S)	You're The Reason I'm Living	1963	8.00	20.00
Capitol T-1942	(M)	18 Yellow Roses	1963	6.00	15.00
Capitol ST-1942	(S)	18 Yellow Roses	1963	8.00	20.00
Capitol T-2007	(M)	Golden Folk Hits	1963	6.00	15.00
Capitol ST-2007	(S)	Golden Folk Hits	1963	8.00	20.00
Capitol T-2194	(M)	From "Hello Dolly" To "Goodbye Charlie"	1964	6.00	15.00
Capitol ST-2194	(S)	From "Hello Dolly" To "Goodbye Charlie"	1964	8.00	20.00
Capitol T-2322	(M)	Venice Blue	1965	6.00	15.00
Capitol ST-2322	(S)	Venice Blue	1965	8.00	20.00
Capitol T-2571	(M)	The Best Of Bobby Darin	1966	6.00	15.00
Capitol ST-2571	(S)	The Best Of Bobby Darin	1966	6.00	15.00
Atlantic 8121	(M)	The Shadow Of Your Smile	1966	6.00	15.00
Atlantic SD-8121	(S)	The Shadow Of Your Smile	1966	8.00	20.00
Atlantic 8126	(M)	In A Broadway Bag	1966	6.00	15.00
Atlantic SD-8126	(S)	In A Broadway Bag	1966	8.00	20.00
Atlantic 8135	(M)	If I Were A Carpenter	1966	6.00	15.00
Atlantic SD-8135	(S)	If I Were A Carpenter	1966	20.00	50.00
Atlantic 8142	(M)	Inside Out	1967	6.00	15.00
Atlantic SD-8142	(S)	Inside Out	1967	12.00	30.00
Atlantic 8154	(M)	Bobby Darin Sings Doctor Dolittle	1967	6.00	15.00
Atlantic SD-8154	(S)	Bobby Darin Sings Doctor Dolittle	1967	6.00	15.00
Direction 1936	(S)	Born Walden Robert Cassotto	1968	10.00	25.00
Direction 1937	(S)	Commitment	1969	10.00	25.00
Motown M-753L	(S)	Bobby Darin	1972	6.00	15.00
Motown M-813L	(S)	Darin 1936-1973	1974	4.00	10.00

DARROW, CHRIS

Label & Catalog #		Title	Year	VG+	NM
Fantasy 9403	(S)	Artist Proof	1972	4.00	10.00
United Arts. LA-048F	(S)	Chris Darrow	1973	4.00	10.00
United Arts. LA-242G	(S)	Under My Own Disguise	1974	4.00	10.00
Pacific Arts PAC7-132	(S)	Fretless	197?	4.00	10.00

DARRYL WAY'S WOLF

Label & Catalog #		Title	Year	VG+	NM
London XPS-644	(S)	Darryl Way's Wolf	1973	4.00	10.00

DARTELLS, THE

Label & Catalog #		Title	Year	VG+	NM
Dot DLP-3522	(M)	Hot Pastrami	1963	14.00	35.00
Dot DLP-25522	(S)	Hot Pastrami	1963	20.00	50.00

DARTS, THE

Label & Catalog #		Title	Year	VG+	NM
Del-Fi DF-1244	(M)	Hollywood Drag	1963	14.00	35.00
Del-Fi DFST-1244	(S)	Hollywood Drag	1963	20.00	50.00

DAUGHTERS OF ALBION, THE

Label & Catalog #		Title	Year	VG+	NM
Fontana SRF-68586	(S)	The Daughters Of Albion (With inserts)	1968	6.00	15.00

Walden Robert Cassotto, better known as Bobby Darin, was an ambitious singer with a wide ranging palate: After breaking into the AM market with a series of unimpressive rock'n roll hits, he hit his stride as a cabaret singer with uptempo, Sinatra-ish performances on such standards as "Mack The Knife" and "Beyond The Sea." Things & Other Things kept the pot boiling while his interests moved onward. . . Opting for folk/rock in the latter part of the '60s, he contributed one excellent album to that genre, If I Were A Carpenter.

Label & Catalog #		Title	Year	VG+	NM
DAVE DEE, DOZY, BEAKY, MICK & TICH					
Fontana MGF-27567	(M)	Greatest Hits	1967	12.00	30.00
Fontana SRF-67567	(S)	Greatest Hits	1967	16.00	40.00
		("Bend It" and "Hold Tight" are rechanneled.)			
Imperial LP-12402	(S)	Time To Take Off ("Zabadak" is rechanneled)	1968	16.00	40.00
V.M.C. 124	(S)	Another Day, Another Lifetime	1968	40.00	100.00
DAVIES, DAVE					
Dave Davies is lead guitar and second singer/songwriter for The Kinks.					
RCA Victor AFL1-3603	(S)	Dave Davies	1980	4.00	10.00
RCA Victor AFL1-4036	(S)	Glamour	1981	4.00	10.00
Warner Bros. 23917	(S)	Chosen People	1983	4.00	10.00
DAVIS, JESSE ED					
Atco SD-33-346	(S)	Jesse Ed Davis	1970	6.00	15.00
Atco SD-33-382	(S)	Ululu	1972	6.00	15.00
Epic KE-32133	(S)	Keep On Comin'	1973	5.00	12.00
DAVIS, PAUL					
Paul Davis also recorded with Gracious.					
Bang BLPS-223	(S)	A Little Bit Of Paul Davis	1970	14.00	35.00
DAVIS, SPENCER [THE SPENCER DAVIS GROUP]					
Steve Winwood fronted Spencer Davis' groups on each U.A. album except 6652.					
United Arts. UAL-3578	(M)	Gimme Some Lovin'	1967	20.00	50.00
United Arts. UAS-6578	(E)	Gimme Some Lovin'	1967	16.00	40.00
United Arts. UAL-3589	(M)	I'm A Man	1967	16.00	40.00
United Arts. UAS-6589	(P)	I'm A Man	1967	20.00	50.00
United Arts. UAS-6641	(P)	Spencer Davis' Greatest Hits	1968	10.00	25.00
United Arts. UAS-6652	(S)	With Their New Face On	1968	8.00	20.00
United Arts. UAS-6691	(S)	Heavies	1969	8.00	20.00
Mediarts 4111	(S)	It's Been So Long	1971	4.00	10.00
Vertigo VEL-1015	(S)	Gluggo	1973	4.00	10.00
Vertigo VEL1-21	(S)	Living In A Back Street	1974	4.00	10.00
United Arts. LA-433E	(S)	The Very Best Of The Spencer Davis Group	1975	.80	4.00
DAVIS, TIM					
Tim Davis was a member of The Steve Miller Band.					
Metromedia BML-1054	(S)	Pipe Dream	1972	4.00	10.00
Metromedia BML-1075	(S)	Take Me As I Am	1974	4.00	10.00
DAVIS, TYRONE					
Dakar DK-9005	(S)	Can I Change My Mind	1969	12.00	30.00
Dakar DK-9027	(S)	Turn Back The Hands Of Time	1970	12.00	30.00
Dakar DK-76901	(S)	I Had It All The Time	1972	12.00	30.00
Dakar DK-76902	(S)	Tyrone Davis' Greatest Hits	1972	10.00	25.00
Dakar DK-76904	(S)	Without You In My Life	1973	10.00	25.00
Dakar DK-76909	(S)	It's All In the Game	1974	8.00	20.00
Dakar DK-76915	(S)	Homewrecker	1975	8.00	20.00
Dakar DK-76918	(S)	Turning Point	1976	8.00	20.00
Columbia PC-34268	(S)	Love And Touch	1976	1.00	5.00
Columbia PC-34654	(S)	Let's Be Closer Together	1977	1.00	5.00
Columbia JC-35305	(S)	I Can't Go On This Way	1978	1.00	5.00
Columbia JC-35723	(S)	In The Mood	1979	1.00	5.00
Columbia JC-36230	(S)	Can't You Tell It's Me	1979	1.00	5.00
Columbia JC-36598	(S)	I Just Can't Keep On Going	1980	1.00	5.00
Columbia FC-37366	(S)	Everything In Place	1981	1.00	5.00
Epic PE-38626	(S)	Tyrone Davis' Greatest Hits	1983	1.00	5.00
DAVISON, BRIAN					
Brian Davison also recorded as a member of The Nice.					
Mercury SR-61340	(S)	Every Which Way	1971	4.00	10.00
DAWE, TIM					
Dawe was a member of Iron Butterfly.					
Straight STS-1058	(S)	Penrod	1969	12.00	30.00
Warner Bros. WS-1841	(S)	Penrod	1970	6.00	15.00
DAY, BOBBY					
Bobby Day is a pseudonym for Bobby Byrd.					
Class LP-5002	(M)	Rockin' With Robin	1959	250.00	600.00
Rendezvous M-1312	(M)	Rockin' With Robin	196?	40.00	100.00
		(Rendezvous 1312 is a reissue of Class 5002.)			
DAY BLINDNESS					
Studio 10 DBX-101	(S)	Day Blindness	1969	20.00	50.00

Robert Byrd's name can be found as singer and songwriter on rhythm'n blues records cred-ited to The Hollywood Flames, also known as The Four Flames, The Flames, and/or The Hollywood Four Flames, as well as The Jets, The Tangiers, The Satellites, and Bob & Earl! As Bobby Day he scored a chart-topping smash in 1958 with the delightful "Rock-in' Robin." The album, Rockin' Robin With Bobby Day, features a ridiculous photo of the singer out on a limb surrounded by half-a-dozen stuffed birds, not one of which is a robin!

Label & Catalog #		Title	Year	VG+	NM

DE-FENDERS, THE
The De-Fenders feature Bruce Johnston.

World Pacific WP-1810	(M)	The Big Ones	1963	20.00	50.00
World Pacific ST-1810	(S)	The Big Ones *(Green vinyl)*	1963	60.00	150.00
World Pacific ST-1810	(S)	The Big Ones *(Red vinyl)*	1963	60.00	150.00
World Pacific ST-1810	(S)	The Big Ones	1963	30.00	75.00
Del-Fi DFLP-1242	(M)	Drag Beat	1963	20.00	50.00
Del-Fi DFST-1242	(S)	Drag Beat	1963	30.00	75.00

DEAD BOYS, THE

| Sire SR-6038 | (S) | Young, Loud And Snotty | 1977 | 8.00 | 20.00 |
| Sire SRK-6054 | (S) | We Have Come For Your Children | 1978 | 8.00 | 20.00 |

DEAD KENNEDYS

| I.R.S. SP-70014 | (S) | Fresh Fruit For Rotting Vegetables *(With poster)* | 1981 | 8.00 | 20.00 |
| Alternate Tentacles | (S) | Fresh Fruit For Rotting Vegetables | 1981 | 1.00 | 5.00 |

DEADLY ONES, THE

| Vee Jay LP-1090 | (M) | It's Monster Surfing Time | 1964 | 40.00 | 100.00 |
| Vee Jay VS-1090 | (S) | It's Monster Surfing Time | 1964 | 60.00 | 150.00 |

DEAL, BILL, & THE RHONDELS

| Heritage HTS-35003 | (S) | Vintage Rock | 1968 | 12.00 | 30.00 |
| Heritage HTS-35006 | (P) | The Best Of Bill Deal & The Rhondels | 1969 | 12.00 | 30.00 |

DEAN, AL

| Warrior 506 | (M) | Fragile Heart | 195? | 50.00 | 125.00 |

DEAN, RUSSELL

| Metromedia 1046 | (S) | Russell Dean | 1971 | 4.00 | 10.00 |

DECEMBER'S CHILDREN

| Mainstream S-6128 | (S) | December's Children | 1970 | 20.00 | 50.00 |

DEE, JOEY [JOEY DEE & THE STARLIGHTERS]
Joey Dee can be found on the Roulette soundtrack "Hey Let's Twist" and "Two Tickets To Paris."

Roulette R-25166	(M)	Doin' The Twist	1961	16.00	40.00
Roulette SR-25166	(S)	Doin' The Twist	1961	20.00	50.00
Roulette R-25171	(M)	All The World Is Twistin'	1961	12.00	30.00
Roulette SR-25171	(S)	All The World Is Twistin'	1961	16.00	40.00
Roulette R-25173	(M)	Back To The Peppermint Lounge Twistin'	1961	12.00	30.00
Roulette SR-25173	(S)	Back To The Peppermint Lounge Twistin'	1961	16.00	40.00
Roulette R-25197	(M)	Joey Dee	1962	10.00	25.00
Roulette SR-25197	(S)	Joey Dee	1962	12.00	30.00
Roulette R-25221	(M)	Dance, Dance, Dance	1963	10.00	25.00
Roulette SR-25221	(S)	Dance, Dance, Dance	1963	12.00	30.00
Scepter S-503	(M)	The Peppermint Twisters	1962	10.00	25.00
Scepter SS-503	(S)	The Peppermint Twisters	1962	12.00	30.00
Forum FC-9099	(M)	Joey Dee & The Starlighters	1963	3.20	8.00
Forum FCS-9099	(S)	Joey Dee & The Starlighters	1963	4.00	10.00
Jubilee JLP-8000	(M)	Hitsville	1966	8.00	20.00
Jubilee JLS-8000	(S)	Hitsville	1966	10.00	25.00
Tomorrow TV1-135	(S)	Joey Dee	1977	4.00	10.00
Mohawk 1005	(S)	Joey Dee	1978	4.00	10.00

(Mohawk 1005 is a reissue of Tomorrow 135.)

DEE, KIKI

Liberty LST-7613	(S)	Patterns	1969	4.00	10.00
Tamla TS-303	(S)	Great Expectations	1970	4.00	10.00
Liberty LN-10148	(S)	Patterns	1981	.80	4.00

DEE, MERCY

| Arhoolie 1007 | (M) | Mercy Dee | 1961 | 20.00 | 50.00 |

DEEP, THE

| Parkway P-7051 | (M) | Psychedelic Moods | 1966 | 100.00 | 250.00 |
| Parkway SP-7051 | (S) | Psychedelic Moods | 1966 | 300.00 | 500.00 |

DEEP PURPLE
Deep Purple features Ritchie Blackmore, Ian Paice and Jon Lord. Refer to Green Bullfrog.

Tetragrammaton T-102	(S)	Shades Of Deep Purple	1968	12.00	30.00
Tetragrammaton T-107	(S)	Book Of Taliesyn	1968	12.00	30.00
Tetragrammaton T-119	(S)	Deep Purple	1968	12.00	30.00
Tetragrammaton T-131	(S)	Deep Purple & The Royal Philharmonic	1968	150.00	300.00

—Tetragrammaton albums above do not mention Campbell, Silver, Cosby Corp on the label.—

Tetragrammaton T-102	(S)	Shades Of Deep Purple	198?	4.00	10.00
Tetragrammaton T-107	(S)	Book Of Taliesyn	198?	4.00	10.00
Tetragrammaton T-119	(S)	Deep Purple	198?	4.00	10.00

—Tetragrammaton albums above have "A Division of Campbell, Silver, Cosby Corp" on the label.—

CUSTOM HIGH FIDELITY
Mercury MG 20314

THEY SING...THEY SWING

FAMOUS FOR THEIR HITS OF COME GO WITH ME • WHISPERING BELLS • COOL SHAKE

DEL VIKINGS

* COME ALONG WITH ME
* SUMMERTIME
* YOURS
* HEART AND SOUL
* A SUNDAY KIND OF LOVE
* OVER THE RAINBOW

* IS IT ANY WONDER
* MY FOOLISH HEART
* THE WHITE CLIFFS OF DOVER
* DOWN IN BERMUDA
* I'M SITTIN' ON TOP OF THE WORLD
* NOW IS THE HOUR

The Del Vikings were originally an all-black group consisting of U.S. Air Force members Corinthian "Kripp" Johnson, Samuel Patterson, Don Jackson, Clarence Quick and Bernard Robertson. Their acapella recordings, with overdubbed instruments, appear on the Luniverse album despite the cover photo showing the later, integrated group. Patterson and Robertson were assigned to Germany, replaced by Norman Wright and first white member, Dave Lerchey. The group then moved to Fee Bee and cut "Come Go With Me," one of the most prominent rock'n roll/rhythm'n blues hits of the '50s. When Jackson was also shipped to Germany, he was replaced by a second white member, Donald "Gus" Backus. When their manager signed the group to Mercury, Backus, Lerchey, Quick, Wright followed and picked up William Blakely as a fifth member (shown here on They Sing. . . They Swing). Johnson was contractually forced to remain with Fee Bee and formed a second Del Vikings with Don Jackson. When Kripp's contract with Fee Bee expired he rejoined his original partners and disbanded the second group. . .

Label & Catalog #		Title	Year	VG+	NM
Warner Bros. WS-1860	(S)	Deep Purple & The Royal Philharmonic	1970	4.00	10.00
Warner Bros. WS-1877	(S)	Deep Purple In Rock	1970	4.00	10.00
Warner Bros. BS-2564	(S)	Fireball	1971	4.00	10.00
Warner Bros. BS-2607	(S)	Machine Head	1972	4.00	10.00
Warner Bros. BS4-2607	(Q)	Machine Head	1974	10.00	25.00
Warner Bros. 2LS-2644	(S)	Purple Passages (2 LPs)	1972	1.20	6.00
Warner Bros. BS-2678	(S)	Who Do We Think We Are	1972	1.00	5.00
Warner Bros. 2BS-2701	(S)	Made In Japan (2 LPs)	1973	1.20	6.00
Warner Bros. BS-2766	(S)	Burn	1974	1.00	5.00
Warner Bros. PRK-2832	(S)	Stormbringer	1974	1.00	5.00
Warner Bros. PR4-2832	(Q)	Stormbringer	1974	10.00	25.00
Warner Bros. PRK-2895	(S)	Come Taste The Band	1975	1.00	5.00
Warner Bros. PRK-2995	(S)	Made in Europe	1976	1.00	5.00
		—Warner Bros. albums above have green "WB" labels.—			
Warner Bros. BSK-3100	(S)	Machine Head	1977	.80	4.00
Warner Bros. PRK-3223	(S)	When We Rock, We Rock	1978	1.00	5.00
Warner Bros. PRK-3486	(S)	Deepest Purple (Best Of Deep Purple)	1980	.80	4.00
Scepter CTN-18010	(S)	The Best Of Deep Purple	1972	1.00	5.00
Harvest SHVL-751	(S)	Book Of Taliesyn	197?	60.00	150.00
Harvest SHVL-777	(S)	Deep Purple In Rock	197?	60.00	150.00

(Harvest 751 and 777 are US discs inside UK jackets manu-factured
for export during the early '70s. While the label and catalog number
are British, the label reads "Made in USA.")

DEEP SIX, THE

Liberty LRP-3475	(M)	The Deep Six	1966	5.00	12.00
Liberty LST-7475	(S)	The Deep Six	1966	6.00	15.00

DEKKER, DESMOND

Uni 73059	(S)	Israelites	1969	12.00	30.00

("Tip Of My Finger," "Too Much Too Soon,"
and "Nincompoop" are rechanneled.)

DEL SATINS, THE

B.T. Puppy BTS-1019	(S)	Out To Lunch	1972	150.00	300.00

DEL VIKINGS, THE

The original all-black Del Vikings were Corinthian "Kripp" Johnson and Samuel Patterson with Don Jackson,
Clarence Quick and Bernard Robertson. Jackson, Patterson and Robertson were replaced by Norman Wright and white
members Dave Lerchey and Donald "Gus" Backus. The all-black group recorded the material that showed up on the
Luniverse album, even though the cover depicts the later, racially integrated group. When their manager signed them
to Mercury, Johnson formed a second group, for Fee Bee. The group on the Mercury albums consisted of Backus,
Lerchey, Quick, Wright and William Blakely; the group on the Dot album was original members Kripp Johnson and
Don Jackson with Arthur Budd, Eddie Everette and Chuck Jackson. Refer to The Chantels.

Luniverse LP-1000	(M)	Come Go With The Del Vikings	1957	500.00	750.00
		(Original copies of LP-1000 have eight tracks. The cover slick is pasted on			
		the jacket. Counterfeits have ten or twelve tracks with a wraparound cover.)			
Mercury MG-20314	(M)	They Sing-They Swing	1957	150.00	300.00
Mercury MG-20353	(M)	A Swinging, Singing Record Session	1958	150.00	300.00
Dot DLP-3695	(M)	Come Go With Me	1966	150.00	300.00
Dot DLP-25695	(E)	Come Go With Me	1966	150.00	300.00

DEL VIKINGS, THE / THE SONNETS

Crown CLP-5368	(M)	The Del Vikings And The Sonnets	1963	16.00	40.00
Crown CST-368	(E)	The Del Vikings And The Sonnets	1963	8.00	20.00
		—Crown albums above have gray labels.—			

DELANEY & BONNIE

Delaney and Bonnie Bramlett.

Elektra EKS-74039	(S)	Accept No Substitutes	1969	6.00	15.00
Stax STS-2026	(S)	Home	1969	6.00	15.00
Crescendo GNPS-2054	(S)	Genesis	1970	4.00	10.00
Atco SD-33-326	(S)	On Tour With Eric Clapton & Friends	1970	6.00	15.00
Atco SD-33-341	(S)	To Bonnie From Delaney	1970	4.00	10.00
Atco SD-33-358	(S)	Motel Shot	1971	4.00	10.00
Atco SD-33-383	(S)	Country Life	1972	4.00	10.00
Atco SD-33-7014	(S)	The Best Of Delaney & Bonnie	1972	3.20	8.00
Columbia KC-31377	(S)	D&B Together	1972	3.20	8.00

DELFONICS, THE

The Delfonics feature Major Harris.

Philly Groove 1150	(S)	La La Means I Love You	1968	30.00	75.00
Philly Groove 1151	(S)	The Sexy Sound Of Soul	1969	30.00	75.00
Philly Groove 1152	(S)	The Delfonics' Super Hits	1969	20.00	50.00
Philly Groove 1153	(S)	The Delfonics	1970	20.00	50.00
Philly Groove 1154	(S)	Tell Me This Is A Dream	1972	20.00	50.00
Philly Groove 1501	(S)	Alive & Kicking	1974	20.00	50.00
Kory 1002	(S)	The Best Of The Delfonics	1977	4.00	10.00
Poogie 121680	(S)	The Delfonics Return	1981	4.00	10.00

Jackie DeShannon had established herself as a songwriter with several minor hits when she toured with The Beatles. Breakin' It Up On The Beatles Tour attempts to capitalize on that bit of fortune and hints at a live album. It is not. Rather, it is her second studio album and includes two of her earliest [and very minor] chart hits, "Needles And Pins" and "When You Walk In The Room." Like too many under-appreciated artists, her early albums remain much harder to find than their assigned values indicate.

Label & Catalog #		Title	Year	VG+	NM

DELLS, THE

Label & Catalog #		Title	Year	VG+	NM
Vee Jay LP-1010	(M)	Oh What A Nite	1959	500.00	750.00
		—Vee Jay albums above have maroon labels.—			
Vee Jay LP-1010	(M)	Oh What A Nite	1959	150.00	300.00
Vee Jay LPS-1141	(M)	It's Not Unusual	1965	20.00	50.00
Vee Jay LPS-1141	(S)	It's Not Unusual	1965	40.00	100.00
		—Vee Jay albums above have black rainbow labels.—			
Vee Jay Inter. 7305	(S)	The Dells In Concert	197?	1.00	5.00
Upfront UPF-105	(S)	Stay In My Corner	1968	4.00	10.00
Buddah BDS-5053	(S)	The Dells	1969	4.00	10.00
Cadet LPS-804	(S)	There Is	1968	20.00	50.00
Cadet LPS-822	(S)	Musical Menu/Always Together	1969	20.00	50.00
Cadet LPS-824	(S)	The Dells' Greatest Hits	1969	20.00	50.00
Cadet LPS-829	(S)	Love Is Blue	1969	20.00	50.00
Cadet LPS-837	(S)	Like It Is, Like It Was	1970	20.00	50.00
Cadet CADJ-3	(S)	The Dells (Promo sampler)	1973	8.00	20.00
Cadet 50004	(S)	Freedom Means	1971	8.00	20.00
Cadet 50017	(S)	The Dells Sing Dionne Warwick's Greatest Hits	1972	8.00	20.00
Cadet 50021	(S)	Sweet As Funk Can Be	1972	8.00	20.00
Cadet 60027	(S)	The Dells Vs. The Dramatics	1974	6.00	15.00
Cadet 50037	(S)	Give Your Baby A Standing Ovation	1973	14.00	35.00
Cadet 50046	(S)	The Dells	1973	14.00	35.00
Cadet 60030	(S)	The Mighty, Mighty Dells	1974	10.00	25.00
Cadet 60036	(S)	The Dells' Greatest Hits, Vol. 2	1975	1.00	5.00
Trip TLX-9503	(S)	The Dells' Greatest Hits	1973	1.00	5.00
Mercury SRM-1145	(S)	They Said It Couldn't Be Done	1977	1.00	5.00
ABC AA-1100	(S)	New Beginnings	1978	1.00	5.00
ABC AA-1113	(S)	Face To Face	1978	1.00	5.00
20th Cent.-Fox 618	(S)	I Touched A Dream	1980	1.00	5.00
20th Cent.-Fox 633	(S)	Whatever Turns You On	1981	1.00	5.00
Lost-Nite LLP-21	(10")	The Dells (Red vinyl)	1981	4.00	10.00
Solid Smoke 8029	(S)	Breezy Ballads And Tender Tunes	1984	1.00	5.00

DELTA MERCHANT

Label & Catalog #		Title	Year	VG+	NM
Excello LPS-8014	(S)	Moog Blues	1970	10.00	25.00

DEMENSIONS, THE

Label & Catalog #		Title	Year	VG+	NM
Coral CRL-57430	(M)	My Foolish Heart	1963	50.00	150.00
Coral CRL-757430	(S)	My Foolish Heart	1963	100.00	300.00

DEMIAN

Demian originally recorded as Bubble Puppy.

Label & Catalog #		Title	Year	VG+	NM
ABC ABCS-718	(S)	Demian	1970	30.00	75.00

DENNY, SANDY

Ms Denny was former lead vocalist with Fairport Convention and Fotheringay. Refer to The Bunch.

Label & Catalog #		Title	Year	VG+	NM
A&M SP-4317	(S)	The Northstar Grassman And The Ravens	1971	6.00	15.00
A&M SP-4371	(S)	Sandy	1972	6.00	15.00
Island ILPS-9340	(S)	Like An Old Fashioned Waltz	1973	6.00	15.00
Carthage CGLP-440?	(S)	Rendezvous	1985	3.20	8.00

DEPENDABLES, THE

Label & Catalog #		Title	Year	VG+	NM
United Arts. UAS-6799	(S)	Klatu Berrada Niktu	1971	6.00	15.00

DEREK & THE DOMINOS

Derek is Eric Clapton while the Dominos feature Duane Allman.

Label & Catalog #		Title	Year	VG+	NM
Atco 2-704	(M)	Layla (2 LPs. White label promo)	1970	150.00	300.00
Atco SD-2-704	(S)	Layla (2 LPs. White label promo)	1970	80.00	200.00
Atco SD-2-704	(S)	Layla (2 LPs)	1970	12.00	30.00
RSO 2-8800	(S)	Derek & The Dominos In Concert (2 LPs)	1973	8.00	20.00
Polydor 2-3501	(S)	Layla (2 LPs)	1974	4.00	10.00

DERRINGER, RICK

Rick Derringer originally recorded with The McCoys. Refer to Edgar Winter.

Label & Catalog #		Title	Year	VG+	NM
Blue Sky BZ-32481	(S)	All American Boy	1973	1.00	5.00
Blue Sky ZQ-32481	(Q)	All American Boy	1974	8.00	20.00
Blue Sky BZ-33423	(S)	Spring Fever	1975	1.00	5.00
Blue Sky BZ-34181	(S)	Derringer	1976	1.00	5.00
Blue Sky BZ-34470	(S)	Sweet Evil	1977	1.00	5.00
Blue Sky PRO-265	(DJ)	Live In Cleveland	1977	8.00	20.00
Blue Sky BZ-34848	(S)	Rock Derringer Live	1977	1.00	5.00

DeSHANNON, JACKIE

Ms DeShannon can be found on the RCA soundtrack "Together."

Label & Catalog #		Title	Year	VG+	NM
Liberty LRP-3320	(M)	Jackie DeShannon	1963	16.00	40.00
Liberty LRP-7320	(S)	Jackie DeShannon	1963	20.00	50.00
Liberty LRP-3390	(M)	Breakin' It Up On The Beatles Tour	1964	16.00	40.00
Liberty LRP-7390	(S)	Breakin' It Up On The Beatles Tour	1964	20.00	50.00

Label & Catalog #		Title	Year	VG+	NM
Imperial LP-9286	(M)	This Is Jackie DeShannon	1965	8.00	20.00
Imperial LP-12286	(S)	This Is Jackie DeShannon	1965	10.00	25.00
Imperial LP-9294	(M)	You Won't Forget Me	1965	8.00	20.00
Imperial LP-12294	(S)	You Won't Forget Me	1965	10.00	25.00
Imperial LP-9296	(M)	In The Wind	1965	8.00	20.00
Imperial LP-12296	(S)	In The Wind	1965	10.00	25.00
		—Imperial albums above have black, white & pink labels.—			
Imperial LP-9328	(M)	Are You Ready For This?	1966	6.00	15.00
Imperial LP-12328	(S)	Are You Ready For This?	1966	8.00	20.00
Imperial LP-9344	(M)	New Image	1967	6.00	15.00
Imperial LP-12344	(S)	New Image	1967	8.00	20.00
Imperial LP-9352	(M)	For You	1967	6.00	15.00
Imperial LP-12352	(S)	For You	1967	8.00	20.00
Imperial LP-9386	(M)	Me About You	1967	6.00	15.00
Imperial LP-12386	(S)	Me About You	1967	6.00	15.00
Imperial LP-9404	(M)	What The World Needs Now Is Love	1967	6.00	15.00
Imperial LP-12404	(S)	What The World Needs Now Is Love	1967	6.00	15.00
		("What The World Needs Now Is Love" is rechanneled.)			
Imperial LP-12415	(S)	Laurel Canyon	1968	6.00	15.00
Imperial LP-12442	(S)	Put A Little Love In Your Heart	1969	6.00	15.00
Imperial LP-12453	(S)	To Be Free	1970	6.00	15.00
Sunset SUS-5225	(S)	Lonely Girl	1968	4.00	10.00
Sunset SUS-5322	(S)	Jackie DeShannon	1970	4.00	10.00
Capitol ST-772	(S)	Songs	1971	1.20	6.00
Atlantic SD-7231	(S)	Jackie	1972	1.20	6.00
Atlantic SD-7303	(S)	Your Baby Is A Lady	1974	1.00	5.00
Columbia PC-33500	(S)	New Arrangement	1975	1.20	6.00
United Artists LA-434E	(S)	The Very Best Of Jackie DeShannon	1975	1.00	5.00
Amherst AMH-1010	(S)	You're The Only Dancer	1977	1.00	5.00
Liberty LN-10179	(S)	The Very Best Of Jackie DeShannon	1982	.80	4.00

DESIGN

Epic E-30224	(S)	Design	1971	4.00	10.00

DeSANTO, SUGAR PIE

Checker LP-2979	(M)	Sugar Pie DeSanto	1961	80.00	200.00

DETERGENTS, THE
The Detergents feature Ron Dante.

Roulette R-25308	(M)	The Many Faces Of The Detergents	1965	60.00	150.00
Roulette SR-25308	(E)	The Many Faces Of The Detergents	1965	40.00	100.00

DETROIT: *Refer to* MITCH RYDER

DETROIT CITY LIMITS, THE

OKeh 14127	(S)	98¢ + Tax	1968	12.00	30.00

DETROIT EMERALDS, THE

Westbound WB-2013	(S)	You Want It, You Got It	197?	20.00	50.00

DEUCE COUPES, THE

Del Fi DFLP-1243	(M)	Hotrodder's Choice	1963	20.00	50.00
Del Fi DFS-1243	(S)	Hotrodder's Choice	1963	30.00	75.00

DEUCE COUPES, THE

Crown CLP-5393	(M)	The Shut Downs	1963	8.00	20.00
Crown CST-393	(S)	The Shut Downs	1963	10.00	25.00
		—Crown albums above have gray labels.—			

DEVIANTS, THE

Sire SES-97001	(S)	Ptooff	1968	24.00	60.00
Sire SES-97005	(S)	Disposable	1969	24.00	60.00
Sire SES-97016	(S)	No. 3	1969	24.00	60.00

DEVILED HAM

Super-K SKS-6003	(M)	I Had Too Much To Dream Last Night	1968	8.00	20.00

DEVIL'S ANVIL, THE
Rock with a desert feeling courtesy of Felix Pappalardi.

Columbia CL-2664	(M)	Hard Rock From The Middle East	1967	10.00	25.00
Columbia CS-9464	(S)	Hard Rock From The Middle East	1967	14.00	35.00

DEVO

Warner Bros. 3329	(S)	Q: Are We Not Men? A: We Are Devo!	1978	1.00	5.00
Warner Bros. 3337	(S)	Duty Now For The Future	1979	1.00	5.00
Warner Bros. 3435	(S)	Freedom Of Choice	1980	1.00	5.00
Warner Bros. WBMS-115	(DJ)	DEV-O Live	1980	16.00	40.00
Warner Bros. 3548	(S)	DEV-O Live	1981	1.00	5.00

Label & Catalog #		Title	Year	VG+	NM
Warner Bros. 3595	(S)	New Traditionalists	1981	1.00	5.00
Warner Bros. 23741	(S)	Oh, No! It's Devo	1982	1.00	5.00
Warner Bros. 25097	(S)	Shout	1984	1.00	5.00

DIABLOS, THE: *Refer to* **NOLAN STRONG & THE DIABLOS**

DIALS, THE

Time 52100	(M)	It's Monkey Time	1964	10.00	25.00
Time S-2100	(S)	It's Monkey Time	1964	12.00	30.00

DIAMOND, NEIL
Refer to The Band; Diana Ross / Neil Diamond.

Bang BLP-214	(M)	The Feel Of Neil Diamond	1966	20.00	50.00
		(Some copies of BLP-214 erroneously play stereo. These must be heard to be identified and would be worth $10 more than the mono.)			
Bang BLPS-214	(P)	The Feel Of Neil Diamond	1966	30.00	75.00
		("Solitary Man," "Do It," and "I'll Come Running" are rechanneled.)			
Bang BLP-217	(M)	Just For You	1967	14.00	35.00
Bang BLPS-217	(S)	Just For You	1967	20.00	50.00
		(First pressings of Bang 217 promote "Thank The Lord For The Nighttime" on the cover. "The Long Way Home," "You'll Forget," and "Solitary Man" are rechanneled.)			
Bang BLP-217	(M)	Just For You	1967	12.00	30.00
Bang BLPS-217	(S)	Just For You	1967	16.00	40.00
		(Later first pressings of Bang 217 have a sticker promoting "Shilo" pasted over the blurb for "Thank The Lord For The Nighttime" on the cover.)			
Bang BLPS-217	(S)	Just For You	1970	6.00	15.00
		(Second pressings of Bang 217 promote "Shilo" on the cover.)			
Bang BLPS-219	(S)	Neil Diamond's Greatest Hits	1968	12.00	30.00
		("Do It," "Kentucky Woman" and the single version of "Solitary Man" are rechanneled on this LP.)			
Bang BLPS-219	(S)	Neil Diamond's Greatest Hits	196?	6.00	15.00
		("Solitary Man" is rerecorded in stereo on later pressings.)			
Bang BLPS-221	(S)	Shilo	1970	12.00	30.00
Bang BLPS-224	(S)	Do It!	1971	10.00	25.00
		(While the cover and label list "Hanky Panky," the record plays "The Long Way Home." "Some Day Baby" is mono while "Shot Down," "You'll Forget" and "The Long Way Home" are rechanneled.)			
Bang BLPS-227	(S)	Double Gold (2 LPs)	1973	10.00	25.00
		—Bang albums above have red & white labels.—			
Bang BLPS-217	(S)	Just For You	197?	4.00	10.00
Bang BLPS-219	(S)	Neil Diamond's Greatest Hits	197?	4.00	10.00
Bang BLPS-221	(S)	Shilo	197?	4.00	10.00
Bang BLPS-224	(S)	Do It!	197?	4.00	10.00
Bang BLPS-227	(S)	Double Gold (2 LPs)	197?	4.00	10.00
		—Bang albums above have yellow labels.—			
Bang BLPS-221	(S)	Shilo	197?	1.00	5.00
Bang BLPS-224	(S)	Do It!	197?	1.00	5.00
Bang BLPS-227	(S)	Double Gold (2 LPs)	197?	1.00	5.00
		—Bang albums above have blue labels.—			
Uni ST-73030	(S)	Velvet Gloves And Spit	1968	8.00	20.00
		(Gatefold cover without "Shilo.")			
Uni ST-73030	(S)	Velvet Gloves And Spit	1970	4.00	10.00
		(Gatefold cover with "Shilo.")			
Uni ST-73047	(S)	Brother Love's Traveling Salvation Show	1969	8.00	20.00
		(Gatefold cover without "Sweet Caroline.")			
Uni ST-73047	(S)	Brother Love's Traveling Salvation Show	1970	4.00	10.00
		(Gatefold cover with "Sweet Caroline.")			
Uni ST-73071	(S)	Touching You, Touching Me	1969	4.00	10.00
Uni ST-73084	(S)	Neil Diamond/Gold	1970	4.00	10.00
Decca/CBS 245012	(S)	Neil Diamond/Gold (Columbia Record Club)	1971	12.00	30.00
Uni ST-73092	(S)	Tap Root Manuscript	1970	8.00	20.00
Uni ND-11	(S)	Neil Diamond (Radio sampler)	1970	80.00	200.00
Uni ST-1913	(S)	Open-End Interview (Promo)	1971	150.00	300.00
Uni ST-93030	(S)	Velvet Gloves And Spit	1971	1.00	5.00
Uni ST-93047	(S)	Brother Love's Traveling Salvation Show	1971	1.00	5.00
Uni ST-93071	(S)	Touching You Touching Me	1971	1.00	5.00
Uni ST-93084	(S)	Neil Diamond Gold	1971	1.00	5.00
Uni ST-93092	(S)	Tap Root Manuscript	1971	1.00	5.00
Uni ST-93106	(S)	Stones	1971	1.00	5.00
Uni ST-93136	(S)	Moods	1972	1.00	5.00
MCA SM-734727	(S)	It's Happening!	1972	20.00	50.00
MCA 2005	(S)	Moods	197?	.80	4.00
MCA 2006	(S)	Touching You Touching Me	197?	.80	4.00
MCA 2007	(S)	Neil Diamond/Gold	197?	.80	4.00
MCA 2008	(S)	Stones	197?	.80	4.00
MCA 2011	(S)	Sweet Caroline	197?	.80	4.00
MCA 2013	(S)	Tap Root Manuscript	197?	.80	4.00

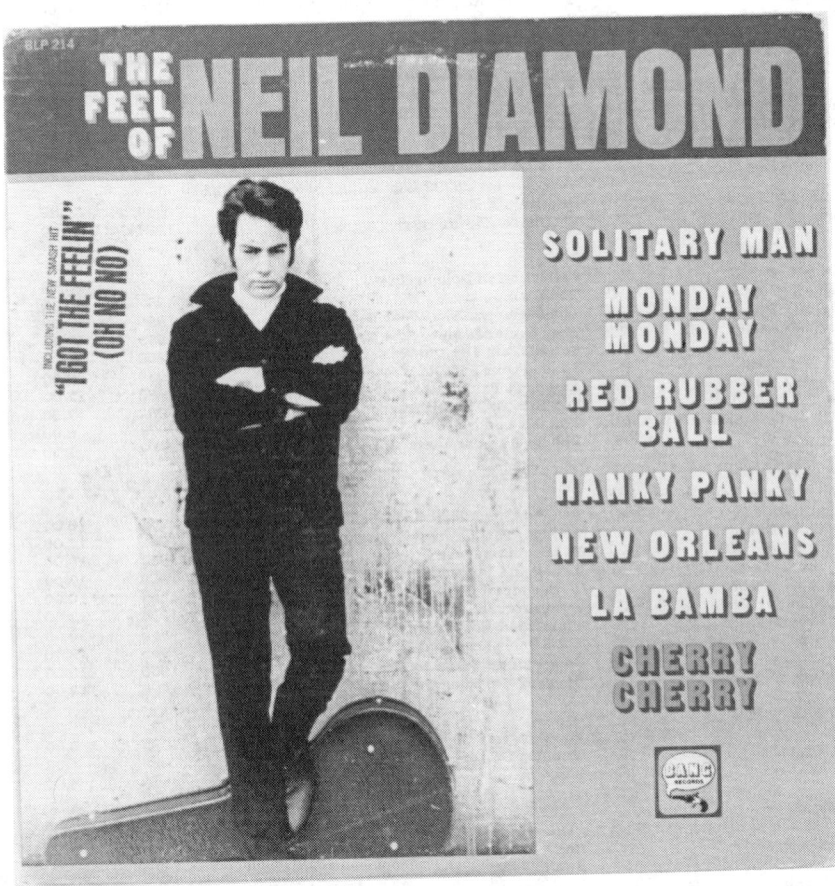

The Feel Of Neil Diamond *remains a hard to find and undervalued piece of '60s pop, especially the improbably rare—and vastly undervalued—stereo pressing. The mono pressing shown here has a sticker affixed to the cover calling the potential customer's attention to the inclusion of the hit single, "I Got The Feelin' (Oh No No)."*

Label & Catalog #		Title	Year	VG+	NM
MCA 8000	(S)	Hot August Night (2 LPs. Photo labels)	1972	4.00	10.00
MCA 8000	(S)	Hot August Night (2 LPs. Plain labels)	1973	1.00	5.00
MCA 2103	(S)	Rainbow	1974	.80	4.00
MCA 2106	(S)	Neil Diamond/His 12 Greatest Hits	1974	.80	4.00
MCA 2227	(S)	And The Singer Sings His Song	1976	.80	4.00
MCA 5239	(S)	Love Songs	1981	.80	4.00
Frog King AAR-1	(S)	Early Classics (Includes songbook)	1972	10.00	25.00
Frog King AAR-1	(S)	Early Classics (Without songbook)	1972	6.00	15.00
		("Kentucky Woman" is in stereo on this while "Do It" is mono.)			
Columbia KC-32550	(S)	Jonathan Livingston Seagull	1973	.80	4.00
Columbia HC-42550	(S)	Jonathan Livingston Seagull (Half-speed)	1982	20.00	50.00
Columbia PC-32919	(S)	Serenade	1974	.80	4.00
Columbia PCQ-32919	(Q)	Serenade	1974	10.00	25.00
Columbia PC-33965	(S)	Beautiful Noise	1976	.80	4.00
Columbia KC2-34404	(S)	Love At The Greek (2 LPs)	1977	1.00	5.00
Columbia JC-34990	(S)	I'm Glad You're Here With Me Tonight	1977	.80	4.00
Columbia FC-35625	(S)	You Don't Bring Me Flowers	1982	.80	4.00
Columbia HC-45625	(S)	You Don't Bring Me Flowers (Half-speed)	1982	10.00	30.00
Columbia FC-36121	(S)	September Morn	1980	.80	4.00
Capitol 12120	(S)	The Jazz Singer (Soundtrack)	1980	.80	4.00
Columbia PC-37628	(S)	On The Way To The Sky	1981	.80	4.00
Columbia HC-47628	(S)	On The Way To The Sky (Half-speed)	1982	10.00	30.00
Columbia PC-38068	(S)	12 Greatest Hits, Volume II	1982	.80	4.00
Columbia HC-48068	(S)	12 Greatest Hits, Volume II (Half-speed)	1982	10.00	30.00
Columbia PC-38359	(S)	Heartlight	1982	.80	4.00
Columbia HC-48359	(S)	Heartlight (Half-speed master)	1982	10.00	30.00
Columbia 38792	(S)	Classics—The Early Years	1983	.80	4.00
		(Columbia 38792 is a reissue of Frog King 1.)			
Columbia 39915	(S)	Primitive	1984	.80	4.00
Columbia 9C9-39915	(S)	Primitive (Picture disc)	1984	6.00	15.00

DIAMONDS, THE

Mercury MG-20213	(M)	Collection Of Golden Hits	1956	60.00	150.00
Mercury MG-20309	(M)	The Diamonds	1957	60.00	150.00
Mercury MG-20368	(M)	The Diamonds Meet Pete Rugolo	1958	30.00	75.00
Mercury SR-60076	(S)	The Diamonds Meet Pete Rugolo	1958	40.00	100.00
Mercury MG-20480	(M)	Songs From The Old West	1959	30.00	75.00
Mercury SR-60159	(S)	Songs From The Old West	1959	40.00	100.00
Wing MGW-12114	(M)	America's Famous Song Stylists	1962	12.00	30.00
Wing MGW-12178	(M)	Pop Hits By The Diamonds	1962	12.00	30.00
Sound Recorders SRS-4644	(S)	The Diamonds '70	1971	8.00	20.00
Rhino RNDF-209	(M)	The Best Of The Diamonds	1984	1.00	5.00

DICK & DEE DEE
Dick St. John and Dee Dee Sperling.

Liberty LRP-3236	(M)	Tell Me/The Mountain's High	1962	16.00	40.00
Liberty LST-7236	(E)	Tell Me/The Mountain's High	1962	12.00	30.00
Warner Bros. W-1500	(M)	Young And In Love	1963	10.00	25.00
Warner Bros. WS-1500	(S)	Young And In Love	1963	12.00	30.00
Warner Bros. W-1538	(M)	Turn Around	1964	10.00	25.00
Warner Bros. WS-1538	(S)	Turn Around	1964	12.00	30.00
Warner Bros. W-1586	(M)	Thou Shalt Not Steal	1965	10.00	25.00
Warner Bros. WS-1586	(S)	Thou Shalt Not Steal	1965	12.00	30.00
Warner Bros. W-1623	(M)	Songs We've Sung On "Shindig"	1966	10.00	25.00
Warner Bros. WS-1623	(S)	Songs We've Sung On "Shindig"	1966	12.00	30.00

DICTATORS, THE

Epic KE-033348	(S)	The Dictators Go Girl Crazy	1975	6.00	15.00
Asylum 7E-1109	(S)	Manifest Destiny	1977	4.00	10.00
Asylum 6E-147	(S)	Bloodbrothers	1978	4.00	10.00

DIDDLEY, BO
Bo Diddley is a pseudonym for Ellas McDaniel.

Checker LP-1431	(M)	Bo Diddley (White label promo)	1958	250.00	600.00
Checker LP-1431	(M)	Bo Diddley	1958	80.00	200.00
Chess LP-1431	(M)	Bo Diddley	1958	150.00	300.00
Checker LP-1436	(M)	Go Bo Diddley (White label promo)	1959	250.00	600.00
Checker LP-1436	(M)	Go Bo Diddley	1959	60.00	150.00
Checker LP-2974	(M)	Have Guitar, Will Travel (White label promo)	1960	200.00	500.00
Checker LP-2974	(M)	Have Guitar, Will Travel	1960	60.00	150.00
Checker LP-2976	(M)	Spotlight On Bo Diddley (White label promo)	1960	250.00	600.00
Checker LP-2976	(M)	Spotlight On Bo Diddley	1960	80.00	200.00
Checker LP-2977	(M)	Bo Diddley Is A Gunslinger (White label promo)	1960	200.00	500.00
Checker LP-2977	(M)	Bo Diddley Is A Gunslinger	1960	60.00	150.00
Checker LP-2980	(M)	Bo Diddley Is A Lover (White label promo)	1961	250.00	600.00
Checker LP-2980	(M)	Bo Diddley Is A Lover	1961	80.00	200.00
Checker LP-2982	(M)	Bo Diddley's A Twister (White label promo)	1962	200.00	500.00
Checker LP-2982	(M)	Bo Diddley's A Twister	1962	40.00	100.00

The covers of Dick and Dee Dee's albums, such as Young And In Love *and* Tell Me, *depict them as the modicum of the then popular "boy/girl next door" fixation of American parents everywhere. Despite the image, Richard St. John was a rather progressive record maker and many of the duo's finest sides stand as testaments to his ability to mold a classic pop single.*

Label & Catalog #		Title	Year	VG+	NM
Checker LP-2984	(M)	Bo Diddley (White label promo)	1962	200.00	500.00
Checker LP-2984	(M)	Bo Diddley	1962	40.00	100.00
Checker LP-2985	(M)	Bo Diddley And Company (White label promo)	1963	200.00	500.00
Checker LP-2985	(M)	Bo Diddley And Company	1963	60.00	150.00
Checker LP-2987	(M)	Surfin' With Bo Diddley (White label promo)	1964	150.00	300.00
Checker LP-2987	(M)	Surfin' With Bo Diddley	1964	40.00	100.00
Checker LPS-2987	(E)	Surfin' With Bo Diddley	1964	24.00	60.00
Checker LP-2988	(M)	Bo Diddley's Beach Party (White label promo)	1963	150.00	300.00
Checker LP-2988	(M)	Bo Diddley's Beach Party	1963	40.00	100.00
Checker LPS-2988	(E)	Bo Diddley's Beach Party	1963	24.00	60.00
Checker LP-2989	(M)	16 All Time Greatest Hits (White label promo)	1965	80.00	200.00
Checker LP-2989	(M)	16 All Time Greatest Hits	1964	20.00	50.00
Checker LPS-2989	(E)	16 All Time Greatest Hits	1964	16.00	40.00
Checker LP-2992	(M)	Hey! Good Lookin' (White label promo)	1965	150.00	300.00
Checker LP-2992	(M)	Hey! Good Lookin'	1965	24.00	60.00
Checker LPS-2992	(E)	Hey! Good Lookin'	1965	16.00	40.00
Checker LP-2996	(M)	500% More Man (White label promo)	1965	150.00	300.00
Checker LP-2996	(M)	500% More Man	1965	24.00	60.00
Checker LPS-2996	(E)	500% More Man	1965	16.00	40.00
		—Checker albums above have black or maroon labels with silver print—			
Checker LP-2987	(M)	Surfin' With Bo Diddley	196?	See note below	
		(A copy of this album was found with a gold version of the original Checker label. Rare with no established value.)			
Checker LPS-2992	(E)	Hey! Good Lookin'	1966	12.00	30.00
Checker LPS-2996	(E)	500% More Man	1966	12.00	30.00
		—Checker albums above have blue labels with checkers on top.—			
Checker LP-2982	(M)	Road Runner	1967	30.00	75.00
Checker LP-2982	(E)	Road Runner	1967	20.00	50.00
		("Road Runner" is a repackage of "Bo Diddley's A Twister.")			
Checker LP-3001	(M)	The Originator	1966	12.00	30.00
Checker LPS-3001	(S)	The Originator	1966	16.00	40.00
Checker LP-3006	(M)	Go Bo Diddley	1967	20.00	50.00
Checker LPS-3006	(E)	Go Bo Diddley	1967	16.00	40.00
Checker LP-3007	(M)	Boss Man	1967	30.00	75.00
Checker LPS-3007	(E)	Boss Man	1967	20.00	50.00
		(Checker 3006 and 3007 are reissues of 1436 and 1431.)			
		—Checker albums above have blue labels with checkers on top.—			
Checker LPS-3013	(S)	The Black Gladiator	1968	12.00	30.00
Chess CH-50001	(S)	Another Dimension	1971	16.00	40.00
Chess 2CH-60005	(E)	Got My Own Bag Of Tricks (2 LPs)	1972	10.00	25.00
Chess CH-50016	(S)	Where It All Began	1972	16.00	40.00
Chess CH-50029	(S)	The London Bo Diddley Sessions	1973	10.00	25.00
Chess CH-50047	(S)	Big Bad Bo	1974	10.00	25.00
Chess 9106	(M)	Bo Diddley: His Greatest Sides	1983	1.00	5.00
Chess 9169	(S)	Super, Super Blues Band	1983	1.00	5.00
Chess 9185	(E)	Two Great Guitars	1984	1.00	5.00
		—Chess 9000 albums above list Sugar Hill as the parent company on the back cover.—			
Chess 9106	(M)	Bo Diddley: His Greatest Sides	198?	.80	4.00
Chess 9169	(S)	Super, Super Blues Band	198?	.80	4.00
Chess 9185	(E)	Two Great Guitars	198?	.80	4.00
		—Chess 9000 albums above list MCA as the parent company on the back cover.—			
Check Mate 1960	(S)	Give Me A Break	1988	6.00	15.00
RCA Victor APL1-1229	(S)	The 20th Anniversary Of Rock N' Roll	1976	8.00	20.00
M.F. 2002	(S)	I'm A Man (2 LPs)	1977	40.00	100.00
Accord SN-7812	(S)	Toronto Rock And Roll Revival, Volume 5	1982	8.00	20.00
Check Mate 1960	(S)	Give Me A Break	1988	6.00	15.00
JVC VDPZ1329	(S)	Live At The Ritz (With Ron Wood)	1989	1.00	5.00
Triple X 51017	(S)	Breakin' Through The BS	1989	.80	4.00
MCA/Chess 9264	(M)	In The Spotlight	1987	.80	4.00
MCA/Chess CH-9194	(M)	Bo Diddley	1988	.80	4.00
MCA/Chess CH-9196	(M)	Go Bo Diddley	1988	.80	4.00
MCA/Chess 9187	(M)	Have Gun, Will Travel	1989	.80	4.00
MCA/Chess 9285	(M)	Bo Diddley Is A Gunslinger	1989	.80	4.00
MCA/Chess 3-19502	(M)	Bo Diddley: The Chess Box	1990	.80	4.00

DIDDLEY, BO, & CHUCK BERRY

Label & Catalog #		Title	Year	VG+	NM
Checker LP-2991	(M)	Two Great Guitars	1964	30.00	75.00
Checker LPS-2991	(E)	Two Great Guitars	1964	20.00	50.00
		—Checker albums above have black labels with silver print.—			
Checker LPS-2991	(E)	Two Great Guitars	1966	12.00	30.00
		—Checker albums above have blue labels with checkers on top.—			

DIGA RHYTHM BAND, THE
The Digas are Mickey Hart and Bill Kreutzmann of The Grateful Dead.

Label & Catalog #		Title	Year	VG+	NM
Round RX-110	(S)	The Diga Rhythm Band	1976	12.00	30.00

DILLARD & BOYCE
Doug Dillard and Tommy Boyce.

Label & Catalog #		Title	Year	VG+	NM
Mercury SRM-1-3826	(S)	We're In This Together	1977	4.00	10.00

Ellas McDaniel took his moniker from a single-stringed African instrument known as a "bo diddley." After hitting big with the single of the same name, he just up and called the rhythmic progression, based squarely on that of the vaudevillian "shave-and-a-haircut" pattern, bo diddley. Both Have Guitar Will Travel *and* Two Great Guitars *illustrate the good humor with which Mr Diddley has always been associated.*

Label & Catalog #		Title	Year	VG+	NM

DILLARD & CLARK
Doug Dillard, formerly of The Dillards, and Gene Clark, formerly of The Byrds.

A&M SP-4158	(S)	The Fantastic Expedition Of Dillard & Clark	1969	10.00	25.00
		—A&M albums above have brown labels.—			
A&M SP-4158	(S)	The Fantastic Expedition Of Dillard & Clark	1970	6.00	15.00
A&M SP-4158	(S)	Through The Morning, Through The Night	1970	6.00	15.00
		—A&M albums above have silver labels.—			

DILLARDS, THE
The original group was Doug and Rodney Dillard with Mitch Jayne and Dean Webb. They played straight bluegrass and their first few albums are not included here. Herb Pederson replaced Doug in 1966 with Paul York joining in 1969. Pederson was replaced by Billy Ray Latham in 1972.

Elektra EKS-74035	(S)	Wheatstraw Suite	1968	8.00	20.00
Elektra EKS-74054	(S)	Copperfields	1969	8.00	20.00
Anthem ANS-5901	(S)	Roots And Branches	1972	4.00	10.00
Poppy LA-175F	(S)	Tribute To The Great American Duck	1973	4.00	10.00
Crystal Clear CCS-5007	(S)	Mountain Rock	1979	8.00	20.00
Flying Fish FF-27040	(S)	The Dillards Vs. The Incredible L.S. Time Machine	1978	3.20	8.00
Flying Fish FF-27082	(S)	Decade Waltz	1979	1.20	6.00
Flying Fish FF-215	(S)	The Dillards Homecoming And Family Reunion	1980	1.20	6.00

DING DONGS, THE

Motown 716	(S)	Gimme Dat Ding	1970	6.00	15.00

DINNING, MARK
Mark's sisters recorded as The Dinning Sisters (below).

MGM E-3828	(M)	Teen Angel	1960	40.00	100.00
MGM SE-3828	(S)	Teen Angel	1960	80.00	200.00
MGM E-3855	(M)	Wanderin'	1960	40.00	100.00
MGM SE-3855	(S)	Wanderin'	1960	60.00	150.00

DINNING SISTERS, THE

Capitol H-318	(10")	The Dinning Sisters	195?	16.00	40.00

DINO, DESI & BILLY
Dino Martin, Desi Arnaz Jr, and Billy Hinsche. They can be found on the Uni soundtrack "Follow Me."

Reprise R-6176	(M)	I'm A Fool	1965	8.00	20.00
Reprise RS-6176	(S)	I'm A Fool	1965	10.00	25.00
Reprise R-6194	(M)	Our Times Are Coming	1966	8.00	20.00
Reprise RS-6194	(S)	Our Times Are Coming	1966	10.00	25.00
Reprise R-6198	(M)	Memories Are Made Of This	1966	8.00	20.00
Reprise RS-6198	(S)	Memories Are Made Of This	1966	10.00	25.00
Reprise R-6224	(M)	Souvenir (With sheet of bonus photos)	1966	10.00	25.00
Reprise RS-6224	(S)	Souvenir (With sheet of bonus photos)	1966	12.00	30.00
Reprise R-6224	(M)	Souvenir (Without the photos)	1966	8.00	20.00
Reprise RS-6224	(S)	Souvenir (Without the photos)	1966	10.00	25.00

DION
Dion DiMucci originally recorded with The Belmonts (above).

Laurie LLP-2004	(M)	Alone With Dion (Gatefold cover)	1960	80.00	200.00
		(Cover includes four wallet-size bonus cards on inside strip.)			
Laurie LLP-2009	(M)	Runaround Sue (Blue vinyl)	1961	500.00	1,000.00
Laurie LLP-2009	(M)	Runaround Sue (Green vinyl)	1961	500.00	1,000.00
Laurie LLP-2009	(M)	Runaround Sue (Yellow vinyl)	1961	500.00	1,000.00
Laurie LLP-2009	(M)	Runaround Sue	1961	40.00	100.00
Laurie T-91027	(M)	Runaround Sue (Capitol Record Club)	196?	60.00	150.00
Laurie DT-91027	(E)	Runaround Sue (Capitol Record Club)	196?	60.00	150.00
Laurie LLP-2012	(M)	Lovers Who Wander	1962	30.00	75.00
Laurie LLP-2013	(M)	Dion Sings His Greatest Hits	1959	30.00	75.00
Laurie SLP-2013	(E)	Dion Sings His Greatest Hits	196?	30.00	75.00
Laurie T-90386	(M)	His Greatest Hits (Capitol Record Club)	196?	60.00	150.00
Laurie DT-90386	(E)	His Greatest Hits (Capitol Record Club)	196?	60.00	150.00
Laurie LLP-2015	(M)	Love Came To Me	1963	30.00	75.00
Laurie LLP-2017	(M)	Dion Sings To Sandy (& All Other Girls)	1963	30.00	75.00
Laurie LLP-2019	(M)	Dion Sings The 15 Million Sellers	1963	30.00	75.00
Laurie SLP-2019	(E)	Dion Sings The 15 Million Sellers	1963	30.00	75.00
Laurie LLP-2022	(M)	More Of Dion's Greatest Hits	1963	30.00	75.00
Laurie SLP-2022	(E)	More Of Dion's Greatest Hits	1963	30.00	75.00
Laurie T-91128	(M)	More Of Dion's Greatest Hits (Capitol Rec. Club)	196?	60.00	150.00
Laurie DT-91128	(E)	More Of Dion's Greatest Hits (Capitol Rec. Club)	196?	60.00	150.00
		—Laurie albums above have gold & white labels with large benday dots.—			
Columbia CL-2010	(M)	Ruby Baby	1963	12.00	30.00
Columbia CS-8810	(S)	Ruby Baby	1963	16.00	40.00
Columbia CL-2107	(M)	Donna The Prima Donna	1963	12.00	30.00
Columbia CS-8907	(S)	Donna The Prima Donna	1963	16.00	40.00
Laurie SLP-2047	(S)	Dion	1968	8.00	20.00
Laurie DT-91577	(S)	Dion (Capitol Record Club)	1968	10.00	25.00
Columbia CS-9773	(S)	Wonder Where I'm Bound	1969	8.00	20.00
		—Columbia albums above have "360 Sound" labels.—			

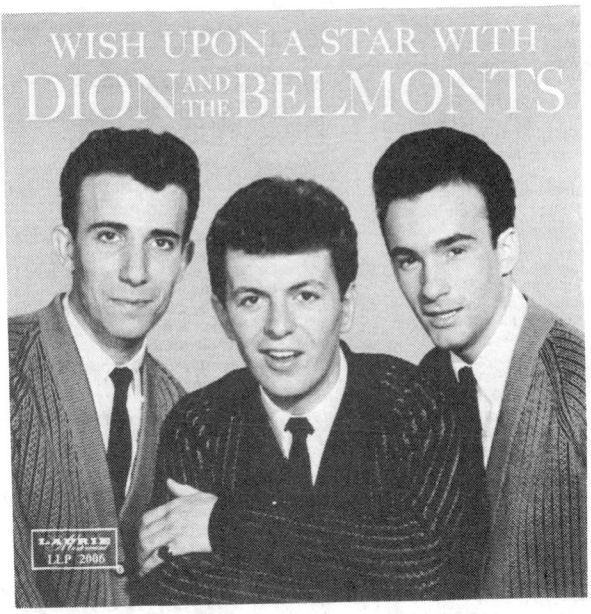

After achieving massive success as a doo-wop group with The Belmonts, illustrated here by When You Wish Upon A Star, Dion DiMucci branched out into a lucrative solo career, first with Laurie, illustrated by Love Came To Me, and then with Columbia. As the quintessential Italian kid making good, Dion was the idol of virtually every white kid on the streets of New York, much the same role that Frankie Lymon played for every black kid in New York. (Elvis wasn't the king everywhere, at least not then.)

Label & Catalog #		Title	Year	VG+	NM
Warner Bros. WS-1826	(S)	Sit Down, Old Friend	1969	8.00	20.00
Warner Bros. WS-1872	(S)	You're Not Alone	1971	6.00	15.00
Warner Bros. WS-1945	(S)	Sanctuary	1971	6.00	15.00
Warner Bros. BS-2642	(S)	Suite For Late Summer	1972	5.00	12.00
Columbia KC-31942	(E)	Dion's Greatest Hits	1973	1.00	5.00
Warner Bros. BS-2954	(S)	Streetheart	1976	4.00	10.00
Roxbury RX3-300	(S)	The Bitter End Years (3 LPs)	1976	10.00	25.00
Dayspring DST-4022	(S)	Inside Job	1980	1.00	5.00

DION & THE BELMONTS
Refer to The Belmonts.

Laurie LLP-1002	(M)	Presenting Dion & The Belmonts	1959	200.00	400.00
		(Original covers have "Mastersound" in the upper right corner.)			
		— Laurie albums above have gold labels—			
Laurie LLP-2002	(M)	Presenting Dion & The Belmonts	1959	60.00	150.00
Laurie LLPS-2002	(E)	Presenting Dion & The Belmonts	196?	500.00	750.00
Laurie LLP-2006	(M)	Wish Upon A Star	1959	150.00	300.00
Laurie LLP-2016	(M)	'Together' On Records	1959	30.00	75.00
		— Laurie albums above have gold & white labels with large benday dots.—			
ABC ABC-599	(M)	Together Again	1967	12.00	30.00
ABC ABCS-599	(S)	Together Again	1967	15.00	40.00
Warner Bros. BS-2664	(S)	Reunion—Live At Madison Square Garden	1973	12.00	30.00
Laurie SLP-6000	(P)	60 Greatest Hits (3 LPs in box)	197?	8.00	20.00
Laurie SLP-6000	(P)	60 Greatest Hits (3 LPs in cover)	197?	4.00	10.00
		(Tracks are in mono and stereo as recorded.)			
Laurie SLP-4002	(E)	Everything You Always Wanted To Hear By Dion & The Belmonts	197?	4.00	10.00
		(LES-4002 contains "The Wanderer," "The Majestic," "A Teenager In Love," and "When You Wish Upon A Star" in stereo.)			
Pickwick SPC-3521	(S)	Doo Wop	1975	4.00	10.00
		(Pickwick 3521 is a reissue of ABC 599.)			
GRT 2103707	(P)	The Dion Years (1958-1963) (2 LPs)	1975	4.00	10.00
Lifesong JZ-35356	(S)	Return Of The Wanderer	1978	4.00	10.00

DIRE STRAITS

Warner Bros. 3266	(S)	Dire Straits	1979	1.00	5.00
Warner Bros. 3330	(S)	Communique	1979	1.00	5.00
Warner Bros. 3480	(S)	Making Movies	1980	1.00	5.00
Warner Bros. WBMS-109	(DJ)	Dire Straits Live	1980	20.00	50.00
Warner Bros. 23728	(DJ)	Love Over Gold (Quiex II vinyl)	1982	20.00	50.00
Warner Bros. 23728	(S)	Love Over Gold	1982	1.00	5.00
Warner Bros. 29800	(S)	Twisting By The Pool	1983	1.00	5.00
Warner Bros. 25085	(DJ)	Dire Straits Live—Alchemy (2 LPs. Quiex II vinyl)	1984	20.00	50.00
Warner Bros. 25085	(S)	Dire Straits Live—Alchemy (2 LPs)	1984	1.20	6.00
Warner Bros. 25264	(DJ)	Brothers In Arms (2 LPs. Quiex II vinyl)	1985	20.00	50.00
Warner Bros. 25264	(S)	Brothers In Arms (2 LPs)	1985	1.20	6.00

DIRTY BLUES BAND, THE

BluesWay BLS-6010	(S)	The Dirty Blues Band	1968	10.00	25.00
BluesWay BLS-6020	(S)	Stone Dirt	1968	10.00	25.00

DIRTY OLD MEN, THE

Nocturne 902	(S)	The Dirty Old Men	1969	6.00	15.00

DISTANT GALAXY

Verve V6-5063	(S)	Distant Galaxy	1968	6.00	15.00

DIXIE CUPS, THE

Red Bird RB-20-100	(M)	Chapel Of Love	1964	30.00	75.00
Red Bird RBS-20-100	(S)	Chapel Of Love	1964	40.00	100.00
Red Bird RB-20-103	(M)	Iko Iko	1965	60.00	150.00
ABC-Paramount 525	(M)	Riding High	1965	30.00	75.00
ABC-Paramount S-525	(S)	Riding High	1965	40.00	100.00

DIXIEBELLES, THE

Sound Stage-7 SSM-5000	(M)	Down At Papa Joe's	1963	20.00	50.00
Sound Stage-7 SSS-15000	(E)	Down At Papa Joe's	1963	16.00	40.00

DIXON, WILLIE

Bluesville BVLP-1003	(M)	Willie's Blues	1960	60.00	150.00
		— Bluesville albums above have bright blue labels with silver print.—			
Bluesville BVLP-1003	(M)	Willie's Blues	1964	16.00	40.00
		— Bluesville albums above have blue labels with a trident logo on the right side.—			
Columbia CS-9987	(S)	I Am The Blues	1970	10.00	25.00
		— Columbia albums above have "360 Sound" labels.—			
Columbia CS-9987	(S)	I Am The Blues	197?	1.00	5.00
Ovation QD-1433	(S)	Catalyst	1974	4.00	10.00
Chess CH3-16500	(M)	Willie Dixon (3 LP box)	1988	12.00	30.00
Bug C1-90595	(S)	Hidden Charms	1988	6.00	15.00

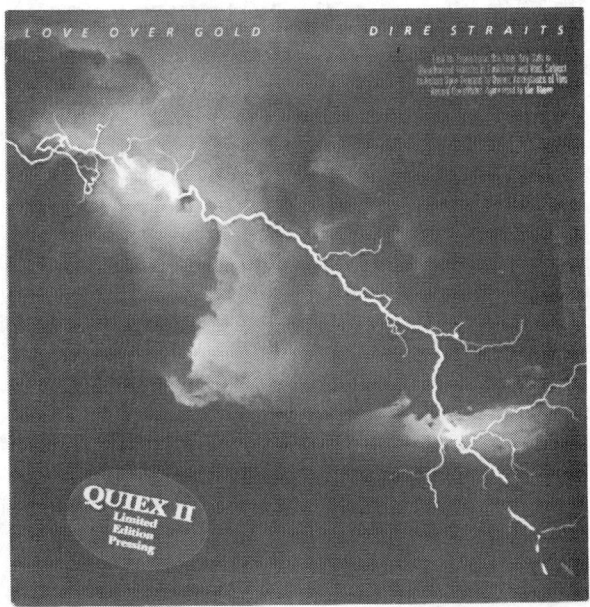

These two by Dire Straits, Brothers In Arms *and* Love Over Gold, *along with their sixth album,* Dire Straits Live/Alchemy, *were issued promotionally as "Limited Edition Pressings" on Quiex II virgin vinyl and are very hot with audiophiles.*

Label & Catalog #		Title	Year	VG+	NM
DIXON, WILLIE, & MEMPHIS SLIM					
Verve MGV-3007	(M)	**Blues Every Which Way**	1960	**50.00**	**125.00**
— Verve albums above have "Verve Records, Inc." on the bottom of the label.—					
Battle BV-6122	(M)	**In Paris**	1963	**8.00**	**20.00**
Battle BVS-6122	(S)	**In Paris**	1963	**10.00**	**25.00**
DOBKINS, CARL, JR.					
Decca DL-8938	(M)	**Carl Dobkins, Jr.**	1959	**40.00**	**100.00**
Decca DL-78938	(S)	**Carl Dobkins, Jr.**	1959	**60.00**	**150.00**
DOC HOLLIDAY					
Metromedia 1017	(S)	**Doc Holliday**	1973	**8.00**	**20.00**
DR. FEELGOOD & THE INTERNS					
Dr. Feelgood also recorded as Piano Red.					
OKeh OKM-12101	(M)	**Doctor Feelgood & The Interns**	1962	**40.00**	**100.00**
OKeh OKS-14101	(S)	**Doctor Feelgood & The Interns**	1962	**80.00**	**200.00**
DR. JOHN					
Dr. John is a pseudonym for Mac Rebennack. Refer to Mike Bloomfield & Dr. John & John Hammond.					
Atco SD-33-234	(S)	**Gris-Gris**	1968	**12.00**	**30.00**
— Atco albums above have purple & brown labels.—					
Atco SD-33-234	(S)	**Gris-Gris**	1968	**6.00**	**15.00**
Atco SD-33-270	(S)	**Babylon**	1969	**6.00**	**15.00**
Atco SD-33-316	(S)	**Remedies**	1970	**6.00**	**15.00**
Atco SD-33-362	(S)	**The Sun, Moon And Herbs**	1971	**6.00**	**15.00**
— Atco albums above have yellow labels with an 1841 Broadway address.—					
Atco SD-7006	(S)	**Gumbo**	1972	**1.00**	**5.00**
Atco SD-7018	(S)	**In The Right Place**	1973	**1.00**	**5.00**
Atco SD-7043	(S)	**Destively Bonnaroo**	1974	**1.00**	**5.00**
Springboard SPB-4018	(S)	**Dr. John**	1972	**1.00**	**5.00**
Barometer BRM-67001	(S)	**Anytime, Anyplace**	1974	**1.00**	**5.00**
United Arts. LA-552G	(S)	**Hollywood Be Thy Name**	1975	**1.00**	**5.00**
Trip TLX-350	(S)	**Dr. John Superpak** (2 LPs)	1975	**1.00**	**5.00**
Trip TLP-9518	(S)	**Zu Zu Man**	1975	**1.00**	**5.00**
Trip TOP-16-1	(S)	**Dr. John's 16 Greatest Hits**	1976	**1.00**	**5.00**
Karate 5404	(S)	**One Night Late**	1978	**1.00**	**5.00**
A&M SP-732	(S)	**City Lights**	1979	**1.00**	**5.00**
A&M SP-740	(S)	**Love Potion**	1979	**1.00**	**5.00**
Accord SN-7118	(S)	**Love Potion**	1981	**1.00**	**5.00**
Cleancuts 705	(S)	**Dr. John Plays Mac Rebennack**	1982	**1.00**	**5.00**
DR. K'S BLUES BAND					
World Pacific WPS-21903	(S)	**Dr. K's Blues Band**	1970	**6.00**	**15.00**
DR. MARIGOLD'S PRESCRIPTION					
Alshire 5159	(S)	**Doctor Marigold's Prescription**	1969	**5.00**	**12.00**
DR. ROSS					
Fortune F-3011	(M)	**Doctor Ross, The Harmonica Boss**	1962	**20.00**	**50.00**
Fortune FS-3011	(S)	**Doctor Ross, The Harmonica Boss**	1962	**40.00**	**100.00**
Testament 2206	(M)	**Doctor Ross**	196?	**8.00**	**20.00**
DR. WEST'S MEDICINE SHOW & JUG BAND					
Dr. West's Band features Norman Greenbaum.					
Go Go 22-17-002	(M)	**The Eggplant That Ate Chicago**	1967	**10.00**	**25.00**
Go Go 22-17-002	(E)	**The Eggplant That Ate Chicago**	1967	**8.00**	**20.00**
Gregar GG-101	(E)	**Norman Greenbaum**	1970	**8.00**	**20.00**
		(Gregar 101 contains earlier material.)			
DOCTORS OF MADNESS, THE					
United Arts. LA871	(S)	**The Doctors Of Madness** (2 LPs)	1976	**6.00**	**15.00**
DODD, DICK					
Dodd was a member of The Standells.					
Tower ST-5142	(S)	**First Evolution Of Dick Dodd**	1968	**20.00**	**50.00**
DOGGETT, BILL					
King 295-82	(10")	**Bill Doggett—His Organ And Combo**	1955	**60.00**	**150.00**
King 295-83	(10")	**Bill Doggett—His Organ And Combo, Volume 2**	1955	**60.00**	**150.00**
King 295-89	(10")	**All-Time Christmas Favorites**	1955	**150.00**	**300.00**
		(King 89 is often referred to as the first R&B Christmas album. . .)			
King 295-102	(10")	**Sentimentally Yours**	1956	**60.00**	**150.00**
King 395-502	(M)	**Moondust**	1957	**30.00**	**75.00**
King 395-514	(M)	**Hot Doggett**	1957	**30.00**	**75.00**
King 395-523	(M)	**As You Desire**	1958	**30.00**	**75.00**
King 395-531	(M)	**Everybody Dance To The Honky Tonk**	1958	**30.00**	**75.00**
King 395-532	(M)	**Dame Dreaming**	1958	**30.00**	**75.00**
King 395-533	(M)	**A Salute To Ellington**	1958	**30.00**	**75.00**

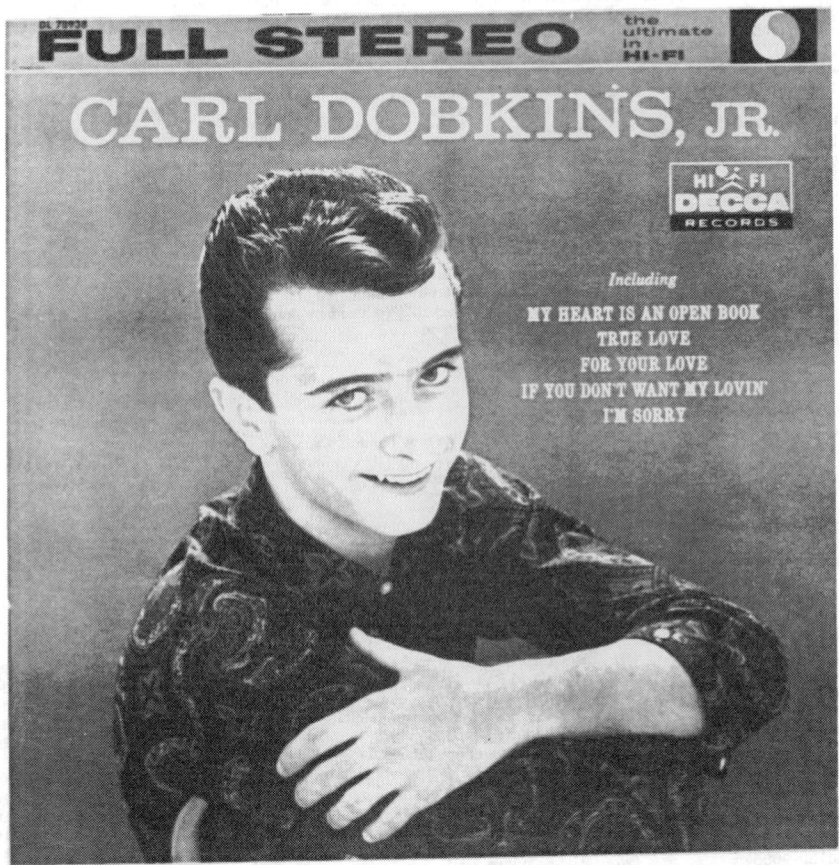

Carl Dobkins Jr hit the upper regions of the national charts in 1959 with "My Heart Is An Open Book," and then watched as his next single, "If You Don't Want My Lovin'," squeaked into the Top 100. Still, Decca followed with an album that included both charters in stereo.

Label & Catalog #		Title	Year	VG+	NM
King 395-557	(M)	The Doggett Beat For Dancing Feet	1958	30.00	75.00
King 395-563	(M)	Candle Glow	1958	30.00	75.00
King 395-582	(M)	Swingin' Easy	1959	30.00	75.00
King 395-585	(M)	Dance Awhile	1959	30.00	75.00
King 395-600	(M)	Bill Doggett Christmas	1959	30.00	75.00
King 395-609	(M)	Hold It	1959	30.00	75.00
King 633	(M)	High And Wide	1959	20.00	50.00
King 641	(M)	Big City Dance Party	1959	20.00	50.00
King 667	(M)	Bill Doggett On Tour	1959	20.00	50.00
King 706	(M)	For Reminiscent Lovers, Romantic Songs	1960	20.00	50.00
King 723	(M)	Back Again With More	1960	20.00	50.00
King 759	(M)	Bonanza Of 24 Songs	1960	20.00	50.00
King 778	(M)	The Many Moods Of Bill Doggett	1963	16.00	40.00
King 830	(M)	American Songs In The Bossa Nova Style	1963	16.00	40.00
King 868	(S)	Impressions	1964	16.00	40.00
King 908	(S)	The Best Of Bill Doggett	1964	16.00	40.00
King 959	(S)	Bonanza Of 24 Hit Songs	1966	16.00	40.00

—King albums above have crownless black or blue labels. The logo on the covers have a crown with "King" in open capital block letters below.—

Warner Bros. W-1404	(M)	3,046 People Danced 'Til 4 AM	1960	8.00	20.00
Warner Bros. WS-1404	(M)	3,046 People Danced 'Til 4 AM	1960	10.00	25.00
Warner Bros. W-1421	(M)	The Band With The Beat	1961	8.00	20.00
Warner Bros. W-1421	(S)	The Band With The Beat	1961	10.00	25.00
Warner Bros. WS-1452	(M)	Bill Doggett Swings	1962	8.00	20.00
Warner Bros. WS-1452	(S)	Bill Doggett Swings	1962	10.00	25.00
Columbia CL-1814	(M)	Oops!	1962	8.00	20.00
Columbia CS-8614	(S)	Oops!	1962	10.00	25.00
Columbia CL-1942	(M)	Prelude To The Blues	1963	8.00	20.00
Columbia CS-8742	(S)	Prelude To The Blues	1963	10.00	25.00
Columbia CL-2082	(M)	Fingertips	1963	8.00	20.00
Columbia CS-8882	(S)	Fingertips	1963	10.00	25.00
ABC-Paramount 507	(M)	Wow!	1965	8.00	20.00
ABC-Paramount S-507	(S)	Wow!	1965	10.00	25.00
Roulette R-25330	(M)	Honky Tonk Ala Mod	1966	8.00	20.00
Roulette SR-25330	(S)	Honky Tonk Ala Mod	1966	10.00	25.00
King 1078	(S)	Honky Tonk Popcorn (Produced by James Brown)	1969	20.00	50.00
King 1097	(S)	The Nearness Of You	1970	10.00	25.00
King 1101	(S)	Ram Bunk Shush	1970	10.00	25.00
King 1104	(S)	Sentimental Journey	1970	10.00	25.00
King 1108	(S)	Soft	1970	10.00	25.00

DOHERTY, DENNY
Mr. Doherty was a member of The Mugwumps; The Mama's & The Papa's.

Dunhill DS-50096	(S)	Watcha' Gonna Do?	1970	6.00	15.00
Ember EMS-1036	(S)	Waiting For A Song	1975	4.00	10.00

DOJO

Eclipse ES-7309	(S)	Down For The Last Time	1971	10.00	25.00

DOLENZ, JONES, BOYCE & HART
Mickey Dolenz, Davey Jones, Tommy Boyce and Bobby Hart. Refer to The Monkees.

Capitol ST-11513	(S)	Dolenz, Jones, Boyce And Hart	1976	6.00	15.00

DOMINO, FATS

Imperial LP-9004	(M)	Rock And Rollin' With Fats Domino	1956	150.00	300.00
Imperial LP-9009	(M)	Rock And Rollin'	1956	150.00	300.00
Imperial LP-9028	(M)	This Is Fats Domino!	1957	150.00	300.00
Imperial LP-9038	(M)	Here Stands Fats Domino	1957	150.00	300.00
Imperial LP-9040	(M)	This Is Fats	1957	150.00	300.00

— Original Imperial albums above have maroon labels.—

Imperial LP-9004	(M)	Rock And Rollin' With Fats Domino	1958	40.00	100.00
Imperial LP-9009	(M)	Rock And Rollin'	1958	40.00	100.00
Imperial LP-9028	(M)	This Is Fats Domino!	1958	40.00	100.00
Imperial LP-9038	(M)	Here Stands Fats Domino	1958	40.00	100.00
Imperial LP-9040	(M)	This Is Fats	1958	40.00	100.00
Imperial LP-9055	(M)	The Fabulous Mr. D	1958	40.00	100.00
Imperial LP-9062	(M)	Fats Domino Swings	1959	40.00	100.00
Imperial LP-9065	(M)	Let's Play Fats Domino	1959	40.00	100.00
Imperial LP-9103	(M)	Million Record Hits	1960	40.00	100.00
Imperial LP-9127	(M)	A Lot Of Dominos	1961	40.00	100.00
Imperial LP-12066	(S)	A Lot Of Dominos	1961	60.00	150.00
Imperial LP-9138	(M)	I Miss You So	1961	40.00	100.00
Imperial LP-12398	(E)	I Miss You So	1961	30.00	75.00
Imperial LP-9153	(M)	Let The Four Winds Blow	1961	40.00	100.00
Imperial LP-12073	(S)	Let The Four Winds Blow	1961	60.00	150.00
Imperial LP-9164	(M)	What A Party	1962	30.00	75.00
Imperial LP-9170	(M)	Twistin' The Stomp	1962	30.00	75.00
Imperial LP-9195	(M)	Million Sellers By Fats	1962	24.00	60.00
Imperial LP-9208	(M)	Just Domino	1962	24.00	60.00

Antoine "Fats" Domino has apparently always been playing the same slowly shuffling rhythms that are now all but synonymous with New Orleans. He was the most successful single black artist of the '50s and early '60s with more than 60 sides having reached the national pop charts prior to the onslaught of Beatlemania, a record surpassed only by Elvis! Yet he was almost forgotten after the British Invasion. Still playing today, he claims that what he played before rock'n roll they called rhythm'n blues and the same things he played after rock'n roll they called. . . rock'n roll!

Label & Catalog #		Title	Year	VG+	NM
Imperial LP-9227	(M)	Walking To New Orleans	1963	20.00	50.00
Imperial LP-9239	(M)	Let's Dance With Domino	1963	20.00	50.00
Imperial LP-9248	(M)	Here He Comes Again	1963	20.00	50.00

— Imperial mono albums above have black labels with colored stars on top; stereo album have black labels with silver print. —

Label & Catalog #		Title	Year	VG+	NM
Imperial LP-9004	(M)	Rock And Rollin' With Fats Domino	1964	12.00	30.00
Imperial LP-12087	(E)	Rock And Rollin' With Fats Domino	1964	8.00	20.00
Imperial LP-9009	(M)	Rock And Rollin'	1964	12.00	30.00
Imperial LP-12088	(E)	Rock And Rollin'	1964	8.00	20.00
Imperial LP-9028	(M)	This Is Fats Domino!	1964	12.00	30.00
Imperial LP-12089	(E)	This Is Fats Domino!	1964	8.00	20.00
Imperial LP-9038	(M)	Here Stands Fats Domino	1964	12.00	30.00
Imperial LP-12090	(E)	Here Stands Fats Domino	1964	8.00	20.00
Imperial LP-9040	(M)	This Is Fats	1964	12.00	30.00
Imperial LP-12091	(E)	This Is Fats	1964	8.00	20.00
Imperial LP-9055	(M)	The Fabulous Mr. D	1964	12.00	30.00
Imperial LP-12094	(E)	The Fabulous Mr. D	1964	8.00	20.00
Imperial LP-9062	(M)	Fats Domino Swings	1964	12.00	30.00
Imperial LP-12091	(E)	Fats Domino Swings	1964	8.00	20.00
Imperial LP-9065	(M)	Let's Play Fats Domino	1964	12.00	30.00
Imperial LP-12095	(E)	Let's Play Fats Domino	1964	8.00	20.00
Imperial LP-9103	(M)	Million Record Hits	1964	12.00	30.00
Imperial LP-12103	(E)	Million Record Hits	1964	8.00	20.00
Imperial LP-9127	(M)	A Lot Of Dominos	1964	12.00	30.00
Imperial LP-12066	(S)	A Lot Of Dominos	1964	14.00	35.00
Imperial LP-9138	(M)	I Miss You So	1964	12.00	30.00
Imperial LP-12098	(E)	I Miss You So	1964	8.00	20.00
Imperial LP-9153	(M)	Let The Four Winds Blow	1964	12.00	30.00
Imperial LP-12073	(S)	Let The Four Winds Blow	1964	16.00	40.00
Imperial LP-9195	(M)	Million Sellers By Fats	1964	12.00	30.00
Imperial LP-12195	(E)	Million Sellers By Fats	1964	8.00	20.00
Imperial LP-9227	(M)	Walking To New Orleans	1964	12.00	30.00
Imperial LP-12227	(E)	Walking To New Orleans	1964	8.00	20.00
Imperial LP-9239	(M)	Let's Dance With Domino	1964	12.00	30.00
Imperial LP-12239	(E)	Let's Dance With Domino	1964`	8.00	20.00
Imperial LP-9248	(M)	Here He Comes Again	1964	12.00	30.00
Imperial LP-12248	(E)	Here He Comes Again	1964	8.00	20.00

— Imperial albums above have black, white & pink labels. —

Label & Catalog #		Title	Year	VG+	NM
Imperial LP-9004	(M)	Rock And Rollin' With Fats Domino	1967	8.00	20.00
Imperial LP-12087	(E)	Rock And Rollin' With Fats Domino	1967	6.00	15.00
Imperial LP-9009	(M)	Rock And Rollin'	1967	8.00	20.00
Imperial LP-12088	(E)	Rock And Rollin'	1967	6.00	15.00
Imperial LP-9028	(M)	This Is Fats Domino!	1967	8.00	20.00
Imperial LP-12089	(E)	This Is Fats Domino!	1967	6.00	15.00
Imperial LP-9038	(M)	Here Stands Fats Domino	1967	8.00	20.00
Imperial LP-12090	(E)	Here Stands Fats Domino	1967	6.00	15.00
Imperial LP-9040	(M)	This Is Fats	1967	8.00	20.00
Imperial LP-12091	(E)	This Is Fats	1967	6.00	15.00
Imperial LP-9055	(M)	The Fabulous Mr. D	1967	8.00	20.00
Imperial LP-12094	(E)	The Fabulous Mr. D	1967	6.00	15.00
Imperial LP-9062	(M)	Fats Domino Swings	1967	8.00	20.00
Imperial LP-12091	(E)	Fats Domino Swings	1967	6.00	15.00
Imperial LP-9065	(M)	Let's Play Fats Domino	1967	8.00	20.00
Imperial LP-12095	(E)	Let's Play Fats Domino	1967	6.00	15.00
Imperial LP-9103	(M)	Fats Domino Sings Million Record Hits	1967	8.00	20.00
Imperial LP-12103	(E)	Fats Domino Sings Million Record Hits	1967	6.00	15.00
Imperial LP-9127	(M)	A Lot Of Dominos	1967	8.00	20.00
Imperial LP-12066	(S)	A Lot Of Dominos	1967	6.00	15.00
Imperial LP-9138	(M)	I Miss You So	1967	8.00	20.00
Imperial LP-12098	(E)	I Miss You So	1967	6.00	15.00
Imperial LP-9153	(M)	Let The Four Winds Blow	1967	8.00	20.00
Imperial LP-12073	(S)	Let The Four Winds Blow	1967	10.00	25.00
Imperial LP-9195	(M)	Million Sellers By Fats	1967	8.00	20.00
Imperial LP-12195	(S)	Million Sellers By Fats	1967	10.00	25.00
Imperial LP-9227	(M)	Walking To New Orleans	1967	8.00	20.00
Imperial LP-12227	(E)	Walking To New Orleans	1967	6.00	15.00
Imperial LP-9239	(M)	Let's Dance With Domino	1967	8.00	20.00
Imperial LP-12239	(E)	Let's Dance With Domino	1967	6.00	15.00
Imperial LP-9248	(M)	Here He Comes Again	1967	8.00	20.00
Imperial LP-12248	(E)	Here He Comes Again	1967	6.00	15.00

— Imperial albums above have black, white & green labels. —

Label & Catalog #		Title	Year	VG+	NM
ABC Paramount ABC-455	(M)	Here Comes Fats Domino	1963	8.00	20.00
ABC Paramount ABCS-455	(S)	Here Comes Fats Domino	1963	10.00	25.00
ABC Paramount ABC-479	(M)	Fats On Fire	1964	8.00	20.00
ABC Paramount ABCS-479	(S)	Fats On Fire	1964	10.00	25.00
ABC Paramount ABC-510	(M)	Getaway With Fats Domino	1965	8.00	20.00
ABC Paramount ABCS-510	(S)	Getaway With Fats Domino	1965	10.00	25.00
ABC Paramount T-90167	(M)	Getaway With Fats Domino	1965	10.00	25.00

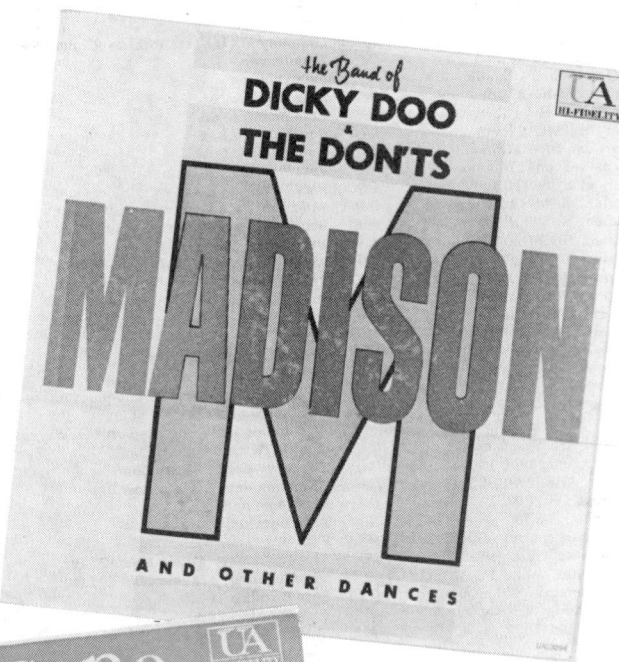

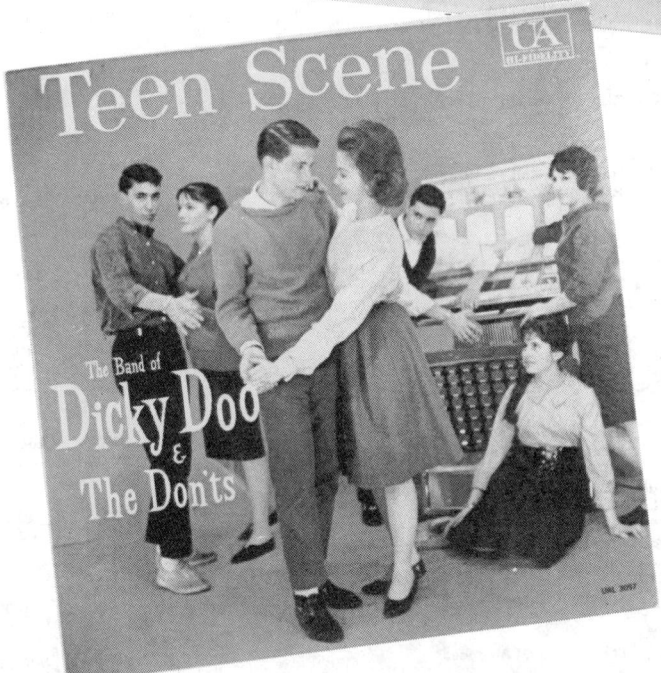

Most collectors and Top 40 enthusiasts always figured that, as the leader, Jerry Grant (a.k.a. Jerry Granahan) played the role of Mr Doo in the humorously named Dicky Doo & The Don'ts. Actually, Dicky Doo was the nickname of drummer Dave Alldred, formerly a member of Jimmy Bowen's Rhythm Orchids. The group had several chart hits for the then fledgling Swan Records before signing with the newly formed United Artists. These two albums, Madison and Teen Scene, the group's only on a major, were issued in 1959. A few years later they were recorded live in Wilkes-Barre, PA, and a record pressed, although it is doubtful that it was released.

Label & Catalog #		Title	Year	VG+	NM
ABC Paramount ST-90167	(S)	Getaway With Fats Domino (Capitol Record Club)	1965	10.00	25.00
Grand Award G-267	(M)	Fats Domino	196?	8.00	20.00
Grand Award GS-267	(E)	Fats Domino	196?	4.00	10.00
Mercury MG-21039	(M)	Fats Domino '65	1965	10.00	25.00
Mercury SR-61039	(S)	Fats Domino '65	1965	16.00	40.00
Mercury MG-21065	(M)	Southland U.S.A.	1966	Unreleased	
Mercury SR-61065	(S)	Southland U.S.A.	1966	Unreleased	
Sunset SUM-1103	(M)	Fats Domino	1966	5.00	12.00
Sunset SUS-5103	(E)	Fats Domino	1966	5.00	12.00
Sunset SUM-1158	(M)	Stompin' Fats Domino	1967	5.00	12.00
Sunset SUS-5158	(E)	Stompin' Fats Domino	1967	5.00	12.00
Sunset SUS-5200	(P)	Trouble In Mind	1968	8.00	20.00
Sunset SUS-5299	(E)	Ain't That A Shame	1970	5.00	12.00
Reprise RS-6304	(S)	Fats Is Back	1968	8.00	20.00
Reprise RS-6439	(S)	Fats (Test pressing)	1971	150.00	300.00
Reprise RS-6439	(S)	Fats (Stock copy without a cover)	1971	250.00	500.00
Reprise RS-6439	(S)	Fats	1971	Unreleased	
United Arts. UAS-9958	(M)	Legendary Masters (2 LPs)	1971	6.00	15.00
United Arts. UAMG-104	(DJ)	The Fats Domino Sound	1973	14.00	35.00
		(Promo only with edited versions of 30 tracks.)			
United Arts. LA-122	(DJ)	Cookin' With Fats (2 LPs)	1974	300.00	500.00
		(Promos have one disc on black vinyl and one on colored vinyl.)			
United Arts. LA-122	(M)	Cookin' With Fats (2 LPs)	1974	12.00	30.00
United Arts. LA-233G	(M)	The Very Best Of Fats Domino	1974	4.00	10.00
United Arts. LA-380E	(M)	The Very Best Of Fats Domino	1975	3.20	8.00
Everest FS-280	(E)	Fats Domino	1974	3.20	8.00
Everest FS-330	(E)	Fats Domino, Volume 2	1975	3.20	8.00
Harlem Hitparade 5005	(P)	Fats' Hits	1975	3.20	8.00
Candlelite Music P2-13197	(E)	The Legendary Music Man (2 LPs)	1976	6.00	15.00
Candlelite Music P2-13197	(P)	The Legendary Music Man (2 LPs)	1976	6.00	15.00
"FD" Records WB-8000	(S)	Fats Domino 1980	1980	6.00	15.00
FD Records WB-8000	(S)	Fats Domino 1980	1980	6.00	15.00
Liberty LM-1027	(M)	Million Sellers By Fats	1981	1.00	5.00

DON & DEWEY
Don "Sugarcane" Harris and Dewey Terry.

Specialty SPS-2131	(E)	They're Rockin' Til Midnight, Rollin' Til Dawn	1970	20.00	50.00
		("Pink Champagne" and "Mammer Jammer" are stereo.)			

DON & EDDIE

Modern PLP-814	(M)	Rock And Roll Party	1963	20.00	50.00
Modern PLP-814S	(S)	Rock And Roll Party	1963	20.00	50.00

DON & THE GOOD TIMES
Don & The Good Times also recorded with Jim Valley.

Burdette 300	(M)	Don & The Goodtimes' Greatest Hits	1966	60.00	150.00
Burdette 300S	(S)	Don & The Goodtimes' Greatest Hits	1966	150.00	300.00
Burdette 300S	(E)	Don & The Goodtimes' Greatest Hits	1966	40.00	100.00
Epic LN-24311	(M)	So Good	1967	6.00	15.00
Epic BN-26311	(S)	So Good	1967	8.00	20.00
Wand WDS-679	(S)	Where The Action Is	1969	12.00	30.00
Picadilly	(S)	Goodtime Rock 'n Roll	1980	10.00	25.00

DON, DICK & JIMMY

Modern LMP-1205	(M)	Spring Fever	195?	60.00	150.00
Crown CLP-5005	(M)	Spring Fever	1959	20.00	50.00
		(Crown 5005 is a reissue of Modern 1205.)			
		—Crown albums above have black labels with a silver "Crown" logo.—			
Verve MGV-2084	(M)	Medium Rare	1958	16.00	40.00
Verve MGV-2107	(M)	Songs For The Hearth	1959	16.00	40.00
		—Verve albums above have "Verve Records, Inc" on the bottom of the label.—			

DONALDSON, BO, & THE HEYWOODS

Family Prod. FPS-2711	(S)	Special Someone	1973	4.00	10.00

DONNER, RAL

Gone LP-5012	(M)	Takin' Care Of Business	1961	150.00	300.00

DONNER, RAL / RAY SMITH / BOBBY DALE

Crown CLP-5335	(M)	Ral Donner, Ray Smith And Bobby Dale	1963	16.00	40.00
Crown CST-335	(E)	Ral Donner, Ray Smith And Bobby Dale	1963	8.00	20.00
		—Crown albums above have gray labels.—			

DONNIE & THE DELCHORDS & THE NEONS

Taurus 1000	(S)	Sing With Triple Stereo	1967	150.00	300.00

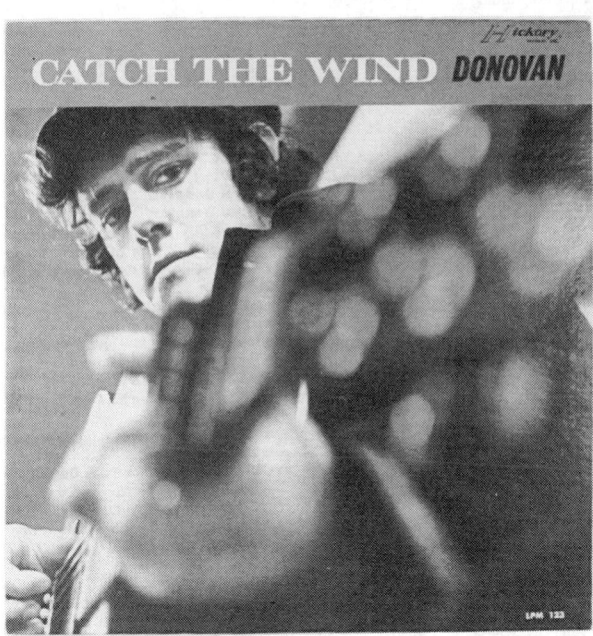

Another talent often treated with contempt by writers who should know better, Donovan Leitch began as "England's answer to Dylan," as evidenced by such early Hickory albums ~s Catch The Wind and Like It Is. He evolved into a unique artist whose obsessions with th of antiquity appeared a bit too early to have caught the fancy of the "new age" mov Through 1976 he had seen twenty of his albums make the charts and received a pair Gold Record awards.

Label & Catalog #		Title	Year	VG+	NM

DONOVAN

Billed as "Great Britain's answer to Dylan," singer, songwriter and guitar player Donovan Leitch's early work was in the contemporary folk vein. By 1966 he was working in an eclectic pop style.

Label & Catalog #		Title	Year	VG+	NM
Hickory LPM-123	(M)	Catch The Wind	1965	10.00	25.00
Hickory LPS-123	(E)	Catch The Wind	1965	8.00	20.00
Hickory LPM-127	(M)	Fairy Tale	1965	8.00	20.00
Hickory LPS-127	(S)	Fairy Tale ("Colours" is rechanneled)	1965	10.00	25.00
Hickory LPM-135	(M)	The Real Donovan	1966	8.00	20.00
Hickory LPS-135	(P)	The Real Donovan	1966	10.00	25.00
		(While this compilation features rechanneled stereo tracks from Hickory 127, the other tracks, including "Colours," are stereo.)			
Hickory LPS-143	(P)	Like It Is, Was And Evermore Shall Be	1968	8.00	20.00
Hickory LPS-149	(P)	The Best Of Donovan	1969	8.00	20.00
Epic LN-24217	(M)	Sunshine Superman	1966	12.00	30.00
Epic BN-26217	(E)	Sunshine Superman	1966	6.00	15.00
Epic LN-24239	(M)	Mellow Yellow	1967	12.00	30.00
Epic BN-26239	(E)	Mellow Yellow	1967	6.00	15.00
Epic LN-24349	(M)	Wear Your Love Like Heaven	1967	4.00	10.00
Epic BN-26349	(S)	Wear Your Love Like Heaven	1967	5.00	12.00
Epic LN-24350	(M)	For Little Ones	1967	4.00	10.00
Epic BN-26350	(S)	For Little Ones	1967	5.00	12.00
Epic L2N-171	(M)	A Gift From A Flower To A Garden	1968	16.00	40.00
Epic B2N-171	(S)	A Gift From A Flower To A Garden	1968	8.00	20.00
		(Boxed set of the two previous albums, "Wear Your Love Like Heaven" and "For Little Ones." Issued with a portfolio of lyrics, drawings, and poetry, which are included in the price.)			
Epic BN-26386	(S)	Donovan In Concert	1968	5.00	12.00
Epic BN-26420	(S)	The Hurdy Gurdy Man	1969	5.00	12.00
Epic BXN-26439	(S)	Donovan's Greatest Hits	1969	4.00	10.00
		("Catch The Wind" and "Colours" were rerecorded in stereo while "Mellow Yellow" is rechanneled.)			
Epic BN-26481	(S)	Barabajagal	1969	5.00	12.00
Epic E-30125	(S)	Open Road	1970	5.00	12.00
Epic E-31210	(S)	The World Of Donovan	1972	5.00	12.00
		—Epic albums above have yellow labels.—			
Epic BXN-26439	(S)	Donovan's Greatest Hits	197?	1.00	5.00
Epic KE-32156	(S)	Cosmic Wheels (Includes poster)	1973	6.00	15.00
Epic KE-32800	(S)	Essence To Essence	1974	4.00	10.00
Epic PE-33245	(S)	7-Tease	1974	4.00	10.00
Epic BG-33731	(S)	The Hurdy Gurdy Man / Barabajagal (2 LPs)	1975	4.00	10.00
Epic BG-33734	(P)	In Concert / Sunshine Superman (2 LPs)	1975	4.00	10.00
Epic PE-33945	(S)	Slow Down World	1976	4.00	10.00
		—Epic albums above have orange labels.—			
Epic B2N-171	(S)	A Gift From A Flower To A Garden	197?	4.00	10.00
Epic BXN-26439	(S)	Donovan's Greatest Hits	197?	.80	4.00
		—Epic albums above have black labels.—			
Janus 3022	(S)	Donovan P. Leitch	1970	4.00	10.00
Janus 3025	(S)	Hear Me Now	1971	4.00	10.00
Bell 1135	(P)	Early Treasures	1973	4.00	10.00
Pye 502	(P)	The Pye History Of British Music:	1975	4.00	10.00
Pye 502	(P)	The Pye History Of British Music, Vol. 2	1976	4.00	10.00
Kory 3010	(P)	Early Treasures	1977	1.00	5.00
Arista 8B-4143	(S)	Donovan	1980	1.00	5.00
Allegiance AV-437	(S)	Lady Of The Stars	1983	1.00	5.00
Great Northern Arts 61007	(S)	The Classics Live	1991	1.00	5.00

DOO, DICKY, & THE DON'TS

United Arts. UAL-3094	(M)	The Madison & Other Dances	1959	16.00	40.00
United Arts. UAS-6094	(S)	The Madison & Other Dances	1959	20.00	50.00
United Arts. UAL-3097	(M)	Teen Scene	1959	16.00	40.00
United Arts. UAS-6097	(S)	Teen Scene	1959	20.00	50.00
(No label)	(DJ)	Dicky Doo & The Don'ts Live	1962	See note below	
		(Private pressing has a suggested NM value of $500-1,000.)			

DOOBIE BROTHERS, THE

Warner Bros. WS-1919	(S)	The Doobie Brothers	1971	3.20	8.00
Warner Bros. BS-2634	(S)	Toulouse Street	1972	3.20	8.00
Warner Bros. BS-2694	(S)	The Captain And Me	1973	3.20	8.00
		—Warner Bros. albums above have green "WB" labels.—			
Warner Bros. WS-1919	(S)	The Doobie Brothers	197?	.80	4.00
Warner Bros. BS-2634	(S)	Toulouse Street	197?	.80	4.00
Warner Bros. BS4-2634	(Q)	Toulouse Street	1974	6.00	15.00
Warner Bros. BS-2694	(S)	The Captain And Me	197?	.80	4.00
Warner Bros. BS4-2694	(Q)	The Captain And Me	1974	6.00	15.00
Warner Bros. BS-2750	(S)	What Were Once Vices Are Now Habits	1974	.80	4.00
Warner Bros. BS4-2750	(Q)	What Were Once Vices Are Now Habits	1974	6.00	15.00
Warner Bros. BS-2835	(S)	Stampede	1975	.80	4.00
Warner Bros. BS4-2835	(Q)	Stampede	1975	6.00	15.00
?ck SPC-3721	(S)	Introducing The Doobie Brothers	1980	4.00	10.00

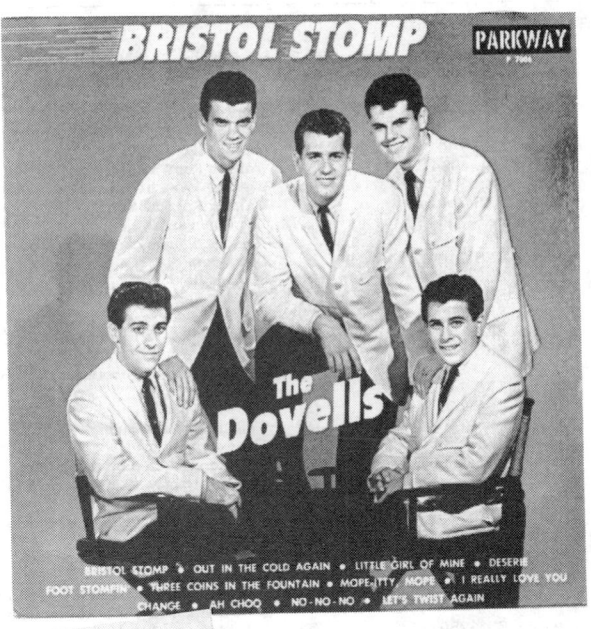

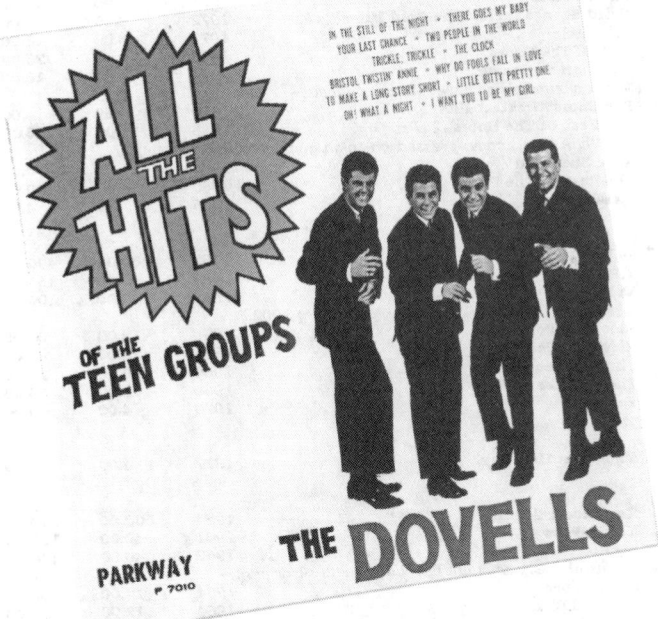

Philadelphia's Dovells featured Len Barry (born Leonard Borisoff) with Danny Brooks (Born Jim Meeley), Mike Dennis (born Mike Freda) Jerry Summers (born Jerry Gross) and Arnie Silver (born Arnie Silver). The uptempo jive group scored several hits, including two biggies with 1961's "Bristol Stomp" and '63's "You Can't Sit Down." By the time their singles stopped making the charts, both Brooks and Barry had left, the latter for a brief spell in the spotlight as a solo. The other members later recorded as The Magistrates on MGM. Dovells' LPs, such as Bristol Stomp and All The Hits Of The Teen Groups, are hard to find in NM condition but not a lot of collectors seem to care about white groups from Philly. . .

Label & Catalog #		Title	Year	VG+	NM

DOORS, THE

The Doors were John Densmore, Robbie Kreiger, Ray Manzarek and Jim Morrison. After Morrison's death in 1971, the trio recorded 75017 and 75038. Refer to The Butts Band.

Label & Catalog #		Title	Year	VG+	NM
Elektra EKL-4007	(M)	The Doors	1967	60.00	150.00
Elektra EKS-74007	(S)	The Doors	1967	20.00	50.00
Elektra EKL-4014	(M)	Strange Days	1967	80.00	200.00
Elektra EKS-74014	(S)	Strange Days	1967	12.00	30.00
Elektra EKL-4024	(M)	Waiting For The Sun	1968	150.00	300.00
Elektra EKS-74024	(S)	Waiting For The Sun *(White label promo)*	1968	60.00	150.00
Elektra EKS-74024	(S)	Waiting For The Sun	1968	12.00	30.00
Elektra EKS-75005	(S)	The Soft Parade	1969	20.00	50.00
		— Elektra albums above have brown labels.—			
Elektra EKS-74007	(S)	The Doors	1969	4.00	10.00
Elektra EKS-74014	(S)	Strange Days	1969	4.00	10.00
Elektra EKS-74024	(S)	Waiting For The Sun	1969	4.00	10.00
Elektra EKS-75005	(S)	The Soft Parade	1969	6.00	15.00
Elektra EKS-75007	(S)	Morrison Hotel/Hard Rock Cafe *(White label)*	1970	50.00	125.00
Elektra EKS-75007	(S)	Morrison Hotel/Hard Rock Cafe	1970	8.00	20.00
		— Elektra albums above have red labels.—			
Elektra EKS-74007	(S)	The Doors	1971	1.00	5.00
Elektra EKS-74014	(S)	Strange Days	1971	1.00	5.00
Elektra EKS-74024	(S)	Waiting For The Sun	1971	1.00	5.00
Elektra EKS-75005	(S)	The Soft Parade	1971	1.00	5.00
Elektra EKS-75007	(S)	Morrison Hotel/Hard Rock Cafe	1971	1.00	5.00
Elektra EKS-2-9002	(S)	Absolutely Live *(2 LPs. White label promo)*	1970	30.00	75.00
Elektra EKS-2-9002	(S)	Absolutely Live *(2 LPs)*	1970	10.00	25.00
Elektra EKS-74079	(S)	The Doors 13 *(White label promo)*	1970	16.00	40.00
Elektra EKS-74079	(S)	The Doors 13	1970	6.00	15.00
Elektra EKS-75011	(S)	L.A. Woman *(White label promo)*	1971	40.00	100.00
Elektra EKS-75011	(S)	L.A. Woman	1971	20.00	50.00
		(Originally issued in a cover with a die-cut window and a yellow inner sleeve with a photo of the group.)			
Elektra EKS-75011	(S)	L.A. Woman *(Standard cover)*	197?	4.00	10.00
Elektra EKS-75017	(S)	Other Voices	1971	6.00	15.00
Elektra EKS-2-6001	(S)	Weird Scenes Inside The Gold Mine *(2 LPs)*	1972	6.00	15.00
Elektra EKS-75038	(S)	Full Circle	1972	6.00	15.00
Elektra EQ-5035	(Q)	Best Of The Doors	1973	10.00	25.00
Elektra SE-502	(S)	An American Prayer	1978	4.00	10.00
		— Elektra albums above have "butterfly" labels.—			
Elektra 5E-515	(S)	The Doors' Greatest Hits	1980	.80	4.00
Elektra 60345	(S)	The Best Of The Doors *(2 LPs)*	1985	16.00	40.00
		(White label promo pressed on "high quality audiophile vinyl.")			
Elektra 60269	(S)	Alive She Cried	1984	1.00	5.00
Elektra 60345	(S)	The Best Of The Doors *(2 LPs)*	1985	4.00	10.00
Elektra 60417	(S)	Classics	1985	.80	4.00

DORSEY, LEE

Label & Catalog #		Title	Year	VG+	NM
Fury 1002	(M)	Ya Ya	1962	200.00	400.00
Sphere Sound SR-7003	(M)	Ya Ya	1963	60.00	150.00
Sphere Sound SSR-7003	(E)	Ya Ya	1963	40.00	100.00
		(Sphere Sound 7003 is a reissue of Fury 1002.)			
Amy 8010	(M)	Ride Your Pony	1966	12.00	30.00
Amy S-8010	(S)	Ride Your Pony	1966	16.00	40.00
Amy 8011	(M)	The New Lee Dorsey	1966	10.00	25.00
Amy S-8011	(S)	The New Lee Dorsey	1966	12.00	30.00
Polydor 24-4024	(S)	Yes We Can	1970	4.00	10.00

DOUCETTE

Label & Catalog #		Title	Year	VG+	NM
Mushroom MRS-5009	(S)	Mama, Let Him Play	1977	4.00	10.00

DOUGLAS, K. C.

Label & Catalog #		Title	Year	VG+	NM
Cook LP-5002	(M)	Road Recordings	1954	500.00	750.00
Bluesville BVLP-1023	(M)	K. C.'s Blues	1961	40.00	100.00
Bluesville BVLP-1050	(M)	Big Road Blues	1962	40.00	100.00
		— Bluesville albums above have bright blue labels with silver print.—			
Bluesville BVLP-1023	(M)	K. C.'s Blues	1964	12.00	30.00
Bluesville BVLP-1050	(M)	Big Road Blues	1964	12.00	30.00
		— Bluesville albums above have blue labels with a trident logo on the right side.—			

DOUGLAS, STEVE, & THE REBEL ROUSERS

Label & Catalog #		Title	Year	VG+	NM
Crown CLP-5251	(M)	Twist With Steve Douglas & The Rebel Rousers	1962	8.00	20.00
Crown CST-251	(S)	Twist With Steve Douglas & The Rebel Rousers	1962	12.00	30.00
		— Crown albums above have gray labels.—			

DOVELLS, THE

The Dovells feature Len Barry. Refer to the Orlons.

Label & Catalog #		Title	Year	VG+	NM
Parkway P-7006	(M)	The Bristol Stomp	1961	40.00	100.00
		— Parkway albums above have plain orange labels.—			
Parkway P-7006	(M)	The Bristol Stomp	1962	20.00	50.00

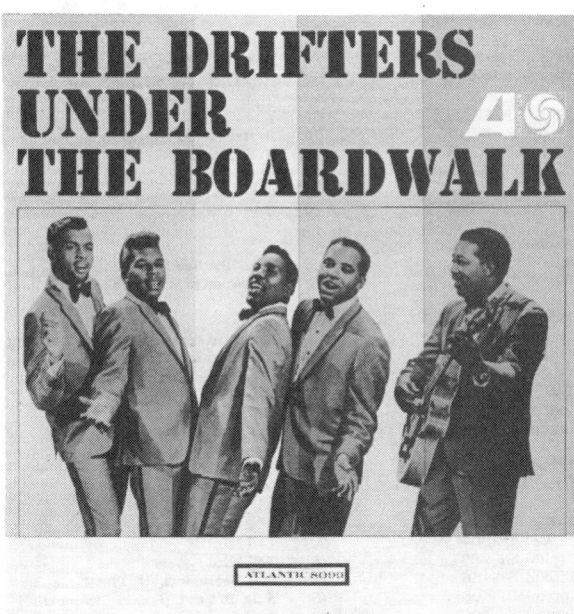

The ground-breaking Drifters were an influential rhythm'n blues vocal group. Originally formed under lead vocalist Clyde McPhatter, they set the standard for '50s groups, influencing almost every black singer to follow and more than a few white ones, including Elvis, who idolized Clyde. By the time of the Save The Last Dance For Me album, there were all new members, including a new lead singer in Benjamin Nelson, better known as Ben. E. King, and the group was geared towards pop. An entirely different set of pipes paced Under The Boardwalk, especially lead singer Johnny Moore. Over the course of their career, there were more personnel changes than most readers would want to read about in this caption.

Label & Catalog #		Title	Year	VG+	NM
Parkway P-7010	(M)	All The Hits Of The Teen Groups	1962	20.00	50.00
Parkway P-7021	(M)	For Your Hully Gully Party	1963	20.00	50.00
Parkway P-7025	(M)	You Can't Sit Down	1963	20.00	50.00
—Parkway albums above have orange & yellow labels with the date on the bottom.—					
Parkway P-7006	(M)	The Bristol Stomp	196?	12.00	30.00
Parkway P-7010	(M)	All The Hits Of The Teen Groups	196?	12.00	30.00
Parkway P-7011	(M)	Don't Knock The Twist (Soundtrack)	196?	12.00	30.00
Parkway P-7021	(M)	For Your Hully Gully Party	196?	12.00	30.00
Parkway P-7025	(M)	You Can't Sit Down	196?	12.00	30.00
—Parkway albums above have orange & yellow labels without a date.—					
Cameo C-1082	(M)	Len Barry Sings With The Dovells	1965	12.00	30.00
Cameo CS-1082	(S)	Len Barry Sings With The Dovells	1965	20.00	50.00
Wyncote W-9052	(M)	Discotheque	1965	6.00	15.00
Wyncote SW-9052	(E)	Discotheque	1965	4.00	10.00
Wyncote 9114	(M)	The Dovells' Biggest Hits	1965	6.00	15.00
Wyncote SW-9114	(E)	The Dovells' Biggest Hits	1965	4.00	10.00

DOWELL, JOE

Smash MGS-27000	(M)	Wooden Heart	1961	20.00	50.00
Smash SRS-67000	(S)	Wooden Heart	1961	30.00	75.00
Smash MGS-27011	(M)	German American Hits	1962	10.00	25.00
Smash SRS-67011	(S)	German American Hits	1962	12.00	30.00
Wing MGW-12328	(M)	Wooden Heart	196?	8.00	20.00
Wing MGS-16328	(S)	Wooden Heart	196?	10.00	25.00
(Wing 12/16328 is a reissue of Smash 2/67000.)					

DOYLE, MIKE

Fleetwood FLP-3018	(M)	The Secrets Of Surfing	1963	60.00	150.00

DOZIER, GENE, & THE BROTHERHOOD

Minit 40010	(M)	Blues Power	1967	12.00	30.00
Minit 240010	(S)	Blues Power	1967	12.00	30.00

DRAGSTERS, THE
The Dragsters are a product of Gary Usher.

Wing MGW-12269	(M)	Hey Little Cobra/Drag City	1964	30.00	75.00
Wing SRW-16269	(S)	Hey Little Cobra/Drag City	1964	40.00	100.00

DRAKE, NICK

Island OLPS-9134	(S)	Bryter Layter	1971	10.00	25.00
Island SMAS-9307	(S)	Nick Drake	1971	10.00	25.00
Island SMAS-9318	(S)	Pink Moon	1972	10.00	25.00
Antilles AN-7010	(S)	Five Leaves Left	1973	6.00	15.00
Antilles AN-7028	(S)	Bryter Layter	1973	6.00	15.00

DRAMATICS, THE

Volt VOS-6018	(S)	Whatcha See Is Whatcha Get	1972	10.00	25.00
Volt VOS-6019	(S)	A Dramatic Experience	1973	10.00	25.00

DREAMLOVERS, THE

Columbia CL-2020	(M)	The Bird & Other Golden Dancing Grooves	1963	20.00	50.00
Columbia CS-8820	(S)	The Bird & Other Golden Dancing Grooves	1963	30.00	75.00

DREAMS

Columbia CS-30225	(S)	Dreams	1970	4.00	10.00
Columbia CS-30960	(S)	Imagine My Surprise	1971	4.00	10.00

DREAMS & ILLUSIONS

Verve/Forecast FTV-3040	(S)	Dreams And Illusions	1968	8.00	20.00

DREW, PATTI

Capitol T-2804	(M)	Tell Him	1967	12.00	30.00
Capitol ST-2804	(S)	Tell Him	1967	16.00	40.00
Capitol ST-156	(S)	I've Been Here All The Time	1969	8.00	20.00
Capitol ST-408	(S)	Wild Is Love (Promo picture disc)	1969	16.00	40.00
Capitol ST-408	(S)	Wild Is Love	1969	8.00	20.00

DRIFTERS, THE
Originally formed under Clyde McPhatter, the constantly changing line-up featured many lead singers over the years, including Johnny Moore, Bobby Hendricks and Ben E. King.

Atlantic 8003	(M)	Clyde McPhatter & The Drifters	1956	300.00	600.00
Atlantic 8022	(M)	Rockin' And Driftin'	1958	300.00	600.00
Atlantic 8041	(M)	The Drifters' Greatest Hits	1959	300.00	600.00
—Atlantic albums above have black labels.—					
Atlantic 8022	(M)	Rockin' And Driftin'	1959	250.00	500.00
—Atlantic albums above have white "bullseye" labels.—					
Atlantic 8003	(M)	Clyde McPhatter & The Drifters	196?	80.00	200.00
Atlantic 8022	(M)	Rockin' And Driftin'	196?	80.00	200.00
Atlantic 8041	(M)	The Drifters' Greatest Hits	1959	80.00	200.00

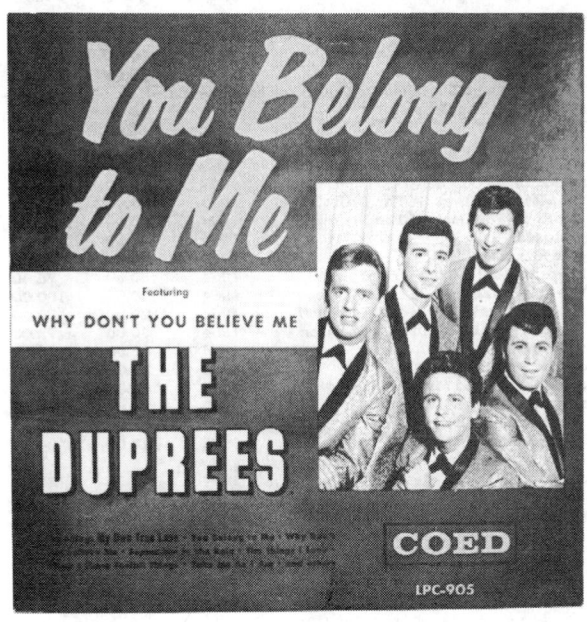

Jersey City's Duprees hit big in 1962 with a remake of Jo Stafford's "You Belong To Me" and then scored three more hits and a few chart entries before disbanding. Both of their Coed albums are sought after by collectors of early '60s white vocal groups and are hard to find. Later in the decade, as their image paled, members of the group, including lead singer Joey Vann (born Joseph Canzano), formed The Italian Asphalt & Pavement Company.

Label & Catalog #		Title	Year	VG+	NM
Atlantic 8059	(M)	Save The Last Dance For Me	1962	60.00	150.00
Atlantic SD-8059	(S)	Save The Last Dance For Me	1962	100.00	250.00
—Atlantic albums above multi-color labels with a white "fan" logo on the right side.—					
Atlantic 8003	(M)	Clyde McPhatter & The Drifters	1963	40.00	100.00
Atlantic 8022	(M)	Rockin' And Driftin'	1963	40.00	100.00
Atlantic 8041	(M)	The Drifters' Greatest Hits	1963	30.00	75.00
Atlantic 8059	(M)	Save The Last Dance For Me	1963	30.00	75.00
Atlantic SD-8059	(S)	Save The Last Dance For Me	1963	40.00	100.00
Atlantic 8073	(M)	Up On The Roof (The Best Of The Drifters)	1963	40.00	100.00
Atlantic SD-8073	(S)	Up On The Roof (The Best Of The Drifters)	1963	60.00	150.00
Atlantic 8093	(M)	Our Biggest Hits	1964	30.00	75.00
Atlantic SD-8093	(S)	Our Biggest Hits	1964	40.00	100.00
Atlantic 8099	(M)	Under The Boardwalk (White cover)	1964	30.00	75.00
Atlantic SD-8099	(S)	Under The Boardwalk (White cover)	1964	40.00	100.00
Atlantic 8099	(M)	Under The Boardwalk (Multi-colored cover)	1964	20.00	50.00
Atlantic SD-8099	(S)	Under The Boardwalk (Multi-colored cover)	1964	30.00	75.00
Atlantic 8103	(M)	The Good Life With The Drifters	1965	20.00	50.00
Atlantic SD-8103	(S)	The Good Life With The Drifters	1965	30.00	75.00
Atlantic 8113	(M)	I'll Take You Where The Music's Playing	1965	20.00	50.00
Atlantic SD-8113	(S)	I'll Take You Where The Music's Playing	1965	30.00	75.00
Atlantic 8153	(M)	The Drifters' Golden Hits	1968	10.00	25.00
Atlantic SD-8153	(P)	The Drifters' Golden Hits	1968	12.00	30.00
—Atlantic albums above multi-color labels with a black "fan" logo on the right side.—					
Clarion 608	(M)	The Drifters	1964	8.00	20.00
Clarion SD-608	(P)	The Drifters	1964	12.00	30.00
Atco SD-33-375	(E)	Their Greatest Recordings-The Early Years	1971	4.00	10.00

DRIFTERS, THE / THE COASTERS

TPP 1002	(E)	The Drifters Meet The Coasters	197?	4.00	10.00

DRIFTIN' SLIM
Driftin' Slim is a pseudonym for Elmon Mickle.

Milestone MLS-93004	(M)	Driftin' Slim And His Blues Band (2 LPs)	1968	8.00	20.00

DRISCOLL, JULIE "JOOLS": *Refer to* BRIAN AUGER

DRUIDS OF STONEHENGE, THE

Uni 3004	(M)	Creation	1967	20.00	50.00
Uni 73004	(S)	Creation	1967	30.00	75.00

DRY CITY SCAT BAND

Elektra EKL-292	(M)	Dry City Scat Band	1965	10.00	25.00
Elektra EKS-7292	(S)	Dry City Scat Band	1965	12.00	30.00

DRY DOCK COUNTY

Mercury SR-61286	(S)	Dry Dock County	1970	6.00	15.00

DUALS, THE

Sue LP-2002	(M)	Stick Shift (Cartoon cover)	1961	250.00	500.00
Sue LP-2002	(M)	Stick Shift (Photo cover)	1964	150.00	300.00

DUBS, THE / THE SHELLS

Josie JM-4001	(M)	The Dubs Meet The Shells	1962	150.00	300.00
Josie JSS-4001	(P)	The Dubs Meet The Shells	1962	300.00	600.00

DUBS, THE

Candlelite 1003	(M)	You've Got To Be Good To Make It In NYC	197?	4.00	10.00
Candlelite 1004	(M)	The Best Of The Dubs	197?	4.00	10.00

DUCKS, THE

Just Sunshine 6	(S)	The Ducks	1973	4.00	10.00

DULCIMER

Mercury SR-61355	(S)	And I Turned As I Had Turned As A Boy	1971	10.00	25.00

DUNBAR, AYNSLEY
Aynsley Dunbar also recorded as a Bluesbreaker with John Mayall and as a Mother with Frank Zappa.

Blue Thumb BTS-4	(S)	Retaliation	1968	10.00	25.00
Blue Thumb BTS-6	(S)	Doctor Dunbar's Prescription	1969	10.00	25.00
Blue Thumb BTS-16	(S)	To Mum, From Aynsley And The Boys	1970	10.00	25.00

DUPREE, "CHAMPION" JACK
Refer to King Curtis & Jack Dupree.

Atlantic 8019	(M)	Blues From The Gutter	1959	80.00	200.00
Atlantic SD-8019	(S)	Blues From The Gutter	1959	150.00	300.00
—Atlantic mono albums above have black labels; stereos have green labels.—					
Atlantic 8019	(M)	Blues From The Gutter	196?	20.00	50.00
Atlantic SD-8019	(S)	Blues From The Gutter	196?	30.00	75.00

The bulk of Blonde On Blonde, one of those records that can intelligently be argued as the "Greatest Rock Album of All Time," was recorded in Nashville in a matter of days. Dylan's unorthodox recording method—especially to the country music capitol's picky pickers—consisted of allowing his sidemen to know as little as possible about the song they were recording! Except for the key and meter, he expected them to use their skills to follow his lead, improvising as they were moved by the music. While this allowed for a great degree of play and contributed to the success of the album, some of the musicians thought the whole thing was just plain shit! Many of the Nashville cats were openly contemptuous at the time but, as recent interviews show, they now credit him with opening up their views on recording and inspiring a new approach to cutting country.

Label & Catalog #		Title	Year	VG+	NM
Atlantic 8045	(S)	Natural And Soulful Blues	196?	20.00	50.00
Atlantic SD-8045	(S)	Natural And Soulful Blues	196?	30.00	75.00
Atlantic 8056	(M)	Champion Of The Blues	1961	20.00	50.00
—Atlantic albums above have multi-colored labels with a white "fan" logo on the right side.—					
Atlantic 8019	(M)	Blues From The Gutter	196?	8.00	20.00
Atlantic SD-8019	(S)	Blues From The Gutter	196?	10.00	25.00
Atlantic 8045	(S)	Natural And Soulful Blues	196?	8.00	20.00
Atlantic SD-8045	(S)	Natural And Soulful Blues	196?	10.00	25.00
Atlantic 8056	(M)	Champion Of The Blues	196?	10.00	25.00
—Atlantic albums above have multi-colored labels with a black "fan" logo on the right side.—					
King LP-735	(M)	Champion Jack Dupree Sings The Blues	1961	175.00	350.00
Continental CLP-16002	(M)	Low Down Blues	1961	100.00	250.00
Folkways FS-3825	(M)	Women Blues Of Champion Jack Dupree	1961	10.00	25.00
OKeh OKM-12103	(M)	Cabbage Greens	1963	12.00	30.00
Archive of Folk Music 217	(E)	Champion Jack Dupree	1968	1.00	5.00
Blue Horizon 7702	(S)	When You Feel The Feeling	1969	10.00	25.00
London PS-553	(S)	From New Orleans To Chicago	1969	8.00	20.00
Atlantic SD-8255	(S)	Blues From The Gutter	1970	6.00	15.00
King KS-1084	(S)	Walking The Blues	1970	6.00	15.00
Everest 217	(E)	Champion Jack Dupree	197?	.80	4.00
Crescendo GNPS-10001	(S)	Tricks	1974	1.00	5.00
Crescendo GNPS-10005	(S)	Happy To Be Free	1974	1.00	5.00
DUPREE, "CHAMPION" JACK, & MICKEY BAKER					
Sire SES-97010	(S)	In Heavy Blues	1969	14.00	35.00
DUPREE, "CHAMPION" JACK / JIMMY RUSHING					
Audio Lab AL-1512	(M)	Two Shades Of Blue	1959	80.00	200.00
DUPREE, SIMON, & THE BIG SOUND					
Tower ST-5097	(S)	Without Reservations	1968	20.00	50.00
DUPREES, THE					
Coed LPC-905	(M)	You Belong To Me	1962	200.00	400.00
Coed LPC-906	(M)	Have You Heard	1963	150.00	300.00
Heritage HTS-35002	(S)	Total Recall	1968	12.00	30.00
Post 1000	(E)	The Duprees Sing	196?	12.00	30.00
Colossus 5000	(S)	Dupree's Gold	1970	12.00	30.00
(Colossus 5000 is a compilation that credits Italian Asphalt & Pavement Co.)					
DURAN DURAN					
Harvest ST-12111	(S)	Rio	1982	1..00	5.00
Harvest ST-15006	(S)	Carnival	1982	1..00	5.00
Harvest ST-12158	(S)	Duran Duran	1983	1.00	5.00
Harvest ST-12310	(S)	Seven And The Ragged Tiger	1983	1..00	5.00
Harvest ST-12374	(S)	Arena	1994	1..00	5.00
Capitol SPRO-79097/8	(DJ)	Duran Duran Goes Dutch	1987	12.00	30.00
DUROCS, THE					
Capitol ST-11981	(S)	The Durocs	1979	6.00	15.00
DUST					
Kama Sutra KSBS-2041	(S)	Dust (Gatefold jacket)	1971	10.00	25.00
Kama Sutra KSBS-2059	(S)	Hard Attack (Gatefold jacket)	1972	10.00	25.00
—Kama Sutra albums above have pink labels.—					
Kama Sutra KSBS-2041	(S)	Dust	1973	4.00	10.00
Kama Sutra KSBS-2059	(S)	Hard Attack	1973	4.00	10.00
—Kama Sutra albums above have blue labels.—					
DUST & ASHES					
Avant Garde 134	(S)	A Different Shade Of Blue	1972	4.00	10.00
Avant Garde 137	(S)	Lives We Share	1972	4.00	10.00
DYKE & THE BLAZERS					
Original Sound LP-8876	(M)	The Funky Broadway	1967	20.00	50.00
Original Sound LPS-8876	(S)	The Funky Broadway	1967	30.00	75.00
Original Sound LPS-8877	(S)	Dyke's Greatest Hits	1968	30.00	75.00
DYLAN, BOB					
Refer to The Band; Barry Goldberg; George Harrison & Friends; Doug Sahm; Victoria Spivey; The Traveling Wilburys.					
Columbia CL-1779	(M)	Bob Dylan	1962	200.00	400.00
(The label is hand-stamped "Promo-Not For Sale" and the cover has a "A New Star On Columbia" sticker.)					
Columbia CL-1779	(M)	Bob Dylan	1962	150.00	300.00
Columbia CS-8579	(S)	Bob Dylan	1962	300.00	500.00
(The label is hand-stamped "Promo-Not For Sale" and the cover has a "A New Star On Columbia" sticker.)					
Columbia CS-8579	(S)	Bob Dylan	1962	200.00	400.00
—Columbia albums above have six white-on-black "eye" logos on each label.—					

Surely no one would confuse Nashville Skyline, Dylan's loving tribute to Nashville's country music machine, for rock'n roll. The "Bard of the 60s" can certainly be accused of manipulating a string of country cliches so that many of the songs sound like parodies (including a ridiculously campy Elvis ending on "Peggy Day"). Still, the contribution of "Lay Lady lay" to the idiom's catalog made people sit up and take notice. This half-speed mastered version was issued years after the album's chart run and did not sell well (none of the CBS half-speeds did) and is consequently much more difficult to find than the original.

Label & Catalog #		Title	Year	VG+	NM
Columbia CL-1779	(M)	**Bob Dylan**	1963	**16.00**	**40.00**
Columbia CS-8579	(S)	**Bob Dylan**	1965	**16.00**	**40.00**
Columbia CL-1986	(M)	**The Freewheelin' Bob Dylan**	1963	See note below	
		(First pressings of CL-1986 contain four songs deleted from subsequent pressings, including "Let Me Die In My Footsteps." As all known mono copies list the later songs on the label, the record must be played to identify. Rare with a suggested NM value of $10,000-20,000.)			
Columbia CS-8786	(S)	**The Freewheelin' Bob Dylan**	1963	See note below	
		(First pressings of CS-8786 contain four songs deleted from subsequent pressings, including "Let Me Die In My Footsteps." Stereo copies list these songs on the label. For more information on this record, refer to the article "The World's Most Valuable Album." Rare with a suggested NM value of $20,000-30,000.)			
Columbia CL-1986	(DJ)	**The Freewheelin' Bob Dylan** *(White label)*	1963	See note below	
		(White label promo with both the label and the title & timing strip on the cover listing the deleted tracks. The record plays the replacements. Rare with a suggested NM value of $3,000-5,000.)			
Columbia 1986		**The Freewheelin' Bob Dylan Insert**	1963	**200.00**	**400.00**
		(Some white label promos included an insert approximately 4" x 11" that reads "NOTICE: Please note that on Side 1, Band 3 and Band 6 are reversed." This is in reference to the original track line-up where those songs, "Let Me Die In My Footsteps" and "A Hard Rain's A-Gonna Fall," were transposed after the labels had been printed.)			
Columbia CL-1986	(DJ)	**The Freewheelin' Bob Dylan** *(White label)*	1963	**1,000.00**	**2,000.00**
		(White label promo with the label listing the deleted tracks. The title & timing strip lists, and the record plays, the replacement tracks.)			
Columbia CL-1986	(DJ)	**The Freewheelin' Bob Dylan** *(White label)*	1963	**500.00**	**750.00**
		(White label promo with the title & timing strip listing the deleted tracks. The label lists, and the record plays, the replacement tracks.)			
Columbia CL-1986	(DJ)	**The Freewheelin' Bob Dylan** *(White label)*	1963	**300.00**	**500.00**
		(White label promo with the label and title & timing strip listing, and the record playing, the replacement tracks.)			
Columbia CL-1986	(M)	**The Freewheelin' Bob Dylan**	1963	**12.00**	**30.00**
Columbia CS-8786	(S)	**The Freewheelin' Bob Dylan**	1963	**16.00**	**40.00**
Columbia CL-2105	(DJ)	**The Times They Are A-Changin'** *(White label)*	1964	**200.00**	**400.00**
Columbia CL-2105	(M)	**The Times They Are A-Changin'**	1964	**12.00**	**30.00**
		(Issued with a sheet continuing "11 Outlined Epitaphs.")			
Columbia CS-8905	(S)	**The Times They Are A-Changin'**	1964	**16.00**	**40.00**
		(Issued with a sheet continuing "11 Outlined Epitaphs.")			
Columbia CL-2193	(DJ)	**Another Side Of Bob Dylan** *(White label)*	1964	**300.00**	**500.00**
Columbia CL-2193	(M)	**Another Side Of Bob Dylan**	1964	**16.00**	**40.00**
Columbia CS-8993	(S)	**Another Side Of Bob Dylan**	1964	**16.00**	**40.00**
Columbia CL-2302	(M)	**Bob Dylan In Concert**	1965	Unreleased	
Columbia CS-9102	(S)	**Bob Dylan In Concert**	1965	Unreleased	
		(Front cover slicks exist for this cancelled title and have a suggested Near Mint value of $3,000-5,000.)			
Columbia CL-2328	(DJ)	**Bringing It All Back Home** *(White label)*	1965	**200.00**	**400.00**
Columbia CL-2328	(M)	**Bringing It All Back Home**	1965	**20.00**	**50.00**
Columbia CS-9128	(S)	**Bringing It All Back Home**	1965	**16.00**	**40.00**

—Columbia mono albums above have "Guaranteed High Fidelity" or " 360 Sound Stereo" in black on the bottom of the labels.—

Label & Catalog #		Title	Year	VG+	NM
Columbia CL-1779	(M)	**Bob Dylan**	1965	**12.00**	**30.00**
Columbia CS-8579	(S)	**Bob Dylan**	1965	**10.00**	**25.00**
Columbia CL-1986	(M)	**The Freewheelin' Bob Dylan**	1965	**12.00**	**30.00**
Columbia CS-8786	(S)	**The Freewheelin' Bob Dylan**	1965	**10.00**	**25.00**
Columbia CL-2105	(M)	**The Times They Are A-Changin'**	1965	**12.00**	**30.00**
Columbia CS-8905	(S)	**The Times They Are A-Changin'**	1965	**10.00**	**25.00**
Columbia CL-2193	(M)	**Another Side Of Bob Dylan**	1965	**12.00**	**30.00**
Columbia CS-8993	(S)	**Another Side Of Bob Dylan**	1965	**10.00**	**25.00**
Columbia CL-2328	(M)	**Bringing It All Back Home**	1965	**16.00**	**40.00**
Columbia CS-9128	(S)	**Bringing It All Back Home**	1965	**10.00**	**25.00**
Columbia CL-2389	(M)	**Highway 61 Revisited** *(White label promo)*	1965	**200.00**	**400.00**
Columbia CL-2389	(M)	**Highway 61 Revisited**	1965	**30.00**	**75.00**
Columbia CS-9189	(S)	**Highway 61 Revisited**	1965	**80.00**	**200.00**
		(First pressings of CS-9189 were erroneously mastered with an alternate take of "From A Buick 6." The matrix number in the trail-off vinyl on the first side must end with a "— 1.")			
Columbia CS-9189	(S)	**Highway 61 Revisited**	1965	**12.00**	**30.00**
		(Second pressings have the "regular" version of "From A Buick 6.")			
Columbia		**Highway 61 Revisited Poster**	1965	**100.00**	**300.00**
		(Album-size ink line drawing of Dylan by Lambert. This may have been included with other Dylan albums during 1965.)			
Columbia C2L-41	(M)	**Blonde On Blonde** *(2 LPs. White label)*	1966	See note below	
		(White label promos have a suggested NM value of $1,000-2,000.)			
Columbia C2L-41	(M)	**Blonde On Blonde** *(2 LPs)*	1966	**40.00**	**100.00**
Columbia C2S-841	(S)	**Blonde On Blonde** *(2 LPs)*	1966	**20.00**	**50.00**
		(Original covers have nine photos on the inside, including one of actress Claudia Cardinale.)			

Label & Catalog #		Title	Year	VG+	NM
Columbia C2L-41	(M)	**Blonde On Blonde** (2 LPs)	1966	150.00	300.00
Columbia C2S-841	(S)	**Blonde On Blonde** (2 LPs)	1966	12.00	30.00
		(Later covers delete two of the inner photos, including the one of Ms. Cardinale. The remaining seven photos were rearranged.)			
Columbia KCL-2663	(M)	**Bob Dylan's Greatest Hits**	1967	20.00	50.00
Columbia KCS-9463	(S)	**Bob Dylan's Greatest Hits**	1967	6.00	15.00
		(Virtually all pressings of this album through the '70s were issued with a fold-open poster by Milton Glaser worth an additional $3.)			
Warner/7-Arts. 221567	(DJ)	**Bob Dylan**	1967	1,000.00	1,500.00
		(One-sided album in a plain cardboard jacket compiled by Wittmark Publishers to showcase twelve of Dylan's [then] unreleased.)			
Columbia CL-2804	(DJ)	**John Wesley Harding**	1968	See note below	
		(Contrary to previous listings, a white label promo for this album does not exist. Mono copies with DJ title & timing strips on the cover have a suggested NM value of $100-200.)			
Columbia CL-2804	(M)	**John Wesley Harding**	1968	60.00	150.00
Columbia CS-9604	(S)	**John Wesley Harding**	1968	8.00	20.00
Columbia KCS-9825	(S)	**Nashville Skyline**	1969	12.00	30.00
Columbia C2X-30050	(S)	**Self Portrait** (2 LPs)	1970	60.00	150.00
—Columbia albums above have "360 Sound" in white on the bottom of the labels.—					
Columbia CS-8579	(S)	**Bob Dylan**	1970	.80	4.00
Columbia KC-8579	(S)	**Bob Dylan**	1972	.80	4.00
Columbia PC-8579	(S)	**Bob Dylan**	1979	.80	4.00
Columbia CS-8786	(S)	**The Freewheelin' Bob Dylan**	1970	1.00	5.00
Columbia CS-8786	(S)	**The Freewheelin' Bob Dylan** (Red vinyl)	197?	660.00	1,000.00
Columbia KC-8786	(S)	**The Freewheelin' Bob Dylan**	1972	.80	4.00
Columbia PC-8786	(S)	**The Freewheelin' Bob Dylan**	1979	.80	4.00
Columbia CS-8905	(S)	**The Times They Are A-Changin'**	1970	1.00	5.00
Columbia KC-8905	(S)	**The Times They Are A-Changin'**	1972	.80	4.00
Columbia PC-8905	(S)	**The Times They Are A-Changin'**	1979	.80	4.00
Columbia CS-8993	(S)	**Another Side Of Bob Dylan**	1970	1.00	5.00
Columbia CS-8993	(S)	**Another Side Of Bob Dylan** (Blue vinyl)	197?	660.00	1,000.00
Columbia KC-8993	(S)	**Another Side Of Bob Dylan**	1972	.80	4.00
Columbia PC-8993	(S)	**Another Side Of Bob Dylan**	1979	.80	4.00
Columbia CS-9128	(S)	**Bringing It All Back Home**	1970	1.00	5.00
Columbia KC-9128	(S)	**Bringing It All Back Home**	1972	.80	4.00
Columbia JC-9128	(S)	**Bringing It All Back Home**	1977	.80	4.00
Columbia PC-9128	(S)	**Bringing It All Back Home**	1979	.80	4.00
Columbia CS-9189	(S)	**Highway 61 Revisited**	1970	1.00	5.00
Columbia KC-9189	(S)	**Highway 61 Revisited**	1972	.80	4.00
Columbia JC-9189	(S)	**Highway 61 Revisited**	1977	.80	4.00
Columbia C2S-841	(S)	**Blonde On Blonde** (2 LPs)	1970	4.00	10.00
Columbia CG-841	(S)	**Blonde On Blonde** (2 LPs)	198?	2.40	6.00
Columbia CS-9463	(S)	**Bob Dylan's Greatest Hits**	1970	.80	4.00
Columbia JC-9463	(S)	**Bob Dylan's Greatest Hits**	1977	.80	4.00
Columbia CS-9604	(S)	**John Wesley Harding**	1970	1.00	5.00
Columbia KC-9604	(S)	**John Wesley Harding**	1972	.80	4.00
Columbia JC-9604	(S)	**John Wesley Harding**	1977	.80	4.00
Columbia CQ-32825	(Q)	**Nashville Skyline**	1973	12.00	30.00
Columbia KCS-9825	(S)	**Nashville Skyline**	1970	1.00	5.00
Columbia KC-9825	(S)	**Nashville Skyline**	1972	.80	4.00
Columbia JC-9825	(S)	**Nashville Skyline**	1977	.80	4.00
Columbia HE-49825	(S)	**Nashville Skyline** (Half-speed master)	1975	25.00	75.00
Columbia C2X-30050	(S)	**Self Portrait** (2 LPs)	1970	4.00	10.00
Columbia P2X-30050	(S)	**Self Portrait** (2 LPs)	1979	2.40	6.00
Columbia CG-30050	(S)	**Self Portrait** (2 LPs)	198?	2.40	6.00
Columbia KC-30290	(S)	**New Morning**	1970	3.20	8.00
Columbia PC-30290	(S)	**New Morning**	1979	.80	4.00
Columbia KG-31120	(S)	**Bob Dylan's Greatest Hits, Vol. 2** (2 LPs)	1972	4.00	10.00
Columbia PG-31120	(S)	**Bob Dylan's Greatest Hits, Vol. 2** (2 LPs)	1979	2.40	6.00
Columbia CG-31120	(S)	**Bob Dylan's Greatest Hits, Vol. 2** (2 LPs)	198?	2.40	6.00
Columbia KC-32460	(S)	**Pat Garrett And Billy The Kid**	1973	6.00	15.00
		(The title on the front cover is in raised black letters.)			
Columbia PC-32460	(S)	**Pat Garrett And Billy The Kid**	1979	.80	4.00
Columbia PC-32747	(S)	**Dylan**	1974	.80	4.00
—Columbia albums above have red labels with gold print.—					
Asylum 7E-1003	(S)	**Planet Waves** (White label promo)	1974	20.00	50.00
Asylum 7E-1003	(S)	**Planet Waves**	1974	8.00	20.00
		(With The Band. Issued with a wraparound second cover.)			
Asylum EQ-1003	(Q)	**Planet Waves**	1974	20.00	50.00
Island AB-201	(S)	**Before The Flood** (2 LPs)	1974	16.00	40.00
Asylum AB-201	(S)	**Before The Flood** (2 LPs. White label promo)	1974	16.00	40.00
Asylum AB-201	(S)	**Before The Flood** (2 LPs)	1974	6.00	15.00
		("Before The Flood" also features The Band.)			
Columbia PC-33235	(DJ)	**Blood On The Tracks** (Test pressing)	1975	See note below	
		(Original test pressings include completely different recordings of "Idiot Wind," "Lily, Rosemary And The Jack Of Hearts," "Tangled Up In Blue," "If You See Her Say Hello" and "You're A Big Girl Now." Rare with a suggested NM value of $4,000-6,000.)			

Label & Catalog #		Title	Year	VG+	NM
Columbia PC-33235	(S)	**Blood On The Tracks** (White label promo)	1975	**12.00**	**30.00**
Columbia PC-33235	(S)	**Blood On The Tracks**	1975	**4.00**	**10.00**
		(Original covers of PC-33235 have black liner notes on the back.)			
Columbia PC-33235	(S)	**Blood On The Tracks** ("Mural cover")	1976	**6.00**	**15.00**
		(Second pressing covers feature a full-cover drawing on the back.)			
Columbia HC-43235	(S)	**Blood On The Tracks** (Half-speed master)	1975	**25.00**	**75.00**
Columbia JC-33235	(S)	**Blood On The Tracks**	197?	**.80**	**4.00**
		(Later pressings have the liner notes in white print.)			
Columbia CS2-33682	(S)	**The Basement Tapes** (2 LPs. White label)	1975	**16.00**	**40.00**
Columbia CS2-33682	(S)	**The Basement Tapes** (2 LPs)	1975	**5.00**	**12.00**
Columbia CG-33682	(S)	**The Basement Tapes** (2 LPs)	198?	**2.40**	**6.00**
		("The Basement Tapes" also feature The Band.)			
Columbia PC-33893	(S)	**Desire** (White label promo)	1976	**12.00**	**30.00**
Columbia PC-33893	(S)	**Desire**	1976	**2.40**	**6.00**
Columbia PCQ-33893	(Q)	**Desire**	1976	**14.00**	**35.00**
Columbia JC-33893	(S)	**Desire**	1978	**.80**	**4.00**
Columbia PC-34349	(S)	**Hard Rain** (White label promo)	1976	**12.00**	**30.00**
Columbia PC-34349	(S)	**Hard Rain**	1976	**2.40**	**6.00**
Columbia JC-34349	(S)	**Hard Rain**	1978	**.80**	**4.00**
Columbia AS-422	(DJ)	**Renaldo And Clara**	1976	**20.00**	**50.00**
		(Originals have a title sticker on the front cover;			
		counterfeits have the title printed on the front.)			
Columbia JC-35453	(S)	**Street Legal** (White label promo)	1978	**10.00**	**25.00**
Columbia JC-35453	(S)	**Street Legal**	1978	**2.40**	**6.00**
Columbia PC-35453	(S)	**Street Legal**	198?	**.80**	**4.00**
Columbia PC2-36067	(S)	**Bob Dylan At Budokan** (2 LPs. White label)	1979	**12.00**	**30.00**
Columbia PC2-36067	(S)	**Bob Dylan At Budokan** (2 LPs)	1979	**3.20**	**8.00**
Columbia CG-36067	(S)	**Bob Dylan At Budokan** (2 LPs)	198?	**2.40**	**6.00**
Columbia FC-36120	(S)	**Slow Train Coming** (White label promo)	1979	**8.00**	**20.00**
Columbia FC-36120	(S)	**Slow Train Coming**	1979	**1.00**	**5.00**
Columbia PC-36120	(S)	**Slow Train Coming**	198?	**.80**	**4.00**
Columbia AS-798	(S)	**Saved** (White label promo)	1980	**10.00**	**25.00**
Columbia FC-36553	(S)	**Saved**	1980	**1.00**	**5.00**
Columbia PC-36553	(S)	**Saved**	198?	**.80**	**4.00**
Columbia TC-37496	(S)	**Shot Of Love**	1981	**1.00**	**5.00**
Columbia TC-37496	(S)	**Shot Of Love**	198?	**.80**	**4.00**
Columbia AS-1259	(DJ)	**The Dylan London Interview, July 1981**	1981	**8.00**	**20.00**
Columbia AS-1471	(DJ)	**Electric Lunch** (Sampler)	1982	**6.00**	**15.00**
Columbia PC-37637	(S)	**Planet Waves**	1983	**.80**	**4.00**
Columbia CG-37661	(S)	**Before The Flood**	1983	**2.40**	**6.00**
Columbia QC-38819	(S)	**Infidels**	1983	**1.00**	**5.00**
Columbia FC-39944	(S)	**Real Live**	1985	**.80**	**4.00**
Columbia C5S-38830	(P)	**Biograph** (5 LPs)	1985	**10.00**	**25.00**
Columbia CAS-2222	(S)	**Time Passes Slowly** (Promo sampler)	1985	**10.00**	**25.00**
Columbia CK-40110	(S)	**Empire Burlesque**	1986	**1.00**	**5.00**
Columbia OC-40439	(S)	**Knocked Out Loaded**	1987	**1.00**	**5.00**
Columbia FC-40957	(S)	**Down In The Groove**	1988	**1.00**	**5.00**
Columbia OC-45056	(S)	**Dylan And The Dead**	1989	**1.00**	**5.00**
		(Columbia OC-45056 features backing by The Grateful Dead.)			
Columbia C-46794	(S)	**Under A Blood Red Sky**	1990	**6.00**	**15.00**
Columbia 474000	(S)	**Bob Dylan 30th Anniversary**			
		Concert Celebration (3 LPs)	1993	**12.00**	**30.00**
		(474000 is a various artists live tribute to the poet of his generation.)			
Columbia C-53000	(S)	**Good As I Been To You**	1992	**6.00**	**15.00**
Columbia C-57099	(S)	**Unplugged** (2 LPs)	1995	**4.00**	**10.00**

—Columbia albums above have red labels with gold print.—

DYLAN, BOB, & ALAN J. WEBERMAN

Folkways FB-5322	(M)	**Bob Dylan Versus A. J. Weberman**	1977	**150.00**	**300.00**
		(This album consists of a poorly taped telephone conversation			
		between Mr Weberman. and his hero.)			

DYNAMICS, THE

Bolo BLP-8001	(M)	**The Dynamics With Jimmy Hanna**	1963	**20.00**	**50.00**

DYNAMICS, THE

Cotillion SD-9009	(S)	**First Landing**	1969	**6.00**	**15.00**

DYNAMICS, THE

Black Gold 5001	(S)	**What A Shame**	1973	**4.00**	**10.00**

DYNATONES, THE

HBR HLP-8509	(M)	**The Fife Piper**	1966	**6.00**	**15.00**
HBR HST-9509	(S)	**The Fife Piper**	1966	**8.00**	**20.00**

EAGLE
Eagle originally recorded as The Beacon Street Union.

Janus JLS-3011	(S)	Come Under Nancy's Tent	1970	**8.00**	**20.00**

EAGLES, THE
Don Henley, Glenn Frey, Bernie Leadon, and Randy Meisner formed The Eagles after working as Linda Ronstadt's backing group for several months (and one album). Don Felder joined in 1974, Leadon left in 1975, replaced by Joe Walsh, formerly of The James Gang. Meisner left in 1977, replaced by Timothy Schmidt. Refer to The James Gang; Poco; Linda Ronstadt; Shiloh.

Asylum SD-5054	(S)	Eagles (Gatefold cover)	1972	**3.20**	**8.00**
Asylum SD-5054	(S)	Eagles (Regular cover)	1973	**1.00**	**5.00**
Asylum SD-5068	(S)	Desperado	1973	**1.00**	**5.00**
Asylum 7E-1004	(S)	On The Border	1974	**1.00**	**5.00**
Asylum EQ-1004	(Q)	On The Border	1975	**6.00**	**15.00**
Asylum 7E-1039	(S)	One Of These Nights	1975	**1.00**	**5.00**
Asylum EQ-1039	(Q)	One Of These Nights	1975	**6.00**	**15.00**
Asylum 7E-1052	(S)	Their Greatest Hits 1971-1975	1976	**1.00**	**5.00**
Asylum 7E-1084	(S)	Hotel California	1976	**1.00**	**5.00**
Asylum 6E-103	(S)	Hotel California	1976	**.80**	**4.00**
Asylum 6E-105	(S)	Their Greatest Hits 1971-1975	1976	**.80**	**4.00**
Asylum 5E-508	(S)	The Long Run	1979	**.80**	**4.00**
Asylum BB-705	(S)	Eagles Live	1980	**.80**	**4.00**
Asylum 9-60205-1	(S)	Eagles Greatest Hits, Volume 2	1982	**.80**	**4.00**

EARLS, THE

Old Town LP-104	(M)	Remember Me Baby	1963	**300.00**	**600.00**
		(Original records have blue labels on thick vinyl. The run-off vinyl is less than 1" on both sides with the numbers stamped into the wax. Counterfeits have run-off areas of more than 1" per side and the numbers are etched in.)			

EARTH & FIRE

Red Bullet PRBLP-3000	(S)	Earth And Fire	1977?	**6.00**	**15.00**

EARTH, WIND & FIRE

Warner Bros. WS-1905	(S)	Earth, Wind & Fire	1971	**3.20**	**8.00**
Warner Bros. WS-1958	(S)	The Need Of Love	1971	**3.20**	**8.00**
Warner Bros. WZS-2798	(S)	Another Time (2 LPs)	1974	**1.20**	**6.00**
Columbia KC-31702	(S)	Last Days And Time	1972	**3.20**	**8.00**
Columbia KC-32194	(S)	Head To The Sky	1973	**3.20**	**8.00**
Columbia CQ-32194	(Q)	Head To The Sky	1974	**6.00**	**15.00**
Columbia KC-32712	(S)	Open Our Eyes	1974	**3.20**	**8.00**
Columbia CQ-32712	(Q)	Open Our Eyes	1974	**6.00**	**15.00**
Columbia KC-33280	(S)	That's The Way Of The World	1975	**3.20**	**8.00**
Columbia KC-33694	(S)	Gratitude	1975	**3.20**	**8.00**
Columbia KC-34242	(S)	Spirit	1976	**3.20**	**8.00**
Columbia JC-34905	(S)	All 'N All	1977	**1.20**	**6.00**
Columbia AS-457	(S)	Greatest Hits (Promo)	1978	**6.00**	**15.00**
Columbia FC-35647	(S)	Best Of Earth, Wind & Fire	1978	**1.20**	**6.00**
Columbia FC-35647	(DJ)	Best Of Earth, Wind & Fire (Picture disc)	1979	**6.00**	**15.00**
Columbia HC-45647	(S)	Best Of Earth, Wind & Fire (Half-speed)	1981	**12.00**	**36.00**
Columbia FC-35730	(S)	I Am	1979	**1.20**	**6.00**
Columbia HC-45730	(S)	I Am (Half-speed master)	1981	**10.00**	**30.00**
Columbia KC2-36795	(S)	Faces (2 LPs)	1980	**1.20**	**6.00**
Columbia TC-37548	(S)	Raise	1981	**1.00**	**5.00**
Columbia HC-47548	(S)	Raise (Half-speed master)	1982	**10.00**	**30.00**
Columbia TC-38367	(S)	Powerlight	1983	**1.00**	**5.00**
Columbia HC-48367	(S)	Powerlight (Half-speed master)	1983	**15.00**	**45.00**

EARTH ISLAND

Philips 600-340	(S)	We Must Survive	1970	**10.00**	**25.00**

EARTH OPERA
Earth Opera features David Grisman and Peter Rowan. Refer to Old & In The Way; The Rowan Brothers.

Elektra EKS-74016	(S)	Earth Opera	1968	**8.00**	**20.00**
Elektra EKS-74038	(S)	The Great American Eagle Tragedy	1969	**8.00**	**20.00**

Label & Catalog #		Title	Year	VG+	NM

EARTH QUAKE
| A&M SP-4308 | (S) | Earth Quake | 1971 | 6.00 | 15.00 |
| A&M SP-4337 | (S) | Why Don't You Try Me? | 1972 | 6.00 | 15.00 |

EARTHQUIRE
| Natural Resources 106 | (S) | Earthquire | 1972 | 6.00 | 15.00 |

EARTHY SIDE
| P.I.P. 6804 | (S) | Earthy Side | 1971 | 4.00 | 10.00 |

EAST
| Capitol ST-11083 | (S) | East | 1971 | 10.00 | 25.00 |

EAST OF EDEN
Deram DES-18023	(S)	Mercator Projected	1969	8.00	20.00
Deram DES-18043	(S)	Snafu	1970	8.00	20.00
Harvest SW-806	(S)	East Of Eden	1971	8.00	20.00

EAST SIDE KIDS, THE
| Uni 73032 | (S) | The Tiger And The Lamb | 1968 | 8.00 | 20.00 |

EASYBEATS, THE
United Arts. UAL-3588	(M)	Friday On My Mind	1967	16.00	40.00
United Arts. UAS-6588	(S)	Friday On My Mind	1967	20.00	50.00
		("Make You Feel Alright" is rechanneled)			
United Arts. UAS-6667	(S)	Falling Off The Edge Of The World	1968	16.00	40.00
		("Women" is rechanneled)			
Rare Earth 517	(S)	Easy Ridin'	1970	Unreleased	
Rhino RNLP-124	(S)	Best Of The Easybeats	1985	1.00	5.00

EBONY RHYTHM FUNK CAMPAIGN, THE
| Uni 73142 | (S) | The Ebony Rhythm Funk Campaign | 1970 | 6.00 | 15.00 |

EBONYS, THE
| Phila. Inter. KZ-32419 | (S) | The Ebonys | 1973 | 4.00 | 10.00 |

ECLECTION
| Elektra EKS-74023 | (S) | Eclection | 1968 | 6.00 | 15.00 |

EDDY, DUANE
Jamie JLP-3000	(M)	Have "Twangy" Guitar-Will Travel	1958	50.00	125.00
Jamie JLPS-3000	(S)	Have "Twangy" Guitar-Will Travel	1958	150.00	300.00
		(Green cover with Eddy sitting with his guitar case. The title on the cover is in white print.)			
Jamie JLP-3000	(M)	Have "Twangy" Guitar-Will Travel	1958	40.00	100.00
Jamie JLPS-3000	(S)	Have "Twangy" Guitar-Will Travel	1958	100.00	250.00
		(Green cover with Eddy sitting with his guitar case. The title on the cover is in green and red print.)			
		—Jamie albums above have yellow/gold labels.—			
Jamie JLPM-3000	(M)	Have "Twangy" Guitar-Will Travel	1959	20.00	50.00
Jamie JLPS-3000	(S)	Have "Twangy" Guitar-Will Travel	1959	40.00	100.00
Jamie JLPS-3000	(E)	Have "Twangy" Guitar-Will Travel	196?	20.00	50.00
		(Red cover with Eddy standing with his guitar.)			
Jamie T-90682	(M)	Have "Twangy" Guitar-Will Travel	196?	20.00	50.00
Jamie ST-90682	(S)	Have "Twangy" Guitar-Will Travel	196?	30.00	75.00
		(Capitol Record Club)			
Jamie JLPM-3006	(M)	Especially For You....	1959	24.00	60.00
Jamie JLPS-3006	(S)	Especially For You....	1959	40.00	100.00
Jamie JLPM-3009	(M)	The "Twangs" The "Thang"	1959	24.00	60.00
Jamie JLPS-3009	(S)	The "Twangs" The "Thang"	1959	40.00	100.00
Jamie T-91301	(M)	The "Twangs" The "Thang"	1965	24.00	60.00
Jamie ST-91301	(S)	The "Twangs" The "Thang"	1965	24.00	60.00
		(Capitol Record Club)			
Jamie JLPM-3011	(M)	Songs Of Our Heritage (Gatefold cover)	1960	40.00	100.00
Jamie JLPS-3011	(S)	Songs Of Our Heritage (Gatefold cover)	1960	60.00	150.00
Jamie JLPS-3011	(S)	Songs Of Our Heritage (Gatefold cover. Blue vinyl)	1960	300.00	500.00
Jamie JLPS-3011	(S)	Songs Of Our Heritage (Gatefold cover. Red vinyl)	1960	300.00	500.00
		(Original pressings of Jamie 301 on black and colored vinyl above have gatefold covers with a fold-open poster bound to the inside. Subtract 20-30% if the poster has been removed.)			
Jamie JLPM-3011	(M)	Songs Of Our Heritage (Standard cover)	1960	12.00	30.00
Jamie JLPS-3011	(S)	Songs Of Our Heritage (Standard cover)	1960	16.00	40.00
Jamie JLPM-3014	(M)	$1,000,000 Worth Of Twang	1960	20.00	50.00
Jamie JLPS-3014	(E)	$1,000,000 Worth Of Twang	1960	16.00	40.00
Jamie JLPM-3019	(M)	Girls! Girls! Girls!	1961	20.00	50.00
Jamie JLPS-3019	(E)	Girls! Girls! Girls!	1961	16.00	40.00
Jamie JLPM-3021	(M)	$1,000,000 Worth Of Twang, Volume 2	1962	20.00	50.00
Jamie JLPS-3021	(E)	$1,000,000 Worth Of Twang, Volume 2	1962	16.00	40.00

Label & Catalog #		Title	Year	VG+	NM
Jamie JLPM-3022	(M)	Twistin' With Duane Eddy	1962	16.00	40.00
Jamie JLPS-3022	(S)	Twistin' With Duane Eddy	1962	20.00	50.00
		("Rebel Rouser Twist," "Cannon Ball Twist," "Movin' 'N Groovin'			
		Twist," "Ramrod Twist" and "Twisting Up & Down" are rechanneled.)			
Jamie JLPM-3024	(M)	Surfin'	1963	20.00	50.00
Jamie JLPS-3024	(S)	Surfin'	1963	30.00	75.00
Jamie JLPM-3025	(M)	Duane Eddy & The Rebels-In Person	1963	16.00	40.00
Jamie JLPS-3025	(S)	Duane Eddy & The Rebels-In Person	1963	20.00	50.00
Jamie T-90663	(M)	Duane Eddy & The Rebels-In Person	1964	24.00	60.00
Jamie ST-90663	(S)	Duane Eddy & The Rebels-In Person	1964	24.00	60.00
		(Capitol Record Club)			
Jamie JLPM-3026	(M)	16 Greatest Hits	1964	20.00	50.00
Jamie JLPS-3026	(E)	16 Greatest Hits	1964	16.00	40.00
		—Jamie albums above have gold & white labels.—			
RCA Victor LPM-2525	(M)	Twistin' And Twangin'	1962	12.00	30.00
RCA Victor LSP-2525	(S)	Twistin' And Twangin'	1962	16.00	40.00
RCA Victor LPM-2576	(M)	Twangy Guitar, Silky Strings	1962	12.00	30.00
RCA Victor LSP-2576	(S)	Twangy Guitar, Silky Strings	1962	16.00	40.00
RCA Victor LPM-2648	(M)	Dance With The Guitar Man	1962	12.00	30.00
RCA Victor LSP-2648	(S)	Dance With The Guitar Man	1962	16.00	40.00
RCA Victor LPM-2681	(M)	Twang A Country Song	1963	12.00	30.00
RCA Victor LSP-2681	(S)	Twang A Country Song	1963	16.00	40.00
RCA Victor LPM-2700	(M)	Twangin' Up A Storm	1963	12.00	30.00
RCA Victor LSP-2700	(S)	Twangin' Up A Storm	1963	16.00	40.00
		—RCA albums above have black "Long Play" or "Living Stereo" labels.—			
RCA Victor LPM-2798	(M)	Lonely Guitar	1964	8.00	20.00
RCA Victor LSP-2798	(S)	Lonely Guitar	1964	12.00	30.00
RCA Victor LPM-2918	(M)	Water Skiing	1964	8.00	20.00
RCA Victor LSP-2918	(S)	Water Skiing	1964	12.00	30.00
RCA Victor LPM-2993	(M)	Twangin' The Golden Hits	1965	8.00	20.00
RCA Victor LSP-2993	(S)	Twangin' The Golden Hits	1965	12.00	30.00
		—RCA albums above have black "Mono" or "Stereo" labels.—			
RCA Victor LPM-3432	(M)	Twangsville	1965	8.00	20.00
RCA Victor LSP-3432	(S)	Twangsville	1965	12.00	30.00
RCA Victor LPM-3477	(M)	The Best Of Duane Eddy	1966	8.00	20.00
RCA Victor LSP-3477	(P)	The Best Of Duane Eddy	1966	10.00	25.00
		—RCA albums above have black "Monaural" or "Stereo" labels.—			
RCA Victor LSP-3477	(P)	The Best Of Duane Eddy	1969	6.00	15.00
		—RCA albums above have orange labels on non-flexible vinyl.—			
Colpix CP-490	(M)	Duane A-Go-Go	1965	12.00	30.00
Colpix CPS-490	(S)	Duane A-Go-Go	1965	16.00	40.00
Colpix CP-494	(M)	Duane Eddy Does Bob Dylan	1965	12.00	30.00
Colpix CPS-494	(S)	Duane Eddy Does Bob Dylan	1965	16.00	40.00
Reprise R-6218	(M)	The Biggest Twang Of Them All	1966	2.00	30.00
Reprise RS-6218	(S)	The Biggest Twang Of Them All	1966	16.00	40.00
Reprise R-6240	(M)	The Roaring Twangies	1967	8.00	20.00
Reprise RS-6240	(S)	The Roaring Twangies	1967	10.00	25.00
Sire SASH-3707	(P)	Vintage Years (2 LPs)	1975	10.00	25.00
EDEN'S CHILDREN					
ABC 624	(M)	Eden's Children	1968	8.00	20.00
ABC S-624	(S)	Eden's Children	1968	10.00	25.00
ABC S-652	(S)	Sure Looks Real	1968	8.00	20.00
EDGE, THE					
Nose NRS-48003	(S)	The Edge	1970	16.00	40.00
EDGE, GRAEME					
Refer to The Moody Blues.					
Threshold THS-15	(S)	Kick Off Your Muddy Boots	1975	1.00	5.00
London PS-686	(S)	Paradise Ballroom	1977	1.00	5.00
EDGEWOOD					
TMI 30971	(S)	Ship Of Labor	1972	4.00	10.00
EDISON ELECTRIC BAND, THE					
Cotillion SD-9022	(S)	Bless You, Dr. Woodward	1970	4.00	10.00
EDMUNDS, DAVE					
Edmunds was a member of Love Sculpture and later of Rockpile.					
MAM 3	(S)	Rockpile (Counterfeits exist)	1972	10.00	25.00
RCA Victor LPL1-5003	(S)	Subtle As Flying Mallet	1975	4.00	10.00
Swan Song SS-8418	(S)	Get It	1977	1.00	5.00
Atlantic PR-320	(DJ)	College Network Interview (Colored label)	1978	12.00	30.00
Swan Song SS-8505	(S)	Trax On Wax 4	1979	1.00	5.00
Swan Song SS-8507	(S)	Repeat When Necessary	1979	1.00	5.00
Swan Song SS-16034	(S)	Twangin...	1981	1.00	5.00
Swan Song SS-8510	(S)	The Best Of Dave Edmunds	1982	1.00	5.00
RCA Victor AYL1-4238	(S)	Subtle As Flying Mallet	1982	.80	4.00

Label & Catalog #		Title	Year	VG+	NM
Columbia FC-37930	(S)	D.E. 7th	1982	1.00	5.00
Columbia 38651	(S)	Information	1983	1.00	5.00
Columbia AS-	(DJ)	Information (Picture disc)	1983	6.00	15.00
Columbia 39273	(S)	Riff Raff	1984	1.00	5.00

EDWARD BEAR

Capitol SKAO-426	(S)	Bearings	1970	1.00	5.00
Capitol ST-580	(S)	Eclipse	1971	1.00	5.00
Capitol ST-11157	(S)	Edward Bear	1972	1.00	5.00
Capitol SMAS-11192	(S)	Close Your Eyes	1973	1.00	5.00

EDWARD'S HAND

GRT 1005	(S)	Edward's Hand	1969	6.00	15.00
RCA Victor LSP-4452	(S)	Stranded	1970	4.00	10.00

EGG

Deram DES-18039	(S)	Egg	1970	5.00	12.00
Deram DES-18056	(S)	The Polite Force	1971	5.00	12.00

EGGS OVER EASY

A&M SP-4366	(S)	Good 'N' Cheap	1972	4.00	10.00

801

801 features Brian Eno and Phil Manzanera.

Polydor PD1-6148	(S)	801 Live	1978	4.00	10.00

18TH CENTURY CYCLE, THE

Sidewalk T-5909	(M)	Off On A 20th Century Cycle	1967	6.00	15.00
Sidewalk ST-5909	(S)	Off On A 20th Century Cycle	1967	8.00	20.00
United Arts. UAS-6697	(S)	Bacharach Baroque	1969	5.00	12.00

EIRE APPARENT

Buddah BDS-5031	(S)	Sunrise (Produced by Jimi Hendrix)	1969	14.00	35.00

EKSEPTION

Philips PHS-600334	(S)	Ekseption	1970	4.00	10.00
Philips PHS-600348	(S)	Begger Julias Time Trip	1970	4.00	10.00

EL CAMPO JADES, THE

Golden Eagle LP-101	(M)	The El Campo Jades	1966	20.00	50.00

EL CHICANO

Kapp KS-3632	(S)	Viva Tirado	1970	4.00	10.00
Kapp KS-3640	(S)	Revolution	1971	4.00	10.00
Kapp KS-3643	(S)	Golden Soul	1971	4.00	10.00
Kapp KS-3663	(S)	Celebration	1972	4.00	10.00
MCA 69	(S)	Revolution	1972	1.00	5.00
MCA 401	(S)	Cinco	1972	1.00	5.00

EL DORADOS, THE / THE ELDORADOS

Vee Jay VJLP-1001	(M)	Crazy Little Mama	1959	400.00	750.00
		(Vee Jay 1001 contains two tracks by The Magnificents.)			
		—*Vee Jay albums above have maroon labels with a thick silver band around the perimeter.*—			
Vee Jay VJLP-1001	(M)	Crazy Little Mama	1960	200.00	500.00
		—*Vee Jay albums above have maroon labels with a thin silver band around the perimeter.*—			
Vee Jay VJLP-1001	(M)	Crazy Little Mama	196?	150.00	300.00
		—*Vee Jay albums above have black rainbow labels.*—			
Lost-Nite LLP-20	(10")	The Eldorados (Red vinyl)	1981	4.00	10.00
Solid Smoke 8025	(M)	Low Mileage/High Octane	1984	1.00	5.00

ELBERT, DONNIE

King 629	(M)	The Sensational Donnie Elbert Sings	1959	150.00	400.00
Deluxe DLP-12003	(S)	Have I Sinned	1971	10.00	25.00
Trip TLP-9524	(S)	Stop In The Name Of Love	1972	10.00	25.00
All Platinum AP-3007	(S)	Where Did Our Love Go	1972	10.00	25.00
All Platinum AP-3019	(S)	Dancin' The Night Away	1977	10.00	25.00
Sugarhill 256	(S)	From The Git Go	1981	1.00	5.00

ELECTRIC FLAG, THE

The original Electric Flag includes Mike Bloomfield, Barry Goldberg and Nick Gravenites. The Flag can be found on the Sidewalk soundtrack "The Trip."

Columbia CS-9597	(S)	A Long Time Comin'	1968	6.00	15.00
Columbia CS-9714	(S)	The Electric Flag	1968	6.00	15.00
		—*Columbia albums above have "360 Sound" on the bottom of the label.*—			
Columbia CS-9597	(S)	A Long Time Comin'	197?	.80	4.00
Columbia CS-9714	(S)	The Electric Flag	197?	.80	4.00
Columbia C-30422	(S)	The Best Of The Electric Flag	1971	1.00	5.00
Atlantic SD-18112	(S)	The Band Kept Playing	1974	1.00	5.00

Electric Light Orchestra's Face The Music *was issued commercially with an uninterrupted series of grooves on both sides of the record. To assist willing FM jocks with playing songs, United Artists issued promo copies of the album banded for air-play. These promotional copies are not identified on the front cover but have a sticker on the back that reads "Face The Music is a complete and conceptual album, however, this special D.J. copy has been banded for easy cueing." While the record is very hard to find, not many of today's collectors are all that enthusiatic about ELO. . .*

Label & Catalog #		Title	Year	VG+	NM

ELECTRIC INDIAN

| United Arts. UAS-6728 | (S) | Keem 'O Sabe | 1969 | 6.00 | 15.00 |

ELECTRIC JUNKYARD

| RCA Victor LSP-4158 | (S) | The Electric Junkyard | 1969 | 6.00 | 15.00 |

ELECTRIC LIGHT ORCHESTRA [ELO]

ELO was founded by former members of The Move, Roy Wood and Jeff Lynne, although Wood left soon after the group's formation. Refer to The Idle Race; Olivia Newton-John / ELO; The Traveling Wilburys.

United Arts. UAS-5573	(S)	No Answer	1972	1.00	5.00
United Arts. LA-040F	(S)	Electric Light Orchestra II	1973	1.00	5.00
United Arts. LA-188F	(S)	On The Third Day	1973	1.00	5.00
United Arts. LA-339G	(S)	Eldorado	1974	1.00	5.00
United Arts. LA-546DJ	(S)	Face The Music (Banded for air-play)	1975	6.00	15.00
United Arts. LA-546G	(S)	Face The Music	1975	1.00	5.00
U.A./Jet SP-123	(S)	Ole ELO (Gold vinyl in black & white cover)	1976	40.00	100.00
U.A./Jet SP-123	(S)	Ole ELO (Gold vinyl & no cover)	1976	20.00	50.00
U.A./Jet SP-123	(S)	Ole ELO (Red vinyl & no cover)	1976	30.00	75.00
U.A./Jet SP-123	(S)	Ole ELO (Blue vinyl & no cover)	1976	30.00	75.00
U.A./Jet SP-123	(S)	Ole ELO (White vinyl & no cover)	1976	30.00	75.00

("Ole" was first issued promotionally on gold vinyl in a black & white photo cover. It was then issued on gold, red, white and blue vinyl in plain cardboard jackets. U.A. finally issued the album commercially with the same cover as the original gold vinyl LP except in color.)

| U.A./Jet LA-630G | (S) | Ole ELO | 1976 | 1.00 | 5.00 |
| U.A./Jet LA-679G | (S) | A New World Record | 1976 | 1.00 | 5.00 |

— U.A. albums above have light brown labels.—

U.A./Jet LA-823L2	(S)	Out Of The Blue (2 LPs. Blue vinyl promo)	1977	10.00	25.00
U.A./Jet LA-823L2	(S)	Out Of The Blue (2 LPs. Blue vinyl)	1977	4.00	10.00
Jet JZ-35524	(S)	No Answer	1978	.80	4.00
Jet PZ-35524	(S)	No Answer	1981	.80	4.00
Jet JZ-35525	(S)	On The Third Day	1978	.80	4.00
Jet PZ-35525	(S)	On The Third Day	1981	.80	4.00
Jet JZ-35526	(S)	Eldorado	1978	.80	4.00
Jet PZ-35526	(S)	Eldorado	1981	.80	4.00
Jet JZ-35527	(S)	Face The Music	1978	.80	4.00
Jet PZ-35527	(S)	Face The Music	1981	.80	4.00
Jet JZ-35528	(S)	Ole ELO	1978	.80	4.00
Jet PZ-35528	(S)	Ole ELO	1981	.80	4.00
Jet JZ-35529	(S)	A New World Record	1978	.80	4.00
Jet PZ-35529	(S)	A New World Record	1981	.80	4.00
Jet JZ-35530	(S)	Out Of The Blue (2 LPs)	1978	1.00	5.00
Jet PZ-35530	(S)	Out Of The Blue (2 LPs)	1981	1.00	5.00
Jet JZ-35533	(S)	Electric Light Orchestra II	1978	.80	4.00
Jet PZ-35533	(S)	Electric Light Orchestra II	1981	.80	4.00
Jet FZ-35769	(S)	Discovery	1979	.80	4.00
Jet HZ-45769	(S)	Discovery (Half-speed master)	1981	10.00	30.00
Jet FZ-36310	(S)	ELO's Greatest Hits	1979	.80	4.00
Jet HZ-46310	(S)	ELO's Greatest Hits (Half-speed master)	1981	13.00	40.00
Jet Z4X-36966	(S)	Box Of Their Best (4 LP box)	1980	6.00	15.00
Jet FZ-37371	(S)	Time	1981	.80	4.00
Jet HZ-47371	(S)	Time (Half-speed master)	1981	10.00	30.00
Jet FZ-38490	(S)	Secret Messages	1983	.80	4.00
Jet HZ-48490	(S)	Secret Messages (Half-speed master)	1983	16.00	50.00

ELECTRIC PRUNES, THE

Reprise R-6248	(M)	The Electric Prunes	1967	20.00	50.00
Reprise RS-6248	(S)	The Electric Prunes	1967	24.00	60.00
Reprise R-6262	(M)	Underground	1967	16.00	40.00
Reprise RS-6262	(S)	Underground	1967	20.00	50.00
Reprise R-6275	(M)	Mass In F Minor	1967	14.00	35.00
Reprise RS-6275	(S)	Mass In F Minor	1967	10.00	25.00
Reprise RS-6316	(S)	Release Of An Oath	1968	10.00	25.00

—Reprise albums above have pink, gold & green labels.—

| Reprise RS-6275 | (S) | Mass In F Minor | 1969 | 6.00 | 15.00 |
| Reprise RS-6342 | (S) | Just Good Rock N' Roll | 1969 | 10.00 | 25.00 |

—Reprise albums above have brown labels.—

ELECTRIC UNDERGROUND, THE

| Premier P-9060 | (M) | Guitar Explosion | 196? | 8.00 | 20.00 |
| Premier PS-9060 | (S) | Guitar Explosion | 196? | 10.00 | 25.00 |

ELECTROMAGNETS, THE

The Electromagnets feature Eric Johnson, formerly of Mariani.

| E.C.M. 1001 | (S) | The Electromagnets (Green cover) | 197? | 60.00 | 150.00 |
| E.C.M. 1001 | (S) | The Electromagnets (Red/orange cover) | 197? | 50.00 | 125.00 |

Label & Catalog #		Title	Year	VG+	NM

ELEPHANT'S MEMORY
Refer to Stan Bronstein; John Lennon & Yoko Ono.

Label & Catalog #		Title	Year	VG+	NM
Buddah BDS-5033	(S)	Elephant's Memory	1969	6.00	15.00
Buddah BDS-5038	(S)	Songs From "Midnight Cowboy"	1969	6.00	15.00
Metromedia MD-1035	(S)	Take It To The Streets	1970	8.00	20.00
Apple SMAS-3389	(S)	Elephants Memory *(Prod. by John & Yoko)*	1972	10.00	25.00
RCA Victor APL1-0569	(S)	Angel's Forever	1974	1.00	5.00

ELF

Epic KE-31789	(S)	Elf	1972	10.00	25.00
MGM M3G-4974	(S)	L.A. 59	1974	6.00	15.00
MGM M3G-4994	(S)	Trying To Burn The Sun	1975	6.00	15.00

ELGINS, THE

V.I.P. 400	(M)	Darling Baby	1966	20.00	50.00
V.I.P. S-400	(S)	Darling Baby	1966	30.00	75.00

ELIGIBLES, THE

Capitol T-1310	(M)	The Eligibles	1960	6.00	15.00
Capitol ST-1310	(S)	The Eligibles	1960	8.00	20.00

ELIJAH

United Arts. UAS-5590	(S)	Elijah	1972	1.00	5.00
Sounds Of The South 377	(S)	Fanfares	1973	1.00	5.00

ELIMINATORS, THE

Liberty LRP-3365	(M)	Liverpool! Dragsters! Cycles! Surfing!	1964	30.00	75.00
Liberty LST-7365	(S)	Liverpool! Dragsters! Cycles! Surfing!	1964	50.00	125.00

ELIZABETH

Vanguard VSD-6501	(S)	Elizabeth	1968	10.00	25.00

ELLERINE

Mainstream 377	(S)	Ellerine	1972	10.00	25.00

ELLIE POP

Mainstream S-6115	(S)	Ellie Pop	1968	12.00	30.00

ELLINGTON, MARC
Marc Ellington was a member of Fairport Convention.

Ampex A-10131	(S)	Rains/Reins Of Change	1971	5.00	12.00

ELLIOT, "MAMA" CASS
Cass Elliot was one of The Mama's & The Papa's. Refer to The Big Three; The Mugwumps; Dave Mason & Cass Elliot.

Dunhill DS-50040	(S)	Dream A Little Dream	1968	6.00	15.00
Dunhill DS-50055	(S)	Bubble Gum, Lemonade & Something For Mama	1969	6.00	15.00
Dunhill DS-50071	(S)	Make Your Own Kind Of Music	1970	6.00	15.00
Dunhill DS-50093	(S)	Mama's Big Ones	1970	4.00	10.00
RCA Victor LSP-4619	(S)	Cass Elliot	1971	4.00	10.00
RCA Victor LSP-4753	(S)	The Road Is No Place For A Lady	1972	4.00	10.00
RCA Victor APL1-0303	(S)	Don't Call Me Mama No More	1973	4.00	10.00
		—RCA albums above have orange labels.—			

ELLIOT, RON
Ron Elliot was a member of the Beau Brummels.

Warner Bros. WS-1833	(S)	Candlestickmaker *(With booklet)*	1969	6.00	15.00

ELLIS, JIMMY
Jimmy Ellis also recorded as Orion.

Boblo 78-829	(S)	Ellis Sings Elvis By Request	1978	20.00	50.00

ELLIS, SHIRLEY

Congress CGL-3002	(M)	Shirley Ellis In Action	1964	10.00	25.00
Congress CGS-3002	(S)	Shirley Ellis In Action	1964	12.00	30.00
Congress CGL-3003	(M)	The Name Game	1965	10.00	25.00
Congress CGS-3003	(S)	The Name Game	1965	12.00	30.00
Columbia CL-2679	(M)	Sugar, Let's Shing-A-Ling	1967	8.00	20.00
Columbia CS-9479	(S)	Sugar, Let's Shing-A-Ling	1967	10.00	25.00

ELMER GANTRY'S VELVET OPERA

Epic BN-26415	(S)	Elmer Gantry's Velvet Opera	1968	20.00	50.00

EMERALD CHOIR, THE

Boat 1017	(S)	Timber Timbre Burn	198?	5.00	12.00

EMERSON, LAKE & PALMER
Keith Emerson, Greg Lake and Carl Palmer. Refer to The Nice.

Cotillion SD-9040	(S)	Emerson, Lake & Palmer	1971	3.20	8.00
Cotillion SD-9900	(S)	Tarkus	1971	3.20	8.00

Label & Catalog #		Title	Year	VG+	NM
Cotillion SD-9903	(S)	Trilogy	1972	3.20	8.00
Cotillion SMAS-94773	(S)	Trilogy (Capitol Record Club)	1972	4.00	10.00
Cotillion ELP-66666	(S)	Pictures At An Exhibition	1972	3.20	8.00
Manticore ELP-66669	(S)	Brain Salad Surgery	1973	3.20	8.00
Manticore 3-200	(S)	Ladies And Gentlemen (2 LPs)	1974	3.20	8.00
Atlantic SD-19120	(S)	Emerson, Lake & Palmer	1977	.80	4.00
Atlantic SD-19121	(S)	Trilogy	1977	.80	4.00
Atlantic SD-19122	(S)	Pictures At An Exhibition	1977	.80	4.00
Atlantic SD-19123	(S)	Trilogy	1977	.80	4.00
Atlantic SD-19124	(S)	Brain Salad Surgery	1977	.80	4.00
Atlantic PR-277	(DJ)	Works, Volume 1 (Sampler)	1977	4.00	10.00
Atlantic 7000	(S)	Works, Volume 1 (2 LPs)	1977	1.00	5.00
Atlantic SD-19147	(S)	Works, Volume 2	1977	.80	4.00
Atlantic SD-19211	(S)	Love Beach	1978	.80	4.00
Atlantic PR-281	(DJ)	On Tour With Emerson, Lake & Palmer	1979	16.00	40.00
Atlantic SD-19255	(S)	Emerson, Lake & Palmer In Concert	1979	.80	4.00
Atlantic SD-19283	(S)	The Best Of Emerson, Lake & Palmer	1980	.80	4.00

EMERSON'S OLD TIMEY CUSTARD-SUCKIN' BAND

ESP-Disk' 2006	(S)	Emerson's Old Timey Custard-Suckin' Band	196?	12.00	30.00

EMOTIONS, THE

Volt VOS-6008	(S)	So I Can Love You	1971	10.00	25.00
Volt VOS-6015	(S)	Untouched	1972	10.00	25.00

ENCHANTMENTS, THE

Rogue 1000	(M)	The Enchantments Present Accapella	196?	20.00	50.00

END, THE

London PS-560	(S)	Introspection (Produced by Bill Wyman)	1969	20.00	50.00

ENDLE ST. CLOUD
ESC also recorded as Potter St. Cloud.

International Arts. 12	(S)	Thank You All Very Much	1968	12.00	30.00

ENGEL, SCOTT, & JOHN STEWART
Scott Engel and John Stewart later recorded as Scott and John Walker as part of The Walker Brothers.

Tower T-5026	(M)	I Only Came To Dance With You	1966	6.00	15.00
Tower ST-5026	(S)	I Only Came To Dance With You	1966	10.00	25.00

ENGEMANN, BOBBY

Capitol ST-221	(S)	My Own Thing	1969	4.00	10.00

ENGLISH GYPSY: *Refer to GYPSY*

ENO
Brian Eno was a member of Roxy Music. Robert Fripp plays on several albums below and is co-credited on Antilles 7001 and 7018. Refer to David Bowie; 801; Talking Heads.

Antilles AN-7001	(S)	No Pussyfooting	1973	6.00	15.00
Island ILPS-9268	(S)	Here Come The Warm Jets	1974	6.00	15.00
Island ILPS-9309	(S)	Taking Tiger Mountain By Strategy	1974	6.00	15.00
Island ILPS-9351	(S)	Another Green World (With lithos)	1975	12.00	30.00
		(LPS-9351 was issued with four lithographs.)			
Island ILPS-9351	(S)	Another Green World (Without lithos)	1975	6.00	15.00
Antilles ANM-7018	(S)	Evening Star	1975	4.00	10.00
Antilles AN-7030	(S)	Discreet Music	1975	4.00	10.00
Island ILPS-9478	(S)	Before And After Science	1977	4.00	10.00
Antilles AN-7070	(S)	Music For Films	1978	4.00	10.00
PVC 7908	(S)	Music For Airports	1979	4.00	10.00
Editions EG ENO-1	(S)	Here Come The Warm Jets	1980	1.00	5.00
Editions EG ENO-2	(S)	Taking Tiger Mountain By Strategy	1980	1.00	5.00
Editions EG ENO-3	(S)	Another Green World	1980	1.00	5.00
Editions EG ENO-4	(S)	Before And After Science	1980	1.00	5.00
Editions EG EGS-102	(S)	No Pussyfooting	1980	1.00	5.00
Editions EG EGS-103	(S)	Evening Star	1980	1.00	5.00
Editions EG EGS-201	(S)	Music For Airports	1980	1.00	5.00
Editions EG EGS-202	(S)	Possible Music	1980	1.00	5.00
Editions EG EGS-303	(S)	Discreet Music	1980	1.00	5.00
Editions EG EGS-105	(S)	Music For Films	1980	1.00	5.00
Editions EG EGS-107	(S)	The Plateaux Of Mirrors	1980	1.00	5.00
Editions EG EGD-20	(S)	Ambient 4: On Land	1982	1.00	5.00
Editions EG EGD-37	(S)	The Pearl	198?	1.00	5.00
Editions EG EGD-53	(S)	Apollo (Atmospheres & Soundtracks)	198?	1.00	5.00
Editions EG EGBS-2	(S)	Working Backwards 1983-1973 (11 LP box)	1983	24.00	60.00

ENTWISTLE, JOHN
Mr. Entwistle is a member of The Who.

Decca DL-79183	(S)	Smash Your Head Against The Wall	1971	10.00	25.00
Decca DL-79190	(S)	Whistle Rhymes	1972	10.00	25.00

Label & Catalog #		Title	Year	VG+	NM
MCA/Track 321	(S)	Rigor Mortis Sets In	1973	6.00	15.00
MCA/Track 1926	(S)	Who's Ox (Promo sampler)	1975	20.00	50.00
MCA/Track 2129	(S)	Mad Dog	1975	6.00	15.00
Atco SD-38-142	(S)	Too Late The Hero	1981	.80	4.00
EPPS, PRESTON					
Original Sound LPM-5002	(M)	Bongo, Bongo, Bongo	1960	20.00	50.00
Original Sound LPS-8851	(S)	Bongo, Bongo, Bongo	1960	30.00	75.00
		("Bongo Rock" is rechanneled)			
Top Rank RM-349	(M)	Bongola	1961	14.00	35.00
Top Rank RS-649	(S)	Bongola	1961	20.00	50.00
EPPS, PRESTON / THE BONGO TEENS					
Original Sound OS-8872	(M)	Surfin' Bongos	1963	14.00	35.00
Original Sound OSS-8872	(S)	Surfin' Bongos	1963	20.00	50.00
EQUALS, THE					
Laurie LP-2045	(M)	Unequalled	1967	10.00	25.00
Laurie SLP-2045	(S)	Unequalled	1967	12.00	30.00
RCA Victor LSP-4078	(S)	Baby Come Back	1968	10.00	25.00
		— RCA albums above have orange labels on non-flexible vinyl.—			
President PTL-1015	(S)	Equal Sensation	1968	10.00	25.00
President PTL-1020	(S)	The Sensational Equals	1968	10.00	25.00
President PTL-1025	(S)	Equals Supreme	1968	10.00	25.00
President PTL-1030	(S)	Strikeback	1969	10.00	25.00
ERIC, MARK					
Revue 7210	(S)	A Midsummer's Day Dream	1969	4.00	10.00
ERICA					
ESP-Disk' 1099	(S)	You Used To Think	1968	20.00	50.00
ERIK					
Vanguard VRS-9267	(M)	Look Where I Am	1967	6.00	15.00
Vanguard VSD-79267	(S)	Look Where I Am	1967	8.00	20.00
ERIK & THE VIKINGS					
Karate 1401	(M)	Sing Along Rock 'N Roll	1965	8.00	20.00
ESQUERITA					
Capitol T-1186	(M)	Esquerita	1959	1,000.00	1,600.00
ESQUIRES, THE					
Bunky 300	(S)	Get On Up And Get Away	1968	14.00	35.00
ESSEX, THE					
Roulette R-25234	(M)	Easier Said Than Done	1963	16.00	40.00
Roulette SR-25234	(S)	Easier Said Than Done	1963	20.00	50.00
Roulette R-25235	(M)	A Walkin' Miracle	1963	16.00	40.00
Roulette SR-25235	(S)	A Walkin' Miracle	1963	20.00	50.00
Roulette R-25246	(M)	Young And Lively	1964	16.00	40.00
Roulette SR-25246	(S)	Young And Lively	1964	20.00	50.00
ESSEX, DAVID					
Columbia C-32560	(S)	Rock On	1973	4.00	10.00
Columbia CQ-32560	(Q)	Rock On	1974	6.00	15.00
ESTABLISHMENT, THE					
King KS-1123	(S)	The Establishment	1971	4.00	10.00
ESTES, "SLEEPY" JOHN					
Singer, guitar player and songwriter John Estes is one of the few bluesmen to have been recorded prior to WWII.					
Delmark DL-603	(M)	The Legend Of Sleepy John Estes	1966	20.00	50.00
Delmark DS-603	(E)	The Legend Of Sleepy John Estes	1966	12.00	30.00
Delmark DL-608	(M)	Broke And Hungry	1966	20.00	50.00
Delmark DS-608	(E)	Broke And Hungry	1966	12.00	30.00
Delmark DS-613	(E)	Sleepy John Estes	1969	12.00	30.00
Delmark DS-619	(E)	Electric Sheep	1969	12.00	30.00
ETC.					
Windi WLPS-1011	(S)	Etc. Is The Name Of The Band!	1976	24.00	60.00
ETERNITY'S CHILDREN					
Tower ST-5123	(S)	Eternity's Children	1968	10.00	25.00
Tower ST-5144	(S)	Timeless (Canadian)	1968	12.00	30.00
EUPHONIOUS WAIL					
Kapp KS-3668	(S)	Euphonious Wail	1973	6.00	15.00

Label & Catalog #		Title	Year	VG+	NM
EUPHORIA					
Heritage HTS-35,005	(S)	Euphoria	1969	6.00	15.00
EUPHORIA					
Capitol SKAO-363	(S)	A Gift From Euphoria	1969	50.00	125.00
EVANS, PAUL					
Guaranteed GUL-1000	(M)	Fabulous Teens	1960	30.00	75.00
Guaranteed GUS-1000	(S)	Fabulous Teens	1960	40.00	100.00
Carlton TLP-129	(M)	Hear Paul Evans In Your Home Tonight	1961	20.00	50.00
Carlton STLP-129	(S)	Hear Paul Evans In Your Home Tonight	1961	30.00	75.00
		("Seven Little Girls" is rechanneled on this album.)			
Carlton TLP-130	(M)	Folk Songs Of Many Lands	1961	20.00	50.00
Carlton STLP-130	(S)	Folk Songs Of Many Lands	1961	30.00	75.00
Kapp KL-1346	(M)	21 Years In A Tennessee Jail	1964	10.00	25.00
Kapp KS-3346	(S)	21 Years In A Tennessee Jail	1964	12.00	30.00
Kapp KL-1475	(M)	Another Town, Another Jail	1966	10.00	25.00
Kapp KS-3475	(S)	Another Town, Another Jail	1966	12.00	30.00
EVE					
LHI 3100	(S)	Take It And Smile	1970	6.00	15.00

EVEN DOZEN JUG BAND, THE
Formed by Stefan Grossman and Peter Siegel, The Jug Band included—at one time or another—Maria D'Amato (a.k.a. Maria Muldaur), David Grisman, Steve Katz, Joshua Rifkin, and John Sebastian.

Elektra EKL-246	(M)	The Even Dozen Jug Band	1965	12.00	30.00
Elektra ES-7246	(S)	The Even Dozen Jug Band	1965	20.00	50.00
Everest FS-339	(S)	Jug Band Music And Rags	197?	6.00	15.00
		(Everest 339 is a reissue of Elektra 7246.)			

EVERETT, BETTY
Ms. Everett also recorded with Jerry Butler.

Vee Jay LP-1077	(M)	You're No Good	1964	20.00	50.00
Vee Jay LPS-1077	(S)	You're No Good	1964	30.00	75.00
Vee Jay LP-1077	(M)	It's In His Kiss	1964	14.00	35.00
Vee Jay VJS-1077	(S)	It's In His Kiss	1964	20.00	50.00
		("It's In His Kiss" is a reissue of "You're No Good.")			
Vee Jay LP-1122	(M)	The Very Best Of Betty Everett	1965	14.00	35.00
Vee Jay VJS-1122	(S)	The Very Best Of Betty Everett	1965	20.00	50.00
Sunset SUS-5220	(S)	I Need You So	1968	6.00	15.00
Uni 73048	(S)	There"ll Come A Time	1969	10.00	25.00
EVERGREEN BLUE SHOES					
Amos 7002	(S)	The Ballad Of Evergreen Blue Shoes	1968	6.00	15.00
EVERGREEN BLUES, THE					
Mercury SR-61157	(S)	7 Do 11	1968	6.00	15.00
ABC 669	(S)	Comin' On	1969	6.00	15.00

EVERLY BROTHERS, THE
The EBs are brothers Don and Phil Everly. Note: Of the duo's Cadence repertoire, only "Let It Be Me," "Like Strangers," "Love Of My Life," "Poor Jenny," "Take A Message To Mary," "Til I Kissed You," and "When Will I Be Loved" were released in stereo.

Cadence CLP-3003	(M)	The Everly Brothers	1958	50.00	125.00
Cadence CLP-3016	(M)	Songs Our Daddy Taught Us	1958	50.00	125.00
Cadence CLP-3025	(M)	The Everly Brothers' Best	1959	50.00	125.00
Cadence CLP-3040	(M)	The Fabulous Style Of The Everly Brothers	1960	50.00	125.00
Cadence CLP-25040	(P)	The Fabulous Style Of The Everly Brothers	1960	80.00	200.00
		—Cadence albums above have burgundy labels with silver print.—			
Cadence CLP-3003	(M)	The Everly Brothers	1963	20.00	50.00
Cadence CLP-3016	(M)	Songs Our Daddy Taught Us	1963	20.00	50.00
Cadence CLP-3025	(M)	The Everly Brothers' Best	1963	20.00	50.00
Cadence CLP-3040	(M)	The Fabulous Style Of The Everly Brothers	1963	20.00	50.00
Cadence CLP-25040	(P)	The Fabulous Style Of The Everly Brothers	1963	30.00	75.00
Cadence CLP-3059	(M)	Folk Songs Of The Everly Brothers	1963	20.00	50.00
Cadence CLP-25059	(E)	Folk Songs Of The Everly Brothers	1963	16.00	40.00
		(Cadence 3/25059 is a reissue of 3106.)			
Cadence CLP-3062	(M)	15 Everly Hits 15	1963	16.00	40.00
Cadence CLP-25062	(P)	15 Everly Hits 15	1963	20.00	50.00
		—Cadence albums above have red labels with black print.—			
Warner Bros. PRO-134	(DJ)	It's Everly Time Souvenir Sampler	1960	300.00	600.00
		(10" promotional sampler from their Warner Bros. debut.)			
Warner Bros. W-1381	(M)	It's Everly Time	1960	12.00	30.00
Warner Bros. WS-1381	(S)	It's Everly Time	1960	16.00	40.00
Warner Bros. W-1395	(M)	A Date With The Everly Brothers (Gatefold cover)	1960	20.00	50.00
Warner Bros. WS-1395	(S)	A Date With The Everly Brothers (Gatefold cover)	1960	30.00	75.00
		(WB 1395 was issued with cut-out poster and a sheet of eight wallet-size, color photos.)			

After scoring a dozen massive hits for Cadence, Don and Phil Everly signed with Warner Bros. in 1960, the label's first real stab at the "new music." They rewarded their new company's daring with six top ten sides in their first two years. Unfortunately, after that their career went into a tailspin and their singles slowly stopped having any impact on the charts. Worse was the almost complete lack of consumer attention their albums brought. Consequently, many of their Warner Bros. albums are more difficult to find than their earlier Cadence LPs, especially their Christmas offering. Oddly, while four of their Warner Bros. albums made the charts, their sole RIAA Gold Record was awarded to The Very Best Of The Everly Brothers, a 1964 album that didn't make the charts.

Label & Catalog #		Title	Year	VG+	NM
Warner Bros. W-1395	(M)	A Date With The Everly Brothers *(Gatefold cover)*	1960	16.00	40.00
Warner Bros. WS-1395	(S)	A Date With The Everly Brothers *(Gatefold cover)*	1960	20.00	50.00
		(The prices above do not include the poster or wallet cards.)			
Warner Bros. W-1395	(M)	A Date With The Everly Brothers *(Standard cover)*	1961	12.00	30.00
Warner Bros. WS-1395	(S)	A Date With The Everly Brothers *(Standard cover)*	1961	16.00	40.00
Warner Bros. W-1418	(M)	Both Sides Of An Evening	1961	12.00	30.00
Warner Bros. WS-1418	(S)	Both Sides Of An Evening	1961	16.00	40.00
Warner Bros. W-1430	(M)	Instant Party	1962	12.00	30.00
Warner Bros. WS-1430	(S)	Instant Party	1962	16.00	40.00
Warner Bros. W-1471	(M)	The Everly Brothers' Golden Hits	1962	10.00	25.00
Warner Bros. WS-1471	(S)	The Everly Brothers' Golden Hits	1962	14.00	35.00
		—Warner mono albums above have grey labels; stereo albums have gold labels.—			
Warner Bros. W-1483	(M)	Christmas With The Everly Brothers	1962	16.00	40.00
Warner Bros. WS-1483	(S)	Christmas With The Everly Brothers	1962	20.00	50.00
Warner Bros. W-1513	(M)	Great Country Hits	1963	16.00	40.00
Warner Bros. WS-1513	(S)	Great Country Hits	1963	20.00	50.00
Warner Bros. W-1554	(M)	Very Best Of The Everly Brothers *(Yellow cover)*	1964	12.00	30.00
Warner Bros. WS-1554	(S)	Very Best Of The Everly Brothers *(Yellow cover)*	1964	16.00	40.00
Warner Bros. W-1554	(M)	Very Best Of The Everly Brothers *(White cover)*	1965	8.00	20.00
Warner Bros. WS-1554	(S)	Very Best Of The Everly Brothers *(White cover)*	1965	10.00	25.00
Warner Bros. ST-91343	(S)	Very Best Of The Everly Brothers *(Cap. Rec. Club)*	1965	16.00	40.00
Warner Bros. W-1578	(M)	Rock N' Soul	1965	16.00	40.00
Warner Bros. WS-1578	(S)	Rock N' Soul	1965	20.00	50.00
Warner Bros. W-1585	(M)	Gone, Gone, Gone	1965	16.00	40.00
Warner Bros. WS-1585	(S)	Gone, Gone, Gone	1965	20.00	50.00
Warner Bros. W-1605	(M)	Beat N' Soul	1965	16.00	40.00
Warner Bros. WS-1605	(S)	Beat N' Soul	1965	20.00	50.00
Warner Bros. W-1620	(M)	In Our Image	1966	16.00	40.00
Warner Bros. WS-1620	(S)	In Our Image	1966	20.00	50.00
		—Warner albums above have grey labels with a black & white logo.—			
Warner Bros. W-1646	(M)	Two Yanks In London	1966	16.00	40.00
Warner Bros. WS-1646	(S)	Two Yanks In London	1966	20.00	50.00
		(Although uncredited, the Hollies back up the Everlys throughout this album.)			
Warner Bros. W-1676	(M)	The Hit Sound Of The Everly Brothers	1967	16.00	40.00
Warner Bros. WS-1676	(S)	The Hit Sound Of The Everly Brothers	1967	20.00	50.00
Warner Bros. W-1708	(M)	The Everly Brothers Sing	1967	16.00	40.00
Warner Bros. WS-1708	(S)	The Everly Brothers Sing	1967	20.00	50.00
		—Warner albums above have gold labels.—			
Warner Bros. WS-1752	(S)	Roots	1968	12.00	30.00
Warner Bros. ST-91601	(S)	Roots *(Capitol Record Club)*	1968	16.00	40.00
Warner Bros. WS-1858	(S)	The Everly Brothers' Show	1970	8.00	20.00
Capitol STBO-93286	(S)	The Everly Brothers' Show *(Capitol Record Club)*	1970	10.00	25.00
Harmony HS-11304	(S)	The Everly Brothers	1968	6.00	15.00
Harmony HS-11350	(S)	Christmas With The Everly Brothers	1969	6.00	15.00
Harmony HS-11388	(S)	Chained To A Memory	1970	4.00	10.00
Barnaby BGP-350	(E)	The Original Greatest Hits *(2 LPs)*	1970	5.00	12.00
Barnaby 30260	(E)	The End Of An Era	1971	4.00	10.00
RCA Victor LSP-4781	(S)	Pass The Chicken And Listen	1972	6.00	15.00
RCA Victor LSP-4620	(S)	Stories We Could Tell	1972	6.00	15.00
Barnaby 2BR-15008	(E)	The History Of The Everly Brothers *(2 LPs)*	1973	5.00	12.00
Barnaby 2BR-6006	(E)	The Everly Brothers' Greatest Hits *(2 LPs)*	1974	5.00	12.00
Pair PDL-1063	(S)	Living Legends *(2 LPs)*	1976	1.00	5.00
Candlelite OP-2505	(P)	Magical Golden Hits *(2 LPs)*	1976	8.00	20.00
Barnaby BR-4004	(E)	The Everly Brothers' Greatest Hits, Vol. 1	1977	4.00	10.00
Barnaby BR-4005	(E)	The Everly Brothers' Greatest Hits, Vol. 2	1977	4.00	10.00
Barnaby BR-4006	(E)	The Everly Brothers' Greatest Hits, Vol. 3	1977	4.00	10.00
Passport 4006DJ	(S)	Reunion Concert *(Promo label)*	1983	20.00	50.00
Passport 11001	(S)	The Everly Brothers Reunion Concert *(2 LPs)*	1983	4.00	10.00
Mercury 822431	(S)	EB 84	1984	1.00	5.00
Polydor 832520-1	(S)	Some Hearts	1985	1.00	5.00
Arista AL9-8207	(P)	24 Original Classics *(2 LPs)*	1985	4.00	10.00
Rhino RNLP-210	(M)	Folk Songs Of The Everly Brothers	1985	1.00	5.00
Rhino RNLP-211	(M)	The Everly Brothers	1985	1.00	5.00
Rhino RNLP-212	(M)	Songs Our Daddy Taught Us	1985	1.00	5.00
Rhino RNLP-213	(M)	The Fabulous Style Of The Everly Brothers	1985	1.00	5.00
Rhino RNLP-214	(P)	All They Had To Do Is Dream	1985	1.00	5.00
Rhino RNLP-258	(M)	Heartaches And Harmonies *(Picture disc)*	1985	1.00	5.00

EVERLY, DON

Label & Catalog #		Title	Year	VG+	NM
Ode 77005	(S)	Don Everly	1970	6.00	15.00
Ode 77023	(S)	Sunset Towers	1974	5.00	12.00
Hickory AH-44003	(S)	Brother Jukebox	1976	4.00	10.00

EVERLY, PHIL

Label & Catalog #		Title	Year	VG+	NM
RCA Victor APL1-0092	(S)	Star Spangled Banner	1973	6.00	15.00
Pye 12104	(S)	Phil's Diner	1975	6.00	15.00
Pye 12121	(S)	Mystic Line	1976	5.00	12.00
Elektra 6E-213	(S)	Living Alone	1979	4.00	10.00

Label & Catalog #		Title	Year	VG+	NM
EVERPRESENT FULLNESS					
White Whale 7132	(S)	Everpresent Fullness	1970	10.00	25.00
EVERY MOTHER'S SON					
MGM E-4471	(M)	Every Mother's Son	1967	5.00	12.00
MGM SE-4471	(S)	Every Mother's Son	1967	6.00	15.00
MGM E-4504	(M)	Every Mother's Son's Back	1967	4.00	10.00
MGM SE-4504	(S)	Every Mother's Son's Back	1967	4.00	10.00
EVERYDAY PEOPLE					
Paramount PAS-6021	(S)	Everyday People	1972	4.00	10.00
EVERYTHING IS EVERYTHING					
Vanguard VSD-6512	(S)	Everything Is Everything	1969	10.00	25.00
EXCEPTIONS, THE					
Flair 6444	(S)	Rock 'N' Roll Mass	1968	6.00	15.00
EXCITERS, THE					
United Arts. UAL-3264	(M)	Tell Him	1963	20.00	50.00
United Arts. UAS-6264	(S)	Tell Him	1963	40.00	100.00
Roulette R-25326	(M)	The Exciters	1966	16.00	40.00
Roulette RS-25326	(S)	The Exciters	1966	20.00	50.00
RCA Victor LSP-4211	(S)	Caviar And Chitlin's	1969	10.00	25.00
EXUMA					
Mercury SR-61265	(S)	Exuma	1970	4.00	10.00
Mercury SR-61314	(S)	Exuma II	1970	4.00	10.00
Kama Sutra KLS-2040	(S)	Do Wah Nanny	1971	4.00	10.00
Kama Sutra KLS-2052	(S)	Snake	1972	4.00	10.00
Kama Sutra KLS-2074	(S)	Life	1973	4.00	10.00
EYES OF BLUE, THE					
Mercury SR-61184	(S)	Crossroads Of Time	1968	12.00	30.00
Mercury SR-61220	(S)	In Fields Of Ardath	1969	12.00	30.00

FABIAN

Chancellor CHL-5003	(M)	Hold That Tiger	1959	40.00	100.00
Chancellor CHLS-5003	(S)	Hold That Tiger	1959	60.00	150.00
		—Chancellor albums above have pink labels.—			
Chancellor CHL-5003	(M)	Hold That Tiger	1959	20.00	50.00
Chancellor CHLS-5003	(S)	Hold That Tiger	1959	30.00	75.00
Chancellor CHL-5005	(M)	The Fabulous Fabian	1959	20.00	50.00
Chancellor CHLX-5005	(S)	The Fabulous Fabian	1959	30.00	75.00
Chancellor CHL-5012	(M)	The Good Old Summertime	1960	20.00	50.00
Chancellor CHLS-5012	(S)	The Good Old Summertime	1960	30.00	75.00
Chancellor CHL-69802	(M)	The Fabian Facade: Young And Wonderful	1960	30.00	75.00
		(Felt-covered, gatefold jacket with a die-cut window allowing the photo inner sleeve to show through.)			
Chancellor CHL-5019	(M)	Rockin' Hot	1961	30.00	75.00
Chancellor CHL-5024	(M)	Fabian's 16 Fabulous Hits	1962	30.00	75.00
		—Chancellor albums above have black labels.—			
ABC X-806	(E)	16 Greatest Hits	1973	4.00	10.00
United Arts. LA-449E	(M)	The Very Best Of Fabian	1975	1.00	5.00
Trip TOP-16-20	(E)	16 Greatest Hits	1977	1.00	5.00

FABIAN / FRANKIE AVALON

Chancellor CHL-5009	(M)	The Hit Makers	1960	30.00	75.00
		—Chancellor albums above have black labels.—			
Tele-House CD-2041	(S)	Double Dynamite (2 LPs)	197?	5.00	12.00

FABULOUS COUNTS, THE

Cotillion SD-9011	(S)	Jan Jan	1969	6.00	15.00

FABULOUS FLIPPERS, THE

Veritas VS-2570	(S)	Something Tangible	107?	8.00	20.00

FABULOUS JOKERS, THE

Monument MLP-8059	(M)	Guitars Extraordinaire	1966	40.00	100.00
Monument SLP-18059	(S)	Guitars Extraordinaire	1966	60.00	150.00

FABULOUS RHINESTONES, THE

Just Sunshine 9	(S)	Freewheelin'	1973	4.00	10.00

FACES, THE

After the break-up of The Small Faces, members Ronnie Lane, Kenny Jones and Ian McLagen added Rod Stewart and Ron Wood and signed with Warner Bros. as The Faces, even though the first album, 1851, is credited to The Small Faces. When Stewart achieved success in 1971 (with Wood as a pivotal contributor on his solo albums), the touring group was billed as Rod Stewart & The Faces. By 1975 The Faces were through. Refer to Jeff Beck; The Who.

Warner Bros. PRO	(DJ)	First Step Box	1970	200.00	400.00
		(Promotional box contains a copy of the album, a badge, a sheet of cutouts with a pair of scissors, and a press kit with photos, etc.)			
Warner Bros. WS-1851	(S)	First Step	1970	6.00	15.00
Warner Bros. WS-1892	(S)	Long Player	1971	3.20	8.00
Warner Bros. ST-93718	(S)	Long Player (Capitol Record Club)	1971	4.00	10.00
Warner Bros. BS-2574	(S)	A Nod Is As Good As A Wink... To A Blind Horse	1971	3.20	8.00
Warner Bros. BS-2665	(S)	Ooh La La	1973	3.20	8.00
Warner Bros. BS-2897	(S)	Snakes & Ladders	1976	3.20	8.00

FAGEN, DONALD

Donald Fagen is one-half of Steely Dan.

Warner Bros. 23696	(S)	The Nightfly (Promo on Quiex II vinyl)	1982	6.00	15.00
Warner Bros. 23696	(S)	The Nightfly	1982	1.00	5.00

FAIRPORT CONVENTION

The original group was Ashley Hutchings, Martin Lamble, Simon Nicol, and Richard Thompson with vocalists Judy Dyble and Ian Matthews. Dyble left in 1968, replaced by Sandy Denny. Matthews departed in '69, followed by Lamble's death. Both Denny and Hutchings left in '70, followed by Thompson's departure in '71. Other members included Dave Mattacks, Dave Swarbrick, Trevor Lucas, and Jerry Donahue. Refer to The Bunch; Fotheringay; Steeleye Span.

Cotillion SO-9024	(S)	Fairport Convention	1969	10.00	25.00
A&M SP-4185	(S)	Fairport Convention	1969	6.00	15.00
		(SP-4185 is the release of the UK "What We Did On Our Holidays.")			

Fabian Forte was one of the post-Presley pretty boys from Philadelphia. That he was signed
based exclusively on his good looks is now part of his story. That he also cut some decent
rock'n roll has been generally overlooked by the obsessed. The entire success of his career
lasted less than twenty-four months with ten charting singles in 1959-60, three of which
made the Top 10. His first album, Hold That Tiger, shown here, was based around the 1959
hit, "Tiger." It must have been difficult to sell an album with this cover to anyone but girls.

Label & Catalog #		Title	Year	VG+	NM
A&M SP-4206	(S)	Unhalfbricking	1969	6.00	15.00
A&M SP-4257	(S)	Leige And Lief	1970	6.00	15.00
A&M SP-4265	(S)	Full House	1970	6.00	15.00
A&M SP-4319	(S)	Angel Delight	1971	6.00	15.00
A&M SP-4333	(S)	"Babbacombe" Lee	1972	6.00	15.00
A&M SP-4386	(S)	Rosie	1973	6.00	15.00
A&M SP-4407	(S)	Fairport Nine	1973	6.00	15.00
A&M SP-3530	(S)	Fairport Chronicles	1976	4.00	10.00
A&M SP-3603	(S)	Fairport Nine	1976	4.00	10.00
Island ILPS-9286	(S)	Fairport Live/A Movable Feast	1974	5.00	12.00
Island ILPS-9313	(S)	Rising For The Moon	1975	5.00	12.00
Island HELP-28	(S)	Live At The Troubador, 1970	1976	5.00	12.00
Carthage CGLP-4417	(S)	Full House	198?	3.20	8.00
		(Carthage 4417 is a reissue of A&M 4265.)			
Carthage CGLP-4418	(S)	Unhalfbricking	198?	3.20	8.00
		(Carthage 4418 is a reissue of A&M 4206.)			
Carthage CGLP-4430	(S)	What We Did On Our Holidays	198?	3.20	8.00
		(Carthage 4430 is a reissue of A&M 4185.)			
Hannibal HNBL-1319	(S)	House Full	1986	3.20	8.00
Hannibal HNBL-1329	(S)	Heyday	1987	3.20	8.00

FAIRWEATHER

Label & Catalog #		Title	Year	VG+	NM
Neon 1	(S)	Beginning From An End	1971	6.00	15.00

FAITH

Label & Catalog #		Title	Year	VG+	NM
Brown Bag LA085	(S)	Faith	1973	6.00	15.00
		(Originally issued as "Limousine" by Limousine.)			

FAITH, ADAM

Label & Catalog #		Title	Year	VG+	NM
MGM E-3951	(M)	England's Top Singer	1961	16.00	40.00
MGM SE-3951	(S)	England's Top Singer	1961	20.00	50.00
Amy 8005	(M)	Adam Faith	1965	10.00	25.00
Amy S-8005	(S)	Adam Faith	1965	12.00	30.00

FAITHFULL, MARIANNE

Label & Catalog #		Title	Year	VG+	NM
London LL-3423	(M)	Marianne Faithfull	1965	8.00	20.00
London PS-423	(E)	Marianne Faithfull	1965	8.00	20.00
		(Original covers for PS-423 read "Stereo" in the upper right corner.)			
London PS-423	(E)	Marianne Faithfull	196?	6.00	15.00
		(Later covers read "Stereo Electronically Re-Processed.")			
London LL-3452	(M)	Go Away From My World	1965	6.00	15.00
London PS-452	(S)	Go Away From My World	1965	8.00	20.00
		("Summer Nights" is rechanneled.)			
London LL-3482	(M)	Faithfull Forever	1966	6.00	15.00
London PS-482	(S)	Faithfull Forever	1966	8.00	20.00
London PS-547	(S)	Marianne Faithfull's Greatest Hits	1969	4.00	10.00
		("As Tears Go By," "This Little Bird," "Summer Nights," "Come And Stay With Me" and "In My Time Of Sorrow" are rechanneled.)			
Island 9570	(S)	Broken English	1979	1.00	5.00
Island 9648	(S)	Dangerous Acquaintances	1981	1.00	5.00
Island 90039	(S)	Broken English	1983	.80	4.00
Island 90066	(S)	A Child's Adventure (Quiex II vinyl)	1983	6.00	15.00
Island 90066	(S)	A Child's Adventure	1983	1.00	5.00

FALCONAIRES, THE

The Falconaires feature Steve Alaimo, Keith Allison and Mark Lindsay of Paul Revere's Raiders.

Label & Catalog #		Title	Year	VG+	NM
USAF 70-3/4	(S)	Something From The Falconaires	1970	20.00	50.00

FALCONE, VINCENT

Label & Catalog #		Title	Year	VG+	NM
Pianissimo 2001	(S)	You Again	197?	4.00	10.00

FALCONS, THE

Former members include Eddie Floyd and Wilson Pickett.

Label & Catalog #		Title	Year	VG+	NM
Relic 8005	(M)	You're So Fine	1985	4.00	10.00
Relic 8006	(M)	I Found A Love	1985	4.00	10.00

FALLEN ANGELS, THE

Label & Catalog #		Title	Year	VG+	NM
Roulette R-25358	(M)	The Fallen Angels	1967	12.00	30.00
Roulette SR-25358	(S)	The Fallen Angels	1967	16.00	40.00
Roulette SR-42011	(S)	It's A Long Way Down	1968	100.00	250.00

FALLENROCK

Label & Catalog #		Title	Year	VG+	NM
Capricorn CP-0143	(S)	Watch For Fallenrock	1974	4.00	10.00

FAME, GEORGIE

Refer to Shorty.

Label & Catalog #		Title	Year	VG+	NM
Imperial LP-9282	(M)	Yeh, Yeh	1965	10.00	25.00
Imperial LP-12282	(S)	Yeh, Yeh ("Yeh Yeh" is rechanneled)	1965	12.00	30.00

The Fendermen's Mule Skinner Blues ranks as one of the "All-Time Most Over-Rated Rare Records" in that the album is, in fact, quite rare and more than a little in demand. The problem is that, after shelling out four figures for a clean copy, it invariably inspires the proud new owner to ask him/her self "Just why the @#!% did I shell out big bucks for this!" While the hit single remains a classic of its kind, the rest of the album is not likely to inspire a new generation of musicians to Fendermania.

Label & Catalog #		Title	Year	VG+	NM
Imperial LP-9331	(M)	Get Away	1966	10.00	25.00
Imperial LP-12331	(E)	Get Away	1966	8.00	20.00
Epic BN-26368	(S)	The Ballad Of Bonnie And Clyde	1968	10.00	25.00
Island ILPS-9293	(S)	Georgie Fame	1975	4.00	10.00
FAME GANG, THE					
Fame SKAO-4200	(S)	Solid Gold From Muscle Shoals	1969	10.00	25.00
FAMILY					
Reprise RS-6312	(S)	Music In A Doll's House	1968	8.00	20.00
Reprise RS-6340	(S)	Family Entertainment	1969	6.00	15.00
Reprise RS-6384	(S)	A Song For Me	1970	6.00	15.00
United Arts. UAS-5527	(S)	Anyway	1971	6.00	15.00
		—U.A. albums above have brown labels.—			
United Arts. UAS-5562	(S)	Fearless	1971	4.00	10.00
United Arts. UAS-5644	(S)	Bandstand	1972	4.00	10.00
United Arts. LA181	(S)	It's Only A Movie	1973	4.00	10.00
FAMILY DOGG, THE					
Buddah BDS-5100	(S)	The View From Rowland's Head	1972	10.00	25.00
FAMILY TREE, THE					
RCA Victor LSP-3955	(S)	Miss Butters	1968	5.00	12.00
FANNY					
Reprise RS-6416	(S)	Fanny	1970	3.20	8.00
Reprise RS-6456	(S)	Charity Ball	1971	3.20	8.00
Reprise MS-2058	(S)	Fanny Hill	1972	3.20	8.00
Reprise MS-2137	(S)	Mother's Pride	1973	3.20	8.00
Casablanca NBLP-7007	(S)	Rock & Roll Survivors	1974	3.20	8.00
FANNY ADAMS					
Kapp KS-3644	(S)	Fanny Adams	1971	4.00	10.00
FANTASTIC BAGGYS, THE					
The Baggys are the creation of Steve Barri and Phil Sloan.					
Imperial LP-9270	(M)	Tell 'Em I'm Surfin'	1964	60.00	150.00
Imperial LP-12270	(S)	Tell 'Em I'm Surfin'	1964	80.00	200.00
Liberty LN-10192	(S)	Tell 'Em I'm Surfin' (Abridged reissue)	1982	4.00	10.00
FANTASTIC FOUR, THE					
Soul 717	(P)	Best Of The Fantastic Four	1969	16.00	40.00
Soul 722	(S)	How Sweet He Is	1970	Unreleased	
Westbound 201	(S)	Alvin Stone	1975	6.00	15.00
Westbound 226	(S)	Night People	1976	6.00	15.00
Westbound 306	(S)	Got To Have Your Love	1977	6.00	15.00
Westbound 6108	(S)	B. Y. O. F. (Bring Your Own Funk)	1978	6.00	15.00
FANTASTIC JOHNNY C, THE					
Phil-L.A. Of Soul 4000	(S)	Boogaloo Down Broadway	1968	30.00	75.00
FANTASY					
Liberty LSP-7643	(S)	Fantasy	1970	8.00	20.00
FAR CRY					
Vanguard VSD-6510	(S)	Far Cry	1969	10.00	25.00
FAR EAST FAMILY BAND					
Muland 7002	(S)	The Cave Down To The Earth	197?	6.00	15.00
Muland 7139	(S)	Parallel World	197?	6.00	15.00
All Ears FE-11479	(S)	Tenkujin	197?	6.00	15.00
FARDON, DON					
Crescendo GNPS-2044	(S)	Indian Reservation	1968	6.00	15.00
Decca DL-75225	(S)	I've Paid My Dues	1970	6.00	15.00
FARGO					
RCA Victor LSP-4178	(S)	I See It Now	1969	4.00	10.00
FARLOW, STAN					
Checker 3015	(S)	Hot Wheels	1970	6.00	15.00
FARLOWE, CHRIS					
Columbia CL-2593	(M)	The Fabulous Chris Farlowe	1966	14.00	35.00
Columbia CS-9393	(E)	The Fabulous Chris Farlowe	1966	10.00	25.00
Immediate Z12-52010	(S)	Paint It Farlowe	1968	8.00	20.00
Polydor 24-4041	(S)	From Here To Mama Rosa With The Hill	1970	4.00	10.00

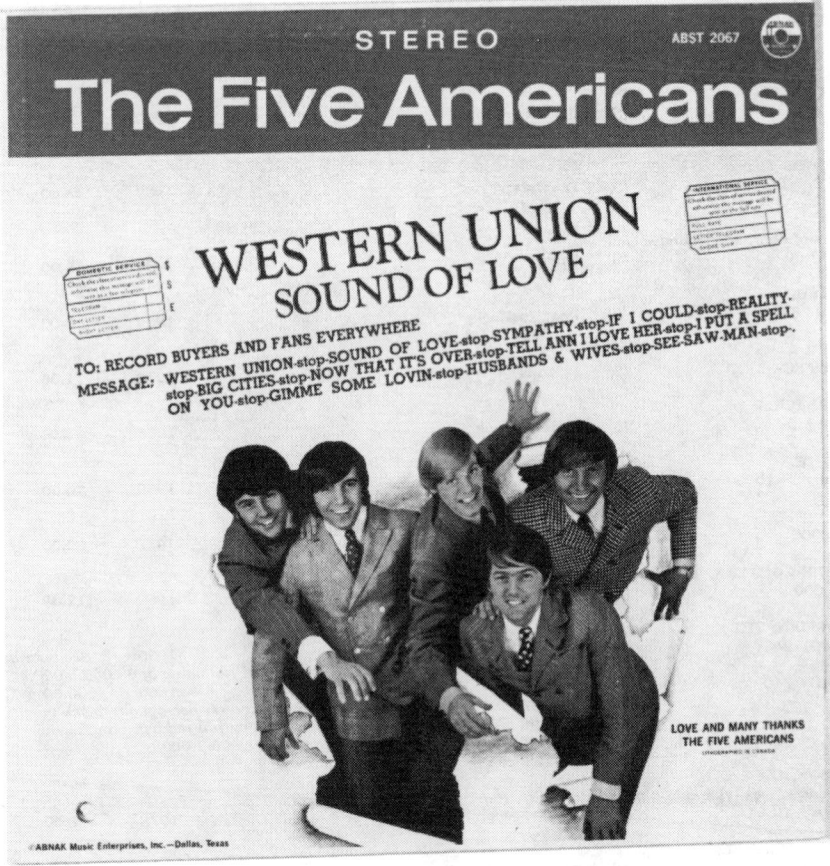

The Five Americans, hailing from Dallas, Texas, and featuring the lead vocals of Michael Rabon, had a pair of modest hits for Hanna-Barbera Records before moving over to Abnak. Put in the hands of Dale Hawkins as producer, the ol' rocker steered them straight into the national Top 10 in 1967 with "Western Union," a clever record with an excellent pop sound. Hawkins and the group followed with two more Top 40 hits before their association ended, one of which, "Sound Of Love," was used as part of the title for their first album, Western Union/Sound Of Love, on their new label (shown here).

Label & Catalog #		Title	Year	VG+	NM

FARNER, MARK, & DON BREWER
Refer to Grand Funk Railroad; Terry Knight & The Pack.

| Quadico 7401 | (S) | **Monumental Funk** | 1979 | 4.00 | 10.00 |
| Quadico 7401 | (S) | **Monumental Funk** *(Picture disc)* | 1979 | 6.00 | 15.00 |

FARQUAHR

| Verve/Forecast FTS-3053 | (S) | **Fabulous Farquahr** | 1969 | 4.00 | 10.00 |
| Elektra EKS-74083 | (S) | **Farquahr** | 1970 | 4.00 | 10.00 |

FAT

| RCA Victor LSP-4368 | (S) | **Fat** | 1970 | 4.00 | 10.00 |

FAT

| Dream Merchant O-812 | (S) | **Footloose** | 1976 | 10.00 | 25.00 |

FAT CHANCE

| RCA Victor LSP-4626 | (S) | **Fat Chance** | 1972 | 4.00 | 10.00 |

FAT CITY
Fat City features Bill and Taffy Danoff.

| ABC/Probe CPLP-4508 | (S) | **Reincarnation** | 1969 | 6.00 | 15.00 |
| Paramount PAS-6028 | (S) | **Welcome To Fat City** | 1972 | 6.00 | 15.00 |

FAT MATTRESS

| Atco SD-33-309 | (S) | **Fat Mattress** | 1969 | 4.00 | 10.00 |
| Atco SD-33-347 | (S) | **Fat Mattress II** | 1970 | 4.00 | 10.00 |

FAT WATER

| MGM SE-4660 | (S) | **Fat Water** | 1969 | 4.00 | 10.00 |

FAUN
Members of Faun later founded Journey.

| Gregar 7000 | (S) | **Faun** | 1969 | 12.00 | 30.00 |

FEAR ITSELF

| Dot DLP-25942 | (S) | **Fear Itself** | 1969 | 8.00 | 20.00 |

FEATHER

| Columbia KC-30127 | (S) | **Friends** | 1970 | 1.00 | 5.00 |

FEDERAL DUCK

| Musicor MS-3162 | (S) | **Federal Duck** | 1968 | 8.00 | 20.00 |

FELICE, DEE

| Bethlehem B-10000 | (S) | **In Heat** *(Produced by James Brown)* | 1969 | 20.00 | 50.00 |

FELT

| Nasco 9006 | (S) | **Felt** | 1971 | 30.00 | 75.00 |

FEMININE COMPLEX, THE

| Athena 600 | (S) | **The Feminine Complex** | 1969 | 12.00 | 30.00 |

FENDERMEN, THE

Soma MG-1240	(M)	**Mule Skinner Blues** *(Blue vinyl)*	1960	*See note below*	
		(MG 1240 on blue vinyl has a suggested NM value of $3,000-5,000.)			
Soma MG-1240	(M)	**Mule Skinner Blues** *(Opaque black vinyl)*	1960	500.00	1,000.00
		(Some copies of Soma 1240 were pressed on non-opaque black vinyl: Light will shine through the black vinyl with a reddish brown glow. These have a suggested NM value of $1,000-1,600.)			

FERGUSON, JAY
Jay Ferguson was originally a member of Spirit. Refer to Jo Jo Gunne; Magic.

| Asylum AS-11394 | (S) | **Jay Ferguson Live** *(Promo)* | 1978 | 8.00 | 20.00 |

FERRIS WHEEL, THE

| Uni 73093 | (S) | **The Ferris Wheel** | 1970 | 5.00 | 12.00 |

FETCHIT, STEPPIN

| Motown M-619 | (M) | **My Son The Sit-In** | 1963 | *Unreleased?* | |

FEVER TREE
Fever Tree can also be found on the Uni soundtrack "Angels Die Hard."

Uni 73024	(S)	**The Fever Tree**	1968	10.00	25.00
Uni 73040	(S)	**Another Time, Another Place**	1968	10.00	25.00
Uni 73067	(S)	**Creation**	1970	10.00	25.00
Ampex A-10113	(S)	**For Sale**	1970	10.00	25.00
MCA 551	(S)	**The Fever Tree**	1973	1.00	5.00

The Five Keys were arguably the most important of the early rhythm'n blues vocal groups, laying the foundations for the many that followed. While their early recordings, especially the Aladdin sides, are still revered, by the time of rock'n roll's ascendence, the group was basically a middle-of-the-road ballad group. The Five Keys On Stage! is a legendary collectible in the wrong sort of way: The cover photo of the group shows the man on the left with his right hand behind him and along his right side in such a manner that just the top of one member shows. Unfortunately, it shows at such an angle—the reader can plainly see it at the bottom of the suit coat—that it looks entirely like a different member. This gaffe forced Capitol to withdraw the album and have their art department touch up the photo with an airbrush. While most collectors who want this record seek out this, the "penis cover," it is the air-brushed cover that is by far the rarer of the two!

Label & Catalog #		Title	Year	VG+	NM

FI-TONES, THE

| Relic 5010 | (M) | The Fi-Tones | 197? | 4.00 | 10.00 |

FIELDS

| Uni 73050 | (S) | Fields | 1969 | 20.00 | 50.00 |

FIFTH AVENUE BAND, THE

| Reprise RS-6369 | (S) | The Fifth Avenue Band | 1969 | 4.00 | 10.00 |

FIFTH DIMENSION, THE

Soul City SC-92000	(M)	Up, Up And Away	1967	5.00	12.00
Soul City SCS-92000	(S)	Up, Up And Away	1967	6.00	15.00
Soul City SC-92001	(M)	The Magic Garden	1967	5.00	12.00
Soul City SCS-92001	(S)	The Magic Garden	1967	6.00	15.00
Soul City SCS-92002	(S)	Stoned Soul Picnic	1968	5.00	12.00
Soul City SCS-92005	(S)	The Age Of Aquarius	1969	5.00	12.00
Soul City SCS-33900	(S)	The Fifth Dimension/Greatest Hits	1970	4.00	10.00
Soul City SCS-33901	(S)	The July 5th Album	1970	4.00	10.00
Bell 6045	(S)	Portrait	1970	3.20	8.00
Bell 6060	(S)	Love's Lines, Angles And Rhymes	1971	3.20	8.00
Bell 9000	(S)	The Fifth Dimension/Live! (2 LPs)	1971	3.20	8.00
Bell 6065	(S)	Reflections	1971	3.20	8.00
Bell 6073	(S)	Individually & Collectively	1972	3.20	8.00
Bell 1106	(S)	Greatest Hits On Earth	1972	3.20	8.00
Bell 1116	(S)	Living Together, Growing Together	1971	3.20	8.00
Bell 1315	(S)	Soul And Inspiration	1974	3.20	8.00
ABC 897	(S)	Earthbound	1975	1.50	6.00

FIFTH ESTATE, THE

| Jubilee JGM-8005 | (M) | Ding Dong The Witch Is Dead | 1967 | 6.00 | 15.00 |
| Jubilee JGS-8005 | (S) | Ding Dong The Witch Is Dead | 1967 | 8.00 | 20.00 |

FIFTY FOOT HOSE

| Limelight 86062 | (S) | Cauldron | 1969 | 40.00 | 100.00 |

FIRE

| ABC S-661 | (S) | Fire | 1969 | 8.00 | 20.00 |

FIRE & ICE, LTD.

| Capitol T-2577 | (M) | The Happening | 1966 | 12.00 | 30.00 |
| Capitol ST-2577 | (S) | The Happening | 1966 | 16.00 | 40.00 |

FIRE ESCAPE, THE

Crescendo GNP-2034	(M)	Psychotic Reaction	1967	12.00	30.00
Crescendo GNPS-2034	(S)	Psychotic Reaction	1967	12.00	30.00
		—GNP albums above have red labels.—			
Crescendo GNPS-2034	(S)	Psychotic Reaction	196?	4.00	10.00
		—GNP albums above have blue labels.—			

FIREBALLS, THE [JIMMY GILMER & THE FIREBALLS]

Top Rank RM-324	(M)	The Fireballs	1960	80.00	200.00
Top Rank RM-343	(M)	Vaquero	1960	80.00	200.00
Top Rank RS-643	(S)	Vaquero	1960	150.00	300.00
Warwick W-2042	(M)	Here Are The Fireballs	1961	80.00	200.00
Warwick WST-2042	(S)	Here Are The Fireballs	1961	150.00	300.00
Dot DLP-3512	(M)	Torquay	1963	20.00	50.00
Dot DLP-25512	(S)	Torquay	1963	30.00	75.00
Dot DLP-3545	(M)	Sugar Shack	1963	16.00	40.00
Dot DLP-25545	(S)	Sugar Shack	1963	24.00	60.00
Dot DLP-3577	(M)	Buddy's Buddy	1964	20.00	50.00
Dot DLP-25577	(S)	Buddy's Buddy	1964	30.00	75.00
Dot DLP-3643	(M)	Lucky 'Leven	1965	12.00	30.00
Dot DLP-25643	(S)	Lucky 'Leven	1965	16.00	40.00
Dot DLP-3668	(M)	Folkbeat	1965	12.00	30.00
Dot DLP-25668	(S)	Folkbeat	1965	16.00	40.00
Dot DLP-3709	(M)	Campusology	1966	12.00	30.00
Dot DLP-25709	(S)	Campusology	1966	16.00	40.00
Dot DLP-25856	(S)	Firewater	1968	10.00	25.00
		("Daisy Petal Pickin'" is rechanneled)			
Crown CLP-5376	(M)	Jimmy Gilmer & The Fireballs & The Sugar Shackers	196?	10.00	25.00
Crown CST-376	(S)	Jimmy Gilmer & The Fireballs & The Sugar Shackers	196?	10.00	25.00
Crown CLP-5387	(M)	The Sensational Jimmy Gilmer & The Fireballs	196?	10.00	25.00
Crown CST-387	(S)	The Sensational Jimmy Gilmer & The Fireballs	196?	10.00	25.00
		—Crown albums above have gray labels.—			
Atco SD-33-239	(S)	Bottle Of Wine	1968	10.00	25.00
Atco SD-33-275	(S)	Come On, React!	1969	10.00	25.00

The Five Satins, under the leadership of Fred Parris, recorded, under less than ideal conditions one of the quintessential vocal classics with their enormous hit of 1956. If the group had disbanded and gone their separate ways immediately thereafter, they would live eternally on every "oldies but goodies" show or chart in the country because of that one record: "In The Still Of The Nite" is invariably voted the #1 Oldie Of All-Time, unless it's beaten out for the top spot by The Penguins' "Earth Angel."

Label & Catalog #		Title	Year	VG+	NM

FIREBIRDS, THE
| Crown CST-589 | (S) | Light My Fire | 1968 | 30.00 | 75.00 |

FIREFLIES, THE
| Taurus S-1002 | (S) | You Were Mine | 1967 | 150.00 | 300.00 |

(The 1959 hit, "You Were Mine," was rerecorded in stereo.)

FIRST EDITION, THE
The First Edition features Kenny Rogers. The majority of their LPs are country/pop and not included in this edition.
Reprise R-6276	(M)	The First Edition	1967	10.00	25.00
Reprise RS-6276	(S)	The First Edition	1967	12.00	30.00
Reprise RS-6302	(S)	The First Edition's Second	1968	6.00	15.00
Reprise RS-6328	(S)	The First Edition '69	1969	6.00	15.00

FISCHER, WILD MAN
Bizarre 2XS-6332	(S)	An Evening With Wild Man Fischer			
		(2 LPs produced by Frank Zappa)	1969	20.00	50.00
Rhino RNLP-021	(S)	Pronounced Normal	1981	1.00	5.00

FISHER, CHIP
| RCA Victor LPM-1797 | (M) | Chipper At The Sugar Bowl | 1958 | 14.00 | 35.00 |
| RCA Victor LSP-1797 | (S) | Chipper At The Sugar Bowl | 1958 | 20.00 | 50.00 |

FIVE AMERICANS, THE
HBR HLP-8503	(S)	I See The Light	1966	12.00	30.00
		(HBR 8503 is in compatible mono/stereo.)			
Abnak AB-1967	(M)	Western Union/Sound Of Love	1967	8.00	20.00
Abnak ABST-2067	(S)	Western Union/Sound Of Love	1967	10.00	25.00
Abnak AB-1969	(M)	Progressions	1967	6.00	15.00
Abnak ABST-2069	(S)	Progressions ("Evol-Not Love" is rechanneled)	1967	8.00	20.00
Abnak ABST-2071	(P)	Now And Then (2 LPs)	1968	8.00	20.00

FIVE BY FIVE
| Paula LPS-2202 | (S) | Next Exit | 1969 | 10.00 | 25.00 |

FIVE DOLLAR SHOES, THE
| Neighborhood 47002 | (S) | Five Dollar Shoes | 1972 | 4.00 | 10.00 |

FIVE JADES, THE
| Relic 107 | (M) | The Five Jades Acapella | 197? | 4.00 | 10.00 |

FIVE KEYS, THE
Refer to Jack Teagarden.
Aladdin LP-806	(M)	The Best Of The Five Keys	1956	1,000.00	2,000.00
		(Should a copy of Aladdin 806 exist with a blue label, it would have a suggested NM value of $3,000-6,000.)			
		—Aladdin albums above have maroon labels.—			
Aladdin SLP-806	(M)	The Best Of The Five Keys	1956		*Bootleg*
Score LP-4003	(M)	The Five Keys On The Town	1957	350.00	750.00
Capitol T-828	(M)	The Five Keys On Stage (Yellow label promo)	1957	300.00	600.00
Capitol T-828	(M)	The Five Keys On Stage (Black label promo)	1957	300.00	600.00
Capitol T-828	(M)	The Five Keys On Stage	1957	150.00	300.00
		(The cover photo has the first member's hand against his body so that his thumb has a phallic appearance.)			
Capitol T-828	(M)	The Five Keys On Stage	1957	250.00	500.00
		(The cover has the thumb airbrushed out.)			
King 688	(M)	The Five Keys	1960	350.00	750.00
King 692	(M)	Rhythm & Blues Hits Past And Present	1960	300.00	600.00
		—King albums above have crownless black labels.—			
Capitol T-1769	(M)	The Fantastic Five Keys	1962	150.00	300.00

FIVE MAN ELECTRICAL BAND
Capitol ST-165	(S)	Five Man Electrical Band	1969	6.00	15.00
Lionel LRS-1100	(S)	Good-byes & Butterflies	1970	15.00	30.00
Lionel LRS-1101	(S)	Coming Of Age	1971	6.00	15.00
Lion LN-1009	(S)	Sweet Paradise	1973	6.00	15.00

FIVE ROYALS, THE [THE FIVE ROYALES]
Apollo LP-488	(M)	The Rockin' 5 Royals	1956	*See note below*	
		(Apollo 488 is rare with the following suggested NM values: First pressings with a purple label are $4,000-6,000. Second pressings with a green label, $2,000-3,000. Later pressings with a yellow label, $750-1,500. Counterfeits exist.)			
King 580	(M)	Dedicated To You	1957	250.00	500.00
King 616	(M)	The 5 Royales Sing For You	1959	200.00	400.00
King 678	(M)	The Five Royales	1960	80.00	200.00
King 955	(M)	24 All Time Hits	1966	40.00	100.00
		—King albums above have crownless black labels.—			

By the time The Flamingos made it onto the national pop charts in 1959, the group consisted of original members Johnny Carter and cousins Jake and Zeke Carey along with Tommy Hunt, Terry Johnson and lead singer Nate Nelson. While the original group had recorded such gems as "Golden Teardrops" (called "the Mona Lisa of group ballads" by collector/dealer/author Louis Silvani), the new group placed nine sides on the Top 100 in the '50s, including the classic "I Only Have Eyes For You." Their first two albums for End, Flamingo Serenade and Flamingo Favorites, are shown here, the latter with a cover that depicts their growing popularity with white teenagers.

Label & Catalog #		Title	Year	VG+	NM

FIVE SATINS, THE
Refer to Fred Parris & The Satins.

Label & Catalog #		Title	Year	VG+	NM
Ember ELP-100	(M)	The Five Satins Sing *(Red photo cover. Blue vinyl)*	1957	1,000.00	2,000.00
Ember ELP-100	(M)	The Five Satins Sing *(Red photo cover)*	1957	200.00	500.00
		—Ember albums above have red labels.—			
Ember ELP-100	(M)	The Five Satins Sing *(Red photo cover)*	1959	100.00	300.00
Ember ELP-100	(M)	The Five Satins Sing *(Black & gold title cover)*	1959	80.00	200.00
Ember ELP-401	(M)	Encore, Volume 2	1960	80.00	200.00
		—Ember albums above have "logs logo" labels.—			
Ember ELP-100	(M)	The Five Satins Sing	1961	40.00	100.00
Ember ELP-401	(M)	Encore, Volume 2	1961	40.00	100.00
		—Ember albums above have black labels.—			
Mt. Vernon 108	(M)	The Five Satins Sing	196?	12.00	30.00
Celebrity Show. JB-7671	(M)	The Best Of The Five Satins	1970	10.00	25.00
Lost Nite LLP-8	(10")	The Five Satins *(Red vinyl)*	1981	4.00	10.00
Lost Nite LLP-9	(10")	The Five Satins *(Red vinyl)*	1981	4.00	10.00
Relic 5008	(M)	The Five Satins' Greatest Hits, Vol. 1	197?	4.00	10.00
Relic 5013	(M)	The Five Satins' Greatest Hits, Vol. 2	197?	4.00	10.00
Relic 5024	(M)	The Five Satins' Greatest Hits, Vol. 3	197?	4.00	10.00

FIVE STAIRSTEPS, THE [THE STAIRSTEPS]

Label & Catalog #		Title	Year	VG+	NM
Windy C 6000	(M)	The Five Stairsteps	1967	8.00	20.00
Windy C S-6000	(S)	The Five Stairsteps	1967	10.00	25.00
Buddah BSD-5008	(S)	Our Family Portrait	1968	6.00	15.00
Curtom 8002	(S)	Love's Happening	1969	6.00	15.00
Buddah BSD-5061	(S)	The Stairsteps	1970	6.00	15.00
Buddah BSD-5068	(S)	Step By Step By Step	1970	6.00	15.00

FLACK, ROBERTA

Label & Catalog #		Title	Year	VG+	NM
Atlantic SD-8230	(S)	First Take	1969	3.20	8.00
Atlantic SD-1569	(S)	Chapter Two	1970	3.20	8.00
Atlantic SD-1594	(S)	Quiet Fire	1971	3.20	8.00
		—Atlantic albums above have green & orange labels with "1841 Broadway" on the bottom.—			
Atlantic SD-7271	(S)	Killing Me Softly	1973	1.00	5.00
Atlantic QD-7271	(Q)	Killing Me Softly	1974	6.00	15.00
Atlantic SD-18131	(S)	Feel Like Makin' Love	1975	1.00	5.00
Atlantic SD-19149	(S)	Blue Lights In The Basement	1978	1.00	5.00
Atlantic SD-19186	(S)	Roberta Flack	1978	1.00	5.00
Atlantic SD-7004	(S)	Live & More *(2 LPs)*	1980	1.00	5.00
MCA 5141	(S)	Bustin' Loose	1981	1.00	5.00
Atlantic SD-19354	(S)	I'm The One	1982	1.00	5.00

FLACK, ROBERTA, & DONNY HATHAWAY

Label & Catalog #		Title	Year	VG+	NM
Atlantic SD-7216	(S)	Roberta Flack & Donny Hathaway	1972	3.20	8.00
		—Atlantic albums above have green & orange labels with "1841 Broadway" on the bottom.—			
Atlantic SD-16013	(S)	Roberta Flack Featuring Donny Hathaway	1980	1.00	5.00

FLAIRS, THE

Label & Catalog #		Title	Year	VG+	NM
Crown CLP-5356	(M)	The Flairs	1963	24.00	60.00
Crown CST-356	(E)	The Flairs	1963	12.00	30.00
		—Crown albums above have gray labels.—			

FLAME, THE
Features Blondie Chaplin And Rickie Fataar, later of The Beach Boys.

Label & Catalog #		Title	Year	VG+	NM
Brother BR-2500	(S)	Flame *(With poster)*	1970	10.00	25.00
		(Brother 2500 was recorded in compatible stereo/quadraphonic.)			

FLAMIN' GROOVIES, THE

Label & Catalog #		Title	Year	VG+	NM
Snazz R-2371	(S)	Sneekers *(10" album. Counterfeits exist)*	1969	30.00	75.00
Epic BN-26487	(S)	Supersnazz	1969	20.00	50.00
Kama Sutra KSBS-2021	(S)	Flamingo *(Gatefold cover)*	1970	12.00	30.00
Kama Sutra KSBS-2031	(S)	Teenage Head	1971	12.00	30.00
		—Kama Sutra albums above have pink labels.—			
Kama Sutra KSBS-2021	(S)	Flamingo	1972	6.00	15.00
Kama Sutra KSBS-2031	(S)	Teenage Head	1972	6.00	15.00
		—Kama Sutra albums above have blue labels.—			
Sire SASD-7521	(S)	Shake Some Action	1976	6.00	15.00
Buddah BDS-5683	(S)	Still Shakin'	1977	6.00	15.00
Sire SRK-6059	(S)	The Flamin' Groovies Now *(12 tracks)*	1978	6.00	15.00
Sire SRK-6059	(S)	The Flamin' Groovies Now *(14 tracks)*	1978	4.00	10.00
Sire SRK-6067	(S)	Jumpin' In The Night	1979	4.00	10.00

FLAMING EMBER

Label & Catalog #		Title	Year	VG+	NM
Hot Wax HA-702	(S)	Westbound #9	1970	6.00	15.00
Hot Wax HA-705	(S)	Sunshine	1970	5.00	12.00

FLAMING YOUTH
Flaming Youth features Phil Collins.

Label & Catalog #		Title	Year	VG+	NM
Uni 73075	(S)	Ark 2	1969	12.00	30.00

Label & Catalog #		Title	Year	VG+	NM

FLAMINGOS, THE

Checker LP-1433	(M)	The Flamingos	1959	250.00	500.00
		—Checker albums above have black labels.—			
Checker LP-1433	(M)	The Flamingos	1965	60.00	150.00
Checker LPS-1433	(E)	The Flamingos	1965	30.00	75.00
Checker LPS-3005	(E)	The Flamingos	196?	10.00	25.00
		(Chess 3005 is a reissue of 1433.)			
		—Checker albums above have blue labels.—			
End LP-304	(M)	Flamingo Serenade	1959	80.00	200.00
End LPS-304	(S)	Flamingo Serenade	1959	200.00	400.00
		(Original covers correctly list the record as Stereo. "But Not For Me" is rechanneled on this and all subsequent pressings.)			
End STLP-304	(S)	Flamingo Serenade	196?	80.00	200.00
		(Later covers incorrectly read Rechanneled Stereo.)			
End LP-307	(M)	Flamingo Favorites	1960	40.00	100.00
End LPS-307	(E)	Flamingo Favorites	1960	30.00	75.00
End LP-308	(M)	Requestfully Yours	1960	40.00	100.00
End LPS-308	(E)	Requestfully Yours	1960	30.00	75.00
End LP-316	(M)	The Sound Of The Flamingos	1962	40.00	100.00
End LPS-316	(S)	The Sound Of The Flamingos	1962	100.00	250.00
		(Stereo copies read "Stereo" in the upper right corner of the cover.)			
End LPS-316	(E)	The Sound Of The Flamingos	1962	30.00	75.00
Constellation CS-3	(M)	Collectors Showcase: The Flamingos	1964	40.00	100.00
		(First pressings have "hot flamingo" pink lettering on the cover.)			
Constellation CS-3	(M)	Collectors Showcase: The Flamingos	1964	20.00	50.00
		(Second pressings have cooler, dark pink lettering on the cover.)			
Philips PHM-200-206	(M)	Their Hits-Then And Now	1966	10.00	25.00
Philips PHS-600-206	(S)	Their Hits-Then And Now	1966	14.00	35.00
Ronze RLP-1001	(S)	The Flamingos Today	1972	6.00	15.00
Chess 702	(M)	The Flamingos	1975	4.00	10.00
Lost Nite LLP-7	(M)	The Flamingos (10" LP on red vinyl)	1981	4.00	10.00
Solid Smoke 8018	(M)	Golden Teardrops	1984	1.00	5.00
Roulette SR-59018	(S)	Serenade	1984	1.00	5.00

FLAMINGOS, THE / THE MOONGLOWS

Vee Jay LP-1052	(M)	The Flamingos Meet The Moonglows	1962	60.00	150.00

FLANDERS, TOMMY

Flanders was a member of The Blues Project.

Verve/Forecast FTS-3075	(S)	Moonstone	1970	8.00	20.00

FLARES, THE

Press PR-73001	(M)	Encore Of Foot Stompin' Hits	1965	30.00	75.00
Press PRS-83001	(S)	Encore Of Foot Stompin' Hits	1965	50.00	125.00

FLEETWOOD MAC

Over the years Mick Fleetwood and John McVie have hosted a continually changing roster of members including Peter Green, Jeremy Spencer, Christine McVie, Bob Welch, Lindsey Buckingham and Stevie Nicks. Refer to Buckingham-Nicks; John Mayall.

Epic LN-24402	(M)	Fleetwood Mac (White label promo)	1968	40.00	100.00
Epic BN-26402	(S)	Fleetwood Mac	1968	12.00	30.00
Epic LN-24446	(M)	English Rose (White label promo)	1969	40.00	100.00
Epic BN-26446	(S)	English Rose	1969	12.00	30.00
Epic KE-30632	(S)	Black Magic Woman (2 LPs)	1971	6.00	15.00
		(Epic 30632 repackages 26402 and 26445.)			
		—Epic albums above have yellow labels.—			
Epic KE-33740	(S)	Fleetwood Mac / English Rose (2 LPs)	1974	4.00	10.00
		—Epic albums above have orange labels.—			
Blue Horizon BH-3801	(S)	Fleetwood Mac In Chicago (2 LPS)	1970	12.00	30.00
		(BH-3801 is a jam taped in 1969 with several Chicago blues artists. It was also issued as two separate albums, below)			
Blue Horizon BH-4802	(S)	Blues Jam In Chicago, Volume 1	1970	6.00	15.00
Blue Horizon BH-4803	(S)	Blues Jam In Chicago, Volume 2	1970	6.00	15.00
Sire SASH-3706	(S)	Vintage Years (2 LPs)	1975	6.00	15.00
Sire SASH-3715	(S)	Fleetwood Mac In Chicago (2 LPs)	1975	6.00	15.00
		(Sire 3716 is a reissue of Blue Horizon 3801.)			
Sire 2XS-6006	(S)	Vintage Years (2 LPs)	1977	4.00	10.00
Sire 2XS-6009	(S)	Fleetwood Mac In Chicago (2 LPs)	1977	4.00	10.00
Sire 2XS-6045	(S)	The Original Fleetwood Mac (2 LPs)	1977	4.00	10.00
Reprise RS-6368	(S)	Then Play On	1969	8.00	20.00
		(Original pressings of 6368 have "When You Say" and "My Dream.")			
Reprise RS-6368	(S)	Then Play On (With "O Well")	1970	6.00	15.00
Reprise RS-6408	(S)	Kiln House	1970	6.00	15.00
Reprise RS-6465	(S)	Future Games (Yellow cover)	1971	10.00	25.00
Reprise RS-6465	(S)	Future Games (Green cover)	1972	6.00	15.00
Reprise MS-2080	(S)	Bare Trees	1972	6.00	15.00
Reprise MS-2138	(S)	Penguin	1973	6.00	15.00
Reprise MS-2158	(S)	Mystery To Me	1973	8.00	20.00
		(Original pressings have "Good Things Come To Those Who Wait.")			

Label & Catalog #		Title	Year	VG+	NM
Reprise MS-2158	(S)	Mystery To Me (With "For Your Love")	1973	5.00	12.00
Reprise MS-2196	(S)	Heroes Are Hard To Find	1974	5.00	12.00
		—Reprise albums above have brown labels.—			
Reprise MS-2225	(S)	Fleetwood Mac	1975	.80	4.00
Reprise MSK-2278	(S)	Bare Trees	1977	.80	4.00
Reprise MSK-2279	(S)	Mystery To Me	1977	.80	4.00
Reprise MSK-2281	(S)	Fleetwood Mac	1977	.80	4.00
Warner Bros. PRO-652	(S)	Rumours (Embossed promo cover)	1977	20.00	50.00
Warner Bros. BSK-3010	(S)	Rumours	1977	.80	4.00
Warner Bros. 2HS-3350	(S)	Tusk (2 LPs)	1979	6.00	15.00
Warner Bros. PRO-866	(S)	Tusk Remix (Promo)	1979	6.00	15.00
Warner Bros. PRO-???	(S)	The Fleetwood Mac Story (Promo. 2 LPs)	1979	20.00	50.00
Warner Bros. 2WB-3500	(S)	Fleetwood Mac Live (2 LPs)	1980	1.00	5.00
Warner Bros. 23607	(S)	Mirage (Qutex II vinyl promo)	1982	6.00	15.00
Warner Bros. 23607	(S)	Mirage	1982	.80	4.00

FLEETWOODS, THE

Dolton BLP-2001	(M)	Mr. Blue	1959	30.00	75.00
Dolton BST-8001	(S)	Mr. Blue ("Mr. Blue" is rechanneled)	1959	40.00	100.00
Dolton BLP-2002	(M)	The Fleetwoods	1960	20.00	50.00
Dolton BST-8002	(S)	The Fleetwoods	1960	30.00	75.00
Dolton BLP-2005	(M)	Softly	1961	20.00	50.00
Dolton BST-8005	(S)	Softly ("Come Softly To Me" is rechanneled)	1961	30.00	75.00
Dolton BLP-2007	(M)	Deep In A Dream	1961	16.00	40.00
Dolton BST-8007	(S)	Deep In A Dream	1961	20.00	50.00
Dolton BLP-2011	(M)	The Best Of The Oldies	1962	16.00	40.00
Dolton BST-8011	(S)	The Best Of The Oldies	1962	20.00	50.00
		—Dolton albums above have light blue labels with the fish logo above the spindle hole.—			
Dolton BLP-2001	(M)	Mr. Blue	1962	8.00	20.00
Dolton BST-8001	(S)	Mr. Blue ("Mr. Blue" is rechanneled)	1962	10.00	25.00
Dolton BLP-2002	(M)	The Fleetwoods	1962	8.00	20.00
Dolton BST-8002	(S)	The Fleetwoods	1962	10.00	25.00
Dolton BLP-2005	(M)	Softly	1962	8.00	20.00
Dolton BST-8005	(S)	Softly ("Come Softly To Me" is rechanneled)	1962	10.00	25.00
Dolton BLP-2007	(M)	Deep In A Dream	1962	8.00	20.00
Dolton BST-8007	(S)	Deep In A Dream	1962	10.00	25.00
Dolton BLP-2011	(M)	The Best Of The Oldies	1962	8.00	20.00
Dolton BST-8011	(S)	The Best Of The Oldies	1962	10.00	25.00
Dolton BLP-2018	(M)	The Fleetwoods' Greatest Hits	1962	10.00	25.00
Dolton BST-8018	(P)	The Fleetwoods' Greatest Hits	1962	12.00	30.00
Dolton BLP-2025	(M)	Goodnight My Love	1963	12.00	30.00
Dolton BST-8025	(S)	Goodnight My Love	1963	16.00	40.00
Dolton BLP-2020	(M)	The Fleetwoods Sing For Lovers By Night	1963	12.00	30.00
Dolton BST-8020	(S)	The Fleetwoods Sing For Lovers By Night	1963	16.00	40.00
Dolton BLP-2030	(M)	Before And After	1965	12.00	30.00
Dolton BST-8030	(S)	Before And After	1965	16.00	40.00
Dolton BLP-2039	(M)	Folk Rock	1965	12.00	30.00
Dolton BST-8039	(S)	Folk Rock	1965	16.00	40.00
		—Dolton albums above have dark blue labels with a color logo on the left side.—			
Sunset SUM-5131	(M)	In A Mellow Mood	1966	5.00	12.00
Sunset SUS-1131	(S)	In A Mellow Mood	1966	6.00	15.00
United Arts. LA334E	(S)	The Very Best Of The Fleetwoods	1975	4.00	10.00
		("Come Softly To Me" is in stereo on this album.)			
Liberty LN-10159	(S)	The Fleetwoods' Greatest Hits	1982	.80	4.00
Liberty LN-10160	(S)	The Best Goodies Of The Oldies	1982	.80	4.00
Liberty LN-10199	(S)	Buried Treasure	1983	.80	4.00

FLEMONS, WADE

Vee Jay LP-1011	(M)	Wade Flemons	1959	60.00	150.00
		—Vee Jay albums above have maroon labels.—			
Vee Jay LP-1011	(M)	Wade Flemons	196?	30.00	75.00
		—Vee Jay albums above have black rainbow labels.—			

FLINT

Flint features Don Brewer, Mel Schacher and Craig Frost, formerly of Grand Funk.

Columbia JC-35574	(S)	Flint	1978	4.00	10.00

FLIRTATIONS, THE

Deram DES-18028	(S)	Nothing But A Heartache	1969	8.00	20.00

FLO & EDDIE

Flo & Eddie are Mark Volman and Howard Kaylan, formerly of The Turtles. Refer to Barry Mann; Frank Zappa.

Reprise MS-2099	(S)	The Phlorescent Leech And Eddie	1972	8.00	20.00
Reprise MS-2141	(S)	Flo And Eddie	1973	8.00	20.00
Columbia PC-33554	(S)	Illegal, Immoral And Fattening	1975	5.00	12.00
Columbia PC-34262	(S)	Moving Targets	1976	5.00	12.00
Epiphany ELP-4010	(S)	Rock Steady With Flo & Eddie	1981	4.00	10.00
Rhino RNTA-1998	(S)	The History Of Flo & Eddie (3 LP box)	1973	4.00	10.00

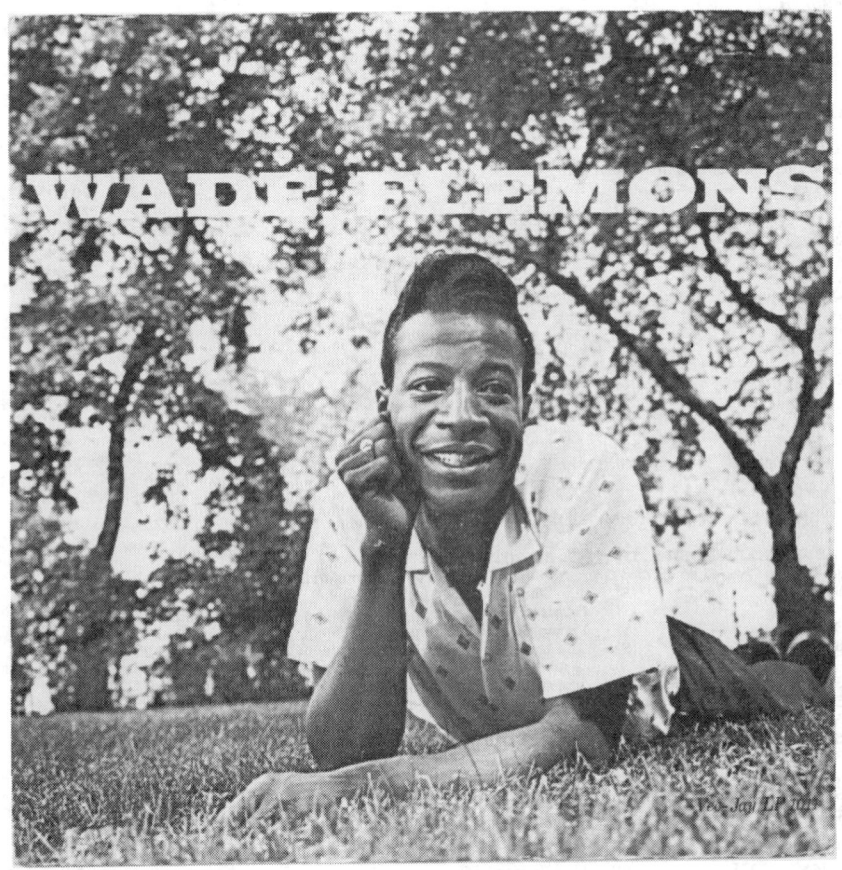

As a solo artist for Vee Jay, Wade Flemons placed three modest hits on the pop charts in 1959-60. The label issued one LP, which did not sell particularly well. For most observers, it would have appeared that Mr Flemons' career had come to an end. But he resurfaced in 1969 as one of the founding members of Earth, Wind & Fire, a group that burned up the charts through the '70s.

Label & Catalog #		Title	Year	VG+	NM
FLOATING BRIDGE, THE					
Vault VS-124	(S)	The Floating Bridge	1969	12.00	30.00
FLOATING HOUSE BAND, THE					
Takoma 1029	(S)	The Floating House Band	1969	6.00	15.00
FLOATING OPERA, THE					
Embryo 730	(S)	The Floating Opera	1971	6.00	15.00
FLOCK, THE					
Columbia CS-9911	(S)	The Flock	1969	8.00	20.00
Columbia C-30007	(S)	Dinosaur Swamps	1970	8.00	20.00
		— Columbia albums above have "360 Sound" labels.—			
Mercury SRM-1-1035	(S)	Inside Out	1975	4.00	10.00
FLOW					
CTI 1003	(S)	Flow	1970	10.00	25.00
FLOWERS, PHIL					
Guest Star G-1456	(M)	I Am The Greatest	196?	14.00	35.00
Guest Star GS-1456	(S)	I Am The Greatest	196?	20.00	50.00
Guest Star G-1457	(M)	Phil Flowers Sings A Tribute	196?	14.00	35.00
Guest Star GS-1457	(S)	Phil Flowers Sings A Tribute	196?	20.00	50.00
Mt. Vernon 154	(M)	Rhythm 'N' Blues	196?	10.00	25.00
Dot DLP-25849	(S)	Our Man In Washington	1968	6.00	15.00
FLOYD, EDDIE					
Eddie Floyd was formerly with The Falcons.					
Stax ST-714	(M)	Knock On Wood	1967	20.00	50.00
Stax STS-714	(S)	Knock On Wood	1967	20.00	50.00
Stax STS-2002	(S)	I've Never Found A Girl	1968	12.00	30.00
Stax STS-2011	(S)	Rare Stamps	1969	10.00	25.00
		("Big Bird" and "Things Get Better" are rechanneled.)			
Stax STS-2017	(S)	You've Got To Have Eddie	1969	10.00	25.00
Stax STS-2029	(S)	California Girl	1970	10.00	25.00
Stax ST-2041	(M)	Down To Earth *(White label promo)*	1971	12.00	30.00
Stax STS-2041	(S)	Down To Earth	1971	10.00	25.00
Stax STS-3016	(S)	Baby Lay Your Head Down	1973	10.00	25.00
Stax STS-5512	(S)	Soul Street	1974	10.00	25.00
Stax STS-4122	(S)	Chronicle	1979	4.00	10.00
Malaco 6352	(S)	Experience	1977	4.00	10.00
FLUDD					
Warner Bros. B-2578	(S)	Fludd	1972	4.00	10.00
FLUFF					
Roulette SR-3011	(S)	Fluff	1972	4.00	10.00
FLYING BURRITO BROTHERS, THE [THE BURRITO BROTHERS]					
The FBB feature Chris Hillman and Gram Parsons among a cast of thousands.					
A&M SP-4175	(S)	The Gilded Palace Of Sin	1969	8.00	20.00
A&M SP-4258	(S)	Burrito Deluxe	1970	6.00	15.00
A&M SP-4295	(S)	Flying Burrito Brothers	1971	4.00	10.00
A&M SP-4343	(S)	The Last Of The Red Hot Burritos	1972	4.00	10.00
		—A&M albums above have brown labels.—			
A&M SP-4175	(S)	The Gilded Palace Of Sin	197?	1.00	5.00
A&M SP-4258	(S)	Burrito Deluxe	197?	1.00	5.00
A&M SP-4295	(S)	Flying Burrito Brothers	197?	1.00	5.00
A&M SP-4343	(S)	The Last Of The Red Hot Burritos	197?	1.00	5.00
A&M SP-3631	(S)	Close Up The Honky-Tonks *(2 LPs)*	1974	1.20	6.00
A&M SP-8070	(DJ)	Hot Burrito *(Sampler)*	1975	12.00	30.00
A&M SP-4578	(S)	Sleepless Nights	1976	1.00	5.00
Columbia PC-33817	(S)	Flying Again	1975	1.00	5.00
Columbia PC-34222	(S)	Airborne	1976	1.00	5.00
Regency REG-79001	(S)	Live From Tokyo	1980	1.00	5.00
Ariola 86439	(S)	Live In Amsterdam	198?	1.00	5.00
FLYING CIRCUS, THE					
Capitol ST-11147	(S)	The Flying Circus	1973	4.00	10.00
Capitol ST-11240	(S)	Last Laugh	1974	4.00	10.00
FLYING MACHINE, THE: *Refer to* JAMES TAYLOR					
FLYING MACHINE, THE					
Janus JLS-3007	(P)	The Flying Machine	1969	5.00	12.00
FOCUS					
Polydor 2442-118	(S)	Focus At The Rainbow	1973	10.00	25.00
		(Polydor 2442-119 has a US disc housed in a UK jacket.)			

Label & Catalog #		Title	Year	VG+	NM

FOGELBERG, DAN
Dan Fogelberg is a contemporary singer-songwriter with a folkie/pop bent.

Label & Catalog #		Title	Year	VG+	NM
Full Moon PE-33137	(S)	Souvenirs	1974	.80	4.00
Full Moon PE-33499	(S)	Captured Angel *(2 LPs)*	1975	1.20	6.00
Full Moon PEQ-33499	(Q)	Captured Angel *(2 LPs)*	1975	8.00	20.00
Full Moon PE-34185	(S)	Nether Lands	1975	.80	4.00
Full Moon PE-35634	(S)	Phoenix	1979	.80	4.00
Full Moon HE-45634	(S)	Phoenix *(Half-speed master)*	1982	5.00	15.00
Full Moon PE-37393	(S)	The Innocent Age *(2 LPs)*	1981	.80	4.00
Full Moon PE-38308	(S)	Greatest Hits	1982	.80	4.00
Full Moon HE-48308	(S)	Greatest Hits *(Half-speed master)*	1982	5.00	15.00
Full Moon A2S-1335	(DJ)	Interchords *(2 LPs)*	1982	10.00	25.00
Full Moon PE-39004	(S)	Windows And Walls	1984	.80	4.00

FOGELBERG, DAN, & TIM WEISBURG

Label & Catalog #		Title	Year	VG+	NM
Full Moon PE-35339	(S)	Twin Sons Of Different Mothers	1978	.80	4.00
Full Moon HE-45339	(S)	Twin Sons Of Different Mothers *(Half-speed)*	1982	5.00	15.00

FOGERTY, JOHN
Refer to The Blue Ridge Rangers; Creedence Clearwater; The Golliwogs.

Label & Catalog #		Title	Year	VG+	NM
Asylum 7E-1046	(S)	John Fogerty	1975	1.00	5.00
Warner Bros. 25203	(S)	Centerfield *(Quiex II vinyl promo)*	1985	8.00	20.00
Warner Bros. 25203	(S)	Centerfield *(With "Zanz Kant Danz")*	1985	1.00	5.00
Warner Bros. 25203	(S)	Centerfield	1985	.80	4.00

FOGERTY, TOM
Refer to Creedence Clearwater; The Golliwogs; Ruby; Merl Saunders & Jerry Garcia & Tom Fogerty.

Label & Catalog #		Title	Year	VG+	NM
Fantasy F-9407	(S)	Tom Fogerty	1972	6.00	15.00
Fantasy F-9413	(S)	Excalibur	1972	6.00	15.00
Fantasy F-9448	(S)	Zephyr National	1974	5.00	12.00
Fantasy F-9469	(S)	Myopia	1974	5.00	12.00
Fantasy F-9611	(S)	Deal It Out	1981	4.00	10.00

FOGHAT

Label & Catalog #		Title	Year	VG+	NM
Bearsville 2077	(S)	Foghat	1972	1.20	6.00
Bearsville 2136	(S)	Foghat	1973	1.00	5.00
Bearsville BRK-6950	(S)	Energized	1974	1.00	5.00
Bearsville BRK-6956	(S)	Rock And Roll Outlaws	1974	1.00	5.00
Bearsville BRK-6959	(S)	A Fool For The City	1974	1.00	5.00
Bearsville BRK-6962	(S)	Night Shift	1976	1.00	5.00
Bearsville BRK-6971	(S)	Foghat Live	1977	1.00	5.00
Bearsville BRK-6977	(S)	Stone Blue	1978	1.00	5.00
Bearsville BRK-6990	(S)	Boogie Motel	1979	1.00	5.00
Bearsville BRK-6999	(S)	Tight Shoes	1980	1.00	5.00
Bearsville 3578	(S)	Girls To Chat & Boys To Bounce	1980	.80	4.00
Bearsville 23747	(S)	In The Mood For Something Rude	1982	.80	4.00
Bearsville 23888	(S)	Zig-Zag Walk	1983	.80	4.00

FOLKSWINGERS, THE

Label & Catalog #		Title	Year	VG+	NM
World Pacific WP-1812	(M)	12 String Guitar	1963	10.00	25.00
World Pacific ST-1812	(S)	12 String Guitar *(Red vinyl)*	1963	24.00	60.00
World Pacific ST-1812	(S)	12 String Guitar	1963	12.00	30.00
World Pacific WP-1814	(M)	12 String Guitar, Volume 2	1963	10.00	25.00
World Pacific ST-1814	(S)	12 String Guitar, Volume 2	1963	12.00	30.00
World Pacific WP-1846	(M)	Raga Rock	1966	10.00	25.00
World Pacific ST-1846	(S)	Raga Rock	1966	12.00	30.00

FONTANA, WAYNE, & THE MINDBENDERS
Refer to The Mindbenders.

Label & Catalog #		Title	Year	VG+	NM
Fontana MGF-27542	(M)	The Game Of Love	1965	12.00	30.00
Fontana SRF-67542	(E)	The Game Of Love	1965	10.00	25.00

FONTANA, WAYNE

Label & Catalog #		Title	Year	VG+	NM
MGM E-4459	(M)	Wayne Fontana	1967	8.00	20.00
MGM SE-4459	(S)	Wayne Fontana	1967	10.00	25.00

FOOD

Label & Catalog #		Title	Year	VG+	NM
Capitol ST-304	(S)	Forever Is A Dream	1969	30.00	75.00

FOOL, THE

Label & Catalog #		Title	Year	VG+	NM
Mercury SR-61178	(S)	The Fool	1968	8.00	20.00

FORD, FRANKIE

Label & Catalog #		Title	Year	VG+	NM
Ace LP-1005	(M)	Let's Take A Sea Cruise	1959	150.00	300.00
Briarmede BR-5002	(S)	Frankie Ford	197?	4.00	10.00

FORD, NEAL, & THE FANATICS

Label & Catalog #		Title	Year	VG+	NM
Hickory LPS-141	(S)	Neal Ford & The Fanatics	1968	10.00	25.00

Label & Catalog #		Title	Year	VG+	NM
FORD THEATRE, THE					
ABC S-658	(S)	Trilogy For The Masses	1968	6.00	15.00
ABC S-681	(S)	Time Changes	1969	6.00	15.00
FOREIGNER					
Atlantic SD-18215	(S)	Foreigner	1977	1.00	5.00
Atlantic SD-19999	(S)	Double Vision	1978	1.00	5.00
Atlantic SD-129999	(S)	Head Games	1979	1.00	5.00
Atlantic SD-116999	(S)	Foreigner 4	1981	1.00	5.00
Atlantic SD-180999	(S)	Foreigner Records	1982	1.00	5.00
Atlantic SD-81999	(S)	Agent Provocateur	1985	1.00	5.00
FOREST					
Harvest SKAO-419	(S)	Forest	1970	20.00	50.00
FOREVERMORE					
RCA Victor LSP-4272	(S)	Yours Forever More	1969	5.00	12.00
RCA Victor LSP-4425	(S)	Words On Black Plastic	1970	4.00	10.00
FORMULA V					
Burlinguen	(S)	Formula V	197?	10.00	25.00
Miami 6076	(S)	Volume IV	197?	10.00	25.00
20th Cent.-Fox 630	(S)	Phase 1	1977	4.00	10.00
FORT MUDGE MEMORIAL DUMP					
Mercury SR-61256	(S)	Fort Mudge Memorial Dump	1970	12.00	30.00
FORTUNE, JOHNNY					
Park Avenue P-1301	(M)	Soul Surfer	1963	50.00	125.00
Park Avenue PS-401	(S)	Soul Surfer	1963	80.00	200.00
FORTUNES, THE					
Press PR7-3002	(M)	The Fortunes	1965	14.00	35.00
Press PRS-83002	(S)	The Fortunes	1965	20.00	50.00
Coca-Cola (No number)	(DJ)	It's The Real Thing	1969	24.00	60.00
World Pacific WPS-21904	(S)	That Same Old Feeling	1970	6.00	15.00
Capitol ST-647	(S)	Freedom	1971	6.00	15.00
Capitol ST-809	(S)	Here Comes That Rainy Day Feeling Again	1971	8.00	20.00
FORUM, THE					
Mira MLP-301	(M)	The River Is Wide	1967	6.00	15.00
Mira MLPS-301	(S)	The River Is Wide	1967	8.00	20.00
		("The River Is Wide" is rechanneled)			
FORUM QUORUM, THE					
Decca DL-75030	(S)	The Forum Quorum	1968	8.00	20.00
FOTHERINGAY					
Fotheringay featured Sandy Denny, Trevor Lucas and Jerry Donahue. Refer to Fairport Convention.					
A&M SP-4289	(S)	Fotheringay	1970	10.00	25.00
FOUNDATIONS, THE					
Uni 73016	(S)	Baby, Now That I've Found You	1968	12.00	30.00
		("Baby, Now That I've Found You" is rechanneled.)			
Uni 73043	(S)	Build Me Up Buttercup	1969	12.00	30.00
		(Side 1 is in stereo; side 2 is rechanneled.)			
Uni 73058	(S)	Digging The Foundations	1969	12.00	30.00
FOUR JACKS & A JILL					
RCA Victor LSP-4019	(S)	Master Jack	1968	6.00	15.00
RCA Victor LSP-4103	(S)	Fables	1968	6.00	15.00
FOUR LOVERS, THE					
The Lovers were Frankie Valli with Hank Majewski and brothers Nick and Tommy DeVito. Frankie and Tommy later formed the nucleus of The Four Seasons.					
RCA Victor LPM-1317	(M)	Joyride	1956	400.00	750.00
FOUR SEASONS, THE [FRANKIE VALLI & THE FOUR SEASONS]					
Original members were Frankie Valli and Tommy DeVito with Nick Massi and Bob Gaudio. As a songwriter, Gaudio teamed with producer Bob Crewe for many of the group's hits. Massi left in '65, replaced by Joe Long. DeVito retired in 1971, replaced by Demetri Callas. Refer to The Beatles; Bob Crewe; The Four Lovers; Frankie Valli.					
Vee Jay LP-1053	(M)	Sherry And 11 Others	1962	12.00	30.00
Vee Jay SR-1053	(P)	Sherry And 11 Others	1962	16.00	40.00
Vee Jay LP-1055	(M)	Four Seasons' Greetings	1963	12.00	30.00
Vee Jay SR-1055	(S)	Four Seasons' Greetings	1963	16.00	40.00
Vee Jay LP-1056	(M)	Big Girls Don't Cry	1963	12.00	30.00
Vee Jay SR-1056	(P)	Big Girls Don't Cry	1963	16.00	40.00
Vee Jay LP-1059	(M)	Ain't That A Shame	1963	10.00	25.00
Vee Jay SR-1059	(P)	Ain't That A Shame	1963	16.00	40.00

Under the leadership of Glen Dale and Barry Pritchard, The Fortunes were a brief part of the British Invasion with their distinctive 1965 hit "You've Got Your Troubles." This was followed later the same year by the not quite as big "Here It Comes Again." Both of these Top 40 hits were included on their first album, which did not help the eponymous debut to dent the charts in a significant manner. The mono version pictured here and the much rarer stereo pressing are more difficult to find than their assigned values indicate but, except for chart-single collectors, the group has not weathered the years well with finicky LP buyers.

Label & Catalog #		Title	Year	VG+	NM
Vee Jay LP-1065	(M)	Golden Hits Of The Four Seasons	1963	14.00	35.00
Vee Jay SR-1065	(P)	Golden Hits Of The Four Seasons	1963	20.00	50.00
Vee Jay LP-1082	(M)	Folk-Nanny	1963	10.00	25.00
Vee Jay SR-1082	(S)	Folk-Nanny	1963	16.00	40.00
		("Connie-O," "Soon," "Silver Wings." "Star Maker" are rechanneled.)			
Vee Jay LP-1082	(M)	Stay & Other Great Hits	1964	8.00	20.00
Vee Jay SR-1082	(S)	Stay & Other Great Hits	1964	12.00	30.00
		("Stay" is a repackage of "Folk-Nanny.")			
Vee Jay LP-1088	(M)	More Golden Hits By The Four Seasons	1964	12.00	30.00
Vee Jay SR-1088	(P)	More Golden Hits By The Four Seasons	1964	16.00	40.00
		(First pressings include "Long Lonely Nights.")			
Vee Jay LP-1088	(M)	More Golden Hits By The Four Seasons	1965	6.00	15.00
Vee Jay SR-1088	(P)	More Golden Hits By The Four Seasons	1965	8.00	20.00
		(Later pressings replace "Nights" with "Apple Of My Eye.")			
Vee Jay LP-1121	(M)	We Love Girls	1965	12.00	30.00
Vee Jay LP-1121	(S)	We Love Girls	1965	16.00	40.00
Vee Jay LP-1154	(M)	Recorded Live On Stage	1965	12.00	30.00
Vee Jay SR-1154	(S)	Recorded Live On Stage	1965	16.00	40.00
Coca-Cola TX-94	(DJ)	The Four Seasons Swing The Jingle	1964	100.00	250.00
		(Both sides contain identical 90, 60, 60, 30 and 10 second spots.)			
Philips PHM-200-124	(M)	Dawn (Go Away) & 11 Other Great Songs	1964	8.00	20.00
Philips PHS-600-124	(S)	Dawn (Go Away) & 11 Other Great Songs	1964	10.00	25.00
Philips PHM-200-129	(M)	Born To Wander	1964	8.00	20.00
Philips PHS-600-129	(S)	Born To Wander	1964	10.00	25.00
Philips PHM-200-146	(M)	Rag Doll	1964	8.00	20.00
Philips PHS-600-146	(P)	Rag Doll	1964	10.00	25.00
Philips PHM-200-146	(M)	Rag Doll	1964	8.00	20.00
Philips PHS-600-146	(P)	Rag Doll	1964	10.00	25.00
		(Second pressings of Philips 146 have a yellow seal noting "Save It For Me" on the cover. "Rag Doll" is in mono on this album.)			
Philips PHM-200-164	(M)	The Four Seasons Entertain You	1965	8.00	20.00
Philips PHS-600-164	(S)	The Four Seasons Entertain You	1965	10.00	25.00
		(The cover has an orange seal noting "Bye Bye Baby.")			
Philips PHM-200-164	(M)	The Four Seasons Entertain You	1965	8.00	20.00
Philips PHS-600-164	(S)	The Four Seasons Entertain You	1965	10.00	25.00
		(Cover has an orange seal noting "Bye Bye Baby" and "Toy Soldier.")			
Philips PHM-200-164	(M)	The Four Seasons Entertain You	1965	6.00	15.00
Philips PHS-600-164	(S)	The Four Seasons Entertain You	1965	8.00	20.00
		(The cover has a blue seal noting "Bye Bye Baby" and "Toy Soldier.")			
Philips PHM-200-193	(M)	Big Hits By Bacharach, David & Dylan	1965	8.00	20.00
Philips PHS-600-193	(S)	Big Hits By Bacharach, David & Dylan	1965	10.00	25.00
		(The cover has a medieval motif.)			
Philips PHM-200-193	(M)	Big Hits By Bacharach, David & Dylan	1965	12.00	30.00
Philips PHS-600-193	(S)	Big Hits By Bacharach, David & Dylan	1965	16.00	40.00
		(The cover features photos of the group.)			
Philips PHM-200-196	(M)	Gold Vault Of Hits	1965	8.00	20.00
Philips PHS-600-196	(S)	Gold Vault Of Hits	1965	10.00	25.00
		(The title on the cover is in unadorned red print; the group photo on the back cover features Charlie Calello.)			
Philips PHM-200-196	(M)	Gold Vault Of Hits	1965	6.00	15.00
Philips PHS-600-196	(S)	Gold Vault Of Hits	1965	8.00	20.00
		(The title on the cover is in red print outlined in black; the group photo on the back cover features Charlie Calello.)			
Philips PHM-200-196	(M)	Gold Vault Of Hits	196?	5.00	12.00
Philips PHS-600-196	(S)	Gold Vault Of Hits	196?	6.00	15.00
		(Later pressings the title is red with black trim or solid black; the group photo on the back cover features Joe Long.)			
Philips PHM-200-201	(M)	Working My Way Back To You	1966	8.00	20.00
Philips PHS-600-201	(S)	Working My Way Back To You	1966	10.00	25.00
Philips PHM-200-221	(M)	2nd Gold Vault Of Hits	1966	6.00	15.00
Philips PHS-600-221	(S)	2nd Gold Vault Of Hits	1966	8.00	20.00
Philips PHM-200-222	(M)	Lookin' Back	1966	8.00	20.00
Philips PHS-600-222	(S)	Lookin' Back	1966	10.00	25.00
Philips PHM-200-223	(M)	The Four Seasons' Christmas Album	1966	10.00	25.00
Philips PHS-600-223	(S)	The Four Seasons' Christmas Album	1966	12.00	30.00
Philips PHM-200-243	(M)	New Gold Hits	1967	6.00	15.00
Philips PHS-600-243	(S)	New Gold Hits	1967	8.00	20.00
Philips PHS-2-6501	(P)	Edizone D'Oro (2 LPs)	1969	10.00	25.00
		(The "4" on the cover is in unadorned red on a gold foil. "Rag Doll" is in stereo on all pressings of this album.)			
Philips PHS-2-6501	(P)	Edizone D'Oro (2 LPs)	1969	12.00	30.00
		(The "4" on the cover is in white or red with black trim on gold foil.)			
Philips PHS-2-6501	(P)	Edizone D'Oro (2 LPs)	1969	10.00	25.00
		(The "4" on the cover is in white print on a gold board.)			
Philips PHS-600-290	(S)	Genuine Imitation Life Gazette	1969	10.00	25.00
		(Original covers are yellow newspaper.)			
Philips PHS-600-290	(S)	Genuine Imitation Life Gazette	1969	5.00	12.00
		(Later covers are white newspaper.)			
Philips PHS-600341	(S)	Half And Half	1970	6.00	15.00

Frankie Valli, Hank Majewski and brothers Nick and Tommy DeVito scored one hit, "The Apple Of My Eye," for RCA Victor in 1956 as The Four Lovers. The group kept plugging along through their career, making the necessary changes in style, songs and personnel until they resurfaced in 1962 on the basically rhythm 'n blues Vee Jay label as. . . The Four Seasons!

Label & Catalog #		Title	Year	VG+	NM
Sears SPS-609	(S)	Brotherhood Of Man	1970	10.00	25.00
Pickwick SPC-3223	(S)	Brotherhood Of Man	1970	4.00	10.00
		(Pickwick 3223 is a reissue of Sears 609.)			
Longines Sym. 95833	(P)	The Greatest Hits Of Frankie Valli			
		& The Four Seasons (4 LPs)	197?	10.00	25.00
		(The cover reads "As seen on TV.")			
Longines Sym. 95833	(P)	The Greatest Hits Of Frankie Valli			
		& The Four Seasons (4 LPs)	197?	8.00	20.00
		(The cover reads "As seen on TV." and "4 Record Collection.")			
Longines Sym. 95833	(P)	The Greatest Hits Of Frankie Valli			
		& The Four Seasons (4 LPs)	197?	6.00	15.00
		(The cover makes no mention of the TV offer.)			
Mowest 108	(S)	Chameleon	1972	3.20	8.00
Motown S-788	(S)	Inside Out	1973	Unreleased	
Warner Bros. BS-2900	(S)	Who Loves You?	1975	1.00	5.00

FOUR TOPS, THE
The Four Tops feature the lead vocals of Levi Stubbs. They can also be found on the ABC soundtrack "Shaft In Africa."
Refer to The Supremes & The Four Tops.

Label & Catalog #		Title	Year	VG+	NM
Workshop 217	(M)	Jazz Impressions	1962	Unreleased	
Motown 622	(M)	The Four Tops	1964	12.00	30.00
Motown MS-622	(S)	The Four Tops	1964	16.00	40.00
Motown 634	(M)	The Four Tops, No. 2	1964	12.00	30.00
Motown MS-634	(S)	The Four Tops, No. 2	1965	16.00	40.00
Motown 647	(M)	The Four Tops On Top	1966	12.00	30.00
Motown MS-647	(S)	The Four Tops On Top	1966	16.00	40.00
Motown 654	(M)	The Four Tops Live	1966	10.00	25.00
Motown MS-654	(S)	The Four Tops Live	1966	12.00	30.00
Motown 657	(M)	The Four Tops On Broadway	1967	8.00	20.00
Motown MS-657	(S)	The Four Tops On Broadway	1967	10.00	25.00
Motown 660	(M)	Reach Out	1967	8.00	20.00
Motown MS-660	(S)	Reach Out	1967	10.00	25.00
Motown 662	(M)	The Four Tops' Greatest Hits	1967	6.00	15.00
Motown MS-662	(S)	The Four Tops' Greatest Hits	1967	8.00	20.00
Motown M-669	(M)	Yesterday Dreams	1968	12.00	30.00
Motown MS-669	(S)	Yesterday Dreams	1968	6.00	15.00
Motown MS-675	(S)	The Four Tops Now	1969	6.00	15.00
Motown MS-695	(S)	Soul Spin	1969	6.00	15.00
Motown MS-704	(S)	Still Waters Run Deep	1970	6.00	15.00
Motown MS-721	(S)	Changing Times	1970	6.00	15.00
Motown MS-740	(S)	The Four Tops' Greatest Hits, Volume 2	1971	5.00	12.00
Motown MS-748	(S)	Nature Planned It	1972	5.00	12.00
Motown MS-764	(S)	The Best Of The Four Tops (2 LPs)	1973	5.00	12.00
Dunhill DX-50129	(S)	Keeper Of The Castle	1972	4.00	10.00
Dunhill DX-50144	(S)	Main Street People	1973	4.00	10.00
Dunhill DX-50166	(S)	Meeting Of The Minds	1974	4.00	10.00
Dunhill DX-50188	(S)	Live & In Concert	1974	4.00	10.00
Command QD-40011	(Q)	Keeper Of The Castle	1974	8.00	20.00
Command QD-40012	(Q)	Main Street People	1974	8.00	20.00
ABC D-862	(S)	Night Lights Harmony	1975	1.00	5.00
ABC AA-011014	(S)	The Show Must Go On	1977	1.00	5.00
ABC AA-1092	(S)	At The Top	1978	1.00	5.00
Natural Resources 4008	(S)	Reach Out	1978	4.00	10.00
Casablanca NBLP-7258	(S)	Tonight	1981	1.00	5.00
Casablanca NBLP-7266	(S)	One More Mountain	1982	1.00	5.00

FOUR TUNES, THE

Label & Catalog #		Title	Year	VG+	NM
Jubilee LP-1039	(M)	12 X 4	1957	100.00	250.00

FOURTH WAY, THE

Label & Catalog #		Title	Year	VG+	NM
Capitol ST-317	(S)	The Fourth Way	1969	8.00	20.00
Harvest SKAO-423	(S)	Sun And Moon Have Come Together	1970	6.00	15.00
Harvest ST-666	(S)	Werewolf	1971	6.00	15.00

FOWLEY, KIM

Label & Catalog #		Title	Year	VG+	NM
Tower T-5080	(M)	Love Is Alive And Well	1967	12.00	30.00
Tower ST-5080	(S)	Love Is Alive And Well	1967	16.00	40.00
Imperial LP-12413	(S)	Born To Be Wild	1968	16.00	40.00
Imperial LP-12423	(S)	Outrageous	1969	16.00	40.00
Imperial LP-12443	(S)	Good Clean Fun	1969	16.00	40.00
Capitol ST-11075	(S)	I'm Bad	1972	4.00	10.00
Capitol ST-11159	(S)	International Heroes	1973	4.00	10.00
Capitol ST-11248	(S)	Automatic	1974	4.00	10.00
PVC 7906	(S)	Sunset Boulevard	1978	4.00	10.00
Antilles AN-7075	(S)	Snake Document Masquerade	1979	4.00	10.00

FOX, THE

Label & Catalog #		Title	Year	VG+	NM
Crewe CR-1336	(S)	For Fox Sake	1970	6.00	15.00

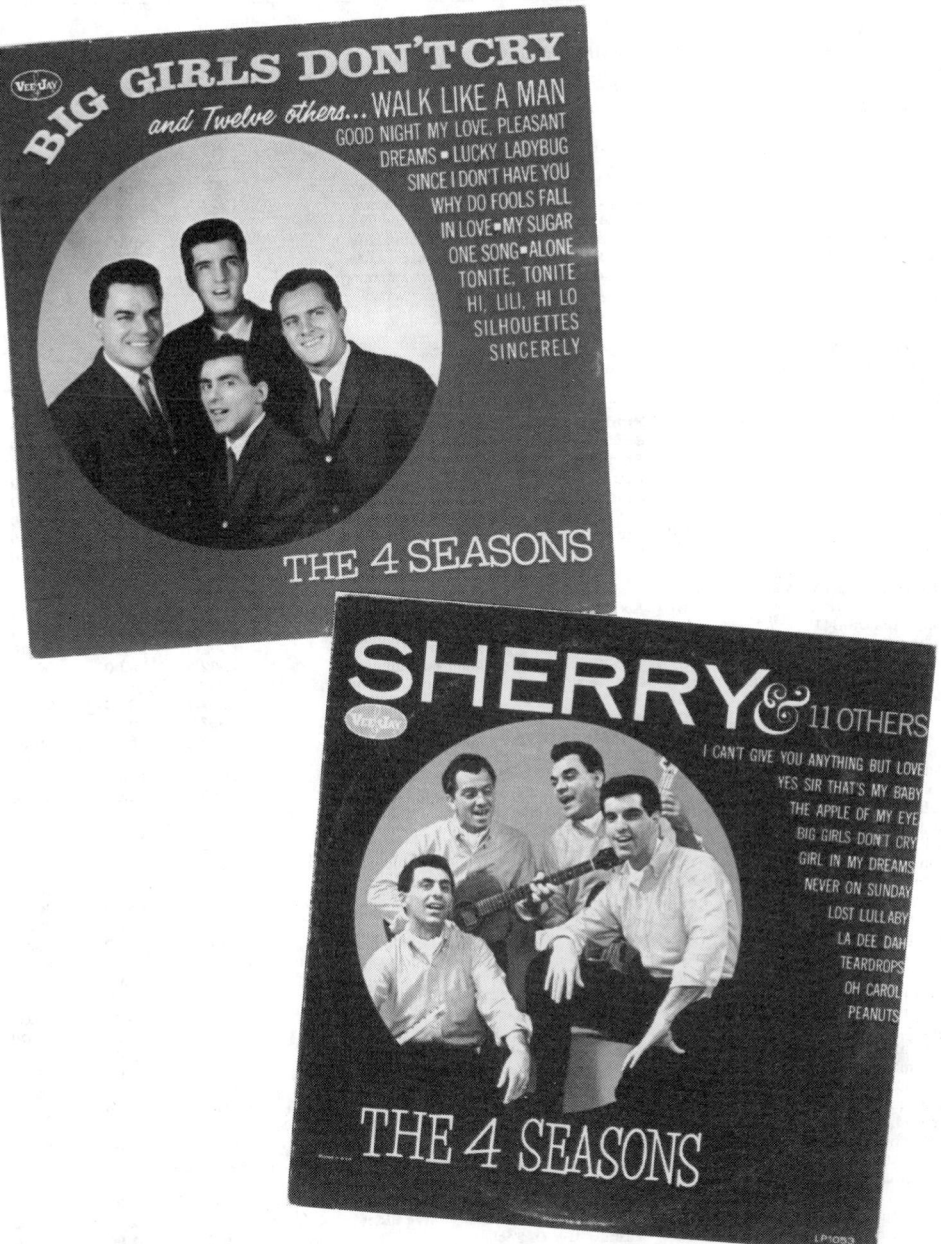

The original Four Seasons that struck gold in 1962 with three chart-toppers in the group's first six months were Frankie Valli and Tommy DeVito, both formerly of The Four Lovers, with Bob Gaudio and Nick Massi. With producer and fifth Season Bob Crewe, they created a unique, '50s-like sound that kept them at the top of the charts through 1967, by which time their sound and image had become [temporarily] dated. In fifteen years The Seasons placed nearly two-dozen albums on the best-seller lists, two of which, Sherry and Big Girls Don't Cry, are pictured here. While they never moved the numbers that The Beatles did for Vee Jay, a comparison of the listings for both groups implies that there should be many more label variations listed under The Four Seasons. Unfortunately, the eye for detail that marks the true Beatles collector is not [yet] associated with Four Seasons collectors.

Label & Catalog #		Title	Year	VG+	NM

FOXX, INEZ

Label & Catalog #		Title	Year	VG+	NM
Symbol SYM-4400	(M)	Mockingbird	1963	80.00	200.00
Sue LP-1027	(M)	Mockingbird	1964	40.00	100.00
		(Sue 1027 is a reissue of Symbol 4400.)			
Volt VOS-6022	(S)	Inez Foxx In Memphis	1973	10.00	25.00

FOXX, INEZ & CHARLIE

Label & Catalog #		Title	Year	VG+	NM
Sue LP-1037	(M)	Inez And Charlie Foxx	1966	40.00	100.00
Sue LP-1037	(S)	Inez And Charlie Foxx	1966	60.00	150.00
Dynamo D-7000	(M)	Come By Here	1967	12.00	30.00
Dynamo DS-8000	(S)	Come By Here	1967	16.00	40.00
Dynamo D-700?	(M)	Inez And Charlie Foxx's Greatest Hits	1967	12.00	30.00
Dynamo DS-800?	(S)	Inez And Charlie Foxx's Greatest Hits	1967	16.00	40.00
		(Contains rerecorded stereo versions of earlier Symbol material.)			
Dynamo D-7003	(M)	Swinging Mackin' Band	1967	12.00	30.00
Dynamo DS-8003	(S)	Swinging Mackin' Band	1967	16.00	40.00

FRAMPTON, PETER
Peter Frampton formerly recorded with The Herd.

Label & Catalog #		Title	Year	VG+	NM
A&M PR-4348	(S)	Winds Of Change	1972	1.00	5.00
A&M PR-4389	(S)	Frampton's Camel (Includes a poster)	1973	4.00	10.00
A&M PR-4389	(S)	Frampton's Camel (Without the poster)	1973	1.00	5.00
A&M PR-3619	(S)	Something's Happening	1974	1.00	5.00
A&M PR-4512	(S)	Frampton	1975	1.00	5.00
A&M SP-3703	(S)	Frampton Comes Alive (2 LPs)	1978	1.20	6.00
A&M PR-3703	(S)	Frampton Comes Alive (Picture disc)	1978	4.00	10.00
A&M SP-4704	(S)	I'm In You	1978	1.00	5.00
A&M SP-4704	(DJ)	I'm In You (Picture disc)	1978	6.00	15.00
A&M SP-27200	(DJ)	The Peter Frampton Radio Special	197?	10.00	25.00

FRANKLIN, ARETHA

Label & Catalog #		Title	Year	VG+	NM
Columbia CL-1612	(M)	Aretha	1961	20.00	50.00
Columbia CS-8412	(S)	Aretha	1961	30.00	75.00
Columbia CL-1761	(M)	The Electrifying Aretha Franklin	1962	16.00	40.00
Columbia CS-8561	(S)	The Electrifying Aretha Franklin	1962	20.00	50.00
—Columbia albums above have three white "eye" logos on each side of the spindle hole.—					
Columbia CL-1612	(M)	Aretha	196?	8.00	20.00
Columbia CS-8412	(S)	Aretha	196?	10.00	25.00
Columbia CL-1761	(M)	The Electrifying Aretha Franklin	196?	8.00	20.00
Columbia CS-8561	(S)	The Electrifying Aretha Franklin	196?	10.00	25.00
Columbia CL-1876	(M)	The Tender... Swinging Aretha Franklin	1962	10.00	25.00
Columbia CS-8676	(S)	The Tender... Swinging Aretha Franklin	1962	12.00	30.00
Columbia CL-2079	(M)	Laughing On The Outside	1963	10.00	25.00
Columbia CS-8879	(S)	Laughing On The Outside	1963	12.00	30.00
Columbia CL-2163	(M)	Unforgettable	1964	10.00	25.00
Columbia CS-8963	(S)	Unforgettable	1964	12.00	30.00
Columbia CL-2281	(M)	Runnin' Out Of Fools	1964	10.00	25.00
Columbia CS-9081	(S)	Runnin' Out Of Fools	1964	12.00	30.00
Columbia CL-2351	(M)	Yeah!!!	1965	10.00	25.00
Columbia CS-9151	(S)	Yeah!!!	1965	12.00	30.00
—Columbia albums above have "Guaranteed High Fidelity" or "360 Sound Stereo" in black on the bottom of the label.—					
Columbia CL-2521	(M)	Soul Sister	1966	8.00	20.00
Columbia CS-9321	(S)	Soul Sister	1966	8.00	20.00
Columbia CL-2629	(M)	Take It Like You Give It	1967	8.00	20.00
Columbia CS-9429	(S)	Take It Like You Give It	1967	8.00	20.00
Columbia CL-2673	(M)	Aretha Franklin's Greatest Hits	1967	6.00	15.00
Columbia CS-9473	(S)	Aretha Franklin's Greatest Hits	1967	6.00	15.00
Columbia CL-2754	(M)	Take A Look	1967	6.00	15.00
Columbia CS-9554	(S)	Take A Look	1967	6.00	15.00
Columbia CS-9601	(S)	Aretha Franklin's Greatest Hits, Volume 2	1968	6.00	15.00
Columbia CS-9776	(S)	Soft And Beautiful	1969	6.00	15.00
—Columbia albums above have "360 Sound" in white on the bottom of the label.—					
Columbia KG-31355	(S)	In The Beginning—The World Of Aretha Franklin 1960-1967 (2 LPs)	1972	1.20	6.00
Columbia KC-31953	(S)	Aretha Franklin's First Twelve Sides	1972	1.00	5.00
Columbia LE-10069	(S)	Runnin' Out Of Fools	1973	1.00	5.00
Columbia LE-10070	(S)	Aretha Franklin's Greatest Hits	1973	1.00	5.00
Columbia C2-37377	(S)	The Legendary Queen Of Soul (2 LPs)	1981	1.00	5.00
Columbia PC-38042	(S)	Sweet Bitter Love	1982	.80	4.00
Harmony HS-11274	(S)	Queen Of Soul	1968	1.00	5.00
Harmony HS-11349	(S)	Once In A Lifetime	1969	1.00	5.00
Harmony HS-11418	(S)	Two Sides Of Love	1970	1.00	5.00
Harmony KH-30606	(S)	Aretha Franklin's Greatest Hits 1960-1965	1971	1.00	5.00
Candlelite DP-2507	(S)	Heart And Soul (2 LPs)	1977	1.20	6.00
Atlantic 8139	(M)	I Never Loved A Man (The Way I Love You)	1967	10.00	25.00
Atlantic SD-8139	(S)	I Never Loved A Man (The Way I Love You)	1967	8.00	20.00
Atlantic 8150	(M)	Aretha Arrives	1967	10.00	25.00
Atlantic SD-8150	(S)	Aretha Arrives	1967	8.00	20.00

After struggling through a series of misguided efforts with Columbia, who had her singing some Broadway, a little jazz, a touch of gospel, and a lot of pop tunes, Aretha Franklin jumped to Atlantic, headed for Muscle Shoals and, with one album, I Never Loved A Man The Way I Love You, all but redefined soul music! By her third album, her new label believed that it could comfortably bill her as Lady Soul, which, considering the fact that she was already the undisputed "Queen of Soul," seems a bit subdued for Atlantic's PR department.

Label & Catalog #		Title	Year	VG+	NM
Atlantic 8176	(M)	**Lady Soul**	1968	12.00	30.00
Atlantic SD-8176	(S)	**Lady Soul**	1968	8.00	20.00
Atlantic SD-8186	(S)	**Aretha Now**	1968	8.00	20.00
		— *Atlantic stereo albums above have green & blue labels.*—			
Atlantic SD-8150	(S)	**Aretha Arrives**	1969	8.00	20.00
		— *Atlantic stereo albums above have brown & purple labels.*—			
Atlantic SD-8207	(S)	**Aretha In Paris**	1968	8.00	20.00
Atlantic SD-8212	(S)	**Soul '69**	1969	8.00	20.00
Atlantic SD-8227	(S)	**Aretha's Gold**	1969	6.00	15.00
Atlantic SD-8248	(S)	**This Girl's In Love With You**	1970	5.00	12.00
Atlantic SD-8265	(S)	**Spirit In The Dark**	1970	5.00	12.00
Atlantic SD-8295	(S)	**Aretha's Greatest Hits**	1971	4.00	10.00
Atlantic SD-7205	(S)	**Live At The Fillmore West**	1971	4.00	10.00
Atlantic QD-7205	(Q)	**Live At Fillmore West**	1974	8.00	20.00
Atlantic SD-7213	(S)	**Young, Gifted And Black**	1972	4.00	10.00
Atlantic SD-2-906	(S)	**Amazing Grace** (2 LPs)	1972	4.00	10.00
		— *Atlantic albums above have green & orange labels with "1841 Broadway" on the bottom.*—			
Atlantic SD-7265	(S)	**Hey Now Hey (The Other Side Of The Sky)**	1973	1.00	5.00
Atlantic SD-7292	(S)	**Let Me In Your Life**	1974	1.00	5.00
Atlantic QD-8305	(Q)	**The Best Of Aretha Franklin**	1974	8.00	20.00
Atlantic SD-18116	(S)	**With Everything I Feel In Me**	1974	1.00	5.00
Atlantic SD-18151	(S)	**You**	1975	1.00	5.00
Atlantic SD-18176	(S)	**Sparkle**	1976	1.00	5.00
Atlantic SD-18204	(S)	**Ten Years Of Gold**	1976	1.00	5.00
Atlantic SD-19102	(S)	**Sweet Passion**	1977	1.00	5.00
Atlantic SD-19161	(S)	**Almighty Fire**	1978	1.00	5.00
Atlantic SD-19248	(S)	**La Diva**	1979	1.00	5.00
FRANKLIN, CAROLYN					
RCA Victor LSP-4160	(S)	**Baby Dynamite**	1969	10.00	25.00
RCA Victor LSP-4317	(S)	**Chain Reaction**	1969	10.00	25.00
RCA Victor LSP-4411	(S)	**I'd Rather Be Lonely**	1970	10.00	25.00
		— *RCA albums above have orange labels on non-flexible vinyl.*—			
FRANKLIN, ERMA					
Epic LN-3824	(S)	**Her Name Is Erma**	1962	12.00	30.00
Epic BN-619	(S)	**Her Name Is Erma**	1962	16.00	40.00
Brunswick BL-754147	(S)	**Soul Sister**	1969	10.00	25.00
FRANKLIN, PETE					
Bluesville BVLP-1068	(M)	**Guitar Pete's Blues**	1963	40.00	100.00
		— *Bluesville albums above have bright blue labels with silver print.*—			
Bluesville BVLP-1068	(M)	**Guitar Pete's Blues**	1964	10.00	25.00
		— *Bluesville albums above have blue labels with a trident logo on the right side.*—			
FRANTIC					
Lizard 20103	(S)	**Conception**	197?	8.00	20.00
FRATERNITY OF MAN, THE					
ABC S-647	(S)	**The Fraternity Of Man**	1968	12.00	30.00
Dot DLP-25955	(S)	**Get It On**	1969	12.00	30.00
FREAK SCENE, THE					
Columbia CL-2656	(M)	**Psychedelic Psoul**	1967	30.00	75.00
Columbia CS-9456	(S)	**Psychedelic Psoul**	1967	50.00	125.00
FREAKOUT GUITARS					
Spin-o-rama M-190	(M)	**Freakout!**	196?	10.00	25.00
Spin-o-rama S-190	(S)	**Freakout!**	196?	12.00	30.00
FRED, JOHN [JOHN FRED & HIS PLAYBOY BAND]					
Paula LP-2191	(M)	**John Fred And His Playboys**	1966	8.00	20.00
Paula LPS-2191	(S)	**John Fred And His Playboys**	1966	10.00	25.00
Paula LP-2193	(M)	**34:40 Of John Fred And His Playboys**	1967	8.00	20.00
Paula LPS-2193	(S)	**34:40 Of John Fred And His Playboys**	1967	10.00	25.00
Paula LP-2197	(M)	**Agnes English**	1967	10.00	25.00
Paula LPS-2197	(S)	**Agnes English**	1967	10.00	25.00
Paula LPS-2197	(S)	**Judy In Disguise With Glasses**	1968	8.00	20.00
		("*Judy*" *is a repackage of* "*Agnes.*")			
Paula LPS-2201	(S)	**Permanently Stated**	1968	6.00	15.00
Uni 73077	(S)	**Love In My Soul**	1970	16.00	40.00
Guiness BNS-36022	(S)	**Juke Box**	1977	6.00	15.00
FREDDIE & THE DREAMERS					
Tower T-5003	(M)	**I'm Telling You Now**	1965	10.00	25.00
Tower DT-5003	(E)	**I'm Telling You Now**	1965	8.00	20.00
		(*While Tower 5003 pictures Freddie & The Dreamers on the cover, it is actually a various artists comp with only two tracks by F&TDs.*)			

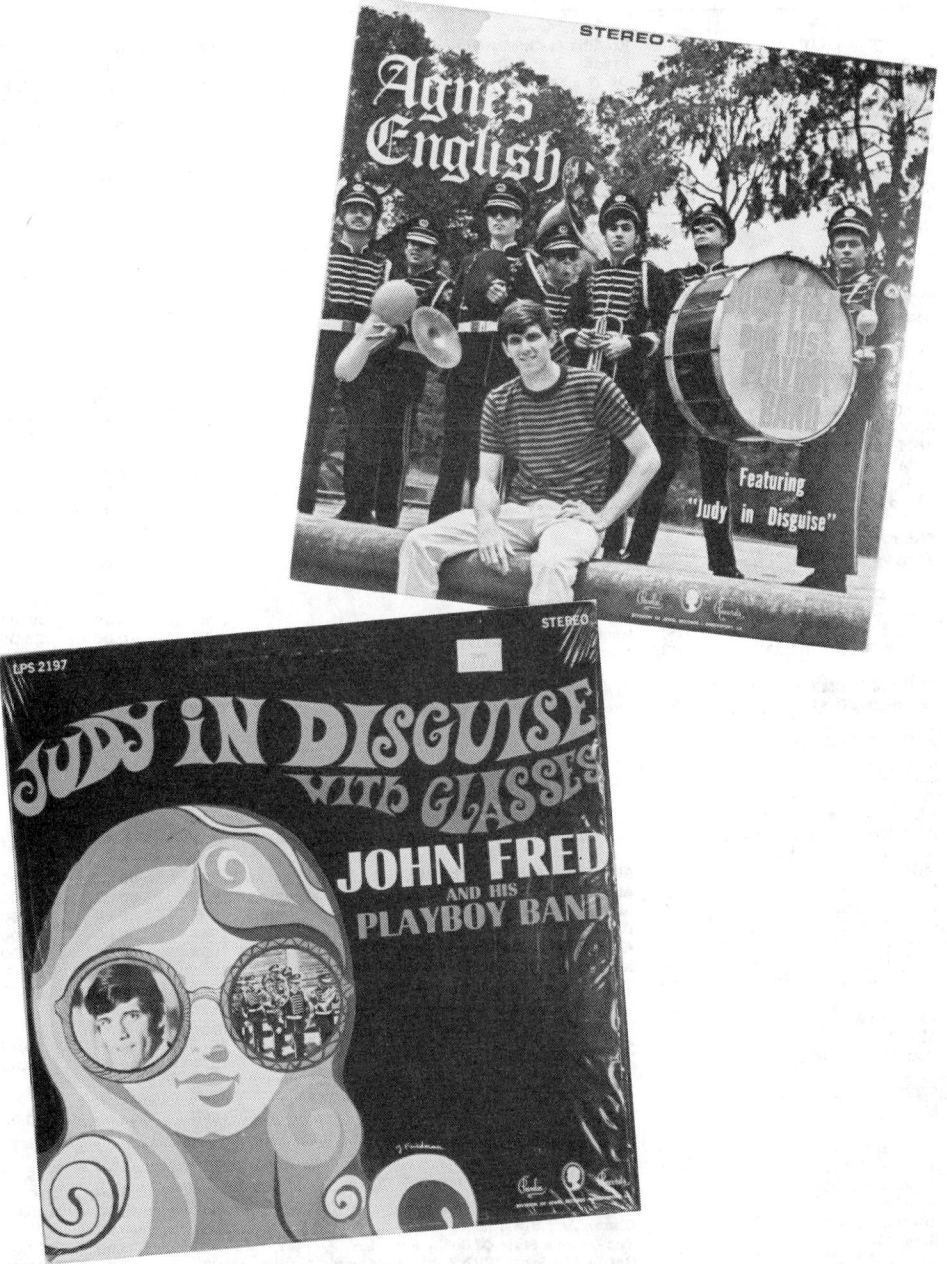

John Fred Gourrier had been a regional success for more than a decade when the delightful spoof of The Beatles and Sgt. Pepper, "Judy In Disguise (With Glasses)," was lifted from the Agnes English album and soared to the top of the charts. After the single's unexpected success, the album was retitled to, what else, Judy In Disguise, and given new cover art that was a noticeably mod improvement over the drab original. It was sent back out for retail exposure, where it sold modestly in the first months of 1968.

Label & Catalog #		Title	Year	VG+	NM
Mercury MG-21017	(M)	Freddie & The Dreamers	1965	10.00	25.00
Mercury SR-61017	(E)	Freddie & The Dreamers	1965	8.00	20.00
Mercury MG-21026	(M)	Do The Freddie	1965	8.00	20.00
Mercury SR-61026	(S)	Do The Freddie	1965	10.00	25.00
Mercury MG-21031	(M)	Seaside Swingers	1965	8.00	20.00
Mercury SR-61031	(S)	Seaside Swingers	1965	10.00	25.00
Mercury MG-21053	(M)	Frantic Freddie	1965	6.00	15.00
Mercury SR-61053	(S)	Frantic Freddie	1965	8.00	20.00
Mercury MG-21061	(M)	Fun Lovin' Freddie	1966	6.00	15.00
Mercury SR-61061	(S)	Fun Lovin' Freddie	1966	8.00	20.00
Capitol SM-11896	(M)	The Best Of Freddie & The Dreamers	1976	1.00	5.00

("I'm Telling You Now," "You Were Made For Me", "Over You,"
"I Just Don't Understand" and "A Little You" are in stereo.)

FREDERICK, JESSE

Bearsville 2043	(S)	Jesse Frederick	1971	4.00	10.00

FREE

A&M SP-4198	(S)	Tons Of Sobs	1969	3.20	8.00
A&M SP-4204	(S)	Free	1969	3.20	8.00
A&M SP-4268	(S)	Fire And Water	1970	1.20	6.00
A&M SP-4287	(S)	Highway	1971	1.20	6.00
A&M SP-4306	(S)	Free Live!	1971	1.20	6.00
A&M SP-4349	(S)	Free At Last	1972	1.20	6.00
A&M SP-3663	(S)	Best Of Free	1972	1.20	6.00
Island SW-9324	(S)	Heartbreaker	1973	1.20	6.00

FREE BAND, THE

Vanguard VSD-6507	(S)	The Free Band	1969	8.00	20.00

FREE DESIGN

Project-3 PR-5031SD	(S)	You Can Be Born Again	1968	10.00	25.00
Project-3 PR-5037SD	(S)	Heaven/Earth	1971	10.00	25.00
Project-3 PR-5061SD	(S)	One By One	1972	10.00	25.00

FREE MOVEMENT, THE

Columbia KC-31136	(S)	I've Found Someone Of My Own	1972	6.00	15.00

FREE SPIRITS, THE

ABC 593	(M)	Out Of Sight And Sound	1967	6.00	15.00
ABC S-593	(S)	Out Of Sight And Sound	1967	8.00	20.00

FREED, ALAN
Alan Freed was an influential disc jockey often credited for assisting the development of rock'n roll through exposing
white listeners to black music.

MGM E-293	(10")	Alan Freed Presents The Big Beat	1956	80.00	200.00
Coral CRL-57063	(M)	Alan Freed's Rock 'N Roll Dance Party, Volume 1	1956	60.00	150.00
Coral CRL-57115	(M)	Alan Freed's Rock 'N Roll Dance Party, Volume 2	1957	60.00	150.00
Coral CRL-57177	(M)	Go Go Go—Alan Freed's TV Record Hop	1957	60.00	150.00
Coral CRL-57213	(M)	Alan Freed's Rock Around The Block	1958	60.00	150.00
Coral CRL-57216	(M)	Alan Freed Presents The King's Henchmen	1958	60.00	150.00
Brunswick BL-54043	(M)	The Alan Freed Rock & Roll Show	1959	60.00	150.00

FREEDOM

ABC S-708	(S)	Freedom	1970	4.00	10.00
Cotillion SD-9064	(S)	Through The Years	1971	4.00	10.00

FREEDOM EXPRESS, THE

Mercury SR-61250	(S)	Easy Ridin'	1970	24.00	60.00

FREEMAN, BOBBY

Jubilee JLP-1086	(M)	Do You Wanna Dance?	1959	50.00	125.00
Jubilee JLPS-1086	(S)	Do You Wanna Dance?	1959	80.00	200.00
Jubilee JGM-5010	(M)	Twist With Bobby Freeman	1962	40.00	100.00
Autumn LP-102	(M)	C'mon And S-W-I-M	1964	20.00	50.00
King 930	(M)	The Lovable Style Of Bobby Freeman	1965	150.00	300.00
Josie JM-4007	(M)	Get In The Swim With Bobby Freeman	1965	12.00	30.00
Josie JGS-4007	(E)	Get In The Swim With Bobby Freeman	1965	10.00	25.00

FREEMAN, BOBBY / CHUCK JACKSON

Grand Prix K-430	(M)	Bobby Freeman And Chuck Jackson	196?	4.00	10.00
Grand Prix K-430	(E)	Bobby Freeman And Chuck Jackson	196?	1.00	5.00

FREEPORT

Mainstream S-6130	(S)	Freeport	1970	20.00	50.00

FREHLEY, ACE: Refer to KISS

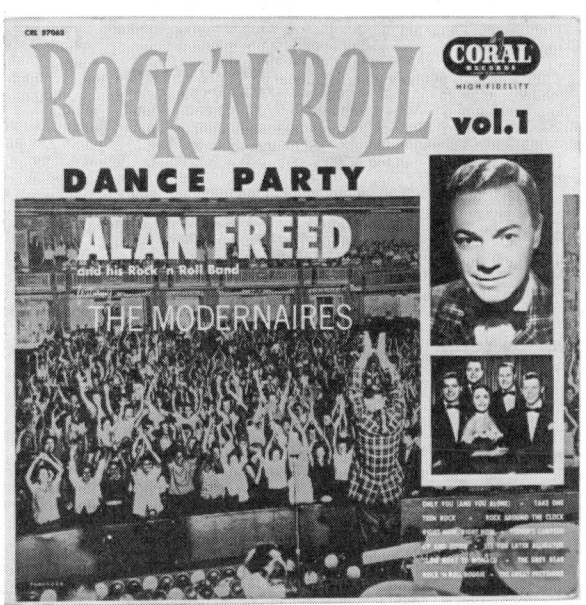

One of the many ways rock'n roll impresario Alan Freed attempted to cash in on the phenomenon he played a major part in developing was issuing record albums in his name. These two volumes of Coral's Rock'n Roll Dance Party credit Alan Freed and His Rock 'N Roll Band, although the first volume also features the pop vocal group, The Modernaires, while the second volume features Jimmy Cavello.

Label & Catalog #		Title	Year	VG+	NM

FRESH

| RCA Victor LSP-4328 | (S) | Fresh Out Of Borstal | 1970 | 4.00 | 10.00 |
| RCA Victor LSP-4427 | (S) | Fresh Today | 1970 | 4.00 | 10.00 |

FRESH AIR

| Columbia KC-32282 | (S) | Fresh Air | 1970 | 1.00 | 5.00 |

FREY, GLENN

Frey was a member of The Eagles. Refer to Longbranch Pennywhistle.

| MCA 5501 | (S) | The Allnighter (Quiex II vinyl promo) | 1984 | 6.00 | 15.00 |
| MCA 5501 | (S) | The Allnighter | 1984 | .80 | 4.00 |

FRIAR TUCK

| Mercury MG-21111 | (M) | Friar Tuck & His Psychedelic Guitar | 1967 | 20.00 | 50.00 |
| Mercury SR-61111 | (S) | Friar Tuck & His Psychedelic Guitar | 1967 | 30.00 | 75.00 |

FRIEND & LOVER

| Verve/Forecast FTS-3055 | (S) | Reach Out Of The Darkness | 1968 | 8.00 | 20.00 |

FRIENDS

Probe 4511	(S)	From Here To There	1969	6.00	15.00
Oblivion 3	(S)	Friends	1972	6.00	15.00
MGM SE-4901	(S)	Friends	1973	4.00	10.00

FRIENDS OF DISTINCTION, THE

RCA Victor LSP-4149	(S)	Grazin'	1969	6.00	15.00
RCA Victor LSP-4212	(S)	Highly Distinct	1969	6.00	15.00
RCA Victor LSP-4313	(S)	Real Friends	1970	6.00	15.00
RCA Victor LSP-4408	(S)	Whatever	1970	6.00	15.00
		—RCA albums above have orange labels on non-flexible vinyl.—			
RCA Victor LSP-4492	(S)	Friends & People	1971	4.00	10.00
RCA Victor LSP-4814	(S)	Friends Of Distinction's Greatest Hits	1972	4.00	10.00
RCA Victor APD1-0276	(Q)	Friends Of Distinction's Greatest Hits	1973	8.00	20.00
RCA Victor LSP-4829	(S)	Love Can Make It Easier	1973	4.00	10.00
		—RCA albums above have orange labels on flexible vinyl.—			

FRIENDSOUND

Friendsound is Phil Volk, Drake Levin and Mike Smith of Paul Revere's Raiders. Refer to Brotherhood.

| RCA Victor LSP-4114 | (S) | Joyride | 1969 | 6.00 | 15.00 |

FRIJID PINK

Parrot PAS-71033	(S)	Frijid Pink	1970	10.00	25.00
Parrot PAS-71041	(S)	Frijid Pink Defrosted	1970	10.00	25.00
		(The inner sleeve is a full-color photo of the group.)			
Lion LN-1004	(S)	Earth Omen	1972	8.00	20.00
Fantasy F-9464	(S)	All Pink Inside	1974	6.00	15.00

FRIPP, ROBERT

Robert Fripp was the leader of King Crimson. Refer to Brian Eno; Giles, Giles & Fripp; Andy Summers & Robert Fripp; Toyah & Robert Fripp.

Polydor PD-6201	(S)	Exposure	1979	3.20	8.00
Polydor PD-6266	(S)	God Save The Queen/Under Heavy Manners	1980	3.20	8.00
Polydor PD-6317	(S)	The League Of Gentlemen	1981	3.20	8.00
E.G. EGS-110	(S)	Let The Power Fall	1981	1.00	5.00
E.G. EGMLP-4	(S)	Network (Mint-LP compilation)	1985	1.00	5.00
E.G. EGED-9	(S)	God Save The Queen	1985	1.00	5.00
E.G. EGLP-41	(S)	Exposure (Remixed)	1985	1.00	5.00
E.G. EGED-43	(S)	Live!	1986	1.00	5.00

FRITH, FRED

| Ralph 8106 | (S) | Speechless | 1981 | 3.20 | 8.00 |

FROM BRITAIN WITH BEAT

| Modern Sound M-544 | (M) | From Britain With Beat | 1965 | 20.00 | 50.00 |
| Modern Sound MS-544 | (S) | From Britain With Beat | 1965 | 30.00 | 75.00 |

FROST

Vanguard VSD-6520	(S)	Frost Music	1969	6.00	15.00
Vanguard VSD-6541	(S)	Rock And Roll Music	1969	6.00	15.00
Vanguard VSD-6556	(S)	Through The Eyes Of Music	1970	6.00	15.00
Vanguard VSD-79392	(S)	Early Frost	1978	6.00	15.00

FROST, FRANK, & THE NIGHTHAWKS

Phillips Int. PLP-1975	(M)	Hey Boss Man!	1961	See note below	
		(Rare with a suggested NM value of $3,000-5,000.)			
Jewel LPS-5013	(S)	Frank Frost	1973	6.00	15.00
Earwig LPS-4901	(S)	Rockin' The Juke Joint Down	1979	4.00	10.00
Earwig LPS-4914	(S)	Midnight Prowler	198?	4.00	10.00

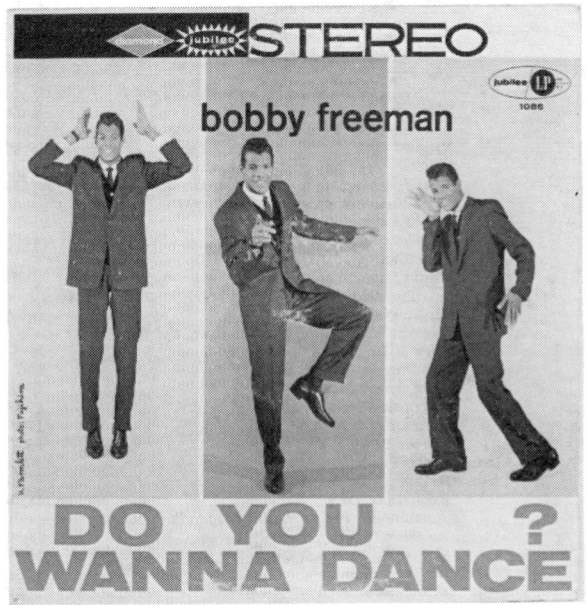

After singing with The Romancers and The Vocaleers as a teenager, Bobby Freeman went solo and scored with "Do You Wanna Dance," a huge hit in 1958. While Mr Freeman placed several more sides on the national pop charts (including such novelty dance numbers as "I Do The Shimmy Shimmy" for King and "C'mon And Swim" for Autumn), it is the exuberant quality of his first big hit that keeps his name on oldies stations around the country. The fact that it has found its way back onto those same charts as covers by Del Shannon (1964), The Beach Boys (1965), The Mama's & The Papa's (1968), Bette Midler (1973), and The Ramones (1978) certainly argues for the enduring attraction of the song for both artists and record buyers alike.

Label & Catalog #		Title	Year	VG+	NM

FROST, MAX, & THE TROOPERS
For additional listings refer to the Tower soundtrack "Wild In The Streets."

Label & Catalog #		Title	Year	VG+	NM
Tower ST-5147	(S)	**Shape Of Things To Come**	1968	20.00	50.00

FROST, THOMAS & RICHARD

Uni 73124	(S)	**Thomas And Richard Frost**	1972	4.00	10.00

FRUMMOX

Probe 4511	(S)	**From Here To There**	1969	6.00	15.00

FRUMPY

Billingsgate 1003	(S)	**By The Way**	1973	4.00	10.00

FUGS, THE
The Fugs were Tuli Kupferberg, Ed Sanders and Ken Weaver. The Broadside and ESP albums feature backing by Peter Stampfel and Steve Weber, later The Holy Modal Rounders.

Broadside 304	(M)	**The Village Fugs Sings Ballads Of Contemporary Protest** (With insert)	1966	175.00	350.00
Broadside 304	(M)	**The Village Fugs Sings Ballads Of Contemporary Protest** (Without insert)	1966	150.00	300.00
ESP-Disk' 1018	(M)	**The Fugs First Album**	1966	16.00	40.00
		(Cover reads "Reissue of Broadside 304.)			
ESP-Disk' 1018	(M)	**The Fugs First Album**	1966	60.00	150.00
		(Turquoise & black cover with different back cover)			
ESP-Disk' 1017	(M)	**The Fugs First Album**	196?	12.00	30.00
		(The cover makes no mention of the Broadside original.)			
ESP-Disk' 1017	(M)	**The Fugs First Album**	196?	20.00	50.00
		(Psychedelic wizard cover)			
ESP-Disk' 1028	(S)	**The Fugs**	196?	20.00	50.00
		(Black & white cover with the photos on the back staggered.)			
ESP-Disk' 1028	(S)	**The Fugs**	196?	14.00	35.00
		(Black & white cover with the photos on the back straight.)			
ESP-Disk' 1028	(S)	**The Fugs**	196?	30.00	75.00
		(The cover is a psychedelic color shield.)			
ESP-Disk' 1038	(S)	**Virgin Fugs**	1967	40.00	100.00
		(The cover has a sticker that reads " For Adult Minds Only" and was issued with a poster, a flip book, and stickers. This and all subsequent pressings are in partial mono and partial stereo.)			
ESP-Disk' 1038	(S)	**Virgin Fugs**	1967	20.00	50.00
		(The cover has a sticker that reads " For Adult Minds Only" without the inserts.)			
ESP-Disk' 1038	(S)	**Virgin Fugs**	1967	20.00	50.00
		("For Adult Minds" is stamped on the back cover.)			
ESP-Disk' 1038	(S)	**Virgin Fugs**	1967	14.00	35.00
		("For Adult Minds" printed on the front cover.)			
ESP-Disk' 2018	(S)	**Fugs 4, Rounders Score**	1967	30.00	75.00
Reprise R-6280	(M)	**Tenderness Junction**	1967	14.00	35.00
Reprise RS-6280	(S)	**Tenderness Junction**	1967	10.00	25.00
Reprise RS-6305	(S)	**It Crawled Into My Hand, Honest**	1968	10.00	25.00
Reprise RS-6359	(S)	**Belle Of Avenue A**	1969	10.00	25.00
Reprise RS-6396	(S)	**Golden Filth**	1970	10.00	25.00
PVC 8914	(S)	**Proto Punk** (With insert)	1982	6.00	15.00
Olufsen 5006	(S)	**Refuse To Be Burnt Out**	1985	6.00	15.00
Olufsen 5009	(S)	**Buckets Of Love**	1985	20.00	50.00
		(Banned due to the breast-fondling cover.)			
Olufsen 5011	(S)	**No More Slavery**	1986	3.00	8.00
New Rose 56	(S)	**Refuse To Be Burnt Out**	1985	6.00	15.00
New Rose 79	(S)	**No More Slavery**	1986	6.00	15.00
New Rose 115	(S)	**Star Peace**	1987	6.00	15.00

FULL MOON

Douglas KZ-31904	(S)	**Full Moon**	1972	6.00	15.00

FULLER, BOBBY [THE BOBBY FULLER FOUR]

Mustang M-900	(M)	**KRLA King Of The Wheels**	1965	30.00	75.00
Mustang MS-900	(S)	**KRLA King Of The Wheels**	1965	60.00	150.00
Mustang M-901	(M)	**I Fought The Law**	1966	20.00	50.00
Mustang MS-901	(S)	**I Fought The Law**	1966	40.00	100.00
Rhino RNDF-201	(S)	**The Best Of The Bobby Fuller Four**	1982	1.00	5.00
Rhino RNLP-057	(S)	**Bobby Fuller Tapes**	1984	1.00	5.00
Voxx LP-100	(S)	**Bobby Fuller Tapes, Vol. 2**	1985	1.00	5.00

FULLER, JERRY

Lin LP-100	(M)	**Teenage Love**	1960	150.00	300.00

FULSON, LOWEL

Arhoolie R-2003	(M)	**Early Recordings**	1962	16.00	40.00
Jewel LP-5003	(M)	**In A Heavy Bag**	1965	16.00	40.00
Jewel LPS-5003	(S)	**In A Heavy Bag**	1965	20.00	50.00

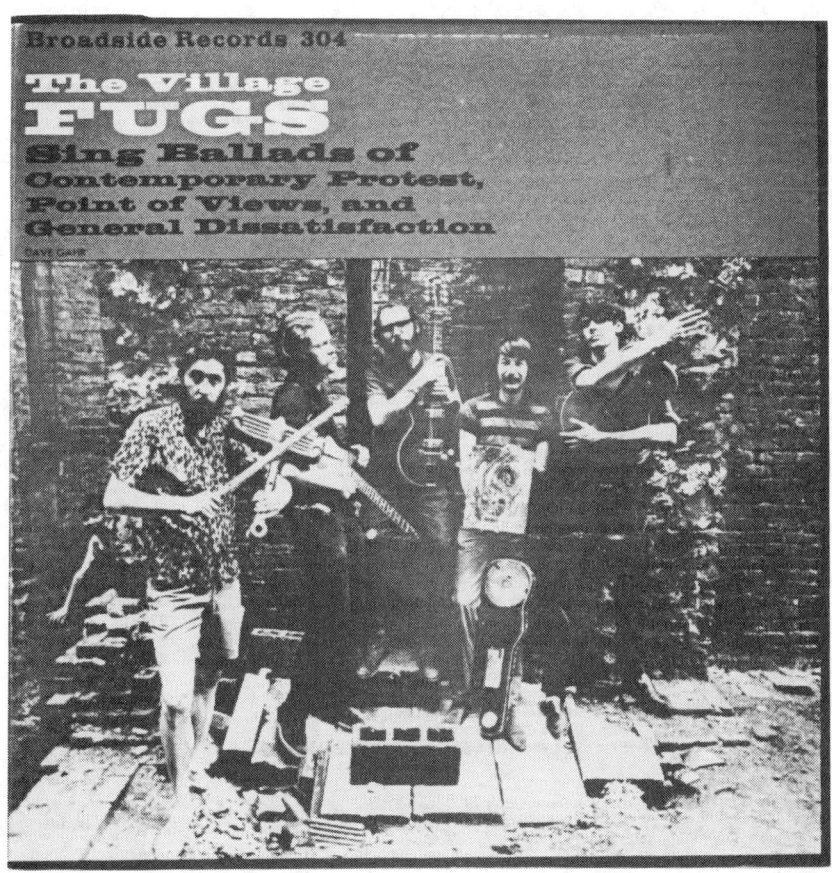

The Village Fugs were basically a pair of East Village, post-Beat poets, Ed Sanders and Tuli Kupferberg, with drummer Ken Weaver. They recorded their first attempt at "making music" for the local folkie label, Broadside, with Peter Stampfel and Steve Weber, better known as The Holy Modal Rounders. Moving over to the avant garde ESP-Disk', they shortened their moniker to The Fugs and preceded to delight teenage girls with their mod appearance and charming tales of tender love. But classic rock'n roll was not their only claim to fame: Kupferberg achieved a sort of literary immortality by being referred to in Allen Ginsberg's Howl! as "the person who jumped off the Brooklyn Bridge and survived." Years later, Sanders went to California intent on proving that poor Charlie Manson was the patsy in an elaborate conspiracy by the White House to discredit the counter-culture. [Should this seem too spacey for my younger readers, Nixon and his minions did, in fact, engage in any manner of underhanded means to achieve that stated goal.] Sanders returned, more than a little frightened, and wrote what may be one of the most chilling books of its time, The Family.

		Title	Year	VG+	NM
	(M)	I've Got The Blues	1965	16.00	40.00
	(S)	I've Got The Blues	1965	20.00	50.00
Kent KST-516	(M)	Lowell Fulson	1965	12.00	30.00
Kent KST-516	(S)	Lowell Fulson	1965	16.00	40.00
Kent KLP-5020	(M)	Tramp	1967	12.00	30.00
Kent KST-520	(S)	Tramp	1967	16.00	40.00
Kent KST-531	(S)	Lowell Fulson Now	1969	12.00	30.00
Chess CH-408	(P)	Head Hung Down	197?	4.00	10.00
Chess 2-205	(P)	Chess Blues Masters Series (2 LPs)	1976	6.00	15.00
Big Town 1008	(S)	Lovemaker	1876	4.00	10.00

FUN & GAMES

Uni 73042	(S)	Elephant Candy	1968	10.00	25.00

FUNKADELIC
Funkadelic, who also recorded as Parliament, is the brainchild of George Clinton.

Westbound 2000	(S)	Funkadelic	1970	20.00	50.00
Westbound 2001	(S)	Free Your Mind And Your Ass Will Follow	1970	20.00	50.00
Westbound 2007	(S)	Maggot Brain	1971	20.00	50.00
Westbound 2020	(S)	America Eats Its Young	1972	20.00	50.00
Westbound 2022	(S)	Cosmic Slop	1973	20.00	50.00
Westbound 1001	(S)	Standing On The Verge Of Getting It On	1974	20.00	50.00
Westbound 1004	(S)	Funkadelic's Greatest Hits	1975	20.00	50.00
Westbound 215	(S)	Let's Take It To The Stage	1975	20.00	50.00
Westbound 216	(S)	Funkadelic	1975	14.00	35.00
		(Westbound 216 is a reissue of 2000.)			
Westbound 227	(S)	Tales Of Kidd Funkadelic	1976	20.00	50.00
Westbound 303	(S)	The Best Of The Early Years	1977	16.00	40.00
		—*Westbound albums above have thick vinyl and thick cardboard covers.*—			
Westbound 2001	(S)	Free Your Mind And Your Ass Will Follow	197?	10.00	25.00
Westbound 2007	(S)	Maggot Brain	197?	10.00	25.00
Westbound 2020	(S)	America Eats Its Young	197?	10.00	25.00
Westbound 2022	(S)	Cosmic Slop	197?	10.00	25.00
Westbound 1001	(S)	Standing On The Verge Of Getting It On	197?	10.00	25.00
Westbound 1004	(S)	Funkadelic's Greatest Hits	197?	10.00	25.00
Westbound 215	(S)	Let's Take It To The Stage	197?	10.00	25.00
Westbound 216	(S)	Funkadelic	1975	10.00	25.00
Westbound 227	(S)	Tales Of Kidd Funkadelic	197?	10.00	25.00
Westbound 303	(S)	The Best Of The Early Years	197?	10.00	25.00
		—*Westbound reissues above have thinner vinyl and thinner cardboard jackets with a space for the UPC bar code on the back cover.*—			
20th Century 208	(S)	Standing On The Verge Of Getting It On	198?	8.00	20.00
20th Century 215	(S)	Let's Take It To The Stage	198?	8.00	20.00
20th Century 216	(S)	Funkadelic	1975	8.00	20.00
20th Century 217	(S)	Free Your Mind And Your Ass Will Follow	198?	8.00	20.00
20th Century 218	(S)	Maggot Brain	198?	8.00	20.00
20th Century 221	(S)	America Eats Its Young	198?	8.00	20.00
20th Century 223	(S)	Cosmic Slop	198?	8.00	20.00
20th Century 227	(S)	Tales Of Kidd Funkadelic	198?	8.00	20.00
Warner Bros. BS-2973	(S)	Hardcore Jollies	1976	12.00	30.00
Warner Bros. BS-3209	(S)	One Nation Under A Groove	1978	12.00	30.00
Warner Bros. BSK-3371	(S)	Uncle Jam Wants You	1979	12.00	30.00
Warner Bros. 3BSK-482	(S)	The Electric Spanking Of War Babies	1981	12.00	30.00

FUSE
Fuse features Rick Nielson And Tom Peterson, later of Cheap Trick.

Epic BN-26502	(S)	Fuse (Counterfeits exist)	1970	30.00	75.00

FUSION

Atco SD-33-295	(S)	Border Town	1969	6.00	15.00

FUTURE

Shamley 703	(S)	Down The Country Road	1969	8.00	20.00

FUZZ, THE

Calla SD-2001	(S)	The Fuzz	1971	4.00	10.00

G. T. O. 'S
Girls Together Outrageously were produced by Frank Zappa.

Straight STS-1059	(S)	Permanent Damage *(With booklet)*	1969	40.00	100.00
Straight STS-1059	(S)	Permanent Damage *(Without booklet)*	1969	30.00	75.00
Reprise RS-6390	(S)	Permanent Damage *(With booklet)*	1970	30.00	75.00
Reprise RS-6390	(S)	Permanent Damage *(Without booklet)*	1970	20.00	50.00

GABRIEL, PETER
Gabriel was the leader of Genesis.

Atco SD-36-147	(S)	Peter Gabriel	1977	1.00	5.00
Atlantic SD-19181	(S)	Peter Gabriel	1978	1.00	5.00
Mercury 3848	(S)	Peter Gabriel	1980	1.00	5.00
Geffen GHS-2011	(DJ)	Peter Gabriel (Security) *(Quiex II vinyl)*	1982	8.00	20.00
Geffen GHS-2011	(S)	Peter Gabriel (Security)	1982	1.00	5.00
Geffen PRO-???	(DJ)	Peter Gabriel Plays Live	1983	10.00	25.00
Geffen GHS-4012	(S)	Peter Gabriel Plays Live	1983	1.00	5.00

GAINSBOROUGH GALLERY, THE

Evolution 2012	(S)	Life Is A Song	1970	5.00	12.00

GALAHADS, THE

Liberty LRP-3371	(M)	The Galahads	1964	8.00	20.00
Liberty LST-7371	(S)	The Galahads	1964	10.00	25.00

GALE, SUNNY

RCA Victor LPM-1277	(M)	Sunny And Blue	1956	16.00	40.00
Warwick W-2018	(M)	Sunny	1960	16.00	40.00

GALLAGHER, RORY
Rory originally recorded with Taste.

Atco SD-33-368	(S)	Rory Gallagher	1971	5.00	12.00
Atlantic SD-7004	(S)	Deuce	1971	5.00	12.00
Polydor PD-5513	(S)	Live In Europe	1972	4.00	10.00
Polydor PD-5522	(S)	Blueprint	1973	4.00	10.00
Polydor PD-5539	(S)	Tattoo	1973	4.00	10.00
Polydor PD-9501	(S)	Irish Tour 1974	1974	4.00	10.00
Polydor PD-6510	(S)	Sinner... And Saint	1975	4.00	10.00
Polydor PD-6519	(S)	The Story So Far	1975	4.00	10.00
Springboard 4056	(S)	In The Beginning	197?	1.00	5.00
Springboard 4056	(S)	Take It Easy Baby	197?	1.00	5.00
Chrysalis CHR-1098	(S)	Against The Grain	1975	3.20	8.00
Chrysalis CHR-1124	(S)	Calling Card	1976	3.20	8.00
Chrysalis CHR-1170	(S)	Photo Finish	1978	3.20	8.00
Chrysalis CHR-1235	(S)	Top Priority	1979	3.20	8.00
Chrysalis CHR-1280	(S)	Stage Struck	1980	3.20	8.00
Mercury SRM-1-4051	(S)	Jinx	1982	3.20	8.00
IRS/Capo 13071	(S)	Defender	1989	1.00	5.00
IRS/Capo 13070	(S)	Fresh Evidence	1990	1.00	5.00

GALLERY

Sussex SUX-7017	(S)	Nice To Be With You	1972	5.00	12.00
Sussex SUX-7026	(S)	Jim Gold And Gallery	1973	4.00	10.00

GALS & PALS

Fontana MGF-27538	(M)	Gals And Pals	1965	6.00	15.00
Fontana SRS-67538	(S)	Gals And Pals	1965	8.00	20.00

GAME

Faithful Virtue 2003	(S)	Game	1969	8.00	20.00
Evolution 2021	(S)	Game	1970	5.00	12.00
Evolution 3008	(S)	Long Hot Summer	1970	5.00	12.00

GANDALF

Capitol ST-121	(S)	Gandalf	1969	80.00	200.00

Label & Catalog #		Title	Year	VG+	NM
GANT, CECIL					
Red Mill *(No number)*	*(M)*	**Cecil Gant** *(Red vinyl)*	1956	**250.00**	**500.00**
King 671	*(M)*	**Cecil Gant**	1958	**60.00**	**150.00**
Sound 601	*(M)*	**The Incomparable Cecil Gant**	1958	**40.00**	**100.00**
GANTS, THE					
Liberty LRP-3432	*(M)*	**Road Runner**	1965	**12.00**	**30.00**
Liberty LST-7432	*(S)*	**Road Runner**	1965	**16.00**	**40.00**
		("Road Runner" is rechanneled on this album.)			
Liberty LRP-3455	*(M)*	**The Gants Galore**	1966	**12.00**	**30.00**
Liberty LST-7455	*(S)*	**The Gants Galore**	1966	**16.00**	**40.00**
Liberty LRP-3473	*(M)*	**The Gants Again**	1966	**12.00**	**30.00**
Liberty LST-7473	*(S)*	**The Gants Again**	1966	**16.00**	**40.00**
GARCIA, JERRY					

Jerry "Captain Trips' Garcia was the heart and soul of the world's most psychedelic band, The Grateful Dead. Refer to Old & In The Way; Merl Saunders & Jerry Garcia; Howard Wales & Jerry Garcia.

Warner Bros. BS-2582	*(S)*	**Garcia**	1972	**10.00**	**25.00**
Round RX-102	*(S)*	**Garcia**	1974	**10.00**	**25.00**
Round RX-107	*(S)*	**Reflections**	1975	**10.00**	**25.00**
United Arts. LA565	*(S)*	**Reflections**	1976	**6.00**	**15.00**
		(U.A. 565 is a reissue of Round 107.)			
Arista AB-4160	*(S)*	**Cats Under The Stars**	1978	**1.00**	**5.00**
Arista 9603	*(S)*	**Run For The Roses**	1982	**1.00**	**5.00**
GARDNER, DON, & DEE DEE FORD					
Fire LP-105	*(M)*	**Need Your Lovin'**	1962	**300.00**	**500.00**
Sue LP-1044	*(M)*	**Don Gardner & Dee Dee Ford In Sweden**	1965	**60.00**	**150.00**
GARFUNKEL, ART					

Refer to Simon & Garfunkel.

Columbia C-31474	*(S)*	**Angel Clare**	1973	**.80**	**4.00**
Columbia CQ-31474	*(Q)*	**Angel Clare**	1974	**4.00**	**10.00**
Columbia C-33700	*(S)*	**Breakaway**	1975	**.80**	**4.00**
Columbia CQ-33700	*(Q)*	**Breakaway**	1975	**4.00**	**10.00**
Columbia JC-34975	*(DJ)*	**Watermark** *(Test press. with "Fingerpaint")*	1977	**20.00**	**50.00**
Columbia JC-34975	*(S)*	**Watermark** *(With "Fingerpaint")*	1977	**40.00**	**100.00**
		(Original test pressings and a few stock copies of JC-34975 above contain "Fingerpaint.")			
Columbia JC-34975	*(S)*	**Watermark**	1978	**.80**	**4.00**
		(Later pressings released for sale have a remastered second side replacing "Fingerpaint" with "What A Wonderful World.")			
Columbia JC-35780	*(S)*	**Fate For Breakfast**	1979	**.80**	**4.00**
Columbia JC-37392	*(S)*	**Scissors Cut**	1981	**.80**	**4.00**
GARNETT, GALE					
RCA Victor LPM-2833	*(M)*	**My Kind Of Folk Songs** *(Blue-toned cover)*	1964	**16.00**	**40.00**
RCA Victor LSP-2833	*(S)*	**My Kind Of Folk Songs** *(Blue-toned cover)*	1964	**20.00**	**50.00**
		(Original covers for RCA 2833 have a black & white photo with a blue tone.)			
RCA Victor LPM-2833	*(M)*	**My Kind Of Folk Songs** *(Color cover)*	1965	**8.00**	**20.00**
RCA Victor LSP-2833	*(S)*	**My Kind Of Folk Songs** *(Color cover)*	1965	**10.00**	**25.00**
		(Later covers have a different photo in full-color.)			
RCA Victor LSP-3305	*(M)*	**Lovin' Place**	1965	**8.00**	**20.00**
RCA Victor LSP-3305	*(S)*	**Lovin' Place**	1965	**10.00**	**25.00**
RCA Victor LPM-3325	*(M)*	**The Many Faces Of Gale Garnett**	1965	**8.00**	**20.00**
RCA Victor LSP-3325	*(S)*	**The Many Faces Of Gale Garnett**	1965	**10.00**	**25.00**
RCA Victor LPM-3498	*(M)*	**Variety Is The Spice Of Gale Garnett**	1966	**8.00**	**20.00**
RCA Victor LSP-3498	*(S)*	**Variety Is The Spice Of Gale Garnett**	1966	**10.00**	**25.00**
RCA Victor LPM-3586	*(M)*	**New Adventures**	1966	**8.00**	**20.00**
RCA Victor LSP-3586	*(S)*	**New Adventures**	1966	**10.00**	**25.00**
RCA Victor LPM-3747	*(M)*	**Flying And Rainbows And Love**	1967	**10.00**	**25.00**
RCA Victor LSP-3747	*(S)*	**Flying And Rainbows And Love**	1967	**10.00**	**25.00**
Columbia CL-2825	*(M)*	**An Audience With The King Of Wands**	1968	**6.00**	**15.00**
Columbia CS-9625	*(S)*	**An Audience With The King Of Wands**	1968	**6.00**	**15.00**
Columbia CS-9760	*(S)*	**Sausalito Heliport**	1969	**6.00**	**15.00**
GARRETT, JOANN					
Chess LP-1548	*(S)*	**Just A Taste**	1969	**6.00**	**15.00**
GARVIN, REX, & THE MIGHTY CRAVERS					
Tower ST-5130	*(S)*	**Raw Funky Earth**	1968	**8.00**	**20.00**
GAS MASK					
Tonsil 4001	*(S)*	**Gas Mask**	1970	**8.00**	**20.00**
GASCA, LOUIS					
Blue Thumb BTS-5985	*(S)*	**For Those Who Chant**	1972	**4.00**	**10.00**

After leaving the safe, if constricting, confines of Genesis in 1975, Peter Gabriel issued a series of self-titled albums for several labels. This, the fourth, is subtitled Security, and was issued promotionally as a "Limited Edition Pressing" on Quiex II vinyl. This patented version of virgin vinyl was an attempt by several companies to attract added exposure via FM play by programmers with an audiophile bent. Whether or not it achieved its desired goals is a moot point today. What it did do was create a number of collectibles for vinyl junkies everywhere!

Label & Catalog #		Title	Year	VG+	NM
GATES, DAVID					
Gates was a member of Bread.					
Elektra EKS-75066	(S)	**David Gates' First**	1973	1.00	5.00
Elektra EQ-5066	(Q)	**David Gates' First**	1973	4.00	10.00
Elektra 7E-1028	(S)	**Never Let Her Go**	1975	.80	4.00
Elektra 6E-148	(S)	**Goodbye Girl**	1978	.80	4.00
Elektra 6E-251	(S)	**Falling In Love Again**	1980	.80	4.00
Arista AL-9563	(S)	**Take Me Now**	1981	.80	4.00
GATES, HEN, & HIS GATERS					
Masterseal MLP-700	(M)	**Let's All Dance To Rock And Roll**	195?	30.00	75.00
Masterseal MSLP-5005	(S)	**Let's All Dance To Rock And Roll**	195?	30.00	75.00
		(Apparently, all copies of MSLP-5005 play mono.)			
Plymouth R12-144	(M)	**Rock And Roll**	1956	30.00	75.00
Paris 3	(M)	**Rock 'N' Roll Festival**	1957	30.00	75.00
		(Paris 3 contains one side by Hen Gates and the other by Sarah Vaughan and Dizzie Gillespie.)			
GATORCREEK					
Gatorcreek features Kenny Loggins.					
Mercury SR-61311	(S)	**Gatorcreek**	1970	5.00	12.00
GAUCHOS, THE					
ABC-Paramount ABC-506	(M)	**The Gauchos Featuring Jim Doval**	1965	10.00	25.00
ABC-Paramount ABCS-506	(S)	**The Gauchos Featuring Jim Doval**	1965	12.00	30.00
GAYE, MARVIN					
Refer to Diana Ross & Marvin Gaye; Mary Wells & Marvin Gaye.					
Tamla T-221	(M)	**Soulful Moods Of Marvin Gaye**	1961	600.00	1,200.00
Tamla T-239	(M)	**That Stubborn Kind Of Fella**	1963	300.00	600.00
Tamla T-242	(M)	**Recorded Live On Stage**	1963	150.00	300.00
Tamla T-251	(M)	**When I'm Alone I Cry**	1964	60.00	150.00
Tamla T-252	(M)	**Marvin Gaye's Greatest Hits**	1964	12.00	30.00
Tamla TS-252	(S)	**Marvin Gaye's Greatest Hits**	1964	16.00	40.00
Tamla T-258	(M)	**How Sweet It Is To Be Loved By You**	1965	16.00	40.00
Tamla TS-258	(S)	**How Sweet It Is To Be Loved By You**	1965	20.00	50.00
Tamla T-259	(M)	**Hello Broadway, This Is Marvin**	1965	16.00	40.00
Tamla TS-259	(S)	**Hello Broadway, This Is Marvin**	1965	20.00	50.00
Tamla T-261	(M)	**Tribute To The Great Nat King Cole**	1965	16.00	40.00
Tamla TS-261	(S)	**Tribute To The Great Nat King Cole**	1965	20.00	50.00
Tamla T-266	(M)	**Moods Of Marvin Gaye**	1966	12.00	30.00
Tamla TS-266	(S)	**Moods Of Marvin Gaye**	1966	16.00	40.00
Tamla T-278	(M)	**Marvin Gaye's Greatest Hits, Volume 2**	1967	6.00	15.00
Tamla TS-278	(S)	**Marvin Gaye's Greatest Hits, Volume 2**	1967	8.00	20.00
		—*Tamla albums above have two side-by-side circles at the top of the label.*—			
Tamla T-285	(M)	**In The Groove**	1968	20.00	50.00
Tamla TS-285	(S)	**In The Groove**	1968	10.00	25.00
Tamla TS-285	(S)	**I Heard It Through The Grapevine**	1968	8.00	20.00
		("Grapevine" is a repackage of "In The Groove.")			
Tamla TS-292	(S)	**M. P. G.**	1969	8.00	20.00
Tamla TS-293	(S)	**Marvin Gaye And His Girls**	1969	8.00	20.00
		(Duets with Tammi Terrell and Kim Weston.)			
Tamla TS-299	(S)	**That's The Way Love Is**	1970	6.00	15.00
Tamla TS-300	(S)	**Marvin Gaye's Super Hits**	1970	6.00	15.00
Tamla TS-310	(S)	**What's Going On**	1971	4.00	10.00
Tamla TS-322	(S)	**Trouble Man** *(Soundtrack)*	1972	4.00	10.00
Tamla TS-329	(S)	**Let's Get It On**	1973	4.00	10.00
Motown M9-791A3	(S)	**Anthology** *(3 LPs)*	1974	6.00	15.00
Tamla TS-333	(S)	**Marvin Gaye Live!**	1974	4.00	10.00
Tamla T6-342S1	(S)	**I Want You**	1976	4.00	10.00
Tamla T6-348	(S)	**Marvin Gaye's Greatest Hits**	1976	4.00	10.00
Tamla T7-352R2	(S)	**Live (At The London Palladium)** *(2 LPs)*	1977	6.00	15.00
Tamla TS-364	(S)	**Hear, My Dear** *(2 LPs)*	1979	6.00	15.00
Tamla TS-374	(S)	**In Our Lifetime**	1981	4.00	10.00
Kory 1011	(S)	**Marvin Gaye's Greatest Hits, Vol. 2**	1976	4.00	10.00
Natural Resources 4007	(S)	**Soulful Moods Of Marvin Gaye**	1978	4.00	10.00
Motown M5-125V1	(S)	**M. P. G.**	1983	1.00	5.00
Motown M5-181V1	(S)	**Live (At The London Palladium)** *(2 LPs)*	1983	1.00	5.00
Motown M5-191V1	(S)	**Marvin Gaye's Greatest Hits**	1983	1.00	5.00
Motown M5-192V1	(S)	**Let's Get It On**	1983	1.00	5.00
Motown M5-216V1	(S)	**Tribute To The Great Nat King Cole**	1983	1.00	5.00
Motown M5-218V1	(M)	**That Stubborn Kind Of Fella**	1983	1.00	5.00
Motown 5292	(S)	**I Want You**	1983	1.00	5.00
Motown 5295	(S)	**Hear, My Dear** *(2 LPs)*	1983	1.00	5.00
Motown 5296	(S)	**Moods Of Marvin Gaye**	1983	1.00	5.00
Motown 5301	(S)	**Marvin Gaye's Super Hits**	1983	1.00	5.00
Motown 6058	(S)	**Every Great Motown Hit Of Marvin Gaye**	1983	1.00	5.00
Columbia FC-38197	(S)	**Midnight Love**	1982	1.00	5.00
Columbia HC-48197	(S)	**Midnight Love** *(Half-speed master)*	1984	16.00	50.00

The passing of Jerry Garcia from this plane of endeavor sparked a most interesting reaction from right-winged pundits. These writers, who normally reserve their vitriol for "liberal" Democratic candidates in the field of politics, felt an apparently undeniable urge to drop their cover and expose themselves for what they truly are: Frustrated record reviewers for Rolling Stone! The ranting approached the bizarre with one inspired writer condescendingly referring to Garcia merely as "a third-tier rock guitar player." Which inspires the retort, "Who, pray tell, are the first and second-tier players?" The only other thing that arouses the same reaction is an Oliver Stone movie. . .

Label & Catalog #		Title	Year	VG+	NM

GAYE, MARVIN, & TAMMI TERRELL

Label & Catalog #		Title	Year	VG+	NM
Tamla T-277	(M)	United	1967	10.00	25.00
Tamla TS-277	(S)	United	1967	12.00	30.00
		—Tamla albums above have two side-by-side circles at the top of the label.—			
Tamla T-284	(M)	You're All I Need	1968	20.00	50.00
Tamla TS-284	(S)	You're All I Need	1968	8.00	20.00
Tamla TS-294	(S)	Easy	1969	8.00	20.00
Tamla TS-302	(S)	Greatest Hits	1970	6.00	15.00
Motown M5-142V1	(S)	You're All I Need	1983	1.00	5.00
Motown M5-225V1	(S)	Greatest Hits	1983	1.00	5.00

GAYE, MARVIN, & KIM WESTON

Tamla T-260	(M)	Side By Side	1965	Unreleased	
Tamla TS-260	(S)	Side By Side	1965	Unreleased	
Tamla T-270	(M)	Take Two	1966	12.00	30.00
Tamla TS-270	(S)	Take Two	1966	16.00	40.00
		—Tamla albums above have two side-by-side circles at the top of the label.—			

GEDDES, DAVID

| Big Tree 89511 | (S) | Run Joey, Run | 197? | 4.00 | 10.00 |

GENE & DEBBIE

| T.R.X. LPS-1001 | (S) | Hear And Now | 1968 | 10.00 | 25.00 |

GENESIS

This Genesis is an American band.

Mercury SR-61175	(S)	In The Beginning	1968	14.00	35.00
		—Mercury albums above have red labels with Mercury head on top—			
London LC-50006	(S)	In The Beginning	1977	1.00	5.00

GENESIS

This Genesis is a UK band and features Peter Gabriel and Phil Collins.

Impulse ASD-9205	(S)	Trespass	1971	10.00	25.00
ABC X-816	(S)	Trespass	1971	4.00	10.00
MCA X-816	(S)	Trespass	1978	.80	4.00
Fam. Charisma CAS-1052	(S)	Nursery Cryme (Pink label)	1971	4.00	10.00
Fam. Charisma CAS-1058	(S)	Foxtrot (Pink label)	1972	4.00	10.00
Fam. Charisma CAS-6060	(S)	Selling England By The Pound	1973	4.00	10.00
Fam. Charisma CA-1066	(S)	Genesis Live	1974	4.00	10.00
Fam. Charisma CA-2701	(S)	Nursery Cryme / Foxtrot (2 LPs)	1976	4.00	10.00
London PS-643	(S)	From Genesis To Revelation	1974	8.00	20.00
		(This is the first American release of Genesis' 1969 debut album.)			
Buddah BDS-5659	(S)	The Best Of Genesis (2 LPs)	1976	4.00	10.00
Atco SD-2-401	(S)	The Lamb Lies Down On Broadway (2 LPs)	1974	4.00	10.00
Atco SD-36-129	(S)	A Trick Of The Tail	1976	4.00	10.00
Atco SD-36-144	(S)	Wind And Wuthering	1977	4.00	10.00
Atco SD-38-100	(S)	Wind And Wuthering	1979	.80	4.00
Atco SD-38-101	(S)	A Trick Of The Tail	1979	.80	4.00
Atlantic 1800	(S)	Spot The Pigeon	1977	.80	4.00
Atlantic SD-9002	(S)	Seconds Out (2 LPs)	1977	1.00	5.00
Atlantic SD-19173	(S)	And Then There Were Three	1978	.80	4.00
Atlantic SD-16014	(S)	Duke	1980	.80	4.00
Atlantic SD-19313	(S)	Abacab	1981	.80	4.00
Atlantic SD-2000	(S)	Three Sides Live (2 LPs)	1982	1.00	5.00
Atlantic 80116	(S)	Genesis	1983	.80	4.00
Atlantic 80030	(S)	Nursery Cryme	1983	.80	4.00

GENTLE GIANT

Vertigo VE-1005	(S)	Acquiring The Taste	1971	6.00	15.00
Columbia KC-31649	(S)	Three Friends	1972	4.00	10.00
Columbia KC-32022	(S)	Octopus	1973	4.00	10.00
Capitol ST-11337	(S)	The Power And The Glory	1974	4.00	10.00
Capitol ST-11428	(S)	Free Hand	1975	4.00	10.00
Capitol ST-11532	(S)	Interview	1976	4.00	10.00
Capitol ST-11592	(S)	Playing The Fool	1977	4.00	10.00
Capitol ST-11696	(S)	The Missing Piece	1977	4.00	10.00
Capitol ST-11813	(S)	Giant For A Day	1978	4.00	10.00
Capitol SN-16044	(S)	The Power And The Glory	1980	.80	4.00
Capitol SN-16045	(S)	Giant For A Day	1980	.80	4.00
Capitol SN-16046	(S)	The Missing Piece	1980	.80	4.00
Capitol SN-16047	(S)	Interview	1980	.80	4.00
Capitol SN-16048	(S)	Free Hand	1980	.80	4.00

GENTLE SOUL

| Epic BN-26374 | (S) | Gentle Soul | 1968 | 60.00 | 150.00 |

GENTRYS, THE

| MGM E-4336 | (M) | Keep On Dancing | 1965 | 8.00 | 20.00 |
| MGM SE-4336 | (P) | Keep On Dancing | 1965 | 10.00 | 25.00 |

The cover for Capitol's Dracula's Deuce *credits "Monstrous Vocals and Instrumentals by The Ghouls," yet another pseudonym for Gary Usher and his talented group of musicians. On this outing, Usher exploited two fads at once: The explosion of interest in automobile and classic movie monsters, spurred on by magazines such as "Car Model" and Forrest J. Acker-man's "Famous Monsters Of Filmland." Unfortunately, the idea didn't catch on, the record didn't sell, and, thirty years later, the field has a major collectible.*

Label & Catalog #		Title	Year	VG+	NM
MGM E-4346	(M)	Gentry Time	1966	8.00	20.00
MGM SE-4346	(S)	Gentry Time	1966	10.00	25.00
MGM GAS-127	(S)	The Gentrys	1970	8.00	20.00
Sun 117	(S)	The Gentrys	1970	12.00	30.00
GEORDIE					
MGM SE-4903	(S)	Hope You Like It	1973	12.00	30.00
GEORGE, BARBARA					
A.F.O. 5001	(M)	I Know (You Don't Love Me Anymore)	1962	100.00	250.00
GEORGE, LOWELL					
Lowell was the founder of Little Feat.					
Warner Bros. 3194	(S)	Thanks, I'll Eat It Here	1979	4.00	10.00
GERONIMO BLACK					
Uni 73132	(S)	Geronimo Black	1972	10.00	25.00
Helios 4405	(S)	Welcome Back	1980	5.00	12.00
GERRY & THE PACEMAKERS					
Laurie LLP-2024	(M)	Don't Let The Sun Catch You Crying	1964	12.00	30.00
Laurie SLP-2024	(E)	Don't Let The Sun Catch You Crying	1964	10.00	25.00
Laurie T-90555	(M)	Don't Let The Sun Catch You Crying	1965	12.00	30.00
Laurie DT-90555	(E)	Don't Let The Sun Catch You Crying	1965	12.00	30.00
		(Capitol Record Club)			
Laurie LLP-2027	(M)	Gerry & The Pacemakers' Second Album	1964	12.00	30.00
Laurie SLLP-2027	(E)	Gerry & The Pacemakers' Second Album	1964	12.00	30.00
Laurie LLP-2030	(M)	I'll Be There	1964	10.00	25.00
Laurie SLLP-2030	(E)	I'll Be There	1964	12.00	30.00
United Arts. UAL-3387	(M)	Ferry Cross The Mersey	1965	10.00	25.00
United Arts. UAS-6387	(S)	Ferry Cross The Mersey	1965	16.00	40.00
		(This soundtrack also has background music by George Martin)			
United Arts. T-90812	(M)	Ferry Cross The Mersey (Capitol Rec. Club)	196?	16.00	40.00
United Arts. ST-90812	(M)	Ferry Cross The Mersey (Capitol Rec. Club)	196?	20.00	50.00
		(The Capitol Record Club pressings have different cover art.)			
Laurie LLP-2031	(M)	Greatest Hits	1965	10.00	25.00
Laurie SLLP-2031	(E)	Greatest Hits	1965	6.00	15.00
Laurie T-90384	(M)	Greatest Hits (Capitol Record Club)	1965	10.00	25.00
Laurie DT-90384	(E)	Greatest Hits (Capitol Record Club)	1965	10.00	25.00
Laurie LLP-2037	(M)	Girl On A Swing	1966	10.00	25.00
Laurie SLP-2037	(E)	Girl On A Swing	1966	8.00	20.00
Capitol SM-11898	(S)	The Best Of Gerry & The Pacemakers	1979	1.00	5.00
		("I Like It," "I'm The One" and "Away From You" are in mono.)			
GHENT, TOM					
Tetragrammaton 113	(S)	Tom Ghent	1969	4.00	10.00
GHOULS, THE					
The Ghouls are a creation of Gary Usher & Co.					
Capitol T-2215	(M)	Dracula's Deuce	1965	60.00	150.00
Capitol ST-2215	(S)	Dracula's Deuce	1965	80.00	200.00
GIANT					
Mercury SR-61285	(S)	What's In This Life For You	1970	4.00	10.00
GIANT CRAB					
Uni 73037	(S)	A Giant Crab Comes Forth	1968	10.00	25.00
Uni 73057	(S)	Cool It, Helios	1969	10.00	25.00
GIBB, ROBIN					
Robin Gibb is a member of The Bee Gees.					
Atco SD-33-323	(S)	Robin's Reign	1970	8.00	20.00
GIBSON, HARRY					
Sutton SSU-313	(M)	Rockin' Rhythm	196?	6.00	15.00
GIBSON, STEVE, & THE RED CAPS					
Mercury MG-25115	(10")	You're Driving Me Crazy	1954	200.00	400.00
Mercury MG-25116	(10")	Blueberry Hill	1954	200.00	400.00
GIDEON & POWER					
Bell 1104	(S)	I Gotta Be Me	1972	4.00	10.00
GILES, GILES & FRIPP					
GG&F features Robert Fripp.					
Deram DES-18019	(S)	The Cheerful Insanity Of Giles, Giles And Fripp	1968	30.00	75.00

Label & Catalog #		Title	Year	VG+	NM
GILLESPIE, DANA					
London PS-540	(S)	Foolish Seasons	1968	12.00	30.00
GILMER, JIMMY, & THE FIREBALLS: Refer to THE FIREBALLS					
GIRARD, CHUCK					
Chuck was the lead singer for The Hondells. Refer to Lovesong.					
Good News GNR-001	(DJ)	The Chuck Girard Radio Special	1979	6.00	15.00
Good News 8110	(S)	Take A Hand (Picture disc)	1979	4.00	10.00
GLACIERS, THE					
Mercury MG-20895	(M)	From Sea To Ski	1964	20.00	50.00
Mercury SR-60895	(S)	From Sea To Ski	1964	30.00	75.00
GLAD					
ABC S-655	(S)	Feelin' Glad	1969	10.00	25.00
GLASS FAMILY ELECTRIC BAND, THE					
Warner Bros. WS-1776	(S)	The Glass Family Electric Band	1969	6.00	15.00
GLASS HARP, THE					
The Glass Harp features lead guitarist Phil Keaggy.					
Decca DL-75261	(S)	Glass Harp	1971	10.00	25.00
Decca DL-75306	(S)	Synergy	1971	12.00	30.00
Decca DL-75358	(S)	It Makes Me Glad	1972	12.00	30.00
MCA 293	(S)	Glass Harp	1977	4.00	10.00
		(MCA 293 is a reissue of Decca 75261.)			
GLASS HOUSE, THE					
Kirshner KES-108	(S)	Globetrotters	1971	5.00	12.00
Invictus ST-7305	(S)	Inside The Glass House	1971	4.00	10.00
Invictus ST-9810	(S)	Thanks, I Needed That	1972	4.00	10.00
GLASS PRISM, THE					
RCA Victor LSP-4201	(S)	Poe Through The Glass Prism	1969	6.00	15.00
RCA Victor LSP-4270	(S)	On Joy And Sorrow	1970	6.00	15.00
GLENN, LLOYD					
Swing Time 1901	(10")	Lloyd Glenn	1954	See note below	
		(Swing Time 1901 has a suggested NM value of $3,000-4,000.)			
Aladdin LP-808	(M)	Chica Boo (Red vinyl)	1956	1,000.00	2,000.00
Aladdin LP-808	(M)	Chica Boo	1956	500.00	1,000.00
Score SLP-4006	(M)	Lloyd Glenn	1957	500.00	1,000.00
Score SLP-4020	(M)	After Hours	1958	500.00	1,000.00
Imperial LP-9174	(M)	Chica Boo	1962	60.00	150.00
Imperial LP-12174	(S)	Chica Boo	1962	80.00	200.00
Imperial LP-9175	(M)	After Hours	1962	60.00	150.00
Imperial LP-12175	(S)	After Hours	1962	80.00	200.00
Black & Blue 33077	(S)	Old Time Shuffle	1977	4.00	10.00
GLITTER, GARY					
Bell 1108	(S)	Gary Glitter	1972	4.00	10.00
GLITTER BAND, THE					
Gary Glitter's former mates.					
Arista 207	(S)	Makes You Blind	1976	4.00	10.00
GLITTERHOUSE					
Dynovoice 31905	(S)	Color Blind	1968	6.00	15.00
GLORY					
Avalanche LA148	(S)	Glory	1973	6.00	15.00
GNARLY, PHIL & THE TOUGH GUYS					
Flaming Pie 319	(S)	Philville	1987	4.00	10.00
GO-GO'S, THE					
RCA Victor LPM-2930	(M)	Swim With The Go-Go's	1964	6.00	15.00
RCA Victor LSP-2930	(S)	Swim With The Go-Go's	1964	8.00	20.00
GO-GO'S, THE					
I.R.S. 70021	(S)	Beauty And The Beat (Blue cover)	1981	.80	4.00
I.R.S. 70021	(S)	Beauty And The Beat (Pink cover)	1981	.80	4.00
I.R.S. 70031	(S)	Vacation	1981	.80	4.00
I.R.S. 70041	(S)	Talk Show	1981	.80	4.00
GO ZOO BAND					
Go Go 22170004	(S)	Sounds That Are Happening	196?	6.00	15.00

Label & Catalog #		Title	Year	VG+	NM

GODCHAUX, KEITH & DONNA
Refer to The Grateful Dead; The Heart Of Gold Band.

| Round RX-104 | (S) | **Keith And Donna** | 1975 | 12.00 | 30.00 |

GODLEY & CREME
Kevin Godley and Lol Creme, formerly of 10CC.

Mercury MK-41	(DJ)	**Musical Excerpts From Consequences**	1977	4.00	10.00
Mercury SRM-3-1700	(S)	**Consequences** *(3 LPs)*	1977	3.00	10.00
Polydor PD-6177	(S)	**'L'**	1978	1.00	5.00
Polydor PD-6257	(S)	**Freeze Frame**	1979	1.00	5.00

GODFREY DANIEL
Godfrey Daniel consists of members of The Amboy Dukes setting '60s hits to '50s white doo-woppy arrangements.

| Atlantic SD-7219 | (S) | **Take A Sad Song** | 1971 | 6.00 | 15.00 |

GODZ, THE

ESP-Disk' 1037	(M)	**Contact High With The Godz**	1967	30.00	75.00
ESP-Disk' 1037	(S)	**Contact High With The Godz**	1967	20.00	50.00
ESP-Disk' 1047	(S)	**Godz 2**	1968	20.00	50.00
ESP-Disk' 1077	(S)	**Third Testament**	1969	20.00	50.00
ESP-Disk' 2017	(S)	**Godzundheit**	1970	20.00	50.00
Millennium 8003	(S)	**The Godz**	1978	10.00	25.00
Casablanca NBLP-7134	(S)	**Nothing Is Sacred**	1979	10.00	25.00

GOEDERT, RON

| Polydor PD-1-6265 | (S) | **Breaking All The Rules** | 1980 | 6.00 | 15.00 |

GOGGLES, THE

| Audio Fidelity AFSD-6244 | (S) | **The Goggles** | 1971 | 6.00 | 15.00 |

GOLDBERG, BARRY
Refer to The Electric Flag.

Epic LN-24199	(M)	**Blowing My Mind**	1966	12.00	30.00
Epic BN-26199	(S)	**Blowing My Mind**	1966	16.00	40.00
Buddah BDS-5012	(S)	**The Barry Goldberg Reunion**	1968	10.00	25.00
Buddah BDS-5029	(S)	**Barry Goldberg Recorded Live**	1970	10.00	25.00
Buddah BDS-5051	(S)	**Street Man**	1970	6.00	15.00
Buddah BDS-5081	(S)	**Blast From My Past**	1971	6.00	15.00
Record Man 5015	(S)	**Barry Goldberg And Friends**	1972	6.00	15.00
Atco SD-36-7040	(S)	**Barry Goldberg**	1974	5.00	12.00
		(SD-7040 features Bob Dylan on backing vocals/percussion.)			

GOLDEN, LOTTI

| Atlantic SD-8223 | (S) | **Motor-Cycle** | 1969 | 4.00 | 10.00 |

GOLDEN DAWN

International Art. 4	(S)	**Power Plant**	1968	30.00	75.00
International Art. 4	(S)	**Power Plant**	1979	6.00	15.00
		(Reissues have "Masterfonics" stamped in the trail-off vinyl.)			

GOLDEN EARRING

Capitol T-2823	(M)	**Winter Harvest**	1967	20.00	50.00
Capitol ST-2823	(E)	**Winter Harvest**	1967	10.00	25.00
Capitol ST-164	(S)	**Miracle Mirror**	1969	16.00	40.00
Capitol ST-11315	(S)	**Golden Earring**	1974	5.00	12.00
Atlantic SD-8244	(S)	**Eight Miles High**	1969	10.00	25.00
Track 396	(S)	**Moontan** *(Nude dancer cover)*	1973	6.00	15.00
Track 396	(S)	**Moontan**	1973	1.00	5.00
Track 2139	(S)	**Switch**	1975	1.00	5.00
MCA 2183	(S)	**To The Hilt**	1976	1.00	5.00
MCA 2254	(S)	**Mad Love**	1977	1.00	5.00
MCA 2353	(S)	**Moontan**	1977	.80	4.00
MCA 8009	(S)	**Golden Earring Live!** *(2 LPs)*	1977	1.20	6.00
MCA 3057	(S)	**Grab It For A Second**	1978	1.00	5.00
MCA 703	(S)	**Grab It For A Second**	1978	.80	4.00
MCA 6004	(S)	**Golden Earring Live!** *(2 LPs)*	1981	1.00	5.00
Polydor PD-6223	(S)	**No Promises... No Debts**	1979	1.00	5.00
Polydor PD-6303	(S)	**Long Blond Animal**	1980	1.00	5.00
"21" 9004	(S)	**Cut**	1982	.80	4.00
"21" 9008	(S)	**N.E.W.S.**	1984	.80	4.00
"21" 823717	(S)	**Something Heavy Going Down**	1984	.80	4.00

GOLDMARK, ANDY

| Warner Bros. BS-2703 | (S) | **Andy Goldmark** *(Produced by Gary Usher)* | 1973 | 5.00 | 12.00 |

GOLDSBORO, BOBBY

| United Arts. UAL-3358 | (M) | **The Bobby Goldsboro Album** | 1964 | 8.00 | 20.00 |
| United Arts. UAS-6358 | (S) | **The Bobby Goldsboro Album** | 1964 | 10.00 | 25.00 |

Lesley Gore was a teenage singing sensation, topping the charts with her first single and following with three more Top Tenners in a row! As an album artist, she was rather less successful, although her LPs are uniformly well-crafted and impeccably performed. Oddly, as the '60s progressed, Ms. Gore's albums became increasingly harder to find in stereo, generally the opposite of what one should expect. Possibly, as they sold poorly, initial press runs were primarily mono, the demand not justifying later runs, where the bulk of the stereo pressings would have been. California Nights is one such album sought after by stereo collectors. Rarer still is the second volume of Golden Hits, an album which many collectors have never seen!

Label & Catalog #		Title	Year	VG+	NM
United Arts. UAL-3381	(M)	I Can't Stop Loving You	1964	8.00	20.00
United Arts. UAS-6381	(S)	I Can't Stop Loving You	1964	10.00	25.00
United Arts. UAL-3425	(M)	Little Things	1965	8.00	20.00
United Arts. UAS-6425	(S)	Little Things	1965	10.00	25.00
United Arts. UAL-3471	(M)	Broomstick Cowboy	1966	8.00	20.00
United Arts. UAS-6471	(S)	Broomstick Cowboy	1966	10.00	25.00
United Arts. UAL-3486	(M)	It's Too Late	1966	8.00	20.00
United Arts. UAS-6486	(S)	It's Too Late	1966	10.00	25.00
United Arts. UAL-3552	(M)	Blue Autumn	1966	8.00	20.00
United Arts. UAS-6552	(S)	Blue Autumn	1966	10.00	25.00
United Arts. UAL-3561	(M)	Solid Goldsboro/Greatest Hits	1967	5.00	12.00
United Arts. UAS-6561	(S)	Solid Goldsboro/Greatest Hits	1967	6.00	15.00
United Arts. UAL-3599	(M)	Romantic, Soulful, Wacky	1967	5.00	12.00
United Arts. UAS-6599	(S)	Romantic, Soulful, Wacky	1967	6.00	15.00
United Arts. UAL-3615	(M)	Our Way Of Life	1967	5.00	12.00
United Arts. UAS-6615	(S)	Our Way Of Life	1967	6.00	15.00
United Arts. UAS-6642	(S)	Honey	1968	6.00	15.00
United Arts. UAS-6657	(S)	Word Pictures	1968	6.00	15.00
United Arts. UAS-6704	(S)	Today	1969	6.00	15.00
United Arts. UAS-6735	(S)	Muddy Mississippi Line	1970	6.00	15.00
United Arts. UAS-5502	(S)	Bobby Goldsboro's Greatest Hits	1970	5.00	12.00
United Arts. UAS-6777	(S)	We Gotta Start Lovin'	1971	5.00	12.00
United Arts. UAS-5516	(S)	Come Back Home	1971	4.00	10.00
United Arts. SP-58	(S)	Family Album (Promo compilation)	1971	20.00	50.00
United Arts. UAS-5578	(S)	California Wine	1972	4.00	10.00
United Arts. LA-019	(S)	Brand New Kind Of Love	1972	3.20	8.00
United Arts. LA-124	(S)	Summer (The First Time)	1973	3.20	8.00
United Arts. LA-311	(S)	10th Anniversary Album (2 LPs)	1975	4.00	10.00
United Arts. LA-424G	(S)	Through The Eyes Of A Man	1975	3.20	8.00
United Arts. LA-639G	(S)	Butterfly For Bucky	1976	1.00	5.00
Sunset SUS-5284	(S)	Pledge Of Love	1970	3.20	8.00
Doral	(S)	Doral Presents Bobby Goldsboro	1971	6.00	15.00
		(Promotional compilation of previously released material.)			
Epic PE-34703	(S)	Goldsboro	1977	1.00	5.00

GOLDTONES, THE

LaBrea L-8011	(M)	The Goldtones	1961	16.00	40.00
LaBrea LS-8011	(S)	The Goldtones	1961	20.00	50.00

GOLIATH

ABC S-702	(S)	Goliath	1979	5.00	12.00

GOLLIWOGS, THE

The Golliwogs was an early incarnation of Creedence Clearwater Revival.

Fantasy F-9474	(M)	Pre-Creedence	1975	12.00	30.00

GOOD & PLENTY

Senate 21001	(S)	The World Of Good & Plenty	196?	12.00	30.00

GOOD GUYS, THE

The Good Guys is a pseudonym for The Challengers.

Crescendo GNP-2001	(M)	Sidewalk Surfing	1964	10.00	25.00
Crescendo GNPS-2001	(S)	Sidewalk Surfing	1964	12.00	30.00
		—GNP albums above have red labels.—			

GOOD GUYS, THE

United Arts. UAL-3370	(M)	The Good Guys Sing	1964	5.00	12.00
United Arts. UAS-6370	(S)	The Good Guys Sing	1964	6.00	15.00

GOOD OLD BOYS, THE

Round 576	(S)	Pistol Packin' Mama	1976	10.00	25.00

GOOD RATS, THE

Kapp KS-3580	(S)	The Good Rats	1969	10.00	25.00
Warner Bros. BS-2813	(S)	Tasty	1974	5.00	12.00
Platinum RCR-8001	(S)	Rat City In Blue	1976	6.00	15.00
Passport SP-20	(DJ)	Rats The Way You Like It-Live	1978	6.00	30.00
Passport PB-9825	(S)	From Rats To Riches	1978	4.00	10.00
Passport PB-9830	(S)	Birth Comes To Us All	1978	1.00	5.00
Rat City RCR-998	(S)	Live At Last (2 LPs)	1980	1.20	6.00
Rat City 8002	(S)	Tasty	1978	1.00	5.00
Rat City 8003	(S)	Great American Music	1981	1.00	5.00

GOOD, THE BAD & THE UGLY, THE

Mercury SR-61253	(S)	The Good, The Bad & The Ugly	1970	4.00	10.00

GOOD TIMES, THE

Kama Sutra KLP-8052	(M)	The Good Times	1966	6.00	15.00
Kama Sutra KLPS-8052	(S)	The Good Times	1966	8.00	20.00

Label & Catalog #		Title	Year	VG+	NM
GOODIES, THE					
Hip HIS-7002	(S)	Candy Coated Goodies	1969	10.00	25.00
GOODNESS & MERCY					
MGM SE-4730	(S)	Goodness & Mercy	1970	4.00	10.00
GOODTHUNDER					
Elektra EKS7-5041	(S)	Goodthunder	1972	6.00	15.00
GOOSE CREEK SYMPHONY					
Capitol ST-444	(S)	Goose Creek Symphony	1970	4.00	10.00
Capitol ST-690	(S)	Welcome To Goose Creek	1971	4.00	10.00
Capitol ST-11044	(S)	Words Of Earnest	1972	4.00	10.00
Columbia KC-32918	(S)	Do Your Thing But Don't Touch Mine	1974	1.20	6.00
GORDIAN KNOT, THE					
Verve V-5062	(M)	Tones	1968	5.00	12.00
Verve V6-5062	(S)	Tones	1968	6.00	15.00
GORDON, ROBERT					
Private Stock 2030	(S)	Robert Gordon With Link Wray	1977	4.00	10.00
Private Stock 7008	(S)	Fresh Fish Special	1978	4.00	10.00
RCA Victor AFL1-3294	(DJ)	Rock Billy Boogie (White vinyl)	1979	4.00	10.00
RCA Victor AFL1-3294	(S)	Rock Billy Boogie	1979	1.00	5.00
RCA Victor DJL1-3411	(DJ)	The Essential Robert Gordon	1979	4.00	10.00
RCA Victor AFL1-3523	(S)	Bad Boy	1980	1.00	5.00
RCA Victor AFL1-3773	(S)	Are You Gonna Be The One	1981	1.00	5.00
GORDON 'N ROGERS					
Capitol STAO-276	(S)	Bug In!	1969	8.00	20.00
GORE, LESLEY					
Mercury MG-20805	(M)	I'll Cry If I Want To	1963	12.00	30.00
Mercury SR-60805	(S)	I'll Cry If I Want To	1963	16.00	40.00
		(Original covers for Mercury 2/60805 have a plain white border.)			
Mercury MG-20805	(M)	I'll Cry If I Want To	1964	6.00	15.00
Mercury SR-60805	(S)	I'll Cry If I Want To	1964	8.00	20.00
		(Later covers have a green blurb in the border for "It's My Party.")			
Mercury MG-20849	(M)	Lesley Gore Sings Of Mixed Up Hearts	1963	12.00	30.00
Mercury SR-60849	(S)	Lesley Gore Sings Of Mixed Up Hearts	1963	16.00	40.00
Mercury MG-20901	(M)	Boys, Boys, Boys	1964	12.00	30.00
Mercury SR-60901	(S)	Boys, Boys, Boys	1964	16.00	40.00
Mercury MG-20943	(M)	Girl Talk	1964	12.00	30.00
Mercury SR-60943	(S)	Girl Talk	1964	16.00	40.00
Mercury MG-21024	(M)	The Golden Hits Of Lesley Gore (12 tracks)	1965	8.00	20.00
Mercury SR-61024	(S)	The Golden Hits Of Lesley Gore (12 tracks)	1965	12.00	30.00
		(SR-61024 contains different takes of "You Don't Own Me," "I Don't Wanna Be A Loser," and "Look Of Love" from those on MG-21024.)			
Mercury SR-61024	(S)	The Golden Hits Of Lesley Gore (10 tracks)	196?	6.00	15.00
Mercury MG-21042	(M)	My Town, My Guy And Me	1965	8.00	20.00
Mercury SR-61042	(S)	My Town, My Guy And Me	1965	12.00	30.00
Mercury MG-21066	(M)	All About Love	1966	8.00	20.00
		(MG-21066 covers have an earlier photo of Ms Gore with short hair. The liner notes are by Carol Myntner.)			
Mercury SR-61066	(S)	All About Love	1966	12.00	30.00
		(SR-61066 covers have a newer photo of Lesley with long hair. The liner notes are by Anthony DeFilipps.)			
Mercury MG-21120	(M)	California Nights	1967	8.00	20.00
Mercury SR-61120	(S)	California Nights	1967	16.00	40.00
Mercury SR-61185	(S)	The Golden Hits Of Lesley Gore, Volume 2	1968	16.00	40.00
Wing SRW-16350	(S)	Girl Talk	1968	6.00	15.00
		(Wing SRW-16350 is a reissue of 60943.)			
Wing SRW-16382	(S)	Love, Love, Love	1968	6.00	15.00
		(Wing 16382 is an abridged reissue of 61066 with the same cover photo.)			
Wing PKW-2-119	(S)	The Sound Of Young Love (2 LPs)	1969	12.00	30.00
		(Wing 119 repackages 16350 and 16382.)			
Mowest MW-117L	(S)	Someplace Else Now	1972	6.00	15.00
A&M SP-4564	(S)	Love Me By Name	1975	6.00	15.00
GOULDMAN, GRAHAM					
Mr Gouldman was later a member of Hotlegs and 10CC.					
RCA Victor LPM-3954	(M)	Graham Gouldman Thing	1968	20.00	50.00
RCA Victor LSP-3954	(S)	Graham Gouldman Thing	1968	20.00	50.00
GRACIOUS					
Gracious features Paul Davis.					
Capitol ST-602	(S)	Gracious	1970	16.00	40.00

Label & Catalog #		Title	Year	VG+	NM

GRAFFITI

| ABC ABCS-663 | (S) | Graffiti | 1968 | 80.00 | 200.00 |

GRAHAM, DAVY

| London PS-552 | (S) | Large As Life And Twice As Natural | 1968 | 16.00 | 40.00 |

GRAHAM CENTRAL STATION [LARRY GRAHAM & GRAHAM CENTRAL STATION]
Larry Graham originally recorded as a member of Sly's Family Stone.

Warner Bros. 2763	(S)	Graham Central Station	1974	4.00	10.00
Warner Bros. BS4-2763	(Q)	Graham Central Station	1975	8.00	20.00
Warner Bros. 2814	(S)	Release Yourself	1974	4.00	10.00
Warner Bros. 2876	(S)	Ain't No 'Bout-A-Doubt It	1975	4.00	10.00
Warner Bros. BS4-2876	(Q)	Ain't No 'Bout-A-Doubt It	1975	8.00	20.00
Warner Bros. 2937	(S)	Mirror	1976	4.00	10.00
Warner Bros. 3041	(S)	Now Do-U-Wanta Dance	1977	4.00	10.00
Warner Bros. 3175	(S)	My Radio Sure Sounds Good To Me	1978	4.00	10.00
Warner Bros. 3322	(S)	Star Walk	1979	4.00	10.00
Warner Bros. 3447	(S)	One In A Million	1980	1.20	6.00
Warner Bros. 3554	(S)	Just Be My Lady	1981	1.20	6.00
Warner Bros. 3668	(S)	Sooner Or Later	1982	1.20	6.00
Warner Bros. 23878	(S)	Victory	1983	1.20	6.00

GRAND FUNK RAILROAD [GRAND FUNK]
Grand Funk was Mark Farner, Don Brewer, Mel Schacher and Craig Frost under the wing of producer and manager Terry Knight . Refer to Flint; Terry Knight & The Pack.

Capitol ST-307	(S)	On Time	1969	6.00	15.00
Capitol SKAO-406	(S)	Grand Funk	1969	6.00	15.00
Capitol SKAO-471	(S)	Closer To Home	1970	6.00	15.00
Capitol SWBB-633	(S)	Grand Funk/Live Album	1970	6.00	15.00
Capitol SW-764	(S)	Survival	1971	6.00	15.00
Capitol SW-853	(S)	E Pluribus Funk	1971	6.00	15.00
		— Capitol albums above have green labels.—			
Capitol ST-307	(S)	On Time	1972	1.00	5.00
Capitol SKAO-406	(S)	Grand Funk	1972	1.00	5.00
Capitol SKAO-471	(S)	Closer To Home	1972	1.00	5.00
Capitol SWBB-633	(S)	Grand Funk/Live Album	1972	1.00	5.00
Capitol SW-764	(S)	Survival	1972	1.00	5.00
Capitol SW-853	(S)	E Pluribus Funk	1972	1.00	5.00
Capitol SABB-11042	(S)	Mark, Don And Mel 1969-71 (2 LPs)	1972	4.00	10.00
Capitol SMAS-11099	(S)	Phoenix	1972	4.00	10.00
Capitol SMAS-11207	(S)	We're An American Band	1973	4.00	10.00
Capitol SMAS-11207	(DJ)	We're An American Band (Gold vinyl)	1973	10.00	25.00
Capitol SMAS-11207	(S)	We're An American Band (Gold vinyl)	1973	4.00	10.00
		(Both the DJ and stock copies include a sheet of four stickers.)			
Capitol SWAE-11278	(S)	Shinin' On	1974	4.00	10.00
Capitol SO-11356	(S)	All The Girls In The World Beware (With poster)	1974	6.00	15.00
Capitol SO-11356	(S)	All The Girls In The World Beware (Without poster)	1974	4.00	10.00
Capitol SABB-11445	(S)	Caught In The Act	1975	4.00	10.00
Capitol ST-11482	(S)	Born To Die	1975	4.00	10.00
Capitol ST-11579	(S)	Grand Funk/Hits	1976	4.00	10.00
MCA 2216	(S)	Good Singin,' Good Playin'	1976	4.00	10.00
		(MCA 2216 was produced by Frank Zappa.)			
Full Moon FMH-3625	(S)	Grand Funk Lives	1981	1.00	5.00
Full Moon 23750	(S)	What's Funk	1983	1.00	5.00

GRANDMOTHERS, THE
The Grandmothers consist of, naturally, former members of Frank Zappa's Mothers Of Invention.

| Rhino RWSP-302 | (S) | The Grandmothers | 1980 | 1.00 | 5.00 |
| Rhino RNLP-804 | (S) | Lookin' Up Granny's Dress | 1984 | 1.00 | 5.00 |

GRANFALLOON

| Takoma 9021 | (S) | Lazer Pace | 1973 | 4.00 | 10.00 |

GRANICUS

| RCA Victor AFL1-0321 | (S) | Granicus | 1973 | 6.00 | 15.00 |

GRANMAX

| Panam 1002 | (S) | A Ninth Alive (White vinyl) | 1977 | 6.00 | 15.00 |
| Panam 1023 | (S) | Kiss Heaven Goodbye | 1978 | 6.00 | 15.00 |

GRAPEFRUIT

| Dunhill DS-50050 | (S) | Around Grapefruit | 1968 | 8.00 | 20.00 |
| RCA Victor LSP-4215 | (S) | Deep Water | 1969 | 6.00 | 15.00 |

GRASS ROOTS, THE
The Grass Roots were originally (on Dunhill 50011) a studio concoction of Steve Barri and Phil Sloan's. Their success led to the formation of a "real" group based around vocalist Rob Grill.

| Dunhill D-50011 | (M) | Where Were You When I Needed You? | 1966 | 20.00 | 50.00 |
| Dunhill DS-50011 | (S) | Where Were You When I Needed You? | 1966 | 30.00 | 75.00 |

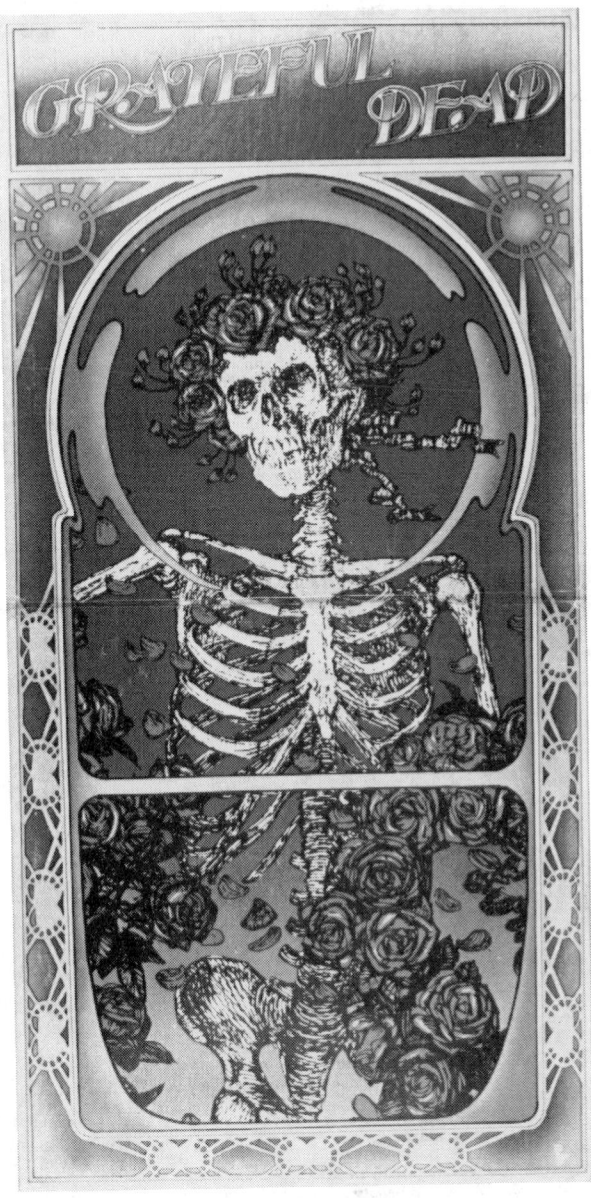

This live double album, tentatively titled Skullfuck by the group for its 1971 release, was changed simply to Grateful Dead after persuasive negotiations by Warner's head Joe Smith. The album is referred to as the "Skull & Roses" album in deference to the beautiful artwork of Alton Kelley, one of the original—and finest—of the San Francisco psychedelic poster artists. While the Dead are the epitome of artists who haven't "sold out" they have nonetheless sold well with two dozen charting albums and eight RIAA Gold Records.

Label & Catalog #		Title	Year	VG+	NM
Dunhill D-50020	(M)	Let's Live For Today	1967	12.00	30.00
Dunhill DS-50020	(S)	Let's Live For Today	1967	16.00	40.00
Dunhill D-50027	(M)	Feelings	1968	12.00	30.00
Dunhill DS-50027	(S)	Feelings	1968	8.00	20.00
Dunhill DS-50047	(S)	Golden Grass	1968	8.00	20.00
Dunhill DS-50052	(S)	Lovin' Things	1969	6.00	15.00
Dunhill DS-50067	(S)	Leavin' It All Behind	1969	6.00	15.00
Dunhill DS-50087	(S)	More Golden Grass	1970	6.00	15.00
Dunhill DSX-50107	(S)	Their 16 Greatest Hits	1971	4.00	10.00
Command QD-40013	(Q)	Their 16 Greatest Hits	1974	10.00	25.00
Dunhill DSX-50112	(S)	Move Along	1972	4.00	10.00
Dunhill DXS-50137	(S)	A Lotta' Mileage	1973	4.00	10.00
Haven ST-9204	(S)	The Grass Roots	1975	4.00	10.00
ABC AC-30003	(S)	The ABC Collection	1976	1.00	5.00
MCA 5331	(S)	Powers Of The Night	1982	1.00	5.00

GRATEFUL DEAD, THE

Original recording members were Jerry Garcia, Bill Kreutzmann, Phil Lesh, Ron "Pig Pen" McKernan (who died in 1973) and Bob Weir with lyricist Robert Hunter. Mickey Hart joined in 1967, left 1970 and rejoined permanently in 1974. Tom Constanten was a member from 1968 through '70. Keith and Donna Godchaux joined 1971 and left in 1978. Brent Mydland was a member from 1979 through his death in 1990. Jerry's death in 1995 ended the group's career as The Grateful Dead. Refer to Bob Dylan; Kingfish; The Rhythm Devils; Touchstone.

Warner Bros. W-1689	(M)	The Grateful Dead	1967	30.00	75.00
Warner Bros. WS-1689	(S)	The Grateful Dead	1967	20.00	50.00
		—Warner albums above have gold labels.—			
Warner Bros. WS-1689	(S)	The Grateful Dead	1968	8.00	20.00
Warner Bros. WS-1749	(S)	Anthem Of The Sun (Purple cover)	1968	10.00	25.00
Warner Bros. WS-1790	(S)	Aoxomoxoa	1969	10.00	25.00
Warner Bros. 2WS-1830	(S)	Live/Dead (2 LPs with booklet)	1970	14.00	35.00
		— Warner albums above have green labels with a "W7" logo on top.—			
Warner Bros. WS-1689	(S)	The Grateful Dead	197?	4.00	10.00
Warner Bros. WS-1749	(S)	Anthem Of The Sun (Purple cover)	197?	4.00	10.00
Warner Bros. WS-1749	(S)	Anthem Of The Sun (White cover)	197?	20.00	50.00
		(Copies of WS-1749 with a white background on the cover contain a radically remixed album within, courtesy of Mr Lesh.)			
Warner Bros. WS-1790	(S)	Aoxomoxoa	197?	4.00	10.00
Warner Bros. 2WS-1830	(S)	Live/Dead (2 LPs)	1970	6.00	15.00
Warner Bros. WS-1869	(S)	Workingman's Dead	1970	6.00	15.00
		(Original covers for WS-1869 are textured and the art on the back is upside down.)			
Warner Bros. WS-1893	(S)	American Beauty	1970	6.00	15.00
Warner Bros. 2WS-1935	(S)	Grateful Dead (2 LPs with sticker)	1971	10.00	25.00
		(WS-1935 was originally issued with a "Skull & Roses" sticker.)			
Warner Bros. 2WS-1935	(S)	Grateful Dead (2 LPs without sticker)	1971	8.00	20.00
Warner Bros. 3WX-2668	(S)	Europe '72 (3 LPs with booklet)	1972	8.00	20.00
		—Warner albums above have green labels with a "WB" logo on top.—			
Warner Bros. WS-1689	(S)	The Grateful Dead	1977	1.00	5.00
Warner Bros. WS-1749	(S)	Anthem Of The Sun	1977	1.00	5.00
Warner Bros. WS-1790	(S)	Aoxomoxoa	1977	1.00	5.00
Warner Bros. 2WS-1830	(S)	Live/Dead (2 LPs)	1977	3.20	8.00
Warner Bros. WS-1869	(S)	Workingman's Dead	1977	1.00	5.00
Warner Bros. WS-1893	(S)	American Beauty	1977	1.00	5.00
Warner Bros. 2WS-1935	(S)	The Grateful Dead (2 LPs)	1977	3.20	8.00
Warner Bros. 3WS-2668	(S)	Europe '72 (3 LPs)	1977	4.00	10.00
Warner Bros. BS-2721	(S)	The History Of The Grateful Dead, Vol. 1 (Bear's Choice)	1977	1.00	5.00
Warner Bros. W-2764	(S)	Skeletons From The Closet/ The Best Of The Grateful Dead	1977	1.00	5.00
Warner Bros. 2W-3091	(S)	What A Long Strange Trip It's Been (2 LPs)	1977	3.20	8.00
		— Warner Bros. albums above have a Burbank street scene on the label.—			
Warner Bros. WS-1689	(S)	The Grateful Dead	1985	.80	4.00
Warner Bros. WS-1749	(S)	Anthem Of The Sun	1985	.80	4.00
Warner Bros. WS-1790	(S)	Aoxomoxoa	1985	.80	4.00
Warner Bros. 2WS-1830	(S)	Live/Dead (2 LPs)	1985	.80	4.00
Warner Bros. WS-1869	(S)	Workingman's Dead	1985	1.20	6.00
Warner Bros. WS-1893	(S)	American Beauty	1985	.80	4.00
Warner Bros. 2WS-1935	(S)	The Grateful Dead (2 LPs)	1985	.80	4.00
Warner Bros. 3WS-2668	(S)	Europe '72 (3 LPs)	1985	1.20	6.00
Warner Bros. BS-2721	(S)	The History Of The Grateful Dead, Vol. 1 (Bear's Choice)	1985	3.20	8.00
Warner Bros. W-2764	(S)	Skeletons From The Closet/ The Best Of The Grateful Dead	1985	.80	4.00
Warner Bros. 2W-3091	(S)	What A Long Strange Trip It's Been (2 LPs)	1985	1.20	6.00
		—Warner Bros. albums above have tan labels.—			
Sunflower SUN-5001	(S)	Vintage Dead	1970	12.00	30.00
		(Counterfeits are 1/4" shorter than normal album covers.)			
Sunflower SNF-5004	(S)	Historic Dead	1971	12.00	30.00
Pride PRD-0016	(S)	History Of The Grateful Dead	1972	12.00	30.00

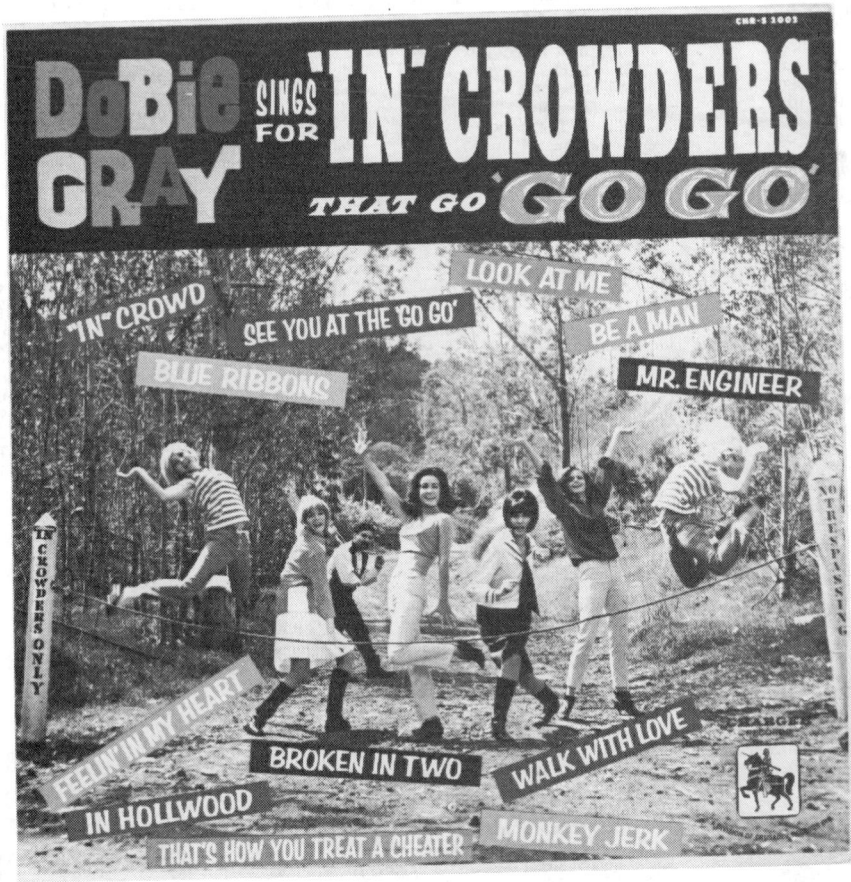

Dobie Gray's "The In Crowd" defined for millions of not-so-popular teenaged listeners including wallflowers, bookworms, art students, record collectors (this is getting a bit too autobiographical here. . .) and other such nebbishes just what it was that they were missing. The album that followed is rare enough in stereo that many collectors have never seen it, although sheer rarity has never been the defining factor in a collectible's worth. Without demand, and there is relatively little for Mr Gray's efforts, collectibles can remain undervalued for years. As for Mr Gray's career, he has been anything but quiet: He was part of the Los Angeles production of "Hair;" recorded with the rock group, Pollution; and received his first RIAA Gold Record Award for 1973's "Drift Away," one of the finest singles of the '70s.

Label & Catalog #		Title	Year	VG+	NM
Verve V6-5093	(S)	Grateful Dead	1972	Unreleased	
		(As Verve was owned by MGM, this may have been a reissue of the Sunflower material or additional live recordings from 1966.)			
Grateful Dead GD-01	(S)	Wake Of The Flood (Green vinyl)	1973	200.00	400.00
		(The green vinyl was issued to members of the fan club. Most of the copies were damaged by local flooding!)			
Grateful Dead GD-01	(S)	Wake Of The Flood	1973	6.00	15.00
		(Original covers of GD-01 do not have the artists on the back.)			
Grateful Dead GD-01	(S)	Wake Of The Flood	1975	8.00	20.00
		(Second pressings have contributing artists listed on the back.)			
Grateful Dead GD-102	(S)	From The Mars Hotel	1974	10.00	25.00
Grateful Dead LA-494	(S)	Blues For Allah	1975	8.00	20.00
United Arts. SP-114	(DJ)	For Dead Heads	1975	16.00	40.00
Grateful Dead LA-620	(S)	Steal Your Face (2 LPs)	1976	6.00	15.00
Arista SP-35	(DJ)	Grateful Dead Sampler	1977	12.00	30.00
Arista AL-7001	(DJ)	Terrapin Station (Banded for air-play)	1977	20.00	50.00
Arista AL-7001	(S)	Terrapin Station	1977	1.00	5.00
Arista AB-4198	(S)	Shakedown Street	1978	1.00	5.00
Arista AL-9508	(S)	Go To Heaven	1980	1.00	5.00
Arista A2L-8604	(S)	Reckoning (2 LPs)	1981	10.00	25.00
Arista A2L-8606	(S)	Dead Set (2 LPs)	1981	6.00	15.00
Pair ARP2-1053	(S)	For The Faithful (2 LPs)	1984	1.20	6.00
Arista AL-8452	(S)	In The Dark	1988	1.00	5.00

GRAVENITES, NICK
Refer to Big Brother & The Holding Company; Mike Bloomfield & Nick Gravenites; The Electric Flag;.

Columbia CS-9899	(S)	My Labors	1969	6.00	15.00
		—Columbia albums above have "360 Sound" labels.—			

GRAVY TRAIN

Polydor 24-4056	(S)	Gravy Train	1970	16.00	40.00
Bell 1121	(S)	Second Birth	1973	8.00	20.00

GRAY, DOBIE
Dobie Gray later recorded with Pollution.

Stripe LPM-2001	(M)	Look-Dobie Gray	1963	40.00	100.00
Charger CHR-M-2002	(M)	Dobie Gray Sings For In Crowders	1965	20.00	50.00
Charger CHR-S-2002	(S)	Dobie Gray Sings For In Crowders	1965	30.00	75.00
Decca DL-75397	(S)	Drift Away	1973	5.00	12.00
MCA 371	(S)	Loving Arms	1973	4.00	10.00
MCA 449	(S)	Hey Dixie	1974	4.00	10.00
Capricorn CP-0163	(S)	New Ray Of Sunshine	1976	4.00	10.00

GREASE BAND, THE
The Grease Band was Joe Cocker's backing band on his early albums.

Shelter 8904	(S)	The Grease Band	1971	5.00	12.00

GREAT BEAR

Scepter SS-585	(S)	Great Bear	1971	4.00	10.00

GREAT JONES

Tonsil 4002	(S)	All Bowed Down!	1970	6.00	15.00

GREAT METROPOLITAN STEAM BAND, THE

Decca DL-75143	(S)	The Great Metropolitan Steam Band	1970	4.00	10.00

GREAT SOCIETY, THE
The Great Society features Grace Slick, later of Jefferson Airplane.

Columbia CS-9624	(S)	Conspicuous Only In Its Absence	1968	10.00	25.00
Columbia CS-9702	(S)	How It Was	1968	10.00	25.00
		—Columbia albums above have "360 Sound" labels.—			
Harmony KH-30391	(S)	Somebody To Love	1970	3.20	8.00
Columbia G-30459	(S)	The Great Society/Collectors Item (2 LPs)	1971	3.20	8.00
		(Columbia 30459 repackages 9624 and 9702.)			

GREAT SPECKLED BIRD
GSB features Ian and Sylvia Tyson.

Ampex A-10103	(S)	Great Speckled Bird	197?	8.00	20.00

GREATEST SHOW ON EARTH, THE

Harvest SKAO-351	(S)	Horizons	1970	5.00	12.00

GREAVES, R.B.

Atco SD-33-311	(S)	R.B. Greaves	1969	6.00	15.00

GREEK FOUNTAIN RIVER FRONT BAND, THE

Montel LLP-110	(M)	The Greek Fountain River Front Band Takes Requests	1965	50.00	125.00

Ronald Bertram Greaves was born on a United States Air Force base. His mother was the sister of Sam Cooke while his father was a Native American. He was raised on a Seminole reservation. While I can't really say for sure that this means much of anything, it certainly could be viewed as portentous by those who believe such things. And he did take his first hit single, "Take A Letter Maria," to the top of most of the nation's charts in 1969.

Label & Catalog #		Title	Year	VG+	NM
GREEN					
Atco SD-33-282	(S)	Green	1969	6.00	15.00
Atco SD-33-366	(S)	To Help Somebody	1971	4.00	10.00
GREEN, AL					
Hot Line 1500	(M)	Back Up Train	1967	20.00	50.00
Hot Line 1500	(S)	Back Up Train	1967	30.00	75.00
		(Al Green's name is spelled "Al Greene" on this album.)			
Bell 6076	(S)	Al Green	1971	8.00	20.00
Kory 1005	(S)	Al Green	1977	4.00	10.00
		(Bell 6076 and Kory 1005 are reissues of Hot Line 1500.)			
Hi SHL-32055	(S)	Green Is Blues	1969	6.00	15.00
Hi SHL-32062	(S)	Al Green Gets Next To You	1971	6.00	15.00
Hi SHL-32070	(S)	Let's Stay Together	1972	6.00	15.00
Hi SHL-32074	(S)	I'm Still In Love With You	1972	6.00	15.00
Hi SHL-32077	(S)	Call Me	1973	6.00	15.00
Hi SHL-32082	(S)	Livin' For You	1973	6.00	15.00
Hi SHL-32087	(S)	Al Green Explores Your Mind	1974	6.00	15.00
Hi SHL-2	(S)	Al Green Radio Special *(Promo interview)*	1974	40.00	100.00
Hi SHL-32089	(S)	Al Green's Greatest Hits	1975	6.00	15.00
		—Hi albums above have orange & white labels.—			
Hi SHL-32055	(S)	Green Is Blues	197?	1.00	5.00
Hi SHL-32062	(S)	Al Green Gets Next To You	197?	1.00	5.00
Hi SHL-32070	(S)	Let's Stay Together	197?	1.00	5.00
Hi SHL-32074	(S)	I'm Still In Love With You	197?	1.00	5.00
Hi SHL-32077	(S)	Call Me	197?	1.00	5.00
Hi SHL-32082	(S)	Livin' For You	197?	1.00	5.00
Hi SHL-32087	(S)	Al Green Explores Your Mind	197?	1.00	5.00
Hi SHL-32089	(S)	Al Green's Greatest Hits	197?	1.00	5.00
Hi SHL-32092	(S)	Al Green Is Love	1975	4.00	10.00
Hi SHL-32097	(S)	Full Of Fire	1976	4.00	10.00
Hi SHL-32103	(S)	Have A Good Time	1976	4.00	10.00
Hi SHL-32105	(S)	Al Green's Greatest Hits, Volume 2	1977	4.00	10.00
		—Hi albums above have gray labels.—			
Hi SHL-8000	(S)	Tired Of Being Alone	1977	4.00	10.00
Hi SHL-6004	(S)	The Belle Album	1977	4.00	10.00
Hi SHL-6009	(S)	Truth 'N' Time	1978	4.00	10.00
Myrrh 6661	(S)	Highway To Heaven	1981	4.00	10.00
Myrrh 6674	(S)	Higher Plane	1981	4.00	10.00
Motown 5290	(S)	Let's Stay Together	1982	.80	4.00
Motown 5284	(S)	I'm Still In Love With You	1982	.80	4.00
Motown 5286	(S)	Call Me	1982	.80	4.00
Motown 5287	(S)	Al Green Explores Your Mind	1982	.80	4.00
Motown 5283	(S)	Al Green's Greatest Hits	1982	.80	4.00
Motown 5285	(S)	Full Of Fire	1982	.80	4.00
Motown 5291	(S)	Al Green's Greatest Hits, Volume 2	1982	.80	4.00
Motown 5302	(S)	Tokyo... Live *(2 LPs)*	1983	1.20	6.00
GREEN, PETER					
Green was a member of Fleetwood Mac.					
Reprise RS-6436	(S)	The End Of The Game	1971	8.00	20.00
GREEN, VERNON, & THE MEDALLIONS					
Dooto DLT-857	(M)	Vernon Green & The Medallions	197?	12.00	30.00
GREEN BULLFROG					
Green Bullfrog features Richie Blackmore and Jon Lord of Deep Purple.					
Decca DL-75269	(S)	Green Bullfrog	1971	10.00	25.00
GREEN LYTE SUNDAY					
RCA Victor LSP-4327	(S)	Green Lyte Sunday	1970	4.00	10.00
GREENBAUM, NORMAN					
Reprise RS-6365	(S)	Spirit In The Sky	1969	8.00	20.00
Reprise RS-6422	(S)	Back Home Again	1970	4.00	10.00
Reprise MS-2048	(S)	Petaluma	1972	4.00	10.00
GREENE, RICHARD					
Reprise BS-2787	(S)	Muleskinner	197?	4.00	10.00
GREENSLADE					
Warners BS-2698	(S)	Greenslade	1973	5.00	12.00
Mercury SRM-1-1015	(S)	Spy Guest	1974	4.00	10.00
Mercury SRM-1-1025	(S)	Time And Tide	1975	4.00	10.00
GREENWICH, ELLIE					
Ms. Greenwich was a member of The Raindrops.					
United Arts. UAS-6648	(S)	Composes, Produces And Sings	1968	20.00	50.00
Verve V6-5091	(S)	Let It Be Written, Let It Be Sung	1973	10.00	25.00

Label & Catalog #		Title	Year	VG+	NM
GRIER, ROOSEVELT					
Ric M-1008	(M)	Soul City	1964	8.00	20.00
Ric S-1008	(S)	Soul City	1964	8.00	20.00
GREGG, BOBBY					
Epic LN-24051	(M)	"Let's Stomp" And "Wild Weekend"	1963	14.00	35.00
Epic BN-26051	(S)	"Let's Stomp" And "Wild Weekend"	1963	20.00	50.00
GRIFFIN					
Romar 2001	(S)	Griffin	1972	4.00	10.00
GRIFFIN, JIMMY					
Jimmy Griffin later recorded as James Griffin with Bread.					
Reprise R-6091	(M)	Summer Holiday	1963	20.00	50.00
Reprise R9-6091	(S)	Summer Holiday	1963	30.00	75.00
GRIFFITH, SHIRLEY					
Bluesville BVLP-1087	(M)	The Blues Of Shirley Griffith	1964	30.00	75.00
—Bluesville albums above have bright blue labels with silver print.—					
Bluesville BVLP-1087	(M)	The Blues Of Shirley Griffith	1964	10.00	25.00
—Bluesville albums above have blue labels with a trident logo on the right side.—					
GRIN					
Grin features Nils Lofgren.					
Spindizzy 257-30321	(S)	Grin	1971	4.00	10.00
Spindizzy 257-31038	(S)	1 Plus 1	1971	4.00	10.00
Spindizzy KZ-31701	(S)	All Out	1972	4.00	10.00
Columbia LE-10265	(S)	All Out *(Remixed)*	1973	1.00	5.00
A&M SP-4415	(S)	Gone Crazy	1973	1.00	5.00
GRINGO					
Decca DL-75314	(S)	Gringo	1971	4.00	10.00
GROOTNA					
Grootna features Marty Balin.					
Columbia C-31033	(S)	Grootna	1971	6.00	15.00
GROOV-U					
Gateway GLP-3010	(M)	Groov-U On Campus	196?	16.00	40.00
GROOVIE GOOLIES, THE					
RCA Victor LSP-4420	(S)	The Groovie Goolies	1970	10.00	25.00
GROUNDHOGS, THE					
Cleve CH-82871	(S)	The Groundhogs With John Lee Hooker And John Mayall	1968	60.00	150.00
World Pacific WPS-21892	(S)	Scratching The Surface	1968	16.00	40.00
Imperial LP-12452	(S)	Blues Obituary	1969	16.00	40.00
Liberty LST-7644	(S)	Thank Christ For The Bomb *(Promo)*	1970	60.00	150.00
(Promos of LSP-7644 with 12" x 12" folder, booklet and press kit.)					
Liberty LST-7644	(S)	Thank Christ For The Bomb	1970	14.00	35.00
United Arts. SP-??	(S)	Live At Leeds *(Promo only with script)*	1971	80.00	200.00
United Arts. UAS-5513	(S)	The Groundhogs Split *(Promo)*	1971	30.00	75.00
(Promos with 12" x 12" folder, press kit and leather pouch.)					
United Arts. UAS-5513	(S)	The Groundhogs Split	1971	10.00	25.00
United Arts. UAS-5570	(S)	Who Will Save The World	1972	10.00	25.00
United Arts. LA008	(S)	Hogwash	1973	10.00	25.00
United Arts. LA603	(S)	Crosscut Saw	1976	10.00	25.00
United Arts. LA680	(S)	Black Diamond	1976	10.00	25.00
GROUP, THE					
RCA Victor LPM-2663	(M)	The Group	1963	8.00	20.00
RCA Victor LSP-2663	(S)	The Group	1963	10.00	25.00
GROUP, THE					
Bell 6038	(S)	The Group	1970	8.00	20.00
GROUP IMAGE, THE					
Community A-101	(S)	A Mouth In The Clouds	1968	12.00	30.00
GROUP ONE					
RCA Victor LPM-3524	(M)	Brothers Go To Mothers And Others	1966	6.00	15.00
RCA Victor LST-3524	(S)	Brothers Go To Mothers And Others	1966	8.00	20.00
GROUP THERAPY					
RCA Victor LSP-3976	(S)	People Get Ready For Group Therapy	1968	8.00	20.00
Philips PHS-600-303	(S)	37 Minutes Of Group Therapy	1969	6.00	15.00

Label & Catalog #		Title	Year	VG+	NM

GROWING CONCERN, THE

Label & Catalog #		Title	Year	VG+	NM
Mainstream 56108	(M)	Growing Concern	1968	30.00	75.00
Mainstream S-6108	(S)	Growing Concern	1968	40.00	100.00

GROWL

DiscReet 2209	(S)	Growl	1974	8.00	20.00

GRYPHON
Gryphon features Steve Howe.

Bell 1316	(S)	Red Queen To Gryphon Three	1974	6.00	15.00

GUESS WHO, THE
The original group—Chad Allan, Bob Ashley, Randy Bachman, Jim Kale, and Garry Peterson—from Winnipeg, Canada, was known as Chad Allan & The Reflections, then as The Expressions. Ashley quit in 1965, replaced by Burton Cummings, by which time the group had become The Guess Who. Chad Allan left in '66. Bachman's departed in 1970 and Kale in '72. Refer to Bachman Turner Overdrive; Brave Belt.

Scepter SP-533	(M)	Shakin' All Over	1966	16.00	40.00
Scepter SPS-533	(P)	Shakin' All Over	1966	8.00	20.00
		(While the cover reads Chad Allan & The Expressions, the label credits The Guess Who. "Shakin' All Over," "Clock On The Wall" and "Till We Kissed" are rechanneled.)			
Wand WDS-691	(P)	Born In Canada	1969	6.00	15.00
		(Wand 691 is a reissue of Scepter 533.)			
MGM SE-4645	(S)	The Guess Who	1969	6.00	15.00
Springboard SPB-4022	(P)	Shakin' All Over	1972	1.00	5.00
Pride 0012	(E)	The History Of The Guess Who	1973	4.00	10.00
RCA Victor LSP-4141	(S)	Wheatfield Soul	1969	8.00	20.00
RCA Victor LSP-4157	(S)	Canned Wheat	1969	8.00	20.00
RCA Victor LSP-4266	(S)	American Woman	1970	8.00	20.00
RCA Victor LSP-4359	(S)	Share The Land	1970	8.00	20.00
		—RCA albums above have orange labels on flexible vinyl.—			
RCA Victor LSP-4141	(S)	Wheatfield Soul	1971	3.20	8.00
RCA Victor LSP-4157	(S)	Canned Wheat	1971	3.20	8.00
RCA Victor LSP-4266	(S)	American Woman	1971	3.20	8.00
RCA Victor LSP-4359	(S)	Share The Land	1971	3.20	8.00
RCA Victor LSP-4574	(S)	So Long, Bannatyne	1971	4.00	10.00
RCA Victor LSPX-1004	(S)	The Best Of The Guess Who	1974	4.00	10.00
RCA Victor LSP-4602	(S)	Rockin'	1972	6.00	15.00
RCA Victor LSP-4779	(S)	Live At The Paramount	1972	12.00	30.00
RCA Victor LSP-4830	(S)	Artificial Paradise *(With paper bag)*	1972	10.00	25.00
RCA Victor LSP-4830	(S)	Artificial Paradise *(Without paper bag)*	1972	4.00	10.00
RCA Victor AFD1-0130	(S)	Guess Who No. 10	1973	4.00	10.00
RCA Victor APD1-0130	(Q)	Guess Who No. 10	1973	10.00	25.00
RCA Victor AFD1-0269	(S)	The Best Of The Guess Who, Volume 2	1974	4.00	10.00
RCA Victor APD1-0269	(Q)	The Best Of The Guess Who, Volume 2	1974	10.00	25.00
RCA Victor AFD1-0405	(S)	Road Food	1974	4.00	10.00
RCA Victor APD1-0405	(Q)	Road Food	1974	10.00	25.00
RCA Victor AFD1-0636	(S)	Flavours	1975	4.00	10.00
RCA Victor APD1-0636	(Q)	Flavours	1975	10.00	25.00
		—RCA albums above have orange labels on flexible vinyl.—			
RCA Victor LSP-4141	(S)	Wheatfield Soul	197?	1.00	5.00
RCA Victor LSP-4157	(S)	Canned Wheat	197?	1.00	5.00
RCA Victor LSP-4266	(S)	American Woman	197?	1.00	5.00
RCA Victor LSP-4359	(S)	Share The Land	197?	1.00	5.00
RCA Victor LSP-4574	(S)	So Long, Bannatyne	197?	1.00	5.00
RCA Victor LSPX-1004	(S)	The Best Of The Guess Who	197?	1.00	5.00
RCA Victor LSP-4602	(S)	Rockin'	197?	1.00	5.00
RCA Victor LSP-4779	(S)	Live At The Paramount	197?	1.00	5.00
RCA Victor LSP-4830	(S)	Artificial Paradise	197?	1.00	5.00
RCA Victor AFD1-0130	(S)	Guess Who No. 10	197?	1.00	5.00
RCA Victor AFD1-0269	(S)	The Best Of The Guess Who, Volume 2	197?	1.00	5.00
RCA Victor AFD1-0405	(S)	Road Food	197?	1.00	5.00
RCA Victor AFD1-0636	(S)	Flavours	1975	1.00	5.00
RCA Victor AFD1-0995	(S)	Power In The Music	1975	1.00	5.00
		—RCA albums above have brown labels.—			
RCA Victor APL1-2253	(S)	The Greatest Of The Guess Who	1977	.80	4.00
RCA Victor ANL1-2683	(S)	Rockin'	1978	.80	4.00
RCA Victor AYL1-3662	(S)	The Best Of The Guess Who	1980	.80	4.00
RCA Victor AYL1-3673	(S)	American Woman	1980	.80	4.00
RCA Victor AYL1-3746	(S)	The Greatest Of The Guess Who	1980	.80	4.00
		—RCA albums above have black labels.—			
Pickwick SPC-3246	(S)	Wild One	197?	3.20	8.00
Pickwick ACL-7069	(S)	Wheatfield Soul	1975	3.20	8.00
Hilltak HT-19227	(S)	All This For A Song	1979	3.20	8.00
Hilltak PR-331	(DJ)	Track And Dialogue	1979	10.00	25.00

GUILD, THE
The Guild is a creation of Gary Usher & Co.

Elektra EKS-	(S)	The Guild	1972	10.00	25.00

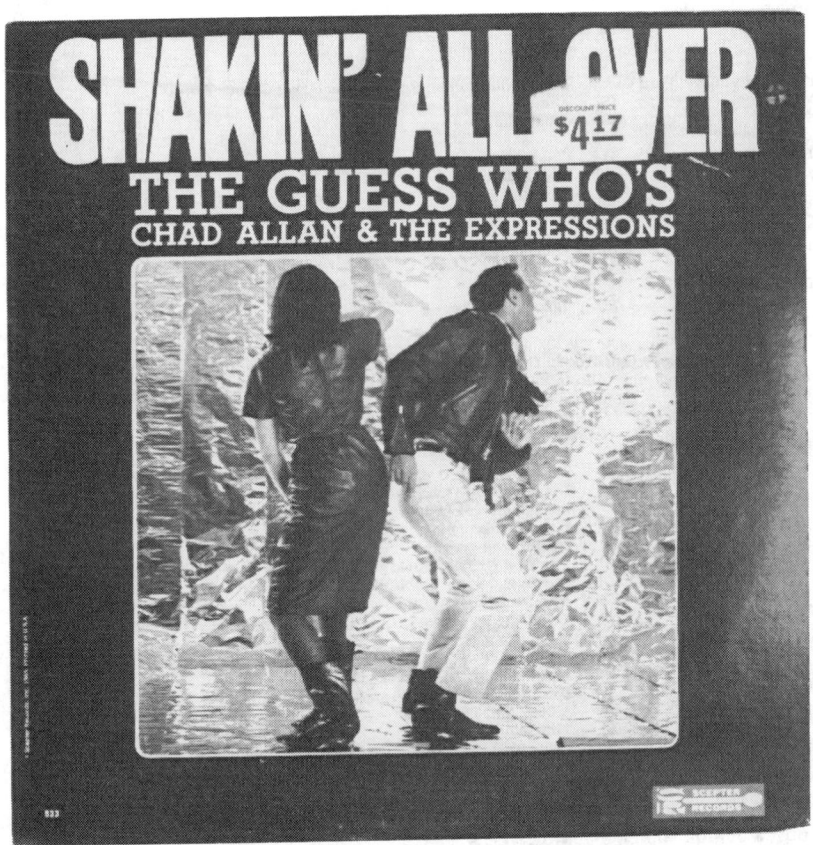

This album's cover would seem to indicate that the record is credited to Chad Allan & The Expressions, which is appropriate, given that that was the name of the group who cut the sides contained within, including the breathtaking version of the title tune. But the label on the record credits Guess Who?, which is also apt, as that was the name applied to the initial pressings of the single of the title tune when issued in Canada in 1965. That the label joke was taken to heart, and that the single was an enormous hit, caused the group to change their name to. . . The Guess Who!

Label & Catalog #		Title	Year	VG+	NM

GUILLORY, ISAAC
Guillory was a member of The Cryan' Shames.

| Atlantic SD-7307 | (S) | Isaac Guillory | 1974 | 5.00 | 12.00 |

GUILLOTINE

| Ampex A-10122 | (S) | Guillotine | 1971 | 6.00 | 15.00 |

GUITAR SLIM
Guitar Slim is a pseudonym for Lee Baker.

Capitol ST-403	(S)	Broke And Hungry	1969	8.00	20.00
Specialty SP-2120	(E)	Things That I Used To Do	1969	8.00	20.00
Arhoolie 2205	(S)	Carolina Blues	197?	4.00	10.00
United US-7764	(E)	Stone Down Blues	197?	3.20	8.00

GULLIVER
Gulliver features Daryl Hall.

| Elektra EKS-74070 | (S) | Gulliver | 1970 | 4.00 | 10.00 |

GUN
Gun features Adrian and Paul Gurvitz (a.k.a. Paul Curtis). Refer to The Baker-Gurvitz Army.

| Epic BN-26468 | (S) | Gun | 1969 | 8.00 | 20.00 |
| Epic BN-26551 | (S) | Gunsight | 1970 | 10.00 | 25.00 |

GUN HILL ROAD

| Mercury SR-61341 | (S) | Gun Hill Road | 1971 | 5.00 | 12.00 |
| Kama Sutra KLS-2061 | (S) | Gun Hill Road | 1972 | 4.00 | 10.00 |

GUNS & BUTTER

| Cotillion SD-9901 | (S) | Guns & Butter | 1972 | 4.00 | 10.00 |

GUNTER, ARTHUR

| Excello LPS-8017 | (E) | Black And Blues | 1971 | 10.00 | 25.00 |

GUTHRIE, ARLO
Arlo Guthrie, son of the legendary Woody Guthrie, is a guitar player, singer and writer in a topical mode. He can also be found on the U.A. soundtrack "Alice's Restaurant."

Reprise R-6267	(M)	Alice's Restaurant	1967	6.00	15.00
Reprise RS-6267	(S)	Alice's Restaurant	1967	6.00	15.00
		—Reprise albums above have green, gold & pink labels.—			
Reprise RS-6267	(S)	Alice's Restaurant	1968	1.00	5.00
Reprise RS-6299	(S)	Arlo	1968	1.00	5.00
Reprise RS-6346	(S)	Running Down The Road	1969	1.00	5.00
		—Reprise albums above have orange & brown labels.—			
Reprise MS-2060	(S)	Hobo's Lullabye	1970	1.00	5.00
Reprise RS-6411	(S)	Washington County	1971	1.00	5.00
Reprise MS-2142	(S)	The Last Of The Brooklyn Cowboys	1972	1.00	5.00
Reprise MS4-2142	(Q)	The Last Of The Brooklyn Cowboys	1973	6.00	15.00
Reprise MS-2183	(S)	Arlo Guthrie	1973	1.00	5.00
Reprise 2R-2214	(S)	Together In Concert (2 LPs with Pete Seeger)	197?	3.20	8.00

GUY, BUDDY

Chess LP-1527	(M)	Left My Blues In San Francisco	1967	12.00	30.00
Chess LPS-1527	(S)	Left My Blues In San Francisco	1967	16.00	40.00
Vanguard VSD-79272	(S)	A Man And The Blues	1968	12.00	30.00
Vanguard VSD-79290	(S)	This Is Buddy Guy	1969	12.00	30.00
Chess LPS-409	(S)	I Was Walking Through the Woods	1970	6.00	15.00
Vanguard VSD-79323	(S)	Hold That Plane!	1972	6.00	15.00
Alligator 4723	(S)	Stone Crazy!	1981	4.00	10.00
Silvertone 1462	(S)	Damn Right, I've Got The Blues	1991	4.00	10.00

GUY, BUDDY, & JUNIOR MANCE & JUNIOR WELLS

| Blue Thumb BYS-20 | (S) | Buddy And The Juniors (Colored vinyl) | 1970 | 20.00 | 50.00 |
| Blue Thumb BYS-20 | (S) | Buddy And The Juniors | 1970 | 10.00 | 25.00 |

GUY, BUDDY, & JUNIOR WELLS

Atco SD-33-364	(S)	Buddy Guy & Junior Wells Play The Blues	1972	6.00	15.00
Blind Pig 1182	(S)	Drinkin' TNT 'N' Smokin' Dynamite	198?	4.00	10.00
Alligator 4802	(S)	Alone And Acoustic	1991	4.00	10.00
Evidence 26002	(S)	Live In Montreux	1992	4.00	10.00

GYPSY

Metromedia 1031	(S)	Gypsy (2 LPs)	1970	6.00	15.00
Metromedia 1044	(S)	In The Garden	1971	5.00	12.00
RCA Victor LSP-4775	(S)	Antithesis	1972	4.00	10.00
RCA Victor APL1-0093	(S)	Unlock The Gate	1973	4.00	10.00

GYPSY

| Decca DL-75299 | (S) | English Gypsy | 1971 | 6.00 | 15.00 |

H. P. LOVECRAFT [LOVECRAFT]

Philips PHM-200-252	(M)	H. P. Lovecraft	1967	8.00	20.00
Philips PHS-600-252	(S)	H. P. Lovecraft	1967	10.00	25.00
Philips PHS-600-279	(S)	Lovecraft II	1968	10.00	25.00
Reprise RS-6419	(S)	Valley Of The Moon	1970	8.00	20.00
Mercury SRM-1-1031	(S)	We Love You	1976	6.00	15.00

(The Reprise and Mercury albums credit Lovecraft.)

HABIBAYYA

Island 9305	(S)	If Man But Knew	1972	5.00	12.00

HACKAMORE BRICK

Kama Sutra KSBS-2025	(S)	One Kiss Leads To Another	1971	5.00	12.00

HAIRCUTS & THE IMPOSSIBLES

Somerset SF-27100	(M)	Beat '66	1966	16.00	40.00
Somerset SF-33100	(S)	Beat '66	1966	20.00	50.00
Somerset SF-27400	(M)	Call It Soul!	1967	16.00	40.00
Somerset SF-33400	(S)	Call It Soul!	1967	20.00	50.00

HALEY, BILL, & HIS COMETS
Bill Haley's first recordings for Essex/Holiday are plainly western swing. But his covers of rhythm'n blues hits "Rocket 88" and "Rock That Joint" and his own "Crazy Man Crazy" are just as plainly among the first "real" rock'n roll records. Signing with Decca in 1954, he cut "Rock Around The Clock," the first international, monster #1 success for the fledgling field. His contributions as one of rock'n roll's progenitors continues to be under-appreciated.

1. Essex Sides

Essex LP-202	(M)	Rock With Bill Haley And The Comets	1955	250.00	600.00
Trans World 202	(M)	Rock With Bill Haley And The Comets	1956	150.00	300.00
Somerset P-4600	(M)	Rock With Bill Haley And The Comets	1957	50.00	150.00

2. Decca Recordings

Decca DL-5560	(10")	Shake, Rattle And Roll	1955	400.00	750.00
Decca DL-8225	(M)	Rock Around The Clock	1956	60.00	150.00
Decca DL-78225	(E)	Rock Around The Clock	1958	30.00	75.00
Decca DL-8315	(M)	Music For The Boyfriend	1956	60.00	150.00
Decca DL-8345	(M)	Rock And Roll Stage Show	1956	80.00	200.00
Decca DL-8569	(M)	Rockin' The Oldies	1957	60.00	150.00
Decca DL-8692	(M)	Rockin' Around The World	1958	60.00	150.00
Decca DL-8775	(M)	Rockin' The Joint	1958	60.00	150.00
Decca DL-8821	(M)	Bill Haley's Chicks	1959	40.00	100.00
Decca DL-78821	(S)	Bill Haley's Chicks	1959	60.00	150.00
Decca DL-8964	(M)	Strictly Instrumental	1960	40.00	100.00
Decca DL-78964	(S)	Strictly Instrumental	1960	60.00	150.00

—Decca albums above have black labels with silver print.—

Decca DL-8225	(M)	Rock Around The Clock	1960	20.00	50.00
Decca DL-78225	(E)	Rock Around The Clock	1960	10.00	25.00

—Decca albums above have black rainbow label with "Mfrd. by Decca Records Inc New York."—

Decca DL-8225	(M)	Rock Around The Clock	1967	12.00	30.00
Decca DL-78225	(E)	Rock Around The Clock	1967	6.00	15.00
Decca DL-5027	(M)	Bill Haley's Greatest Hits	1967	12.00	30.00
Decca DL-75027	(P)	Bill Haley's Greatest Hits	1967	6.00	15.00

—Decca albums above have black rainbow label with "Mfrd. by Decca Records. A division of MCA."—

Decca DL-78225	(E)	Rock Around The Clock	1972	4.00	10.00
Decca DXSE-211	(P)	Golden Hits (2 LPs)	1972	6.00	15.00

—Decca albums above have black rainbow label with "Mfrd. by MCA Records."—

Vocalion VL-3696	(M)	Bill Haley And The Comets	1963	10.00	25.00
MCA/Coral CP55	(S)	Rock Around The Clock	1970	4.00	10.00
MCA/Coral 20015	(S)	Rockin'	1973	4.00	10.00
MCA 161	(DJ)	Bill Haley's Greatest Hits	1973	4.00	10.00
MCA 161	(S)	Bill Haley's Greatest Hits	1973	3.20	8.00

(MCA 161 is a reissue of Decca 75027.)

MCA 78225	(S)	Rock Around The Clock	1973	1.00	5.00

—MCA albums above have black rainbow labels.—

Label & Catalog #		Title	Year	VG+	NM
MCA 78225	(S)	Rock Around The Clock	1978	1.00	5.00
		—MCA albums above have tan & brown labels.—			
MCA 78225	(S)	Rock Around The Clock	1980	1.00	5.00
MCA MCM5004	(E)	Bill Haley's Golden Hits (2 LPs)	1985	1.20	6.00
MCA MCL-1617	(E)	Bill Haley & His Comets	1988	1.00	5.00
		—MCA albums above have blue & white clouds labels.—			

3. Post-Decca Recordings

Label & Catalog #		Title	Year	VG+	NM
Warner Bros. W-1378	(M)	Bill Haley And His Comets	1960	20.00	50.00
Warner Bros. WS-1378	(S)	Bill Haley And His Comets	1960	30.00	75.00
Warner Bros. W-1391	(M)	Bill Haley's Jukebox	1960	20.00	50.00
Warner Bros. WS-1391	(S)	Bill Haley's Jukebox	1960	30.00	75.00
		—WB albums above have gray mono and gold stereo labels.—			
Roulette R-25174	(M)	Twistin' Knights At The Roundtable	1962	30.00	75.00
Roulette SR-25174	(S)	Twistin' Knights At The Roundtable	1962	40.00	100.00
Kama Sutra KLPS-2014	(S)	Scrapbook/Live At The Bitter End	1970	12.00	30.00
Ambassador 98089	(S)	Bill Haley & His Comets	1970	8.00	20.00
Valiant WS-1831	(S)	Rock 'N' Roll Revival	1970	10.00	25.00
Warner Bros. WS-1831	(S)	Rock 'N' Roll Revival	1970	6.00	15.00
		(WB 1831 is a reissue of Valiant 1831.)			
Janus JX25-7003	(S)	Razzle Dazzle (2 LPs)	1971	6.00	15.00
		(Janus 7003 contains previously released sides.)			
Janus JLS-3035	(S)	Travelin' Band	1972	10.00	25.00
Crescendo GNPS-2077	(S)	Rock 'N' Roll	1973	4.00	10.00
Crescendo GNPS-2097	(S)	Rock Around The Country	1976	4.00	10.00
		(GNPS-2097 is a reissue of an album of the same title issued on Sonet in Great Britain in 1971.)			
Springboard SPB-4066	(S)	Greatest Hits Live In London	1977	4.00	10.00
		(SPB-4066 was recorded at London's Hammersmith Palais.)			
Sun SLP-143	(S)	Recorded At Muscle Shoals	1980	4.00	10.00
		(Sun 143 is a reissue of "Bill Haley & His Comets" issued on Sonet in Great Britain in 1976.)			
Great NW Music 4015	(M)	Bill Haley Interviewed By Red Robinson	1981	4.00	10.00
Silhouette SM-10006	(E)	Dedications, Volume 1	1981	4.00	10.00
		(SM-10006 contains live recordings from Alan Freed's 1956 shows.)			
Accord SN-7960	(S)	Live From N.Y.C.	1983	4.00	10.00
		(SN-7960 is a reissue of "Real Live Rock 'N' Roll" released on Ember in Great Britain in 1967.)			
Buddah BDS-69008	(S)	Bill Haley's Scrapbook	1984	4.00	10.00
		(Buddah 69008 is a reissue of Kama Sutra 2014.)			
Ambassador A-98100	(E)	Bill Haley's Rarities	1987	1.00	5.00

4. Budget Reissues, Etc.

Label & Catalog #		Title	Year	VG+	NM
Guest Star GS-1499	(M)	Trini Lopez And Scott Gregory	1964	8.00	20.00
Guest Star GSS-1499	(E)	Trini Lopez And Scott Gregory	1964	4.00	10.00
		(G.S. 1499 contains tracks by Haley credited to "Scott Gregory.")			
Guest Star GS-1454	(M)	Rock Around The Clock King	1964	8.00	20.00
Guest Star GSS-1454	(E)	Rock Around The Clock King	1964	4.00	10.00
Pickwick SHM 3207	(E)	The Original Hits '54-'57	1969	3.20	8.00
Pickwick SPC-3256	(S)	Rockin'	1970	3.20	8.00
Pickwick 2077-2	(E)	Rock 'N' Roll (2 LPs)	1974	4.00	10.00
Pickwick PDA-006	(S)	The Bill Haley Collection (2 LPs)	1976	4.00	10.00
Tellerhouse 78-362	(S)	Rock Around The Clock	197?	3.20	8.00
Piccadilly PIC-3408	(S)	Bill Haley & The Comets	197?	10.00	25.00
51-West 46120	(S)	Greatest Hits	197?	3.20	8.00
Everest 010	(E)	20 Greatest Hits	197?	3.20	8.00
AEI 3106	(S)	Rock Around The Clock	197?	3.20	8.00
Koala AW-14132	(S)	Rock Around The Clock	1979	3.20	8.00
Exact EX-207	(E)	King Of Rock'n'Roll	1980	3.20	8.00
Joker SM-3869	(S)	Rock Around The Clock	1981	3.20	8.00
Phoenix 306	(E)	Bill Haley & The Comets' Greatest Hits	1981	3.20	8.00
Accord SN-7125	(E)	Rockin' And Rollin'	1981	3.20	8.00
Accord SJA-7902	(S)	Mr. Rock 'N' Roll	1982	1.00	5.00
Pair MSM2-35069	(E)	Rock And Roll Giant (2 LPs)	1986	1.00	5.00
Connoisseur VSOP-115	(E)	Bill Haley's Greatest Hits (2 LPs)	1988	1.00	5.00
Connoisseur VSOP-116	(E)	Rip It Up (2 LPs)	1988	1.00	5.00
Everest 4110	(E)	Everest Golden Greats: Bill Haley & The Comets	1988	1.00	5.00

HALFNELSON
Halfnelson is Ron and Russell Mael, later of Sparks.

Label & Catalog #		Title	Year	VG+	NM
Bearsville BV-2048	(S)	Halfnelson (Reissued as "Sparks")	1971	8.00	20.00

HALL, DARYL, & JOHN OATES
Daryl Hall originally recorded with Gulliver.

Label & Catalog #		Title	Year	VG+	NM
Atlantic SD-7242	(S)	Whole Oats	1972	1.20	6.00
Atlantic SD-7269	(S)	Abandoned Luncheonette	1973	1.00	5.00
Atlantic SD-18109	(S)	War Babies	1974	1.00	5.00

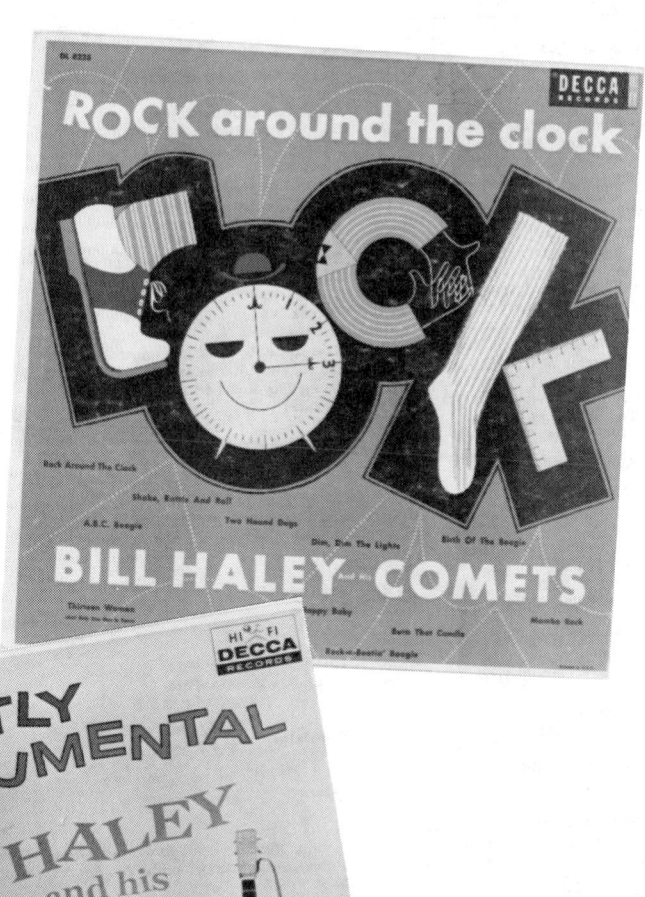

While historians have tended to be less than understanding of Bill Haley's place in the pantheon of rock 'n roll deities, he remains nonetheless a pivotal figure, the first white artist to be able to sell rhythm 'n blues to a white audience in large numbers. . .and get played on the radio! While Rock Around The Clock enjoys some fame, his other Decca albums, such as Strictly Instrumental, rarely receive the attention from collectors they deserve, and finding them in nearly mint condition may be more difficult than the current market values imply.

Label & Catalog #		Title	Year	VG+	NM
Atlantic SD-18123	(S)	No Goodbyes	1977	1.00	5.00
Atlantic SD-19139	(S)	Abandoned Luncheonette	1978	.80	4.00
Chelsea CHL-547	(S)	Past Times Behind	1977	1.00	5.00
RCA Victor APL1-1144	(S)	Daryl Hall & John Oates	1975	1.00	5.00
RCA Victor APL1-1467	(S)	Bigger Than Both Of Us	1976	1.00	5.00
RCA Victor AFL1-2300	(S)	Beauty On A Back Street	1977	1.00	5.00
RCA Victor AFL1-2802	(S)	Livetime	1978	1.00	5.00
RCA Victor AFL1-2804	(S)	Along The Red Ledge (Red vinyl)	1978	4.00	10.00
RCA Victor AFL1-2804	(S)	Along The Red Ledge	1978	1.00	5.00
RCA Victor ANL1-3463	(S)	Daryl Hall & John Oates	1979	.80	4.00
RCA Victor AFL1-3494	(S)	X-Static	1979	1.00	5.00
RCA Victor DJL1-3832	(DJ)	RCA Radio Special Interview Series	1980	4.00	10.00
RCA Victor AYl1-3836	(S)	Daryl Hall & John Oates	1980	.80	4.00
RCA Victor AYL1-3866	(S)	Bigger Than Both Of Us	1980	.80	4.00
RCA Victor AQL1-3646	(S)	Voices	1980	1.00	5.00
RCA Victor AFL1-4028	(S)	Private Eyes	1981	1.00	5.00
RCA Victor DJL1-4179	(DJ)	RCA Radio Special Interview Series	1981	4.00	10.00
RCA Victor AYL1-4230	(S)	Beauty On A Back Street	1981	.80	4.00
RCA Victor AYL1-4231	(S)	Along The Red Ledge	1981	.80	4.00
RCA Victor AYL1-4301	(S)	X-Static	1981	.80	4.00
RCA Victor AFL1-4383	(S)	H2O	1982	.80	4.00
RCA Victor AFL1-4848	(S)	Rock 'N Soul, Part 1	1983	.80	4.00
RCA Victor AFL1-5309	(S)	Big Bam Boom	1984	.80	4.00

HALL, JUANITA

Counterpoint 556	(M)	Juanita Hall Sings The Blues	1958	80.00	200.00

(Counterpoint 556 was issued in compatible mono/stereo.)

HALL, LARRY

Strand SL-1005	(M)	Sandy	1960	80.00	200.00
Strand SLS-1005	(S)	Sandy	1960	150.00	300.00

HALLYDAY, JOHNNY

Philips PHM-200-019	(M)	America's Rockin' Hits	1961	40.00	100.00
Philips PHS-600-019	(S)	America's Rockin' Hits	1961	60.00	150.00

HALOS, THE

Warwick W-2046	(M)	The Halos	1962	250.00	500.00

HAMILTON, RUSS

Kapp KL-1076	(M)	Rainbow	1957	30.00	75.00

HAMILTON, JOE FRANK & REYNOLDS

Dan Hamilton, Joe Frank Carollo and Tommy Reynolds, all formerly of The T-Bones. Reynolds left in 1972, replaced by Alan Dennison, although the trio continued under the old name on Playboy Records.

Dunhill 4276	(S)	Don't Pull Your Love	1971	1.20	6.00
Dunhill 4287	(S)	Annabella	1971	1.20	6.00
Dunhill 4296	(S)	Daisy Mae	1971	1.20	6.00

HAMILTON, ROY

Epic LN-1103	(10")	The Voice Of Roy Hamilton	195?	80.00	200.00
Epic LN-3176	(M)	Roy Hamilton	1955	20.00	50.00
Epic LN-3294	(M)	You'll Never Walk Alone	1956	20.00	50.00
Epic BN-632	(E)	You'll Never Walk Alone	1962	8.00	20.00
Epic LN-3364	(M)	Golden Boy	1957	20.00	50.00
Epic LN-3519	(M)	With All My Love	1958	12.00	30.00
Epic BN-518	(S)	With All My Love	1959	16.00	40.00
Epic LN-3545	(M)	Why Fight The Feeling?	1959	10.00	25.00
Epic BN-525	(S)	Why Fight The Feeling?	1959	12.00	30.00
Epic LN-3561	(M)	Come Out Swingin'	1959	10.00	25.00
Epic BN-530	(S)	Come Out Swingin'	1959	12.00	30.00
Epic LN-3580	(M)	Have Blues, Must Travel	1959	12.00	30.00
Epic BN-535	(S)	Have Blues, Must Travel	1959	12.00	30.00
Epic LN-3628	(M)	Roy Hamilton At His Best	1960	20.00	50.00
Epic LN-3654	(M)	Spirituals	1960	10.00	25.00
Epic BN-551	(S)	Spirituals	1960	12.00	30.00
Epic LN-3717	(M)	Soft 'N Warm	1960	10.00	25.00
Epic BN-578	(S)	Soft 'N Warm	1960	12.00	30.00
Epic LN-3775	(M)	You Can Have Her	1961	12.00	30.00
Epic BN-595	(S)	You Can Have Her	1961	16.00	40.00
Epic LN-3807	(M)	Only You	1962	10.00	25.00
Epic BN-610	(S)	Only You	1962	12.00	30.00
Epic LN-24000	(M)	Mr. Rock And Soul	1962	10.00	25.00
Epic BN-26000	(S)	Mr. Rock And Soul	1962	12.00	30.00
Epic LN-24009	(M)	Roy Hamilton's Greatest Hits	1962	8.00	20.00
Epic BN-26009	(S)	Roy Hamilton's Greatest Hits	1962	10.00	25.00
Epic LN-24316	(M)	Roy Hamilton's Greatest Hits, Vol. 2	1963	8.00	20.00
Epic BN-26316	(S)	Roy Hamilton's Greatest Hits, Vol. 2	1963	10.00	25.00

—Epic albums above have yellow labels with black spokes along the perimeter.—

Illustrated here is an attempt by a smaller label to overcome the financial hurdle of issuing albums in two different formats: Juanita Hall's album on Counterpoint was issued in "compatible mono/stereo," meaning that the grooves were cut to allow either a mono or stereo stylus to pick up the appropriate waves and replay either monophonically or stereophonically. This system did not go over well and separate mono and stereo pressings continued through the late '60s, when mono was simply dumped by the industry.

Label & Catalog #		Title	Year	VG+	NM
MGM E-4139	(M)	Warm And Soul	1963	6.00	15.00
MGM SE-4139	(S)	Warm And Soul	1963	8.00	20.00
MGM E-4233	(M)	Sentimental, Lonely & Blue	1964	6.00	15.00
MGM SE-4233	(S)	Sentimental, Lonely & Blue	1964	8.00	20.00
RCA Victor LPM-3532	(M)	The Impossible Dream	1966	6.00	15.00
RCA Victor LSP-3532	(S)	The Impossible Dream	1966	8.00	20.00

HAMILTON FACE BAND, THE

Philips PHS-600-308	(S)	The Hamilton Face Band	1969	4.00	10.00
Bell 6042	(S)	Ain't Got No Time	1970	4.00	10.00

HAMILTON STREETCAR

Dot DLP-25939	(S)	Hamilton Streetcar	1969	6.00	15.00

HAMMER

San Francisco SD-203	(S)	Hammer	1970	8.00	20.00

HAMMIL, PETER
Hammil was a member of Van Der Graaf Generator.

Charisma CHS-1037	(S)	Fool's Mate	1972	6.00	15.00

HAMMOND, JOHN, JR.
Singer, songwriter, guitar and harp player John Hammond Jr is the son of record executive/producer extraordinaire John Hammond Sr. Refer to Mike Bloomfield & Dr. John & John Hammond; Larry Johnson. Mr Hammond also appears on the Columbia soundtrack "Little Big Man."

Vanguard VRS-9132	(M)	John Hammond	1963	12.00	30.00
Vanguard VSD-2148	(S)	John Hammond	1963	16.00	40.00
Vanguard VRS-9153	(M)	Big City Blues	1964	12.00	30.00
Vanguard VSD-79153	(S)	Big City Blues	1964	16.00	40.00
Vanguard VRS-9178	(M)	So Many Roads	1966	12.00	30.00
Vanguard VSD-79178	(S)	So Many Roads	1966	16.00	40.00
Vanguard VRS-9198	(M)	Country Blues	1966	12.00	30.00
Vanguard VSD-79198	(S)	Country Blues	1966	16.00	40.00
Vanguard VRS-9245	(M)	Mirrors	1967	16.00	40.00
Vanguard VSD-79245	(S)	Mirrors	1967	20.00	50.00
		(Vanguard 9178 and 9245 feature Levon Helm, Garth Hudson and Robbie Robertson of The Band.)			
Atlantic 8152	(M)	I Can Tell	1967	12.00	30.00
Atlantic SD-8152	(S)	I Can Tell	1967	16.00	40.00
		(Atlantic 8152 features Robbie Robertson and Rick Danko of The Band and Bill Wyman of The Rolling Stones.)			
Atlantic SD-8206	(S)	Sooner Or Later	1968	6.00	15.00
Atlantic SD-8251	(S)	Southern Fried	1969	6.00	15.00
Vanguard VSD-11/12	(S)	The Best Of John Hammond (2 LPs)	1970	4.00	10.00
Columbia C-30458	(S)	Source Point	1970	4.00	10.00
Columbia KC-31318	(S)	I'm Satisfied	1972	4.00	10.00
Capricorn CP-0153	(S)	Can't Beat The Kid	1975	4.00	10.00
Vanguard VSD-79380	(S)	John Hammond Solo	1976	1.00	5.00
Vanguard VSD-79400	(S)	Footwork	1978	1.00	5.00
Vanguard VSD-79424	(S)	Hot Tracks	1979	1.00	5.00
Rounder 3042	(S)	Mileage	1980	1.00	5.00
Rounder 3060	(S)	Frogs For Snakes	1982	1.00	5.00
Rounder 3074	(S)	John Hammond Live	1983	1.00	5.00
Flying Fish FF-502	(S)	Nobody But You	1987	1.00	5.00

HAMPTON GREASE BAND, THE

Columbia KC-30555	(S)	Music To Eat (2 LPs)	1971	5.00	12.00

HANGMEN, THE

Monument MLP-8077	(M)	Bitter Sweet	1967	8.00	20.00
Monument SLP-18077	(S)	Bitter Sweet	1967	10.00	25.00

HANSON

Manticore 66672	(S)	Magic Dragon	1974	4.00	10.00
Manticore 66670	(S)	Now Hear This	1973	5.00	12.00

HANSSON, BO

Fam. Charisma CAS-1059	(S)	Lord Of The Rings	1972	4.00	10.00
Fam. Charisma CAS-6062	(S)	Magician's Hat	1973	4.00	10.00
Sire 7525	(S)	Attic Thoughts	1976	4.00	10.00

HAPPENINGS, THE

B.T. Puppy BT-1001	(M)	The Happenings	1966	10.00	25.00
B.T. Puppy BTS-1001	(S)	The Happenings	1966	12.00	30.00
B.T. Puppy BT-1003	(M)	Psycle	1967	10.00	25.00
B.T. Puppy BTS-1003	(S)	Psycle	1967	12.00	30.00
B.T. Puppy BTS-1004	(S)	The Happenings' Golden Hits!	1968	16.00	40.00
Jubilee JGS-8028	(S)	Piece Of Mind	1969	10.00	25.00
Jubilee JGS-8030	(S)	The Happenings' Greatest Hits!	1969	10.00	25.00

The Happenings were Bob Miranda with Tom Giuliano, Dave Libert, and Ralph DeVito. They had originally recorded for Rust Records as The Four Graduates. After signing with The Tokens' B.T. Puppy label and changing their name, they placed themselves in the hands of their mentors. This enabled them to ring up a series of chart singles, including several major hits. By the time DeVito left in 1968 and was replaced by Bernie LaPorta, the group's hit-making days were all but over.

Label & Catalog #		Title	Year	VG+	NM
HAPPENINGS, THE / THE TOKENS					
B.T. Puppy BT-1002	(M)	**Back To Back**	1967	6.00	15.00
B.T. Puppy BTS-1002	(S)	**Back To Back**	1967	8.00	20.00
HAPSHASH & THE COLOURED COAT					
Imperial LP-9377	(M)	**Hapshash & The Coloured Coat**	1968	20.00	50.00
Imperial LP-12377	(S)	**Hapshash & The Coloured Coat**	1968	16.00	40.00
Imperial LP-12430	(S)	**Western Flyer**	1969	16.00	40.00
HARBUS					
Evolution 3018	(S)	**Harbus**	1973	4.00	10.00
HARD MEAT					
Warner Bros. WS-1852	(S)	**Hard Meat**	1969	6.00	15.00
Warner Bros. WS-1879	(S)	**Through A Window**	1970	6.00	15.00
HARD STUFF					
Mercury SRM-1-663	(S)	**Bolex Dementia**	1973	6.00	15.00
HARD TIMES, THE					
World Pacific WP-1867	(M)	**Blew Mind**	1968	10.00	25.00
World Pacific ST-1867	(S)	**Blew Mind**	1968	12.00	30.00
HARDIN, TIM					
Tim Hardin is a guitar player, singer and songwriter in the contemporary folk vein.					
Verve/Folkways FT-3004	(M)	**Tim Hardin 1**	1966	8.00	20.00
Verve/Folkways FTS-3004	(S)	**Tim Hardin 1**	1966	10.00	25.00
Atco 33-210	(M)	**Tim Hardin**	1967	12.00	30.00
Atco SD-33-210	(E)	**Tim Hardin**	1967	6.00	15.00
Verve/Forecast FTS-3022	(S)	**Tim Hardin 2**	1967	6.00	15.00
Verve/Forecast FTS-3049	(S)	**Tim Hardin 3—Live In Concert**	1968	6.00	15.00
Verve/Forecast FTS-3064	(S)	**Tim Hardin 4**	1969	6.00	15.00
Verve/Forecast FTS-3078	(S)	**The Best Of Tim Hardin**	1969	6.00	15.00
HARDIN & YORK					
Bell 6043	(S)	**Through A Window**	1970	4.00	10.00
London XPS-602	(S)	**For The World**	1971	4.00	10.00
HARDWATER					
Hardwater originally recorded as The Astronauts.					
Capitol ST-2954	(S)	**Hardwater**	1968	16.00	40.00
HARMONICA FRANK					
Harmonica Frank is a pseudonym for Frank Floyd.					
Puritan 3003	(M)	**Great Original Recordings Of Harmonica Frank**	196?	6.00	15.00
HARPER, ARTHUR LEE					
Mr. Harper also recorded as Arthur.					
Nocturne NRS-905	(S)	**Love Is The Revolution**	1975	300.00	500.00
HARPERS BIZARRE					
Warner Bros. W-1693	(M)	**Feelin' Groovy**	1967	6.00	15.00
Warner Bros. WS-1693	(S)	**Feelin' Groovy**	1967	6.00	15.00
		— *W.B. albums above have gold labels.* —			
Warner Bros. WS-1693	(S)	**Feelin' Groovy**	1968	4.00	10.00
Warner Bros. WS-1716	(S)	**Anything Goes**	1968	4.00	10.00
Warner Bros. ST-91351	(S)	**Anything Goes** *(Capitol Record Club)*	1968	4.00	10.00
Warner Bros. WS-1739	(S)	**Secret Life Of Harpers Bizarre**	1968	4.00	10.00
Warner Bros. WS-1784	(S)	**Harpers Bizarre**	1969	4.00	10.00
Forest Bay BS-7545LP	(S)	**As Time Goes By**	1976	4.00	10.00
HARPTONES, THE					
Refer to The Crows; The Paragons.					
Harlem Hitparade 5006	(M)	**The Harptones**	197?	5.00	12.00
Ambient Sound 37718	(S)	**Love Needs**	1982	4.00	10.00
Relic LP-5001	(M)	**The Greatest Hits Of The Harptones, Vol. 1**	197?	4.00	10.00
Relic LP-5003	(M)	**The Greatest Hits Of The Harptones, Vol. 2**	197?	4.00	10.00
HARRIS, MAJOR					
Major Harris was formerly the lead singer with The Delfonics.					
Atlantic SD-18119	(S)	**My Way**	1974	8.00	20.00
HARRIS, SHAUN					
Harris was a member of The West Coast Pop Art Experimental Band.					
Capitol ST-11168	(S)	**Shaun Harris**	1973	12.00	30.00
HARRIS, THURSTON					
Score LP-4037	(M)	**Little Bitty Pretty One**	1958	*Unreleased?*	

Label & Catalog #		Title	Year	VG+	NM

HARRIS, WYNONIE / JOE TURNER
Score LP-4036 (M) **Battle Of The Blues** 1958 *Unreleased?*

HARRIS, WYNONIE
Refer to Roy Brown; Amos Milburn.
King KS-1086 (E) **Good Rockin' Blues** 1970 10.00 25.00

HARRISON, GEORGE
Mr Harrison was the lead guitarist for the greatest rock band the world will ever know. Refer to Jackie Lomax; Billy Preston; The Radha Krsna Temple; Leon Russell; Ravi Shankar; The Traveling Wilburys; Doris Troy.

Label & Catalog #		Title	Year	VG+	NM
Apple ST-3350	(S)	**Wonderwall Music** (With bonus photo)	1969	60.00	150.00
		— *Apple albums above have labels with "A Subsidiary of Capitol."* —			
Apple ST-3350	(S)	**Wonderwall Music** (With bonus photo)	1969	10.00	25.00
Apple ST-3350	(S)	**Wonderwall Music** (Without photo)	1969	8.00	20.00
		— *Apple albums above have labels with "Manufactured by Apple."* —			
Zapple ST-3358	(S)	**Electronic Sound**	1969	16.00	40.00
Apple STCH-639	(S)	**All Things Must Pass** (3 LP box)	1970	16.00	40.00
		(First pressings have orange Apple labels on the first two LPs and a custom label on the third with "Mfd. by Apple" on the inside front cover. Includes a poster and a lyric sheet. Produced by Phil Spector)			
Apple STCH-639	(S)	**All Things Must Pass** (3 LP box)	1983	20.00	50.00
		(Capitol box contains LPs with original Apple label but have a large "S" in the trail-off vinyl.)			
Apple STCH-639	(S)	**All Things Must Pass** (3 LP box)	1983	30.00	75.00
		(Capitol box contains LPs with original Apple label but have a large "S" in the trail-off vinyl. Some copies printed with a special sticker with titles and credits affixed to the back cover.)			
Apple SMAS-3410	(S)	**Living In The Material World** (Laminated cover)	1973	6.00	15.00
Apple SMAS-3410	(S)	**Living In The Material World** (Standard cover)	1973	4.00	10.00
Apple SMAS-3418	(S)	**Dark Horse** (Blue & white label)	1974	8.00	20.00
Apple SMAS-3418	(S)	**Dark Horse** (Black & white label)	1974	8.00	20.00
Apple SW-3420	(S)	**Extra Texture** (Die-cut title cover)	1975	5.00	12.00
Apple SW-3492	(S)	**Somewhere In England**	1981	4.00	10.00
Dark Horse (No number)	(DJ)	**Dark Horse Radio Special**	1975	200.00	400.00
Dark Horse PRO-649	(DJ)	**Personal Music Dialogue At 33 & 1/3**	1976	20.00	50.00
Dark Horse DH-3005	(S)	**Thirty Three And 1/3**	1976	1.00	5.00
Dark Horse DHK-3255	(S)	**George Harrison**	1979	1.00	5.00
Dark Horse DHK-3492	(S)	**Somewhere In England**	1981	1.00	5.00
Dark Horse 23734	(DJ)	**Gone Troppo** (Quiex II vinyl promo)	1982	12.00	30.00
Dark Horse 23734	(S)	**Gone Troppo**	1982	1.00	5.00
Dark Horse 25643	(S)	**Cloud Nine**	1987	1.00	5.00
Dark Horse W1-25643	(S)	**Cloud Nine** (Columbia Record Club)	1987	6.00	15.00
Dark Horse R-172348	(S)	**Cloud Nine** (RCA Record Club)	1987	6.00	15.00
Dark Horse 25726	(S)	**The Best Of Dark Horse** (Tan label)	1989	6.00	15.00
Dark Horse W1-25726	(S)	**The Best Of Dark Horse** (Columbia Rec. Club)	1989	6.00	15.00
Dark Horse R-180307	(S)	**The Best Of Dark Horse** (RCA Record Club)	1989	6.00	15.00
Capitol ST-11578	(S)	**Best Of George Harrison**	1976	1.00	5.00
		(Custom photo label. Original covers do not have UPC bar code on the back.)			
Capitol ST-11578	(S)	**Best Of George Harrison**	1988	4.00	10.00
		(Custom photo label. Reissue with a large "S" in the trail-off vinyl.)			
		— *Capitol albums above have photo labels.* —			
Capitol STCH-639	(S)	**All Things Must Pass**	1976	12.00	30.00
Capitol ST-11578	(S)	**Best Of George Harrison**	1976	80.00	200.00
		— *Capitol albums above have orange labels.* —			
Capitol STCH-639	(S)	**All Things Must Pass**	1978	10.00	25.00
		(The third LP in the box is titled "Apple Jam.")			
Capitol STCH-639	(S)	**All Things Must Pass**	1978	6.00	15.00
		(The third LP in the box has been retitled "All Things Must Pass.")			
Capitol ST-11578	(S)	**Best Of George Harrison**	1978	12.00	30.00
Capitol ST-11578	(S)	**Best Of George Harrison**	1989	30.00	75.00
		— *Capitol albums above have purple labels with "Manufactured" in perimeter print.* —			
Capitol SN-16055	(S)	**Dark Horse**	1980	3.00	15.00
Capitol SN-16216	(S)	**Living In The Material World**	1980	10.00	25.00
Capitol SN-16217	(S)	**Extra Texture**	1980	10.00	25.00
		— *Capitol albums above have green labels.* —			
Capitol STCH-639	(S)	**All Things Must Pass**	1983	40.00	100.00
Capitol ST-11578	(S)	**Best Of George Harrison**	1983	3.00	15.00
		— *Capitol albums above have black labels.* —			

HARRISON, GEORGE, & FRIENDS
While Apple 3385 is a various artists album, the concert was done under the auspices of Mr Harrison and it is generally referred to as "his" album. Also features performances by Ravi Shankar, Billy Preston, Ringo, Leon Russell, and Bob Dylan, all backed by Badfinger. Produced by Harrison and Phil Spector.

Label & Catalog #		Title	Year	VG+	NM
Apple STCX-3385	(S)	**The Concert For Bangla Desh** (3 LP box)	1972	12.00	30.00
		— *Apple albums above have labels with "Manufactured by Apple."* —			
Apple STCX-3385	(S)	**The Concert For Bangla Desh** (3 LP box)	197?	20.00	50.00
		— *Apple albums above have labels with ""All rights reserved."* —			
Capitol SABB-12248	(S)	**The Concert For Bangla Desh** (2 LPs)	1982	200.00	400.00

Label & Catalog #		Title	Year	VG+	NM
HARRISON, MIKE					
Harrison was a member of Spooky Tooth.					
Island SW-9321	(S)	Smoke Stack Lightning	1972	5.00	12.00
Island ILPS-9359	(S)	Rainbow Rider	1975	4.00	10.00
HARRISON, WILBERT					
Sphere Sound SSR-7000	(M)	Kansas City	1965	100.00	250.00
Sphere Sound SSSR-7000	(E)	Kansas City	1965	80.00	200.00
Sue SSLP-8801	(S)	Let's Work Together	1970	20.00	50.00
Juggernaut ST-8803	(S)	Shoot You Full Of Love	1971	20.00	50.00
Buddah BDS-5092	(S)	Wilbert Harrison	1971	14.00	35.00
Wet Soul 1001	(S)	Anything You Want	197?	20.00	50.00
HART, MICKEY					
Mickey Hart was a member of The Grateful Dead. Refer to The Diga Rhythm Band; The Heart Of Gold Band. Mr Hart's "world music" recordings are not included in this edition.					
Warner Bros. BS-2635	(S)	Rolling Thunder *(With insert)*	1972	12.00	30.00
Relix RRLP-2026	(S)	Rolling Thunder	1987	.80	4.00
HARTLEY, KEEF					
Deram DES-18024	(S)	Halfbreed	1969	6.00	15.00
Deram DES-18035	(S)	Battle Of North West Six	1970	6.00	15.00
Deram DES-18047	(S)	Time Is Near	1970	6.00	15.00
Deram DES-18070	(S)	Lancashire Hustler	1971	6.00	15.00
Deram DES-18057	(S)	Overdog	1972	6.00	15.00
Deram DES-18065	(S)	72nd Brave	1973	6.00	15.00
HARUMI					
Verve/Forecast FTS-3030	(S)	Harumi	1968	10.00	25.00
HARVEY, ALEX [THE SENSATIONAL ALEX HARVEY BAND]					
Vertigo VEL-1017	(S)	Next	1973	3.20	8.00
Vertigo VEL-2000	(S)	The Impossible Dream	1974	3.20	8.00
Vertigo VEL-2004	(S)	Tomorrow Belongs To Me	1975	3.20	8.00
Atlantic SD-18248	(S)	Live	1975	3.20	8.00
HASSLES, THE					
The Hassles feature Billy Joel.					
United Arts. UAS-6631	(S)	The Hassles	1968	6.00	15.00
United Arts. UAS-6699	(S)	The Hour Of The Wolf	1969	6.00	15.00
Liberty LN-10138	(S)	The Hassles	1981	.80	4.00
Liberty LN-10139	(S)	The Hour Of The Wolf	1981	.80	4.00
HATE					
Paramount PAS-5031	(S)	Hate Kills	1970	14.00	35.00
HATFIELD, BOBBY					
Hatfield was one half of The Righteous Brothers.					
MGM SE-4727	(S)	Messin' In Muscle Shoals	1971	4.00	10.00
HATHAWAY, DONNY					
Refer to Roberta Flack & Donny Hathaway.					
Atco SD-33-332	(S)	Everything Is Everything	1970	4.00	10.00
Atco QD-33-332	(Q)	Everything Is Everything	1974	6.00	15.00
Atco SD-33-360	(S)	Donny Hathaway	1971	4.00	10.00
Atco SD-33-7010	(S)	Donny Hathaway Live	1971	4.00	10.00
Atco SD-33-7029	(S)	Extension Of A Man	1973	4.00	10.00
Atco SD-38-107	(S)	The Best Of Donny Hathaway	1978	3.20	8.00
Atlantic SD-19278	(S)	Donny Hathaway In Performance	1980	3.20	8.00
HAVENS, RICHIE					
Richie Havens is a guitar player, singer and writer of contemporary folk-based music.					
Douglas D-779	(M)	Richie Havens' Record	1966	5.00	12.00
Douglas SD-779	(S)	Richie Havens' Record	1966	6.00	15.00
Douglas D-780	(M)	Electric Havens	1966	5.00	12.00
Douglas SD-780	(S)	Electric Havens	1966	6.00	15.00
Verve/Forecast FT-3006	(M)	Mixed Bag	1966	5.00	12.00
Verve/Forecast FTS-3006	(S)	Mixed Bag	1966	6.00	15.00
Verve/Forecast FTS-3034	(S)	Somethin' Else Again	1968	5.00	12.00
Verve/Forecast FTS-3047	(S)	Richard P. Havens, 1983 *(2 LPs)*	1968	6.00	15.00
Verve/Forecast FTS-3061	(S)	Richie Havens	1969	Unreleased	
MGM SE-4698	(M)	Mixed Bag	1970	1.00	5.00
MGM SE-4699	(M)	Somethin' Else Again	1970	1.00	5.00
MGM SE-4700	(M)	Richard P. Havens, 1983 *(2 LPs)*	1970	1.00	5.00
Stormy Forest SFS-6001	(S)	Stonehenge	1969	4.00	10.00
Stormy Forest SFS-6005	(S)	Alarm Clock	1970	4.00	10.00
Stormy Forest SFS-6010	(S)	The Great Blind Degree	1971	4.00	10.00
Stormy Forest SFS-6012	(S)	On Stage *(2 LPs)*	1972	4.00	10.00

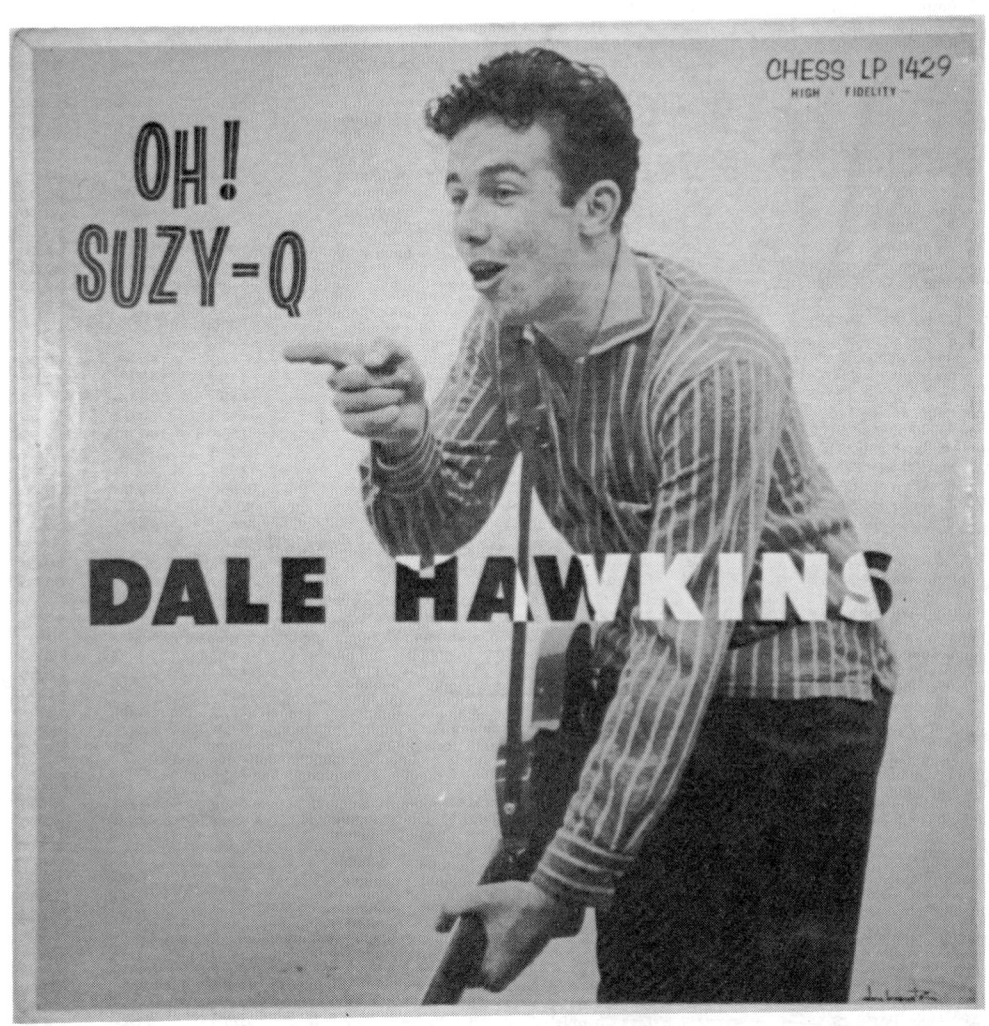

Dale Hawkins achieved lasting rock'n roll fame with one single, "Suzy-Q," featuring one of the most distinctive guitar solos of the pre-Beatles era from James Burton. As one of only a handful of white artists signed to the Chess/Checker label, he managed three more chart appearances, none of which helped this album sell more than a few thousand copies.

Label & Catalog #		Title	Year	VG+	NM
Stormy Forest SFS-6013	(S)	Portfolio	1973	3.20	8.00
Stormy Forest SFS-6201	(S)	Mixed Bag 2	1974	3.20	8.00
A&M SP-4641	(S)	Mirage	1977	1.00	5.00
Elektra 6E-242	(S)	Connections	1980	1.00	5.00
HAWKINS, DALE					
Chess LP-1429	(M)	Oh! Suzie-Q	1958	1,000.00	1,500.00
Roulette R-25175	(M)	Let's All Twist			
		At The Miami Beach Peppermint Lounge	1962	80.00	200.00
Roulette SR-25175	(S)	Let's All Twist			
		At The Miami Beach Peppermint Lounge	1962	150.00	300.00
Bell 6036	(S)	L.A., Memphis And Tyler, Texas	1969	16.00	40.00
Chess 703	(M)	Dale Hawkins	1976	6.00	15.00
		(Outtakes from the '50's Chess sessions.)			
HAWKINS, "SCREAMIN'" JAY					
Epic LN-3448	(M)	At Home With Screamin' Jay Hawkins	1958	800.00	1,200.00
Epic LN-3457	(M)	I Put A Spell On You	1959	300.00	600.00
Epic BN-26457	(E)	I Put A Spell On You	1969	30.00	75.00
		(Epic 26457 is a reissue of 3457.)			
Philips PHS-600-319	(S)	What That Is	1969	16.00	40.00
Philips PHS-600-336	(S)	Screamin' Jay Hawkins	1970	16.00	40.00
Sounds Of Hawaii 5015	(S)	A Night At Forbidden City	196?	20.00	50.00
HAWKINS, RONNIE					
Ronnie's group on many of the Roulette sides, The Hawks, later recorded as The Band.					
Roulette R-25078	(M)	Ronnie Hawkins	1959	60.00	150.00
Roulette SR-25078	(S)	Ronnie Hawkins	1959	100.00	250.00
Roulette SR-25078	(S)	Ronnie Hawkins (Red vinyl)	1959	500.00	1,000.00
Roulette R-25102	(M)	Mr. Dynamo	1960	60.00	150.00
Roulette SR-25102	(S)	Mr. Dynamo	1960	100.00	250.00
Roulette SR-25102	(S)	Mr. Dynamo (Red vinyl)	1960	500.00	1,000.00
Roulette R-25120	(M)	The Folk Ballads Of Ronnie Hawkins	1960	40.00	100.00
Roulette SR-25120	(S)	The Folk Ballads Of Ronnie Hawkins	1960	80.00	200.00
Roulette R-25137	(M)	The Songs Of Hank Williams	1960	40.00	100.00
Roulette SR-25137	(S)	The Songs Of Hank Williams	1960	80.00	200.00
		—Roulette albums above have white labels with crossed color bars.—			
Roulette R-25078	(M)	Ronnie Hawkins	196?	20.00	50.00
Roulette SR-25078	(S)	Ronnie Hawkins	196?	40.00	100.00
		—Roulette albums above have orange labels.—			
Roulette SR-42045	(S)	The Best Of Ronnie Hawkins & His Band	1970	10.00	25.00
		(Roulette 42045 contains early '60s recordings with The Band.)			
Cotillion SD-9019	(S)	Ronnie Hawkins	1970	1.00	5.00
Cotillion SD-9039	(S)	The Hawk	1971	1.00	5.00
Monument KZ-31330	(S)	Rock & Roll Resurrection	1972	1.00	5.00
Monument KZ-32940	(S)	The Giant Of Rock & Roll	1974	1.00	5.00
Monument KZ-33855	(S)	Rock & Roll Resurrection /			
		The Giant Of Rock & Roll (2 LPs)	1976	1.20	6.00
United Arts. LA-968H	(S)	The Hawk	1979	1.00	5.00
Accord SN-7213	(S)	Premonition	1983	1.00	5.00
Silver Eagle SE4-10873	(S)	Ronnie Hawkins' Greatest Hits (Mail order)	1989	1.00	5.00
Rhino R21S-70966	(S)	The Best Of Ronnie Hawkins & The Hawks (2 LPs)	1990	4.00	10.00
HAWKWIND					
United Arts. UAS-5519	(S)	Hawkwind	1971	6.00	15.00
United Arts. UAS-5567	(S)	In Search Of Space	1972	6.00	15.00
United Arts. LA-001F	(S)	Doremi Fasol Latido	1973	5.00	12.00
United Arts. LA-120H	(S)	Space Ritual Alive (2 LPs)	1973	6.00	15.00
United Arts. LA-328G	(S)	Hall Of The Mountain Grill	1974	5.00	12.00
Atco SD-36-115	(S)	Warrior On The Edge Of Time	1975	4.00	10.00
Sire SRK-6047	(S)	Quark Strangeness And Charm	1978	4.00	10.00
Charisma CA-12203	(S)	Hawklords 25 Years On	1978	4.00	10.00
Profile PAL-1237C	(S)	Live Chronicles	1987	3.20	8.00
Enigma 7-75407-1	(S)	The Xenon Codex	1989	3.20	8.00
Road Racer RR-9347	(S)	Space Bandits	1990	3.20	8.00
Road Racer RR-9303	(S)	Palace Springs	1991	3.20	8.00
HAYDEN, WILLIE					
Dooto DTL-293	(M)	Blame It On The Blues	1960	250.00	500.00
		—Dooto albums above have maroon labels.—			
Dooto DTL-293	(M)	Blame It On The Blues	196?	80.00	200.00
		—Dooto albums above have multi-color labels.—			
HAYES, ISAAC					
Enterprise E-100	(M)	Presenting Isaac Hayes	1968	12.00	30.00
Enterprise ES-100	(S)	Presenting Isaac Hayes	1968	16.00	40.00
Enterprise ENS-1001	(S)	Hot Buttered Soul	1969	8.00	20.00
Enterprise ENS-1010	(S)	The Isaac Hayes Movement	1970	8.00	20.00
Enterprise ENS-1014	(S)	To Be Continued	1970	8.00	20.00

Original pressings of Magazine on Mushroom were issued during a dispute between the company and the band. The album bore a contractual dispute disclaimer on the back notifying the public of the situation. Subsequent pressings have a radically different content and mix and lack the disclaimer. The audiophile label Nautilus made Dreamboat Annie one of the first selections for their "Super Disc" series. Today, almost fifteen years later, Ann and Nancy Wilson and their cohorts have virtually slipped from the attention of all but their most devoted collectors.

Label & Catalog #		Title	Year	VG+	NM
Enterprise ENS-5002	(S)	**Shaft** (2 LPs.)	1971	8.00	20.00
Enterprise ENS-5003	(S)	**Black Moses** (2 LPs)	1971	8.00	20.00
Atlantic SD-1599	(S)	**In The Beginning**	1972	6.00	15.00
		(Atlantic 1599 is a reissue of Enterprise 100.)			
Enterprise ENS-5005	(S)	**Live At Sahara Tahoe** (2 LPs)	1973	5.00	12.00
Enterprise ENS-5007	(S)	**Joy**	1973	4.00	10.00
Enterprise ENS-7504	(S)	**Tough Guys**	1974	4.00	10.00
Enterprise ENS-7507	(S)	**Truck Turner** (2 LPs)	1974	6.00	15.00
Enterprise ENS-7510	(S)	**The Best Of Isaac Hayes**	1975	4.00	10.00
ABC D-874	(S)	**Chocolate Chip**	1975	1.00	5.00
ABC D-925	(S)	**Groove-A-Thon**	1976	1.00	5.00
ABC D-996	(S)	**A Man And A Woman** (2 LPs)	1977	1.20	6.00
		(The "Woman" is Dionne Warwick.)			
Polydor PD-6120	(S)	**New Horizon**	1977	1.00	5.00
Polydor PD-6164	(S)	**For The Sake Of Love**	1978	1.00	5.00
Polydor PD-6224	(S)	**Don't Let Go**	1979	1.00	5.00
Polydor PD-6269	(S)	**And Once Again**	1980	1.00	5.00
Polydor PD-6329	(S)	**Lifetime Thing**	1981	1.00	5.00
Stax 4102	(S)	**Hot Bed**	1978	1.00	5.00
Stax 4129	(S)	**The Isaac Hayes Movement**	1977	1.00	5.00
Stax 88003	(S)	**His Greatest Hits** (2 LPs)	1980	1.20	6.00
Stax 8509	(S)	**Black Moses**	1981	1.00	5.00

HAYSTACKS BALBOA

Polydor 24-4032	(S)	**Haystacks Balboa**	1970	5.00	12.00

HAYWARD, JUSTIN, & JOHN LODGE
Hayward and Lodge are members of The Moody Blues.

Threshold THSX-1	(S)	**Blue Jays** (Open-end interview with script)	1975	20.00	50.00
Threshold THS-14	(S)	**Blue Jays**	1975	1.00	5.00
Deram DES-18073	(S)	**Songwriter**	1977	1.00	5.00
Deram DRL-4801	(S)	**Night Flight**	1980	1.00	5.00

HAZEL, EDDIE
Eddie Hazel is a member of the Parliament/Funkadelic community.

Warner Bros. 3058	(S)	**Games, Dames And Guitar Thangs**	1977	20.00	50.00

HEAD

Buddah BDS-5062	(S)	**Head** (With coloring book)	1970	6.00	15.00
Buddah BDS-5062	(S)	**Head** (Without coloring book)	1970	4.00	10.00

HEAD OVER HEELS

Capitol ST-797	(S)	**Head Over Heels**	1970	12.00	30.00

HEAD SHOP, THE

Epic BN-26476	(S)	**The Head Shop**	1969	24.00	60.00

HEADS, THE

Liberty LST-7581	(S)	**Heads Up**	1968	8.00	20.00

HEADS, HANDS & FEET
HH&F features Albert Lee.

Capitol SVBB-680	(S)	**Heads, Hands & Feet** (2 LPs)	1971	8.00	20.00
Capitol ST-11051	(S)	**Tracks**	1972	8.00	20.00
Atco SD-7025	(S)	**Old Soldiers Never Die**	1973	8.00	20.00

HEADS OF THE FAMILY

Alshire 5166	(S)	**Heads Of The Family**	1969	4.00	10.00

HEAR & NOW

Pompeii 6009	(S)	**Hear And Now**	1971	4.00	10.00

HEART

Look LLP-11000	(S)	**Heart**	1969	5.00	12.00
King KS-1119	(S)	**Have A Heart**	1970	4.00	10.00

HEART
Heart features Ann and Nancy Wilson. Refer to Bordersong.

Mushroom MRS-5005	(S)	**Dreamboat Annie**	1976	1.00	5.00
Mushroom MRS-5008	(S)	**Magazine**	1977	6.00	15.00
		(Original pressings have a contractual dispute disclaimer printed on the back cover.)			
Mushroom MRS-5008	(S)	**Magazine** (Without the disclaimer)	1977	1.00	5.00
Mushroom MRS-5008	(S)	**Magazine** (Picture disc)	1978	12.00	30.00
Mushroom MRS-1-SP	(S)	**Magazine** (Picture disc)	1978	6.00	15.00
Mushroom MRS-2-SP	(S)	**Dreamboat Annie** (Picture disc)	1979	8.00	20.00
Columbia AS-884	(DJ)	**Heart** (Sampler)	197?	8.00	20.00
Portrait JR-34799	(S)	**Little Queen**	1977	1.00	5.00
Portrait HR-44799	(S)	**Little Queen** (Half-speed master)	1981	10.00	30.00

Label & Catalog #		Title	Year	VG+	NM
Portrait FR-35555	(S)	Dog And Butterfly	1978	1.00	5.00
Epic FE-36371	(S)	Bebe Le Strange	1980	1.00	5.00
Epic KE-36888	(S)	Greatest Hits/Live (2 LPs)	1980	1.00	5.00
Epic FE-38049	(S)	Private Audition	1982	1.00	5.00
Epic FE-38800	(S)	Passionworks	1983	1.00	5.00

HEART OF GOLD BAND, THE
Heart Of Gold features Keith and Donna Godchaux with Mickey Hart of The Grateful Dead.

Whirled 01967	(S)	Ghosts Playing In The Heart Of Gold Band	1985	6.00	15.00
Relix 2020	(S)	Heart Of Gold Band	1986	3.20	8.00

HEARTBEATS, THE
The Heartbeats are James "Shep" Sheppard with Albert Crump, Wally Roker, Vernon Sievers and Robbie Tatum.
Refer to Shep & The Limelites.

Roulette R-25107	(M)	A Thousand Miles Away	1960	150.00	300.00
Roulette SR-25107	(E)	A Thousand Miles Away	1960	80.00	200.00
		— Roulette albums above have white labels with four crossed color bars.—			
Emus ES-12033	(E)	A Thousand Miles Away	1980	10.00	25.00
		(Emus 12033 is a reissue of Roulette 25107.)			

HEARTBEATS, THE / SHEP & THE LIMELITES

Roulette RE-115	(E)	Echoes Of A Rock Era: The Groups (2 LPs)	1972	6.00	15.00

HEARTS, THE
The Hearts feature Baby Washington.

Zells 337	(M)	I Feel So Good	195?	200.00	400.00

HEARTS & FLOWERS
Hearts & Flowers features Rick Cunha with Linda Ronstadt on backing vocals.

Capitol T-2762	(M)	Now Is The Time For Hearts And Flowers	1967	12.00	30.00
Capitol ST-2762	(S)	Now Is The Time For Hearts And Flowers	1967	16.00	40.00
Capitol ST-2868	(S)	Of Horses, Kids And Forgotten Women	1968	20.00	50.00

HEARTSTOPPERS, THE

All Platinum 3005	(S)	The Heartstoppers	1971	6.00	15.00

HEAVEN & EARTH

Ovation QD-1428	(S)	Refuge	1973	4.00	10.00

HEAVY BALLOON, THE

Elephant EVS-104	(S)	32,000 Lbs.	196?	20.00	50.00

HEAVY CRUISER

Family 2706	(S)	Heavy Cruiser	1972	6.00	15.00
Family 2712	(S)	Lucky Dog	1973	6.00	15.00
Tiger Lily 14034	(S)	Heavy Cruiser II	197?	4.00	10.00

HEAVY REGGAE MACHINE, THE

Reggae 15004	(S)	Doin' The Reggae	1970	6.00	15.00

HEBB, BOBBY

Philips PHM-200-212	(M)	Sunny	1966	10.00	25.00
Philips PHS-600-212	(S)	Sunny	1966	12.00	30.00
Epic BN-26523	(S)	Love Games	1970	4.00	10.00

HELL, RICHARD, & THE VOIDOIDS
Richard Hell originally recorded under his real name, Richard Lloyd, with Television.

Sire SR-6037	(S)	Blank Generation	1977	10.00	25.00

HELLO PEOPLE, THE

Philips PHS-600-265	(S)	The Hello People	1968	6.00	15.00
Philips PHS-600-276	(S)	Fusion	1968	6.00	15.00
Mediarts 41-8	(S)	Have You Seen The Light	1970	5.00	12.00
Dunhill D-50184	(S)	The Handsome Devils	1974	4.00	10.00
ABC D-882	(S)	Bricks	1975	4.00	10.00

HELM, LEVON
Levon Helm was a member of The Band.

ABC AA-1017	(S)	Levon Helm & The RCO All Stars	1977	1.00	5.00
ABC AA-1089	(S)	Levon Helm	1978	1.00	5.00
ABC SPPD-45	(DJ)	Levon Helm (Picture disc)	1978	4.00	10.00
MCA 5120	(S)	American Son	1980	1.00	5.00
Capitol ST-12201	(S)	Levon Helm	1982	1.00	5.00

HELP

Decca DL-75257	(S)	Help	1971	10.00	25.00
Decca DL-75304	(S)	Second Coming	1971	10.00	25.00

Label & Catalog #		Title	Year	VG+	NM

HELP YOURSELF

United Arts. UAS-5583	(S)	Help Yourself	1972	4.00	10.00
United Arts. UAS-5591	(S)	Strange Affair	1972	4.00	10.00
United Arts. LA079	(S)	Beware The Shadow	1973	4.00	10.00

HENDERSON, JOE

Todd MT-2701	(M)	Snap Your Fingers	1962	20.00	50.00
Todd ST-2701	(S)	Snap Your Fingers	1962	30.00	75.00

HENDERSON, WILLIE, & THE SOUL EXPLOSIONS

Brunswick BL7-54163	(S)	Funky Chicken	1969	6.00	15.00
Brunswick BL7-54202	(S)	Dance With The Master	1970	6.00	15.00

HENDRICKS, JAMES

Hendricks was a member of the Big Three and The Mugwumps.

Soul City SCS-92003	(S)	The Songs Of James Hendricks	1968	8.00	20.00
MGM SE-4768	(S)	James Hendricks	1971	6.00	15.00

HENDRIX, JIMI [THE JIMI HENDRIX EXPERIENCE]

Prior to forming the Experience, Seattle's James Hendrix, often working as "Jimmy James," backed a number of artists on record, including Little Richard and Lonnie Youngblood. These early recordings are listed in Section 1. Note: While the Maple album contains Jimi backing Youngblood, the other albums crediting Hendrix and Youngblood contain doctored tapes using a Hendrix imitator. These are marked with an asterisk. To settle a contract dispute, Hendrix recorded with Curtis Knight during 1967. These LPs are listed in Section 2. The Jimi Hendrix Experience also featured Great Britain's Mitch Mitchell and Noel Redding through 1969 with Redding replaced by Billy Cox in '70. The Experience recordings take up Section 3. Hendrix, Cox and Buddy Miles recorded in '69 as the "Band Of Gypsys." Their efforts are listed in Section 4. Refer to Eire Apparent; The Isley Brothers; Love; Martha Velez.

1. Early Recordings

MFP 5278	(S)	What'd I Say (U.S. record in U.K. jacket)	1970	16.00	40.00
Maple LPM-6004	(S)	Two Great Experiences Together	1971	20.00	50.00
ALA 1972	(S)	Friends From The Beginning (With Little Richard)	1972	6.00	15.00
Shout 502	(S)	In The Beginning	1972	6.00	15.00
Thunderbird TDR-300*	(S)	Free Spirit	1972	6.00	15.00
Trip TLP-9500*	(S)	Rare Hendrix	1972	4.00	10.00
Trip TLP-9501*	(S)	The Roots Of Hendrix	1972	4.00	10.00
Trip TLP-9512*	(S)	Moods	1973	4.00	10.00
Trip TLP-9522*	(S)	The Genius Of Jimi Hendrix	1973	4.00	10.00
Trip TLP-16-22*	(S)	Jimi Hendrix's 16 Greatest Hits	1973	4.00	10.00
Pickwick SPC-3347	(S)	Jimi Hendrix/Little Richard Together	1973	6.00	15.00
Everest 296	(S)	Roots Of Rock (With Little Richard)	1974	4.00	10.00
Springboard SPB-4010*	(S)	Jimi Hendrix	1974	4.00	10.00
Springboard SPB-4042*	(S)	Rock Guitar Greats	1974	4.00	10.00
United Artists LA-505	(S)	The Very Best Of Jimi Hendrix	1975	6.00	15.00
51 West Q-160-28*	(S)	Flashback	1974	4.00	10.00
Nutmeg NUT-1001	(S)	High, Live 'N' Dirty (Red vinyl)	1978	10.00	25.00
Nutmeg NUT-1001	(S)	High, Live 'N' Dirty (Black vinyl)	1978	10.00	25.00
Nutmeg NUT-1002*	(S)	Cosmic Turnaround	1981	4.00	10.00
Nutmeg NUT-1003*	(S)	Kaleidoscope	1982	4.00	10.00
Accord SN-7101*	(S)	Before London	1981	4.00	10.00
Accord SN-7112*	(S)	Free Spirit	1981	4.00	10.00
Accord SN-7139*	(S)	Cosmic Feeling	1981	4.00	10.00
Audio Fidelity GAS-701*	(S)	Jimi Hendrix, Vol. 1	1982	4.00	10.00
Audio Fidelity GAS-732*	(S)	Jimi Hendrix, Vol. 2	1982	4.00	10.00
Kaleidoscope 19026*	(S)	Original Hits	1982	4.00	10.00
Starday/King N5-2153*	(S)	From This Day On	1985	4.00	10.00
Topline TOP-124*	(S)	Gangster Of Love	1985	4.00	10.00
Baron LP-105	(S)	Early Jimi Hendrix	198?	6.00	15.00

2. Curtis Knight

Capitol T-2856	(M)	Get That Feeling	1967	30.00	75.00
Capitol ST-2856	(S)	Get That Feeling	1967	20.00	50.00
Capitol T-2894	(M)	Flashing	1968	40.00	100.00
Capitol ST-2894	(S)	Flashing	1968	20.00	50.00
		—Capitol albums above have black rainbow labels.—			
Capitol SWBB-659	(S)	Get That Feeling / Flashing (2 LPs)	1971	10.00	25.00
		—Capitol albums above have green labels.—			
MF Productions 001/002	(S)	Get That Feeling / Flashing (2 LPs)	1976	10.00	25.00
51-West Q-16114	(S)	Flashing	1981	6.00	15.00
51-West Q-16115	(S)	Get That Feeling	1981	6.00	15.00
Pair SPDL2-1155	(S)	Historic Hendrix (2 LPs)	1986	4.00	10.00

3. The Reprise Years

Reprise R-6261	(M)	Are You Experienced? (White label promo)	1967	250.00	500.00
Reprise R-6261	(M)	Are You Experienced?	1967	60.00	150.00
Reprise RS-6261	(S)	Are You Experienced?	1967	16.00	40.00

Label & Catalog #		Title	Year	VG+	NM
Reprise R-6281	(M)	**Axis: Bold As Love** (White label promo)	1968	300.00	600.00
Reprise RS-6281	(S)	**Axis: Bold As Love**	1968	16.00	40.00
		—Reprise albums have pink, gold & green labels.—			
Reprise RS-6261	(S)	**Are You Experienced?**	1968	8.00	20.00
Reprise R-6281	(M)	**Axis: Bold As Love**	1968	1,400.00	2,000.00
Reprise RS-6281	(S)	**Axis: Bold As Love**	1968	8.00	20.00
Reprise 2R-6307	(M)	**Electric Ladyland** (2 LPs. White label promo)	1968	*See note below*	
		(Promos for 2R-6037 have a suggested NM value of $2,000-3,000.)			
Reprise 2RS-6307	(S)	**Electric Ladyland** (2 LPs. White label promo)	1968	80.00	200.00
Reprise 2RS-6307	(S)	**Electric Ladyland** (2 LPs)	1968	16.00	40.00
Reprise MS-2025	(S)	**Smash Hits** (White label promo)	1969	50.00	125.00
Reprise MS-2025	(P)	**Smash Hits** (With poster)	1969	24.00	60.00
Reprise MS-2025	(P)	**Smash Hits** (Without poster)	1969	8.00	20.00
		(Original covers for MS-2025 have a printed advertisement			
		for the bonus poster in the lower right corner.)			
Reprise MS-2034	(S)	**The Cry Of Love** (White label promo)	1971	20.00	50.00
Reprise MS-2034	(S)	**The Cry Of Love**	1971	250.00	500.00
		—Reprise albums above have brown & orange labels.—			
Reprise RS-6261	(P)	**Are You Experienced?**	1971	1.20	6.00
Reprise RS-6281	(S)	**Axis: Bold As Love**	1971	1.20	6.00
Reprise 2RS-6307	(S)	**Electric Ladyland** (2 LPs)	1971	3.20	8.00
Reprise MS-2025	(S)	**Smash Hits**	1971	1.20	6.00
Reprise MS-2025	(P)	**Smash Hits**	1971	8.00	20.00
Reprise MS-2029	(DJ)	**Historic Performances Recorded At The Monterey**			
		International Pop Festival (White label)	1970	20.00	50.00
Reprise MS-2029	(S)	**Historic Performances Recorded At The Monterey**			
		International Pop Festival	1970	6.00	15.00
Reprise MS-2034	(S)	**The Cry Of Love**	1971	6.00	15.00
Reprise MS-2040	(S)	**Rainbow Bridge**	1971	10.00	25.00
Reprise SMAS-93972	(S)	**Rainbow Bridge** (Capitol Record Club)	1971	20.00	50.00
Reprise MS-2049	(S)	**Hendrix In The West**	1972	10.00	25.00
Reprise MS-2103	(S)	**War Heroes** (White label promo)	1972	20.00	50.00
Reprise MS-2103	(S)	**War Heroes**	1972	8.00	20.00
Reprise 2RS-6481	(S)	**Soundtrack Recordings**			
		From The Film "Jimi Hendrix" (2 LPs)	1973	10.00	25.00
Reprise MS-2204	(S)	**Crash Landing** (Promo label)	1975	10.00	25.00
Reprise MS-2204	(S)	**Crash Landing**	1975	4.00	10.00
Reprise MS-2229	(S)	**Midnight Lightning** (Promo label)	1975	10.00	25.00
Reprise MS-2229	(S)	**Midnight Lightning**	1975	4.00	10.00
Reprise 2RS-2245	(S)	**The Essential Jimi Hendrix** (2 LPs)	1978	3.20	8.00
Reprise HS-2293	(S)	**The Essential Jimi Hendrix, Volume 2**	1979	1.20	6.00
Reprise PRO-A-840	(DJ)	**The Jimi Hendrix Medley**	1979	30.00	75.00
Reprise HS-2299	(S)	**Nine To The Universe**	1980	1.20	6.00
Reprise 22306	(S)	**The Jimi Hendrix Concerts** (2 LPs)	1982	3.20	8.00
Reprise 25119	(S)	**Kiss The Sky**	1985	1.20	6.00
Reprise 25358	(S)	**Jimi Plays Monterey**	1986	1.20	6.00
		—Reprise albums above have brown labels.—			
Crawdaddy 5-1975	(DJ)	**The Jimi Hendrix Interview LP**	1975	80.00	200.00
Rhino RNDF-254	(DJ)	**Jimi Hendrix Interview** (Black vinyl test pressing)	1982	10.00	25.00
Rhino RNDF-254	(M)	**Jimi Hendrix Interview** (Picture disc)	1982	10.00	25.00
Analogue RALP-0051	(S)	**Live At Winterland** (2 LPs)	1987	6.00	15.00
Analogue RALP-20078	(S)	**Radio One** (2 LPs)	1988	6.00	15.00
Rykodisc RALP-20078	(S)	**Radio One** (2 LPs on clear vinyl. Capitol Rec. Club)	1988	6.00	15.00

4. Band Of Gypsies

Capitol STAO-472	(S)	**Band Of Gypsys**	1970	6.00	15.00
		—Capitol albums above have green labels.—			
Capitol STAO-472	(S)	**Band Of Gypsys**	1970	10.00	25.00
		—Capitol albums above have red labels.—			
Capitol R-104148	(S)	**Band Of Gypsys** (RCA Record Club)	1970	14.00	35.00
		(Band Of Gypsies are Hendrix with Billy Cox and Buddy Miles.)			
Capitol SJ-12416	(S)	**Band Of Gypsys 2** (Mispressing)	1986	60.00	150.00
		(Some pressings were erroneously mastered with a completely			
		different second side consisting of four unreleased tracks. The cover			
		and label list the normal three tracks. so the disc must be viewed.)			
Capitol SJ-12416	(S)	**Band Of Gypsys 2**	1986	4.00	10.00
EMI America 17171	(S)	**Band Of Gypsys 2** (Colored vinyl)	198?	175.00	350.00
		(Prototype pressings to test colored vinyl for Kate Bush's "Hounds			
		Of Love". While the labels credit the Bush album, the record plays			
		one side of "Band Of Gypsys 2" on both sides.)			
EMI America 17171	(S)	**Band Of Gypsys 2**	198?	1.00	5.00
Capitol MLP-15022	(S)	**Johnny B. Goode**	1986	3.20	8.00

HENLEY, LARRY

Henley was a member of The Newbeats.

Capricorn 0152	(S)	**Piece A' Cake**	1974	4.00	10.00

Label & Catalog #		Title	Year	VG+	NM

HENRI, ADRIAN, & ROGER McGOUGH: *Refer to* THE LIVERPOOL SCENE

HENRY, CLARENCE "FROGMAN"
Argo LP-4009	(M)	You Always Hurt The One You Love	1961	100.00	250.00
Cadet LP-4009	(M)	You Always Hurt The One You Love	1966	20.00	50.00
Roulette SR-42039	(S)	Alive And Well And Living In New Orleans	1969	10.00	25.00

HENRY TREE
| Mainstream S-6129 | (S) | Electric Holy Man | 1968 | 10.00 | 25.00 |

HENSKE & YESTER
Judy Henske and hubby Jerry Yester. Refer to The Lovin' Spoonful; The Modern Folk Quartet.
Straight STS-1052	(S)	Farewell Aldebaran	1968	12.00	30.00
Reprise RS-6388	(S)	Farewell Aldebaran	1971	6.00	15.00
Reprise RS-6426	(S)	Rosebud	1971	6.00	15.00

HEPTONES, THE
Studio One SO-1108	(S)	The Best Of The Heptones	1976	14.00	35.00
Mango MLPS-9381	(S)	Night Food	1976	4.00	10.00
Mango MLPS-9456	(S)	Party Time	1977	4.00	10.00

HERD, THE
The Herd features Peter Frampton.
| Fontana SRF-67579 | (S) | Lookin' Thru You | 1968 | 10.00 | 25.00 |
| | | ("Understand Me" and "William" are rechanneled on this album.) | | | |

HERMAN'S HERMITS
Herman is Peter Noone and The 'Ermits are Derek Lekenby, Karl Green, Keith Hopwood and Barry Whitman. They can also be found on the MGM soundtrack "When The Boys Meet The Girls."
MGM E-4282	(M)	Introducing Herman's Hermits	1965	10.00	25.00
MGM SE-4282	(E)	Introducing Herman's Hermits	1965	8.00	20.00
		(Original covers for MGM 4282 read "Including Their Hit Single I'm Into Something Good.")			
MGM E-4282	(M)	Introducing Herman's Hermits	1965	8.00	20.00
MGM SE-4282	(E)	Introducing Herman's Hermits	1965	6.00	15.00
		(Second pressings have the original cover with a sticker that reads erroneously "Featuring Mrs. Brown You Have A Lovely Daughter.")			
MGM E-4282	(M)	Introducing Herman's Hermits	1965	6.00	15.00
MGM SE-4282	(E)	Introducing Herman's Hermits	1965	4.00	10.00
		(Later covers correctly read "Including Mrs. Brown You've Got A Lovely Daughter.")			
MGM E-4295	(M)	On Tour: Their Second Album	1965	4.00	10.00
MGM SE-4295	(E)	On Tour: Their Second Album	1965	4.00	10.00
MGM E-4315	(M)	The Best Of Herman's Hermits	1965	4.00	10.00
MGM SE-4315	(E)	The Best Of Herman's Hermits	1965	4.00	10.00
MGM T-90613	(M)	The Best Of Herman's Hermits (Capitol Rec. Club)	1965	6.00	15.00
MGM DT-90613	(E)	The Best Of Herman's Hermits (Capitol Rec. Club)	1965	6.00	15.00
MGM E-4342	(M)	Hold On!	1966	1.00	5.00
MGM SE-4342	(S)	Hold On!	1966	1.00	5.00
MGM E-4386	(M)	Both Sides Of Herman's Hermits	1966	1.00	5.00
MGM SE-4386	(E)	Both Sides Of Herman's Hermits	1966	1.00	5.00
MGM E-4416	(M)	Best Of Herman's Hermits, Volume 2	1966	4.00	10.00
MGM SE-4416	(E)	Best Of Herman's Hermits, Volume 2	1966	4.00	10.00
		("Hold On" and "Leaning On A Lamp Post" are in stereo. Issued with a color photo of 'Erman, worth an additional $5.)			
MGM E-4438	(M)	There's A Kind Of Hush All Over The World	1967	1.00	5.00
MGM SE-4438	(E)	There's A Kind Of Hush All Over The World	1967	1.00	5.00
MGM E-4478	(M)	Blaze	1967	1.00	5.00
MGM SE-4478	(S)	Blaze ("Moonshine Man" is rechanneled)	1967	1.00	5.00
MGM E-4505	(M)	The Best Of Herman's Hermits, Volume III	1967	1.20	6.00
MGM SE-4505	(E)	The Best Of Herman's Hermits, Volume III	1967	1.00	5.00
		("Museum," "Mum And Dad," "Last Bus Home" and "Don't Go Out Into The Rain" are in stereo.)			
MGM E-4548	(M)	Mrs. Brown You've Got A Lovely Daughter	1968	1.20	6.00
MGM SE-4548	(S)	Mrs. Brown You've Got A Lovely Daughter	1968	1.00	5.00
		("Mrs. Brown You've Got A Lovely Daughter" and "There's A Kind Of Hush All Over The World" are rechanneled.)			
Abkco AB-4227	(P)	Herman's Hermits XX (2 LPs)	1973	4.00	10.00
Abkco AB-4227	(P)	Herman's Hermits XX (1 LP)	1976	1.00	5.00

HERMETO
| Buddah BDS-9000 | (S) | Cobblestone | 1972 | 4.00 | 10.00 |

HERON, MIKE
Mike Heron was a member of The Incredible String Band.
| Elektra EKS-74093 | (S) | Smiling Men With Bad Reputations | 1971 | 6.00 | 15.00 |

You can argue over The Beatles and Stones in the beat battle of the world that took place in 1964-65, but on this side of the Atlantic it was Herman's Hermits that fought for chart supremacy with the Fab Four, scoring eighteen straight Top 40 hits before their popularity waned in 1967. Each of their first ten albums made the charts, five achieving RIAA Gold status. Original pressings of their first album read "Including Their Hit Single I'm Into Something Good." The copy shown here has a sticker applied to the cover noting, and mis-titling, their next single. After the unexpected success of "Mrs. Brown You've Got A Lovely Daughter," the cover of all subsequent pressings was amended to call attention to the hit.

Label & Catalog #		Title	Year	VG+	NM
HESITATIONS, THE					
Kapp KL-1525	(M)	**Soul Superman**	1967	10.00	25.00
Kapp KS-3525	(S)	**Soul Superman**	1967	10.00	25.00
Kapp KS-3548	(S)	**The New Born Free**	1968	10.00	25.00
Kapp KS-3561	(S)	**Where We're At**	1968	10.00	25.00
Kapp KS-3574	(S)	**Solid Gold**	1968	10.00	25.00
HI-LITES, THE					
Dandee DLP-206	(M)	**For Your Precious Love** *(Counterfeits exist)*	1961	1,000.00	2,000.00
HI-TONES, THE					
Hi HL-31011	(M)	**Raunchy Sounds**	1963	8.00	20.00
Hi SHL-32011	(S)	**Raunchy Sounds**	1963	10.00	25.00
HICKS, DAN, & HIS HOT LICKS					
Epic BN-26464	(S)	**Original Recordings**	1969	6.00	15.00
		— Epic albums above have yellow labels.—			
Epic BN-26464	(S)	**Original Recordings**	197?	1.00	5.00
		— Epic albums above have orange labels.—			
Epic BN-26464	(S)	**Original Recordings**	197?	.80	4.00
		— Epic albums above have black labels.—			
Blue Thumb BTS-29	(S)	**Where's The Money**	1971	6.00	15.00
Blue Thumb BTS-36	(S)	**Striking It Rich** *(Fold-open cover)*	1972	6.00	15.00
Warner Bros. BSK-3158	(S)	**It Happened One Bite**	1978	4.00	10.00
MCA 51	(S)	**Last Train To Hicksville**	1980	4.00	10.00
HICKS, JOE					
Enterprise ENS-1028	(S)	**Mighty**	1971	6.00	15.00
HIGGINS, CHUCK					
Combo LP-300	(M)	**Pachuko Hop**	1960	400.00	800.00
		(Original pressing covers feature a delightfully naked woman.)			
Combo LP-300	(M)	**Pachuko Hop**	1961	200.00	400.00
		(Later pressings feature a photo of a fully attired Higgins.)			
HIGGINS, CHUCK / ROY MILTON					
Dooto DTL-223	(M)	**Rock 'N' Roll Versus Rhythm And Blues**	1959	200.00	400.00
Authentic AUL-223	(M)	**Rock 'N' Roll Versus Rhythm And Blues**	196?	60.00	150.00
		(Authentic 223 is a reissue of Dooto 223.)			
HIGH, MARTHA					
Salsoul	(S)	**He's My Ding Dong Man** *(Prod. by James Brown)*	1979	6.00	15.00
HIGH COUNTRY					
Warner Bros. WS-1937	(S)	**High Country**	1971	4.00	10.00
Warner Bros. BS-2608	(S)	**Dreams**	1972	4.00	10.00
HIGH TIDE					
Liberty LST-7638	(S)	**Sea Shanties**	1969	20.00	50.00
HIGH TREASON					
Abbott ABS-1209	(S)	**High Treason**	197?	20.00	50.00
HIGH VOLTAGE					
Columbia KC-31376	(S)	**High Voltage**	1972	4.00	10.00
HILL, BARBARA, & CHRIS ETHRIDGE					
Atco SD-33-357	(S)	**L.A. Getaway**	1971	4.00	10.00
HILL, VINCE					
Tower T-5064	(M)	**At The Club**	1966	4.00	10.00
HILLAGE, STEVE					
Steve Hillage was a member of Arzachel and Gong.					
Virgin VR-3-118	(S)	**Fish Rising**	1975	5.00	12.00
HILLMAN, CHRIS					
Chris Hillman was a member of The Byrds. Refer to The Flying Burrito Brothers.					
Asylum 7E-1062	(S)	**Slippin' Away**	1976	1.00	5.00
Asylum 7E-1104	(S)	**Clear Sailin'**	1976	1.00	5.00
HILLMEN, THE					
These 1963-64 recordings are actually by The Golden State Boys: Chris Hillman, brothers Vern and Rex Gosdin, and Don Parmley. The album was named The Hillmen after Hillman's success.					
Together STT-1012	(S)	**The Hillmen**	1970	20.00	50.00
Sugar Hill SH-3719	(S)	**The Hillmen**	1981	4.00	10.00
		(Sugar Hill 3719 is a reissue of Together 1012.)			

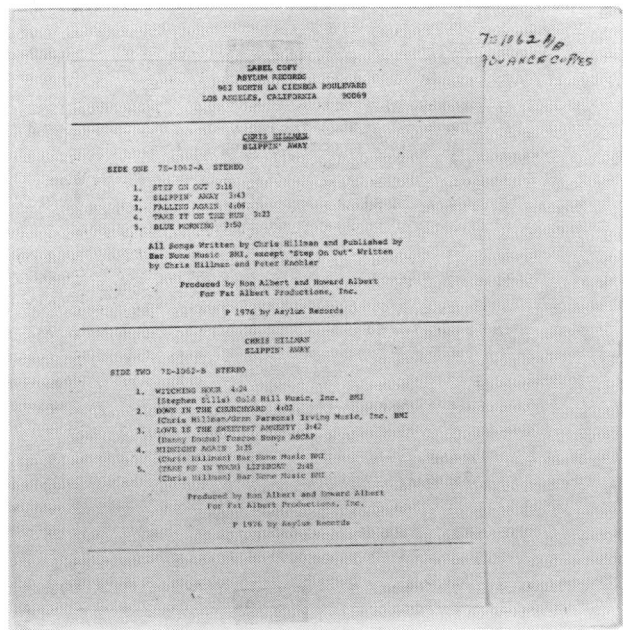

This is an example of what a collector might expect a test-pressing to look like when finger-ing through boxes of LPs. Like most such discs, it was issued in a plain white cardboard jacket with a sheet of 8 1/2" x 11" paper hand-taped to the front. In this case, it is from Asy-lum Records and holds Chris Hillman's Slippin' Away. The sheet supplies all the necessary data for the handler: Titles, times, publishing info, etc. Test pressings can be worth thou-sands or just a few bucks but they are always worth more than the commercially issued ver-sions to collectors of the artist!

Label & Catalog #		Title	Year	VG+	NM
HIM, HE & ME					
Metromedia 1025	(S)	**Him, He And Me**	1970	4.00	10.00
HINE, RUPERT, & DAVID McIVER					
Capitol/Purple SMAS-879	(S)	**Pick Up A Bone**	1972	5.00	12.00
HINTON, JOE					
Backbeat B-60	(M)	**Funny (How Time Slips Away)**	1965	20.00	50.00
Backbeat B-60	(S)	**Funny (How Time Slips Away)**	1965	30.00	75.00
Duke DLPS-91	(M)	**Duke-Peacock Remembers**	1969	8.00	20.00
ABC	(S)	**Joe Hinton**	1973	6.00	15.00
HOBBITS, THE					
Decca DL-4290	(M)	**Down To Middle Earth**	1967	16.00	40.00
Decca DL-74290	(S)	**Down To Middle Earth**	1967	20.00	50.00
Decca DL-5009	(M)	**Men And Doors**	1968	12.00	30.00
Decca DL-75009	(S)	**Men And Doors**	1968	12.00	30.00
Perception	(S)	**Return To Middle Earth**	1971	12.00	30.00
HODGE, CATFISH					
Epic E-26505	(S)	**Get Down**	1970	4.00	10.00
Epic E-30361	(S)	**Live Catfish With Bob Hodge**	1971	4.00	10.00
Westbound W-202	(S)	**Soap Operas**	197?	4.00	10.00
HOG HEAVEN					
Hog Heaven is comprised of members of Tommy James' Shondells.					
Roulette SR-42057	(S)	**Hog Heaven**	1971	8.00	20.00
HOGAN SILAS					
Excello LPS-8019	(S)	**Trouble**	1972	8.00	20.00
HOGG, ANDREW "SMOKEY"					
Time 6	(M)	**Smokey Hogg**	1962	60.00	150.00
Crown CLP-5226	(M)	**Smokey Hogg Sings The Blues**	1962	20.00	50.00
		—Crown albums above have gray labels.—			
Kent LP-5???	(M)	**Original Folk Blues**	1966	6.00	15.00
Kent LP-5??	(E)	**Original Folk Blues**	1966	4.00	10.00
United US-7745	(E)	**Smokey Hogg**	1970	4.00	10.00
		(Both the Kent and United albums are reissues of Crown 5226.)			
HOKUS POKUS					
Romar RM-2002	(S)	**Hokus Pokus**	1972	5.00	12.00
HOLDEN, RON					
Donna DLP-2111	(M)	**I Love You So**	1960	150.00	300.00
Donna DLPS-2111	(S)	**I Love You So**	1960	360.00	600.00
HOLDER, RAM JAM					
Philips PHS-600-324	(S)	**Black London Blues**	1969	4.00	10.00
HOLIDAY, JIMMY					
Minit LP-40005	(M)	**Turning Point**	1966	8.00	20.00
Minit LP-24005	(S)	**Turning Point**	1966	10.00	25.00
HOLLAND, EDDIE					
Motown 604	(M)	**Eddie Holland**	1963	200.00	400.00
HOLLAND, ROSCOE					
Dooto DTL-812	(M)	**For A Piece**	1962	8.00	20.00

HOLLIES, THE

Original recording members were vocalists Allan Clarke and Graham Nash with Tony Hicks, Eric Haydock and Donald Rathbone. Rathbone was replaced by Bobby Elliott in 1963. Haydock left in 1966, replaced by Bernie Calvert. Nash's much ballyhooed departure in 1968 to team up with David Crosby and Steve Stills, opened the door for Terry Sylvester. For a brief spell in 1972-73, Clarke quit for a solo career and was replaced by Mikael Rikfors (on "Romany"). The Hollies can also be found on the U.A. soundtrack "After The Fox." Refer to The Everly Brothers.

Imperial LP-9265	(M)	**Here I Go Again**	1964	40.00	100.00
Imperial LP-12265	(E)	**Here I Go Again**	1964	30.00	75.00
—Imperial albums above have black labels with colored stars and rays on top.—					
Imperial LP-9265	(M)	**Here I Go Again**	1964	20.00	50.00
Imperial LP-12265	(E)	**Here I Go Again**	1964	12.00	30.00
Imperial LP-9299	(M)	**Hear Here!**	1965	20.00	50.00
Imperial LP-12299	(E)	**Hear Here!**	1965	12.00	30.00
Imperial LP-9312	(M)	**The Hollies—Beat Group**	1966	12.00	30.00
Imperial LP-12312	(S)	**The Hollies—Beat Group**	1966	16.00	40.00
Imperial LP-9330	(M)	**Bus Stop**	1966	12.00	30.00
Imperial LP-12330	(E)	**Bus Stop**	1966	10.00	25.00
—Imperial albums above have black, pink & white labels.—					

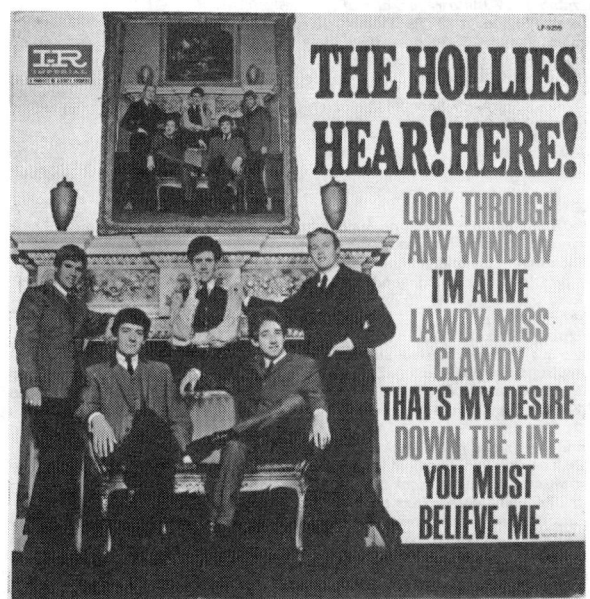

The Hollies—here vocalists Alan Clarke and Graham Nash with Tony Hicks, Bobby Elliott and Eric Haydock—ran up an impressive string of hits on the UK charts, ranking them with The Beatles and The Rolling Stones among Great Britain's hit-makers of the late '60s. Like other British groups of the time, their American LPs were pieced together from various sources (45s, EPs and LPs), often to the bewilderment of the group. In The Hollies' case, they benefited greatly in one respect: Imperial took their second UK album and replaced the two weakest cuts with a pair of wondrous singles, "Look Through Any Window" and "I'm Alive." The resulting assemblage, Hear! Here!, comfortably stands with Meet The Beatles as the definitive Merseybeat album for American listeners. The differences that exist between released material—and, of course, the piles of unreleased sides—make collecting albums from an artist's country of origin both interesting and educational!

Label & Catalog #		Title	Year	VG+	NM
Imperial LP-9330	(M)	**Bus Stop**	1966	8.00	20.00
Imperial LP-12330	(E)	**Bus Stop**	1966	6.00	15.00
Imperial LP-9339	(M)	**Stop! Stop! Stop!**	1966	10.00	25.00
Imperial LP-12339	(S)	**Stop! Stop! Stop!**	1966	12.00	30.00
Imperial LP-9350	(M)	**The Hollies' Greatest Hits**	1967	8.00	20.00
Imperial LP-12350	(P)	**The Hollies' Greatest Hits**	1967	10.00	25.00
		—Imperial albums above have black, green & white labels.—			
Epic LN-24315	(M)	**Evolution**	1967	10.00	25.00
Epic BN-26315	(S)	**Evolution**	1967	12.00	30.00
Epic LN-24344	(M)	**Dear Eloise/King Midas In Reverse**	1967	10.00	25.00
Epic BN-26344	(S)	**Dear Eloise/King Midas In Reverse**	1967	12.00	30.00
Epic BN-26447	(S)	**Words And Music By Bob Dylan**	1969	6.00	15.00
Epic BN-26538	(S)	**He Ain't Heavy, He's My Brother**	1969	8.00	20.00
Epic KE-30255	(S)	**Moving Finger**	1970	8.00	20.00
Epic KE-30958	(S)	**Distant Light**	1971	4.00	10.00
Epic KE-31992	(S)	**Romany**	1972	4.00	10.00
Epic KE-32061	(S)	**The Hollies' Greatest Hits**	1973	4.00	10.00
		—Epic albums above have yellow labels.—			
Epic BN-26447	(S)	**Words And Music By Bob Dylan**	1974	1.00	5.00
Epic KE-30958	(S)	**Distant Light**	1974	1.00	5.00
Epic KE-31992	(S)	**Romany**	1974	1.00	5.00
Epic KE-32061	(P)	**The Hollies' Greatest Hits**	1974	1.00	5.00
Epic KE-32574	(S)	**Hollies**	1974	4.00	10.00
Epic PE-33387	(S)	**Another Night**	1975	4.00	10.00
Epic AS-138	(DJ)	**Everything You Always Wanted To Hear By The Hollies But Were Afraid To Ask For** (*Sampler*)	1976	6.00	15.00
Epic PE-2V-8026	(P)	**The Hollies, Volume 1 & 2** (*2 LPs*)	1976	3.20	8.00
Epic PE-34714	(S)	**Clarke, Hicks, Sylvester, Calvert & Elliot**	1977	1.00	5.00
Epic JE-35334	(S)	**A Crazy Steal**	1978	1.00	5.00
		—Epic albums above have orange labels.—			
United Artists LA-329E	(P)	**The Very Best Of The Hollies**	1975	.80	4.00
Columbia LE-10178	(S)	**He Ain't Heavy, He's My Brother**	1976	1.00	5.00
		(Columbia 10178 is a repackage of Epic 26538.)			
Realm 2V-8026	(P)	**The Hollies, Volume 1** (*2 LPs. TV advertised*)	1976	6.00	15.00
Realm 1V-8027	(P)	**The Hollies, Volume 2** (*TV advertised*)	1976	4.00	10.00
Capitol N-16056	(S)	**Hollies' Greatest**	1980	.80	4.00
Liberty LN-10216	(S)	**Pay You Back With Interest**	1982	.80	4.00
Atlantic 80076-1	(S)	**What Goes Around...**	1983	1.00	5.00

HOLLOWAY, BRENDA

Tamla T-257	(M)	**Every Little Bit Hurts**	1964	100.00	250.00
Tamla TS-257	(E)	**Every Little Bit Hurts**	1964	80.00	200.00

HOLLY, BUDDY [BUDDY HOLLY & THE CRICKETS]
Buddy Holly originally signed with Decca, who tried to record him as a country singer. These are collected on DL-8707, released after his rock'n roll success. He signed with his group, The Crickets, with Brunswick and as a solo artist to the sister label, Coral, although his recordings with and without the group appeared on Coral. In the wake of Holly's death, The Crickets continued without him (and are listed separately). Producer Norman Petty took Buddy's unreleased demo tapes and over-dubbed backing tracks by The Fireballs onto them for continued releases. Refer to Buddy Knox; Jimmy Bowen; The Crickets; Terry Noland.

Brunswick BL-54038	(DJ)	**The Chirping Crickets** (*Yellow label promo*)	1957	*See note below*	
		(Yellow label promos have a suggested NM value of $3,000-5,000.)			
Brunswick BL-54038	(M)	**The Chirping Crickets** (*Textured cover*)	1957	400.00	800.00
Brunswick BL-54038	(M)	**The Chirping Crickets** (*Standard cover*)	1958	300.00	600.00
Decca DL-8707	(DJ)	**That'll Be The Day** (*Pink label promo*)	1958	1,000.00	1,500.00
Decca DL-8707	(M)	**That'll Be The Day**	1958	1,400.00	2,000.00
		(Original pressings have black labels with silver print.)			
Decca DL-8707	(M)	**That'll Be The Day**	196?	150.00	300.00
		(Later pressings have a black label with a rainbow band through the center and were pressed on thick vinyl. Counterfeits from the '70s have poor cover reproduction and were pressed on thin vinyl.)			
Coral CRL-57210	(DJ)	**Buddy Holly** (*Blue label promo*)	1958	500.00	1,000.00
Coral CRL-57210	(M)	**Buddy Holly**	1958	200.00	400.00
Coral CRL-57279	(DJ)	**The Buddy Holly Story** (*Blue label promo*)	1959	500.00	750.00
Coral CRL-57279	(M)	**The Buddy Holly Story**	1959	150.00	300.00
		(The print on the back cover is in red and black.)			
Coral CRL-57279	(M)	**The Buddy Holly Story**	1959	80.00	200.00
Coral CRL-757279	(E)	**The Buddy Holly Story**	1959	70.00	175.00
		(The print on the back cover is in black only.)			
Coral CRL-57326	(DJ)	**The Buddy Holly Story, Vol. 2** (*Blue label*)	1959	500.00	750.00
Coral CRL-57326	(M)	**The Buddy Holly Story, Vol. 2**	1959	80.00	200.00
Coral CRL-57405	(DJ)	**Buddy Holly & The Crickets** (*Blue label*)	1962	500.00	750.00
Coral CRL-57405	(M)	**Buddy Holly & The Crickets**	1962	80.00	200.00
Coral CRL-757405	(E)	**Buddy Holly & The Crickets**	1962	60.00	150.00
		(Coral 57405 is a reissue of Brunswick 54038.)			
Coral CRL-57426	(M)	**Reminiscing** (*Yellow label promo*)	1963	300.00	500.00
Coral CRL-57426	(M)	**Reminiscing**	1963	80.00	200.00
Coral CRL-757426	(E)	**Reminiscing**	1963	60.00	150.00
		—Coral albums above have maroon labels.—			

By the early '70s, The Hollies were original members Alan Clark, Tony Hicks and Bobby Elliott with Bernie Calvert, who joined in 1966, and Terry Sylvester, who replaced Graham Nash in 1968. One of the still unsung pleasures of the pre-disco '70s is Hollies, a pop/rock gem which contained their glorious reading of "The Air That I Breathe." This was followed by the tougher Another Night, which featured two failed hits, the title tune and one of the first—and arguably the best—covers of a Bruce Springsteen song, "Sandy." Both of these albums were shipped to radio stations with title & timing strips affixed to the cover to let the station programmers know exactly what they needed to know to ease the album onto the turntable. While such "promos" can generate big bucks when found on a major collectible artist, these albums usually bring only a nominal premium from collectors of lesser artists, such as The Hollies.

Label & Catalog #		Title	Year	VG+	NM
Coral CRL-57210	(M)	**Buddy Holly**	1963	40.00	100.00
Coral CRL-57279	(M)	**The Buddy Holly Story**	1963	30.00	75.00
Coral CRL-757279	(E)	**The Buddy Holly Story**	1963	20.00	50.00
Coral CRL-57326	(M)	**The Buddy Holly Story, Vol. 2**	1963	30.00	75.00
Coral CRL-757326	(E)	**The Buddy Holly Story, Vol. 2**	1963	20.00	50.00
Coral CRL-57426	(M)	**Reminiscing**	1964	30.00	75.00
Coral CRL-757426	(E)	**Reminiscing**	1964	20.00	50.00
Coral CRL-57450	(DJ)	**Showcase** (Yellow label promo)	1964	100.00	250.00
Coral CRL-57450	(M)	**Showcase**	1964	40.00	100.00
Coral CRL-757450	(E)	**Showcase**	1964	30.00	75.00
Coral CRL-57463	(DJ)	**Holly In The Hills** (Yellow label promo)	1965	100.00	250.00
Coral CRL-57463	(M)	**Holly In The Hills**	1965	50.00	125.00
Coral CRL-757463	(E)	**Holly In The Hills**	1965	40.00	100.00
Coral CXB-8	(DJ)	**The Best Of Buddy Holly** (Yellow label)	1966	100.00	200.00
Coral CXB-8	(M)	**The Best Of Buddy Holly**	1966	30.00	75.00
Coral CXSB-8	(E)	**The Best Of Buddy Holly**	1966	20.00	50.00
Coral CRL-57492	(M)	**Buddy Holly's Greatest Hits**	1967	30.00	75.00
Coral CRL-757492	(P)	**Buddy Holly's Greatest Hits**	1967	20.00	50.00
Coral CRL-757504	(DJ)	**Giant** (Yellow label promo)	1969	60.00	150.00
Coral CRL-757504	(S)	**Giant**	1969	20.00	50.00
		—Coral albums above have black labels that read "A subsidiary of Decca."—			
Vocalion VL-3811	(M)	**The Great Buddy Holly**	1967	30.00	75.00
Vocalion VL-73811	(E)	**The Great Buddy Holly**	1967	20.00	50.00
		(Vocalion 3811 is a repackage of "That'll Be The Day.")			
Vocalion VL-73923	(E)	**Good Rockin'**	1971	40.00	100.00
Decca DXSE-207	(P)	**A Rock & Roll Collection** (2 LPs)	1972	16.00	40.00
MCA 2-4009	(M)	**A Rock & Roll Collection** (2 LPs with liner notes)	1973	8.00	20.00
MCA 2-4009	(P)	**A Rock & Roll Collection** (2 LPs without notes)	1972	1.20	6.00
MCA CD-20101	(M)	**The Great Buddy Holly**	1975	1.20	6.00
MCA 3040	(M)	**20 Golden Greats**	1978	1.00	5.00
MCA 6-8000	(M)	**The Complete Buddy Holly** (6 LP box)	1981	16.00	40.00
MCA 27059	(M)	**For The First Time Anywhere**	1983	.80	4.00
MCA 2-4184	(M)	**Legend**	198?	.80	4.00
MCA 25170	(M)	**The Chirping Crickets**	1988	.80	4.00
Cricket C001000	(M)	**Buddy Holly Live—Volume 1**	197?	8.00	20.00
Cricket C001001	(M)	**Buddy Holly Live—Volume 2**	197?	8.00	20.00
Solid Smoke 8002	(M)	**A Portrait In Music, Volume 1** (Picture disc)	1979	6.00	15.00
Solid Smoke 8003	(M)	**A Portrait In Music, Volume 2** (Picture disc)	1979	6.00	15.00

HOLLYWOOD ARGYLES, THE
The Argyles feature Gary Paxton. Note: It is possible that two pressings with two catalog numbers exist or that covers designate the album L-101 while the record's label carries the L-9001 number.

Lute L-101	(M)	**The Hollywood Argyles**	1960	500.00	750.00
Lute L-9001	(M)	**The Hollywood Argyles**	1960	500.00	750.00

HOLLYWOOD PERSUADERS, THE

Original Sound LPM-5013	(M)	**Drums A Go-Go**	1965	20.00	50.00
Original Sound LPS-8874	(S)	**Drums A Go-Go**	1965	30.00	75.00

HOLLYWOOD SURFERS, THE: Refer to DICK DALE / THE HOLLYWOOD SURFERS

HOLMAN, EDDIE

ABC S-701	(S)	**I Love You**	1969	12.00	30.00
Salsoul 5511	(S)	**A Night To Remember**	1977	1.00	5.00

HOLMBERG, JIM

ESP-Disk' 1098	(S)	**MIJ**	196?	8.00	20.00

HOLMES, MARVIN, & THE UPTIGHTS [MARVIN HOLMES & JUSTICE]

Uni 73046	(S)	**Ooh Ooh The Dragon & Other Monsters**	1969	8.00	20.00
Brown Door MH-6573	(S)	**Summer Of '73**	1973	10.00	25.00
Brown Door MH-6581	(S)	**Honor Thy Father**	1975	10.00	25.00

HOLTS, ROOSEVELT

Blue Horizon 7704	(S)	**Presenting The Country Blues**	1969	4.00	10.00

HOLY LIGHTS

Savoy 14293	(S)	**Holy Lights**	1972	4.00	10.00

HOLY MACKEREL
Holy Mackerel features Paul Williams.

Reprise RS-6311	(S)	**Holy Mackerel**	1968	10.00	25.00

HOLY MODAL ROUNDERS, THE
The Rounders were Peter Stampfel and Steve Weber. Refer to The Fugs.

Folklore FRLP-14031	(M)	**The Holy Modal Rounders**	1964	30.00	75.00
Prestige PRLP-7410	(M)	**The Holy Modal Rounders 2**	1966	14.00	35.00
Prestige PRLP-7451	(M)	**The Holy Modal Rounders**	1966	14.00	35.00
		(Prestige 7451 is a reissue of Folklore 14031.)			

When The Crickets signed with Brunswick, their contract allowed them to record as a group for the parent label, and their singer, guitarist and songwriter, Charles Hardin Holley, known professionally as Buddy Holly, to record as a solo for their Coral subsidiary. The Chirping Crickets was the only album released by the group during Buddy's life, cut short by the now legendary airplane crash in the winter of 1959 that also took the lives of Ritchie Valens and The Big Bopper ("the day the music died"). The group continued without Holly and their work is listed separately.

Label & Catalog #		Title	Year	VG+	NM
ESP-Disk' 1068	(M)	Indian War Whoop	1967	16.00	40.00
ESP-Disk' 1068	(S)	Indian War Whoop	1967	16.00	40.00
Elektra EKS-74026	(S)	The Moray Eels Eat The Holy Modal Rounders	1968	12.00	30.00
Metromedia MD-1039	(S)	Good Taste Is Timeless	1971	12.00	30.00
Fantasy F-24711	(S)	Stampfel And Weber	1972	6.00	15.00
Prestige PR-7720	(M)	The Holy Modal Rounders	1972	6.00	15.00
		(Prestige 7720 is a reissue of Folklore 14031.)			
Rounder 3004	(S)	Alleged In Their Own Time	1975	6.00	15.00
Rounder 3010	(S)	Have Moicy!	1975	6.00	15.00
Adelphi 1030	(S)	Last Round	1978	6.00	15.00
Rounder 3051	(S)	Going Nowhere Fast	1981	6.00	15.00

HOLY MOSES

Label & Catalog #		Title	Year	VG+	NM
RCA Victor LSP-4523	(S)	Holy Moses	1971	6.00	15.00

HOMBRES, THE

Label & Catalog #		Title	Year	VG+	NM
Verve/Forecast FT-3036	(M)	Let It Out	1967	10.00	25.00
Verve/Forecast FTS-3036	(S)	Let It Out	1967	12.00	30.00
Verve/Forecast FTS-3068	(S)	The Hombres	1969	Unreleased	

HOME

Label & Catalog #		Title	Year	VG+	NM
Epic KE-31146	(S)	Pause For A Hoarse Horse	1972	1.00	5.00

HOME SWEET HOME

Label & Catalog #		Title	Year	VG+	NM
Capitol ST-652	(S)	Home Sweet Home	1972	1.00	5.00

HOMEGAS

Label & Catalog #		Title	Year	VG+	NM
Takoma 1026	(S)	Homegas	1971	1.00	5.00

HOMESICK JAMES

Label & Catalog #		Title	Year	VG+	NM
Prestige PRST-7388	(M)	Blues On The South Side	197?	6.00	15.00
BluesWay BLS-6071	(S)	Ain't Sick No More	1973	5.00	12.00

HONDELLS, THE
The Hondells are a creation of Gary Usher & Co. featuring Chuck Girard.

Label & Catalog #		Title	Year	VG+	NM
Mercury MG-20940	(M)	Go Little Honda	1964	16.00	40.00
Mercury SR-60940	(S)	Go Little Honda	1964	30.00	75.00
Mercury MG-20982	(M)	The Hondells	1965	20.00	50.00
Mercury SR-60982	(S)	The Hondells	1965	40.00	100.00

HONEY & THE BEES

Label & Catalog #		Title	Year	VG+	NM
Josie JOS-4013	(S)	Honey And The Bees	197?	6.00	15.00

HONEY CONE

Label & Catalog #		Title	Year	VG+	NM
Hot Wax HA-701	(S)	Take Me With You	1970	4.00	10.00
Hot Wax HA-706	(S)	Sweet Replies	1971	4.00	10.00
Hot Wax HA-707	(S)	Soulful Tapestry	1971	4.00	10.00
Hot Wax HA-713	(S)	Love, Peace & Soul	1972	4.00	10.00

HONEYCOMBS, THE

Label & Catalog #		Title	Year	VG+	NM
Vee Jay IN-88001	(M)	Here Are The Honeycombs	1964	20.00	50.00
Vee Jay IN-88001	(E)	Here Are The Honeycombs	1964	16.00	40.00
Interphon IN-88001	(M)	Here Are The Honeycombs	1964	16.00	40.00
Interphon IN-88001	(E)	Here Are The Honeycombs	1964	12.00	30.00
		(Interphon 88001 and VJ 88001 are the same album.)			

HONK

Label & Catalog #		Title	Year	VG+	NM
20th Century 406	(S)	Honk	1973	5.00	12.00
Epic KE-33094	(S)	Honk	1974	4.00	10.00

HOODOO RHYTHM DEVILS, THE

Label & Catalog #		Title	Year	VG+	NM
Capitol ST-842	(S)	The Hoodoo Rhythm Devils	1971	8.00	20.00
Blue Thumb BTS-42	(S)	The Barbeque Of DeVille	1972	6.00	15.00
Blue Thumb BTS-57	(S)	What The Kids Want	1973	6.00	15.00
Fantasy F-9522	(S)	Safe In Their Homes	1977	1.00	5.00
Fantasy F-9543	(S)	All Kidding Aside	1977	1.00	5.00

HOOK

Label & Catalog #		Title	Year	VG+	NM
Uni 73023	(S)	The Hook Will Grab You	1968	5.00	12.00
Uni 73038	(S)	Hooked	1968	5.00	12.00

HOOKER, EARL

Label & Catalog #		Title	Year	VG+	NM
Cuca KS-3400	(S)	The Genius Of Earl Hooker	196?	60.00	150.00
Blue Thumb BTS-12	(S)	Sweet Black Angel	1969	8.00	20.00
BluesWay BLS-6032	(S)	Don't Have To Worry	1969	8.00	20.00
BluesWay BLS-6038	(S)	If You Miss Him	1970	6.00	20.00
BluesWay BLS-6072	(S)	Do You Remember The Great Earl Hooker	1973	6.00	15.00
Arhoolie 1044	(S)	Two Bugs And A Roach	1975	4.00	10.00

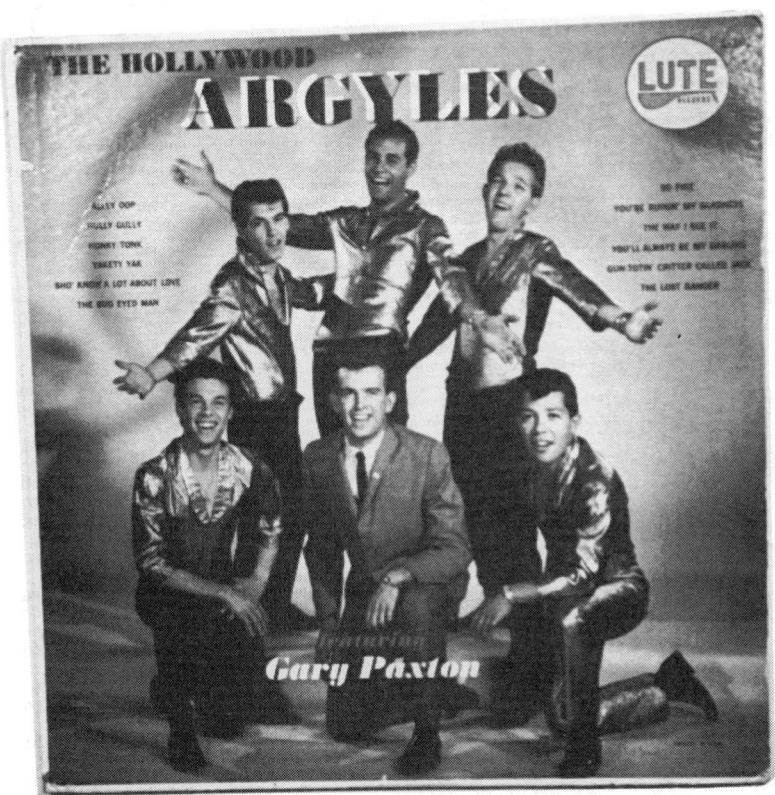

Gary Paxton recorded "Alley Oop" by himself as a respite from his work as Flip in the duo, Skip & Flip (the other half was Skip Battin, later of the latter day Byrds). Due to contractual obligations, he was convinced to issue the single as a "group" effort, credited to the non-existent Hollywood Argyles. After the single topped the charts, Paxton put together a group and the album followed. Like so many albums on tiny labels, it sold next to nothing at the time of release and those that did buy it, partied to it.

Label & Catalog #		Title	Year	VG+	NM
Arhoolie 1051	(S)	Hooker And Steve	1975	4.00	10.00
Arhoolie 1066	(S)	His First And Last Recordings	1975	4.00	10.00
Antilles 7024	(S)	Last Of The Great Earl Hooker	1977	4.00	10.00

HOOKER, JOHN LEE

Refer to Canned Heat; The Groundhogs; Albert King & John Lee Hooker; Sticks McGhee; Big Maceo Merriweather.

Label & Catalog #		Title	Year	VG+	NM
Vee Jay LP-1007	(M)	I'm John Lee Hooker	1959	80.00	200.00
		—*Vee Jay albums above have maroon labels.—*			
Vee Jay LP-1007	(M)	I'm John Lee Hooker	1960	30.00	75.00
Vee Jay LP-1023	(M)	Travelin'	1960	30.00	75.00
Vee Jay LP-1033	(M)	The Folk Lore Of John Lee Hooker	1961	20.00	50.00
Vee Jay SR-1033	(S)	The Folk Lore Of John Lee Hooker	1961	30.00	75.00
Vee Jay LP-1043	(M)	Burnin'	1962	20.00	50.00
Vee Jay SR-1043	(S)	Burnin'	1962	60.00	150.00
Vee Jay LP-1049	(M)	The Best Of John Lee Hooker	1962	20.00	50.00
Vee Jay LP-1049	(P)	The Best Of John Lee Hooker	1962	30.00	75.00
Vee Jay LP-1058	(M)	The Big Soul Of John Lee Hooker	1963	20.00	50.00
Vee Jay SR-1058	(S)	The Big Soul Of John Lee Hooker	1963	60.00	150.00
Vee Jay LP-1066	(M)	John Lee Hooker On Campus	1963	20.00	50.00
Vee Jay SR-1066	(S)	John Lee Hooker On Campus	1963	60.00	150.00
Vee Jay LP-1078	(M)	John Lee Hooker At Newport	1964	20.00	50.00
Vee Jay SR-1078	(S)	John Lee Hooker At Newport	1964	60.00	150.00
Vee Jay LP-8502	(M)	Is He The World's Greatest Folk/Blues Singer	1965	16.00	40.00
		—*Vee Jay albums above have black rainbow labels.—*			
Riverside RLP-12-838	(M)	The Country Blues Of John Lee Hooker	1959	40.00	100.00
Riverside RLP-12-321	(M)	That's My Story	1960	40.00	100.00
King 727	(M)	John Lee Hooker Sings The Blues	1960	200.00	500.00
		—*King albums above have crownless black labels.—*			
King KS-1085	(E)	Moanin' And Stompin' Blues	1970	10.00	25.00
Chess LP-1438	(M)	House Of The Blues	1960	150.00	300.00
Chess LP-1454	(M)	John Lee Hooker Plays And Sings The Blues	1961	150.00	300.00
		—*Chess albums above have black labels.—*			
Chess LPS-1438	(E)	House Of The Blues	196?	20.00	50.00
Chess LP-1454	(M)	John Lee Hooker Plays And Sings The Blues	196?	20.00	50.00
Chess LP-1508	(M)	Real Folk Blues	1966	20.00	50.00
Chess LPS-1508	(E)	Real Folk Blues	1966	14.00	35.00
Chess 2SC-60011	(M)	Mad Man's Blues (2 LPs)	1973	6.00	15.00
		—*Chess albums above have blue & white labels.—*			
Crown CLP-5157	(M)	The Blues	1960	40.00	100.00
Crown CLP-5232	(M)	John Lee Hooker Sings The Blues	1962	40.00	100.00
	—*Crown albums above have black labels with a silver "Crown" on top.—*				
Crown CLP-5157	(M)	The Blues	1960	12.00	30.00
Crown CLP-5232	(M)	John Lee Hooker Sings The Blues	1962	12.00	30.00
Crown CST-???	(E)	John Lee Hooker Sings The Blues	1962	8.00	20.00
Crown CLP-5295	(M)	Folk Blues	1962	12.00	30.00
Crown CST-295	(E)	Folk Blues	1962	8.00	20.00
Crown CLP-5353	(M)	The Great John Lee Hooker	1963	12.00	30.00
Crown CST-353	(E)	The Great John Lee Hooker	1963	8.00	20.00
		—*Crown albums above have gray labels.—*			
Crown CLP-5157	(M)	The Blues	196?	4.00	10.00
Crown CLP-5232	(M)	John Lee Hooker Sings The Blues	196?	4.00	10.00
Crown CST-???	(E)	John Lee Hooker Sings The Blues	196?	4.00	10.00
Crown CLP-5295	(M)	Folk Blues	196?	1.00	5.00
Crown CST-???	(E)	Folk Blues	196?	4.00	10.00
Crown CLP-5333	(M)	The Great John Lee Hooker	196?	1.00	5.00
Crown CST-???	(E)	The Great John Lee Hooker	196?	4.00	10.00
	—*Crown albums above have black labels with a multi-color "Crown" on top.—*				
Battle BLP-6113	(M)	John Lee Hooker	196?	60.00	150.00
Battle BLP-6114	(M)	How Long Blues	196?	60.00	150.00
Galaxy 8201	(M)	I'm John Lee Hooker	1962	100.00	250.00
Galaxy 8205	(M)	Live At Sugar Hill	1962	100.00	250.00
Atco 33-151	(M)	Don't Turn Me From Your Door (White label promo)	1963	100.00	250.00
Atco 33-151	(M)	Don't Turn Me From Your Door	1963	40.00	100.00
Atco SD-33-151	(E)	Don't Turn Me From Your Door	1967	20.00	50.00
Verve/Folkways FT-3003	(M)	John Lee Hooker And Seven Nights	1965	10.00	25.00
Verve/Folkways FTS-3003	(S)	John Lee Hooker And Seven Nights	1965	14.00	35.00
Exodus 325	(M)	Is He The World's Greatest Blues Singer?	1966	10.00	25.00
Impulse A-9103	(M)	It Serve You Right To Suffer	1966	12.00	30.00
Impulse AS-9103	(S)	It Serve You Right To Suffer	1966	16.00	40.00
		—*Impulse albums above have orange & brown labels.—*			
BluesWay BL-6002	(M)	Live At Cafe Au-Go-Go	1966	8.00	20.00
BluesWay BLS-6002	(S)	Live At Cafe Au-Go-Go	1966	10.00	25.00
BluesWay BL-6012	(M)	Urban Blues	1967	8.00	20.00
BluesWay BLS-6012	(S)	Urban Blues	1967	10.00	25.00
BluesWay BLS-6023	(S)	Simply The Truth	1968	10.00	25.00
BluesWay BLS-6038	(S)	If You Miss 'Im	1969	10.00	25.00
BluesWay BLS-6052	(S)	Live At Kabuki Wuki	1973	6.00	15.00

Peter Stampfel and Steve Weber, a.k.a. The Holy Modal Rounders, recorded some of the *downright weirdest music of their time (no small claim to fame, given the times), combining an eclectic mix of basically American sounds with their unorthodox folkie sensibilities. This led to such musiacl assualts on a listener's integrity as* Alleged In Their Own Time *and ther Beefheartian mini-masterpiece,* The Moray Eels Eat The Holy Modal Rounders. *Neither to credit nor lay blame, but they were also responsible for creating the aural backdrop on* The Fugs' *early albums.*

Label & Catalog #		Title	Year	VG+	NM
Kent KLP-5025	(M)	The Original Folk Blues	1967	10.00	25.00
Kent KST-525	(E)	The Original Folk Blues	1967	6.00	15.00
Kent KST-559	(E)	John Lee Hooker's Greatest Hits	1971	6.00	15.00
United UM-729	(M)	Folk Blues	1967	6.00	15.00
United US-729	(E)	Folk Blues	1967	4.00	10.00
United UM-731	(M)	The Great Blues Sounds Of John Lee Hooker	1967	6.00	15.00
United US-731	(E)	The Great Blues Sounds Of John Lee Hooker	1967	4.00	10.00
United US-7710	(E)	Driftin' Through The Blues	197?	4.00	10.00
United US-7725	(E)	The Blues	197?	4.00	10.00
United US-7729	(E)	Folk Blues	197?	4.00	10.00
United US-7746	(E)	John Lee Hooker's Greatest Hits	197?	4.00	10.00
United US-7769	(E)	Original Folk Blues	197?	4.00	10.00
Custom CS-2048	(E)	Driftin' Through The Blues	196?	4.00	10.00
Archive of Folk Music 222	(M)	John Lee Hooker	1968	4.00	10.00
Buddah BDS-4002	(P)	The Very Best Of John Lee Hooker	1969	6.00	15.00
Buddah BDS-7506	(S)	Big Band Blues	1969	6.00	15.00
Tradition 2089	(E)	Real Blues	1970	6.00	15.00
Wand WDS-689	(S)	John Lee Hooker On The Waterfront	1970	6.00	15.00
Stax STS-2013	(S)	That's Where It's At	1970	14.00	35.00
Specialty SPS-2125	(M)	Alone	1970	12.00	30.00
Specialty SPS-2127	(M)	Goin' Down Highway 51	1970	12.00	30.00
		(Specialty 2125 and 2127 contain 1948-54 recordings.)			
Specialty SPS-5005	(S)	Alone	1974	4.00	10.00
Red Lightnin' 003	(S)	No Friend Around	1970	4.00	10.00
ABC S-720	(S)	Endless Boogie (2 LPs)	1970	8.00	20.00
ABC X-736	(S)	Never Get Out Of These Blues Alive	1972	10.00	25.00
ABC S-761	(S)	Live At Soledad Prison	1972	10.00	25.00
ABC S-768	(S)	Born In Mississippi, Raised Up In Tennessee	1973	8.00	20.00
ABC XQ-768	(Q)	Born In Mississippi, Raised Up In Tennessee	1973	10.00	25.00
ABC S-838	(S)	Free Beer And Chicken	1974	6.00	15.00
Jewel 5005	(S)	I Feel Good	1971	6.00	15.00
United Arts. UAS-5512	(S)	Coast To Coast Blues Band	1971	6.00	15.00
United Arts. LA-127	(S)	John Lee Hooker's Detroit (2 LPs)	1973	6.00	15.00
Atlantic SD-7728	(S)	Detroit Special	1972	8.00	20.00
Fantasy F-24706	(S)	Boogie Chillun' (2 LPs)	1972	6.00	15.00
Greene Bottle 4002	(M)	John Lee, Vol. 1	1973	4.00	10.00
Greene Bottle 3130	(M)	Johnny Lee	1972	4.00	10.00
Trip X-9504	(E)	Whiskey And Wimmen	1973	4.00	10.00
Crescendo GNPS-10007	(E)	The Best Of John Lee Hooker	1974	3.20	8.00
Vee Jay 1004	(S)	Gold	1974	3.20	8.00
Bellaphon 5523	(S)	Dusty Road	197?	3.20	8.00
Intercord 128607	(S)	Don't Want Nobody	197?	3.20	8.00
Tomato 7009	(S)	The Cream	1978	3.20	8.00
Lunar 2008	(S)	John Lee Hooker Live In 1978	1978	3.20	8.00
Labor 4	(S)	Hooker Alone (Volume One)	197?	3.20	8.00
Ornament 104	(S)	Live & Well	197?	3.20	8.00
Stax 4134	(S)	That's Where It's At	1979	3.20	8.00
Muse 5205	(S)	Sittin' Here And Thinkin'	1980	3.20	8.00
Fantasy 24722	(M)	Black Snake Blues	1980	1.00	5.00
MCA 1365	(S)	Lonesome Mood	1983	1.00	5.00
MCA 1686	(S)	Tantalizing With The Blues	198?	1.00	5.00
MCA 31361	(S)	Never Get Out Of These Blues Alive	198?	1.00	5.00
Pausa 7197	(S)	Jealous	1986	1.00	5.00
Chess 9199	(M)	John Lee Hooker Plays And Sings The Blues	1986	1.00	5.00
Chess 9214	(M)	Mad Man Blues	1986	1.00	5.00
Chess 9258	(M)	House Of The Blues	1987	1.00	5.00
Chess 9271	(M)	The Real Folk Blues	1987	1.00	5.00
DCC 042	(S)	John Lee Hooker 40th Anniversary Album	1989	1.00	5.00
Chameleon 74794	(S)	The Hook: 20 Years Of Hits And Boogie	1989	4.00	10.00
Chameleon 74808	(S)	The Healer	1989	1.00	5.00
Chameleon 282	(S)	The Folk Blues Of John Lee Hooker	1990	1.00	5.00
Chameleon 287	(S)	John Lee Hooker Live At Sugar Hill	1990	1.00	5.00
Chameleon 298	(S)	John Lee Hooker Live At Sugar Hill, Vol. 2	1990	1.00	5.00
King 727	(M)	John Lee Hooker Sings The Blues	1990	1.00	5.00

HOOVER

Label & Catalog #		Title	Year	VG+	NM
Epic BN-26537	(S)	Hoover	1970	4.00	10.00

HOPE, LYNN

Label & Catalog #		Title	Year	VG+	NM
Aladdin LP-707	(10")	Lynn Hope And His Tenor Sax	1953	300.00	600.00
Aladdin LP-805	(M)	Lynn Hope And His Tenor Sax	1955	200.00	500.00
Aladdin LP-820	(M)	Lynn Hope	1957	Unreleased	
Score SLP-4015	(M)	Tenderly	1957	80.00	200.00
King 717	(M)	Maharaja Of The Saxophone	1961	60.00	150.00
Imperial LP-9177	(M)	Tenderly	1962	20.00	50.00
Imperial LP-12177	(S)	Tenderly	1962	30.00	75.00

John Lee Hooker is a prime mover in the transition from the classic acoustic blues of the pre-World War II era to the electronically amplified blues of the post-war period, which led directly to the formation of "rhythm'n blues." John Lee Hooker Plays & Sings The Blues is a classic from the early '60s; had it not contained the excellent music within, its beautiful cover alone could have made it a collectible!

Label & Catalog #		Title	Year	VG+	NM

HOPKIN, MARY

Ms Hopkin can also be heard on soundtracks for American International's "Kidnapped" and Paramount's "Where's Jack." Her first album was produced by Paul McCartney.

Label & Catalog #		Title	Year	VG+	NM
Apple SW-3351	(S)	Postcard	1969	10.00	25.00
Apple SW-53351	(S)	Postcard (Record club)	1969	12.00	30.00
		("Those Were The Days" is in stereo on both versions of "Postcard.")			
Apple SMAS-3381	(S)	Earth Song/Ocean Song	1969	10.00	25.00
Apple SW-3395	(S)	Those Were The Days	1972	16.00	40.00
		("Those Were The Days," "Temma Harbour," "Think About Your Children" and "Knock Knock Who's There?" are in mono.)			

HOPKINS, LIGHTNIN'

Sam "Lightnin'" Hopkins is a guitar player, singer and songwriter in the country/blues mode. He can also be found on the Columbia soundtrack "Sounder."

Label & Catalog #		Title	Year	VG+	NM
Score SLP-4022	(M)	Lightnin' Hopkins Strums The Blues	1958	600.00	1,200.00
Herald LP-1012	(M)	Lightnin' And The Blues	1959	750.00	1,500.00
		—Herald albums above have black albums.—			
Herald LP-1012	(M)	Lightnin' And The Blues	196?	500.00	1,000.00
		—Herald albums above have yellow albums.—			
Herald LP-1012	(M)	Lightnin' And The Blues	196?	250.00	500.00
		—Herald albums above have multi-color albums.—			
Fire LP-104	(M)	Mojo Hand	1960	600.00	1,200.00
		—Fire albums above have red labels.—			
Dart D-8000	(M)	Lightning Strikes Again	1960	250.00	500.00
Dart D-8000	(M)	Blues Underground	196?	80.00	200.00
		("Underground" is a reissue of "Strikes Again" with a new cover.)			
Tradition TLP-1035	(M)	Country Blues	1960	10.00	25.00
Tradition TLP-1040	(M)	Autobiography In Blues	1961	10.00	25.00
Tradition TLP-2056	(M)	The Best Of Lightnin' Hopkins	1964	8.00	20.00
Tradition TLP-2103	(M)	Lightnin' Strikes	1972	6.00	15.00
Time 1	(M)	Blues/Folk	196?	60.00	150.00
Time 3	(M)	Blues/Folk, Volume 2	196?	60.00	150.00
Time T-70004	(M)	Last Of The Great Blues Singers	1960	60.00	150.00
Time ST-70004	(S)	Last Of The Great Blues Singers	1960	60.00	150.00
Candid CM-8010	(M)	Lightnin' In New York	1961	60.00	150.00
Candid CS-9010	(S)	Lightnin' In New York	1961	60.00	150.00
Bluesville BVLP-1019	(M)	Lightnin'	1961	40.00	100.00
Bluesville BVLP-1029	(M)	Last Night Blues	1961	40.00	100.00
Bluesville BVLP-1045	(M)	Blues In My Bottle	1962	40.00	100.00
Bluesville BVLP-1057	(M)	Walkin' This Street	1962	40.00	100.00
Bluesville BVLP-1061	(M)	Lightnin' & Co.	1963	40.00	100.00
Bluesville BVLP-1070	(M)	Smokes Like Lightnin'	1963	40.00	100.00
Bluesville BVLP-1073	(M)	Goin' Away	1963	40.00	100.00
		—Bluesville albums above have bright blue labels with silver print.—			
Bluesville BVLP-1019	(M)	Lightnin'	1964	12.00	30.00
Bluesville BVLP-1045	(M)	Blues In My Bottle	1964	12.00	30.00
Bluesville BVLP-1057	(M)	Walkin' This Street	1964	12.00	30.00
Bluesville BVLP-1061	(M)	Lightnin' & Co.	1964	12.00	30.00
Bluesville BVLP-1070	(M)	Smokes Like Lightnin'	1964	12.00	30.00
Bluesville BVLP-1073	(M)	Goin' Away	1964	12.00	30.00
Bluesville BVLP-1081	(M)	Gotta Move Your Baby	1964	16.00	40.00
		(Bluesville 1081 is a reissue of 1029.)			
Bluesville BVLP-1084	(M)	Lightnin' Hopkins' Greatest Hits	1964	16.00	40.00
Bluesville BVLP-1086	(M)	Down Home Blues	1964	10.00	25.00
		—Bluesville albums above have blue labels with a trident logo on the right side.—			
Crown CLP-5224	(M)	Lightnin' Hopkins Sings The Blues	1962	40.00	100.00
		—Crown albums above have black labels with a silver "Crown" on top.—			
Crown CLP-5224	(M)	Lightnin' Hopkins Sings The Blues	196?	20.00	50.00
		—Crown albums above have gray labels.—			
Crown CLP-5224	(M)	Lightnin' Hopkins Sings The Blues	196?	10.00	25.00
		—Crown albums above have black labels with a multi-color "Crown" on top.—			
Vee Jay LP-1044	(M)	Lightnin' Strikes	1962	24.00	60.00
		—Vee Jay albums above have black "rainbow" labels with an oval logo on top.—			
Verve V-8453	(M)	Fast Life Woman	1962	20.00	50.00
		(Verve 8453 is a reissue of Dart 8000.)			
Folkways FS-3822	(M)	Lightnin' Hopkins	1962	20.00	50.00
Imperial LP-9180	(M)	Lightnin' Hopkins On Stage	1962	150.00	300.00
Imperial LP-9186	(M)	Lightnin' Hopkins Sings The Blues	1962	150.00	300.00
Imperial LP-9211	(M)	Lightnin' Hopkins And The Blues	1963	80.00	200.00
Imperial LP-12211	(E)	Lightnin' Hopkins And The Blues	1963	40.00	100.00
		(Imperial 92111 is a reissue of 9135.)			
World Pacific WP-1817	(M)	First Meetin'	1963	12.00	30.00
World Pacific ST-1817	(S)	First Meetin' (Red vinyl)	1963	30.00	75.00
World Pacific ST-1817	(S)	First Meetin'	1963	16.00	40.00
Guest Star G-1458	(M)	"Live" At The Bird Lounge, Houston, Texas	1964	12.00	30.00
Guest Star GS-1458	(E)	"Live" At The Bird Lounge, Houston, Texas	1964	8.00	20.00
Mt. Vernon 104	(M)	Nothin' But The Blues	196?	10.00	25.00
		(Mt. Vernon 104 is a reissue of Herald 1012.)			

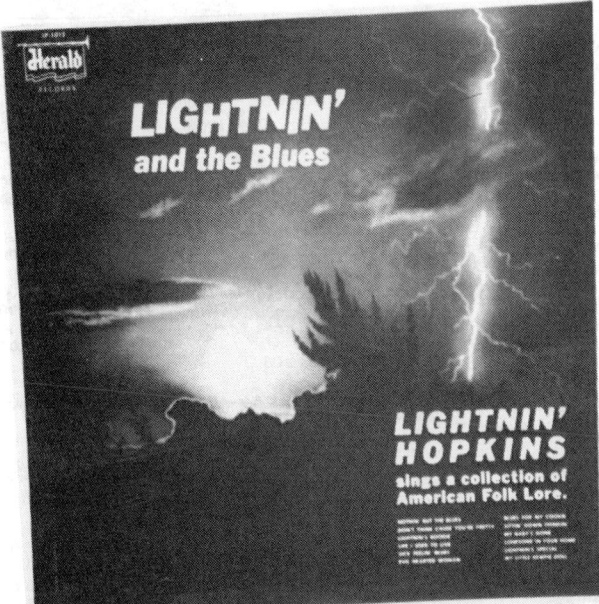

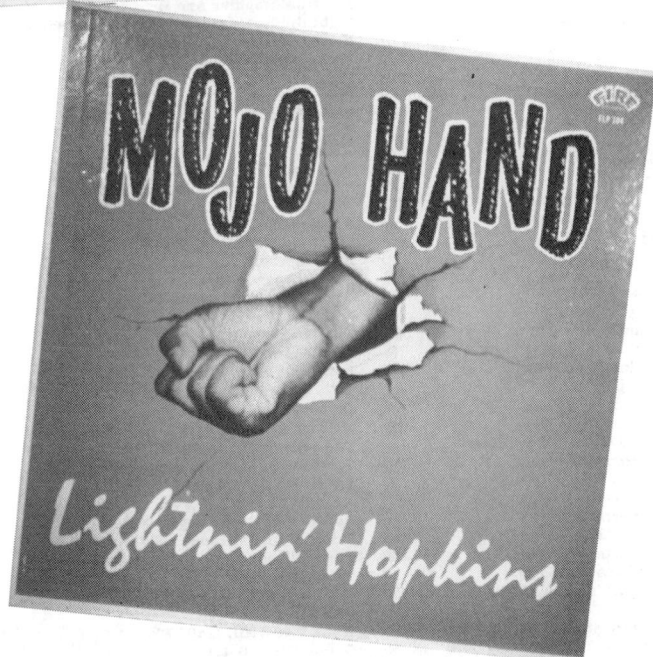

Lightnin' And The Blues *has become what many believe to be the most sought-after blues album in the hobby; the listed value may be conservative for a truly near mint copy.* Mojo Hand *is close behind in both rarity and demand. And there's some pretty good music between the grooves of all three of them.*

Label & Catalog #		Title	Year	VG+	NM
Sphere Sound SSR-7001	(M)	Lightnin' Hopkins	1964	200.00	400.00
Sphere Sound SSSR-7001	(E)	Lightnin' Hopkins	1964	150.00	300.00
Verve/Folkways FV-9000	(M)	The Roots Of Lightnin' Hopkins	1965	10.00	25.00
Verve/Folkways FVS-9000	(S)	The Roots Of Lightnin' Hopkins	1965	12.00	30.00
Verve/Folkways FV-9022	(M)	Lightnin' Strikes	1965	10.00	25.00
Verve/Folkways FVS-9022	(S)	Lightnin' Strikes	1965	12.00	30.00
Verve/Folkways FT-3013	(M)	Something Blue	1967	8.00	20.00
Verve/Folkways FTS-3013	(S)	Something Blue	1967	10.00	25.00
Verve/Folkways FTS-3031	(S)	Lightnin' Strikes	1968	8.00	20.00
		(Folkways 3031 is a reissue of 9022.)			
Folklore FRLP-14021	(M)	Hootin' The Blues	1964	24.00	60.00
Folklore FRST-14021	(S)	Hootin' The Blues	1964	30.00	75.00
Prestige PRLP-7370	(M)	My Life With The Blues (2 LPs)	1965	24.00	60.00
Prestige PRST-7370	(S)	My Life With The Blues (2 LPs)	1965	30.00	75.00
Prestige PRLP-7377	(M)	Soul Blues	1966	20.00	50.00
Prestige PRST-7377	(S)	Soul Blues	1966	24.00	60.00
Prestige PRST-7592	(S)	Lightnin' Hopkins' Greatest Hits	1969	6.00	15.00
		(Prestige 7592 is a reissue of Bluesville 1084.)			
Prestige PRST-7714	(S)	The Best Of Lightnin' Hopkins & His Texas Blues Band	1969	6.00	15.00
		(Prestige 7592 is a reissue of Bluesville 1084.)			
Prestige PRST-7806	(S)	Hootin' The Blues	1969	6.00	15.00
		(Prestige 7806 is a reissue of Folklore 14021.)			
Prestige PRST-7811	(S)	The Blues Of Lightnin' Hopkins	1969	6.00	15.00
		(Prestige 7811 is a reissue of Bluesville 1019.)			
International Art. LP-6	(S)	Free Form Patterns	1968	80.00	200.00
		(Original covers for I.A. 6 have a photo of Hopkins.)			
International Art. LP-6	(S)	Free Form Patterns	1968	20.00	50.00
		(Later covers have inappropriate psychedelic artwork.)			
Vault 129	(S)	California Mudslide	1969	10.00	25.00
Poppy 60002	(S)	Lightnin'	1969	10.00	25.00
Arhoolie 1011	(M)	Lightnin' Hopkins And His Guitar	196?	8.00	20.00
Arhoolie 1022	(M)	Lightnin' Hopkins, His Brother And Barbara Dane	196?	8.00	20.00
Arhoolie 1030	(M)	Blues Festival	196?	6.00	15.00
Arhoolie 1034	(M)	Texas Blues Man	1968	6.00	15.00
Arhoolie 1063	(M)	Lightnin' Hopkins In Berkeley	196?	6.00	15.00
Arhoolie 1087	(M)	Poor Lightnin'	197?	6.00	15.00
Arhoolie 2007	(M)	Early Recordings	197?	6.00	15.00
Arhoolie 2010	(M)	Early Recordings Vol. 2	197?	6.00	15.00
Blues Classics 30	(M)	Historic Recordings 1952-1953	196?	6.00	15.00
Bulldog 1010	(M)	The Texas Bluesman	1965	6.00	15.00
United US-7713	(E)	Lightnin' Hopkins Sings The Blues	196?	6.00	15.00
United US-7744	(E)	Original Folk Blues	196?	6.00	15.00
United US-7785	(E)	A Legend In His Time	196?	6.00	15.00
Everest 241	(S)	Lightnin' Hopkins	1969	6.00	15.00
Jewel 5000	(M)	Blue Lightnin'	1967	6.00	15.00
Jewel 5001	(S)	Talkin' Some Sense	1968	6.00	15.00
Jewel 5015	(S)	Great Electric Show And Dance	1970	6.00	15.00
Trip TLP-8015	(E)	Lightnin' Hopkins	1971	4.00	10.00
Mainstream 311	(S)	The Blues	1971	6.00	15.00
Mainstream 326	(S)	Dirty Blues	1971	6.00	15.00
Mainstream 405	(S)	Low Down Dirty Blues	1974	6.00	15.00
Barnaby Z-30247	(S)	Lightnin' Hopkins In New York	1971	6.00	15.00
Fantasy F-24702	(S)	Double Blues	1972	6.00	15.00
Fantasy F-24725	(S)	How Many More Years I Got?	1981	4.00	10.00
Crescendo GNPS-10022	(M)	The Legacy Of The Blues, Vol. 12	197?	3.20	8.00
Harlem Hit Parade 5013	(M)	The Best Of Lightnin' Hopkins	197?	6.00	15.00
Rhino RNLP-103	(M)	Los Angeles Blues	198?	3.20	8.00
Collectables 5111	(M)	Mojo Hand	198?	3.20	8.00
Collectables 5121	(M)	The Herald Recordings 1954	1989	3.20	8.00
Collectables 5143	(M)	Drinkin' In The Blues	1990	3.20	8.00
Collectables 5144	(M)	Prison Blues	1990	3.20	8.00
Collectables 5145	(M)	Mama And Papa Hopkins	1990	3.20	8.00
Collectables 5146	(M)	Nothin' But The Blues	1990	3.20	8.00

HOPKINS, LIGHTNIN,'' & SONNY TERRY & BROWNIE McGHEE

Vee Jay LP-1138	(M)	Coffee House Blues	1965	20.00	50.00

—Vee Jay albums above have black "rainbow" labels with a brackets logo on top.—

HOPKINS, NICKY

Mr Hopkins is the session pianist who has played on hundreds of records. Refer to Jeff Beck; Steve Miller; and Quicksilver Messenger Service

Columbia KC-32074	(S)	The Tin Man Was A Dreamer	1973	8.00	20.00

HORNETS, THE

Liberty LRP-3348	(M)	Motorcycles U.S.A.	1963	16.00	40.00
Liberty LST-7348	(S)	Motorcycles U.S.A.	1963	20.00	50.00
Liberty LRP-3364	(M)	Big Drag Boats U.S.A.	1964	20.00	50.00
Liberty LST-7364	(S)	Big Drag Boats U.S.A.	1964	30.00	75.00

Label & Catalog #		Title	Year	VG+	NM

HORSES, THE
Horses features soon-to-be actor Don Johnson.

White Whale WWS-7121	(S)	**Horses**	1970	16.00	40.00

HORTON, WALTER "SHAKEY"
Refer to Elmore James & Walter Horton.

Argo LP-4037	(M)	**The Soul Of Blues Harmonica**	1964	40.00	100.00
Argo LPS-4037	(S)	**The Soul Of Blues Harmonica**	1964	60.00	150.00
Alligator AL-4702	(S)	**Big Walter Horton**	1972	4.00	10.00

HOT BUTTER

Musicor MS-3242	(S)	**Popcorn** *(Die-cut shaped cover)*	1972	8.00	20.00
Musicor MS-3242	(S)	**Popcorn** *(Standard cover)*	1972	6.00	15.00

HOT DOGGERS, THE
The Hot Doggers feature Bruce Johnston.

Epic LN-24054	(M)	**Surfin' USA**	1963	60.00	150.00
Epic BN-26054	(S)	**Surfin' USA**	1963	80.00	200.00

HOT DOGS, THE

Ardent ADS=2805	(S)	**Say What You Mean**	1973	4.00	10.00

HOT RODDERS, THE

Crown CLP-5378	(M)	**Big Hot Rod**	1963	6.00	15.00
Crown CST-378	(S)	**Big Hot Rod**	1963	8.00	20.00
		—Crown albums above have gray labels.—			

HOT TUNA
Hot Tuna is Jorma Kaukonen and Jack Cassady of Jefferson Airplane.

RCA Victor LSP-4353	(S)	**Hot Tuna**	1970	8.00	20.00
		—RCA albums above have orange labels on non-flexible vinyl.—			
RCA Victor LSP-4353	(S)	**Hot Tuna**	1971	4.00	10.00
RCA Victor LSP-4550	(S)	**First Pull Up Then Pull Down**	1971	4.00	10.00
		—RCA albums above have orange labels on flexible vinyl.—			
Grunt BFL1-1004	(S)	**Burgers**	1972	1.00	5.00
Grunt BFL1-0348	(S)	**The Phosphorescent Rat**	1974	1.00	5.00
Grunt BFL1-0820	(S)	**America's Choice**	1975	1.00	5.00
Grunt BFD1-0820	(Q)	**America's Choice**	1975	6.00	15.00
Grunt BFL1-1238	(S)	**Yellow Fever**	1975	1.00	5.00
Grunt BFD1-1238	(Q)	**Yellow Fever**	1975	6.00	15.00
Grunt BFL1-1920	(S)	**Hoppkorv**	1976	1.00	5.00
Grunt CYL2-2545	(S)	**Double Dose** *(2 LPs)*	1978	1.20	6.00
Grunt BXL1-2591	(S)	**Burgers**	1978	.80	4.00
Grunt DJL1-2852	(S)	**The Last Interview** *(Promo with poster)*	1978	8.00	20.00
		(Features a live track by Janis Joplin.)			
Grunt BXL1-3357	(S)	**Final Vinyl**	1979	.80	4.00
RCA Victor AYL1-3684	(S)	**Hot Tuna**	1981	.80	4.00
RCA Victor AYL1-3685	(S)	**First Pull Up Then Pull Down**	1981	.80	4.00
RCA Victor AYL1-3950	(S)	**Hoppkorv**	1981	.80	4.00
RCA Victor AYL1-3951	(S)	**Burgers**	1981	.80	4.00

HOTLEGS
Hotlegs was Lol Creme, Kevin Godley, Graham Gouldman, and Eric Stewart, later 10CC.

Capitol ST-587	(S)	**Hotlegs Thinks: School Stinks**	1971	10.00	25.00

HOUR GLASS, THE
Hour Glass features Duane and Gregg Allman.

Liberty LRP-3536	(M)	**The Hour Glass**	1967	10.00	25.00
Liberty LST-7536	(S)	**The Hour Glass**	1967	12.00	30.00
Liberty LRP-3555	(M)	**The Power Of Love**	1968	12.00	30.00
Liberty LST-7555	(S)	**The Power Of Love**	1968	12.00	30.00
United Artists LA-013G2	(S)	**The Hour Glass** *(2 LPs)*	1973	6.00	15.00
		(U.A. 013 repackages the two Liberty albums.)			
Springboard SPB-4046	(S)	**Duane And Gregg Allman**	1976	1.00	5.00

HOUSE

Liberty LSP-7648	(S)	**Shuffle Brothers**	1970	4.00	10.00

HOUSE, SON
Son House is a Delta blues singer, guitar player and songwriter and a forerunner of Robert Johnson and Muddy Waters.

Columbia CL-2417	(M)	**Father Of The Folk Blues**	1965	8.00	20.00
Columbia CS-9217	(S)	**Father Of The Folk Blues**	1965	10.00	25.00
		—Columbia albums above have "360 Sound" labels.—			
Columbia CS-9217	(S)	**Father Of The Folk Blues**	197?	1.00	5.00
Blue Goose 2016	(M)	**The Real Delta Blues**	197?	4.00	10.00

HOUSE, SON, & J. D. SHORT

Verve/Folkways FV-9035	(M)	**Blues From The Mississippi Delta**	1966	16.00	40.00
Verve/Folkways FVS-9035	(E)	**Blues From The Mississippi Delta**	1966	8.00	20.00

Label & Catalog #		Title	Year	VG+	NM
HOUSTON					
SSS International 19	(S)	Houston	1971	6.00	15.00
HOUSTON, JOE					
Modern LMP-1206	(M)	Joe Houston Blows All Night Long	1960	150.00	300.00
Tops L-1518	(M)	Rock And Roll	1958	20.00	50.00
Crown CLP-5006	(M)	Joe Houston Rocks & Rolls All Nite Long	1958	80.00	200.00
Crown CLP-5006	(M)	Joe Houston Blows All Nite Long (Black cover)	1958	40.00	100.00
		(Crown 5006 is a reissue of Modern 1206.)			
		— Crown albums above have black labels with a silver "Crown" logo.—			
Combo LP-100	(M)	Joe Houston (Silver cover with saxophone)	1960	200.00	500.00
Combo LP-100	(M)	Joe Houston (Photo cover)	1960	150.00	300.00
Combo LP-400	(M)	Rockin' At The Drive In	1960	150.00	350.00
		(Original covers for LP-400 have black ink on front and back.)			
Combo LP-400	(M)	Rockin' At The Drive In	196?	100.00	250.00
		(Later covers have blue ink on front and back.)			
Crown CLP-5203	(M)	Wild Man Of The Tenor Sax	1962	30.00	75.00
Crown CLP-5246	(M)	Doin' The Twist	1962	30.00	75.00
Crown CLP-5273	(M)	Rockin' And Rollin"	1962	30.00	75.00
		— Crown albums above have black labels with a silver "Crown" logo.—			
Crown CLP-5006	(M)	Joe Houston Blows All Nite Long	1963	16.00	40.00
Crown CLP-5203	(M)	Wild Man Of The Tenor Sax	1963	16.00	40.00
Crown CLP-5246	(M)	Doin' The Twist	1963	16.00	40.00
Crown CLP-5273	(M)	Rockin' And Rollin"	1963	16.00	40.00
Crown CST-273	(E)	Rockin' And Rollin"	1963	16.00	40.00
Crown CLP-5313	(M)	Surf Rockin'	1963	16.00	40.00
Crown CST-313	(E)	Surf Rockin'	1963	16.00	40.00
Crown CLP-5319	(M)	Limbo	1963	16.00	40.00
Crown CST-319	(E)	Limbo	1963	16.00	40.00
		— Crown albums above have gray labels.—			
Big Town 1004	(S)	Looking Back	1978	4.00	10.00
HOUSTON, THELMA, & PRESSURE COOKER					
Mowest 102	(S)	Thelma Houston	1972	4.00	10.00
HOUSTON FEARLESS					
Imperial LP-12421	(S)	Houston Fearless	1969	8.00	20.00
HOWL THE GOOD					
Rare Earth 537	(S)	Howl The Good	1972	8.00	20.00
HOWLIN' WOLF					
Howlin' Wolf is a pseudonym for Chester Burnett. Refer to The Super Blues Band.					
Chess LP-1434	(DJ)	Moanin' In The Moonlight (White label promo)	1958	800.00	1,600.00
Chess LP-1434	(M)	Moanin' In The Moonlight	1958	300.00	600.00
Chess LP-1469	(DJ)	Howlin' Wolf (White label promo)	1962	800.00	1,600.00
Chess LP-1469	(M)	Howlin' Wolf	1962	300.00	600.00
		— Chess albums above have black & silver labels.—			
Crown CLP-5240	(M)	Howlin' Wolf Sings The Blues	1962	10.00	25.00
		— Crown albums above have gray labels.—			
Chess LP-1502	(M)	The Real Folk Blues	1966	20.00	50.00
Chess LP-1512	(M)	More Real Folk Blues	1967	20.00	50.00
		— Chess albums above have dark blue labels with a color logo on top.—			
Custom CM-2055	(M)	Big City Blues	196?	14.00	35.00
Custom CS-2055	(E)	Big City Blues	196?	8.00	20.00
Kent KLP-526	(M)	Original Folk Blues	1967	6.00	15.00
Kent KST-526	(E)	Original Folk Blues	1967	4.00	10.00
Kent KST-527	(E)	Howlin' Wolf's Twenty Greatest R&B Hits	1967	4.00	10.00
Kent KST-535	(E)	Underground Blues	1967	4.00	10.00
United US-7717	(E)	Big City Blues	1969	4.00	10.00
United US-7747	(E)	Original Folk Blues	1969	4.00	10.00
Cadet 319	(S)	This Is Howlin' Wolf's New Album	1969	10.00	25.00
Chess LP-1540	(M)	Evil	1969	10.00	25.00
Chess CH-50015	(S)	Live And Cookin'	1972	8.00	20.00
Chess CH-60008	(S)	The London Howlin' Wolf Sessions	1971	8.00	20.00
		(Features Ian Stewart, Charlie Watts and Bill Wyman.)			
Chess CH-50045	(M)	The Back Door Wolf	1974	8.00	20.00
Chess CH-60016	(E)	Howlin' Wolf A.K.A. Chester Burnett (2 LPs)	1972	10.00	25.00
		— Chess albums above have blue & white labels.—			
Chess CH-201	(S)	Howlin' Wolf (2 LPs)	1976	5.00	12.00
Chess CH-418	(S)	Change My Way	1977	5.00	12.00
Chess CH509332	(S)	Howlin' Wolf (5 LP box)	1991	16.00	40.00
HUGHES, FREDDIE					
Wand WD-664	(M)	Send My Baby Back	1965	8.00	20.00
Wand WDS-664	(S)	Send My Baby Back	1965	10.00	25.00
Brunswick BL-754157	(S)	Baby Boy	1970	5.00	12.00

Joe Houston Blows All Nite Long *was originally issued on Modern (top) and then reissued on Crown when Modern went belly up. Original covers for the initial Crown pressings were red; later covers were black. Rockin' At The Drive In (below) on Combo also went through a cover change: Original covers had black ink on both the front and the back. Later covers switched to blue ink for both sides.*

Label & Catalog #		Title	Year	VG+	NM
HUGHES, JIMMY					
Vee Jay VJ-1102	(M)	**Steal Away**	1965	10.00	25.00
Vee Jay SR-1102	(E)	**Steal Away**	1965	10.00	25.00
Atco 33-209	(M)	**Why Not Tonight**	1967	10.00	25.00
Atco SD-33-209	(E)	**Why Not Tonight**	1967	10.00	25.00
Volt VOS-6003	(S)	**Something Special**	1969	10.00	25.00
HUGHES, LYNN					
Ms. Hughes was a member of Tongue & Groove.					
Fontana SRF-67611	(S)	**Freeway Gypsy**	1970	5.00	12.00
HULLABALOOS, THE					
Roulette R-25297	(M)	**England's Newest Singing Sensations**	1965	20.00	50.00
Roulette SR-25297	(S)	**England's Newest Singing Sensations**	1965	30.00	75.00
		("Can't You Tell," "I'm Gonna Love You Too," "Party Doll" and "Why Do Fools Fall In Love" are rechanneled.)			
Roulette R-25310	(M)	**The Hullabaloos On Hullabaloo**	1965	20.00	50.00
Roulette SR-25310	(S)	**The Hullabaloos On Hullabaloo**	1965	30.00	75.00
		("Don't Cha Know," "Learning The Game," "Rave On" and "That'll Be The Day" are rechanneled..)			
HUMAN BEINZ, THE / THE MAMMALS					
Gateway GLP-3012	(S)	**Nobody But Me**	1968	16.00	40.00
HUMAN BEINZ, THE					
Capitol ST-2906	(S)	**Nobody But Me**	1968	12.00	30.00
Capitol ST-2926	(S)	**Evolutions**	1968	16.00	40.00
HUMBLE PIE					
Humble Pie featured Peter Frampton (1969-71) and Steve Marriott. Refer to The Small Faces.					
A&M SP-4270	(S)	**Humble Pie**	1970	1.20	6.00
A&M SP-4301	(S)	**Rock On** *(Blue cover)*	1971	1.20	6.00
A&M SP-4342	(S)	**Smokin'**	1972	1.20	6.00
A&M SP-3506	(S)	**Performance—Rockin' The Fillmore** *(2 LPs)*	1972	3.20	8.00
A&M SP-3513	(S)	**Lost And Found** *(2 LPs)*	1972	3.20	8.00
		(A&M 3513 reissues the group's first two UK albums, "As Safe As Yesterday Is" and "Town And Country.")			
A&M SP-3701	(S)	**Eat It** *(2 LPs)*	1973	3.20	8.00
A&M SP-4424	(S)	**Thunderbox**	1973	1.20	6.00
A&M SP-4514	(S)	**Street Rats**	1975	1.20	6.00
A&M SP-3127	(S)	**Humble Pie**	1980	.80	4.00
A&M SP-4301	(S)	**Rock On**	1980	.80	4.00
A&M SP-3132	(S)	**Smokin'**	1980	.80	4.00
A&M SP-6008	(S)	**Performance—Rockin' The Fillmore** *(2 LPs)*	1980	1.00	5.00
A&M SP-6009	(S)	**Lost And Found** *(2 LPs)*	1980	1.00	5.00
A&M SP-6503	(S)	**Eat It** *(2 LPs)*	1980	1.00	5.00
A&M SP-3611	(S)	**Thunderbox**	1980	.80	4.00
A&M SP-3208	(S)	**The Best Of Humble Pie**	1982	.80	4.00
Atco SD-38-122	(S)	**On To Victory**	1980	.80	4.00
Atco SD-38-131	(S)	**Go For The Throat**	1981	.80	4.00
Compleat 672009	(S)	**A Slice Of Humble Pie** *(2 LPs)*	1985	1.20	6.00
HUMBLEBUMS, THE					
The Humblebums feature Gerry Rafferty and Billy Connolly.					
Liberty LST-7636	(S)	**The Humblebums**	1970	12.00	30.00
Liberty LST-7656	(S)	**Open Up The Doors**	1970	12.00	30.00
HUNGRY CHUCK					
Bearsville BR-2071	(S)	**Hungry Chuck**	1972	6.00	15.00
HUNT, TOMMY					
Hunt was formerly a member of the Flamingos.					
Scepter 506	(M)	**I Just Don't Know What To Do With Myself**	1962	20.00	50.00
Scepter SS-506	(S)	**I Just Don't Know What To Do With Myself**	1962	30.00	75.00
Dynamo D-7001	(M)	**Tommy Hunt's Greatest Hits**	1967	8.00	20.00
Dynamo DS-8001	(S)	**Tommy Hunt's Greatest Hits**	1967	10.00	25.00
		(Dynamo 7/8001 contains rerecordings of Hunt's former glories.)			
HUNTER, IVORY JOE					
MGM E-3488	(M)	**I Get That Lonesome Feeling**	1957	200.00	400.00
Atlantic 8008	(M)	**Ivory Joe Hunter**	1957	100.00	250.00
Atlantic 8015	(M)	**The Old & The New**	1958	100.00	250.00
		—Atlantic albums above have black labels.—			
Atlantic 8008	(M)	**Ivory Joe Hunter**	1960	40.00	100.00
Atlantic 8015	(M)	**The Old & The New**	1960	40.00	100.00
		—Atlantic albums above have purple & orange labels.—			
King 605	(M)	**16 Of His Greatest Hits**	1958	200.00	400.00
		—King albums above have crownless black labels.—			
Sound M-603	(M)	**Ivory Joe Hunter**	1959	60.00	150.00

Brian Hyland broke the charts wide open in 1960 with an obnoxious ditty that had everyone singing along, even if they hated it. "Itsy Bitsy Teenie Weenie Yellow Polkadot Bikini" may be seen as an example of the destruction of the impetus of rock'n roll at the hands of the industry hacks who equated such fluff as the equivalent of the real creativity that had preceded it. ("Hey, it sells! We must be doin' something right!") The young singer failed at numerous other attempts to duplicate his initial success until two years later, when the lovely, if a bit overweening, "Sealed With A Kiss" reached the Top 5. The album of the same name (picture here) is also a perfect example of its time: The blonde-haired, good-looking boy next door posing for his senior picture. Nonetheless, the stereo pressing is sought after, even if the hit title tune appears in rechanneled stereo.

Label & Catalog #		Title	Year	VG+	NM
Lion L-70068	(M)	I Need You So	1959	30.00	75.00
Goldisc 403	(M)	The Fabulous Ivory Joe Hunter	1961	30.00	75.00
Strand SL-1123	(M)	The Artistry Of Ivory Joe Hunter	196?	16.00	40.00
Strand SLS-1123	(S)	The Artistry Of Ivory Joe Hunter	196?	20.00	50.00
Smash MGS-27037	(M)	Ivory Joe Hunter's Golden Hits	1963	16.00	40.00
Smash SRS-67037	(S)	Ivory Joe Hunter's Golden Hits	1963	20.00	50.00
Dot DLP-3569	(M)	This Is Ivory Joe Hunter	1964	16.00	40.00
Dot DLP-25569	(S)	This Is Ivory Joe Hunter	1964	20.00	50.00
Epic SE-30348	(S)	The Return Of Ivory Joe Hunter	1971	8.00	20.00
		—Epic albums above have yellow labels.—			
Everest 289	(S)	Ivory Joe Hunter	1974	4.00	10.00
Paramount PAS-6080	(S)	I've Always Been Country	1974	5.00	12.00

HUNTER, ROBERT
Refer to The Grateful Dead.

Round RX-101	(S)	Tales Of The Great Rum Runners	1974	16.00	40.00
Round RX-105	(S)	Tiger Rose	1975	16.00	40.00
Relix RRLP-2001	(S)	Jack O' Roses	1981	1.00	5.00
Relix RRLP-2002	(S)	Promontory Rider—A Retrospective Collection	1982	1.00	5.00
Relix RRLP-2002	(S)	Promontory Rider (Picture disc)	1982	8.00	20.00
Relix RRLP-2003	(S)	Amagamalin Street	1984	1.00	5.00
Relix RRLP-2???	(S)	Tales Of The Great Rum Runners	1985	1.00	5.00
Relix RRLP-2???	(S)	Tiger Rose	1985	1.00	5.00
Relix RRLP-2006	(S)	Live '85	1985	1.00	5.00
Relix RRLP-2009	(S)	Flight Of The Marie Helena	1985	1.00	5.00
Relix RRLP-2019	(S)	Rock Columbia	1986	1.00	5.00
Relix RRLP-2029	(S)	Liberty	1987	1.00	5.00

HURT, MISSISSIPPI JOHN
John Hurt is a blues guitar player, singer and songwriter.

Piedmont PLP-13157	(M)	Folk Songs And Blues	1963	30.00	75.00
Piedmont PLP-13161	(M)	Worried Blues	1964	30.00	75.00
Vanguard VRS-9145	(M)	Blues At Newport	1965	10.00	25.00
Vanguard VSD-79145	(S)	Blues At Newport	1965	12.00	30.00
Vanguard VRS-9220	(M)	Mississippi John Hurt/Today	1966	10.00	25.00
Vanguard VSD-79220	(S)	Mississippi John Hurt/Today	1966	12.00	30.00
Vanguard VRS-9248	(M)	The Immortal Mississippi John Hurt (2 LPs)	1967	10.00	25.00
Vanguard VSD-79248	(S)	The Immortal Mississippi John Hurt (2 LPs)	1967	12.00	30.00
Vanguard VSD-79327	(S)	The Last Session	1972	10.00	25.00
Vanguard VSD-19/20	(S)	The Best Of Mississippi John Hurt (2 LPs)	197?	8.00	20.00
Biograph BLP-C4	(M)	1928 His First Recordings	1972	10.00	25.00

HURVITZ, SANDY

Verve V6-5064	(S)	Sandy's Album Is Here At Last (Produced by Frank Zappa.)	1969	12.00	30.00

HUTTO, J. B., & THE HAWKS

Delmark DL-617	(S)	Hawk Squat	1972	8.00	20.00
Delmark DL-636	(S)	Sidewinder	1973	8.00	20.00

HUTTON, DANNY
Danny Hutton was a member of Three Dog Night.

MGM SE-4664	(S)	Pre-Dog Night	1970	12.00	30.00

HYLAND, BRIAN

Kapp KL-1202	(M)	The Bashful Blonde	1960	20.00	50.00
Kapp KS-3202	(S)	The Bashful Blonde	1960	30.00	75.00
ABC-Paramount 400	(M)	Let Me Belong To You	1961	14.00	35.00
ABC-Paramount S-400	(S)	Let Me Belong To You	1961	20.00	50.00
ABC-Paramount 431	(M)	Sealed With A Kiss	1962	14.00	35.00
ABC-Paramount S-431	(S)	Sealed With A Kiss ("Sealed..." is rechanneled)	1962	20.00	50.00
ABC-Paramount 463	(M)	Country Meets Folk	1964	12.00	30.00
ABC-Paramount S-463	(S)	Country Meets Folk	1964	16.00	40.00
Philips PHM-200-136	(M)	Here's To Our Love	1964	8.00	20.00
Philips PHS-600-136	(S)	Here's To Our Love	1964	10.00	25.00
Philips PHM-200-158	(M)	Rockin' Folk	1965	8.00	20.00
Philips PHS-600-158	(S)	Rockin' Folk	1965	10.00	25.00
Philips PHM-200-217	(M)	The Joker Went Wild	1966	8.00	20.00
Philips PHS-600-217	(S)	The Joker Went Wild	1966	10.00	25.00
Wing MGW-12341	(M)	Here's To Our Love	1967	4.00	10.00
Wing SRW-16341	(S)	Here's To Our Love	1967	4.00	10.00
Dot DLP-25926	(S)	Tragedy	1969	6.00	15.00
Dot DLP-25954	(S)	Stay And Love Me All Summer	1969	6.00	15.00
Uni 73097	(S)	Brian Hyland ("Gypsy Woman" is rechanneled)	1971	6.00	15.00
Private Stock PS-7003	(S)	In A State Of Bayou	1977	4.00	10.00

HYPSTRZ, THE

Voxx	(S)	Hypstrization	1980	6.00	15.00

IAN, JANIS

Janis Ian can also be found on the Inner City soundtrack "Betrayal."

Label/Number		Title	Year		
Verve V-5027	(M)	Janis Ian	1967	6.00	15.00
Verve VS-5027	(S)	Janis Ian	1967	6.00	15.00
Verve/Forecast FT-3017	(M)	Janis Ian/Society's Child	1967	4.00	10.00
Verve/Forecast FTS-3017	(S)	Janis Ian/Society's Child	1967	4.00	10.00
		(Forecast 3017 is a reissue of Verve 5027.)			
Verve/Forecast FTS3024	(M)	For All The Seasons Of Your Mind	1967	4.00	10.00
Verve/Forecast FTS-3024	(S)	For All The Seasons Of Your Mind	1967	4.00	10.00
Verve/Forecast FTS-3048	(S)	The Secret Life Of J. Eddy Fink	1968	4.00	10.00
Verve/Forecast FTS-3063	(S)	Who Really Cares?	1969	4.00	10.00
		— Forecast albums above have brown labels.—			
Capitol STKAO-683	(S)	Present Company	1971	4.00	10.00
Polydor PD-6058	(S)	Janis Ian	1975	1.00	5.00
Columbia KC-32857	(S)	Stars	1974	.80	4.00
Columbia PC-33394	(S)	Between The Lines	1975	.80	4.00
Columbia PCQ-33394	(Q)	Between The Lines	1975	4.00	10.00
Columbia PC-33919	(S)	Aftertones	1976	.80	4.00
Columbia PCQ-33919	(Q)	Aftertones	1976	4.00	10.00
Columbia PC-34440	(S)	Miracle Row	1977	.80	4.00
Columbia PCQ-34440	(Q)	Miracle Row	1977	4.00	10.00
Columbia JC-35325	(S)	Janis Ian	1978	.80	4.00
Columbia JC-36139	(S)	Night Rains	1979	.80	4.00
Columbia FC-37360	(S)	Restless Eyes	1981	.80	4.00

IAN & SYLVIA

Ian Tyson and Sylvia Fricker-Tyson also recorded as The Great Speckled Bird.

Label/Number		Title	Year		
Vanguard VRS-9109	(M)	Ian And Sylvia	1963	10.00	25.00
Vanguard VSD-2113	(S)	Ian And Sylvia	1963	12.00	30.00
Vanguard VRS-9133	(M)	Four Strong Winds	1963	8.00	20.00
Vanguard VSD-2149	(S)	Four Strong Winds	1963	10.00	25.00
Vanguard VRS-9154	(M)	Northern Journey	1964	8.00	20.00
Vanguard VSD-79154	(S)	Northern Journey	1964	10.00	25.00
Vanguard VRS-9175	(M)	Early Morning Rain	1965	8.00	20.00
Vanguard VSD-79175	(S)	Early Morning Rain	1965	10.00	25.00
Vanguard VRS-9215	(M)	Play One More	1966	8.00	20.00
Vanguard VSD-79215	(S)	Play One More	1966	10.00	25.00
Vanguard VRS-9241	(M)	So Much For Dreaming	1967	8.00	20.00
Vanguard VSD-79241	(S)	So Much For Dreaming	1967	10.00	25.00
Vanguard VSD-79269	(S)	The Best Of Ian & Sylvia	1968	6.00	15.00
Vanguard VSD-79284	(S)	Nashville	1968	6.00	15.00
Vanguard VSD-5/6	(S)	Ian & Sylvia's Greatest Hits *(2 LPs)*	197?	5.00	12.00
Vanguard VSD-23/4	(S)	Ian & Sylvia's Greatest Hits, Vol. 2 *(2 LPs)*	197?	5.00	12.00
MGM E-4388	(M)	Lovin' Sound	1967	8.00	20.00
MGM SE-4388	(S)	Lovin' Sound	1967	10.00	25.00
MGM SE-4550	(S)	Full Circle	1968	8.00	20.00
MGM GAS-121	(S)	Ian & Sylvia	1970	6.00	15.00
Columbia C-30736	(S)	Ian & Sylvia	1971	4.00	10.00
Columbia KC-31337	(S)	You Were On My Mind	1972	4.00	10.00
Columbia G-32516	(S)	The Best Of Ian & Sylvia *(2 LPs)*	1973	4.00	10.00

IAN & THE ZODIACS

Label/Number		Title	Year		
Philips PHM-200-176	(M)	Ian And The Zodiacs	1965	16.00	40.00
Philips PHS-600-176	(S)	Ian And The Zodiacs	1965	20.00	50.00

ICE MAN'S BAND, THE

Jerry Butler's band sans the Man.

Label/Number		Title	Year		
Mercury SRM-1-648	(S)	Introducing The Ice Man's Band	1972	6.00	15.00

ID, THE

Label/Number		Title	Year		
RCA Victor LPM-3805	(M)	The Inner Sounds Of The Id	1967	12.00	30.00
RCA Victor LSP-3805	(S)	The Inner Sounds Of The Id	1967	10.00	25.00
		("The Rake" is rechanneled on this album.)			
Aura 1000	(S)	Where Are We Going?	1976	12.00	30.00

Label & Catalog #		Title	Year	VG+	NM
IDES OF MARCH, THE					
Warner Bros. WS-1863	(S)	Vehicle	1970	6.00	15.00
Warner Bros. WS-1896	(S)	Common Bond	1971	5.00	12.00
RCA Victor LSP-4812	(S)	World Woven	1972	4.00	10.00
RCA Victor APL1-0143	(S)	Midnight Oil	1973	4.00	10.00
IDLE, ERIC, & NEIL INNES					
Refer to The Rutles.					
Passport PPSD-98018	(S)	The Rutland Weekend Television Songbook	1976	10.00	25.00
IDLE RACE, THE					
The Idle Race features Jeff Lynne. "Sitting In My Tree" is in mono on this album.					
Liberty LST-7603	(S)	Birthday Party	1969	20.00	50.00
IF					
Capitol ST-539	(S)	If	1969	8.00	20.00
Capitol SW-676	(S)	If 2	1970	8.00	20.00
Capitol SMAS-820	(S)	If 3	1971	8.00	20.00
		—*Capitol albums above have green labels.*—			
Metromedia BML1-057	(S)	Waterfall	1972	5.00	12.00
Metromedia BML1-074	(S)	Double Diamond	1973	5.00	12.00
Capitol ST-11299	(S)	Not Just Another Bunch Of Pretty Faces	1974	4.00	10.00
Capitol ST-11344	(S)	Tea-Break Over-Back On Your 'Eads!	1974	4.00	10.00
IGUANA					
Lion 1011	(S)	Iguana	1972	5.00	12.00
IKETTES, THE					
The Ikettes backed Ike & Tina Turner during the '60s.					
Modern M-102	(M)	Soul Hits	1965	12.00	30.00
Modern MST-102	(S)	Soul Hits	1965	16.00	40.00
United Arts. LA-190F	(S)	The Ikettes' (G)old & New	1975	4.00	10.00
ILL WIND					
ABC S-641	(S)	Flashes	1968	40.00	100.00
ILLINOIS SPEED PRESS, THE					
Columbia CS-9792	(S)	Illinois Speed Press	1969	6.00	15.00
Columbia CS-9976	(S)	Duet	1970	6.00	15.00
ILLUSION, THE					
Steed ST-37003	(S)	The Illusion	1969	4.00	10.00
Steed ST-37005	(S)	Together	1969	4.00	10.00
Steed ST-37006	(S)	If It's So	1970	4.00	10.00
ILLUSTRATION					
Janus 3010	(S)	Illustration	1969	10.00	25.00
ILMO SMOKEHOUSE					
Roulette SR-3002	(S)	Ilmo Smokehouse	1971	6.00	15.00
IMPACS, THE					
King 886	(M)	Impact!	1964	80.00	200.00
King KS-886	(S)	Impact!	1964	150.00	300.00
King 916	(M)	Weekend With The Impacs	1964	80.00	200.00
King KS-916	(S)	Weekend With The Impacs	1964	150.00	300.00
IMPACTS, THE					
The Impacts feature Merrell Fankhauser.					
Del-Fi DFLP-1234	(M)	Wipe Out	1963	30.00	75.00
Del-Fi DFS-1234	(S)	Wipe Out	1963	40.00	100.00
IMPALAS, THE					
Cub 8003	(M)	Sorry (I Ran All The Way Home)	1959	200.00	400.00
Cub S-8003	(S)	Sorry (I Ran All The Way Home)	1959	300.00	600.00
IMPRESSIONS, THE					
Initially, The Impressions were fronted by Jerry Butler. After his solo success, the group was under the leadership of Curtis Mayfield. They can also be found on the Curtom soundtrack "Three The Hard Way."					
ABC-Paramount 450	(M)	The Impressions	1963	12.00	30.00
ABC-Paramount S-450	(S)	The Impressions	1963	16.00	40.00
ABC-Paramount 468	(M)	Never Ending Impressions	1964	12.00	30.00
ABC-Paramount S-468	(S)	Never Ending Impressions	1964	16.00	40.00
ABC-Paramount 493	(M)	Keep On Pushing	1964	12.00	30.00
ABC-Paramount S-493	(S)	Keep On Pushing	1964	16.00	40.00
ABC-Paramount 505	(M)	People Get Ready	1965	12.00	30.00
ABC-Paramount S-505	(S)	People Get Ready	1965	16.00	40.00
ABC-Paramount 515	(M)	The Impressions' Greatest Hits	1965	8.00	20.00
ABC-Paramount S-515	(S)	The Impressions' Greatest Hits	1965	10.00	25.00

The Impalas, an integrated group hailing from Brooklyn, consisted of lead singer Joe "Speedo" Frazier with Tony Carlucci, Lenny Renda, and Richard Wagner. Their sole pop hit, "Sorry (I Ran All The Way Home)," sold enough copies for the MGM subsidiary Cub to encourage the parent label to record an album in stereo, an almost unheard of act for a vocal group on a small label in 1959.

Label & Catalog #		Title	Year	VG+	NM
ABC-Paramount 523	(M)	One By One	1965	8.00	20.00
ABC-Paramount S-523	(S)	One By One	1965	10.00	25.00
ABC-Paramount T-90520	(M)	One By One (Capitol Record Club)	1965	10.00	25.00
ABC-Paramount ST-90520	(S)	One By One (Capitol Record Club)	1965	10.00	25.00
ABC-Paramount 545	(M)	Ridin' High	1966	10.00	25.00
ABC-Paramount S-545	(S)	Ridin' High	1966	12.00	30.00
ABC-Paramount 606	(M)	The Fabulous Impressions	1967	8.00	20.00
ABC-Paramount S-606	(S)	The Fabulous Impressions	1967	10.00	25.00
ABC-Paramount S-635	(S)	We're A Winner	1968	6.00	15.00
ABC-Paramount S-654	(S)	The Best Of The Impressions	1968	6.00	15.00
ABC-Paramount S-668	(S)	The Versatile Impressions	1969	6.00	15.00
ABC-Paramount S-727	(S)	16 Greatest Hits	1970	5.00	12.00
Curtom CRS-8001	(S)	This Is My Country	1968	6.00	15.00
Curtom CRS-8004	(S)	Best Impressions—Curtis, Sam & Fred	1969	6.00	15.00
Curtom CRS-8006	(S)	Check Out Your Mind	1970	6.00	15.00
Curtom CRS-8012	(S)	Times Have Changed	1972	6.00	15.00
Curtom CRS-8016	(S)	Preacher Man	1973	6.00	15.00
Curtom CRS-8019	(S)	Finally Got Myself Together	1974	6.00	15.00
Curtom CRS-5003	(S)	First Impressions	1975	4.00	10.00
Curtom CRS-5009	(S)	Loving Power	1976	4.00	10.00
Sire SASH-3717	(P)	The Vintage Years (2 LPs)	1975	8.00	20.00
Cotillion SD-9912	(S)	It's About Time	1976	4.00	10.00
Scepter CTN-18018	(S)	The Best Of Curtis Mayfield & The Impressions	197?	1.00	5.00
20th Cent.-Fox 596	(S)	Come To My Party	1979	1.00	5.00
20th Cent.-Fox 624	(S)	Fan The Fire	1981	1.00	5.00
Lost-Nite LLP-22	(10")	Jerry Butler & The Impressions (Red vinyl)	1981	4.00	10.00
MCA 1500	(S)	The Impressions' Greatest Hits	1982	.80	4.00

IN GROUP, THE
The In Group features Glen Campbell.

In I-1002	(M)	Swinging 12 String	1964	8.00	20.00
In IS-1002	(S)	Swinging 12 String	1964	10.00	25.00

IN-SECT, THE

Camden CAL-909	(M)	Introducing The In-Sect	1965	16.00	40.00
Camden CAS-909	(S)	Introducing The In-Sect	1965	20.00	50.00

INCORPORATED THANG BAND, THE
The Thangs are members of the Parliament/Funkadelic community.

Warner Bros. 925617	(S)	Lifestyles Of The Roach And Famous	1988	4.00	10.00

INCREDIBLE STRING BAND, THE
The ISB was Mike Heron and Robin Williamson. They can also be found on the Decca soundtrack "Taking Off."

Elektra EKL-322	(M)	The Incredible String Band	1967	8.00	20.00
Elektra EKS-7322	(S)	The Incredible String Band	1967	6.00	15.00
Elektra EKL-4010	(M)	The 5,000 Spirits	1967	8.00	20.00
Elektra EKS-74010	(S)	The 5,000 Spirits	1967	6.00	15.00
Elektra EKS-4021	(M)	The Hangman's Beautiful Daughter	1968	8.00	20.00
Elektra EKS-74021	(S)	The Hangman's Beautiful Daughter	1968	6.00	15.00
Elektra EKS-74036	(S)	Wee Tam	1969	6.00	15.00
Elektra EKS-74037	(S)	The Big Huge	1969	6.00	15.00
		—Elektra albums above have brown labels.—			
Elektra EKS-7322	(S)	The Incredible String Band	197?	1.00	5.00
Elektra EKS-74010	(S)	The 5,000 Spirits	197?	1.00	5.00
Elektra EKS-74021	(S)	The Hangman's Beautiful Daughter	197?	1.00	5.00
Elektra EKS-74036	(S)	Wee Tam	197?	1.00	5.00
Elektra EKS-74037	(S)	The Big Huge	197?	1.00	5.00
Elektra EKS-74057	(S)	Changing Horses	1969	4.00	10.00
Elektra EKS-74061	(S)	I Looked Up	1970	4.00	10.00
		—Elektra albums above have red labels.—			
Elektra EKS-2002	(S)	"U" (2 LPs)	1971	5.00	12.00
Elektra EKS-2004	(S)	Relics Of The Incredible String Band (2 LPs)	1971	4.00	10.00
Elektra EKS-74112	(S)	Liquid Acrobat As Regards The Air	1972	4.00	10.00
Reprise MS-2122	(S)	Earthspan	1972	4.00	10.00
Reprise MS-2198	(S)	Hard Rope And Silver Twine	1974	4.00	10.00
Reprise MS-2129	(S)	No Ruinous Feud	1973	4.00	10.00

INCREDIBLES, THE

Audio Arts AAS-7000	(S)	Heart And Soul	1970	8.00	20.00

INDEPENDENTS, THE

Wand WDS-694	(S)	The First Time We Met	1972	10.00	25.00
Wand WDS-696	(S)	The Independents	1973	10.00	25.00
Wand WDS-699	(S)	Discs Of Gold	1974	10.00	25.00

INDIAN SUMMER

RCA/Neon NE-3	(S)	Indian Summer	1971	8.00	20.00

O' Kelly, Ronald and Rudolph Isley first hit the pop charts in 1959 with "Shout" (RCA Victor 47-7588). As one of the few records released on RCA's Gold Standard Series that was not by Elvis Presley, it made the charts a second time in 1962 (447-0589). This was followed within months by the even bigger "Twist And Shout" for Wand. Both of these songs played pivotal roles in the revised perception of rock'n roll music that occurred in the mid-'60s. . . While The Beatles' cover of "Twist And Shout" is famous around the world, the fact that "Shout" was a mainstay in their live shows through the early years is not. In fact, when the Fabs did their '64 television special, "The Beatles Around The World," it was "Shout" that was the show's centerpiece. Of course the brothers Isley went on to success as a lesser part of Berry Gordy's stable of talent in the mid-'60s before starting their own label, T-Neck. Adding siblings Ernie and Marvin and their brother-in-law Chris Jasper, they continued hitting the soul and pop charts well into the '80s.

Label & Catalog #		Title	Year	VG+	NM
INDIGO GIRLS, THE					
Epic E-57621	(DJ)	**Swamp Ophelia** *(Green vinyl)*	1994	**20.00**	**50.00**
		(Limited edition with both members' autographs on the label.)			
INFLUENCE					
ABC S-630	(S)	**Influence**	1968	**12.00**	**30.00**
INGRAM, LUTHER					
Koko KOS-2201	(S)	**I've Been Here All The Time**	1971	**6.00**	**15.00**
Koko KOS-2202	(S)	**If Loving You Is Wrong** *(With bonus photo)*	1972	**8.00**	**20.00**
Koko KOS-2202	(S)	**If Loving You Is Wrong** *(Without photo)*	1972	**6.00**	**15.00**
INNOCENCE, THE					
The Innocence is Pete Anders and Vinnie Poncia.					
Kama Sutra KLP-8059	(M)	**The Innocence**	1967	**6.00**	**15.00**
Kama Sutra KLPS-8059	(S)	**The Innocence**	1967	**12.00**	**30.00**
INNOCENTS, THE					
The Innocents also recorded with Kathy Young.					
Indigo 503	(M)	**Innocently Yours**	1961	**400.00**	**800.00**
		(Advance copies designated as promos were issued in plain white covers with "The Innocents" printed in blue letters on the front.)			
Indigo 503	(M)	**Innocently Yours**	1961	**150.00**	**300.00**
INSECT TRUST, THE					
Capitol SKAO-109	(S)	**The Insect Trust**	1968	**16.00**	**40.00**
Atco SD-33-313	(S)	**Hoboken Saturday Night**	1970	**14.00**	**35.00**
INTERNATIONAL SUBMARINE BAND, THE					
The I.S.B. features Gram Parsons and Kevin Kelley, both of whom later recorded as Byrds.					
L.H.I. 12001	(S)	**Safe At Home** *(Multicolor label)*	1968	**40.00**	**100.00**
		(Counterfeits have white labels.)			
Shiloh SLP-4008	(S)	**Gram Parsons**	1973	**4.00**	**10.00**
		(Shiloh 4008 is a reissue of LHI 12001.)			
INTRUDERS, THE					
Gamble 5001	(M)	**The Intruders Are Together**	1967	**16.00**	**40.00**
Gamble KZ-5001	(P)	**The Intruders Are Together**	1967	**20.00**	**50.00**
Gamble KZ-5004	(P)	**Cowboys To Girls**	1968	**20.00**	**50.00**
Gamble KZ-5005	(P)	**The Intruders' Greatest Hits**	1969	**16.00**	**40.00**
Gamble KZ-5008	(S)	**When We Get Married**	1970	**20.00**	**50.00**
Gamble KZ-32131	(S)	**Intruders' Super Hits**	1973	**6.00**	**15.00**
TSOP KZ-33149	(S)	**Energy Of Love**	1975	**1.00**	**5.00**
IRON BUTTERFLY					
Refer to Buffalo Springfield / Iron Butterfly.					
Atco 33-227	(M)	**Heavy**	1967	**12.00**	**30.00**
Atco SD-33-227	(S)	**Heavy**	1967	**10.00**	**25.00**
Atco 33-250	(M)	**In-A-Gadda-Da-Vida**	1968	**20.00**	**50.00**
Atco SD-33-250	(S)	**In-A-Gadda-Da-Vida**	1968	**10.00**	**25.00**
		—Atco stereo albums above have purple & brown labels.—			
Atco SD-33-227	(S)	**Heavy**	1969	**1.00**	**5.00**
Atco SD-33-250	(S)	**In-A-Gadda-Da-Vida**	1969	**1.00**	**5.00**
Atco SD-33-280	(S)	**Ball**	1969	**1.00**	**5.00**
Atco SD-33-318	(S)	**Iron Butterfly Live**	1970	**1.00**	**5.00**
Atco SD-33-339	(S)	**Metamorphosis**	1970	**1.00**	**5.00**
Atco SD-33-318	(S)	**Evolution/The Best Of Iron Butterfly Live**	1971	**1.00**	**5.00**
		—Atco albums above yellow labels with "Atlantic Recording Co." on the bottom.—			
MCA 465	(S)	**Scorching Beauty**	1975	**1.00**	**5.00**
MCA 2164	(S)	**Sun And Steel**	1975	**1.00**	**5.00**
IRON MAIDEN					
Harvest ST-12141	(S)	**Killers**	1981	**1.00**	**5.00**
Harvest ST-15000	(S)	**Maiden Japan**	1981	**1.00**	**5.00**
Harvest ST-12202	(S)	**Number Of The Beast**	1982	**1.00**	**5.00**
Harvest SEAX-12219	(S)	**Number Of The Beast** *(Picture disc)*	1982	**20.00**	**50.00**
Capitol ST-12274	(S)	**Piece Of Mind**	1983	**1.00**	**5.00**
Capitol SEAX-12306	(S)	**Piece Of Mind** *(Picture disc)*	1983	**20.00**	**50.00**
		(Contains one bonus track, "Cross Eyed Mary.")			
Capitol ST-12321	(S)	**Powerslave**	1984	**1.00**	**5.00**
IRONMEN, THE					
Reggae 15003	(S)	**Reggae Thing**	1970	**6.00**	**15.00**
ISLEY BROTHERS, THE					
Refer to Jimi Hendrix / The Isley Brothers.					
RCA Victor LPM-2156	(M)	**Shout!**	1959	**60.00**	**150.00**
RCA Victor LSP-2156	(S)	**Shout!**	1959	**150.00**	**300.00**
		—RCA albums above have black "Long Play" or "Living Stereo" labels.—			

Label & Catalog #		Title	Year	VG+	NM
Wand WD-653	(M)	Twist And Shout	1962	30.00	75.00
Wand WDS-653	(S)	Twist And Shout	1962	40.00	100.00
United Arts. UAL-3313	(M)	The Famous Isley Brothers	1963	20.00	50.00
United Arts. UAS-6313	(S)	The Famous Isley Brothers	1963	30.00	75.00
Scepter SC-552	(M)	Take Some Time Out For The Isley Brothers	1966	12.00	30.00
Scepter SCS-552	(S)	Take Some Time Out For The Isley Brothers	1966	16.00	40.00
Tamla T-269	(M)	This Old Heart Of Mine	1966	8.00	20.00
Tamla TS-269	(S)	This Old Heart Of Mine	1966	10.00	25.00
Tamla 275	(M)	Soul On The Rocks	1967	8.00	20.00
Tamla TS-275	(S)	Soul On The Rocks	1967	10.00	25.00
Tamla TS-287	(S)	Doin' Their Thing	1969	8.00	20.00
Sunset SUS-5257	(S)	The Isley Brothers Do Their Thing	1969	6.00	15.00
		(Sunset 5257 is a reissue of United Artists 6313.)			
Camden ACL1-0126	(S)	Rock On, Brother	1973	4.00	10.00
		(Camden 0126 is a repackage of RCA 2156.)			
T-Neck TNS-3001	(S)	It's Our Thing	1969	8.00	20.00
T-Neck TNS-3002	(S)	The Brothers Isley	1969	8.00	20.00
T-Neck TNS-3004	(S)	Live At Yankee Stadium (2 LPs)	1969	12.00	30.00
		(The first side is The Isleys; side 2 is The Edwin Hawkins Singers; side 3 is The Brooklyn Bridge; and side 4, various artists.)			
T-Neck TNS-3006	(S)	Get Into Something	1970	6.00	15.00
T-Neck TNS-3007	(S)	In The Beginning (With Jimi Hendrix)	1971	8.00	20.00
T-Neck TNS-3008	(S)	Givin' It Back	1971	6.00	15.00
T-Neck TNS-3009	(S)	Brother, Brother, Brother	1972	6.00	15.00
T-Neck TNS-3010	(S)	The Isley Brothers Live (2 LPs)	1973	6.00	15.00
T-Neck TNS-3011	(S)	The Isleys' Greatest Hits	1973	4.00	10.00
T-Neck KZ-32453	(S)	3 + 3	1974	3.20	8.00
T-Neck ZQ-32453	(Q)	3 + 3	1974	6.00	15.00
T-Neck KZ-33070	(S)	The Isley Brothers Live It Up	1974	3.20	8.00
T-Neck ZQ-33070	(Q)	The Isley Brothers Live It Up	1974	6.00	15.00
T-Neck PZ-33536	(S)	The Heat Is On	1975	3.20	8.00
T-Neck PZQ-33536	(Q)	The Heat Is On	1975	6.00	15.00
T-Neck PZ-33809	(S)	Harvest For The World	1976	3.20	8.00
T-Neck PZQ-33809	(Q)	Harvest For The World	1976	6.00	15.00
T-Neck A5Z-137	(DJ)	Everything You Always Wanted To Hear By The Isley Brothers But Were Afraid To Ask For	1976	6.00	15.00
T-Neck PZ-34432	(S)	Go For Your Guns	1977	3.20	8.00
T-Neck PZQ-34432	(Q)	Go For Your Guns	1977	6.00	15.00
T-Neck PZ-34452	(S)	Forever Gold	1977	3.20	8.00
T-Neck PZ-34930	(S)	Showdown	1978	3.20	8.00
T-Neck KZ2-35650	(S)	Timeless (2 LPs)	1978	4.00	10.00
T-Neck PZ-36077	(S)	Winner Takes All (2 LPs)	1979	4.00	10.00
T-Neck PZ-36305	(S)	Go All The Way	1980	3.20	8.00
T-Neck FC-37080	(S)	Grand Slam	1981	3.20	8.00
T-Neck FC-37533	(S)	Inside You	1981	3.20	8.00
T-Neck FC-38047	(S)	The Real Deal	1982	3.20	8.00
T-Neck FC-38674	(S)	Between The Sheets	1983	3.20	8.00
T-Neck PZ-39240	(S)	The Isley Brothers' Greatest Hits	1984	3.20	8.00
Pickwick SPC-3331	(S)	Soul Shout	1973	3.20	8.00
United Arts. LA-500E	(S)	The Very Best Of The Isley Brothers	1975	1.00	5.00
Buddah BDS-5652	(S)	The Best Of The Isley Brothers (2 LPs)	1976	6.00	15.00
Trip TOP-16-8	(S)	The Isley Brothers' 16 Greatest Hits	1976	1.00	5.00
Motown M5-106	(S)	Superstar Series, Volume 6	1980	1.00	5.00
Motown M5-196V1	(S)	Soul On The Rocks	1981	1.00	5.00
Motown M5-128V1	(S)	This Old Heart Of Mine	1982	1.00	5.00
Motown M5-143V1	(S)	Doin' Their Thing	1982	1.00	5.00
CBS 39873	(S)	Broadway's Closer To Sunset Blvd.	1985	1.00	5.00
CBS 40118	(S)	Caravan Of Love	1985	1.00	5.00
CBS 40409	(S)	Different Drummer	1987	1.00	5.00
		(The CBS albums credit Isley Jasper Isley.)			
Warner Bros. 25347	(S)	Masterpiece	1985	1.00	5.00
Warner Bros. 25586	(S)	Smooth Sailin'	1987	1.00	5.00
Warner Bros. 25940	(S)	Spend The Night	1989	1.00	5.00

ISLEY BROTHERS, THE / THE CHIFFONS

Refer to The Chiffons.

Spin-O-Rama SP-127	(M)	The Isley Brothers And The Chiffons	1964	12.00	30.00
Spin-O-Rama SPS-127	(E)	The Isley Brothers And The Chiffons	1964	6.00	15.00

ISLEY BROTHERS, THE / MARVIN & JOHNNY

Refer to Marvin & Johnny.

Crown CLP-5352	(M)	The Isley Brothers And Marvin & Johnny	1963	12.00	30.00
Crown CST-352	(E)	The Isley Brothers And Marvin & Johnny	1963	6.00	15.00
		—Crown albums above have gray labels.—			

IT'S A BEAUTIFUL DAY

Columbia CS-9768	(S)	It's A Beautiful Day	1969	12.00	30.00
Columbia CS-1058	(S)	Marrying Maiden	1970	12.00	30.00
		—Columbia albums above gave "360 Sound" labels.—			

Label & Catalog #		Title	Year	VG+	NM
Columbia CS-9768	(S)	It's A Beautiful Day	1970	8.00	20.00
Columbia CS-1058	(S)	Marrying Maiden	1970	6.00	15.00
Columbia C-30734	(S)	Choice Quality Stuff/Anytime	1971	6.00	15.00
Columbia KC-31338	(S)	Live At Carnegie Hall	1972	6.00	15.00
Columbia KC-32181	(S)	It's A Beautiful Day Today	1973	6.00	15.00
San Francisco Sound 11790	(S)	It's A Beautiful Day (Half-speed master)	1985	10.00	25.00
San Francisco Sound 04800	(S)	Marrying Maiden (Half-speed master)	1985	10.00	25.00

ITALIAN ASPHALT & PAVEMENT CO., THE: *Refer to* **THE DUPREES**

IVEYS, THE
The Iveys later recorded as Badfinger.

Apple SAPCOR-8S	(S)	Maybe Tomorrow (Italian. Green label)	1968	1,000.00	1,600.00
		(Copies of this album with a black label are counterfeits. This album was also issued in other countries, including Japan and Germany)			
Apple ST-3355	(S)	Maybe Tomorrow (US cover slick)	1968	1,000.00	1,600.00
		(Cover slicks for a US pressing of ST-3355 were manufactured.)			

IVORY

Tetragrammaton T-104	(S)	Ivory	1968	8.00	20.00
Playboy 115	(S)	Ivory	1973	5.00	12.00

IVORY, JACKIE

Atco 33-178	(M)	Soul Discovery	1965	8.00	20.00
Atco SD-33-178	(S)	Soul Discovery	1965	10.00	25.00

IVORY LIBRARY

Dairyland	(S)	Ivory Library	1985	5.00	12.00

IVY LEAGUE, THE

Cameo C-2000	(M)	Tossing And Turning	1965	12.00	30.00
Cameo CS-2000	(E)	Tossing And Turning	1965	12.00	30.00

J. C.					
Perception 1	(S)	J. C. Life	1969	6.00	15.00
J. GEILS BAND, THE					
Atlantic SD-8275	(S)	The J. Geils Band	1971	.80	4.00
Atlantic SD-8297	(S)	The Morning After	1971	.80	4.00
Atlantic SD-7241	(S)	"Live"—Full House	1972	.80	4.00
Atlantic SD-7260	(S)	Bloodshot *(Red vinyl)*	1973	6.00	15.00
Atlantic SD-7260	(S)	Bloodshot	1973	.80	4.00
Atlantic QD-7260	(Q)	Bloodshot	1973	6.00	15.00
Atlantic SD-7286	(S)	Ladies Invited	1973	.80	4.00
Atlantic QD-7286	(Q)	Ladies Invited	1973	6.00	15.00
Atlantic SD-18107	(S)	Nightmares & Other Tales From The Vinyl Jungle	1974	.80	4.00
Atlantic QD-18107	(Q)	Nightmares & Other Tales From The Vinyl Jungle	1974	6.00	15.00
Atlantic SD-18147	(S)	Hotline	1975	.80	4.00
Atlantic SD-507	(S)	Live—Blow Your Face Out *(2 LPs)*	1976	1.20	6.00
Atlantic SD-19103	(S)	Monkey Island	1977	.80	4.00
Atlantic SD-19234	(S)	Best Of The J. Geils Band	1979	.80	4.00
Atlantic SD-19284	(S)	Best Of The J. Geils Band Two	1980	.80	4.00
EMI 17006	(S)	Sanctuary *(Picture disc)*	1979	6.00	15.00
EMI 17006	(S)	Sanctuary	1979	.80	4.00
EMI 17016	(S)	Love Stinks	1980	.80	4.00
EMI 17062	(S)	Freeze Frame	1981	.80	4.00
EMI 17087	(S)	Showtime!!	1983	.80	4.00
EMI 17137	(S)	You're Gettin' Even While I'm Gettin' Old	1984	.80	4.00
J. K. & CO.					
White Whale WWS-7117	(S)	Suddenly One Summer	1969	10.00	25.00
JACKIE & THE STARLIGHTS					
Lost-Nite LLP-12	(10")	Jackie & The Starlights *(Red vinyl)*	1981	4.00	10.00
JACKS, THE					
The Jacks also recorded as The Cadets. Refer to Aaron Collins.					
RPM LRP-3006	(M)	Jumpin' With The Jacks	1956	1,000.00	2,000.00
Crown CLP-5021	(M)	Jumpin' With The Jacks	1960	100.00	250.00
		—Crown albums above have black labels with a silver "Crown" on top.—			
Crown CLP-5372	(M)	Jumpin' With The Jacks	1962	40.00	100.00
Crown CST-372	(E)	Jumpin' With The Jacks	1962	20.00	50.00
		(Crown 5021 and 5372 are reissues of RPM 3006.)			
		—Crown albums above have gray labels.—			
United US-7797	(E)	Rock 'N' Roll Hits Of The '50's	197?	8.00	20.00
Relic 5023	(M)	The Jacks' Greatest Hits	197?	4.00	10.00
JACKSON, BULL MOOSE					
Audio Lab LP-1524	(M)	Bull Moose Jackson	1959	400.00	800.00
JACKSON, CHUCK					
Wand WD-650	(M)	I Don't Want To Cry	1961	16.00	40.00
Wand WDS-650	(S)	I Don't Want To Cry	1961	20.00	50.00
Wand WD-654	(M)	Any Day Now	1962	16.00	40.00
Wand WDS-654	(S)	Any Day Now	1962	20.00	50.00
Wand WD-655	(M)	Encore	1963	12.00	30.00
Wand WDS-655	(S)	Encore	1963	16.00	40.00
Wand WD-658	(M)	Chuck Jackson On Tour	1964	12.00	30.00
Wand WDS-658	(S)	Chuck Jackson On Tour	1964	16.00	40.00
Wand WD-667	(M)	Mr. Everything	1965	12.00	30.00
Wand WDS-667	(S)	Mr. Everything	1965	16.00	40.00
Wand WD-673	(M)	A Tribute To Rhythm & Blues	1966	12.00	30.00
Wand WDS-673	(S)	A Tribute To Rhythm & Blues	1966	16.00	40.00
Wand WD-676	(M)	A Tribute To Rhythm & Blues, Volume 2	1966	12.00	30.00
Wand WDS-676	(S)	A Tribute To Rhythm & Blues, Volume 2	1966	16.00	40.00
Wand WD-680	(M)	Dedicated To The King!!	1966	12.00	30.00
Wand WDS-680	(S)	Dedicated To The King!!	1966	16.00	40.00
Wand WD-683	(M)	Chuck Jackson's Greatest Hits	1967	8.00	20.00
Wand WDS-683	(S)	Chuck Jackson's Greatest Hits	1967	10.00	25.00

Label & Catalog #		Title	Year	VG+	NM
Strand SL-1125	(M)	The Great Chuck Jackson	196?	10.00	25.00
Strand SLS-1125	(S)	The Great Chuck Jackson	196?	12.00	30.00
Guest Star GS-1912	(M)	Chuck Jackson	196?	8.00	20.00
Guest Star GSS-1912	(S)	Chuck Jackson	196?	4.00	10.00
Spinorama 123	(M)	Starring Chuck Jackson	196?	8.00	20.00
Spinorama 123	(E)	Starring Chuck Jackson	196?	4.00	10.00
Motown M-667	(M)	Chuck Jackson Arrives!	1968	16.00	40.00
Motown MS-667	(S)	Chuck Jackson Arrives!	1968	10.00	25.00
Motown MS-687	(S)	Goin' Back To Chuck Jackson	1969	10.00	25.00
V.I.P. 403	(S)	Teardrops Keep Fallin' On My Heart	1970	10.00	25.00
ABC X-798	(S)	Through All Times	1973	6.00	15.00
Scepter 5100	(S)	A Tribute To Burt Bacharach	1972	6.00	15.00
United Arts. LA-499E	(S)	The Very Best Of Chuck Jackson	1975	1.00	5.00
All Platinum AP-3014	(S)	Needing You, Wanting You	1976	6.00	15.00
EMI SW-17031	(S)	I Wanna Give You Some Love	1980	1.00	5.00

JACKSON, CHUCK, & MAXINE BROWN

Wand WD-669	(M)	Saying Something	1965	12.00	30.00
Wand WDS-669	(S)	Saying Something	1965	16.00	40.00
Wand WD-678	(M)	Hold On, We're Coming	1966	12.00	30.00
Wand WDS-678	(S)	Hold On, We're Coming	1966	16.00	40.00

JACKSON, CHUCK, & TAMMI TERRELL

Wand LP-682	(M)	The Early Show	1967	12.00	30.00
Wand WDS-682	(S)	The Early Show	1967	16.00	40.00

JACKSON, CHUCK / YOUNG JESSIE

Crown CLP-5354	(M)	Chuck Jackson & Young Jessie	196?	12.00	30.00
Crown CST-354	(E)	Chuck Jackson & Young Jessie	196?	8.00	20.00
		—Crown albums above have gray labels.—			

JACKSON, DEON

Atco 33-188	(M)	Love Makes The World Go Round	1966	14.00	35.00
Atco SD-33-188	(S)	Love Makes The World Go Round	1966	20.00	50.00
Solid Smoke 8020	(S)	His Greatest Recordings	1983	1.00	5.00

JACKSON, J. J.

Calla C-1101	(M)	But It's Alright/I Dig Girls	1967	8.00	20.00
Calla CS-1101	(S)	But It's Alright/I Dig Girls	1967	10.00	25.00
Congress CS-7000	(S)	The Greatest Little Soul Band In The World	1968	10.00	25.00
Warner Bros. WS-1797	(S)	The Great J. J. Jackson	1969	6.00	15.00
Perception 3	(S)	J. J. Jackson's Dilemma	1969	6.00	15.00

JACKSON, JACKIE
Jackie is a member of The Jacksons.

Motown M-785	(S)	Jackie Jackson	1973	5.00	12.00

JACKSON, JERMAINE
Jermaine is a member of The Jacksons.

Motown M-752L	(S)	Jermaine	1972	4.00	10.00
Motown M-775L	(S)	Come Into My Life	1973	3.20	8.00
Motown M6-842S	(S)	My Name Is Jermaine	1976	3.20	8.00
Motown M6-888S	(S)	Feel The Fire	1977	3.20	8.00
Motown M7-898	(S)	Frontiers	1978	3.20	8.00
Motown M8-948	(S)	Jermaine	1980	1.00	5.00
Motown M8-952	(S)	Like Your Style	1981	1.00	5.00
Motown M5-117	(S)	Superstar Series, Vol. 17	1981	1.00	5.00
Motown 6017	(S)	Let Me Tickle Your Fancy	1982	1.00	5.00

JACKSON, JOE

A&M SP-3666	(10")	Look Sharp!	1979	3.20	8.00
A&M SP-4743	(S)	Look Sharp!	1979	1.00	5.00
A&M SP-4794	(S)	I'm The Man	1979	1.00	5.00
A&M SP-4837	(S)	Beat Crazy	1980	.80	4.00
A&M SP-4871	(S)	Jumpin' Jive!	1981	.80	4.00
A&M SP-4096	(S)	Night And Day	1982	.80	4.00
A&M SP-4931	(S)	Mike's Murder	1983	.80	4.00
A&M SP-5000	(S)	Body And Soul	1984	.80	4.00

JACKSON, LIL' SON

Arhoolie 1004	(M)	Lil' Son Jackson	1960	6.00	15.00
Imperial LP-9142	(M)	Rockin' And Rollin'	1961	250.00	500.00

JACKSON, MICHAEL
Michael was a member of The Jacksons. He can also be found on the Motown soundtrack "Ben."

Motown M-747	(S)	Got To Be There	1972	4.00	10.00
Motown M-767	(S)	Music And Me	1973	4.00	10.00
Motown M6-825S	(S)	Forever Michael	1975	4.00	10.00
Motown M6-851S	(S)	The Best Of Michael Jackson	1975	1.00	5.00

Label & Catalog #		Title	Year	VG+	NM
Motown 956	(S)	One Day In Your Life	1981	1.00	5.00
Motown M5-107V	(S)	Michael Jackson—Superstar Series, Vol. 7	1980	1.00	5.00
Motown M5-130V	(S)	Got To Be There	1981	.80	4.00
Motown M5-153V	(S)	Ben	1982	.80	4.00
Motown 6101	(S)	Farewell My Summer Love	1984	.80	4.00
Epic FE-37545	(S)	Off The Wall	1982	.80	4.00
Epic HE-47545	(S)	Off The Wall (Half-speed master)	1982	12.00	30.00
Epic GE-38112	(S)	Thriller	1982	.80	4.00
Epic HE-48112	(S)	Thriller (Half-speed master)	1982	12.00	30.00
Epic 8E8-38867	(S)	Thriller (Picture disc)	1983	2.00	10.00
Epic 34043	(S)	Bad	1987	.80	4.00
Epic 9E9-44043	(S)	Bad (Picture disc)	1987	2.00	10.00
JACKSON, MILLIE					
Spring SPR-5703	(S)	Millie Jackson	1972	4.00	10.00
Spring SPR-5706	(S)	It Hurts So Good	1973	4.00	10.00
Spring SPR-6701	(S)	Millie	1974	4.00	10.00
Spring SPR-6703	(S)	Caught Up	1974	4.00	10.00
Spring SPR-6708	(S)	Still Caught Up	1975	4.00	10.00
Spring SPR-6712	(S)	Lovingly Yours	1977	4.00	10.00
Spring SPR-6715	(S)	Feelin' Bitchy	1977	4.00	10.00
Spring SPR-6719	(S)	Get It Out'cha System	1978	4.00	10.00
Spring SPR-6722	(S)	A Moment's Pleasure	1979	4.00	10.00
Spring SPR-6725	(S)	Live & Uncensored (2 LPs)	1979	4.00	10.00
Spring SPR-6727	(S)	For Men Only	1980	4.00	10.00
Spring SPR-6730	(S)	I Had To Say It	1981	4.00	10.00
Spring SPR-6735	(S)	Live And Outrageous (Rated XXX)	1982	4.00	10.00
JACKSON, PYTHON LEE					
Crescendo GNPS-2066	(S)	In A Broken Dream	1972	4.00	10.00
JACKSON, SAMMY					
Arvee M-434	(M)	Ladies' Man	1962	24.00	60.00
JACKSON, WALTER					
OKeh OKM-12107	(M)	It's All Over	1965	10.00	25.00
OKeh OKS-14107	(S)	It's All Over	1965	12.00	30.00
OKeh OKM-12108	(M)	Welcome Home	1965	10.00	25.00
OKeh OKS-14108	(S)	Welcome Home	1965	12.00	30.00
OKeh OKM-12120	(M)	Speak Her Name	1967	10.00	25.00
OKeh OKS-14120	(S)	Speak Her Name	1967	12.00	30.00
OKeh OKS-14128	(S)	Walter Jackson's Greatest Hits	1969	6.00	15.00
Chi-Sound 656	(S)	Feeling Good	1976	1.00	5.00
Chi-Sound 733	(S)	I Want To Come Back As A Song	1977	1.00	5.00
Chi-Sound 844	(S)	Good To See You	1977	1.00	5.00
Epic E-34657	(S)	Walter Jackson's Greatest Hits	1978	1.00	5.00
20th Cent.-Fox 586	(S)	Send In The Clowns	1979	1.00	5.00
Columbia FC-37132	(S)	Tell Me Where It Hurts	1981	1.00	5.00
JACKSON FIVE, THE [THE JACKSONS]					
The Jacksons feature Jackie, Jermaine and Michael Jackson.					
Musico MDS-1047	(S)	Getting Together With The Jackson Five	1970	14.00	35.00
		(This is actually a various artists album with two from the Five.)			
Motown MS-700	(S)	Diana Ross Presents The Jackson Five	1970	10.00	25.00
Motown MS-709	(S)	ABC	1970	10.00	25.00
Motown MS-713	(S)	Christmas Won't Be The Same This Year	1970	10.00	25.00
Motown MS-718	(S)	The Jackson Five's Third Album	1970	6.00	15.00
Motown MS-735	(S)	Maybe Tomorrow	1971	6.00	15.00
Motown M-741L	(S)	The Jackson Five's Greatest Hits	1971	4.00	10.00
Motown M-742L	(S)	Goin' Back To Indiana	1971	4.00	10.00
Motown M-750L	(S)	Looking Through The Windows	1972	4.00	10.00
Motown M-761L	(S)	Skywriter	1973	4.00	10.00
Motown M6-780S	(S)	Dancing Machine	1974	4.00	10.00
Motown M6-783V	(S)	Get It Together	1973	4.00	10.00
Motown M6-829S	(S)	Moving Violation	1975	4.00	10.00
Motown M-865P	(S)	Joyful Jukebox Music	1976	4.00	10.00
Motown M7-868RB	(S)	Anthology (2 LPs)	1976	5.00	12.00
Natural Resources 4013T1	(S)	Boogie (Withdrawn compilation)	1979	80.00	200.00
Motown M5-112V	(S)	Superstar Series, Vol. 12	1980	.80	4.00
Motown M5-152V	(S)	ABC	1982	.80	4.00
Motown M5-157V	(S)	Third Album	1982	.80	4.00
Motown M5-201V	(S)	The Jackson Five's Greatest Hits	1982	.80	4.00
Motown M5-228V	(S)	Maybe Tomorrow	1982	.80	4.00
Motown 6099ML	(S)	14 Greatest Hits	1984	.80	4.00
Motown 6099ML	(S)	14 Greatest Hits (Picture disc)	1984	2.00	10.00
Epic 34229	(S)	The Jacksons	1976	.80	4.00
Epic 34835	(S)	Goin' Places	1978	.80	4.00
Epic PAL-34835	(S)	Goin' Places (Promo picture disc)	1978	12.00	30.00
Epic FE-35552	(S)	Destiny	1978	.80	4.00

Label & Catalog #		Title	Year	VG+	NM
Epic FE-36424	(S)	Triumph	1981	.80	4.00
Epic HE-46424	(S)	Triumph (Half-speed master)	1981	12.00	30.00
Epic KE2-37545	(S)	The Jacksons Live (2 LPs)	1981	.80	4.00
Epic 39576	(S)	Victory	1984	.80	4.00
Epic 8E8-39576	(S)	Victory (Picture disc)	1984	4.00	10.00
JACKSON HEIGHTS					
Mercury SR-61331	(S)	King Progress	1970	10.00	25.00
Verve V6-5089	(S)	Jackson Heights	1973	8.00	20.00
JACOB'S CREEK					
Columbia CS-9829	(S)	Jacob's Creek	1969	4.00	10.00
JACOBS, HANK					
Sue LP-1023	(M)	So Far Away	1964	40.00	100.00
JADE WARRIOR					
Vertigo VEL-1007	(S)	Jade Warrior	1971	4.00	10.00
Vertigo VEL-1009	(S)	Released	1971	4.00	10.00
Vertigo VEL-1012	(S)	Last Autumn's Dream	1972	4.00	10.00
Island ILPS-9290	(S)	Floating World	1974	1.20	6.00
Island ILPS-9318	(S)	Waves	1975	1.20	6.00
Island ILPS-9393	(S)	Kites	1976	1.20	6.00
Antilles AN-7068	(S)	Way Of The Sun	1978	1.20	6.00
JAGGER, CHRIS					
Asylum SD-5069	(S)	Chris Jagger	197?	6.00	15.00
Asylum 7E-1009	(S)	The Adventures Of Valentine Vox The Ventriloquist	197?	6.00	15.00

JAGGER, MICK
Mick Jagger is a member of The Rolling Stones. He can also be found on the soundtracks for U.A.'s "Ned Kelly" and Warner Bros.' "Performance."

Columbia FC-39940	(S)	She's The Boss	1985	.80	4.00
Columbia OC-40919	(S)	Primitive Cool	1987	.80	4.00
JAGGERZ, THE					
Gamble SG-5006	(S)	Introducing The Jaggerz	196?	6.00	15.00
Kama Sutra KSBS-2017	(S)	We Went To Different Schools Together	1970	6.00	15.00
JAKE & THE FAMILY JEWELS					
Polydor 24-5024	(S)	Big Moose Calls His Baby Sweet Lorraine	1972	4.00	10.00
JALOPY FIVE, THE					
Modern Sound M-525	(M)	Draggin' & Surfin'	196?	20.00	50.00
Modern Sound MS-525	(S)	Draggin' & Surfin'	196?	20.00	50.00
Modern Sound M-536	(M)	Draggin' & Surfin'	196?	20.00	50.00
Modern Sound MS-536	(S)	Draggin' & Surfin'	196?	20.00	50.00
Modern Sound M-561	(M)	I Love That West Coast Sound	1965	20.00	50.00
Modern Sound MS-561	(S)	I Love That West Coast Sound	1965	20.00	50.00
JAM FACTORY, THE					
Epic 26521	(S)	Sittin' In The Trap	1970	5.00	12.00
JAMES, ELMORE					
Crown CLP-5168	(M)	Blues After Hours	1961	100.00	250.00
		—Crown albums above have black labels with a silver "Crown" on top.—			
Crown CLP-5168	(M)	Blues After Hours	196?	20.00	50.00
		—Crown albums above have gray labels.—			
Sphere Sound SR-7002	(M)	The Sky Is Crying	1965	80.00	200.00
Sphere Sound SSR-7002	(E)	The Sky Is Crying	1965	60.00	150.00
Sphere Sound SR-7008	(M)	I Need You	1966	80.00	200.00
Sphere Sound SSR-7008	(E)	I Need You	1966	60.00	150.00
		—Sphere Sound albums above have red labels.—			
Sphere Sound SSR-7008	(S)	I Need You	196?	20.00	50.00
		—Sphere Sound albums above have yellow labels.—			
Kent KLP-5022	(M)	Original Folk Blues	1964	16.00	40.00
Kent KST-522	(E)	Original Folk Blues	1964	10.00	25.00
Kent KLP-9001	(M)	Anthology Of The Blues Legend	196?	10.00	25.00
Kent KLP-9010	(M)	The Resurrection Of Elmore James	196?	10.00	25.00
Kent KLP-4003	(M)	The Best Of Elmore James	1985	3.20	8.00
Kent KLP-4004	(M)	King Of The Slide Guitar	1985	3.20	8.00
Chess LP-1537	(S)	Whose Muddy Shoes	1969	10.00	25.00
Bell 6037	(S)	Elmore James	1969	10.00	25.00
Upfront UP-122	(E)	The Great Elmore James	1970	4.00	10.00
Ember LP-3397	(M)	Elmore James	1971	4.00	10.00
Trip TLP-8007	(E)	History Of Elmore James, Vol. 1	1972	4.00	10.00
Trip TLP-9511	(E)	History Of Elmore James, Vol. 2	1972	4.00	10.00
United ULS-7716	(E)	The Rhythm Of My Heart, The Blues In My Soul	1974	4.00	10.00
United ULS-7743	(E)	Original Folk Blues	1975	4.00	10.00

The above pair of LPs by the extraordinary Etta James (both on Crown), serve to illustrate the deft art-work of Fazzio. The Best Of Etta James (CLP-5234) from 1962 features a photo of Ms James with her naturally dark hair short and curly. The later Etta James (from 1963 and shown here in its stereo version, CST-360) is graced with a cover painting of Ms James by Fazzio based squarely on the earlier album's cover photo, except that the artist has substituted a bouffant blonde wig (I assume it's supposed to be a wig). Even more interesting, there are two variations on the CST-360 cover painting: On one she is smiling and on the other she is not! Finally, that such a collectible artist as Fazzio did the bulk of his work for such a cheesy label as Crown is one of life's myriad mysteries. . .

Label & Catalog #		Title	Year	VG+	NM
United ULS-7778	(E)	The Legend Of Elmore James	1975	4.00	10.00
United ULS-7787	(E)	The Resurrection Of Elmore James	1975	4.00	10.00
Harlem Hit Parade 5014	(M)	Screaming Blues	197?	4.00	10.00
Blue Horizon 46021	(M)	Blues Masters, Vol. 1—Elmore James	197?	4.00	10.00
DJM 8008	(M)	All Them Blues	1975	4.00	10.00
Globe 5004	(M)	Dust My Blues	1980	4.00	10.00
Oxford 3238	(M)	One Way Out	1981	4.00	10.00
Intermedia 5034	(M)	Red Hot Blues	1982	1.00	5.00
Deja Vu 2035	(M)	The Elmore James Collection	1985	1.00	5.00
Blue Moon 008	(M)	Red Hot Blues	1986	1.00	5.00
Collectables 5112	(M)	Golden Classics	1988	1.00	5.00
Collectables 5184	(M)	The Complete Fire And Enjoy Sessions 1	1989	1.00	5.00
Collectables 5185	(M)	The Complete Fire And Enjoy Sessions 2	1989	1.00	5.00
Collectables 5186	(M)	The Complete Fire And Enjoy Sessions 3	1989	1.00	5.00
Collectables 5187	(M)	The Complete Fire And Enjoy Sessions 4	1989	1.00	5.00
Relic 1021	(M)	The Last Session 2-21-63	1990	1.00	5.00

JAMES, ELMORE, & WALTER HORTON

Label & Catalog #		Title	Year	VG+	NM
Polydor 2383-200	(M)	Cotton Patch Hot Foots	1973	6.00	15.00

JAMES, ELMORE, & EDDIE TAYLOR

Label & Catalog #		Title	Year	VG+	NM
Muse 5087	(M)	Street Talkin'	1975	4.00	10.00

JAMES, ETTA

Label & Catalog #		Title	Year	VG+	NM
Crown CLP-5209	(M)	Miss Etta James	1961	40.00	100.00
		(Original covers for Crown 5209 have a framed picture of Etta on the front.)			
Crown CLP-5209	(M)	Miss Etta James	1962	30.00	75.00
		(Later covers are white and read "Miss Etta James.")			
Crown CLP-5234	(M)	The Best Of Etta James	1962	30.00	75.00
Crown CLP-5250	(M)	Twist With Etta James	1962	30.00	75.00
		—*Crown albums above have black labels with a silver "Crown" on top.*—			
Crown CLP-5234	(M)	The Best Of Etta James	196?	12.00	30.00
Crown CLP-5250	(M)	Twist With Etta James	196?	12.00	30.00
Crown CLP-5360	(M)	Etta James (Smiling Etta cover)	1963	12.00	30.00
Crown CST-360	(E)	Etta James (Smiling Etta cover)	1963	8.00	20.00
Crown CLP-5360	(M)	Etta James (Somber Etta cover)	1963	12.00	30.00
Crown CST-360	(E)	Etta James (Somber Etta cover)	1963	8.00	20.00
		—*Crown albums above have gray labels.*—			
Kent KLP-5000	(M)	Miss Etta James	1964	12.00	30.00
Kent KST-500	(E)	Miss Etta James (Red vinyl)	1964	30.00	75.00
Kent KST-500	(E)	Miss Etta James	1964	10.00	25.00
		(Kent 5000 is a reissue of Crown 5209.)			
Argo LP-4003	(M)	At Last	1961	12.00	30.00
Argo LPS-4003	(S)	At Last	1961	16.00	40.00
Argo LP-4011	(M)	The Second Time Around	1961	12.00	30.00
Argo LPS-4011	(S)	The Second Time Around	1961	16.00	40.00
Argo LP-4013	(M)	Etta James	1962	12.00	30.00
Argo LPS-4013	(S)	Etta James	1962	16.00	40.00
		("Spoonful" and "If I Can't Have You" are rechanneled on this album.)			
Argo LP-4018	(M)	Etta James Sings For Lovers	1962	12.00	30.00
Argo LPS-4018	(S)	Etta James Sings For Lovers	1962	16.00	40.00
Argo LP-4025	(M)	Top Ten	1963	12.00	30.00
Argo LPS-4025	(S)	Top Ten	1963	16.00	40.00
Argo LP-4032	(M)	Etta James Rocks The House	1964	40.00	100.00
Argo LPS-4032	(S)	Etta James Rocks The House	1964	60.00	150.00
Argo LP-4040	(M)	The Queen Of Soul	1965	12.00	30.00
Argo LPS-4040	(S)	The Queen Of Soul	1965	16.00	40.00
Cadet LP-802	(M)	Tell Mama	1967	8.00	20.00
Cadet LPS-802	(S)	Tell Mama	1967	10.00	25.00
Cadet LPS-4003	(S)	At Last	1969	6.00	15.00
Cadet LPS-4011	(S)	The Second Time Around	1969	6.00	15.00
Cadet LPS-4013	(P)	Etta James	1969	6.00	15.00
Cadet LPS-4018	(S)	Etta James Sings For Lovers	1969	6.00	15.00
Cadet LPS-4025	(S)	Top Ten	1969	6.00	15.00
Cadet LPS-4040	(S)	The Queen Of Soul	1969	6.00	15.00
Cadet LPS-4055	(S)	Call My Name	1969	6.00	15.00
United US-7712	(E)	Etta James Sings	197?	4.00	10.00
Chess 2CH-60004	(P)	Peaches (2 LPs)	1971	8.00	20.00
Chess CH-50042	(S)	Etta James	1973	6.00	15.00
Chess 2CH-60029	(S)	Come A Little Bit Closer (2 LPs)	1974	8.00	20.00
Westbound 203	(S)	Etta James	1974	10.00	25.00
Warner Bros. BSK-3156	(S)	Deep In The Night	1978	1.00	5.00

JAMES, JIMMY, & THE VAGABONDS

Label & Catalog #		Title	Year	VG+	NM
Atco 33-222	(M)	The New Religion	1967	6.00	15.00
Atco SD-33-222	(S)	The New Religion	1967	8.00	20.00

JAMES, KEEF

Label & Catalog #		Title	Year	VG+	NM
Rare Earth 539	(S)	One Tree Or Another	1972	4.00	10.00

Label & Catalog #		Title	Year	VG+	NM
JAMES, LEONARD					
Decca DL-8772	(M)	Boppin' And A Strollin'	1958	20.00	50.00
JAMES, NICKY					
James was a member of Rare Bird.					
Threshold 10	(S)	Every Home Should Have One	1972	5.00	12.00
Threshold 19	(DJ)	Thunderthroat	1976	8.00	20.00
JAMES, SKIP					
Skip James was a blues guitar player, pianist, singer and songwriter.					
Melodeon MLP-7321	(M)	Greatest Of The Delta Blues Singers	196?	30.00	75.00
Vanguard VSR-9219	(M)	Skip James Today!	1966	10.00	25.00
Vanguard VSD-79219	(S)	Skip James Today!	1966	12.00	30.00
Vanguard VSD-79273	(S)	Devil Got My Woman	1968	8.00	20.00
Biograph 12027	(M)	This Old World	197?	4.00	10.00
Biograph 12029	(M)	Early Recordings	197?	4.00	10.00
Melodeon MLP-7321	(M)	Greatest Of The Delta Blues Singers	197?	4.00	10.00
JAMES, TOMMY					
Tommy James was originally the leader of The Shondells (below). Refer to Alive 'N Kickin'.					
Roulette SR-42051	(S)	Tommy James	1970	3.20	8.00
Roulette SR-3001	(S)	Christian Of The World	1971	3.20	8.00
Roulette SR-3007	(S)	My Head, My Bed, My Red Guitar	1972	3.20	8.00
Big-7 TJ1	(DJ)	Hits By A Super Writer	1972	10.00	25.00
		(The Big-7 disc is a publishers demo with title cover.)			
Fantasy F-9509	(S)	In Touch	1976	1.00	5.00
Fantasy F-9532	(S)	Midnight Rider	1977	1.00	5.00
Millennium 7748	(S)	Three Times In Love	1980	1.00	5.00
Aegis 1600	(S)	Hi-Fi	1990	1.00	5.00
JAMES, TOMMY, & THE SHONDELLS					
Members of The Shondells also recorded as Hog Heaven.					
Roulette R-25336	(M)	Hanky Panky	1966	10.00	25.00
Roulette SR-25336	(S)	Hanky Panky ("Hanky..." is rechanneled)	1966	12.00	30.00
Roulette R-25344	(M)	It's Only Love	1967	12.00	30.00
Roulette SR-25344	(S)	It's Only Love	1967	10.00	25.00
Roulette R-25353	(M)	I Think We're Alone Now (Footprint cover)	1967	12.00	30.00
Roulette SR-25353	(S)	I Think We're Alone Now (Footprint cover)	1967	10.00	25.00
Roulette SR-25353	(S)	I Think We're Alone Now (Photo cover)	1968	6.00	15.00
		("I Think We're Alone Now" is rechanneled on both versions of SR-25353.)			
Roulette SR-25355	(P)	Something Special! The Best Of			
		Tommy James & The Shondells	1968	10.00	25.00
Roulette SR-25357	(S)	Gettin' Together	1968	10.00	25.00
Roulette SR-42005	(P)	Something Special! The Best Of			
		Tommy James & The Shondells	1968	6.00	15.00
Roulette SR-42012	(P)	Mony Mony	1968	8.00	20.00
Roulette SR-42023	(S)	Crimson And Clover	1969	8.00	20.00
Roulette SR-42030	(S)	Cellophane Symphony	1969	8.00	20.00
Roulette SR-42040	(P)	The Best Of Tommy James & The Shondells	1969	4.00	10.00
Roulette SR-42044	(S)	Travelin'	1970	4.00	10.00
JAMES & THE GOOD BROTHERS					
Columbia CS-30889	(S)	James And The Good Brothers	1971	4.00	10.00
JAMES GANG, THE					
The James Gang features Joe Walsh, later of The Eagles.					
BluesWay BLS-6034	(S)	Yer' Album	1969	6.00	15.00
ABC S-688	(S)	Yer' Album	1969	1.20	6.00
ABC S-711	(S)	The James Gang Rides Again (With "Bolero")	1970	4.00	10.00
ABC S-711	(S)	The James Gang Rides Again (Without "Bolero")	1970	1.20	6.00
ABC X-721	(S)	Thirds	1971	1.20	6.00
ABC X-733	(S)	Live In Concert	1971	1.20	6.00
ABC X-741	(S)	Straight Shooter	1972	1.20	6.00
ABC X-760	(S)	Passin' Thru	1972	1.20	6.00
ABC X-774	(S)	Best Of The James Gang	1973	1.20	6.00
MCA 774	(S)	Best Of The James Gang	1977	.80	4.00
MCA 3711	(S)	The James Gang Rides Again	1977	.80	4.00
Atco SD-36-102	(S)	Miami	1974	.80	4.00
Atco QD-36-102	(Q)	Miami	1974	6.00	15.00
Atco SD-36-112	(S)	Newborn	1975	.80	4.00
Atco SD-36-141	(S)	Jesse Come Home	1976	.80	4.00
JAMME					
Dunhill DS-50072	(S)	Jamme	1970	8.00	20.00
JAMUL					
Lizard 20101	(S)	Jamul	1970	6.00	15.00

Label & Catalog #		Title	Year	VG+	NM

JAN & DEAN

Jan Berry and Dean Torrence. Refer to The Bel-Aire Pops Orchestra; Mike Love & Dean Torrence.

Label & Catalog #		Title	Year	VG+	NM
Dore LP-101	(M)	Jan & Dean	1960	150.00	300.00
Dore LP-101		Jan & Dean Bonus Photo	1960	40.00	100.00
		—Dore albums above have light blue labels.—			
Liberty LRP-3248	(M)	Jan & Dean's Golden Hits	1962	12.00	30.00
Liberty LST-7248	(S)	Jan & Dean's Golden Hits	1962	16.00	40.00
		("Baby Talk," "We Go Together," "Heart And Soul" and "Jenny Lee" are rechanneled.)			
Liberty LRP-3294	(M)	Jan & Dean Take Linda Surfing	1963	20.00	50.00
Liberty LST-7294	(S)	Jan & Dean Take Linda Surfing	1963	30.00	75.00
		(The Beach Boys provide vocal and instrumental backing on both "Surfin'" and "Surfin' Safari.")			
Liberty LRP-3314	(M)	Surf City	1963	16.00	40.00
Liberty LST-7314	(S)	Surf City	1963	20.00	50.00
Liberty LRP-3339	(M)	Drag City	1963	16.00	40.00
Liberty LST-7339	(S)	Drag City	1963	20.00	50.00
		(The Beach Boys provide backing on "Little Deuce Coupe..")			
Liberty LRP-3361	(M)	Dead Man's Curve/New Girl In School	1964	16.00	40.00
Liberty LST-7361	(S)	Dead Man's Curve/New Girl In School	1964	20.00	50.00
		(Original covers on Liberty 3/7361 are black & white with pink overtones.)			
Liberty LRP-3361	(M)	Dead Man's Curve/New Girl In School	1964	12.00	30.00
Liberty LST-7361	(S)	Dead Man's Curve/New Girl In School	1964	16.00	40.00
		(Second pressing covers are in full color.)			
Liberty LRP-3361	(M)	New Girl In School/Dead Man's Curve	1964	12.00	30.00
Liberty LST-7361	(S)	New Girl In School/Dead Man's Curve	1964	16.00	40.00
		(Third pressings flip-flop the title.)			
Columbia FLP-177	(DJ)	Ride The Wild Surf (Radio spots)	1964	150.00	300.00
		(Columbia 177 is a one-sided promo with a short segment with J&D.)			
Columbia FLP-177 A/B	(DJ)	Ride The Wild Surf (Radio spots)	1964	150.00	300.00
		(Columbia 177 A/B is two-sided with Frank Gifford voice-overs on the second side. This does not feature J&D's voices!)			
Liberty LRP-3368	(M)	Ride The Wild Surf	1964	12.00	30.00
Liberty LST-7368	(S)	Ride The Wild Surf	1964	16.00	40.00
Liberty LRP-3377	(M)	Little Old Lady From Pasadena	1964	12.00	30.00
Liberty LST-7377	(S)	Little Old Lady From Pasadena	1964	16.00	40.00
Liberty LRP-3403	(M)	Command Performance	1965	12.00	30.00
Liberty LST-7403	(S)	Command Performance	1965	16.00	40.00
Liberty LRP-3417	(M)	Jan & Dean's Golden Hits, Volume 2	1965	10.00	25.00
Liberty LST-7417	(S)	Jan & Dean's Golden Hits, Volume 2	1965	12.00	30.00
Liberty CRC-LST-7417	(S)	Jan & Dean's Golden Hits, Volume 2	1965	12.00	30.00
		(Columbia Record Club)			
Liberty LRP-3431	(M)	Folk 'N' Roll	1965	12.00	30.00
Liberty LST-7431	(S)	Folk 'N' Roll	1965	16.00	40.00
Liberty LRP-3441	(M)	Filet Of Soul (A "Live" One)	1966	12.00	30.00
Liberty LST-7441	(S)	Filet Of Soul (A "Live" One)	1966	16.00	40.00
Liberty LRP-3444	(M)	Jan & Dean Meet Batman	1966	20.00	50.00
Liberty LST-7444	(S)	Jan & Dean Meet Batman	1966	30.00	75.00
Liberty LRP-3458	(M)	Popsicle	1966	12.00	30.00
Liberty LST-7458	(S)	Popsicle	1966	16.00	40.00
Liberty LRP-3460	(M)	Jan & Dean's Golden Hits, Volume 3	1966	10.00	25.00
Liberty LST-7460	(S)	Jan & Dean's Golden Hits, Volume 3	1966	12.00	30.00
L-J 101	(M)	Jan & Dean With The Soul Surfers	1963	10.00	25.00
Coca-Cola TX-98	(DJ)	Jan & Dean Swing The Jingle	1965	300.00	500.00
		(Both sides contain the same five 10 to 90 second spots.)			
Columbia CL-2661	(M)	Save For A Rainy Day	1967		Unreleased
Columbia CS-9461	(S)	Save For A Rainy Day	1967		Unreleased
		(While there was no official US release of this album, it did make it to the acetate stage, which has a suggested NM value of $2,000-4,000.)			
J&D 101	(M)	Save For A Rainy Day	1967	150.00	300.00
		(J&D 101 is a "reissue" of the album intended for Columbia above.)			
Sunset SUM-1156	(M)	Jan & Dean	1967	5.00	12.00
Sunset SUS-5156	(S)	Jan & Dean	1967	6.00	15.00
United Arts. UAS-9961	(P)	The Jan & Dean Anthology Album (2 LPs)	1971	10.00	25.00
United Arts. UA-341	(P)	Gotta Take That One Last Ride (2 LPs)	1974	6.00	15.00
		(The Sunset and U.A. albums above contain Liberty recordings.)			
United Arts. LA-443E	(S)	The Very Best Of Jan & Dean, Vol. 1	1975	.80	4.00
United Arts. LA-515E	(S)	The Very Best Of Jan & Dean, Vol. 2	1975	.80	4.00
Deadman's Curve	(M)	Live At The Keystone Berkeley	1981	20.00	50.00
		(Authorized private pressing taken from an audience tape and Originally issued in plain jackets with front and back cover inserts.)			
Deadman's Curve	(M)	Live At The Keystone Berkeley	1981	10.00	25.00
		(Reissued with the front and backs pasted on.)			
Liberty LN-10115	(S)	The Best Of Jan & Dean	1981	.80	4.00
Liberty LN-10151	(S)	The Little Old Lady From Pasadena	1982	.80	4.00

JAN & DEAN / THE SATELLITES

Label & Catalog #		Title	Year	VG+	NM
Inter. Award AKL-250	(M)	Jan & Dean And The Satellites	196?	6.00	15.00
Inter. Award AKS-250	(S)	Jan & Dean And The Satellites	196?	6.00	15.00

The Jaynetts had an enormous hit at the end of 1963 with "Sally Go 'Round The Roses." Long associated with the "girl group" sound of the early '60s, the trio's lone hit sounds nothing like the majority of singles in this genre: While most of the girl group songs were poppy and upbeat, "Sally 'Go Round The Roses" sounded like it had creeped onto the radio via the Twilight Zone. Tuff Records followed with an album that went nowhere and is a desirable artifact from that era and a tough record to find. In 1966 the song was reintroduced to the burgeoning counter-culture of the Bay Area as a staple of the live sets of The Great Society featuring Grace Slick.

Label & Catalog #		Title	Year	VG+	NM
Design DLP-181	(M)	Jan & Dean And The Satellites	196?	6.00	15.00
Design DLPS-181	(S)	Jan & Dean And The Satellites	196?	6.00	15.00

JAN & LORRAINE

ABC S-691	(S)	Gypsy People	1969	4.00	10.00

JANIS, JOHNNY

ABC-Paramount ABC-140	(M)	For The First Time	1956	20.00	50.00
Columbia CL-1674	(M)	The Start Of Something New	1961	6.00	15.00
Columbia CS-8474	(S)	The Start Of Something New	1961	8.00	20.00
Monument MLP-8036	(M)	Once In A Blue Moon	1965	6.00	15.00
Monument SLP-18036	(S)	Once In A Blue Moon	1965	8.00	20.00

JANUARY TYME

Enterprise ENS-1004	(S)	First Time From Memphis	1970	10.00	25.00

JASPER WRATH

Sunflower SNF-5003	(S)	Jasper Wrath (With insert)	1971	10.00	25.00

JAY, BOB, & THE HAWKS

Warner Bros. W-1562	(M)	Everybody's Doing The Watusi	1964	5.00	12.00
Warner Bros. WS-1562	(S)	Everybody's Doing The Watusi	1964	6.00	15.00
Warner Bros. W-1563	(M)	Everybody's Doing The Ska	1964	5.00	12.00
Warner Bros. WS-1563	(S)	Everybody's Doing The Ska	1964	6.00	15.00
Warner Bros. W-1564	(M)	Everybody's Doing The Monkey	1964	5.00	12.00
Warner Bros. WS-1564	(S)	Everybody's Doing The Monkey	1964	6.00	15.00

JAY & THE AMERICANS

The original lead singer was John "Jay" Traynor, who had recorded as a member of The Mystics. After the first two albums, Traynor left to pursue solo stardom. David Blatt was recruited from The Empires and renamed Jay Black. Note that the group was under the direction of Leiber & Stoller.

United Arts. UAL-3222	(M)	She Cried	1962	20.00	50.00
United Arts. UAS-6222	(S)	She Cried	1962	40.00	100.00
United Arts. UAL-3300	(M)	At The Cafe Wha?	1963	20.00	50.00
United Arts. UAS-6300	(S)	At The Cafe Wha?	1963	40.00	100.00
United Arts. UAL-3407	(M)	Come A Little Bit Closer	1964	10.00	25.00
United Arts. UAS-6407	(S)	Come A Little Bit Closer	1964	12.00	30.00
United Arts. UAL-3417	(M)	Blockbusters	1965	10.00	25.00
United Arts. UAS-6417	(S)	Blockbusters	1965	12.00	30.00
United Arts. UAL-3453	(M)	Jay & The Americans' Greatest Hits	1965	8.00	20.00
United Arts. UAS-6453	(P)	Jay & The Americans' Greatest Hits	1965	10.00	25.00
United Arts. ST-90814	(P)	Jay & The Americans' Greatest Hits (Capitol Record Club)	196?	12.00	30.00
United Arts. UAL-3474	(M)	Sunday And Me	1966	8.00	20.00
United Arts. UAS-6474	(S)	Sunday And Me	1966	10.00	25.00
United Arts. UAL-3534	(M)	Livin' Above Your Head	1966	8.00	20.00
United Arts. UAS-6534	(S)	Livin' Above Your Head	1966	10.00	25.00
United Arts. UAL-3555	(M)	Jay & The Americans' Greatest Hits, Vol. 2	1966	8.00	20.00
United Arts. UAS-6555	(S)	Jay & The Americans' Greatest Hits, Vol. 2	1966	8.00	20.00
United Arts. ST-90815	(S)	Jay & The Americans' Greatest Hits, Vol. 2 (Capitol Record Club)	1966	10.00	25.00
United Arts. UAL-3562	(M)	Try Some Of This	1967	6.00	15.00
United Arts. UAS-6562	(S)	Try Some Of This	1967	8.00	20.00
		— U.A. albums above have black labels.—			
Unart M-20018	(M)	Jay & The Americans!!	1968	4.00	10.00
Unart MS-21018	(S)	Jay & The Americans!!	1968	5.00	12.00
Sunset SUS-5278	(S)	Early American Hits	1969	6.00	15.00
		(The Unart and Sunset albums above contain U.A. recordings.)			
United Arts. UAS-6671	(S)	Sands Of Time	1969	8.00	20.00
United Arts. UAS-6719	(S)	Wax Museum	1970	6.00	15.00
United Arts. UAS-6751	(S)	Wax Museum, Volume 2	1970	6.00	15.00
		(U.A. 6751 is a reissue of 6671.)			
United Arts. UAS-6762	(S)	Jay & The Americans Capture The Moment	1970	10.00	25.00
Doral	(S)	Doral Presents Jay & The Americans	1971	8.00	20.00
		(Promotional compilation of previously released material.)			
United Arts. LA-357E	(S)	The Very Best Of Jay & The Americans	1975	.80	4.00

JAY & THE TECHNIQUES

Smash MGS-27095	(M)	Apples, Peaches, Pumpkin Pie	1967	12.00	30.00
Smash SRS-67095	(S)	Apples, Peaches, Pumpkin Pie	1967	12.00	30.00
		(Original covers for SRS-67095 have a photo of the group on stage.)			
Smash SRS-67095	(S)	Apples, Peaches, Pumpkin Pie	1968	8.00	20.00
		(Later covers have a photo of a posed group.)			
Smash SRS-67102	(S)	Love Lost And Found	1968	12.00	30.00

JAYNETTES, THE

Tuff LP-13	(M)	Sally Go Round The Roses	1963	200.00	400.00

JEFFERSON AIRPLANE TAKES OFF   Mono LPM-3584
Produced by Matthew Katz and Tommy Oliver   Stereo LSP-3584

SIDE 1

Blues from an Airplane (BMI 2:10)

Let Me In (EMI 2:55)

Bringing Me Down (BMI 2:22)

It's No Secret (BMI 2:37)

Tobacco Road (ASCAP 3:26)

Runnin' 'Round This World (BMI 2:20)

SIDE 2

Come Up the Years (BMI 2:30)

Run Around (BMI 2:35)

Let's Get Together (BMI 3:32)

Don't Slip Away (BMI 2:31)

Chauffeur Blues (ASCAP 2:25)

And I Like It (BMI 3:16)

JET AGE SOUND

hand and grab you.   Listening to rock bands has convinced me—and I'm old enough   Recorded in RCA Victor's Music Center of

Original pressings of Jefferson Airplane Takes Off! contained twelve tracks, six per side, with the closer on side 1 being "Runnin' 'Round This World." For reasons never explained, the album was remastered with "Runnin'" deleted, leaving fans with an eleven-track album. Shortly afterwards, someone at RCA Victor took notice of the questionable lyrics in "Let Me In" and "Run Around." It was again returned and remastered, this time with the two songs replaced by rerecorded versions. These were then shipped and the album, while never a hit, was a perennial seller for the group. Pictured here is the original back cover with twelve songs. Collectors should note that many covers with this listing do not contain the twelve-track album but the regular eleven-track reissue, so always check the first side label. (Note: "Runnin' 'Round This World" was eventually reissued in 1974 on Early Flight while the original versions of "Let Me In" and "Run Around" had to wait until 1992's boxed CD set, Jefferson Airplane Loves You.)

Label & Catalog #		Title	Year	VG+	NM

JB'S, THE [THE JB'S INTERNATIONAL]
The JB's are James Brown's backing group and were produced by JB. Refer to Fred Wesley.

People PE-5601	(S)	**Food For Thought**	1972	20.00	50.00
People PE-5603	(S)	**Doing It To Death**	1973	20.00	50.00
Polydor PD-6153	(S)	**Disco Fever**	1978	8.00	20.00
		(Polydor 6153 credits The JB's International.)			
Drive DR-111	(S)	**Groove Machine**	1979	8.00	20.00

JEFFERSON

| Janus JLS-3006 | (S) | **Baby, Take Me In Your Arms** | 1969 | 10.00 | 25.00 |

JEFFERSON, BLIND LEMON
Jefferson was a blues guitar player, singer and songwriter.

Riverside 1014	(10")	**The Folk Blues Of Blind Lemon Jefferson**	1953	150.00	300.00
Riverside 1053	(10")	**Penitentiary Blues**	1955	150.00	300.00
Riverside RLP-12-125	(M)	**Blind Lemon Jefferson—Classic Folk Blues**	1957	60.00	150.00
Riverside RLP-12-136	(M)	**Blind Lemon Jefferson, Volume 2**	1958	60.00	150.00
		—Riverside albums above have white labels.—			
Milestone MLP-2004	(M)	**The Immortal Blind Lemon Jefferson**	1968	10.00	25.00
Milestone MLP-2007	(M)	**The Immortal Blind Lemon Jefferson, Volume 2**	1969	10.00	25.00
Milestone MLP-2013	(M)	**Black Snake Moan**	1970	10.00	25.00
Biograph BLP-12015	(M)	**Blind Lemon Jefferson 1926-1929**	197?	8.00	20.00
Yazoo L-1069	(M)	**King Of The Country Blues**	197?	6.00	15.00

JEFFERSON AIRPLANE
The original group was Marty Balin with Signe Andersson, Jack Casady, Paul Kantner, Jorma Kaukonen, and Alexander "Skip" Spence. Andersson and Spence left in late '66, replaced by Grace Slick from The Great Society and Spencer Dryden. "Papa" John Creach joined in 1970. Dryden left and was replaced in 1970 by Joey Covington who was replaced by John Barbata in '72. Balin left in 1971 and by '74, what was left of the Airplane became (shudder) Jefferson Starship. Refer to Hot Tuna; Moby Grape.

RCA Victor LPM-3584	(M)	**Jefferson Airplane Takes Off!** (12 tracks)	1966	See note below	
RCA Victor LSP-3584	(S)	**Jefferson Airplane Takes Off!** (12 tracks)	1966	See note below	
		(First pressings of RCA 3584 have six tracks on the first side with "Runnin' Round This World" as the sixth song. The album features the original versions of "Let Me In" and "Run Around;" see below. The mono pressing has a suggested NM value of $2,000-4,000. The stereo pressing has a suggested NM value of $4,000-8,000.)			
RCA Victor LPM-3584	(M)	**Jefferson Airplane Takes Off!** (11 tracks)	1966	See note below	
RCA Victor LSP-3584	(S)	**Jefferson Airplane Takes Off!** (11 tracks)	1966	See note below	
		(Second pressings have five tracks on the first side with "Runnin' Round This World" deleted from this and all subsequent pressings. The album features the original versions of "Let Me In," with the line "don't tell me you want money," and "Run Around," with "that sway as you lay under me." While the back cover has an "RE" in the upper right corner, the two songs must be listened to for verification. The mono pressing has a suggested NM value of $500-1,500. The stereo pressing has a suggested NM value of $1,500-3,000.)			
RCA Victor LPM-3584	(M)	**Jefferson Airplane Takes Off!** (11 tracks)	1966	10.00	25.00
RCA Victor LSP-3584	(S)	**Jefferson Airplane Takes Off!** (11 tracks)	1966	8.00	20.00
		(Third pressings have five tracks on the first side. The other two songs have been rerecorded: "Let Me In" has changed the line to "don't tell me it's so funny" while "Run Around" has changed the line to "that sway as you stay here by me." The back cover has "LPM/LSP-3584 RE" in the upper right corner.)			
RCA Victor LPM-3766	(M)	**Surrealistic Pillow**	1967	24.00	60.00
RCA Victor LSP-3766	(S)	**Surrealistic Pillow**	1967	10.00	25.00
RCA Victor LOP-1511	(M)	**After Bathing At Baxter's**	1967	20.00	50.00
RCA Victor LSO-1511	(S)	**After Bathing At Baxter's**	1967	8.00	20.00
RCA Victor LSP-4058	(S)	**Crown Of Creation**	1968	12.00	30.00
		—RCA albums above have black labels with Nipper on top.—			
RCA Victor LSP-3584	(S)	**Jefferson Airplane Takes Off!**	1969	4.00	10.00
RCA Victor LSP-3766	(S)	**Surrealistic Pillow**	1969	4.00	10.00
RCA Victor LSO-1511	(S)	**After Bathing At Baxter's**	1969	4.00	10.00
RCA Victor LSP-4058	(S)	**Crown Of Creation**	1969	4.00	10.00
RCA Victor LSP-4133	(S)	**Bless Its Pointed Little Head**	1969	4.00	10.00
RCA Victor LSP-4238	(S)	**Volunteers**	1969	4.00	10.00
		—RCA albums above have orange labels on non-flexible vinyl.—			
RCA Victor LSP-4459	(S)	**The Worst Of Jefferson Airplane**	1970	4.00	10.00
		—RCA albums above have custom black labels on non-flexible vinyl.—			
RCA Victor LSP-3584	(S)	**Jefferson Airplane Takes Off!**	1971	1.00	5.00
RCA Victor LSP-3766	(S)	**Surrealistic Pillow**	1971	1.00	5.00
RCA Victor LSO-1511	(S)	**After Bathing At Baxter's**	1971	1.00	5.00
RCA Victor LSP-4058	(S)	**Crown Of Creation**	1971	1.00	5.00
RCA Victor LSP-4133	(S)	**Bless Its Pointed Little Head**	1971	1.00	5.00
RCA Victor LSP-4238	(S)	**Volunteers**	1971	1.00	5.00
RCA Victor APD1-0320	(Q)	**Volunteers** *(Yellow/orange label)*	1973	30.00	75.00
		("Volunteers," "We Can Be Together," "Wooden Ships" and "Hey Frederick" are alternate takes from the stereo album.)			
		—RCA albums above have orange labels on flexible vinyl.—			

A few years ago, an album like this by The Jelly Bean Bandits would not have a snowball's chance in Hades of attracting serious collector attention. It looks like the group's chosen image is that of "the Fugs of bubblegum music." In fact, like many overlooked titles on the Mainstream label ("Looks like something from those Kasenetz-Katz guys. . ."), the cover does not tell the story. This has become a highly sought-after item among pop/psych collectors and should continue to rise in value as its real rarity becomes obvious.

Label & Catalog #		Title	Year	VG+	NM
RCA Victor LSP-3584	(S)	Jefferson Airplane Takes Off!	1975	1.00	5.00
RCA Victor LSP-3766	(S)	Surrealistic Pillow	1975	1.00	5.00
RCA Victor LSO-1511	(S)	After Bathing At Baxter's	1975	1.00	5.00
RCA Victor LSP-4058	(S)	Crown Of Creation	1975	1.00	5.00
RCA Victor LSP-4133	(S)	Bless Its Pointed Little Head	1975	1.00	5.00
RCA Victor LSP-4238	(S)	Volunteers	1975	1.00	5.00
RCA Victor APD1-0320	(Q)	Volunteers	1975	20.00	50.00
		—RCA albums above have brown labels.—			
Grunt FTR-1001	(S)	Bark *(Issued in a brown paper bag)*	1971	6.00	15.00
Grunt FTR-1001	(S)	Bark *(Without the bag)*	1971	3.20	8.00
Grunt FTR-1007	(S)	Long John Silver	1972	3.20	8.00
Grunt BFL1-0147	(S)	Thirty Seconds Over Winterland	1973	3.20	8.00
Grunt CYL1-0437	(S)	Early Flight	1974	3.20	8.00
Grunt CYL2-1255	(S)	Flight Log 1966-1976 *(2 LPs)*	1977	1.20	6.00
RCA Victor AYL1-3661	(S)	The Worst Of Jefferson Airplane	1980	.80	4.00
RCA Victor AYL1-3738	(S)	Surrealistic Pillow	1980	.80	4.00
RCA Victor AYL1-3739	(S)	Jefferson Airplane Takes Off!	1980	.80	4.00
RCA Victor AYL1-3797	(S)	Crown Of Creation	1980	.80	4.00
RCA Victor AYL1-3798	(S)	Bless Its Pointed Little Head	1980	.80	4.00
RCA Victor AYL1-3867	(S)	Volunteers	1980	.80	4.00
Grunt Victor AYL-4368	(S)	Bark	1980	.80	4.00
Grunt AYL1-4391	(S)	Thirty Seconds Over Winterland	1980	.80	4.00
Grunt AFL1-4545	(S)	After Bathing At Baxter's	1980	.80	4.00
RCA Victor 5724-1-R	(S)	2400 Fulton Street—An Anthology *(2 LPs)*	1987	6.00	15.00
Epic OE-45271	(S)	Jefferson Airplane	1989	4.00	10.00

JEFFERSON STARSHIP
The Starship evolved out of the remains of the Airplane and revolved around Paul Kantner and Grace Slick. Refer to Paul Kantner & The Jefferson Starship.

Grunt BFL1-0717	(S)	Dragonfly	1974	.80	4.00
Grunt BFD1-0717	(Q)	Dragonfly	1974	6.00	15.00
Grunt BFL1-0999	(S)	Red Octopus	1975	.80	4.00
Grunt BFD1-0999	(Q)	Red Octopus	1975	6.00	15.00
Grunt BFL1-1557	(S)	Spitfire	1976	.80	4.00
Grunt BFD1-1557	(Q)	Spitfire	1976	6.00	15.00
Grunt BXL1-2515	(S)	Earth	1978	.80	4.00
Grunt BZL1-3247	(S)	Gold	1979	.80	4.00
Grunt DJL1-3363	(S)	Gold *(Picture disc)*	1979	4.00	10.00
Grunt BZL1-3452	(S)	Freedom At Point Zero	1979	.80	4.00
Grunt AYL1-3660	(S)	Red Octopus	1980	.80	4.00
Grunt AYL1-3796	(S)	Dragonfly	1980	.80	4.00
Grunt BZL1-3848	(S)	Modern Times	1981.	.80	4.00
Grunt AYL1-3953	(S)	Spitfire	1981	.80	4.00
Grunt AYL1-4172	(S)	Earth	1981	.80	4.00
Grunt BXL1-4372	(S)	Winds Of Change	1982	.80	4.00
Grunt DJL1-4569	(S)	RCA Radio Series Special Interview, Vol. 19	1982	4.00	10.00

JEFFREY, JOE

Wand WDS-686	(S)	My Pledge Of Love	1969	14.00	35.00

JELLY BEAN BANDITS, THE

Mainstream 56103	(M)	Jelly Bean Bandits	1967	40.00	100.00
Mainstream S-6103	(S)	Jelly Bean Bandits	1967	60.00	150.00

JELLYBREAD

Blue Horizon BH-4801	(S)	First Slice	1970	14.00	35.00

JELLYROLL

Kapp KS-3626	(S)	Jellyroll	1971	6.00	15.00

JENSEN, KRIS

Hickory LPM-110	(M)	Torture	1963	20.00	50.00

JEREMIAH

Uni 73098	(S)	Jeremiah	1971	6.00	15.00

JEREMY & THE SATYRS

Reprise RS-6282	(S)	Jeremy & The Satyrs	1968	4.00	10.00

JERICHO

Ampex A-10112	(S)	Jericho	1971	10.00	25.00

JETHRO TULL

Reprise RS-6336	(S)	This Was	1969	4.00	10.00
Reprise RS-6360	(S)	Stand Up *(Gatefold cover with stand-up inside)*	1969	6.00	15.00
Reprise RS-6400	(S)	Benefit	1970	4.00	10.00
		—Reprise albums above have brown labels with a "W7" and ":r" logos on top.—			
Reprise RS-6336	(S)	This Was	197?	1.00	5.00
Reprise RS-6360	(S)	Stand Up	197?	1.00	5.00

Label & Catalog #		Title	Year	VG+	
Reprise RS-6400	(S)	Benefit	197?	1.00	
Reprise MS-2035	(S)	Aqualung	1971	1.00	5.00
Reprise MS-2072	(S)	Thick As A Brick (Promo sampler)	1972	12.00	30.00
Reprise MS-2072	(S)	Thick As A Brick (With booklet)	1972	1.20	6.00
Chrysalis MS-2106	(S)	Living In The Past (2 LPs with booklet)	1972	1.20	6.00
		—Reprise albums above have brown labels.—			
Chrysalis CHR-1003	(S)	Thick As A Brick	1973	.80	4.00
Chrysalis CHR-1035	(S)	Living In The Past (2 LPs)	1973	1.00	5.00
Chrysalis CHR-1040	(S)	A Passion Play (Promo edited for airplay)	1973	10.00	25.00
Chrysalis CHR-1040	(S)	A Passion Play (With booklet)	1973	1.00	5.00
Chrysalis CHR-1041	(S)	This Was	1973	.80	4.00
Chrysalis CHR-1042	(S)	Stand Up	1973	.80	4.00
Chrysalis CHR-1043	(S)	Benefit	1973	.80	4.00
Chrysalis CHR-1044	(S)	Aqualung	1973	.80	4.00
Chrysalis CH4-1044	(Q)	Aqualung	1973	16.00	40.00
Chrysalis CHR-1067	(S)	War Child	1974	1.00	5.00
Chrysalis CH4-1067	(Q)	War Child	1974	16.00	40.00
Chrysalis PRO-623	(S)	The Jethro Tull Radio Show	1975	20.00	50.00
Chrysalis CHR-1078	(S)	M.U.—The Best Of Jethro Tull	1975	.80	4.00
Chrysalis CHR-1082	(S)	Minstrel In The Gallery	1975	1.00	5.00
Chrysalis CHR-1111	(S)	Too Old To Rock N' Roll: Too Young To Die	1976	1.00	5.00
Chrysalis CHR-1132	(S)	Songs From The Wood	1977	1.00	5.00
Chrysalis CHR-1135	(S)	Repeat—The Best Of Jethro Tull, Vol. II	1977	.80	4.00
Chrysalis CHR-1175	(S)	Heavy Horses	1978	1.00	5.00
Chrysalis CH2-1201	(S)	Jethro Tull Live—Bursting Out (2 LPs)	1978	3.20	8.00
Chrysalis CHR-12338	(S)	Stormwatch	1979	1.00	5.00
Chrysalis CHR-1301	(S)	"A"	1980	1.00	5.00
Chrysalis CHR-1380	(S)	The Broadsword And The Beast	1982	1.00	5.00

JETT, JOAN, & THE BLACKHEARTS
Ms Jett was a member of The Runaways. Her first album was pressed privately before being released by Boardwalk.

Boardwalk 37065	(S)	Bad Reputation	1981	1.00	5.00
Boardwalk 33243	(S)	I Love Rock-n-Roll	1981	1.00	5.00
MCA/Blackheart 5437	(S)	Joan Jett Album	1983	1.00	5.00
MCA 5476	(S)	Glorious Results Of A Misspent Youth	1984	1.00	5.00

JIMMY G & THE TACKHEADS
Jimmy and The 'Heads are members of the Parliament/Funkadelic community.

Capitol ST-12392	(S)	Federation Of Tackheads	1985	4.00	10.00

JINNIE & VELLA

Imperial LP-12419	(S)	Heartbeat	1969	4.00	10.00

JIVE FIVE, THE

United Arts. UAL-3455	(M)	The Jive Five	1965	20.00	50.00
United Arts. UAS-6455	(S)	The Jive Five	1965	30.00	75.00
Ambient Sound 37717	(S)	Here We Are	1982	6.00	15.00
Relic 5020	(M)	The Jive Five's Greatest Hits	198?	1.00	5.00

JO JO GUNNE
Jo Jo features Jay Ferguson of Spirit.

Asylum SD-5053	(S)	Jo Jo Gunne	1972	6.00	15.00
Asylum SD-5065	(S)	Bite Down Hard	1973	6.00	15.00
Asylum SD-5071	(S)	Jumpin' The Gunne (Gatefold cover)	1973	6.00	15.00
Asylum SD-5071	(S)	Jumpin' The Gunne	1974	4.00	10.00
Asylum 7E-1022	(S)	So Where Is The Show	1974	4.00	10.00

JO MAMA

Atlantic SD-8269	(S)	Jo Mama	1970	4.00	10.00
Atlantic SD-8288	(S)	J Is For Jump	1971	4.00	10.00

JOBRIATH

Elektra EKS-75070	(S)	Jobriath	1975	4.00	10.00
Elektra 7E-1010	(S)	Creatures Of The Street	1976	4.00	10.00

JODE

Vanguard VSD-6564	(S)	Jode	1971	4.00	10.00

JODO

Decca DL-75268	(S)	Guts	1970	14.00	35.00

JODY GRIND

United Arts. UAS-6774	(S)	One Step On	1969	12.00	30.00

JOEL, BILLY
Billy Joel originally recorded as a member of The Hassle and Attila.

Family Prod. 2700	(S)	Cold Spring Harbor (Full color label)	1971	10.00	25.00
		(Copies of Family Prod. 2700 with white labels are counterfeits.)			
Columbia KC-32544	(S)	Piano Man	1973	.80	4.00

Label & Catalog #		Title	Year	VG+	NM
Columbia CQ-32544	(Q)	Piano Man	1974	6.00	15.00
Columbia PC-33146	(S)	Streetlife Serenade	1974	.80	4.00
Columbia PCQ-33146	(Q)	Streetlife Serenade	1974	6.00	15.00
Columbia PC-33848	(S)	Turnstiles	1976	.80	4.00
Columbia PCQ-33848	(Q)	Turnstiles	1976	6.00	15.00
Columbia AS-326	(S)	Souvenir (One-sided live promo album)	1976	6.00	15.00
April-Blackwood ABS-1	(DJ)	Billy Joel (Boxed set of five albums with book)	1979	12.00	30.00
Columbia JC-34987	(S)	The Stranger	1977	.80	4.00
Columbia HC-34987	(S)	The Stranger (Half-speed master)	1981	12.00	30.00
Columbia HC-44987	(S)	The Stranger (Half-speed master)	1982	10.00	25.00
Columbia FC-35609	(S)	52nd Street	1978	.80	4.00
Columbia HC-45609	(S)	52nd Street (Half-speed master)	1982	10.00	25.00
Columbia FC-36384	(S)	Glass House	1980	.80	4.00
Columbia TC-37461	(S)	Songs In The Attic	1981	.80	4.00
Columbia HC-47461	(S)	Songs In The Attic (Half-speed master)	1982	10.00	25.00
Columbia QC-38200	(S)	Nylon Curtain	1982	.80	4.00
Columbia AS-1343	(S)	Billy Joel Interview (Promo)	1982	6.00	15.00
Columbia 38837	(S)	An Innocent Man	1983	.80	4.00
Columbia HC-48837	(S)	An Innocent Man (Half-speed master)	1983	12.00	30.00
Columbia 38984	(S)	Cold Spring Harbor	1984	.80	4.00

JOHN, ELTON
EJ can also be found on the soundtracks for Viking's "The Games" and Paramount's "Friends."

Label & Catalog #		Title	Year	VG+	NM
Uni 73090	(S)	Elton John	1970	4.00	10.00
Uni 73096	(S)	Tumbleweed Connection (With booklet)	1971	4.00	10.00
Uni 93090	(S)	Elton John	1971	3.20	8.00
Uni 93096	(S)	Tumbleweed Connection (With booklet)	1971	3.20	8.00
Uni 93105	(S)	11-17-70	1971	3.20	8.00
Uni 93120	(S)	Madman Across The Water (With booklet)	1971	3.20	8.00
Uni 93135	(S)	Honky Chateau	1972	3.20	8.00
MCA 2012	(S)	Elton John	1973	1.00	5.00
MCA 2014	(S)	Tumbleweed Connection (With booklet)	1973	1.00	5.00
MCA 2105	(S)	11-17-70	1973	1.00	5.00
MCA 2016	(S)	Madman Across The Water (With booklet)	1973	1.00	5.00
MCA 2017	(S)	Honky Chateau	1973	1.00	5.00
		—MCA albums above have black rainbow labels.—			
MCA 2100	(S)	Don't Shoot Me, I'm Only The Piano Player (With booklet)	1972	6.00	15.00
		—MCA albums above have solid black labels.—			
MCA 2100	(S)	Don't Shoot Me, I'm Only The Piano Player (With booklet)	1972	1.00	5.00
MCA 10003	(S)	Goodbye Yellow Brick Road (2 LPs)	1973	1.20	6.00
MCA 2116	(S)	Caribou	1974	1.00	5.00
MCA 2128	(S)	Greatest Hits	1974	1.00	5.00
MCA 2130	(S)	Empty Sky	1975	1.00	5.00
MCA 2142	(DJ)	Capt. Fantastic & The Brown Dirt Cowboy	1975	150.00	300.00
		(All promo copies on brown vinyl are autographed by Elton and Bernie.)			
MCA 2142	(S)	Capt. Fantastic & The Brown Dirt Cowboy	1975	1.00	5.00
MCA 2163	(S)	Rock Of The Westies	1975	1.00	5.00
MCA 2197	(S)	Here And There	1976	1.00	5.00
		—MCA albums above have black rainbow labels.—			
MCA 11004	(S)	Blue Moves (2 LPs)	1976	1.20	6.00
MCA 3027	(S)	Greatest Hits, Vol. 2	1977	1.00	5.00
MCA 3065	(S)	A Single Man	1978	1.00	5.00
MCA L33-1995	(S)	A Single Man (Promo picture disc)	1979	16.00	40.00
MCA 14591	(S)	A Single Man	1979	4.00	10.00
MCA 13921	(S)	The Thom Bell Sessions (3 track EP)	1979	.80	4.00
MCA 5121	(S)	21 At 33	1980	.80	4.00
MCA 619	(S)	11-17-70	1979	.80	4.00
MCA 620	(S)	Empty Sky	1979	.80	4.00
MCA 621	(S)	Rock Of The Westies	1979	.80	4.00
MCA 622	(S)	Here And There	1979	.80	4.00
MCA 3001	(S)	Tumbleweed Connection	1979	.80	4.00
MCA 3003	(S)	Madman Across The Water	1979	.80	4.00
MCA 5224	(S)	Greatest Hits	1979	.80	4.00
MCA 5225	(S)	Greatest Hits, Vol. 2	1979	.80	4.00
MCA 6011	(S)	Blue Moves (2 LPs)	1979	1.00	5.00
MCA 37064	(S)	Honky Chateau	1979	.80	4.00
MCA 37065	(S)	Caribou	1979	.80	4.00
MCA 37066	(S)	Capt. Fantastic & The Brown Dirt Cowboy	1979	.80	4.00
MCA 37067	(S)	Elton John	1979	.80	4.00
MCA 37068	(S)	A Single Man	1979	.80	4.00
MCA 37113	(S)	Don't Shoot Me, I'm Only The Piano Player	1979	.80	4.00
Geffen 2002	(S)	The Fox	1981	.80	4.00
Geffen 2013	(S)	Jump Up!	1982	.80	4.00
Geffen 4006	(S)	Too Low For Zero	1983	.80	4.00
Geffen GHS-24031	(S)	Breaking Hearts (Quiex II vinyl promo)	1984	6.00	15.00
Geffen GHS-24031	(S)	Breaking Hearts	1984	.80	4.00

Label & Catalog #		Title	Year	VG+	NM
JOHN, ROBERT					
Columbia CS-9687	(S)	**If You Don't Want My Love**	1968	8.00	20.00
JOHN, LITTLE WILLIE					
King 564	(M)	**Fever**	1956	600.00	1,200.00
		(Original covers are brown with a nurse holding a thermometer.)			
King 564	(M)	**Fever**	1957	300.00	600.00
		(Later covers are white with "Fever" in large colored letters.)			
King 596	(M)	**Talk To Me**	1958	150.00	300.00
King 603	(M)	**Mister Little Willie John**	1958	150.00	300.00
King 691	(M)	**Little Willie John In Action**	1960	175.00	350.00
King 739	(M)	**Sure Things**	1961	80.00	200.00
King 767	(M)	**The Sweet, The Hot, The Teenage Beat**	1961	80.00	200.00
King 802	(M)	**Come On And Join Little Willie John**	1962	80.00	200.00
King 895	(M)	**These Are My Favorite Songs**	1964	40.00	100.00
King 949	(M)	**Little Willie Sings All Originals**	1966	40.00	100.00
King KS-949	(S)	**Little Willie Sings All Originals**	1966	60.00	150.00
		—King albums above have crownless black labels.—			
King KS-1081	(M)	**Free At Last**	1970	16.00	40.00
		("Leave My Kitten Alone" and "Free At Last" are in stereo.)			
BluesWay BLS-6069	(P)	**Free At Last**	1970	10.00	25.00
JOHN'S CHILDREN					
White Whale WWS-7128	(S)	**Orgasm**	1970	80.00	200.00
JOHNNY & THE BLUE BEATS					
Winsor RL-1001	(S)	**Smile**	1968	14.00	35.00
JOHNNY & THE HURRICANES					
Warwick W-2007	(M)	**Johnny & The Hurricanes**	1959	80.00	200.00
Warwick W-2007ST	(S)	**Johnny & The Hurricanes**	1959	150.00	300.00
		("Red River Rock" is rechanneled on this album.)			
Warwick W-2010	(M)	**Stormsville**	1960	80.00	200.00
Warwick W-2010ST	(S)	**Stormsville**	1960	150.00	300.00
Big Top 12-1302	(M)	**Big Sound Of Johnny & The Hurricanes**	1960	150.00	300.00
Big Top ST-1302	(S)	**Big Sound Of Johnny & The Hurricanes**	1960	200.00	400.00
Attila 1030	(M)	**Live At The Star Club**	1965	200.00	400.00
JOHNSON, BETTY					
Atlantic 8017	(M)	**Betty Johnson**	1958	20.00	50.00
Atlantic 8027	(M)	**The Song You Heard When You Fell In Love**	1959	20.00	50.00
Atlantic SD-8027	(S)	**The Song You Heard When You Fell In Love**	1959	30.00	75.00
		—Atlantic mono albums above have black labels; stereo albums have green labels.—			
Atlantic 8027	(M)	**The Song You Heard When You Fell In Love**	196?	8.00	20.00
Atlantic SD-8027	(S)	**The Song You Heard When You Fell In Love**	196?	10.00	25.00
		—Atlantic albums above have multi-colored labels with a white "fan" logo on the right side.—			
JOHNSON, BUBBER					
King 569	(M)	**Come Home**	1957	100.00	250.00
King 624	(M)	**Sings Sweet Love Songs**	1959	60.00	150.00
JOHNSON, BUD, & THE VOICES FIVE					
Stereocraft RTN-1000	(M)	**Rock N Roll Dance Party**	1958	300.00	500.00
Stereocraft RTN-1000S	(S)	**Rock N Roll Dance Party**	1958	500.00	750.00
JOHNSON, CANDY					
Canjo LP-1001	(M)	**The Candy Johnson Show**	1964	16.00	40.00
Canjo LP-1002	(M)	**Bikini Beach**	1964	12.00	30.00
JOHNSON, COLONEL JUBILATION B., & HIS MYSTIC KNIGHTS BAND					
Columbia CL-2532	(M)	**Moldy Goldies**	1966	12.00	30.00
Columbia CS-9332	(S)	**Moldy Goldies**	1966	16.00	40.00
JOHNSON, LONNIE					
King 520	(M)	**Lonesome Road**	1958	1,000.00	2,000.00
		—King albums above have crownless black labels.—			
Bluesville BVLP-1007	(M)	**Blues By Lonnie**	1960	150.00	300.00
Bluesville BVLP-1011	(M)	**Blues And Ballads**	1960	150.00	300.00
Bluesville BVLP-1024	(M)	**Losing Game**	1961	150.00	300.00
Bluesville BVLP-1062	(M)	**Another Night To Cry**	1963	150.00	300.00
		—Bluesville albums above have bright blue labels with silver print.—			
Bluesville BVLP-1007	(M)	**Blues By Lonnie**	1964	30.00	75.00
Bluesville BVLP-1011	(M)	**Blues And Ballads**	1964	30.00	75.00
Bluesville BVLP-1024	(M)	**Losing Game**	1964	30.00	75.00
Bluesville BVLP-1062	(M)	**Another Night To Cry**	1964	30.00	75.00
		—Bluesville albums above have blue labels with a trident logo on the right side.—			
King K-958	(M)	**Lonnie Johnson 24 Twelve Bar Blues**	1966	30.00	75.00
King KS-958	(S)	**Lonnie Johnson 24 Twelve Bar Blues**	1966	40.00	100.00
King KS-1083	(S)	**Tomorrow Night**	1970	10.00	25.00

Label & Catalog #		Title	Year	VG+	NM
Prestige PRST-7724	(E)	The Blues Of Lonnie Johnson	1969	8.00	20.00
		(Prestige 7724 reissues Bluesville material.)			

JOHNSON, LONNIE, & VICTORIA SPIVEY
Lonnie Johnson also recorded with Victoria Spivey.

Bluesville BVLP-1044	(M)	Idle Hours	1962	60.00	150.00
Bluesville BVLP-1054	(M)	Woman Blues	1962	60.00	150.00
—*Bluesville albums above have bright blue labels with silver print.*—					
Bluesville BVLP-1044	(M)	Idle Hours	1964	12.00	30.00
Bluesville BVLP-1054	(M)	Woman Blues	1964	12.00	30.00
—*Bluesville albums above have blue labels with a trident logo on the right side.*—					

JOHNSON, LOU

Cotillion SD-9008	(S)	Sweet Southern Soul	1969	6.00	15.00
Volt VOS-6016	(S)	With You In Mind	1971	6.00	15.00

JOHNSON, MARV

United Arts. UAL-3081	(M)	Marvelous Marv Johnson	1960	60.00	150.00
United Arts. UAS-6081	(P)	Marvelous Marv Johnson	1960	80.00	200.00
United Arts. UAL-3118	(M)	More Marv Johnson	1961	60.00	150.00
United Arts. UAS-6118	(P)	More Marv Johnson	1961	80.00	200.00
United Arts. UAL-3187	(M)	I Believe	1962	60.00	150.00
United Arts. UAS-6187	(S)	I Believe	1962	80.00	200.00

JOHNSON, OLLIE

RCA Victor LPM-1369	(M)	A Bit Of The Blues	1957	16.00	40.00

JOHNSON, RANDY

Amaret ST-5003	(S)	The Gift Of Randy Johnson	1969	10.00	25.00

JOHNSON, ROBERT

Columbia CL-1654	(M)	King Of The Delta Blues Singers	1961	300.00	500.00
—*Columbia albums above have six white-on-black "eye" logos around the perimeter of the label.*—					
Columbia CL-1654	(M)	King Of The Delta Blues Singers	1963	20.00	50.00
—*Columbia albums above have "Guaranteed High Fidelity" labels.*—					
Columbia CL-1654	(M)	King Of The Delta Blues Singers	1965	10.00	25.00
—*Columbia albums above have "360 Sound Mono" labels.*—					
Columbia CL-1654	(M)	King Of The Delta Blues Singers	1970	4.00	10.00
Columbia C-30034	(M)	King Of The Delta Blues Singers, Volume 2	1970	4.00	10.00
—*Columbia albums above have "Columbia" in gold around the perimeter of the label.*—					
Columbia C3-46222	(M)	The Complete Recordings Of Robert Johnson (3 LP box)	1990	16.00	40.00

JOHNSON, SYL

Twinight LPS-1002	(S)	Is It Because I'm Black?	1972	16.00	40.00
Hi SHL-32081	(S)	Back For A Taste Of Your Love	1973	8.00	20.00
Hi SHL-32085	(S)	Diamond In The Rough	1974	8.00	20.00
Hi SHL-32096	(S)	Total Explosion	1975	8.00	20.00

JOHNSON, "BLIND" WILLIE

Folkways FG-3585	(M)	Blind Willie Johnson: His Story	195?	40.00	100.00
RBF 10	(M)	Blind Willie Johnson 1927-1930	1965	30.00	75.00
Yazoo L-1058	(M)	Praise God I'm Satisfied	197?	6.00	15.00
Yazoo L-1078	(M)	Sweeter As The Years Go By	197?	6.00	15.00

JOHNSTON, BRUCE
Mr Johnston has been a member of The Beach Boys since 1966. Refer to The Catalinas; The De-Fenders; The Hot Doggers; The Rip Chords; The Vettes.

Del-Fi DFLP-1228	(M)	Surfers' Pajama Party	1963	40.00	100.00
Del-Fi DFST-1228	(S)	Surfers' Pajama Party	1963	80.00	200.00
		(Del-Fi 1228 was also issued by Del-Fi credited to The Centurions. It was reissued as 1236 credited to The Surf Stompers.)			
Columbia CL-2057	(M)	Surfin' 'Round The World	1963	50.00	125.00
Columbia CS-8857	(S)	Surfin' 'Round The World	1963	100.00	250.00
Columbia KC-34459	(S)	Going Public (Produced by Gary Usher)	1976	6.00	15.00

JOHNSTONS, THE

Tetragrammaton 110	(S)	Both Sides Now	1969	6.00	15.00
Vanguard VSD-6572	(S)	Colours Of The Dawn	1971	5.00	12.00
Mercury SRM-1-640	(S)	The Johnstons	1972	5.00	12.00

JOLLIVER ARKANSAS

Bell 6031	(S)	Home	1969	6.00	15.00

JON & ROBIN

Abnak AB-M2068	(M)	Soul Of A Boy And Girl	1967	4.00	10.00
Abnak ABST-M2068	(P)	Soul Of A Boy And Girl	1967	4.00	10.00
Abnak ABST-M2070	(S)	Elastic Event	1968	4.00	10.00

The recording career of Bruce Johnston includes solo albums for Del-Fi and Columbia and as the impetus for a potpourri of groups such as The De-Fenders (on World Pacific), The Hot Doggers (Epic), The Catalinas (Ric) and, with Terry Melcher, as Bruce & Terry and The Rip Chords (Columbia). He was therefore more than qualified when the opportunity to join the fabled Beach Boys presented itself in 1965, after which he quickly became the seventh "official" member. Surfin' 'Round The World has been sought after by surf and Beach Boys collectors for decades and the demand shows no signs of abating.

Label & Catalog #		Title	Year	VG+	NM
JONES, BRIAN					
Brian Jones was a member of The Rolling Stones.					
Roll. Stones RSR-49100	(S)	**Pipes Of Pan At Joujouka** (With inserts)	1971	24.00	60.00
JONES, CURTIS					
Bluesville BVLP-1022	(M)	**Trouble Blues**	1961	30.00	75.00
		—Bluesville albums above have bright blue labels with silver print.—			
Bluesville BVLP-1022	(M)	**Trouble Blues**	1964	10.00	25.00
		—Bluesville albums above have blue labels with a trident logo on the right side.—			
Delmar DL-605	(M)	**Lonesome Bedroom Blues**	1963	16.00	40.00
Blue Horizon BH-7703	(S)	**New Resident In Europe**	1972	1.20	6.00
JONES, DAVY [DAVID JONES]					
Davy Jones was a member of The Monkees. Refer to Dolenz, Jones, Boyce & Hart.					
Colpix CP-493	(M)	**David Jones**	1965	10.00	25.00
Colpix SCP-493	(S)	**David Jones**	1965	16.00	40.00
Bell 6067	(S)	**Davy Jones**	1971	8.00	20.00
JONES, JIM, & THE CHAUNTEYS					
Sunglow SLP-113	(S)	**Soul Clap**	196?	20.00	50.00
JONES, JIMMY					
MGM E-3847	(M)	**Good Timin'**	1960	60.00	150.00
MGM SE-3847	(E)	**Good Timin'**	1960	80.00	200.00
		("I Just Go For You" is in stereo on this album.)			
Jen Jillus 1001	(S)	**The Handy Man's Back In Town**	1977	4.00	10.00
JONES, JOE					
Roulette R-25143	(M)	**You Talk Too Much**	1961	60.00	150.00
Roulette SR-25143	(E)	**You Talk Too Much**	1961	40.00	100.00
JONES, JOHN PAUL					
Columbia KC-32047	(S)	**John Paul Jones**	1973	4.00	10.00
JONES, LINDA					
Loma 5907	(S)	**Hypnotized**	1967	10.00	25.00
Turbo 7007	(S)	**Your Precious Love**	196?	10.00	25.00
JONES, MORDECAI					
Polydor PD-5010	(S)	**Mordecai Jones** (With Link Wray)	197?	6.00	15.00
JONES, PAUL					
Mr Jones was a member of Manfred Mann. He can also be found on the Uni soundtrack "Privilege."					
Capitol T-2795	(M)	**Songs From The Film "Privilege"**	1967	12.00	30.00
Capitol ST-2795	(S)	**Songs From The Film "Privilege"**	1967	12.00	30.00
London XPS-605	(S)	**Crucifix In A Horseshoe**	1971	4.00	10.00
JONES, RICKIE LEE					
Warner Bros. 3296	(S)	**Rickie Lee Jones**	1979	1.00	5.00
Warner Bros. 3432	(S)	**Pirates**	1981	1.00	5.00
Warner Bros. 23805	(S)	**Girl At Her Volcano** (10")	1983	3.20	8.00
Warner Bros. 25117	(S)	**The Mafazine**	1984	1.00	5.00
JONES, RUBY					
Curtom CRS-8011	(S)	**Ruby Jones**	1971	4.00	10.00
JONES, RUFUS					
Cameo C-1076	(M)	**Five On Eight**	1964	10.00	25.00
Cameo SC-1076	(S)	**Five On Eight**	1964	16.00	40.00
JOPLIN, JANIS					
Janis was a member of Big Brother & The Holding Company. Refer to Hot Tuna.					
Columbia KCS-9913	(S)	**I Got Dem Ol' Kozmic Blues Again Mama!**	1969	6.00	15.00
		—Columbia albums above have "360 Sound" labels.—			
Columbia KCS-9913	(S)	**I Got Dem Ol' Kozmic Blues Again Mama!**	1970	.80	4.00
Columbia KC-30322	(S)	**Pearl**	1971	3.20	8.00
Columbia PC-30322	(S)	**Pearl**	1975	.80	4.00
Columbia CQ-30322	(Q)	**Pearl**	1974	6.00	15.00
Columbia KC-31160	(S)	**Janis Joplin In Concert** (2 LPs)	1972	3.20	8.00
Columbia PC-31160	(S)	**Janis Joplin In Concert** (2 LPs)	1972	1.00	5.00
Columbia KC-32168	(S)	**Janis Joplin's Greatest Hits**	1973	1.00	5.00
Columbia PC-32168	(S)	**Janis Joplin's Greatest Hits**	1975	.80	4.00
Columbia KC-31160	(S)	**Janis Joplin In Concert** (2 LPs)	1972	3.20	8.00
Columbia Sp. Prod. 13792	(S)	**The Greatest Hits Of Janis Joplin** (2 LPs)	1977	6.00	15.00
Columbia PG-33345	(M)	**Early Performances** (2 LPs)	1975	1.20	6.00
Columbia PC-37569	(S)	**A Farewell Song** (Banded for air-play)	1982	14.00	35.00
Columbia PC-37569	(S)	**A Farewell Song**	1982	1.00	5.00
Columbia AS-1377	(S)	**A Collection** (Promo sampler)	1982	8.00	20.00

After leaving his vocal group background (he had been the lead with *The Savoys* and *The Pretenders*), Jimmy Jones hit the Top 5 on the national pop charts in 1960 with the perennially popular "Handy Man." This was quickly followed by "Good Timin.'" When MGM collected these sides on LP, they rechanneled the mono tapes into ersatz stereo, although the customer would not know that from the cover. While it is generally the mono pressing that collectors seek out when fake stereo was used, in some cases the stereo pressing is so much rarer that it commands a higher price. Such as with Mr Jones' Good Timin' album.

Label & Catalog #		Title	Year	VG+	NM
JORDAN, CLIFFORD					
Vortex 2010	(S)	Soul Fountain	1970	4.00	10.00
JORDAN, KING					
Coral CRL-57372	(M)	Phantom Guitar	1962	8.00	20.00
Coral CRL-757372	(S)	Phantom Guitar	1962	10.00	25.00
JOSEFUS					
Josefus' first album was privately pressed.					
Mainstream 6127	(S)	Josefus	1970	60.00	150.00
JOSEPH					
Scepter 574	(S)	Stoned Age Man	1970	30.00	75.00
JOSEPH, MARGIE					
Volt VOS-6012	(S)	Margie Joseph Makes A New Impression	1971	12.00	30.00
Volt VOS-6016	(S)	Phase II	1971	12.00	30.00
Atlantic SD-7248	(S)	Margie Joseph	1973	4.00	10.00
Atlantic SD-7277	(S)	Sweet Surrender	1974	4.00	10.00
JOSHUA FOX					
Tetragrammaton 125	(S)	Joshua Fox	1968	8.00	20.00
JOURNEY					
Members of this seminal '70s corporate-rock band originally recorded with Faun.					
Columbia PC-33388	(S)	Journey	1975	.80	4.00
Columbia AS-914	(S)	Journey (Promo sampler)	1975	4.00	10.00
Columbia PC-33904	(S)	Look Into The Future	1976	.80	4.00
Columbia PCQ-33904	(Q)	Look Into The Future	1976	4.00	10.00
Columbia PC-34311	(S)	Next	1977	.80	4.00
Columbia AS-1606	(S)	A Candid Conversation (Promo)	197?	4.00	10.00
Columbia JC-34912	(S)	Infinity	1978	.80	4.00
Columbia HC-44912	(S)	Infinity (Half-speed master)	1981	6.00	15.00
Columbia FC-35797	(S)	Evolution	1979	.80	4.00
Columbia FC-36324	(S)	In The Beginning (2 LPs)	1980	1.00	5.00
Columbia FC-36339	(S)	Departure	1980	.80	4.00
Columbia HC-46339	(S)	Departure (Half-speed master)	1981	6.00	15.00
Columbia KC2-37016	(S)	Captured (2 LPs)	1981	1.00	5.00
Columbia TC-37408	(S)	Escape	1981	.80	4.00
Columbia HC-47408	(S)	Escape (Half-speed master)	1981	6.00	15.00
Columbia QC-38504	(S)	Frontiers	1983	.80	4.00
Columbia FC-37998	(S)	Dream After Dream	1982	.80	4.00
Columbia HC-47998	(S)	Dream After Dream (Half-speed master)	1982	6.00	15.00
JOURNEYMEN, THE					
The vocal and instrumental Journeymen were John Phillips, Scott McKenzie and Dick Weissman.					
Capitol T-1629	(M)	The Journeymen	1961	10.00	25.00
Capitol ST-1629	(S)	The Journeymen	1961	12.00	30.00
Capitol T-1770	(M)	Coming Attraction—Live!	1962	10.00	25.00
Capitol ST-1770	(S)	Coming Attraction—Live!	1962	12.00	30.00
Capitol T-1951	(M)	New Directions In Folk Music	1963	10.00	25.00
Capitol ST-1951	(S)	New Directions In Folk Music	1963	12.00	30.00
JOY					
Paula LPS-2217	(S)	Thunderfoot	1972	6.00	15.00
JOY DIVISION					
Members of Joy Division later recorded as New Order.					
Rough Trade FACT-1	(S)	Unknown Pleasures	1979	4.00	10.00
Rough Trade FACT-6	(S)	Closer (Purple tinted vinyl)	1980	20.00	50.00
Rough Trade FACT-6	(S)	Closer (Red tinted vinyl)	1980	10.00	25.00
JOY OF COOKING					
JOC features Toni Browne and Terry Garthwaite.					
Capitol ST-661	(S)	Joy Of Cooking	1970	6.00	15.00
Capitol SMAS-828	(S)	Closer To The Ground	1971	6.00	15.00
Capitol ST-11050	(S)	Castles	1972	4.00	10.00
JOY UNLIMITED					
Mercury SRM-61283	(S)	Joy Unlimited	1970	10.00	25.00
B.A.S.F. 21090	(S)	Butterflies	1972	10.00	25.00
JOYFULL NOISE					
RCA Victor LSP-3963	(S)	Joyfull Noise	1968	6.00	15.00
JOYOUS NOISE					
Capitol SMAS-844	(S)	Joyous Noise	1971	6.00	15.00

Label & Catalog #		Title	Year	VG+	NM
JUAREZ					
Decca DL-75189	(S)	**Juarez**	1970	4.00	10.00
JUBAL					
Jubal features Dennis Linde.					
Elektra EKS-75033	(S)	**Jubal**	1972	4.00	10.00
JUDAS JUMP					
Capitol SKAO-645	(S)	**Scorch**	1970	4.00	10.00
Pride 003	(S)	**Scorch**	1970	4.00	10.00
JUDAS PRIEST					
Visa IMP-7001	(S)	**Rocka-Rolla**	1974	10.00	25.00
Ovation 1751	(S)	**Sad Wines Of Destiny**	1976	10.00	25.00
Columbia 35296	(S)	**Stained Glass**	1978	1.00	5.00
Columbia 35706	(S)	**Hell Bent For Leather**	1979	1.00	5.00
Columbia 36179	(S)	**Unleashed In The East—Live In Japan**	1979	1.00	5.00
Columbia 36443	(S)	**British Steel**	1980	1.00	5.00
Columbia 37052	(S)	**Point Of Entry**	1981	1.00	5.00
Columbia 38160	(S)	**Screaming For Vengeance**	1982	1.00	5.00
Columbia 39219	(S)	**Defenders Of The Faith**	1984	1.00	5.00
Columbia 9C9-39926	(DJ)	**Screaming For Vengeance** *(Picture disc)*	1984	8.00	20.00
		(Mispressing plays Neil Diamond's "Heartlight" album.)			
Columbia 9C9-39926	(DJ)	**Screaming For Vengeance** *(Picture disc)*	1984	5.00	12.00
JUICY LUCY					
Atco SD-33-325	(S)	**Juicy Lucy**	1970	6.00	15.00
Atco SD-33-345	(S)	**Lie Back And Enjoy It**	1970	6.00	15.00
Atco SD-33-367	(S)	**Get A Whiff Of This**	1971	6.00	15.00
JUKIN' BONE					
RCA Victor LSP-4621	(S)	**Whiskey Woman**	1972	4.00	10.00
RCA Victor LSP-4768	(S)	**Way Down East**	1972	4.00	10.00
JULIAN, DON					
Refer to The Larks.					
Amazon 1009	(M)	**Greatest Oldies**	1963	24.00	60.00
JULIAN'S TREATMENT					
Decca DL-75224	(S)	**A Time Before This**	1970	10.00	25.00
JULY					
Epic BN-26416	(E)	**July**	1969	100.00	250.00
JUMP					
Janus 3029	(S)	**Jump**	1971	4.00	10.00
JUNIOR'S EYES					
A&M SP-4189	(S)	**Junior's Eyes**	1970	12.00	30.00
JUPITER					
Jupiter 1005	(S)	**Multiple Choice**	1980	20.00	50.00
JUSTICE, JIMMY					
Kapp KL-1308	(M)	**Justice For All**	1964	10.00	25.00
Kapp KS-3308	(S)	**Justice For All**	1964	14.00	35.00

K-DOE, ERNIE

Minit LP-4002	(M)	Mother-In-Law	1961	80.00	200.00
Minit LP-24002	(E)	Mother-In-Law	1961	150.00	300.00
Janus JLS-3030	(S)	Ernie K-Doe	1971	10.00	25.00

KAK

Epic BN-26429	(S)	Kak	1969	100.00	250.00

KALB, DANNY, & STEFAN GROSSMAN
Kalb and Grossman were members of The Blues Project.

Cotillion SD-90007	(S)	Crosscurrents	1969	6.00	15.00

KALEIDOSCOPE
Kaleidoscope displays the multi-instrumental virtuosity of David Lindley.

Epic LN-24304	(M)	Side Trips	1967	12.00	30.00
Epic BN-26304	(S)	Side Trips	1967	16.00	40.00
Epic LN-24333	(M)	Beacon From Mars	1967	24.00	60.00
Epic BN-26333	(S)	Beacon From Mars	1967	40.00	100.00
Epic BN-26467	(S)	Incredible Kaleidoscope	1969	10.00	25.00
Epic BN-26508	(S)	Bernice	1970	10.00	25.00
Pacific Arts 102	(S)	When Scopes Collide	1978	4.00	10.00

KALIN TWINS, THE

Decca DL-8812	(M)	The Kalin Twins	1959	40.00	100.00

KAMEN, MICHAEL
Michael Kamen also recorded with The New York Rock Ensemble.

Atco SD-7020	(S)	New York Rock	1973	4.00	10.00

KANGAROO
Kangaroo features Barbara Keith.

MGM SE-4586	(S)	Kangaroo	1968	10.00	25.00

KANNIBAL KOMIX

Colossus 1004	(S)	Kannibal Komix	1970	8.00	20.00

KANSAS

Kirshner KZ-32817	(S)	Kansas	1974	1.00	5.00
Kirshner PZ-33385	(S)	Song For America	1975	1.00	5.00
Kirshner PZ-33806	(S)	Masque	1975	1.00	5.00
Kirshner JZ-34224	(S)	Leftoverture	1976	1.00	5.00
Kirshner HZ-44224	(S)	Leftoverture (Half-speed master)	1982	12.00	35.00
Kirshner JZ-34929	(S)	Point Of Know Return	1977	1.00	5.00
Kirshner JZ-34929	(DJ)	Point Of Know Return (Picture disc)	1979	20.00	50.00
Kirshner HZ-44929	(S)	Point Of Know Return (Half-speed master)	1982	15.00	45.00
Kirshner AS-555	(DJ)	Two For The Show (Sampler)	1978	6.00	15.00
Kirshner PZ2-35660	(S)	Two For The Show (2 LPs)	1978	1.00	5.00
Kirshner FZ-36008	(S)	Monolith	1979	1.00	5.00
Kirshner HZ-46008	(S)	Monolith (Half-speed master)	1982	15.00	45.00
Kirshner FZ-36588	(S)	Audio-Visions	1980	1.00	5.00
Kirshner JZ-38002	(S)	Vinyl Confessions	1982	1.00	5.00
Kirshner HZ-48002	(S)	Vinyl Confessions (Half-speed master)	1982	10.00	30.00

KANTNER, PAUL, & JEFFERSON STARSHIP
Mr Kantner called his band on this science fiction-ish concept album Jefferson Starship to dissociate it with his regular group, Jefferson Airplane. Upon the Airplane's demise, he continued with the newly named Starship.

RCA Victor LSP-4448	(DJ)	Blows Against The Empire (Clear vinyl)	1970	60.00	150.00
RCA Victor LSP-4448	(S)	Blows Against The Empire	1970	6.00	15.00
		—RCA albums above have orange labels on non-flexible vinyl.—			
RCA Victor LSP-4448	(S)	Blows Against The Empire	1972	1.00	5.00
		—RCA albums above have orange labels on flexible vinyl.—			

KANTNER, PAUL, & GRACE SLICK
Kantner and Slick are members of Jefferson Airplane and Jefferson Starship.

Grunt FTR-1002	(S)	Sunfighter (With booklet)	1971	6.00	15.00
Grunt BXL1-0148	(S)	Baron Von Tollbooth And The Chrome Nun	1973	4.00	10.00

Label & Catalog #		Title	Year	VG+	NM

KASENETZ-KATZ CIRCUS, THE
Writers and producers Jerry Kasenetz and Jeff Katz were the creative impetus behind the Buddah-based "bubble gum music" of the late '60s. The two projects below consist of K&K with latter-day Shadows Of Knight backing members of such rock'n roll luminaries as The 1910 Fruitgum Company, The Ohio Express, and The Music Explosion.

Buddah BDS-5020	(S)	Kasenetz-Katz Singing Orchestral Circus	1968	4.00	10.00
Buddah BDS-5028	(S)	Kasenetz-Katz Super Circus	1968	4.00	10.00

KATMANDO

Mainstream 6131	(S)	Katmando	1971	16.00	40.00

KAUKONEN, JORMA
Jorma was a member of Jefferson Airplane. Refer to Jefferson Starship; Hot Tuna.

Grunt BFL1-0209	(S)	Quah	1973	4.00	10.00
Relix 2027	(S)	Quah (Picture disc)	1987	4.00	10.00

KAUKONEN, PETER
Peter is Jorma's brother.

Grunt FTR-1006	(S)	Black Kangaroo	1972	4.00	10.00

KAY, JOHN
John Kay is the former lead singer for Steppenwolf.

Dunhill DSX-50120	(S)	Forgotten Songs And Unsung Heros	1972	4.00	10.00
Dunhill DSX-50147	(S)	My Sportin' Life	1973	4.00	10.00
Mercury SRM-1-3715	(S)	All In Good Time	1978	4.00	10.00

KAY, JOHN, & SPARROW
Sparrow became Steppenwolf. The tracks on this album were recorded in 1966-67.

Columbia CS-9758	(S)	John Kay & Sparrow	1970	14.00	35.00
		—Columbia albums above have "360 Sound" labels.—			

KAYE, THOMAS JEFFERSON

Dunhill DSX-50142	(S)	First Grade	1974	6.00	15.00

KAZ, ERIC
Eric Kaz also recorded with The Blues Magoos; American Flyer.

Atlantic SD-7246	(S)	If You're Lonely	1973	4.00	10.00
Atlantic SD-7290	(S)	Cul-De-Sac	1973	4.00	10.00

KEACK, ALEX

Crown CLP-5315	(M)	For Surfers Only/Surfer's Paradise	1963	6.00	15.00
Crown CST-315	(S)	For Surfers Only/Surfer's Paradise	1963	8.00	20.00
		—Crown albums above have gray labels.—			

KEEN, SPEEDY
Speedy was a member of Thunderclap Newman.

Track/MCA 331	(S)	Previous Convictions	1973	6.00	15.00
Island ILPS-9338	(S)	Y' Know Wot I Mean	1975	4.00	10.00

KEITH

Mercury MG-21102	(M)	98.6/Ain't Gonna Lie	1967	6.00	15.00
Mercury SR-61102	(S)	98.6/Ain't Gonna Lie	1967	8.00	20.00
Mercury MG-21129	(M)	Out Of Crank	1967	6.00	15.00
Mercury SR-61129	(S)	Out Of Crank	1967	8.00	20.00
RCA Victor LSP-4143	(S)	The Adventures Of Keith	1969	6.00	15.00

KEITH, BARBARA
Ms. Keith also recorded with Kangaroo.

Verve/Forecast FTS-3062	(S)	Barbara Keith	1970	8.00	20.00
Warner Bros. MS-2087	(S)	Barbara Keith	1972	20.00	50.00

KELLER, JERRY

Kapp KL-1178	(M)	Here Comes Jerry Keller	1960	14.00	35.00
Kapp KS-3178	(S)	Here Comes Jerry Keller	1960	20.00	50.00

KELLY, CASEY

Elektra EKS-75040	(S)	Casey Kelly	1972	4.00	10.00

KELLY, PAUL

Happy Tiger 1015	(S)	Stealing In The Name Of The Lord	1970	6.00	15.00

KELLY BROTHERS, THE

King 810	(M)	The Kelly Brothers Sing A Page Of Songs From The Good Book	1962	40.00	100.00
Excello 8007	(M)	Sweet Soul	196?	20.00	50.00

KENDRICKS, EDDIE
Eddie Kendricks was the lead singer for The Temptations.

Tamla T6-309	(S)	All By Myself	1971	3.20	8.00
Tamla T6-315	(S)	People Hold On	1972	3.20	8.00

Label & Catalog #		Title	Year	VG+	NM
Tamla T6-327	(S)	**Eddie Kendricks**	1973	**3.20**	**8.00**
Tamla T6-330	(S)	**Boogie Down**	1974	**3.20**	**8.00**
Tamla T6-335	(S)	**For You**	1974	**3.20**	**8.00**
Tamla T6-338	(S)	**Hit Man**	1975	**3.20**	**8.00**
Tamla T6-343	(S)	**He's A Friend**	1976	**3.20**	**8.00**
Tamla T6-346	(S)	**Goin' Up In Smoke**	1976	**3.20**	**8.00**
Tamla T7-354	(S)	**Eddie Kendricks At His Best**	1978	**3.20**	**8.00**
Tamla T8-356	(S)	**Slick**	1977	**3.20**	**8.00**
Arista AB-4170	(S)	**Vintage '78**	1978	**1.00**	**5.00**
Atlantic SD-19294	(S)	**Love Keys**	1981	**1.00**	**5.00**
Motown M5-119V	(S)	**Superstsr Series, Vol. 19**	1981	**.80**	**4.00**
Motown M5-196V	(S)	**He's A Friend**	1982	**.80**	**4.00**

KENNEDY, HARRISON
Invictus 9806	(S)	**Hypnotic Music**	1972	**4.00**	**10.00**

KENNEDY, MIKE
Mike Kennedy was the lead singer for Los Bravos.
ABC X-754	(S)	**Louisiana**	1972	**6.00**	**15.00**

KENNEDY, RAY
Cream 9001	(S)	**Raymond Louis Kennedy**	1972	**4.00**	**10.00**

KENNER, CHRIS
Atlantic 8117	(M)	**Land Of 1,000 Dances**	1965	**30.00**	**75.00**

KENSINGTON MARKET
Warner Bros. WS-1754	(S)	**Avenue Road** *(Bordered cover)*	1968	**6.00**	**15.00**
Warner Bros. WS-1754	(S)	**Avenue Road**	1968	**4.00**	**10.00**
Warner Bros. WS-1780	(S)	**Aardvark**	1969	**4.00**	**10.00**

KENTUCKY EXPRESS
Cream 9002	(S)	**That's Not What Lovin' Is**	1971	**4.00**	**10.00**

KEYMEN, THE
Coral CRL-57112	(M)	**Vocal Sounds Of The Keymen**	1957	**14.00**	**35.00**
ABC-Paramount ABC-288	(M)	**Dance With Dick Clark**	1958	**14.00**	**35.00**
ABC-Paramount ABCS-288	(S)	**Dance With Dick Clark**	1958	**20.00**	**50.00**
ABC-Paramount ABC-288	(M)	**Dance With Dick Clark, Volume 2**	1959	**14.00**	**35.00**
ABC-Paramount ABCS-288	(S)	**Dance With Dick Clark, Volume 2**	1959	**20.00**	**50.00**
		(Both of the ABC albums feature Mr Clark solely on the cover.)			
Goldust LPS-153	(S)	**The Keymen Live**	196?	**20.00**	**50.00**

KICKSTANDS, THE
The Kickstands are a creation of Gary Usher & Co.
Capitol T-2078	(M)	**Black Boots And Bikes**	1964	**60.00**	**150.00**
Capitol ST-2078	(S)	**Black Boots And Bikes**	1964	**80.00**	**200.00**
		(Capitol 2078 included a fold-open, 12" x 10" color photo of a bike with a hot rod catalog on the back. This is priced separately below.)			
Capitol 2078		**Black Boots And Bikes Bonus Photo**	1964	**20.00**	**50.00**

KID GLOVES
Buddah BDS-5124	(S)	**Kid Gloves**	1972	**4.00**	**10.00**

KIHN, GREG
Beserkley 0046	(S)	**Greg Kihn**	1976	**4.00**	**10.00**
Beserkley 0052	(S)	**Greg Kihn Again**	1977	**4.00**	**10.00**
Beserkley 0056	(S)	**Next Of Kihn**	1978	**4.00**	**10.00**
Beserkley BZ-10063	(S)	**With The Naked Eye**	1979	**1.00**	**5.00**
Beserkley BZ-10068	(S)	**Glasshouse Rock**	1980	**1.00**	**5.00**
Beserkley AS-11506	(S)	**The Greg Kihn Band** *(Promo)*	1981	**4.00**	**10.00**
Beserkley BZ-10069	(S)	**Rockihnroll**	1981	**1.00**	**5.00**
Beserkley E1-60101	(S)	**Kihntinued**	1982	**1.00**	**5.00**
Beserkley E1-60116	(S)	**Next Of Kihn**	1982	**1.00**	**5.00**
Beserkley E1-60117	(S)	**Greg Kihn Again**	1982	**1.00**	**5.00**
Beserkley E1-60224	(S)	**Kihnspiracy**	1983	**1.00**	**5.00**
Beserkley E1-60354	(S)	**Kihntagious**	1984	**1.00**	**5.00**

KILLING FLOOR
Killing Floor features Rory Gallagher.
Sire SES-97019	(S)	**Killing Floor**	1970	**20.00**	**50.00**

KIM, ANDY
Steed STS-37001	(S)	**How'd We Ever Get This Way**	1968	**6.00**	**15.00**
Steed STS-37002	(S)	**Rainbow Ride**	1969	**6.00**	**15.00**
Steed STS-37004	(S)	**Baby I Love You**	1969	**6.00**	**15.00**
Uni 73137	(S)	**Andy Kim**	1972	**4.00**	**10.00**

Label & Catalog #		Title	Year	VG+	NM
Steed STS-37008	(S)	Andy Kim's Greatest Hits	1973	4.00	10.00
Capitol ST-11318	(S)	Andy Kim	1974	4.00	10.00
Dunhill DSDP-50193	(S)	Andy Kim's Greatest Hits	1974	4.00	10.00
KINDRED					
Warner Bros. BS-1931	(S)	Kindred	1971	4.00	10.00
Warner Bros. BS-2640	(S)	Next Of Kin	1972	4.00	10.00
KING, ALBERT					
King 852	(M)	Big Blues	1963	200.00	400.00
Stax ST-723	(M)	Born Under A Bad Sign	1967	40.00	100.00
Stax STS-723	(S)	Born Under A Bad Sign	1967	60.00	150.00
Stax STS-2003	(S)	Live Wire/Blues Power	1968	20.00	50.00
King KS-1060	(S)	Travelin' To California	1969	10.00	25.00
Atlantic SD-8213	(S)	King Of The Blues Guitar	1969	10.00	25.00
Stax STS-2010	(S)	Years Gone By	1969	10.00	25.00
Stax STS-2015	(S)	King Does The King's Thing	1969	10.00	25.00
Stax STS-2040	(S)	Love Joy	1971	10.00	25.00
Stax STS-3009	(S)	I'll Play The Blues For You	1972	10.00	25.00
Stax STL-4101	(S)	The Pinch	1977	6.00	15.00
Stax STS-5505	(S)	I Wanna Get Funky	1974	6.00	15.00
Stax MPS-8513	(S)	I'll Play The Blues For You	198?	3.20	8.00
Stax MPS-8522	(S)	Years Gone By	198?	3.20	8.00
Stax MPS-8534	(S)	The Lost Session	198?	3.20	8.00
Stax MPS-8536	(S)	I Wanna Get Funky	198?	3.20	8.00
Stax MPS-8546	(S)	Blues At Sunrise	1988	3.20	8.00
Stax MPS-8556	(S)	Wednesday Night In San Francisco	1990	3.20	8.00
Stax MPS-8557	(S)	Thursday Night In San Francisco	1990	3.20	8.00
Utopia BUL1-1387	(S)	Truckload Of Lovin'	1975	3.20	8.00
Utopia BUL1-1731	(S)	Albert	1976	3.20	8.00
Utopia CYL2-2205	(S)	Albert Live (2 LPs)	1976	4.00	10.00
Tomato TOM-6002	(S)	King Albert	1977	3.20	8.00
Tomato TOM-7022	(S)	New Orleans Heat	1978	3.20	8.00
Atlantic AD-2-4402	(S)	Masterworks (2 LPs)	1982	4.00	10.00
Fantasy F-9627	(S)	San Francisco '83	1983	3.20	8.00
Fantasy F-9633	(S)	I'm In A Phone Booth, Baby	1984	3.20	8.00
KING, ALBERT, & JOHN LEE HOOKER					
Tomato 2696142	(S)	I'll Play The Blues For You	1989	3.20	8.00
KING, ALBERT, & LITTLE MILTON					
Stax STX-4123	(S)	Chronicle	1979	4.00	10.00
KING, ALBERT, & STEVE CROPPER, & POP STAPLES					
Stax STS-2020	(S)	Jammed Together	1971	10.00	25.00
KING, ALBERT, & OTIS RUSH					
Chess LPS-1538	(S)	Door To Door	1969	10.00	25.00
KING, ANNA					
Ms King's soul outing was produced by James Brown.					
Smash MGS-27059	(M)	**Back To Soul**	1964	40.00	100.00
Smash SRS-67059	(S)	**Back To Soul**	1964	60.00	150.00

KING, B. B.

Riley "Blues Boy" King is the definitive blues guitarist and singer. His early recordings from the '50s were for RPM. These sides were issued— and continually resissued— on such less than stellar labels as Crown, Kent, Custom and United (among others). His affiliation with ABC-Paramount and its BluesWay subsidiary began in 1961. Refer to Bobby Bland / B. B. King.

Crown CLP-5020	(M)	Singin' The Blues	1957	40.00	100.00
Crown CLP-5063	(M)	The Blues	1958	40.00	100.00
Crown CLP-5115	(M)	B. B. King Wails	1959	40.00	100.00
Crown CLP-5119	(M)	B. B. King Sings Spirituals	1960	30.00	75.00
Crown CLP-5143	(M)	The Great B. B. King	1961	30.00	75.00
Crown CLP-5167	(M)	King Of The Blues	1961	30.00	75.00
Crown CLP-5188	(M)	My Kind Of Blues	1961	30.00	75.00
Crown CLP-5230	(M)	More B. B. King	1962	30.00	75.00
Crown CLP-5248	(M)	Twist With B. B. King	1962	30.00	75.00
Crown CLP-5286	(M)	Easy Listening Blues	1962	30.00	75.00
— Crown albums above have black labels with a silver "Crown" on top.—					
Crown CLP-5020	(M)	Singin' The Blues	196?	8.00	20.00
Crown CST-???	(E)	Singin' The Blues	196?	4.00	10.00
Crown CLP-5063	(M)	The Blues	196?	8.00	20.00
Crown CST-???	(E)	The Blues	196?	4.00	10.00
Crown CLP-5115	(M)	B. B. King Wails	196?	8.00	20.00
Crown CST-147	(E)	B. B. King Wails (Red vinyl)	196?	20.00	50.00
Crown CST-147	(E)	B. B. King Wails	196?	4.00	10.00
Crown CLP-5119	(M)	B. B. King Sings Spirituals	196?	8.00	20.00
Crown CST-152	(E)	B. B. King Sings Spirituals (Red vinyl)	196?	20.00	50.00

Label & Catalog #		Title	Year	VG+	NM
Crown CLP-5143	(M)	The Great B. B. King	1961	8.00	20.00
Crown CST-???	(E)	The Great B. B. King	1961	4.00	10.00
Crown CLP-5167	(M)	King Of The Blues	1961	8.00	20.00
Crown CST-195	(E)	King Of The Blues (Red vinyl)	1961	20.00	50.00
Crown CST-5195	(E)	King Of The Blues	1961	4.00	10.00
Crown CLP-5188	(M)	My Kind Of Blues	1961	8.00	20.00
Crown CST-212	(E)	My Kind Of Blues	1961	4.00	10.00
Crown CLP-5230	(M)	More B. B. King	1962	8.00	20.00
Crown CST-???	(E)	More B. B. King	1962	4.00	10.00
Crown CLP-5248	(M)	Twist With B. B. King	1962	8.00	20.00
Crown CST-???	(E)	Twist With B. B. King	1962	4.00	10.00
Crown CLP-5286	(M)	Easy Listening Blues	1962	8.00	20.00
Crown CST-???	(E)	Easy Listening Blues	1962	4.00	10.00
Crown CLP-5309	(M)	Blues In My Heart	1962	8.00	20.00
Crown CST-309	(E)	Blues In My Heart	1962	4.00	10.00
Crown CLP-5359	(M)	B. B. King	1963	8.00	20.00
Crown CST-359	(E)	B. B. King	1963	4.00	10.00
		—Crown albums above have gray labels.—			
Crown CLP-5020	(M)	Singin' The Blues	1957	4.00	10.00
Crown CST-???	(E)	Singin' The Blues	196?	1.00	5.00
Crown CLP-5063	(M)	The Blues	1958	4.00	10.00
Crown CST-???	(E)	The Blues	196?	1.00	5.00
Crown CLP-5115	(M)	B. B. King Wails	1959	4.00	10.00
Crown CST-147	(E)	B. B. King Wails	196?	1.00	5.00
Crown CLP-5119	(M)	B. B. King Sings Spirituals	196?	4.00	10.00
Crown CST-152	(E)	B. B. King Sings Spirituals	196?	1.00	5.00
Crown CLP-5143	(M)	The Great B. B. King	196?	4.00	10.00
Crown CST-???	(E)	The Great B. B. King	196?	1.00	5.00
Crown CLP-5167	(M)	King Of The Blues	196?	4.00	10.00
Crown CST-195	(E)	King Of The Blues	196?	1.00	5.00
Crown CLP-5188	(M)	My Kind Of Blues	196?	4.00	10.00
Crown CST-212	(E)	My Kind Of Blues	196?	1.00	5.00
Crown CLP-5230	(M)	More B. B. King	196?	4.00	10.00
Crown CST-???	(E)	More B. B. King	196?	1.00	5.00
Crown CLP-5248	(M)	Twist With B. B. King	196?	4.00	10.00
Crown CST-???	(E)	Twist With B. B. King	196?	1.00	5.00
Crown CLP-5286	(M)	Easy Listening Blues	196?	4.00	10.00
Crown CST-???	(E)	Easy Listening Blues	196?	1.00	5.00
Crown CLP-5309	(M)	Blues In My Heart	196?	4.00	10.00
Crown CST-309	(E)	Blues In My Heart	196?	1.00	5.00
Crown CLP-5359	(M)	B. B. King	196?	4.00	10.00
Crown CST-359	(E)	B. B. King	196?	1.00	5.00
		—Crown albums above have black labels with a multi-color "Crown" on top.—			
Kent KLP-5012	(M)	Rock Me Baby	1964	8.00	20.00
Kent KST-512	(E)	Rock Me Baby	1964	6.00	15.00
Kent KLP-5013	(M)	Let Me Love You	1965	8.00	20.00
Kent KST-513	(E)	Let Me Love You	1965	6.00	15.00
Kent KLP-5015	(M)	B. B. King Live On Stage	1965	8.00	20.00
Kent KST-515	(E)	B. B. King Live On Stage	1965	6.00	15.00
Kent KLP-5016	(M)	The Soul Of B. B. King	1966	8.00	20.00
Kent KST-516	(E)	The Soul Of B. B. King	1966	6.00	15.00
Kent KLP-517	(M)	Pure Soul	1966	8.00	20.00
Kent KST-517	(E)	Pure Soul	1966	6.00	15.00
Kent KLP-5021	(M)	The Jungle	1967	8.00	20.00
Kent KST-521	(E)	The Jungle	1967	6.00	15.00
Kent KLP-5029	(M)	Boss Of The Blues	1968	8.00	20.00
Kent KST-529	(E)	Boss Of The Blues	1968	6.00	15.00
Kent KST-533	(E)	From The Beginning	1969	6.00	15.00
Kent KST-535	(E)	Underground Blues	1969	6.00	15.00
Kent KST-539	(E)	The Incredible Soul Of B. B. King	1970	6.00	15.00
Kent KST-543	(E)	Let Me Love You	1970	6.00	15.00
Kent KST-548	(E)	Turn On With B. B. King	1971	6.00	15.00
Kent KST-552	(E)	Greatest Hits, Volume 1	1971	6.00	15.00
Kent KST-561	(E)	Better Than Ever	1971	6.00	15.00
Kent KST-563	(E)	Doing My Thing, Lord	1971	6.00	15.00
Kent KST-565	(E)	B. B. King Live	1972	6.00	15.00
Kent KST-568	(E)	The Original Sweet Sixteen	1972	6.00	15.00
Kent 9011	(S)	B. B. King Anthology	197?	4.00	10.00
Custom CM-2049	(M)	I Love You So	196?	4.00	10.00
Custom CM-2046	(M)	Blues For Me	196?	4.00	10.00
Custom CM-2052	(M)	The Soul Of B. B. King	196?	4.00	10.00
United US-7703	(E)	Heart Full Of Blues	197?	1.20	6.00
United US-7705	(E)	Easy Listening Blues	197?	1.20	6.00
		(United 7705 is a reissue of Crown 5286.)			
United US-7708	(M)	Blues For Me	197?	1.20	6.00
		(United 7708 is a reissue of Custom 2046.)			
United US-7711	(E)	I Love You So	197?	1.20	6.00
		(United 7711 is a reissue of Custom 2049.)			

Label & Catalog #		Title	Year	VG+	NM
United US-7714	(E)	The Soul Of B.B. King	197?	1.20	6.00
		(United 7714 is a reissue of Custom 2052.)			
United US-7721	(E)	Swing Low	197?	1.20	6.00
		(United 7721 is a reissue of Crown 5519.)			
United US-7724	(E)	My Kind Of Blues	197?	1.20	6.00
		(United 7724 is a reissue of Crown 5188.)			
United US-7726	(E)	Singin' The Blues	197?	1.20	6.00
		(United 7721 is a reissue of Crown 5520.)			
United US-7728	(E)	The Great B.B. King	197?	1.20	6.00
		(United 7728 is a reissue of Crown 5143.)			
United US-7732	(E)	The Blues	197?	1.20	6.00
		(United 7732 is a reissue of Crown 5063.)			
United US-7733	(E)	Rock Me, Baby	197?	1.20	6.00
		(United 7733 is a reissue of Kent 5012.)			
United US-7734	(E)	Let Me Love You	197?	1.20	6.00
		(United 7734 is a reissue of Kent 513.)			
United US-7736	(E)	B.B. King Live On Stage	197?	1.20	6.00
		(United 7736 is a reissue of Kent 515.)			
United US-7742	(E)	The Jungle	197?	1.20	6.00
		(United 7742 is a reissue of Kent 521.)			
United US-7750	(E)	Boss Of The Blues	197?	1.20	6.00
		(United 7750 is a reissue of Kent 529.)			
United US-7756	(E)	The Incredible Soul Of B.B. King	197?	1.20	6.00
		(United 7756 is a reissue of Kent 539.)			
United US-7763	(E)	Turn On With B.B. King	197?	1.20	6.00
		(United 7763 is a reissue of Kent 548.)			
United US-7766	(E)	Greatest Hits, Vol. 1	197?	1.20	6.00
		(United 7766 is a reissue of Kent 552.)			
United US-7773	(E)	The Original Sweet Sixteen	197?	1.20	6.00
		(United 7773 is a reissue of Kent 568.)			
United US-7788	(E)	9 X 9	197?	1.20	6.00
Galaxy 202	(M)	16 Greatest Hits	1962	30.00	75.00
Galaxy 8202	(S)	16 Greatest Hits	1962	40.00	100.00
ABC-Paramount 456	(M)	Mr. Blues	1963	12.00	30.00
ABC-Paramount S-456	(S)	Mr. Blues	1963	16.00	40.00
ABC-Paramount 509	(M)	Live At The Regal	1965	16.00	40.00
ABC-Paramount S-509	(S)	Live At The Regal	1965	20.00	50.00
ABC-Paramount 528	(M)	Confessin' The Blues	1965	12.00	30.00
ABC-Paramount S-528	(S)	Confessin' The Blues	1965	16.00	40.00
BluesWay BL-6001	(S)	Blues Is King	1967	10.00	25.00
BluesWay BLS-6001	(S)	Blues Is King	1967	10.00	25.00
BluesWay BLS-6011	(S)	Blues On Top Of Blues	1968	10.00	25.00
BluesWay BLS-6016	(S)	Lucille	1968	10.00	25.00
BluesWay BLS-6022	(S)	His Best/The Electric B. B. King	1968	8.00	20.00
BluesWay BLS-6031	(S)	Live And Well	1969	8.00	20.00
BluesWay BLS-6037	(S)	Completely Well	1969	8.00	20.00
BluesWay BLS-6050	(S)	Back In The Alley	1970	8.00	20.00
ABC ABCD-704	(S)	Blues Is King	1970	4.00	10.00
		(ABC 704 is a reissue of BluesWay 6001.)			
ABC ABCD-709	(S)	Blues On Top Of Blues	1970	4.00	10.00
		(ABC 709 is a reissue of BluesWay 6011.)			
ABC ABCD-712	(S)	Lucille	1970	4.00	10.00
		(ABC 712 is a reissue of BluesWay 6016.)			
ABC ABCD-713	(S)	Indianola Mississippi Seeds	1970	6.00	15.00
ABC ABCD-723	(S)	Live In Cook County Jail	1971	6.00	15.00
ABC ABCD-724	(S)	Live At The Regal	1971	6.00	15.00
		(ABC ABC724 is a reissue of ABC-Paramount 509.)			
ABC ABCD-730	(S)	B.B. King In London	1971	6.00	15.00
ABC ABCD-743	(S)	L.A. Midnight	1972	6.00	15.00
ABC ABCX-759	(S)	Guess Who?	1972	6.00	15.00
ABC ABCX-767	(S)	The Best Of B.B. King	1973	6.00	15.00
ABC ABCD-794	(S)	To Know You Is To Love You	1973	6.00	15.00
ABC ABCD-813	(S)	The Electric B.B. King	1973	6.00	15.00
ABC ABCD-819	(S)	Live & Well	1974	4.00	10.00
		(ABC 819 is a reissue of BluesWay 6031.)			
ABC ABCD-825	(S)	Friends	1974	4.00	10.00
ABC ABCD-868	(S)	Completely Well	1974	4.00	10.00
		(ABC 868 is a reissue of BluesWay 6037.)			
ABC ABCD-878	(S)	Back In The Alley	1974	4.00	10.00
		(ABC 878 is a reissue of BluesWay 6050.)			
ABC ABCD-898	(S)	Lucille Talks Back	1975	4.00	10.00
ABC AB-977	(S)	King Size	1977	3.20	8.00
ABC AA-1061	(S)	Midnight Believer	1978	3.20	8.00
MCA 3151	(S)	Take It Home	1979	1.00	5.00
MCA 2-8016	(S)	"Now Appearing" At Ole Miss (2 LPs)	1980	3.20	8.00
MCA 5162	(S)	There Must Be A Better World Somewhere	1981	1.00	5.00
MCA 5307	(S)	Love Me Tender	1982	1.00	5.00
MCA 5413	(S)	Blues 'N' Jazz	1983	1.00	5.00

Label & Catalog #		Title	Year	VG+	NM

KING, BEN E.

Ben E. King was formerly a member of The Drifters.

Label & Catalog #		Title	Year	VG+	NM
Atco SD-33-133	(M)	**Spanish Harlem** (White label promo)	1961	100.00	250.00
Atco SD-33-133	(M)	**Spanish Harlem**	1961	40.00	100.00
Atco SD-33-133	(S)	**Spanish Harlem**	1961	60.00	150.00
		—Atco albums above have yellow "harp" labels.—			
Atco SD-33-133	(M)	**Spanish Harlem**	1962	16.00	40.00
Atco SD-33-133	(S)	**Spanish Harlem**	1962	20.00	50.00
Atco SD-33-137	(M)	**Ben E. King Sings For Soulful Lovers**	1962	20.00	50.00
Atco SD-33-137	(S)	**Ben E. King Sings For Soulful Lovers**	1962	30.00	75.00
Atco SD-33-142	(M)	**Don't Play That Song**	1962	20.00	50.00
Atco SD-33-142	(S)	**Don't Play That Song**	1962	30.00	75.00
Atco SD-33-165	(M)	**Ben E. King's Greatest Hits**	1964	12.00	30.00
Atco SD-33-165	(S)	**Ben E. King's Greatest Hits**	1964	16.00	40.00
Atco SD-33-174	(M)	**Seven Letters**	1965	18.00	45.00
Atco SD-33-174	(S)	**Seven Letters**	1965	24.00	60.00
		—Atco mono albums above have gold & gray labels; stereo albums have purple & brown labels.—			
Clarion 606	(M)	**Young Boy Blues**	1964	10.00	25.00
Clarion 606	(S)	**Young Boy Blues**	1964	12.00	30.00
Mandala MLP-3008	(M)	**Audio Biography** (Promotional radio interview)	1972	10.00	25.00
Atlantic SD-18132	(S)	**Supernatural**	1975	1.00	5.00
Atlantic SD-18169	(S)	**I Have A Love**	1976	1.00	5.00
Atlantic SD-18191	(S)	**Rhapsody**	1976	1.00	5.00
Atlantic SD-19200	(S)	**Let Me Live In Your Life**	1978	1.00	5.00
Atlantic SD-19269	(S)	**Music Trance**	1980	1.00	5.00
Atlantic SD-19300	(S)	**Street Tough**	1981	1.00	5.00

KING, CAROLE

Ms King was part of New York's acclaimed Brill Building team of songwriters in the '60s. Refer to City; The Cookies / Little Eva / Carole King.

Label & Catalog #		Title	Year	VG+	NM
Ode SP-77006	(S)	**Writer**	1970	1.20	6.00
Ode SP-77009	(S)	**Tapestry** (Textured cover)	1971	1.20	6.00
Ode SP-77009	(S)	**Tapestry** (Standard cover)	1971	1.00	5.00
Ode SP-77013	(S)	**Carole King Music**	1973	1.00	5.00
Ode SQ-88013	(Q)	**Carole King Music**	1974	4.00	10.00
Ode SP-77016	(S)	**Rhymes & Reasons**	1972	1.00	5.00
Ode SP-77018	(S)	**Fantasy**	1973	1.00	5.00
Ode SP-77024	(S)	**Wrap Around Joy**	1974	1.00	5.00
Ode SP-77027	(S)	**Really Rosie**	1975	1.00	5.00
Ode SP-77034	(S)	**Thoroughbred**	1976	1.00	5.00
Epic PE-34944	(S)	**Writer**	1977	.80	4.00
Epic PE-34946	(S)	**Tapestry**	1977	.80	4.00
Epic HE-44946	(S)	**Tapestry** (Half-speed master)	1980	25.00	75.00
Epic PE-34949	(S)	**Carole King Music**	1977	.80	4.00
Epic PE-34950	(S)	**Rhymes & Reasons**	1977	.80	4.00
Epic PE-34953	(S)	**Wrap Around Joy**	1977	.80	4.00
Epic PE-34955	(S)	**Really Rosie**	1977	.80	4.00
Epic PE-34962	(S)	**Fantasy**	1977	.80	4.00
Epic PE-34963	(S)	**Thoroughbred**	1977	.80	4.00
Epic JE-34967	(S)	**Her Greatest Hits**	1978	.80	4.00
Capitol SMAS-11667	(S)	**Simple Things**	1977	1.00	5.00
Capitol SW-11785	(S)	**Welcome Home**	1978	1.00	5.00
Capitol SWAK-11963	(S)	**Touch The Sky**	1979	1.00	5.00
Capitol SOO-12073	(S)	**Pearls (Songs Of Goffin & King)**	1980	1.00	5.00
Capitol SN-16057	(S)	**Simple Things**	1980	.80	4.00
Capitol SN-16058	(S)	**Welcome Home**	1980	.80	4.00
Capitol SN-16059	(S)	**Touch The Sky**	1980	.80	4.00
Capitol SN-16060	(S)	**Pearls (Songs Of Goffin & King)**	1980	.80	4.00
Atlantic SD-19344	(S)	**One To One**	1982	.80	4.00

KING, CLYDE

Label & Catalog #		Title	Year	VG+	NM
Ampex A-20104	(S)	**Direct Me**	197?	4.00	10.00

KING, FREDDIE

Label & Catalog #		Title	Year	VG+	NM
King 762	(M)	**Freddie King Sings The Blues**	1961	150.00	300.00
King 773	(M)	**Let's Hide Away And Dance Away**	1961	100.00	250.00
King 821	(M)	**Bossa Nova And Blues**	1962	80.00	200.00
King 856	(M)	**Freddie King Goes Surfin'**	1963	30.00	75.00
King 856	(S)	**Freddie King Goes Surfin'**	1963	40.00	100.00
King 928	(M)	**A Bonanza Of Instrumentals**	1965	20.00	50.00
King 928	(S)	**A Bonanza Of Instrumentals**	1965	30.00	75.00
		—King albums above have crownless black labels.—			
King 964	(M)	**24 Vocals And Instrumentals**	1966	10.00	25.00
King KS-1059	(S)	**Hide Away**	1969	6.00	15.00
Cotillion SD-9004	(S)	**Freddie King Is A Blues Master**	1969	10.00	25.00
Cotillion SD-9016	(S)	**My Feeling For The Blues**	1970	10.00	25.00
Shelter SW-8905	(S)	**Getting Ready**	1971	5.00	12.00
Shelter SW-8913	(S)	**Texas Cannonball**	1972	5.00	12.00
Shelter SW-8919	(S)	**Woman Across The River**	1973	5.00	12.00

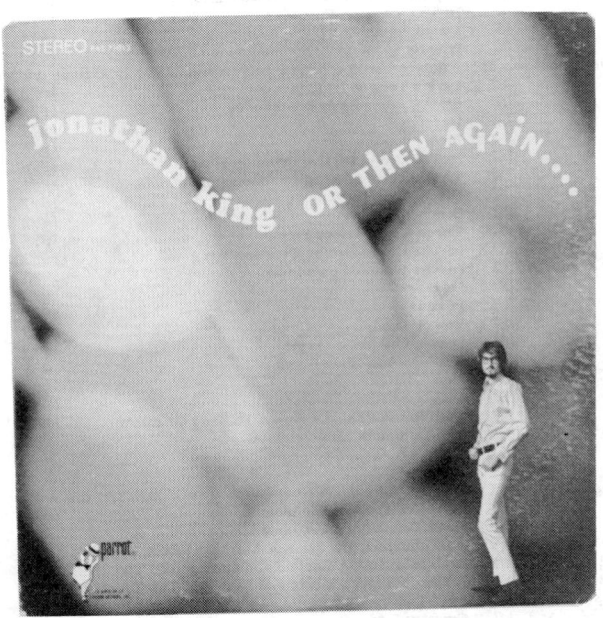

After recording with Hedgehoppers Anonymous (a wondrously bent, pre-psychedelic group name), Jonathon King had a major hit with the sublime "Everyone's Gone To The Moon." His album from these sessions, Or Then Again, included both of his US chart singles with the aforementioned in stereo while "Where The Sun Has Never Shone" appears in rechanneled stereo. Several years later, Mr King formed UK Records and encouraged a group of his studio musicians— Graham Gouldman, Eric Stewart, Lol Creme and Kevin Godley— as a new pop group, whom he ingenuously named 10CC.

Label & Catalog #		Title	Year	VG+	NM
Shelter 2140	(S)	The Best Of Freddie King	1975	1.00	5.00
MCA 690	(S)	The Best Of Freddie King	197?	.80	4.00
RSO 4803	(S)	Burglar	1974	4.00	10.00
RSO 4811	(S)	Larger Than Life	1975	4.00	10.00
RSO 3025	(S)	Freddie King	1977	4.00	10.00

KING, FREDDIE, & LULA REED & SONNY THOMPSON

King 777	(M)	Boy-Girl-Boy	1962	100.00	250.00
		—King albums above have crownless black labels.—			

KING, JONATHAN

Parrot PA-61013	(M)	Or Then Again	1967	16.00	40.00
Parrot PAS-71013	(S)	Or Then Again	1967	20.00	50.00
		("Where The Sun Has Never Shown" is rechanneled on this album.)			
UK S-53101	(S)	Bubble Rock Is Here To Stay	1972	10.00	25.00
UK S-53104	(S)	Pandora's Box	1973	10.00	25.00

KING, TYLER, & THE TWISTEENS

Startime TW-100	(M)	Twistin' Time	1961	8.00	20.00

KING BISCUIT BOY

Paramount PAR-6023	(S)	Gooduns	1972	4.00	10.00
Paramount PAR-6030	(S)	Official Music (With Crowbar)	1973	4.00	10.00
Epic KE-32891	(S)	King Biscuit Boy	1974	3.20	8.00

KING CRIMSON

Original members were Raymond Burrell, Mel Collins, Robert Fripp, Peter Sinfield and Ian Wallace.

Atlantic SD-8245	(S)	In The Court Of The Crimson King	1969	8.00	20.00
Atlantic SD-8266	(S)	In The Wake Of Poseidon	1970	6.00	15.00
Atlantic SD-8278	(S)	Lizard	1971	6.00	15.00
Atlantic SD-7212	(S)	Islands	1972	6.00	15.00
		—Atlantic albums above have green & orange labels with an 1841 Broadway address.—			
Atlantic SD-7263	(S)	Lark's Tongue In Aspic	1973	1.00	5.00
Atlantic SD-7298	(S)	Starless And Bible Black	1974	1.00	5.00
Atlantic SD-18110	(S)	Red	1974	1.00	5.00
Atlantic SD-18135	(S)	USA	1975	1.00	5.00
Atlantic SD-19155	(S)	In The Court Of The Crimson King	1978	1.00	5.00
Warner Bros. WBMS-119	(DJ)	The Return Of King Crimson (Interview)	1981	20.00	50.00
Warner Bros. BSK-3629	(S)	Discipline	1981	1.00	5.00
Warner Bros. 23692	(S)	Beat	1982	1.00	5.00
Warner Bros. 25071	(S)	Three Of A Perfect Pair	1984	1.00	5.00
Editions EG EGKC-1	(S)	In The Court Of The Crimson King	1983	1.00	5.00
Editions EG EGKC-2	(S)	In The Wake Of Poseidon	1983	1.00	5.00
Editions EG EGKC-3	(S)	Lizard	1983	1.00	5.00
Editions EG EGKC-4	(S)	Islands	1983	1.00	5.00
Editions EG EGKC-5	(S)	Earthbound	1983	Unreleased	
Editions EG EGKC-6	(S)	Lark's Tongue In Aspic	1983	1.00	5.00
Editions EG EGKC-7	(S)	Starless And Bible Black	1983	1.00	5.00
Editions EG EGKC-8	(S)	Red	1983	1.00	5.00
Editions EG EGKC-9	(S)	USA	1983	1.00	5.00
Editions EG EGKC-10	(S)	The Young Person's Guide To King Crimson	1983	1.00	5.00
Editions EG EGLP-68	(S)	The Compact King Crimson	1986	1.00	5.00

KING CURTIS

Refer to Buffalo Springfield / King Curtis; The Shirelles & King Curtis. Curts' jazz LPs are not included in this edition.

Atco 33-113	(M)	Have Tenor Sax, Will Blow	1959	40.00	100.00
Atco SD-33-113	(M)	Have Tenor Sax, Will Blow	1959	60.00	150.00
		—Atco albums above have yellow harp labels.—			
RCA Victor LPM-2492	(M)	Arthur Murray's Music For Dancing: The Twist!	1962	10.00	25.00
RCA Victor LSM-2492	(S)	Arthur Murray's Music For Dancing: The Twist!	1962	12.00	30.00
Enjoy ENLP-2001	(M)	Soul Twist	1962	40.00	100.00
Capitol T-1756	(M)	Country Soul	1963	12.00	30.00
Capitol ST-1756	(S)	Country Soul	1963	16.00	40.00
Capitol T-2095	(M)	Soul Serenade	1964	12.00	30.00
Capitol ST-2095	(S)	Soul Serenade	1964	16.00	40.00
Capitol T-2341	(M)	King Curtis Plays The Hits Made Famous By Sam Cooke	1965	12.00	30.00
Capitol ST-2341	(S)	King Curtis Plays The Hits Made Famous By Sam Cooke	1965	16.00	40.00
Capitol ST-2858	(S)	The Best Of King Curtis	1968	10.00	25.00
Capitol SM-11963	(S)	The Best Of King Curtis	1979	1.00	5.00
Clarion 615	(M)	The Great "K" Curtis	1964	10.00	25.00
Clarion SD-615	(S)	The Great "K" Curtis	1964	12.00	30.00
		(Clarion 615 is a reissue of Atco 113.)			
Atco 33-189	(M)	That Lovin' Feeling	1966	10.00	25.00
Atco SD-33-189	(S)	That Lovin' Feeling	1966	12.00	30.00
Atco 33-198	(M)	Live At Small's Paradise	1966	10.00	25.00
Atco SD-33-198	(S)	Live At Small's Paradise	1966	12.00	30.00

The King Pins never saw any of their records make the national pop charts, but their popularity with rhythm'n blues buyers merited an LP from King. The cover is a classic period piece and makes no attempt to pander to a white market. Rhythm'n blues records such as this—especially by smaller, independent labels—were often marketed exclusively in a handful of cities with a large black population. Hence, records by black artists could come and go with the majority of white record buyers never even seeing a copy!

Label & Catalog #		Title	Year	VG+	NM
Atco SD-33-198	(S)	Live At Small's Paradise	1966	12.00	30.00
Atco 33-211	(M)	King Curtis Plays The Great Memphis Hits	1967	10.00	25.00
Atco SD-33-211	(S)	King Curtis Plays The Great Memphis Hits	1967	12.00	30.00
Atco 33-231	(M)	King Size Soul	1967	10.00	25.00
Atco SD-33-231	(S)	King Size Soul	1967	12.00	30.00
Atco 33-247	(M)	Sweet Soul	1968	10.00	25.00
Atco SD-33-247	(S)	Sweet Soul	1968	8.00	20.00
Atco SD-33-266	(S)	The Best Of King Curtis	1968	8.00	20.00
Atco SD-33-293	(S)	Instant Groove	1969	8.00	20.00
Atco SD-33-338	(S)	Get Ready	1970	8.00	20.00
Atco SD-33-359	(S)	Live At Fillmore West	1971	6.00	15.00
Atco SD-33-385	(S)	Everybody's Talkin'	1972	6.00	15.00
Camden CAS-2242	(S)	Sax In Motion	1968	6.00	15.00
		(Camden 2242 is a reissue of RCA Victor 2492.)			
Springboard	(S)	Take The Last Train Home	1973	4.00	10.00
Harlem Hitparade 8001	(S)	Soul On Soul	197?	4.00	10.00
Pickwick SPC-3293	(S)	Watermelon Man	197?	4.00	10.00
Trip TLP-8017	(S)	King Curtis	197?	4.00	10.00
Mt. Vernon MVM-119	(S)	The Soul Of King Curtis	197?	4.00	10.00

KING CURTIS & CHAMPION JACK DUPREE

Label & Catalog #		Title	Year	VG+	NM
Atlantic SD-1637	(S)	Blues At Montreux	1973	8.00	20.00

KING HANNIBAL

Label & Catalog #		Title	Year	VG+	NM
Aware 1001	(S)	Truth	1973	6.00	20.00

KING HARVEST

Label & Catalog #		Title	Year	VG+	NM
Perception 36	(S)	Dancing In The Moonlight	1973	4.00	10.00
A&M SP-4540	(S)	King Harvest	1975	1.00	5.00

KING PINS, THE

Label & Catalog #		Title	Year	VG+	NM
King 865	(M)	It Won't Be This Way Always	1963	150.00	300.00

KINGDOM

Label & Catalog #		Title	Year	VG+	NM
Specialty SPS-2135	(S)	Kingdom	1970	24.00	60.00

KINGFISH

Kingfish features Bob Weir of The Grateful Dead.

Label & Catalog #		Title	Year	VG+	NM
Round RX-108	(S)	Kingfish	1976	10.00	25.00
Jet LA732-G	(S)	Live 'N' Kickin'	1977	4.00	10.00
Accord SN-7128	(S)	Live 'N' Kickin'	198?	1.00	5.00
Relix RRLP-2005	(S)	Kingfish	198?	.80	4.00

KINGSMEN, THE

Label & Catalog #		Title	Year	VG+	NM
Wand WD-657	(M)	The Kingsmen In Person	1964	12.00	30.00
Wand WDS-657	(P)	The Kingsmen In Person	1964	16.00	40.00
Wand WD-659	(M)	More Great Sounds	1964	12.00	30.00
Wand WDS-659	(S)	More Great Sounds	1964	16.00	40.00
		(Wand 659 was originally issued with "Death Of An Angel".)			
Wand WD-659	(M)	More Great Sounds	1965	10.00	25.00
Wand WDS-659	(S)	More Great Sounds	1965	12.00	30.00
		(On later pressings, "Death Of An Angel" was replaced by an uncredited instrumental.)			
Wand WD-662	(M)	The Kingsmen, Volume 3	1965	10.00	25.00
Wand WDS-662	(S)	The Kingsmen, Volume 3	1965	12.00	30.00
Wand WD-670	(M)	The Kingsmen On Campus	1965	10.00	25.00
Wand WDS-670	(S)	The Kingsmen On Campus	1965	12.00	30.00
Wand WD-674	(M)	15 Great Hits	1966	8.00	20.00
Wand WDS-674	(P)	15 Great Hits	1966	10.00	25.00
Wand WD-675	(M)	Up And Away	1966	8.00	20.00
Wand WDS-675	(S)	Up And Away	1966	10.00	25.00
Wand ST-91011	(S)	Up And Away (Capitol Record Club)	1966	10.00	25.00
Wand WD-681	(M)	The Kingsmen's Greatest Hits	1967	6.00	15.00
Wand WDS-681	(P)	The Kingsmen's Greatest Hits	1967	8.00	20.00
Chime 611	(S)	Suddenly There's A Valley	196?	10.00	25.00
Scepter CTN-18002	(S)	The Best Of The Kingsmen	197?	1.00	5.00
Heartwarming 3734	(S)	Kingsmen Live... Naturally	1981	4.00	10.00
Rhino RNLP-126	(S)	The Best Of The Kingsmen	1985	.80	4.00

KINKS, THE

The original Kinks were brothers Ray and Dave Davies, Mick Avory and Pete Quaife, who left in 1969 and was replaced by John Dalton. John Gosling joined in 1970 only to leave in '78. With Dalton's departure in 1976, he was replaced by Andy Pyle (1976-78). Other Kinks have been Gordon Edwards, Jim Rodford, and Ian Gibbons.

Label & Catalog #		Title	Year	VG+	NM
Reprise R-6143	(M)	You Really Got Me (White label promo)	1965	200.00	400.00
Reprise R-6143	(M)	You Really Got Me	1965	16.00	40.00
Reprise RS-6143	(S)	You Really Got Me	1965	20.00	50.00
Reprise R-6158	(M)	Kinks Size (White label promo)	1965	80.00	200.00
Reprise R-6158	(M)	Kinks Size	1965	20.00	50.00
Reprise RS-6158	(E)	Kinks Size	1965	16.00	40.00

Label & Catalog #		Title	Year	VG+	NM
Reprise R-6173	(M)	Kinda Kinks (White label promo)	1965	80.00	200.00
Reprise R-6173	(M)	Kinda Kinks	1965	20.00	50.00
Reprise RS-6173	(E)	Kinda Kinks	1965	16.00	40.00
Reprise R-6184	(M)	Kinks' Kinkdom (White label promo)	1965	80.00	200.00
Reprise R-6184	(M)	Kinks' Kinkdom	1965	20.00	50.00
Reprise RS-6184	(E)	Kinks' Kinkdom	1965	16.00	40.00
Reprise R-6197	(M)	Kink Kontroversy (White label promo)	1966	80.00	200.00
Reprise R-6197	(M)	Kink Kontroversy	1966	20.00	50.00
Reprise RS-6197	(E)	Kink Kontroversy	1966	16.00	40.00
Reprise R-6217	(M)	The Kinks' Greatest Hits	1966	14.00	35.00
Reprise RS-6217	(E)	The Kinks' Greatest Hits	1966	10.00	25.00
Reprise RS-6217	(E)	The Kinks' Greatest Hits (RCA Record Club)	1966	12.00	30.00
Reprise R-6228	(M)	Face To Face	1967	16.00	40.00
Reprise RS-6228	(P)	Face To Face	1967	12.00	30.00
		(1/3 of this album is in bad stereo while the rest is rechanneled.)			
Reprise R-6260	(M)	Live Kinks	1967	14.00	35.00
Reprise RS-6260	(S)	Live Kinks	1967	10.00	25.00
Reprise R-6272	(M)	Something Else By The Kinks (White label promo)	1968	150.00	300.00
Reprise RS-6272	(S)	Something Else By The Kinks	1968	12.00	30.00
—Reprise albums above have pink, gold & green labels.—					
Reprise RS-6327	(S)	The Kinks Are The Village Green Preservation Society	1969	12.00	30.00
Reprise PRO-328	(P)	God Save The Kinks (Boxed set)	1969	250.00	500.00
		(PRO-328 is a boxed set sold through the mail to promote RS-6327. The box includes a postcard, a decal, a bag of grass from the village green, a Union Jack pin, a letter, a Kinks consumer guide, a "God Save The Kinks" button and an album, "Then, Now And In Between", all included in the price.)			
Reprise PRO-328	(P)	Then, Now And In Between	1969	20.00	50.00
		(Issued as part of the "God Save The Kinks" box above.)			
Reprise RS-6366	(S)	Arthur (Or The Decline & Fall Of The British Empire)	1969	10.00	25.00
Reprise RS-6423	(S)	Lola Versus Powerman And The Moneygoround, Part One (Blue-on-white cover)	1970	6.00	15.00
—Reprise albums above have brown & orange labels with a "W7" and ":r" logos on top.—					
Reprise SMAS-93034	(S)	Arthur (Or The Decline & Fall Of The British Empire) (Capitol Rec. Club)	1971	14.00	35.00
Reprise RS-6454	(P)	The Kink Kronikles (2 LPs)	1972	5.00	12.00
Reprise MS-2127	(P)	The Great Lost Kinks Album	1973	20.00	50.00
Reprise RS-6143	(P)	You Really Got Me	197?	3.20	8.00
Reprise RS-6217	(E)	The Kinks' Greatest Hits	197?	3.20	8.00
Reprise RS-6228	(E)	Face To Face	197?	3.20	8.00
Reprise RS-6260	(S)	Live Kinks	197?	3.20	8.00
Reprise RS-6279	(S)	Something Else By The Kinks	197?	3.20	8.00
Reprise RS-6327	(S)	The Kinks Are The Village Green Preservation Society	197?	3.20	8.00
Reprise RS-6366	(S)	Arthur	197?	3.20	8.00
Reprise RS-6423	(S)	Lola Versus Powerman And The Moneygoround, Part One (Black-on-white cover)	197?	3.20	8.00
—Reprise albums above have brown labels with an ":r" logo on top.—					
RCA Victor LSP-4644	(S)	Muswell Hillbillies	1971	12.00	30.00
RCA Victor VPS-6065	(S)	Everybody's In Show Biz (2 LPs)	1972	8.00	20.00
RCA Victor LPL1-5002	(S)	Preservation, Act 1	1973	6.00	15.00
RCA Victor CPL2-5040	(S)	Preservation, Act 2 (2 LPs)	1974	8.00	20.00
RCA Victor APL1-5081	(S)	Soap Opera	1975	6.00	15.00
—RCA albums above have orange labels.—					
RCA Victor VPS-6065	(S)	Everybody's In Show Biz (2 LPs)	1975	1.20	6.00
RCA Victor APL1-5081	(S)	Soap Opera	1975	1.00	5.00
RCA Victor LPL1-5102	(S)	Schoolboys In Disgrace	1975	1.20	6.00
—RCA albums above have brown labels.—					
RCA Victor APL1-1743	(S)	Celluloid Heroes (The Kinks' Greatest)	1976	.80	4.00
RCA Victor APL1-3520	(S)	Second Time Around	1980	.80	4.00
RCA Victor AYL1-3749	(S)	Schoolboys In Disgrace	1980	.80	4.00
RCA Victor AYL1-3750	(S)	Soap Opera	1980	.80	4.00
RCA Victor AYL1-3869	(S)	Celluloid Heroes (The Kinks' Greatest)	1981	.80	4.00
RCA Victor AYL1-4558	(S)	Muswell Hillbillies	1982	.80	4.00
Pickwick ACL-7072	(S)	Preservation, Act 1	1980	6.00	15.00
Pickwick ACL-7074	(S)	Muswell Hillbillies	1980	6.00	15.00
Pye 505	(M)	History Of British Pop Music—The Kinks	1975	4.00	10.00
Pye 509	(M)	History Of British Pop Music—The Kinks, Vol. 2	1976	4.00	10.00
Arista AL-4106	(S)	Sleepwalker (White label promo)	1977	12.00	30.00
Arista AL-4106	(S)	Sleepwalker	1977	.80	4.00
Arista AL-4167	(S)	Misfits (White label promo)	1978	12.00	30.00
Arista AL-4167	(S)	Misfits	1978	.80	4.00
Arista AL-4240	(S)	Low Budget	1979	.80	4.00
Arista SP-69	(DJ)	Low Budget Radio Interview	1979	16.00	40.00
Arista AL-8401	(S)	One For The Road (2 LPs)	1980	3.20	8.00
Arista AL-8609	(S)	One For The Road (2 LPs)	1982	1.20	6.00

Label & Catalog #		Title	Year	VG+	NM
Arista AL-8018	(S)	State Of Confusion	1983	.80	4.00
Arista AL-8264	(S)	Word Of Mouth (Virgin vinyl promo)	1984	4.00	10.00
		(Advance copies of AL:-8264 are on non-opaque vinyl: Light will shine through with a reddish tinge.)			
Arista AL-8264	(S)	Word Of Mouth	1984	.80	4.00
Compleat CPL2-2001	(P)	A Compleat Collection (2 LPs)	1984	1.20	6.00
MCA 5822	(S)	Think Visual	1986	.80	4.00
MCA 17281	(S)	A Look At "Think Visual" (Plain jacket)	1986	20.00	50.00
MCA 6337	(S)	UK Jive	1987	.80	4.00
MCA 42107	(S)	Road (Live)	1989	.80	4.00

KISS

The original Kiss consisted of Peter Criss, Ace Frehley, Gene Simmons and Paul Stanley. Criss was replaced by Eric Carr in 1981 while Frehley was replaced by Vinnie Vincent in 1982.

Casablanca NBLP-9001	(S)	Kiss (White label promo)	1974	80.00	200.00
Casablanca NBLP-9001	(S)	Kiss (Without "Kissin' Time")	1974	30.00	75.00
Casablanca NBLP-7001	(S)	Kiss	1974	10.00	25.00
Casablanca NBLP-7006	(S)	Hotter Than Hell	1974	10.00	25.00
Casablanca NBLP-7016	(S)	Dressed To Kill (Embossed cover)	1975	10.00	25.00
Casablanca NBLP-7020	(S)	Alive!	1975	10.00	25.00
Casablanca NBLP-7025	(S)	Destroyer	1976	10.00	25.00
—Casablanca albums above have blue/grey with a smoking man on the left.—					
Casablanca NBLP-7001	(S)	Kiss	1976	6.00	15.00
Casablanca NBLP-7006	(S)	Hotter Than Hell	1976	6.00	15.00
Casablanca NBLP-7016	(S)	Dressed To Kill	1976	6.00	15.00
Casablanca NBLP-7020	(S)	Alive!	1976	6.00	15.00
Casablanca NBLP-7025	(S)	Destroyer	1976	6.00	15.00
Casablanca NBLP-7032	(S)	Kiss: The Originals	1976	60.00	150.00
		(Issued with a bonus booklet, four Kiss cards and a Kiss Army sticker. Repackages 7001, 7006 and 7016.)			
Casablanca NBLP-7032	(S)	Kiss: The Originals (Without inserts)	1976	40.00	100.00
Casablanca NBLP-7037	(S)	Rock And Roll Over	1976	6.00	15.00
—Casablanca albums above have labels with a desert scene with three camels and "Casablanca" on top.—					
Casablanca NBLP-7001	(S)	Kiss	1977	5.00	12.00
Casablanca NBLP-7006	(S)	Hotter Than Hell	1977	5.00	12.00
Casablanca NBLP-7016	(S)	Dressed To Kill	1977	5.00	12.00
Casablanca NBLP-7020	(S)	Alive!	1977	5.00	12.00
Casablanca NBLP-7025	(S)	Destroyer	1977	5.00	12.00
Casablanca NBLP-7032	(S)	Kiss: The Originals (Includes inserts)	1977	40.00	100.00
Casablanca NBLP-7032	(S)	Kiss: The Originals (Without inserts)	1977	30.00	75.00
Casablanca NBLP-7037	(S)	Rock And Roll Over	1977	5.00	12.00
Casablanca NBLP-7057	(S)	Love Gun (Includes a punchout sheet)	1977	10.00	25.00
Casablanca NBLP-7057	(S)	Love Gun (Without the punchout sheet)	1977	5.00	12.00
Casablanca NBLP-7076	(S)	Alive II (Includes booklet and "tattoos.")	1977	40.00	100.00
		(Original pressing covers of Casablanca 7076 erroneously list "Take Me," "Hooligan" and "Do You Love Me" on the back.)			
Casablanca NBLP-7076	(S)	Alive II (With booklet and "tattoos.")	1977	10.00	25.00
Casablanca NBLP-7076	(S)	Alive II (Without the booklet and "tattoos.")	1977	5.00	12.00
Casablanca NBLP-7100	(S)	Double Platinum (2 LPs)	1978	12.00	30.00
		(Issued with a bonus cardboard platinum album award.)			
Casablanca NBLP-7100	(S)	Double Platinum (2 LPs without the bonus)	1978	8.00	20.00
Casablanca NBLP-7122	(S)	Gene Simmons (Picture disc)	1978	20.00	50.00
Casablanca NBLP-7120	(S)	Gene Simmons (With poster)	1978	10.00	25.00
Casablanca NBLP-7120	(S)	Gene Simmons (Without poster)	1978	6.00	15.00
Casablanca NBLP-7121	(S)	Ace Frehley(Picture disc)	1978	20.00	50.00
Casablanca NBLP-7121	(S)	Ace Frehley (With poster)	1978	10.00	25.00
Casablanca NBLP-7121	(S)	Ace Frehley (Without poster)	1978	6.00	15.00
Casablanca NBLP-7122	(S)	Peter Criss (Picture disc)	1978	20.00	50.00
Casablanca NBLP-7122	(S)	Peter Criss (With poster)	1978	10.00	25.00
Casablanca NBLP-7122	(S)	Peter Criss (Without poster)	1978	6.00	15.00
Casablanca NBLP-7123	(S)	Paul Stanley(Picture disc)	1978	20.00	50.00
Casablanca NBLP-7123	(S)	Paul Stanley (With poster)	1978	10.00	25.00
Casablanca NBLP-7123	(S)	Paul Stanley (Without poster)	1978	6.00	15.00
Casablanca NBLP-7152	(S)	Dynasty (With poster)	1979	6.00	15.00
Casablanca NBLP-7152	(S)	Dynasty (Without poster)	1979	4.00	10.00
Casablanca NBLP-7225	(S)	Unmasked (With poster)	1980	6.00	15.00
Casablanca NBLP-7225	(S)	Unmasked (Without poster)	1980	4.00	10.00
—Casablanca albums above have labels with a desert scene with a film crew and "Manufactured by Casablanca" on the bottom.—					
Casablanca NBLP-7001	(S)	Kiss	1981	4.00	10.00
Casablanca NBLP-7006	(S)	Hotter Than Hell	1981	4.00	10.00
Casablanca NBLP-7016	(S)	Dressed To Kill	1981	4.00	10.00
Casablanca NBLP-7020	(S)	Alive!	1981	4.00	10.00
Casablanca NBLP-7025	(S)	Destroyer	1981	4.00	10.00
Casablanca NBLP-7037	(S)	Rock And Roll Over	1981	4.00	10.00
Casablanca NBLP-7057	(S)	Love Gun	1981	4.00	10.00
Casablanca NBLP-7076	(S)	Alive II	1981	4.00	10.00
Casablanca NBLP-7100	(S)	Double Platinum	1981	4.00	10.00
Casablanca NBLP-7152	(S)	Dynasty	1981	4.00	10.00

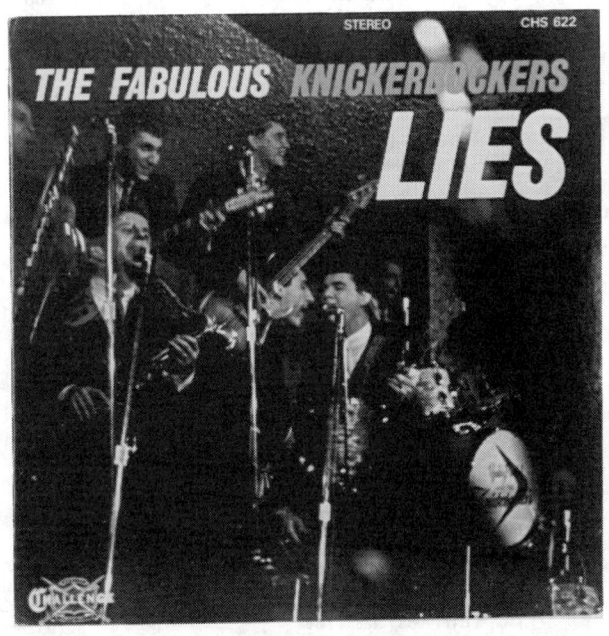

The Knickerbockers, featuring former Royal Teen Buddy Randell as lead singer, were able to imitate many of the '60s rock and soul greats: Their live shows often featured impeccably righteous versions of "You've Lost That Lovin' Feeling." Their second— and rarest— album is Jerk And Twine Time and, while no stereo copies are known to exist, most of the other Challenge albums of this period were issued in both mono and stereo. Their third album contains their big hit, "Lies," a remarkable Beatles sound-alike that convinced more than a few people that it was the Fab Four's follow-up to "Yesterday."

Label & Catalog #		Title	Year	VG+	NM
Casablanca NBLP-7225	(S)	Unmasked	1981	4.00	10.00
		(Includes a paper inner sleeve with lyrics on it.)			
Casablanca NBLP-7261	(S)	Music From The Elder	1981	8.00	20.00
		(Includes a paper inner sleeve with lyrics on it.)			
Casablanca NBLP-7270	(S)	Creatures Of The Night	1982	8.00	20.00
		—Casablanca albums above have labels with a desert scene with a film crew and "Manufactured by Polygram" on the bottom.—			
Mercury 814 297-1	(S)	Lick It Up	1983	4.00	10.00
Mercury 822 495-1	(S)	Animalize	1984	4.00	10.00
Mercury 824 154-1	(S)	Creatures Of The Night	1984	4.00	10.00
Mercury 826 099-1	(S)	Asylum	1985	4.00	10.00
Mercury 832 626-1	(S)	Crazy Nights	1987	4.00	10.00
Mercury 832 903-1	(S)	Crazy Nights (Picture disc)	1987	4.00	10.00
Mercury 836 8871-	(S)	Smashes, Thrashes And Hits (Picture disc)	1988	14.00	35.00
Mercury 836 427-1	(S)	Smashes, Thrashes And Hits	1988	4.00	10.00
Mercury 838 913-1	(S)	Hot In The Shade	1989	4.00	10.00
		—Special Promotional Albums—			
Integrity Entertainment	(S)	Wherehouse Albums Of The Week 5/5/78	1978	30.00	75.00
		(In-store sampler features tracks from "Double Platinum" on one side and tracks from the "FM" soundtrack on the other.)			
Casablanca Kiss-76	(DJ)	Special Album For Their Summer Tour	1978	30.00	75.00
Casablanca NB 20128	(DJ)	A Taste Of Platinum	1978	16.00	40.00
Casablanca NB 20137	(DJ)	Solo Album Sampler	1978	16.00	40.00
Mercury 792	(DJ)	First Kiss, Last Licks	1990	40.00	100.00

KIT KATS, THE

Label & Catalog #		Title	Year	VG+	NM
Jamie LPM-3029	(M)	It's Just A Matter Of Time	1966	10.00	25.00
Jamie LPS-3029	(E)	It's Just A Matter Of Time	1966	10.00	25.00
Jamie LPM-3032	(M)	Do Their Thing Live	1967	10.00	25.00
Jamie LPS-3032	(S)	Do Their Thing Live	1967	10.00	25.00

KITARO

Label & Catalog #		Title	Year	VG+	NM
Geffen GHS-24163	(S)	The Light Of The Spirit	198?	1.00	5.00

KITCHEN CINQ, THE

Label & Catalog #		Title	Year	VG+	NM
L.H.I. 12000	(M)	Everything But The Kitchen Cinq	1967	12.00	30.00
L.H.I. 12000	(S)	Everything But The Kitchen Cinq	1967	16.00	40.00

KLOWNS, THE

Label & Catalog #		Title	Year	VG+	NM
RCA Victor LSP-4438	(S)	Ringling Brothers Barnum & Bailey	1970	4.00	10.00

KNICKERBOCKERS, THE

Label & Catalog #		Title	Year	VG+	NM
Challenge LP-12664	(M)	Sing And Sync Along With Lloyd Thaxton	1965	100.00	200.00
Challenge CH-621	(M)	Jerk And Twine Time	1965	200.00	400.00
Challenge CHS-621	(S)	Jerk And Twine Time	1965	Unreleased	
Challenge CH-622	(M)	Lies (White label promo)	1966	100.00	200.00
Challenge CH-622	(M)	Lies	1966	40.00	100.00
Challenge CHS-622	(S)	Lies	1966	100.00	200.00
Sundazed LP-5000	(S)	The Great Lost Knickerbockers Album (Blue vinyl)	1989	4.00	10.00

KNIGHT, FREDERICK

Label & Catalog #		Title	Year	VG+	NM
Stax STS-3011	(S)	I've Been Lonely So Long	1973	10.00	25.00

KNIGHT, GLADYS, & THE PIPS

Ms Knight and her Pips can also be found on the Buddah soundtrack "Claudine."

Label & Catalog #		Title	Year	VG+	NM
Fury 1003	(M)	Letter Full Of Tears	1962	400.00	800.00
Maxx 3000	(M)	Gladys Knight & The Pips	1964	80.00	200.00
Sphere Sound SR-7006	(M)	Gladys Knight & The Pips	1965	80.00	200.00
Sphere Sound SSR-7006	(E)	Gladys Knight & The Pips	1965	60.00	150.00
Bell 6013	(S)	Tastiest Hits	1968	6.00	15.00
Bell 1323	(S)	In The Beginning	1969	6.00	15.00
Soul S-706	(M)	Everybody Needs Love	1967	8.00	20.00
Soul SS-706	(S)	Everybody Needs Love	1967	10.00	25.00
Soul S-707	(M)	Feelin' Bluesy (Promo label)	1968	16.00	40.00
Soul SS-707	(S)	Feelin' Bluesy	1968	8.00	20.00
Soul SS-711	(S)	Silk And Soul	1968	8.00	20.00
Soul SS-713	(S)	The Nitty Gritty	1969	6.00	15.00
Soul SS-723	(S)	Gladys Knight & The Pips' Greatest Hits	1970	6.00	15.00
Soul SS-730	(S)	All In A Night's Work	1971	5.00	12.00
Soul SS-731	(S)	If I Were Your Woman	1971	5.00	12.00
Soul SS-736	(S)	Standing Ovation	1972	5.00	12.00
Soul SS-737	(S)	Neither One Of Us	1973	5.00	12.00
Soul SS-739	(S)	All I Need Is Time	1973	5.00	12.00
Soul SS-741	(S)	Knight Time	1974	5.00	12.00
Soul SS-744	(S)	A Little Knight Music	1975	5.00	12.00
Motown M-792S	(S)	Anthology (2 LPs)	1974	4.00	10.00
Motown M5-113V	(S)	Superstar Series, Vol. 13	1980	.80	4.00
Motown M5-126V	(S)	Everybody Needs Love	1982	.80	4.00
Motown M5-148V	(S)	The Nitty Gritty	1982	.80	4.00

Label & Catalog #		Title	Year	VG+	NM
Motown M5-148V	(S)	The Nitty Gritty	1982	.80	4.00
Buddah BGS-5141	(S)	Imagination	1973	1.00	5.00
Buddah BDS-5612	(S)	I Feel A Song	1974	1.00	5.00
Buddah BDS-5639	(S)	Second Anniversary	1975	1.00	5.00
Buddah BDS-5651	(S)	Bless This House	1975	1.00	5.00
Buddah BDS-5653	(S)	Greatest Hits	1976	1.00	5.00
Buddah BDS-5676	(S)	Pipe Dreams	1976	1.00	5.00
Buddah BDS-5689	(S)	Love Is Always On Your Mind	1977	1.00	5.00
Buddah BDS-5701	(S)	One And Only	1978	1.00	5.00
Buddah BDS-5714	(S)	Miss Gladys Knight	1978	1.00	5.00
Springboard SPB-4035	(S)	Early Hits	1972	.80	4.00
Springboard SPC-4050	(S)	How Do You Say Goodbye	1973	.80	4.00
Pickwick SPC-3349	(S)	Every Beat Of My Heart	1973	.80	4.00
Trip TLP-9509	(S)	It Hurts Me So Bad	1973	.80	4.00
Trip TSK-3500	(S)	Super Pak (2 LPs)	1974	1.00	5.00
United Arts. LA-503E	(S)	The Very Best Of Gladys Knight & The Pips	1975	.80	4.00
MCP 8028	(S)	The Best Of Gladys Knight & The Pips	1976?	.80	4.00
Upfront UPF-130	(S)	Gladys Knight & The Pips	197?	.80	4.00
Upfront UPF-165	(S)	Gladys Knight & The Pips	197?	.80	4.00
Columbia JC-35704	(S)	Gladys Knight	1979	1.00	5.00
Columbia JC-36387	(S)	About Love	1980	1.00	5.00
Columbia FC-37086	(S)	Touch	1981	1.00	5.00
Columbia FC-38114	(S)	That Special Time Of Year	1982	1.00	5.00
Lost-Nite LLP-17	(10")	Gladys Knight & The Pips (Red vinyl)	1981	4.00	10.00
Accord SN-7103	(S)	Every Beat Of My Heart	1981	.80	4.00
Accord SN-7105	(S)	Letter Full Of Tears	1981	.80	4.00
Accord SN-7131	(S)	I Feel A Song	1981	.80	4.00
Accord SN-7188	(S)	It's Showtime	1982	.80	4.00

KNIGHT, JEAN

Stax STS-2045	(S)	Mr. Big Stuff	1971	14.00	35.00

KNIGHT, LONNIE

Symposium 2004	(S)	Family In The Wind	1974	6.00	15.00
Flashlight 3002	(S)	Song For A City Mouse	1975	6.00	15.00

KNIGHT, ROBERT

Sound Stage-7 SSM-7000	(M)	Everlasting Love	1967	14.00	35.00
Sound Stage-7 SM-17000	(S)	Everlasting Love	1967	20.00	50.00

KNIGHT, SONNY

Aura AR-3001	(M)	If You Want This Love	1964	8.00	20.00
Aura AS-3001	(S)	If You Want This Love	1964	10.00	25.00

KNIGHT, TERRY, & THE PACK
The Pack features Mark Farner and Don Brewer, later of Grand Funk Railroad.

Lucky Eleven LE-8000	(M)	Terry Knight & The Pack	1966	10.00	25.00
Lucky Eleven LES-8000	(E)	Terry Knight & The Pack	1966	8.00	20.00
Lucky Eleven LE-8001	(M)	Reflections	1966	10.00	25.00
Lucky Eleven LES-8001	(S)	Reflections	1966	12.00	30.00
Cameo C-2007	(M)	Reflections	1967	6.00	15.00
Cameo CS-2007	(S)	Reflections	1967	8.00	20.00
		(Cameo 2007 is a reissue of Lucky Eleven 8001.)			
Abkco AB-4217	(S)	Mark, Don And Terry 1966-67 (2 LPs)	1972	5.00	12.00

KNIGHTS, THE
The Knights are a creation of Gary Usher & Co.

Capitol T-2189	(M)	Hot Rod High	1964	200.00	400.00
Capitol DT-2189	(E)	Hot Rod High	1964	200.00	400.00

KNOWBODY ELSE
Members of Knowbody Else later recorded as Black Oak Arkansas.

Hip HIS-7003	(S)	Knowbody Else	1969	16.00	40.00

KNOX, BUDDY

Roulette R-25003	(M)	Buddy Knox (White label promo)	1957	100.00	400.00
Roulette R-25003	(M)	Buddy Knox	1957	80.00	200.00
		—Roulette albums above have black & silver labels.—			
Roulette R-25003	(M)	Buddy Knox	1957	40.00	100.00
		—Roulette albums above have black & red labels.—			
Liberty LRP-3251	(M)	Buddy Knox's Golden Hits	1962	12.00	30.00
Liberty LSP-7251	(P)	Buddy Knox's Golden Hits	1962	16.00	40.00
		(Contains rerecorded versions of the Roulette material.)			
United Arts. UAS-6689	(S)	Gypsy Man	1969	10.00	25.00
Accord SN-7218	(S)	Party Doll & Other Hits	1982	.80	4.00

KNOX, BUDDY, & JIMMY BOWEN
Buddy Holly plays guitar on "All For You".

Roulette R-25048	(M)	Buddy Knox & Jimmy Bowen	1958	80.00	200.00

Label & Catalog #		Title	Year	VG+	NM
		—Roulette albums above have black labels.—			
Roulette R-25048	(M)	**Buddy Knox & Jimmy Bowen**	196?	4.00	100.00
		—Roulette albums above have white labels.—			
KOALA, THE					
Capitol SKAO-176	(S)	The Koala	1969	30.00	75.00
KODAKS, THE					
Lost-Nite LLP-14	(10")	The Kodaks (Red vinyl)	1981	4.00	10.00
KODAKS, THE / THE STARLITES					
Sphere Sound SR-7005	(M)	The Kodaks Vs. The Starlites	1965	100.00	250.00
Sphere Sound SRR-7005	(E)	The Kodaks Vs. The Starlites	1965	80.00	200.00
KOLE, JERRY, & THE STROKERS					
Jerry Kole is a pseudonym for Jerry Cole. Refer to Ritchie Valens / Jerry Kole.					
Crown CLP-5385	(M)	Hot Rod Alley	1963	12.00	30.00
Crown CST-385	(S)	Hot Rod Alley	1963	16.00	40.00
		—Crown albums above have gray labels.—			
KOOL & THE GANG					
De-Lite DSR-2003	(S)	Kool & The Gang	1969	10.00	25.00
De-Lite DSR-2008	(S)	Live At The Sex Machine	1971	4.00	10.00
De-Lite DSR-2009	(S)	The Best Of Kool & The Gang	1971	4.00	10.00
De-Lite DSR-2010	(S)	Live At PJ's	1971	4.00	10.00
De-Lite DSR-2011	(S)	Music Is The Message	1972	4.00	10.00
De-Lite DSR-2012	(S)	Good Times	1973	4.00	10.00
De-Lite DSR-4001	(S)	Kool Jazz	1973	4.00	10.00
De-Lite DSR-2013	(S)	Wild And Peaceful	1974	4.00	10.00
De-Lite DSR-2014	(S)	Light Of Worlds	1974	4.00	10.00
De-Lite DSR-2015	(S)	Kool & The Gang's Greatest Hits	1975	4.00	10.00
De-Lite DSR-2016	(S)	Spirit Of The Boogie	1975	4.00	10.00
De-Lite DSR-2018	(S)	Love And Understanding	1976	4.00	10.00
De-Lite DSR-2023	(S)	Open Sesame	1976	4.00	10.00
De-Lite DSR-9507	(S)	Kool & The Gang Spin Their Top Ten Hits	1978	4.00	10.00
De-Lite DSR-9509	(S)	Everybody's Dancin'	1978	4.00	10.00
De-Lite DSR-9513	(S)	Ladies Night	1979	4.00	10.00
De-Lite MK-48	(S)	History Of Kool & The Gang (Promo)	1979	6.00	15.00
De-Lite DSR-9518	(S)	Celebrate	1980	4.00	10.00
De-Lite DSR-8502	(S)	Something Special	1981	4.00	10.00
De-Lite DSR-8505	(S)	As One	1982	4.00	10.00
KOOPER, AL					
Al Kooper was a member of The Blues Project and formed the original Blood, Sweat & Tears. Refer to Mike Bloomfield & Al Kooper; Mike Bloomfield, Al Kooper & Steve Stills. He can also be found on the U.A. soundtrack "The Landlord."					
Columbia CS-9718	(S)	I Stand Alone	1969	4.00	10.00
Columbia CS-9855	(S)	You Never Know Who Your Friends Are	1969	4.00	10.00
Columbia CS-9951	(S)	Kooper Session	1969	4.00	10.00
		—Columbia albums above have "360 Sound" labels.—			
Columbia CS-9718	(S)	I Stand Alone	197?	.80	4.00
Columbia CS-9855	(S)	You Never Know Who Your Friends Are	197?	.80	4.00
Columbia CS-9951	(S)	Kooper Session	197?	.80	4.00
Columbia KC-30031	(S)	Easy Does It (2 LPs)	1970	1.20	6.00
Columbia KV-30506	(S)	New York City (You're A Woman)	1971	1.00	5.00
Columbia KC-31189	(S)	Possible Projection Of The Future	1972	1.00	5.00
Columbia KC-31723	(S)	Naked Songs	1972	1.00	5.00
Columbia PG-33169	(S)	Unclaimed Freight (Al's Big Deal)	1975	1.00	5.00
United Arts. LA-702G	(S)	Act Like Nothing's Wrong	1976	1.00	5.00
Columbia FC-38137	(S)	Championship Wrestling	1982	1.00	5.00
KORNER, ALEXIS					
Warner Bros. 2XS-1966	(S)	Bootleg Him (2 LPs with Charlie Watts)	1972	10.00	25.00
Warner Bros. BS-2647	(S)	Accidently Borne In New Orleans	1972	6.00	15.00
Just Sunshine 13	(S)	All Stars Blues Incorporated	1974	4.00	10.00
Columbia PC-33427	(S)	Get Off Of My Cloud (With Keith Richards)	1975	6.00	15.00
KORTCHMAR, DANNY					
Kortchmar was a member of The Blues Project.					
Warner Bros. BS-2711	(S)	Kootch	1973	4.00	10.00
KOSSOFF, PAUL					
Paul Kossof was a member of Free and later formed Back Street Crawler.					
Island ILPS-9264	(S)	Back Street Crawler	1975	1.00	5.00
DJM 300	(S)	Koss (2 LPs)	1977	4.00	10.00
KRAFTWERK					
Vertigo VEL-2003	(S)	Autobahn	1975	3.20	8.00
Vertigo VEL-2006	(S)	Ralf And Florian	1975	1.00	5.00
Capitol ST-11457	(S)	Radio-Activity	1975	.80	4.00

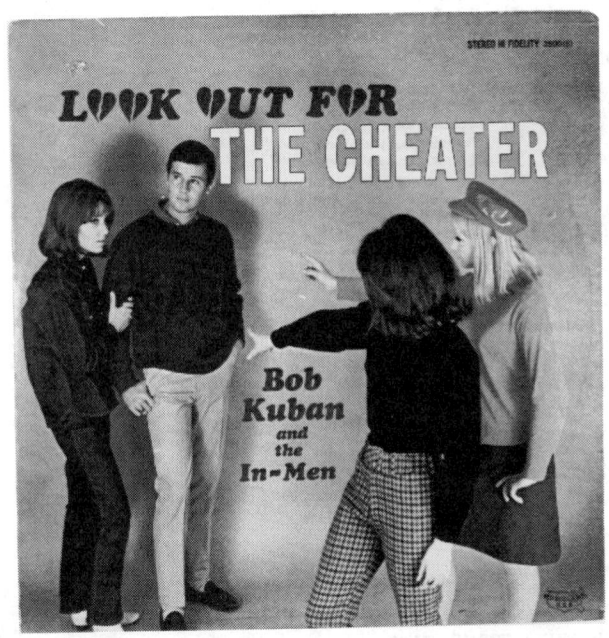

Bob Kuban & The In-Men had a national hit in 1966 with "The Cheater" on Musicland. The group followed with two more charting singles, including a daring version of The Beatles' "Drive My Car." This led to their sole album, which sports this great period-piece of a cover: Three attractively mod chicks and one wimpy looking guy dressed in the eternally accept-able "preppy/collegiate" fashion, consisting of loafers, sweater, and button-down collar.

Label & Catalog #		Title	Year	VG+	NM
Capitol ST-11603	(S)	**Trans-Europe Express**	1977	.80	4.00
Capitol ST-11728	(S)	**The Man-Machine**	1978	.80	4.00
Mercury SRM-3704	(S)	**Autobahn**	1977	.80	4.00
Warner Bros. HS-3549	(S)	**Computer-World**	1981	.80	4.00

KRAMER, BILLY J., & THE DAKOTAS

Imperial LP-9267	(M)	Little Children	1964	20.00	50.00
Imperial LP-12267	(P)	Little Children	1964	30.00	75.00
		—Imperial mono albums above have black labels with stars on top; stereo albums are black with silver print.—			
Imperial LP-9267	(M)	Little Children	1964	12.00	30.00
Imperial LP-12267	(P)	Little Children	1964	16.00	40.00
Imperial LP-9273	(M)	I'll Keep You Satisfied/From A Window	1964	12.00	30.00
Imperial LP-12273	(S)	I'll Keep You Satisfied/From A Window	1964	16.00	40.00
		("I'll Keep You Satisfied," "Sugar Babe," "I'll Be On My Way," "From A Window," "Second To None," and "The Cruel Surf" are rechanneled.)			
Imperial LP-9291	(M)	Trains And Boats And Planes	1965	12.00	30.00
Imperial LP-12291	(E)	Trains And Boats And Planes	1965	10.00	25.00
		—Imperial albums above have black & pink labels.—			
Capitol SM-11897	(M)	The Best Of Billy J., Kramer & The Dakotas	1979	1.00	5.00
		("Trains And Boats And Planes" and "From A Window" are stereo.)			

KRISTOFFERSON, KRIS
Kris Kristofferson is a singer and writer of popular songs with a folk and country flavor.

Monument SLP-18139	(S)	Kristofferson	1970	6.00	15.00
Monument KZ-30679	(S)	The Silver-Tongued Devil And I	1971	1.00	5.00
Monument ZQ-30679	(Q)	The Silver-Tongued Devil And I	1973	6.00	15.00
Monument KZ-30817	(S)	Me & Bobby McGhee	1971	1.00	5.00
		(Monument 30817 is a reissue of 18139.)			
Monument KZ-31302	(S)	Border Lord	1972	1.00	5.00
Monument KZ-31909	(S)	Jesus Was A Capricorn	1972	1.00	5.00
Monument ZQ-31909	(Q)	Jesus Was A Capricorn	1973	6.00	15.00
Monument PZ-32914	(S)	Spooky Lady's Sideshow	1974	1.00	5.00
Monument PZQ-32914	(Q)	Spooky Lady's Sideshow	1974	6.00	15.00
Monument PZ-33278	(S)	Breakaway	1974	1.00	5.00
Monument PZ-33379	(S)	Who's To Bless... And Who's To Blame	1975	1.00	5.00
Monument PZ-34254	(S)	Surreal Thing	1976	1.00	5.00
Monument PZ-34687	(S)	Songs Of Kristofferson	1977	1.00	5.00
Monument JZ-35310	(S)	Easter Island	1978	1.00	5.00
Monument JZ-36135	(S)	Shake Hands With The Devil	1979	1.00	5.00
Monument JZ-36885	(S)	To The Bone	1981	1.00	5.00

KUBAN, BOB, & THE IN-MEN

Musicland LP-3500	(M)	Look Out For The Cheater	1966	10.00	25.00
Musicland SLP-3500	(S)	Look Out For The Cheater	1966	12.00	30.00

KUPER, GARY

Polydor 24-4058	(S)	Shoot For The Moon	1971	4.00	10.00

KUPFERBERG, TULI
Tuli was a member of The Fugs.

ESP-Disk' 1035	(M)	No Deposit No Return *(Gold vinyl)*	1967	24.00	60.00
ESP-Disk' 1035	(M)	No Deposit No Return	1967	16.00	40.00
Shimmy Disc	(S)	Tuli And Friends	1989	4.00	10.00

KUSTOM KINGS, THE

Smash MGS-27051	(M)	Kustom City, U.S.A.	1964	50.00	125.00
Smash SRS-67051	(S)	Kustom City, U.S.A.	1964	80.00	200.00

KWESKIN, JIM [JIM KWESKIN & THE JUG BAND]
The Jug Band consisted of Maria D'Amato (later Maria Muldauer), Richard Greene, Bill Keith, Mel Lyman, Geoff Muldauer and Fritz Richmond.

Vanguard VRS-9139	(M)	Jim Kweskin & The Jug Band	1965	8.00	20.00
Vanguard VSD-2158	(S)	Jim Kweskin & The Jug Band	1965	10.00	25.00
Vanguard VRS-9163	(M)	Jug Band Music	1966	8.00	20.00
Vanguard VSD-79163	(S)	Jug Band Music	1966	10.00	25.00
Vanguard VRS-9188	(M)	Relax Your Mind	1966	8.00	20.00
Vanguard VSD-79188	(S)	Relax Your Mind	1966	10.00	25.00
Vanguard VRS-9234	(M)	See Reverse Side For Title	1966	8.00	20.00
Vanguard VSD-79234	(S)	See Reverse Side For Title	1966	10.00	25.00
Vanguard VRS-9243	(M)	Jump For Joy	1967	8.00	20.00
Vanguard VSD-79243	(S)	Jump For Joy	1967	6.00	15.00
Vanguard VSD-79270	(S)	The Best Of Jim Kweskin & The Jug Band	1968	6.00	15.00
Vanguard VSD-79278	(S)	Whatever Happened To Those Good Old Days	1968	6.00	15.00
Reprise R-6266	(M)	Garden Of Joy	1967	6.00	15.00
Reprise RS-6266	(S)	Garden Of Joy	1967	6.00	15.00
Vanguard VSD-13/14	(S)	Greatest Hits *(2 LPs)*	1970	4.00	10.00

LA LUPE

Roulette SR-42024	(S)	The Queen Does Her Own Thing	1968	12.00	30.00

LaBELLE, PATTI & THE BLUEBELLES [THE BLUEBELLES]

Newtown 631	(M)	Sweethearts Of The Apollo	1963	200.00	400.00
Newtown 632	(M)	Sleigh Bells, Jingle Bells And Bluebelles	1963	200.00	400.00
Parkway P-7043	(M)	The Bluebelles On Stage (With bonus single)	1965	60.00	150.00
Parkway P-7043	(M)	The Bluebelles On Stage (Without single)	1965	50.00	125.00
Atlantic 8119	(M)	Over The Rainbow	1966	12.00	30.00
Atlantic SD-8119	(S)	Over The Rainbow	1966	16.00	40.00
Atlantic 8147	(M)	Dreamer	1967	12.00	30.00
Atlantic SD-8147	(S)	Dreamer	1967	16.00	40.00
Upfront UPF-129	(E)	Patti Labelle & The Bluebelles At The Apollo	197?	1.00	5.00
Trip TLX-3508	(E)	Patti Labelle & The Bluebelles	197?	1.00	5.00
Trip TLP-9525	(E)	Early Hits	197?	1.00	5.00
Trip TLP-8000	(E)	Patti Labelle & The Bluebelles's Greatest Hits	197?	1.00	5.00
Mistletoe 1204	(E)	Merry Christmas From Labelle	197?	1.00	5.00
United Arts. LA-504E	(E)	The Very Best Of Patti Labelle & The Bluebelles	1974	1.00	5.00

LACEWING

Mainstream 6132	(S)	Lacewing	1971	20.00	50.00

LAINE, DENNY

Denny Laine was an original member of The Moody Blues. Refer to Ginger Baker.

Wizard/Reprise-MS-2190	(S)	Ah, Laine!	1972	4.00	10.00
Capitol ST-11588	(DJ)	Holly Days (Produced by Paul McCartney)	1976	10.00	25.00
		(Original copies of ST-11588 were issued as promos in plain white jackets and have a 1976 copyright date on the label.)			
Capitol ST-11588	(M)	Holly Days	1977	4.00	10.00
Takoma 71034	(S)	Japanese Tears	1983	4.00	10.00

LAKE, GREG

Refer to Emerson, Lake & Palmer.

Chrysalis 1357	(S)	Greg Lake	1981	1.00	5.00

LAMB

Fillmore F-30003	(S)	Sign Of Change	1970	6.00	15.00
Warner Bros. WS-1920	(S)	Cross Between	1971	6.00	15.00
Warner Bros. WS-1952	(S)	Bring Out The Sun	1972	6.00	15.00

LAMONT

Uni 73076	(S)	A Legend In His Own Mind	1970	4.00	10.00

LAMPLIGHTERS, THE

Federal 510	(M)	The Best Of The Lamplighters (Red vinyl)	195?	See note below	
		(Federal 510 by The Lamplighters is a bootleg worth $25-35.)			

LANCE, BOBBY

Cotillion SD-9041	(S)	First Peace	1971	4.00	10.00
Atlantic SD-7218	(S)	Rollin' Man	1972	4.00	10.00

LANCE, MAJOR

OKeh OKM-12105	(M)	The Monkey Time	1963	14.00	35.00
OKeh OKS-14105	(S)	The Monkey Time	1963	20.00	50.00
		("Monkey Time" and "Mama Didn't Know" are rechanneled.)			
OKeh OKM-12106	(M)	Um, Um, Um, Um, Um, Um	1964	14.00	35.00
OKeh OKS-14106	(P)	Um, Um, Um, Um, Um, Um	1964	20.00	50.00
OKeh OKM-12110	(M)	Major Lance's Greatest Hits	1965	12.00	30.00
OKeh OKS-14110	(S)	Major Lance's Greatest Hits	1965	16.00	40.00
		("Monkey Time" is rechanneled on this album.)			

LANCELOT LINK

ABC S-715	(S)	Lancelot Link & The Evolution Revolution	1970	16.00	40.00

Label & Catalog #		Title	Year	VG+	NM
LANDSLIDE					
Capitol ST-11006	(S)	Two-Sided Fantasy	1972	1.00	5.00
LARAMIE					
Mercury SR-61292	(S)	Laramie	1970	1.00	5.00
LARKS, THE					
The Larks feature Don Julian.					
Money MY-1102	(M)	The Jerk	1965	14.00	35.00
Money MS-1102	(S)	The Jerk	1965	20.00	50.00
Money MY-1107	(M)	Soul Kaleidoscope	1966	14.00	35.00
Money MS-1107	(S)	Soul Kaleidoscope	1966	20.00	50.00
Money MY-1110	(M)	Superslick	1967	16.00	40.00
Money MS-1110	(S)	Superslick	1967	16.00	40.00
LAST POETS, THE					
Juggernaut 8802	(S)	Right On	1971	20.00	50.00
Douglas Z-30583	(S)	This Is Madness	1971	20.00	50.00
Douglas Z-30811	(S)	Last Poets	1971	20.00	50.00
Douglas NBLP-7051	(S)	Delights Of The Garden	1977	10.00	25.00
LAST RITUAL					
Capitol SKAO-206	(S)	The Last Ritual	1969	5.00	12.00
LAST WORDS, THE					
Atco SD-33-235	(S)	The Last Words	1968	6.00	15.00
LATIN SOULS, THE					
Kapp KL-1524	(M)	Boo-Go-Loo And Shing-A-Ling	1967	8.00	20.00
Kapp KS-3524	(S)	Boo-Go-Loo And Shing-A-Ling	1967	8.00	20.00
LAUPER, CYNDI					
Portrait 38930	(S)	She's So Unusual	1983	.60	4.00
Portrait 9R9-39610	(S)	She's So Unusual *(Picture disc)*	1984	4.00	10.00
LAURA					
Ovation 14-11	(S)	Laura	1970	4.00	10.00
LAUREN, ROD					
RCA Victor LPM-2176	(M)	I'm Rod Lauren	1961	14.00	35.00
RCA Victor LSP-2176	(S)	I'm Rod Lauren	1961	20.00	50.00
LAWRENCE, VICKI					
Bell 1120	(S)	The Night The Lights Went Out In Georgia	1973	3.20	8.00
LAY, SAM					
Blue Thumb BTS-14	(S)	Sam Lay In Bluesland	1968	10.00	25.00
LAZARUS					
Amazon 1001	(S)	Lazarus	1970	8.00	20.00
LAZARUS					
Bearsville 2044	(S)	Lazarus	1971	4.00	10.00
Bearsville 2135	(S)	Fool's Paradise	1973	4.00	10.00
LAZARUS, KEN					
Steady 100	(S)	Reggae's Greatest Hits	1970	6.00	15.00
Steady 102	(S)	Scorcher	1970	6.00	15.00
Steady 105	(S)	Reggae's Greatest Hits, Volume 2	1970	6.00	15.00
LAZY LESTER					
Excello LP-8006	(M)	True Blues	1966	200.00	400.00
Excello LPS-8006	(M)	True Blues	1966	30.00	75.00
		(Later "Electronic Stereo" covers contain mono records.)			
LEAGUE OF GENTLEMEN, THE: *Refer to* **ROBERT FRIPP**					
LEATHERCOATED MINDS, THE					
The Minds feature J.J. Cale.					
Viva V-36003	(M)	Trip Down Sunset Strip	1967	20.00	50.00
Viva VS-36003	(S)	Trip Down Sunset Strip	1967	30.00	75.00
LEAVES, THE					
Mira LP-3005	(M)	Hey Joe	1966	16.00	40.00
Mira LPS-3005	(S)	Hey Joe	1966	20.00	50.00
Surrey LPS-3005	(S)	Hey Joe *(Issued in a Mira jacket)*	196?	60.00	150.00
Capitol T-2638	(M)	All The Good That's Happening	1967	10.00	25.00
Capitol ST-2638	(S)	All The Good That's Happening	1967	12.00	30.00

The Larks, better known to rhythm'n blues fans as Don Julian & The Meadowlarks, had a Top 10 hit with "The Jerk," one of countless dance records attempting to replace the twist in the early '60s. America's Newest Dance Craze was Money's second LP release and, like the majority of the early '60s dance records, does not command the respect of enough collectors.

Label & Catalog #		Title	Year	VG+	NM

LED ZEPPELIN

Led Zeppelin was Jimmy Page, Robert Plant, John Bonham and John Paul Jones. Refer to Eric Clapton/ Jeff Beck / Jimmy Page; Lord Sutch; The Yardbirds.

Label & Catalog #		Title	Year	VG+	NM
Atlantic SD-8216	(S)	Led Zeppelin	1969	150.00	300.00
		—Atlantic albums above have purple & brown, Atco-style labels.—			
Atlantic 8216	(M)	Led Zeppelin (White label promo)	1969	200.00	400.00
Atlantic SD-8216	(S)	Led Zeppelin (White label promo)	1969	100.00	250.00
Atlantic SD-8216	(S)	Led Zeppelin	1968	8.00	20.00
Atlantic 8236	(M)	Led Zeppelin II (White label promo)	1969	200.00	400.00
Atlantic SD-8236	(S)	Led Zeppelin II (White label promo)	1969	100.00	250.00
Atlantic SD-8236	(S)	Led Zeppelin II (Textured cover)	1969	8.00	20.00
Atlantic 7201	(M)	Led Zeppelin III (White label promo)	1970	200.00	400.00
Atlantic SD-7201	(S)	Led Zeppelin III (White label promo)	1970	100.00	250.00
Atlantic SD-7201	(S)	Led Zeppelin III (Die-cut cover)	1970	4.00	10.00
Atlantic 7208	(M)	Led Zeppelin IV (White label promo)	1971	200.00	400.00
Atlantic SD-7208	(S)	Led Zeppelin IV (White label promo)	1971	100.00	250.00
Atlantic SD-7208	(S)	Led Zeppelin IV	1971	4.00	10.00
Atlantic 7255	(M)	Houses Of The Holy (White label promo)	1973	660.00	1,000.00
Atlantic SD-7255	(S)	Houses Of The Holy	1973	4.00	10.00
		—Atlantic albums above have green & orange labels with "1841 Broadway" on the bottom.—			
Atlantic SD-8216	(S)	Led Zeppelin	197?	1.00	5.00
Atlantic SD-8236	(S)	Led Zeppelin II (Glossy cover)	197?	1.00	5.00
Atlantic SD-7201	(S)	Led Zeppelin III	197?	1.00	5.00
Atlantic SD-7208	(S)	Led Zeppelin IV	197?	1.00	5.00
Atlantic SD-7255	(S)	Houses Of The Holy	197?	1.00	5.00
		—Atlantic albums above have green & orange labels with "75 Rockefeller Plaza" on the bottom.—			
Atlantic SD-8216	(S)	Led Zeppelin (Laminated cover)	1970	80.00	200.00
Atlantic SD-8236	(S)	Led Zeppelin II (Laminated cover)	1970	80.00	200.00
Atlantic SD-7201	(S)	Led Zeppelin III (Laminated cover)	1970	80.00	200.00
		—Atlantic albums above have green & orange "GEMA" label manufactured for export to Germany.—			
Atlantic SD-19126	(S)	Led Zeppelin	197?	.80	4.00
Atlantic SD-19127	(S)	Led Zeppelin II	197?	.80	4.00
Atlantic SD-19128	(S)	Led Zeppelin III	197?	.80	4.00
Atlantic SD-19129	(S)	Led Zeppelin IV	197?	.80	4.00
Atlantic SD-19130	(S)	Houses Of The Holy	197?	.80	4.00
Swan Song SS-2-200	(S)	Physical Graffiti (2 LPs)	1975	4.00	10.00
Swan Song SS-8416	(S)	Presence	1976	1.00	5.00
Swan Song SS-2-201	(S)	The Song Remains The Same (2 LPs)	1975	4.00	10.00
Swan Song SS-16002	(S)	In Through The Out Door (Without bag)	1979	1.00	5.00
		(SS 16002 was issued with six different cover variations. Each came in a brown paper bag-like second cover, worth an additional $5.)			
Swan Song 79-00511	(S)	Coda	1982	1.00	5.00

LED ZEPPELIN / DUSTY SPRINGFIELD

Label & Catalog #		Title	Year	VG+	NM
Atlantic SP-135	(DJ)	Led Zeppelin / Dusty In Memphis	1969	80.00	200.00
		(Album sampler with one side devoted to each artist's new album. This is known among collectors as "Climb Aboard Led Zeppelin.")			

LEE, ALVIN

Lee originally recorded as the leader of Ten Years After.

Label & Catalog #		Title	Year	VG+	NM
Columbia PC-32729	(S)	On The Road To Freedom	1974	1.20	6.00
Columbia PC-33187	(S)	In Flight	1975	1.20	6.00
Columbia PC-33796	(S)	Pump Iron!	1975	1.20	6.00
RSO 3033	(S)	Rocket Fuel	1978	1.20	6.00
RSO 3049	(S)	Ride On	1979	1.20	6.00
Atlantic SD-19287	(S)	Free Fall	1980	1.20	6.00
Atlantic SD-19036	(S)	RX5	1981	1.20	6.00

LEE, ARTHUR

Mr. Lee was the leader of Love.

Label & Catalog #		Title	Year	VG+	NM
A&M SP-4356	(S)	Vindicator	1972	12.00	30.00
Rhino RNLP-020	(S)	Arthur Lee	1981	.80	4.00

LEE, BRENDA

Label & Catalog #		Title	Year	VG+	NM
Decca DL-8873	(M)	Grandma, What Great Songs You Sang	1960	10.00	25.00
Decca DL-78873	(S)	Grandma, What Great Songs You Sang	1960	12.00	30.00
Decca DL-4039	(M)	Brenda Lee	1960	10.00	25.00
Decca DL-74039	(S)	Brenda Lee	1960	12.00	30.00
Decca DL-4082	(M)	This Is Brenda	1960	10.00	25.00
Decca DL-74082	(S)	This Is Brenda	1960	12.00	30.00
Decca DL-4104	(M)	Emotions	1961	8.00	20.00
Decca DL-74104	(S)	Emotions	1961	10.00	25.00
Decca DL-4176	(M)	All The Way	1961	8.00	20.00
Decca DL-74176	(S)	All The Way	1961	10.00	25.00
Decca DL-4216	(M)	Sincerely, Brenda Lee	1962	8.00	20.00
Decca DL-74216	(S)	Sincerely, Brenda Lee	1962	10.00	25.00
Decca DL-4326	(M)	That's All	1962	8.00	20.00
Decca DL-74326	(S)	That's All	1962	10.00	25.00

Label & Catalog #		Title	Year	VG+	NM
Decca DL-4370	(M)	All Alone Am I	1963	8.00	20.00
Decca DL-74370	(S)	All Alone Am I	1963	10.00	25.00
Decca DL-4439	(M)	Let Me Sing	1963	8.00	20.00
Decca DL-74439	(S)	Let Me Sing	1963	10.00	25.00
—Decca albums above have black labels with silver print.—					
Decca DL-8873	(M)	Grandma, What Great Songs You Sang	196?	4.00	10.00
Decca DL-78873	(S)	Grandma, What Great Songs You Sang	196?	5.00	12.00
Decca DL-4039	(M)	Brenda Lee	196?	4.00	10.00
Decca DL-74039	(S)	Brenda Lee	196?	5.00	12.00
Decca DL-4082	(M)	This Is Brenda	196?	4.00	10.00
Decca DL-74082	(S)	This Is Brenda	196?	5.00	12.00
Decca DL-4104	(M)	Emotions	196?	4.00	10.00
Decca DL-74104	(S)	Emotions	196?	5.00	12.00
Decca DL-4176	(M)	All The Way	196?	4.00	10.00
Decca DL-74176	(S)	All The Way	196?	5.00	12.00
Decca DL-4216	(M)	Sincerely, Brenda Lee	196?	4.00	10.00
Decca DL-74216	(S)	Sincerely, Brenda Lee	196?	5.00	12.00
Decca DL-4326	(M)	That's All	196?	4.00	10.00
Decca DL-74326	(S)	That's All	196?	5.00	12.00
Decca DL-4370	(M)	All Alone Am I	196?	4.00	10.00
Decca DL-74370	(S)	All Alone Am I	196?	5.00	12.00
Decca DL-4439	(M)	Let Me Sing	196?	4.00	10.00
Decca DL-74439	(S)	Let Me Sing	196?	5.00	12.00
Decca DL-4509	(M)	By Request	1964	6.00	15.00
Decca DL-74509	(S)	By Request	1964	8.00	20.00
Decca DL-4583	(M)	Merry Christmas From Brenda Lee	1964	6.00	15.00
Decca DL-74583	(S)	Merry Christmas From Brenda Lee	1964	8.00	20.00
Decca DL-4626	(M)	Top Teen Hits	1965	6.00	15.00
Decca DL-74626	(S)	Top Teen Hits	1965	8.00	20.00
Decca DL-4661	(M)	The Versatile Brenda Lee	1965	5.00	12.00
Decca DL-74661	(S)	The Versatile Brenda Lee	1965	6.00	15.00
Decca DL-4684	(M)	Too Many Rivers	1965	5.00	12.00
Decca DL-74684	(S)	Too Many Rivers	1965	6.00	15.00
Decca DL-4755	(M)	Bye, Bye Blues	1966	5.00	12.00
Decca DL-74755	(S)	Bye, Bye Blues	1966	6.00	15.00
Decca DL-4757	(M)	Ten Golden Years (Gatefold cover)	1966	6.00	15.00
Decca DL-74757	(S)	Ten Golden Years (Gatefold cover)	1966	8.00	20.00
Decca DL-4825	(M)	Coming On Strong	1966	5.00	12.00
Decca DL-74825	(S)	Coming On Strong	1966	6.00	15.00
—Decca albums above have black "rainbow" labels with "Mfrd by Decca" beneath the rainbow.—					
Decca DL-4941	(M)	Reflections In Blue	1967	5.00	12.00
Decca DL-74941	(S)	Reflections In Blue	1967	5.00	12.00
Decca DL-74955	(S)	For The First Time	1968	5.00	12.00
Decca DL-75111	(S)	Johnny One Time	1969	5.00	12.00
Decca ST-92062	(S)	Johnny One Time (Capitol Record Club)	1969	5.00	12.00
Decca DL-75232	(S)	Memphis Portrait	1970	5.00	12.00
Vocalion VL-3795	(M)	Here's Brenda Lee	1967	5.00	12.00
Vocalion VL-73795	(S)	Here's Brenda Lee	1967	5.00	12.00
Vocalion VL-73890	(S)	Let It Be Me	1970	5.00	12.00
Coral CB-20044	(S)	Let It Be Me	197?	1.00	5.00
MCA 4012	(S)	The Brenda Lee Story (2 LPs)	1973	4.00	10.00
MCA 305	(S)	Brenda	1973	1.00	5.00
MCA 373	(S)	A New Sunrise	1973	1.00	5.00
MCA 433	(S)	Brenda Lee Now	1974	1.00	5.00
MCA 477	(S)	Sincerely	1975	1.00	5.00
MCA 2233	(S)	The L.A. Sessions	1976	1.00	5.00
MCA 3211	(S)	Even Better	1980	1.00	5.00
MCA 758	(S)	Even Better	1980	1.00	5.00
MCA 812	(S)	Take Me Back	1980	1.00	5.00
MCA 824	(S)	Only When I Laugh	1981	1.00	5.00
MCA 5342	(S)	Brenda Lee's Greatest Country Hits	1982	1.00	5.00

LEE, BRENDA / TENNESSEE ERNIE FORD

Decca MG-9226	(M)	The Show For Christmas Seals	1962	12.00	30.00
Decca MG-79226	(S)	The Show For Christmas Seals	1962	16.00	40.00

LEE, BYRON, & THE DRAGONAIRES

Jad JS-1004	(S)	Byron Lee & The Dragonaires	196?	8.00	20.00
BMN BLP-004	(M)	Dance The Ska	196?	8.00	20.00
Towers Hall LP-006	(M)	The Sounds Of Jamaica	196?	8.00	20.00

LEE, DICKIE

Smash MGS-27020	(M)	Tales Of Patches	1962	14.00	35.00
Smash SRS-67020	(S)	Tales Of Patches	1962	20.00	50.00
TCF Hall T-9001	(M)	"Laurie" And "The Girl From Peyton Place"	1965	8.00	20.00
TCF Hall ST-9001	(S)	"Laurie" And "The Girl From Peyton Place"	1965	10.00	25.00

Label & Catalog #		Title	Year	VG+	NM

LEE, JACKIE

| Mirwood MW-7000 | (M) | The Duck | 1966 | 8.00 | 20.00 |
| Mirwood SW-7000 | (S) | The Duck | 1966 | 10.00 | 25.00 |

LEE, LEAPY

| Decca DL-75076 | (S) | Little Arrows | 1968 | 3.20 | 8.00 |
| Decca DL-75237 | (S) | Leapy Lee | 1970 | 3.20 | 8.00 |

LEE, LAURIE
Ms. Lee was formerly a member of The Meditation Singers.

Chess CH-50031	(S)	Love More Than Pride	1969	6.00	15.00
Hot Wax HA-708	(S)	Women's Love Rights	1971	6.00	15.00
Hot Wax HA-714	(S)	Two Sides Of Laura Lee	1972	6.00	15.00
Invictus KZ-33133	(S)	I Can't Make It Alone	1973	6.00	15.00
Hot Wax HA-715	(S)	The Rip Off	1984	3.20	8.00
Myrrh MSB-6722	(S)	Jesus Is The Light Of The World	1983	3.20	8.00
Becket 017	(S)	All Power	1984	3.20	8.00

LEFT BANKE, THE
The Left Banke features Michael Brown. Refer to The Beckies; Montage; Stories.

Smash MGS-27088	(M)	Walk Away Renee/Pretty Ballerina	1967	24.00	60.00
Smash SRS-67088	(P)	Walk Away Renee/Pretty Ballerina	1967	24.00	60.00
Smash SRS-67113	(P)	Left Banke, Too	1968	24.00	60.00
		(Both stereo albums have been poorly counterfeited.)			
Rhino RNLP-123	(S)	The Best Of The Left Banke	1984	1.00	5.00

LEGEND

| Bell 6027 | (S) | Legend | 1969 | 16.00 | 40.00 |

LEGENDS, THE

| Columbia CL-1707 | (M) | Hit Sounds Of Today's Smash Hit Combos | 1961 | 12.00 | 30.00 |
| Columbia CS-8507 | (S) | Hit Sounds Of Today's Smash Hit Combos | 1961 | 16.00 | 40.00 |

LEGENDS, THE

Ermine LP-101	(M)	The Legends Let Loose	1963	80.00	200.00
Capitol T-1925	(M)	The Legends Let Loose	1963	16.00	40.00
Capitol ST-1925	(S)	The Legends Let Loose	1963	20.00	50.00
		(Capitol 1925 is a reissue of Ermine 101.)			

LEIBER, JERRY

Zephyr 12002	(M)	Scooby-Doo	1956	60.00	150.00
Kapp KL-1127	(M)	Scooby-Doo	1959	20.00	50.00
		(Kapp 1127 is a reissue of Zephyr 12002.)			

LEIBER & STOLLER BIG BAND, THE
Jerry Leiber and Mike Stoller were the first, and most influential, of the independent production teams in the field of rock'n roll. The Big Band is Atlantic's house band under the direction of the two.

Atlantic 8047	(M)	Yakety Yak	1960	16.00	40.00
Atlantic SD-8047	(S)	Yakety Yak	1960	20.00	50.00
		—Atlantic albums above have multi-colored labels with a white "fan" logo on the right side.—			
Atlantic 8047	(M)	Yakety Yak	196?	8.00	20.00
Atlantic SD-8047	(S)	Yakety Yak	196?	10.00	25.00
		—Atlantic albums above have multi-colored labels with a black "fan" logo on the right side.—			

LEMON PIPERS, THE
Refer to 1910 Fruitgum Co. / The Lemon Pipers.

Buddah BD-5009	(M)	Green Tambourine	1968	8.00	20.00
Buddah BDS-5009	(S)	Green Tambourine	1968	10.00	25.00
Buddah BDS-5016	(S)	Jungle Marmalade	1968	8.00	20.00

LENNEAR, CLAUDIA

| Warner Bros. BS-2654 | (S) | Phew! | 1973 | 6.00 | 15.00 |

LENNON, JOHN
Mr Lennon was the leader and rhythm guitar player for the greatest rock group the world will ever know. Refer to Elephant's Memory; Nilsson; Yoko Ono; David Peel.

Apple SW-3362	(S)	Live Peace In Toronto (With 1970 calendar)	1969	16.00	40.00
Apple SW-3362	(S)	Live Peace In Toronto (Without calendar)	1969	12.00	30.00
		—Apple albums above read "A Subsidiary of Capitol" on the bottom.—			
Apple SW-3362	(S)	Live Peace In Toronto (Without calendar)	197?	6.00	15.00
Apple SW-3372	(S)	John Lennon/Plastic Ono Band	1970	8.00	20.00
Apple SW-3379	(S)	Imagine (With inserts)	1971	12.00	30.00
		(Issued with poster and a postcard.)			
Apple SW-3379	(S)	Imagine (Without inserts)	1971	8.00	20.00
Apple SW-3379	(S)	Imagine Bonus Poster	1974	.80	4.00
Apple SW-3414	(S)	Mind Games	1973	8.00	20.00
Apple SW-3416	(S)	Walls And Bridges (With book)	1974	8.00	20.00
		—Apple albums above read "Manufactured by Apple" on the bottom.—			

The John Lennon Collection *was a posthumous compilation, supposedly of his post-Beatles hits. But it inexplicably omitted such chart-makers as* "Cold Turkey," "Mother," "Woman Is The Nigger Of The World," *and* "Stand By Me." *Instead, the compiler(s) chose to use album tracks* "Jealous Guy," "Love," "Dear Yoko," *and* "I'm Losing You." *The promo was issued as a* "Limited Edition Pressing" *on* Quiex II *vinyl, making it desirable both as a Lennon item and as an audiophile collectible.*

Label & Catalog #		Title	Year	VG+	NM
Adam VIII 8018	(S)	**Roots: John Lennon Sings** **The Great Rock & Roll Hits**	1975	**500.00**	1,000.00
		(Original front covers for Adam 8018 have the graphics printed on the cardboard. The back has ads for other albums: The song titles for "20 Solid Gold Hits" must be legible. The print on the spine reads "John Lennon Sings The Great Rock & Roll Hits." Copies with cover slicks, illegible print, or spines that read "John Lennon Sings The Greatest Rock & Roll Hits" are repros. Finally, original records must have "A-8018" hand etched into the actual paper label.)			
Apple SK-3419	(S)	Rock 'N' Roll	1975	8.00	20.00
Apple SW-3421	(S)	Shaved Fish	1975	6.00	15.00
		—Apple albums above read "Manufactured by Apple" on the bottom.—			
Apple SW-3379	(S)	Imagine	1974	8.00	20.00
		—Apple labums ahave an "All Rights Reserved" disclaimer.—			
Capitol SW-3362	(S)	Live Peace In Toronto 1969	1978	4.00	10.00
Capitol SW-3372	(S)	John Lennon/Plastic Ono Band	1978	4.00	10.00
Capitol SW-3379	(S)	Imagine (With poster)	1978	4.00	10.00
Capitol SW-3414	(S)	Mind Games	1978	16.00	40.00
Capitol SW-3416	(S)	Walls And Bridges	1978	4.00	10.00
Capitol SK-3419	(S)	Rock 'N' Roll	1978	16.00	40.00
Capitol SW-3421	(S)	Shaved Fish	1978	4.00	10.00
		—Capitol albums above have purple labels with "Mfd. by Capitol" on top.—			
Capitol SW-3372	(S)	John Lennon/Plastic Ono Band	1988	6.00	15.00
Capitol SW-3379	(S)	Imagine (With poster)	1986	4.00	10.00
Capitol SW-3416	(S)	Walls And Bridges	1989	6.00	15.00
Capitol SW-3421	(S)	Shaved Fish	1989	6.00	15.00
		—Capitol albums above have purple labels with "Manufactured. by Capitol" on top.—			
Capitol SW-3362	(S)	Live Peace In Toronto 1969	1983	20.00	50.00
Capitol SW-3372	(S)	John Lennon/Plastic Ono Band	1983	6.00	15.00
Capitol SW-3379	(S)	Imagine	1983	6.00	15.00
Capitol SW-3379	(S)	Imagine (Digitally remastered with poster)	1983	8.00	20.00
Capitol SW-3421	(S)	Shaved Fish	1983	6.00	15.00
Capitol SV-12239	(S)	Live In New York City	1986	1.00	5.00
Capitol SV-12451	(S)	Live In New York City	1986	1.00	5.00
Capitol R-144497	(S)	Live In New York City (RCA Record Club)	1986	6.00	15.00
Capitol SV-512451	(S)	Live In New York City (Columbia Rec. Club)	1986	6.00	15.00
Capitol SJ-12533	(S)	Menlove Ave.	1986	1.00	5.00
Capitol R-144136	(S)	Menlove Ave. (RCA Record Club)	1986	20.00	50.00
		—Capitol albums above have black labels.—			
Capitol SN-16068	(S)	Mind Games	1980	4.00	10.00
Capitol SN-16069	(S)	Rock 'N' Roll	1980	4.00	10.00
		—Capitol albums above have green labels.—			
Capitol C1-90803	(S)	Imagine: Music From The Original Motion Picture (2 LPs)	1988	10.00	25.00
Geffen GHSP-2023	(DJ)	The John Lennon Collection (Quiex II vinyl)	1982	20.00	50.00
Geffen GHSP-2023	(S)	The John Lennon Collection	1982	5.00	12.00
LENNON, JOHN, & YOKO ONO					
Apple T-5001	(S)	Two Virgins: Unfinished Music No. 1	1968	60.00	150.00
		(Issued in a brown paper outer sleeve that is the same size as the album jacket and opens on the right. Records have glossy labels with "MR" machine-stamped in the trail-off vinyl.)			
Apple T-5001	(S)	Two Virgins: Unfinished Music No. 1	1968	60.00	150.00
		(Issued in a brown paper outer sleeve that is the same size as the album jacket and opens on the right. Originals have glossy labels with "MR" machine-stamped in the trail-off vinyl. Reissued in 1985 with non-glossy labels; these are worth $10-15.)			
Apple T-5001	(S)	Two Virgins: Unfinished Music No. 1	1985	6.00	15.00
		(Issued in a brown paper outer sleeve that is the same size as the album jacket and opens on the right. Non- glossy labels with "MR" machine-stamped in the trail-off vinyl.)			
Zapple ST-3357	(S)	Unfinished Music #2: Life With The Lions	1969	10.00	25.00
Apple 3361	(S)	Wedding Album	1969	80.00	200.00
		(Boxed set contains photos, postcard, poster of wedding photos, poster of lithographs, a booklet of press clippings, duplicate of marriage certificate, a "bagism" bag.)			
Apple SVBB-3392	(DJ)	Some Time In New York City (2 LPs)	1972	600.00	900.00
		(White label promo)			
Apple SVBB-3392	(S)	Some Time In New York City (2 LPs)	1972	12.00	30.00
		(The label credits John & Yoko/Plastic Ono Band With Elephant's Memory And Invisible Strings. It was issued with a bonus photo and a petition to the U.S. government to allow John to stay in the States. The second record contains a live jam with Frank Zappa's Mothers.)			
Capitol SVBB-3392	(S)	Some Time In New York City	1978	10.00	25.00
		(2 LPs in double pocket, gatefold jacket.)			
Capitol SVBB-3392	(S)	Some Time In New York City	1978	100.00	250.00
		(2 LPs in single pocket, gatefold jacket)			
		—Capitol albums above have purple labels with "Mfd. by Capitol" on top.—			

Label & Catalog #		Title	Year	VG+	NM
Geffen GHS-2001	(S)	**Double Fantasy**	*1980*	4.00	10.00
	—Geffen albums above have off-white labels with print along the perimeter.—				
Geffen GHS-2001	(S)	**Double Fantasy**	*1980*	20.00	50.00
	—Geffen albums above have off-white labels without perimeter print.—				
Geffen GHS-2001	(S)	**Double Fantasy**	*1986*	20.00	50.00
	—Geffen albums above have black labels.—				
Geffen GHS-2001	(S)	**Double Fantasy** *(Columbia Record Club)*	*1980*	30.00	75.00
		(Record Club release with "CH" on the label .)			
Geffen GHS-2001	(S)	**Double Fantasy** *(Columbia Record Club)*	*1980*	6.00	15.00
		(Record Club release without the "CH" on the label .)			
Geffen R-104689	(S)	**Double Fantasy** *(RCA Record Club)*	*1980*	16.00	40.00
Capitol C1-91425	(S)	**Double Fantasy**	*1989*	6.00	15.00
Capitol C1-591425	(S)	**Double Fantasy** *(Columbia Record Club)*	*1989*	24.00	60.00
Polydor 1Y817-238-1	(DJ)	**Heart Play** *(With letter from Yoko)*	*1983*	16.00	40.00
		(Label has minimal print but does not state that it is a promo.)			
Polydor 1Y817-238-1	(S)	**Heart Play** *(With letter from Yoko)*	*1983*	2.00	10.00
		(Red label reads "Side 1" and "Side 2.")			
Polydor 1Y817-238-1	(S)	**Heart Play**	*1983*	6.00	15.00
		(Red label reads "Side A" and "Side B.")			
Polydor 1Y817-160-1	(S)	**Milk And Honey**	*1984*	.80	4.00
Polydor 1Y817-160-1	(S)	**Milk And Honey** *(Green vinyl)*	*1984*	60.00	150.00
Polydor 1Y817-160-1	(S)	**Milk And Honey** *(Gold vinyl)*	*1984*	60.00	150.00
		(These are unauthorized pressings done by a Polydor company employee "after hours." Issued without a cover.)			
Polydor 1Y817-160-1	(S)	**Milk And Honey** *(Columbia Record Club)*	*1984*	30.00	75.00
Silhouette SM-10012	(DJ)	**Reflections And Poetry** *(2 LPs with poster)*	*1984*	20.00	50.00
Silhouette SM-10012	(S)	**Reflections And Poetry** *(2 LPs with poster)*	*1984*	10.00	25.00
LENOIR, J. B.					
Chess LP-410	(M)	**Natural Man**	*1970*	6.00	15.00
Polydor 24-4011	(S)	**J. B. Lenoir**	*1970*	6.00	15.00
LEONDA					
Epic BN-26383	(S)	**Woman In The Sun**	*1969*	4.00	10.00
LEORME					
Peters Int. 9008	(S)	**Beyond Leng**	*1974*	6.00	15.00
LESTER, KETTY					
Era EL-108	(M)	**Love Letters**	*1963*	20.00	50.00
Era ES-108	(S)	**Love Letters**	*1963*	30.00	75.00
RCA Victor LPM-2945	(M)	**Soul Of Me**	*1964*	10.00	25.00
RCA Victor LSP-2945	(S)	**Soul Of Me**	*1964*	12.00	30.00
RCA Victor LPM-3326	(M)	**Where Is Love**	*1965*	10.00	25.00
RCA Victor LSP-3326	(S)	**Where Is Love**	*1965*	12.00	30.00
Tower T-5029	(M)	**When A Woman Loves A Man**	*1967*	10.00	25.00
Tower ST-5029	(S)	**When A Woman Loves A Man**	*1967*	10.00	25.00
LETTA					
Capitol ST-2929	(S)	**Free Soul**	*1968*	5.00	12.00
Chisa 805	(S)	**Letta**	*1970*	1.00	5.00
Chisa 809	(S)	**Mosadi**	*1971*	1.00	5.00
Fantasy F-9428	(S)	**Naturally**	*1973*	1.00	5.00
A&M SP-4609	(S)	**There's Music In The Air**	*1976*	1.00	5.00
LEVIATHAN					
Mach XMA-12501	(S)	**Leviathan**	*1974*	14.00	35.00
LEWIS, BARBARA					
Atlantic 8086	(M)	**Hello Stranger**	*1963*	14.00	35.00
Atlantic SD-8086	(S)	**Hello Stranger**	*1963*	20.00	50.00
Atlantic 8090	(M)	**Snap Your Fingers**	*1964*	14.00	35.00
Atlantic SD-8090	(S)	**Snap Your Fingers**	*1964*	20.00	50.00
Atlantic 8110	(M)	**Baby, I'm Yours**	*1965*	12.00	30.00
Atlantic SD-8110	(S)	**Baby, I'm Yours**	*1965*	16.00	40.00
Atlantic 8118	(M)	**It's Magic**	*1966*	12.00	30.00
Atlantic SD-8118	(S)	**It's Magic**	*1966*	16.00	40.00
Atlantic SD-8173	(S)	**Workin' On A Groovy Thing**	*1968*	10.00	25.00
Enterprise ENS-1006	(S)	**The Many Grooves Of Barbara Lewis**	*1970*	10.00	25.00
Atlantic SD-8286	(S)	**The Best Of Barbara Lewis**	*1971*	8.00	20.00
LEWIS, BOBBY					
Beltone 4000	(M)	**Tossin' And Turnin'**	*1961*	80.00	200.00
R.P.A. 1002	(S)	**Portrait In Love**	*1976*	4.00	10.00
R.P.A. 1013	(S)	**Soul Full Of Music**	*1977*	4.00	10.00

Label & Catalog #		Title	Year	VG+	NM

LEWIS, FURRY
Refer to Mississippi Fred McDowell / Furry Lewis.

Label & Catalog #		Title	Year	VG+	NM
Bluesville BVLP-1036	(M)	**Back On My Feet Again**	1961	40.00	100.00
Bluesville BVLP-1037	(M)	**Done Changed My Mind**	1961	40.00	100.00
		—Bluesville albums above have bright blue labels with silver print.—			
Bluesville BVLP-1036	(M)	**Back On My Feet Again**	1964	12.00	30.00
Bluesville BVLP-1037	(M)	**Done Changed My Mind**	1964	12.00	30.00
		—Bluesville albums above have blue labels with a trident logo on the right side.—			
Prestige PRST-7810	(S)	**Back On My Feet Again**	1970	6.00	15.00
		(Prestige 7810 is a reissue of Bluesville 1036.)			
Biograph 12017	(M)	**When I Lay My Burden Down**	1970	4.00	10.00
Adelphi 1007	(S)	**On The Road Again**	1970	6.00	15.00
Ampex A-10140	(S)	**Live At The Gaslight**	1971	10.00	25.00
Fantasy F-24709	(S)	**Shake 'Em On Down** *(2 LPs)*	1972	6.00	15.00
Southland 3	(S)	**American Blues Heritage, Vol. 3**	1976	4.00	10.00

LEWIS, GARY [GARY LEWIS & THE PLAYBOYS]

Label & Catalog #		Title	Year	VG+	NM
Liberty LRP-3408	(M)	**This Diamond Ring**	1965	6.00	15.00
Liberty LST-7408	(S)	**This Diamond Ring**	1965	8.00	20.00
Liberty LRP-3419	(M)	**A Session With Gary Lewis**	1965	5.00	12.00
Liberty LST-7419	(S)	**A Session With Gary Lewis**	1965	6.00	15.00
Liberty LRP-3428	(M)	**Everybody Loves A Clown**	1965	5.00	12.00
Liberty LST-7428	(S)	**Everybody Loves A Clown**	1965	6.00	15.00
Liberty LRP-3435	(M)	**She's Just My Style**	1966	5.00	12.00
Liberty LST-7435	(S)	**She's Just My Style**	1966	6.00	15.00
Liberty LRP-3452	(M)	**Hits Again!**	1966	5.00	12.00
Liberty LST-7452	(S)	**Hits Again!**	1966	6.00	15.00
Liberty LRP-3468	(M)	**Gary Lewis' Golden Greats**	1966	5.00	12.00
Liberty LST-7468	(S)	**Gary Lewis' Golden Greats**	1966	6.00	15.00
Liberty LRP-3487	(M)	**You Don't Have To Paint Me A Picture**	1967	8.00	20.00
Liberty LST-7487	(S)	**You Don't Have To Paint Me A Picture**	1967	8.00	20.00
		(Some copies of Liberty 3/7487 were erroneously mastered with "Ice Melts The Sun" as the fourth song on the first side, although the cover and label list "Tina." This must be heard to be identified.)			
Liberty LRP-3487	(M)	**You Don't Have To Paint Me A Picture**	1967	5.00	12.00
Liberty LST-7487	(S)	**You Don't Have To Paint Me A Picture**	1967	6.00	15.00
Liberty LRP-3519	(M)	**New Directions**	1967	5.00	12.00
Liberty LST-7519	(S)	**New Directions**	1967	6.00	15.00
Liberty LRP-3524	(M)	**Listen**	1967	5.00	12.00
Liberty LST-7524	(S)	**Listen**	1967	6.00	15.00
Liberty LST-7568	(S)	**Gary Lewis Now!**	1968	4.00	10.00
Liberty LST-7589	(S)	**More Golden Greats**	1968	4.00	10.00
Liberty LST-7606	(S)	**Close Cover Before Playing**	1969	4.00	10.00
Liberty LST-7623	(S)	**Rhythm Of The Rain**	1969	4.00	10.00
Liberty LST-7633	(S)	**I'm On The Right Road Now**	1969	4.00	10.00
Sunset SUM-1168	(M)	**Gary Lewis & The Playboys**	1967	4.00	10.00
Sunset SUS-5168	(M)	**Gary Lewis & The Playboys**	1967	4.00	10.00
Sunset SUS-5262	(M)	**Rhythm!**	1968	4.00	10.00
United Arts. LA-430	(S)	**Very Best Of Gary Lewis & The Playboys**	1975	.80	4.00
United Arts. LM-1003	(S)	**This Diamond Ring**	1980	.80	4.00

LEWIS, HUEY, & THE NEWS

Label & Catalog #		Title	Year	VG+	NM
Chrysalis 1340	(S)	**Picture This**	1982	80	4.00
Chrysalis 1412	(S)	**Sports**	1983	80	4.00
Chrysalis 8V8-42795A	(S)	**'84 Sports Tour** *(Picture disc)*	1984	4.00	10.00

LEWIS, JERRY LEE
By the early months of 1958, "The Killer" had established himself as Elvis' heir apparent. By the end of '58, Jerry Lee's career plummeted into limbo. After his tenure with Sun Records, he signed with Mercury's Smash in 1963 and continued his rock'n roll career, to no avail. But by the second half of the '60s, he had reestablished himself as one of country'n western's most distinctive stylists. The first section below lists titles with Sun sides; the second, his Smash rockers. The records from his country career are not included in this edition. For additional listings refer to Johnny Cash / Jerry Lee Lewis; Johnny Cash, Jerry Lee Lewis & Carl Perkins; Class Of '55.

1. The Sun Sides

Label & Catalog #		Title	Year	VG+	NM
Sun SLP-1230	(M)	**Jerry Lee Lewis**	1958	80.00	200.00
Sun SLP-1265	(M)	**Jerry Lee's Greatest** *(White label promo)*	1961	400.00	750.00
Sun SLP-1265	(M)	**Jerry Lee's Greatest**	1961	100.00	250.00
Design DLP-165	(M)	**Rockin' With Jerry Lee Lewis**	1963	10.00	25.00
Design DSP-165	(E)	**Rockin' With Jerry Lee Lewis**	1963	8.00	20.00
Sun LP-102	(E)	**Original Golden Hits, Volume 1**	1969	3.20	8.00
Sun LP-103	(E)	**Original Golden Hits, Volume 2**	1969	3.20	8.00
Sun LP-107	(E)	**Rockin' Rhythm & Blues**	1969	3.20	8.00
Sun LP-108	(E)	**The Golden Cream Of The Country**	1969	3.20	8.00
Sun LP-114	(E)	**A Taste Of Country**	1970	3.20	8.00
Sun LP-124	(E)	**Monsters**	1971	3.20	8.00
Sun LP-128	(E)	**Original Golden Hits, Volume 3**	1971	3.20	8.00

While Jerry Lee has yet to receive an RIAA Gold Record, he has placed twenty albums on the charts, although the bulk of the long-revered Sun material had to wait until Shelby Singleton's series of repackages in 1969 to see the best-seller lists. Collectors should note that a white label promo exists for Sun 1265, Jerry Lee's Greatest that commands big buckaroos.

Label & Catalog #		Title	Year	VG+	NM
Sun LP-145	(E)	**Roots**	1971	3.20	8.00
Sears SPS-610	(E)	**Hound Dog**	1970	8.00	20.00
Pickwick SPC-3224	(E)	**High Heel Sneakers**	1970	1.00	5.00
Pickwick SPC-3344	(E)	**Drinkin' Wine Spo Dee-O-Dee**	1973	1.00	5.00
Pickwick PTP-2055	(E)	**Breathless** (2 LPs)	197?	1.20	6.00
Pickwick TRS-1002	(E)	**Breathless** (2 LPs. Special Market)	197?	1.20	6.00
Pickwick/Hilltop JS-6110	(E)	**Roll Over Beethoven**	1972	1.00	5.00
Pickwick/Hilltop JS-6120	(E)	**Rural Route #20**	1972	1.00	5.00
Trip TLX-8501	(E)	**The Best Of Jerry Lee Lewis** (2 LPs)	1974	1.20	6.00
Power Pak PO-247	(E)	**From The Vaults Of Sun**	1974	1.00	5.00
Everest FS-298	(E)	**Jerry Lee Lewis**	1975	1.00	5.00
Sun Inter. 1011	(E)	**Duets** (Gold vinyl)	1978	3.20	8.00
Sun Inter. 1018	(E)	**Trio +** (Gold vinyl)	1978	3.20	8.00
Koala AW-14109	(E)	**Great Balls Of Fire**	1981	1.00	5.00
Koala AW-14120	(E)	**A Whole Lot Of Shakin'**	1982	1.00	5.00
Accord SN-7903	(E)	**Doin' Just Fine**	1982	1.00	5.00
Aura 1021	(E)	**The Louisiana Fireball**	1982	1.00	5.00
Rhino RNDF-255	(M)	**Original Sun Greatest Hits** (Picture disc)	1983	4.00	10.00

2. Smash Rock'n Roll

Label & Catalog #		Title	Year	VG+	NM
Smash MGS-27040	(M)	**The Golden Hits Of Jerry Lee Lewis**	1964	10.00	25.00
Smash SRS-67040	(S)	**The Golden Hits Of Jerry Lee Lewis**	1964	12.00	30.00
Smash SRS-67040	(S)	**The Golden Rock Hits Of Jerry Lee Lewis**	1969	6.00	15.00
		("Golden Rock Hits" is a reissue of "Golden Hits.")			
Smash MGS-27056	(M)	**The Greatest Live Show On Earth**	1964	40.00	100.00
Smash SRS-67056	(S)	**The Greatest Live Show On Earth**	1964	60.00	150.00
Smash MGS-27063	(M)	**The Return Of Rock**	1965	14.00	35.00
Smash SRS-67063	(S)	**The Return Of Rock**	1965	20.00	50.00
Smash MGS-27079	(M)	**Memphis Beat**	1966	8.00	20.00
Smash SRS-67079	(S)	**Memphis Beat**	1966	12.00	30.00
Smash MGS-27086	(M)	**By Request—** **More Of The Greatest Live Show On Earth**	1966	12.00	30.00
Smash SRS-67086	(S)	**By Request—** **More Of The Greatest Live Show On Earth**	1966	16.00	40.00
Smash MGS-27097	(M)	**Soul My Way**	1967	14.00	35.00
Smash SRS-67097	(S)	**Soul My Way**	1967	20.00	50.00
Wing MGW-12340	(M)	**The Return Of Rock**	1967	4.00	10.00
Wing SRW-16340	(S)	**The Return Of Rock**	1967	4.00	10.00
		(Wing 12/16340 is an abridged reissue of Smash 2/67063.)			
Wing SRW-16340	(S)	**In Demand**	1968	4.00	10.00
		("In Demand" is a reissue of "The Return Of Rock.")			
Wing SRW-16406	(S)	**Unlimited**	1968	4.00	10.00
Wing PKW2-125	(S)	**The Legend Of Jerry Lee Lewis** (2 LPs)	1969	4.00	10.00
		(Wing 125 is a repackage of 16340 and 16405.)			

LEWIS, JERRY LEE / ROGER MILLER / ROY ORBISON

Label & Catalog #		Title	Year	VG+	NM
Pickwick CPS-3027	(E)	**Jerry Lee Lewis-Roger Miller-Roy Orbison**	197?	1.00	5.00

LEWIS, JOHNNY

Label & Catalog #		Title	Year	VG+	NM
Camelot 201M	(M)	**Johnny Lewis Sings And Plays**	1966	20.00	50.00
Camelot 201S	(S)	**Johnny Lewis Sings And Plays**	1966	24.00	60.00

LEWIS, SMILEY

Label & Catalog #		Title	Year	VG+	NM
Imperial LP-9141	(M)	**I Hear You Knocking** (Green vinyl)	1961	See note below	
		(Green vinyl copies have a suggested NM value of $3,000-6,000.)			
Imperial LP-9141	(M)	**I Hear You Knocking**	1961	300.00	600.00

LEWIS & CLARKE EXPEDITION

Label & Catalog #		Title	Year	VG+	NM
Colgems COM-105	(M)	**The Lewis & Clarke Expedition**	1967	10.00	25.00
Colgems COS-105	(S)	**The Lewis & Clarke Expedition**	1967	12.00	30.00

LEXIA

Label & Catalog #		Title	Year	VG+	NM
Verve 5086	(S)	**Lexia**	1972	4.00	10.00

LIBERATION STREET BAND, THE

Label & Catalog #		Title	Year	VG+	NM
Pentagram 10002	(S)	**Down On The Corner**	1970	4.00	10.00

LT. GARCIA'S MAGIC MUSIC BOX

Label & Catalog #		Title	Year	VG+	NM
Kama Sutra KLPS-8071	(S)	**Cross The Border**	1968	6.00	15.00

LIFEGUARDS, THE

Label & Catalog #		Title	Year	VG+	NM
Time 2163	(M)	**Today's 1,000,000 Sellers**	1964	10.00	25.00
Time S-2163	(S)	**Today's 1,000,000 Sellers**	1964	14.00	35.00

LIFEGUARDS, THE

Label & Catalog #		Title	Year	VG+	NM
Wyncote W-9043	(M)	**C'Mon And Swim**	1964	1.00	5.00
Wyncote WS-9043	(S)	**C'Mon And Swim**	1964	1.20	6.00

Each edition of this book has presented the reader—nay, the very hobby itself—with listings of rare records not even believed to have existed during the time of the previous edition. For the fourth edition—slaved over throughout 1994 by indentured servants locked away in the belly of my manse and fed those table scraps rejected by my cats—Smiley Lewis' I Hear You Knocking was listed for the first time as having been pressed on green vinyl. That copy, nearly mint, sold for $6,000. As none have surfaced since, it remains the sole copy known to be in the hands of collectors. While a "suggested NM value" is proffered in this edition, its value remains, ultimately, in the hands of the collector who plunked down the six big ones. . . regardless of anyone else's opinion!

Label & Catalog #		Title	Year	VG+	NM

LIGGINS, JOE

Mercury MG-20731	(M)	Honeydripper	1962	30.00	75.00
Mercury SR-60731	(S)	Honeydripper	1962	40.00	100.00

LIGHTFOOT, GEORGE

Vault 130	(S)	Natchez Trace	1969	5.00	12.00

LIGHTFOOT, GORDON
Canadian Gordon Lightfoot is a guitar player, singer and writer of pop songs with a folkie background.

United Arts. UAL-3487	(M)	Lightfoot	1965	8.00	20.00
United Arts. UAS-6487	(S)	Lightfoot	1965	10.00	25.00
United Arts. UAL-3587	(M)	The Way I Feel	1967	8.00	20.00
United Arts. UAS-6587	(S)	The Way I Feel	1967	10.00	25.00
United Arts. UAS-6649	(S)	Lightfoot	1968	8.00	20.00
United Arts. UAS-6672	(S)	Back Here On Earth	1968	8.00	20.00
United Arts. UAS-6714	(S)	Sunday Concert	1969	8.00	20.00
United Arts. UAS-5510	(S)	Classic Lightfoot	1971	1.00	5.00
United Arts. LA-381E	(S)	The Very Best Of Gordon Lightfoot	1974	1.00	5.00
United Arts. LA-445E	(S)	The Very Best Of Gordon Lightfoot, Vol. 2	1974	1.00	5.00
Reprise RS-6392	(S)	Sit Down, Young Stranger	1970	1.20	6.00
Reprise RS-6392	(S)	If You Could Read My Mind	1970	1.00	5.00
		(Repackage of "Sit Down, Young Stranger.")			
Reprise MS-2037	(S)	Summer Side Of Life	1971	1.00	5.00
Reprise MS-2056	(S)	Don Quixote	1972	1.00	5.00
Reprise MS-2116	(S)	Old Dan's Records	1972	1.00	5.00
Reprise MS-2177	(S)	Sundown	1974	1.00	5.00
Reprise MS4-2177	(Q)	Sundown	1974	6.00	15.00
Reprise MS-2206	(S)	Cold On The Shoulder	1975	1.00	5.00
Reprise MS4-2206	(Q)	Cold On The Shoulder	1975	6.00	15.00
Reprise 2MS-2237	(S)	Gord's Gold (2 LPs)	1975	1.00	5.00
Reprise MS-2246	(S)	Summertime Dream	1976	1.00	5.00

LIGHTHOUSE

RCA Victor LSP-4173	(S)	Lighthouse	1969	6.00	15.00
RCA Victor LSP-4241	(S)	Suite Feeling	1969	6.00	15.00
RCA Victor LSP-4325	(S)	Peacing It All Together	1970	6.00	15.00
Evolution 3007	(S)	One Fine Morning	1971	6.00	15.00
Evolution 3010	(S)	Thoughts Of Movin' On	1972	4.00	10.00
Evolution 3014	(S)	Lighthouse Live! (2 LPs)	1972	4.00	10.00
Evolution 3016	(S)	Sunny Days	1972	6.00	15.00
Polydor PD-5056	(S)	Can You Feel It	1973	5.00	12.00
Polydor PD-6028	(S)	Good Day	1974	5.00	12.00
Janus JSX-7025	(S)	The Best Of Lighthouse	1976	1.00	5.00

LIGHTMAN, AARON

Poppy 4010	(S)	Aaron Lightman	1970	4.00	10.00

LIGHTNIN' SLIM

Excello LP-8000	(M)	Rooster Blues	1960	200.00	400.00
Excello LPS-8000	(M)	Rooster Blues	1968	20.00	50.00
		(Later "Electronic Stereo" covers contain mono records.)			
Excello LP-8004	(M)	Lightnin' Slim's Bell Ringer	1965	100.00	250.00
Excello LPS-8004	(M)	Lightnin' Slim's Bell Ringer	1968	20.00	50.00
		(Later "Electronic Stereo" covers contain mono records.)			
Excello LPS-8018	(S)	High And Low Down	1971	6.00	15.00
Excello LPS-8023	(S)	London Gumbo	1972	6.00	15.00

LIGHTNING

P.I.P. 6807	(S)	Lightning	1971	12.00	30.00

LIMOUSINE

G.S.F 1002	(S)	Limousine	1972	6.00	15.00

LINCOLN, PHILAMORE
The uncredited backing group for Lincoln is Jimmy Page's Yardbirds.

Epic BN-26497	(S)	North Wind Blew South	1970	10.00	25.00

LINCOLN STREET EXIT
Lincoln Street Exit later recorded as Xit.

Mainstream S-6126	(S)	Drive It	1970	60.00	150.00

LIND, BOB
Bob Lind is a singer of folk-based pop songs.

Verve/Forecast FT-3005	(M)	Elusive Bob Lind	1966	10.00	25.00
Verve/Forecast FTS-3005	(S)	Elusive Bob Lind	1966	12.00	30.00
World Pacific WP-1841	(M)	Don't Be Concerned	1966	10.00	25.00
World Pacific ST-21841	(S)	Don't Be Concerned	1966	12.00	30.00

After going through several incarnations and name changes, The Imperials were born. As evidenced by their first album for End. they were "The Imperials featuring Little Anthony." By their second LP, they were "Little Anthony & The Imperials," which is how they are best remembered forty years later.

Label & Catalog #		Title	Year	VG+	NM
World Pacific WP-1851	(M)	Photographs Of Feeling	1966	6.00	15.00
World Pacific ST-21851	(S)	Photographs Of Feeling	1966	8.00	20.00
Capitol ST-780	(S)	Since There Were Circles	1971	10.00	25.00
LINDE, DENNIS					
Intrepid 4004	(M)	Linde Manor	1966	8.00	20.00
Intrepid 74004	(S)	Linde Manor	1966	10.00	25.00
LINDESFARNE					
Elektra EKS-74099	(S)	Nicely Out Of Tune	1971	4.00	10.00
Elektra EKS-75021	(S)	Fog On The Tyne	1972	4.00	10.00
Elektra EKS-75043	(S)	Dingly Dell	1972	4.00	10.00
Elektra EKS-75077	(S)	Roll On, Ruby	1974	4.00	10.00
Atco SD-38-108	(S)	Back And Forth	1978	1.00	5.00
LINDSAY, MARK					
Lindsay was a member of Paul Revere's Raiders.					
Columbia CS-9986	(S)	Arizona	1970	4.00	10.00
		— Columbia albums above have "360 Sound" labels.—			
Columbia CS-9986	(S)	Arizona	1970	1.00	5.00
Columbia CS-30111	(S)	Silver Bird	1970	3.20	8.00
Columbia CS-30735	(S)	You've Got A Friend	1971	1.00	5.00
LINHART, BUZZY					
Buzzy Linhart originally recorded with The Seventh Sons.					
Philips PHS-600-029	(S)	Buzzy	1969	4.00	10.00
Kama Sutra KSBS-2037	(S)	The Time To Live Is Now	1971	3.20	8.00
Kama Sutra KSBS-2042	(S)	Buzzy Linhart Is Music	1972	3.20	8.00
Kama Sutra KSBS-2053	(S)	Buzzy	1972	3.20	8.00
Atco SD-36-7044	(S)	Pussycats Can Go Far	1974	3.20	8.00
LINN COUNTY					
Mercury SR-61181	(S)	Proud Flesh Soothseer	1968	8.00	20.00
Mercury SR-61218	(S)	Fever Shot	1969	8.00	20.00
Philips PHS-600-326	(S)	Till The Break Of Dawn	1970	6.00	15.00
LINTON, SHERWOOD, & THE COTTON KINGS					
Re-Car 2108	(S)	Sherwood Linton & The Cotton Kings	1968	30.00	75.00
LIPSCOMB, MANCE					
Mance Lipscomb was a blues guitar player and singer.					
Arhoolie 1001	(M)	Texas Sharecropper And Songster	1960	20.00	50.00
Reprise R-2012	(M)	Trouble In Mind	1961	40.00	100.00
Reprise R-92012	(S)	Trouble In Mind	1961	60.00	150.00
Arhoolie 1023	(M)	Texas Songster, Vol. 2	1963	14.00	35.00
Arhoolie 1026	(M)	Texas Songster In A Live Performance	1965	14.00	35.00
Arhoolie 1033	(M)	Mance Lipscomb, Vol. 4	1966	14.00	35.00
Arhoolie 10??	(M)	Mance Lipscomb, Vol. 5	196?	8.00	20.00
Arhoolie 1069	(M)	Mance Lipscomb, Vol. 6	197?	8.00	20.00
Reprise RS-6404	(S)	Trouble In Mind	1969	12.00	30.00
		(Reprise 6404 is a reissue of 92012 with a new cover.)			
LIQUID SMOKE					
Avco Embassy AVE-33005	(S)	Liquid Smoke	196?	10.00	25.00
LIQUIDATORS, THE					
Reggae 15002	(S)	Super Reggae	1970	6.00	15.00
LISTENING					
Vanguard VSD-6504	(S)	Listening	1968	16.00	40.00
LITTER, THE					
The Litter originally released two LPs privately.					
Probe CPLP-4504	(S)	Emerge	1969	16.00	40.00
LITTLE ANTHONY & THE IMPERIALS					
Little Anthony is Anthony Gourdine. Refer to The Chantels.					
End 303	(M)	We Are Little Anthony & The Imperials	1959	150.00	300.00
End 311	(M)	Shades Of The 40's	1960	80.00	200.00
DCP DCL-3801	(M)	I'm On The Outside Looking In	1964	10.00	25.00
DCP DCS-6801	(S)	I'm On The Outside Looking In	1964	12.00	30.00
DCP DCL-3808	(M)	Goin' Out Of My Head	1965	10.00	25.00
DCP DCS-6808	(S)	Goin' Out Of My Head	1965	12.00	30.00
DCP DCL-3809	(M)	Best Of Little Anthony & The Imperials	1966	8.00	20.00
DCP DCS-6809	(S)	Best Of Little Anthony & The Imperials	1966	10.00	25.00
Roulette R-25294	(M)	Little Anthony & The Imperials' Greatest Hits	1965	10.00	25.00
Roulette SR-25294	(E)	Little Anthony & The Imperials' Greatest Hits	1965	10.00	25.00
		(Roulette 25294 reissues End recordings.)			

Label & Catalog #		Title	Year	VG+	NM
Forum F-9107	(S)	Little Anthony & The Imperials' Greatest Hits	196?	4.00	10.00
Forum FS-9107	(E)	Little Anthony & The Imperials' Greatest Hits	196?	4.00	10.00
Veep VP-13510	(M)	I'm On The Outside Looking In	1966	6.00	15.00
Veep VPS-16510	(S)	I'm On The Outside Looking In	1966	8.00	20.00
Veep VP-13512	(M)	The Best Of Little Anthony & The Imperials	1966	5.00	12.00
Veep VPS-16512	(S)	The Best Of Little Anthony & The Imperials	1966	6.00	15.00
Veep VP-13513	(M)	Payin' Our Dues	1966	6.00	15.00
Veep VPS-16513	(S)	Payin' Our Dues	1966	8.00	20.00
Veep VP-13514	(M)	Reflections	1967	6.00	15.00
Veep VPS-16514	(S)	Reflections	1967	8.00	20.00
Veep VP-13516	(M)	Movie Grabbers	1967	6.00	15.00
Veep VPS-16516	(S)	Movie Grabbers	1967	8.00	20.00
Veep VPS-16519	(S)	The Best Of Little Anthony, Volume 2	1968	6.00	15.00
United Arts. UAS-6720	(S)	Out Of Sight, Out Of Mind	1969	8.00	20.00
Sunset SUS-5287	(S)	Little Anthony & The Imperials	1970	6.00	15.00
United Arts. LA-026G	(S)	Legendary Masters (2 LPs)	1973	10.00	25.00
United Arts. LA-255G	(S)	The Very Best Of Little Anthony & The Imperials	1974	.80	4.00
United Arts. LA-382E	(S)	The Very Best Of Little Anthony & The Imperials	1975	.80	4.00
Avco AV-11012	(S)	On A New Street	1973	8.00	20.00
MCA/Songbird 3245	(S)	Daylight	1980	1.00	5.00
Liberty LN-10133	(S)	Little Anthony & The Imperials	1981	.80	4.00
United Arts. LM-1017	(S)	Out Of Sight, Out Of Mind	1981	.80	4.00
Accord SN-7216	(S)	Tears On My Pillow	1983	.80	4.00

LITTLE ANTHONY & THE IMPERIALS / THE PLATTERS

Exact 231	(S)	Little Anthony & The Imperials / The Platters	1980	.80	4.00

LITTLE BOY BLUES

Fontana MGF-27578	(M)	In The Woodland Of Weir	1967	10.00	25.00
Fontana SRF-67578	(S)	In The Woodland Of Weir	1967	12.00	30.00

LITTLE CAESAR & THE ROMANS

Del-Fi DFLP-1218	(M)	Memories Of Those Oldies But Goodies	1961	200.00	400.00

LITTLE EVA

Little Eva is Eva Boyd. Refer to The Cookies / Little Eva / Carole King.

Dimension DLP-6000	(M)	L-L-L-L-Loco-Motion	1962	60.00	150.00
Dimension DLPS-6000	(E)	L-L-L-L-Loco-Motion	1962	60.00	150.00
		(First pressings do not contain "Keep Your Hands Off Of My Baby.")			
Dimension DLP-6000	(M)	L-L-L-L-Loco-Motion	1962	80.00	200.00
Dimension DLPS-6000	(E)	L-L-L-L-Loco-Motion	1962	80.00	200.00
		(Later pressings contain "Keep Your Hands Off Of My Baby.")			

LITTLE FEAT

The Feat were formed and led by Lowell George. For additional listings refer to Kathy Dalton.

Warner Bros. WS-1890	(S)	Little Feat (With photo on back cover)	1971	6.00	15.00
Warner Bros. WS-1890	(S)	Little Feat (Without photo on back cover)	1971	4.00	10.00
Warner Bros. BS-2600	(S)	Sailin' Shoes	1972	4.00	10.00
Warner Bros. BS-2686	(S)	Dixie Chicken	1972	4.00	10.00
Warner Bros. BS-2784	(S)	Feats Don't Fail Me Now	1972	4.00	10.00
Warner Bros. BS-2884	(S)	The Last Record Album	1972	4.00	10.00
		—Warner Bros. albums above have green "W7" labels.—			
Warner Bros. WS-1890	(S)	Little Feat	197?	.80	4.00
Warner Bros. BS-2600	(S)	Sailin' Shoes	197?	.80	4.00
Warner Bros. BS-2686	(S)	Dixie Chicken	197?	.80	4.00
Warner Bros. BS-2784	(S)	Feats Don't Fail Me Now	197?	.80	4.00
Warner Bros. BS-2884	(S)	The Last Record Album	197?	.80	4.00
Warner Bros. BS-3015	(S)	Time Loves A Hero	1977	1.00	5.00
Warner Bros. 2BS-3140	(S)	Waiting For Columbus (2 LPs)	1977	20.00	60.00
Warner Bros. HS-3345	(S)	Down On The Farm	1979	1.00	5.00
Warner Bros. PRO-984	(DJ)	Hoy-Hoy! (2 LPs)	1981	6.00	15.00
Warner Bros. 2BSK-3538	(S)	Hoy-Hoy! (2 LPs)	1981	1.20	6.00

LITTLE JOHN

Epic PE-26531	(S)	Up And Down	1970	4.00	10.00
Epic PE-30414	(S)	Little John	1971	4.00	10.00

LITTLE MILTON

Little Milton is a pseudonym for Milton Campbell. Refer to Albert King & Little Milton.

Checker LP-2995	(M)	We're Gonna Make It	1965	60.00	150.00
		—Checker albums above have black labels.—			
Checker LP-3002	(M)	Little Milton Sings Big Blues	1966	30.00	75.00
Checker LP-3011	(S)	Grits Ain't Groceries	1969	10.00	25.00
Checker LP-3012	(S)	If Walls Could Talk	1970	10.00	25.00
Chess CH-50013	(S)	Little Milton's Greatest Hits	1972	6.00	15.00
Chess 2ACMB-204	(S)	Little Milton (2 LPs)	1976	4.00	10.00
Stax STS-3012	(S)	Waiting For Little Milton	1973	10.00	25.00
Stax STS-5514	(S)	Blues N' Soul	1974	10.00	25.00

Label & Catalog #		Title	Year	VG+	NM
Glades 7508	(S)	Friend Of Mine	1976	4.00	10.00
Glades 7511	(S)	Me For You, You For Me	1977	4.00	10.00
Stax 4123	(S)	Chronicle	1979	4.00	10.00
Stax 8514	(S)	Walking The Back Streets	1981	1.00	5.00

LITTLE MISS CORNSHUCKS

Chess LP-1453	(M)	Little Miss Cornshucks (White label promo)	1961	250.00	500.00
Chess LP-1453	(M)	Little Miss Cornshucks	1961	80.00	200.00

LITTLE RICHARD

The ever-raucous, flamboyantly joyous "Little Richard" Penniman is a progenitor and an archetype of rock & roll. Refer to Canned Heat & Little Richard; Jimi Hendrix & Little Richard.

Camden CAL-420	(M)	Little Richard	1956	80.00	200.00
Specialty 100	(M)	Here's Little Richard	1957	250.00	500.00
		—Specialty albums above have black & yellow labels.—			
Specialty SP-2100	(M)	Here's Little Richard	1957	80.00	200.00
Specialty SP-2103	(M)	Little Richard	1957	80.00	200.00
		(Original jackets have a full-cover front photo.)			
Specialty SP-2103	(M)	Little Richard	196?	40.00	100.00
		(Later jackets have a large black triangle in the upper right corner.)			
Specialty SP-2104	(M)	The Fabulous Little Richard	1958	80.00	200.00
Specialty SP-2111	(M)	Little Richard—His Biggest Hits	1963	20.00	50.00
Specialty SP-2111	(E)	Little Richard—His Biggest Hits	1963	20.00	50.00
Specialty SP-2113	(E)	Little Richard's Grooviest 17 Original Hits	1968	10.00	25.00
Specialty SP-2136	(M)	Well Alright!	1970	10.00	25.00
		("Poor Boy Paul," "Bama-Lama Bama-Loo," "Annie Is Back" and "Shake A Hand" are in stereo on this album.)			
		—Specialty albums above have thick vinyl with black & gold labels that read "Stereo Natural Sound."—			
Specialty SP-2100	(M)	Here's Little Richard	197?	8.00	20.00
Specialty SP-2103	(M)	Little Richard	197?	8.00	20.00
Specialty SP-2104	(M)	The Fabulous Little Richard	197?	8.00	20.00
Specialty SP-2111	(E)	Little Richard—His Biggest Hits	197?	8.00	20.00
Specialty SP-2113	(E)	Little Richard's Grooviest 17 Original Hits	197?	8.00	20.00
Specialty SP-2136	(M)	Well Alright!	197?	8.00	20.00
		—Specialty albums above have thin vinyl on black & gold labels that read "Natural Sound."—			
20th Century FXG-5010	(M)	Little Richard Sings Gospel	1959	40.00	100.00
20th Century SGM-5010	(S)	Little Richard Sings Gospel	1959	60.00	150.00
Mercury MG-20656	(M)	It's Real	1961	20.00	50.00
Mercury SR-60656	(S)	It's Real	1961	30.00	75.00
Crown CLP-5362	(M)	Little Richard Sings Freedom Songs	1963	8.00	20.00
Crown CST-362	(S)	Little Richard Sings Freedom Songs	1963	8.00	20.00
		—Crown albums above have gray labels.—			
Coral CRL-57446	(M)	Coming Home	1963	16.00	40.00
Coral CRL-757446	(S)	Coming Home	1963	20.00	50.00
Wing MGW-12288	(M)	King Of The Gospel Singers	1964	6.00	15.00
Wing SRW-16288	(S)	King Of The Gospel Singers	1964	8.00	20.00
		(Wing 12288 is an abridged reissue of Mercury 20656.)			
Vee Jay LP-1107	(M)	Little Richard Is Back	1964	16.00	40.00
Vee Jay SR-1107	(S)	Little Richard Is Back	1964	20.00	50.00
		(Vee Jay 1107 reputedly features Jimi Hendrix on guitar on "Whole Lotta Shakin'," "Hound Dog," "Going Home Tomorrow," "Goodnight Irene," "Money Honey" and "Lawdy Miss Clawdy.")			
Vee Jay LP-1124	(M)	Little Richard's Greatest Hits	1965	10.00	25.00
Vee Jay SR-1124	(S)	Little Richard's Greatest Hits	1965	16.00	40.00
		—Vee Jay albums above have black rainbow labels.—			
Vee Jay VJS-2-100	(S)	Little Richard's Gold (2 LPs)	196?	10.00	25.00
Spin-O-Rama 119	(M)	Clap Your Hands	196?	4.00	10.00
Spin-O-Rama 119	(E)	Clap Your Hands	196?	4.00	10.00
Guest Star GS-1429	(M)	Little Richard With Sister Rosetta Tharpe	196?	4.00	10.00
Guest Star GSS-1429	(E)	Little Richard With Sister Rosetta Tharpe	196?	4.00	10.00
Modern 100	(M)	His Greatest Hits/Recorded Live	196?	6.00	15.00
Modern 1000	(S)	His Greatest Hits/Recorded Live	196?	6.00	15.00
Modern 103	(M)	The Wild And Frantic Little Richard	196?	6.00	15.00
Modern 1003	(S)	The Wild And Frantic Little Richard	196?	6.00	15.00
Custom 2061	(M)	Little Richard Sings Spirituals	196?	6.00	15.00
OKeh OKM-12121	(M)	Greatest Hits Recorded Live	1967	8.00	20.00
OKeh OKS-14121	(S)	Greatest Hits Recorded Live	1967	12.00	30.00
OKeh OKM-12117	(M)	The Explosive Little Richard	1967	8.00	20.00
OKeh OKS-14117	(S)	The Explosive Little Richard	1967	12.00	30.00
Roulette RS-42007	(S)	Forever Yours	1968	10.00	25.00
Buddah BDS-7501	(S)	Little Richard	1969	10.00	25.00
Kama Sutra NSBS-2023	(S)	Little Richard	1970	10.00	25.00
Camden CAS-2430	(E)	Every Hour With Little Richard	1970	4.00	10.00
Reprise RS-6406	(S)	The Rill Thing	1970	8.00	20.00
Epic EG-3042	(S)	Cast A Long Shadow	1971	8.00	20.00
Reprise RS-6462	(S)	The King Of Rock And Roll	1971	8.00	20.00
Reprise MS-2107	(S)	The Second Coming	1972	8.00	20.00
Scepter 18020	(S)	The Best Of Little Richard	1971	6.00	15.00

Label & Catalog #		Title	Year	VG+	NM
Trip 8013	(E)	Little Richard's Greatest Hits	1971	1.00	5.00
Trip TOP-16-46	(E)	16 Greatest Hits	1978	1.00	5.00
Pickwick SPC-3258	(S)	King Of The Gospel Singers	1972	1.00	5.00
United Arts. LA-497E	(E)	The Very Best Of Little Richard	1975	.80	4.00
GRT 2103	(E)	The Original Little Richard	1977	1.00	5.00
United US-7775	(S)	His Greatest Hits/Recorded Live	197?	1.00	5.00
United US-7777	(S)	The Wild And Frantic Little Richard	197?	1.00	5.00
Upfront UPF-123	(E)	The Best Of Little Richard	197?	1.00	5.00
Upfront UPF-197	(E)	Little Richard Sings Gospel	197?	1.00	5.00
Vee Jay DYS-730	(E)	Talkin' 'Bout Soul	197?	4.00	10.00
Audio Encores 1002	(S)	Little Richard	1980	10.00	25.00
Exact 206	(E)	The Best Of Little Richard	1980	.80	4.00
Accord SN-7123	(E)	Tutti Frutti	1981	.80	4.00
Everest 4114	(E)	Little Richard's Greatest Hits	1982	.80	4.00

LITTLE RIVER BAND, THE [LRB]

Label & Catalog #		Title	Year	VG+	NM
Harvest ST-11512	(S)	Little River Band	1976	.80	4.00
Harvest ST-11645	(S)	Diamantina Cocktail	1977	.80	4.00
Harvest ST-11783	(S)	Sleeper Catcher	1978	.80	4.00
Capitol ST-11954	(S)	First Under The Wire	1979	.80	4.00
Capitol ST-12061	(S)	Backstage Pass (2 LPs)	1980	1.00	5.00
Capitol ST-12163	(S)	Time Exposure	1981	.80	4.00
Capitol ST-12247	(S)	Greatest Hits	1982	.80	4.00
Capitol ST-12273	(S)	The Net	1983	.80	4.00
Capitol ST-12365	(S)	Playing To Win	1985	.80	4.00

LITTLE ROYAL

Label & Catalog #		Title	Year	VG+	NM
King KS-1145	(S)	Jealous	1972	6.00	15.00

LITTLE SONNY

Label & Catalog #		Title	Year	VG+	NM
Enterprise ENS-1005	(S)	New King Of The Blues Harmonica	1970	14.00	35.00
Enterprise ENS-1018	(S)	Black And Blue	1971	14.00	35.00
Enterprise ENS-1036	(S)	Hard Goin' Up	1973	14.00	35.00

LITTLE WALTER
Refer to The Super Blues Band.

Label & Catalog #		Title	Year	VG+	NM
Checker LP-1428	(M)	The Best Of Little Walter	1958	300.00	600.00
		—Checker albums above have black labels.—			
Checker LP-3005	(M)	The Best Of Little Walter	1967	20.00	50.00
Checker LPS-3005	(E)	The Best Of Little Walter	1967	14.00	35.00
		(Checker 3004 is a reissue of 1428.)			
		—Checker albums above have blue labels with checkers on top.—			
Chess LPS-1535	(S)	Hate To See You Go	1969	10.00	25.00
Chess 2CH-60014	(S)	Boss Blues Harmonica (2 LPs)	1972	6.00	15.00
Chess LP-416	(S)	Confessin' The Blues	1974	4.00	10.00
Delmark DL-648	(M)	The Blues World Of Little Walter	1986	1.00	5.00
Chess 9192	(M)	The Best Of Little Walter	1986	1.00	5.00
		(Chess 9192 is a reissue of Checker 1428.)			
Chess 9292	(S)	The Best Of Little Walter, Vol. 2	1990	1.00	5.00

LIVELY ONES, THE

Label & Catalog #		Title	Year	VG+	NM
Del-Fi DFLP-1226	(M)	Surf-Rider	1963	12.00	30.00
Del-Fi DFST-1226	(S)	Surf-Rider	1963	16.00	40.00
Del-Fi DFLP-1231	(M)	Surf Drums	1963	12.00	30.00
Del-Fi DFST-1231	(S)	Surf Drums	1963	16.00	40.00
Del-Fi DFLP-1237	(M)	This Is Surf City	1963	12.00	30.00
Del-Fi DFST-1237	(S)	This Is Surf City	1963	16.00	40.00
Del-Fi DFLP-1238	(M)	Great Surf Hits	1963	12.00	30.00
Del-Fi DFLP-1238	(S)	Great Surf Hits	1963	16.00	40.00
Del-Fi DFLP-1240	(M)	Surfin' South Of The Border	1964	12.00	30.00
Del-Fi DFST-1240	(S)	Surfin' South Of The Border	1964	16.00	40.00
MGM E-4449	(M)	Bugalu Party	1967	8.00	20.00
MGM SE-4449	(S)	Bugalu Party	1967	10.00	25.00

LIVERPOOL BEATS, THE [THE BEATS]

Label & Catalog #		Title	Year	VG+	NM
Rondo 2026	(M)	The New Merseyside Sound	1964	6.00	15.00
Rondo 2026	(S)	The New Merseyside Sound	1964	6.00	15.00
		(Rondo 2006 credits The Liverpool Beats.)			
Design DLP-170	(M)	The New Merseyside Sound	1964	6.00	15.00
Design DLPS-170	(S)	The New Merseyside Sound	1964	6.00	15.00
		(Design 170, a reissue of Rondo 2026, credits The Beats.)			

LIVERPOOL FIVE, THE
Refer to The Astronauts / The Liverpool Five.

Label & Catalog #		Title	Year	VG+	NM
RCA Victor LPM-3583	(M)	Arrive	1966	10.00	25.00
RCA Victor LSP-3583	(S)	Arrive	1966	12.00	30.00
RCA Victor LPM-3682	(M)	Out Of Sight	1967	10.00	25.00
RCA Victor LSP-3682	(S)	Out Of Sight	1967	12.00	30.00

Label & Catalog #		Title	Year	VG+	NM

LIVERPOOL KIDS, THE
While the cover credits The Liverpool Lads, the label lists the artists as The Schoolboys.

| Palace 777 | (M) | Beatle Mash | 1964 | 6.00 | 15.00 |

LIVERPOOL SCENE, THE
The Scene is Adrian Henri and Roger McGough.

Epic LN-24336	(M)	The Incredible New Liverpool Scene	1967	8.00	20.00
Epic BN-26336	(S)	The Incredible New Liverpool Scene	1967	10.00	25.00
		(Epic 24/26336 credits Henri & McGough.)			
RCA Victor LSP-4189	(S)	The Amazing Adventures			
		Of The Liverpool Scene	1969	6.00	15.00
RCA Victor LSP-4267	(S)	Bread On The Night	1970	6.00	15.00

LIVERPOOLS, THE

Wyncote W-9001	(M)	Beatlemania In The U.S.A.	1964	6.00	15.00
Wyncote SW-9001	(S)	Beatlemania In The U.S.A.	1964	6.00	15.00
Wyncote W-9061	(M)	The Hit Sounds From England	1964	6.00	15.00
Wyncote SW-9061	(S)	The Hit Sounds From England	1964	6.00	15.00

LIVIN' BLUES

| Dwarf 2003 | (S) | Dutch Treat | 1971 | 12.00 | 30.00 |

LOADING ZONE, THE
The Loading Zone originally released an album privately.

| RCA Victor LSP-3959 | (S) | The Loading Zone | 1968 | 10.00 | 25.00 |

LOCKWOOD, JR., ROBERT

| Trix 3307 | (S) | Contrasts | 197? | 8.00 | 20.00 |

LOCOMOTIVE

| MGM SE-4653 | (S) | Locomotive | 1970 | 5.00 | 12.00 |

LODGE, JOHN
John Lodge is a member of The Moody Blues.

| London PS-683 | (S) | Natural Avenue | 1976 | 1.00 | 5.00 |

LODI

| Mowest 101 | (S) | Lodi | 1972 | 10.00 | 25.00 |

LOFGREN, NILS
Refer to Crazy Horse; Grin.

A&M SP-4509	(S)	Nils Lofgren	1975	1.00	5.00
A&M SP-8362	(DJ)	Authorized Bootleg (Counterfeits exist)	1976	10.00	25.00
A&M SP-4573	(S)	Cry Tough	1976	1.00	5.00
A&M SP-4576	(S)	Nils	1976	1.00	5.00
A&M SP-4628	(S)	I Came To Dance	1977	1.00	5.00
A&M SP-3707	(S)	Night After Night (2 LPs)	1977	1.20	6.00
A&M SP-3201	(S)	The Best Of Nils Lofgren	1981	1.00	5.00
Backstreet 5251	(S)	Night Fades Away	1981	1.00	5.00

LOGGINS, KENNY

Columbia PC-34655	(S)	Celebrate Me Home	1977	.80	4.00
Columbia JC-35387	(S)	Nightwatch	1978	.80	4.00
Columbia HC-45387	(S)	Nightwatch (Half-speed master)	1981	8.00	25.00
Columbia JC-36172	(S)	Keep The Fire	1979	.80	4.00
Columbia C2X-36738	(S)	Kenny Loggins Alive (2 LPs)	1980	1.00	5.00
Columbia AS-946	(DJ)	Kenny Loggins (Radio sampler)	1981	4.00	10.00
Columbia TC-38127	(S)	High Adventure	1982	.80	4.00

LOGGINS & MESSINA
Kenny Loggins and Jim Messina. Refer to Buffalo Springfield.

Columbia KC-31044	(S)	Sittin' In	1972	.80	4.00
Columbia KC-31748	(S)	Loggins And Messina	1972	.80	4.00
Columbia KC-32540	(S)	Full Sail	1973	.80	4.00
Columbia CQ-32540	(Q)	Full Sail	1974	4.00	10.00
Columbia PG-32848	(S)	On Stage (2 LPs)	1974	1.00	5.00
Columbia PC-33175	(S)	Mother Lode	1974	.80	4.00
Columbia PC-33810	(S)	So Fine	1975	.80	4.00
Columbia PC-33578	(S)	Native Sons	1976	.80	4.00
Columbia PCQ-33578	(Q)	Native Sons	1976	4.00	10.00
Columbia FC-34388	(S)	The Best Of Friends	1976	.80	4.00
Columbia HC-44388	(S)	The Best Of Friends (Half-speed master)	1982	8.00	25.00
Columbia JG-34167	(S)	Finale (2 LPs)	1977	1.00	5.00

LOLLIPOP SHOPPE, THE
The Lollipop Shoppe can also be found on the Tower soundtrack "Angels From Hell."

| Uni 73019 | (S) | The Lollipop Shoppe | 1968 | 30.00 | 75.00 |

Label & Catalog #		Title	Year	VG+	NM

LOMAX, JACKIE
Apple ST-3354	(S)	Is This What You Want *(Prod. by George Harrison)*	1969	10.00	25.00
Warner Bros. WS-1914	(S)	Home Is In My Head	1971	4.00	10.00
Warner Bros. PRO-520	(DJ)	An Interview With Jackie Lomax	1972	16.00	40.00
Warner Bros. BS-2591	(S)	Three	1972	4.00	10.00

LONESOME SUNDOWN
| Excello LPS-8012 | (M) | Lonesome Lonely Blues | 1970 | 10.00 | 25.00 |
| Joliet 6002 | (S) | Been Gone Too Long | 1979 | 4.00 | 10.00 |

LONG, SHORTY
Soul S-709	(M)	Here Comes The Judge	1968	12.00	30.00
Soul SS-709	(S)	Here Comes The Judge	1968	6.00	15.00
Soul SS-719	(S)	The Prime Of Shorty Long	1969	6.00	15.00

LONGBRANCH PENNYWHISTLE
LP includes J.D. Souther, Glenn Frey, James Burton, Ry Cooder, Doug Kershaw and Buddy Emmons.
| Amos AAS-7007 | (S) | Longbranch Pennywhistle | 1969 | 20.00 | 50.00 |

LOOKING GLASS, THE
| Epic KE-31320 | (S) | The Looking Glass | 1972 | 4.00 | 10.00 |
| Epic KE-32167 | (S) | Subway Serenade | 1973 | 4.00 | 10.00 |

LOOSE
| Nocturne 906 | (S) | Freaky Billie, The Wheelie King | 1970 | 12.00 | 30.00 |

LORD, JON
Lord is a member of Deep Purple.
| Capitol ST-870 | (S) | Gemini Suite | 1970 | 4.00 | 10.00 |
| Warner Bros. BS-2717 | (S) | Gemini Suite | 1973 | 1.00 | 5.00 |

LORD SITAR
| Capitol ST-3916 | (S) | Lord Sitar | 1968 | 12.00 | 30.00 |

LORD SUTCH
Cotillion SD-9015	(S)	Lord Sutch And His Heavy Friends	1972	12.00	30.00
		(SD-9015 features Jimmy Page and John Bonham with Jeff Beck.)			
Cotillion SD-9049	(S)	Hands Of Jack The Ripper	1972	12.00	30.00
		(SD-9015 features members of Deep Purple and The Who.)			

LOREN, DONNA
| Capitol T-2323 | (M) | Beach Blanket Bingo | 1965 | 16.00 | 40.00 |
| Capitol ST-2323 | (S) | Beach Blanket Bingo | 1965 | 20.00 | 50.00 |

LOS BLUES
| United Arts. UAS-5542 | (S) | Los Blues | 1971 | 4.00 | 10.00 |

LOS BRAVOS
Los Bravos features Mike Kennedy.
Press PR-73003	(M)	Black Is Black	1966	20.00	50.00
Press PAS-83003	(E)	Black Is Black	1966	14.00	35.00
Parrot PAS-71021	(S)	Bring A Little Lovin'	1968	30.00	75.00
		(PAS-71021 contains "Black Is Black" in stereo.)			

LOS LOBOS
The all-Chicano Los Lobos del Este de Los Angeles pressed their first two albums privately.
| Slash 25177 | (S) | How Will The Wolf Survive? | 1984 | 1.00 | 5.00 |

LOS SEVEN DAYS
| Eco 314 | (M) | Sha-La-La | 196? | 20.00 | 50.00 |

LOST & FOUND
International Art. 3	(S)	Everybody's Here	1968	20.00	50.00
International Art. 3	(S)	Everybody's Here	1979	6.00	15.00
		(Reissues have "Masterfonics" stamped in the trail-off vinyl.)			
Tempo 7064	(S)	Number Two	1973	Unreleased	

LOST GENERATION, THE
| Brunswick BL-75164 | (S) | Sly, Slick And The Wicked | 1970 | 4.00 | 10.00 |

LOST NATION
| Rare Earth RS-518 | (S) | Paradise Lost | 1970 | 8.00 | 20.00 |

LOTHAR & THE HAND PEOPLE
Capitol ST-2997	(S)	Presenting Lothar & The Hand People	1968	16.00	40.00
Capitol SM-2997	(S)	Presenting Lothar & The Hand People	1977	1.00	5.00
Capitol ST-247	(S)	Space Hymn	1969	16.00	40.00

Label & Catalog #		Title	Year	VG+	NM
LOUDERMILK, JOHN D.					
Mr Loudermilk is singer and writer of folk-based pop songs.					
RCA Victor LPM-2434	(M)	Language Of Love	1961	8.00	20.00
RCA Victor LSP-2434	(S)	Language Of Love	1961	10.00	25.00
RCA Victor LPM-2539	(M)	Twelve Sides Of Loudermilk	1962	8.00	20.00
RCA Victor LSP-2539	(S)	Twelve Sides Of Loudermilk	1962	10.00	25.00
—RCA albums above have black "Long Play" or "Living Stereo" labels.—					
RCA Victor LPM-3497	(M)	A Bizarre Collection Of... Unusual Songs	1965	6.00	15.00
RCA Victor LSP-3497	(S)	A Bizarre Collection Of... Unusual Songs	1965	8.00	20.00
RCA Victor LPM-3807	(M)	Suburban Attitudes In Country Verse	1967	6.00	15.00
RCA Victor LSP-3807	(S)	Suburban Attitudes In Country Verse	1967	6.00	15.00
—RCA albums above have black "Monaural" or "Stereo" labels.—					
RCA Victor LSP-4040	(S)	Country Love Songs	1968	6.00	15.00
RCA Victor LSP-4097	(S)	The Open Mind Of John D. Loudermilk	1968	6.00	15.00
—RCA albums above have orange labels on non-flexible vinyl.—					
Warner Bros. WS-1922	(S)	Volume 1: Elloree	1971	4.00	10.00
Music Is Medicine 9009	(S)	Just Passing Through	1977	4.00	10.00
LOUIE & THE LOVERS					
Epic KE-30026	(S)	Rise	1970	8.00	20.00
LOUISIANA RED					
Roulette R-25200	(M)	The Lowdown Back Porch Blues	1963	14.00	35.00
Atco SD-33-389	(S)	Louisiana Red Sings The Blues	1972	6.00	15.00
LOVE					
Love features Arthur Lee with Bryan MacLean, John Echols, Ken Forssi, and Snoopy Pfisterer. For the second album, Tjay and Cantrelli and Michael Stuart join, after which Cantrelli and Pfisterer leave. After the third album, Lee replaces all the members with a revolving cast of backing musicians.					
Elektra EKL-4001	(DJ)	Love (White label)	1966	150.00	300.00
Elektra EKL-4001	(M)	Love	1966	16.00	40.00
Elektra EKS-74001	(S)	Love	1966	8.00	20.00
Elektra EKL-4005	(M)	Da Capo	1966	16.00	40.00
Elektra EKS-74005	(S)	Da Capo	1966	8.00	20.00
Elektra EKL-4013	(DJ)	Forever Changes (White label)	1967	60.00	150.00
Elektra EKL-4013	(M)	Forever Changes	1967	20.00	50.00
Elektra EKS-74013	(S)	Forever Changes	1967	10.00	25.00
—Elektra albums above have brown labels.—					
Elektra EKS-74001	(S)	Love	197?	3.20	8.00
Elektra EKS-74005	(S)	Da Capo	197?	3.20	8.00
Elektra EKS-74013	(S)	Forever Changes	197?	3.20	8.00
Elektra EKS-74049	(DJ)	Four Sail (White label)	1969	30.00	75.00
Elektra EKS-74049	(S)	Four Sail	1969	6.00	15.00
Elektra EKS-74058	(S)	Love Revisited	1970	6.00	15.00
—Elektra albums above have red labels.—					
Elektra EKS-74001	(S)	Love	197?	1.00	5.00
Elektra EKS-74005	(S)	Da Capo	197?	1.00	5.00
Elektra EKS-74013	(S)	Forever Changes	197?	1.00	5.00
Elektra EKS-74049	(S)	Four Sail	197?	1.00	5.00
Elektra EKS-74058	(S)	Love Revisited	197?	1.00	5.00
—Elektra albums above have butterfly labels.—					
Blue Thumb BTS-9000	(S)	Out Here (2 LPs)	1969	6.00	15.00
Blue Thumb BTS-8822	(S)	False Start (With Jimi Hendrix on one track)	1970	6.00	15.00
RSO 4804	(S)	Reel To Real	1974	1.00	5.00
Rhino RNLP-800	(S)	Best Of Love	1980	1.00	5.00
Rhino RNDF-251	(S)	Love Live/1978 Reunion (Picture disc)	1981	6.00	15.00
MCA 27025	(S)	Studio / Live	1982	1.00	5.00
Rhino RNLP-70175	(S)	Golden Archive (The Best Of Love)	1986	1.00	5.00
LOVE, HOLLY					
Ace LP-1022	(M)	My Love Confessions	1962	12.00	30.00
LOVE, MIKE					
Mike Love is a member of The Beach Boys. Refer to Celebration.					
Boardwalk NB1-33242	(S)	Looking Back With Love	1981	1.00	5.00
LOVE, MIKE, & DEAN TORRENCE					
Refer to Jan & Dean.					
Premore PL-1083	(S)	Rock N' Roll Is Here Again	1983	4.00	10.00
LOVE, PRESTON					
Kent KST-540	(S)	Omaha Bar-B-Q	1968	8.00	20.00
LOVE EXCHANGE, THE					
Tower ST-5115	(S)	The Love Exchange	1968	10.00	25.00

The Lovin' Spoonful was one of the great American bands of the '60s who responded to the British Invasion with a brand of music so American that it could never be mistaken for anything else. They combined many elements already common to rock'n roll, including a healthy grounding in folk-blues, and mixed in a little jugband and lunacy. They remain under-appreciated by critics and collectors and their LPs are much more difficult to find in NM than the values assigned indicate. Do You Believe In Magic and Hums Of The Lovin' Spoonful are the best, the latter a singular display of John Sebastian's prodigious songwriting and singing abilities.

Label & Catalog #		Title	Year	VG+	NM

LOVE GENERATION, THE

Label & Catalog #		Title	Year	VG+	NM
Imperial LP-9351	(M)	The Love Generation	1967	6.00	15.00
Imperial LP-12351	(S)	The Love Generation	1967	8.00	20.00
Imperial LP-12364	(S)	A Generation Of Love	1968	8.00	20.00
Imperial LP-12408	(S)	Montage	1968	8.00	20.00

LOVE IS A HEART-ON

Heavy	(S)	Love Is A Heart-On	1970	60.00	150.00

LOVE, PEACE & HAPPINESS

RCA Victor LSP-4535	(S)	Love Is Stronger	1971	4.00	10.00

LOVE SCULPTURE

Love Sculpture features Dave Edmunds.

Rare Earth RS-505	(S)	Blues Helping	1969	16.00	40.00
Parrot PAS-71035	(S)	Forms And Feeling	1970	10.00	25.00

LOVECRAFT: *Refer to H.P. LOVECRAFT*

LOVESONG

Lovesong features Chuck Girard of The Hondells.

Good News 8100	(S)	Lovesong	197?	5.00	12.00
Good News 8101	(S)	The Final Touch	197?	5.00	12.00
Good News 8104	(S)	Feel The Touch	197?	5.00	12.00

LOVIN' SPOONFUL, THE

The original Spoonful were Steve Boone, Joe Butler, John Sebastian and Zal Yanovsky, replaced in 1967 by Jerry Yester, formerly of The Modern Folk Quartet. By 1969 Boone was the only original member left.

Kama Sutra KLP-8050	(M)	Do You Believe In Magic?	1965	8.00	20.00
Kama Sutra KLPS-8050	(S)	Do You Believe In Magic?	1965	12.00	30.00
Kama Sutra T-90597	(M)	Do You Believe In Magic? *(Capitol Rec. Club)*	1965	12.00	30.00
Kama Sutra ST-90597	(S)	Do You Believe In Magic? *(Capitol Rec. Club)*	1965	12.00	30.00
Kama Sutra KLP-8051	(M)	Daydream	1966	8.00	20.00
Kama Sutra KLPS-8051	(S)	Daydream	1966	12.00	30.00
Kama Sutra KLP-8053	(M)	What's Up, Tiger Lily?	1966	8.00	20.00
Kama Sutra KLPS-8053	(S)	What's Up, Tiger Lily?	1966	12.00	30.00
Kama Sutra KLP-8054	(M)	Hums Of The Lovin' Spoonful	1966	8.00	20.00
Kama Sutra KLPS-8054	(S)	Hums Of The Lovin' Spoonful	1966	12.00	30.00
Kama Sutra KLP-8056	(M)	The Best Of The Lovin' Spoonful	1967	4.00	10.00
Kama Sutra KLPS-8056	(S)	The Best Of The Lovin' Spoonful	1967	4.00	10.00
		(K.S. 8056 was issued with four full-color photos, priced separately below.)			
Kama Sutra 8056		The Best Of The Lovin' Spoonful Bonus Photos	1967	4.00	10.00
Kama Sutra KLP-8058	(M)	You're A Big Boy Now	1967	8.00	20.00
Kama Sutra KLPS-8058	(S)	You're A Big Boy Now	1967	8.00	20.00
Kama Sutra KLPS-8061	(S)	Everything's Playing	1968	6.00	15.00
Kama Sutra KLPS-8064	(S)	The Best Of The Lovin' Spoonful, Volume 2	1968	4.00	10.00
Kama Sutra KOPS-750-2	(S)	24 Karat Hits *(2 LPs)*	1968	6.00	15.00
Kama Sutra KLPS-8073	(S)	Revelations: Revolution '69	1969	10.00	25.00
Kama Sutra KLPS-2011	(S)	The John Sebastian Songbook	1970	4.00	10.00
Kama Sutra KSBS-2013	(S)	The Very Best Of The Lovin' Spoonful	1970	4.00	10.00
Kama Sutra KLPS-2029	(S)	Once Upon A Time	1971	4.00	10.00
Arista BLS-8084	(S)	The Best Of The Lovin' Spoonful	1983	.80	4.00
Rhino RNLP-855	(S)	The Best Of The Lovin' Spoonful, Vol. 2	1985	.80	4.00

LOWE, JIM

Mercury MG-20246	(M)	The Door Of Fame	1957	60.00	150.00
Dot DLP-3114	(M)	Wicked Women	1958	40.00	100.00
Dot DLP-3881	(M)	Songs They Sing Behind The Green Door	1965	60.00	150.00
Dot DLP-25681	(E)	Songs They Sing Behind The Green Door	1965	60.00	150.00

LOWE, NICK

Aside from being one of the wittiest rock'n rollers of the post-'60s era (as writer, arranger, singer and bass player), Mr Lowe is also a producer (refer to then main mate Carlene Carter or good mate Dave Edmunds) and a leader of the group Rockpile. Refer to Brinsley Schwarz.

Columbia 35329	(S)	Pure Pop For Now People	1978	1.00	5.00
Columbia 36087	(S)	Labour Of Lust	1979	1.00	5.00
Columbia AS-1400	(DJ)	An Interrogation Of Nick Lowe	1982	6.00	15.00
Columbia 37932	(S)	Nick The Knife	1982	1.00	5.00
Columbia 38589	(S)	The Abominable Showman	1983	1.00	5.00
Columbia 39371	(S)	Nick Lowe And His Cowboy Outfit	1984	1.00	5.00

LUCEY, CHRIS

Surrey SS-1027	(S)	Song Of Protest And Anti-Protest	197?	16.00	40.00

LUCIFER

Uni 73111	(S)	Black Mass By Lucifer	1971	6.00	15.00
Invictus ST-7309	(S)	Lucifer	1971	6.00	15.00

Frankie Lymon left the confines of his group, The Teenagers, where he had recorded one of the definitive group rockers of the '50s, "Why Do Fools Fall In Love," for a shot at solo stardom. Unfortunately, this move did not bring the rewards expected. The best-selling hit, "Little Bitty Pretty One," noted on the cover of the Rock'n Roll album, did not reach the national Top 40 pop charts and it was his only single to make the Top 100. The man who was bigger than Elvis to black kids all over New York City died at the age of 25, another loss to the insanities of drug abuse and its attendant prohibition.

Label & Catalog #		Title	Year	VG+	NM

LULU

Marie Lawrie achieved success as a singer and actor under the name of Lulu. She can also be found on the Fontana soundtrack "To Sir With Love."

Parrot PA-61016	(M)	From Lulu With Love	1967	10.00	25.00
Parrot PAS-71016	(S)	From Lulu With Love	1967	12.00	30.00
Epic LN-24339	(M)	To Sir With Love	1967	10.00	25.00
Epic BN-26339	(S)	To Sir With Love	1967	12.00	30.00
		("Morning Dew" and "Let's Pretend" are rechanneled.)			
Epic BN-26396	(P)	Boy	1968	Unreleased	
Atco 33-310	(M)	New Routes (White label promo)	1970	12.00	30.00
Atco SD-33-310	(S)	New Routes	1970	4.00	10.00
Epic BN-26536	(S)	It's Lulu	1970	4.00	10.00
Atco 33-330	(M)	Melody Fair	1970	12.00	30.00
Atco SD-33-330	(S)	Melody Fair	1970	4.00	10.00
		(Atco 330 was produced by hubby Maurice Gibb of The Bee Gees.)			
Harmony H-30249	(P)	To Love Somebody	1970	8.00	20.00
		(Harmony 30249 is a repackage of the unreleased Epic 26396.)			
Pickwick SPC-3237	(S)	Lulu	1973	1.00	5.00
Chelsea BCL1-0144	(S)	Lulu	1973	4.00	10.00
Chelsea CHL-518	(S)	Heaven And Earth And The Stars	1976	8.00	20.00
		(CHL-518 has two tracks arranged and produced by David Bowie.)			
Rocket BXL1-3073	(S)	Don't Take Love For Granted	1978	4.00	10.00
Alfa 10006	(S)	Lulu	1981	4.00	10.00

LYMON, FRANKIE

Frankie Lymon originally recorded with The Teenagers.

Roulette R-25013	(M)	Frankie Lymon At The London Palladium	1958	200.00	400.00
Roulette R-25036	(M)	Rock 'N Roll	1958	200.00	400.00
		—Roulette albums above have black labels.—			
Guest Star G-1406	(M)	Teen Time Tunes Starring Frankie Lymon	1959	20.00	50.00
Guest Star GS-1406	(E)	Teen Time Tunes Starring Frankie Lymon	1959	12.00	30.00
		(Guest Star 1406 is actually a various artists compilation with a full color cover.)			
Guest Star G-1406	(M)	Rock & Roll Party Starring Frankie Lymon	196?	12.00	30.00
Guest Star GS-1406	(E)	Rock & Roll Party Starring Frankie Lymon	196?	8.00	20.00
		("Rock & Roll Party" is a repackage of "Teen Time Tunes" with a black & white cover.)			

LYMON, LEWIS, & THE TEENCHORDS

| Lost-Nite LLP-13 | (10") | Lewis Lymon & The Teenchords (Red vinyl) | 1981 | 4.00 | 10.00 |

LYNN, BARBARA

Jamie JLP-3023	(M)	You'll Lose A Good Thing	1962	20.00	50.00
Jamie JLPS-3023	(E)	You'll Lose A Good Thing	1962	20.00	50.00
Jamie JLP-3026	(M)	Sister Of Soul	1963	Unreleased?	
Jamie JLPS-3026	(S)	Sister Of Soul	1963	Unreleased?	
Atlantic 8171	(M)	Here Is Barbara Lynn	1968	20.00	50.00
Atlantic SD-8171	(S)	Here Is Barbara Lynn	1968	20.00	50.00

LYNN, DONNA

Capitol T-2085	(M)	Java Jones/			
		My Boyfriend Got A Beatle Haircut	1964	8.00	20.00
Capitol ST-2085	(S)	Java Jones/			
		My Boyfriend Got A Beatle Haircut	1964	12.00	30.00

LYNN, TAMI

| Cotillion SD-9052 | (S) | Love Is Here And Now You're Gone | 1972 | 4.00 | 10.00 |

LYNOTT, PHIL

Phillip Lynott was a member of Thin Lizzy.

Warner Bros. BSK-3405	(S)	Solo In Soho	1980	3.20	8.00
Warner Bros. 23745	(S)	The Phillip Lynott Album	1982	3.20	8.00
MCA 5354	(S)	Making Love From Memory	1982	Unreleased?	

LYNYRD SKYNYRD

The original recording band, was Ronnie Van Zandt with Gary Rossington, Allen Collins, Billy Powell, Leon Wilkeson, Bob Burns, and Ed King. Both Van Zandt and Gaines are killed in an airplane crash in 1977 with surviving members reforming as The Rossington-Collins Band.

Sounds of the South 363	(S)	Pronounced Leh-nerd Skin-nerd	1973	6.00	15.00
Sounds of the South 413	(S)	Second Helping	1974	6.00	15.00
		—Sounds of the South albums above have yellow labels.—			
MCA 2137	(S)	Nothin' Fancy	1975	3.20	8.00
MCA 2170	(S)	Gimme Back My Bullets	1976	3.20	8.00
MCA 3019	(S)	Pronounced Leh-nerd Skin-nerd	1976	1.00	5.00
MCA 3020	(S)	Second Helping	1976	1.00	5.00
MCA 3021	(S)	Nothin' Fancy	1976	1.00	5.00
MCA 3022	(S)	Gimme Back My Bullets	1976	1.00	5.00

Label & Catalog #		Title	Year	VG+	NM
MCA 1946	(DJ)	One More From The Road (Black vinyl)	1976	6.00	15.00
MCA 1946	(DJ)	One More From The Road (Blue vinyl)	1976	20.00	50.00
MCA 1946	(DJ)	One More From The Road (Gold vinyl)	1976	20.00	50.00
MCA 1946	(DJ)	One More From The Road (Purple vinyl)	1976	20.00	50.00
MCA 1946	(DJ)	One More From The Road (Red vinyl)	1976	20.00	50.00
MCA2-6001	(S)	One More From The Road (2 LPs)	1976	3.20	8.00
		—MCA albums above have black rainbow labels.—			
MCA 3019	(S)	Pronounced Leh-nerd Skin-nerd	1977	.80	4.00
MCA 3020	(S)	Second Helping	1977	.80	4.00
MCA 3021	(S)	Nothin' Fancy	1977	.80	4.00
MCA 3022	(S)	Gimme Back My Bullets	1977	.80	4.00
MCA2-6001	(S)	One More From The Road (2 LPs)	1977	1.00	5.00
MCA 3029	(S)	Street Survivors (With inserts)	1977	6.00	15.00
		(Original covers have the group in flames)			
MCA 3029	(S)	Street Survivors (With inserts)	197?	3.20	8.00
		(Later covers have a new cover with the flames airbrushed out.)			
MCA L33-1988	(DJ)	Skynyrd's First And... Last (Sampler)	1978	6.00	15.00
MCA 3047	(S)	Skynyrd's First And... Last	1978	1.00	5.00
MCA 37071	(S)	Skynyrd's First And... Last	1978	.80	4.00
		—MCA albums above have tan labels.—			
MCA 3019	(S)	Pronounced Leh-nerd Skin-nerd	1979	.80	4.00
MCA 5221	(S)	Pronounced Leh-nerd Skin-nerd	1979	.80	4.00
MCA 37212	(S)	Second Helping	1979	.80	4.00
MCA 5222	(S)	Second Helping	1979	.80	4.00
MCA 3022	(S)	Gimme Back My Bullets	1979	.80	4.00
MCA2-8001	(S)	One More From The Road (2 LPs)	1979	1.00	5.00
MCA 11008	(S)	Gold & Platinum (Embossed cover)	1979	1.00	5.00
MCA 11008	(S)	Gold & Platinum (Plain cover)	1979	.80	4.00
MCA 6898	(S)	Gold & Platinum	1980	.80	4.00
MCA 5370	(S)	Best Of The Rest	1982	.80	4.00
MCA 42084	(S)	Legend	1987	.80	4.00
MCA 2-8027	(S)	Southern By The Grace Of God	1988	.80	4.00
		—MCA albums above have clouds labels.—			

MAC-KAC

Atlantic 8012	(M)	Mac-Kac & His French Rock & Roll	1956	20.00	50.00

— Atlantic albums above have black labels.—

MACEO

Maceo Parker from James Brown's band.

El Cello 8022	(S)	Funky Music Machine	1972	10.00	25.00
People PE-6601	(S)	Us (Produced by James Brown)	1973	12.00	30.00
House Of Fox LP-1	(S)	Doing Their Own Thing	197?	10.00	25.00

MACK, LONNIE

Fraternity SF-1014	(M)	The Wham Of That Memphis Man	1963	60.00	150.00
Fraternity SSF-1014	(S)	The Wham Of That Memphis Man	1963	150.00	300.00
Elektra EKS-74050	(S)	Whatever's Right	1969	10.00	25.00
Elektra EKS-74040	(S)	Glad I'm In The Band	1969	10.00	25.00
Elektra EKS-74077	(M)	For Collectors Only	1970	10.00	25.00
Elektra EKS-74102	(S)	The Hills Of Indiana	1971	10.00	25.00
Trip TLX-9522	(P)	The Memphis Sound Of Lonnie Mack	1975	1.00	5.00
Capitol ST-11703	(S)	Lonnie Mack And Pismo	1977	1.00	5.00

MacKAY, RABBIT

Uni 73026	(S)	Bug Cloth	1968	5.00	12.00
Uni 73064	(S)	Passing Through	1969	5.00	12.00

MAD LADS, THE

Volt 414	(M)	The Mad Lads In Action	1966	12.00	30.00
Volt S-414	(S)	The Mad Lads In Action	1966	16.00	40.00
Volt VOS-6005	(S)	The Mad Mad Mad Mad Mad Mad Lads	1969	12.00	30.00
Volt VOS-6020	(S)	A New Beginning	1973	8.00	20.00

MAD RIVER

Capitol ST-2985	(S)	Mad River	1968	20.00	50.00
Capitol ST-185	(S)	Paradise Bar And Grill	1969	16.00	40.00

(Counterfeits of 185, and perhaps 2985, exist.)

MADHOUSE

Today 1010	(S)	Serve 'Em	1972	4.00	10.00

MADONNA

Sire 23867	(S)	Madonna	1983	12.00	30.00

(Original pressings of 23867 have a 4:48 version of "Burning Up.")

Sire 23867	(S)	Madonna	1983	1.00	5.00

(Later pressings have a remixed, 3:41 version of "Burning Up.")

Sire 25157	(DJ)	Like A Virgin (White vinyl)	1984	12.00	30.00
Sire 25157	(S)	Like A Virgin	1984	1.00	5.00
Sire PRO-A-2892	(S)	You Can Dance (Single edits of LP remixes)	1987	12.00	30.00
Sire 25442	(S)	True Blue (Clear vinyl)	198?	See note below	
Sire 25442	(S)	True Blue (Picture disc)	198?	See note below	

(Both the clear vinyl and picdisc of 25442 are imported bootlegs.)

Sire 25442	(S)	True Blue	1986	1.00	5.00
Sire 25611	(S)	Who's That Girl?	1987	1.00	5.00
Sire 25535	(S)	You Can Dance	1987	1.00	5.00
Sire 25844	(S)	Like A Prayer	1989	1.00	5.00
Sire 26440	(S)	The Immaculate Collection	1990	1.00	5.00
Sire 26209	(S)	I'm Breathless	1990	6.00	15.00
Sire 26464	(S)	The Royal Box	1990	12.00	30.00

(Special box with "The Immaculate Collection" and VHS video.)

Sire PRO-A-5904	(DJ)	Erotica (2 LPs. 1,500 copies pressed)	198?	20.00	50.00

MADRIGAL

SSS International	(S)	Madrigal	1971	12.00	30.00

MADURA

Columbia G-30794	(S)	Madura (2 LPs)	1971	5.00	12.00
Columbia KC-32545	(S)	Madura II	1973	4.00	10.00

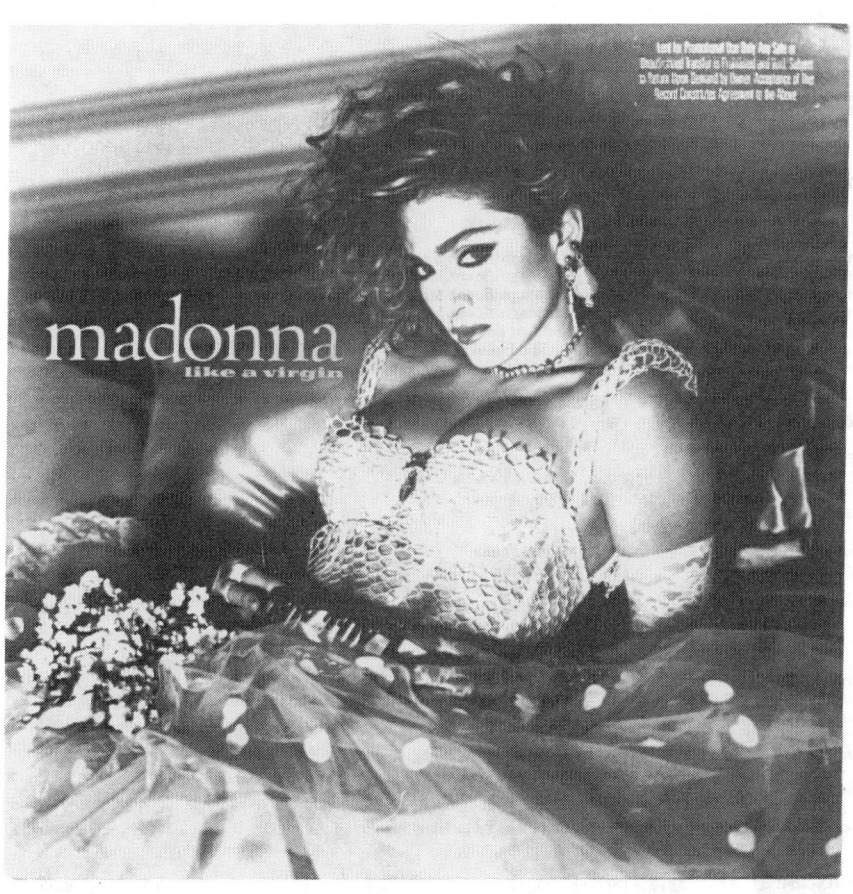

Madonna is the single most successful female singer of the past two decades. She owes this to a combination of talent, savvy, ambition and intelligence. While the supply-and-demand end of the equation for value means that it will be years before her commercial releases attain even negligible value, the market for special items such as the white vinyl Like A Virgin shown above, will grow readily with time.

Label & Catalog #		Title	Year	VG+	NM

MAESTRO, JOHNNY
Johnny Maestro was the lead singer for The Crests; The Brooklyn Bridge.

| Buddah BDS-5091 | (P) | **The Johnny Maestro Story** *(With inserts)* | 1971 | 10.00 | 25.00 |

MAFFITT & DAVIES

| Capitol ST-2999 | (S) | **The Rise And Fall Of Honesty** | 1968 | 5.00 | 12.00 |

MAGENTA

| Magenta 100 | (S) | **Magenta** | 1976 | 5.00 | 12.00 |

MAGIC
Magic features Jay Ferguson.

| Rare Earth 527 | (S) | **Magic** | 1971 | 10.00 | 25.00 |

MAGIC LANTERNS, THE
The Magic Lanterns feature what appears to be Mr Ozzy Osbourne.

| Atlantic SD-8217 | (S) | **Shame Shame** | 1969 | 8.00 | 20.00 |

MAGIC SAM

| Delmark DL-615 | (S) | **West Side Soul** | 1968 | 20.00 | 50.00 |
| Delmark DL-620 | (S) | **Black Magic** | 1969 | 20.00 | 50.00 |

MAGIC SAND

| Uni 73094 | (S) | **Magic Sand** | 1971 | 10.00 | 25.00 |

MAGMA

| Polydor ???? | (S) | **Magma** | 1970 | 30.00 | 75.00 |

MAGMA

A&M SP-4397	(S)	**Mekanik Destruktin Commandoh**	1973	3.20	8.00
A&M SP-3650	(S)	**Kohn Tarkosz**	1974	3.20	8.00
Tomato 7021	(S)	**Attahk**	1978	1.00	5.00

MAGNA CARTA

| Dunhill DS-50091 | (S) | **Seasons** | 1970 | 3.20 | 8.00 |

MAGNIFICENT MEN, THE

Capitol T-2678	(M)	**The Magnificent Men**	1967	4.00	10.00
Capitol ST-2678	(S)	**The Magnificent Men**	1967	4.00	10.00
Capitol T-2775	(M)	**The Magnificent Men "Live!"**	1967	4.00	10.00
Capitol ST-2775	(S)	**The Magnificent Men "Live!"**	1967	4.00	10.00
Capitol T-2846	(M)	**World Of Soul**	1968	4.00	10.00
Capitol ST-2846	(S)	**World Of Soul**	1968	4.00	10.00
Mercury SR-61252	(S)	**Better Than A Ten Cent Movie**	1970	4.00	10.00

MAGNIFICENTS, THE / THE RHYTHM ACES

| Solid Smoke 8030 | (S) | **15 Cool Jewels** | 1983 | 4.00 | 10.00 |

MAH-NA MAH-NA

| GRT 20003 | (S) | **Mah-Na Mah-Na** | 1971 | 3.20 | 8.00 |

MAHAL, TAJ

Columbia CS-9579	(S)	**Taj Mahal**	1968	10.00	25.00
Columbia CS-9698	(S)	**Natch'l Blues**	1969	10.00	25.00
Columbia GP-18	(S)	**Giant Step** *(2 LPs)*	1969	8.00	20.00
—Columbia albums above have "360 Sound" labels.—					
Columbia CS-9579	(S)	**Taj Mahal**	197?	1.00	5.00
Columbia CS-9698	(S)	**Natch'l Blues**	197?	1.00	5.00
Columbia GP-18	(S)	**Giant Step** *(2 LPs)*	197?	1.00	5.00
Columbia KC-30619	(S)	**The Real Thing**	1971	1.00	5.00
Columbia KC-30767	(S)	**Happy To Be Just Like I Am**	1971	1.00	5.00
Columbia KC-31605	(S)	**Recycling The Blues And Other Related Stuff**	1972	1.00	5.00
Columbia KC-32600	(S)	**Oooh So Good 'N Blues**	1973	1.00	5.00
Columbia KC-33051	(S)	**Mo' Roots**	1974	1.00	5.00
Columbia PC-33801	(S)	**Music Keeps Me Together**	1975	1.00	5.00
Columbia PC-34103	(S)	**Satisfied 'N Tickled, Too**	1976	1.00	5.00
Columbia PC-34466	(S)	**The Taj Mahal Anthology**	1977	1.00	5.00
Columbia FE-36528	(S)	**The Best Of Taj Mahal**	1981	.80	4.00
Warner Bros. BS-2994	(S)	**Music For Ya (Misica Para Tu)**	1977	1.00	5.00

MAHOGANY

| Epic BN-26498 | (S) | **Mahogany** | 1970 | 4.00 | 10.00 |

MAHOGANY RUSH [FRANK MARINO & MAHOGANY RUSH]

20th Century S-451	(S)	**Child Of Novelty**	1973	8.00	20.00
20th Century S-463	(S)	**Maxoom**	1975	8.00	20.00
20th Century S-482	(S)	**Strange Universe**	1975	8.00	20.00
Columbia PC-34190	(S)	**Mahogany Rush IV**	1976	3.20	8.00

Label & Catalog #		Title	Year	VG+	NM
Columbia PC-34677	(S)	World Anthem	1977	3.20	8.00
Columbia JC-35257	(S)	Frnk Marino & Mahogany Rush Live	1978	3.20	8.00
Columbia FC-35753	(S)	Tales Of The Unexpected	1979	3.20	8.00
Columbia FC-36204	(S)	What's Next	1980	3.20	8.00
Columbia FC-37099	(S)	The Power Of Rock And Roll	1981	3.20	8.00
Columbia FC-38023	(S)	Juggernaut	1982	3.20	8.00

MAIDEN, SIDNEY

Bluesville BVLP-1035	(M)	Trouble An' Blues	1961	30.00	75.00
		—Bluesville albums above have bright blue labels with silver print.—			
Bluesville BVLP-1035	(M)	Trouble An' Blues	1964	10.00	25.00
		—Bluesville albums above have blue labels with a trident logo on the right side.—			

MAILER MacKENZIE BAND

Ampex A-10114	(S)	The Mailer MacKenzie Band	1971	5.00	12.00

MAIN ATTRACTION, THE

Tower ST-5177	(S)	And Now	1968	10.00	25.00

MAINHORSE

Visa/Import IMP-1001	(S)	Mainhorse	1971	3.20	8.00

MAJIC SHIP

Bel Ami BA-711	(S)	Majic Ship	1968	300.00	500.00

MAJORS, THE

Imperial LP-9222	(M)	Meet The Majors	1963	60.00	150.00
Imperial LP-12222	(P)	Meet The Majors	1963	150.00	300.00

MALCOLM & CHRIS

Blues Time 9008	(S)	Just The Blues	1970	4.00	10.00

MALDOON

Warner Bros. BS-2706	(S)	Maldoon	1973	1.20	6.00

MALLARD

Mallard features Bill Harkleroad and Mark Boston, also known as Zoot Horn Rollo and Rockette Morton, respectively, and Art Tripp, all former members of Capt. Beefheart's Magic Band.

Virgin PZ-34489	(S)	In A Different Climate	1977	6.00	15.00

MALO

Warner Bros. BS-2584	(S)	Malo	1972	3.20	8.00
Warner Bros. BS-2652	(S)	Dos	1972	3.20	8.00
Warner Bros. BS-2702	(S)	Evolution	1973	3.20	8.00
Warner Bros. BS-2769	(S)	Ascension	1974	3.20	8.00

MAMA LION

Mama Lion features Lynn Carey. Refer to Neil Merryweather & Lynn Carey.

Family 2702	(S)	Mama Lion	1972	8.00	20.00
Family 2713	(S)	Give It Everything I've Got	1973	8.00	20.00

MAMAS & THE PAPAS, THE

The Mama's were Michelle Phillips and Cass Elliot; the Papa's were John Phillips and Denny Doherty, all of whom recorded solo. Refer to Barry McGuire; The Mugwumps..

Dunhill D-50006	(M)	If You Can Believe Your Eyes And Ears	1966	20.00	50.00
Dunhill DS-50006	(S)	If You Can Believe Your Eyes And Ears	1966	30.00	75.00
		(Original covers for Dunhill 50006 plainly show the toilet in the lower right corner. On all subsequent pressings a scroll with the titles of the album's hit singles has been placed over the toilet.)			
Dunhill D-50006	(M)	If You Can Believe Your Eyes And Ears	1966	8.00	20.00
Dunhill DS-50006	(S)	If You Can Believe Your Eyes And Ears	1966	10.00	25.00
		(The toilet on the cover is concealed by a scroll.)			
Dunhill DS-50006	(S)	If You Can Believe Your Eyes And Ears	1968	20.00	50.00
		(Some later pressings have a black border on all four sides of the cover, eliminating all but the faces of the four members. The label reads "A Subsidiary of ABC" on the bottom.)			
Dunhill D-50010	(M)	The Mama's & The Papa's	1966	8.00	20.00
Dunhill DS-50010	(S)	The Mama's & The Papa's	1966	10.00	25.00
Dunhill D-50014	(M)	The Mama's & The Papa's Deliver	1967	8.00	20.00
Dunhill DS-50014	(S)	The Mama's & The Papa's Deliver	1967	10.00	25.00
		—Dunhill albums above read "Dist. by ABC-Paramount" on the bottom of the label.—			
Dunhill D-50025	(M)	Farewell To The First Golden Era	1967	5.00	12.00
Dunhill DS-50025	(S)	Farewell To The First Golden Era	1967	6.00	15.00
Dunhill DS-50031	(S)	The Papa's And The Mama's (Gatefold cover)	1968	8.00	20.00
		—Dunhill albums above read "A Subsidiary of ABC Records" on the bottom of the label.—			
Dunhill DS-50006	(S)	If You Can Believe Your Eyes And Ears	196?	3.20	8.00
Dunhill DS-50010	(S)	The Mama's & The Papa's	196?	3.20	8.00
Dunhill DS-50014	(S)	The Mama's & The Papa's Deliver	196?	3.20	8.00

Label & Catalog #		Title	Year	VG+	NM
Dunhill DS-50025	(S)	Farewell To The First Golden Era	196?	3.20	8.00
Dunhill DS-50031	(S)	The Papa's And The Mama's	196?	3.20	8.00
Dunhill DS-50032	(S)	Book Of Songs	1968	4.00	10.00
Dunhill DS-50038	(S)	Golden Era, Volume 2	1968	4.00	10.00
Dunhill DS-50064	(S)	16 Of Their Greatest Hits	1969	4.00	10.00
Dunhill DS-50073	(S)	A Gathering Of Flowers (2 LP box with book)	1970	10.00	25.00
Dunhill DSX-50100	(S)	Monterey International Pop Festival	1970	4.00	10.00
Dunhill DSX-50106	(S)	People Like Us	1971	4.00	10.00
		—Dunhill albums above have black labels with "Dunhill/ABC" on top and "Dunhill Records is a subsidiary" on the bottom.—			
Pickwick SPC-3352	(S)	California Dreaming	1972	1.00	5.00
Dunhill DSX-50145	(S)	20 Golden Hits (2 LPs)	1973	3.20	8.00
MCA 709	(S)	Farewell To The First Golden Era	1980	.80	4.00
MCA 710	(S)	The Papa's & The Mama's	1980	.80	4.00
MCA 37145	(S)	16 Of Their Greatest Hits	1980	.80	4.00
MCA 6019	(S)	The Best Of The Mama's & Papa's (2 LPs)	1982	1.00	5.00

MAMMALS, THE: *Refer to* THE HUMAN BEINZ / THE MAMMALS

MAN [MANPOWER]

Label & Catalog #		Title	Year	VG+	NM
Philips PHS-600-313	(S)	Revelation	1969	8.00	20.00
		(Philips 313 credits Manpower.)			
Liberty LST-9803	(S)	Man	1970	4.00	10.00
Liberty 1032	(S)	Do You Like It Here, Are You Settling In	1971	4.00	10.00
United Artists LA-O77F	(S)	Be Good To Yourself	1973	4.00	10.00
United Artists LA-179H	(S)	Back Into The Future (2 LPs)	1973	5.00	12.00
United Artists LA-247	(S)	Rhinos, Winos And Lunatics	1974	4.00	10.00
United Artists LA-345	(S)	Slow Motion	1975	4.00	10.00
MCA 2190	(S)	Welsh Connection	1976	1.00	5.00

MANASSAS: *Refer to* STEPHEN STILLS

MANCHESTER, MELISSA

Label & Catalog #		Title	Year	VG+	NM
Bell 1123	(S)	Home To Myself	1973	1.20	6.00
Bell 1303	(S)	Bright Eyes	1974	1.20	6.00
Arista AL-4031	(S)	Melissa	1975	1.00	5.00
Arista AQ-4031	(Q)	Melissa	1975	4.00	10.00
Arista AL-4067	(S)	Better Days And Happy Endings	1976	1.00	5.00
Arista AQ-4067	(Q)	Better Days And Happy Endings	1976	4.00	10.00
Arista AL-4095	(S)	Help Is On The Way	1976	1.00	5.00
Arista AL-4136	(S)	Singin'	1977	1.00	5.00
Arista AL-4186	(S)	Don't Cry Out Loud	1978	1.00	5.00
Arista AL-9506	(S)	Melissa Manchester	1979	1.00	5.00
Arista AL-9533	(S)	For The Working Girl	1980	1.00	5.00
Arista AL-9574	(S)	Hey Ricky	1982	1.00	5.00
Arista AL-9611	(S)	Melissa Manchester's Greatest Hits	1983	1.00	5.00
Arista AL-8094	(S)	Emergency	1983	1.00	5.00

MANCHESTERS, THE

The Manchesters is a pseudonym for The Chartbusters and the albums include Beatles covers and Chartbusters' singles!

Label & Catalog #		Title	Year	VG+	NM
Diplomat D-2307	(M)	Beatlerama	1964	6.00	15.00
Diplomat DS-2307	(B)	Beatlerama	1964	8.00	20.00
		(Original pressings for Diplomat 2307 do not credit The Manchesters on the cover or the label.)			
Diplomat D-2307	(M)	Beatlerama	1964	6.00	15.00
Diplomat DS-2307	(B)	Beatlerama	1964	8.00	20.00
Guest Star G-2307	(M)	Beatlerama	1964	6.00	15.00
Guest Star GS-2307	(S)	Beatlerama	1964	8.00	20.00

MANDEL, HARVEY

Label & Catalog #		Title	Year	VG+	NM
Philips PHS-600-281	(S)	Cristo Redentor	1968	10.00	25.00
Philips PHS-600-306	(S)	Righteous	1969	10.00	25.00
Philips PHS-600-325	(S)	Games Guitars Play	1969	10.00	25.00
Janus JLS-3017	(S)	Baby Batter	1970	4.00	10.00
Janus JLS-3037	(S)	The Snake	1972	4.00	10.00
Janus JLS-3047	(S)	Shangrenade	1973	4.00	10.00
Janus JSX-3067	(S)	Feel The Sound	1974	4.00	10.00
Janus JXS-7014	(S)	The Best Of Harvey Mandel	1975	4.00	10.00

MANDO & THE CHILI PEPPERS

Label & Catalog #		Title	Year	VG+	NM
Golden Crest CR-3023	(M)	On The Road With Rock & Roll	195?	20.00	50.00

MANDRAKE MEMORIAL

Label & Catalog #		Title	Year	VG+	NM
Poppy PYS-40,002	(S)	Mandrake Memorial	1968	16.00	40.00
Poppy PYS-40,003	(S)	Medium	1969	16.00	40.00
Poppy PYS-40,006	(S)	Puzzle	1970	16.00	40.00

The Manhattans were George "Smitty" Smith backed by Edward "Sonny" Bivins, Kenneth "Wally" Kelly, Winfred "Blue" Lovett, and Richard Taylor. This group placed four sides on the national pop charts in the '60s, two of which, "Follow Your Heart" and "Baby I Need You," can be found on their first album, Dedicated To You. Following the death of Smitty in 1970, the group found their new lead in Gerald Alston. After signing with Columbia, The Manhattans became part of the '70s renaissance of lushly romantic black vocal groups.

Label & Catalog #		Title	Year	VG+	NM

MANDRILL

Label & Catalog #		Title	Year	VG+	NM
Polydor 24-4050	(S)	Mandrill	1971	4.00	10.00
Polydor PD1-5025	(S)	Mandrill Is	1972	1.00	5.00
Polydor PD1-5043	(S)	Composite Truth	1973	1.00	5.00
Polydor PD1-5059	(S)	Just Outside Of Town	1973	1.00	5.00
Polydor PD2-9002	(S)	Mandrilland (2 LPs)	1974	1.00	5.00
Polydor PD1-6047	(S)	The Best Of Mandrill	1975	1.00	5.00
United Arts. LA-408G	(S)	Solid	1975	1.00	5.00
Arista 4144	(S)	We Are One	1977	1.00	5.00
Arista 4195	(S)	New Worlds	1978	1.00	5.00
Arista 9527	(S)	Getting In The Mood	1980	1.00	5.00

MANFRED MANN

Manfred Mann is vocalist Paul Jones backed by Manfred Mann, Mike Vickers, Tom McGuinnes and Mike Hugg. Vickers left in 1965, replaced by Jack Bruce. Both Jones and Bruce departed in 1966, replaced by Mike D'abo and Klaus Voorman. The group split in 1969 with Mann and Hugg forming Manfred Mann Chapter Three. The group can also be found on the soundtracks for U.A.'s "Charge Of The Light Brigade" and Mercury's "Up The Junction."

Label & Catalog #		Title	Year	VG+	NM
Ascot ALM-13015	(M)	The Manfred Mann Album	1964	16.00	40.00
Ascot ALS-16015	(P)	The Manfred Mann Album	1964	20.00	50.00
Ascot ALM-13018	(M)	The Five Faces Of Manfred Mann	1965	16.00	40.00
Ascot ALS-16018	(P)	The Five Faces Of Manfred Mann	1965	20.00	50.00
Ascot ALM-13021	(M)	My Little Red Book Of Winners	1965	16.00	40.00
Ascot ALS-16021	(S)	My Little Red Book Of Winners	1965	20.00	50.00
Ascot ALM-13024	(M)	Mann Made	1966	16.00	40.00
Ascot ALS-16024	(S)	Mann Made	1966	20.00	50.00
United Arts. UAL-94	(DJ)	Manfred Mann Interview	1966	80.00	200.00
		(Promotional interview issued in a plain cardboard jacket.)			
United Arts. UAL-3549	(M)	Pretty Flamingo	1966	12.00	30.00
United Arts. UAS-6549	(S)	Pretty Flamingo	1966	16.00	40.00
United Arts. UAL-3551	(M)	Manfred Mann's Greatest Hits	1966	12.00	30.00
United Arts. UAS-6551	(P)	Manfred Mann's Greatest Hits	1966	16.00	40.00
		("Do Wah Diddy Diddy," "Sha La La," "I Got You Babe," and "Satisfaction" are rechanneled.)			
Mercury SR-61168	(S)	The Mighty Quinn	1968	10.00	25.00
Janus JLS-3064	(S)	The Best Of Manfred Mann	1974	4.00	10.00
Capitol M-11688	(S)	The Best Of Manfred Mann	1977	1.20	6.00
Capitol N-16073	(S)	The Best Of Manfred Mann	1980	1.00	5.00

MANFRED MANN CHAPTER THREE

Chapter Three is Manfred Mann and Mike Hugg with session players.

Label & Catalog #		Title	Year	VG+	NM
Polydor 24-4013	(S)	Manfred Mann Chapter 3	1970	1.00	5.00

MANFRED MANN'S EARTH BAND

Earth Band is Mann with Colin Pattenden, Chris Slade and Mick Rogers, who left in '76, replaced by Chris Thompson.

Label & Catalog #		Title	Year	VG+	NM
Polydor PD-5015	(S)	Manfred Mann's Earth Band	1972	1.00	5.00
Polydor PD-5031	(S)	Glorified, Magnified	1972	1.00	5.00
Polydor PD-5050	(S)	Get Your Rocks Off	1973	1.00	5.00
Polydor PD-6019	(S)	Solar Fire	1973	1.00	5.00
Warner Bros. BS-2826	(S)	The Good Earth	1974	1.00	5.00
Warner Bros. BS-2877	(S)	Nightingales And Bombers	1975	1.00	5.00
Warner Bros. BS-2965	(S)	The Roaring Silence	1976	1.00	5.00
Warner Bros. BSK-3055	(S)	The Roaring Silence	1977	.80	4.00
		(WB 3055 is a reissue of 2965 with "Spirit In The Night-Version 2")			
Warner Bros. BSK-3157	(S)	Watch	1978	.80	4.00
Warner Bros. BSK-3302	(S)	Angel Station	1979	.80	4.00
Warner Bros. BSK-3498	(S)	Chance	1981	.80	4.00
Arista AL8-8194	(S)	Somewhere In Afrika	1983	.80	4.00

MANHATTANS, THE

Label & Catalog #		Title	Year	VG+	NM
Carnival CLP-201	(M)	Dedicated To You	1966	100.00	250.00
Carnival CLPS-201	(S)	Dedicated To You	1966	150.00	500.00
Carnival CLP-202	(M)	For You And Yours	1967	60.00	150.00
Carnival CLPS-202	(S)	For You And Yours	1967	150.00	300.00
Deluxe DLP-12000	(S)	With These Hands	1971	8.00	20.00
Deluxe DLP-12004	(S)	A Million To One	1972	8.00	20.00
Columbia KC-32444	(S)	There's No Me Without You	1973	1.00	5.00
Columbia KC-33064	(S)	That's How Much I Love You	1975	1.00	5.00
Columbia PC-34450	(S)	It Feels So Good	1977	1.00	5.00
Columbia PCQ-34450	(Q)	It Feels So Good	1977	6.00	15.00
Columbia PC-35252	(S)	There's No Good In Goodbye	1978	1.00	5.00
Columbia JC-35693	(S)	Love Talk	1979	1.00	5.00
Columbia JC-36411	(S)	After Midnight	1980	1.00	5.00
Columbia JC-36861	(S)	The Manhattans' Greatest Hits	1980	1.00	5.00
Columbia FC-37156	(S)	Black Tie	1981	1.00	5.00
Solid Smoke 8007	(S)	Follow Your Heart	1981	1.00	5.00

Barry Iberman, a.k.a. Barry Mann, was a staple in the Brill Building stable of songwriters, usually paired with Cynthia Weil. His attempts at a career as a singer were limited: He scored a huge hit—and a perennial favorite on oldies stations—with "Who But The Bomp (In The Bomp, Bomp, Bomp)," but that basically remains his sole claim to fame.

Label & Catalog #		Title	Year	VG+	NM

MANN, BARRY
Mr Mann is part of the famed Brill Building staff of songwriters, usually paired with Cynthia Weill.

Label & Catalog #		Title	Year	VG+	NM
ABC-Paramount 399	(M)	Who Put The Bomp	1963	50.00	125.00
ABC-Paramount S-399	(S)	Who Put The Bomp	1963	80.00	200.00
New Design Z-30876	(S)	Lay It All Out	1971	4.00	10.00
RCA Victor DJL1-1162	(DJ)	Flo & Eddie Interview Barry Mann	1973	20.00	50.00
RCA Victor APL1-0860	(DJ)	Survivor	1975	4.00	10.00
Casablanca NBLP-7226	(S)	Barry Mann	1980	1.00	5.00

MANN, CARL

Phillips Inter. PLP-1960	(M)	Like Mann	1960	300.00	600.00

MANN, STEVE

Custom Fidelity CFS-1675	(S)	Straight Life	196?	4.00	10.00

MANNA

Columbia KC-31623	(S)	Manna	1972	4.00	10.00

MANNING, TERRY

Enterprise ENS-1008	(S)	Home Sweet Home	1969	16.00	40.00

MANPOWER: *Refer to MAN*

MANZANERA, PHIL
Phil Manzanera was a member of Roxy Music. Refer to 801.

Antilles AN-7008	(S)	Mainstream	1974	1.00	5.00
Atco SD-36-113	(S)	Diamond Head	197?	1.00	5.00
Polydor PD1-6147	(S)	Listen Now	1978	1.00	5.00
Polydor PD1-6178	(S)	K-Scope	1978	1.00	5.00
Editions E.G. 114	(S)	Primitive Guitars	1982	1.00	5.00

MANZAREK, RAY
Manzarek was a member of The Doors.

Mercury SRM-1-703	(S)	The Golden Scarab	1974	4.00	10.00
Mercury SRM-1-1014	(S)	The Whole Thing Started With Rock & Roll	1976	4.00	10.00

MAR-KETS, THE [THE MARKETTS]
On their first two Liberty albums they were The Mar-Kets; afterwards, The Marketts.

Liberty LRP-3226	(M)	Surfer's Stomp *(With insert)*	1962	20.00	50.00
Liberty LST-7226	(S)	Surfer's Stomp *(With insert)*	1962	24.00	60.00
		(*Liberty 3226 included a two-page insert, "Learn the new dance sensation. . ."The Surfers Stomp" as recorded by The Mar-Kets."*)			
Liberty LRP-3226	(M)	Surfer's Stomp *(Without insert)*	1962	16.00	40.00
Liberty LST-7226	(S)	Surfer's Stomp *(Without insert)*	1962	20.00	50.00
Liberty LRP-3226	(M)	The Surfing Scene	196?	12.00	30.00
Liberty LST-7226	(S)	The Surfing Scene	196?	16.00	40.00
		(*"Surfing Scene" is a reissue of "Surfer's Stomp."*)			
Warner Bros. T-1509	(M)	The Marketts Take To Wheels	1963	16.00	40.00
Warner Bros. ST-1509	(S)	The Marketts Take To Wheels	1963	20.00	50.00
Warner Bros. T-1537	(M)	Out Of Limits	1964	12.00	30.00
Warner Bros. ST-1537	(S)	Out Of Limits	1964	16.00	40.00
Warner Bros. T-1642	(M)	Batman Theme	1966	16.00	40.00
Warner Bros. ST-1642	(S)	Batman Theme	1966	20.00	50.00
World Pacific WP-1870	(M)	Sun Power	1967	8.00	20.00
World Pacific ST-1870	(S)	Sun Power	1967	10.00	25.00
Mercury SRM-1-679	(S)	AM, FM, Etc.	1973	6.00	15.00

MAR-KEYS, THE

Atlantic 8055	(M)	Last Night	1961	40.00	100.00
—*Atlantic albums above multi-color labels with a white "fan" logo on the right side.*—					
Atlantic 8055	(M)	Last Night	1962	20.00	50.00
Atlantic SD-8055	(E)	Last Night	1966	16.00	40.00
Atlantic 8062	(M)	Do The Pop-Eye With The Mar-Keys	1962	20.00	50.00
Atlantic SD-8062	(E)	Do The Pop-Eye With The Mar-Keys	1966	16.00	40.00
—*Atlantic albums above multi-color labels with a black "fan" logo on the right side.*—					
Stax ST-707	(M)	Great Memphis Sound	1966	20.00	50.00
Stax STS-707	(E)	Great Memphis Sound	1966	16.00	40.00
Stax STS-2025	(S)	Damifiknew	1969	8.00	20.00
Stax STS-2036	(S)	Memphis Experience	1971	8.00	20.00

MAR-KEYS, THE / BOOKER T. & THE M.G.'S

Stax ST-720	(M)	Back To Back	1967	8.00	20.00
Stax STS-720	(S)	Back To Back	1967	10.00	25.00

MARATHONS, THE

Arvee A-428	(M)	Peanut Butter	1961	80.00	200.00

In 1963 Margaret Battavio, known professionally as Little Peggy March, became the youngest female singer to top the charts when the fifteen year old hit with the pre-liberation "I Will Follow Him." (The precocious singer was fourteen when she put the tracks on wax.) Of course—and I know this one is going to get me in hot water—this record, a staple of oldies stations nationwide, must be a formidable obstacle to the pleasures of nostalgia for those [unflexible] feminists who came of age in the early '60s. . .

Label & Catalog #		Title	Year	VG+	NM
MARBLES, THE					
Cotillion SD-9029	(S)	The Marbles	1970	4.00	10.00
MARCELS, THE					
Colpix CP-416	(M)	Blue Moon	1961	150.00	300.00
		—Colpix albums above have gold labels.—			
Colpix CP-416	(M)	Blue Moon	196?	50.00	150.00
		—Colpix albums above have blue labels.—			
MARCH, PEGGY [LITTLE PEGGY MARCH]					
RCA Victor LPM-2732	(M)	I Will Follow Him	1963	14.00	35.00
RCA Victor LSP-2732	(S)	I Will Follow Him	1963	20.00	50.00
RCA Victor LPM-3883	(M)	No Foolin'	1968	14.00	35.00
RCA Victor LSP-3883	(S)	No Foolin'	1968	10.00	25.00
MARCH, PEGGY, & BENNIE THOMAS					
RCA Victor LPM-3408	(M)	In Our Fashion	1965	14.00	35.00
RCA Victor LSP-3408	(S)	In Our Fashion	1965	20.00	50.00
		(*RCA 3408 features four tracks by each artist with four duets.)			
MARCHAN, BOBBY					
Sphere Sound SR-7004	(M)	There's Something On Your Mind	1964	80.00	200.00
Sphere Sound SSR-7004	(S)	There's Something On Your Mind	1964	150.00	300.00
MARCUS					
Kinetic Z-30207	(S)	Marcus	1970	6.00	15.00
MARESCA, ERNIE					
Seville SV-77001	(M)	Shout! Shout! Knock Yourself Out	1962	50.00	125.00
Seville SV-87001	(S)	Shout! Shout! Knock Yourself Out	1962	80.00	200.00
MARIANO & THE UNBELIEVABLES					
Capitol T-2831	(M)	Mariano And The Unbelievables	1967	5.00	12.00
Capitol ST-2831	(S)	Mariano And The Unbelievables	1967	5.00	12.00
MARINO, FRANK: *Refer to* **MAHOGANY RUSH**					
MARK-ALMOND BAND					
Blue Thumb 27	(S)	Mark-Almond	1970	4.00	10.00
Blue Thumb 32	(S)	Mark-Almond II	1971	4.00	10.00
Columbia KC-31917	(S)	Rising	1972	4.00	10.00
Columbia KC-32486	(S)	Mark-Almond '73	1973	4.00	10.00
A&M SP-4730	(S)	Other People's Rooms	1978	1.00	5.00
Pacific Arts 142	(S)	The Best Of The Mark-Almond Band Live	1981	1.00	5.00
MARKETTS, THE: *Refer to* **THE MAR-KETS**					

MARLEY, BOB, & THE WAILERS
The various albums listed below prior to the Island Records listings are albums that collect Wailers' sides recorded prior to their 1973 signing with Island. For additional listings refer to Johnny Nash.

Studio One	(M)	The Wailing Wailers	196?	80.00	200.00
Studio One/Buddah	(S)	The Best Of Bob Marley & The Wailers	1976	1.00	5.00
Calla CAS-1240	(S)	The Birth Of A Legend (2 LPs)	1976	1.00	5.00
ALA 1982	(S)	Shakedown	197?	1.00	5.00
ALA 1986	(S)	Soul Captives	197?	1.00	5.00
		(ALA 1986 is a reissue of 1982.)			
Cotillion SD-5228	(S)	Chances Are	1980	1.00	5.00
Pressure Disc LPS-507	(S)	Soul Revolution	1981	1.00	5.00
Pressure Disc LPS-50028	(S)	Reggae Revolution, Vol. 2	198?	1.00	5.00
		(Pressure Disb 50028 is a reissue of 507.)			
Pressure Disc LPS-50029	(S)	Reggae Revolution, Vol. 3	198?	1.00	5.00
Phoenix 10	(S)	Marley	1982	1.00	5.00
Accord SN-7211	(S)	Jamaican Storm	1982	.80	4.00
Island ILPS-9241	(S)	Catch A Fire	1973	20.00	50.00
		(The cover is shaped like a cigarette lighter with a hinge that allows the top to flip open.)			
Island ILPS-9241	(S)	Catch A Fire (Standard cover)	1973	1.00	5.00
Island ILPS-9256	(S)	Burnin'	1973	1.00	5.00
Island ILPS-9281	(S)	Natty Dread	1974	1.00	5.00
Island ILPS-9376	(S)	Live! Bob Marley & The Wailers	1975	1.00	5.00
Island ILPS-9383	(S)	Rastaman Vibration	1976	40.00	100.00
		(Issued promotionally in a burlap box with a press kit.)			
Island ILPS-9383	(S)	Rastaman Vibration	1976	4.00	10.00
		—Original Island albums above have black labels with an "i" on the bottom.—			
Island ILPS-9498	(S)	Exodus	1977	.80	4.00
Island ILPS-9517	(S)	Kaya	1978	.80	4.00
Island ISLD-11	(S)	Babylon By Bus (2 LPs)	1978	1.20	6.00
Island ILPS-9542	(S)	Survival	1979	.80	4.00

It is interesting to note the difference in artwork that a little success can bring a label. The Marvelettes' Please Mr. Postman features a cover that almost anyone with the ability to draw a straight line might have accomplished. Looking at this album, it would be hard to tell that this was anything but a privately pressed album. Three years later Berry Gordy's tastes—and finances—allowed this stunningly kinetic bit of cartooning for Martha & The Vandella's Dance Party. The only thing wrong I can see in it at all is the complete lack of black folk on the dance floor.

Label & Catalog #		Title	Year	VG+	NM
Island ILPS-9596	(S)	Uprising	1980	.80	4.00
Mango BMSP-100	(S)	Bob Marley & The Wailers-The Box Set	1982	40.00	100.00
		(Boxed set of nine Island albums: 9241, 9256, 9281, 9376, 9383, 9498, 9517, 9542 and 9596.)			
Mango MLPS-9795	(S)	Reggae Greats-The Wailers	1984	.80	4.00
Island 7-90085	(S)	Confrontation (Picture disc)	1984	1.20	6.00
Island 7-90085	(S)	Confrontation	1984	.80	4.00
Island 7-90169	(S)	Legend	1984	.80	4.00
Island 7-90250	(S)	Rebel Music	1986	.80	4.00

MARMALADE

Epic BN-26553	(S)	The Best Of Marmalade	1970	8.00	20.00
London PS-575	(P)	Reflections Of My Life	1970	8.00	20.00

MARSHMALLOW WAY

United Arts. UAS-6708	(S)	Marshmallow Way	1969	8.00	20.00

MARTHA & THE VANDELLAS
Martha is Martha Reeves.

Gordy G-902	(M)	Come And Get These Memories	1963	150.00	300.00
Gordy GS-902	(S)	Come And Get These Memories	1963	300.00	500.00
Gordy G-907	(M)	Heat Wave	1963	80.00	200.00
Gordy G-907	(E)	Heat Wave	1963	60.00	150.00
		(Copies of Gordy G-907 issued in "Stereo" covers are rechanneled.)			
Gordy GS-907	(S)	Heat Wave	1963	150.00	400.00
		(Copies in mono covers with a black "Stereo" sticker are real stereo.)			
Gordy G-915	(M)	Dance Party	1965	14.00	35.00
Gordy GS-915	(S)	Dance Party	1965	20.00	50.00
Gordy G-917	(M)	Martha & The Vandellas' Greatest Hits	1966	10.00	25.00
Gordy GS-917	(S)	Martha & The Vandellas' Greatest Hits	1966	10.00	25.00
Gordy G-920	(M)	Watchout!	1967	10.00	25.00
Gordy GS-920	(S)	Watchout!	1967	10.00	25.00
Gordy G-925	(M)	Martha & The Vandellas' Live!	1967	10.00	25.00
Gordy GS-925	(S)	Martha & The Vandellas' Live!	1967	10.00	25.00
Gordy G-926	(M)	Ridin' High (Promo)	1968	12.00	30.00
Gordy GS-926	(S)	Ridin' High	1968	6.00	15.00
Gordy GS-944	(S)	Sugar 'N Spice	1969	6.00	15.00
Gordy GS-952	(S)	Natural Resources	1970	6.00	15.00
Gordy GS-958	(S)	Black Magic	1972	6.00	15.00
Motown 778	(S)	Anthology (2 LPs)	1974	4.00	10.00
Motown M5-111V	(S)	Superstar Series, Vol. 11	1981	1.00	5.00
Motown M<5-145V	(S)	Heat Wave	1981	1.00	5.00
Motown M5-204V	(S)	Martha & The Vandellas' Greatest Hits	1982	1.00	5.00

MARTIN, DEWEY
Dewey Martin was a member of Buffalo Springfield.

Uni 73088	(S)	Dewey Martin And Medicine Ball	1970	10.00	25.00

MARTIN & NEIL
Vince Martin & Fred Neil.

Elektra EKL-248	(M)	Tear Down The Walls	1965	20.00	50.00
Elektra EKS-7248	(S)	Tear Down The Walls	1965	30.00	75.00

MARTYN, JOHN

Warner Bros. WS-1854	(S)	Stormbringers	1970	4.00	10.00
Island SW-9325	(S)	Solid Air	1973	4.00	10.00

MARVELETTES, THE

Tamla T-228	(M)	Please Mr. Postman	1961	300.00	600.00
		—Tamla albums above have white labels.—			
Tamla T-229	(M)	The Marveletts Sing Smash Hits Of '62	1962	600.00	1,200.00
		(Original covers are white with a large "M" and a "62" inside a circle and the group's name is mis-spelled. The title on the record is "The Marvelettes Sing,. with the group's name correctly spelled)			
Tamla T-229	(M)	The Marveletts Sing	1962	250.00	500.00
		(Later covers are black with the titles of the hits inside circles and the group's name mis-spelled. The title on the record is "The Marvelettes Sing".)			
Tamla T-231	(M)	Playboy	1962	250.00	500.00
		—Tamla albums above have a disc over-lapping a globe at the top of the label.—			
Tamla T-228	(M)	Please Mr. Postman	1963	150.00	300.00
Tamla T-229	(M)	The Marvelettes Sing	1963	100.00	250.00
Tamla T-231	(M)	Playboy	1963	100.00	250.00
Tamla T-237	(M)	The Marvelous Marvelettes	1963	80.00	200.00
Tamla T-243	(M)	Recorded Live On Stage	1963	30.00	75.00
Tamla T-253	(M)	The Marvelettes' Greatest Hits (Yellow cover)	1966	12.00	30.00
Tamla TS-253	(S)	The Marvelettes' Greatest Hits (Yellow cover)	1966	12.00	30.00

Barbara Mason placed seven sides on the pop charts for Arctic Records in the latter half of the '60s, writing each one. The first, "Yes, I'm Ready," was the biggest and, like so many artists who run up against the tight guidelines of oldies stations, it is the only one that is still played. Her second hit, "Sad, Sad Girl," made the Top 30 and is included on her first album (shown here). Ms Mason did not have any similar success until signing with Buddah in the early '70s.

Label & Catalog #		Title	Year	VG+	NM
Tamla T-253	(M)	The Marvelettes' Greatest Hits (Green cover)	1967	10.00	25.00
Tamla TS-253	(S)	The Marvelettes' Greatest Hits (Green cover)	1967	8.00	20.00
Tamla T-274	(M)	The Marvelettes	1967	10.00	25.00
Tamla TS-274	(S)	The Marvelettes	1967	8.00	20.00
Tamla T-286	(M)	Sophisticated Soul	1968	12.00	30.00
Tamla TS-286	(S)	Sophisticated Soul	1968	6.00	15.00
Tamla TS-288	(S)	The Marvelettes In Full Bloom	1969	6.00	15.00
Tamla TS-305	(S)	Return Of The Marvelettes	1970	6.00	15.00
—Tamla albums above have yellow labels with two side-by-side circles at the top.—					
Motown M7-827	(S)	The Marvelettes/Anthology (2 LPs)	1975	6.00	15.00
Motown M5-180V	(S)	The Marvelettes' Greatest Hits	1981	1.00	5.00

MARVIN & JOHNNY
For additional listings refer to The Isley Brothers / Marvin & Johnny.

Crown CLP-5381	(M)	Marvin & Johnny	1963	12.00	30.00
Crown CST-381	(E)	Marvin & Johnny	1963	8.00	20.00
—Crown albums above have gray labels.—					

MARVIN, WELCH & FARRAR [MARVIN & FARRAR]
Hank Marvin and Bruce Welch, the twin guitars behind Britain's Shadows, with John Farrar.

Capitol ST-760	(S)	Marvin, Welch And Farrar	1971	4.00	10.00
Sire SAS-7403	(S)	Second Opinion	1972	4.00	10.00
EMI ST-11403	(S)	Hank Marvin And John Farrar	1973	4.00	10.00

MASHMAKAN

Epic E-30235	(S)	Mashmakan	1970	3.20	8.00
Epic E-30813	(S)	The Family	1971	3.20	8.00

MASKED MARAUDERS, THE
A bogus "review" of a non-existent supergroup that had Dylan, Lennon, and Jagger and others jamming together led to this, a spoof of a spoof.

Reprise/Deity RS-6378	(S)	The Masked Marauders	1969	6.00	15.00

MASON, BARBARA

Arctic ALP-1000	(M)	Yes, I'm Ready	1965	14.00	35.00
Arctic ALPS-1000	(P)	Yes, I'm Ready	1965	20.00	50.00
Arctic ALPS-1004	(S)	Oh, How It Hurts	1968	12.00	30.00
National General 2001	(S)	If You Knew Him Like I Do	1970	12.00	30.00
Buddah BDS-5117	(S)	Give Me Your Love	1972	4.00	10.00
Buddah BDS-5140	(S)	Lady Love	1974	4.00	10.00
Buddah BDS-5610	(S)	Transition	1974	4.00	10.00
Buddah BDS-5628	(S)	Love's The Thing	1975	4.00	10.00
Warner Bros. 5014	(S)	Locked In This Position	1977	4.00	10.00
Prelude 12159	(S)	I Am Your Woman, She Is Your Wife	1978	4.00	10.00

MASON, DAVE
Dave Mason was a member of Traffic.

Blue Thumb BTS-19	(S)	All Together ((Pink marbled vinyl)	1970	100.00	200.00
		(Original pressings of the record were erroneously titled "All Together", most of which were withdrawn and destroyed.)			
Blue Thumb BTS-19	(S)	Alone Together (Multi-colored vinyl)	1970	6.00	15.00
Blue Thumb BTS-19	(S)	Alone Together (Black vinyl)	1971	20.00	50.00
Blue Thumb BTS-34	(S)	Headkeeper	1972	4.00	10.00
Blue Thumb BTS-54	(S)	Dave Mason Is Alive	1973	4.00	10.00
Blue Thumb BTS-880	(S)	Dave Mason At His Best	1974	1.00	5.00
Columbia PC-31721	(S)	It's Like You Never Left	1974	.80	4.00
Columbia PCQ-31721	(Q)	It's Like You Never Left	1974	4.00	10.00
Columbia PC-33096	(S)	Dave Mason	1974	.80	4.00
Columbia PCQ-33096	(Q)	Dave Mason	1974	4.00	10.00
Columbia PC-33698	(S)	Split Coconut	1976	.80	4.00
Columbia PCQ-33698	(Q)	Split Coconut	1976	4.00	10.00
Columbia PG-34174	(S)	Certified Live (2 LPs)	1976	.80	4.00
Columbia PC-34680	(S)	Let It Flow	1977	.80	4.00
Columbia JC-35285	(S)	Mariposa De Oro	1978	.80	4.00
Columbia FC-37089	(S)	The Best Of Dave Mason	1981	.80	4.00
ABC TD-6013	(S)	Dave Mason At His Very Best	1985	.80	4.00

MASON, DAVE, & CASS ELLIOT
Refer to Dave (above) and, for Ms Elliot, The Big Three; The Mugwumps; The Mama's & The Papa's.

Blue Thumb BTS-25	(S)	Dave Mason And Cass Elliot	1969	10.00	25.00
Blue Thumb BTS-8825	(S)	Dave Mason And Cass Elliot	1971	3.20	8.00
		(Blue Thumb 8825 is a reissue of 25.)			

MASON & DIXON

Tower ST-5136	(S)	Our Thing	1969	5.00	12.00

MASON PROFFIT

Happy Tiger HT-1009	(S)	Wanted! Mason Proffit	1970	6.00	15.00
Happy Tiger HT-1019	(S)	Movin' Toward Happiness	1971	6.00	15.00

Label & Catalog #		Title	Year	VG+	NM
Ampex A-10138	(S)	Last Night I Had The Strangest Dream	1971	4.00	10.00
Warner Bros. BS-2657	(S)	Rockfish Crossing	1972	3.20	8.00
Warner Bros. BS-2704	(S)	Bareback Rider	1973	3.20	8.00
Warner Bros. 2LS-2746	(S)	Come And Gone	1973	3.20	8.00
MATCHING MOLE					
Columbia KC-32148	(S)	Little Red Record	1972	3.20	8.00
MATRIX					
Rare Earth R-542L	(S)	Matrix	1972	6.00	15.00
MATTHEWS' SOUTHERN COMFORT					
Decca DL-75191	(S)	Matthews' Southern Comfort	1970	4.00	10.00
Decca DL-75242	(S)	Second Spring	1970	4.00	10.00
Decca DL-75264	(S)	Later That Same Year	1971	4.00	10.00
MAUDS, THE					
Mercury MG-21135	(M)	The Mauds Hold On	1967	6.00	15.00
Mercury SR-61135	(S)	The Mauds Hold On	1967	8.00	20.00
MAXWELL, DIANE					
Challenge CHL-607	(M)	Almost Seventeen	1959	10.00	25.00
Challenge CHS-2501	(S)	Almost Seventeen	1959	14.00	35.00
MAY BLITZ					
Paramount PAS-5020	(S)	May Blitz	1970	8.00	20.00

MAYALL, JOHN [JOHN MAYALL'S BLUESBREAKERS]
Mayall was a prime mover in the '60s British blues scene. His influence on that decade's rock music is explained by some, but by no means all, of the musicians who played, although not alays recording, as Bluesbreakers. These include John McVie (1963-67), Hughie Flint (1964-66), Eric Clapton (1965-66), Jack Bruce (1965-66), Peter Green (1966-67, Aynsley Dunbar (1966-68), Mick Fleetwood (1967), and Mick Taylor (1967-69). Refer to the Groundhogs.

London LL-3492	(M)	Blues Breakers With Eric Clapton	1966	10.00	25.00
London PS-492	(S)	Blues Breakers With Eric Clapton	1966	12.00	30.00
London LL-3502	(M)	A Hard Road	1967	8.00	20.00
London PS-502	(S)	A Hard Road	1967	8.00	20.00
London LL-3529	(M)	Crusade	1967	8.00	20.00
London PS-529	(S)	Crusade	1967	8.00	20.00
London PS-534	(S)	The Blues Alone	1968	6.00	15.00
London PS-537	(S)	Bare Wires	1968	6.00	15.00
London PS-543	(S)	Raw Blues	1968	6.00	15.00
London PS-545	(S)	Blues From Laurel Canyon	1969	6.00	15.00
London PS-562	(S)	Looking Back	1969	6.00	15.00
London PS-570	(S)	The Diary Of A Band	1970	4.00	10.00
London PS-589	(S)	Live In Europe	1971	4.00	10.00
London 2PS-600	(S)	Through The Years (2 LPs)	1971	4.00	10.00

—London mono albums above have red labels with a red "London" on top in a silver box; stereo albums above have deep blue labels with a blue "London" on top in a silver box.—

London 2BP-618	(S)	Down The Line (2 LPs)	1973	1.20	6.00
London LC-50009	(S)	Blues Breakers With Eric Clapton	1977	1.00	5.00
London 820 320	(S)	Primal Solos	1977	1.00	5.00
Polydor 24-4004	(S)	The Turning Point	1970	1.20	6.00
Polydor 24-4010	(S)	Empty Rooms	1970	1.20	6.00
Polydor 24-4022	(S)	U.S.A. Union	1970	1.20	6.00
Polydor 25-3002	(S)	Back To The Roots (2 LPs)	1971	3.20	8.00
Polydor PD-5012	(S)	Memories	1971	1.20	6.00
Polydor PD-5027	(S)	Jazz-Blues Fusion	1972	1.20	6.00
Polydor PD-5036	(S)	Moving On	1972	3.20	8.00
Polydor PD-23006	(S)	The Best Of John Mayall	1973	1.20	6.00
Polydor PD-3005	(S)	Ten Years Are Gone (2 LPs)	1973	1.20	6.00
Polydor PD-6030	(S)	The Latest Edition	1974	3.20	8.00
Blue Thumb BTS-6019	(S)	New Year, New Band, New Company	1975	1.20	6.00
ABC D-926	(S)	Notice To Appear	1975	1.20	6.00
ABC D-958	(S)	A Banquet In Blues	1976	1.20	6.00
ABC D-992	(S)	Lots Of People	1977	1.20	6.00
ABC D-1039	(S)	A Hard Core Package	1977	1.20	6.00
ABC D-1086	(S)	Last Of The British Blues	1978	1.20	6.00
DJM 23	(S)	The Bottom Line	1979	1.20	6.00
DJM 29	(S)	No More Interviews	1979	1.20	6.00
Accord SN-7209	(S)	Roadshow Blues Band	1982	1.00	5.00
Crescendo GNPS-2184	(S)	Behind The Iron Curtain	1986	1.00	5.00
Decal LIK-1	(S)	Some Of My Best Friends Are Blues	1986	1.00	5.00
Polydor 422-837-127	(S)	Archives To The Eighties Featuring Eric Clapton And Mick Taylor	1988	1.00	5.00
Island ILS-91005	(S)	Chicago Line	1988	1.00	5.00

Label & Catalog #		Title	Year	VG+	NM

MAYER, NATHANIEL

Fortune 8014	(M)	**Going Back To The Village Of Love**	1962	150.00	300.00
		—Fortune albums above have light blue labels on thick vinyl.—			
Fortune 8014	(M)	**Going Back To The Village Of Love**	196?	60.00	150.00
		—Fortune albums above have purple labels on thick vinyl.—			
Fortune 8014	(M)	**Going Back To The Village Of Love**	196?	30.00	75.00
		—Fortune albums above have yellow labels on thick vinyl.—			
Fortune 8014	(M)	**Going Back To The Village Of Love**	197?	6.00	15.00
		—Fortune albums above have bluish purple labels on thin vinyl.—			

MAYFIELD, CURTIS
Curtis Mayfield was a founding member of The Impressions.

Curtom CRS-8005	(S)	**Curtis**	1970	6.00	15.00
Curtom CRS-8008	(S)	**Curtis Mayfield Live** (2 LPs)	1971	6.00	15.00
Curtom CRS-8009	(S)	**Roots**	1971	6.00	15.00
Curtom CRS-8014	(S)	**Superfly**	1972	4.00	10.00
Curtom CRS-8015	(S)	**Back To The World**	1973	6.00	15.00
Curtom CRS-8018	(S)	**Curtis Mayfield In Chicago**	1973	6.00	15.00
Curtom CRS-SP	(DJ)	**Rapping** (Interview)	1973	10.00	25.00
ABC AC-30009	(S)	**Curtis Mayfield—The ABC Collection**	1976	4.00	10.00
RSO 3053	(S)	**Heartbeat**	1979	1.00	5.00
RSO 3077	(S)	**Something To Believe In**	1980	1.00	5.00
RSO 3084	(S)	**Right Combination**	1980	1.00	5.00
Boardwalk NB1-33239	(S)	**Love Is The Place**	1981	1.00	5.00
Boardwalk NB1-33256	(S)	**Honesty**	1982	1.00	5.00

MAYFIELD, PERCY

Tangerine TRC-1505	(M)	**My Jug And I**	1966	8.00	20.00
Tangerine TRCS-1505	(S)	**My Jug And I**	1966	10.00	25.00
Tangerine TRC-1510	(M)	**Bought Blues**	1967	8.00	20.00
Tangerine TRCS-1510	(S)	**Bought Blues**	1967	10.00	25.00
Brunswick BL7-54145	(S)	**Walking On A Tightrope**	1969	8.00	20.00
Specialty SPS-2186	(E)	**The Best Of Percy Mayfield**	1970	8.00	20.00
RCA Victor LSP-4269	(S)	**Percy Mayfield Sings Percy Mayfield**	1970	6.00	15.00
RCA Victor LSP-4444	(S)	**Weakness Is A Thing Called Man**	1970	6.00	15.00
RCA Victor LSP-4558	(S)	**Blues And Then Some**	1971	6.00	15.00

MAYPOLE

Colossus CS-1007	(S)	**Maypole**	1971	24.00	60.00

MC-5, THE

Elektra EKS-74042	(S)	**Kick Out The Jams** (White label promo)	1969	60.00	150.00
Elektra EKS-74042	(S)	**Kick Out The Jams**	1969	30.00	75.00
		(Original pressings open side one with the anthem, "Kick out the jams, motherfuckers!" and feature liner notes on the inside of the gatefold cover.)			
		—Elektra albums above have brown labels.—			
Elektra EKS-74042	(S)	**Kick Out The Jams**	1970	20.00	50.00
		(Later pressings replace the expletive with "Kick out the jams, brothers and sisters!" and delete the liner notes.)			
		—Elektra albums above have red labels.—			
Atlantic SD-8247	(S)	**Back In The U.S.A.**	1970	20.00	50.00
Atlantic SD-8285	(S)	**High Time**	1971	20.00	50.00

McCALL, TOUSSAINT

Ronn 7527	(M)	**Nothing Can Take The Place Of You**	1967	12.00	30.00
Ronn 7527S	(S)	**Nothing Can Take The Place Of You**	1967	16.00	40.00
		("Nothing Can Take The Place..." and "Shimmy" are rechanneled.)			

McCARTNEY, PAUL [PAUL McCARTNEY & WINGS]
Mac was once the premier bass player in rock as a member of the world's greatest band, The Beatles. The albums below may be credited to any of the following: Paul McCartney, Paul & Linda McCartney, Paul McCartney & Wings, or just Wings. After the fall of Apple, all of Mac's albums were reissued by Capitol, often with several label variations. When Paul moved to Columbia, he took his catalog with him and all of the Apple and Capitol albums were reissued first on Columbia's regular line (with a "JC" prefix) and then on their budget line ("PC"). Those reissues and variations that have significant value are listed below. Refer to The Beatles; The Crickets; Mary Hopkin; Denny Laine; Percy Thrillington. He can also be found on the London soundtrack "The Family Way."

Apple STAO-3363	(S)	**McCartney**	1970	8.00	20.00
		(The label has "McCartney" and "Paul McCartney" on two lines at the top. The Apple address on the back cover is in New York. Counterfeits have inferior reproductions of the labels and cover.)			
Apple STAO-3363	(S)	**McCartney**	1970	12.00	30.00
		(The label has both "McCartney" and "Paul McCartney" on two lines at the top. The Apple address on the back cover is in California. Counterfeits have inferior reproductions of the labels and cover.)			
Apple STAO-3363	(S)	**McCartney**	1970	12.00	30.00
		(The label has "McCartney" only at the top but the back cover reads "An ABKCO managed company.")			

From 1963 through at least 1970, Paul McCartney could claim that he was not only one of two singers and songwriters for the world's greatest rock'n roll band, but that he was also the field's most creative bassist. Even if Sgt Pepper's Lonely Hearts Club Band did not, in fact, contain the treasures that it does, it would remain a constant source of inspiration—and, perhaps, awe—for students of the electric bass as well as that of fledgling drummers, as the performance by The Beatles' rhythm section reached heights unmatched since. Unfortunately, with his necessary but much maligned declaration of independence, Mac jump-started a solo career that has made him one of the wealthiest entertainers in the world, but has left behind a paucity of memorable music. Band On The Run is generously considered his masterpiece. This half-speed mastered reissue from CBS is in demand by Beatles/McCartney collectors as well as audiophiles who place form over content.

Label & Catalog #		Title	Year	VG+	NM
Apple STAO-3363	(S)	McCartney	1970	8.00	20.00
		(The label has "McCartney" only at the top.)			
Apple SMAS-3363	(S)	McCartney	197?	12.00	30.00
Apple SPRO-6210	(DJ)	Brung To Ewe By	1971	200.00	400.00
		(Radio spots for "Ram." Originals have even spacing between the tracks; counterfeits are uneven.)			
Apple MAS-3375	(M)	Ram	1971	See note below	
		(Mono pressing issued to radio stations in standard stereo cover. Rare with a suggested Near Mint value of $3,000-6,000.)			
Apple SMAS-3375	(S)	Ram	1971	6.00	15.00
		(The Apple is unsliced on one side while sliced on the other.)			
Apple SMAS-3375	(S)	Ram	1971	10.00	25.00
		(The Apple label is unsliced on both sides.)			
		—Apple albums above have "Manufactured by Apple" on the bottom of the label.—			
Apple STAO-3363	(S)	McCartney	1970	40.00	100.00
Apple SMAS-3375	(S)	Ram	1971	20.00	50.00
Apple SW-3386	(S)	Wild Life	1971	6.00	15.00
Apple SMAL-3409	(S)	Red Rose Speedway (With booklet)	1973	6.00	15.00
Apple SO-3415	(S)	Band On The Run (With poster)	1973	6.00	15.00
		—Apple albums above have "A Subsidiary of Capitol" on the bottom of the label.—			
Apple SMAS-3363	(S)	McCartney	1975	40.00	100.00
Apple SMAS-3375	(S)	Ram	1975	40.00	100.00
		—Apple albums above have an "All Rights Reserved" disclaimer on the label.—			
Capitol SMAS-3363	(S)	McCartney	197?	10.00	25.00
Capitol SMAS-3375	(S)	Ram	197?	10.00	25.00
Capitol SW-3386	(S)	Wild Life	197?	10.00	25.00
Capitol SMAL-3409	(S)	Red Rose Speedway (With booklet)	197?	10.00	25.00
		—Capitol albums above have black labels with "Manufactured by McCartney Music."—			
Capitol SMAS-3363	(S)	McCartney	197?	8.00	20.00
Capitol SMAS-3375	(S)	Ram	197?	8.00	20.00
Capitol SW-3386	(S)	Wild Life	197?	8.00	20.00
Capitol SMAL-3409	(S)	Red Rose Speedway (With booklet)	197?	8.00	20.00
Capitol SMAL-3409	(S)	Red Rose Speedway (With booklet)	197?	16.00	40.00
		(The cover has the Capitol logo on the back.)			
		—Capitol albums above have black labels with "Manufactured by MPL Communications."—			
Capitol SMAS-3375	(S)	Ram	197?	16.00	40.00
Capitol PRO-2955/56	(DJ)	Band On The Run Radio Interview	1973	1,000.00	1,500.00
		(White label with a script and two photos in a plain cardboard jacket. Counterfeits have yellow labels.)			
Capitol SO-3415	(S)	Band On The Run (With poster)	1973	16.00	40.00
		—Capitol albums above have black labels with "Manufactured by Capitol."—			
Capitol SO-3415	(S)	Band On The Run (With poster)	197?	10.00	25.00
		—Capitol albums above have photo labels with "Manufactured by MPL Communications."—			
Capitol SO-3415	(S)	Band On The Run (With poster)	197?	8.00	20.00
		—Capitol albums above have black labels with "Manufactured by MPL Communications."—			
Capitol SEAX-11901	(S)	Band On The Run (Picture disc)	1975	14.00	35.00
Capitol SMAS-11419	(S)	Venus And Mars (With inserts)	1975	5.00	12.00
		(SMAS-11419 was issued with two posters and two stickers.)			
Capitol SMAS-11419	(S)	Venus And Mars (Without inserts)	1975	3.20	8.00
Capitol SW-11525	(DJ)	Wings At The Speed Of Sound (White label)	1976	150.00	300.00
Capitol SW-11525	(S)	Wings At The Speed Of Sound	1976	3.20	8.00
Capitol SWCO-11593	(S)	Wings Over America (3 LPs with poster)	1976	6.00	15.00
Capitol SW-11777	(S)	London Town (With poster)	1978	1.00	5.00
Capitol SOO-11905	(S)	Wings' Greatest (White label promo)	1978	200.00	400.00
Capitol SOO-11905	(S)	Wings' Greatest	1978	1.00	5.00
Capitol SMAS-3363	(S)	McCartney (Black label)	197?	6.00	15.00
Columbia C3X-37990	(S)	Wings Over America	1976	16.00	40.00
Columbia JC-36478	(S)	McCartney	1979	6.00	15.00
Columbia PC-36478	(S)	McCartney	1982	6.00	15.00
Columbia JC-36479	(S)	Ram	1979	6.00	15.00
Columbia PC-36479	(S)	Ram	1982	6.00	15.00
Columbia JC-36480	(S)	Wild Life	1979	6.00	15.00
Columbia PC-36480	(S)	Wild Life	1982	6.00	15.00
Columbia JC-36481	(S)	Red Rose Speedway	1979	6.00	15.00
Columbia PC-36481	(S)	Red Rose Speedway	1982	6.00	15.00
Columbia JC-36482	(S)	Band On The Run	1981	6.00	15.00
Columbia JC-36482	(S)	Band On The Run	1981	40.00	100.00
		(The cover has the "MPL" logo in lower left)			
Columbia PC-36482	(S)	Band On The Run	1984	8.00	20.00
Columbia HC-46482	(S)	Band On The Run (Half-speed master)	1981	30.00	75.00
Columbia FC-36057	(DJ)	Back To The Egg (Promo label)	1979	16.00	40.00
Columbia FC-36057	(S)	Back To The Egg	1979	1.00	5.00
Columbia PC-36057	(S)	Back To The Egg	1982	10.00	25.00
Columbia FC-36511	(DJ)	McCartney II (White label)	1980	12.00	30.00
Columbia FC-36511	(S)	McCartney II (With single)	1980	6.00	15.00
		(FC-36511 was issued with a promo single, "Coming Up.")			
Columbia FC-36511	(S)	McCartney II (Without single)	1980	6.00	15.00
Columbia PC-36511	(S)	McCartney II	1982	30.00	75.00

In a witty display of his other talents, Paul McCartney, needing another LP to satisfy the demands of his contract with Capitol before departing for Columbia, assembled a cast of studio musicians and led them through MOR renditions of the tunes from Ram. Quite rare, the listing for Thrillington in this book can be found under Percy "Thrills" Thrillington, the artist credited on the album.

Label & Catalog #		Title	Year	VG+	NM
Columbia JC-36801	(S)	Venus And Mars (With inserts)	1980	6.00	15.00
Columbia PC-36801	(S)	Venus And Mars	1982	6.00	15.00
Columbia AS2-821	(DJ)	The McCartney Interview (2 LP promo)	1980	12.00	30.00
		(Originals have white labels with black print in a glossy cover. Counterfeits have blank white labels.)			
Columbia AS2-821	(DJ)	The McCartney Interview (Single stock LP)	1980	4.00	10.00
Columbia FC-37409	(S)	Wings At The Speed Of Sound	1980	6.00	15.00
Columbia PC-37409	(S)	Wings At The Speed Of Sound	1982	6.00	15.00
Columbia TC-37462	(S)	Tug Of War	1980	1.00	5.00
Columbia PC-37462	(S)	Tug Of War	1980	30.00	75.00
Columbia PC-37990	(S)	Wings Over America (3 LPs)	1980	20.00	50.00
Columbia QC-39149	(S)	Pipes Of Peace	1983	1.00	5.00
Columbia SC-39613	(S)	Give My Regards To Broad Street	1984	1.00	5.00
Capitol PJAS-12475	(S)	Press To Play	1986	1.00	5.00
Capitol CLW-48287	(S)	All The Best (2 LPs)	1988	8.00	20.00
Capitol C1-91653	(S)	Flowers In The Dirt	1989	4.00	10.00
Capitol C1-94778	(S)	Tripping The Live Fantastic (3 LPs)	1990	20.00	50.00
Capitol C1-95379	(S)	Highlight! Tripping The Live Fantastic	1990	10.00	25.00
		(Capitol Record Club single album sampler.)			

McCLINTON, O. B. "OBIE"

Enterprise ENS-1023	(S)	Country	1972	14.00	35.00
Enterprise ENS-1029	(S)	Obie From Senatobie	1973	14.00	35.00
Enterprise ENS-1037	(S)	Live At Randy's Rodeo	1973	14.00	35.00
Enterprise ENS-7506	(S)	If You Loved Her That Way	1974	10.00	25.00

McCOO, MARILYN, & BILLY DAVIS, JR.
Marilyn and Billy were formerly members of The Fifth Dimension.

ABC 952	(S)	I Hope We Get To Love In Time	1976	1.00	5.00
ABC 1026	(S)	The Two Of Us	1977	1.00	5.00
Columbia JC-35603	(S)	Marilyn And Billy	1978	1.00	5.00

McCORMICK, GAYLE
Ms. McCormick was a member of Smith.

Dunhill DS-50109	(S)	Gayle McCormick	1971	4.00	10.00
Decca DL-75364	(S)	Flesh And Blood	1972.	4.00	10.00
Fantasy FS-9467	(S)	One More Hour	1974	4.00	10.00

McCOY, VAN

Columbia CL-2497	(M)	Night Time Is Lonely Time	1966	8.00	20.00
Columbia CS-9297	(S)	Night Time Is Lonely Time	1966	10.00	25.00
Buddah BDS-5103	(S)	Soul Improvisations	1972	6.00	15.00
Buddah BDS-5648	(S)	From Disco To Love	1976	1.00	5.00
Avco 69001	(S)	Love Is The Answer	1974	1.00	5.00
Avco 69006	(S)	Disco Baby	1975	1.00	5.00
Avco 69009	(S)	Disco Kid	1975	1.00	5.00
H&L 69012	(S)	Real McCoy	1976	1.00	5.00
H&L 69014	(S)	Rhythms Of The World	1976	1.00	5.00
H&L 69016	(S)	The Hustle (& Best Of Van McCoy)	1976	1.00	5.00
MCA 3036	(S)	My Favorite Fantasy	1977	1.00	5.00
MCA 3071	(S)	Lovely Dancer	1979	1.00	5.00

McCOYS, THE
The McCoys feature Rick Derringer.

Bang BLP-212	(M)	Hang On Sloopy	1965	12.00	30.00
Bang BLPS-212	(S)	Hang On Sloopy	1965	16.00	40.00
		("Hang On Sloopy" is rechanneled.)			
Bang BLP-213	(M)	You Make Me Feel So Good	1966	12.00	30.00
Bang BLPS-213	(S)	You Make Me Feel So Good	1966	16.00	40.00
Mercury SR-61163	(S)	Infinite McCoys	1968	10.00	25.00
Mercury SR-61207	(S)	Human Ball	1969	10.00	25.00

McCRACKLIN, JIMMY

Chess LP-1464	(M)	Jimmy McCracklin Sings	1961	60.00	150.00
Crown CLP-5244	(M)	Twist With Jimmy McCracklin	1962	20.00	50.00
		—Crown albums above have black labels with a silver "Crown" on top.—			
Crown CLP-5244	(M)	Twist With Jimmy McCracklin	196?	8.00	20.00
		—Crown albums above have gray labels.—			
Crown CLP-5244	(M)	Twist With Jimmy McCracklin	196?	4.00	10.00
		—Crown albums above have black labels with a multi-color "Crown" on top.—			
Imperial LP-9219	(M)	I Just Gotta Know	1964	10.00	25.00
Imperial LP-12219	(S)	I Just Gotta Know	1964	12.00	30.00
Imperial LP-9285	(M)	Every Night, Every Day	1965	10.00	25.00
Imperial LP-12285	(S)	Every Night, Every Day	1965	12.00	30.00
Imperial LP-9297	(M)	Think	1965	10.00	25.00
Imperial LP-12297	(S)	Think	1965	12.00	30.00
Imperial LP-9306	(M)	My Answer	1966	10.00	25.00
Imperial LP-12306	(S)	My Answer	1966	12.00	30.00

Gene McDaniels placed a half-dozen sides in the national Top 40 in 1961-62 with a sophisti-cated blend of rhythm'n blues and pop. Liberty capitalized on his two biggest with LPs: 100 Lbs. Of Clay and Tower Of Strength. (His second Top 40 hit, "A Tear," can also be found on his second album.) By '63 he was considered passe amidst the explosion of new soul sounds emanating from Detroit and the deep South and was unable to score another major pop hit.

Label & Catalog #		Title	Year	VG+	NM
Imperial LP-9316	(M)	New Soul Of Jimmy McCracklin	1966	10.00	25.00
Imperial LP-12316	(S)	New Soul Of Jimmy McCracklin	1966	12.00	30.00
Minit LP-40009	(M)	The Best Of Jimmy McCracklin	1967	10.00	25.00
Minit LP-24009	(S)	The Best Of Jimmy McCracklin	1967	14.00	35.00
Minit LP-24011	(S)	Let's Get Together	1968	14.00	35.00
Minit LP-24017	(S)	Stinger Man	1969	14.00	35.00
Stax STS-2047	(S)	Yesterday Is Gone	1972	10.00	25.00

McCRAE, GEORGE

TK 501	(S)	Rock Your Baby	1974	4.00	10.00
TK 602	(S)	George McCrae	1975	4.00	10.00
TK 606	(S)	Diamond Touch	1977	4.00	10.00

McCRAE, GWEN

Cat 2603	(S)	Gwen McCrae	1974	4.00	10.00
Cat 2605	(S)	Rockin' Chair	1975	4.00	10.00
Cat 2606	(S)	Together (With George McCrae)	1976	4.00	10.00
Cat 2608	(S)	Something So Right	1976	4.00	10.00

McCULLOCH, DANNY
Danny was a member of Eric Burdon & The Animals.

Verve/Forecast FTS-3058	(S)	Danny McCulloch	1968	Unreleased?	
Capitol ST-174	(S)	Wings Of A Man	1969	8.00	20.00

McDANIELS, GENE

Liberty LRP-3146	(M)	In Times Like These	1960	14.00	35.00
Liberty LST-7146	(S)	In Times Like These (Blue vinyl)	1960	80.00	200.00
Liberty LST-7146	(S)	In Times Like These	1960	20.00	50.00
Liberty LRP-3175	(M)	Sometimes I'm Happy, Sometimes I'm Blue	1960	14.00	35.00
Liberty LST-7175	(S)	Sometimes I'm Happy, Sometimes I'm Blue	1960	20.00	50.00
Liberty LRP-3191	(M)	100 Lbs. Of Clay	1961	12.00	30.00
Liberty LST-7191	(S)	100 Lbs. Of Clay	1961	16.00	40.00
Liberty LRP-3204	(M)	Gene McDaniels Sings Movie Memories	1962	12.00	30.00
Liberty LST-7204	(S)	Gene McDaniels Sings Movie Memories	1962	16.00	40.00
Liberty LRP-3215	(M)	Tower Of Strength	1962	12.00	30.00
Liberty LST-7215	(S)	Tower Of Strength	1962	16.00	40.00
Liberty LRP-3258	(M)	Hit After Hit	1962	10.00	25.00
Liberty LST-7258	(S)	Hit After Hit	1962	12.00	30.00
Liberty LRP-3275	(M)	Spanish Lace	1963	10.00	25.00
Liberty LST-7275	(S)	Spanish Lace	1963	12.00	30.00
Liberty LRP-3311	(M)	The Wonderful Word Of Gene McDaniels	1963	10.00	25.00
Liberty LST-7311	(S)	The Wonderful Word Of Gene McDaniels	1963	12.00	30.00
Sunset SUM-1122	(M)	Facts Of Life	1967	5.00	12.00
Sunset SUS-5122	(S)	Facts Of Life	1967	6.00	15.00
Atlantic SD-8259	(S)	Outlaw	1970	4.00	10.00
United Arts. LA-447E	(S)	The Very Best Of Gene McDaniels	1975	.80	4.00
Ode 77028	(S)	Natural Juices	1975	1.00	5.00

McDONALD, "COUNTRY" JOE: *Refer to* **COUNTRY JOE (McDONALD)**

McDONALD, KATHY

Capitol ST-11224	(S)	Insane Asylum	1974	12.00	30.00

McDONALD, MICHAEL
Michael McDonald was the lead singer for The Doobie Brothers from 1975 on.

Warner Bros. 23703	(S)	If That's What It Takes	1982	.80	4.00

McDONALD & GILES

Cotillion SD-9042	(S)	McDonald And Giles	1971	4.00	10.00

McDONOUGH, MEGAN

Wooden Nickel 1002	(S)	In The Megan Manner	1972	1.00	5.00

McDOWELL, "MISSISSIPPI" FRED
Fred McDowell was a blues guitar player and singer.

Arhoolie F-1021	(M)	Delta Blues	1964	20.00	50.00
Arhoolie F-1027	(M)	Delta Blues, Volume 2	1966	20.00	50.00
Milestone MLP-3003	(M)	Long Way From Home	1966	12.00	30.00
Milestone MLS-93003	(S)	Long Way From Home	1966	16.00	40.00
Arhoolie F-1046	(S)	Mississippi Fred McDowell & His Blues Boys	1970	14.00	35.00
Sire SASH 97018	(S)	Mississippi Fred McDowell In London	1970	12.00	30.00
Everest 253	(S)	Mississippi Fred McDowell	1971	8.00	20.00
Capitol ST-403/409	(DJ)	I Do Not Play No Rock & Roll (Picture disc)	1973	30.00	75.00
Capitol ST-403	(S)	I Do Not Play No Rock & Roll	1973	10.00	25.00
Just Sunshine JSS-4	(S)	Mississippi Fred McDowell 1904-1972	1973	6.00	15.00
Arhoolie F-1068	(S)	Keep Your Lamp Trimmed and Burning	1973	8.00	20.00
Original Jazz Library 8051	(S)	Levee Camp Blues	1980	6.00	15.00

Label & Catalog #		Title	Year	VG+	NM

McDOWELL, "MISSISSIPPI" FRED / FURRY LEWIS

| Biograph BLP-12017 | (M) | When I Lay My Burden Down | 1970 | 8.00 | 20.00 |

McGEAR, MIKE
Mike McGear also recorded as a member of Scaffold.

| Warner Bros. BS-2825 | (S) | McGear | 1974 | 4.00 | 10.00 |

McGHEE, BROWNIE
Walter Brown McGhee is a blues guitar and piano player, singer and writer of traditional style folk-blues. His entire career is linked with partner Sonny Terry. Refer to Sonny Terry & Brownie McGhee.

Folkways FP-30	(10")	Brownie McGhee Blues	1951	60.00	150.00
Folkways FA-2030	(10")	Brownie McGhee Blues	1951	60.00	150.00
Bluesville BVLP-1042	(M)	Brownie's Blues	1962	30.00	75.00

— Bluesville albums above have bright blue labels with silver print.—

| Bluesville BVLP-1042 | (M) | Brownie's Blues | 1964 | 10.00 | 25.00 |

— Bluesville albums above have blue labels with a trident logo on the right side.—

McGHEE, STICKS, & JOHN LEE HOOKER

| Audio Lab AL-1520 | (M) | Highway Of Blues | 1959 | 150.00 | 300.00 |

McGOVERN, MAUREEN
Ms McGovern can also be found on the Warner Bros soundtrack "The Towering Inferno."

20th Century 419	(S)	The Morning After	1973	1.20	6.00
20th Century 439	(S)	Nice To Be Around	1974	1.00	5.00
20th Century 474	(S)	Academy Award Performance	1975	1.00	5.00
Warner Bros. K-3327	(S)	Maureen McGovern	1979	1.00	5.00

McGRATH, BAT

| Epic BN-26499 | (S) | Introducing Bat McGrath | 1969 | 4.00 | 10.00 |

McGRATH, SUNI

| Adelphi AD-1002 | (S) | Cornflower Suite | 1970 | 6.00 | 15.00 |
| Adelphi AD-1014 | (S) | The Call Of The Morning Dove | 1971 | 6.00 | 15.00 |

McGUINN, ROGER
James McGuinn was a founder of The Byrds. He changed his name to Roger in 1967. He can also be found backing The Chad Mitchell Trio and Judy Collins and on a number of guitar albums.

Columbia KC-31946	(S)	Roger McGuinn	1973	1.00	5.00
Columbia PC-35154	(S)	Cardiff Rose	1974	1.00	5.00
Columbia PC-33541	(S)	Roger McGuinn And Band	1975	1.00	5.00
Columbia KC-32956	(S)	Peace On You	1975	1.00	5.00
Columbia PC-34656	(S)	Thunderbyrd	1976	1.00	5.00
Columbia AS-353	(DJ)	The Roger McGuinn Airplay Anthology	1977	8.00	20.00

(AS-353 is a compilation of Byrds and solo material.)

McGUINN, CLARK & HILLMAN
Roger McGuinn, Gene Clark and Chris Hillman, all formerly of The Byrds.

Capitol SW-11910	(S)	McGuinn, Clark & Hillman	1979	.80	4.00
Capitol ST-12043	(S)	City	1980	.80	4.00
Capitol SOO-12108	(S)	McGuinn And Hillman	1980	.80	4.00
Capitol SN-16280	(S)	McGuinn, Clark & Hillman	1982	.80	4.00

McGUINNESS-FLINT
Tom McGuinness and Hughie Flint. Refer to Mannfred Mann; John Mayall.

| Capitol SMAS-625 | (S) | McGuinness-Flint | 1970 | 6.00 | 15.00 |
| Capitol ST-794 | (S) | Happy Birthday, Ruthy Baby | 1971 | 6.00 | 15.00 |

McGUIRE, BARRY
Barry originally recorded as a member of The New Christy Minstrels. Refer to Barry & Barry; the Various Artists section under Surrey.

Horizon WP-1636	(M)	The Barry McGuire Album	1963	12.00	30.00
Horizon ST-1636	(S)	The Barry McGuire Album	1963	16.00	40.00
Mira LP-3000	(M)	The Barry McGuire Album	1965	8.00	20.00
Mira LPS-3000	(S)	The Barry McGuire Album	1965	10.00	25.00

(Mira 3000 is a reissue of Horizon 1636.)

Dunhill D-50003	(M)	Barry McGuire	1966	12.00	30.00
Dunhill DS-50003	(S)	Barry McGuire	1966	16.00	40.00
Dunhill D-50005	(M)	This Precious Time	1966	10.00	25.00
Dunhill DS-50005	(S)	This Precious Time	1966	12.00	30.00

(50005 features backing vocals by The Mama's & The Papa's.)

Dunhill DS-50033	(S)	The World's Last Private Citizen	1968	10.00	25.00
Ode SP-77004	(S)	Barry McGuire And The Doctor	1970	6.00	15.00
Myrrh MSA-6519	(S)	Seeds	1974	4.00	10.00
Myrrh MSA-6531	(S)	Lighten Up	1975	4.00	10.00
Myrrh MSX-6548	(S)	To The Bride	1975	4.00	10.00
Myrrh MSA-6555	(S)	Jubilation	1975	4.00	10.00
Myrrh MSA-6568	(S)	Jubilation Too	1976	4.00	10.00
Sparrow SPR-1007	(S)	C'mon Along	1976	4.00	10.00

Label & Catalog #		Title	Year	VG+	NM
Sparrow SPR-10??	(S)	Firewind	1976	4.00	10.00
Sparrow SPR-1013	(S)	Have You Heard?	1977	4.00	10.00
Sparrow SPR-1023	(S)	Cosmic Cowboy	1978	4.00	10.00
Sparrow SPR-1031	(S)	Inside Out	197?	4.00	10.00
Sparrow SPR-10??	(S)	Polka Dot Bear	1980	4.00	10.00
Sparrow SPR-10??	(S)	The Best Of	1980	4.00	10.00
Sparrow SPR-10??	(S)	Finer Than Gold	1981	4.00	10.00
Birdwing ????	(S)	Bullfrogs And Butterflies	1978	4.00	10.00
Light ????	(S)	The Witness	1978	4.00	10.00

McILWAINE, ELLEN
Ms. McIlwaine was a member of Fear Itself.

Polydor PD-5044	(S)	We The People	1973	6.00	15.00

McKAY, SCOTTY

Ace LP-1017	(M)	Tonight In Person	1961	30.00	75.00

McKENDREE SPRING

Decca DL-75104	(S)	McKendree Spring	1969	4.00	10.00
Decca DL-75230	(S)	Second Thoughts	1970	4.00	10.00
Decca DL-75332	(S)	McKendree Spring	1972	4.00	10.00
Decca DL-75385	(S)	Tracks	1972	4.00	10.00
MCA 44	(S)	McKendree Spring	1973	.80	4.00
MCA 60	(S)	Tracks	1973	.80	4.00
MCA 277	(S)	McKendree Spring	1973	.80	4.00
MCA 370	(S)	Spring Suite	1973	.80	4.00

McKENZIE, SCOTT
Scott McKenzie formerly recorded as a member of The Journeymen.

Ode Z12-44001	(M)	The Voice Of Scott McKenzie	1967	8.00	20.00
Ode Z12-44002	(S)	The Voice Of Scott McKenzie	1967	10.00	25.00
Ode SP-77007	(S)	Stained Glass Morning	1970	6.00	15.00

McLAUCHLAN, MURRAY
Canadian Murray McLauchlan is a guitar player, singer and writer of contemporary folk based material.

Epic E-31166	(S)	Songs From The Street	1972	4.00	10.00
Epic KE-31902	(S)	Murray McLauchlan	1973	4.00	10.00
Epic KE-32859	(S)	One Day To Dust	1973	4.00	10.00
Epic KE-33344	(S)	Sweeping The Spotlight Away	1974	4.00	10.00

McLEAN, DON

Mediarts 41-4	(S)	Tapestry	1970	6.00	15.00
United Arts. UAS-5522	(S)	Tapestry	1971	1.00	5.00
United Arts. UAS-5535	(S)	American Pie	1971	1.00	5.00
United Arts. UAS-5651	(S)	Don McLean	1972	1.00	5.00
United Arts. LA-161	(S)	Playing Favorites	1972	1.00	5.00
United Arts. LA-315	(S)	Homeless Brother	1974	1.00	5.00
United Arts. LA-652	(S)	Solo	1976	1.00	5.00
Arista AS-4149	(S)	Prime Time	1977	1.00	5.00
Millennium DJL1-3933	(DJ)	RCA Special Radio Series (With insert)	197?	4.00	10.00
Millennium 7756	(S)	Chain Lightning	1981	1.00	5.00
Millennium 7762	(S)	Believers	1981	1.00	5.00

McLOLLIE, OSCAR, & HIS HONEYJUMPERS

Crown CLP-5016	(M)	Oscar McLollie And His Honeyjumpers	195?	Unreleased?	

McLUHAN

Brunswick BL-754177	(S)	Anomaly	1972	8.00	20.00

McNAIR, BARBARA

Warner Bros. W-1541	(M)	I Enjoy Being A Girl	1964	8.00	20.00
Warner Bros. WS-1541	(S)	I Enjoy Being A Girl	1964	10.00	25.00
Warner Bros. W-1570	(M)	Livin' End	1964	8.00	20.00
Warner Bros. WS-1570	(S)	Livin' End	1964	10.00	25.00
Motown 644	(M)	Here I Am	1966	8.00	20.00
Motown S-644	(S)	Here I Am	1966	10.00	25.00
Motown S-680	(S)	The Real Barbara McNair	1969	8.00	20.00
Audio Fidelity AFSD-6222	(S)	More Today Than Yesterday	1969	6.00	15.00

McNAMARA, ROBIN

Steed STS-37007	(S)	Lay A Little Lovin' On Me	1970	1.20	6.00

McNEELY, BIG JAY

Federal 295-96	(10")	Big Jay McNeely	1954	See note below	
		(Federal 96 has a suggested NM value of $3,000-6,000.)			
Savoy MG-15045	(10")	A Rhythm And Blues Concert	1955	See note below	
		(Savoy 15045 has a suggested NM value of $1,000-3,000.)			

After playing Eddie in the cult film phenomenon "The Rocky Horror Picture Show," Marvin Lee Aday, better known as Meatloaf, struck platinum with *Bat Out Of Hell*. The album is notable in that the songs are very much in the vein of those from the film, and the cover features the glorious work of former underground comix artist Richard Corben. The album came out at just the right time to be a part of the picture disc mania of the late '70s (above) and lasted long enough in its popularity to see a half-speed mastered reissue emerge during that craze a few years later (below).

Label & Catalog #		Title	Year	VG+	NM
Federal 395-530	(M)	Big Jay McNeely In 3-D	1956	500.00	1,000.00
King 650	(M)	Big Jay McNeely In 3-D	1959	300.00	600.00
		(King 650 is a reissue of Federal 530.)			
Warner Bros. W-1523	(M)	Big Jay McNeely	1963	30.00	75.00
Warner Bros. WS-1523	(S)	Big Jay McNeely	1963	40.00	100.00

McPHATTER, CLYDE
Clyde was formerly the lead singer for Billy Ward & The Dominoes; The Drifters.

Label & Catalog #		Title	Year	VG+	NM
Atlantic 8024	(M)	Love Ballads	1958	250.00	500.00
Atlantic 8031	(M)	Clyde	1959	250.00	500.00
		—*Atlantic albums above have black labels.*—			
Atlantic 8031	(M)	Clyde	1960	200.00	400.00
		—*Atlantic albums above have white "bullseye" labels.*—			
Atlantic 8024	(M)	Love Ballads	1960	80.00	200.00
Atlantic 8031	(M)	Clyde	1960	80.00	200.00
Atlantic 8077	(M)	The Best Of Clyde McPhatter	1963	80.00	200.00
		—*Atlantic albums above have orange & purple labels.*—			
MGM E-3775	(M)	Let's Start Over Again	1959	60.00	150.00
MGM SE-3775	(S)	Let's Start Over Again	1959	80.00	200.00
MGM E-3866	(M)	Clyde McPhatter's Greatest Hits	1960	30.00	75.00
MGM SE-3866	(S)	Clyde McPhatter's Greatest Hits	1960	40.00	100.00
Mercury MG-20597	(M)	Ta Ta	1960	20.00	50.00
Mercury SR-60262	(S)	Ta Ta	1960	30.00	75.00
Mercury MG-20655	(M)	Golden Blues Hits	1962	20.00	50.00
Mercury SR-60655	(S)	Golden Blues Hits	1962	30.00	75.00
Mercury MG-20711	(M)	Lover Please	1962	20.00	50.00
Mercury SR-60711	(S)	Lover Please	1962	30.00	75.00
Mercury MG-20750	(M)	Rhythm And Soul	1962	20.00	50.00
Mercury SR-60750	(S)	Rhythm And Soul	1962	30.00	75.00
Wing MGW-12224	(M)	May I Sing For You?	1962	8.00	20.00
Wing SRW-16224	(S)	May I Sing For You?	1962	10.00	25.00
Mercury MG-20783	(M)	Clyde McPhatter's Greatest Hits	1963	12.00	30.00
Mercury SR-60783	(S)	Clyde McPhatter's Greatest Hits	1963	16.00	40.00
Mercury MG-20902	(M)	Songs Of The Big City	1964	12.00	30.00
Mercury SR-60902	(S)	Songs Of The Big City	1964	16.00	40.00
Mercury MG-20915	(M)	Live At The Apollo	1964	12.00	30.00
Mercury SR-60915	(S)	Live At The Apollo	1964	16.00	40.00
Decca DL-75231	(S)	Welcome Home	1970	10.00	25.00

McTELL, RALPH

Label & Catalog #		Title	Year	VG+	NM
Capitol ST-240	(S)	Eight Frames A Second	1969	8.00	20.00
20th Century T-486	(S)	Streets Of London	1975	6.00	15.00

McTELL, "BLIND" WILLIE

Label & Catalog #		Title	Year	VG+	NM
Melodeon 7323	(M)	1940	1956	150.00	300.00
Bluesville BVLP-1040	(M)	Last Session	1962	60.00	150.00
		—*Bluesville albums above have bright blue labels with silver print.*—			
Bluesville BVLP-1040	(M)	Last Session	1964	12.00	30.00
		—*Bluesville albums above have blue labels with a trident logo on the right side.*—			
Prestige PRST-7809	(E)	Last Session	1970	6.00	15.00
		(Prestige 7809 is a reissue of Bluesville 1040.)			
Atlantic SD-7224	(M)	Atlanta 12 String	1972	6.00	15.00
Yazoo L-1005	(M)	The Early Years 1927-1933	197?	8.00	20.00
Yazoo L-1037	(M)	Doin' That Alabama Strut	197?	8.00	20.00

McVIE, CHRISTINE
Miss Perfect of Chickenshack later recorded as Mrs McVie with Fleetwood Mac after marrying Mr McVie.

Label & Catalog #		Title	Year	VG+	NM
Sire SASD-7522	(S)	The Legendary Christine Perfect Album	1976	6.00	15.00
Sire SR-6022	(S)	The Legendary Christine Perfect Album	1977	1.00	5.00
Warner Bros. 25059	(S)	Christine McVie (Quiex II vinyl promo)	1984	6.00	15.00
Warner Bros. 25059	(S)	Christine McVie	1984	1.00	5.00

MEAT LOAF
Refer to Stoney & Meat Loaf

Label & Catalog #		Title	Year	VG+	NM
Epic E-34974	(S)	Bat Out Of Hell	1977	1.00	5.00
Epic E99-34974	(S)	Bat Out Of Hell (Picture disc)	1979	8.00	20.00
Epic HE-44974	(S)	Bat Out Of Hell (Half-speed master)	1981	10.00	30.00
Epic AS-409	(DJ)	Live At Father's Place (Black vinyl)	1978	12.00	30.00
		(Counterfeits on red vinyl exist.)			
Epic FE-36007	(S)	Dead Ringer	1981	1.00	5.00
Epic FE-38444	(S)	Midnight At The Lost And Found	1983	1.00	5.00

MECKI MARK MEN, THE

Label & Catalog #		Title	Year	VG+	NM
Limelight LS-86054	(S)	The Mecki Mark Men	1968	10.00	25.00
Limelight LS-86068	(S)	Running In The Summer Night	1969	10.00	25.00

MEDICINE HEAD

Label & Catalog #		Title	Year	VG+	NM
Polydor PD-5532	(S)	One And One Is One	1973	1.20	6.00

Label & Catalog #		Title	Year	VG+	NM

MEDLEY, BILL
Mr. Medley is one half of The Righteous Brothers. Bill can also be found on the Paramount soundtrack "The Hard Ride." Refer to Sonny & Cher.

MGM SE-4583	(S)	Bill Medley 100%	1968	6.00	15.00
MGM SE-4603	(S)	Soft And Soulful	1969	6.00	15.00
MGM SE-4640	(S)	Someone Is Standing Outside	1969	6.00	15.00
MGM SE-4702	(S)	Nobody Knows	1970	6.00	15.00
MGM SE-4741	(S)	Gone	1970	6.00	15.00
A&M SP-3505	(S)	A Song For You	1971	4.00	10.00
A&M SP-3517	(S)	Smile	1973	4.00	10.00
United Arts. LA929	(S)	Another Beginning	1978	4.00	10.00
United Arts. LT-1024	(S)	Sweet Thunder	1980	4.00	10.00

MEL & TIM
Mel Hardin and Tim McPherson.

Bamboo BMS-8001	(S)	Good Guys Only Win In The Movies	1970	10.00	25.00
Stax STS-3007	(S)	Starting All Over Again	1972	10.00	25.00
Stax STS-5501	(S)	Mel And Tim	1974	10.00	25.00

MELANIE
Melanie Safka is a singer and writer of folk-based pop music. She can also be found on the Bell soundtrack "R.P.M."

Buddah BDS-5024	(S)	Born To Be	1969	3.20	8.00
Buddah BDS-5041	(S)	Melanie	1969	3.20	8.00
Buddah BDS-5060	(S)	Candles In The Rain	1970	3.20	8.00
Buddah BDS-5066	(S)	Leftover Wine	1970	1.20	6.00
Buddah BDS-5074	(S)	My First Album	1970	1.20	6.00
Buddah BDS-5095	(S)	Garden In The City	1971	1.20	6.00
Buddah BDS-5132	(S)	All The Right Noises	1971	1.20	6.00
Buddah BDS-95000	(S)	The Good Book (2 LPs)	1971	3.20	8.00
Buddah BDS-95005	(S)	The Four Sides Of Melanie (2 LPs)	1972	3.20	8.00
Buddah 5664	(S)	The Best Of Melanie (2 LPs)	1976	3.20	8.00
Neighborhood 47001	(S)	Gather Me	1971	1.00	5.00
Neighborhood 47005	(S)	Stoneground Words	1972	1.00	5.00
Neighborhood 49001	(S)	Melanie At Carnegie Hall	1973	1.00	5.00
Neighborhood 48001	(S)	Madrugada	1974	1.00	5.00
Neighborhood 3000	(S)	As I See It Now	1974	1.00	5.00
Neighborhood 3001	(S)	Sunsets And Other Beginnings	1975	1.00	5.00
Pickwick SPC-3317	(S)	Try The Real Thing	1971	.80	4.00
ABC D-879	(S)	From The Beginning	1975	.80	4.00
Atlantic SD-18190	(S)	Photograph	1976	.80	4.00
Midsong 3033	(S)	Photogenic—Not Just Another Pretty Face	1977	.80	4.00
Tomato 9003	(S)	Ballroom Streets (2 LPs)	1979	1.00	5.00
Accord SN-7109	(S)	What Have They Done To My Song, Ma	1981	.80	4.00
Accord SN-7191	(S)	Beautiful People	1982	.80	4.00
Blanche 6177	(S)	Arabesque	1982	.80	4.00

MELCHER, TERRY
Terry Melcher also recorded with Bruce Johnston under a number of guises, including Bruce & Terry, The Catalinas, and The Rip Chords. He was also a Columbia producer, notably Paul Revere & The Raiders.

Reprise MS-2185	(S)	Terry Melcher	1974	6.00	15.00

MELLENCAMP, JOHN COUGAR [JOHN COUGAR]

MCA 2225	(S)	Chestnut Street Incident	1977	8.00	20.00
Riva 7401	(S)	John Cougar	1979	1.00	5.00
Riva 7403	(S)	Nothin' Matters And What If It Did	1980	1.00	5.00
Riva 7501	(S)	American Fool	1982	1.00	5.00
Riva 7504	(S)	Uh-Huh	1983	1.00	5.00
Riva	(DJ)	The Kid Inside (Picture disc)	198?	12.00	30.00
Riva	(S)	The Kid Inside	198?	1.00	5.00

MELLO-KINGS, THE

Herald H-1013	(M)	Tonight-Tonight	1960	300.00	600.00
		—Herald albums above have yellow labels.—			
Herald H-1013	(M)	Tonight-Tonight	196?	150.00	300.00
		—Herald albums above have multi-color labels.—			

MELTING POT, THE

Ampex A-10111	(S)	Fire Burn, Cauldron Bubble	1971	4.00	10.00

MELTON, BARRY
Mr Melton was a member of Country Joe & The Fish.

Vanguard VSD-6551	(S)	Bright Sun Is Shining	1970	6.00	15.00
Columbia KC-31279	(S)	Melton, Levy And The Dey Brothers	1972	6.00	15.00
Firesign FSA-8702	(S)	The Fish	1977	3.20	8.00
Music Is Medicine 9007	(S)	We Are Like The Ocean	1977	3.20	8.00
Music Is Medicine 9014	(S)	Level With Me	1978	3.20	8.00

Label & Catalog #		Title	Year	VG+	NM

MELTZER, DAVID & TINA
David and Tina Meltzer originally recorded with Serpent Power.

Vanguard VSD-6519	(S)	**Poet Song**	1969	8.00	20.00

MELVIN, HAROLD, & THE BLUENOTES
Harold Melvin's Blue Notes featured lead singer Teddy Pendergrass.

Phila. Int. PZ-31648	(S)	**I Miss You (Original cover)**	1972	16.00	40.00
Phila. Int. PZ-31648	(S)	**I Miss You**	1972	3.20	8.00
Phila. Int. PZ-32407	(S)	**Black And Blue**	1973	3.20	8.00
Phila. Int. PZQ-32407	(Q)	**Black And Blue**	1974	6.00	15.00
Phila. Int. PZ-33148	(S)	**To Be True**	1975	3.20	8.00
Phila. Int. PZ-33808	(S)	**Wake Up Everybody**	1975	3.20	8.00
Phila. Int. PZQ-33808	(Q)	**Wake Up Everybody**	1975	6.00	15.00
Phila. Int. PZ-34230	(S)	**All Their Greatest Hits**	1976	3.20	8.00
ABC 969	(S)	**Reaching For The World**	1977	1.00	5.00
ABC 1041	(S)	**Now Is The Time**	1977	1.00	5.00

MELVIN, MICHAEL

Dot DLP-25961	(S)	**The Plastic Cow Goes Moooooog**	1969	10.00	25.00

MEMPHIS SLIM
Memphis Slim is a pseudonym for Peter Chapman. Refer to Willie Dixon; Sonny Boy Williamson & Memphis Slim..

Vee Jay VJLP-1012	(M)	**Memphis Slim At The Gate Of The Horn**	1959	200.00	400.00
		—Vee Jay albums above have maroon labels.—			
Vee Jay VJLP-1012	(M)	**Memphis Slim At The Gate Of The Horn**	196?	80.00	200.00
		—Vee Jay albums above have black rainbow labels.—			
Strand SL-1046	(M)	**The World's Foremost Blues Singer**	1959	16.00	40.00
Strand SLS-1046	(S)	**The World's Foremost Blues Singer**	1959	20.00	50.00
Folkways FG-3254	(M)	**The Real Boogie Woogie**	1960	40.00	100.00
Folkways FG-3535	(M)	**The Real Honky Tonk Piano Solos**	1961	40.00	100.00
Folkways FG-3536	(M)	**Chicago Blues**	1961	40.00	100.00
Chess LP-1455	(M)	**Memphis Slim**	1961	80.00	200.00
		—Chess albums above have black labels.—			
United Arts. UAL-3137	(M)	**Broken Soul Blues**	1961	30.00	75.00
United Arts. UAS-6137	(S)	**Broken Soul Blues**	1961	40.00	100.00
Candid CM-8023	(M)	**Tribute To Big Bill Broonzy**	1961	30.00	75.00
Candid CS-9023	(S)	**Tribute To Big Bill Broonzy**	1961	40.00	100.00
Candid CM-8024	(M)	**Memphis Slim, U.S.A.**	1962	30.00	75.00
Candid CS-9024	(S)	**Memphis Slim, U.S.A.**	1962	40.00	100.00
Bluesville BVLP-1018	(M)	**Just Blues**	1961	40.00	100.00
Bluesville BVLP-1031	(M)	**No Strain**	1961	40.00	100.00
Bluesville BVLP-1053	(M)	**All Kinds Of Blues**	1962	40.00	100.00
Bluesville BVLP-1075	(M)	**Steady Rollin' Blues**	1963	40.00	100.00
		—Bluesville albums above have bright blue labels with silver print.—			
Bluesville BVLP-1018	(M)	**Just Blues**	1964	12.00	30.00
Bluesville BVLP-1031	(M)	**No Strain**	1964	12.00	30.00
Bluesville BVLP-1053	(M)	**All Kinds Of Blues**	1964	12.00	30.00
Bluesville BVLP-1075	(M)	**Steady Rollin' Blues**	1964	12.00	30.00
		—Bluesville albums above have blue labels with a trident logo on the right side.—			
Battle BM-6118	(M)	**Alone With My Friends**	1963	20.00	50.00
Battle BM-6122	(M)	**Baby Please Come Home**	1963	20.00	50.00
Disc D-105	(M)	**If The Rabbit Had A Gun**	1964	20.00	50.00
King LP-885	(M)	**Memphis Slim**	1964	20.00	50.00
Chess LP-1510	(M)	**Real Folk Blues**	1966	40.00	100.00
Scepter SM-535	(M)	**Self Portrait**	1966	8.00	20.00
Scepter SMS-535	(S)	**Self Portrait**	1966	10.00	25.00
Jubilee JGM-8003	(M)	**Legend Of The Blues**	1967	10.00	25.00
Jubilee JGS-8003	(S)	**Legend Of The Blues**	1967	10.00	25.00
Everest FS-215	(E)	**Memphis Slim**	1968	4.00	10.00
Buddah BDS-7505	(S)	**Mother Earth**	1969	6.00	15.00
King KS-1082	(S)	**Messin' Around With The Blues**	1970	6.00	15.00
Jewell 5004	(S)	**Born With The Blues**	1971	4.00	10.00
Warner Bros. WS-1899	(S)	**Blue Memphis**	1971	6.00	15.00
Warner Bros. BS-2646	(S)	**South Side Reunion**	1972	6.00	15.00
Everest FS-286	(E)	**Memphis Slim, Volume 2**	1974	4.00	10.00
Fantasy 24705	(S)	**Raining The Blues (2 LPs)**	1972	5.00	12.00
Black Lion 155	(S)	**Rock Me Baby**	1974	3.20	8.00
Crescendo GNPS-10002	(S)	**The Blues Is Everywhere**	1974	1.20	6.00
Folkways 2387	(S)	**Favorite Blues Singers**	1974	1.20	6.00
Pearl 10	(S)	**Memphis Slim, U.S.A.**	1978	1.20	6.00
Muse 5219	(S)	**I'll Just Keep On Singing The Blues**	1981	1.20	6.00

MEMPHIS SLIM & ROOSEVELT SYKES

Olympic 7136	(S)	**Memphis Blues**	1975	1.20	6.00

MEMPHIS SOUL BAND, THE

Minit 24028	(S)	**Soul Cowboy**	1970	6.00	15.00

The Merry-Go-Round, a pop/rock group featuring a very youthful Emitt Rhodes, is presented on the cover of their sole long-player as appropriately dressed and perfectly coifed young gentlemen. The album peaked in value a few years ago—as did Mr Rhodes' solo albums—and has settled comfortably into a value range of $20-30 for NM mono or stereo copies.

Label & Catalog #		Title	Year	VG+	NM

MEMPHIS WILLIE B.

Bluesville BVLP-1034	(M)	Introducing Memphis Willie B.	1961	40.00	100.00
Bluesville BVLP-1048	(M)	Hard Working Man Blues	1962	40.00	100.00

—Bluesville albums above have bright blue labels with silver print.—

Bluesville BVLP-1034	(M)	Introducing Memphis Willie B.	1964	12.00	30.00
Bluesville BVLP-1048	(M)	Hard Working Man Blues	1964	12.00	30.00

—Bluesville albums above have blue labels with a trident logo on the right side.—

MEN AT WORK

Epic E-37978	(S)	Business As Usual	1982	.80	4.00
Epic HE-47978	(S)	Business As Usual (Half-speed master)	1982	5.00	15.00
Epic PAL-37978	(DJ)	Business As Usual (Picture disc)	1983	16.00	40.00
Epic E-38660	(S)	Cargo	1983	.80	4.00
Epic HE-48660	(S)	Cargo (Half-speed master)	1983	5.00	15.00

MER-DA

Janus JSX-3042	(S)	Long Burn The Fire	1972	3.20	8.00

MERCHANTS OF DREAM, THE

Capitol ST-102	(S)	Soul Knight	1968	6.00	15.00

MERCY, THE

Sundi SRLP-803	(S)	Love (Can Make You Happy)	1969	6.00	15.00
Warner Bros. WS-1799	(S)	Love (Can Make You Happy)	1969	4.00	10.00

MERMAIDS, THE

Chattahoochie CHLP-628	(M)	The Mermaids Resurface!	197?	14.00	35.00

MERRIWEATHER, BIG MACEO, & JOHN LEE HOOKER

Fortune LP-3002	(M)	Big Maceo Merriweather & John Lee Hooker	1961	60.00	150.00

MERRY-GO-ROUND, THE
The Merry-Go-Round features Emitt Rhodes.

A&M LP-132	(M)	The Merry-Go-Round	1967	10.00	25.00
A&M SP-4132	(S)	The Merry-Go-Round	1967	12.00	30.00
Rhino RNLP-126	(S)	The Best Of The Merry-Go-Round	1985	.80	4.00

MERRYWEATHER, NEIL [MERRYWEATHER]

Capitol SKAO-220	(S)	Merryweather	1969	6.00	15.00
Capitol STBB-278	(S)	Word Of Mouth	1969	6.00	15.00
		(Capitol 220 and 278 credit Merryweather.)			
Kent KST-546	(S)	Neil Merryweather And The Boers	1972	8.00	20.00
Mercury SRM-1007	(S)	Space Rangers	1974	4.00	10.00
Mercury SRM-1024	(S)	Kryptonite	1975	4.00	10.00

MERRYWEATHER & CAREY
Neil Merryweather with Lynn Carey of Mama Lion.

RCA Victor LSP-4442	(S)	Ivar Avenue Reunion	1970	6.00	15.00
RCA Victor LSP-4485	(S)	Vacuum Cleaner	1971	6.00	15.00

MERSEYBOYS, THE

Vee Jay VJ-1101	(M)	15 Greatest Songs Of The Beatles	1964	40.00	100.00
Vee Jay VJS-1101	(S)	15 Greatest Songs Of The Beatles	1964	60.00	150.00

MESMERIZING EYE, THE

Smash MGS-27090	(M)	Psychedelia/A Musical Light Show	1967	20.00	50.00
Smash SRS-67090	(S)	Psychedelia/A Musical Light Show	1967	30.00	75.00

MESSENGERS, THE

Rare Earth RS-509	(S)	The Messengers	1969	8.00	20.00

MESSINA, JIM [JIM MESSINA & HIS JESTERS]
Refer to Buffalo Springfield; Loggins & Messina.

Audio Fidelity DFM-3037	(M)	The Dragsters	1964	30.00	75.00
Audio Fidelity DFS-7037	(S)	The Dragsters	1964	40.00	100.00
		(The Audio Fidelity album credits Jim Messina & His Jesters.)			
Thimble TLP-3	(S)	Jim Messina	197?	6.00	15.00
		(Thimble 3 is a reissue of Audio Fidelity 7037.)			
Warner Bros. 3559	(DJ)	Messina (Quiex II vinyl)	1981	6.00	15.00
Warner Bros. 3559	(S)	Messina	1981	.80	4.00

METAMORPHOSIS

London PS-588	(S)	Dynamic Arena	1971	1.20	6.00

METERS, THE

Josie JOS-4010	(S)	The Meters	1969	30.00	75.00
Josie JOS-4011	(S)	Look-Ka Py Py	1970	30.00	75.00
Josie JOS-4012	(S)	Struttin'	1970	30.00	75.00

In 1957, Mickey Baker and Sylvia Vanderpool recorded and released their only album for RCA Victor's Vik subsidiary, New Sounds. The cover featured a photo of the duo on stage. In 1965, RCA's budget subsidiary, Camden, issued Love Is Strange, a collection of 45 sides plus tracks from the Vik album. The cover boasts a nice painting based on the photo on the earlier album. RCA again reissued the material in 1973, this time as part of its standard catalog and titled Do It Again (not shown).

Label & Catalog #		Title	Year	VG+	NM
Reprise MS-2076	(S)	Cabbage Alley	1972	30.00	75.00
Reprise MS-2200	(S)	Rejuvenation	1972	30.00	75.00
Virgo 12002	(S)	Best Of The Meters	1975	20.00	50.00
Island 9250	(S)	Cissy Strut	1975	20.00	50.00
Warner Bros. B-3042	(S)	New Directions	1977	20.00	50.00
METHUSELAH					
Elektra EKS-70452	(S)	Matthew, Mark, Luke And John	1969	6.00	15.00
METROS, THE					
RCA Victor LPM-3776	(M)	Sweetest One	1967	30.00	75.00
RCA Victor LSP-3776	(S)	Sweetest One	1967	40.00	100.00
METROTONES, THE					
Columbia CL-6341	(10")	Tops In Rock And Roll	1955	100.00	250.00
MEYERS, AUGIE					
Mr. Meyers is a member of Sir Douglas' Quintet.					
Paramount 6065	(S)	You Ain't Rollin' Your Roll Rite	1973	3.20	8.00
Polydor 24-4069	(S)	Western Head Music Co.	197?	3.20	8.00
Texas Re-cord LP-1002	(S)	Live At The Longneck	1977	3.20	8.00
Texas Re-cord LP-1005	(S)	Finally In Lights	1977	3.20	8.00
MFSB					
Phila. Inter. PZ-32046	(S)	MFSB	1973	3.20	8.00
Phila. Inter. PZ-32707	(S)	Love Is The Message	1974	3.20	8.00
Phila. Inter. PZQ-32707	(Q)	Love Is The Message	1975	6.00	15.00
Phila. Inter. PZ-31358	(S)	Universal Love	1975	3.20	8.00
Phila. Inter. PZ-33845	(S)	Philadelphia Freedom	1975	3.20	8.00
Phila. Inter. PZQ-33845	(Q)	Philadelphia Freedom	1975	6.00	15.00
Phila. Inter. PZ-34238	(S)	Summertime	1976	3.20	8.00
MICHAELANGELO					
Columbia CS-30686	(S)	One Voice Many	1971	4.00	10.00
MICHAELS, DANNY					
Chambers BB-205	(M)	On The Bandstand	196?	60.00	150.00
Vistone 654	(S)	On The Bandstand	196?	60.00	150.00
MICHAELS, LEE					
A&M LP-140	(M)	Carnival Of Life	1967	12.00	30.00
A&M SP-4140	(S)	Carnival Of Life	1967	16.00	40.00
A&M SP-4152	(S)	Recital	1968	6.00	15.00
A&M SP-4199	(S)	Lee Michaels	1969	6.00	15.00
A&M SP-4249	(S)	Barrel	1970	5.00	12.00
A&M SP-4302	(S)	5th	1971	5.00	12.00
A&M SP-4336	(S)	Space And First Takes	1972	5.00	12.00
A&M SP-3518	(S)	Live (2 LPs)	1973	6.00	15.00
		—A&M albums above have brown labels.—			
Columbia KC-32275	(S)	Nice Day For Something	1973	1.00	5.00
Columbia CQ-32275	(Q)	Nice Day For Something	1973	6.00	15.00
Columbia KC-32846	(S)	Tailface	1974	1.00	5.00
Columbia	(DJ)	Lee Michaels In Hawaii	1975	10.00	25.00
MICHAELS, LINDY					
Vault 123	(S)	Ragamuffin Child	1969	5.00	12.00
MICHELLE					
ABC D-684	(S)	Saturn Rings	1969	4.00	10.00
MICKEY & SYLVIA					
Mickey Baker and Sylvia Vanderpool.					
Vik LX-1102	(M)	New Sounds	1957	250.00	500.00
Camden CAL-863	(M)	Love Is Strange	1965	20.00	50.00
Camden CAS-863	(E)	Love Is Strange	1965	12.00	30.00
RCA Victor APM1-0327	(M)	Do It Again	1973	4.00	10.00
		(RCA 0327 is a reissue of Vik 1102.)			
MIDAS TOUCH, THE					
Decca DL-75151	(S)	Midas Touch	1969	6.00	15.00
Decca DL-75240	(S)	Color My World With Love	1970	5.00	12.00
MIDDLE OF THE ROAD, THE					
RCA Victor LSP-4674	(S)	Acceleration	1972	1.20	6.00
MIDNIGHT SUN					
Kapp KS-3667	(S)	Midnight Sun	1972	1.20	6.00

Rhythm'n blues belter Amos Milburn, a mainstay of bands in the '40s and '50s, was given a new lease on life when Berry Gordy signed him to Motown in 1963. This album was assembled and released, apparently to little or no reception at the stores. The Blues Boss remains one of the legendarily rare Motown albums.

Label & Catalog #		Title	Year	VG+	NM

MIDNIGHTERS, THE
The Midnighters eventually became Hank Ballard & The Midnighters. Material they recorded under this name appeared on albums that King sold more or less as Ballard solo vehicles, which is where they are listed in this book.

Label & Catalog #		Title	Year	VG+	NM
Federal 295-90	(10")	**Their Greatest Hits**	1954		See note below
		(Federal 90 has a suggested NM value of $10,000-20,000.)			
Federal 395-541	(M)	**Their Greatest Hits**	1955		See note below
		(Federal 541 with a red cover has a suggested NM value of $3,000-5,000. Later pressings with a yellow cover, $2,000-3,000)			
Federal 395-581	(M)	**The Midnighters, Volume 2**	1955		See note below
		(Federal 581 has a suggested NM value of $2,000-3,000.)			
King 541	(M)	**Their Greatest Jukebox Hits**	1958	300.00	600.00
King 581	(M)	**The Midnighters, Volume 2**	1958	300.00	600.00
		(King 541 and 581 are reissues of Federal 541 and 581.)			
		—*King albums above have crownless black labels with a small, 2" wide "KING" on top.*—			
King 541	(M)	**Their Greatest Jukebox Hits** *(Girl cover)*	196?	200.00	400.00
King 541	(M)	**Their Greatest Jukebox Hits** *(Ballard cover)*	196?	100.00	250.00
King 581	(M)	**The Midnighters, Volume 2**	196?	200.00	400.00
		—*King albums above have crownless black labels with a large, 3" wide "KING" on top.*—			

MIGHTY SPARROW

Warner Bros. BS-2771	(S)	**Hot And Sweet**	1974	8.00	20.00

MILBURN, AMOS

Aladdin LP-704	(10")	**Rockin' The Boogie** *(Red vinyl in blue cover)*	1955		See note below
		(Red vinyl LPs in blue covers have a suggested NM value of $4,000-8,000.)			
Aladdin LP-704	(10")	**Rockin' The Boogie**	1955		See note below
		(Black vinyl copies have a suggested NM value of $2,000-3,000.)			
Aladdin LP-810	(M)	**Rockin' The Boogie**	1958		Unreleased
Score LP-4012	(M)	**Let's Have A Party**	1957	350.00	700.00
Score LP-4035	(M)	**Amos Milburn Sings The Blues**	1958		Unreleased
Imperial LP-9176	(M)	**Million Sellers**	1962	200.00	400.00
Motown 608	(M)	**The Blues Boss**	1963	500.00	1,000.00

MILBURN, AMOS / WYNONIE HARRIS / CROWN PRINCE WATERFORD

Aladdin LP-703	(10")	**Party After Hours** *(Red vinyl in blue cover)*	1955		See note below
		(Red vinyl LPs in blue covers have a suggested NM value of $4,000-8,000.)			
Aladdin LP-703	(10")	**Party After Hours**	1955		See note below
		(Black vinyl copies have a suggested NM value of $2,000-3,000.)			

MILES, BUDDY [THE BUDDY MILES EXPRESS]
Refer to Carlos Santana & Buddy Miles.

Mercury SR-61196	(S)	**Expressway To Your Skull**	1968	8.00	20.00
Mercury SR-61222	(S)	**Electric Church**	1969	8.00	20.00
Mercury SPM-2-7500	(S)	**Live** *(2 LPs)*	1971	6.00	15.00
Mercury SR-61313	(S)	**We've Got To Live Together**	1972	3.20	8.00
Columbia CS-32048	(S)	**Chapter VII**	1973	1.00	5.00
Columbia CS-33089	(S)	**All The Faces Of Buddy Miles**	1973	1.00	5.00
Columbia CS-34694	(S)	**Booger Bear**	1973	1.00	5.00
Columbia CQ-34694	(Q)	**Booger Bear**	1974	8.00	20.00
Casablanca NBLP-7019	(S)	**More Miles Per Gallon**	1975	1.00	5.00

MILES, LONG GONE

World Pacific WP-1820	(M)	**Country Born**	1964	10.00	25.00
World Pacific ST-1820	(S)	**Country Born**	1964	12.00	30.00

MILKWOOD

A&M SP-4226	(S)	**Under Milkwood**	1969	500.00	750.00

MILKWOOD

Paramount PAS-6046	(S)	**How's The Weather?**	1973	12.00	30.00

MILKWOOD TAPESTRY

Metromedia	(S)	**Milkwood Tapestry**	1969	20.00	50.00

MILLENIUM
Millenium features Curt Boetcher with Gary Usher as executive producer.

Columbia CS-9663	(S)	**Begin**	1968	12.00	30.00

MILLER, STEVE [THE STEVE MILLER BAND]
The original recording Steve Miller Band was Miller with Boz Scaggs, Curley Cooke, Tim Davis, Jim Peterman, and Lonnie Turner. Cooke left and the remaing quintet signed with Capitol. They can also be found on the U.A. soundtrack "Revolution." After the second album, both Scaggs and Peterman left. Nicky Hopkins joined in 1969, stayed for two albums, and quit. Miller has used cast of thousands since. Refer to Chuck Berry.

Capitol SKAO-2920	(S)	**Children Of The Future**	1968	10.00	25.00
Capitol ST-2984	(S)	**Sailor**	1968	10.00	25.00
Capitol STBB-177	(S)	**Children Of The Future/Sailor** *(2 LPs)*	1969	8.00	20.00
Capitol ST-184	(S)	**Brave New World**	1969	8.00	20.00
		—*Capitol albums above have black rainbow labels.*—			

The Miracles first album, Hi! We're The Miracles, featured an almost unbelievably amateurish cover that, along with the bold credit for producer Berry Gordy, Jr., fully captures the ambience of the fledgling Tamla/Motown corporation. The later Greatest Hits From The Beginning is a two-disc compilation, basically the group's first two albums, that adequately captures the beauty of their early work. Mono pressings are preferred as all stereo pressings are horrendously rechanneled.

Label & Catalog #		Title	Year	VG+	NM
Capitol SKAO-2920	(S)	Children Of The Future	1970	4.00	10.00
Capitol ST-2984	(S)	Sailor	1970	4.00	10.00
Capitol STBB-177	(S)	Children Of The Future/Sailor (2 LPs)	1970	4.00	10.00
Capitol ST-184	(S)	Brave New World	1970	4.00	10.00
Capitol ST-436	(S)	Number Five	1970	4.00	10.00
Capitol ST-331	(S)	Your Saving Grace	1970	4.00	10.00
Capitol SW-748	(S)	Rock Love	1971	4.00	10.00
Capitol SMAS-11022	(S)	Recall The Beginning	1972	4.00	10.00
		—Capitol albums above have green labels.—			
Capitol SVBB-11114	(S)	Anthology (2 LPs)	1972	1.00	5.00
Capitol R-223186	(S)	Anthology (2 LPs. Capitol Record Club)	1973	4.00	10.00
Capitol SMAS-11235	(S)	The Joker	1973	.80	4.00
Capitol ST-11497	(S)	Fly Like An Eagle	1976	.80	4.00
Capitol SO-11630	(S)	Book Of Dreams	1977	.80	4.00
Capitol SOO-11872	(DJ)	Greatest Hits 1974-78 (Blue vinyl)	1978	12.00	30.00
Capitol SOO-11872	(S)	Greatest Hits 1974-78	1978	.80	4.00
Capitol SEAX-11903	(S)	Book Of Dreams (Picture disc)	1978	4.00	10.00
Capitol ST-12121	(S)	Circle Of Love	1981	.80	4.00
Capitol ST-12216	(S)	Abracadabra	1982	.80	4.00
Capitol ST-12263	(S)	Steve Miller Live	1983	.80	4.00
Capitol SN-16078	(S)	Brave New World	1980	.80	4.00
Capitol SN-16079	(S)	Your Saving Grace	1980	.80	4.00
Capitol SN-16262	(S)	Children Of The Future	1970	.80	4.00
Capitol SN-16263	(S)	Sailor	1982	.80	4.00
Mobile Fidelity MFSL-021	(S)	Fly Like An Eagle	1976	12.00	35.00

MILLER, STEVE / QUICKSILVER MESSENGER SERVICE / THE BAND

Capitol STCR-288	(S)	Sailor / Quicksilver Messenger Service / Music From Big Pink (3 LP boxed set)	1969	16.00	40.00

MILTON, ROY
Refer to Chuck Higgins / Roy Milton.

Kent KLP-5054	(M)	The Great Roy Milton	1963	20.00	50.00
Kent KST-554	(E)	The Great Roy Milton	1963	12.00	30.00
United US-7767	(E)	Roots Of Rock, Vol. 1	197?	6.00	15.00

MIMMS, GARNET, & THE ENCHANTERS

United Arts. UAL-3305	(M)	Cry Baby And 11 Other Hits	1963	30.00	75.00
United Arts. UAS-6305	(S)	Cry Baby And 11 Other Hits	1963	40.00	100.00
United Arts. UAL-3396	(M)	As Long As I Have You	1964	20.00	50.00
United Arts. UAS-6396	(S)	As Long As I Have You	1964	30.00	75.00
United Arts. UAL-3498	(M)	I'll Take Good Care Of You	1966	20.00	50.00
United Arts. UAS-6498	(S)	I'll Take Good Care Of You	1966	30.00	75.00

MIND EXPANDERS, THE

Dot DLP-3773	(M)	What's Happening	1967	20.00	50.00
Dot DLP-25773	(S)	What's Happening	1967	30.00	75.00

MIND GARAGE

RCA Victor LSP-4218	(S)	Mind Garage	1969	8.00	20.00
RCA Victor LSP-4319	(S)	Mind Garage Again!	1970	8.00	20.00

MINDBENDERS, THE
The Mindbenders originally recorded with Wayne Fontana.

Fontana MGF-27554	(M)	A Groovy Kind Of Love	1966	12.00	30.00
Fontana SRF-67554	(E)	A Groovy Kind Of Love	1966	10.00	25.00
		(First pressings have "Don't Cry No More.")			
Fontana MGF-27554	(M)	A Groovy Kind Of Love	1966	10.00	25.00
Fontana SRF-67554	(E)	A Groovy Kind Of Love	1966	8.00	20.00
		(Later pressings have "Ashes To Ashes.")			

MINNESODA

Capitol ST-11102	(S)	Minnesoda	1972	1.20	6.00

MINT TATTOO

Dot DLP-25918	(S)	Mint Tattoo	1969	10.00	25.00

MIRACLES, THE [SMOKEY ROBINSON & THE MIRACLES]
Tamla 220-254 credit The Miracles, although they are obviously Smokey's group. 267-318 credit Smokey Robinson & The Miracles. With Robinson's departure in 1973, the group again recorded as The Miracles.

Tamla 220	(M)	Hi! We're The Miracles	1961	400.00	750.00
Tamla 223	(M)	Cookin' With The Miracles	1962	400.00	750.00
Tamla 230	(M)	I'll Try Something New	1962	400.00	750.00
		—Tamla albums above have a disc overlapping a globe at the top of the label.—			
Tamla 236	(M)	Christmas With The Miracles	1963	150.00	300.00
Tamla 238	(M)	The Fabulous Miracles	1963	150.00	300.00
Tamla 238	(M)	You've Really Got A Hold On Me	1963	80.00	200.00
		(Repackage of "The Fabulous Miracles.")			

The mid-'60s was an interesting time for the recording industry as they attempted to exploit fads from other forms. This trio of albums—Hot Rod Hootenanny, Rods n' Ratfinks and Surfink—played upon the then popular custom-car creations and related cartoon work of Ed "Big Daddy" Roth, who also supplied the cover art and the voice of Mr. Gasser. Roth also bestowed the ever lovable "Ratfink" on American lore. The first two rod-oriented albums credit The Weirdos and the voice of Mr. Gasser while the final, surf LP credits Mr. Gasser and The Weirdos, which is how they are listed in this book.

Label & Catalog #		Title	Year	VG+	NM
Tamla 241	(M)	Recorded Live On Stage	1963	80.00	200.00
Tamla 245	(M)	The Miracles Doin' Mickey's Monkey	1963	80.00	200.00
Tamla T-245	(S)	The Miracles Doin' Mickey's Monkey	1963	150.00	300.00
Tamla 2-254	(M)	Greatest Hits From The Beginning (2 LPs)	1965	20.00	50.00
Tamla T-2-254	(P)	Greatest Hits From The Beginning (2 LPs)	1965	14.00	35.00
		(The first disc of 254 is rechanneled; the second is stereo.)			
Tamla 267	(M)	Going To A Go-Go	1965	12.00	30.00
Tamla T-267	(S)	Going To A Go-Go	1965	16.00	40.00
Tamla 271	(M)	Away We A Go-Go	1966	10.00	25.00
Tamla T-271	(S)	Away We A Go-Go	1966	12.00	30.00
Tamla 276	(M)	Make It Happen	1967	10.00	25.00
Tamla T-276	(S)	Make It Happen	1967	12.00	30.00
Tamla T-276	(S)	Tears Of A Clown	1970	8.00	20.00
		("Tears Of A Clown" is a repackage of "Make It Happen.")			
Tamla T-280	(S)	Greatest Hits, Volume 2	1968	8.00	20.00
		—Tamla albums above have two side-by-side circles at the top of the label.—			
Tamla T-289	(S)	Smokey Robinson & The Miracles Live!	1969	8.00	20.00
Tamla T-290	(S)	Special Occasion	1968	8.00	20.00
Tamla T-295	(S)	Time Out	1969	6.00	15.00
Tamla T-297	(S)	Four In Blue	1969	6.00	15.00
Tamla T-301	(S)	What Love Has Joined Together	1970	6.00	15.00
Tamla T-306	(S)	A Pocketful Of Miracles	1970	6.00	15.00
Tamla T-307	(S)	The Season For Miracles	1970	6.00	15.00
Tamla T-312	(S)	One Dozen Roses	1971	6.00	15.00
Tamla T-318	(S)	Flying High Together	1972	6.00	15.00
Tamla T-320	(P)	The Miracles 1957-1972 (2 LPs)	1973	6.00	15.00
Tamla T6-325	(S)	Renaissance	1973	3.20	8.00
Tamla T6-334	(S)	Do It Baby	1974	3.20	8.00
Motown 793	(P)	Anthology (3 LPs)	1974	6.00	15.00
Tamla T6-339	(S)	City Of Angels	1975	3.20	8.00
Tamla T6-336	(S)	Don't Cha Love It	1975	3.20	8.00
Tamla T6-344	(S)	Power Of Music	1976	3.20	8.00
Columbia PC-34460	(S)	Love Crazy	1977	1.00	5.00
Columbia PCQ-34460	(Q)	Love Crazy	1977	6.00	15.00
Columbia JC-34910	(S)	The Miracles	1977	1.00	5.00
Natural Resources 4009	(S)	I'll Try Something New	1978	6.00	15.00
Motown M5-133V	(S)	Do It Baby	1982	.80	4.00

MIRETTES, THE

Revue RS-7205	(S)	In The Midnight Hour	1968	5.00	12.00
Uni 73062	(S)	Whirlpool	1969	5.00	12.00

MR. FLOOD'S PARTY

Cotillion SD-9003	(S)	Mr. Flood's Party	1969	6.00	15.00

MR. GASSER & THE WEIRDOS [THE WEIRDOS FEATURING MR. GASSER]
Mr. Gasser is a pseudonym for Ed "Big Daddy" Roth. The Weirdos are a creation of Gary Usher & Co.

Capitol T-2010	(M)	Hot Rod Hootenanny	1963	40.00	100.00
Capitol ST-2010	(S)	Hot Rod Hootenanny	1963	60.00	150.00
Capitol T-2057	(M)	Rods N' Ratfinks (With ratfink decal)	1963	50.00	125.00
Capitol ST-2057	(S)	Rods N' Ratfinks (With ratfink decal)	1963	70.00	175.00
Capitol T-2057	(M)	Rods N' Ratfinks (Without decal)	1963	40.00	100.00
Capitol ST-2057	(S)	Rods N' Ratfinks (Without decal)	1963	60.00	150.00
Capitol T-2114	(M)	Surfink! (With bonus single)	1964	60.00	150.00
Capitol ST-2114	(S)	Surfink! (With bonus single)	1964	80.00	200.00
		(Includes the bonus single "Santa Barbara" / "Midnight Run" by The Super Stocks in a special "pocket" on the cover.			
Capitol T-2114	(M)	Surfink! (Without single)	1964	40.00	100.00
Capitol ST-2114	(S)	Surfink! (Without single)	1964	60.00	150.00

MR. SHORTSTUFF

Spivey 1005	(M)	Mr. Shortstuff	196?	8.00	20.00

MITCHELL, JONI
Joni Mitchell is a guitar player, singer and writer of contemporary folk-based pop music.

Reprise RS-6293	(S)	Joni Mitchell	1968	4.00	10.00
Reprise RS-6341	(S)	Clouds	1969	10.00	25.00
		(Original pressings of RS-6341 have a highly visible paste-up blemish running up the back cover artwork.)			
Reprise RS-6341	(S)	Clouds	1970	4.00	10.00
		(Later pressings have the blemish touched up.)			
Reprise RS-6376	(S)	Ladies Of The Canyon	1970	4.00	10.00
		—Reprise albums above have brown & orange labels with a "W7" logo on top.—			
Reprise RS-6293	(S)	Joni Mitchell	1971	2.00	5.00
Reprise RS-6341	(S)	Clouds	1971	2.00	5.00
Reprise RS-6376	(S)	Ladies Of The Canyon	1971	2.00	5.00
Reprise MS-2038	(S)	Blue	1971	4.00	10.00
Asylum SD-5057	(S)	For The Roses	1972	2.00	5.00

Label & Catalog #		Title	Year	VG+	NM
Asylum 7E-1001	(S)	Court And Spark	1974	2.00	5.00
Asylum EQ-1001	(Q)	Court And Spark	1974	8.00	20.00
Asylum 202	(S)	Miles Of Aisles	1974	2.00	5.00
Asylum 7E-1051	(S)	The Hissing Of Summer Lawns	1975	2.00	5.00
Asylum EQ-1051	(Q)	The Hissing Of Summer Lawns	1975	8.00	20.00
Asylum 7E-1087	(S)	Hejira	1976	2.00	5.00
Asylum BB-701	(S)	Don Juan's Reckless Daughter (2 LPs)	1978	1.20	6.00
Asylum SE-505	(S)	Mingus	1979	2.00	5.00
Asylum 704	(S)	Shadows And Light (2 LPs)	1980	1.20	6.00
Geffen 2019	(DJ)	Wild Things Run Fast (Qutex II vinyl)	1982	10.00	25.00
Geffen 2019	(S)	Wild Things Run Fast	1982	2.00	5.00

MITCHELL, WILLIE

Hi HL-32010	(M)	Sunrise Serenade	1963	16.00	40.00
Hi SHL-32010	(E)	Sunrise Serenade	1963	12.00	30.00
Hi HL-32021	(M)	Hold It	1964	10.00	25.00
Hi SHL-32021	(S)	Hold It	1964	12.00	30.00
Hi HL-32026	(M)	It's Dance Time	1965	10.00	25.00
Hi SHL-32026	(S)	It's Dance Time	1965	12.00	30.00
Hi HL-32029	(M)	Driving Beat	1966	10.00	25.00
Hi SHL-32029	(S)	Driving Beat	1966	12.00	30.00
Hi HL-32034	(M)	Hit Sound Of Willie Mitchell	1967	10.00	25.00
Hi SHL-32034	(S)	Hit Sound Of Willie Mitchell	1967	12.00	30.00
Hi HL-32039	(M)	Ooh Baby, You Turn Me On	1967	10.00	25.00
Hi HL-32039	(S)	Ooh Baby, You Turn Me On	1967	12.00	30.00
Hi SHL-32042	(S)	Willie Mitchell Live	1968	10.00	25.00
Hi SHL-32045	(S)	Solid Soul	1968	10.00	25.00
Hi SHL-32048	(S)	On Top	1969	10.00	25.00
Hi SHL-32050	(S)	Soul Bag	1969	10.00	25.00
Hi SHL-32056	(S)	The Many Moods Of Willie Mitchell	1970	10.00	25.00
Hi SHL-32058	(S)	Robbin's Nest	1971	10.00	25.00
		—Hi albums above have orange & white labels.—			

MOB, THE

Colossus CS-1006	(S)	The Mob	1971	6.00	15.00

MOB, THE

Private Stock 2005	(S)	The Mob	1975	1.00	5.00

MOBY GRAPE

Moby Grape was Alexander "Skip" Spence, Bob Mosley, Jerry Miller, Peter Lewis and Don Stephenson.

Columbia CL-2698	(M)	Moby Grape	1967	16.00	40.00
Columbia CS-9498	(S)	Moby Grape	1967	16.00	40.00
		(Original covers for Columbia 26/9498 feature Don Stephenson "giving the finger" while holding a washboard. Issued with a poster, priced separately below.)			
Columbia 26/9498		Moby Grape Bonus Poster #1	1967	6.00	15.00
		(The poster also features Stephenson "giving the finger.")			
Columbia CL-2698	(M)	Moby Grape	1967	8.00	20.00
Columbia CS-9498	(S)	Moby Grape	1967	8.00	20.00
		(Later covers have Stephenson's offending member removed via the airbrush. Issued with a poster, priced separately below.)			
Columbia 26/9498		Moby Grape Bonus Poster #2	1967	1.00	5.00
		(The second poster also has Stephenson's finger airbrushed out.)			
Columbia CS-9613	(S)	Wow	1968	8.00	20.00
Columbia MGS-1	(S)	Grape Jam	1968	4.00	10.00
		("Grape Jam" was issued as bonus album with "Wow.")			
Columbia CS-9696	(S)	Moby Grape '69	1969	8.00	20.00
Columbia CS-9912	(S)	Truly Fine Citizen	1969	8.00	20.00
		—Columbia albums above have "360 Sound" on the bottom of the label.—			
Columbia CS-9498	(S)	Moby Grape (With poster #2)	1970	4.00	10.00
Columbia CS-9498	(S)	Moby Grape (Without poster)	1970	1.00	5.00
Harmony KH-30392	(M)	Omaha	1971	4.00	10.00
Reprise RS-6460	(S)	20 Granite Creek	1971	8.00	20.00
Columbia AS-31098	(S)	Great Grape	1972	4.00	10.00
Escape ESA1A	(S)	Live Grape (Marble vinyl)	1978	5.00	12.00
Escape JAM95018	(S)	Live Grape (Purple vinyl)	1978	4.00	10.00
San Francisco Sound 04801	(S)	Wow / Grape Jam (2 LPs. Half-speed master)	1983	8.00	20.00
San Francisco Sound 04805	(S)	Moby Grape (Half-speed master)	1983	6.00	15.00
San Francisco Sound 04830	(S)	Moby Grape '84 (Half-speed master)	1984	6.00	15.00

MOCCASIN

MGM SE-4728	(S)	Moccasin	1971	3.50	8.00

MOD-MODS, THE

The Mod-Mods feature future talkshow host Morton Downey, Jr.

Rel LP-102	(M)	Heaven's Door	196?	12.00	30.00

Label & Catalog #		Title	Year	VG+	NM

MODERN FOLK QUARTET, THE
The MFQ features Jerry Yester. Refer to Henske & Yester; The Lovin' Spoonful.

Warner Bros. W-1511	(M)	**Modern Folk Quartet**	*1963*	**10.00**	**25.00**
Warner Bros. WS-1511	(S)	**Modern Folk Quartet**	*1963*	**12.00**	**30.00**
Warner Bros. W-1546	(M)	**Changes**	*1964*	**10.00**	**25.00**
Warner Bros. WS-1546	(S)	**Changes**	*1964*	**12.00**	**30.00**

MODERN LOVERS, THE: *Refer to* **JONATHAN RICHMAN & THE MODERN LOVERS**

MOLLAND, JOEY
Joey Molland originally recorded as a member of The Iveys and Badfinger. Refer to Natural Gas.

Earth Tone ET-01002	(S)	**After The Pearl**	*1983*	**5.00**	**12.00**

MOLLY HATCHET

Epic PE-35347	(S)	**Molly Hatchet**	*1978*	**.80**	**4.00**
Epic PJE-35347	(DJ)	**Molly Hatchet** *(Picture disc)*	*1979*	**10.00**	**25.00**
Epic AS-528	(DJ)	**Molly Hatchet Live**	*1979*	**10.00**	**25.00**
Epic PE-36110	(S)	**Flirtin' With Disaster**	*1979*	**.80**	**4.00**
Epic AS-99-694	(DJ)	**Flirtin' With Disaster** *(Picture disc)*	*1979*	**8.00**	**20.00**
Epic PE-36572	(S)	**Beatin' The Odds**	*1980*	**.80**	**4.00**
Epic AS-99-884	(DJ)	**Beatin' The Odds** *(Picture disc)*	*1980*	**6.00**	**15.00**
Epic PE-37480	(S)	**Take No Prisoners**	*1981*	**.80**	**4.00**
Epic AS-99-1320	(DJ)	**Take No Prisoners** *(Picture disc)*	*1981*	**5.00**	**12.00**
Epic PE-38429	(S)	**No Guts... No Glory**	*1983*	**.80**	**4.00**
Epic PE-39621	(S)	**The Deed Is Done**	*1984*	**.80**	**4.00**

MOLOCH

Enterprise ENS-1002	(S)	**Moloch**	*1969*	**8.00**	**20.00**

MOM'S APPLE PIE

Brown Bag 14200	(S)	**Mom's Apple Pie**	*1972*	**1.00**	**5.00**
		(Original covers for 14200 feature a vagina in mom's apple pie.)			
Brown Bag 14200	(S)	**Mom's Apple Pie**	*1972*	**4.00**	**10.00**
		(Later covers replace the vagina with a barbed wire wall!)			
Brown Bag LA-073F	(S)	**Mom's Apple Pie #2**	*1973*	**4.00**	**10.00**

MOMENTS, THE

Stang ST-1003	(S)	**Not On The Outside, But On The Inside Strong**	*1969*	**12.00**	**30.00**
Stang ST-1003	(S)	**A Moment With The Moments**	*1970*	**10.00**	**25.00**
Stang ST-1004	(S)	**Greatest Hits**	*1971*	**8.00**	**20.00**
Stang ST-1006	(S)	**Live At The New York State Women's Prison**	*1971*	**10.00**	**25.00**
Stang ST-1009	(S)	**The Other Side Of The Moments**	*1972*	**10.00**	**25.00**
Stang ST-1015	(S)	**Live At The Miss Black America Contest**	*1972*	**8.00**	**20.00**
Stang ST-1019	(S)	**The Best Of The Moments**	*1973*	**6.00**	**15.00**
Stang ST-1022	(S)	**My Thing**	*1974*	**6.00**	**15.00**
Stang ST-1023	(S)	**Those Sexy Moments**	*1974*	**6.00**	**15.00**
Stang ST-1026	(S)	**Look At Me**	*1975*	**6.00**	**15.00**
Stang ST-1034	(S)	**Sharp**	*1978*	**6.00**	**15.00**

MONDAY BLUES

Vault 133	(S)	**The Phil Spector Song Book**	*1970*	**8.00**	**20.00**

MONITORS, THE

Soul SS-714	(S)	**Greetings, We're The Monitors**	*1969*	**14.00**	**35.00**

MONKEES, THE
The Monkees were Michael Nesmith, Micky Dolenz, Peter Tork and Davy Jones. Monkees albums outsold everyone for several years, usually ending up in the hands of post-pubescent fans who played the beecheeses out of 'em! Copies of the earlier albums are so common in less than NM condition that they are all but unsellable. Try 25-50¢ apiece. . .

Colgems COM-101	(M)	**The Monkees**	*1966*	**6.00**	**24.00**
Colgems COS-101	(S)	**The Monkees**	*1966*	**6.00**	**24.00**
		(Colgems 101 was originally issued with the cover erroneously listing "Papa Jean's Blues.")			
Colgems COM-101	(M)	**The Monkees**	*1967*	**5.00**	**20.00**
Colgems COS-101	(S)	**The Monkees**	*1967*	**5.00**	**20.00**
		(Later pressings correctly list "Papa Gene's Blues.")			
Colgems COM-102	(M)	**More Of The Monkees**	*1967*	**5.00**	**20.00**
Colgems COS-102	(S)	**More Of The Monkees**	*1967*	**5.00**	**20.00**
Colgems COS-102	(S)	**More Of The Monkees** *(Clear vinyl)*	*1967*	**300.00**	**500.00**
Colgems COM-103	(M)	**Headquarters**	*1967*	**5.00**	**20.00**
Colgems COS-103	(S)	**Headquarters**	*1967*	**5.00**	**20.00**
Colgems COM-104	(M)	**Pisces, Aquarius, Capricorn & Jones, Ltd.**	*1967*	**10.00**	**40.00**
Colgems COS-104	(S)	**Pisces, Aquarius, Capricorn & Jones, Ltd.**	*1967*	**5.00**	**20.00**
		—*Colgems albums above read "TM of Colgems Records" at the top of the label.*—			
Colgems COM-101	(M)	**The Monkees**	*1968*	**7.50**	**30.00**
Colgems COS-101	(S)	**The Monkees**	*1968*	**4.00**	**16.00**
Colgems COM-102	(M)	**More Of The Monkees**	*1968*	**7.50**	**30.00**
Colgems COS-102	(S)	**More Of The Monkees**	*1968*	**4.00**	**16.00**

Label & Catalog #		Title	Year	VG+	NM
Colgems COM-103	(M)	**Headquarters**	1968	**7.50**	**30.00**
Colgems COS-103	(S)	**Headquarters**	1968	**4.00**	**16.00**
		(The back cover has a photo of Mike, Pete and Mickey with beards.)			
Colgems COM-104	(M)	**Pisces, Aquarius, Capricorn & Jones, Ltd.**	1968	**15.00**	**60.00**
Colgems COS-104	(S)	**Pisces, Aquarius, Capricorn & Jones, Ltd.**	1968	**4.00**	**16.00**
		—Colgems albums above do not have "TM of Colgems Records" on the label and "RE" on the cover.—			
Colgems COM-109	(M)	**The Birds, The Bees And The Monkees**	1968	**40.00**	**100.00**
Colgems COS-109	(S)	**The Birds, The Bees And The Monkees**	1968	**5.00**	**20.00**
Colgems COSO-5008	(S)	**Head**	1968	**20.00**	**50.00**
Colgems COS-113	(S)	**Instant Replay**	1969	**10.00**	**25.00**
Colgems COS-115	(S)	**The Monkees' Greatest Hits**	1969	**10.00**	**25.00**
Colgems COS-117	(S)	**The Monkees Present**	1969	**10.00**	**25.00**
Colgems COS-119	(S)	**Changes**	1970	**30.00**	**75.00**
Colgems SCOS-1001	(S)	**A Barrel Full Of Monkees** (2 LPs)	1971	**30.00**	**75.00**
		—Colgems albums above delete "TM of Colgems Records" from the label.—			
Colgems PRS-329	(S)	**The Monkees' Golden Hits**	1972	**30.00**	**75.00**
Bell 6081	(S)	**Refocus**	1973	**12.00**	**30.00**
Arista AL-4089	(S)	**The Monkees' Greatest Hits**	1976	**4.00**	**10.00**
		(Arista 4089 is a reissue of Bell 6081.)			
Laurie House LH-8009	(P)	**The Monkees** (TV advertised)	1974	**8.00**	**20.00**
RCA/Pair DPL2-0188	(S)	**The Monkees** (2 LPs)	1976	**10.00**	**25.00**
Rhino RNLP-701	(S)	**Monkee Business** (Picture disc)	1982	**1.00**	**5.00**
Rhino RNLP-113	(S)	**Monkee Flips**	1984	**1.00**	**5.00**
Rhino RNLP-140	(S)	**The Monkees**	1985	**1.00**	**5.00**
Rhino RNLP-141	(S)	**More Of The Monkees**	1985	**1.00**	**5.00**
Rhino RNLP-142	(S)	**Headquarters**	1985	**1.00**	**5.00**
Rhino RNLP-143	(S)	**Pieces, Aquarius, Capricorn & Jones, Ltd.**	1985	**1.00**	**5.00**
Rhino RNLP-144	(S)	**The Birds, The Bees And The Monkees**	1985	**12.00**	**30.00**
		(Pressings with "RE-1" etched in the trail-off vinyl contain an alternate take of "Valleri.")			
Rhino RNLP-144	(S)	**The Birds, The Bees And The Monkees**	1985	**1.00**	**5.00**
Rhino RNLP-145	(S)	**Head**	1985	**1.00**	**5.00**
Rhino RNLP-146	(S)	**Instant Replay**	1985	**1.00**	**5.00**
Rhino RNLP-147	(S)	**The Monkees Present Micky, David And Michael**	1985	**1.00**	**5.00**
Rhino RNLP-148	(S)	**Changes**	1986	**1.00**	**5.00**
Rhino RNLP-70139	(S)	**Live 1967**	1987	**1.00**	**5.00**
Rhino RNIN-70706	(S)	**Pool It!**	1987	**1.00**	**5.00**
Rhino RNLP-70150	(S)	**Missing Links**	1987	**1.00**	**5.00**
FSH 71110	(S)	**20th Anniversary Tour 1986**	1987	**8.00**	**20.00**
		(Live album sold during Micky, Peter and Davy's 1987 tour.)			
Silhouette SM-10012	(S)	**Tails Of The Monkees** (Picture disc)	197?	**4.00**	**10.00**
Arista AL9-9432	(S)	**Then And Now... The Best Of The Monkees**	1986	**3.20**	**8.00**
(No label) FSH-71110	(S)	**Live, 20th Anniversary Tour** (2 LPs)	1986	**6.00**	**15.00**
Silver Eagle SE-1048	(S)	**The Best Of The Monkees** (2 LPs TV advertised)	1986	**6.00**	**15.00**

MONKEES, THE
These Monkees are not those Monkees!

Wyncote W-9199	(M)	**Monkey Business**	1966	**4.00**	**10.00**
Wyncote WS-9199	(S)	**Monkey Business**	1966	**5.00**	**12.00**

MONN, JEFF

Vanguard VSD-79291	(S)	**Reality**	1968	**5.00**	**12.00**

MONROE, VAUGHN
The rest of Mr Monroe's recordings are in the MOR field.

Dot DLP-3419	(M)	**Surfers Stomp**	1962	**12.00**	**30.00**
Dot DLP-25419	(S)	**Surfers Stomp**	1962	**16.00**	**40.00**

MONROES, THE

Alpha AAE-15015	(S)	**The Monroes** (EP)	198?	**12.00**	**30.00**

MONTAGE
Montage features Michael Brown of The Left Banke.

Laurie SLP-2049	(S)	**Montage**	1969	**8.00**	**20.00**

MONTEZ, CHRIS
Refer to The Chantels.

Monogram M-100	(M)	**Let's Dance And Have Some Kinda' Fun!!!**	1963	**250.00**	**500.00**
A&M LP-115	(M)	**The More I See You/Call Me**	1966	**8.00**	**20.00**
A&M SP-4115	(S)	**The More I See You/Call Me**	1966	**10.00**	**25.00**
		("Call Me" is rechanneled.)			
A&M LP-120	(M)	**Time After Time**	1966	**5.00**	**12.00**
A&M SP-4120	(S)	**Time After Time**	1966	**6.00**	**15.00**
A&M LP-128	(M)	**Foolin' Around**	1967	**5.00**	**12.00**
A&M SP-4128	(S)	**Foolin' Around**	1967	**6.00**	**15.00**
A&M LP-157	(M)	**Watch What Happens**	1967	**5.00**	**12.00**
A&M SP-4157	(S)	**Watch What Happens**	1967	**6.00**	**15.00**

Label & Catalog #		Title	Year	VG+	NM

MOODY BLUES

The original Moodys were Graeme Edge, Denny Laine, Mike Pinder, Ray Thomas, and Clint Warwick. From the second album on, Laine and Warwick were replaced by Justin Hayward and John Lodge.

Label & Catalog #		Title	Year	VG+	NM
London LL-3428	(M)	Go Now/Moody Blues #1	1965	20.00	50.00
London PS-428	(E)	Go Now/Moody Blues #1	1965	14.00	35.00
Deram DE-16012	(M)	Days Of Future Passed	1968	100.00	250.00
Deram DES-18012	(S)	Days Of Future Passed	1968	8.00	20.00
Deram DES-18017	(S)	In Search Of The Lost Chord	1968	8.00	20.00
Deram DES-18025	(S)	On The Threshold Of A Dream	1969	8.00	20.00
Deram DES-18051	(E)	In The Beginning	1971	4.00	10.00
		(Deram 18051 is a repackage of London 428.)			
		— Deram albums above have the "London" logo beneath Deram at the top of the label.—			
Threshold THS-1	(S)	To Our Children's Children's Children	1969	4.00	10.00
Threshold THS-3	(S)	A Question Of Balance	1970	4.00	10.00
Threshold SMAS-93329	(S)	A Question Of Balance (Capitol Record Club)	1973	8.00	20.00
Threshold THX-100	(DJ)	Special Interview Kit (Includes script)	1971	60.00	150.00
Threshold THS-5	(S)	Every Good Boy Deserves Favour	1971	3.20	8.00
Threshold THS-7	(S)	Seventh Sojourn	1972	3.20	8.00
		— Threshold albums above have white labels with a purple logo on top.—			
Threshold THS-12/13	(S)	This Is The Moody Blues (2 LPs)	1974	1.20	6.00
London PS-690/1	(S)	Caught Live + 5 (2 LPs)	1977	1.20	6.00
London PS-708	(S)	Octave (Blue vinyl)	1978	4.00	10.00
London PS-708	(S)	Octave	1978	1.00	5.00
Threshold TRL-2901	(S)	Long Distance Voyager	1981	1.00	5.00
Threshold TRL-2902	(S)	The Present	1983	1.00	5.00
Threshold 820155	(S)	Voices In The Sky—The Best Of The Moody Blues	1985	1.00	5.00

MOOG MACHINE, THE

The Moog Synthesizer is operated by Ken Ascher.

Columbia CS-9921	(S)	Switched-On Rock	1969	6.00	15.00

MOON, THE

The Moon features David Marks, formerly of The Beach Boys.

Imperial LP-9381	(M)	Without Earth	1968	16.00	40.00
Imperial LP-12381	(S)	Without Earth	1968	16.00	40.00
Imperial LP-12444	(S)	The Moon	1969	16.00	40.00

MOON, CHRIS

Kinetic 30228	(S)	The Chris Moon Group	1970	6.00	15.00
Barnaby 30228	(S)	The Chris Moon Group	1970	4.00	10.00

MOON, KEITH

Keith Moon was a member of The Who.

MCA 2136	(S)	Two Sides Of The Moon	1975	16.00	40.00

MOON, ROGER

Capitol ST-11370	(S)	Nobody Knows My Name	1975	1.20	6.00

MOONGLOWS, THE

Refer to The Flamingos / The Moonglows.

Chess LP-1430	(M)	Look, It's The Moonglows	1959	300.00	600.00
Chess LP-1471	(DJ)	The Best Of Bobby Lester & The Moonglows (White label promo)	1962	500.00	1,000.00
Chess LP-1471	(M)	The Best Of Bobby Lester & The Moonglows	1962	200.00	400.00
		—Chess albums above have black labels.—			
Chess LP-1471	(M)	The Best Of Bobby Lester & The Moonglows	196?	20.00	50.00
		—Chess albums above have blue & white labels.—			
Constellation C-2	(M)	Collectors Showcase—The Moonglows	1962	40.00	100.00
		(Original covers have a light, electric blue lettering on the front.)			
Constellation C-2	(M)	Collectors Showcase—The Moonglows	1962	20.00	50.00
		(Later covers have a cooler, dark blue lettering.)			
RCA Victor LSP-4722	(S)	The Return Of The Moonglows	1972	6.00	15.00
Chess ACRR-701	(S)	The Moonglows	197?	6.00	15.00
Lost-Nite LP-23	(10")	The Moonglows (Red vinyl)	1981	4.00	10.00

MOONLIGHTERS

Century 29132	(M)	An Evening With The Moonlighters	197?	6.00	15.00

MOONQUAKE

Fantasy F-9450	(S)	Moonquake	1974	1.20	6.00
Fantasy F-9486	(S)	Starstruck	1974	1.20	6.00

MOONLIGHTERS, THE

Century 29132	(M)	An Evening With The Moonlighters	197?	6.00	15.00

MOONRIDER

Anchor 2010	(S)	Moonrider	1975	3.50	8.00

On their first long-player, The Moonglows are apparently mistaking something in the middle of the day ("Look! Up in the sky! It's a bird! It's a plane!") as the moon a-glowin'. Perhaps it was a flying saucer? They were rather common back then. . .

Label & Catalog #		Title	Year	VG+	NM
MOORE, ALEX					
Arhoolie 1008	(M)	Whistling Alex Moore	196?	5.00	12.00
MOORE, BOBBY, & THE RHYTHM ACES					
Checker LP-3000	(M)	Searching For My Love	1966	12.00	30.00
Checker LPS-3000	(E)	Searching For My Love	1966	10.00	25.00
MOORE, GATEMOUTH					
King 684	(M)	Gatemouth Moore Sings The Blues	1960	See note below	
		(King 684 has a suggested NM value of $3,000-5,000.)			
Audio Fidelity AFLP-1921	(M)	Revival!	1960	30.00	75.00
Audio Fidelity AFSD-5921	(S)	Revival!	1960	40.00	100.00
MOORE, SCOTTY					
Scotty was Elvis' lead guitar player from 1954 through 1968.					
Epic LN-24103	(M)	The Guitar That Changed The World	1964	30.00	75.00
Epic BN-26103	(S)	The Guitar That Changed The World	1964	40.00	100.00
Guinness GNS-36038	(S)	What's Left	1977	6.00	15.00
MORGAN, DAVE					
Ampex A-10118	(S)	Morgan	197?	6.00	15.00
MORGEN, STEVE					
Probe CPLP-4507	(M)	Morgen (With insert)	1969	60.00	150.00
MORNING					
Vault 138	(S)	Morning	1970	8.00	20.00
Fantasy 9402	(S)	Struck Like Silver	1972	6.00	15.00
MORNING DEW					
Roulette R-41045	(M)	Morning Dew	1967	70.00	175.00
Roulette RS-41045	(S)	Morning Dew	1967	100.00	250.00
MORNING GLORY					
Fontana MGF-27573	(M)	Two Suns Worth	1967	8.00	20.00
Fontana SRF-67573	(S)	Two Suns Worth	1967	10.00	25.00
MORRILL, KENT					
Kent Morrill was a member of The Wailers.					
Cream CR-5001	(S)	The Dream Maker	197?	5.00	12.00
MORRISON, VAN					
Van The Man was the original lead singer for Them. Refer to The Band.					
Bang BLP-218	(M)	Blowin' Your Mind	1967	12.00	30.00
Bang BLPS-218	(S)	Blowin' Your Mind	1967	16.00	40.00
		(Bang 218 was originally issued with the complete "Brown-Eyed Girl" that includes the line "Making love in the green grass.")			
Bang BLPS-218	(S)	Blowin' Your Mind	1968	8.00	20.00
		(Second pressings contain a censored version of "Brown-Eyed Girl" that deletes "Making love in the green grass.")			
Bang BLPS-222	(S)	The Best Of Van Morrison	1970	4.00	10.00
		—*Bang albums above have red & white labels.*—			
Bang BLPS-218	(S)	Blowin' Your Mind	197?	1.00	5.00
Bang BLPS-222	(S)	The Best Of Van Morrison	197?	1.00	5.00
Bang BLPS-400	(S)	T. B. Sheets	1973	6.00	15.00
		—*Bang albums above have yellow labels.*—			
Warner Bros. WS-1768	(S)	Astral Weeks	1968	10.00	25.00
Warner Bros. WS-1835	(S)	Moondance	1970	8.00	20.00
		—*Warner albums above have green "W7" labels.*—			
Warner Bros. WS-1768	(S)	Astral Weeks	197?	4.00	10.00
Warner Bros. WS-1835	(S)	Moondance	197?	4.00	10.00
Warner Bros. WS-1885	(S)	Van Morrison, His Band And Street Choir	1970	4.00	10.00
Warner Bros. WS-1950	(S)	Tupelo Honey (With poster)	1971	6.00	15.00
Warner Bros. WS-1950	(S)	Tupelo Honey (Without poster)	1971	4.00	10.00
Warner Bros. WS-2633	(S)	St. Dominic's Preview	1972	4.00	10.00
		—*Warner albums above have green "WB" labels.*—			
Warner Bros. WS-1768	(S)	Astral Weeks	197?	1.00	5.00
Warner Bros. WS-1835	(S)	Moondance	197?	1.00	5.00
Warner Bros. WS-1885	(S)	Van Morrison, His Band And Street Choir	197?	1.00	5.00
Warner Bros. WS-1950	(S)	Tupelo Honey	197?	1.00	5.00
Warner Bros. WS-2633	(S)	St. Dominic's Preview	197?	1.00	5.00
Warner Bros. BS-2712	(S)	Hard Nose The Highway	1973	1.00	5.00
Warner Bros. 2ES-2760	(S)	It's Too Late To Stop Now (2 LPs)	1974	4.00	10.00
Warner Bros. BS-2805	(S)	Vleedon Fleece	1974	1.00	5.00
Warner Bros. BS-2987	(S)	A Period Of Transition	1977	1.00	5.00
		—*Warner albums above have palm-tree labels.*—			
Warner Bros. BSK-3212	(S)	Wavelength	1978	1.00	5.00

To assist in the promotion of Van the Man's latest album, Wavelength, his most commercial in years, his label taped him Live At The Roxy as part of their "Warner Bros. Music Show" series. Issued to radio stations in an omnibus red jacket with a die-cut hole for the info to show, this album was an excellent set and a perfect partner to his live double, It's Too Late To Stop Now, issued four years earlier.

Label & Catalog #		Title	Year	VG+	NM
Warner Bros. WBMS-102	(DJ)	Live At The Roxy (Blue vinyl)	1978	60.00	150.00
Warner Bros. WBMS-102	(DJ)	Live At The Roxy	1978	20.00	50.00
Warner Bros. HS-3390	(S)	Into The Music	1979	1.00	5.00
Warner Bros. BSK-3462	(S)	Common One	1980	1.00	5.00
Warner Bros. BSK-3652	(S)	Beautiful Vision	1982	1.00	5.00
Warner Bros. 23802	(S)	Inarticulate Speech Of The Heart	1983	1.00	5.00

MORTIMER

| Philips PHS-600-267 | (S) | Mortimer | 1968 | 10.00 | 25.00 |

MOSLEY, BOB
Bob Mosley was a member of Moby Grape.

| Reprise RS-2068 | (S) | Bob Mosley | 1972 | 8.00 | 20.00 |

MOTHER EARTH
Mother Earth features Tracy Nelson.

Mercury SR-61194	(S)	Living With The Animals	1968	12.00	30.00
Mercury SR-61226	(S)	Make A Joyful Noise	1969	6.00	15.00
Mercury SR-61230	(S)	Tracy Nelson Country	1969	6.00	15.00
Mercury SR-61270	(S)	Satisfied	1970	6.00	15.00
Reprise RS-6431	(S)	Bring Me Home	1971	6.00	15.00
Reprise MS-2054	(S)	Tracy Nelson/Mother Earth	1972	6.00	15.00

MOTHER LOVE

| Epic BN-26520 | (S) | Carousel Of Dreams | 1970 | 3.50 | 8.00 |

MOTHERLODE

| Buddah BDS-5046 | (S) | When I Die | 1969 | 4.00 | 10.00 |
| Buddah BDS-5108 | (S) | Tapped Out | 1972 | 4.00 | 10.00 |

MOTHERS OF INVENTION, THE: Refer to FRANK ZAPPA

MOTIONS, THE

| Philips PHS-600-317 | (S) | Electric Baby | 1969 | 8.00 | 20.00 |

MOTLEY CRUE
Motley Crue's first album was privately pressed.

Elektra 60174	(S)	Too Fast For Love	1981	1.00	5.00
Elektra 60289	(S)	Shout At The Devil	1983	1.00	5.00
Elektra 60395	(S)	Helter Skelter (Picture disc with poster)	1984	14.00	35.00
Elektra 60395	(S)	Helter Skelter	1984	1.00	5.00

MOTIONS, THE

| Philips PHS-600-317 | (S) | Electric Baby | 1969 | 8.00 | 20.00 |

MOTT THE HOOPLE
Mott The Hoople features Ian Hunter.

Atlantic SD-8272	(S)	Mad Shadows	1970	4.00	10.00
Atlantic SD-8258	(S)	Mott The Hoople	1970	4.00	10.00
Atlantic SD-8284	(S)	Wildlife	1971	4.00	10.00
Atlantic SD-8304	(S)	Brain Capers	1972	4.00	10.00
Atlantic SD-7297	(S)	Rock And Roll Queen	1974	4.00	10.00
Columbia KC-31750	(S)	All The Young Dudes (Prod. by David Bowie)	1972	1.00	5.00
Columbia KC-32425	(S)	Mott	1973	1.00	5.00
Columbia PC-32871	(S)	The Hoople	1974	1.00	5.00
Columbia PCQ-32871	(Q)	The Hoople	1974	8.00	20.00
Columbia PC-33282	(S)	Mott The Hoople Live	1974	1.00	5.00
Columbia PC-33705	(S)	Drive On	1975	1.00	5.00
Columbia PC-34236	(S)	Shouting And Pointing	1976	1.00	5.00
Columbia PC-34368	(S)	Mott The Hoople's Greatest Hits	1976	1.00	5.00

MOUNT RUSHMORE

| Dot DLP-25898 | (S) | High On Mount Rushmore | 1968 | 6.00 | 15.00 |
| Dot DLP-25934 | (S) | Mount Rushmore '69 | 1969 | 6.00 | 15.00 |

MOUNTAIN
Mountain features Leslie West.

Windfall 4500	(S)	Leslie West	1969	3.20	8.00
Windfall 4501	(S)	Climbing!	1970	3.20	8.00
Windfall 5500	(S)	Nantucket Sleighride (With inserts)	1971	4.00	10.00
Windfall 5500	(S)	Nantucket Sleighride (Without inserts)	1971	3.20	8.00
Windfall 5501	(S)	Flowers Of Evil	1971	3.20	8.00
Windfall 5002	(S)	The Road Goes Ever On	1972	3.20	8.00
Columbia PC-32079	(S)	The Best Of Mountain	1973	1.00	5.00
Columbia CQ-32079	(Q)	The Best Of Mountain	1973	6.00	15.00
Columbia PC-33088	(S)	Avalanche	1974	1.00	5.00
Columbia CQ-33088	(Q)	Avalanche	1974	6.00	15.00

While Frank Zappa had a long and distinctive career, for collectors—and, more than likely historians—it was his early work with the original Mothers Of Invention for Verve Records that will maintain his reputation as a rock genius. . . Absolutely Free was a collage of iconoclastic noises with appropriate cover art. Many fans were made aware of this record through ads in the back of comic books in the mid-'60s. Due to the fact that all aspects of creativity were the [all but] exclusive domain of Zappa, the original albums on Verve, although clearly credited to The Mothers Of Invention as a group, are listed under Frank Zappa, along with his solo work and his other Mothers.

Label & Catalog #		Title	Year	VG+	NM

MOUTH & MacNEAL

Philips PHS-700000	(S)	How Do You Do	1972	3.20	8.00
Philips PHS-700003	(S)	Mouth & MacNeal	1973	1.00	5.00

MOVE, THE

Formed in 1966, The Move was Roy Wood with Carl Wayne, Bev Bevan, Trevor Burton, and Chris Kefford, who left in 1968. Burton opted out in '69 and was replaced by Rick Price. Jeff Lynne joined in 1970. By '71 Wood, and Lynne were in the process of transforming the group into The Electric Light Orchestra. Refer to Sheridan-Price.

A&M SP-4259	(S)	Shazam	1969	12.00	30.00
Capitol ST-658	(S)	Looking On	1971	8.00	20.00
Capitol ST-811	(S)	Message From The Country	1971	8.00	20.00
		— Capitol albums above have green labels.—			
United Arts. UAS-5666	(S)	Split Ends	1973	4.00	10.00
A&M SP-3181	(S)	Shazam	1974	1.00	5.00
A&M SP-3625	(P)	Best Of The Move/First Move (2 LPs)	1974	4.00	10.00

MUDD

Uni 73089	(S)	Mud On Mudd	1970	4.00	10.00
Uni 73110	(S)	Mudd	1971	4.00	10.00

MUDDY WATERS

Muddy Waters is a pseudonym for McKinley Morganfield. Refer to The Super Blues Band.

Chess LP-1427	(DJ)	The Best Of Muddy Waters (White label promo)	1957	1,000.00	1,500.00
Chess LP-1427	(M)	The Best Of Muddy Waters	1957	250.00	500.00
Chess LP-1444	(DJ)	Muddy Waters Sings Big Bill (White label promo)	1960	600.00	1,000.00
Chess LP-1444	(M)	Muddy Waters Sings Big Bill	1960	200.00	400.00
Chess LP-1449	(DJ)	Muddy Waters At Newport (White label promo)	1963	200.00	400.00
Chess LP-1449	(M)	Muddy Waters At Newport	1963	70.00	175.00
Chess LP-1483	(DJ)	Folk Singer (White label promo)	1964	200.00	400.00
Chess LP-1483	(M)	Folk Singer	1964	70.00	175.00
		—Chess albums above have black & silver labels.—			
Chess LP-1501	(M)	The Real Folk Blues Of Muddy Waters	1965	20.00	50.00
Chess LPS-1501	(E)	The Real Folk Blues Of Muddy Waters	1965	14.00	35.00
Chess LP-1507	(M)	Muddy, Brass And Blues	1966	14.00	35.00
Chess LPS-1507	(S)	Muddy, Brass And Blues	1966	20.00	50.00
Chess LP-1511	(M)	More Real Folk Blues	1967	20.00	50.00
Chess LPS-1511	(E)	More Real Folk Blues	1967	10.00	25.00
Chess LP-1533	(M)	Blues From Big Bill's Copacabana	1968	20.00	50.00
Chess LPS-1533	(S)	Blues From Big Bill's Copacabana	1968	16.00	40.00
Cadet Concept 314	(S)	Electric Mud	1968	10.00	25.00
Cadet Concept 320	(S)	After The Rain	1969	10.00	25.00
Chess LPS-1539	(S)	Sail On	1969	10.00	25.00
Chess LPS-1553	(S)	They Call Me Muddy Waters	1971	8.00	20.00
Chess 2CH-60006	(S)	McKinley Morganfield A.K.A. Muddy Waters (2 LPs)	1971	10.00	25.00
Chess CH-50012	(S)	Muddy Waters Live	1972	8.00	20.00
Chess CH-60013	(S)	The London Muddy Waters Sessions	1972	8.00	20.00
		—Chess albums above have blue labels.—			
Chess CH-50023	(S)	Can't Get No Grindin'	1973	8.00	20.00
Chess CH-60026	(S)	London Revisited	1974	6.00	15.00
Chess CH-60031	(S)	Unk In Funk	1974	6.00	15.00
Chess CH-127	(S)	Fathers And Sons (2 LPs)	1975	12.00	30.00
Chess CH-50033	(S)	Fathers And Sons (2 LPs)	1976	8.00	20.00
Chess CH-50035	(S)	The Muddy Waters Woodstock Album	1976	8.00	20.00
Chess CH6-80002	(M)	Muddy Waters (6 LP box)	1989	16.00	40.00

MUGWUMPS, THE

The Mugwumps were Cass Elliot, Denny Doherty, Jim Hendricks and Zal Yanovsky. They also appear on the Tower soundtrack "Riot On Sunset Strip."

Warner Bros. W-1697	(M)	The Mugwumps	1967	10.00	25.00
Warner Bros. WS-1697	(S)	The Mugwumps	1967	12.00	30.00

MULDAUR, GEOFF

Folklore FRLP-14004	(M)	Sleepy Man Blues	1964	12.00	30.00
Folklore FRST-14004	(S)	Sleepy Man Blues	1964	16.00	40.00
Prestige PRST-7727	(S)	Sleepy Man Blues	1969	6.00	15.00
		(Prestige 7727 is a reissue of Folklore 14004.)			

MULDAUR, GEOFF & MARIA

Reprise MS-2073	(S)	Sweet Potatoes	1972	4.00	10.00

MULDAUR, MARIA

The former Maria D'Amato recorded with The Even Dozen Jug Band;. The Jim Kweskin Jug Band.

Reprise MS-2148	(S)	Maria Muldauer	1973	1.00	5.00
Reprise MS-2194	(S)	Waitress In A Donut Shop	1974	1.00	5.00
Reprise MS4-2194	(Q)	Waitress In A Donut Shop	1974	6.00	15.00
Reprise MS-2235	(S)	Sweet Harmony	1976	1.00	5.00
Warner Bros. BS-3162	(S)	Southern Winds	1978	1.00	5.00

Label & Catalog #		Title	Year	VG+	NM
MULESKINNER					
The Muleskinner is Richard Greene, David Grisman, Bill Keith and Clarence White.					
Warner Bros. BS-2787	(S)	Muleskinners	1972	6.00	15.00
MUNGO JERRY					
Janus JXS-7000	(S)	Mungo Jerry	1970	4.00	10.00
Janus JLS-3027	(S)	Memoirs Of A Stockbroker	1970	4.00	10.00
MURIETTA					
Cherry Red 5103	(S)	Murietta	1971	4.00	10.00
MURPHY, ELLIOTT					
Polydor PD-5061	(S)	Aquashow	1973	8.00	20.00
		(Original pressings list "Like A Great Gatsby" on label and cover.)			
Polydor PD-5061	(S)	Aquashow	1974	4.00	10.00
		(Later pressings list "Like A Crystal Microphone.)			
RCA Victor APL1-0916	(S)	Lost Generation	1975	10.00	25.00
RCA Victor APL1-1318	(S)	Night Lights	1976	10.00	25.00
		—*RCA albums above have orange labels.*—			
Columbia PC-34653	(S)	Just A Story From America	1977	4.00	10.00
Courtisane MUR-101	(S)	Affairs *(6 song EP)*	1980	8.00	20.00
Courtisane KMH-709232	(S)	Murph The Surf	1982	8.00	20.00
EMIS 101459	(S)	Milwaukee	1986	8.00	20.00
MURPHY, J. F., & SALT					
Elektra EKS-75024	(S)	J. F. Murphy And Salt Live	1972	1.20	6.00
MUSIC ASYLUM					
United Arts. UAS-6778	(S)	Commit Thyself	1970	8.00	20.00
MUSIC COMPANY, THE					
Crestview CRS-3057	(S)	Hard & Heavy	196?	10.00	25.00
MUSIC EXPLOSION, THE					
Refer to The Kasenetz-Katz Circus.					
Laurie LLP-2040	(M)	A Little Bit O' Soul	1967	6.00	15.00
Laurie SLLP-2040	(S)	A Little Bit O' Soul	1967	8.00	20.00
MUSIC MACHINE, THE [BONNIWELL'S MUSIC MACHINE]					
The Music Machine features Sean Bonniwell. Refer to T.S. Bonniwell.					
Original Sound 5015	(M)	Turn On The Music Machine	1966	12.00	30.00
Original Sound 8875	(S)	Turn On The Music Machine	1966	20.00	50.00
Warner Bros. W-1732	(M)	Bonniwell's Music Machine	1967	10.00	25.00
Warner Bros. WS-1732	(S)	Bonniwell's Music Machine	1967	16.00	40.00
MUSICAL THEATRE					
Metromedia 1015	(S)	Revolutionary Revelation	1969	5.00	12.00
MUSSELWHITE, CHARLIE					
Vanguard VRS-9232	(M)	Stand Back! Here Comes Charlie Musselwhite's South Side Band	1966	8.00	20.00
Vanguard VSD-79232	(S)	Stand Back! Here Comes Charlie Musselwhite's South Side Band	1966	10.00	25.00
Vanguard VSD-79287	(S)	Charlie Musselwhite	1968	8.00	20.00
Vanguard VSD-6258	(S)	Tennessee Woman	1969	8.00	20.00
Cherry Red 5102	(S)	Louisiana Fog	1968	6.00	15.00
Cherry Red 5104	(S)	Blues From Chicago	1968	6.00	15.00
Arhoolie 1056	(S)	Takin' My Time	1971	4.00	10.00
Arhoolie 1074	(S)	Goin' Back Down South	1974	4.00	10.00
Paramount PAS-5012	(S)	Memphis, Tennessee	197?	6.00	15.00
Capitol ST-11450	(S)	Leave The Blues To Us	1975	4.00	10.00
Kicking Mule 305	(S)	The Harmonica According To Charlie Musselwhite	1978	3.20	8.00
Crystal Clear 5005	(S)	Time's Gettin' Tougher Than Tough	1978	6.00	15.00
Crosscut CCR-1008	(S)	Memphis, Tennessee	1985	3.20	8.00
		(Crosscut 1008 is a reissue of Paramount 5012.)			
Crosscut CCR-1013	(S)	Mellow-Dee	1986	3.20	8.00
Blue Horizon 005	(S)	Cambridge Blues	1988	3.20	8.00
Alligator 4781	(S)	Ace Of Harps	1990	3.20	8.00
Alligator 49801	(S)	Signature	1991	3.20	8.00
MUTZIE					
Sussex 7001	(S)	Light Of Your Shadow	1970	10.00	25.00
MX-80					
Ralph MX-8002	(S)	Out Of The Tunnel	1980	4.00	10.00
Ralph MX-8102	(S)	Crowd Control	1980	4.00	10.00

Label & Catalog #		Title	Year	VG+	NM

MYERS, DAVE [DAVE MYERS & THE SURFTONES]

Del-Fi DFLP-1239	(M)	Hangin' Twenty	1963	20.00	50.00
Del-Fi DFST-1239	(S)	Hangin' Twenty	1963	30.00	75.00
		(Del-Fi 1239 credits Dave Myers & The Surftones.)			
Carole CAR-8002	(M)	Greatest Racing Themes	1966	20.00	50.00

MYLON

| Columbia KC-31085 | (S) | Mylon With Holy Smoke | 1972 | 4.00 | 10.00 |
| Columbia KC-31472 | (S) | Over The Influence | 1972 | 4.00 | 10.00 |

MYRTH

| RCA Victor LSP-4210 | (S) | Myrth | 1969 | 4.00 | 10.00 |

MYSTIC ASTROLOGIC CRYSTAL BAND, THE

Carole 8001	(M)	Mystic Astrologic Crystal Band	1967	10.00	25.00
Carole S-8001	(S)	Mystic Astrologic Crystal Band	1967	12.00	30.00
Carole S-8003	(S)	Clip Out, Put On Book	1968	12.00	30.00

MYSTIC NUMBER NATIONAL BANK, THE

| Probe CPLPS-4501 | (S) | The Mystic Number National Bank | 1969 | 6.00 | 15.00 |

NAGLE, RON

Warner Bros. WS-1902	(S)	Bad Rice	1970	8.00	20.00

NASH, GRAHAM
Refer to Crosby & Nash; Crosby, Stills & Nash; Crosby, Stills, Nash & Young; The Hollies.

Atlantic SD-7204	(S)	Songs For Beginners	1971	1.20	6.00

—Atlantic albums above have green & orange labels with an 1841 Broadway address.—

Atlantic SD-7288	(S)	Wild Tales	1974	.80	4.00
Capitol ST-12014	(S)	Earth & Sky	1980	.80	4.00
Atlantic 81633	(S)	Innocent Eyes	1986	.80	4.00

NASH, JOHNNY

ABC-Paramount 244	(M)	Johnny Nash	1958	12.00	30.00
ABC-Paramount S-244	(S)	Johnny Nash	1958	16.00	40.00
ABC-Paramount 276	(M)	Quiet Hour	1959	12.00	30.00
ABC-Paramount S-276	(S)	Quiet Hour	1959	16.00	40.00
ABC-Paramount 299	(M)	I Got Rhythm	1959	12.00	30.00
ABC-Paramount S-299	(S)	I Got Rhythm	1959	16.00	40.00
ABC-Paramount 344	(M)	Let's Get Lost	1960	10.00	25.00
ABC-Paramount S-344	(S)	Let's Get Lost	1960	12.00	30.00
ABC-Paramount 383	(M)	Studio Time	1961	10.00	25.00
ABC-Paramount S-383	(S)	Studio Time	1961	12.00	30.00
Argo LP-4038	(M)	Composer's Choice	1964	6.00	15.00
Argo LPS-4038	(S)	Composer's Choice	1964	8.00	20.00
Jad JS-1207	(S)	Hold Me Tight	1968	6.00	15.00
Jad JS-1001	(S)	Prince Of Peace	1969	6.00	15.00
Jad JS-1006	(S)	Folk Soul	1969	6.00	15.00
Epic KE-31607	(S)	I Can See Clearly Now	1972	4.00	10.00

(Although uncredited, Nash is backed by Bob Marley & The Wailers.)
—Epic albums above have yellow labels.—

Epic KE-31607	(S)	I Can See Clearly Now	1973	1.00	5.00
Epic KE-32158	(S)	My Merry-Go-Round	1973	1.00	5.00
Epic KE-32828	(S)	Celebrate Life	1974	1.00	5.00

—Epic albums above have orange labels.—

NASH THE SLASH

Ralph NS-8409	(S)	Million Year Picnic (Clear vinyl)	1984	8.00	20.00

NASHVILLE TEENS, THE

London LL-3407	(M)	Tobacco Road	1964	40.00	100.00
London PS-407	(E)	Tobacco Road	1964	30.00	75.00

NATURAL FOUR, THE

Curtom CRT-8600	(S)	The Natural Four	1974	4.00	10.00

NATURAL GAS

Firebird 18	(S)	Natural Gas	1970	5.00	12.00

NATURAL GAS
This Gas features Joey Molland of Badfinger.

Private Stock PS-2011	(S)	Natural Gas	1976	4.00	10.00

NAVARRO, TONY, & THE SUNDIALERS

Urania UR-900	(M)	Twist Around The Town	1961	40.00	100.00
Urania US-5900	(S)	Twist Around The Town	1961	80.00	200.00

NAVASOTA

ABC-Paramount X-757	(S)	Rootin'	1972	6.00	15.00

NAZZ
Nazz features Todd Rundgren. Poorly reproduced counterfeits of each of the SGC albums exist.

SGC SD-5001	(S)	Nazz	1968	12.00	30.00
SGC 5002	(M)	Nazz Nazz (White label promo on red vinyl)	1969	30.00	75.00
SGC SD-5002	(S)	Nazz Nazz (Red vinyl)	1969	12.00	30.00

—SGC albums above have orange & red label with a blue logo.—

Label & Catalog #		Title	Year	VG+	NM
SGC SD-5002	(S)	Nazz Nazz (Red vinyl)	1969	12.00	30.00
SGC SD-5002	(S)	Nazz Nazz (Black vinyl)	1970	30.00	75.00
SGC SD-5004	(S)	Nazz III	1971	12.00	30.00
		—SGC albums above have orange & red label with a purple logo.—			
Rhino RNLP-109	(S)	Nazz	1984	1.00	5.00
Rhino RNLP-110	(S)	Nazz Nazz (Red vinyl)	1984	1.00	5.00
Rhino RNLP-111	(S)	Nazz III	1984	1.00	5.00
Rhino RNLP-116	(S)	The Best Of The Nazz	1984	1.00	5.00
NEGATIVELAND					
SST 133	(S)	Escape From Noise	1987	4.00	10.00
NEIGHBORHOOD					
Big Tree 2001	(S)	Debut	1970	5.00	12.00
NEIGHB'RHOOD CHILDR'N, THE					
Acta 8005	(M)	The Neighb'rhood Childr'n	1968	30.00	75.00
Acta 38005	(S)	The Neighb'rhood Childr'n	1968	40.00	100.00
NEIL, FRED					
Refer to Martin & Neil.					
Elektra EKL-293	(M)	Bleecker And MacDougal	1965	12.00	30.00
Elektra EKS-7293	(S)	Bleecker And MacDougal	1965	16.00	40.00
		—Elektra albums above have gold labels.—			
Elektra EKS-7293	(S)	Bleecker And MacDougal	1969	6.00	15.00
		—Elektra albums above have red labels.—			
Capitol T-2665	(M)	Fred Neil	1966	8.00	20.00
Capitol ST-2665	(S)	Fred Neil	1966	10.00	25.00
		(Original covers of ST-2665 have a color photo of Neil on the back.)			
Capitol ST-2665	(S)	Fred Neil	1967	8.00	20.00
		(Later covers have a black & white photo on the back.)			
Capitol T-2862	(M)	Fred Neil: Sessions	1967	8.00	20.00
Capitol ST-2862	(S)	Fred Neil: Sessions	1967	10.00	25.00
		—Capitol albums above have black "rainbow" labels.—			
Capitol ST-294	(S)	Everybody's Talkin'	1969	4.00	10.00
		(Capitol 274 is a reissue of 2665.)			
		—Capitol albums above have green labels.—			
Elektra EKS-74073	(S)	Little Bit Of Rain	1970	6.00	15.00
		(Elektra 74073 is a reissue of 7293.)			
NELSON, LADY, & THE LORDS					
Dunhill 50028	(S)	Picadilly Pickle	1968	5.00	12.00
NELSON, RICKY [RICK NELSON]					
Rick can also be found on the Decca soundtrack "On The Flip Side." Refer to Appletree Theatre.					
Verve V-2083	(M)	Teen Time	1957	100.00	250.00
		(This is actually a various artists album containing Ricky's first three sides for Verve but, as it gets its hefty value from the great shot of Ricky on the cover, it is listed here.)			
Imperial LP-9048	(M)	Ricky	1957	40.00	100.00
Imperial LP-9050	(M)	Ricky Nelson	1958	40.00	100.00
Imperial LP-9061	(M)	Ricky Sings Again	1959	40.00	100.00
Imperial LP-12090	(S)	Ricky Sings Again	1962	60.00	150.00
Imperial LP-9082	(M)	Songs By Ricky	1959	30.00	75.00
Imperial LP-12030	(S)	Songs By Ricky	1959	80.00	200.00
Imperial LP-9122	(M)	More Songs By Ricky	1960	30.00	75.00
Imperial LP-12059	(DJ)	More Songs By Ricky (Blue vinyl)	1960	660.00	1,000.00
		(Promo copies were issued with a fold-open poster, priced separately below)			
Imperial LP-12059		More Songs By Ricky Bonus Poster	1960	100.00	200.00
Imperial LP-12059	(S)	More Songs By Ricky	1960	40.00	100.00
Imperial LP-9152	(M)	Rick Is 21	1961	16.00	40.00
Imperial LP-12071	(S)	Rick Is 21	1961	40.00	100.00
Imperial LP-9167	(M)	Album Seven By Rick	1962	16.00	40.00
Imperial LP-12082	(S)	Album Seven By Rick	1962	40.00	100.00
Imperial LP-9218	(M)	Best Sellers	1963	16.00	40.00
Imperial LP-9223	(M)	It's Up To You	1963	16.00	40.00
Imperial LP-9232	(M)	Million Sellers	1963	16.00	40.00
Imperial LP-9244	(M)	A Long Vacation	1963	16.00	40.00
Imperial LP-9251	(M)	Rick Nelson Sings For You	1964	16.00	40.00
Imperial LP-12251	(E)	Rick Nelson Sings For You	1964	10.00	25.00
		—Imperial mono albums above have black labels with stars on top; stereo albums have black labels with silver print.—			
Imperial LP-9048	(M)	Ricky	1964	10.00	25.00
Imperial LP-9050	(M)	Ricky Nelson	1964	10.00	25.00
Imperial LP-9061	(M)	Ricky Sings Again	1964	10.00	25.00
Imperial LP-12090	(M)	Ricky Sings Again	1964	16.00	40.00
Imperial LP-9082	(M)	Songs By Ricky	1964	10.00	25.00
Imperial LP-12030	(S)	Songs By Ricky	1964	16.00	40.00

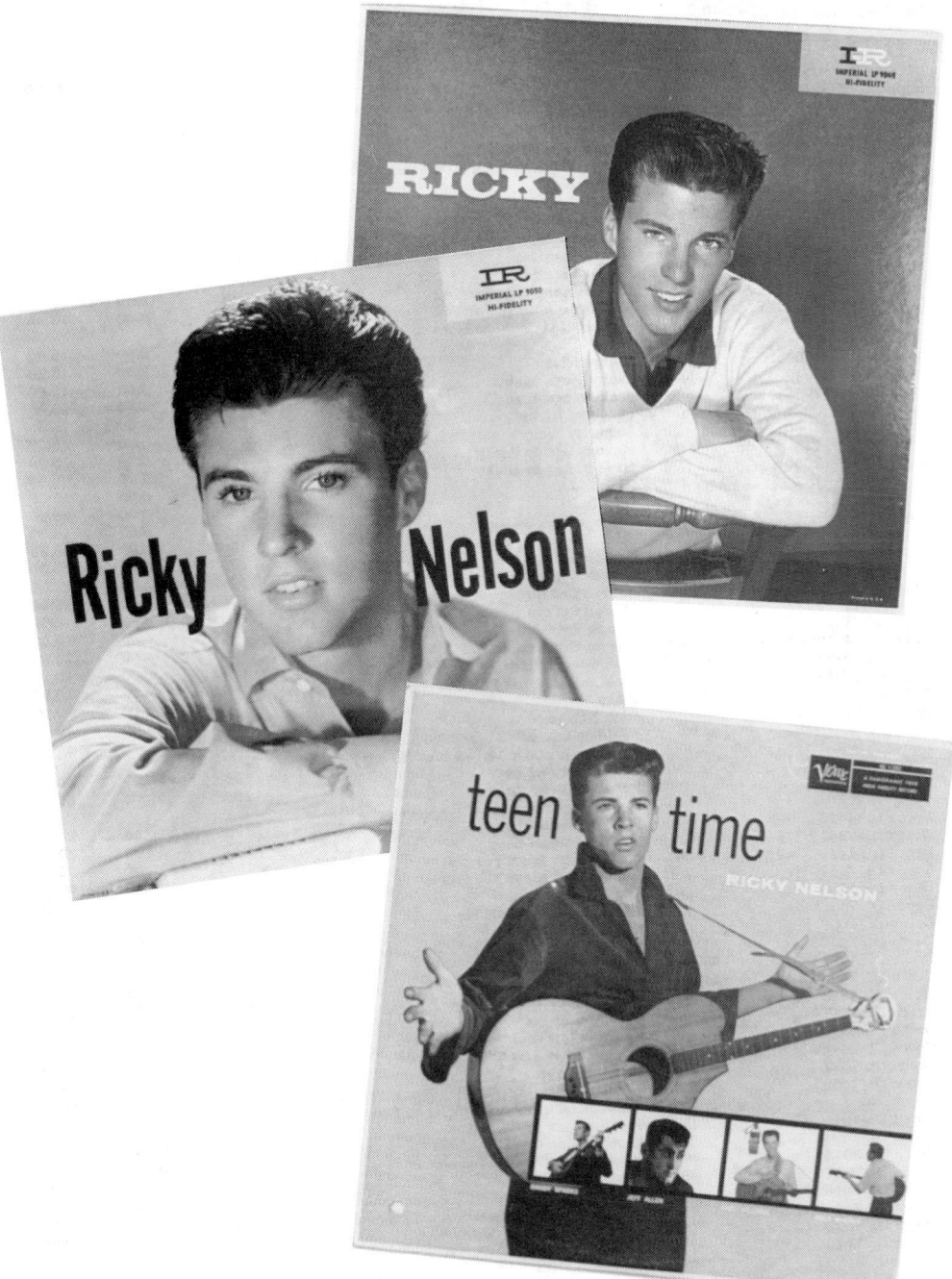

Ricky's first album ain't his album. That is, while almost everyone refers to this as his first, Teen Time is a various artists album that features the kid on the cover (if he's supposed to look appealing, he looks like he's appealing for help) and the three sides he cut for Verve prior to moving to Imperial. Note the shot of Randy Sparks in the box on the extreme left.

Label & Catalog #		Title	Year	VG+	NM
Imperial LP-9122	(M)	More Songs By Ricky	1964	10.00	25.00
Imperial LP-12059	(S)	More Songs By Ricky	1964	16.00	40.00
Imperial LP-9152	(M)	Rick Is 21	1964	10.00	25.00
Imperial LP-12071	(S)	Rick Is 21	1964	16.00	40.00
Imperial LP-9167	(M)	Album Seven By Rick	1964	10.00	25.00
Imperial LP-12082	(S)	Album Seven By Rick	1964	16.00	40.00
Imperial LP-9218	(M)	Best Sellers	1964	10.00	25.00
Imperial LP-12218	(E)	Best Sellers	1964	6.00	15.00
Imperial LP-9232	(M)	Million Sellers	1964	10.00	25.00
Imperial LP-12232	(E)	Million Sellers	1964	6.00	15.00
Imperial LP-9244	(M)	A Long Vacation	1964	10.00	25.00
Imperial LP-12244	(E)	A Long Vacation	1964	6.00	15.00
Imperial LP-9251	(M)	Rick Nelson Sings For You	1964	10.00	25.00
Imperial LP-12251	(E)	Rick Nelson Sings For You	1964	6.00	15.00
		—Imperial albums above have black, white & pink labels.—			
Imperial LP-9048	(M)	Ricky	1966	6.00	15.00
Imperial LP-9050	(M)	Ricky Nelson	1966	6.00	15.00
Imperial LP-9061	(M)	Ricky Sings Again	1966	6.00	15.00
Imperial LP-12090	(M)	Ricky Sings Again	1966	10.00	25.00
Imperial LP-9082	(M)	Songs By Ricky	1966	6.00	15.00
Imperial LP-12030	(S)	Songs By Ricky	1966	10.00	25.00
Imperial LP-9122	(M)	More Songs By Ricky	1966	6.00	15.00
Imperial LP-12059	(S)	More Songs By Ricky	1966	10.00	25.00
Imperial LP-9152	(M)	Rick Is 21	1966	6.00	15.00
Imperial LP-12071	(S)	Rick Is 21	1966	10.00	25.00
Imperial LP-9167	(M)	Album Seven By Rick	1966	6.00	15.00
Imperial LP-12082	(S)	Album Seven By Rick	1966	10.00	25.00
Imperial LP-9218	(M)	Best Sellers	1966	6.00	15.00
Imperial LP-12218	(E)	Best Sellers	1966	4.00	10.00
Imperial LP-9232	(M)	Million Sellers	1966	6.00	15.00
Imperial LP-12232	(E)	Million Sellers	1966	4.00	10.00
Imperial LP-9244	(M)	A Long Vacation	1966	6.00	15.00
Imperial LP-12244	(E)	A Long Vacation	1966	4.00	10.00
Imperial LP-9251	(M)	Rick Nelson Sings For You	1966	6.00	15.00
Imperial LP-12251	(E)	Rick Nelson Sings For You	1966	4.00	10.00
Imperial LP-12392	(E)	Ricky	1966	4.00	10.00
Imperial LP-12393	(E)	Rick Nelson	1966	4.00	10.00
		(Imperial 12392 and 12393 are reissues of 9048 and 9050.)			
		—Imperial albums above have black, white & green labels.—			
Decca DL-4419	(M)	For Your Sweet Love	1963	16.00	40.00
Decca DL-74419	(S)	For Your Sweet Love	1963	20.00	50.00
		—Decca albums above have black & silver labels.—			
Decca DL-4419	(M)	For Your Sweet Love	1963	10.00	25.00
Decca DL-74419	(S)	For Your Sweet Love	1963	12.00	30.00
Decca DL-4479	(M)	Rick Nelson Sings For You	1963	12.00	30.00
Decca DL-74479	(S)	Rick Nelson Sings For You	1963	16.00	40.00
Decca DL-4559	(M)	The Very Thought Of You	1964	12.00	30.00
Decca DL-74559	(S)	The Very Thought Of You	1964	16.00	40.00
Decca DL-4608	(M)	Spotlight On Rick	1964	12.00	30.00
Decca DL-74608	(S)	Spotlight On Rick	1964	16.00	40.00
Decca DL-4660	(M)	Best Always	1965	12.00	30.00
Decca DL-74660	(S)	Best Always	1965	16.00	40.00
Decca DL-4678	(M)	Love And Kisses	1965	12.00	30.00
Decca DL-74678	(S)	Love And Kisses	1965	16.00	40.00
Decca DL-4779	(M)	Bright Lights And Country Music	1966	8.00	20.00
Decca DL-74779	(S)	Bright Lights And Country Music	1966	10.00	25.00
Decca DL-4827	(M)	Country Fever	1967	8.00	20.00
Decca DL-74827	(S)	Country Fever	1967	10.00	25.00
		—Decca albums above have black labels with "Mfrd by Decca" beneath the rainbow.—			
Decca DL-4944	(M)	Another Side Of Rick	1967	8.00	20.00
Decca DL-74944	(S)	Another Side Of Rick	1967	10.00	25.00
Decca DL-5014	(M)	Perspective (White label promo)	1968	20.00	50.00
Decca DL-75014	(S)	Perspective	1968	14.00	35.00
Decca DL-75162	(S)	Rick Nelson In Concert (Gatefold cover)	1970	8.00	20.00
Decca DL-75162	(S)	Rick Nelson In Concert (Standard cover)	197?	4.00	10.00
Decca DL-75236	(S)	Rick Sings Nelson (With poster)	1970	8.00	20.00
Decca DL-75236	(S)	Rick Sings Nelson (Without poster)	1970	6.00	15.00
Decca DL-75297	(S)	Rudy The Fifth	1971	6.00	15.00
Decca DL-75391	(S)	Garden Party	1972	4.00	10.00
Sunset SUM-1118	(M)	Ricky Nelson	1966	6.00	15.00
Sunset SUS-5118	(P)	Ricky Nelson	1966	8.00	20.00
Sunset SUS-5205	(S)	I Need You	1968	6.00	15.00
United Arts. UAS-960	(M)	Legendary Masters (2 LPs, Brown label)	1971	12.00	30.00
United Arts. UAS-960	(M)	Legendary Masters (2 LPs, Gold label)	197?	6.00	15.00
MCA 2-4004	(S)	Rick Nelson Country (2 LPs)	1973	6.00	15.00
		(MCA collects Decca 74827 and 74779.)			
MCA 383	(S)	Windfall	1974	4.00	10.00
Capitol SOO-12109	(S)	Playing To Win	197?	4.00	10.00

Label & Catalog #		Title	Year	VG+	NM
Epic KE-34420	(S)	Intakes	1977	4.00	10.00
Epic 3E-36868	(S)	Four You *(10" LP)*	1981	4.00	10.00
MCA 1517	(S)	The Decca Years	1982	1.20	6.00

NELSON, SANDY
Drummer Sandy Nelson can also be found on the RCA soundtrack "Wild On The Beach."

Imperial LP-9105	(M)	Sandy Nelson Plays Teen Beat	1960	12.00	30.00
Imperial LP-12044	(S)	Sandy Nelson Plays Teen Beat	1962	16.00	40.00
Imperial LP-9136	(M)	He's A Drummer Boy	1962	16.00	40.00
Imperial LP-12089	(E)	He's A Drummer Boy	1962	12.00	30.00
Imperial LP-9159	(M)	Let There Be Drums	1962	16.00	40.00
Imperial LP-12080	(E)	Let There Be Drums	1962	12.00	30.00
Imperial LP-9168	(M)	Drums Are My Beat!	1962	8.00	20.00
Imperial LP-12083	(S)	Drums Are My Beat!	196?	12.00	30.00
Imperial LP-9189	(M)	Drummin' Up A Storm	1962	8.00	20.00
Imperial LP-12189	(S)	Drummin' Up A Storm	1962	10.00	25.00
Imperial LP-9202	(M)	Golden Hits	1962	8.00	20.00
Imperial LP-12202	(P)	Golden Hits	1962	10.00	25.00
Imperial LP-9203	(M)	Country Style	1962	8.00	20.00
Imperial LP-12203	(S)	Country Style	1962	10.00	25.00
Imperial LP-9203	(M)	On The Wild Side	1966	6.00	15.00
Imperial LP-12203	(S)	On The Wild Side	1966	8.00	20.00
		("On The Wild Side" is a repackage of "Country Style"			
		with the original records in new jackets.)			
Imperial LP-9204	(M)	...And Then There Were Drums	1962	6.00	15.00
Imperial LP-12204	(S)	...And Then There Were Drums	1962	8.00	20.00
Imperial LP-9215	(M)	Teenage House Party	1962	8.00	20.00
Imperial LP-12215	(S)	Teenage House Party	1962	10.00	25.00
Imperial LP-9224	(M)	The Best Of The Beats	1963	6.00	15.00
Imperial LP-12224	(S)	The Best Of The Beats	1963	8.00	20.00
Imperial LP-9237	(M)	Beat That Drum	1963	6.00	15.00
Imperial LP-12237	(S)	Beat That Drum	1963	8.00	20.00
Imperial LP-9249	(M)	Sandy Nelson Plays	1963	6.00	15.00
Imperial LP-12249	(S)	Sandy Nelson Plays	1963	8.00	20.00
Imperial LP-9258	(M)	Be True To Your School	1963	6.00	15.00
Imperial LP-12258	(S)	Be True To Your School	1963	8.00	20.00
		—Imperial mono albums above have black labels with stars on top;			
		stereo albums have black labels with silver print.—			
Imperial LP-9272	(M)	Live! In Las Vegas	1964	8.00	20.00
Imperial LP-12272	(E)	Live! In Las Vegas	1964	6.00	15.00
Imperial LP-9278	(M)	Teen Beat '65	1965	5.00	12.00
Imperial LP-12278	(S)	Teen Beat '65	1965	6.00	15.00
Imperial LP-9283	(M)	Drum Discotheque	1965	5.00	12.00
Imperial LP-12283	(S)	Drum Discotheque	1965	6.00	15.00
Imperial LP-9287	(M)	Drums A Go-Go	1965	5.00	12.00
Imperial LP-12287	(S)	Drums A Go-Go	1965	6.00	15.00
Imperial LP-9298	(M)	Boss Beat	1966	5.00	12.00
Imperial LP-12298	(S)	Boss Beat	1966	6.00	15.00
Imperial LP-9305	(M)	"In" Beat	1966	5.00	12.00
Imperial LP-12305	(S)	"In" Beat	1966	6.00	15.00
Imperial LP-9314	(M)	Super Drums	1966	5.00	12.00
Imperial LP-12314	(S)	Super Drums	1966	6.00	15.00
		—Imperial albums above have black, white & pink labels.—			
Imperial LP-9329	(M)	Beat That #!!@* Drum	1966	5.00	12.00
Imperial LP-12329	(S)	Beat That #!!@* Drum	1966	6.00	15.00
Imperial LP-9340	(M)	Cheetah Beat	1967	5.00	12.00
Imperial LP-12340	(S)	Cheetah Beat	1967	6.00	15.00
Imperial LP-9345	(M)	The Beat Goes On	1967	5.00	12.00
Imperial LP-12345	(S)	The Beat Goes On	1967	6.00	15.00
Imperial LP-9362	(M)	Soul Drums	1967	5.00	12.00
Imperial LP-12362	(S)	Soul Drums	1967	6.00	15.00
Imperial LP-12367	(S)	Boogaloo Beat	1968	5.00	12.00
Imperial LP-12400	(S)	Rock And Roll Revival	1968	5.00	12.00
Imperial LP-12424	(S)	Rebirth Of The Beat	1969	5.00	12.00
Imperial LP-12439	(S)	Manhattan Spiritual	1969	5.00	12.00
Imperial LP-12451	(S)	Groovy	1969	5.00	12.00
		—Imperial albums above have black, white & green labels.—			
Sunset SUM-1114	(M)	Walking Beat	1966	4.00	10.00
Sunset SUS-5114	(S)	Walking Beat	1966	5.00	12.00
Sunset SUM-1166	(M)	Teen Drums	1967	4.00	10.00
Sunset SUS-5166	(S)	Teen Drums	1967	5.00	12.00
Sunset SUS-5224	(S)	And There Were Drums *(Drums & More Drums)*	1968	4.00	10.00
Sunset SUS-5261	(S)	Heavy Drums	1969	4.00	10.00
Sunset SUS-5291	(S)	Sandy Nelson Plays Fats Domino Hits	1970	4.00	10.00

NELSON, TRACY
Ms. Nelson was also a member of Mother Earth.

Prestige PRLP-7393	(M)	Deep Are The Roots	1965	10.00	25.00

Label & Catalog #		Title	Year	VG+	NM
Prestige PRST-7393	(S)	Deep Are The Roots	1965	12.00	30.00
Prestige PRST-7726	(S)	Deep Are The Roots	1969	6.00	15.00
		(Prestige 7726 is a reissue of 7393.)			
Columbia KC-31759	(S)	Poor Man's Paradise	1973	3.20	8.00
Atlantic SD-7310	(S)	Tracy Nelson	1974	1.20	6.00
MCA 494	(S)	Sweet Soul Music	1975	1.20	6.00
Flying Fish FF-052	(S)	Homemade Songs	1978	1.00	5.00
Flying Fish 209	(S)	Come See About Me	1980	1.00	5.00
NEMETZ, SHELLY					
Fantasy F-8424	(S)	Shelly Nemetz	1972	3.20	8.00
NEON					
Paramount PAS-5024	(S)	Neon	1971	3.20	8.00
NEON PHILHARMONIC					
Warner Bros. WS-1769	(S)	The Moth Confesses	1969	10.00	25.00
Warner Bros. WS-1804	(S)	Neon Philharmonic	1969	6.00	15.00
NEP-TUNES, THE					
Family FLP-152	(M)	Surfer's Holiday	1963	80.00	200.00
Family SFLP-552	(S)	Surfer's Holiday	1963	150.00	300.00
NESMITH, MICHAEL					

Nesmith was a member of The Monkees. Refer to Wichita Train Whistle.

Label & Catalog #		Title	Year	VG+	NM
RCA Victor LSP-4371	(S)	Magnetic South	1970	10.00	25.00
RCA Victor LSP-4415	(S)	Loose Salute	1970	8.00	20.00
RCA Victor LSP-4497	(S)	Nevada Fighter	1971	8.00	20.00
RCA Victor LSP-4563	(S)	Tantamount To Treason	1971	8.00	20.00
RCA Victor LSP-4695	(S)	And The Hits Just Keep On Comin'	1972	8.00	20.00
Pacific Arts 7-101	(S)	The Prison (Box with booklet)	1978	16.00	40.00
Pacific Arts 7-101	(S)	The Prison (Standard cover)	1978	4.00	10.00
Pacific Arts 7-106	(S)	Michael Nesmith Compilation	1978	4.00	10.00
Pacific Arts 7-107	(S)	From A Radio Engine To The Photon Wing	1978	4.00	10.00
Pacific Arts 7-116	(S)	And The Hits Just Keep On Comin'	1978	4.00	10.00
Pacific Arts 7-117	(S)	Pretty Much Your Standard Ranch Stash	1978	4.00	10.00
Pacific Arts 7-118	(S)	Live At The Palais	1978	4.00	10.00
Pacific Arts 7-130	(S)	Infinite Rider On The Big Dogma	1979	4.00	10.00
Pacific Arts	(DJ)	The Michael Nesmith Radio Special	1979	16.00	40.00
NEU					
Billingsgate 1001	(S)	Neu	1973	5.00	12.00
Capitol ST-11423	(S)	Neu '75	1975	5.00	12.00
NEVILLE, AARON					
Par-Lo LP-1	(M)	Tell It Like It Is	1967	30.00	75.00
Par-Lo LP-1	(S)	Tell It Like It Is	1967	80.00	200.00
Minit LP-40007	(M)	Like It 'Tis	1967	16.00	40.00
Minit LP-24007	(E)	Like It 'Tis	1967	12.00	30.00
		(Minit 40007 is a reissue of Par-Lo 1.)			
NEW BIRTH					
RCA Victor APL1-0285	(S)	It's Been A Long Time	1973	1.00	5.00
RCA Victor APD1-0285	(Q)	It's Been A Long Time	1974	4.00	10.00
NEW CACTUS BAND, THE					
Atco SD-36-7017	(S)	Son Of Cactus	1973	1.20	6.00
NEW CENSATION, THE					
Pride 6012	(S)	New Censation	1974	3.20	8.00
NEW COLONY SIX, THE					
Sentar LP-101	(M)	Breakthrough	1966	250.00	500.00
Sentar ST-3001	(M)	Colonization	1967	12.00	30.00
Sentar SST-3001	(S)	Colonization	1967	16.00	40.00
Mercury SR-61165	(S)	Revelations	1968	6.00	15.00
Mercury SR-61228	(S)	Attacking A Straw Man	1969	6.00	15.00
NEW DIMENSIONS, THE					
Sutton SU-331	(M)	Deuces And Eights	1963	30.00	75.00
Sutton SSU-331	(S)	Deuces And Eights	1963	40.00	100.00
Sutton SU-332	(M)	Surf 'N' Bongos	1963	14.00	35.00
Sutton SSU-332	(S)	Surf 'N' Bongos	1963	20.00	50.00
Sutton SU-336	(M)	Soul Surf	1964	14.00	35.00
Sutton SSU-336	(S)	Soul Surf	1964	20.00	50.00
NEW DIRECTION					
Neptune 200	(S)	New Direction	1970	3.20	8.00

Label & Catalog #		Title	Year	VG+	NM
NEW HEAVENLY BLUE					
RCA Victor LSP-4439	(S)	Educated Homegrown	1970	4.00	10.00
Atlantic SD-7247	(S)	New Heavenly Blue	1972	3.20	8.00
NEW HOPE					
Jamie LPS-3034	(S)	To Understand Is To Love	1970	8.00	20.00
Light 5590	(S)	Good Fallofus	1972	4.00	10.00
NEW LIFE					
Amaret 5004	(S)	Sidehackers	1970	4.00	10.00
NEW LONDON RHYTHM 'N BLUES BAND, THE					
Vocalion VL-73880	(S)	Soul Cookin'	1969	4.00	10.00
NEW MIX, THE					
United Arts. UAS-6678	(S)	The New Mix	1968	4.00	10.00
NEW ORDER					
New Order is made up of surviving members of Joy Division.					
Rough Trade FACT-50	(S)	Movement (Purple tinted vinyl)	1981	16.00	40.00
Rough Trade FACT-50	(S)	Movement (Red tinted vinyl)	1981	8.00	20.00
Rough Trade FACT-12	(S)	Power, Corruption And Lies	1983	5.00	12.00
Qwest	(S)	Power, Corruption And Lies	198?	1.20	6.00
NEW RIDERS OF THE PURPLE SAGE, THE					
Columbia KC-30888	(S)	New Riders Of The Purple Sage	1971	1.20	6.00
Columbia KC-31284	(S)	Powerglide	1972	1.20	6.00
Columbia KC-31930	(S)	Gypsy Cowboy	1972	1.20	6.00
Columbia KC-32450	(S)	Adventures Of Panama Red	1973	1.20	6.00
Columbia CQ-32450	(Q)	Adventures Of Panama Red	1974	6.00	15.00
Columbia PC-32870	(S)	Home, Home On The Road	1974	1.00	5.00
Columbia PC-33145	(S)	Brujo	1974	1.00	5.00
MCA 2307	(S)	Marin County Line	1977	1.00	5.00
A&M SP-4818	(S)	Feelin' All Right	1981	1.00	5.00
Relix RRLP-2024	(S)	Before Time Began	1986	.80	4.00
Relix RRLP-2025	(S)	Vintage NRPS	1987	.80	4.00
Relix 2025	(S)	Vintage NRPS (Picture disc)	1987	4.00	10.00
NEW ROTARY CONNECTION, THE: *Refer to* **THE ROTARY CONNECTION**					
NEW SEEKERS, THE					
The New Seekers were formed out of the ashes of The Seekers by original member Keith Potger.					
Elektra EKS-74088	(S)	Beautiful People	1971	3.20	8.00
Elektra EKS-74108	(S)	New Colors	1971	3.20	8.00
Elektra EKS-74115	(S)	We'd Like To Teach The World To Sing	1972	4.00	10.00
		(Elektra 74115 is a repackage of 74108 with the hit single added as the title tune.)			
Elektra EKS-75034	(S)	Circles	1972	3.20	8.00
Elektra EKS-75051	(S)	The Best Of The New Seekers	1973	3.20	8.00
Elektra EQ-75051	(Q)	The Best Of The New Seekers	1973	6.00	15.00
Verve V6-5090	(S)	Come Softly To Me	1972	3.20	8.00
Verve V6-5095	(S)	The History Of The New Seekers	1973	3.20	8.00
NEW SOCIETY, THE					
RCA Victor LPM-3676	(M)	The Barock Sound Of The New Society	1966	5.00	12.00
RCA Victor LSP-3676	(S)	The Barock Sound Of The New Society	1966	6.00	15.00
NEW VAUDEVILLE BAND, THE					
The NVB were session musicians having a lark. They can be found on the RCA soundtrack "The Bliss Of Mrs Blossom."					
Fontana MGF-27560	(M)	Winchester Cathedral	1966	6.00	15.00
Fontana SRF-67560	(S)	Winchester Cathedral	1966	6.00	15.00
		(Original pressings of Fontana 2/67560 have "Whatever Happened To Phyllis Puke" and "Diana Goodbye," while the back cover features three paragraphs of liner notes. "Winchester Cathedral," "Lili Marlene," "A Nightingale Sang In Berkeley Square," "Your Love Ain't What It Used To Be" and "That's All For Now, Sugar Baby" are rechanneled on this version and the repressing below.)			
Fontana MGF-27560	(M)	Winchester Cathedral	1966	4.00	10.00
Fontana SRF-67560	(S)	Winchester Cathedral	1966	4.00	10.00
		(Later pressings have "Oh, Donna Clara." The back cover features a single paragraph of liner notes.)			
Fontana MGF-27688	(M)	The New Vaudeville Band On Tour	1967	4.00	10.00
Fontana SRF-67588	(P)	The New Vaudeville Band On Tour	1967	4.00	10.00
		("Thoroughly Modern Millie," "Peek-A-Boo," "Shirl;," "Sadie Moonshine" and "Amy" are rechanneled on this album.)			
NEW WAVE, THE					
Canterbury CLPS-1501	(S)	The New Wave	1967	10.00	25.00

Label & Catalog #		Title	Year	VG+	NM

NEW YORK DOLLS, THE
Both Dolls albums were originally issued with custom dolls labels and inner sleeves.

Mercury SRM-1-675	(S)	New York Dolls	1973	20.00	50.00
Mercury SRM-1-1001	(S)	Too Much, Too Soon	1974	20.00	50.00
		—Mercury albums above have custom "doll" labels and inner sleeves.—			
Mercury SRM-1-675	(S)	New York Dolls	197?	6.00	15.00
Mercury SRM-1-1001	(S)	Too Much, Too Soon	197?	6.00	15.00

NEW YORK ROCK & ROLL ENSEMBLE, THE [THE NEW YORK ROCK ENSEMBLE]
The Ensemble features Michael Kamen. Refer to Cream / The New York Rock & Roll Ensemble.

Atco SD-33-240	(S)	New York Rock & Roll Ensemble	1968	6.00	15.00
Atco SD-33-294	(S)	Faithful Friends	1969	6.00	15.00
Atco SD-33-312	(S)	Reflections	1970	6.00	15.00
Columbia KC-30033	(S)	Roll Over	1970	5.00	12.00
Columbia KC-31317	(S)	Freedomburger	1972	5.00	12.00

NEWBEATS, THE
Larry Henley, Dean Mathis and Mark Mathis.

Hickory LP-120	(M)	Bread And Butter	1964	40.00	100.00
Hickory LPS-120	(E)	Bread And Butter	1964	60.00	150.00
		("Everything's Alright" and "Pink Dolly Rue" are in stereo.)			
Hickory T-90701	(M)	Bread And Butter (Capitol Record Club)	196?	60.00	150.00
Hickory DT-90701	(E)	Bread And Butter (Capitol Record Club)	196?	60.00	150.00
Hickory ST-90701	(S)	Bread And Butter (Capitol Record Club)	196?	150.00	300.00
Hickory LP-122	(M)	Big Beat Sounds By The Newbeats	1965	30.00	75.00
Hickory LPS-122	(S)	Big Beat Sounds By The Newbeats	1965	40.00	100.00
Hickory LP-128	(M)	Run Baby Run	1965	30.00	75.00
Hickory LPS-128	(S)	Run Baby Run	1965	40.00	100.00

NEWBURY PARK

Cream 9003	(S)	Newbury Park	1971	1.00	5.00

NEWMAN, RANDY

Reprise RS-6286	(S)	Randy Newman	1968	8.00	20.00
		(Original covers of RS-6286 have a collage of a rather staid-looking Mr Newman standing in the clouds.)			
Reprise RS-6286	(S)	Randy Newman	1969	4.00	10.00
		(Later covers have a close-up of Newman's face.)			
Reprise RS-6373	(S)	12 Songs	1970	4.00	10.00
		—Reprise albums above have brown & orange labels with a "W7" and ":r" logos on top.—			
Reprise PRO-484	(DJ)	Randy Newman Live	1970	20.00	50.00
Reprise RS-6459	(S)	Randy Newman Live	1971	1.00	5.00
Reprise MS-2064	(S)	Sail Away (With poster)	1972	4.00	10.00
		(Original covers for MS-2064 do not list the song titles on the back.)			
Reprise MS-2064	(S)	Sail Away (With poster)	1972	1.00	5.00
		(Later covers list the song titles on the back.)			
Reprise MS-2193	(S)	Good Old Boys	1974	1.00	5.00
Reprise MS4-2193	(Q)	Good Old Boys	1974	6.00	15.00
Warner Bros. K-3079	(S)	Little Criminals	1977	1.00	5.00
Warner Bros. HS-3346	(S)	Born Again	1979	1.00	5.00
Warner Bros. 23755	(S)	Trouble In Paradise	1983	1.00	5.00

NEWTON-JOHN, OLIVIA

Uni 73117	(S)	If Not For You	1971	8.00	25.00
MCA 389	(S)	Let Me Be There	1973	1.00	5.00
MCA 411	(S)	If You Love Me, Let Me Know	1974	1.00	5.00
MCA 2133	(S)	Have You Never Been Mellow	1975	1.00	5.00
MCA 2148	(S)	Clearly Love	1975	1.00	5.00
MCA 2186	(S)	Come On Over	1976	1.00	5.00
MCA 2223	(S)	Don't Stop Believin'	1976	1.00	5.00
MCA 2280	(S)	Making A Good Thing Better	1977	1.00	5.00
MCA 3028	(S)	Olivia Newton-John's Greatest Hits	1977	.80	4.00
MCA 3067	(S)	Totally Hot	1978	1.00	5.00
MCA 5229	(S)	Physical	1981	1.00	5.00
MCA 16011	(S)	Physical (Half-speed master)	1981	8.00	25.00
MCA 5347	(S)	Olivia's Greatest Hits, Vol. 2	1982	.80	4.00

NEWTON-JOHN, OLIVIA / ELO

MCA 6100	(S)	Xanadu	1980	.80	4.00

NEWTON-JOHN, OLIVIA / TOM JONES

Entropy TLA-50138	(S)	Super Stars	1982	20.00	50.00

NEXT WORLD

Era E-604	(S)	Symphonic Rock	1973	16.00	40.00

When Olivia Newton-John proffered a pale reading of Bob Dylan's "If Not For You" as her first "hit," was there anyone who could have predicted that within a few years she would be the physical fantasy of a major portion of America's male population? The two albums pictured here illustrate the transformation from cute sex kitten on her Uni debut (top) and her realization as rock goddess on her multi-platinum Physical, shown here (bottom) in its half-speed mastered "Audiophile" version.

Label & Catalog #		Title	Year	VG+	NM

NICE, THE

The Nice features Keith Emerson, later of Emerson, Lake & Palmer.

Label & Catalog #		Title	Year	VG+	NM
Immediate Z12-52004	(S)	Thoughts of Emerlist Davjack	1968	8.00	20.00
Immediate Z12-52020	(S)	Ars Longa Vita Brevis	1969	8.00	20.00
Immediate Z12-52022	(S)	The Nice	1969	6.00	15.00
Immediate Z12-52026	(S)	Nice	1971	6.00	15.00
Mercury SR-61295	(S)	Five Bridges	1970	4.00	10.00
Mercury SR-61324	(S)	Elegy	1971	4.00	10.00
Mercury SRM2-6500	(S)	Keith Emerson With The Nice (2 LPs)	1972	1.20	6.00
		(Mercury 6500 is a reissue of 61295 and 61324.)			
Sire SASH-3710	(S)	The Immediate Story (2 LPs)	1975	4.00	10.00
Columbia P-11633	(S)	Thoughts of Emerlist Davjack	198?	1.00	5.00
Columbia P-11634	(S)	Ars Longa Vita Brevis	198?	1.00	5.00
Columbia P-11635	(S)	Everything As Nice As Mother Makes It	198?	1.00	5.00

NICHOLS, ROGER

A&M SP-4139	(S)	His Small Circle Of Friends	1968	5.00	12.00

NICKEL

Musicor MS-3205	(S)	Nickel	1971	1.20	6.00

NICKEL BAG, THE

Kama Sutra KLPS-8066	(S)	Doing Their Love Thing	1968	10.00	25.00

NICKS, STEVIE

Refer to Buckingham/Nicks; Fleetwood Mac.

Modern 139	(S)	Bella Donna	1981	.80	4.00
Modern 90048	(S)	The Wild Heart	1983	.80	4.00
Modern PR-2881	(DJ)	Reflections From The Other Side Of The Mirror (Interview with script)	1989	16.00	40.00

NICO

Nico originally recorded with The Velvet Underground.

Verve V-5032	(M)	Chelsea Girl	1967	12.00	30.00
Verve V6-5032	(S)	Chelsea Girl	1967	16.00	40.00
Elektra EKS-74029	(S)	The Marble Index	1968	10.00	25.00
Reprise RS-6424	(S)	Desert Shore	1970	8.00	20.00
Island ILPS-9311	(S)	The End	1975	6.00	15.00

NIGHT OWLS, THE

Valmor 79	(M)	Twisting The Oldies	1962	40.00	100.00

NIGHTCRAWLERS, THE

Kapp KL-1520	(M)	The Little Black Egg	1967	30.00	75.00
Kapp KS-3520	(E)	The Little Black Egg	1967	20.00	50.00

NILSSON

Harry Nelson, aka the idiosyncratically brilliant Nilsson, was named by John Lennon as his "favorite American group of 1968!" Harry can also be found on soundtracks for RCA's "The Point," "Skidoo" and "The World's Greatest Lover;" U.A.'s "Midnight Cowboy;" and Boardwalk's "Popeye."

Tower T-5095	(M)	Spotlight On Nilsson	1968	8.00	20.00
Tower ST-5095	(S)	Spotlight On Nilsson	1968	8.00	20.00
Tower DT-5165	(E)	Spotlight On Nilsson	1969	4.00	10.00
		(Tower 5165 is a reissue of 5095.)			
Musicor MS-2505	(S)	Early Times	1970	4.00	10.00
		(The Tower and Musicor albums collect pre-RCA recordings.)			
RCA Victor LPM-3874	(M)	Pandemonium Shadow Show	1967	16.00	40.00
RCA Victor LSP-3874	(S)	Pandemonium Shadow Show	1967	8.00	20.00
RCA Victor	(DJ)	The True One	1967	80.00	200.00
		(Boxed set includes a copy of LPM-3874, two black & white glossy photos, a button, poster, stickers and bios.)			
RCA Victor LPM-3956	(M)	Aerial Ballet	1968	20.00	50.00
RCA Victor LSP-3956	(S)	Aerial Ballet	1968	8.00	20.00
		—RCA albums above have black "Monaural" or "Stereo" labels.—			
RCA Victor LSP-3956	(S)	Aerial Ballet	1969	4.00	10.00
RCA Victor LSP-4197	(S)	Harry	1969	4.00	10.00
RCA Victor LSP-4289	(S)	Nilsson Sings Newman	1970	6.00	15.00
		—RCA albums above have orange labels on non-flexible vinyl.—			
RCA Victor LSP-4197	(S)	Harry	1971	1.00	5.00
RCA Victor LSP-4289	(S)	Nilsson Sings Newman	1971	1.00	5.00
RCA Victor LSP-4543	(S)	Aerial Pandemonium Ballet	1971	3.20	8.00
		(RCA 4548 is a compilation of remixed tracks from 3874 and 3956 with additional vocals.)			
RCA Victor LSP-4515	(S)	Nilsson Schmilsson	1971	3.20	8.00
RCA Victor LSP-4717	(S)	Son Of Schmilsson	1972	3.20	8.00
RCA Victor APL1-0097	(S)	A Little Touch Of Schmilsson In The Night	1973	3.20	8.00
RCA SPS-33-567	(DJ)	Scatalogue (Sampler with insert)	1974	60.00	150.00
		(Bootlegs titled "Scatalogue" contain unreleased tracks.)			

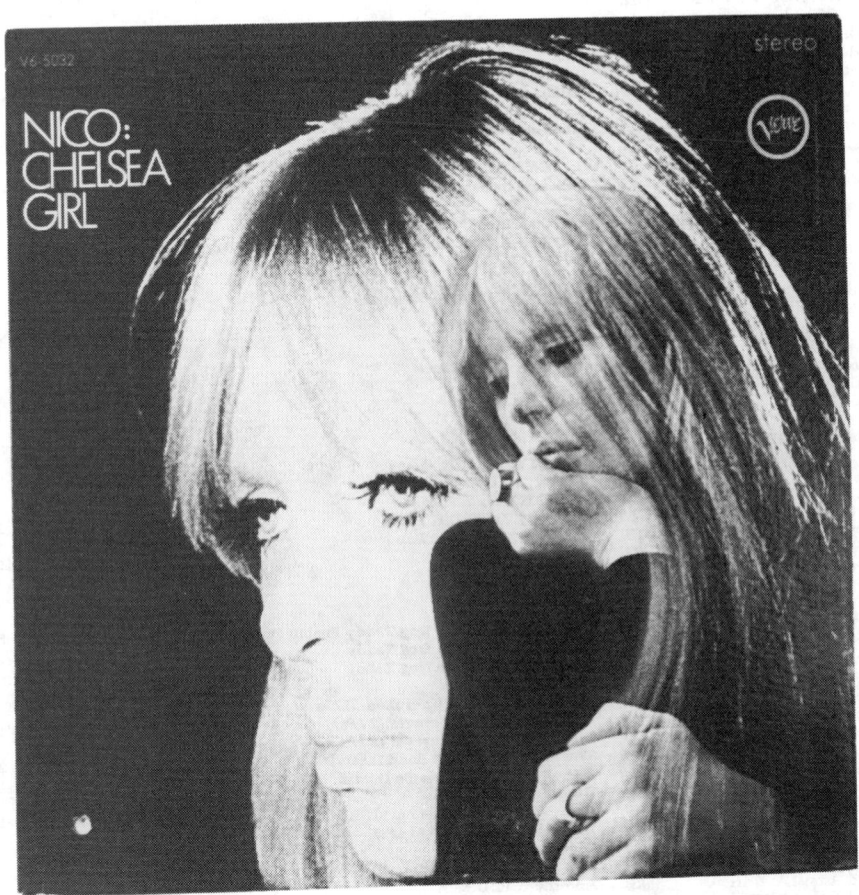

The extraordinarily lovely Nico first attracted attention (outside of the New York circle in which she was a local, if German-born, legend) as the vocalist on The Velvet Underground's first album. This, her solo debut, offers her as a sultry-throated successor to Marlene Dietrich. The cover photo accurately captures the mood of her world-weary, ever-jaded approach to songs.

Label & Catalog #		Title	Year	VG+	NM
Rapple ABL1-0220	(S)	Son Of Dracula	1974	3.20	8.00
RCA Victor APD1-0319	(Q)	Nilsson Schmilsson	1974	6.00	15.00
RCA Victor CPL1-0570	(S)	Pussy Cats	1974	4.00	10.00
RCA Victor APD1-0570	(Q)	Pussy Cats	1974	8.00	20.00
		(RCA 0580 was produced by and features John Lennon.)			
RCA Victor APL1-0817	(S)	Duit On Mon Dei	1975	1.00	5.00
RCA Victor APD1-0817	(Q)	Duit On Mon Dei	1975	6.00	15.00
		—RCA albums above have orange labels.—			
RCA Victor APL1-1031	(S)	Sandman	1976	1.00	5.00
RCA Victor APD1-1031	(Q)	Sandman	1976	6.00	15.00
RCA Victor APL1-1119	(S)	That's The Way It Is	1976	1.00	5.00
RCA Victor AFL1-2276	(S)	Knnilssonn	1977	1.00	5.00
RCA Victor AFL1-2798	(S)	Nilsson's Greatest Hits	1978	1.00	5.00
Solo Music 165	(S)	Schmilsson	197?	20.00	50.00
Pickwick SPC-3321	(S)	Rock 'N' Roll	1977	1.00	5.00

1910 FRUITGUM COMPANY, THE
Refer to The Kasenetz-Katz Circus.

Buddah BDS-5010	(S)	Simon Says	1968	6.00	15.00
Buddah BDS-5022	(S)	1, 2, 3 Red Light	1968	6.00	15.00
Buddah BDS-5027	(S)	Goody, Goody Gumdrops	1969	4.00	10.00
Buddah BDS-5036	(S)	Indian Giver	1969	4.00	10.00
Buddah BDS-5043	(S)	Hard Ride	1969	4.00	10.00
Buddah BDS-5057	(S)	Juiciest Fruitgum	1970	6.00	15.00

1910 FRUITGUM COMPANY, THE / THE LEMON PIPERS

Buddah BDS-5015	(S)	Checkmate	1968	4.00	10.00

98% AMERICAN MOM & APPLE PIE 1929 CRASH BAND, THE

L.H.I. 12001	(S)	The 98% American Mom & Apple Pie Crash Band	1967	6.00	15.00

NIRVANA

Bell 6015	(S)	The Story Of Simon Simopath	1968	10.00	25.00
Bell 6024	(S)	All Of Us	1969	10.00	25.00
Metromedia 1018	(S)	Nirvana	1970	10.00	25.00

NIRVANA SITAR & STRING GROUP, THE

Mr. G G-8001	(M)	Sitar & Strings	1968	8.00	20.00
Mr. G GS-8001	(S)	Sitar & Strings	1968	8.00	20.00

NITECAPS, THE

Sire 1-23756	(S)	Go To The Line	1983	1.20	6.00

NITTY GRITTY DIRT BAND, THE [THE DIRT BAND]

Liberty LRP-3501	(M)	The Nitty Gritty Dirt Band	1967	10.00	25.00
Liberty LST-7501	(S)	The Nitty Gritty Dirt Band	1967	12.00	30.00
Liberty LRP-3516	(M)	Ricochet	1967	10.00	25.00
Liberty LST-7516	(S)	Ricochet	1967	12.00	30.00
Liberty LST-7540	(S)	Rare Junk	1968	10.00	25.00
Liberty LST-7611	(S)	Alive	1969	8.00	20.00
Liberty LST-7642	(DJ)	Uncle Charlie & His Dog Teddy Promo Pack	1970	20.00	50.00
Liberty LST-7642	(S)	Uncle Charlie & His Dog Teddy	1970	6.00	15.00
Liberty LTAO-7642	(S)	Uncle Charlie & His Dog Teddy	198?	.80	4.00
United Arts. UAS-5553	(S)	All The Good Times	1971	1.20	6.00
United Arts. UAS-9801	(S)	Will The Circle Be Unbroken (3 LPs)	1972	6.00	15.00
United Arts. LA-184J2	(S)	Stars And Stripes Forever (2 LPs)	1974	4.00	10.00
United Arts. LWB-184	(S)	Stars And Stripes Forever (2 LPs)	198?	1.20	6.00
United Arts. SP-117	(DJ)	The Nitty Gritty Dirt Band Interview	1975	8.00	20.00
United Arts. LA-469	(DJ)	A Programmers Guide To Dream	1975	6.00	15.00
United Arts. LA-469G	(S)	Dream	1975	1.20	6.00
United Arts. LA-670L3	(S)	Dirt, Silver And Gold (3 LPs)	1977	4.00	10.00
United Arts. LKCL-670	(S)	Dirt, Silver And Gold (3 LPs)	198?	1.20	6.00
United Arts. LA-830H	(S)	Chicken Chronicles	1978	3.20	8.00
United Arts. LA-854H	(S)	Dirt Band	1978	3.20	8.00
United Arts. LA-974H	(S)	An American Dream	1979	3.20	8.00
United Arts. LO-974	(S)	An American Dream	198?	.80	4.00
United Arts. LT-1040	(S)	Make A Little Magic	1980	3.20	8.00
United Arts. LW-1106	(S)	Jealousy	1981	3.20	8.00
Liberty 51146	(S)	Let's Go	1983	3.20	8.00
Warner Bros. 25113	(S)	Plain Dirt Fashion	1984	1.20	6.00
Warner Bros. 25304	(S)	Partners, Brothers And Friends	1985	1.20	6.00
Warner Bros. 25382	(S)	Twenty Years Of Dirt— The Best Of The Nitty Gritty Dirt Band	1986	1.20	6.00
Warner Bros. 25573	(S)	Hold On	1987	1.20	6.00
Warner Bros. 25722	(S)	Workin' Band	1988	1.20	6.00
Warner Bros. 25830	(S)	More Great Dirt— The Best Of The Nitty Gritty Dirt Band, Vol. II	1989	1.20	6.00
Universal UVL-2-12500	(S)	Will The Circle Be Unbroken, Vol. 2 (2 LPs)	1989	3.20	8.00

To promote the Nitty Gritty Dirt Band's Uncle Charlie & His Dog Teddy, Liberty assembled this impressive leatherette folio which included an LP, an interview disc, photos, bios, a stack of photocopied press clippings that dated back to the group's origins, etc. Out of this emerged one Top 10 single, "Mr. Bojangles," and a modest selling album. While this package has a certain value to Dirt Band collectors, had such a folio been put together to promote, say, Sgt. Pepper's Lonely Hearts Club Band, it would fetch four figures in any condition! Such is the difference in the nature of collecting between the stars at the top of the heap and those further down.

Label & Catalog #		Title	Year	VG+	NM

NITZSCHE, JACK

Jack Nitzsche was Phil Spector's arranger during the latter's hit-making years. The albums below qualify as easy-listening but are collected almost exclusively by rock'n roll fans.

Reprise R-6101	(M)	The Lonely Surfer	1963	40.00	100.00
Reprise RS-6101	(S)	The Lonely Surfer	1963	80.00	200.00
Reprise R-6115	(M)	Dance To The Hits Of The Beatles	1964	20.00	50.00
Reprise RS-6115	(S)	Dance To The Hits Of The Beatles	1964	30.00	75.00
Reprise R-6200	(M)	Chopin '66	1966	10.00	25.00
Reprise RS-6200	(S)	Chopin '66	1966	12.00	30.00
		—Reprise albums above have pink, gold & green labels.—			
Reprise RS-6101	(S)	The Lonely Surfer	197?	6.00	15.00
Reprise MS-2092	(S)	St. Giles Cripplegate	1972	8.00	20.00
		—Reprise albums above have brown labels.—			

NOAH

Dunhill DSX-50117	(S)	Peaceman's Farm	1972	4.00	10.00

NOBLES, CLIFF, & COMPANY

Phil L.A. Of Soul 4001	(S)	The Horse	1968	24.00	60.00
Moon Shot 601	(S)	Pony The Horse	1969	14.00	35.00

NOLAN, KENNY

20th Century 532	(S)	Kenny Nolan	1976	.80	4.00
Polydor PD1-6151	(S)	Songs Between Us	1977	.80	4.00
Polydor PD1-6166	(S)	I Like Dreamin'	1977	.80	4.00

NOLAND, TERRY

Brunswick BL-54041	(M)	Terry Noland *(With Buddy Holly on guitar)*	1958	300.00	600.00

NOONAN, STEVE

Elektra EKS-74017	(S)	Steve Noonan	1968	6.00	15.00

NOONE, PETER

Mr. Noone was Herman of Herman's Hermits. Refer to the Tremblers.

Johnson ARZ-37369	(S)	One Of The Glory Boys	1982	1.00	5.00

NORMAN, LARRY

Larry was a member of People.

Capitol ST-446	(S)	Upon This Rock	1969	12.00	30.00
Impact HWS-3121	(S)	Upon This Rock	1970	6.00	15.00
		(Impact 3121 is a reissue of Capitol 446.)			
One Way JC-7397	(S)	Street Level	1970	12.00	30.00
One Way JC-4847	(S)	Bootleg *(Gatefold cover)*	1971	16.00	40.00
One Way 2JC-900	(S)	Bootleg *(Regular cover)*	1971	12.00	30.00
Verve V6-5092	(S)	Only Visiting This Planet *(Tri-fold cover)*	1972	12.00	30.00
Verve V6-5092	(S)	Only Visiting This Planet *(Gatefold cover)*	1972	16.00	40.00
MGM SE-4942	(S)	So Long Ago The Garden	1973	16.00	40.00
Solid Rock SRA-2001	(S)	In Another Land	1976	6.00	15.00
"AB" AB-777	(S)	Streams Of White Light Into Darkened Corners	1977	10.00	25.00
Street Level ROCK-888-5	(S)	Only Visiting This Planet *(Gatefold cover)*	1978	6.00	15.00
Street Level ROCK-888-5	(S)	Only Visiting This Planet *(Regular cover)*	1978	4.00	10.00
		(Street Level 888-5 is a reissue of Verve 5092.)			
Solid Rock SRA-2007	(S)	Something New Under The Son	1981	6.00	15.00
Phydeaux BONE-777-6	(S)	Almost So Long Ago The Garden	1981	6.00	15.00
Phydeaux ARF-777-6	(S)	Almost So Long Ago The Garden	1984	5.00	12.00
		(Phydeaux 777-6 is a reissue of MGM 4942.)			

NORTHCOTT, TOM

Uni 73108	(S)	Upside Downside	1971	8.00	20.00

NORTON BUFFALO

Capitol 11625	(S)	Loving In The Valley On The Moon	1977	1.20	6.00
Capitol 11847	(S)	Desert Horizon	1978	1.20	6.00

NOTES FROM THE UNDERGROUND

Vanguard VSD-6502	(S)	Notes From The Underground	1970	12.00	30.00

NOVA LOCAL

Decca DL-74977	(S)	Nova 1	1968	16.00	40.00

NOVAC

Embryo SD-527	(S)	The Fifth Word	197?	4.00	10.00

NOW GENERATION, THE

Somerset 30800	(S)	Sock It To Me	1968	4.00	10.00
Spar 4806	(S)	Come Together	1970	8.00	20.00
Spar 4807	(S)	Hits Are Our Business	1970	8.00	20.00

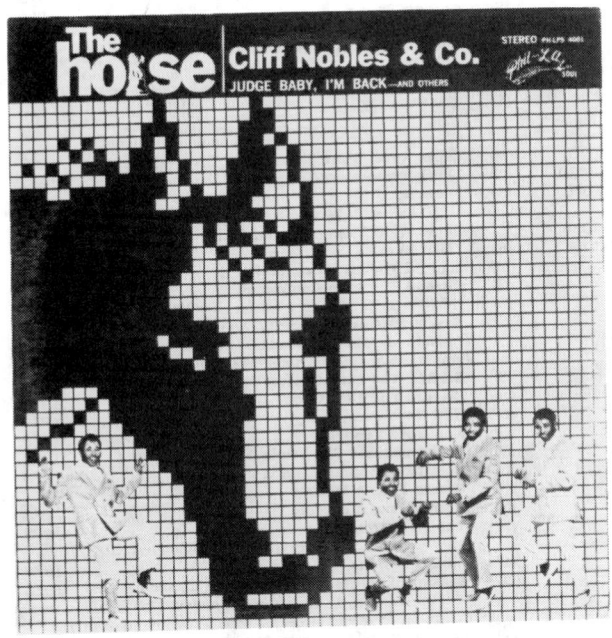

Cliff Nobles & Co. hit the top of the soul and pop charts in 1968 with "The Horse." Issued by the independent Phil-L.A. Of Soul label, it was followed by an LP of the same name. Like the few other albums issued by this label, it is much harder to find than its value indicates.

Label & Catalog #		Title	Year	VG+	NM

NRBQ

The New Rhythm & Blues Quintet also recorded with Carl Perkins. Refer to Wildweeds.

Label & Catalog #		Title	Year	VG+	NM
Columbia CS-9858	(S)	**NRBQ**	1969	10.00	25.00
		—Columbia albums above have "360 Sound" labels.—			
Columbia CS-9858	(S)	**NRBQ**	197?	4.00	10.00
Kama Sutra KSBS-2045	(S)	**Scraps**	1972	12.00	30.00
Kama Sutra KSBS-2065	(S)	**Workshop**	1973	16.00	40.00
Annuit Coeptis 1001	(S)	**Scraps / Workshop** *(2 LPs)*	1976	8.00	20.00
Mercury SRM-1-3712	(S)	**NRBQ At Yankee Stadium**	1978	6.00	15.00
Red Rooster 101	(S)	**All Hopped Up**	1977	6.00	15.00
Red Rooster 3029	(S)	**All Hopped Up**	1979	4.00	10.00
Red Rooster 3030	(S)	**Kick Me Hard**	1979	4.00	10.00
Red Rooster 3048	(S)	**Tiddly Winks**	1980	4.00	10.00
Red Rooster 3055	(S)	**Scraps**	1982	4.00	10.00
Red Rooster 3066	(S)	**Tapdancin' Bats**	1983	4.00	10.00
Bearsville 23187	(S)	**Grooves In Orbit**	1983	4.00	10.00

NUCLEUS

Label & Catalog #		Title	Year	VG+	NM
Mainstream S-6120	(S)	**Nucleus**	1969	14.00	35.00

NUGENT, TED

Nugent was the leader of The Amboy Dukes.

Label & Catalog #		Title	Year	VG+	NM
Epic 33692	(S)	**Ted Nugent**	1975	1.00	5.00
Epic PE-34121	(S)	**Free-For-All**	1976	1.00	5.00
Epic PEQ-34121	(Q)	**Free-For-All**	1976	6.00	15.00
Epic 34700	(S)	**Cat Scratch Fever**	1977	1.00	5.00
Epic 35069	(S)	**Double Live Gonzo!** *(2 LPs)*	1978	3.20	8.00
Epic 35551	(S)	**Weekend Warriors**	1978	1.00	5.00
Epic PE-36000	(S)	**State Of Shock**	1979	1.00	5.00
Epic AS-99-607	(DJ)	**State Of Shock** *(Picture disc)*	1979	6.00	15.00
Epic 36404	(S)	**Scream Dream**	1980	1.00	5.00
Epic 37084	(S)	**Intensities In 10 Cities**	1981	1.00	5.00
Epic 37667	(S)	**Great Gonzos! The Best Of Ted Nugent**	1981	1.00	5.00

NUNNERY, STU

Label & Catalog #		Title	Year	VG+	NM
Evolution 3023	(S)	**Stu Nunnery**	1973	4.00	10.00

NYRO, LAURA

Label & Catalog #		Title	Year	VG+	NM
Verve/Folkways FT-3020	(M)	**Laura Nyro—More Than A New Discovery**	1967	12.00	30.00
Verve/Folkways FTS-3020	(S)	**Laura Nyro—More Than A New Discovery**	1967	12.00	30.00
Verve/Forecast FTS-3020	(S)	**Laura Nyro**	1968	6.00	15.00
		(Forecast 3020 is a reissue of Folkways 3020.)			
Verve/Forecast ST-93036	(S)	**Laura Nyro** *(Capitol Record Club)*	1968	6.00	15.00
Verve/Forecast FTS-3029	(S)	**Laura Nyro**	1968	*Unreleased*	
Columbia CL-2826	(M)	**Eli And The 13th Confession**	1968	12.00	30.00
Columbia CS-9626	(S)	**Eli And The 13th Confession**	1968	4.00	10.00
Columbia CS-9737	(S)	**New York Tendaberry** *(Includes a booklet)*	1969	6.00	15.00
Columbia CS-9737	(S)	**New York Tendaberry** *(Without booklet)*	1969	4.00	10.00
Columbia KC-30259	(S)	**Christmas And The Beads Of Sweat**	1970	10.00	25.00
		—Columbia albums above have "360 Sound" labels.—			
Columbia CS-9626	(S)	**Eli And The 13th Confession**	1970	.80	4.00
Columbia PC-9626	(S)	**Eli And The 13th Confession**	1978	.80	4.00
Columbia CS-9737	(S)	**New York Tendaberry**	1970	.80	4.00
Columbia PC-9737	(S)	**New York Tendaberry**	1978	.80	4.00
Columbia KC-30259	(S)	**Christmas And The Beads Of Sweat**	1970	1.00	5.00
Columbia PC-30259	(S)	**Christmas And The Beads Of Sweat**	1978	.80	4.00
Columbia KC-30987	(S)	**Gonna Take A Miracle**	1971	1.00	5.00
Columbia PC-30987	(S)	**Gonna Take A Miracle**	1978	.80	4.00
Columbia KC-31410	(S)	**The First Songs**	1973	.80	4.00
		(Columbia 31410 is a reissue of Forecast 3020.)			
Columbia JC-33912	(S)	**Smile**	1976	.80	4.00
Columbia JG-34331	(DJ)	**Season Of Lights... Laura Nyro In Concert** *(2 LPs)*	1976	20.00	50.00
		(Issued in a plain cardboard jacket. This album was edited down to a single LP for commercial release in 1977.)			
Columbia JC-34786	(S)	**Season Of Lights... Laura Nyro In Concert**	1977	.80	4.00
Columbia JC-35449	(S)	**Nested**	1978	.80	4.00
Columbia JC-39215	(S)	**Mother's Spiritual**	1984	.80	4.00

O. D. CORRAL				
Wild West 01	(S)	O. D. Corral Live	1975	6.00	15.00
O' DELL, KENNY				
Vegas 401	(S)	Beautiful People	1968	4.00	10.00
O' JAYS, THE				
Imperial LP-9290	(M)	Comin' Through	1965	18.00	45.00
Imperial LP-12290	(S)	Comin' Through	1965	24.00	60.00
Minit LP-40008	(M)	Soul Sounds	1967	14.00	35.00
Minit LP-24008	(S)	Soul Sounds	1967	20.00	50.00
Bell 6014	(S)	Back On Top	1968	6.00	15.00
Sunset SUS-5222	(S)	Full Of Soul	1968	6.00	15.00
		(Sunset 5522 is a reissue of Imperial 12290.)			
Neptune 202	(S)	The O' Jays In Philadelphia	1969	10.00	25.00
United Arts. UAS-5655	(P)	The O' Jays' Greatest Hits	1972	4.00	10.00
Bell 6082	(S)	The O' Jays	1973	4.00	10.00
Stang 1024	(S)	The O' Jays Meet The Moments	1974	4.00	10.00
Kory 1006	(S)	The O' Jays	1977	4.00	10.00
Phila. Inter. KZ-31712	(S)	Back Stabbers	1972	1.20	6.00
Phila. Inter. KZ-32120	(S)	The O' Jays In Philadelphia	1973	1.20	6.00
		(Phila. Inter. 32120 is a reissue of Neptune 202.)			
Phila. Inter. KZ-32408	(S)	Ship Ahoy	1973	1.20	6.00
Phila. Inter. PZQ-32408	(Q)	Ship Ahoy	1974	6.00	15.00
Phila. Inter. KZ-32953	(S)	The O' Jays Live In London	1974	1.20	6.00
Phila. Inter. PZQ-32953	(Q)	The O' Jays Live In London	1974	6.00	15.00
Phila. Inter. KZ-33150	(S)	Survival	1975	1.20	6.00
Phila. Inter. PZ-33807	(S)	Family Reunion	1975	1.20	6.00
Phila. Inter. PZQ-33807	(Q)	Family Reunion	1975	6.00	15.00
Phila. Inter. PZ-34245	(S)	Message In The Music	1975	1.20	6.00
Phila. Inter. ASZ-140	(DJ)	Everything You Always Wanted To Hear By The O' Jays	1975	6.00	15.00
Phila. Inter. PZ-34684	(S)	Travelin' At The Speed Of Thought	1976	1.20	6.00
Phila. Inter. P-35024	(S)	The O' Jays/Collector's Item *(2 LPs)*	1977	3.20	8.00
Phila. Inter. JZ-35355	(S)	So Full Of Love	1978	1.20	6.00
Phila. Inter. FZ-36037	(S)	Identify Yourself	1979	1.20	6.00
Phila. Inter. FZ-36416	(S)	Year 2000	1980	1.20	6.00
Phila. Inter. FZ-37999	(S)	My Favorite Person	1982	1.20	6.00
Phila. Inter. FZ-38518	(S)	When Will I See You Again	1983	1.00	5.00
Phila. Inter. FZ-39251	(S)	The O' Jays' Greatest Hits	1984	1.20	6.00
Phila. Inter. FZ-39367	(S)	Love And More	1984	1.20	6.00
Phila. Inter. FZ-39402	(S)	Close Company	1984	1.20	6.00
Phila. Inter. FZ-53015	(S)	Love Fever	1985	1.00	5.00
Phila. Inter. FZ-53056	(S)	Let Me Touch You	1987	1.00	5.00
Chess CH-9151	(S)	From The Beginning	1984	1.00	5.00
EMI 4-90921	(S)	Serious	1990	1.00	5.00
O' KAYSIONS, THE				
ABC S-664	(S)	Girl Watcher *("Girl Watcher" is rechanneled)*	1968	20.00	50.00
O' KEEFE, DANNY				
Danny O' Keefe originally recorded with Calliope.				
Cotilion SD-9036	(S)	Danny O' Keefe	1970	6.00	15.00
Signpost 8404	(S)	O' Keefe	1972	1.00	5.00
Warner Bros. PRO-760	(DJ)	The O' Keefe File	1977	4.00	10.00
O' SULLIVAN, GILBERT				
Mam 2	(S)	Himself	1971	1.00	5.00
Mam 4	(S)	Himself	1972	1.00	5.00
Mam 5	(S)	Back To Front	1972	1.00	5.00
Mam 10	(S)	Stranger In My Own Backyard	1974	1.00	5.00
OCEAN				
Kama Sutra KSBS-2033	(S)	Put Your Hand In The Hand	1971	4.00	10.00
Kama Sutra KSBS-2064	(S)	Give Tomorrow's Children One More Chance	1972	4.00	10.00

		Title	Year	VG+	NM

r player, singer and writer of topical, folk-based songs. Refer to Sammy Walker.

			Year	VG+	NM
	(M)	All The News That's Fit To Sing	1964	12.00	30.00
	(S)	All The News That's Fit To Sing	1964	16.00	40.00
...-1287	(M)	I Ain't Marching Anymore	1965	12.00	30.00
	(S)	I Ain't Marching Anymore	1965	16.00	40.00
		—Elektra albums above have a guitar player logo on the label.—			
Elektra EKL-269	(M)	All The News That's Fit To Sing	1966	8.00	20.00
Elektra EKS-7269	(S)	All The News That's Fit To Sing	1966	10.00	25.00
Elektra EKL-287	(M)	I Ain't Marching Anymore	1966	8.00	20.00
Elektra EKS-7287	(S)	I Ain't Marching Anymore	1966	10.00	25.00
Elektra EKL-310	(M)	Phil Ochs In Concert	1966	10.00	25.00
Elektra EKS-7310	(S)	Phil Ochs In Concert	1966	12.00	30.00
Folkways FB-5321	(M)	Interviews With Phil Ochs	1967?	20.00	50.00
A&M LP-133	(M)	Pleasures Of The Harbor	1967	8.00	20.00
A&M SP-4133	(S)	Pleasures Of The Harbor	1967	12.00	30.00
A&M SP-4148	(S)	Tape From California	1968	10.00	25.00
A&M SP-4181	(S)	Rehearsals For Retirement	1969	10.00	25.00
A&M SP-4253	(S)	Phil Ochs' Greatest Hits	1970	10.00	25.00
		—A&M albums above have brown labels.—			
A&M SP-4599	(S)	Chords Of Fame (2 LPs)	1976	6.00	15.00

OCTOBER COUNTRY
Epic BN-26381	(S)	October Country	1968	8.00	20.00

ODEGARD, KEVIN
Wooff 4	(S)	Kevin Odegard	1971	5.00	12.00
A.S.I. 209	(S)	Silver Lining	1976	4.00	10.00

OHIO EXPRESS, THE
Refer to The Kasenetz-Katz Circus.
Cameo C-20,000	(M)	Beg, Borrow And Steal	1968	12.00	30.00
Cameo CS-20,000	(S)	Beg, Borrow And Steal	1968	16.00	40.00
Buddah BDS-5018	(S)	The Ohio Express	1968	6.00	15.00
Buddah BDS-5026	(S)	Chewy Chewy	1969	6.00	15.00
Buddah BDS-5037	(S)	Mercy	1969	6.00	15.00
Buddah BDS-5058	(P)	The Very Best Of The Ohio Express	1970	6.00	15.00

OHIO PLAYERS, THE
Capitol ST-192	(S)	Observations In Time	1969	20.00	50.00
Trip 8029	(S)	First Impression	1972	1.00	5.00
Capitol ST-11291	(S)	The Ohio Players	1974	1.00	5.00
		(Capitol 11291 is a reissue of 192.)			
Westbound 2015	(S)	Pain	1972	8.00	20.00
Westbound 2017	(S)	Pleasure	1973	8.00	20.00
Westbound 2021	(S)	Ecstasy	1973	8.00	20.00
Westbound 1003	(S)	Climax	1974	8.00	20.00
Westbound 1005	(S)	Ohio Players Greatest Hits	1975	4.00	10.00
Westbound 211	(S)	Rattlesnake	1975	4.00	10.00
Westbound 219	(S)	Pain	1975	4.00	10.00
Westbound 220	(S)	Pleasure	1975	4.00	10.00
Westbound 222	(S)	Ecstasy	1975	4.00	10.00
United Arts. LA-502E	(S)	The Very Best Of The World Of The Ohio Players	1975	1.00	5.00
Mercury SRM-705	(S)	Skin Tight	1974	1.00	5.00
Mercury SRM-1013	(S)	Fire	1974	1.00	5.00
Mercury SRM-1038	(S)	Honey	1975	1.00	5.00
Mercury SRM-1088	(S)	Contradiction	1976	1.00	5.00
Mercury SRM-1122	(S)	Ohio Players Gold	1976	1.00	5.00
Mercury SRM-3701	(S)	Angel	1977	1.00	5.00
Mercury SRM-3707	(S)	Mr. Mean	1977	1.00	5.00
Mercury SRM-3730	(S)	Jass-Ay-Lay-Dee	1978	1.00	5.00
Arista 4226	(S)	Everybody Up	1979	1.00	5.00
Boardwalk FW-37090	(S)	Tenderness	1981	1.00	5.00
Accord SN-7102	(S)	Young And Ready	1981	.80	4.00

OLA & THE JANGLERS
Crescendo GNPS-2050	(S)	Let's Dance/What A Way To Die	1969	4.00	10.00

OLD & IN THE WAY
O&ITW features Jerry Garcia, David Grisman and Peter Rowan.
Round RX-103	(S)	Old And In The Way	1975	10.00	25.00
Sugar Hill	(S)	Old And In The Way	1987	1.00	5.00

OLDFIELD, MIKE
Mike Oldfield originally recorded with Sallyangie.
Virgin VR13-105	(S)	Tubular Bells	1973	1.00	5.00
Virgin QR13-105	(Q)	Tubular Bells	1974	10.00	25.00
Virgin VR13-109	(DJ)	Hergest Ridge (Banded for air-play)	1974	6.00	15.00

Stereo copies of Roy's first two Monument albums, Lonely And Blue and Crying, creatively produced by Fred Foster and impeccably engineered by Bill Porter, have been difficult to find for decades. The continued interest paid them by the audiophile community, where they are often revered as the finest stereo pop recordings ever made, have pushed the prices far above their mono counterparts. Never a big seller during his life (only nine of his albums made the charts), he received a solitary RIAA Gold Record for his 1962 Greatest Hits compilation. In the wake of his death in 1989 two albums on Virgin, a hits package and his final studio recordings, Mystery Girl, both went gold.

Label & Catalog #		Title	Year	VG+	NM
Virgin VR13-109	(S)	Hergest Ridge	1974	1.00	5.00
Virgin PZ-33913	(S)	Ommadawn	1975	.80	4.00
Virgin PZQ-33913	(Q)	Ommadawn	1975	10.00	25.00
Virgin PZ-34116	(S)	Tubular Bells	1976	.80	4.00
Virgin HE-44116	(S)	Tubular Bells (Half-speed master)	1976	10.00	25.00
Virgin PZ-37358	(S)	QE2	1981	.80	4.00
Virgin PZ-37983	(S)	Five Miles Out	1982	.80	4.00

OLDHAM, SPOONER

Attarack 5002	(S)	Spare Change	1971	6.00	15.00

OLDHAM, ANDREW

Mr Andrew Loog Oldham is best known as the manager of The Rolling Stones through 1967. The albums below, credited to The Andrew Oldham Orchestra, contain instrumental versions of pop/rock songs.

London LL-3457	(M)	The Rolling Stones Songbook	1965	40.00	100.00
London PS-457	(S)	The Rolling Stones Songbook	1965	60.00	150.00
Parrot PA-61003	(M)	East Meets West	1965	30.00	75.00
Parrot PAS-71003	(S)	East Meets West	1965	40.00	100.00

OLENN, JOHNNY

Liberty LRP-3029	(M)	Just Rollin' With Johnny Olenn	1957	300.00	500.00

OLIVE BRANCH

London SP-44152	(S)	Winds Of Chance	1971	1.20	6.00

OLIVER

Crewe 1333	(S)	Good Morning Starshine	1969	4.00	10.00
Crewe 1344	(S)	Oliver Again	1970	4.00	10.00
United Arts. UAS-5511	(S)	Prisms	1971	4.00	10.00

OLIVER & THE TWISTERS

Colpix CP-423	(M)	Look Who's Twistin' Everybody	1961	16.00	40.00

OLLIE & THE NIGHTINGALES

Stax STS-2021	(S)	Ollie And The Nightingales	1969	20.00	50.00

OLYMPIC RUNNERS, THE

London PS-653	(S)	Put The Music Where Your Mouth Is	197?	16.00	40.00

OLYMPICS, THE

Arvee A-423	(M)	Doin' The Hully Gully	1960	150.00	300.00
Arvee A-424	(M)	Dance By The Light Of The Moon	1961	80.00	200.00
Arvee A-429	(M)	Party Time	1961	80.00	200.00
Tri-Disc 1001	(M)	Do The Bounce	1963	30.00	75.00
Mirwood M-7003	(M)	Something Old, Something New	1966	16.00	40.00
Mirwood MS-7003	(S)	Something Old, Something New	1966	20.00	50.00
		(Mirwood 7003 contains rerecorded versions of earlier hits.)			
Post 8000	(E)	The Olympics Sing	196?	10.00	25.00
Everest 4109	(E)	The Olympics	1981	1.00	5.00
Rhino RNDF-207	(M)	The Official Record Album Of The Olympics	1984	1.00	5.00

OMNIBUS

United Arts. UAS-6743	(S)	Omnibus	1970	14.00	35.00

ON THE SEVENTH DAY

Mercury SR-61248	(S)	On The Seventh Day	1970	6.00	15.00

ONE

Grunt FTR-1008	(S)	Come	1972	4.00	10.00

ONO, YOKO

Yoko's first three albums were produced by hubby, John Lennon. Refer to John Lennon & Yoko Ono.

Apple SW-3373	(S)	Yoko Ono/Plastic Ono Band	1971	6.00	15.00
Apple SVBB-3380	(S)	Fly (2 LPs with poster)	1971	10.00	25.00
Apple SVBB-3399	(S)	Approximately Infinite Universe (2 LPs)	1972	8.00	20.00
Apple SW-3412	(S)	Feeling The Space	1973	6.00	15.00

OPEN WINDOW

Vanguard VSD-6515	(S)	The Open Window	1969	6.00	15.00

ORANG-UTAN

Bell 6054	(S)	Orang-Utan	1971	16.00	40.00

ORANGE COLORED SKY

Uni 73031	(S)	Orange Colored Sky	1968	20.00	50.00

ORANGE GROVE

Somerset 34000	(S)	Crystal Blue Persuasion	1969	6.00	15.00

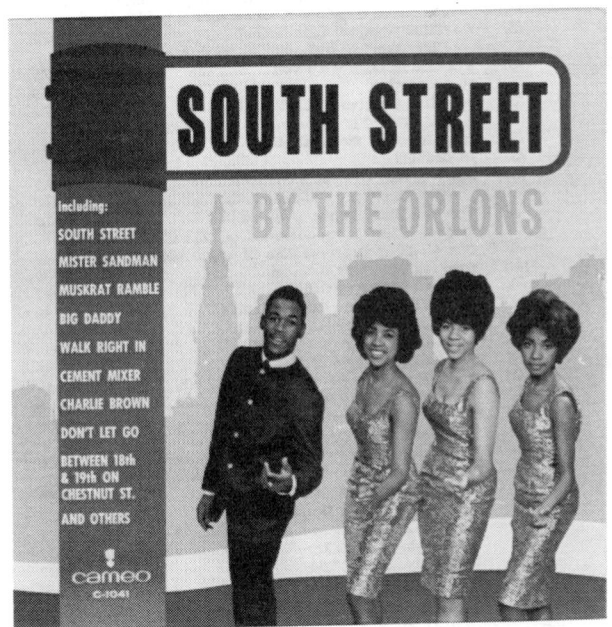

The Orlons were Rosetta Hightower backed by Shirley Brickly, Marlena Davis and Steve Caldwell. Like so many other Philadelphia artists, they signed with the Cameo/Parkway company and blazed onto the charts with a series of dance-oriented singles. Their third straight Top 10 hit inspired their third long-player, South Street. Like too many groups from this era, collectors have tended to slight these records and the amounts paid for copies are not indicative of just how difficult it is to find these records in collectible condition.

Label & Catalog #		Title	Year	VG+	NM

ORANGE WEDGE: *Refer to* WEDGE

ORBISON, ROY

Mr Orbison can also be found on the soundtracks for MGM's "The Fastest Guitar Alive" and Warner Bros' "Roadie."
Refer to Class Of '55; Jerry Lee Lewis / Roger Miller / Roy Orbison; The Traveling Wilburys.

Label & Catalog #		Title	Year	VG+	NM
Sun SLP-1260	(M)	Roy Orbison At The Rockhouse	1961	350.00	750.00
Monument M-4002	(M)	Lonely And Blue	1961	100.00	250.00
Monument SM-14002	(S)	Lonely And Blue	1961	360.00	600.00
Monument M-4007	(M)	Crying	1962	80.00	200.00
Monument SM-14007	(S)	Crying	1962	300.00	500.00
Monument M-4009	(M)	Roy Orbison's Greatest Hits	1962	20.00	50.00
Monument SM-14009	(S)	Roy Orbison's Greatest Hits	1962	30.00	75.00
		—Monument albums above have copper & white swirl labels.—			
Monument MLP-8000	(M)	Roy Orbison's Greatest Hits	1963	12.00	30.00
Monument SLP-18000	(S)	Roy Orbison's Greatest Hits	1963	16.00	40.00
Monument MLP-8003	(M)	In Dreams	1963	60.00	150.00
Monument SLP-18003	(S)	In Dreams	1963	150.00	300.00
		—Monument albums above have rainbow & white swirl labels.—			
Monument MLP-8003	(M)	In Dreams	1964	30.00	75.00
Monument SLP-18003	(S)	In Dreams	1964	60.00	150.00
Monument MLP-8023	(M)	Early Orbison	1964	12.00	30.00
Monument SLP-18023	(S)	Early Orbison	1964	20.00	50.00
Monument MLP-8024	(M)	More Of Roy Orbison's Greatest Hits	1964	12.00	30.00
Monument SLP-18024	(S)	More Of Roy Orbison's Greatest Hits	1964	16.00	40.00
		("It's Over" is in stereo on this album.)			
Monument MLP-8035	(M)	Orbisongs	1965	10.00	25.00
Monument SLP-18035	(S)	Orbisongs	1965	14.00	35.00
Monument MLP-8045	(M)	The Very Best Of Roy Orbison	1966	10.00	25.00
Monument SLP-18045	(S)	The Very Best Of Roy Orbison	1966	14.00	35.00
		("It's Over" is rechanneled on this album.)			
		—Monument albums above have green labels with a gold perimeter.—			
Monument KZG-31484	(S)	All-Time Greatest Hits (2 LPs)	1972	10.00	25.00
		("It's Over" is rechanneled on this album.)			
Mercury SRM-1-1045	(S)	I'm Still In Love With You	1975	5.00	12.00
Monument MG-7600	(S)	Regeneration	1976	5.00	12.00
Monument MP-8600	(S)	All-Time Greatest Hits (2 LPs)	1977	6.00	15.00
		("It's Over" is rechanneled on this album.)			
Monument MC-6619	(S)	Roy Orbison's Greatest Hits	1977	5.00	12.00
Monument MC-6620	(S)	In Dreams	1977	5.00	12.00
Monument MC-6621	(S)	More Of Roy Orbison's Greatest Hits	1977	5.00	12.00
		("It's Over" is in stereo on this album.)			
Monument MC-6622	(S)	The Very Best Of Roy Orbison	1977	5.00	12.00
		("It's Over" is rechanneled on this album.)			
Monument KWG-38389	(S)	The All-Time Greatest Hits Of Roy Orbison	1982	1.00	5.00
Design DLP-164	(M)	Orbiting With Roy Orbison	196?	6.00	15.00
Design DLPS-164	(E)	Orbiting With Roy Orbison	196?	4.00	10.00
MGM E-4308	(M)	There Is Only One Roy Orbison	1965	10.00	25.00
MGM SE-4308	(S)	There Is Only One Roy Orbison	1965	14.00	35.00
MGM E-4322	(M)	The Orbison Way	1965	10.00	25.00
MGM SE-4322	(S)	The Orbison Way	1965	14.00	35.00
MGM T-90631	(M)	The Orbison Way (Capitol Record Club)	1965	14.00	35.00
MGM ST-90631	(S)	The Orbison Way (Capitol Record Club)	1965	14.00	35.00
MGM E-4379	(M)	The Classic Roy Orbison	1966	10.00	25.00
MGM SE-4379	(S)	The Classic Roy Orbison	1966	14.00	35.00
MGM T-90928	(M)	The Classic Roy Orbison (Capitol Record Club)	1966	14.00	35.00
MGM ST-90928	(S)	The Classic Roy Orbison (Capitol Record Club)	1966	14.00	35.00
MGM E-4424	(M)	Roy Orbison Sings Don Gibson	1967	10.00	25.00
MGM SE-4424	(S)	Roy Orbison Sings Don Gibson	1967	14.00	35.00
MGM T-91173	(M)	Roy Orbison Sings Don Gibson (Capitol Rec. Club)	1967	14.00	35.00
MGM ST-91173	(S)	Roy Orbison Sings Don Gibson (Capitol Rec. Club)	1967	14.00	35.00
MGM E-4514	(M)	Cry Softly, Lonely One	1967	10.00	25.00
MGM SE-4514	(S)	Cry Softly, Lonely One	1967	14.00	35.00
		—MGM albums above have black labels.—			
MGM SE-4636	(S)	The Many Moods Of Roy Orbison	1969	10.00	25.00
MGM SE-4659	(S)	The Great Songs Of Roy Orbison	1970	10.00	25.00
MGM SE-4683	(S)	Hank Williams The Roy Orbison Way	1970	10.00	25.00
MGM SE-4835	(S)	Roy Orbison Sings	1972	6.00	15.00
MGM SE-4867	(S)	Memphis	1972	6.00	15.00
MGM SE-4934	(S)	Milestones	1973	6.00	15.00
		—MGM albums above have blue & gold labels.—			
Sun 113	(E)	The Original Sun Sound Of Roy Orbison	1969	4.00	10.00
Candlelite P2-12946	(S)	The Living Legend Of Roy Orbison (2 LPs)	197?	6.00	15.00
Trip TLX-8505	(S)	The Best Of Roy Orbison	197?	1.00	5.00
Buckboard 5-1015	(S)	Roy Orbison's Golden Hits	197?	4.00	10.00
Hallmark SHM-824	(S)	The Exciting Roy Orbison	197?	1.00	5.00
Candlelite P2-12946	(S)	The Living Legend Of Roy Orbison	197?	6.00	15.00
Asylum 6E-198	(S)	Laminar Flow	1979	4.00	10.00
Accord SN-7150	(M)	Ooby Dooby	1981	1.00	5.00

The Osmond Family produced an entertainment machine that rivalled the Jacksons during the '70s. Recording as a group (shown here in their earlier incarnation as the pre-pubescent brother ensemble, The Osmond Brothers) or as various solo acts (illustrated here by Marie's debut) they placed thirty-three LPs on the best-seller list in eight years, fifteen of which received RIAA Gold Records.

Label & Catalog #		Title	Year	VG+	NM
Hits Unlimited 233-0	(S)	My Spell On You	1982	20.00	50.00
Virgin 90604	(S)	In Dreams: The Greatest Hits (2 LPs)	1987	1.20	6.00
Rhino 20574	(S)	For The Lonely (2 LPs)	1988	1.20	6.00

ORBITT III

Beverly Hills 38	(S)	Orbit III	1973	4.00	10.00

ORCHESTRAL MANOEUVRES IN THE DARK [OMD]

Virgin 37721	(S)	Architecture & Morality	1982	1.20	6.00
Virgin AS-1408	(DJ)	A Constructive Conversation With OMD	1982	8.00	20.00
Virgin 38543	(S)	Dazzle Ships	1983	1.20	6.00
A&M SP-5027	(S)	Junk Culture	1984	1.20	6.00

ORCHIDS, THE

Roulette R-25169	(M)	Twistin' At The Roundtable	1962	12.00	30.00
Roulette SR-25169	(S)	Twistin' At The Roundtable	1962	16.00	40.00

ORGAN GRINDERS, THE

Mercury SR-61282	(S)	Out Of The Egg	1970	10.00	25.00

ORIENT EXPRESS, THE

Mainstream S-6117	(S)	The Orient Express	1969	30.00	75.00

ORIGINAL CASTE, THE

T.A. 5003	(S)	One Tin Soldier	1970	5.00	12.00

ORIGINAL SURFARIS, THE

This group of Surfaris lost in a legal bout with the other Surfaris over the group name. As the other band had a national hit ("Wipe Out"), the court awarded them the rights to the name and the original Surfaris here had to bill themselves on record as. . . "The Original Surfaris."

Diplomat D-2309	(M)	Wheels-Shorts-Hot Rods	1963	10.00	25.00
Diplomat DS-2309	(S)	Wheels-Shorts-Hot Rods	1963	14.00	35.00

ORIGINAL TATTOOS, THE

M.P.S. 21143	(S)	The Original Tattoos	1972	4.00	10.00

ORIGINALS, THE

Soul SS-716	(S)	Green Grow The Lilacs	1969	12.00	30.00
Soul SS-716	(S)	Baby, I'm For Real	1969	8.00	20.00
		("Baby, I'm For Real" is a repackage of "Green Grow The Lilacs.")			
Soul SS-724	(S)	Portrait Of The Originals	1970	8.00	20.00
Soul SS-729	(S)	Naturally Together	1970	8.00	20.00
Soul SS-734	(S)	Definitions	1973	6.00	15.00
Soul SS-740	(S)	The Game Called	1973	6.00	15.00
Soul SS-743	(S)	California Sunset	1974	Unreleased	
Motown 826	(S)	California Sunset	1975	4.00	10.00
Soul SS-746	(S)	Communique	1976	4.00	10.00
Soul SS-749	(S)	Down To Love Town	1977	4.00	10.00
Fantasy F-9546	(S)	Another Time, Another Place	1978	1.00	5.00
Fantasy F-9577	(S)	Come Away With Me	1979	1.00	5.00

ORIOLES, THE

Refer to The Cadillacs; Sonny Til & The Orioles.

Parker PLP-816	(M)	Modern Sounds Of The Orioles	1962	20.00	50.00
Parker PLP-816S	(S)	Modern Sounds Of The Orioles	1962	30.00	75.00
Big-A LP-2001	(M)	The Orioles' Greatest All Time Hits	1969	10.00	25.00

ORION, P. J., & THE MAGNATES

Magnate 122459	(M)	P. J. Orion And The Magnates	196?	60.00	150.00

ORLONS, THE

Cameo C-1020	(M)	The Wah Watusi	1962	20.00	50.00
Cameo C-1033	(M)	All The Hits	1962	20.00	50.00
Cameo C-1041	(M)	South Street	1963	20.00	50.00
Cameo C-1054	(M)	Not Me	1963	20.00	50.00
Cameo C-1061	(M)	The Orlons' Biggest Hits	1963	20.00	50.00
Cameo C-1073	(M)	Down Memory Lane	1963	20.00	50.00

ORLONS, THE / THE DOVELLS

Cameo C-1067	(M)	Golden Hits Of The Orlons & The Dovells	1963	20.00	50.00

ORPHAN

London XPS-614	(S)	Everyone Lives To Sing	1972	3.20	8.00
London XPS-630	(S)	Rock And Reflections	1973	3.20	8.00
London XPS-645	(S)	More Orphan Than Not	1974	3.20	8.00

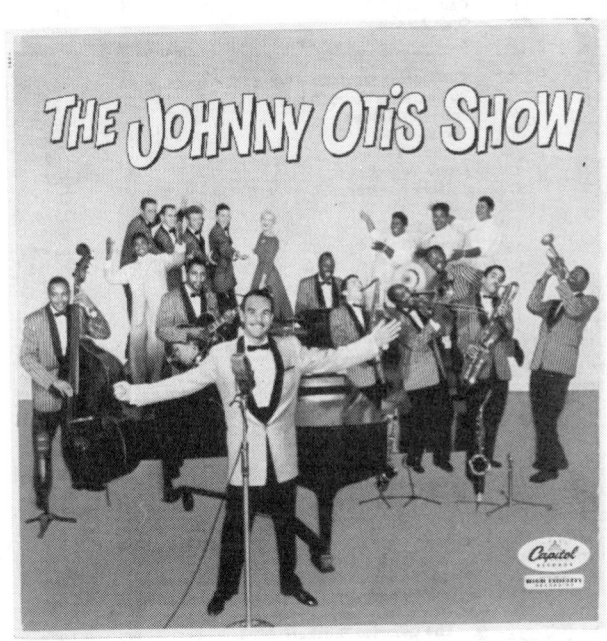

John Veliotes (of Greek descent) became so immersed in the American Negro lifestyle of his time that he reached the point where, as a band-leader and songwriter, he was taken for black. The Johnny Otis Caravan toured the country featuring many of the top rhythm'n blues stars of the time. The Johnny Otis Show, his sole album for Capitol, displays some of those acts in a hoked-up cover photo that is more reminiscent of the pre-WWII troupes than anything we now associate with the early days of rock'n roll.

Label & Catalog #		Title	Year	VG+	NM

ORPHAN EGG

The Orphan Egg can also be found on the American International soundtrack "The Cycle Savages."

| Carole CARS-8004 | (S) | Orphan Egg | 1968 | 16.00 | 40.00 |
| O.M.I. M-7002? | (S) | Don't Say No | 1980 | 20.00 | 50.00 |

ORPHEUS

MGM E-4524	(M)	Orpheus	1968	8.00	20.00
MGM SE-4524	(S)	Orpheus	1968	10.00	25.00
MGM SE-4569	(S)	Ascending	1968	10.00	25.00
MGM SE-4599	(S)	Joyful	1969	10.00	25.00

OSANNA

| Peters Int. 9001 | (S) | Milano Calibro 9 | 1973 | 5.00 | 12.00 |
| Peters Int. 9007 | (S) | Landscape Of Life | 1974 | 4.00 | 10.00 |

OSBOURNE, OZZY

Mr Osbourne was the former lead singer for Black Sabbath. Refer to The Magic Lanterns.

Jet FZ-36812	(S)	Blizzard Of Ozz	1981	1.00	5.00
Jet FZ-37492	(S)	Diary Of A Madman	1981	1.00	5.00
Jet AS-99-1372	(DJ)	Diary Of A Madman (Picture disc)	1981	8.00	20.00
Jet 8Z8-37640	(S)	Mr. Crowley (Picture disc EP)	1982	4.00	10.00
Jet FZ-38350	(S)	Speak Of The Devil	1982	1.00	5.00

OSIBISA

Decca DL-75285	(S)	Osibisa	1971	6.00	15.00
Decca DL-75327	(S)	Woyaya	1972	6.00	15.00
Decca DL-75368	(S)	Heads	1972	6.00	15.00
Buddah BDS-5136	(S)	Super Fly T.N.T.	1973	4.00	10.00
Warner Bros. BS-2732	(S)	Happy Children	1973	4.00	10.00
Warner Bros. BS-2802	(S)	Osibirock	1974	4.00	10.00
Island 9411	(S)	Ojah Awake	1977	4.00	10.00

OSMOND, DONNY

MGM SE-4782	(S)	The Donny Osmond Album (Die-cut cover)	1971	1.20	6.00
MGM SE-4797	(S)	To You With Love, Donny	1971	.80	4.00
MGM SE-34820	(S)	Portrait Of Donny	1972	.80	4.00
MGM SE-4854	(S)	Too Young	1972	.80	4.00
MGM SE-4872	(S)	My Best To You	1972	.80	4.00
MGM SE-4886	(S)	Alone Together	1973	.80	4.00
MGM SE-4930	(S)	A Time For Us	1973	.80	4.00
MGM SE-4978	(S)	Donny	1974	.80	4.00
Polydor PD-6067	(S)	Disco Train	1976	.80	4.00
Polydor PD-6109	(S)	Donald Clark Osmond	1977	.80	4.00

OSMOND, DONNY & MARIE

D&M can also be found on the Polydor soundtrack "Goin' Coconuts."

MGM SE-4968	(S)	I'm Leaving It All Up To You	1974	3.20	8.00
MGM SE-4996	(S)	Make The World Go Away	1975	1.00	5.00
Polydor PD-6068	(S)	Donny & Marie	1976	.80	4.00
Polydor PD-6083	(S)	New Season	1976	.80	4.00
Polydor PD-6127	(S)	Winning Combination	1978	.80	4.00

OSMOND, MARIE

MGM SE-4910	(S)	Paper Roses	1973	4.00	10.00
MGM SE-4944	(S)	In My Little Corner Of The World	1974	3.20	8.00
MGM SE-4979	(S)	Who's Sorry Now	1975	3.20	8.00
Polydor PD-6099	(S)	This Is The Way That I Feel	1977	1.20	6.00

OSMOND BROTHERS, THE

The original Osmond Brothers were Alan, Donny, Jay, Merrill and Wayne.

MGM E-4146	(M)	Songs We Sang On The Andy Williams Show	1963	10.00	25.00
MGM SE-4146	(S)	Songs We Sang On The Andy Williams Show	1963	12.00	30.00
MGM PM-7	(DJ)	AC Spark Plug Division Presents The Osmond Brothers	1963	20.00	50.00
		PM-7 features six tracks from 4146 on one side.)			
MGM E-4187	(M)	We Sing You A Merry Christmas	1963	10.00	25.00
MGM SE-4187	(S)	We Sing You A Merry Christmas	1963	12.00	30.00
MGM E-4235	(M)	All-Time Hymn Favorites	1964	8.00	20.00
MGM SE-4235	(S)	All-Time Hymn Favorites	1964	10.00	25.00
MGM E-4291	(M)	The New Sound Of The Osmond Brothers	1965	8.00	20.00
MGM SE-4291	(S)	The New Sound Of The Osmond Brothers	1965	10.00	25.00
Metro M-543	(M)	We Sing You A Merry Christmas	1965	4.00	10.00
Metro MS-543	(S)	We Sing You A Merry Christmas	1965	6.00	15.00
		(Metro 543 is a reissue of MGM 4137.)			

OSMONDS, THE

The Osmonds were the Brothers above with siblings Jimmy and Marie joining in 1975.

| MGM SE-4724 | (S) | Osmonds | 1971 | 1.00 | 5.00 |

The Outsiders scored a big hit in 1966 with the catchy "Time Won't Let Me." This was followed by three more top 40 hits and commercial oblivion. While these two albums contain three of their hits, only the first one made a splash on the album charts. Lead singer Sonny Geraci abandoned his engaging swagger with The Outsiders to adopt a rather, ahem, wimpy persona as the head of Climax, who topped the charts with "Precious And Few" in 1972.

Label & Catalog #		Title	Year	VG+	NM
MGM SE-4770	(S)	Homemade	1971	1.00	5.00
MGM SE-4796	(S)	Phase-III	1972	1.00	5.00
MGM SE-4826	(S)	The Osmonds "Live" (2 LPs)	1972	3.20	8.00
MGM SE-4851	(S)	Crazy Horses	1972	1.00	5.00
MGM SE-4902	(S)	The Plan	1973	1.00	5.00
MGM SE-4939	(S)	Love Me For A Reason	1974	1.00	5.00
MGM SE-4993	(S)	The Proud One	1975	1.00	5.00
MGM SE-5012	(S)	Around The World—Live In Concert (2 LPs)	1975	3.20	8.00
Polydor PD-6077	(S)	Brainstorm	1976	1.00	5.00
Polydor PD-8001	(S)	The Osmond Christmas Album (2 LPs)	1976	3.20	8.00
Polydor PD-9005	(S)	The Osmonds' Greatest Hits	1978	1.00	5.00

OSMOSIS

RCA Victor LSP-4369	(S)	Osmosis	1970	8.00	20.00

OTHER HALF, THE
This Other Half features Randy Holden, later of Blue Cheer.

Acta 8004	(M)	The Other Half	1968	30.00	75.00
Acta 38004	(S)	The Other Half	1968	40.00	100.00

OTIS, JOHNNY
Refer to Mel Williams.

Dig 104	(M)	Rock And Roll Hit Parade, Volume 1	1957	600.00	1,000.00
		(Original covers for Dig 104 are gold on thick cardboard and have thick vinyl records. Counterfeits with gold covers have thinner board and records.)			
Dig 104	(M)	Rock And Roll Hit Parade, Volume 1	1958	300.00	600.00
		(Later covers are yellow on thick cardboard; the records are on thick vinyl.)			
Capitol T-940	(M)	The Johnny Otis Show	1958	150.00	300.00
Kent KST-534	(S)	Cold Shot	1968	10.00	25.00
Epic BN-26524	(S)	Cuttin' Up	1970	10.00	25.00
Epic EG-30473	(S)	Live At Monterey	1971	10.00	25.00
Savoy 2230	(M)	Original Johnny Otis Show (2 LPs)	1978	6.00	15.00
Savoy 2252	(M)	Original Johnny Otis Show, Vol. 2 (2 LPs)	1980	6.00	15.00

OTIS, SHUGGIE

Epic BN-26511	(S)	Here Comes Shuggie Otis	1970	6.00	15.00
Epic KE-30752	(S)	Freedom Flight	1971	6.00	15.00
Epic KE-33059	(S)	Inspiration Information	1974	4.00	10.00

OUTLAW BLUES BAND, THE

BluesWay BLS-6021	(S)	The Outlaw Blues Band	1968	10.00	25.00

OUTLAWS, THE

Arista AL-4042	(S)	Outlaws	1975	1.00	5.00
Arista AL-4070	(S)	Lady In Waiting	1976	1.00	5.00
Arista AL-4135	(S)	Hurry Sundown	1977	1.00	5.00
Arista 2-8300	(S)	Bring It Back Alive	1978	1.00	5.00
Arista AL-4205	(S)	Playin' To Win	1978	1.00	5.00
Arista 9507	(S)	In The Eye Of The Storm	1979	1.00	5.00
Arista 9542	(S)	Ghost Riders	1980	1.00	5.00
Arista 9584	(S)	Los Hombres Malo	1982	1.00	5.00
Arista 9614	(S)	High Tides Forever—Greatest Hits	1982	1.00	5.00

OUTRAGE

Kama Sutra KLPS-8074	(S)	Outrage	1969	4.00	10.00

OUTSIDERS, THE

Capitol T-2501	(M)	Time Won't Let Me	1966	8.00	20.00
Capitol ST-2501	(S)	Time Won't Let Me	1966	10.00	25.00
Capitol T-2568	(M)	Album #2	1966	8.00	20.00
Capitol ST-2568	(S)	Album #2 ("Respectable" is rechanneled)	1966	10.00	25.00
Capitol T-2636	(M)	In	1967	10.00	25.00
Capitol ST-2636	(S)	In	1967	10.00	25.00
Capitol T-2745	(M)	Happening Live	1967	10.00	25.00
Capitol ST-2745	(S)	Happening Live	1967	10.00	25.00

OVATIONS, THE

Sounds of Memphis 7001	(S)	Hooked On A Feeling	1972	4.00	10.00
MGM SE-4945	(S)	Having A Party	1972	4.00	10.00

OVERLAND STAGE, THE

Epic KE-31319	(S)	The Overland Stage	1972	2.50	6.00

OXPETALS, THE

Mercury SR-61289	(S)	Oxpetals	1970	3.20	8.00

OZUNA, SUNNY, & THE SUNGLOWS: *Refer to* **THE DUNGLOWS**

P. FUNK ALL-STARS, THE
The Pure Funk All-Stars are members of the Parliament/Funkadelic community.

Epic 39168	(S)	Urban Dancefloor Guerilla	1983	8.00	20.00

PABLO CRUISE

A&M SP-4528	(S)	Pablo Cruise	1975	.80	4.00
A&M SP-4575	(S)	Lifeline	1976	.80	4.00
A&M SP-4625	(S)	A Place In The Sun	1977	.80	4.00
A&M SP-4697	(S)	Worlds Away	1978	.80	4.00
A&M SP-3712	(S)	Part Of The Game	1979	.80	4.00
A&M SP-3726	(S)	Reflector	1981	.80	4.00

PACIFIC DRIFT

Deram DES-18040	(S)	Feelin' Free	1970	8.00	20.00

PACIFIC, GAS & ELECTRIC
PG&E can also be found on the Columbia soundtrack "Tell Me That You Love Me Junie Moon."

Power P-701	(S)	Get It On	1968	10.00	25.00
Columbia CS-9900	(S)	Pacific Gas & Electric	1969	4.00	10.00
Columbia CS-1017	(S)	Are You Ready	1970	4.00	10.00
Columbia CS-1048	(S)	Heavy Hands	1970	4.00	10.00
		—Columbia albums above have "360 Sound" labels.—			
Columbia CS-30362	(S)	PG&E	1971	3.20	8.00
Dunhill DSX-50157	(S)	Starring Charlie Allen	197?	3.20	8.00

PACIFIC OCEAN

V.M.C. 135	(S)	Pacific Ocean	1969	8.00	20.00

PACKERS, THE

Imperial LP-12409	(S)	Hitch It Up	1968	5.00	12.00
Pure Soul 1001	(S)	Hole In The Wall	196?	5.00	12.00

PAGE, JIMMY
Jimmy Page is the former guitar player/leader of The Yardbirds and Led Zeppelin. He was a mainstay as a session guitarist throughout the '60s for countless British recordings, some of which are collected on the Springboard album.

Springboard SPB-4038	(S)	Special Early Works	1972	10.00	25.00

PAIR

Liberty LRP-3461	(M)	"In"-Citement	1966	6.00	15.00
Liberty LST-7461	(S)	"In"-Citement	1966	8.00	20.00

PALADIN

Island ILPS-9150	(S)	Paladin	1972	4.00	10.00

PALMER, BRUCE
Palmer was a member of Buffalo Springfield.

Verve/Forecast FTS-3086	(S)	The Cycle Is Complete	1970	8.00	20.00

PALMER, EARL

Liberty LRP-3201	(M)	Drumsville	1961	12.00	30.00
Liberty LST-7201	(S)	Drumsville	1961	16.00	40.00
Liberty LRP-3227	(M)	Percolator Twist	1962	12.00	30.00
Liberty LST-7227	(S)	Percolator Twist	1962	16.00	40.00

PALMER, ROBERT

Island ISLP-9294	(S)	Sneakin' Sally Through The Alley	1975	1.00	5.00
Island ISLP-9372	(S)	Pressure Drop	1975	1.00	5.00
Island ISLP-9420	(S)	Some People Can Do What They Like	1976	1.00	5.00
Island ISLP-9476	(S)	Double Fun	1978	1.00	5.00
Island PRO-819	(DJ)	Secrets *(Picture disc)*	1979	8.00	20.00
Island ISLP-9544	(S)	Secrets	1979	1.00	5.00
Warner Bros. WBMS-111	(DJ)	Live In Boston	1979	12.00	30.00
Island ISLP-9595	(S)	Clues	1980	1.00	5.00
Island ISLP-9665	(S)	Maybe It's Live	1982	1.00	5.00
Island 90065	(S)	Pride	1983	1.00	5.00

Label & Catalog #		Title	Year	VG+	NM
PAN					
Columbia KC-32062	(S)	**Pan**	1973	4.00	10.00
PANAMA LIMITED JUG BAND, THE					
Harvest SKAO-387	(S)	**The Panama Limited Jug Band**	1969	4.00	10.00
PANICS, THE					
Chancellor CHL-5026	(M)	**Panicsville**	1962	16.00	40.00
Chancellor CHLS-5026	(S)	**Panicsville**	1962	20.00	50.00
Phillips PHM-200-159	(M)	**Discotheque Dance Party**	1964	6.00	15.00
Phillips PHS-600-159	(S)	**Discotheque Dance Party**	1964	8.00	20.00
PAPA DOO RUN RUN					
Telarc 70501	(S)	**California Project**	198?	4.00	10.00
PAPA NEBO					
Atlantic SD-8280	(S)	**Papa Nebo**	1970	3.20	8.00
PAPER LACE					
Mercury SRM-1-1008	(S)	**Paper Lace**	1974	4.00	10.00
PAPPALARDI					
Felix Pappalardi is best known as Cream's producer. Refer to The Devil's Anvil.					
A&M SP-4586	(S)	**Creation**	1976	3.20	8.00
A&M SP-4729	(S)	**Don't Worry Ma**	1979	3.20	8.00
PARAGONS, THE					
Lost-Nite LLP-4	(10")	**The Paragons** *(Red vinyl)*	1981	4.00	10.00
PARAGONS, THE / THE JESTERS					
Winley LP-6003	(M)	**War! The Jesters Vs. The Paragons**	195?	250.00	500.00
Jubilee JLP-1098	(M)	**The Paragons Meet The Jesters** *(Multi-color vinyl)*	1959	1,000.00	1,500.00
Jubilee JLP-1098	(M)	**The Paragons Meet The Jesters**	1959	150.00	300.00
		—Jubilee albums above have glossy blue labels.—			
Josie 4008	(M)	**The Paragons Meet The Jesters**	1962	80.00	200.00
		(Josie 4008 is a reissue of Jubilee 1098.)			
Jubilee JLP-1098	(M)	**The Paragons Meet The Jesters**	196?	60.00	150.00
		—Jubilee albums above have flat black labels.—			
Jubilee JLP-1098	(M)	**The Paragons Meet The Jesters**	196?	30.00	75.00
		—Jubilee albums above have black labels with a multi-color logo.—			
PARAGONS, THE / THE HARPTONES					
Musicnote M-8001	(M)	**The Paragons Vs. The Harptones**	1964	14.00	35.00
PARCHMENT					
Myrrh MSA-6551	(S)	**Shamble Jam**	1975	12.00	30.00
PARIS, PRISCILLA					
Priscilla also recorded with her siblings as The Paris Sisters.					
York 4005	(M)	**Priscilla Sings Herself**	1967	14.00	35.00
York 4005-S	(S)	**Priscilla Sings Herself**	1967	20.00	50.00.
		(York 4005 features liner notes by Phil Spector.)			
Happy Tiger HT-1002	(S)	**Priscilla Loves Billy**	1968	16.00	40.00
Out Of Town 8002	(S)	**Love Is**	197?	10.00	25.00
PARIS PILOT					
Hip 7004	(S)	**Paris Pilot**	1970	10.00	25.00
PARIS SISTERS, THE					
The sisters Paris are Albeth, Priscilla and Sherrell.					
Unifilms 505	(M)	**The Paris Sisters Sing Songs From Glass House**	1966	14.00	35.00
Unifilms 505	(S)	**The Paris Sisters Sing Songs From Glass House**	1966	20.00	50.00
Sidewalk T-5906	(M)	**The Hits Of The Paris Sisters**	1967	20.00	50.00
Sidewalk DT-5906	(E)	**The Hits Of The Paris Sisters**	1967	14.00	35.00
Reprise R-6259	(M)	**Everything Under The Sun**	1967	20.00	50.00
Reprise RS-6259	(S)	**Everything Under The Sun**	1967	30.00	75.00
PARISH HALL					
Fantasy 8398	(S)	**Parish Hall**	1969	8.00	20.00
PARKER, GRAHAM, & THE RUMOUR					
Mercury SRM-1117	(S)	**Heat Treatment**	1977	1.00	5.00
Mercury SRM-3706	(S)	**Stick To Me**	1977	1.00	5.00
Mercury SRM-100	(S)	**Parkerilla** *(2 LPs)*	1978	1.00	5.00
Arista A:-4223	(S)	**Squeezing Out Sparks**	1979	1.00	5.00
Arista SP-41	(DJ)	**Live Sparks**	1979	8.00	20.00
Arista 9517	(S)	**The Up Escalator**	1980	1.00	5.00
Arista 9589	(S)	**Another Grey Area**	1982	1.00	5.00

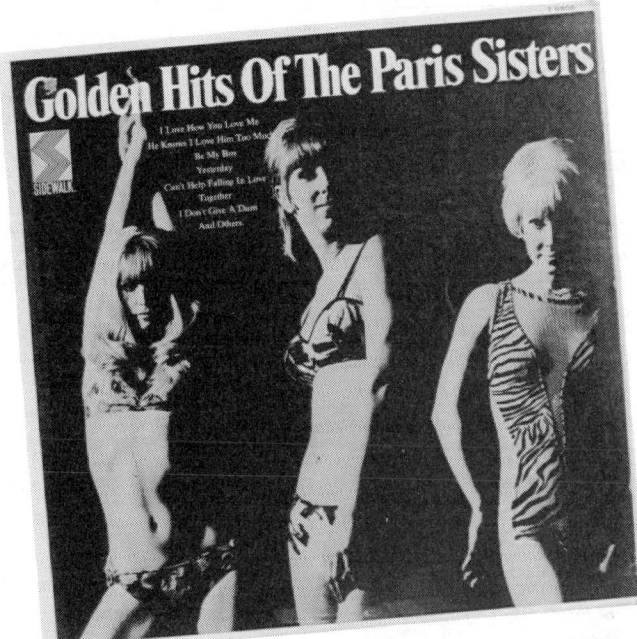

The Paris Sisters—Albeth, Priscilla and Sherrell—came under the wing of Phil Spector when he produced a handful of singles for the trio on the Gregmark label. While four of them charted, "I Love How You Love Me" was a major hit and became an early precursor to the more developed "girl group" sound that Spector would perfect with The Ronettes and The Crystals. Unfortunately, fans had to wait years for this material to be collected on Golden Hits Of The Paris Sisters, *and then it showed up on the Sidewalk label! At the same time, Priscilla launched a solo career that included* Priscilla Loves Billy *with its lovely cover for the even more obscure Happy Tiger label. It is doubtful that many collectors ever saw a copy of either title for sale in 1967 or '68.*

		Title	Year	VG+	NM

...JUNIOR
...ue Bland / Little Junior Parker.

	(M)	**Driving Wheel**	1962	**60.00**	**150.00**
Duke	(M)	**The Best Of Junior Parker**	1967	**20.00**	**50.00**
	(P)	**The Best Of Junior Parker**	1967	**16.00**	**40.00**
		—*Duke albums above have orange labels.*—			
Mercury MG-21101	(M)	**Like It Is**	1967	**12.00**	**30.00**
Mercury SR-61101	(S)	**Like It Is**	1967	**10.00**	**25.00**
Minit 24024	(S)	**Blues Man**	1969	**10.00**	**25.00**
Blue Rock SRB-64004	(S)	**Honey-Drippin' Blues**	1969	**6.00**	**15.00**
Capitol ST-64	(S)	**The Outside Man**	1970	**6.00**	**15.00**
United Arts. UAS-6823	(S)	**I Tell Stories Sad And True**	1971	**6.00**	**15.00**
BluesWay BLS-6066	(S)	**Sometime Tomorrow**	1973	**6.00**	**15.00**
ABC AC-30010	(S)	**Junior Parker - The ABC Collection**	1976	**6.00**	**15.00**

PARKER, LITTLE JUNIOR, & JIMMY McGRIFF

Capitol ST-569	(S)	**Dudes Doin' Business**	1971	**6.00**	**15.00**
United Arts. UAS-6814	(S)	**100 Proof Black Magic**	1971	**6.00**	**15.00**

PARKS, VAN DYKE

Warner Bros. WS-1727	(S)	**Song Cycle**	1968	**10.00**	**25.00**
		—*Warner Bros. albums above have gold labels.*—			
Warner Bros. WS-1727	(S)	**Song Cycle**	1969	**4.00**	**10.00**
Warner Bros. BS-2589	(S)	**Discover America**	1972	**4.00**	**10.00**
Warner Bros. BS-2878	(S)	**Clang Of The Yankee Reaper**	1975	**4.00**	**10.00**
		—*Warner Bros. albums above have green labels.*—			

PARLET
Parlet is a member of the Parliament/Funkadelic community.

Casablanca 7094	(S)	**Pleasure Principle**	1978	**6.00**	**15.00**
Casablanca 7146	(S)	**Invasion Of The Body Snatchers**	1979	**6.00**	**15.00**
Casablanca 7224	(S)	**Play Me Or Trade Me**	1980	**6.00**	**15.00**

PARLIAMENT
Parliament, who also recorded as Funkadelic, is the brainchild of George Clinton.

Invictus 7302	(S)	**Osmium**	1970	**40.00**	**100.00**
Casablanca NBLP-9003	(S)	**Up For The Down Stroke**	1974	**16.00**	**40.00**
Casablanca NBLP-7002	(S)	**Up For The Down Stroke**	1975	**12.00**	**30.00**
Casablanca NBLP-7014	(S)	**Chocolate City**	1975	**12.00**	**30.00**
Casablanca NBLP-7022	(S)	**Mothership Connection**	1976	**12.00**	**30.00**
Casablanca NBLP-7034	(S)	**The Clones Of Dr. Funkenstein**	1976	**12.00**	**30.00**
Casablanca NBLP-7053	(S)	**Parliament Live/P. Funk Earth Tour**	1977	**12.00**	**30.00**
Casablanca NBLP-7084	(S)	**Funkentelechy Vs. The Placebo Syndrome**	1977	**12.00**	**30.00**
Casablanca NBLP-7125	(S)	**Motor-Booty Affair**	1978	**12.00**	**30.00**
Casablanca NBLP-7125	(S)	**Motor Booty Affair** *(Picture disc)*	1979	**16.00**	**40.00**
Casablanca NBLP-7195	(S)	**Gloryhallastoopid**	1979	**12.00**	**30.00**
Casablanca NBLP-7249	(S)	**Trombipulation**	1980	**12.00**	**30.00**
Casablanca 822367	(S)	**Parliament's Greatest Hits**	1984	**6.00**	**15.00**

PARRIS, FRED, & THE SATINS

Elektra E1-60152	(S)	**Fred Parris & The Satins**	1982	**6.00**	**15.00**

PARRISH, PAUL

Music Factory MFS-12,001	(S)	**The Forest Of My Mind**	196?	**6.00**	**15.00**
Warner Bros. WS-1930	(S)	**Songs**	1971	**5.00**	**12.00**
ABC 1013	(DJ)	**Song For A Young Girl** *(Picture disc)*	1979	**4.00**	**10.00**

PARRISH & GURVITZ
Paul Parrish and Adrian Gurvitz. Refer to The Baker-Gurvitz Army; Three Man Army.

Decca DL-75336	(S)	**Parrish And Gurvitz**	1972	**6.00**	**15.00**

PARSONS, ALAN [THE ALAN PARSONS PROJECT]

20th Cent. Fox T-508	(S)	**Tales Of Mystery & Imagination—Edgar Allan Poe**	1976	**1.00**	**5.00**
Arista 7002	(S)	**I Robot**	1977	**.80**	**4.00**
Arista 4180	(S)	**Pyramid**	1978	**.80**	**4.00**
Arista 9504	(S)	**Eve**	1979	**.80**	**4.00**
Arista SP-68	(DJ)	**Audio Guide To The Alan Parsons Project**	1979	**20.00**	**50.00**
		(Boxed set of the first four Project albums with a double-LP set of Parson's work with other artists as engineer, etc.)			
Arista 9518	(S)	**The Turn Of A Friendly Card**	1980	**.80**	**4.00**
Arista 9599	(S)	**Eye In The Sky**	1982	**.80**	**4.00**
Arista SP-140	(DJ)	**Audio Guide To The Alan Parsons Project**	1982	**30.00**	**75.00**
		(Boxed set of the first six Project albums with a special double-LP set of Parson's work with other artists as engineer, etc.)			
Arista 8193	(S)	**The Best Of The Alan Parsons Project**	1983	**.80**	**4.00**
Arista 8204	(S)	**Ammonia Avenue**	1984	**.80**	**4.00**
Arista PD-8263	(S)	**Vulture Culture** *(Promo picture disc)*	1985	**10.00**	**25.00**
Arista 8263	(S)	**Vulture Culture**	1985	**.80**	**4.00**

As the follow-up to the staggering advances made on Pet Sounds and "Good Vibrations," Brian Wilson envisioned an album with themes that transcended anything that had ever been contemplated in rock music. Smile was to incorporate advanced production techniques, [then] hip [at least to Brian] humor, Americana themes such as the old West, and vocal arrangements so complex as to set new standards in all fields of endeavor! And all this was to be held together by the intentionally opaque lyrics of Van Dyke Parks. In the wake of the disaster that Smile was for Wilson and The Beach Boys, Parks was perceived by members of the group and execs at Capitol as one of the bad guys and instead of signed to a contract, was allowed to escape the lunacy and find refuge with the progressive Warner Bros. label. His first album, Song Cycle, was a brilliant journey to some of the places that Brian had been heading for with Smile.

Label & Catalog #		Title	Year	VG+	NM

PARSONS, GRAM

Gram Parsons led The International Submarine Band, recorded as a latter day member of The Byrds, and then founded The Flying Burrito Brothers with Chris Hillman.

Reprise MS-2123	(S)	G.P.	1973	4.00	10.00
Reprise MS-2171	(S)	Grievous Angel	1974	4.00	10.00
Sierra SRS-89702	(S)	Gram Parsons-The Early Years 1963-1965	1979	1.00	5.00
Sierra GP-1973	(S)	Gram Parsons And The Fallen Angels Live	1982	1.00	5.00

PASSING CLOUDS

Pete 1106	(S)	Hawks And Doves	1969	6.00	15.00

PATTO

Mike Patto, formerly of Spooky Tooth.

Vertigo VEL-1001	(S)	Patto	1971	5.00	12.00
Vertigo VEL-1008	(S)	Hold Your Fire	1972	5.00	12.00
Island SW-9322	(S)	Roll 'Em, Smoke 'Em Put Another Line Out	1976	12.00	30.00

PAUL, BILLY

Neptune 201	(S)	Ebony Woman	1970	6.00	15.00
Gamble SG-5002	(S)	Feelin' Good At The Cadillac Club	1971	12.00	30.00
Phila. Inter. KZ-30580	(S)	Going East	1971	1.20	6.00
Phila. Inter. KZ-31793	(S)	360 Degrees Of Billy Paul	1972	1.20	6.00
Phila. Inter. ZQ-31793	(Q)	360 Degrees Of Billy Paul	1973	6.00	15.00
Phila. Inter. KZ-32118	(S)	Ebony Woman	1973	1.20	6.00
		(Philadelphia International 32118 is a reissue of Neptune 201.)			
Phila. Inter. KZ-32409	(S)	War Of The Gods	1973	1.20	6.00
Phila. Inter. ZQ-32409	(Q)	War Of The Gods	1973	6.00	15.00
Phila. Inter. KZ-32952	(S)	Live In Europe	1974	1.20	6.00
Phila. Inter. ZQ-32952	(Q)	Live In Europe	1974	6.00	15.00
Phila. Inter. KZ-33157	(S)	Got My Head On Straight	1975	1.20	6.00
Phila. Inter. KZ-33843	(S)	When Love Is New	1976	1.20	6.00
Phila. Inter. KZ-34389	(S)	Let 'Em In	1977	1.20	6.00
Phila. Inter. KZ-34923	(S)	Only The Strong Survive	1978	1.20	6.00

PAUL & PAULA

Paul & Paula are Ray Hildebrand and Jill Jackson.

Phillips PHM-200-078	(M)	Paul And Paula Sing For Young Lovers	1963	12.00	30.00
Phillips PHS-600-078	(S)	Paul And Paula Sing For Young Lovers	1963	16.00	40.00
Phillips PHM-200-089	(M)	We Go Together	1963	12.00	30.00
Phillips PHS-600-089	(S)	We Go Together	1963	16.00	40.00
Phillips PHM-200-101	(M)	Holiday For Teens	1963	12.00	30.00
Phillips PHS-600-101	(S)	Holiday For Teens	1963	16.00	40.00

PAUPERS, THE

Verve/Forecast FT-3026	(M)	Magic People	1967	6.00	15.00
Verve/Forecast FTS-3026	(S)	Magic People	1967	8.00	20.00
Verve/Forecast FTS-3051	(S)	Ellis Island	1968	6.00	15.00

PAVLOV'S DOG

Pavlov's Dog later recorded as The St. Louis Hounds.

ABC-Paramount D-866	(S)	Pampered Menial	1975	10.00	25.00
Columbia PC-33552	(S)	Pampered Menial	1976	4.00	10.00
		(Columbia 33552 is a reissue of ABC 866.)			
Columbia PC-33964	(S)	At The Sound Of The Bell	1976	4.00	10.00

PAYNE, FREDA

Ms Payne began her recording career as a jazz-based vocalist.

MGM E-4370	(M)	How Do You Say I Don't Love You Anymore	1966	6.00	15.00
MGM SE-4370	(S)	How Do You Say I Don't Love You Anymore	1966	8.00	20.00
MGM GAS-128	(S)	Freda Payne	1970	6.00	15.00
Invictus ST-7301	(S)	Band Of Gold	1970	6.00	15.00
Invictus ST-7307	(S)	Contact	1971	6.00	15.00
Invictus ST-9804	(S)	The Best Of Freda Payne	1972	6.00	15.00
Dunhill DSX-50176	(S)	Payne And Pleasure	1974	6.00	15.00
ABC D-901	(S)	Out Of Payne Comes Love	1976	1.00	5.00
Capitol ST-11700	(S)	Stares And Whispers	1978	1.00	5.00
Capitol ST-11864	(S)	Supernatural High	1978	1.00	5.00
Capitol ST-12003	(S)	Hot	1979	1.00	5.00

PEACE & QUIET

Kinetic 30315	(S)	Peace And Quiet	1971	5.00	12.00

PEACHES & HERB

The original duo is Herb Fame with Francine Barker.

Date TE-3004	(M)	Let's Fall In Love	1967	8.00	20.00
Date TES-4004	(S)	Let's Fall In Love	1967	10.00	25.00
Date TE-3005	(M)	For Your Love	1967	8.00	20.00
Date TES-4005	(S)	For Your Love	1967	10.00	25.00

Label & Catalog #		Title	Year	VG+	NM
Date TES-4007	(S)	Peaches And Herb's Golden Duets	1968	8.00	20.00
Date TES-4012	(S)	Peaches And Herb's Greatest Hits	1968	8.00	20.00
Epic JE-36099	(S)	Peaches And Herb's Greatest Hits	1979	1.00	5.00
Epic E-36089	(S)	Love Is Strange	1979	1.00	5.00
		(The Epic albums repackage Date material.)			

PEACHES & HERB
The later pair is Herb Fame with Linda Greene.

MCA 2261	(S)	Peaches & Herb	1977	1.00	5.00
Polydor 6172	(S)	2 Hot!	1978	1.00	5.00
Polydor 6239	(S)	Twice The Fire	1979	1.00	5.00
Polydor 6298	(S)	Worth The Wait	1980	1.00	5.00
Polydor 6332	(S)	Sayin' Something!	1981	1.00	5.00

PEANUT BUTTER CONSPIRACY, THE
The Conspiracy Columbia albums were produced by Gary Usher.

Columbia CL-2654	(M)	Peanut Butter Conspiracy Is Spreading	1967	12.00	30.00
Columbia CS-9495	(S)	Peanut Butter Conspiracy Is Spreading	1967	12.00	30.00
Columbia CL-2790	(M)	The Great Conspiracy	1968	16.00	40.00
Columbia CS-9590	(S)	The Great Conspiracy	1968	12.00	30.00
Challenge 2000	(M)	For Children Of All Ages	1969	12.00	30.00

PEARLS BEFORE SWINE
Pearls features Tom Rapp.

ESP-Disk' 1054	(M)	One Nation Under Ground *(With poster)*	1967	30.00	75.00
ESP-Disk' 1054	(M)	One Nation Under Ground *(Without poster)*	1967	20.00	50.00
ESP-Disk' 1054	(S)	One Nation Under Ground *(With poster)*	1967	30.00	75.00
ESP-Disk' 1054	(S)	One Nation Under Ground *(Without poster)*	1967	20.00	50.00
		(ESP 1054 was issued simultaneously with three different covers: black & white; sepia-toned black & white with a white border; and sepia-toned black & white without the border. The prices are for any of the three.)			
ESP-Disk' 1054	(S)	One Nation Under Ground *(Full color cover)*	1968	12.00	30.00
ESP-Disk' 1075	(S)	Balaklava	1968	16.00	40.00
Reprise MS-6364	(S)	These Things Too	1969	12.00	30.00
Reprise MS-6405	(S)	The Use Of Ashes	1970	12.00	30.00
Reprise MS-6442	(S)	City Of Gold	1971	16.00	40.00
Reprise MS-6467	(S)	Beautiful Lies You Could Live In	1971	16.00	40.00

PEDICIN, MIKE

Apollo LP-484	(M)	Musical Medicine	1957	60.00	150.00

PEEBLES, ANN

Hi SHL-32059	(S)	Part Time Love	1970	6.00	15.00
Hi SHL-32065	(S)	Straight From The Heart	1972	6.00	15.00
Hi SHL-32079	(S)	I Can't Stand The Rain	1974	6.00	15.00
Hi SHL-32091	(S)	Tellin' It	1975	6.00	15.00
Hi 6002	(S)	If This Is Heaven	197?	4.00	10.00
Hi 6007	(S)	Handwriting Is On The Wall	197?	4.00	10.00
Hi 8009	(S)	Straight From The Heart	197?	4.00	10.00
Motown M5-288V	(S)	I Can't Stand The Rain	198?	.80	4.00

PEEL, DAVID, & THE LOWER EAST SIDE

Elektra EKS-74032	(S)	Have A Marijuana	1968	16.00	40.00
Elektra EKS-74069	(S)	The American Revolution	1970	12.00	30.00
Apple SW-3391	(S)	The Pope Smokes Dope *(Prod. by John & Yoko)*	1972	30.00	75.00

PENDERGRASS, TEDDY
Mr Pendergrass is the former lead singer for Harold Melvin's Blue Notes (1970-76).

Phila. Inter. JZ-34390	(S)	Teddy Pendergrass	1977	1.20	6.00
Phila. Inter. JZ-35095	(DJ)	Life Is A Song Worth Singing *(Picture disc)*	1978	6.00	15.00
Phila. Inter. JZ-35095	(S)	Life Is A Song Worth Singing	1978	1.20	6.00
Phila. Inter. JZ-36003	(S)	Teddy	1979	1.20	6.00
Phila. Inter. JZ-36294	(S)	Teddy Live! Coast To Coast *(2 LPs)*	1979	3.20	8.00
Phila. Inter. JZ-36745	(S)	TP	1980	1.20	6.00
Phila. Inter. JE-37491	(S)	It's Time For Love	1981	1.20	6.00
Phila. Inter. HE-47491	(S)	It's Time For Love *(Half-speed master)*	1981	8.00	20.00
Phila. Inter. JE-38118	(S)	This One's For You	1982	1.20	6.00
Phila. Inter. JE-38646	(S)	Heaven Only Knows	1984	1.20	6.00

PENDULUM

Perception 23	(S)	Pendulum	1972	3.20	8.00

PENGUINS, THE

Dootone DTL-204	(M)	The Best Vocal Groups... Rhythm & Blues *(Red vinyl)*	1959	1,500.00	3,000.00
		(Because all of the first side of this various artists album is by The Penguins, it is generally referred to as the "first Penguins album.")			
		—*Dootone albums above have flat maroon labels.*—			

Label & Catalog #		Title	Year	VG+	NM
Dootone DTL-204	(M)	The Best Vocal Groups... Rhythm & Blues	1959	30.00	600.00
		—Dootone albums above have glossy maroon labels.—			
Dooto DTL-204	(M)	The Best Vocal Groups... Rhythm & Blues	1959	80.00	200.00
		(Dooto 204 is a reissue of Dootone 204.)			
		—Dooto albums above have blue & yellow labels.—			
Dooto DTL-242	(M)	The Cool Cool Penguins	1959	300.00	600.00
		—Dootone albums above have yellow & red labels.—			
Dooto DTL-204	(M)	The Best Vocal Groups... Rhythm & Blues	196?	Counterfeit	
Dooto DTL-242	(M)	The Cool Cool Penguins	196?	80.00	200.00
		—Dooto albums above have multi-color labels.—			
Dootone DTL-242	(M)	The Cool Cool Penguins	196?	Counterfeit	

PENN, DAN

Bell 1127	(S)	Nobody's Fool	1973	6.00	15.00

PENTANGLE, THE

Pentangle is Terry Cox, Bert Jansch, Jacqui McShee, John Renbourn and Danny Thompson.

Reprise RS-6315	(S)	The Pentangle	1968	6.00	15.00
Reprise 2RS-6334	(S)	Sweet Child (2 LPs)	1969	6.00	15.00
Reprise RS-6372	(S)	Basket Of Light	1969	4.00	10.00
		—Reprise albums above have brown & orange labels.—			
Reprise RS-6430	(S)	Cruel Sister	1971	1.00	5.00
Reprise RS-6463	(S)	Reflections	1971	1.00	5.00
Reprise MS-2100	(S)	Solomon's Seal	1972	1.00	5.00

PEOPLE

The Capitol People features Larry Norman.

Capitol ST-2924	(S)	I Love You	1968	16.00	40.00
Capitol ST-151	(S)	Both Sides Of People!	1969	16.00	40.00
Paramount PAS-5013	(S)	There Are People And There Are People	1970	8.00	20.00

PEPPER, JIM

Embryo SD-731	(S)	Pepper's Pow Wow	196?	16.00	40.00

PEPPER TREE, THE

Capitol ST-848	(S)	You're My People	1971	3.20	8.00

PEPPERMINT RAINBOW, THE

Decca DL-75129	(S)	Will You Be Staying After Sunday	1969	6.00	15.00

PEPPERMINT TROLLEY COMPANY, THE

Acta 8007	(M)	The Peppermint Trolley Company	1968	6.00	15.00
Acta 38007	(S)	The Peppermint Trolley Company	1968	8.00	20.00

PERHACS, LINDA

Kapp KS-????	(S)	Parallelograms	197?	80.00	200.00

PERKINS, CARL

Mr Perkins was also a member of Class Of '55.

Sun SLP-1225	(M)	The Dance Album Of Carl Perkins	1957	500.00	750.00
Sun SLP-1225	(M)	Teen Beat—The Best Of Carl Perkins	1961	300.00	500.00
		("Teen Beat" is a repackage of "Dance Album.")			
Columbia CL-1234	(M)	Whole Lotta Shakin' (White label promo)	1958	500.00	750.00
Columbia CL-1234	(M)	Whole Lotta Shakin'	1958	175.00	350.00
Design DLP-611	(M)	Tennessee	1963	12.00	30.00
Design SDLP-611	(E)	Tennessee	1963	8.00	20.00
Dollie 4001	(M)	Country Boy's Dream	196?	12.00	30.00
Dollie ST-91428	(S)	Country Boy's Dream (Capitol Rec. Club)	196?	16.00	40.00
Sun LP-111	(E)	Original Golden Hits	1969	4.00	10.00
Sun LP-112	(E)	Blue Suede Shoes	1969	4.00	10.00
		(Sun 111 and 112 reissue material recorded 1956-57.)			
Columbia CS-9833	(S)	Carl Perkins' Greatest Hits	1969	10.00	25.00
Columbia CS-9931	(S)	Carl Perkins On Top	1969	10.00	25.00
		—Columbia albums above have "360 Sound" labels.—			
Harmony HK-11385	(S)	Carl Perkins	196?	6.00	15.00
Harmony HK-31179	(S)	Brown Eyed Handsome Man	1972	4.00	10.00
Harmony HK-31192	(S)	The Greatest Hits Of Carl Perkins	1972	4.00	10.00
Mercury SRM-1-691	(S)	My Kind Of Country	1973	4.00	10.00
Columbia LE-10117	(S)	Carl Perkins' Greatest Hits	1974	4.00	10.00
Trip TLP-8503	(E)	The Best Of Carl Perkins (2 LPs)	1974	1.20	6.00
U.A./Jet LA-856H	(S)	Ol' Blue Suede's Back	1978	4.00	10.00
Jet KZ-35604	(S)	Ol' Blue Suede's Back	1978	1.00	5.00
Album Globe AG-8118	(S)	Country Soul	1980	1.00	5.00
Album Globe AG-9037	(S)	Goin' Back To Memphis	1980	1.00	5.00
Suede 002	(S)	Live At Austin City Limits	1981	4.00	10.00
Accord SN-7169	(S)	Presenting Carl Perkins	1982	1.00	5.00
Allegiance 5001	(S)	The Heart And Soul Of Carl Perkins	1984	1.00	5.00
Koala AW-14164	(S)	Country Soul	198?	1.00	5.00

Label & Catalog #		Title	Year	VG+	NM
PERKINS, CARL, & NRBQ					
Columbia CS-9981	(S)	Boppin' The Blues	1970	10.00	25.00
		—Columbia albums above have "360 Sound " labels.—			
Columbia CS-9981	(S)	Boppin' The Blues	197?	4.00	10.00
Accord SN-7915	(S)	Boppin' The Blues	1982	1.00	5.00
PERLITCH, MICHAEL					
Atlantic SD-7230	(S)	Keyboard Tales	1972	3.20	8.00
PERSUADERS, THE					
Saturn SAT-5000	(M)	Surfer's Nightmare	1963	150.00	300.00
Saturn SATS-5000	(S)	Surfer's Nightmare	1963	200.00	400.00
PERSUADERS, THE					
Atco SD-36-7021	(S)	The Persuaders	1973	6.00	15.00
Atco SD-36-7046	(S)	Best Thing That Ever Happened To Me	1974	6.00	15.00
Calla PZ-34802	(S)	It's All About Love	1977	4.00	10.00
PERSUASIONS, THE					
Catamount CATA-905	(S)	Stardust	197?	20.00	50.00
Reprise/Straight STS-6394	(S)	Acappella	1970	12.00	30.00
Capitol ST-791	(S)	We Came To Play	1971	8.00	20.00
Capitol ST-872	(S)	Street Corner Symphony	1972	8.00	20.00
Capitol ST-11101	(S)	Spread The Word	1972	6.00	15.00
MCA 326	(S)	We Still Ain't Got No Band	1973	4.00	10.00
A&M SD-3656	(S)	I Just Want To Sing With My Friends	1974	4.00	10.00
A&M SD-3635	(S)	More Than Before	1974	4.00	10.00
Elektra 7E-1099	(S)	Chirpin'	1977	4.00	10.00
PETER & GORDON					
Peter Asher and Gordon Waller. Refer to Linda Ronstadt.					
Capitol T-2115	(M)	A World Without Love	1964	8.00	20.00
Capitol ST-2115	(S)	A World Without Love	1964	10.00	25.00
Capitol T-2220	(M)	I Don't Want To See You Again	1964	8.00	20.00
Capitol ST-2220	(S)	I Don't Want To See You Again	1964	10.00	25.00
Capitol T-2324	(M)	I Go To Pieces	1965	8.00	20.00
Capitol ST-2324	(S)	I Go To Pieces	1965	10.00	25.00
Capitol T-2368	(M)	True Love Ways	1965	8.00	20.00
Capitol ST-2368	(S)	True Love Ways	1965	10.00	25.00
Capitol T-2430	(M)	Peter & Gordon Sing The Hits Of Nashville	1966	8.00	20.00
Capitol ST-2430	(S)	Peter & Gordon Sing The Hits Of Nashville	1966	10.00	25.00
Capitol T-2477	(M)	Woman	1966	8.00	20.00
Capitol ST-2477	(S)	Woman ("Woman" is rechanneled)	1966	10.00	25.00
Capitol T-2549	(M)	The Best Of Peter & Gordon	1966	5.00	12.00
Capitol ST-2549	(S)	The Best Of Peter & Gordon	1966	6.00	15.00
		(First pressings of Capitol 2549 have black "rainbow" labels.)			
Capitol ST-2549	(S)	The Best Of Peter & Gordon	1967	3.20	8.00
Capitol ST-2549	(S)	The Best Of Peter & Gordon	1967	4.00	10.00
		(Later pressings have red & white Starline "bullseye" label. "Woman" is rechanneled on both.)			
Capitol T-2664	(M)	Lady Godiva	1967	6.00	15.00
Capitol ST-2664	(S)	Lady Godiva	1967	8.00	20.00
Capitol T-2729	(M)	A Knight In Rusty Armour	1967	6.00	15.00
Capitol ST-2729	(S)	A Knight In Rusty Armour	1967	8.00	20.00
Capitol T-2747	(M)	In London For Tea	1967	8.00	20.00
Capitol ST-2747	(S)	In London For Tea	1967	10.00	25.00
Capitol T-2882	(M)	Hot, Cold And Custard	1968	8.00	20.00
Capitol ST-2882	(S)	Hot, Cold And Custard	1968	10.00	25.00
PETTY, TOM [TOM PETTY & THE HEARTBREAKERS]					
Refer to Del Shannon; The Traveling Wilburys.					
Shelter SRL-52006	(S)	Tom Petty & The Heartbreakers	1976	6.00	15.00
		(Issued with a sheet of black & white photos.)			
		—Shelter albums above have yellow labels.—			
Shelter/ABC TP-12677	(DJ)	Official Live 'Leg	1976	16.00	40.00
		(TP-12677 is a one-sided promo issued with official letter to DJs. Convincing counterfeits exist.)			
Shelter/ABC SRL-52006	(S)	Tom Petty & The Heartbreakers	1978	.80	4.00
Shelter/ABC DA-52029	(DJ)	You're Gonna Get It! (Red vinyl)	1978	6.00	15.00
Shelter/ABC DA-52029	(S)	You're Gonna Get It!	1978	1.00	5.00
Backstreet BSR-5106	(S)	Damn The Torpedoes	1979	1.00	5.00
Backstreet BSR-5160	(S)	Hard Promises	1981	1.00	5.00
Backstreet BSR-5360	(S)	Long After Dark	1982	1.00	5.00
MCA 37116	(S)	You're Gonna Get It!	1983	.80	4.00
MCA 37143	(S)	Tom Petty & The Heartbreakers	1983	.80	4.00
MCA-37239	(S)	Hard Promises	1983	.80	4.00
MCA-37248	(S)	Damn The Torpedoes	1983	.80	4.00
MCA-5360	(S)	Long After Dark	1983	.80	4.00

Label & Catalog #		Title	Year	VG+	NM
MCA 5486	(S)	Southern Accents	1985	.80	4.00
MCA 8021	(DJ)	Pack Up The Plantation (Sampler)	1985	1.20	6.00
MCA 8021	(S)	Pack Up The Plantation	1985	.80	4.00
MCA 5836	(S)	Let Me Up (I've Had Enough)	1987	.80	4.00
MCA 6253	(S)	Full Moon Fever	1989	.80	4.00

PETERSON, RAY

RCA Victor LPM-2297	(M)	Tell Laura I Love Her	1960	40.00	100.00
RCA Victor LSP-2297	(S)	Tell Laura I Love Her	1960	60.00	150.00

—RCA albums above have black "Long Play" or "Living Stereo" labels.—

MGM E-4250	(M)	The Very Best Of Ray Peterson	1964	10.00	25.00
MGM SE-4250	(S)	The Very Best Of Ray Peterson	1964	12.00	30.00
MGM E-4277	(M)	The Other Side Of Ray Peterson	1965	10.00	25.00
MGM SE-4277	(S)	The Other Side Of Ray Peterson	1965	12.00	30.00
Camden CAM-2119	(M)	Goodnight My Love	1966	5.00	12.00
Camden CAS-2119	(S)	Goodnight My Love	1966	6.00	15.00

(Camden 2119 is a reissue of RCA 2297.)

Uni 73078	(S)	The Best Of Ray Peterson	1969	8.00	20.00

(Uni 73078 contains rerecordings of earlier material.)

Decca DL-75307	(S)	Ray Peterson Country	1971	8.00	20.00

PHANTOM'S DIVINE COMEDY, THE

Capitol ST-11313	(S)	Part One	1974	24.00	60.00

PHARAOHS, THE

Scarab 001	(S)	Awakening	1972	6.00	15.00

PHILLIPS, "LITTLE" ESTHER

King 622	(M)	Memory Lane	1959	1,500.00	3,000.00
Lenox 227	(M)	Release Me	1962	40.00	100.00
Lenox 227	(S)	Release Me	1962	80.00	200.00
Atlantic 8102	(M)	And I Love Him (Pink Cupid cover)	1965	20.00	50.00
Atlantic SD-8102	(S)	And I Love Him (Pink Cupid cover)	1965	30.00	75.00
Atlantic 8102	(M)	And I Love Him (Black photo cover)	1966	12.00	30.00
Atlantic SD-8102	(S)	And I Love Him (Black photo cover)	1966	16.00	40.00
Atlantic 8122	(M)	Esther	1966	12.00	30.00
Atlantic SD-8122	(S)	Esther	1966	16.00	40.00
Atlantic 8130	(M)	The Country Side Of Esther Phillips	1966	12.00	30.00
Atlantic SD-8130	(S)	The Country Side Of Esther Phillips	1966	16.00	40.00

(Atlantic 8130 is a reissue of Lenox 227.)

Atlantic SD-1565	(S)	Burnin'	1970	6.00	15.00
Kudu 05	(S)	From A Whisper To A Scream	1972	4.00	10.00
Kudu 09	(S)	Alone Again Naturally	1972	4.00	10.00
Kudu 14	(S)	Black-Eyed Blues	1973	4.00	10.00
Kudu 18	(S)	Performance	1974	4.00	10.00
Kudu 23	(S)	Esther Phillips And Joe Beck	1975	4.00	10.00
Kudu 28	(S)	For All We Know (With Joe Beck)	1976	4.00	10.00
Kudu 31	(S)	Capricorn Princess	1976	4.00	10.00
Atlantic SD-1680	(S)	Confessing The Blues	1976	4.00	10.00
Mercury SRM-1187	(S)	You've Come A Long Way, Baby	1977	1.00	5.00
Mercury SRM-3733	(S)	All About Esther Philips	1978	1.00	5.00
Mercury SRM-3769	(S)	Here's Esther—Are You Ready?	1979	1.00	5.00
Mercury SRM-4005	(S)	Good Black Is Hard To Crack	1981	1.00	5.00

PHILLIPS, GENE

Crown CLP-5375	(S)	Gene Phillips And The Rockers	1963	12.00	30.00
Crown CST-375	(E)	Gene Phillips And The Rockers	1963	8.00	20.00

—Crown albums above have gray labels.—

PHILLIPS, JOHN

Mr. Phillips was the leader of The Journeymen and The Mama's & The Papa's. He can also be found on MGM's soundtrack "Brewster McCloud."

Dunhill DS-50077	(S)	John Phillips/Wolf King Of L.A.	1970	6.00	15.00

PHILLIPS, MICHELLE

Michelle Phillips was a member of The Mama's & The Papa's.

A&M SP-4651	(S)	Victim Of Romance	1977	6.00	15.00

PHILLIPS, WARREN, & THE ROCKETS

Members of The Rockets later recorded as Foghat.

Parrot PAS-71044	(S)	Rocked Out	1970	12.00	30.00
London 50018	(S)	Barefoot Days	1979	4.00	10.00

PHLUPH

Verve V-5054	(M)	Phluph	1968	8.00	20.00
Verve V6-5054	(S)	Phluph	1968	10.00	25.00

Label & Catalog #		Title	Year	VG+	NM

PIANO RED
Piano Red also recorded as Dr. Feelgood.

Label & Catalog #		Title	Year	VG+	NM
Groove LG-1002	(M)	Piano Red In Concert	1956	300.00	600.00
Mastersound 1116	(S)	Dr. Feelgood Goes To College	196?	20.00	50.00
King KS-1117	(S)	Happiness Is Piano Red	1970	8.00	20.00

PICKETT, BOBBY "BORIS", & THE CRYPT KICKERS

Garpax CPX-57001	(M)	The Monster Mash	1962	60.00	150.00
Garpax SGP-67001	(S)	The Monster Mash	1962	150.00	300.00
Parrott XPAS-71063	(E)	The Original Monster Mash	1973	12.00	30.00
		(Parrot 71063 is a reissue of Garpax 67001.)			

PICKETT, WILSON

Double-L DL-2300	(M)	It's Too Late	1963	16.00	40.00
Double-L SDL-8300	(S)	It's Too Late	1963	20.00	50.00
		("R 'n B Special" is rechanneled on this album.)			
Wand WD-672	(M)	Great Wilson Pickett Hits	1966	12.00	30.00
Wand WDS-672	(E)	Great Wilson Pickett Hits	1966	10.00	25.00
Atlantic 8114	(M)	In The Midnight Hour	1965	16.00	40.00
Atlantic SD-8114	(E)	In The Midnight Hour	1965	12.00	30.00
Atlantic 8129	(M)	The Exciting Wilson Pickett	1966	16.00	40.00
Atlantic SD-8129	(E)	The Exciting Wilson Pickett	1966	12.00	30.00
Atlantic 8138	(M)	The Wicked Pickett	1967	16.00	40.00
Atlantic SD-8138	(E)	The Wicked Pickett	1967	12.00	30.00
Atlantic 8145	(M)	The Sound Of Wilson Pickett	1967	16.00	40.00
Atlantic SD-8145	(P)	The Sound Of Wilson Pickett	1967	12.00	30.00
Atlantic 8151	(M)	The Best Of Wilson Pickett	1967	12.00	30.00
Atlantic SD-8151	(E)	The Best Of Wilson Pickett	1967	8.00	20.00
Atlantic SD-8175	(S)	I'm In Love	1968	10.00	25.00
Atlantic SD-8183	(S)	Midnight Mover	1968	10.00	25.00
Atlantic SD-8215	(S)	Hey Jude	1969	8.00	20.00
Atlantic SD-8250	(S)	Right On	1970	8.00	20.00
Atlantic SD-8270	(S)	Wilson Pickett In Philadelphia	1970	8.00	20.00
Atlantic SD-8290	(S)	The Best Of Wilson Pickett, Volume 2	1971	6.00	15.00
Atlantic SD-8300	(S)	Don't Knock My Love	1971	6.00	15.00
Atlantic SD-2501	(P)	Wilson Pickett's Greatest Hits	1973	5.00	12.00
RCA Victor LSP-4858	(S)	Tonight I'm My Biggest Audience	1973	4.00	10.00
RCA Victor APL1-0312	(S)	Miz Lena's Boy	1973	4.00	10.00
RCA Victor APL1-0495	(S)	Pickett In The Picket	1974	4.00	10.00
RCA Victor APL1-0856	(S)	Join Me And Let's Be Free	1975	4.00	10.00
Wicked 9001	(S)	Chocolate Mountain	1976	10.00	25.00
Big Tree 76011	(S)	Funky Situation	1978	1.00	5.00
EMI SW-17019	(S)	I Want You	1979	1.00	5.00
EMI SW-17043	(S)	Right Track	1981	1.00	5.00

PICKETTYWITCH

Janus JLS-3015	(S)	Pickettywitch	1970	4.00	10.00

PIDGEON

Decca DL-75103	(S)	Pidgeon	1969	5.00	12.00

PIG IRON

Columbia CS-1018	(S)	Pig Iron	1970	1.00	5.00

PILOT

RCA Victor LSP-4730	(S)	Pilot	1972	5.00	12.00
RCA Victor LSP-4825	(S)	Point Of View	1973	8.00	20.00

PINDER, MIKE
Pinder is a member of The Moody Blues.

Threshold THS-18	(S)	The Promise	1976	4.00	10.00

PINK FAIRIES, THE

Polydor PD-5537	(S)	Kings Of Oblivion	1973	8.00	20.00

PINK FLOYD
Pink Floyd's original members were founder Syd Barrett, who completed the first album and was replaced by David Gilmour, along with Nick Mason, Roger Waters and Roger Wright.

Tower T-5093	(M)	Piper At The Gates Of Dawn	1967	60.00	150.00
Tower ST-5093	(S)	Piper At The Gates Of Dawn	1967	24.00	60.00
Tower ST-5131	(S)	A Saucerful Of Secrets	1968	24.00	60.00
		—Tower albums above have flat orange labels.—			
Tower ST-5093	(S)	Piper At The Gates Of Dawn	1968	20.00	50.00
Tower ST-5131	(S)	A Saucerful Of Secrets	1968	20.00	50.00
Tower ST-5169	(DJ)	More (Promo label)	1968	60.00	150.00
Tower ST-5169	(S)	More	1968	20.00	50.00
		—Tower albums above have multi-color striped labels.—			

Label & Catalog #		Title	Year	VG+	NM
Harvest SKAO-382	(S)	**Atom Heart Mother**	1970	10.00	25.00
		(Original covers of SKAO-382 do not have the title on the front.)			
Harvest SKAO-382	(S)	**Atom Heart Mother** *(Title on cover)*	197?	6.00	15.00
Harvest STBB-388	(S)	**Ummagumma** *(2 LPs)*	1970	16.00	40.00
		(Original covers of Harvest 388 have a copy of the "Gigi" soundtrack album leaning against the wall in the lower foreground.)			
Harvest STBB-388	(S)	**Ummagumma** *(2 LPs)*	197?	6.00	15.00
		(The cover has a blank cover leaning against the wall.)			
Harvest SW-759	(S)	**Relics**	1971	6.00	15.00
Harvest SMAS-832	(S)	**Meddle**	1971	6.00	15.00
Harvest ST-11078	(S)	**Obscured By Clouds**	1972	6.00	15.00
Harvest SMAS-11163	(S)	**Dark Side Of The Moon** *(With inserts)*	1973	10.00	25.00
		(SMAS-11163 was issued with posters and 2 stickers)			
Harvest SMAS-11163	(S)	**Dark Side Of The Moon** *(Without inserts)*	1973	6.00	15.00
Harvest SABB-11257	(S)	**Nice Pair** *(2 LPs)*	1973	6.00	15.00
		(Repackages material from Tower 5098, 5131 and Harvest 388.)			
Capitol SPRO-8116	(DJ)	**Pink Floyd Tour '75**	1975	30.00	75.00
Capitol SEAX-11902	(S)	**Dark Side Of The Moon** *(Picture disc)*	1978	12.00	30.00
Capitol ST-12276	(S)	**The Works**	1983	1.00	5.00
Columbia PC-33453	(S)	**Wish You Were Here** *(Banded for air-play)*	1975	100.00	250.00
		(Advance copies were shipped in plain white jackets.)			
Columbia PC-33453	(DJ)	**Wish You Were Here** *(Blue cover)*	1975	150.00	300.00
		(Blue cover with the photo and title printed on the jacket.)			
Columbia PC-33453	(S)	**Wish You Were Here**	1975	10.00	25.00
		(Original pressings of PC-33453 were issued in a blue shrinkwrap with a photo & title sticker affixed to the wrap.)			
Columbia PC-33453	(S)	**Wish You Were Here**	1975	4.00	10.00
Columbia PCQ-33453	(Q)	**Wish You Were Here**	1975	16.00	40.00
Columbia JC-34474	(S)	**Animals** *(Promo label with insert)*	1977	40.00	100.00
Columbia AP-1	(S)	**Animals** *(Advance copy)*	1977	60.00	150.00
		(Advance copy intended for air-play with the word "fuck" edited out of "Pigs". Issued in a plain white jacket.)			
Columbia JC-34474	(S)	**Animals**	1977	4.00	10.00
Columbia PCQ-34474	(Q)	**Animals**	1977	16.00	40.00
Columbia HC-33453	(S)	**Wish You Were Here** *(Half-speed master)*	1981	20.00	60.00
Columbia HC-43453	(S)	**Wish You Were Here** *(Half-speed master)*	1982	15.00	45.00
Columbia PC2-36183	(S)	**The Wall** *(2 LPs)*	1983	4.00	10.00
Columbia HC2-46183	(S)	**The Wall** *(2 LPs. Half-speed master)*	1983	50.00	150.00
Columbia AS-	(DJ)	**Off The Wall**	1983	50.00	125.00
Columbia TC-37680	(S)	**Collection Of Great Dance Songs**	1983	1.20	6.00
Columbia HC-47680	(S)	**Collection Of Great Dance Songs** *(Half-speed)*	1983	30.00	75.00
Columbia AS-1636	(DJ)	**The Final Cut** *(Banded for airplay)*	1983	8.00	20.00
Columbia QC-38243	(S)	**The Final Cut**	1983	1.20	6.00
Columbia CK-40599	(S)	**A Momentary Lapse Of Reason**	1987	1.00	5.00
Columbia C2K-44484	(S)	**Delicate Sound Of Thunder**	1988	1.00	5.00

PINK PUZZ: *Refer to* PAUL REVERE & THE RAIDERS

PINKINY CANANDY

Uni 73049	(S)	**Pinkiny Canandy**	1969	5.00	12.00

PIPE DREAM

RCA Victor LSP-4221	(S)	**Wanderers/Lovers**	1969	4.00	10.00

PIPKINS, THE

Capitol ST-483	(S)	**Gimme Dat Ding**	1970	10.00	25.00

PIRANHAS, THE

Custom Fidelity 1452	(S)	**Somethin' Fishy**	1969	60.00	150.00

PISANI, FRANK

Dellwood DLD-56010	(S)	**Sky**	1977	40.00	100.00

PISANO & RUFF

A&M SP-4276	(S)	**Under The Blanket**	1970	3.50	8.00

PITNEY, GENE

Musicor MM-2001	(M)	**The Many Sides Of Gene Pitney**	1962	20.00	50.00
Musicor MS-3001	(E)	**The Many Sides Of Gene Pitney**	1962	12.00	30.00
Musicor MM-2003	(M)	**Only Love Can Break A Heart** *(Die-cut cover)*	1962	16.00	40.00
Musicor MS-3003	(S)	**Only Love Can Break A Heart** *(Die-cut cover)*	1962	20.00	50.00
		—*Musicor albums above have brown labels.*—			
Musicor MM-2001	(M)	**The Many Sides Of Gene Pitney**	1963	10.00	25.00
Musicor MS-3001	(E)	**The Many Sides Of Gene Pitney**	1963	8.00	20.00
Musicor MM-2003	(M)	**Only Love Can Break A Heart**	1963	10.00	25.00
Musicor MS-3003	(S)	**Only Love Can Break A Heart**	1963	12.00	30.00
Musicor MM-2004	(M)	**Gene Pitney Sings Just For You**	1963	12.00	30.00
Musicor MS-3004	(S)	**Gene Pitney Sings Just For You**	1963	16.00	40.00

Label & Catalog #		Title	Year	VG+	NM
Musicor MM-2005	(M)	Gene Pitney Sings World-Wide Winners	1963	12.00	30.00
Musicor MS-3005	(P)	Gene Pitney Sings World-Wide Winners	1963	16.00	40.00

("Only Love Can Break A Heart," "If I Didn't Have A Dime," "The Man Who Shot Liberty Valance," "Tower Tall" and "Half Heaven-Half Heartache" are in stereo.)

Musicor MM-2006	(M)	Blue Gene	1963	12.00	30.00
Musicor MS-3006	(S)	Blue Gene	1963	16.00	40.00
Musicor MM-2007	(M)	The Fair Young Ladies Of Folkland	1964	12.00	30.00
Musicor MS-3007	(S)	The Fair Young Ladies Of Folkland	1964	16.00	40.00
Musicor MM-2008	(M)	Gene Pitney's Big Sixteen	1964	12.00	30.00
Musicor MS-3008	(S)	Gene Pitney's Big Sixteen	1964	16.00	40.00

("Town Without Pity" and "Take Me Tonight" are rechanneled.)
—Musicor albums above have black labels with "Distributed by United Artists."—

Musicor MM-2015	(M)	Gene Italiano	1964	10.00	25.00
Musicor MS-3015	(S)	Gene Italiano	1964	12.00	30.00
Musicor MM-2019	(M)	It Hurts To Be In Love	1964	10.00	25.00
Musicor MS-3019	(P)	It Hurts To Be In Love	1964	12.00	30.00
Musicor MM-2043	(M)	Gene Pitney's More Big Sixteen, Volume 2	1965	10.00	25.00
Musicor MS-3043	(S)	Gene Pitney's More Big Sixteen, Volume 2	1965	12.00	30.00

("It Hurts To Be In Love," "Today's Teardrops," "Hello, Mary Lou," "Every Breath I Take" and "I Laughed So Hard I Cried" are rechanneled.)

Musicor M-2044	(M)	For The First Time! Two Great Singers	1965	10.00	25.00
Musicor MS-3044	(S)	For The First Time! Two Great Singers	1965	12.00	30.00
Musicor M-2044	(M)	Recorded In Nashville	1965	10.00	25.00
Musicor MS-3044	(S)	Recorded In Nashville	1965	12.00	30.00
Musicor MM-2056	(M)	I Must Be Seeing Things	1965	10.00	25.00
Musicor MS-3056	(S)	I Must Be Seeing Things	1965	12.00	30.00
Musicor M-2065	(M)	It's Country Time Again!	1965	10.00	25.00
Musicor MS-3065	(S)	It's Country Time Again!	1965	12.00	30.00
Musicor MM-2069	(M)	Looking Through The Eyes Of Love	1965	10.00	25.00
Musicor MS-3069	(S)	Looking Through The Eyes Of Love	1965	12.00	30.00
Musicor MM-2072	(M)	Gene Pitney Espanol	1965	10.00	25.00
Musicor MS-3072	(S)	Gene Pitney Espanol	1965	12.00	30.00
Musicor MM-2085	(M)	Gene Pitney's Big Sixteen, Volume 3	1966	8.00	20.00
Musicor MS-3085	(S)	Gene Pitney's Big Sixteen, Volume 3	1966	10.00	25.00
Musicor MM-2095	(M)	Backstage I'm Lonely	1966	8.00	20.00
Musicor MS-3095	(S)	Backstage I'm Lonely	1966	10.00	25.00
Musicor MM-2100	(M)	Messuno Mi Puo Giudicare	1966	8.00	20.00
Musicor MS-3100	(S)	Messuno Mi Puo Giudicare	1966	10.00	25.00
Musicor MM-2101	(M)	The Gene Pitney Show	1966	8.00	20.00
Musicor MS-3101	(S)	The Gene Pitney Show	1966	10.00	25.00
Musicor MM-2102	(M)	Greatest Hits Of All Time	1966	8.00	20.00
Musicor MS-3102	(P)	Greatest Hits Of All Time	1966	10.00	25.00

("Town Without Pity," "Every Breath I Take" and "It Hurts To Be In Love" are rechanneled.)

Musicor MM-2104	(M)	The Country Side Of Gene Pitney	1966	8.00	20.00
Musicor MS-3104	(S)	The Country Side Of Gene Pitney	1966	10.00	25.00
Musicor MM-2108	(M)	Young And Warm And Wonderful	1966	8.00	20.00
Musicor MS-3108	(S)	Young And Warm And Wonderful	1966	10.00	25.00
Musicor MM-2117	(M)	Just One Smile	1967	8.00	20.00
Musicor MS-3117	(S)	Just One Smile	1967	10.00	25.00
Musicor MM-2134	(M)	Golden Greats	1967	8.00	20.00
Musicor MS-3134	(P)	Golden Greats	1967	10.00	25.00
Musicor M2S-3148	(P)	The Gene Pitney Story (2 LPs with bonus photo)	1968	14.00	35.00
Musicor M2S-3148	(P)	The Gene Pitney Story (2 LPs without photo)	1968	10.00	25.00
Musicor MS-3161	(S)	Gene Pitney Sings Burt Bacharach	1968	8.00	20.00
Musicor MS-3164	(S)	She's A Heartbreaker	1968	10.00	25.00
Musicor P2S-5025	(P)	This Is Gene Pitney (2 LPs. Record Club)	1968	10.00	25.00
Musicor MS-3174	(S)	The Greatest Hits Of Gene Pitney	1969	6.00	15.00

("I Wanna Love My Life Away," "Something's Gotten Hold Of My Heart," "Nessuno Mi Puo Giudicare" and "Louisiana Mama" are rechanneled.)

Musicor MS-3183	(S)	Gene Pitney Singing The Platters' Golden Platters	1970	6.00	15.00
Musicor MS-3206	(S)	Ten Years After	1971	6.00	15.00
Musicor MS-3250	(P)	The Golden Hits Of Gene Pitney	1971	6.00	15.00

—Musicor albums above have black labels.—

Music Disc MDS-1003	(S)	The Man Who Shot Liberty Valance	1969	4.00	10.00
Music Disc MDS-1005	(S)	Town Without Pity	1969	4.00	10.00
Music Disc MDS-1006	(S)	America's Greatest Country Songs	1969	4.00	10.00
Music Disc MDS-1008	(S)	Twenty Four Hours From Tulsa	1969	4.00	10.00
Music Disc MDS-1014	(S)	Baby, I Need Your Lovin'	1969	4.00	10.00
Design DLP-160	(M)	Spotlight On Gene Pitney	196?	6.00	15.00
Design DLPS-160	(S)	Spotlight On Gene Pitney	196?	6.00	15.00
Colum. House TVP-2P6397	(P)	The Fabulous Gene Pitney (2 LPs)	197?	6.00	15.00

(This set was offered for sale through TV advertisements.)

Trip TOP-16-16	(P)	Gene Pitney's 16 Greatest Hits	1976	1.00	5.00
West-52 QR-16055	(S)	The Pick Of Gene Pitney	1979	4.00	10.00
Everest 4100	(S)	Gene Pitney	1981	1.00	5.00
Rhino RNLP-1102	(P)	Gene Pitney Anthology 1961-1968 (2 LPs)	198?	4.00	10.00

Label & Catalog #		Title	Year	VG+	NM
PIXIES, THE					
Elektra PR-8127	(DJ)	The Pixies Live (One sided)	1989	20.00	50.00
PIXIES THREE, THE					
Mercury MG-20912	(M)	Party With The Pixies Three	1964	60.00	150.00
Mercury SR-60912	(P)	Party With The Pixies Three	1964	80.00	200.00
PLAIN JANE					
Hobbit 5000	(S)	Plain Jane	1969	8.00	20.00
PLAINSONG					
Elektra EKS-75044	(S)	Plainsong	1972	5.00	12.00
PLANT & SEE					
White Whale S-7120	(S)	Plant And See	1969	8.00	20.00
PLASTER CASTERS, THE					
Bluestime BTS-9001	(S)	The Plaster Casters Blues Band	1969	20.00	50.00
PLASTIC ONO BAND, THE: Refer to JOHN LENNON; YOKO ONO					
PLATTERS, THE					
The original Platters feature Tony Williams.					
Federal 295-549	(10")	The Platters	1955	Unreleased	
Federal 549	(M)	The Platters	195?	1,250.00	2,500.00
King 651	(M)	The Platters	1959	500.00	1,000.00
		(King 651 is a reissue of Federal 549.)			
		—King albums above have crownless black labels.—			
Mercury MG-20146	(M)	The Platters	1956	50.00	100.00
Mercury MG-20216	(M)	The Platters, Volume 2	1956	40.00	100.00
Mercury MG-20298	(M)	Flying Platters	1957	40.00	100.00
Mercury MG-20366	(M)	Flying Platters Around The World	1959	12.00	30.00
Mercury SR-60043	(S)	Flying Platters Around The World	1959	20.00	50.00
Mercury MG-20410	(M)	Remember When?	1959	12.00	30.00
Mercury SR-60087	(S)	Remember When?	1959	20.00	50.00
Mercury MG-20472	(M)	Encore Of Golden Hits	1960	8.00	20.00
Mercury SR-60243	(P)	Encore Of Golden Hits	1960	10.00	25.00
Mercury MG-20481	(M)	Reflections	1960	8.00	20.00
Mercury SR-60160	(S)	Reflections	1960	10.00	25.00
Mercury MG-20589	(M)	Life Is Just A Bowl Of Cherries	1960	8.00	20.00
Mercury SR-60245	(S)	Life Is Just A Bowl Of Cherries	1960	10.00	25.00
Mercury MG-20591	(M)	More Encore Of Golden Hits	1960	8.00	20.00
Mercury SR-60252	(S)	More Encore Of Golden Hits	1960	10.00	25.00
Mercury MG-20613	(M)	Encore Of Broadway Golden Hits	1961	8.00	20.00
Mercury SR-60613	(S)	Encore Of Broadway Golden Hits	1961	10.00	25.00
Mercury MG-20669	(M)	Song For The Lonely	1962	8.00	20.00
Mercury SR-60669	(S)	Song For The Lonely	1962	10.00	25.00
Mercury MG-20759	(M)	Moonlight Memories	1963	8.00	20.00
Mercury SR-60759	(S)	Moonlight Memories	1963	10.00	25.00
Mercury MG-20782	(M)	The Platters Present All-Time Movie Hits	1963	8.00	20.00
Mercury SR-60782	(S)	The Platters Present All-Time Movie Hits	1963	10.00	25.00
Mercury MG-20808	(M)	The Platters Sing Latino	1963	8.00	20.00
Mercury SR-60808	(S)	The Platters Sing Latino	1963	10.00	25.00
Mercury MG-20841	(M)	Christmas With The Platters	1963	8.00	20.00
Mercury SR-60841	(S)	Christmas With The Platters	1963	10.00	25.00
Mercury MG-20893	(M)	Encore Of Golden Hits Of The Groups	1964	8.00	20.00
Mercury SR-60893	(S)	Encore Of Golden Hits Of The Groups	1964	10.00	25.00
Mercury MG-20933	(M)	10th Anniversary Album	1964	6.00	15.00
Mercury SR-60933	(S)	10th Anniversary Album	1964	8.00	20.00
		—Mercury albums above have black & silver labels.—			
Mercury MG-20983	(M)	The New Soul Of The Platters	1965	5.00	12.00
Mercury SR-60983	(S)	The New Soul Of The Platters	1965	6.00	15.00
Wing MGW-12112	(M)	Encores!	1959	12.00	30.00
		(Original covers for 12112 have liner notes on the back.)			
Wing MGW-12112	(M)	Encores!	196?	6.00	15.00
Wing SRW-16112	(E)	Encores!	196?	4.00	10.00
		(Later covers have ads for other Wing albums on the back.)			
Wing MGW-12226	(M)	Flying Platters	1963	5.00	12.00
Wing SRW-16226	(S)	Flying Platters	1963	4.00	10.00
Wing MGW-12272	(M)	Reflections	1964	5.00	12.00
Wing SRW-16272	(S)	Reflections	1964	4.00	10.00
Wing MGW-12346	(M)	10th Anniversary Album	1965	5.00	12.00
Wing SRW-16346	(S)	10th Anniversary Album	1965	4.00	10.00
Musicor MM-2091	(M)	I Love You 1,000 Times	1966	5.00	12.00
Musicor MS-3091	(S)	I Love You 1,000 Times	1966	6.00	15.00
Musicor MM-2111	(M)	The Platters Have The Magic Touch	1966	5.00	12.00
Musicor MS-3111	(S)	The Platters Have The Magic Touch	1966	6.00	15.00

Party With The Pixies Three *illustrates how the record industry viewed the proper presentation of a girl group prior to the introduction of Carnaby Street "mod" via the British Invasion in 1964. 'Love' (Can Make You Happy) by The Mercy shows how the same industry packaged a female threesome in the wake of the "Swinging Sixties" media explosion.*

Label & Catalog #		Title	Year	VG+	NM
Musicor MM-2125	(M)	Going Back To Detroit	1967	5.00	12.00
Musicor MS-3125	(S)	Going Back To Detroit	1967	6.00	15.00
Musicor MM-2141	(M)	New Golden Hits Of The Platters	1967	5.00	12.00
Musicor MS-3141	(S)	New Golden Hits Of The Platters	1967	6.00	15.00
Musicor MS-3156	(S)	Sweet, Sweet Lovin'	1968	6.00	15.00
Musicor MS-3171	(S)	I Get The Sweetest Feeling	1968	6.00	15.00
Musicor MS-3185	(S)	Singing The Great Hits Our Way	1969	6.00	15.00
Music Disc MDS-1002	(S)	Only You	1969	5.00	12.00
Musicor MS-3251	(S)	The Golden Hits Of The Platters	1973	2.00	10.00
Pickwick SPC-3120	(S)	In The Still Of The Night	197?	1.00	5.00
Pickwick SPC-3236	(S)	The Platters' Super Hits	197?	1.00	5.00
Trip 16-11	(E)	The Platters' 16 Greatest Hits	1976	1.00	5.00
Chicago Fire 7401	(S)	Live In Chicago	1974	4.00	10.00
Ram	(S)	Reborn	1978	4.00	10.00

PLATTERS, THE / THE EXOTIC GUITARS

Guest Star G-1419	(M)	Only You	196?	6.00	15.00
Guest Star GS-1419	(E)	Only You	196?	4.00	10.00

PLAYBACKS, THE

Round LP-1111	(M)	Greatest Of The Latest	196?	30.00	75.00

PLAYERS, THE

Minit 40006	(M)	He'll Be Back	1967	10.00	25.00
Minit 24006	(S)	He'll Be Back	1967	12.00	30.00

PLEASURE FAIR, THE

Uni 3009	(M)	The Pleasure Fair	1967	4.00	10.00
Uni 73009	(S)	The Pleasure Fair	1967	6.00	15.00

PLIMSOULS, THE

Beat BE-1001	(S)	Zero Hour	1980	10.00	25.00
Planet P-13	(S)	The Plimsouls	1981	8.00	20.00
Geffen 4002	(S)	Everywhere At Once	1983	1.00	5.00

PLUM NELLY

Capitol ST-692	(S)	Deceptive Lines	1971	3.20	8.00

PLUS

Probe CPLP-4513	(S)	The Seven Deadly Sins	1969	6.00	15.00

POCO

The original Poco was Richie Furay and Jim Messina, both of Buffalo Springfield, with George Grantham, Rusty Young, and Randy Meisner, who quit in 1969, replaced by Timothy Schmidt. After the second album, Messina left and Paul Cotton joined. Furay quit in '73; Schmidt in '77. Refer to The Eagles.

Epic BN-26460	(S)	Pickin' Up The Pieces	1969	6.00	15.00
Epic BN-26522	(S)	Poco	1970	6.00	10.00
Epic KE-30209	(S)	Deliverin'	1971	6.00	10.00
Epic KE-30753	(S)	From The Inside	1971	6.00	10.00
Epic KE-31601	(S)	A Good Feelin' To Know	1972	6.00	10.00
		—Epic albums above have yellow labels.—			
Epic BN-26460	(S)	Pickin' Up The Pieces	1973	.80	4.00
Epic BN-26522	(S)	Poco	1973	.80	4.00
Epic KE-30209	(S)	Deliverin'	1973	.80	4.00
Epic EQ-30209	(Q)	Deliverin'	1974	4.00	10.00
Epic KE-30753	(S)	From The Inside	1973	.80	4.00
Epic KE-31601	(S)	A Good Feelin' To Know	1973	.80	4.00
Epic KE-32354	(S)	Crazy Eyes	1973	1.00	5.00
Epic EQ-32354	(Q)	Crazy Eyes	1974	4.00	10.00
Epic PE-32895	(S)	Poco Seven	1974	1.00	5.00
Epic PE-33192	(S)	Cantamos	1974	1.00	5.00
Epic PEQ-33192	(Q)	Cantamos	1974	4.00	10.00
Epic PE-33537	(S)	The Very Best Of Poco (2 LPs)	1975	1.20	6.00
Epic PE-33336	(S)	Poco Live	1976	1.00	5.00
		—Epic albums above have orange labels.—			
ABC 890	(S)	Head Over Heels	1975	.80	4.00
ABC 946	(S)	Rose Of Cimarron	1976	.80	4.00
ABC 989	(S)	Indian Summer	1977	.80	4.00
ABC 1099	(S)	Legend	1978	.80	4.00
MCA 5132	(S)	Under The Gun	1980	.80	4.00
MCA 5227	(S)	Blue And Gray	1981	.80	4.00
MCA 5288	(S)	Cowboys & Englishmen	1982	.80	4.00
MCA 5363	(S)	Backtracks	1982	.80	4.00
Atlantic 80008	(S)	Ghost Town	1982	.80	4.00
Atlantic 80148	(S)	Inamorata	1984	.80	4.00

PODIPTO

GRT 30002	(S)	Podipto	1970	3.20	8.00

Label & Catalog #		Title	Year	VG+	NM
POE					
Uni 73099	(S)	Up Through The Spiral	1971	4.00	10.00
POET & THE ONE MAN BAND					
Paramount PAS-5010	(S)	Poet And The One Man Band	1969	5.00	12.00
POINTER, BONNIE					
Ms. Pointer is a member of The Pointer Sisters.					
Motown M7-929	(S)	Bonnie Pointer	1979	1.00	5.00
POINTER SISTERS, THE					
The sisters Pointer are Anita, Bonnie, June and Ruth.					
Blue Thumb BTS-48	(S)	The Pointer Sisters	1973	1.00	5.00
Blue Thumb BTS-6009	(S)	That's A Plenty	1974	1.00	5.00
Blue Thumb BTS-8002	(S)	Live At The Opera House *(2 LPs)*	1974	1.20	6.00
Blue Thumb BTS-6021	(S)	Steppin'	1975	1.00	5.00
Blue Thumb BTS-6026	(S)	The Best Of The Pointer Sisters *(2 LPs)*	1976	1.20	6.00
Blue Thumb BTS-6023	(S)	Having A Party	1977	1.00	5.00
Planet 1	(S)	Energy	1978	1.00	5.00
Planet 9003	(S)	Priority	1979	1.00	5.00
Planet 9	(S)	Special Things	1980	1.00	5.00
Planet 18	(S)	Black & White	1981	1.00	5.00
Planet 4355	(S)	So Excited!	1982	1.00	5.00
Planet 60203	(S)	Pointer Sisters' Greatest Hits	1982	1.00	5.00
Planet 4705	(S)	Break Out	1983	1.00	5.00
POLICE					
A&M SP-4753	(S)	Outlandos d'Amour	1979	4.00	10.00
		(Advance copies were pressed on non-opaque purple vinyl.)			
A&M SP-4753	(S)	Outlandos d'Amour	1979	1.00	5.00
A&M SP-4792	(S)	Reggatta de Blanc	1979	1.00	5.00
A&M SP-4831	(S)	Zenyatta Mondatta	1980	1.00	5.00
A&M SP-3730	(S)	Ghost In The Machine	1981	1.00	5.00
A&M SP-3730	(S)	Ghost In The Machine *(Picture disc)*	1981	*See note below*	
		(Prototype picdisc that lights up when placed on a turntable! With less than ten pressed, it has a suggested NM value of $500-1,500.)			
A&M SP-3735	(S)	Synchronicity *(Black & white cover)*	1983	12.00	30.00
A&M SP-3735	(S)	Synchronicity *(Brown & grey cover)*	1983	8.00	20.00
A&M SP-3735	(S)	Synchronicity *(Blue, red & yellow cover)*	1983	1.00	5.00
POLLUTION					
Pollution on Prophecy features Dobie Gray.					
Capitol ST-205	(S)	Heir: Pollution	1970	8.00	20.00
Prophecy SD-6051	(S)	Pollution	1971	10.00	25.00
Prophecy SD-6057	(S)	Pollution II	1972	10.00	25.00
PONDEROSA TWINS PLUS ONE					
Horoscope 5001	(S)	Two + Two + One	1971	4.00	10.00
POOKAH					
United Arts. UAS-6737	(S)	Pookah	1970	4.00	10.00
POOL-PAH					
Greene Bottle 1008	(S)	The Flasher	1973	4.00	10.00
POOLE, BRIAN, & THE TREMELOES					
Brian Poole & The Tremeloes were the group that beat out The Beatles for a Decca recording contract in 1962. The Trems were Alan Blakely, Alan Howard, Dave Munden, and Rick West. In 1965, Poole and the group parted ways, with Howard quitting and Mick Clark joining. Refer to The Tremeloes.					
Audio Fidelity AFLP-2151	(M)	Brian Poole Is Here	1966	20.00	50.00
Audio Fidelity AFSD-6151	(E)	Brian Poole Is Here	1966	16.00	40.00
Audio Fidelity AFLP-2177	(M)	The Tremeloes Are Here!	1967	16.00	40.00
Audio Fidelity AFSD-6177	(E)	The Tremeloes Are Here!	1967	12.00	30.00
		(Audio Fidelity 2177 is a reissue of 2151.)			
POOR BOYS, THE					
Rare Earth 519	(S)	Ain't Nothin' In Our Pocket But Love	1970	6.00	15.00
POP, IGGY					
Pop was a member of The Stooges.					
RCA Victor APL1-2275	(S)	The Idiot *(Produced by David Bowie)*	1977	6.00	15.00
RCA Victor AFL1-2488	(S)	Lust For Life *(Produced by David Bowie)*	1977	6.00	15.00
RCA Victor AFL1-2796	(S)	TV Eye—1977 Live	1978	4.00	10.00
Bomp 1018	(S)	Kill City *(Green vinyl)*	1979	4.00	10.00
Arista AL-4237	(S)	New Values	1979	6.00	15.00
Arista AL-4259	(S)	Soldier	1980	4.00	10.00
Arista 9572	(S)	Party	1981	4.00	10.00

Label & Catalog #		Title	Year	VG+	NM
POPPIES, THE					
Epic LN-24200	(M)	Lullaby Of Love	1966	8.00	20.00
Epic BN-24200	(S)	Lullaby Of Love	1966	10.00	25.00
POPPY FAMILY, THE					
London PS-674	(S)	Which Way Are You Going, Billy?	1970	6.00	15.00
PORCELAIN BEARMEAT					
Dill Pickle 3468	(S)	Free Love, Free Sex, Free Music	1971	6.00	15.00
PORTER, DAVID					
Enterprise ENS-1009	(S)	Gritty, Groovy And Gettin' It	1970	8.00	20.00
Enterprise ENS-1012	(S)	Into A Real Thing	1971	8.00	20.00
Enterprise ENS-1019	(S)	Victim Of The Joke?	1972	8.00	20.00
Enterprise ENS-1026	(S)	Sweat And Love	1973	8.00	20.00
PORTER, JERRY					
Mirror SWB-123	(M)	Don't Bother Me!	1966	40.00	100.00
PORTER, PEPPER					
First American FA-7756	(S)	Invasion	1980	10.00	25.00
POSSUM					
Capitol ST-648	(S)	Possum	1970	4.00	10.00
POSSUM RIVER					
Ovation 14	(S)	Possum River	1971	4.00	10.00
POST, MIKE					
Warner Bros. WS-1809	(S)	Fused	1969	4.00	10.00
POTLIQUOR					
Janus JLS-3002	(S)	First Taste	1970	5.00	12.00
Janus JLS-3033	(S)	Levee Blues	1972	5.00	12.00
Janus JLS-3036	(S)	Louisiana Rock And Roll	1973	5.00	12.00
Capitol ST-11998	(S)	Potliquor	1979	1.00	5.00
POTTER, DON					
Mirror 122	(S)	Over The Rainbow	197?	4.00	10.00
POTTER ST. CLOUD					
D. F. Potter and Endle St. Cloud.					
Mediarts 41-7	(S)	Potter St. Cloud	1970	6.00	15.00
POWELL, JIMMY					
Decca DL-75216	(S)	Jimmy Powell	1970	4.00	10.00
POWER, DUFFY					
G.S.F. 1005	(S)	Duffy Power	197?	4.00	10.00
POWER OF ZEUS					
Rare Earth 516	(S)	The Gospel According To Zeus	1970	12.00	30.00
POWERS OF BLUE, THE					
M.T.A. 1002	(M)	Flipout	1967	10.00	25.00
M.T.A. 5002	(S)	Flipout	1967	12.00	30.00
POZO SECO SINGERS, THE					
The Pozo Seco Singers feature future country star Don Williams.					
Columbia CL-2515	(M)	Time/I'll Be Gone	1966	4.00	10.00
Columbia CS-9315	(S)	Time/I'll Be Gone ("Time" is rechanneled)	1966	4.00	10.00
Columbia CL-2600	(M)	I Can Make It With You	1967	4.00	10.00
Columbia CS-9400	(S)	I Can Make It With You	1967	4.00	10.00
Columbia CS-9656	(S)	Shades Of Time	1968	4.00	10.00
Certron CS-7007	(S)	Spend Some Time With Me	1970	4.00	10.00
PRAIRIE MADNESS					
Columbia KC-31003	(S)	Prairie Madness	1972	1.00	5.00
PREMIERS, THE					
Warner Bros. W-1565	(M)	Farmer John	1964	16.00	40.00
Warner Bros. WS-1565	(S)	Farmer John	1964	20.00	50.00
PRESIDENTS, THE					
Sussex SXBX-7005	(S)	5-10-15-20 (25-30 Years Of Love)	1970	10.00	25.00

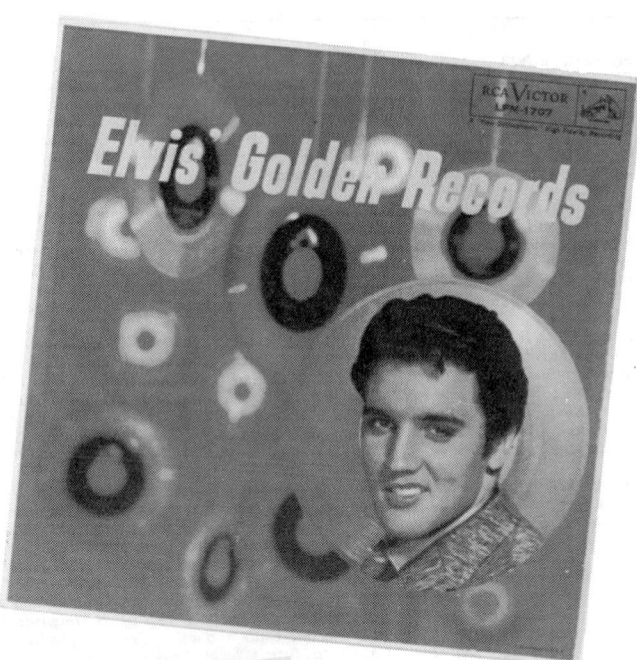

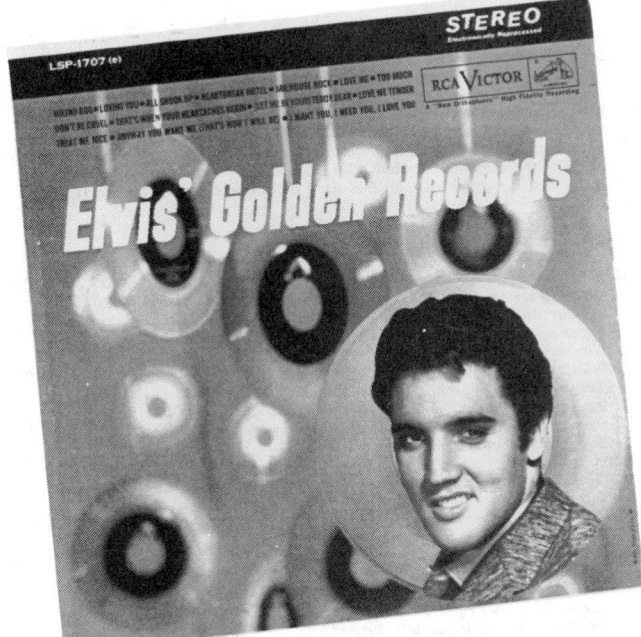

Original pressings of Elvis' Golden Records *from 1958 had the title in light blue print. Later pressings changed the print to white and added the song titles in a black border at the cover's top. This album received an RIAA Gold Record in 1961, indicating sales of approximately 600,000 copies through that period. It received RIAA Platinum certification in 1988, indicating sales of an additional 1,000,000 copies between 1975 and 1988, an astounding accomplishment for a record twenty years old!*

Label & Catalog #		Title	Year	VG+	NM

PRESLEY, ELVIS

Elvis Aron Presley is the single most collectible artist in all of recorded music. With few exceptions, each of his albums remained in print through the vinyl era. To do justice to the enormous amount of label and cover variations that exist for these, the second edition of "A Touch Of Gold," a book devoted exclusively to Elvis, is in the works. For this fifth edition, the listings for those albums issued prior to 1965 include each of the mono and stereo label variations on RCA's glossy black label with Nipper on top listening to "his master's voice." Later pressings with orange, brown and the "new" black label are not listed.

During the 1960s, it was common practice for RCA to have millions of covers printed at once (saving money on a per unit cost) and then using the jackets as the demand arose. Consequently, it's possible that a first pressing jacket could hold a second or third pressing record. As a rule of thumb, mono covers prior to LPM-2756 could hold a first, second, or third pressing album. Stereo albums initially issued from 1968-70 (4088 through 4460, all on the orange label) that are found sealed can be determined by attempting to carefully "bend" the record: If the disc inside is non-flexible, it's an original. But if the disc is flexible, it may be any number of pressings.

Except for the binaural "stereo" on "Essential Elvis, Volume 2," all appearances of the '50s recordings on stereo albums are [hideously] rechanneled. The following soundtrack songs were not released on vinyl in stereo in their original versions: "In My Way," "Forget Me Never," "I Slipped, I Stumbled, I Fell," and the single versions of "Wild In The Country" and "Lonely Man" (all from 1960); "Follow That Dream," "What A Wonderful Life," "I'm Not The Marrying Kind," "A Whistling Tune," "Sound Advice," "King Of The Whole Wide World," "This Is Living," "Riding The Rainbow," "Home Is Where The Heart Is," "I Got Lucky," and "A Whistling Tune" (1961); "Mama" (1962); and "Stay Away" and "Stay Away, Joe" (1967).

In my continuing attempts to make this book as user-friendly as possible, the listings here are noticeably different from previous editions. Section 1 lists albums issued in mono only during the '50s. Section 2 lists the electronically rechanneled stereo versions of the '50s titles. Section 3 collects the LPs issued in the early '60s when monos still carried the "Long 33 1/3 Play" on the label and stereos were known as "Living." Section 4 lists the brief period in 1963-64 when the label carried the "RCA Victor" logo on top in silver print (as it had been since the first LPs were manufactured) and read either "Mono" or "Stereo." Section 5 collects the last few years of the decade when titles were still being released in both mono and stereo. The logo on top switched to white and the designations on the bottom were "Monaural" or "Stereo." Section 6 lists the rest of the releases from 1968 into the '80s. Section 7 is devoted to Camden budgets, RCA Record Club and other "special products" releases, including such mail-order outlets as Reader's Digest and Candlelite Music.

Regarding the musicians that played with Elvis: On his first Sun recordings, he was backed by Scotty Moore on lead guitar and Bill Black on stand-up bass, both of whom have listings as solo artists in this book. They were eventually joined by drummer D.J. Fontana for the later Sun sides. It was this quartet, along with vocal backing by the ubiquitous Jordanaires, that was the backbone of his recordings for RCA through the '50s and into the '60s.

In the wake of Elvis' death in August 1977, pressing plant employees around the country took it upon themselves to create their own collectibles by squeezing a little colored vinyl into the molds they were tending, producing a limited edition of one or two copies for themselves. Several titles exist on the brown label, the later black label with Nipper in the upper right, and on the Pickwick reissues of the original Camden titles. Exactly which titles—and how many of each were pressed—is unknown (and may, in fact, never be known). But each album on colored vinyl carries a suggested Near Mint value of $400-800 each.

1. RCA Victor "Long Play" 1956-1960

Label & Catalog #		Title	Year	VG+	NM
RCA Victor LPM-1254	(M)	**Elvis Presley**	1956	250.00	500.00
		(Original covers for RCA 1254 have the title on the front with "Elvis" in pale pink letters and "Presley" in pale green. The logo box in the upper right corner is the same pale green and holds the catalog number within its borders.)			
RCA Victor LPM-1254	(M)	**Elvis Presley**	1956	200.00	400.00
		(Second covers have the title on the cover with "Elvis" in pale pink letters and "Presley" in a darker, neon-like green. The logo box in the upper right corner is the same dark green and holds the catalog number within its borders.)			
RCA Victor LPM-1254	(M)	**Elvis Presley**	1956	150.00	300.00
		(Third covers have the title on the cover with "Elvis" in pale pink letters and "Presley" in a darker, neon-like green. The logo box in the upper right corner is plain black print and the catalog number is in the lower left corner.)			
RCA Victor LPM-1254	(M)	**Elvis Presley**	195?	60.00	150.00
		(Fourth covers have the title on the cover with "Elvis" in a darker, neon-like pink or red letters and "Presley" in dark green. The logo box in the upper right corner is plain black print and the catalog number is in the lower left corner.)			
RCA Victor LPM-1382	(M)	**Elvis**	1956	150.00	300.00
		(Original covers have ads for other albums along the border of the back.)			
RCA Victor LPM-1382	(M)	**Elvis**	1957	60.00	150.00
		(Later covers delete the ads on the back.)			
RCA Victor LPM-1382	(M)	**Elvis**	195?	500.00	1,000.00
		(Some later pressings contain an alternate take of "Old Shep" in which Elvis sings "he grew old and his eyes were fast growing dim." On all other pressings he sings "he grew old... his eyes were fast growing dim." Copies with the matrix number in the trail-off vinyl ending with "15S," "17S" and "19S" have thus far been identified.)			

As an example of cover stickers there is probably none better than Elvis Is Back!, recorded and released within weeks of Presley's discharge from the U.S. Army in 1960. Since the jacket was printed prior to the recording session (to hasten the process of getting the album on the street), the actual songs that would make the record were not known, so stickers with the titles were affixed to the front after the fact. Original pressings of the album titled the fourth song on the second side as "The Girl Next Door," which appeared on both the label and the sticker (top). All subsequent pressings title the song "The Girl Next Door Went A' Walking" and a new sticker was made up with the title change (bottom).

Label & Catalog #		Title	Year	VG+	NM
RCA Victor LPM-1382	(M)	**Elvis**	1956	**250.00**	**500.00**
		(The label prefixes each track with "Band 1" through "Band 6.")			
RCA Victor LPM-1515	(M)	**Loving You**	1957	**80.00**	**200.00**
		(The title on the front over is in red print.)			
RCA Victor LPM-1515	(M)	**Loving You**	1957	**80.00**	**200.00**
		(The title on the front over is in orange print.)			
RCA Victor LOC-1035	(M)	**Elvis' Christmas Album** *(Red vinyl)*	1957	*See note below*	
		(A single copy of LOC-1035 on translucent red vinyl exists. It has a suggested NM value of $5,000-15,000.)			
RCA Victor LOC-1035	(M)	**Elvis' Christmas Album** *(With sticker)*	1957	**500.00**	**1,000.00**
RCA Victor LOC-1035	(M)	**Elvis' Christmas Album** *(Without sticker)*	1957	**300.00**	**600.00**
		(Original copies of LOC-1035 was issued a special "gift certificate" sticker. This may have been affixed to the cover or to the loose plastic bag in which some distributors packaged the album.)			
RCA Victor LPM-1707	(M)	**Elvis' Golden Records**	1958	**60.00**	**150.00**
		(Original covers for LPM-1707 have the title in light blue print.)			
RCA Victor LPM-1707	(M)	**Elvis' Golden Records**	1959	**40.00**	**100.00**
		(Second covers have the title on the front in light blue print but have "RE" on the back cover.)			
RCA Victor LPM-1884	(M)	**King Creole**	1958	**60.00**	**150.00**
RCA Victor LPM-1884		**King Creole Bonus Photo**	1958	**100.00**	**300.00**
RCA Victor LPM-1951	(M)	**Elvis' Christmas Album**	1958	**40.00**	**100.00**
		(RCA 1951 is a reissue of 1035.)			
RCA Victor LPM-1990	(M)	**For LP Fans Only**	1959	**80.00**	**200.00**
RCA Victor LPM-2011	(M)	**A Date With Elvis** *(With sticker)*	1959	**150.00**	**300.00**
RCA Victor LPM-2011	(M)	**A Date With Elvis** *(Without sticker)*	1959	**80.00**	**200.00**
		(LPM-2011 was originally issued in a gatefold jacket with a 1960 calendar on the back. Most copies have a red sticker affixed to the front that reads "Never Before On LP" and lists the ten song titles.)			
RCA Victor LPM-2075	(M)	**Elvis' Gold Records, Volume 2**	1960	**60.00**	**150.00**

—*RCA albums above have black labels with "Long Play" on the bottom.*—

2. RCA Victor "Stereo Electronically Reprocessed" 1962-1968

RCA Victor LSP-1254	(E)	**Elvis Presley**	1962	**24.00**	**60.00**
RCA Victor LSP-1382	(E)	**Elvis**	1962	**24.00**	**60.00**
RCA Victor LSP-1515	(E)	**Loving You**	1962	**24.00**	**60.00**
RCA Victor LSP-1707	(E)	**Elvis' Golden Records**	1962	**24.00**	**60.00**
RCA Victor LSP-1884	(E)	**King Creole**	1962	**24.00**	**60.00**
RCA Victor LSP-2075	(E)	**Elvis' Gold Records, Volume 2**	1962	**24.00**	**60.00**

—*RCA albums above have black labels with "RCA Victor" in silver on top and "Stereo Electronically Reprocessed" on the bottom.*—

RCA Victor LSP-1254	(E)	**Elvis Presley**	1965	**16.00**	**40.00**
RCA Victor LSP-1382	(E)	**Elvis**	1965	**16.00**	**40.00**
RCA Victor LSP-1515	(E)	**Loving You**	1965	**16.00**	**40.00**
RCA Victor LSP-1707	(E)	**Elvis' Golden Records**	1965	**16.00**	**40.00**
RCA Victor LSP-1884	(E)	**King Creole**	1965	**16.00**	**40.00**
RCA Victor LSP-1951	(E)	**Elvis' Christmas Album**	1965	**20.00**	**50.00**
RCA Victor LSP-1990	(E)	**For LP Fans Only**	1965	**150.00**	**300.00**
		(Some copies of 1990 were erroneously printed with the cover photo of Elvis on the front and back.)			
RCA Victor LSP-1990	(E)	**For LP Fans Only**	1965	**20.00**	**50.00**
RCA Victor LSP-2011	(E)	**A Date With Elvis**	1965	**20.00**	**50.00**
RCA Victor LSP-2075	(E)	**Elvis' Gold Records, Volume 2**	1965	**16.00**	**40.00**

—*RCA albums above have black labels with "RCA Victor" in white on top and "Stereo Electronically Reprocessed" on the bottom.*—

3. RCA Victor "Long Play" / "Living Stereo" 1960-1963

RCA Victor LPM-2231	(M)	**Elvis Is Back!** *(Gatefold with sticker)*	1960	**60.00**	**150.00**
RCA Victor LPM-2231	(M)	**Elvis Is Back!** *(Gatefold without sticker)*	1960	**40.00**	**100.00**
RCA Victor LSP-2231	(S)	**Elvis Is Back!** *(Gatefold with sticker)*	1960	**80.00**	**200.00**
RCA Victor LSP-2231	(S)	**Elvis Is Back!** *(Gatefold without sticker)*	1960	**60.00**	**150.00**
		(Original covers for 2231 do not have the song titles printed on the front. Most copies have a yellow sticker affixed to the cover that lists the twelve song titles. Both the label and the sticker list the fourth song on the second side as "The Girl Next Door.")			
RCA Victor LPM-2231	(M)	**Elvis Is Back!** *(Gatefold with sticker)*	1960	**50.00**	**125.00**
RCA Victor LPM-2231	(M)	**Elvis Is Back!** *(Gatefold without sticker)*	1960	**30.00**	**75.00**
RCA Victor LSP-2231	(S)	**Elvis Is Back!** *(Gatefold with sticker)*	1960	**60.00**	**150.00**
RCA Victor LSP-2231	(S)	**Elvis Is Back!** *(Gatefold without sticker)*	1960	**40.00**	**100.00**
		(Second pressings do not the song titles printed on th front. Most copies have a yellow sticker affixed to the front that lists the twelve song titles. The sticker and the label list "The Girl Next Door Went A-Walking" the title of the song on all subsequent pressings.)			
RCA Victor LPM-2231	(M)	**Elvis Is Back!** *(Gatefold cover)*	1960	**20.00**	**50.00**
RCA Victor LSP-2231	(S)	**Elvis Is Back!** *(Gatefold cover)*	1960	**30.00**	**75.00**
		(Third pressings have the song titles printed on the front cover.)			

Label & Catalog #		Title	Year	VG+	NM
RCA Victor LPM-2256	(M)	G.I. Blues (With sticker)	1960	40.00	100.00
RCA Victor LPM-2256	(M)	G.I. Blues (Without sticker)	1960	20.00	50.00
RCA Victor LSP-2256	(S)	G.I. Blues (With sticker)	1960	50.00	125.00
RCA Victor LSP-2256	(S)	G.I. Blues (Without sticker)	1960	30.00	75.00
		(The cover has a heart-shaped sticker advertising "Wooden Heart.)			
RCA Victor LPM-2328	(M)	His Hand In Mine	1961	20.00	50.00
RCA Victor LSP-2328	(S)	His Hand In Mine	1961	30.00	75.00
RCA Victor LPM-2370	(M)	Something For Everybody	1961	20.00	50.00
RCA Victor LSP-2370	(S)	Something For Everybody	1961	30.00	75.00
		(Original covers for 2370 advertise Compact-33s on the back.)			
RCA Victor LPM-2426	(M)	Blue Hawaii	1961	20.00	50.00
RCA Victor LSP-2426	(S)	Blue Hawaii	1961	30.00	75.00
		(Some later pressings of 2426 had a red sticker on the cover that reads "Contains the Twist Special Rock-A-Hula Baby." Add $25-50 for copies with this sticker.)			
RCA Victor LPM-2523	(M)	Pot Luck With Elvis	1962	20.00	50.00
RCA Victor LSP-2523	(S)	Pot Luck With Elvis	1962	30.00	75.00
RCA Victor LPM-2621	(M)	Girls! Girls! Girls!	1962	20.00	50.00
RCA Victor LSP-2621	(S)	Girls! Girls! Girls!	1962	30.00	75.00
RCA Victor 2621		Girls! Girls! Girls! Bonus Calendar	1962	100.00	300.00
		(1963 calendar with ads for Elvis' EPs and LPs on the back)			
RCA Victor LPM-2697	(M)	It Happened At The World's Fair	1963	20.00	50.00
RCA Victor LSP-2697	(S)	It Happened At The World's Fair	1963	30.00	75.00
RCA Victor 2697		It Happened At The World's Fair Photo	1963	100.00	300.00
		—RCA albums above have black labels with "Long Play" or "Living Stereo" on the bottom.—			

4. RCA Victor "Mono" / "Stereo" 1963-1964

Label & Catalog #		Title	Year	VG+	NM
RCA Victor LPM-1254	(M)	Elvis Presley	1963	20.00	50.00
RCA Victor LPM-1382	(M)	Elvis	1963	20.00	50.00
RCA Victor LPM-1515	(M)	Loving You	1963	20.00	50.00
RCA Victor LPM-1707	(M)	Elvis' Golden Records	1963	20.00	50.00
RCA Victor LPM-1884	(M)	King Creole	1963	20.00	50.00
RCA Victor LPM-1951	(M)	Elvis' Christmas Album	1963	20.00	50.00
RCA Victor LPM-1990	(M)	For LP Fans Only	1963	20.00	50.00
RCA Victor LPM-2011	(M)	A Date With Elvis	1963	20.00	50.00
RCA Victor LPM-2075	(M)	Elvis' Gold Records, Volume 2	1963	20.00	50.00
RCA Victor LPM-2231	(M)	Elvis Is Back! (Gatefold cover)	1963	20.00	50.00
RCA Victor LSP-2231	(S)	Elvis Is Back! (Gatefold cover)	1965	20.00	50.00
RCA Victor LPM-2256	(M)	G.I. Blues	1963	20.00	50.00
RCA Victor LSP-2256	(S)	G.I. Blues	1963	20.00	50.00
RCA Victor LPM-2328	(M)	His Hand In Mine	1963	20.00	50.00
RCA Victor LSP-2328	(S)	His Hand In Mine	1963	20.00	50.00
RCA Victor LPM-2370	(M)	Something For Everybody	1963	20.00	50.00
RCA Victor LSP-2370	(S)	Something For Everybody	1963	20.00	50.00
		(The back cover advertises "Viva Las Vegas.".)			
RCA Victor LPM-2426	(M)	Blue Hawaii	1963	20.00	50.00
RCA Victor LSP-2426	(S)	Blue Hawaii	1963	20.00	50.00
RCA Victor LPM-2523	(M)	Pot Luck With Elvis	1963	20.00	50.00
RCA Victor LSP-2523	(S)	Pot Luck With Elvis	1963	20.00	50.00
RCA Victor LPM-2621	(M)	Girls! Girls! Girls!	1963	20.00	50.00
RCA Victor LSP-2621	(S)	Girls! Girls! Girls!	1963	20.00	50.00
RCA Victor LPM-2756	(M)	Fun In Acapulco	1963	20.00	50.00
RCA Victor LSP-2756	(S)	Fun In Acapulco	1963	24.00	60.00
RCA Victor LPM-2765	(M)	Elvis' Golden Records, Volume 3	1963	20.00	50.00
RCA Victor LSP-2765	(S)	Elvis' Golden Records, Volume 3	1963	24.00	60.00
RCA Victor 2765		Elvis' Golden Records, Volume 3 Folio	1963	25.00	75.00
		(LPM-2765 was issued with a booklet titled "Elvis Full Color Picture Folio Plus Special Giant Size Pin-Up Picture Inside" Subtract $25 if the pin-up is missing.)			
RCA Victor LPM-2894	(M)	Kissin' Cousins	1964	20.00	50.00
RCA Victor LSP-2894	(S)	Kissin' Cousins	1964	24.00	60.00
		(The cover has a small b&w photo of the cast in the lower right.)			
RCA Victor LPM-2894	(M)	Kissin' Cousins	1964	36.00	90.00
RCA Victor LSP-2894	(S)	Kissin' Cousins	1964	40.00	100.00
		(The cover does not have the inset b&w photo.)			
RCA Victor LPM-2999	(M)	Roustabout	1964	20.00	50.00
RCA Victor LSP-2999	(S)	Roustabout	1964	250.00	500.00
		—RCA albums above have black labels with a silver "RCA Victor" on top and "Mono" or "Stereo" on the bottom.—			

5. RCA Victor "Monaural" / "Stereo" 1965-1968

Label & Catalog #		Title	Year	VG+	NM
RCA Victor LPM-1254	(M)	Elvis Presley	1965	16.00	40.00
RCA Victor LPM-1382	(M)	Elvis	1965	16.00	40.00
RCA Victor LPM-1515	(M)	Loving You	1965	16.00	40.00
RCA Victor LPM-1707	(M)	Elvis' Golden Records	1965	16.00	40.00
RCA Victor LPM-1884	(M)	King Creole	1965	16.00	40.00

Label & Catalog #		Title	Year	VG+	NM
RCA Victor LPM-1951	(M)	Elvis' Christmas Album	1965	16.00	40.00
RCA Victor LPM-1990	(M)	For LP Fans Only	1965	150.00	300.00
		(Some copies of 1990 were erroneously printed with the cover photo of Elvis on the front and back.)			
RCA Victor LPM-1990	(M)	For LP Fans Only	1965	16.00	40.00
RCA Victor LPM-2011	(M)	A Date With Elvis	1965	16.00	40.00
RCA Victor LPM-2075	(M)	Elvis' Gold Records, Volume 2	1965	16.00	40.00
RCA Victor LPM-2231	(M)	Elvis Is Back! (Gatefold cover)	1965	16.00	40.00
RCA Victor LSP-2231	(S)	Elvis Is Back! (Gatefold cover)	1965	16.00	40.00
RCA Victor LPM-2256	(M)	G.I. Blues	1965	16.00	40.00
RCA Victor LSP-2256	(S)	G.I. Blues	1965	16.00	40.00
RCA Victor LPM-2328	(M)	His Hand In Mine	1965	16.00	40.00
RCA Victor LSP-2328	(S)	His Hand In Mine	1965	16.00	40.00
RCA Victor LPM-2370	(M)	Something For Everybody	1965	16.00	40.00
RCA Victor LSP-2370	(S)	Something For Everybody	1965	16.00	40.00
RCA Victor LPM-2426	(M)	Blue Hawaii	1965	16.00	40.00
RCA Victor LSP-2426	(S)	Blue Hawaii	1965	16.00	40.00
RCA Victor LPM-2523	(M)	Pot Luck With Elvis	1965	16.00	40.00
RCA Victor LSP-2523	(S)	Pot Luck With Elvis	1965	16.00	40.00
RCA Victor LPM-2621	(M)	Girls! Girls! Girls!	1965	16.00	40.00
RCA Victor LSP-2621	(S)	Girls! Girls! Girls!	1965	16.00	40.00
RCA Victor LPM-2756	(M)	Fun In Acapulco	1965	16.00	40.00
RCA Victor LSP-2756	(S)	Fun In Acapulco	1965	16.00	40.00
RCA Victor LPM-2765	(M)	Elvis' Golden Records, Volume 3	1965	16.00	40.00
RCA Victor LSP-2765	(S)	Elvis' Golden Records, Volume 3	1965	16.00	40.00
RCA Victor LPM-2894	(M)	Kissin' Cousins	1965	16.00	40.00
RCA Victor LSP-2894	(S)	Kissin' Cousins	1965	16.00	40.00
RCA Victor LPM-2999	(M)	Roustabout	1965	16.00	40.00
RCA Victor LSP-2999	(S)	Roustabout	1965	16.00	40.00
RCA Victor LPM-3338	(M)	Girl Happy	1965	16.00	40.00
RCA Victor LSP-3338	(S)	Girl Happy	1965	16.00	40.00
RCA Victor LPM-3450	(M)	Elvis For Everyone	1965	16.00	40.00
RCA Victor LSP-3450	(P)	Elvis For Everyone	1965	16.00	40.00
RCA Victor LPM-3468	(M)	Harum Scarum	1965	12.00	30.00
RCA Victor LSP-3468	(S)	Harum Scarum	1965	12.00	30.00
RCA Victor 3468		Harum Scarum Bonus Photo	1965	12.00	30.00
RCA Victor LPM-3553	(M)	Frankie And Johnny	1966	12.00	30.00
RCA Victor LSP-3553	(S)	Frankie And Johnny	1966	12.00	30.00
RCA Victor 3553		Frankie And Johnny Bonus Print	1966	12.00	30.00
RCA Victor LPM-3643	(M)	Paradise Hawaiian Style	1966	12.00	30.00
RCA Victor LSP-3643	(S)	Paradise Hawaiian Style	1966	12.00	30.00
RCA Victor LPM-3702	(M)	Spinout	1966	12.00	30.00
RCA Victor LSP-3702	(S)	Spinout	1966	12.00	30.00
RCA Victor 3702		Spinout Bonus Photo	1966	12.00	30.00

—RCA albums above have black labels with "RCA Victor" in white on top and "Monaural" or "Stereo" on the bottom.—

Label & Catalog #		Title	Year	VG+	NM
RCA Victor SP-33-461	(M)	Special Palm Sunday Programming	1967	1,000.00	2,000.00
		(Radio program consisting of previously released album tracks issued without a cover. Counterfeits exist!)			
RCA Victor LPM-3758	(M)	How Great Thou Art	1967	30.00	75.00
RCA Victor LSP-3758	(S)	How Great Thou Art	1967	20.00	50.00
		(Original covers do not have the RIAA Gold Record Award on the front.)			
RCA Victor LSP-3758	(S)	How Great Thou Art	1967	12.00	30.00
		(Later covers have the RIAA Gold Record Award on the cover.)			

—RCA albums above have black labels with "Mono/Stereo Dynagroove" on the bottom.—

Label & Catalog #		Title	Year	VG+	NM
RCA Victor LPM-3787	(M)	Double Trouble	1967	20.00	50.00
RCA Victor LSP-3787	(S)	Double Trouble	1967	12.00	30.00
RCA Victor 3787		Double Trouble Bonus Photo	1967	12.00	30.00
		(Original covers for 3787 have a printed announcement for a bonus photo between the two photos of Elvis.)			
RCA Victor LPM-3787	(M)	Double Trouble	1967	20.00	50.00
RCA Victor LSP-3787	(S)	Double Trouble	1967	12.00	30.00
		(Later covers delete the bonus photo announcement.)			
RCA Victor LPM-3893	(M)	Clambake	1967	80.00	200.00
RCA Victor LSP-3893	(S)	Clambake	1967	12.00	30.00
RCA Victor 3893		Clambake Bonus Photo	1967	12.00	30.00
RCA Victor UNMR-5697	(M)	Special Christmas Programming	1967	1,000.00	2,000.00
		(Radio program consisting of previously released album tracks issued without a cover. Counterfeits exist!)			
RCA Victor LPM-3921	(M)	Elvis' Gold Records, Volume 4	1968	800.00	1,200.00
RCA Victor LSP-3921	(S)	Elvis' Gold Records, Volume 4	1968	16.00	40.00
RCA Victor 3921		Elvis' Gold Records, Volume 4 Bonus Photo	1968	60.00	180.00
RCA Victor LPM-3989	(M)	Speedway	1968	800.00	1,200.00
RCA Victor LSP-3989	(S)	Speedway	1968	12.00	30.00
RCA Victor 3989		Speedway Bonus Photo	1968	20.00	60.00

—RCA albums above have black labels with "RCA Victor" in white on top and "Monaural" or "Stereo" on the bottom.—

Label & Catalog #		Title	Year	VG+	NM

6. RCA Victor Non-Flexible Stereo 1969-71

Label & Catalog #		Title	Year	VG+	NM
RCA Victor LPM-4088	(P)	Elvis (NBC TV Special)	1968	10.00	25.00
RCA Victor LSP-4155	(S)	From Elvis In Memphis	1969	10.00	25.00
RCA Victor LSP-4155		From Elvis In Memphis Bonus Photo	1969	5.00	15.00
RCA Victor LSP-6020	(S)	From Memphis To Vegas /			
		From Vegas To Memphis (2 LPs)	1969	12.00	30.00
RCA Victor 6020		From Memphis To Vegas /			
		From Vegas To Memphis Bonus Photos	1969	5.00	15.00
		(LSP-6020 was issued with two of four possible bonus photos. Each has a value of $15.)			
RCA Victor (No number)		International Hotel Presents Elvis, 1969	1969	See note below	
		(This special box was given to those persons who attended Elvis' opening shows in Las Vegas in July 1969. The box includes a copy of LPM-4088; a copy of LSP-4155; three photos; a 1969 Elvis Record Catalog; and a letter of thanks from Elvis and the Colonel. Very rare with a suggested NM value of $2,500-4,500 of which at least 90% is for the box alone.)			
RCA Victor (No number)		International Hotel Presents Elvis, 1970	1970	See note below	
		(This special box was given to those persons who attended Elvis' opening shows in Las Vegas in February 1970. The box includes a copy of LSP-6020; a copy of the single "Kentucky Rain;" one photo; an Elvis 1970 Record Catalog; a 1970 wallet calendar; a hotel menu; a photo album; and a letter of thanks from Elvis and the Colonel. Very rare with a suggested NM value of $2,5000-4,500 of which at least 90% is for the box alone.)			
RCA Victor LSP-4362	(S)	On Stage-February, 1970	1970	10.00	25.00
RCA Victor LPM-6401	(M)	Worldwide 50 Gold Award Hits, Vol. 1	1970	24.00	60.00
		(4 LP box with ad for book on cover.)			
RCA Victor 6401		Worldwide 50 Gold Award Hits, Vol. 1 Book	1970	10.00	30.00
RCA Victor LSP-4428	(S)	Elvis In Person At The International Hotel	1970	10.00	25.00
RCA Victor LSP-4429	(S)	Back In Memphis	1970	10.00	25.00
		(RCA 4428 and 4429 reissue both parts of 6020.)			
RCA Victor LSP-4445	(S)	That's The Way It Is	1970	10.00	25.00
RCA Victor LSP-4460	(S)	Elvis Country	1971	10.00	25.00
RCA Victor 4460		Elvis Country Bonus Photo	1971	4.00	12.00
		—RCA albums above have orange labels on non-flexible vinyl.—			
RCA Victor LPM-4088	(P)	Elvis (NBC TV Special)	1971	4.00	10.00
RCA Victor LSP-4155	(S)	From Elvis In Memphis	1971	4.00	10.00
RCA Victor LSP-6020	(S)	From Memphis To Vegas /			
		From Vegas To Memphis (2 LPs)	1971	6.00	15.00
RCA Victor LSP-4362	(S)	On Stage-February, 1970	1971	4.00	10.00
RCA Victor LPM-6401	(M)	Worldwide 50 Gold Award Hits, Vol. 1 (4 LP)	1971	10.00	25.00
RCA Victor LSP-4428	(S)	Elvis In Person At The International Hotel	1971	4.00	10.00
RCA Victor LSP-4429	(S)	Back In Memphis	1971	4.00	10.00
RCA Victor LSP-4445	(S)	That's The Way It Is	1971	4.00	10.00
RCA Victor LSP-4460	(S)	Elvis Country	1971	4.00	10.00
		—RCA albums above have orange labels on flexible vinyl.—			
RCA Victor LSP-4530	(S)	Love Letters From Elvis	1971	12.00	30.00
		(Original covers for LSP-4530 have the RCA logo and catalog number at the top center on front.)			
RCA Victor LSP-4530	(S)	Love Letters From Elvis	1971	6.00	15.00
		(Later covers have the RCA logo and catalog number in the lower right corner of the cover.)			
RCA Victor LPM-6402	(M)	The Other Sides—			
		Worldwide Gold Award Hits, Vol. 2 (4 LP)	1971	20.00	50.00
		(4 LP box. Original boxes have printed ads on the front for two bonuses: A fold-open print of Elvis and an envelope with a "piece" of Elvis' wardrobe, worth an additional $15 each.)			
RCA Victor LSP-4579	(S)	The Wonderful World Of Christmas	1971	12.00	30.00
RCA Victor 4579		The Wonderful World Of Christmas Photo	1971	10.00	30.00
RCA Victor LSP-4671	(S)	Elvis Now	1972	10.00	25.00
RCA Victor LSP-4690	(S)	He Touched Me	1972	10.00	25.00
RCA SPS-33-571-1	(DJ)	Recorded At Madison Square Garden	1972	80.00	200.00
		(2 LPs banded for air-play and issued in a plain white cover.)			
RCA Victor LSP-4776	(DJ)	Recorded At Madison Square Garden	1972	6.00	15.00
RCA Victor VPSX-6089	(Q)	Aloha From Hawaii Via Satellite (2 LPs)	1973	See note below	
		(RCA provided the Van Camp Co., sponsors of the "Aloha From Hawaii" TV Special, with advance copies of VPSX-6089, to which the company affixed stickers with the "Chicken of the Sea" mermaid. These were distributed among employees and have a suggested NM value of $2,000-4,000.)			
RCA Victor VPSX-6089	(Q)	Aloha From Hawaii Via Satellite (2 LPs)	1973	12.00	30.00
		(Original commercial copies of VPSX-6089 have dark orange labels with a dark "Quadradisc" on top and "RCA" on the bottom.)			
RCA Victor APL1-0283	(S)	Elvis	1973	20.00	50.00
RCA Victor CPL1-0341	(P)	A Legendary Performer, Volume 1	1974	6.00	15.00
		(Black label with gold print in a die-cut cover with a bonus book.)			
RCA Victor APL1-0388	(S)	Raised On Rock/ For Ol' Times Sake	1973	10.00	25.00
RCA Victor CPL1-0475	(S)	Good Times	1974	10.00	25.00

Label & Catalog #		Title	Year	VG+	NM
RCA Victor DJL1-0606	(DJ)	Recorded Live On Stage In Memphis	1974	80.00	200.00
RCA Victor APL1-0606	(S)	Recorded Live On Stage In Memphis	1974	6.00	15.00
RCA Victor APD1-0606	(Q)	Recorded Live On Stage In Memphis	1974	80.00	200.00
Boxcar (No number)	(M)	Having Fun With Elvis On Stage	1974	80.00	200.00
RCA Victor CPM1-0818	(M)	Having Fun With Elvis On Stage	1974	10.00	25.00
RCA Victor APL1-0873	(S)	Promised Land	1975	20.00	50.00
RCA Victor APD1-0873	(Q)	Promised Land (Orange label)	1975	60.00	150.00
RCA Victor APD1-0873	(Q)	Promised Land (Black label)	1976	20.00	50.00
RCA Victor APL1-1039	(S)	Elvis Today	1975	20.00	50.00
RCA Victor APD1-1039	(Q)	Elvis Today (Orange label)	1975	60.00	150.00
RCA Victor APD1-1039	(Q)	Elvis Today (Black label)	1976	20.00	50.00
		—RCA albums above have orange "dynaflex" labels.—			
RCA Victor CPL1-1349	(P)	A Legendary Performer, Volume 2	1976	6.00	15.00
		(Black label with gold print in a die-cut cover with a bonus book.)			
RCA Victor APL1-0873	(S)	Promised Land	1975	4.00	10.00
RCA Victor APL1-1039	(S)	Elvis Today	1975	4.00	10.00
RCA Victor APM1-1675	(M)	The Sun Sessions	1976	4.00	10.00
RCA Victor APL1-1506	(S)	From Elvis Presley Boulevard, Memphis, Tennessee	1976	4.00	10.00
		—RCA albums above have brown labels.—			
RCA Victor APL1-2275	(S)	Welcome To My World	1977	1.00	5.00
RCA Victor AFL1-2428	(S)	Moody Blue (Solid colored vinyl)	1977	800.00	1,200.00
		(Copies of AFL1-2428 were pressed on solid colored vinyl; gold, green, red, and white are known to exist.)			
RCA Victor AFL1-2428	(S)	Moody Blue (Multi-colored vinyl)	1977	1,200.00	1,800.00
		(Copies were also pressed on multi-colored, "splash" vinyl; purple-on-white, yellow-on-white, and red-on-white exist.)			
RCA Victor AFL1-2428	(S)	Moody Blue (Blue vinyl)	1977	1.00	5.00
RCA Victor AFL1-2428	(S)	Moody Blue (Black vinyl)	1977	150.00	300.00
RCA Victor CPL1-3078	(P)	A Legendary Performer, Volume 3	1979	6.00	15.00
		(Black label with gold print in a die-cut cover with a bonus book.)			
RCA Victor DJL1-3455	(S)	Pure Elvis	1979	150.00	300.00
RCA Victor CPL8-3699	(P)	Elvis Aron Presley (8 LP box with book)	1980	30.00	75.00
RCA Victor DJL1-3729	(P)	Elvis Aron Presley In-Store Sampler	1980	60.00	150.00
RCA Victor DJL1-3780	(P)	Elvis Aron Presley Radio Station Sampler	1980	80.00	200.00
RCA Victor CPL1-4848	(P)	A Legendary Performer, Volume 4	1980	6.00	15.00
		(Black label with gold print in a die-cut cover with a bonus book.)			
RCA Victor CPM6-5172	(P)	A Golden Celebration (6 LP box with photo)	1984	16.00	40.00

7. RCA Special Products & Camden, 1968-1973

Label & Catalog #		Title	Year	VG+	NM
RCA Victor PRS-279	(S)	Singer Presents Elvis Singing Flaming Star & Others	1968	10.00	25.00
		(Available through Singer Sewing Centers in preparation for the Singer sponsored NBC-TV Special. With the purchase of an album the fan received several bonuses, priced separately below. This was reissued on Camden.)			
RCA Victor PRS-279		Singer Presents Elvis Bonus #1	1968	40.00	100.00
		(32 page booklet listing all of the stations carrying the TV Special.)			
RCA Victor PRS-279		Singer Presents Elvis Bonus #2	1968	10.00	25.00
		(Full color photo with Elvis in-print catalog on the back and an ad for the TV Special on the bottom.)			
RCA Victor PRS-279		Singer Presents Elvis Bonus #3	1968	6.00	15.00
		(Full color photo with the catalog on the back but without the ad.)			
RCA Victor PRS-279		Singer Presents Elvis Bonus #4	1968	6.00	15.00
		(A 4" x 6" "ticket" inviting the customer to watch the TV Special.)			
		—RCA albums above have light brown labels.—			
Camden CAS-2304	(S)	Elvis Sings Flaming Star	1969	10.00	25.00
Camden CAS-2408	(S)	Let's Be Friends	1970	10.00	25.00
Camden CAS-2440	(S)	Almost In Love	1970	10.00	25.00
Camden CAL-2428	(P)	Elvis' Christmas Album	1970	10.00	25.00
		—Camden albums above have blue labels on non-flexible vinyl.—			
Camden CAS-2304	(S)	Elvis Sings Flaming Star	197?	4.00	10.00
Camden CAS-2408	(S)	Let's Be Friends	197?	4.00	10.00
Camden CAS-2440	(S)	Almost In Love	197?	4.00	10.00
Camden CAL-2428	(M)	Elvis' Christmas Album	197?	4.00	10.00
Camden CAX-2472	(P)	You'll Never Walk Alone	197?	4.00	10.00
Camden CAL-2518	(M)	C'mon Everybody	1971	4.00	10.00
Camden CAL-2533	(M)	I Got Lucky	1971	4.00	10.00
Camden CAS-2567	(S)	Elvis Sings Hits From His Movies, Volume 1	1972	4.00	10.00
Camden CAS-2595	(S)	Burning Love & Hits From His Movies, Vol. 2	1972	10.00	25.00
		(Original pressings of CAS-2595 have a star on the front cover advertising the bonus photo, priced separately below.)			
Camden 2595		Burning Love Bonus Photo	1972	10.00	25.00
Camden CAS-2595	(S)	Burning Love & Hits From His Movies, Vol. 2	1972	10.00	25.00
Camden CAS-2611	(P)	Separate Ways	1973	4.00	10.00
		—Camden albums above have blue labels on flexible vinyl.—	1973	4.00	10.00

John Preston Courville, a.k.a. Johnny Preston, was discovered by J. P. "Big Bopper" Richardson, who wrote "Running Bear" for his protege and, along with country music's then latest singing sensation, George Jones, provided the "Indian sounds" in the background. He then watched it top the charts. Both of Preston's Mercury albums from this era, Running Bear and Come Rock With Me, are rarer in stereo than mono.

Label & Catalog #		Title	Year	VG+	NM
RCA Victor R-213690	(M)	Worldwide Gold Award Hits, Parts 1 & 2	1974	14.00	35.00
		(Record Club. 2 LPs with orange labels.)			
RCA Victor DPL2-0056	(E)	Elvis (2 LPs on blue labels)	1973	12.00	30.00
RCA Victor DPL2-0056	(E)	Elvis Commemorative Album	1978	12.00	30.00
		(Gold vinyl reissue of 0056, "Elvis.")			
RCA Victor DPL2-0168	(P)	Elvis In Hollywood (2 LPs on blue labels)	1976	10.00	25.00
		(Special TV mail-order compilation issued with a bonus book.)			
RCA Victor DML5-0263	(P)	The Elvis Presley Story (5 LPs)	1977	12.00	30.00
		(Issued with a bonus album, DML-0264, priced separately below.)			
RCA Victor DML1-0264	(P)	Elvis-His Songs Of Inspiration	1977	4.00	10.00
RCA Victor DML5-0347	(P)	Memories Of Elvis (5 LPs)	1978	12.00	30.00
		(Issued with a bonus album, DML-0348, priced separately below.)			
RCA Victor DML1-0348	(P)	The Greatest Show On Earth	1978	4.00	10.00
RCA Victor DML6-0412	(P)	The Legendary Recordings			
		Of Elvis Presley (6 LPs with booklet and print)	1980	16.00	40.00
		(Issued with a bonus album, DML-0413, priced separately below.)			
RCA Victor DML1-0413	(P)	Greatest Moments In Music	1980	4.00	10.00
RCA Victor DVL1-0461	(P)	The Legendary Magic Of Elvis Presley	1980	4.00	10.00
RCA Victor RD4A-0101	(P)	Elvis! His Greatest Hits (8 LPs)	1982	150.00	300.00
RCA Victor RD4A-0102	(P)	Elvis! His Greatest Hits (7 LPs)	1982	20.00	50.00
		(Issued with a bonus book and print, included in the price, and an album, RD4A-181, priced separately below.)			
RCA Victor RD4A-181	(P)	Elvis Sings Inspirational Favorites	1982	6.00	15.00
RCA Victor RB4-191	(P)	The Legend Lives On (7 LPs)	1984	16.00	40.00
RCA Victor RDA-242D	(P)	Elvis Sings Country Favorites	1985	20.00	50.00
		(Issued as a bonus album with Reader's Digest's various artists boxed set "The Great Country Entertainers.")			
RCA Victor DVM1-0704	(M)	Elvis (One Night With You)	1985	12.00	30.00
RCA Victor DVM1-0704		Elvis (One Night With You) Bonus Poster	1985	4.00	10.00
RCA Victor DJM1-0835	(M)	An Audio Self Portrait	1985	20.00	50.00
RCA Victor 6313-1-R	(M)	Elvis Talks (Reissue of DJM1-0835)	1988	10.00	25.00

PRESLEY, ELVIS / THE SILVER BEATLES

United Dist. UDL-2382	(M)	Lightning Strikes Twice	1981	30.00	75.00
		(Side 1 contains early live Elvis; side two, The Beatles' Decca tapes.)			

PRESTON, BILLY
Refer to George Harrison & Friends.

Derby LPM-701	(M)	16 Year Old Soul	1963	100.00	250.00
Vee Jay LP-1123	(M)	The Most Exciting Organ Ever	1965	12.00	30.00
Vee Jay LPS-1123	(S)	The Most Exciting Organ Ever	1965	20.00	50.00
Vee Jay LP-1142	(M)	Greatest Hits	1965	12.00	30.00
Vee Jay LPS-1142	(S)	Greatest Hits	1965	20.00	50.00
Exodus EX-304	(M)	Early Hits Of 1965	1965	8.00	20.00
Exodus EX-304	(S)	Early Hits Of 1965	1965	10.00	25.00
Capitol T-2532	(M)	Wildest Organ In Town	1966	8.00	20.00
Capitol ST-2532	(S)	Wildest Organ In Town	1966	10.00	25.00
Buddah BDS-7502	(S)	Billy Preston	1969	6.00	15.00
Apple ST-3359	(S)	That's The Way God Planned It	1969	20.00	50.00
		(Original covers feature a close-up of Preston. Produced by George Harrison.)			
		—Apple albums above have "A Subsidiary of Capitol" on the bottom of the label.—			
Apple ST-3359	(S)	That's The Way God Planned It	1969	8.00	20.00
		(Later covers feature multiple images of Preston.)			
		—Apple albums above have ""Manufactured by Apple" on the bottom of the labels.—			
Apple ST-3370	(S)	Encouraging Words (Prod. by George Harrison)	1970	8.00	20.00
A&M SP-3507	(S)	I Wrote A Simple Song (With George Harrison)	1971	4.00	10.00
A&M SP-3516	(S)	Music Is My Life	1972	1.00	5.00
A&M SP-3526	(S)	Everybody Likes Some Kind Of Music	1973	1.00	5.00
A&M SP-3637	(S)	Live European Tour	1974	1.00	5.00
A&M SP-3645	(S)	Kids And Me	1974	1.00	5.00
A&M SP-4532	(S)	It's My Pleasure	1975	1.00	5.00
A&M SP-4656	(S)	It's A Whole New Thing	1977	1.00	5.00
A&M SP-3205	(S)	The Best Of Billy Preston	1981	1.00	5.00
Trip X-9506	(S)	Goldfingers (2 LPs)	1973	1.00	5.00
Crescendo GNPS-2071	(S)	Soul'd Out (2 LPs)	1973	1.00	5.00
Peacock 179	(S)	Gospel In My Soul	197??	1.00	5.00
Springboard SPB-4034	(S)	The Genius Of Billy Preston	1978	1.00	5.00
Myrrh B-6605	(S)	Behold	1978	1.00	5.00
Motown M7-915	(S)	Fastbreak	1979	1.00	5.00
Motown M7-925	(S)	Late At Night	1979	1.00	5.00
Motown M8-941	(S)	Way I Am	1981	1.00	5.00
Motown 6020	(S)	Pressin' On	1982	1.00	5.00

PRESTON, DON

A&M SP-4155	(S)	Blues	1969	6.00	15.00
A&M SP-4174	(S)	Hot Air Through A Straw	1969	6.00	15.00
Shelter SR-2114	(S)	Been Here All The Time	1974	1.00	5.00

Lloyd Price had one of the primordial rock'n roll hits in 1952 with "Lawdy Miss Clawdy." Not content singing and writing, Mr Price started his own label, KRC, in 1957, and a second, Double-L, in 1963. In between these projects, he signed with ABC-Paramount, with whom he had nine Top 40 hits from 1957 through 1960. While the biggest was the chart-topping "Stagger Lee," he is probably better remembered for "Personality." The success of the latter caused his label to name three albums after it, the first being Mr. Personality, shown here in its rare stereo pressing (bottom). After this succes, his early rhythm'n blues sides were collected by Specialty onto a self-titled LP (top) after his success in the white marketplace.

Label & Catalog #		Title	Year	VG+	NM
PRESTON, JOHNNY					
Mercury MG-20592	(M)	Running Bear	1960	40.00	100.00
Mercury SR-60250	(P)	Running Bear	1960	80.00	200.00
Mercury MG-20609	(M)	Come Rock With Me	1961	40.00	100.00
Mercury SR-60609	(P)	Come Rock With Me	1961	80.00	200.00
Wing MGW-12246	(M)	Running Bear	196?	6.00	15.00
Wing SRW-16246	(S)	Running Bear	196?	12.00	30.00
		(Wing 12246 is an abridged reissue of Mercury 20592.)			
PRETENDERS					
Pretenders features Chrissie Hynde.					
Sire SR-6083	(S)	Pretenders	1980	1.00	5.00
Sire 3563	(S)	Extended Play	1981	1.00	5.00
Sire 3572	(S)	Pretenders II	1981	1.00	5.00
Warner Bros. WBMS-121	(DJ)	Pretenders Live *(Counterfeits exist)*	198?	20.00	50.00
Sire 23980	(DJ)	Learning To Crawl *(Quiex II vinyl)*	1984	10.00	25.00
Sire 23980	(S)	Learning To Crawl	1984	1.00	5.00
PRETTY PEOPLE, THE					
Crestview CRS-3056	(S)	The Pretty People By The Pretty People	197?	6.00	15.00
PRETTY THINGS, THE					
Fontana MGF-27544	(M)	The Pretty Things	1965	40.00	100.00
Fontana SRF-67544	(P)	The Pretty Things	1965	40.00	100.00
Rare Earth RS-506	(S)	S.F. Sorrow *(Round cover)*	1969	20.00	50.00
Rare Earth RS-515	(S)	Parachute	1970	6.00	15.00
Warner Bros. BS-2680	(S)	Freeway Madness	1973	1.20	6.00
Swan Song 8411	(S)	Silk Torpedo	1975	1.20	6.00
Swan Song 8414	(S)	Savage Eye	1976	1.20	6.00
Rare Earth R-459R2	(S)	Real Pretty *(2 LPs)*	1976	6.00	15.00
		(Rare Earth 549 repackages 506 and 515.)			
Sire SASH-3713	(E)	The Vintage Years *(2 LPs)*	1976	6.00	15.00
PRICE, ALAN					
Price was a member of the original Animals. He can also be found on the WB's soundtrack, "O Lucky Man."					
Parrot PA-1018	(M)	The Price Is Right	1968	8.00	20.00
Parrot PAS-71018	(S)	The Price Is Right	1968	12.00	30.00
		("I Put A Spell On You" and "Shame" are rechanneled.)			
Warner Bros. BS-2783	(S)	Between Today And Yesterday	1974	1.00	5.00
Jet LA-809H	(S)	Alan Price	1977	1.00	5.00
Jet JZ-35710	(S)	Lucky Day	1979	1.00	5.00
Jet NJZ-36510	(S)	Rising Sun	1980	1.00	5.00
PRICE, LLOYD					
Specialty SP-2105	(M)	Lloyd Price	1959	60.00	150.00
ABC-Paramount ABC-277	(M)	The Exciting Lloyd Price	1959	20.00	50.00
ABC-Paramount ABCS-277	(S)	The Exciting Lloyd Price	1959	40.00	100.00
ABC-Paramount ABC-297	(M)	Mr. Personality	1959	20.00	50.00
ABC-Paramount ABCS-297	(S)	Mr. Personality	1959	40.00	100.00
ABC-Paramount ABC-315	(M)	Mr. Personality Sings The Blues	1960	20.00	50.00
ABC-Paramount ABCS-315	(S)	Mr. Personality Sings The Blues	1960	40.00	100.00
ABC-Paramount ABC-324	(M)	Mr. Personality's 15 Hits	1960	20.00	50.00
ABC-Paramount ABCS-324	(E)	Mr. Personality's 15 Hits	196?	10.00	25.00
ABC-Paramount ABC-346	(M)	The Fantastic Lloyd Price	1960	20.00	50.00
ABC-Paramount ABCS-346	(E)	The Fantastic Lloyd Price	196?	10.00	25.00
ABC-Paramount ABC-366	(M)	Lloyd Price Sings The Million Sellers	1961	14.00	35.00
ABC-Paramount ABCS-366	(S)	Lloyd Price Sings The Million Sellers	1961	20.00	50.00
ABC-Paramount ABC-382	(M)	Cookin' With Lloyd Price	1961	14.00	35.00
ABC-Paramount ABCS-382	(S)	Cookin' With Lloyd Price	1961	20.00	50.00
Grand Prix KS-422	(M)	Mr. Rhythm & Blues	196?	4.00	10.00
Grand Prix K-422	(E)	Mr. Rhythm & Blues	196?	1.00	5.00
Guest Star G-1910	(M)	Come To Me	196?	4.00	10.00
Guest Star GS-1910	(E)	Come To Me	196?	1.00	5.00
Double-L D-2301	(M)	The Lloyd Price Orchestra	1963	10.00	25.00
Double-L SDL-8301	(S)	The Lloyd Price Orchestra	1963	14.00	35.00
Double-L D-2303	(M)	Misty	1963	10.00	25.00
Double-L SDL-8303	(S)	Misty	1963	14.00	35.00
Monument MLP-8032	(M)	Lloyd Swings For Sammy	1965	10.00	25.00
Monument SMP-18032	(S)	Lloyd Swings For Sammy	1965	14.00	35.00
Jad 1002	(S)	Lloyd Price Now	1969	10.00	25.00
ABC X-763	(P)	Lloyd Price's 16 Greatest Hits	1972	5.00	12.00
ABC AC-30006	(P)	Lloyd Price—The ABC Collection	1976	5.00	12.00
LPG 111	(S)	Music, Music	197?	4.00	10.00
Upfront UPF-126	(S)	Misty	197?	1.00	5.00
Turntable 5001	(S)	Lloyd Price Now	197?	4.00	10.00
Trip 16-5	(P)	Lloyd Price's 16 Greatest Hits	1976	.80	4.00
MCA 1503	(S)	Lloyd Price's Greatest Hits	1982	.80	4.00

Label & Catalog #		Title	Year	VG+	NM
PRIDE					
Warner Bros. RS-1848	(S)	Pride	1970	3.50	8.00
PRIMO PEOPLE, THE					
Capitol ST-695	(S)	The Primo People	1971	4.00	10.00
PRINCE					
Warner Bros. BSK-3150	(S)	For You	1978	1.00	5.00
Warner Bros. BSK-3366	(S)	Prince	1979	1.00	5.00
Warner Bros. BSK-3478	(S)	Dirty Mind	1980	1.00	5.00
Warner Bros. BSK-3601	(S)	Controversy (With poster)	1981	6.00	15.00
Warner Bros. BSK-3601	(S)	Controversy (Without poster)	1981	1.00	5.00
Warner Bros. 23720	(S)	1999	1982	1.00	5.00
Warner Bros. 25110	(S)	Purple Rain	1984	1.00	5.00
Warner Bros. 25110	(DJ)	Purple Rain (Purple vinyl promo)	1984	12.00	30.00
Warner Bros. 25677DJ	(DJ)	The Black Album (2 45RPM LPs)	1987	See note below	
		(Two 45RPM records containing the complete album. Rare with a suggested NM value of $4,000-8,000.)			
Warner Bros. 25677	(S)	The Black Album	1987	See note below	
		(The completed album was withdrawn prior to release and has a suggested NM value of $3,000-6,000. Counterfeits exist.)			
Warner Bros. 45793	(DJ)	The Black Album (Orange marbled vinyl)	1994	60.00	150.00
		(1,000 copies were pressed on orange vinyl in a black jacket.)			
Warner Bros. 45793	(DJ)	The Black Album (White vinyl)	1994	150.00	300.00
		(300 copies were pressed on white vinyl in a white jacket.)			
Warner Bros. 45793	(DJ)	The Black Album (Black & white vinyl)	1994	300.00	500.00
		(50 copies with numbered labels on black & white vinyl in a white jacket.)			
PRINCE BUSTER					
RCA Victor LPM-3792	(M)	Ten Commandments	1967	10.00	25.00
RCA Victor LSP-3792	(S)	Ten Commandments	1967	14.00	35.00
PRIOR, MADDY, & JUNE TABOR					
Maddy Prior also recorded with Steeleye Span.					
Chrysalis CHR-1101	(S)	Silly Sisters	1976	6.00	15.00
PRISCILLA					
Priscilla Coolidge Jones.					
Sussex SXBS-7002	(S)	Gypsy Queen	1970	4.00	10.00
A&M SP-4297	(S)	Gypsy Queen	1971	1.00	5.00
PROBY, P. J.					
Liberty LRP-3406	(M)	Somewhere/Go Go P. J. Proby	1965	6.00	20.00
Liberty LST-7406	(S)	Somewhere/Go Go P. J. Proby	1965	10.00	25.00
Liberty LRP-3421	(M)	P. J. Proby	1965	6.00	20.00
Liberty LST-7421	(S)	P. J. Proby	1965	10.00	25.00
Liberty LRP-3497	(M)	Enigma	1967	8.00	20.00
Liberty LST-7497	(S)	Enigma	1967	10.00	25.00
Liberty LRP-3515	(M)	Phenomenon	1967	8.00	20.00
Liberty LST-7515	(S)	Phenomenon	1967	10.00	25.00
Liberty LRP-3561	(M)	What's Wrong With My World?	1968	8.00	20.00
Liberty LST-7561	(S)	What's Wrong With My World?	1968	10.00	25.00
PROCESSION					
Smash SRS-67122	(S)	Procession	1969	8.00	20.00

PROCOL HARUM

After working as a fledgling r&b band, The Paramounts—including Gary Brooker, Robin Trower, Chris Copping, and B.J. Wilson—break up in 1966. Songwriter Brooker, along with lyricist Keith Reid, recruit Matthew Fisher, Dave Knights, Ray Royer and Bobby Harrison in '67 and form Procol Harum. This is the group that records the monumental "A Whiter Shade Of Pale." After the single hits worldwide, Royer and Harrison are dismissed, replaced by Trower and Wilson. In early '69, both Knights and Fisher left, replaced by Copping, and The Paramounts had essentially reformed!

Deram DE-16008	(M)	Procol Harum	1967	30.00	75.00
Deram DES-18008	(E)	Procol Harum	1967	14.00	35.00
Deram		Procol Harum Bonus Poster	1967	10.00	25.00
A&M SP-4151	(S)	Shine On Brightly	1968	10.00	25.00
A&M SP-4179	(S)	A Salty Dog	1969	6.00	15.00
A&M SP-4261	(S)	Home	1970	4.00	10.00
A&M SP-4294	(S)	Broken Barricades (Gatefold cover)	1971	4.00	10.00
		—A&M albums above have brown labels.—			
A&M SP-4151	(S)	Shine On Brightly	197?	1.00	5.00
A&M SP-4179	(S)	A Salty Dog	197?	1.00	5.00
A&M SP-4261	(S)	Home	197?	1.00	5.00
A&M SP-4294	(S)	Broken Barricades	197?	1.00	5.00
A&M SP-4335	(S)	Procol Harum Live In Concert With The Edmonton Symphony Orchestra	1972	1.00	5.00
A&M SP-4373	(E)	A Whiter Shade Of Pale	1972	1.00	5.00
		(A&M 4373 is a reissue of Deram 18008 plus "Good Captain Clack.")			

Label & Catalog #		Title	Year	VG+	NM
A&M SP-4401	(S)	The Best Of Procol Harum	1973	1.00	5.00
A&M SP-8503	(S)	Procol Harum Lives (Promotional boxed set)	197?	150.00	300.00
		(SP-8503 is a boxed set that includes a press kit, photos, a keychain viewer, and an interview LP, which is also priced separately below.)			
A&M SP-8503	(S)	Procol Harum Lives (Interview)	197?	20.00	50.00
Chrysalis CHR-1037	(S)	Grand Hotel	1973	1.00	5.00
Chrysalis CHT-1058	(S)	Exotic Birds And Fruit	1974	1.00	5.00
Chrysalis CHR-1080	(S)	Procol's Ninth	1975	1.00	5.00
Chrysalis CHR-1130	(S)	Something Magic	1977	1.00	5.00
Pair CRPDL2-1010	(S)	Cornerstone (2 LPs)	197?	1.00	5.00
		(Pair 1020 collects Chrysalis 1037 and 1080.)			

PROFESSOR LONGHAIR
Professor Longhair is a pseudonym for Henry Roland Byrd.

Atlantic SD-7225	(M)	New Orleans Piano	1972	10.00	25.00
Harvest SW-11790	(S)	Live On The Queen Mary	1978	6.00	15.00
Atlantic SD-2-4001	(S)	The Last Mardi Gras (2 LPs)	1982	6.00	15.00
Nighthawk 108	(M)	Mardi Gras In New Orleans	1982	4.00	10.00
Alligator AL-4719	(S)	Crawfish Fiesta	1980	1.00	5.00

PROVIDENCE

Threshold THS-9	(S)	Ever Since The Dawn	1973	6.00	15.00

PRYSOCK, RED

Mercury MG-20088	(M)	Rock 'N' Roll	1955	80.00	200.00
Mercury MG-20211	(M)	Fruit Boots	1957	50.00	125.00
Mercury MG-20307	(M)	The Beat	1957	30.00	75.00
Mercury MG-20512	(M)	Swing Softly Red	1958	20.00	50.00
Mercury SR-60188	(M)	Swing Softly Red	1959	30.00	75.00
		—Mercury albums above have black & silver labels.—			
Wing MGW-12007	(M)	Fruit Boots (With liner notes)	1959	16.00	40.00
Wing MGW-12007	(M)	Fruit Boots (With LP ads on back cover)	196?	8.00	20.00
Wing SRW-16007	(E)	Fruit Boots	196?	4.00	10.00

PRYSOCK, RED, & SIL AUSTIN

Mercury MG-20434	(M)	Battle Royal	1958	20.00	50.00
Mercury SR-60106	(S)	Battle Royal	1959	30.00	75.00
		—Mercury albums above have black & silver labels.—			

PSYCHEDELIC FURS, THE

Columbia 36791	(S)	The Psychedelic Furs	1980	.80	4.00
Columbia ASA-1296	(DJ)	Interchords (Interview)	1981	8.00	20.00
Columbia 37339	(S)	Talk Talk Talk	1981	.80	4.00
Columbia 38261	(S)	Forever Now	1982	.80	4.00
Columbia 39278	(S)	Mirror Moves	1984	.80	4.00

PUCKETT, GARY, & THE UNION GAP

Columbia CS-9612	(S)	The Union Gap	1968	4.00	10.00
Columbia CS-9664	(S)	Young Girl	1968	4.00	10.00
Columbia CS-9715	(S)	Incredible	1968	4.00	10.00
Columbia CS-9935	(S)	The New Gary Pucket & The Union Gap Album	1969	4.00	10.00
Columbia CS-1042	(S)	Greatest Hits	1970	4.00	10.00
		—Columbia albums above have "360 Sound" labels.—			
Columbia CS-9612	(S)	The Union Gap	1972	.80	4.00
Columbia CS-9664	(S)	Young Girl	1972	.80	4.00
Columbia CS-9715	(S)	Incredible	1972	.80	4.00
Columbia CS-9935	(S)	New Album	1972	.80	4.00
Columbia CS-1042	(S)	Greatest Hits	1972	.80	4.00
Columbia KC-340862	(S)	The Gary Puckett Album	1972	1.00	5.00
Harmony FH-31184	(S)	Lady Willpower	1972	.80	4.00

PUFF

MGM SE-4622	(S)	Puff	1969	4.00	10.00

PUGH

Vault 137	(S)	Pugh	1970	4.00	10.00

PULSE

Poison Ring 2237	(S)	Pulse	197?	10.00	25.00

PUNCH

A&M SP-4307	(S)	Punch	1971	4.00	10.00

PURE FOOD & DRUG ACT

Epic KE-3401	(S)	Choice Cuts	1972	6.00	15.00

PURE LOVE & PLEASURE

Dunhill DS-50076	(S)	A Record Of Pure Love And Pleasure	1970	4.00	10.00

Red Prysock was one of the early sax players who had a dramatic impact on popular music by simplifying the elements of jazz into a form of rhythm'n blues that, while looked down upon as a parody by jazz buffs, drew the attention of black and white listeners. With its honking riffs and easy dance rhythms, this music laid the groundwork for what we call rock'n roll.

Label & Catalog #		Title	Year	VG+	NM

PURE PRAIRIE LEAGUE

RCA Victor LSP-4650	(S)	Pure Prairie League	1972	1.00	5.00
RCA Victor LSP-4769	(S)	Bustin' Out	1972	1.00	5.00
RCA Victor APL1-0933	(S)	Two Lane Highway	1975	1.00	5.00
RCA Victor APD1-0933	(Q)	Two Lane Highway	1975	4.00	10.00

PURIFY, JAMES & BOBBY

Bell 6003	(M)	James And Bobby Purify	1967	10.00	25.00
Bell 6003	(S)	James And Bobby Purify	1967	12.00	30.00
Bell 6010	(M)	The Pure Sound Of The Purifys	1967	10.00	25.00
Bell 6010	(S)	The Pure Sound Of The Purifys	1967	12.00	30.00

PURPLE GANG, THE

Sire/London SES-97006	(S)	The Purple Gang Strikes	1969	8.00	20.00

PURPLE IMAGE

Map City 3015	(S)	Purple Image	1971	24.00	60.00

PUSH

Moon 100	(S)	Push	197?	4.00	10.00

PUZZLE

ABC S-671	(S)	Puzzle	1969	4.00	10.00

PYRAMID

Bang 402	(S)	Pyramid	1974	1.00	5.00

PYRAMIDS, THE

Best LPM-1001	(M)	The Original Penetration	1964	100.00	250.00
Best BR-16501	(M)	The Original Penetration	1965	80.00	200.00
Best BRS-36501	(E)	The Original Penetration	1965	60.00	150.00

(16501 is a reissue replacing "Walkin' The Dog" with "Road Runnah")

QUATERMASS					
Harvest SKAO-314	(S)	Quatermass	1970	12.00	30.00
QUATRAIN					
Tetragrammaton T-5002	(S)	Quatrain	1969	10.00	25.00
QUATRO, SUZI					
Bell 1302	(S)	Suzi Quatro	1974	4.00	10.00
Bell 1313	(S)	Quatro	1974	4.00	10.00
Bell 4035	(S)	Your Mama Won't Like Me	1975	4.00	10.00
RSO 3044	(S)	If You Knew Suzi	1978	1.00	5.00
RSO 3064	(S)	Suzi... & Other 4 Letter Words	1979	1.00	5.00
Dreamland 15006	(S)	Rock Hard	1980	1.00	5.00
QUATTLEBAUM, DOUG					
Bluesville BVLP-1065	(M)	Softee Man Blues	1963	30.00	75.00
—Bluesville albums above have bright blue labels with silver print.—					
Bluesville BVLP-1065	(M)	Softee Man Blues	1964	10.00	25.00
—Bluesville albums above have blue labels with a trident logo on the right side.—					
QUEEN					
Elektra EKS-75064	(S)	Queen (White label promo)	1973	20.00	50.00
Elektra EKS-75064	(S)	Queen (Title embossed in gold on the cover)	1973	12.00	30.00
Elektra EKS-75064	(S)	Queen (Title printed on the cover)	1973	1.00	5.00
Elektra EQ-5064	(Q)	Queen	1973	16.00	40.00
Elektra EKS7-5082	(S)	Queen II (White label promo)	1974	20.00	50.00
Elektra EKS7-5082	(S)	Queen II	1974	1.00	5.00
Elektra 7E-1026	(S)	Sheer Heart Attack (White label promo)	1974	20.00	50.00
Elektra 7E-1026	(S)	Sheer Heart Attack	1974	1.00	5.00
Elektra 7E-1053	(S)	A Night At The Opera	1975	1.00	5.00
Elektra 6E-101	(S)	A Day At The Races	1976	1.00	5.00
Elektra 6E-112	(DJ)	News Of The World	1977	60.00	150.00
		(White label promo with 13" x 13" cover and press kit)			
Elektra 6E-112	(S)	News Of The World	1977	1.00	5.00
Elektra 6E-166	(S)	Jazz (With poster of naked girls on bikes)	1978	1.00	5.00
Elektra BB-702	(S)	Live Killers	1979	1.00	5.00
Elektra 5E-513	(S)	The Game (Shiny, mirror cover)	1980	6.00	15.00
Elektra 5E-513	(S)	The Game (Silver-gray cover)	1980	1.00	5.00
Elektra 5E-518	(S)	Flash Gordon	1980	1.00	5.00
Elektra 5E-564	(S)	Queen's Greatest Hits	1981	1.00	5.00
Elektra E1-60128	(S)	Hot Space	1982	1.00	5.00
Capitol 12322	(S)	The Works	1984	1.00	5.00
Capitol ?????	(S)	Kind Of Magic	1986	1.00	5.00
Capitol SV-12476	(S)	The Highlander—There Can Be Only One	1986	*Unreleased*	
Hollywood ED-62005	(S)	Queen At The BBC (Promo picture disc)	1995	40.00	100.00
QUEEN ANNE'S LACE					
Coral CRL-757509	(S)	Queen Anne's Lace	1969	6.00	15.00
QUEEN'S NECTARINE MACHINE					
ABC ABCS-666	(S)	Mystic Powers Of Roving Tarot Gamble	1969	16.00	40.00
QUEENSRYCHE					
Queensryche originally issued a privately pressed 12" EP.					
EMI ST-19006	(S)	Queensryche	1983	4.00	10.00
EMI ST-17134	(DJ)	The Warning (High Quality Vinyl)	1984	16.00	40.00
EMI ST-17134	(S)	The Warning	1984	1.00	5.00
EMI SPRO-1436	(DJ)	Operation Mindcrime (Picture disc)	1988	20.00	50.00
EMI SPRO-9869	(DJ)	Speaking In Digital (Interview)	198?	16.00	40.00
QUESTION MARK & THE MYSTERIANS					
Cameo C-2004	(M)	96 Tears	1966	40.00	100.00
Cameo CS-2004	(E)	96 Tears	1966	30.00	75.00
Cameo C-2006	(M)	Action	1967	60.00	150.00
Cameo SC-2006	(E)	Action	1967	40.00	100.00

Label & Catalog #		Title	Year	VG+	NM

QUICKSILVER MESSENGER SERVICE [QUICKSILVER]

Original recording members were John Cipollina, Gary Duncan, Greg Elmore and David Freiberg. Later members include Nicky Hopkins (Capitol 391) and Dino Valenti (Capitol 498 on). Refer to Steve Miller / Quicksilver Messenger Service / The Band.

Capitol ST-2904	(S)	Quicksilver Messenger Service	1968	20.00	50.00
		(Original covers for ST-2904 are a glossy black with a deep red and foil-like silver graphics.)			
Capitol ST-120	(S)	Happy Trails	1969	12.00	30.00
		—*Capitol albums above have black rainbow labels.*—			
Capitol ST-2904	(S)	Quicksilver Messenger Service	1969	4.00	10.00
Capitol ST-120	(S)	Happy Trails	1969	4.00	10.00
Capitol ST-391	(S)	Shady Grove	1969	6.00	15.00
Capitol ST-498	(S)	Just For Love	1970	6.00	15.00
Capitol ST-630	(S)	What About Me?	1970	6.00	15.00
Capitol ST-819	(S)	Quicksilver	1971	4.00	10.00
		—*Capitol albums above have green labels.*—			
Capitol ST-2904	(S)	Quicksilver Messenger Service	1972	1.00	5.00
Capitol ST-120	(S)	Happy Trails	1972	1.00	5.00
Capitol ST-391	(S)	Shady Grove	1972	1.00	5.00
Capitol ST-498	(S)	Just For Love	1972	1.00	5.00
Capitol ST-630	(S)	What About Me?	1972	1.00	5.00
Capitol ST-819	(S)	Quicksilver	1972	1.00	5.00
Capitol ST-11002	(S)	Comin' Through	1972	1.00	5.00
		—*Capitol albums above have red labels.*—			
Capitol SWBB-11165	(S)	Anthology (2 LPs)	1973	1.20	6.00
Capitol SWBB-11462	(S)	Solid Silver	1975	.80	4.00
Capitol SN-16089	(S)	Quicksilver Messenger Service	1980	.80	4.00
Capitol SN-16090	(S)	Happy Trails	1980	.80	4.00
Capitol SN-16091	(S)	Quicksilver	1980	.80	4.00
Capitol SN-16092	(S)	What About Me?	1980	.80	4.00
Capitol SN-16093	(S)	Just For Love	1980	.80	4.00
Capitol SN-16094	(S)	Shady Grove	1980	.80	4.00

QUIET SUN

Antilles 7008	(S)	Mainstream	1975	4.00	10.00

QUILL

Cotillion SD-9017	(S)	Quill	1970	10.00	25.00

QUINAIMES BAND

Elektra EKS-74096	(S)	Quinaimes Band	1971	1.00	5.00

QUINTESSENCE

Island SMAS-9301	(S)	Quintessence	1971	10.00	25.00
Island ST-9305	(S)	Dive Deep	1971	10.00	25.00

QUINTET

Sir Douglas' Quintet minus Sir Doug.

United Arts. UAS-5514	(S)	Future Tense	1971	3.20	8.00
United Arts. UAS-5599	(S)	The Quintet	1972	3.20	8.00

QUIVER

Warner Bros. BS-1939	(S)	Quiver	1971	1.00	5.00
Warner Bros. BS-2630	(S)	Gone In The Morning	1972	1.00	5.00

RABBIT 1
Bell 6057 · (S) · Rabbit 1 · 1971 · **4.00** · **10.00**

RABBLE, THE
Roulette SR-42010 · (S) · The Rabble · 1968 · **60.00** · **150.00**

RABON, MICHAEL, & CHOCTAW
Uni 73102 · (S) · Michael Rabon And Choctaw · 1971 · **6.00** · **15.00**

RACKET SQUAD, THE
Jubilee JGS-8015 · (S) · The Racket Squad · 1968 · **6.00** · **15.00**
Jubilee JGS-8026 · (S) · Corners Of Your Mind · 1969 · **6.00** · **15.00**

RADHA KRSNA TEMPLE
Produced by George Harrison.
Apple SKAO-3376 · (S) · Radha Krsna Temple · 1971 · **6.00** · **15.00**

RAFEY, SUSAN
Verve V-8636 · (M) · Hurt So Bad · 1965 · **6.00** · **15.00**
Verve V6-8636 · (S) · Hurt So Bad · 1965 · **8.00** · **20.00**

RAFFERTY, GERRY
Gerry Rafferty originally recorded with The Humblebums and Stealers Wheel.
United Arts. 840 · (S) · City To City · 1978 · **.80** · **4.00**
United Arts. 958 · (S) · Night Owl · 1979 · **.80** · **4.00**
United Arts. 1039 · (S) · Snakes And Ladders · 1980 · **.80** · **4.00**

RAIDERS, THE
Liberty LRP-3225 · (M) · Twistin' The Country Classics · 1962 · **10.00** · **25.00**
Liberty LST-7225 · (S) · Twistin' The Country Classics · 1962 · **12.00** · **30.00**

RAIN
Project-3 RS-5072SD · (S) · Rain · 1970 · **10.00** · **25.00**

RAINBOW
Crescendo GNPS-2049 · (S) · After The Storm · 1969 · **10.00** · **25.00**

RAINBOW BAND, THE
Elektra EKS-74092 · (S) · The Rainbow Band · 1971 · **8.00** · **20.00**

RAINBOW PRESS
Mr. G 9003 · (S) · There's A War On · 1968 · **14.00** · **35.00**
Mr. G 9004 · (S) · Sunday Funnies · 1969 · **20.00** · **50.00**

RAINDROPS, THE
The Raindrops feature Jeff Barry and Ellie Greenwich.
Jubilee 5023 · (M) · The Raindrops · 1963 · **80.00** · **200.00**
Jubilee 5023 · (S) · The Raindrops · 1963 · **200.00** · **400.00**

RAINY DAZE
Uni 3002 · (M) · That Acapulco Gold · 1967 · **8.00** · **20.00**
Uni 73002 · (S) · That Acapulco Gold · 1967 · **10.00** · **25.00**

RAITT, BONNIE
Warner Bros. BS-1953 · (S) · Bonnie Raitt · 1971 · **4.00** · **10.00**
Warner Bros. BS-2643 · (S) · Give It Up · 1972 · **4.00** · **10.00**
—*Warner Bros. albums above have green "WB" labels.*—
Warner Bros. BS-1953 · (S) · Bonnie Raitt · 197? · **1.20** · **6.00**
Warner Bros. BS-2643 · (S) · Give It Up · 197? · **1.20** · **6.00**
Warner Bros. BS-2729 · (S) · Takin' My Time · 1973 · **1.20** · **6.00**
Warner Bros. BS-2818 · (S) · Streetlights · 1974 · **1.20** · **6.00**
Warner Bros. BS-2864 · (S) · Home Plate · 1975 · **1.20** · **6.00**
Warner Bros. BS-2990 · (S) · Sweet Forgiveness · 1977 · **1.20** · **6.00**
—*Warner albums above have palm-tree labels.*—
Warner Bros. BS-3369 · (S) · The Glow · 1979 · **1.00** · **5.00**
Warner Bros. BSK-3630 · (S) · Green Light · 1982 · **1.00** · **5.00**

Label & Catalog #		Title	Year	VG+	NM

RAM

Polydor 24-5013	(S)	Where (In Conclusion)	1972	10.00	25.00

RAMBEAU, EDDIE

DynoVoice 9001	(M)	Concrete And Clay	1965	8.00	20.00
DynoVoice DS-9001	(S)	Concrete And Clay	1965	10.00	25.00

RAMONES

Sire SASD-7520	(S)	Ramones	1976	8.00	20.00
Sire SASD-7528	(S)	Ramones Leave Home	1977	12.00	30.00
		(Original pressings of Sire 7528 contain "Carbona Not Glue.")			
Sire SASD-7528	(S)	Ramones Leave Home	1977	8.00	20.00
		(Second pressings have "Sheena Is A Punk Rocker.")			
Sire SR-6020	(S)	Ramones	1977	6.00	15.00
		(Sire 6020 is a reissue of 7520.)			
Sire SR-6031	(S)	Ramones Leave Home	1977	6.00	15.00
		(Sire 6031 is a reissue of 7528 with "Sheena Is A Punk Rocker.")			
Sire SRK-6042	(S)	Rocket To Russia	1977	6.00	15.00
Sire SRK-6063	(S)	Road To Ruin	1978	5.00	12.00
Sire SRK-6077	(S)	End Of The Century (Prod. by Phil Spector)	1980	5.00	12.00
Sire SRK-3571	(S)	Pleasant Dreams	1981	5.00	12.00
Sire 23800	(S)	Subterranean Jungle	1983	4.00	10.00
Sire 25187	(S)	Too Tough To Die	1984	4.00	10.00
Sire 25433	(S)	Animal Boy	1986	4.00	10.00
Sire 25641	(S)	Halfway To Sanity	1987	4.00	10.00
Sire 25709	(S)	Ramonesmania	1988	4.00	10.00
Sire 25905	(S)	Brain Drain	1989	4.00	10.00
Sire 26220	(S)	All The Stuff And More, Vol. 1	1990	4.00	10.00
Sire 26618	(S)	All The Stuff And More, Vol. 2	1991	4.00	10.00

RANDAZZO, TEDDY

Mr Randazzo, formerly of The Three Chuckles, can be found on Roulette's soundtrack "Hey Let's Twist."

Vik LX-1121	(M)	I'm Confessin'	195?	80.00	200.00
ABC-Paramount 352	(M)	Journey To Love	1961	12.00	30.00
ABC-Paramount S-352	(S)	Journey To Love	1961	16.00	40.00
ABC-Paramount 421	(M)	Teddy Randazzo Twists	1962	12.00	30.00
ABC-Paramount S-421	(S)	Teddy Randazzo Twists	1962	16.00	40.00
Colpix CP-445	(M)	Big Wide World	1963	10.00	25.00
Colpix SCP-445	(S)	Big Wide World	1963	16.00	40.00

RANDY & THE RAINBOWS

Ambient Sound 37715	(S)	C'mon Let's Go	1982	5.00	12.00

RANKIN, KENNY

Mercury MG-21141	(M)	Mind-Dusters	1967	5.00	12.00
Mercury SR-61141	(S)	Mind-Dusters	1967	5.00	12.00
Mercury SR-61240	(S)	Family	1969	4.00	10.00

RAPP, TOM

Refer to Pearls Before Swine.

Reprise MS-2069	(S)	Tom Rapp	1972	6.00	15.00
Blue Thumb BTS-44	(S)	Stardancer	1972	6.00	15.00
Blue Thumb BTS-56	(S)	Sunforest	1973	6.00	15.00

RARE BIRD

Rare Bird features Nicky James.

Probe 24-4514	(S)	Rare Bird	1970	8.00	20.00
ABC 716	(S)	As Your Mind Flies By	1972	4.00	10.00
Polydor 24-5530	(S)	Epic Forest	1973	4.00	10.00
Polydor 24-6502	(S)	Somebody's Watching	1974	4.00	10.00
Polydor 24-6506	(S)	Born Again	1974	4.00	10.00

RARE EARTH

Verve V6-5066	(S)	Dreams/Answers	1968	20.00	50.00
Rare Earth 6-507	(S)	Get Ready (Shape cover)	1969	12.00	30.00
Rare Earth 6-507	(S)	Get Ready (Standard cover)	1969	6.00	15.00
Rare Earth 6-510	(S)	Generation	1970		
Rare Earth 6-514	(S)	Ecology	1970	*Unreleased*	
Rare Earth 6-520	(S)	One World	1970	6.00	15.00
Rare Earth 6-534	(S)	Rare Earth In Concert (2 LPs)	1970	6.00	15.00
Rare Earth 6-543	(S)	Willie Remembers	1972	4.00	10.00
Rare Earth 6-546	(S)	Ma	1973	4.00	10.00
Rare Earth 6-548	(S)	Back To Earth	1975	4.00	10.00
Rare Earth 6-550	(S)	Midnight Lady	1976	4.00	10.00
Prodigal P6-10019	(S)	Rare Earth	1978	1.00	5.00
Prodigal P7-10025	(S)	Band Together	1978	1.00	5.00
Prodigal P7-10027	(S)	Grand Slam	1978	1.00	5.00
Motown M5-116V	(S)	Superstar Series, Vol. 16	1981	.80	4.00

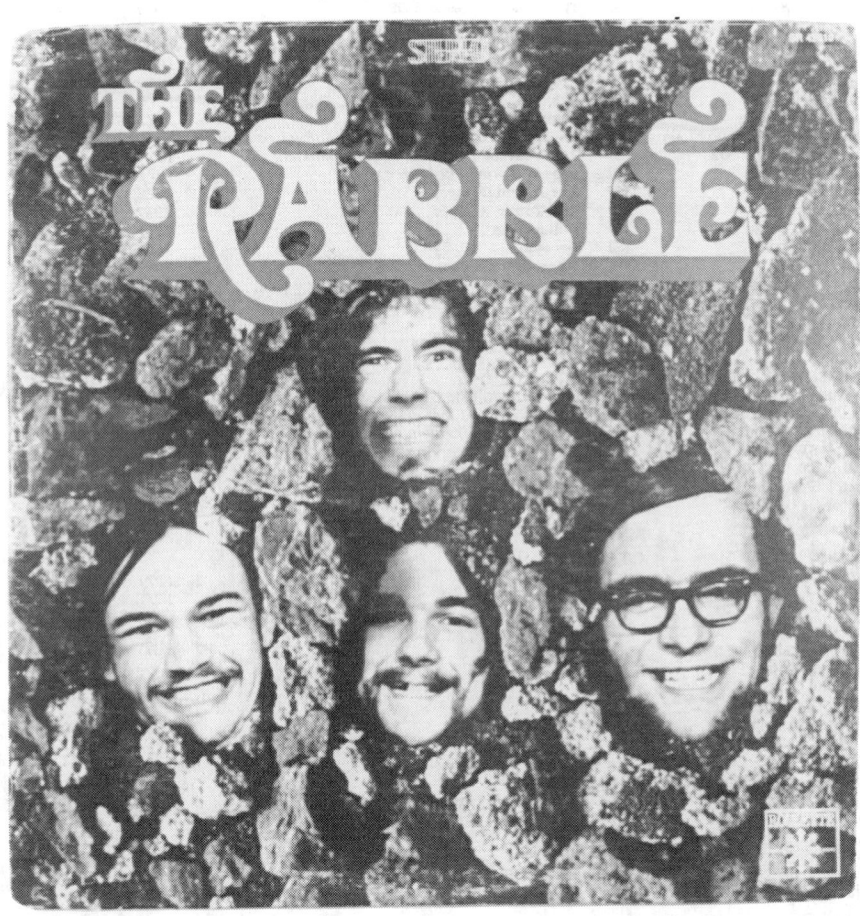

This album by The Rabble depicts the group members sporting the type of schidt-eating grin most of us remember donning for our high school yearbook pictures.

Label & Catalog #		Title	Year	VG+	NM

RASCALS, THE [THE YOUNG RASCALS]

The Young Rascals were Eddie Brigati, Felix Cavaliere, Gene Cornish and Dino Danelli. Brigati left in 1970 followed by Cornish in 1971; they were replaced by Buzzy Fetten, Robert Popwell and Ann Sutton for the Columbia albums. Refer to The Critters / The Young Rascals / Lou Christie.

Label & Catalog #		Title	Year	VG+	NM
Atlantic 8123	(M)	The Young Rascals	1966	12.00	30.00
Atlantic SD-8123	(S)	The Young Rascals	1966	16.00	40.00
Atlantic 8134	(M)	Collections	1967	12.00	30.00
Atlantic SD-8134	(S)	Collections	1967	16.00	40.00
Atlantic 8148	(M)	Groovin'	1967	12.00	30.00
Atlantic SD-8148	(S)	Groovin'	1967	16.00	40.00
Atlantic 8169	(M)	Once Upon A Dream	1968	16.00	40.00
Atlantic SD-8169	(S)	Once Upon A Dream	1968	12.00	30.00
Atlantic 8190	(M)	Time Peace/Greatest Hits (White label promo)	1968	20.00	50.00
Atlantic SD-8190	(S)	Time Peace/Greatest Hits	1968	10.00	25.00
—Atlantic stereo albums above have green & blue labels.—					
Atlantic SD-8123	(S)	The Young Rascals	1966	20.00	50.00
—Atlantic albums above have purple & green labels.—					
Atlantic SD-8190	(S)	Time Peace/Greatest Hits	1968	1.00	5.00
—Atlantic albums above have purple & gold labels.—					
Atlantic ST-	(DJ)	Freedom Suite Narration (Interview)	1969	40.00	100.00
Atlantic ST-137	(DJ)	Freedom Suite (Sampler)	1969	20.00	50.00
Atlantic SD-2-091	(S)	Freedom Suite (2 LPs)	1969	10.00	25.00
Atlantic SD-8246	(S)	See	1970	4.00	10.00
Atlantic SD-8276	(S)	Search And Nearness	1971	4.00	10.00
—Atlantic albums above have green & orange labels with a Broadway address on the bottom.—					
Warner Bros. SP-2502	(S)	24 Greatest Hits (2 LPs. TV advertised)	1971	6.00	15.00
Columbia 30462	(S)	Peaceful World (2 LPs)	1971	8.00	20.00
Columbia 31103	(S)	The Island Of Real	1972	6.00	15.00
Rhino	(S)	The Young Rascals	198?	.80	4.00
Rhino	(S)	Collections	198?	.80	4.00
Rhino	(S)	Groovin'	198?	.80	4.00
Rhino	(S)	Once Upon A Dream	198?	.80	4.00
Rhino	(S)	Time Peace/Greatest Hits	198?	.80	4.00
Rhino	(S)	Freedom Suite (2 LPs)	198?	1.00	5.00
Rhino	(S)	See	198?	.80	4.00
Rhino	(S)	Search And Nearness	198?	.80	4.00

RASPBERRIES, THE

The Raspberries were Jim Bonfanti, Wally Bryson, Eric Carmen and Dave Smalley When Bonfanti and Smalley left in '73, they were replaced by Michael McBride and Scott McCarl. Refer to Bang; Dave Smalley.

Label & Catalog #		Title	Year	VG+	NM
Capitol ST-11036	(S)	Raspberries (Scratch 'n sniff cover)	1972	10.00	25.00
Capitol ST-11036	(S)	Raspberries (Standard cover)	1972	6.00	15.00
Capitol ST-11123	(S)	Fresh Raspberries	1972	6.00	15.00
Capitol SMAS-11220	(S)	Side Three (Shape cover)	1973	10.00	25.00
Capitol ST-11329	(S)	Starting Over	1974	4.00	10.00
Capitol ST-11524	(S)	Raspberries' Best	1976	1.00	5.00

RASTUS

Label & Catalog #		Title	Year	VG+	NM
GRT 30004	(S)	Rastus	1971	4.00	10.00
Neighborhood 47003	(S)	Streamin'	1972	4.00	10.00

RATCHELL

Label & Catalog #		Title	Year	VG+	NM
Decca DL-75330	(S)	Ratchell	1971	4.00	10.00
Decca DL-75365	(S)	Ratchell 2	1972	4.00	10.00

RATIONALS, THE

Label & Catalog #		Title	Year	VG+	NM
Crewe CR-1334	(S)	The Rationals	1968	8.00	20.00

RATTLES, THE

Refer to The Searchers / The Rattles.

Label & Catalog #		Title	Year	VG+	NM
Mercury MG-21127	(M)	The Rattles' Greatest Hits	1967	30.00	75.00
Mercury SR-61127	(E)	The Rattles' Greatest Hits	1967	20.00	50.00

RAVEN

Label & Catalog #		Title	Year	VG+	NM
Discovery 36133	(M)	Live At The Inferno	1967	30.00	75.00
Columbia CS-9903	(S)	Raven	1969	4.00	10.00

RAVENS, THE

The Ravens feature the lead bass lines of Jimmy Ricks.

Label & Catalog #		Title	Year	VG+	NM
Regent MG-6062	(M)	Write Me A Letter	195?	200.00	400.00
—Regent albums above have green labels.—					
Regent MG-6062	(M)	Write Me A Letter	196?	60.00	150.00
—Regent albums above have red labels.—					
Harlem Hitparade 1007	(M)	The Ravens	1975	4.00	10.00
Savoy SJL-2227	(M)	The Greatest Group Of Them All (2 LPs)	1978	5.00	12.00

RAW

Label & Catalog #		Title	Year	VG+	NM
Coral CRL7-57515	(S)	Raw Holly	1971	8.00	20.00

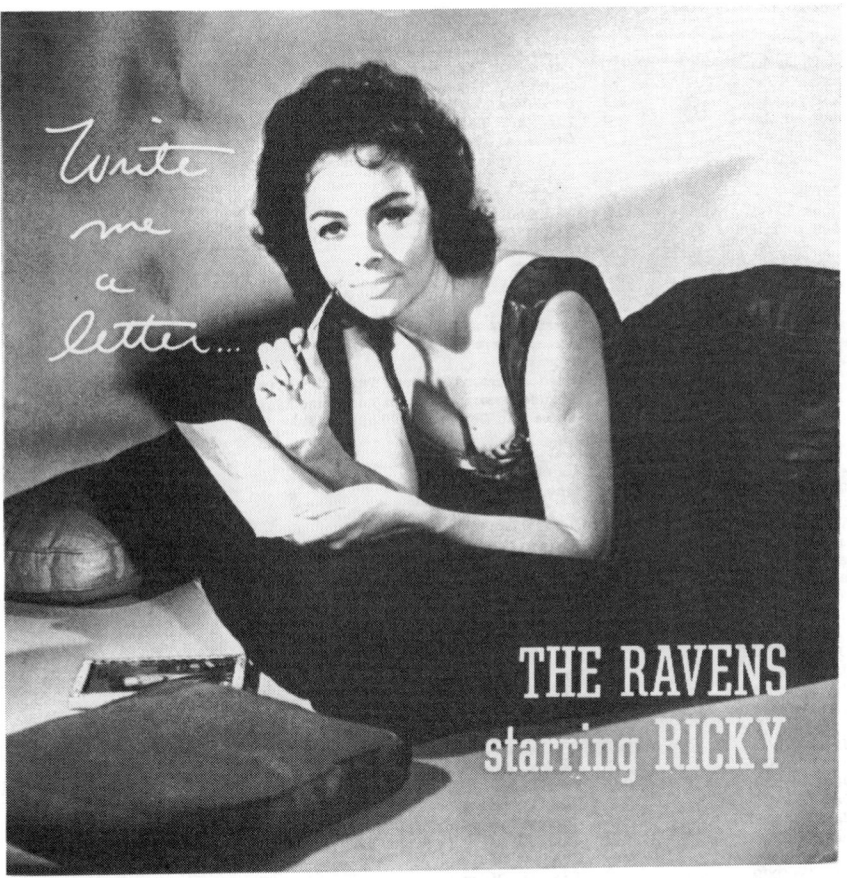

The Ravens were one of the premier rhythm'n blues groups of the late '40s and '50s. While they featured tenor Ollie Jones and, later, Maithe Marshall, it was bass singer Jimmy Ricks that captured listeners' attention, popularizing the lead bass for a period that is now all but forgotten. Write Me A Letter, their sole LP, was not atypical for the time in that the album cover does not feature a picture of the black group but that of a lovely young white woman.

Label & Catalog #		Title	Year	VG+	NM

RAY, DIANE

| Mercury MG-20903 | (M) | The Exciting Years | 1964 | 30.00 | 75.00 |
| Mercury SR-60903 | (S) | The Exciting Years | 1964 | 40.00 | 100.00 |

RAY, JAMES

| Caprice LP-1002 | (M) | James Ray | 1962 | 30.00 | 75.00 |
| Caprice SLP-1002 | (S) | James Ray | 1962 | 40.00 | 100.00 |

RAZMATAZ

| United Arts. UAS-5564 | (S) | For The First Time | 1972 | 4.00 | 10.00 |

REBECCA & THE SUNNYBROOK FARMERS

| Musicor MS-3176 | (S) | Rebecca & The Sunnybrook Farmers | 1969 | 14.00 | 35.00 |
| Musicor MS-3176 | | Rebecca & The Sunnybrook Farmers Bonus Photo | 1969 | 6.00 | 15.00 |

REBIRTH

| Avant Garde AVS-135 | (S) | Rebirth | 1971 | 20.00 | 50.00 |

RED BEANS & RICE

| Epic BN-26461 | (S) | Red Beans And Rice | 1969 | 4.00 | 10.00 |

RED CRAYOLA

International Art.	(M)	Parable Of The Arable Land	1968	40.00	100.00
International Art.	(S)	Parable Of The Arable Land	1968	24.00	60.00
International Art.	(S)	God Bless The Red Crayola	1968	24.00	60.00
International Art.	(S)	Parable Of The Arable Land	1979	6.00	15.00
International Art.	(S)	God Bless The Red Crayola	1979	6.00	15.00

(Reissues have "Masterfonics" stamped in the trail-off vinyl.)

RED HOOK

| Red Hook 523 | (M) | Red Hook | 196? | 8.00 | 20.00 |
| Blue Lion 101 | (M) | Red Hook | 196? | 8.00 | 20.00 |

REDBONE

Redbone features Pat and Lolly Vegas.

Epic KE-30109	(S)	Potlatch	1970	1.00	5.00
Epic KE-30815	(S)	Message From A Drum	1971	1.00	5.00
Epic KE-31598	(S)	Already Here	1972	1.00	5.00
Epic KE-32462	(S)	Wovoka	1973	1.00	5.00
Epic KE-33053	(S)	Beaded Dreams Through Turquoise Eyes	1974	1.00	5.00
Epic EQ-33053	(Q)	Beaded Dreams Through Turquoise Eyes	1974	6.00	15.00
Epic KEG-33456	(S)	Come And Get Your Redbone (2 LPs)	1975	1.00	5.00

REDEYE

| Pentagram PE-10003 | (S) | Games | 1970 | 4.00 | 10.00 |
| Pentagram PE-10006 | (S) | One Man's Poison | 1971 | 4.00 | 10.00 |

REDWING

Fantasy F-8409	(S)	Redwing	1970	3.20	8.00
Fantasy F-9405	(S)	What The Country Needs	1972	3.20	8.00
Fantasy F-9439	(S)	Take Me Home	1973	3.20	8.00
Fantasy F-9459	(S)	Dead Or Alive	1974	3.20	8.00
Fantasy F-9488	(M)	Beyond The Sun And Stars	1975	3.20	8.00

REED, JIMMY

Vee Jay LP-1004	(M)	I'm Jimmy Reed	1958	80.00	200.00
Vee Jay LP-1008	(M)	Rockin' With Reed	1959	80.00	200.00
Vee Jay LP-1022	(M)	Found Love	1959	80.00	200.00

—*Vee Jay albums above have maroon labels with silver print.*—

Vee Jay LP-1004	(M)	I'm Jimmy Reed	196?	30.00	75.00
Vee Jay LP-1008	(M)	Rockin' With Reed	196?	30.00	75.00
Vee Jay LP-1022	(M)	Found Love	1960	30.00	75.00
Vee Jay LP-1025	(M)	Now Appearing	1960	30.00	75.00
Vee Jay 2LP-1035	(M)	Jimmy Reed At Carnegie Hall (2 LPs)	1961	18.00	45.00
Vee Jay 2SR-1035	(P)	Jimmy Reed At Carnegie Hall (2 LPs)	1961	24.00	60.00
Vee Jay LP-1039	(M)	The Best Of Jimmy Reed	1962	14.00	35.00
Vee Jay SR-1039	(P)	The Best Of Jimmy Reed	1962	20.00	50.00
Vee Jay LP-1050	(M)	Just Jimmy Reed	1962	14.00	35.00
Vee Jay LPS-1050	(S)	Just Jimmy Reed	1962	20.00	50.00
Vee Jay LP-1067	(M)	T'Ain't No Big Thing... But He Is Jimmy Reed	1963	14.00	35.00
Vee Jay LPS-1067	(S)	T'Ain't No Big Thing... But He Is Jimmy Reed	1963	20.00	50.00
Vee Jay LP-1072	(M)	The Best Of The Blues	1963	16.00	40.00
Vee Jay LP-1073	(M)	The 12 String Guitar Blues	1963	16.00	40.00
Vee Jay SR-1073	(S)	The 12 String Guitar Blues	1963	60.00	150.00
Vee Jay LP-1080	(M)	More Of The Best Of Jimmy Reed	1964	16.00	40.00
Vee Jay SR-1080	(P)	More Of The Best Of Jimmy Reed	1964	60.00	150.00
Vee Jay LP-1095	(M)	Jimmy Reed At Soul City	1964	16.00	40.00

Label & Catalog #		Title	Year	VG+	NM
Vee Jay LP-8501	(M)	The Legend, The Man	1965	16.00	40.00
Vee Jay VJS-8501	(S)	The Legend, The Man	1964	60.00	150.00
		— Vee Jay albums above have black labels with a rainbow border.—			
BluesWay BL-6004	(M)	The New Jimmy Reed Album	1967	8.00	20.00
BluesWay BLS-6004	(S)	The New Jimmy Reed Album	1967	10.00	25.00
BluesWay BL-6009	(M)	Soulin'	1967	8.00	20.00
BluesWay BLS-6009	(S)	Soulin'	1967	10.00	25.00
BluesWay BLS-6013	(S)	Big Boss Man	1968	8.00	20.00
BluesWay BLS-6024	(S)	Down In Virginia	1969	8.00	20.00
BluesWay BLS-6054	(S)	I Ain't From Chicago	1973	6.00	15.00
BluesWay BLS-6067	(S)	The Ultimate Jimmy Reed	1973	6.00	15.00
BluesWay BLX-6073	(P)	Jimmy Reed At Carnegie Hall (2 LPs)	1973	8.00	20.00
Everest 234	(E)	Jimmy Reed	1969	1.00	5.00
Buddah BDS-4003	(S)	Just Jimmy Reed	197?	1.00	5.00
Exodus EX-307	(S)	Jimmy Reed At Carnegie Hall (2 LPs)	197?	1.00	5.00
Exodus EX-308	(S)	The Best Of Jimmy Reed	197?	1.20	6.00
Exodus EX-310	(S)	Just Jimmy Reed	197?	1.00	5.00
Exodus EX-311	(S)	Jimmy Reed Sings The Best Of The Blues	197?	1.00	5.00
Crescendo GNPS-10006	(S)	The Best Of Jimmy Reed (2 LPs)	1974	1.20	6.00
Trip X-9515	(E)	The History Of Jimmy Reed	1974	1.00	5.00
Tradition TLP-2069	(S)	Wailin' The Blues	197?	1.00	5.00
Trip TIP-16-47	(E)	Jimmy Reed's 16 Greatest Hits	1978	.80	4.00
Blues On Blues 10001	(S)	Let The Bossman Speak	197?	1.00	5.00

REED, LOU
Lou Reed is the former leader of The Velvet Underground.

Label & Catalog #		Title	Year	VG+	NM
RCA Victor LSP-4701	(S)	Lou Reed	1972	6.00	15.00
RCA Victor LSP-4807	(S)	Transformer	1972	4.00	10.00
RCA Victor APL1-0207	(S)	Berlin (With booklet)	1973	4.00	10.00
RCA Victor APL1-0472	(S)	Rock N Roll Animal	1974	4.00	10.00
RCA Victor CPL1-0611	(S)	Sally Can't Dance	1974	4.00	10.00
RCA Victor CPL22-1101	(S)	Metal Machine Music	1975	20.00	50.00
RCA Victor APD2-1101	(Q)	Metal Machine Music	1975	60.00	150.00
		—RCA albums above have orange labels.—			
RCA Victor APL1-0915	(S)	Coney Island Baby	1975	3.20	8.00
RCA Victor APL1-0959	(S)	Lou Reed Live	1975	3.20	8.00
RCA Victor CPL22-1101	(S)	Metal Machine Music	1975	14.00	35.00
		—RCA albums above have brown labels.—			
Arista AL-4100	(S)	Rock And Roll Heart	1976	1.20	6.00
Arista ???	(DJ)	Take No Prisoners (Single LP sampler)	1978	10.00	25.00
Arista A2L-8502	(S)	Take No Prisoners (2 LPs)	1978	3.20	8.00
Arista 4169	(S)	Street Hassle	1978	1.20	6.00
Arista AL-4229	(S)	The Bells	1979	1.20	6.00
Arista AL-9522	(S)	Growing Up In Public	1980	1.20	6.00
Arista A2L-8603	(S)	Rock And Roll Diary 1967-1980 (2 LPs)	1980	1.20	6.00
RCA Victor ANL1-2480	(S)	Coney Island Baby	1977	.80	4.00
RCA Victor AFL1-4807	(S)	Transformer	1977	.80	4.00
RCA Victor AFL1-0472	(S)	Rock N Roll Animal	1977	.80	4.00
RCA Victor AFL1-0611	(S)	Sally Can't Dance	1977	.80	4.00
RCA Victor AFL1-0959	(S)	Lou Reed Live	1977	.80	4.00
RCA Victor APL1-2001	(S)	Walk On The Wild Side/Best Of Lou Reed	1977	1.00	5.00
RCA Victor AFL1-2001	(S)	Walk On The Wild Side/Best Of Lou Reed	1978	.80	4.00
RCA Victor AYL1-3664	(S)	Rock N Roll Animal	1980	.80	4.00
RCA Victor AYL1-3752	(S)	Lou Reed Live	1980	.80	4.00
RCA Victor AYL1-3753	(S)	Walk On The Wild Side/Best Of Lou Reed	1980	.80	4.00
RCA Victor AYL1-3806	(S)	Transformer	1980	.80	4.00
RCA Victor AYL1-3807	(S)	Coney Island Baby	1980	.80	4.00
RCA Victor DJL1-4266	(DJ)	Special Radio Series, Vol. XVII (Interview)	1980	8.00	20.00
RCA Victor AFL1-4221	(S)	Blue Mask	1980	1.00	5.00
RCA Victor DJL1-4267	(DJ)	Blue Mask Interview Album	1980	8.00	20.00
RCA Victor AYL1-4388	(S)	Berlin	1983	.80	4.00
RCA Victor AYL1-4555	(S)	Sally Can't Dance	1983	.80	4.00
RCA Victor AFL1-4568	(S)	Legendary Hearts	1983	1.00	5.00
RCA Victor AFL1-4998	(S)	New Sensations	1984	1.00	5.00

REED, LULA
For additional listings refer to Freddie King & Lula Reed.

Label & Catalog #		Title	Year	VG+	NM
King 604	(M)	Blue And Moody	1959	See note below	
		(King 604 has a suggested NM value of $2,000-3,000.)			

REEVES, MARTHA
Martha Reeves was the former lead singer with Martha & The Vandellas.

Label & Catalog #		Title	Year	VG+	NM
MCA 393	(S)	Martha Reeves	1974	1.00	5.00
Fantasy F-9549	(S)	We Meet Again	1978	1.00	5.00
Fantasy F-9591	(S)	Gotta Keep Moving	1979	1.00	5.00

REFLECTIONS, THE

Label & Catalog #		Title	Year	VG+	NM
Golden World 300	(M)	(Just Like) Romeo And Juliet	1964	60.00	150.00

Label & Catalog #		Title	Year	VG+	NM
REGENTS, THE					
Gee GLP-706	(M)	Barbara Ann	1961	80.00	200.00
Gee SGLP-706	(S)	Barbara Ann	1961	200.00	400.00
		("Barbara Ann" and "I'm So Lonely" are rechanneled .)			
Gee SGLP-706	(S)	Barbara Ann	197?	10.00	25.00
		(Reissue from Publishers Central Bureau licensed through Roulette Records, as noted on the back cover.)			
Capitol KAO-2153	(M)	Live At The AM/PM Discotheque	1964	20.00	50.00
Capitol SKAO-2153	(S)	Live At The AM/PM Discotheque	1964	30.00	75.00
REGGAES, THE					
Sparerib 111	(S)	The Reggaes With Marcia Griffiths	1972	6.00	15.00
REID, TERRY					
Epic BN-26427	(S)	Bang Bang, You're Terry Reid	1968	4.00	10.00
Epic BN-26477	(S)	Move Over For... Terry Reid	1968	4.00	10.00
Epic BN-26477	(S)	Terry Reid	1969	3.20	8.00
		("Terry Reid" is a reissue of "Move Over For...")			
		— Epic albums above have yellow labels.—			
Atlantic SD-7259	(S)	River	1973	3.20	8.00
REJOICE					
Dunhill DS-50049	(S)	Rejoice	1969	4.00	10.00
REMAINS, THE					
Epic LN-24214	(M)	The Remains (White label promo)	1966	200.00	400.00
Epic LN-24214	(M)	The Remains	1966	80.00	200.00
Epic BN-26214	(S)	The Remains	1966	150.00	300.00
Spoonfed SFD-3205	(S)	The Remains (Red vinyl)	1978	6.00	15.00
		(Spoonfed 2305 is a reissue of Epic 26214 plus four tracks)			

RENAISSANCE
Elektra 74068 features Keith Relf and Jim McCarty of The Yardbirds. By the time the group signed with Capitol, it consisted of all new members.

Label & Catalog #		Title	Year	VG+	NM
Elektra EKS-74068	(S)	Renaissance ("Mystic baby" back cover)	1969	10.00	25.00
Elektra EKS-74068	(S)	Renaissance	1970	6.00	15.00
Capitol SMAS-11116	(S)	Prologue	1972	3.20	8.00
Capitol ST-11216	(S)	Ashes Are Burning	1973	3.20	8.00
Capitol SWBC-11871	(S)	In The Beginning (2 LPs)	1978	1.00	5.00
		(Capitol 11871 is a repackage of 11116 and 11216.)			
Sire SASD-7502	(S)	Turns Of The Cards	1974	3.20	8.00
Sire SASD-7510	(S)	Scheherazade & Other Stories	1975	3.20	8.00
Sire SASD-3902	(S)	Live At Carnegie Hall (2 LPs)	1976	4.00	10.00
Sire SASD-7526	(S)	Novella	1977	3.20	8.00
Sire SRK-6015	(S)	Turns Of The Cards	1977	1.00	5.00
Sire SRK-6017	(S)	Scheherazade & Other Stories	1977	1.00	5.00
Sire SRK-6024	(S)	Novella	1977	1.00	5.00
Sire 2XS-6029	(S)	Live At Carnegie Hall (2 LPs)	1977	1.00	5.00
Sire SRK-6049	(S)	A Song For All Seasons	1978	1.00	5.00
Sire 6068	(S)	Azure D'or	1979	1.00	5.00
I.R.S. 70019	(S)	Camera Camera	1981	1.00	5.00
I.R.S. 70033	(S)	Time Line	1983	1.00	5.00
RENAY, DIANE					
20th Century TF-3133	(M)	Navy Blue	1964	40.00	100.00
20th Century TFS-3133	(S)	Navy Blue	1964	80.00	200.00
		("Man Of Mystery," "Navy Blue," "Sooner Or Later" and "Unbelievable Guy" are rechanneled.)			
REO SPEEDWAGON					
Epic E-31089	(S)	R.E.O. Speedwagon	1971	1.20	6.00
Epic KE-31745	(S)	R.E.O. Two	1972	1.20	6.00
		— Epic albums above have yellow labels.—			
Epic E-31089	(S)	R.E.O. Speedwagon	1971	.80	4.00
Epic KE-31745	(S)	R.E.O. Two	1972	.80	4.00
Epic KE-32378	(S)	Ridin' The Storm Out	1974	.80	4.00
Epic PE-32948	(S)	Lost In A Dream	1974	.80	4.00
Epic PE-33338	(S)	This Time We Mean It	1975	.80	4.00
Epic PE-34143	(S)	R.E.O.	1976	.80	4.00
Epic PEG-34494	(S)	You Get What You Play For (2 LPs)	1977	1.00	5.00
Epic JE-35082	(S)	You Can Tune A Piano, But You Can't Tuna Fish	1978	.80	4.00
Epic HE-45082	(S)	You Can Tune A Piano, But You Can't Tuna Fish (Half-speed master)	1982	6.00	15.00
Epic AS-410	(DJ)	Live Again	1978	6.00	15.00
Epic AS-643	(DJ)	Nine Lives	1979	6.00	15.00
Epic JE-35988	(S)	Nine Lives	1979	.80	4.00
Epic JE2-36444	(S)	A Decade Of Rock & Roll 1970-1980 (2 LPs)	1980	1.00	5.00

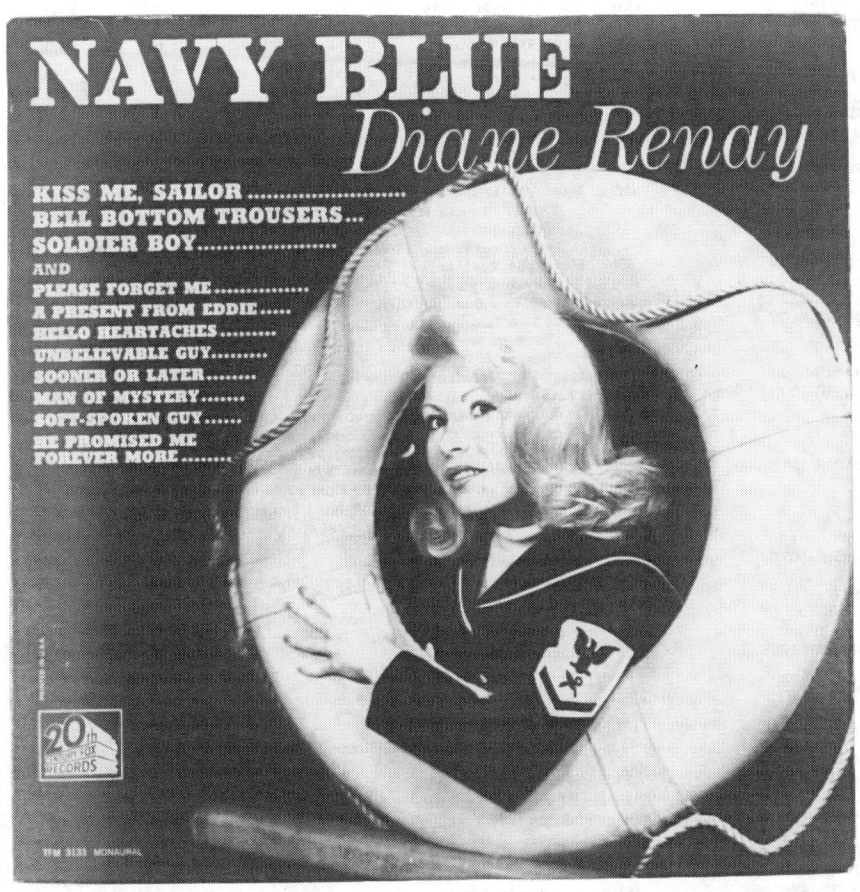

Renee Diane Kushner, a.k.a. Diane Renay, could boast a Top 10 single with "Navy Blue" during the opening salvo of 1964's British Invasion and followed with another Top 30 side in "Kiss Me Sailor." Both of these hits are included on her lone album outing. Pictured here is the more common mono pressing; stereo versions are much rarer.

Label & Catalog #		Title	Year	VG+	NM
Epic FE-36844	(S)	**Hi Infidelity**	1980	.80	4.00
Epic HE-46844	(S)	**Hi Infidelity** *(Half-speed master)*	1982	6.00	15.00
Epic FE-38100	(S)	**Good Trouble**	1982	.80	4.00
Epic HE-48100	(S)	**Good Trouble** *(Half-speed master)*	1982	6.00	15.00
Epic PE-35593	(S)	**Wheels Are Turnin'**	1984	.80	4.00
REPAIRS, THE					
Rare Earth 6-532	(S)	**Already A Household Word**	1971	4.00	10.00
Mowest 121	(S)	**The Repairs**	1972	4.00	10.00
REPARATA & THE DELRONS					
World Artists WAM-2006	(M)	**Whenever A Teenager Cries**	1965	20.00	50.00
World Artists WAS-3006	(S)	**Whenever A Teenager Cries**	1965	30.00	75.00
Avco Embassy AVE-33008	(S)	**Rock And Roll Revolution**	1970	10.00	25.00
REPLACEMENTS, THE					
Twin/Tone TTR-8123	(S)	**Sorry Ma, Forgot To Take Out The Trash**	1981	4.00	10.00
Twin/Tone TTR-8332	(S)	**Hootenanny**	1983	4.00	10.00
Twin/Tone TTR-8441	(S)	**Let It Be**	1984	3.20	8.00
Sire 25330	(S)	**Tim**	1985	1.00	5.00
Sire 25557	(S)	**Pleased To Meet Me**	1987	1.00	5.00
Warner Bros. WBMS-148	(DJ)	**An Interview With Paul Westerberg**	1987	12.00	30.00
Sire/Reprise 25831	(S)	**Don't Tell A Soul**	1989	1.00	5.00
Sire/Reprise 26298	(S)	**All Shook Down**	1990	1.00	5.00
Sire/Reprise PRO-4632	(S)	**Don't Sell Or Buy... It's Crap** *(5 tracks)*	1991	12.00	30.00
RESEARCH					
Flick City 5001	(S)	**In Research**	197?	14.00	35.00
RESIDENTS, THE					
Ralph RR-0274	(M)	**Meet The Residents** *("Defaced Beatles" cover)*	1974	100.00	200.00
		(Original covers feature a reproduction of the "Meet The Beatles" album, graphically "altered" by adding moustaches, teeth, etc. Back cover reads "First Pressing-1,000 Discs-February, 1974.")			
Ralph RR-0274	(S)	**Meet The Residents** *("Defaced Beatles" cover)*	1987	1.00	5.00
		(Remixed reissue with the original cover plus additional music.)			
Ralph RR-0278	(S)	**Duck Stab / Buster & Glen**	1978	1.00	5.00
Ralph RR-0677	(S)	**Meet The Residents**	1977	6.00	15.00
		(Remixed reissue with new cover art of an alien-like crustacean". There is a split "a" in the Ralph logo on the back cover.)			
Ralph RR-0677	(S)	**Meet The Residents** *(Picture disc)*	1987	10.00	25.00
Ralph RR-1075	(S)	**Third Reich 'N' Roll**	1976	20.00	50.00
		(Original covers have a matte finish and depict Dick Clark in Nazi regalia holding an orange and green hand-colored carrot. Back cover reads "First Pressing-1,000 Copies.")			
Ralph RR-1075	(S)	**Third Reich 'N' Roll Collectors Box**	1977	See note below	
		(Limited edition of 25 boxes with a numbered, silk-screened cover given to friends. The velvet-lined box contains a red vinyl record with silk-screened labels and a set of signed, numbered lithographs. Rare with a suggested Near Mint value of $500-1,500.)			
Ralph RR-1075	(S)	**Third Reich 'N' Roll**	1977	1.00	5.00
		(Later pressings have fully printed graphics on a glossy cover.)			
Ralph RR-1276	(S)	**Fingerprince**	1976	30.00	75.00
		(The first 1,000 copies have a textured, chocolate-brown cover that states "First Pressing December 1976" on the back)			
Ralph RR-1276	(S)	**Fingerprince**	1977	8.00	20.00
		(Second pressing of 5,000 copies have a slick, light brown cover.)			
Ralph RR-1276	(S)	**Fingerprince**	198?	4.00	10.00
		(Later pressings have a black cover with pink and green graphics.)			
Ralph RR-1174	(S)	**Not Available**	1978	6.00	15.00
		(The Residents' second album, intentionally made "not available" to the public for four years..)			
Ralph DJ-7901	(DJ)	**Please Do Not Steal It!**	1979	10.00	25.00
		(Promo compilation of 1,000 copies.)			
Ralph ESK-7906	(S)	**Eskimo** *(White vinyl)*	1980	12.00	30.00
Ralph ESK-7906	(S)	**Eskimo**	1980	4.00	10.00
Ralph RZ-7907	(S)	**Eskimo** *(Picture disc)*	1983	8.00	20.00
Ralph RZ-8006	(S)	**Diskomo**	1980	10.00	25.00
Ralph RZ-8052	(S)	**Commercial Album**	1980	6.00	15.00
		(Original covers have incorrect song listing on the back.)			
Ralph RZ-8052	(S)	**Commercial Album** *(Green vinyl)*	1980	20.00	50.00
Ralph RZ-8052	(S)	**Commercial Album**	1980	1.00	5.00
		(Back cover has correct song listings.)			
Ralph RZ-8152	(S)	**Mark Of The Mole** *(Brown vinyl)*	1981	20.00	50.00
		(Edition of 1,000 copies in an autographed, silk-screened cover.)			
Ralph RZ-8152	(S)	**Mark Of The Mole**	1981	4.00	10.00
Ralph RZ-8202	(S)	**The Tunes Of Two Cities**	1982	4.00	10.00
Ralph RZ-8252	(S)	**Intermission**	1982	4.00	10.00

Reparata Aiese with Sheila Reilly and Carol Crobnicki (the Delrons) charted modestly with "Whenever A Teenager Cries" in 1965. Their label, the hit-hungry World Artists, followed with an LP titled after the single and blessed with what is now perceived as outlandishly dated cover art. Of course, anyone with a course in Design 101, a pre-requisite apparently unnoticed by record company graphics departments from then 'til now, would have gagged at this layout. . . Still, a tough girl group record to find.

Label & Catalog #		Title	Year	VG+	NM
Ralph RZ-8302	(S)	Residue	1983	4.00	10.00
Ralph RR-8351	(S)	Title In Limbo	1983	4.00	10.00
Ralph RZ-0001	(S)	The Mole Show	1983	12.00	30.00
Ralph RZ-0001	(S)	The Mole Show (Picture disc)	1983	10.00	25.00
Ralph RZ-0001	(S)	The Mole Show (Ralph bootleg)	1983	20.00	50.00
Ralph RZ-8402	(S)	George & James (100 copies on clear vinyl)	1984	12.00	30.00
Ralph RZ-8402	(S)	George & James	1984	12.00	30.00
		(A first pressing of less than 200 copies was erroneously shipped bearing the matrix number "RZ-8402-A Re-1" in the trail-off vinyl.)			
Ralph RZ-8402	(S)	George & James	1984	4.00	10.00
Ralph RZ-8452	(S)	Whatever Happened To Vileness Fats?	1984	60.00	150.00
		(100 copies of RZ-8452 were pressed on red vinyl.)			
Ralph RZ-8452	(S)	Whatever Happened To Vileness Fats?	1984	4.00	10.00
Episode ED-21	(S)	Census Taker (Soundtrack)	1985	60.00	150.00
		(500 copies of ED-21 were pressed on red vinyl.)			
Episode ED-21	(S)	Census Taker (Soundtrack)	1985	20.00	50.00
Ralph RZ-7707	(S)	Meet The Residents 13th Anniversary Picture Disc	1985	10.00	25.00
Ralph RZ-7707	(S)	Meet The Residents (White vinyl)	1985	20.00	50.00
Ralph RZ-8552	(S)	The Big Bubble/Part Four Of The Mole Trilogy (Marbled pink vinyl)	1985	20.00	50.00
Ralph RZ-8552	(S)	The Big Bubble—Part Four Of The Mole Trilogy	1985	4.00	10.00
Ralph RZ-8681	(S)	Stars And Hank Forever (Blue vinyl)	1986	20.00	50.00
Ralph RZ-8681	(S)	Stars And Hank Forever	1986	1.00	5.00
Ralph 88521	(S)	Meet The Residents	1988	10.00	25.00
		(Reissued "Defaced Beatles" cover.)			
Ryko 20044	(S)	God In Three Persons	1988	1.00	5.00
Enigma 7-73547	(S)	The King And Eye	1989	1.00	5.00
Enigma 7-73608	(S)	Cube-E:The History Of American Music In 3 E-Z Pieces/Live In Holland	1990	1.00	5.00
Cryptic OP-12	(S)	Freak Show	1990	1.00	5.00
RESNICK, ART					
Symposium 2005	(S)	Jungleopolis	197?	6.00	15.00
RESTIVO, JOHNNY					
RCA Victor LPM-2149	(M)	Oh, Johnny	1959	20.00	50.00
RCA Victor LSP-2149	(S)	Oh, Johnny	1959	30.00	75.00
RESTUM, WILLIE					
Gone GLP-5011	(M)	Willie Restum At The Dream Lounge	1959	100.00	250.00
REVELATION					
Mercury SR-61301	(S)	Revelation	1970	4.00	10.00

REVELLS, THE
The Revells are a creation of Gary Usher & Co. Note: The stereo pressing contains alternate takes of some of the tracks on the mono pressing.

Reprise R-6160	(M)	The Go Sound Of The Slots	1965	60.00	150.00
Reprise RS-6160	(S)	The Go Sound Of The Slots	1965	80.00	200.00

REVENGERS, THE

Metro M-565	(M)	Batman And Other Supermen	1966	12.00	30.00
Metro MS-565	(S)	Batman And Other Supermen	1966	16.00	40.00

REVERE, PAUL, & THE RAIDERS [THE RAIDERS]
Revolving around Revere and Mark Lindsay were various Raiders, including the "classic" line-up (1963-67) with Phil Volk, Michael Smith and Drake Levin, who is drafted in 1966 and replaced by Jim Valley. The three members quit as a group in '67 and hired in their place were Charlie Coe, Joe Correro, and Freddy Weller. By 1970 the group has hipped its name to just The Raiders. Refer to Brotherhood; Michael Christian; The Falconaires; Friendsound.

Gardena LP-G1000	(M)	Like, Long Hair	1961	200.00	400.00
Sande S-1001	(M)	Paul Revere & The Raiders	1963	360.00	600.00
		(Original pressings read "Sande" in the trail-off vinyl with no mention of Etiquette Records.)			
Sande S-1001	(M)	Paul Revere & The Raiders	1979	10.00	25.00
		(Reissues have both "Etiquette" and "Sande" in the trail-off vinyl.)			
Jerden JRL-7004	(M)	In The Beginning	1966	20.00	50.00
Jerden JRS-7004	(E)	In The Beginning	1966	14.00	35.00
		(Jerden 7004 is a repackage of Sande 1001.)			
Jerden T-90709	(M)	In The Beginning (Capitol Record Club)	1966	20.00	50.00
Jerden DT-90709	(E)	In The Beginning (Capitol Record Club)	1966	20.00	50.00
Columbia CL-2307	(M)	Here They Come!	1965	12.00	30.00
Columbia CS-9107	(P)	Here They Come!	1965	16.00	40.00
		—Columbia albums above have "Guaranteed High Fidelity" or "360 Sound Stereo" in black on the bottom of the labels.—			
Columbia Cl-2307	(M)	Here They Come!	1966	8.00	20.00
Columbia CS-9107	(P)	Here They Come!	1966	10.00	25.00

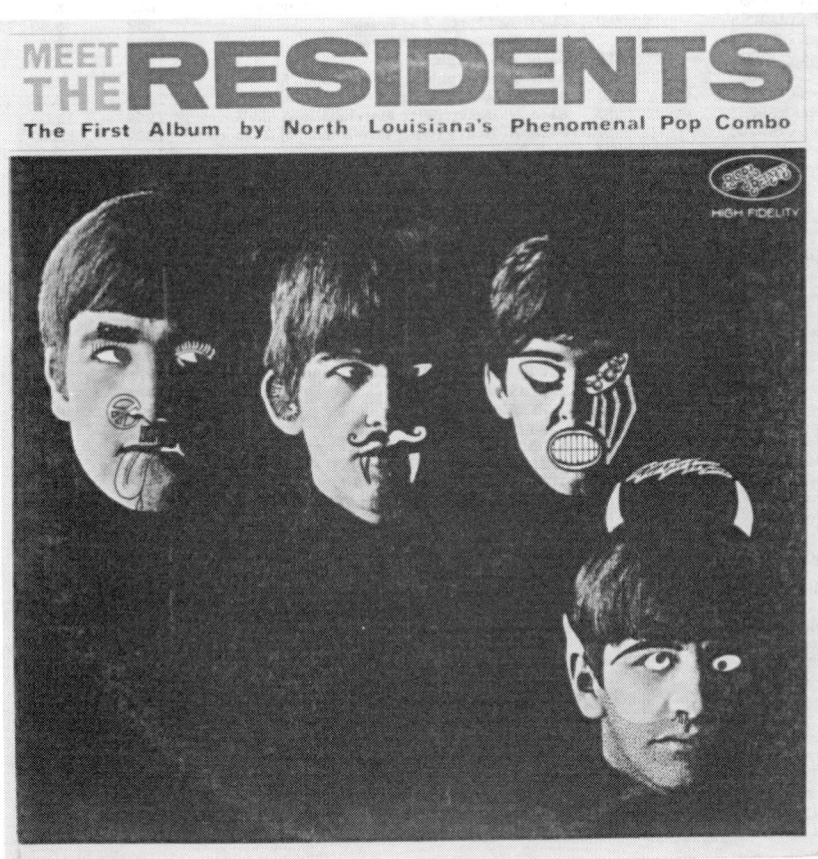

The Bay Area's most well-known unknown group began their lengthy career with a bit of a problem with their first album, Meet The Residents. It seems that the powers-that-be at Capitol Records took a dim view of the group's iconoclastic alteration of their clients' legendary album and convinced Ralph Records to cease and desist. A new cover was substituted, the record was remixed and sent out to the marketplace. . . And years later we have an expensive collectible!

Label & Catalog #		Title	Year	VG+	NM
Columbia CL-2451	(M)	Just Like Us!	1966	8.00	20.00
Columbia CS-9251	(P)	Just Like Us!	1966	10.00	25.00
Columbia CL-2508	(M)	Midnight Ride	1966	8.00	20.00
Columbia CS-9308	(P)	Midnight Ride	1966	10.00	25.00
		(Original covers for 25/9308 have the song titles in hard-to-read black print on the front.)			
Columbia CL-2508	(M)	Midnight Ride	1966	6.00	15.00
Columbia CS-9308	(P)	Midnight Ride	1966	8.00	20.00
		(Later covers have the song titles in bold, readable print.)			
Columbia CL-2595	(M)	The Spirit Of '67	1966	6.00	15.00
Columbia CS-9395	(P)	The Spirit Of '67	1966	8.00	20.00
Columbia 62963	(S)	Good Thing	196?	See note below	
		(Recently unearthed, this album is ten of the tracks from "Spirit Of '67" with two older tracks. Its origins are unknown although it has a '60s type label and was manufactured in the U.S.)			
Columbia KCL-2662	(M)	Greatest Hits (With photo booklet)	1967	6.00	15.00
Columbia KCS-9462	(P)	Greatest Hits (With photo booklet)	1967	6.00	15.00
Columbia KCL-2662	(M)	Greatest Hits (Without booklet)	1967	4.00	10.00
Columbia KCS-9462	(P)	Greatest Hits (Without booklet)	1967	4.00	10.00
Columbia CL-2721	(M)	Revolution!	1967	6.00	15.00
Columbia CS-9521	(S)	Revolution! ("Him Or Me" is rechanneled)	1967	6.00	15.00
Columbia CL-2755	(M)	Christmas Past... And Present	1967	6.00	15.00
Columbia CS-9555	(S)	Christmas Past... And Present	1967	6.00	15.00
Columbia CL-2805	(M)	Goin' To Memphis	1968	4.00	10.00
Columbia CS-9605	(S)	Goin' To Memphis	1968	4.00	10.00
Columbia CS-9665	(S)	Something Happening	1968	6.00	15.00
Columbia CS-9753	(S)	Hard 'N' Heavy (With Marshmallow) (B&W cover)	1969	12.00	30.00
Columbia CS-9753	(S)	Hard 'N' Heavy (With Marshmallow) (Color cover)	1969	6.00	15.00
Columbia (No number)	(DJ)	Pink Puzz	1969	See note below	
		(In an attempt to gain a portion of the FM market that condemned the group as teenyboppers, Lindsay compiled ten tracks from the group's 1967-68 albums and issued it to stations as an "advance copy" of a new album by a new group, Pink Puzz. Whether this album exists as an acetate or a test pressing is unknown.)			
Columbia CS-9905	(S)	Alias Pink Puzz	1969	6.00	15.00
Columbia GP-12	(P)	Two All-Time Great Selling LPs	1970	6.00	15.00
		(GP-12 repackages "Spirit Of '67" and "Revolution.")			
		— Columbia albums above have "360 Sound" labels.—			
Columbia GP-12	(P)	Two All-Time Great Selling LPs	197?	1.00	5.00
Columbia CS-9964	(S)	Collage	1970	1.00	5.00
Columbia CS-30386	(S)	The Raiders' Greatest Hits, Volume II	1971	1.00	5.00
Columbia CS-30768	(S)	Indian Reservation	1971	1.00	5.00
Columbia CQ-30768	(Q)	Indian Reservation	1973	8.00	20.00
Columbia KC-31196	(S)	Country Wine	1972	6.00	15.00
Columbia KG-31464	(S)	All-Time Greatest Hits	1972	1.00	5.00
Columbia LE-10170	(P)	Midnight Ride	197?	1.00	5.00
Columbia P-13512	(S)	Goin' To Memphis (Special Products)	197?	1.00	5.00
Harmony KH-30089	(S)	Paul Revere & The Raiders Featuring Mark Lindsay	1970	1.00	5.00
Harmony KH-30975	(P)	Good Thing	1971	1.00	5.00
		(Harmony 30975 is an abridged reissue of Columbia 9395.)			
Harmony KH-31183	(S)	Movin' On	1972	1.00	5.00
		(Harmony 31183 is an abridged reissue of Columbia 9521.)			
Sears SPS-493	(E)	Paul Revere & The Raiders	1969	10.00	25.00
		(Sears 493 is a repackage of Sande 1001.)			
Pickwick SPC-3176	(E)	Paul Revere & The Raiders	1970	4.00	10.00
		(Pickwick 3175 is a repackage of Sande 1001.)			
Realm 2V-8008	(S)	We Gotta All Get Together (2 LPs)	1976	12.00	30.00
Realm 1V-8009	(S)	Paul Revere & The Raiders Featuring Mark Lindsay's "Arizona"	1976	12.00	30.00
		(Both of the Realm albums above were sold through TV offers only.)			
BacTrac BT-17701	(S)	Paul Revere & The Raiders (Best Of) Vol. 1	1982	.80	4.00
Raider/America	(S)	Special Edition Featuring Michael Bradley	1982	6.00	15.00
Era/K-Tel NU-5880	(S)	Great Raider Reunion With Mark Lindsay	1983	1.00	5.00
Hitbound	(S)	Paul Revere Rides Again	1983	5.00	12.00
No label	(S)	Still Live	1984	6.00	15.00
No label	(S)	Generic Rock Album	1984	6.00	15.00

REVIVAL

Kama Sutra KLPS-2047	(S)	Revival	1972	4.00	10.00

REVOLUTIONARY BLUES BAND, THE

Coral CRL-757506	(S)	The Revolutionary Blues Band	1969	6.00	15.00

REYNOLDS, JODY

Tru-Gems 1002	(S)	Endless Sleep	1978	4.00	10.00

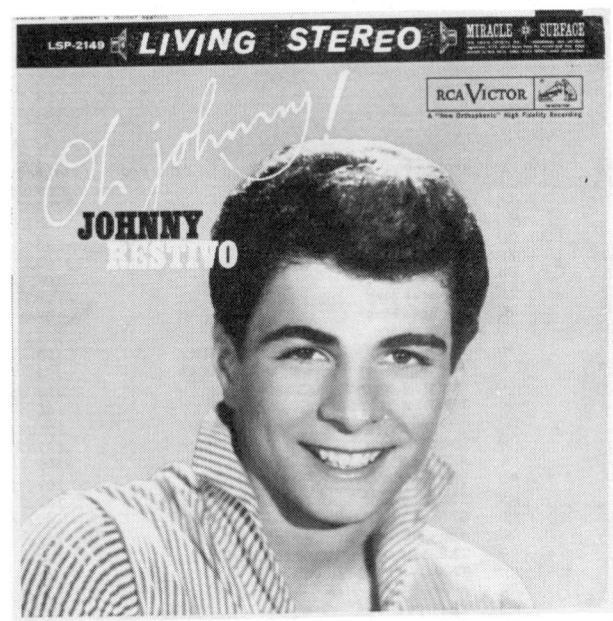

*Johnny Restivo was a 15 year-old hunk from da Bronks with a minor hit in 1959 ("The Shape I'm In")
that moved someone at RCA Victor to give the go ahead on an LP. The cover photo and the title, Oh
Johnny!, would allow even the less imaginative to imagine that someone had a crush on the guy.*

Label & Catalog #		Title	Year	VG+	NM

REYNOLDS, TEDDY, & THE TWISTERS

Crown CLP-5247	(M)	The Twist	1961	8.00	20.00
Crown CST-247	(S)	The Twist	1961	10.00	25.00
		—Crown albums above have gray labels.—			

RHINOCEROUS

Elektra EKS-74030	(S)	Rhinocerous	1968	6.00	15.00
Elektra EKS-74056	(S)	Satin Chickens	1969	6.00	15.00
Elektra EKS-74075	(S)	Better Times Are Coming	1970	6.00	15.00

RHODES, EMITT

Emitt Rhodes was the leader of The Merry-Go-Round.

A&M SP-4254	(S)	American Dream	1970	10.00	25.00
		(First pressings of SP-4254 have a photo of a shirt-sleeved Rhodes posing in front of a paint splattered backdrop on the cover and contains the song "You're A Very Lovely Woman.")			
A&M SP-4254	(S)	American Dream	1970	6.00	15.00
		(Second pressings have a framed photo of a jacketed Rhodes on the cover and replaces "Lovely Woman" with "Saturday Night.")			
Dunhill DS-50089	(S)	Emitt Rhodes	1970	4.00	10.00
Dunhill DS-50111	(S)	Mirror	1971	4.00	10.00
Dunhill DS-50122	(S)	Farewell To Paradise	1973	4.00	10.00

RHODES, TODD

King 295-88	(10")	Todd Rhodes Playing His Greatest Hits	1954	750.00	1,500.00
King 658	(M)	Dance Music	1960	400.00	800.00
		—King albums above have crownless black labels.—			

RHYTHM & NOISE

| Ralph RN-8405 | (S) | Contents Under Notice (Clear vinyl) | 1984 | 8.00 | 20.00 |

RHYTHM DEVILS, THE

The Rhythm Devils were percussionists Mickey Hart and Bill Kreutzmann of The Grateful Dead.

| Passport PB-9844 | (S) | The Rhythm Devils Play River Music | 1980 | 8.00 | 20.00 |

RHYTHM ROCKERS, THE

| Challenge CHL-617 | (M) | Soul Surfin' | 1963 | 30.00 | 75.00 |

RICH, CHARLIE

Charlie Rich could, and did, play just about every kind of music there is. After years of struggling to make it, he opted for country and achieved international success. Albums from this part of his career are not included in this book.

Philips Inter. PLP-1970	(M)	Lonely Weekends	1960	250.00	500.00
Groove G-1000	(M)	Charlie Rich	1964	60.00	150.00
Groove GS-1000	(S)	Charlie Rich	1964	150.00	300.00
RCA Victor LPM-3352	(M)	That's Rich	1965	16.00	40.00
RCA Victor LSP-3352	(S)	That's Rich	1965	20.00	50.00
RCA Victor LPM-3537	(M)	Big Boss Man	1966	16.00	40.00
RCA Victor LSP-3537	(S)	Big Boss Man	1966	20.00	50.00
RCA Victor LSP-4560	(S)	I'm Just Me	1971	6.00	15.00
Smash MGS-27070	(M)	The Many New Sides Of Charlie Rich	1965	12.00	30.00
Smash SRS-67070	(S)	The Many New Sides Of Charlie Rich	1965	16.00	40.00
Smash MGS-27078	(M)	The Best Years	1966	12.00	30.00
Smash SRS-67078	(S)	The Best Years	1966	16.00	40.00
Wing SRW-16375	(S)	A Lonely Weekend	1969	4.00	10.00
Sun LP-110	(S)	Lonely Weekend	1970	3.20	8.00
Sun LP-123	(S)	A Time For Tears	1971	3.20	8.00
Sun LP-132	(S)	The Early Years	1974	3.20	8.00
Sun LP-133	(S)	The Memphis Sound Of Charlie Rich	1974	3.20	8.00
Sun LP-134	(S)	Golden Treasures	1974	3.20	8.00
Sun LP-135	(S)	Sun's Best Of Charlie Rich	1974	3.20	8.00
Trip TLP-8502	(S)	The Best Of Charlie Rich (2 LPs)	1974	1.20	6.00
Power Pak PO-241	(S)	There Won't Be Anymore	1974	1.00	5.00
Power Pak PO-245	(S)	Arkansas Traveler	1974	1.00	5.00
Power Pak PO-252	(S)	The Silver Fox	1974	1.00	5.00
Mercury SRM2-7505	(S)	Fully Realized (2 LPs)	1974	1.20	6.00
Sun Inter. 1003	(S)	20 Golden Hits (Gold vinyl)	1979	1.20	6.00
Sun Inter. 1007	(S)	The Original Charlie Rich	1979	1.00	5.00

RICHARD, CLIFF, & THE SHADOWS

Cliff Richard was the UK's biggest rock'n roll star until The Beatles, after whose emergence he, like so many others, fell from Top 40 grace. He resurrected his career in the '70s and these solo albums are listed separately below. The Shadows also enjoyed success apart from Cliff; their individual releases are also in this edition. Cliff and the group can also be found on the soundtracks for Dot's "Wonderful To Be Young" and Epic's "Swinger's Paradise."

ABC-Paramount 321	(M)	Cliff Sings	1960	30.00	75.00
ABC-Paramount S-321	(S)	Cliff Sings	1960	40.00	100.00
ABC-Paramount 391	(M)	Listen To Cliff	1961	30.00	75.00
ABC-Paramount S-391	(S)	Listen To Cliff	1961	40.00	100.00

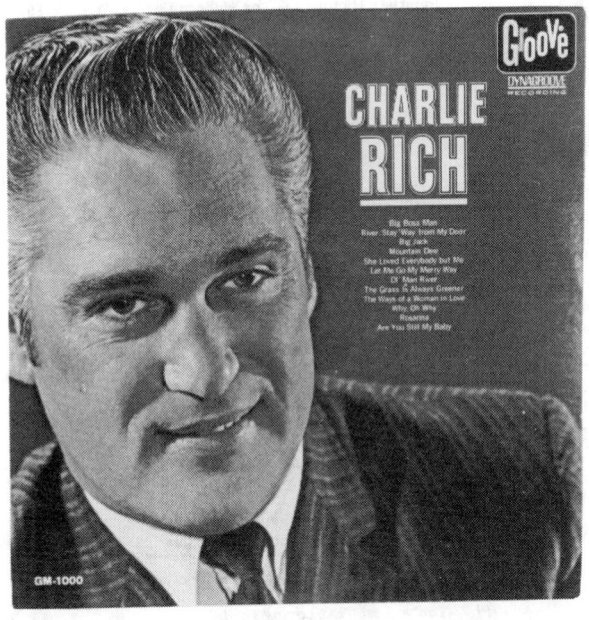

Charlie Rich, one of Sam Phillips' premier proteges in the post-Presley days, issued one album for Phillips International before signing with RCA Victor, who had previously picked up Elvis and another Sun star, Roy Orbison. His self-titled first album for his new label was issued on their Groove subsidiary to little fanfare or sales. He then moved to Mercury's Smash label, where success on a large—and deserving—scale, eluded him, despite quality collections like The Many New Sides Of Charlie Rich. Of course, in his later, more mellow years, he would achieve country'n western superstardom with Epic.

Label & Catalog #		Title	Year	VG+	NM
Epic LN-24063	(M)	**Summer Holiday**	1963	14.00	35.00
Epic BN-26063	(S)	**Summer Holiday**	1963	20.00	50.00
Epic LN-24089	(M)	**It's All In The Game**	1964	12.00	30.00
Epic BN-26089	(S)	**It's All In The Game**	1964	16.00	40.00
Epic LN-24115	(M)	**Cliff Richard In Spain**	1964	12.00	30.00
Epic BN-26115	(S)	**Cliff Richard In Spain**	1964	16.00	40.00

RICHARD, CLIFF
Cliff can also be found on the soundtrack "Two A Penny" on both Uni and Light.

MFP 1420	(S)	**All My Love**	1971	6.00	15.00
		(Manufactured by Capitol for export only.)			
Rocket BXL1-2210	(S)	**I'm Nearly Famous**	1976	4.00	10.00
Rocket BXL1-2268	(S)	**Every Face Tells A Story**	1977	4.00	10.00
Rocket BXL1-2958	(S)	**Green Light**	1978	4.00	10.00
EMI SW-17018	(S)	**We Don't Talk Anymore**	1979	1.00	5.00
EMI SW-17039	(S)	**I'm No Hero**	1980	1.00	5.00
EMI SW-17059	(S)	**Wired For Sound**	1981	1.00	5.00
EMI ST-17081	(S)	**Now You See Me, Now You Don't**	1982	1.00	5.00
EMI SN-16220	(S)	**Green Light**	1981	.80	4.00
EMI SN-16221	(S)	**I'm Nearly Famous**	1981	.80	4.00
EMI SN-16253	(S)	**Every Face Tells A Story**	1981	.80	4.00

RICHARDS, KEITH
Keith Richards is a member of The Rolling Stones.

Virgin 90973	(S)	**Talk Is Cheap**	1988	4.00	10.00

RICHARDSON, WARREN S.
Mr Richardson later recorded as Bill Spooner with The Tubes.

Cotillion SD-9013	(S)	**Warren S. Richardson Jr.**	1970	12.00	30.00

RICHMAN, JONATHAN, & THE MODERN LOVERS

Home Of The Hits HH-1910	(S)	**The Modern Lovers**	1975	20.00	50.00
Beserkley BX-0048	(S)	**Jonathan Richman & The Modern Lovers**	1976	10.00	25.00
Beserkley BZ-0050	(S)	**The Modern Lovers**	1976	10.00	25.00
Beserkley PZ-34800	(S)	**Rock 'N' Roll With The Modern Lovers**	1977	8.00	20.00
Beserkley JBZ-0055	(S)	**Modern Lovers 'Live'**	1978	8.00	20.00
Beserkley JBZ-0060	(S)	**Back In Your Life** *(Distributed by Playboy)*	1979	8.00	20.00
Beserkley BZ-0060	(S)	**Back In Your Life** *(Distributed by Elektra)*	1980	6.00	15.00
Mohawk SCALP-0002	(S)	**The Original Modern Lovers**	1981	8.00	20.00
Sire 23939	(S)	**Jonathan Sings!**	1983	4.00	10.00

RICKS, JIMMY
Mr. Ricks was formerly a member of The Ravens.

Signature SM-1032	(M)	**Jimmy Ricks** *(White label promo)*	1961	100.00	200.00
Signature SM-1032	(M)	**Jimmy Ricks**	1961	150.00	300.00
Mainstream 56050	(M)	**Vibrations**	1965	20.00	50.00
Mainstream S-6050	(S)	**Vibrations**	1965	24.00	60.00
Jubilee JGS-8021	(S)	**Tell Her You Love Her**	1969	24.00	60.00

RIG

Capitol ST-473	(S)	**Rig**	1970	4.00	10.00

RIGHTEOUS BROTHERS, THE
The brothers righteous were Bobby Hatfield and Bill Medley.

Moonglow MLP-1001	(M)	**Right Now!**	1963	14.00	35.00
Moonglow MSP-1001	(S)	**Right Now!**	1963	20.00	50.00
Moonglow MLP-1002	(M)	**Some Blue-Eyed Soul**	1964	14.00	35.00
Moonglow MSP-1002	(S)	**Some Blue-Eyed Soul**	1964	20.00	50.00
Moonglow MLP-1003	(M)	**This Is New!**	1965	14.00	35.00
Moonglow MSP-1003	(S)	**This Is New!**	1965	20.00	50.00
Moonglow MLP-1004	(M)	**The Best Of The Righteous Brothers**	1966	10.00	25.00
Moonglow MSP-1004	(S)	**The Best Of The Righteous Brothers**	1966	12.00	30.00
Philles PHLP-4007	(M)	**You've Lost That Loving Feelin'** *(White label promo)*	1965	80.00	200.00
Philles PHLP-4007	(M)	**You've Lost That Loving Feelin'**	1965	10.00	25.00
Philles PHLP-ST-4007	(P)	**You've Lost That Loving Feelin'**	1965	16.00	40.00
Philles T-90692	(M)	**You've Lost That Loving Feelin'** *(Capitol Rec. Club)*	1965	20.00	50.00
Philles ST-90692	(P)	**You've Lost That Loving Feelin'** *(Capitol Rec. Club)*	1965	20.00	50.00
Philles PHLP-4008	(M)	**Just Once In My Life**	1965	10.00	25.00
Philles PHLP-ST-4008	(P)	**Just Once In My Life**	1965	16.00	40.00
Philles PHLP-4009	(M)	**Back To Back**	1966	8.00	20.00
Philles PHLP-ST-4009	(P)	**Back To Back**	1966	12.00	30.00
		(Portions of the three Philles albums were produced by Phil Spector, the rest by Mr Medley.)			
Verve V-5001	(M)	**Soul And Inspiration**	1966	8.00	20.00
Verve V6-5001	(S)	**Soul And Inspiration**	1966	10.00	25.00
Verve V-5004	(S)	**Go Ahead And Cry**	1966	8.00	20.00
Verve V6-5004	(S)	**Go Ahead And Cry**	1966	10.00	25.00

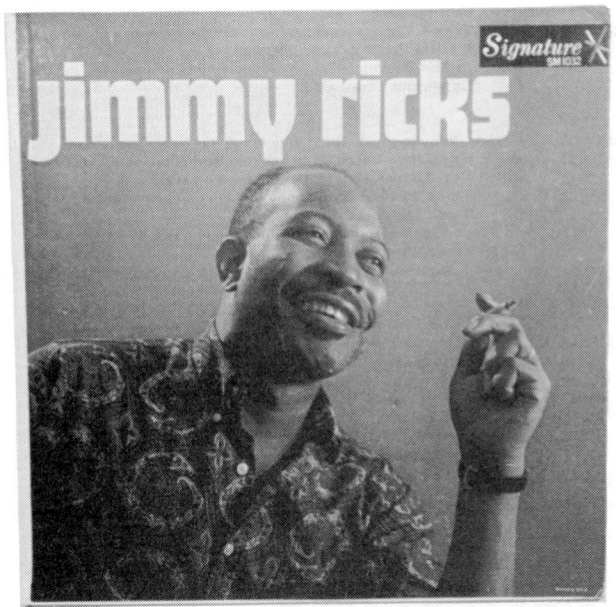

Former bass singer for The Ravens, Jimmy Ricks set out for solo fame and fortune and recorded one eponymous album for the Signature label in 1960. The reader is advised to note that in the listings the white label promo for Signature 1032 is valued at less than the stock copy. This is unusual, quite the opposite of probably 99% of records with promo counterparts. What we are left to assume is that after Signature sent out the promo copies for review and air-play, the response was so slight that it did not justify more than a tiny pressing for commercial use.

Label & Catalog #		Title	Year	VG+	NM
Verve V-5010	(M)	Sayin' Somethin'	1967	6.00	15.00
Verve V6-5010	(S)	Sayin' Somethin'	1967	8.00	20.00
Verve ST-91057	(S)	Sayin' Somethin' (Capitol Record Club)	1967	8.00	20.00
Verve V-5020	(M)	The Righteous Brothers' Greatest Hits	1967	5.00	12.00
Verve V6-5020	(P)	The Righteous Brothers' Greatest Hits	1967	6.00	15.00
Verve V-5031	(M)	Souled Out	1967	6.00	15.00
Verve V6-5031	(S)	Souled Out	1967	6.00	15.00
Verve V-5051	(M)	Standards	1968	8.00	20.00
Verve V6-5051	(S)	Standards	1968	6.00	15.00
Verve V-5058	(M)	One For The Road	1968	12.00	30.00
Verve V6-5058	(S)	One For The Road	1968	10.00	25.00
		(Original covers for Verve 5058 credit The Blossoms on the back .)			
Verve V6-5058	(S)	One For The Road	1968	4.00	10.00
Verve V6-5071	(S)	Greatest Hits, Vol. 2	1969	4.00	10.00
Verve V6-5076	(S)	Re-Birth	1969	4.00	10.00
MGM SE-102	(S)	The Righteous Brothers	1970	5.00	12.00
MGM SE-4885	(S)	The History Of The Righteous Brothers	1973	4.00	10.00
Haven ST-9201	(S)	Give It To The People	1974	1.00	5.00
Haven ST-9203	(S)	Sons Of Mrs. Righteous	1975	1.00	5.00

RINCON SURFSIDE BAND, THE
The Rincons are a creation of Steve Barri and Phil Sloan..

Dunhill D-50001	(M)	Surfing Songbook	1965	80.00	200.00
Dunhill DS-50001	(S)	Surfing Songbook	1965	150.00	300.00

RIOPELLE, JERRY

Capitol ST-732	(S)	Jerry Riopelle	1971	6.00	15.00
Capitol ST-863	(S)	Second Album	1971	6.00	15.00
Capitol SM-732	(S)	Jerry Riopelle	1977	1.00	5.00
Capitol SM-863	(S)	Second Album	1977	1.00	5.00
ABC X-827	(S)	Saving Grace	1974	6.00	15.00
ABC D-886	(S)	Take A Chance	1975	6.00	15.00
Little Eskimo 7	(S)	A Little Bit At A Time	1977	6.00	15.00
Little Eskimo 8	(S)	In The Round	1978	6.00	15.00
Little Eskimo 9	(S)	Dangerous Stranger	1979	6.00	15.00

RIP CHORDS, THE
The Rip Chords are a creation of Bruce Johnston and Terry Melcher & Co.

Columbia CL-2151	(M)	Hey, Little Cobra (& Other Hot Rod Hits)	1964	14.00	35.00
Columbia CS-8951	(S)	Hey, Little Cobra (& Other Hot Rod Hits)	1964	20.00	50.00
Columbia CL-2216	(M)	Three Window Coupe	1964	20.00	50.00
Columbia CS-9016	(S)	Three Window Coupe	1964	30.00	75.00
		(Originally issued with a borderless, full view cover.)			
Columbia CS-9016	(S)	Three Window Coupe	196?	8.00	20.00
		(Special Products reissue with a black border on the cover.)			

RIPPERTON, MINNIE

GRT-30001	(S)	Come To My Garden	1970	4.00	10.00
Janus 7011	(S)	Come To My Garden	1974	1.00	5.00
Epic KE-32561	(S)	Perfect Angel	1974	1.00	5.00
Epic PE-33454	(S)	Adventures In Paradise	1975	1.00	5.00
Epic PEQ-33454	(Q)	Adventures In Paradise	1975	4.00	10.00
Epic PE-34191	(S)	Stay In Love	1976	1.00	5.00
Capitol SN-12004	(S)	Perfect Angel	1979	.80	4.00
Capitol SN-12005	(S)	Adventures In Paradise	1979	.80	4.00
Capitol SN-12006	(S)	Stay In Love	1979	.80	4.00
Capitol SN-16145	(S)	Perfect Angel	1980	.80	4.00
Capitol SN-16146	(S)	Adventures In Paradise	1980	.80	4.00
Capitol SN-16147	(S)	Stay In Love	1980	.80	4.00
Capitol SO-11936	(S)	Minnie	1979	1.00	5.00
Capitol SOO-12097	(S)	Love Lives Forever	1980	1.00	5.00
Capitol ST-12189	(S)	The Best Of Minnie Ripperton	1981	.80	4.00

RISERS, THE

Imperial LP-9269	(M)	She's A Bad Motorcycle	1964	40.00	100.00
Imperial LP-12269	(S)	She's A Bad Motorcycle	1964	60.00	150.00

RIVER CITY

Enterprise ENS-1027	(S)	Anna Divina	1973	4.00	10.00

RIVERS, JOHNNY

Capitol T-2161	(M)	The Sensational Johnny Rivers	1964	8.00	20.00
Capitol STT-2161	(S)	The Sensational Johnny Rivers	1964	10.00	25.00
United Arts. UAL-3386	(M)	Go Johnny, Go	1964	8.00	20.00
United Arts. UAS-6386	(S)	Go Johnny, Go	1964	10.00	25.00
United Arts. T-90813	(M)	Go Johnny, Go (Capitol Record Club)	1966	10.00	25.00
United Arts. ST-90813	(S)	Go Johnny, Go (Capitol Record Club)	1966	10.00	25.00

Label & Catalog #		Title	Year	VG+	NM
Unart M-20007	(M)	The Great Johnny Rivers	1968	4.00	10.00
Unart S-21007	(S)	The Great Johnny Rivers	1968	4.00	10.00
		(Unart 20007 is a reissue of United Arts. 3/6386.)			
Imperial LP-9264	(M)	Johnny Rivers At The Whiskey A-Go-Go	1964	14.00	35.00
Imperial LP-12264	(S)	Johnny Rivers At The Whiskey A-Go-Go	1964	20.00	50.00
		—Imperial mono albums above have black labels with stars on top;			
		stereo albums have black labels with silver print.—			
Imperial LP-9264	(M)	Johnny Rivers At The Whiskey A-Go-Go	1964	8.00	20.00
Imperial LP-12264	(S)	Johnny Rivers At The Whiskey A-Go-Go	1964	10.00	25.00
Imperial LP-9274	(M)	Here We A-Go-Go Again	1964	8.00	20.00
Imperial LP-12274	(S)	Here We A-Go-Go Again	1964	10.00	25.00
Imperial LP-9280	(M)	Johnny Rivers In Action	1965	8.00	20.00
Imperial LP-12280	(S)	Johnny Rivers In Action	1965	10.00	25.00
Imperial LP-9284	(M)	Meanwhile Back At The Whiskey A-Go-Go	1965	8.00	20.00
Imperial LP-12284	(S)	Meanwhile Back At The Whiskey A-Go-Go	1965	10.00	25.00
Imperial LP-9293	(M)	Johnny Rivers Rocks The Folk	1965	8.00	20.00
Imperial LP-12293	(S)	Johnny Rivers Rocks The Folk	1965	10.00	25.00
Imperial LP-9307	(M)	And I Know You Wanna Dance	1966	8.00	20.00
Imperial LP-12307	(S)	And I Know You Wanna Dance	1966	10.00	25.00
Imperial LP-9324	(M)	Johnny Rivers' Golden Hits	1966	6.00	15.00
Imperial LP-12324	(S)	Johnny Rivers' Golden Hits	1966	8.00	20.00
		—Imperial albums above have black, pink & white labels.—			
Imperial LP-9264	(M)	Johnny Rivers At The Whiskey A-Go-Go	196?	4.00	10.00
Imperial LP-12264	(S)	Johnny Rivers At The Whiskey A-Go-Go	196?	5.00	12.00
Imperial LP-9274	(M)	Here We A-Go-Go Again	196?	4.00	10.00
Imperial LP-12274	(S)	Here We A-Go-Go Again	196?	5.00	12.00
Imperial LP-9280	(M)	Johnny Rivers In Action	196?	4.00	10.00
Imperial LP-12280	(S)	Johnny Rivers In Action	196?	5.00	12.00
Imperial LP-9284	(M)	Meanwhile Back At The Whiskey A-Go-Go	196?	4.00	10.00
Imperial LP-12284	(S)	Meanwhile Back At The Whiskey A-Go-Go	196?	5.00	12.00
Imperial LP-9293	(M)	Johnny Rivers Rocks The Folk	196?	4.00	10.00
Imperial LP-12293	(S)	Johnny Rivers Rocks The Folk	196?	5.00	12.00
Imperial LP-9307	(M)	And I Know You Wanna Dance	196?	4.00	10.00
Imperial LP-12307	(S)	And I Know You Wanna Dance	196?	5.00	12.00
Imperial LP-9324	(M)	Johnny Rivers' Golden Hits	196?	4.00	10.00
Imperial LP-12324	(S)	Johnny Rivers' Golden Hits	196?	5.00	12.00
Imperial LP-9334	(M)	Changes	1966	5.00	12.00
Imperial LP-12334	(S)	Changes	1966	6.00	15.00
Imperial LP-9341	(M)	Rewind	1967	5.00	12.00
Imperial LP-12341	(S)	Rewind	1967	6.00	15.00
Imperial LP-9372	(M)	Realization	1968	6.00	15.00
Imperial LP-12372	(S)	Realization	1968	6.00	15.00
Imperial LP-12427	(S)	A Touch Of Gold	1969	4.00	10.00
Imperial LP-16001	(S)	Slim Slo Slider	1969	4.00	10.00
		—Imperial albums above have black, green & white labels.—			
Sunset SUS-5157	(S)	Johnny Rivers	1967	1.20	6.00
Sunset SUS-5251	(S)	The Early Years	1968	1.20	6.00
Sears SPS-417	(S)	Mr. Teenage	1968	10.00	25.00
Sears SPS-487	(S)	Groovin'	1968	12.00	30.00
Pickwick PC-3022	(M)	Johnny Rivers	196?	1.00	5.00
Pickwick SPC-3022	(S)	Johnny Rivers	196?	1.00	5.00
United Arts. X-93	(S)	Johnny Rivers Superpak (2 LPs)	1971	1.00	5.00
United Arts. UAS-5532	(S)	Home Grown	1971	1.00	5.00
U.S. Armed Forces RL-102	(S)	Home Grown	1971	4.00	10.00
United Arts. UAS-5650	(S)	L. A. Reggae	1972	1.00	5.00
U.S. Armed Forces RL-193	(S)	L. A. Reggae	1972	4.00	10.00
United Arts. UXS-93	(S)	Johnny Rivers (2 LPs)	1972	1.00	5.00
United Artists LA-020G	(S)	Rockin' Rivers (Canadian)	1974	8.00	20.00
United Arts. LA-075	(S)	Blue Suede Shoes	1973	1.00	5.00
Atlantic SD-7301	(S)	The Road	1974	1.00	5.00
Epic 50121	(S)	New Lovers And Old Friends	1975	1.00	5.00
United Artists LA-486	(S)	Wild Night	1976	1.00	5.00
Soul City 76004	(S)	Outside Help	1977	1.00	5.00
RSO 3082	(S)	Borrowed Time	1980	1.00	5.00
Priority 38439	(S)	Not A Through Street	1983	.80	4.00
United Artists LA253G	(S)	The Very Best Of Johnny Rivers	1974	.80	4.00
United Artists LA387E	(S)	The Very Best Of Johnny Rivers	1975	.80	4.00
United Artists LA444E	(S)	The Very Best Of Johnny Rivers	1976	.80	4.00
Liberty LN-10154	(S)	Blue Suede Shoes	1982	.80	4.00
Live From Gilley's 83-06	(S)	Johnny Rivers	1983	8.00	20.00
Rhino R2-70793	(S)	Anthology, 1964-1977 (2 LPs)	1991	1.20	6.00

RIVIERAS, THE
This Rivieras is a white rock'n roll group from the '60s.

Riviera 701	(M)	Campus Party	1964	100.00	250.00
U.S.A. 102	(M)	Let's Have A Party	1964	60.00	150.00

Label & Catalog #		Title	Year	VG+	NM

RIVIERAS, THE
This Rivieras is a black '50s rhythm'n blues group from the '50s.

Post 2000	(S)	The Rivieras Sing	196?	20.00	50.00

RIVINGTONS, THE

Liberty LRP-3282	(M)	Doin' The Bird	1963	60.00	150.00
Liberty LST-7282	(S)	Doin' The Bird	1963	80.00	200.00

ROAD, THE

Kama Sutra KSBS-8075	(S)	The Road	1969	6.00	15.00
Kama Sutra KSBS-2012	(S)	The Road	1970	4.00	10.00
Kama Sutra KSBS-2032	(S)	Cognition (2 LPs)	1970	6.00	15.00

ROAD

Natural Resources 105L	(S)	Road	1972	6.00	15.00

ROAD HOME, THE

Dunhill DS-50104	(S)	Peaceful Children	1971	4.00	10.00

ROAD RUNNERS, THE
The Road Runners are a creation of Gary Usher & Co.

London LL-3381	(M)	The New Mustang (& Other Hot Rod Hits)	1964	80.00	200.00
London PS-381	(S)	The New Mustang (& Other Hot Rod Hits)	1964	150.00	300.00

ROBBER, ROBBY, & THE HI-JACKERS

Premier P-156	(M)	The Twist	1961	6.00	15.00
Premier PS-156	(S)	The Twist	1961	8.00	20.00
Coronet CX-157	(M)	Let's Twist Again	1961	6.00	15.00
Coronet CXS-157	(S)	Let's Twist Again	1961	8.00	20.00

ROBBS, THE

Mercury MG-21130	(M)	The Robbs	1967	8.00	20.00
Mercury SR-61130	(S)	The Robbs	1967	10.00	25.00

ROBERTS, ANDY

Ampex A-10117	(S)	With Everyone	1970	6.00	15.00
Ampex A-10120	(S)	Home Grown	1971	6.00	15.00

ROBERTS, AUSTIN

Chelsea BCL1-0199	(S)	Last Thing On My Mind	1972	1.00	5.00
Chelsea BCL1-1004	(S)	Austin Roberts	1972	1.00	5.00

ROBERTS, ROCKY, & THE AIREDALES

Brunswick BL-754133	(S)	Rocky Roberts And The Airedales	1968	6.00	15.00

ROBERTSON, ROBBIE
Robbie Robertson was a member of The Band.

Geffen GHS-24160	(S)	Robbie Robertson	1989	1.00	5.00

ROBINS, THE

Whippet WLP-703	(M)	Rock 'N' Roll With The Robins	1958	400.00	750.00
Crescendo GNPS-9034	(E)	The Best Of The Robins	1975	6.00	15.00

ROBINSON, ANDY

Philips PHS-600-289	(S)	Patterns Of Reality	1969	6.00	15.00

ROBINSON, FENTON

Seventy-7 2001	(S)	Monday Morning Blues 'N' Boogie	1972	6.00	15.00
Alligator AL-4705	(S)	Somebody Loan Me A Dime	1974	4.00	10.00
Alligator AL-4710	(S)	I Hear Some Blues Downstairs	1978	4.00	10.00

ROBINSON, FLOYD

RCA Victor LPM-2162	(M)	Floyd Robinson	1960	30.00	75.00
RCA Victor LSP-2162	(S)	Floyd Robinson	1960	40.00	100.00

ROBINSON, JOHNNY

Epic BN-26528	(S)	Memphis High	1970	4.00	10.00

ROBINSON, L. C.

BluesWay BLS-6082	(S)	House Cleanin' Blues	1974	6.00	15.00
Arhoolie 1062	(S)	Ups And Downs	1972	6.00	15.00

ROBINSON, SMOKEY
Mr Robinson was formerly lead singer for The Miracles.

Tamla T6-328	(S)	Smokey	1973	3.20	8.00
Tamla T6-331	(S)	Pure Smokey	1974	3.20	8.00
Tamla T6-337	(S)	A Quiet Storm	1975	3.20	8.00
Tamla T6-341	(S)	Smokey's Family Robinson	1976	3.20	8.00
Tamla T6-350	(S)	Deep In My Soul	1977	3.20	8.00

The Rock-A-Teens hit the national charts big in 1959: "Woo-Hoo" was one of a few rock'n roll hits that Roulette Records, better known for their jazz line-up, could lay claim to at the time. The label promptly followed with an LP which shows a dancing couple and what one may assume is that he is "woo-hooing" she.

Label & Catalog #		Title	Year	VG+	NM
Tamla T7-359	(S)	Love Breeze	1978	3.20	8.00
Tamla T7-363	(S)	Smokin' (2 LPs)	1979	3.20	8.00
Tamla T7-366	(S)	Where There's Smoke...	1979	3.20	8.00
Tamla T8-367	(S)	Warm Thoughts	1980	3.20	8.00
Tamla T8-375	(S)	Being With You	1981	3.20	8.00
Motown M5-118V	(S)	Superstar Series, Vol. 18	1981	.80	4.00
Motown M5-134V	(S)	Smokey	1981	.80	4.00
Motown M5-154	(S)	Song In My Heart	1982	.80	4.00
Motown M5-168V	(S)	Pure Smokey	1981	.80	4.00
Motown M5-197V	(S)	A Quiet Storm	1981	.80	4.00
Motown M5-230V	(S)	Love Breeze	1981	.80	4.00
Tamla T8-6001T	(S)	Yes It's You, Lady	1982	1.00	5.00
Tamla T8-6030T	(S)	Touch The Sky	1983	1.00	5.00
Tamla T8-6064T	(S)	Blame It On Love & All The Great Hits	1983	1.00	5.00
Tamla T8-6098T	(S)	Essar	1984	1.00	5.00

ROBINSON, TOM

Harvest SPRO-8791	(DJ)	Tom Robinson (Sampler)	1978	1.20	6.00
Harvest STBO-11778	(S)	Power In The Darkness (2 LPs)	1978	1.20	6.00
Harvest STBO-11930	(S)	TRB Two	1979	1.00	5.00

ROCK & ROLL REVIVAL, THE

Dunhill DS-50059	(S)	Great Oldies Done Hear And Now	1969	6.00	15.00

ROCK-A-TEENS, THE

Roulette R-25109	(M)	Woo-Hoo	1960	60.00	150.00
Roulette SR-25109	(S)	Woo-Hoo ("Woo-Hoo" is rechanneled)	1960	80.00	200.00

ROCK CANDY

MGM SE-4703	(S)	Rock Candy	1970	4.00	10.00

ROCK FLOWERS, THE

Wheel WLS-1001	(S)	Rock Flowers	1972	4.00	10.00
Wheel WLS-1002	(S)	Naturally	1972	4.00	10.00

ROCK ISLAND

Project-3 PR-4005SD	(S)	Rock Island	1970	14.00	35.00

ROCKET 88
Rocket 88 is a creation of Charlie Watts of The Rolling Stones.

Atlantic 19293	(S)	Rocket 88	1981	4.00	10.00

ROCKETS, THE
The Rockets feature Ralph Molina and Danny Talbot, later of Crazy Horse.

White Whale WWS-7116	(S)	The Rockets	1968	10.00	25.00

ROCKIN' FOO

Hobbit HB-5001	(S)	Rockin' Foo	1969	8.00	20.00
Uni 73115	(S)	Rockin' Foo	1971	6.00	15.00

ROCKIN' REBELS, THE

Swan SLP-509	(M)	Wild Weekend	1963	100.00	250.00

ROCKPILE
Rockpile features Nick Lowe and Dave Edmunds.

Columbia JC-36886	(S)	Seconds Of Pleasure (With bonus EP)	1980	3.20	8.00

ROCKY FELLERS, THE

Scepter SP-512	(M)	Killer Joe	1963	20.00	50.00
Scepter SPS-512	(S)	Killer Joe	1963	40.00	100.00

ROD & THE COBRAS

Somerset SF-20500	(M)	Drag Race At Surf City	1964	14.00	35.00
Somerset SS-20500	(S)	Drag Race At Surf City	1964	20.00	50.00

RODGERS, JIMMIE
Jimmie Rodgers can also be found on the Roulette soundtrack "The Long Hot Summer."

Roulette R-25020	(M)	Jimmie Rodgers	1958	20.00	50.00
Roulette R-25033	(M)	Number One Ballads	1958	20.00	50.00
Roulette R-25042	(M)	Jimmie Rodgers Sings Folk Songs	1958	20.00	50.00
		— Roulette albums above have black labels.—			
Roulette R-25020	(M)	Jimmie Rodgers	196?	10.00	25.00
Roulette R-25033	(M)	Number One Ballads	196?	10.00	25.00
Roulette R-25042	(M)	Jimmie Rodgers Sings Folk Songs	196?	10.00	25.00
Roulette SR-25042	(E)	Jimmie Rodgers Sings Folk Songs	196?	10.00	25.00
Roulette R-25057	(M)	His Golden Year	1959	10.00	25.00
Roulette R-25071	(M)	TV Favorites	1959	12.00	30.00
Roulette SR-25071	(S)	TV Favorites	1959	20.00	50.00

Label & Catalog #		Title	Year	VG+	NM
Roulette R-25081	(M)	Twilight On The Trail	1959	12.00	30.00
Roulette SR-25081	(S)	Twilight On The Trail	1959	20.00	50.00
Roulette R-25095	(M)	It's Christmas Once Again	1959	12.00	30.00
Roulette SR-25095	(S)	It's Christmas Once Again	1959	20.00	50.00
Roulette R-25103	(M)	When The Spirit Moves You	1960	12.00	30.00
Roulette SR-25103	(S)	When The Spirit Moves You	1960	16.00	40.00
Roulette R-25128	(M)	At Home With Jimmie Rodgers—			
		An Evening Of Folk Songs	1960	12.00	30.00
Roulette SR-25128	(S)	At Home With Jimmie Rodgers—			
		An Evening Of Folk Songs	1960	16.00	40.00
Roulette R-25150	(M)	The Folk Song World Of Jimmie Rodgers	1961	12.00	30.00
Roulette SR-25150	(S)	The Folk Song World Of Jimmie Rodgers	1961	16.00	40.00
Roulette R-25160	(M)	The Best Of Jimmie Rodgers Folk Songs	1961	12.00	30.00
Roulette SR-25160	(S)	The Best Of			
		Jimmie Rodgers Folk Songs (Red vinyl)	1961	100.00	250.00
Roulette SR-25160	(S)	The Best Of Jimmie Rodgers Folk Songs	1961	16.00	40.00
Roulette R-25179	(M)	15 Million Sellers	1962	10.00	25.00
Roulette SR-25179	(P)	15 Million Sellers	1962	12.00	30.00
		—Roulette albums above have white labels.—			
Roulette R-25199	(M)	Folk Songs	1963	8.00	20.00
Roulette SR-25199	(S)	Folk Songs	1963	10.00	25.00
Roulette SR-42006	(S)	Yours Truly	1968	6.00	16.00
Forum F-9025	(M)	At Home With Jimmie Rodgers—			
		An Evening Of Folk Songs	196?	1.00	5.00
Forum SF-9025	(S)	At Home With Jimmie Rodgers—			
		An Evening Of Folk Songs	196?	1.00	5.00
Forum F-9049	(M)	Just For You	196?	1.00	5.00
Forum SF-9049	(S)	Just For You	196?	1.00	5.00
Forum F-9059	(M)	Jimmie Rodgers Sings Folk Songs	196?	1.00	5.00
Forum FS-9059	(S)	Jimmie Rodgers Sings Folk Songs	196?	1.00	5.00
Forum F-16004	(S)	Just For You	197?	1.00	5.00
		(The Forum Circle albums are Roulette reissues.)			
Dot DLP-3453	(M)	No One Will Ever Know	1962	5.00	12.00
Dot DLP-25453	(S)	No One Will Ever Know	1962	6.00	15.00
Dot DLP-3496	(M)	Jimmie Rodgers In Folk Concert	1963	5.00	12.00
Dot DLP-25496	(S)	Jimmie Rodgers In Folk Concert	1963	6.00	15.00
Dot DLP-3502	(M)	My Favorite Hymns	1963	5.00	12.00
Dot DLP-25502	(S)	My Favorite Hymns	1963	6.00	15.00
Dot DLP-3525	(M)	Honeycomb & Kisses Sweeter Than Wine	1963	5.00	12.00
Dot DLP-25525	(S)	Honeycomb & Kisses Sweeter Than Wine	1963	6.00	15.00
Dot DLP-3556	(M)	Town And Country	1964	5.00	12.00
Dot DLP-25556	(S)	Town And Country	1964	6.00	15.00
Dot DLP-3556	(M)	The World I Used To Know	1964	4.00	10.00
Dot DLP-25556	(S)	The World I Used To Know	1964	5.00	12.00
		("The World I Used To Know" is a repackage of "Town And Country.")			
Dot DLP-3579	(M)	12 Great Hits	1964	4.00	10.00
Dot DLP-25579	(S)	12 Great Hits	1964	5.00	12.00
Dot DLP-3614	(M)	Deep Purple	1965	4.00	10.00
Dot DLP-25614	(S)	Deep Purple	1965	5.00	12.00
Dot DLP-3657	(M)	Christmas With Jimmie Rodgers	1965	4.00	10.00
Dot DLP-25657	(S)	Christmas With Jimmie Rodgers	1965	5.00	12.00
Dot DLP-3687	(M)	The Nashville Sound	1966	4.00	10.00
Dot DLP-25687	(S)	The Nashville Sound	1966	5.00	12.00
Dot DLP-3710	(M)	Country Music 1966	1966	4.00	10.00
Dot DLP-25710	(S)	Country Music 1966	1966	5.00	12.00
Dot DLP-3717	(M)	It's Over	1966	4.00	10.00
Dot DLP-25717	(S)	It's Over	1966	5.00	12.00
Dot DLP-3780	(M)	Love Me, Please Love Me	1967	5.00	12.00
Dot DLP-25780	(S)	Love Me, Please Love Me	1967	5.00	12.00
Dot DLP-3815	(M)	Golden Hits/15 Hits Of Jimmie Rodgers	1967	4.00	10.00
Dot DLP-25815	(S)	Golden Hits/15 Hits Of Jimmie Rodgers	1967	4.00	10.00
Hamilton HL-12114	(M)	Favorite Hymns And Favorite Folk Ballads	1964	1.00	5.00
Hamilton HS-12114	(S)	Favorite Hymns And Favorite Folk Ballads	1964	1.20	6.00
A&M LP-130	(M)	Child Of Clay	1967	4.00	10.00
A&M SP-4130	(S)	Child Of Clay	1967	1.20	6.00
A&M SP-4187	(S)	Windmills Of Your Mind	1968	1.20	6.00
A&M SP-4242	(S)	Troubled Times	1970	1.20	6.00
A&M LP-1008	(S)	Both Sides Now	1970	1.20	6.00
Pickwick SPC-3106	(S)	Am I That Easy To Forget?	197?	.80	4.00
Twinset PAS-2-1042	(S)	Honeycomb (2 LPs)	1974	1.20	6.00
Scrimshaw ASP-1001	(S)	Yesterday-Today	1978	1.00	5.00

RODGERS, JIMMIE / THE LIMELITERS

Guest Star G-1405	(M)	Jimmie Rodgers And The Limeliters	196?	4.00	10.00
Guest Star GS-1405	(S)	Jimmie Rodgers And The Limeliters	196?	5.00	12.00

ROE, TOMMY

ABC-Paramount ABC-432	(M)	Sheila	1962	16.00	40.00
ABC-Paramount ABCS-432	(S)	Sheila	1962	20.00	50.00

Label & Catalog #		Title	Year	VG+	NM
ABC-Paramount ABC-467	(M)	**Something For Everybody**	1964	**12.00**	**30.00**
ABC-Paramount ABCS-467	(E)	**Something For Everybody**	1968	**20.00**	**50.00**
		(ABC-Paramount 467 was issued in rechanneled stereo years after its mono debut and is quite rare.)			
ABC-Paramount ABC-575	(M)	**Sweet Pea**	1966	**12.00**	**30.00**
ABC-Paramount ABCS-575	(S)	**Sweet Pea**	1966	**16.00**	**40.00**
ABC-Paramount T-90883	(M)	**Sweet Pea** *(Capitol Record Club)*	1966	**16.00**	**40.00**
ABC-Paramount ST-90883	(S)	**Sweet Pea** *(Capitol Record Club)*	1966	**16.00**	**40.00**
ABC-Paramount ABC-594	(M)	**It's Now Winter's Day**	1967	**8.00**	**20.00**
ABC-Paramount ABCS-594	(S)	**It's Now Winter's Day**	1967	**10.00**	**25.00**
ABC 610	(M)	**Phantasy**	1967	**12.00**	**30.00**
ABC S-610	(S)	**Phantasy**	1967	**16.00**	**40.00**
ABC S-683	(S)	**Dizzy**	1969	**8.00**	**20.00**
ABC S-700	(S)	**12 In A Roe/A Collection Of Greatest Hits**	1969	**4.00**	**10.00**
		("Everybody," "Party Girl" and "Carol" are rechanneled.)			
ABC S-714	(S)	**We Can Make Music**	1970	**4.00**	**10.00**
ABC S-732	(S)	**Beginnings**	1971	**4.00**	**10.00**
ABC X-762	(S)	**Tommy Roe's 16 Greatest Hits**	1972	**1.20**	**6.00**
Monument PZ-34182	(S)	**Energy**	1976	**3.20**	**8.00**
Monument MG-7614	(S)	**Full Bloom**	1977	**3.20**	**8.00**
MCA 1519	(S)	**Tommy Roe's Greatest Hits**	1982	**.80**	**4.00**
Accord SN-7155	(S)	**Sheila**	1981	**.80**	**4.00**

ROE, TOMMY / BOBBY LEE

Crown CLP-5323	(M)	**Tommy Roe And Bobby Lee**	1963	**8.00**	**20.00**
Crown CST-323	(E)	**Tommy Roe And Bobby Lee**	1963	**4.00**	**10.00**
		—Crown albums above have gray labels.—			

ROE, TOMMY / AL TORNELLO

Diplomat D-2474	(M)	**Whirling With Tommy Roe And Al Tornello**	196?	**4.00**	**10.00**
Diplomat DS-2474	(S)	**Whirling With Tommy Roe And Al Tornello**	196?	**4.00**	**10.00**

ROGERS, KENNY, & THE FIRST EDITION: *Refer to* THE FIRST EDITION

ROKES, THE

RCA Victor Int. FPM-185	(M)	**Che Mondo Strano**	1968	**30.00**	**75.00**

ROLLING STONES, THE

The original Rollin' Stones, formed in 1962 through Brian Jones' ambitions, consisted of Jones, Mick Jagger, Keith Richards, Ian Stewart, Dick Taylor, and Tony Chapman. They recorded several sides as demos to no avail. By January of '63, Taylor and Chapman had been replaced by Bill Wyman and Charlie Watts. This group's demos also attracted little industry attention. By May, Andrew Loog Oldham had signed the group to a management deal, changing their name to The Rolling Stones, and dropping Stewart's role—and his more mature, 50s looks—to the less visible position of keyboard player and roadie.

They played grittily realistic rhythm'n blues and had, for the times, extremely long hair, which gave them an almost universally acknowledged [by the straight press] unkempt image. This allowed Oldham to sell them as the bad boys to The Beatles' cultivated boy-next-door image. The immortal line, "Would you allow your daughter to date a Rolling Stone?," was a bit of condescension from the press that acted as a major publicity coup for the group.

Due to a series of unpleasant episodes involving controlled substances and the British police, Jones slowly lost his way and left the group in 1969. He died shortly thereafter. He was replaced by Mick Taylor of John Mayall's band. Taylor quit at the end of '74 and was replaced for the express purpose of touring by Ron Wood, formerly of The Faces. By the end of '75, Ronnie was a full-fledged Stone, a position he continues to hold. In December of 1985, unofficial "sixth Stone" Ian Stewart died of a heart attack.

The two sections below collect the recordings the group did for Decca, issued in the States by London, from 1962 through 1969. The second section consists of the material done on their own, eponymous label, originally distributed by Atlantic/Warner Bros (through 1985) and then CBS. Refer to the various members along with John Hammond; Alexis Korner; Andrew Oldham; Rocket 88.

1. The Rolling Stones On Decca/London

London LL-3375	(DJ)	**The Rolling Stones** *(White label promo)*	1964	*See note below*	
		(White label promos have a suggested NM value of $2,000-3,000.)			
London LL-3375	(M)	**The Rolling Stones**	1964	**100.00**	**200.00**
London PS-375	(E)	**The Rolling Stones**	1964	**150.00**	**300.00**
		(Original covers for 3375/375 have a box in the lower left corner advertising the bonus photo, priced separately below.)			
London		**The Rolling Stones Bonus Photo**	1964	**40.00**	**100.00**
London LL-3402	(M)	**12 X 5**	1965	**100.00**	**200.00**
London PS-402	(E)	**12 X 5**	1965	**150.00**	**300.00**
London LL-3420	(M)	**The Rolling Stones, Now!**	1965	**100.00**	**200.00**
London PS-420	(E)	**The Rolling Stones, Now!**	1965	**150.00**	**300.00**
London LL-3429	(M)	**Out Of Our Heads**	1965	**100.00**	**200.00**
London PS-429	(E)	**Out Of Our Heads**	1965	**150.00**	**300.00**
		—London albums above have maroon or dark blue labels with "Made in England by the Decca Record Co. Ltd" at the very top with the "London/ffrr" logo beneath.—			

Pictured here are two rarities featuring the cover graphics from The Rolling Stones' classic Big Hits (High Tide & Green Grass): The illustration on top is of the original cover design with the title on one line and group's name on one line, all in lower case letters. This version was rejected and the album was issued with the more familiar graphics where the title is on three lines and the artist's credit on two— a total of five lines versus the original two— and the letters are in upper case. These graphics can be seen (below) on the experimental picture disc made up in 1969 to hype the group's second big hits package, Through The Past, Darkly.

Label & Catalog #		Title	Year	VG+	NM
London LL-3375	(M)	The Rolling Stones	1965	24.00	60.00
London PS-375	(E)	The Rolling Stones	1965	10.00	25.00
London LL-3402	(M)	12 X 5 (Blue vinyl)	1965	See note below	
		(LL-3402 on colored vinyl is rare, perhaps a one-of-a-kind, with a suggested NM value of $6,000-12,000.)			
London LL-3402	(M)	12 X 5	1965	24.00	60.00
London PS-402	(E)	12 X 5	1965	10.00	25.00
London LL-3420	(M)	The Rolling Stones, Now!	1965	24.00	60.00
London PS-420	(E)	The Rolling Stones, Now!	1965	10.00	25.00
London LL-3429	(M)	Out Of Our Heads	1965	24.00	60.00
London PS-429	(E)	Out Of Our Heads	1965	10.00	25.00
London LL-3451	(M)	December's Children (And Everybody's)	1965	24.00	60.00
London PS-451	(E)	December's Children (And Everybody's)	1965	10.00	25.00
		—London mono albums above have maroon labels with a silver "London" on top; stereo albums above have deep blue labels with a silver "London" on top.—			
London LL-3375	(M)	The Rolling Stones	1965	16.00	40.00
London PS-375	(E)	The Rolling Stones	1966	4.00	10.00
London LL-3402	(M)	12 X 5	1965	16.00	40.00
London PS-402	(E)	12 X 5	1966	4.00	10.00
London LL-3420	(M)	The Rolling Stones, Now!	1965	16.00	40.00
London PS-420	(E)	The Rolling Stones, Now!	1966	4.00	10.00
London LL-3429	(M)	Out Of Our Heads	1965	16.00	40.00
London PS-429	(E)	Out Of Our Heads	1966	4.00	10.00
London LL-3451	(M)	December's Children (And Everybody's)	1965	16.00	40.00
London PS-451	(E)	December's Children (And Everybody's)	1966	4.00	10.00
London NP-1	(M)	High Tide And Green Grass (Big Hits)	1966	See note below	
		(The original front cover design had the title on one line in radically different type. These were rejected and replaced. Suggested values in collectible condition are $3,000-6,000.)			
London NP-1	(M)	High Tide And Green Grass (Big Hits)	1966	16.00	40.00
London NPS-1	(E)	High Tide And Green Grass (Big Hits)	1966	4.00	10.00
London LL-3476	(M)	Aftermath	1966	16.00	40.00
London PS-476	(S)	Aftermath	1966	4.00	10.00
London LL-3493	(M)	Got Live If You Want It	1966	16.00	40.00
London PS-493	(P)	Got Live If You Want It	1966	4.00	10.00
London LL-3499	(M)	Between The Buttons	1967	16.00	40.00
London PS-499	(S)	Between The Buttons	1967	4.00	10.00
London LL-3509	(M)	Flowers	1967	20.00	50.00
London PS-509	(P)	Flowers	1967	10.00	25.00
London NP-2	(M)	Their Satanic Majesties Request (3-D cover)	1967	100.00	250.00
London NPS-2	(S)	Their Satanic Majesties Request (3-D cover)	1967	16.00	40.00
London PS-539	(S)	Beggar's Banquet ("ffrr" label)	1968	150.00	300.00
London PS-539	(S)	Beggar's Banquet	1968	10.00	25.00
		(First pressings credit all songs to Jagger-Richard.)			
London PS-539	(S)	Beggar's Banquet	1968	6.00	15.00
		(Later pressings credit Rev. Wilkins as writer of "Prodigal Son.")			
London NPS-3	(S)	Through The Past, Darkly— Big Hits, Vol. 2 (Hexagonal cover)	1969	4.00	10.00
London NPS-3	(S)	Through The Past, Darkly— Big Hits, Vol. 2 (Picture disc)	1969	See note below	
		(London pressed up fifteen prototype picture discs to test the viability of a commercial release. Seven copies had the front cover of "High Tide & Green Grass" on both sides The other eight had "High Tide" on one side and Ten Years After's "Sssh" on the other. Suggested NM values of $4,000-8,000.)			
London RSD-1	(DJ)	The Rolling Stones—The Promotional Album	1969	See note below	
		(RSD-1 has a suggested NM value of $2,000-3,000. Counterfeits exist.)			
London NPS-4	(S)	Let It Bleed (Includes a fold-open poster)	1969	6.00	15.00
London NPS-4	(S)	Let It Bleed (Without the poster)	1969	4.00	10.00
London NPS-5	(S)	Get Yer Ya-Ya's Out!	1970	4.00	10.00
London 2PS-606/7	(P)	Hot Rocks 1964-1971 (2 LPs)	1972	500.00	750.00
		(Original pressings of PS-606/607 feature alternate mixes on "Brown Sugar" and "Wild Horses." The word "Shelly" with the date "11-18-71" is etched in the trail-off vinyl.)			
London 2PS-606/7	(P)	Hot Rocks 1964-1971 (2 LPs)	1972	10.00	25.00
		(Second pressings feature the regular mixes on all tracks. "Shelly" with or without a later date is in the trail-off vinyl.)			
London 2PS-606/7	(P)	Hot Rocks 1964-1971 (2 LPs)	197?	6.00	15.00
		(Later pressings feature the regular mixes on all tracks. "Shelly" cannot be found in the trail-off vinyl.)			
London 2PS-626/7	(P)	More Hot Rocks (2 LPs)	1972	6.00	15.00
		—London mono albums above have red labels with a red "London" on top in a silver box; stereo albums above have deep blue labels with a blue "London" on top in a silver box.—			
London PS-375	(E)	The Rolling Stones	197?	1.00	5.00
London PS-402	(E)	12 X 5	197?	1.00	5.00
London PS-420	(E)	The Rolling Stones, Now!	197?	1.00	5.00
London PS-429	(E)	Out Of Our Heads	197?	1.00	5.00
London PS-451	(E)	December's Children (And Everybody's)	197?	1.00	5.00
London NPS-1	(E)	High Tide And Green Grass (Big Hits)	197?	1.00	5.00

Label & Catalog #		Title	Year	VG+	NM
London PS-476	(S)	**Aftermath**	197?	1.00	5.00
London PS-493	(P)	**Got Live If You Want It**	197?	1.00	5.00
London PS-499	(S)	**Between The Buttons**	197?	1.00	5.00
London PS-509	(M)	**Flowers**	197?	1.00	5.00
		(These later stereo pressings of 509 play mono!)			
London NPS-2	(S)	**Their Satanic Majesties Request** (2-D cover)	197?	6.00	15.00
London PS-539	(S)	**Beggar's Banquet**	197?	1.00	5.00
London NPS-3	(S)	**Through The Past, Darkly—**			
		Big Hits, Vol. 2 (Hexagonal cover)	197?	1.00	5.00
London NPS-3	(S)	**Through The Past, Darkly—**			
		Big Hits, Vol. 2 (Square cover)	197?	8.00	20.00
London NPS-4	(S)	**Let It Bleed**	197?	1.00	5.00
London NPS-5	(S)	**Get Your Ya-Ya's Out!**	197?	1.00	5.00
London 2PS-606/7	(P)	**Hot Rocks 1964-1971** (2 LPs)	197?	1.20	6.00
London 2PS-626/7	(P)	**More Hot Rocks** (2 LPs)	197?	1.20	6.00
		—London stereo albums above have lighter blue labels with a blue "London" on top in a silver box			
		and are pressed on thinner vinyl.—			
I.N.S. Radio 1003	(M)	**It's Here Luv!!**	1965	100.00	250.00
		(Originals are on thick vinyl with crisp printing on the cover.)			
Abkco DVL2-0268	(P)	**The Rolling Stones' Greatest Hits** (2 LPs.)	1975	8.00	20.00
Abkco ANA-1	(P)	**Metamorphosis**	1975	4.00	10.00
Abkco MPD-1	(S)	**Songs Of The Rolling Stones**	1975	300.00	500.00
		(Cover photo has a shot of the group in a field.)			
Abkco MPD-1	(S)	**Songs Of The Rolling Stones**	1975	See note below	
		(Orange cover with a shot taken from the "Rock & Roll Circus."			
		Rare with a suggested Near Mint value of $2,000-4,000.)			

2. The Rolling Stones On Rolling Stones

Label & Catalog #		Title	Year	VG+	NM
Rolling Stones COC 59100	(M)	**Sticky Fingers** (White label promo)	1971	250.00	500.00
Rolling Stones COC 59100	(S)	**Sticky Fingers** (White label promo)	1971	100.00	250.00
Rolling Stones COC 59100	(S)	**Sticky Fingers** (Zipper cover)	1971	4.00	10.00
Rolling Stones PRB-164	(DJ)	**Interview With Mick Jagger** (White label)	1971	10.00	250.00
Rolling Stones PRB-164	(DJ)	**Interview With Mick Jagger** (Yellow label)	1971	60.00	150.00
Rolling Stones COC-39100	(S)	**Jamming With Edward** (White label promo)	1972	60.00	150.00
Rolling Stones COC-39100	(S)	**Jamming With Edward**	1972	6.00	15.00
Rolling Stones COC-2-2900	(S)	**Exile On Main Street** (2 LPs)	1972	6.00	15.00
		(Original covers for COC-2900 have a single pocket, Unipak design—			
		the front cover flap has to be opened to remove the records from the			
		inside— and includes a tearsheet of postcards.)			
Rolling Stones COC-2-2900	(S)	**Exile On Main Street** (2 LPs)	1973	3.20	8.00
		(Later covers have two-pockets that open on the outside.)			
Rolling Stones COC 59101	(S)	**Goat's Head Soup** (With bonus photo)	1973	4.00	10.00
Rolling Stones COC 59101	(S)	**Goat's Head Soup** (Without the photo)	1973	1.20	6.00
Rolling Stones COC 79101	(S)	**It's Only Rock 'N' Roll**	1974	1.20	6.00
Rolling Stones COC 79102	(S)	**Made In The Shade**	1975	1.20	6.00
Rolling Stones COC 79104	(S)	**Black And Blue**	1976	1.20	6.00
Rolling Stones COC 2-9001	(S)	**Love You Live**	1977	1.20	6.00
Rolling Stones COC 39108	(S)	**Some Girls**	1978	1.20	6.00
		(Original covers have die-cut holes to display the inner sleeve graphics,			
		which features faces of personalities, including Farrah Fawcett and Lucille			
		Ball. There were at least nine color combinations used on this cover.)			
Rolling Stones COC 39108	(S)	**Some Girls**	1978	1.20	6.00
		(Later covers do not have the die-cut face-holes while			
		the inner sleeve deletes Farrah Fawcett and Lucille Ball.)			
Rolling Stones COC 16015	(S)	**Emotional Rescue** (With poster)	1980	4.00	10.00
Rolling Stones COC 16015	(S)	**Emotional Rescue** (Without poster)	1980	1.00	5.00
Rolling Stones COC 16028	(S)	**Sucking In The Seventies**	1981	1.00	5.00
Rolling Stones COC 16052	(S)	**Tattoo You**	1981	1.00	5.00
Rolling Stones COC 39113	(S)	**Still Life**	1982	1.00	5.00
Rolling Stones COC 39113	(S)	**Still Life** (Picture disc)	1982	16.00	40.00
Rolling Stones 7-90120	(S)	**Undercover**	1983	1.00	5.00
Rolling Stones 7-90176	(S)	**Rewind/1971-1984**	1984	10.00	25.00
Rolling Stones C-40250	(S)	**Dirty Work**	1986	1.00	5.00
Rolling Stones C-45333	(S)	**Steel Wheels**	1989	1.00	5.00
Rolling Stones C-47456	(S)	**Flashpoint**	1991	1.00	5.00

ROMAN, MURRAY

Label & Catalog #		Title	Year	VG+	NM
Tetragrammaton 101	(S)	**You Can't Beat People Up**	1968	6.00	15.00
Tetragrammaton 120	(S)	**Blind Man's Movie**	1969	6.00	15.00

ROMANCERS, THE
Refer to The Chi-Lites / The Romancers.

Label & Catalog #		Title	Year	VG+	NM
Selma 1245	(S)	**Do The Slauson**	1963	8.00	20.00
Selma 1501	(S)	**Let's Do The Swim**	1963	8.00	20.00

ROMEOS, THE

Label & Catalog #		Title	Year	VG+	NM
Mark-II 1001	(M)	**Precious Memories**	1967	10.00	25.00

Label & Catalog #		Title	Year	VG+	NM

RONETTES, THE

The Ronettes are sisters Veronica (aka Ronnie Spector) and Estelle Bennett and cousin Nedra Talley Ross. They are, along with The Shangri-La's, the quintessential "girl group" of the '60s. All of their hits and their second album (below) were the products of producer Phil Spector.

Colpix CLP-486	(M)	The Ronettes Featuring Veronica	1965	100.00	200.00
Colpix CST-486	(S)	The Ronettes Featuring Veronica	1965	150.00	300.00
		— Colpix albums above have gold labels.—			
Colpix CLP-486	(M)	The Ronettes Featuring Veronica	196?	40.00	100.00
Colpix CST-486	(S)	The Ronettes Featuring Veronica	196?	60.00	150.00
		— Colpix albums above have blue labels.—			
Philles PHLP-4006	(M)	Presenting The Fabulous Ronettes	1965	500.00	750.00
		—Philles albums above have blue labels.—			
Philles PHLP-4006	(M)	Presenting The Fabulous Ronettes	1965	150.00	300.00
Philles PHLP-ST-4006	(S)	Presenting The Fabulous Ronettes	1965	300.00	500.00
		—Philles albums above have yellow & red labels.—			
Philles T-90721	(M)	Presenting The Fabulous Ronettes	1965	100.00	250.00
Philles ST-90721	(S)	Presenting The Fabulous Ronettes	1965	200.00	400.00
		(Capitol Record Club)			

RONNIE & THE DEADBEATS

Check 103	(M)	Groovin' With Ronnie & The Deadbeats	197?	8.00	20.00

RONNIE & THE POMONA CASUALS

Donna 2112	(M)	Everybody Jerk	1965	12.00	30.00

RONNY & THE DAYTONAS

Mala 4001	(M)	G. T. O.	1964	60.00	150.00
Mala 4002	(M)	Sandy	1966	30.00	75.00
Mala 4002S	(S)	Sandy	1966	40.00	100.00

RONSTADT, LINDA, & THE STONE PONEYS [THE STONE PONEYS]

The Stone Poneys formed as a folk-based trio consisting of Linda with Bob Kimmel and Kenny Edwards. After their second album the name changed to Linda Ronstadt & The Stone Poneys, after which the group dissolved. This left Linda with a contract to fulfill with Capitol as a solo artist (below).

Capitol T-2666	(M)	The Stone Poneys	1967	10.00	25.00
Capitol ST-2666	(S)	The Stone Poneys	1967	14.00	35.00
Capitol T-2763	(M)	Evergreen, Volume II	1967	10.00	25.00
Capitol ST-2763	(S)	Evergreen, Volume II	1967	14.00	35.00
Capitol ST-2863	(S)	Linda Ronstadt & The Stone Poneys Vol. III	1968	18.00	45.00
Capitol ST-11383	(S)	The Stone Poneys Featuring Linda Ronstadt	1974	1.00	5.00
Pickwick SPC-3298	(S)	Stoney End	1973	1.00	5.00

RONSTADT, LINDA

After her first two albums, Linda recruited a band that consisted of Don Henley, Glenn Frey, Bernie Leadon, and Randy Meisner. After one album, the group leaves and signs with Asylum as The Eagles. At which point, Ms Ronstadt teamed up with manager and producer Peter Asher and realized success as the biggest selling female American singer of the '70s. Refer to Hearts & Flowers; Peter & Gordon.

Capitol ST-208	(S)	Hand Sown... Home Grown	1969	6.00	15.00
		—Capitol albums above have black "rainbow" labels.—			
Capitol ST-208	(S)	Hand Sown... Home Grown	1970	3.20	8.00
Capitol ST-407	(S)	Silk Purse	1970	3.20	8.00
Capitol SMAS-635	(S)	Linda Ronstadt	1972	3.20	8.00
		—Capitol albums above have green labels.—			
Capitol ST-208	(S)	Hand Sown... Home Grown	197?	.80	4.00
Capitol ST-407	(S)	Silk Purse	197?	.80	4.00
Capitol SMAS-635	(S)	Linda Ronstadt	197?	.80	4.00
		—Capitol albums above have red labels.—			
Capitol ST-11269	(S)	Different Drum	1974	1.00	5.00
		(ST-11269 cinsists of Stone Poneys and early solo tracks.)			
Capitol ST-11358	(S)	Heart Like A Wheel	1974	1.00	5.00
Capitol SW-11358	(S)	Heart Like A Wheel	1974	.80	4.00
Capitol SKBB-11629	(S)	A Retrospective (2 LPs)	1977	1.00	5.00
		(SKBB-11629 cinsists of Stone Poneys and early solo tracks.)			
Capitol SN-16130	(S)	Hand Sown, Home Grown	1980	.80	4.00
Capitol SN-16131	(S)	Silk Purse	1980	.80	4.00
Capitol SN-16132	(S)	Linda Ronstadt	1980	.80	4.00
Asylum 5064	(S)	Don't Cry Now	1973	.80	4.00
Asylum 7E-1045	(S)	Prisoner In Disguise	1975	.80	4.00
Asylum 7E-1072	(S)	Hasten Down The Wind	1976	.80	4.00
Asylum 7E-1092	(S)	Greatest Hits	1976	.80	4.00
Asylum 6E-104	(S)	Simple Dreams	1977	.80	4.00
Asylum 6E-106	(S)	Greatest Hits	1977	.80	4.00
Asylum 6E-155	(S)	Living In The USA	1978	.80	4.00
Asylum DP-401	(S)	Living In The U.S.A. (Picture disc)	1978	4.00	10.00
Asylum 5E-510	(S)	Mad Love	1980	.80	4.00
Asylum 5E-516	(S)	Greatest Hits, Volume Two	1980	.80	4.00
Asylum E1-60185	(S)	Get Closer	1982	.80	4.00
Asylum 60260	(S)	What's New	1983	.80	4.00
Asylum 60387	(S)	Lush Life	1984	.80	4.00

STEREO

PLAYABLE ON STEREO & MONO PHONOGRAPHS

Linda Ronstadt
Stone Poneys Vol. III
and Friends

The original Stone Poneys were folkies Bob Kimmel and Ken Edwards backing vocalist
Linda Ronstadt. This, their third and final album, is the most difficult to find. It boasts this
gorgeous photo of the oh so lovely Linda just before she was required to pursue a solo career.

Catalog #		Title	Year	VG+	NM

ROSE, TIM

Columbia CS-9577	(S)	Tim Rose	1968	4.00	10.00
Columbia CS-9772	(S)	Thru Rose Colored Glasses	1969	4.00	10.00
		— Columbia albums above have "360 Sound" labels.—			
Capitol ST-673	(S)	Love, A Kind Of Hate Story	1970	4.00	10.00
Playboy 101	(S)	Tim Rose	1972	4.00	10.00

ROSE GARDEN, THE

Atco SD-33-225	(S)	The Rose Garden	1968	6.00	15.00

ROSIE

Rosie Hamlin, who originally recorded as Rosie & The Originals.

Brunswick BL-54102	(M)	Lonely Blue Nights With Rosie	1961	60.00	150.00
Brunswick BL-754102	(S)	Lonely Blue Nights With Rosie	1961	100.00	250.00

ROSS, DIANA

Diana Ross originally recorded with The Supremes.

Motown 711	(S)	Diana Ross	1970	1.20	6.00
Motown 719	(S)	Diana!	1971	1.20	6.00
Motown 723	(S)	Surrender	1971	1.20	6.00
Motown 724	(S)	Everything Is Everything	1970	1.20	6.00
Motown 758	(S)	Lady Sings The Blues (2 LPs)	1972	3.20	8.00
Motown 772	(S)	Touch Me In The Morning	1973	1.20	6.00
Motown 801	(S)	Live At Caesars Palace	1973	1.20	6.00
Motown M7-812	(S)	Last Time I Saw Him	1973	1.20	6.00
Motown M7-861	(S)	Diana Ross	1976	1.20	6.00
Motown M7-869	(S)	Diana Ross' Greatest Hits	1976	1.00	5.00
Motown M7-877	(S)	An Evening With Diana Ross (2 LPs)	1977	1.20	6.00
Motown M7-890	(S)	Baby It's Me	1977	1.00	5.00
Motown M7-907	(S)	Ross	1978	1.00	5.00
Motown M7-923	(DJ)	The Boss (Gold vinyl)	1979	8.00	20.00
Motown M7-923	(S)	The Boss	1979	1.00	5.00
Motown M8-936	(S)	Diana	1980	1.00	5.00
Motown 951	(S)	To Love Again	1981	1.00	5.00
Motown 960	(S)	All The Great Hits (2 LPs)	1981	1.00	5.00
Motown 6049	(S)	Anthology	1983	1.00	5.00
Kory 1008	(S)	Touch Me In The Morning	1980	.80	4.00
Motown M5-135V	(S)	Diana!	1980	.80	4.00
Motown M5-155V	(S)	Diana	1980	.80	4.00
Motown M5-163V	(S)	Touch Me In The Morning	1980	.80	4.00
Motown M5-169V	(S)	Live At Caesars Palace	1980	.80	4.00
Motown M5-198V	(S)	The Boss	1980	.80	4.00
RCA Victor AFL1-4153	(S)	Why Do Fools Fall In Love	1981	1.00	5.00
RCA Victor AFL1-4384	(S)	Silk Electric	1982	1.00	5.00
RCA Victor AFL1-4677	(S)	Ross	1983	1.00	5.00
RCA Victor AFL1-5009	(S)	Swept Away	1984	1.00	5.00

ROSS, DIANA / NEIL DIAMOND

MCA SM-734727	(S)	It's Happening!	1972	20.00	50.00

ROSS, DIANA, & MARVIN GAYE

Motown M7-803	(S)	Diana & Marvin	1973	3.20	8.00

ROSS, DR. ISAIAH

Testament 2206	(M)	Call The Doctor	196?	30.00	75.00

ROSS, MISS JACKIE

Chess LP-1489	(M)	In Full Bloom	1966	12.00	30.00
Chess LPS-1489	(S)	In Full Bloom	1966	16.00	40.00

ROTARY CONNECTION, THE [THE NEW ROTARY CONNECTION]

Cadet Concept LPS-312	(S)	Rotary Connection	1968	6.00	15.00
Cadet Concept LPS-317	(S)	Aladdin	1968	6.00	15.00
Cadet Concept LPS-318	(S)	Peace	1969	6.00	15.00
Cadet Concept LPS-322	(S)	Songs	1969	6.00	15.00
Cadet Concept LPS-329	(S)	Dinner Music	1970	6.00	15.00
Chess 50006	(S)	Hey Love	1971	4.00	10.00
		(Chess 50006 credits The New Rotary Connection.)			

ROUGH TRADE

True North APHT-5010	(S)	For Those Who Think Young (Half-speed)	198?	10.00	30.00

ROUND, JONATHAN

Westbound 2009	(S)	Jonathan Round (Round cover)	1971	12.00	30.00
Westbound 2009	(S)	Jonathan Round (Standard cover)	1972	6.00	15.00

ROUND ROBIN

Domain 101	(M)	Greatest Hits, Slauson Style	1964	10.00	25.00
Challenge LP-620	(M)	The Land Of 1,000 Dances Featuring Round Robin	1965	10.00	25.00

Rosalie Hamlin made girl group history with the landmark "Angel Baby" in 1961 as the leader of Rosie & The Originals. She then struck out on her own and had a modest chart-maker with "Lonely Blue Nights." Nonetheless, her label commissioned an album and this rarity now stands as an artifact to a time long gone.

Label & Catalog #		Title	Year	VG+	NM
ROUTERS, THE					
Warner Bros. W-1490	(M)	Let's Go With The Routers	1963	10.00	25.00
Warner Bros. WS-1490	(S)	Let's Go With The Routers	1963	12.00	30.00
Warner Bros. W-1524	(M)	1963's Great Instrumental Hits	1964	12.00	30.00
Warner Bros. WS-1524	(S)	1963's Great Instrumental Hits	1964	16.00	40.00
Warner Bros. W-1559	(M)	Charge!	1964	8.00	20.00
Warner Bros. WS-1559	(S)	Charge!	1964	10.00	25.00
Warner Bros. W-1595	(M)	Go Go Go With The Chuck Berry Songbook	1965	8.00	20.00
Warner Bros. WS-1595	(S)	Go Go Go With The Chuck Berry Songbook	1965	10.00	25.00
ROWAN BROTHERS, THE [THE ROWANS]					
The Rowans feature Peter Rowan and David Grisma. Refer to Earth Opera; Old & In The Way.					
Columbia KC-31297	(S)	The Rowan Bros.	1972	1.00	5.00
Asylum 7E-1114	(S)	Jubilation	1975	1.00	5.00
Asylum 7E-1038	(S)	The Rowans	1976	1.00	5.00
Asylum 7E-1073	(S)	Sibling Rivalry	1977	1.00	5.00
ROXY					
Elektra EKS-74063	(S)	Roxy	1969	6.00	15.00
ROXY MUSIC					
The original Roxy Music was Bryan Ferry, Brian Eno, Rik Kenton, Andy MacKay, Phil Manzanera, and Paul Thompson.					
Reprise MS-2114	(S)	Roxy Music	1972	10.00	25.00
Warner Bros. BS-2969	(S)	For Your Pleasure	1973	10.00	25.00
Atlantic SD-7045	(S)	Stranded	1974	1.00	5.00
Atco SD-36-106	(S)	Country Life *(Nearly naked ladies cover)*	1975	6.00	15.00
Atco SD-36-106	(S)	Country Life *(Deleted ladies cover)*	1975	1.00	5.00
Atco SD-36-127	(S)	Siren	1975	1.00	5.00
Atco SD-36-133	(S)	Roxy Music	1975	1.00	5.00
Atco SD-36-134	(S)	For Your Pleasure	1975	1.00	5.00
		(Atco 133 and 134 are reissues of Reprise 2114 and W.B. 2969.)			
Atco SD-36-139	(S)	Viva! Roxy Music	1976	1.00	5.00
Atco SD-38-114	(S)	Manifesto *(Picture disc)*	1979	6.00	15.00
Atco SD-38-114	(S)	Manifesto	1979	1.00	5.00
Atco SD-38-102	(S)	Flesh + Blood	1980	1.00	5.00
Atco SD-90122	(S)	The Atlantic Years 1973-1980	1984	.80	4.00
Warner Bros. 23686	(S)	Avalon	1982	1.00	5.00
Warner Bros. 23808	(S)	Musique/The High Road	1983	1.00	5.00
ROYAL, BILLY JOE					
Columbia CL-2403	(M)	Down In The Boondocks	1965	8.00	20.00
Columbia CS-9203	(S)	Down In The Boondocks	1965	10.00	25.00
Columbia CL-2781	(M)	Billy Joe Royal	1967	8.00	20.00
Columbia CS-9581	(S)	Billy Joe Royal	1967	10.00	25.00
Columbia CS-9974	(S)	Cherry Hill Park	1969	6.00	15.00
Mercury SRM-3837	(S)	Billy Joe Royal	1980	1.00	5.00
ROYAL COUNTS, THE					
Catamount 904	(S)	Acappella Soul	197?	4.00	10.00
ROYAL GUARDSMEN, THE					
Laurie LLP-2038	(M)	Snoopy Vs. The Red Baron	1967	6.00	15.00
Laurie SLLP-2038	(S)	Snoopy Vs. The Red Baron	1967	8.00	20.00
Laurie LLP-2039	(M)	The Return Of The Red Baron	1967	6.00	15.00
Laurie SLLP-2039	(S)	The Return Of The Red Baron	1967	8.00	20.00
Laurie LLP-2042	(M)	Snoopy And His Friends	1967	10.00	25.00
Laurie SLLP-2042	(S)	Snoopy And His Friends	1967	12.00	30.00
		(Issued with a "Merry Snoopy's Christmas" poster attached to the back cover as a tear-off sheet.)			
Laurie LLP-2042	(M)	Snoopy And His Friends *(Without the sheet)*	1967	6.00	15.00
Laurie SLLP-2042	(S)	Snoopy And His Friends *(Without the sheet)*	1967	8.00	20.00
Laurie SLLP-2046	(S)	Snoopy For President	1968	8.00	20.00
ROYAL PLAYBOYS, THE					
Waldorf Music Hall 33-136	(10")	Rock And Roll/New Orleans Blues	195?	250.00	500.00
		(This is actually a various artists album with six of the eight songs featuring The Royal Playboys.)			
ROYAL TEENS, THE					
Tru-Gems TG-1001	(M)	Music Gems: "Short Shorts" & Others	1974	8.00	20.00
ROYALETTES, THE					
MGM E-4332	(M)	It's Gonna Take A Miracle	1965	8.00	20.00
MGM SE-4332	(S)	It's Gonna Take A Miracle	1965	10.00	25.00
MGM E-4366	(M)	The Elegant Sound Of The Royalettes	1966	8.00	20.00
MGM SE-4366	(S)	The Elegant Sound Of The Royalettes	1966	10.00	25.00

Snoopy And His Friends by *The Royal Guardsmen* was issued with a special "Merry Christmas" poster attached to the back cover. Fans were instructed to "Tear me off" along the dotted line. While the group's novelty has long since seen its 15-minutes of fame fade away, finding this album with the poster still attached remains a chore.

Label & Catalog #		Title	Year	VG+	NM
RUBBER BAND, THE					
GRT 10007	(S)	The Jimi Hendrix Songbook	1969	10.00	25.00
GRT 10010	(S)	The Cream Songbook	1969	10.00	25.00
GRT 10015	(S)	The Beatles Songbook	1969	10.00	25.00

RUBEN & THE JETS
The group was formed in response to the Mothers Of Invention's "Crusin' With Ruben & The Jets." Aside from Zappa's producing the first album, none of The Mothers have anything to do with this group.

Label & Catalog #		Title	Year	VG+	NM
Mercury SRM-1-659	(S)	For Real	1973	6.00	15.00
Mercury SRM-1-694	(S)	Cib Safis	1974	4.00	10.00
RUBICON					
20th Cent. Fox 552	(S)	Rubicon	1978	2.40	6.00
20th Cent. Fox 557	(S)	American Dreams	1980	2.40	6.00
RUBY					
Chrysalis CHR-1061	(S)	Red Crystal Fantasies	1974	1.00	5.00

RUBY
Ruby features Tom Fogerty, formerly of Creedence Clearwater.

Label & Catalog #		Title	Year	VG+	NM
PBR International 7001	(S)	Ruby	1976	1.00	5.00
PBR International 7004	(S)	Rock & Roll Madness	1978	1.00	5.00
RUBY & THE ROMANTICS					
Kapp KL-1323	(M)	Our Day Will Come	1963	12.00	30.00
Kapp KS-3323	(S)	Our Day Will Come	1963	16.00	40.00
Kapp KL-1341	(M)	Till Then	1963	10.00	25.00
Kapp KS-3341	(S)	Till Then	1963	12.00	30.00
Kapp KL-1458	(M)	Greatest Hits Album	1966	8.00	20.00
Kapp KS-3458	(S)	Greatest Hits Album	1966	10.00	25.00
Kapp KL-1526	(M)	Ruby And The Romantics	1967	8.00	20.00
Kapp KS-3526	(S)	Ruby And The Romantics	1967	10.00	25.00
ABC S-638	(S)	More Than Yesterday	1968	6.00	15.00

RUFFIN, DAVID
David Ruffin was formerly a member of The Temptations.

Label & Catalog #		Title	Year	VG+	NM
Motown MS-685	(S)	My Whole World Ended	1969	8.00	20.00
Motown MS-696	(S)	Doin' His Thing	1969	6.00	15.00
Motown M-733	(S)	David Ruffin	1971	Unreleased	
Motown M-762	(S)	David Ruffin	1973	4.00	10.00
Motown M-818	(S)	Me 'N' Rock 'N' Roll Are Here To Stay	1974	4.00	10.00
Motwon 849	(S)	Who Am I	1975	4.00	10.00
Motown M-866	(S)	Everything's Coming Up Love	1976	4.00	10.00
Motown M7-885	(S)	In My Stride	1977	4.00	10.00
Motown M7-895	(S)	At His Best	1978	1.00	5.00
Warner Bros. BSK-3306	(S)	So Soon We Change	1977	1.00	5.00
Warner Bros. BSK-3516	(S)	Gentleman Ruffin	1980	1.00	5.00
Motown M5-146V	(S)	My Whole World Ended	1981	.80	4.00
Motown M5-211V	(S)	At His Best	1981	.80	4.00

RUFFIN, JIMMY

Label & Catalog #		Title	Year	VG+	NM
Soul 704	(M)	Jimmy Ruffin Sings Top 10 (Monochrome cover)	1967	20.00	50.00
Soul 704	(M)	Jimmy Ruffin Sings Top 10 (Color cover)	1967	10.00	25.00
Soul S-704	(S)	Jimmy Ruffin Sings Top 10 (Color cover)	1967	10.00	25.00
Soul S-708	(S)	Ruff 'N Ready	1969	6.00	15.00
RSO 3078	(S)	Sunrise	1980	1.00	5.00

RUFFIN, JIMMY & DAVID

Label & Catalog #		Title	Year	VG+	NM
Soul S-728	(S)	I Am My Brother's Keeper	1970	6.00	15.00
Motown M5-108V	(S)	Superstar Series, Vol. 8	1980	.80	4.00

RUFUS
Rufus includes Kevin Murphy, formerly of The American Breed, and lead singer Chaka Khan.

Label & Catalog #		Title	Year	VG+	NM
ABC X-783	(S)	Rufus	1973	3.20	8.00
ABC X-809	(S)	Rags To Rufus	1974	3.20	8.00
Command QD-40024	(Q)	Rags To Rufus	1975	6.00	15.00
ABC D-837	(S)	Rufusized	1975	3.20	8.00
Command QD-40023	(Q)	Rufusized	1975	6.00	15.00
ABC D-909	(S)	Rufus Featuring Chaka Khan	1975	3.20	8.00
ABC 975	(S)	Ask Rufus	1977	3.20	8.00
ABC AA-1049	(DJ)	Street Player (Picture disc)	1979	4.00	10.00
ABC AA-1049	(S)	Street Player	1979	1.00	5.00
ABC AA-1098	(DJ)	Numbers (Picture disc)	1979	4.00	10.00
ABC AA-1098	(S)	Numbers	1979	1.00	5.00
MCA 642	(S)	Rufus	1979	.80	4.00
MCA 37034	(S)	Rags To Rufus	1979	.80	4.00
MCA 37035	(S)	Rufusized	1979	.80	4.00
MCA 37036	(S)	Rufus Featuring Chaka Khan	1979	.80	4.00
MCA 37037	(S)	Ask Rufus	1979	.80	4.00

Label & Catalog #		Title	Year	VG+	NM
MCA 37038	(S)	Street Player	1979	.80	4.00
MCA 5103	(S)	Masterjam	1979	1.00	5.00
MCA 5159	(S)	Party 'Til You're Broke	1981	1.00	5.00
MCA 5270	(S)	Camouflage	1981	1.00	5.00
MCA 5339	(S)	The Very Best Of Rufus	1982	1.00	5.00
Warner Bros. 23679	(S)	Live—Stompin' At The Savoy (2 LPs)	1983	1.00	5.00
Warner Bros. 23753	(S)	Seal In Red	1983	1.00	5.00

RUGBYS, THE

Amazon 1000	(S)	Hot Cargo	1970	4.00	10.00

RUMBLERS, THE

Downey DLP-1001	(M)	Boss!	1963	60.00	150.00
Downey DLPS-1001	(S)	Boss!	1963	80.00	200.00
Dot DLP-3509	(M)	Boss!	1963	20.00	50.00
Dot DLP-25509	(S)	Boss!	1963	30.00	75.00
		(Dot 3/25509 is a reissue of Downey 1001.)			

RUMPLESTILTSKIN

Bell 6047	(S)	Rumplestiltskin	1970	8.00	20.00

RUNAWAYS, THE
The Runaways feature Joan Jett and Lita Ford.

Mercury SRM-1-1090	(S)	The Runaways (Gatefold cover)	1976	8.00	20.00
Mercury SRM-1-1126	(S)	Queens Of Noise	1977	6.00	15.00
Mercury SRM-1-3705	(S)	Waitin' For The Night	1977	6.00	15.00
Mercury SRM-1-3740	(S)	Live In Japan	1977	6.00	15.00
Rhino RNLP-250	(S)	Little Lost Girls (Picture disc)	1982	1.00	5.00
Rhino RNLP-250	(S)	Little Lost Girls	1982	1.00	5.00
Rhino EP-602	(S)	Momma, We're All Crazee Now	1983	1.00	5.00

RUNDGREN, TODD
Mr. Rundgren was a member of The Nazz. Refer to American Dream; Utopia.

Ampex A-10105	(S)	Runt (12 tracks)	1970	60.00	150.00
		(Original pressings of A-10105 have seven tracks on the first side and five on the second although both the cover and the labels only list six on Side 1 and four on Side 2. To identify this pressing the tracks on the record must be counted. Promo copies of this pressing are not known to exist.)			
Ampex A-10105	(DJ)	Runt (10 tracks. White label promo)	1970	40.00	100.00
		(White label promos for a second pressing exist that list and play ten tracks. Stock copies of this pressing are not known to exist.)			
Ampex A-10105	(S)	Runt (10 tracks)	1970	20.00	50.00
		(White label promos and stock copies for a second pressing exist that list and play ten tracks. Counterfeits exist.)			
Bearsville 10105	(S)	Runt (10 tracks)	1972	10.00	25.00
Bearsville 10116	(DJ)	Ballad Of Todd Rundgren (White label)	1972	40.00	100.00
Bearsville 10116	(S)	Ballad Of Todd Rundgren	1972	20.00	50.00
		(Counterfeits of 10116 exist.)			
Bearsville 2BX-2066	(DJ)	Something/Anything (2 LPs. White label)	1972	20.00	50.00
Bearsville 2BX-2066	(S)	Something/Anything (2 LPs. Colored vinyl)	1972	200.00	400.00
		(White label copies exist with one blue and one red vinyl record. This may or may not be a promotional item. . .)			
Bearsville 2BX-2066	(S)	Something/Anything (2 LPs)	1972	10.00	25.00
Bearsville PRO-524	(DJ)	The Todd Rundgren Radio Show	1972	60.00	150.00
Bearsville BRK-2133	(S)	A Wizard/A True Star	1973	3.20	8.00
Bearsville PRO-597	(DJ)	Banded Radio Interview	1974	40.00	100.00
Bearsville 2B-6952	(S)	Todd (2 LPs)	1974	1.20	6.00
Bearsville BRK-6957	(S)	Initiation	1975	.80	4.00
Bearsville BRK-6963	(S)	Faithful	1976	.80	4.00
Bearsville BRK-6981	(S)	Hermit Of Mink Hollow	1978	.80	4.00
Bearsville PRO-788	(DJ)	Back To The Bars Radio Sampler	1978	20.00	50.00
Bearsville 2BRK-6986	(S)	Back To The Bars (2 LPs)	1978	1.00	5.00
Bearsville BHS-3522	(S)	Healing	1981	.80	4.00
Bearsville 23732	(S)	The Ever Popular Tortured Artist Effect	1983	.80	4.00
Warner Bros. 9-25881	(S)	Nearly Human	1989	6.00	15.00

RUSH

Mercury SRM-1011	(S)	Rush	1974	1.20	6.00
Mercury SRM-1023	(S)	Fly By Night	1975	1.20	6.00
Mercury SRM-1046	(S)	Caress Of Steel	1975	1.20	6.00
Mercury MK-32	(DJ)	Everything Your Listener Ever Wanted To Hear By Rush	1975	40.00	100.00
Mercury SRM-1079	(S)	2112	1976	1.00	5.00
Mercury SRM-7508	(S)	All The World's A Stage (2 LPs)	1976	1.20	6.00
Mercury SRM-1184	(S)	A Farewell To Kings	1977	1.00	5.00
Mercury SRM-9200	(S)	Archives (3 LPs)	1978	1.20	6.00
		(Mercury SRM-9200 reissues 1011, 1023 and 1046.)			
Mercury SRM-3743	(S)	Hemispheres	1978	1.00	5.00
Mercury SRP-1300	(S)	Hemispheres (Picture disc)	1979	10.00	25.00

Label & Catalog #		Title	Year	VG+	NM
Mercury SRM-4001	(S)	Permanent Waves	1980	1.00	5.00
Mercury SRM-4013	(S)	Moving Pictures	1981	1.00	5.00
Mercury SRM-7001	(S)	Exit... Stage Left	1981	1.00	5.00
Mercury SRM-4063	(S)	Signals	1982	1.00	5.00
Mercury SRM-818476	(S)	Grace Under Pressure	1984	1.00	5.00

RUSH, MERILEE

Bell 6020	(M)	Angel Of The Morning	1968	6.00	15.00
Bell 6020	(S)	Angel Of The Morning	1968	8.00	20.00
		("Angel Of The Morning" is rechanneled.)			
United Arts. LA-735G	(S)	Merilee Rush	197?	1.00	5.00
Liberty LN-10166	(S)	Merilee Rush	1982	.80	4.00

RUSH, OTIS
Refer to Albert King & Otis Rush.

Blue Horizon BM-4602	(S)	Blues Masters, Volume 2	1968	10.00	25.00
Cotillion SD-9006	(S)	Mourning In The Morning	1969	10.00	25.00
Blue Horizon BM-4805	(S)	Chicago Blues	1970	10.00	25.00
Delmark 638	(S)	Cold Day In Hell	1975	4.00	10.00
Bullfrog 301	(S)	Right Place, Wrong Time	1977	4.00	10.00
Delmark 643	(S)	So Many Roads	1979	4.00	10.00

RUSKIN-SPEAR, ROGER
Ruskin-Spear was a member of The Bonzo Dog Band.

United Arts. LA097	(S)	Electric Shocks	1973	10.00	25.00

RUSSELL, LEON
Refer to Asylum Choir; Joe Cocker; George Harrison & Friends.

Shelter SHE-1001	(S)	Leon Russell (With "Old Masters")	1968	6.00	15.00
Shelter SHE-1001	(S)	Leon Russell (Without "Old Masters")	1970	1.00	5.00
		(SHE-1001 features George Harrison and Ringo Starr.)			
Shelter SW-8903	(S)	Leon Russell & The Shelter People	1971	1.00	5.00
Shelter SW-8911	(S)	Carney	1972	1.00	5.00
Shelter STCO-8917	(S)	Leon Live (3 LPs)	1973	4.00	10.00
Shelter SW-8923	(S)	Hank Wilson's Back, Vol. 1	1972	1.00	5.00
Shelter 2108	(S)	Stop All The Jazz	1974	1.00	5.00
Shelter 2118	(S)	Leon Russell	1974	.80	4.00
Shelter 2121	(S)	Carney	1974	.80	4.00
Shelter 2138	(S)	Will O' The Wisp	1975	.80	4.00
Shelter 52004	(S)	Best Of Leon	1976	.80	4.00
Shelter 52007	(S)	Leon Russell	1976	.80	4.00
Shelter 52008	(S)	Leon Russell & The Shelter People	1976	.80	4.00
Shelter 52011	(S)	Carney	1976	.80	4.00
Shelter 52020	(S)	Will O' The Wisp	1976	.80	4.00
MCA 682	(S)	Leon Russell	1979	.80	4.00
MCA 683	(S)	Leon Russell & The Shelter People	1979	.80	4.00
MCA 685	(S)	Carney	1979	.80	4.00
MCA 686	(S)	Will O' The Wisp	1979	.80	4.00
Paradise 2943	(S)	Wedding Album	1976	.80	4.00
Paradise 3066	(S)	Make Love To The Music	1977	.80	4.00
Paradise 3172	(S)	Americana	1978	.80	4.00
Paradise 3532	(S)	The Live Album	1981	.80	4.00

RUSTIX

Rare Earth RS-508	(S)	Bedlam (Shaped cover)	1969	6.00	15.00
Rare Earth RS-513	(S)	Come On, People	1969	4.00	10.00

RUTLES, THE
The Rutles feature Neil Innes of The Bonzo Dog Band and Eric Idle of Monty Python.

Warner Bros. PRO-723	(DJ)	Meet The Rutles (Sampler on gold vinyl)	1978	10.00	25.00
Warner Bros. H-3151	(S)	Meet The Rutles (With booklet)	1978	10.00	25.00

RYDELL, BOBBY

Cameo C-1006	(M)	We Got Love	1959	20.00	50.00
Cameo C-1007	(M)	Bobby Sings	1960	20.00	50.00
Cameo C-1009	(M)	Biggest Hits (Die-cut cover)	1961	30.00	75.00
		(C-1009 was originally issued with a die-cut cover with a textured photo on inner sleeve.)			
Cameo C-1009	(M)	Biggest Hits (Standard cover)	1961	10.00	25.00
Cameo C-1010	(M)	Bobby Rydell Salutes The "Great Ones"	1961	10.00	25.00
Cameo SC-1010	(S)	Bobby Rydell Salutes The "Great Ones"	1961	14.00	35.00
Cameo C-1011	(M)	Rydell At The Copa	1961	10.00	25.00
Cameo SC-1011	(S)	Rydell At The Copa	1961	14.00	35.00
Cameo C-1019	(M)	All The Hits (Red vinyl)	1962	60.00	150.00
Cameo C-1019	(M)	All The Hits	1962	10.00	25.00
Cameo C-1028	(M)	Biggest Hits, Volume 2	1962	10.00	25.00
Cameo C-1040	(M)	All The Hits, Volume 2	1963	10.00	25.00
Cameo SC-1040	(P)	All The Hits, Volume 2	1963	14.00	35.00
Cameo C-1043	(M)	Bye Bye Birdie	1963	8.00	20.00

Label & Catalog #		Title	Year	VG+	NM
Cameo C-1055	(M)	Wild (Wood) Days	1963	8.00	20.00
Cameo CS-1055	(S)	Wild (Wood) Days	1963	10.00	25.00
Cameo C-1070	(M)	The Top Hits Of '63	1964	8.00	20.00
Cameo CS-1070	(S)	The Top Hits Of '63	1964	10.00	25.00
Cameo C-1080	(M)	Forget Him	1964	8.00	20.00
Cameo CS-1080	(E)	Forget Him	1964	8.00	20.00
Cameo C-2001	(M)	16 Golden Hits	1965	8.00	20.00
Cameo CS-2001	(E)	16 Golden Hits	1965	8.00	20.00
Cameo C-4017	(M)	An Era Reborn	196?	8.00	20.00
Cameo CS-4017	(S)	An Era Reborn	196?	8.00	20.00
Strand SL-1120	(M)	Bobby Rydell Sings	196?	10.00	25.00
Strand SLS-1120	(S)	Bobby Rydell Sings	196?	8.00	20.00
Spinorama 143	(M)	Starring Bobby Rydell	196?	1.00	5.00
Spinorama S-143	(S)	Starring Bobby Rydell	196?	1.00	5.00
Capitol T-2281	(M)	Somebody Loves You	1965	6.00	15.00
Capitol ST-2281	(S)	Somebody Loves You	1965	8.00	20.00

RYDELL, BOBBY, & CHUBBY CHECKER

Label & Catalog #		Title	Year	VG+	NM
Cameo C-1013	(M)	Bobby Rydell / Chubby Checker	1961	12.00	30.00
Cameo C-1063	(M)	Chubby Checker And Bobby Rydell	1963	8.00	20.00

RYDELL, BOBBY / BARRY NORMAN / STEPHEN GARRICK

Label & Catalog #		Title	Year	VG+	NM
Venise 10035	(S)	Twistin' (Gold vinyl)	197?	10.00	25.00

RYDER, MITCH & THE DETROIT WHEELS

Label & Catalog #		Title	Year	VG+	NM
New Voice 2000	(M)	Take A Ride	1966	10.00	25.00
New Voice S-2000	(S)	Take A Ride	1966	12.00	30.00
New Voice 2002	(M)	Breakout!!!	1966	10.00	25.00
New Voice S-2002	(S)	Breakout!!!	1966	12.00	30.00
		(NV 2002 was originally issued without "Devil With A Blue Dress.")			
New Voice 2002	(M)	Breakout!!!	1966	8.00	20.00
New Voice S-2002	(S)	Breakout!!!	1966	10.00	25.00
		(Later pressings include "Devil With A Blue Dress.")			
New Voice 2003	(M)	Sock It To Me!	1967	10.00	25.00
New Voice S-2003	(S)	Sock It To Me!	1967	12.00	30.00
New Voice 2004	(M)	All Mitch Ryder Hits!	1967	8.00	20.00
New Voice S-2004	(S)	All Mitch Ryder Hits!	1967	10.00	25.00
New Voice S-2005	(S)	Mitch Ryder Sings The Hits	1968	6.00	15.00
Crewe CR-1335	(S)	All Mitch Ryder Hits	1968	6.00	15.00
		(Crewe 1335 is a reissue of New Voice 2004.)			

RYDER, MITCH

Label & Catalog #		Title	Year	VG+	NM
DynoVoice 1901	(M)	What Now My Love	1967	6.00	15.00
DynoVoice 31901	(S)	What Now My Love	1967	6.00	15.00
Dot DLP-25963	(S)	The Detroit-Memphis Experiment	1969	6.00	15.00
Paramount PAS-6010	(S)	Detroit	1971	6.00	15.00
Seeds & Stems 7801	(S)	How I Spent My Summer Vacation	1978	3.20	8.00
Seeds & Stems 7804	(S)	Naked But Not Dead	1980	3.20	8.00
Riva 7503	(S)	Never Kick A Sleeping Dog	1983	3.20	8.00

RYE

Label & Catalog #		Title	Year	VG+	NM
Beverly Hills 27	(S)	The Beginning	1971	4.00	10.00

S. C. R. A. [THE SOUTHERN CONTEMPORARY ROCK ASSEMBLY]

Atlantic SD-7235	(S)	The Ship Album	1972	6.00	15.00

SACCO, LOU CHRISTIE: *Refer to* LOU CHRISTIE

SAD CAFE

A&M SP-4737	(S)	Misplaced Ideals	1978	1.20	6.00
A&M SP-4779	(S)	Facades	1979	1.20	6.00
Polydor 5045	(S)	Sad Cafe	1980	1.20	6.00

SADISTIC MIKA BAND, THE

Harvest ST-11375	(S)	The Sadistic Mika Band	1974	1.00	5.00

SAGITTARIUS

Sagittarius features Curt Boetcher with producer/performer Gary Usher..

Columbia CS-9644	(S)	Present Tense	1968	12.00	30.00
Together STT-1002	(S)	The Blue Marble (Includes 2 bonus photos)	1969	20.00	50.00
Together STT-1002	(S)	The Blue Marble (Without the photos)	1969	14.00	35.00

SAHM, DOUG [THE SIR DOUGLAS QUINTET]

Doug Sahm recorded solo for years before forming The Sir Douglas Quintet with Augie Meyers. Personnel from this band play on albums credited both to the group and solely to Sahm. Refer to The Quintet.

Tribe TR-37001	(M)	The Best Of The Sir Douglas Quintet	1966	20.00	50.00
Tribe TRS-47001	(E)	The Best Of The Sir Douglas Quintet	1966	16.00	40.00
Smash SRS-67108	(S)	Sir Douglas Quintet + 2 = (Honkey Blues) (Gatefold cover)	1968	12.00	30.00
Smash SRS-67115	(S)	Mendocino	1969	10.00	25.00
Smash SRS-67130	(S)	Together After Five	1970	10.00	25.00
Philips PHS-600-344	(S)	1+1+1=4 (Gatefold cover)	1970	10.00	25.00
Philips PHS-600-353	(S)	The Return Of Doug Saldana	1971	10.00	25.00
Mercury SRM-1-655	(S)	Rough Edges	1972	12.00	30.00
Atlantic SD-7287	(S)	Texas Tornado	1973	4.00	10.00
Atlantic SD-7254	(S)	Doug Sahm & Band	1973	4.00	10.00
Warner Bros. BS-2810	(S)	Groover's Paradise	1974	6.00	15.00
Dot 2057	(S)	Texas Rock For Country Rollers	1976	6.00	15.00
Takoma TAK-7075	(S)	Hell Of A Spell	1980	3.20	8.00
Takoma TAK-7086	(S)	The Best Of The Sir Douglas Quintet	1980	3.20	8.00
Takoma TAK-7088	(S)	Border Wave	1981	3.20	8.00
Takoma TAK-7095	(S)	Live Texas Tornado	1983	3.20	8.00
R&M UDL-2343	(E)	The Tracker	1981	6.00	15.00
		(R&M 2343 is a repackage of the Tribe material.)			
Accord SN-7905	(S)	Made In Texas	1982	1.00	5.00
Varrack VR-004	(S)	Quintessence	1983	3.20	8.00
Teardrop TD-5000	(S)	The West Side Sound Rolls Again	1983	3.20	8.00
Crazy Cajun CCLP-1003	(S)	The Best Of The Sir Douglas Quintet	1985	1.00	5.00
		(Crazy Cajun 1003 is a reissue of Tribe 37001.)			
Crazy Cajun CCLP-1029	(S)	The Tracker	1985	1.00	5.00
		(Crazy Cajun 1003 is a reissue of R&M 2343.)			

SAILCAT

Elektra EKS-75029	(S)	Motorcycle Mama	1972	1.00	5.00

SAIN, OLIVER

Abat 404	(S)	Main Man	1973	8.00	20.00
Abat 406	(S)	Bus Stop	1974	8.00	20.00

ST. JAMES, ROD

Paula 2218	(S)	Has Anybody Seen The Superstar?	1972	1.00	5.00

ST. JOHN, BRIDGET

Dandelion D9-101	(S)	Ask Me No Questions	1970	6.00	15.00
Elektra EKS-74104	(S)	Songs For The Gentleman	1971	4.00	10.00

ST. JOHN GREEN

Flick Disc FLS-45001	(S)	St. John Green	1968	6.00	15.00

Douglas Sahm, forever Sir Doug to his fans, has maintained a career long after his hit-making years, primarily as an Austin, Texas, legend. These two albums are credited to him but . . . Rough Edges consists of outtakes from previously issued albums by The Sir Douglas Quintet. Groovers Paradise, on the other hand, features Doug backed by Creedence Clearwater's rhythm section, Doug Clifford and Stu Cook.

Label & Catalog #		Title	Year	VG+	NM
ST. LOUIS JIMMY					
Bluesville BVLP-1028	(M)	**Goin' Down Blues**	1961	30.00	75.00
—Bluesville albums above have bright blue labels with silver print.—					
Bluesville BVLP-1028	(M)	**Goin' Down Blues**	1964	10.00	25.00
—Bluesville albums above have blue labels with a trident logo on the right side.—					
ST. PETERS, CRISPIAN					
Jamie JLPM-3027	(M)	**The Pied Piper**	1966	20.00	50.00
Jamie JLPS-3027	(E)	**The Pied Piper**	1966	14.00	35.00
SAINT STEVEN					
Probe CPLP-4506	(S)	**Over The Hills**	1970	20.00	50.00
SALISBURY, SANDY					
Sandy also recorded with Sagittarius.					
Together ST-????	(S)	**Sandy**	1970	*Unreleased*	
SALLOOM, SINCLAIR, & THE MOTHER BEAR					
Cadet Concept 316	(S)	**Sinclair Salloom And The Mother Bear**	1968	5.00	12.00
SALLYANGIE					
Sallyangie is Sally and Mike Oldfield.					
Warner Bros. WS-1783	(S)	**Children Of The Sun**	1969	6.00	15.00
SALT WATER TAFFY					
Buddah BDS-5021	(S)	**Finders Keepers**	1968	8.00	20.00
SALVATION					
ABC S-623	(S)	**Salvation**	1968	8.00	20.00
ABC S-653	(S)	**Gypsy Carnival Caravan**	1968	8.00	20.00
SAM & DAVE					
Sam Moore and Dave Prater.					
Roulette R-25323	(M)	**Sam And Dave**	1966	12.00	30.00
Roulette SR-25323	(P)	**Sam And Dave**	1966	16.00	40.00
(Half of the tracks on SR-25323 are rechanneled.)					
Stax ST-708	(M)	**Hold On I'm Comin'**	1966	16.00	40.00
Stax STS-708	(S)	**Hold On I'm Comin'**	1966	20.00	50.00
("I Take What I Want" is rechanneled)					
Stax ST-712	(M)	**Double Dynamite**	1966	12.00	30.00
Stax STS-712	(S)	**Double Dynamite**	1966	16.00	40.00
Stax ST-725	(M)	**Soul Men**	1967	12.00	30.00
Stax STS-725	(S)	**Soul Men**	1967	16.00	40.00
Atlantic SD-8205	(S)	**I Thank You**	1968	10.00	25.00
Atlantic SD-8218	(S)	**The Best Of Sam And Dave**	1969	8.00	20.00
United Arts. LA262	(S)	**Back At 'Cha!**	1974	6.00	15.00
United Arts. LA524	(S)	**Back At 'Cha!**	1975	4.00	10.00
Gusto 0045	(S)	**Sweet And Funky Gold**	197?	4.00	10.00
SAM APPLE PIE					
Sire SES-97020	(S)	**Sam Apple Pie**	1969	16.00	40.00

SAM THE SHAM [SAM THE SHAM & THE PHARAOHS]
Sam The Sham is a [mocking] pseudonym for Sam Samudio. The group can also be found on the MGM soundtrack "When The Boys Meet The Girls."

MGM E-4297	(M)	**Wooly Bully**	1965	12.00	30.00
MGM SE-4297	(S)	**Wooly Bully**	1965	16.00	40.00
MGM E-4314	(M)	**Their Second Album**	1965	10.00	25.00
MGM SE-4314	(S)	**Their Second Album**	1965	12.00	30.00
MGM E-4347	(M)	**On Tour**	1966	10.00	25.00
MGM SE-4347	(S)	**On Tour**	1966	12.00	30.00
MGM E-4407	(M)	**Lil' Red Riding Hood**	1966	10.00	25.00
MGM SE-4407	(S)	**Lil' Red Riding Hood**	1966	12.00	30.00
("Lil' Red Riding Hood" is rechanneled.)					
MGM E-4422	(M)	**The Best Of Sam The Sham**	1967	8.00	20.00
MGM SE-4422	(S)	**The Best Of Sam The Sham**	1967	10.00	25.00
MGM E-4479	(M)	**Nefertiti**	1967	8.00	20.00
MGM SE-4479	(S)	**Nefertiti**	1967	10.00	25.00
MGM SE-4479	(S)	**Sam The Sham Revue**	1968	8.00	20.00
("Sam The Sham Revue" is a repackage of "Nefertiti.")					
MGM SE-4526	(S)	**Ten Of Pentacles**	1968	8.00	20.00
SAMMY					
Philips PHS-700006	(S)	**Sammy**	1973	6.00	15.00
SAMUDIO, SAM					
Sam Samudio is best known as Sam The Sham.					
Atlantic SD-8271	(S)	**Hard And Heavy**	1971	4.00	10.00

Label & Catalog #		Title	Year	VG+	NM
SANCTUARY			197?	6.00	15.00
Veritas VS-92072	(S)	Sanctuary			
SAND			1973	4.00	10.00
Barnaby 15006	(S)	Sand			
SANDALS, THE [THE SANDELLS]					
The group's first album credits The Sandells; the latter two, The Sandals.					
World Pacific WP-1818	(M)	Scrambler	1964	16.00	40.00
World Pacific ST-1818	(S)	Scrambler *(Red vinyl)*	1964	40.00	100.00
World Pacific ST-1818	(S)	Scrambler	1964	20.00	50.00
World Pacific WP-1832	(M)	The Endless Summer	1966	8.00	20.00
World Pacific ST-1832	(S)	The Endless Summer	1966	10.00	25.00
		(World Pacific 1832 is a repackage of W.P. 1818.)			
World Pacific WPS-21884	(S)	The Last Of The Ski Bums	1969	10.00	25.00
		(Orange cover with three skiers' silhouettes.)			
World Pacific WPS-21884	(S)	The Last Of The Ski Bums	1969	10.00	25.00
		(Blue cover with cartoon skiers in a VW bus.)			
SANDALWOOD			1973	4.00	10.00
Bell 1134	(S)	Sandalwood			
SANDERS, ED					
Mr. Sanders was a member of The Fugs.					
Reprise RS-6374	(S)	Sanders' Truckstop	1969	12.00	30.00
Reprise MS-2105	(S)	Beer Cans On The Moon	1972	12.00	30.00
SANDY COAST: *Refer to* **VANITY FARE**					
SANFORD/TOWNSEND BAND, THE					
Ed Sanford and John Townsend.					
Warner Bros. BS-2966	(S)	The Sanford/Townsend Band	1977	1.20	6.00
Warner Bros. BS-3081	(S)	Duo-Glide	1978	1.20	6.00
Warner Bros. BS-3343	(S)	Nail Me To The Wall	1979	1.20	6.00
SANTA FE					
RTV 301	(S)	Good Earth	1971	12.00	30.00
Ampex A-10135	(S)	Santa Fe	1971	4.00	10.00
SANTANA					
The group was named after its leader, Carlos Santana.					
Columbia CS-9781	(S)	Santana	1969	6.00	15.00
Columbia KC-30130	(S)	Abraxas *(With poster)*	1970	8.00	20.00
Columbia KC-30130	(S)	Abraxas *(Without poster)*	1970	6.00	15.00
		—Columbia albums above have "360 Sound" labels.—			
Columbia CS-9781	(S)	Santana	1970	1.00	5.00
Columbia KC-30130	(S)	Abraxas	1970	1.00	5.00
Columbia PC-30130	(S)	Abraxas	1972	.80	4.00
Columbia PCQ-30130	(Q)	Abraxas	1974	6.00	15.00
Columbia HC-40130	(S)	Abraxas *(Half-speed master)*	1981	25.00	75.00
Columbia C-30595	(S)	Santana III	1971	1.00	5.00
Columbia CQ-30595	(Q)	Santana III	1974	6.00	15.00
Columbia KC-31610	(S)	Caravanserai	1972	1.00	5.00
Columbia PC-31610	(S)	Caravanserai	1972	1.00	5.00
Columbia PCQ-31610	(Q)	Caravanserai	1974	6.00	15.00
Columbia PC-32445	(S)	Welcome	1973	1.00	5.00
Columbia PCQ-32445	(Q)	Welcome	1974	6.00	15.00
Columbia PC-33050	(S)	Santana's Greatest Hits	1974	1.00	5.00
Columbia PCQ-33050	(Q)	Santana's Greatest Hits	1974	6.00	15.00
Columbia PC-33135	(S)	Borboletta	1974	1.00	5.00
Columbia PCQ-33135	(Q)	Borboletta	1974	6.00	15.00
Columbia PC-33576	(S)	Amigos	1976	1.00	5.00
Columbia PCQ-33576	(Q)	Amigos	1976	6.00	15.00
Columbia PC-34423	(S)	Festival	1977	1.00	5.00
Columbia PCQ-34423	(Q)	Festival	1977	6.00	15.00
Columbia C2-34914	(S)	Moonflower *(2 LPs)*	1977	3.20	8.00
Columbia PC-35600	(S)	Inner Secrets	1978	1.00	5.00
Columbia FC-35600	(S)	Inner Secrets	1978	1.00	5.00
Columbia FC-36154	(S)	Marathon	1979	1.00	5.00
Columbia AS-573	(DJ)	The Solo Guitar Of Devadip Carlos Santana	1979	6.00	15.00
Columbia C2-36590	(S)	Swing Of Delight *(2 LPs)*	1980	1.20	6.00
Columbia FC-37158	(S)	Zebop!	1981	1.00	5.00
Columbia HC-47158	(S)	Zebop! *(Half-speed master)*	1981	12.00	36.00
Columbia FC-38122	(S)	Shango	1982	1.00	5.00
Columbia FC-39527	(S)	Beyond Appearances	1985	1.00	5.00

Label & Catalog #		Title	Year	VG+	NM

SANTANA, CARLOS
Carlos Santana is the leader of Santana.

Columbia JC-35686	(S)	Oneness/Silver Dreams-Golden Reality	1979	1.00	5.00
Columbia PC-36590	(S)	The Swing Of Delight *(2 LPs)*	1978	3.20	8.00
Columbia FC-38642	(S)	Havana Moon	1982	1.00	5.00

SANTANA, CARLOS, & ALICE COLTRANE

Columbia PC-32900	(S)	Illuminations	1974	1.00	5.00
Columbia PCQ-32900	(Q)	Illuminations	1974	6.00	15.00

SANTANA, CARLOS, & JOHN McLAUGHLIN

Columbia KC-32034	(S)	Love Devotion Surrender	1973	1.00	5.00

SANTANA, CARLOS, & BUDDY MILES
Refer to Buddy Miles.

Columbia KC-31308	(S)	Live!	1972	1.00	5.00

SAPO

Bell 1301	(S)	Sapo	1974	6.00	15.00

SAPODILLA PUNCH

Philips PHS-600312	(S)	Sapodilla Punch	1969	6.00	15.00

SAPPHIRE THINKERS, THE

Hobbit HB-5003	(S)	From Within	1969	12.00	30.00

SAPPHIRES, THE

Swan LP-513	(M)	Who Do You Love	1964	200.00	400.00

SARAH

Cream 9010	(S)	Sarah Is No Lady	1972	4.00	10.00

SAROFEEN & SMOKE

GWP ST-2029	(S)	Sarofeen And Smoke	1971	6.00	15.00

SARSTEDT, CLIVE

RCA Victor LSP-4375	(S)	Clive Sarstedt	1970	4.00	10.00
RCA Victor LSP-4509	(S)	Freeway Getaway	1971	4.00	10.00

SARSTEDT, PETER

World Pacific WPS-21895	(S)	Where Do You Go To, My Lovely?	1969	4.00	10.00
World Pacific WPS-21899	(S)	As Though It Were A Movie	1969	4.00	10.00
United Arts. UAS-5558	(S)	Every Word You Say Is Written Down	1971	4.00	10.00

SARSTEDT, RICHARD

Evolution 2022	(S)	Another Day Passes By	197?	4.00	10.00

SATAN & THE DECIPLES

Goldband 7750	(S)	Underground	1969	14.00	35.00

SAUNDERS, MERL

Fantasy F-8421	(S)	Heavy Turbulence	1972	6.00	15.00
Crystal Clear	(S)	Do I Move You? *(Direct-to-disc)*	198?	6.00	15.00

SAUNDERS, MERL, & JERRY GARCIA

Fantasy F-79002	(S)	Live At The Keystone	1973	6.00	15.00

SAUNDERS, MERL, & JERRY GARCIA & TOM FOGERTY

Fantasy F-9421	(S)	Fire Up	1973	6.00	15.00

SAVAGE GRACE

Reprise RS-6399	(S)	Savage Grace	1970	4.00	10.00
Reprise RS-6484	(S)	Savage Grace 2	1971	4.00	10.00

SAVAGE RESURRECTION

Mercury MG-21156	(M)	Savage Resurrection *(White label promo)*	1968	40.00	100.00
Mercury SR-61156	(S)	Savage Resurrection	1968	40.00	100.00

SAVAGE ROSE

Polydor ~	(S)	In The Plain *(Gatefold cover)*	1969	8.00	20.00
P⌐¹	(S)	In The Plain *(Standard cover)*	1970	5.00	12.00
	(S)	Your Daily Gift	1970	5.00	12.00
	(S)	Refugee	1971	5.00	12.00

all of the Cameo/Parkway artists at one time or another.

	(M)	The Most Heard Sax In The World	1962	20.00	50.00
	(S)	The Most Heard Sax In The World	1962	40.00	100.00

Label & Catalog #		Title	Year	VG+	NM
SAVOY BROWN					
Parrot PAS-71024	(S)	Getting To The Point	1968	6.00	15.00
Parrot PAS-71027	(S)	Blue Matter	1969	6.00	15.00
Parrot PAS-71029	(S)	A Step Further	1969	6.00	15.00
Parrot PAS-71036	(S)	Raw Sienna	1970	6.00	15.00
Parrot PAS-71042	(S)	Looking In	1970	6.00	15.00
Parrot PAS-71047	(S)	Street Corner Talking	1971	6.00	15.00
—Parrot albums above have black labels with "Distributed by London."—					
Parrot PAS-71024	(S)	Getting To The Point	1972	3.20	8.00
Parrot PAS-71027	(S)	Blue Matter	1972	3.20	8.00
Parrot PAS-71029	(S)	A Step Further	1972	3.20	8.00
Parrot PAS-71036	(S)	Raw Sienna	1972	3.20	8.00
Parrot PAS-71042	(S)	Looking In	1972	3.20	8.00
Parrot PAS-71047	(S)	Street Corner Talking	1972	3.20	8.00
Parrot PAS-71052	(S)	Hellbound Train	1972	3.20	8.00
Parrot PAS-71057	(S)	Lion's Share	1972	3.20	8.00
Parrot PAS-71059	(S)	Jack The Toad	1973	3.20	8.00
—Parrot albums above have black labels with "A Product of London Records."—					
London PS-638	(S)	Boogie Brothers	1974	1.00	5.00
London PS-659	(S)	Wire Fire	1975	1.00	5.00
London PS-670	(S)	Skin 'N' Bone	1976	1.00	5.00
London PS-718	(S)	Savage Return	1977	1.00	5.00
London LC-5000	(S)	London Collector	1977	1.00	5.00
Townhouse ST-7002	(S)	Rock & Roll Warriors	1981	1.00	5.00
SAWBUCK					
Fillmore 2-31248	(S)	Sawbuck	1972	8.00	20.00
SAYER, LEO					
Warner Bros. BS-2738	(S)	Silverbird	1973	1.00	5.00
Warner Bros. BS-2836	(S)	Just A Boy	1975	1.00	5.00
Warner Bros. BS-2885	(S)	Another Year	1975	1.00	5.00
Warner Bros. BS-2962	(S)	Endless Flight	1976	1.00	5.00
Warner Bros. BS-3089	(S)	Thunder In My Heart	1977	1.00	5.00
Warner Bros. BS-3200	(S)	Leo Sayer	1978	1.00	5.00
Warner Bros. BS-3374	(S)	Here	1979	1.00	5.00
Warner Bros. BS-3483	(S)	Living In A Fantasy	1980	1.00	5.00
SCAFFOLD					
Scaffold features Mike McGear.					
Bell 6018	(M)	Thank U Very Much *(White label promo)*	1968	20.00	50.00
Bell 6018	(S)	Thank U Very Much	1968	20.00	50.00
SCAGGS, BOZ					
Boz was a member of The Steve Miller Band.					
Atlantic SD-8239	(S)	Boz Scaggs	1969	3.20	8.00
Atlantic SD-19166	(S)	Boz Scaggs	1978	.80	4.00
Columbia KC-30454	(S)	Moments	1971	1.00	5.00
Columbia PC-30454	(S)	Moments	1978	.80	4.00
Columbia KC-30976	(S)	Boz Scaggs & Band	1971	1.00	5.00
Columbia PC-30976	(S)	Boz Scaggs & Band	1978	.80	4.00
Columbia KC-31384	(S)	My Time	1972	1.00	5.00
Columbia PC-31384	(S)	My Time	1978	.80	4.00
Columbia KC-32760	(S)	Slow Dancer *(Boz Scaggs cover)*	1974	1.00	5.00
Columbia KC-32760	(S)	Slow Dancer *(Male dancer cover)*	1974	.80	4.00
Columbia A2S-71-4	(DJ)	KSAN Live Concert *(2 LPs)*	1974	20.00	50.00
		(Issued in a plain cardboard jacket.)			
Columbia AS-203	(DJ)	The Boz Scaggs Sampler	1974	6.00	15.00
Columbia JC-33920	(S)	Silk Degrees	1976	.80	4.00
Columbia HC-43920	(S)	Silk Degrees *(Half-speed master)*	1981	10.00	30.00
Columbia JC-37429	(S)	Down Two, Then Left	1977	.80	4.00
Columbia FC-36106	(S)	Middle Man	1980	.80	4.00
Columbia FC-36841	(S)	Hits	1980	.80	4.00
SCAMPS, THE					
Project 8002	(M)	Teen Dance And Sing Along Party	1962	16.00	40.00
SCHOOLBOYS, THE: Refer to THE LIVERPOOL KIDS					
SCHULZE, KLAUS					
Klaus Schulze is a member of Tangerine Dream.					
Island ILPS-9510	(S)	Body Love	1971	4.00	10.00
SCORPION					
Tower ST-5171	(S)	Scorpion	1969	20.00	50.00
SCOTT, ALLAN					
Tower ST-5164	(S)	When I Needed A Woman	1969	6.00	15.00

Label & Catalog #		Title	Year	VG+	NM
SCOTT, FREDDIE					
Colpix CP-461	(M)	Freddie Scott Sings	1964	30.00	75.00
Colpix SCP-461	(S)	Freddie Scott Sings	1964	60.00	150.00
		—Colpix albums above have gold labels.—			
Colpix CP-461	(M)	Freddie Scott Sings	1965	16.00	40.00
Colpix SCP-461	(E)	Freddie Scott Sings	1965	12.00	30.00
		—Colpix albums above have blue labels.—			
Columbia CL-2258	(M)	Everything I Have Is Yours	1964	8.00	20.00
Columbia CS-9058	(S)	Everything I Have Is Yours	1964	10.00	25.00
Columbia CL-2660	(M)	Lonely Man	1967	8.00	20.00
Columbia CS-9460	(S)	Lonely Man	1967	10.00	25.00
		—Columbia albums above have "360 Sound" labels.—			
Shout SLP-501	(M)	Are You Lonely For Me	1967	8.00	20.00
Shout SLPS-501	(S)	Are You Lonely For Me	1967	10.00	25.00
Probe CPLP-4517	(S)	I Shall Be Released	1970	10.00	25.00
SCOTT, JACK					
Carlton LP-12-107	(M)	Jack Scott	1959	80.00	200.00
Carlton STLP-12-107	(S)	Jack Scott	1959	200.00	400.00
		(The cover has "Stereo" in felt-like letters pasted vertically along the left side. "My True Love" and "Leroy" are rechanneled on this and each subsequent pressing below.)			
Carlton STLP-12-107	(S)	Jack Scott	1959	150.00	300.00
		(The cover has "Stereo" in felt-like letters across the top.)			
Carlton STLP-12-107	(S)	Jack Scott	1959	100.00	200.00
		(The cover has "Stereo" printed across the top.)			
Carlton LP-12-122	(M)	What Am I Living For	1959	60.00	150.00
Carlton STLP-12-122	(S)	What Am I Living For	1959	150.00	300.00
		("What Am I Living For" is rechanneled on this album.)			
Top Rank RM-319	(M)	I Remember Hank Williams	1960	60.00	150.00
Top Rank RS-619	(S)	I Remember Hank Williams	1960	100.00	250.00
Top Rank RM-326	(M)	What In The World's Come Over You? (White label promo)	1960	150.00	300.00
Top Rank RM-326	(M)	What In The World's Come Over You? (Red label promo)	1960	150.00	300.00
Top Rank RM-326	(M)	What In The World's Come Over You?	1960	60.00	150.00
Top Rank RS-626	(S)	What In The World's Come Over You?	1960	100.00	250.00
Top Rank RM-348	(M)	The Spirit Moves Me	1961	60.00	150.00
Top Rank RS-648	(S)	The Spirit Moves Me	1961	100.00	250.00
Sesac 4201	(M)	Soul Stirring	196?	300.00	600.00
Groove G-1001	(M)	Jack Scott	1964	Unreleased	
Groove GS-1001	(S)	Jack Scott	1964	Unreleased	
Capitol T-2035	(M)	Burning Bridges	1964	40.00	100.00
Capitol ST-2035	(S)	Burning Bridges	1964	80.00	200.00
		—Capitol albums above have black rainbow labels.—			
Capitol ST-2035	(S)	Burning Bridges	1969	20.00	50.00
		—Capitol albums above have green labels.—			
Capitol N-66121	(M)	Burning Bridges	197?	4.00	10.00
		(N-66121 has a stereo cover but plays mono.)			
Ponie 563N1	(S)	Jack Scott	1974	6.00	15.00
Ponie 7055N5	(S)	Jack Scott	1977	6.00	15.00
Jade J33-113	(SO	Jack Is Back	198?	6.00	15.00
Jade J33-114	(S)	The Way I Rock	198?	6.00	15.00
Rock'n Roll 75-001	(M)	Jack Scott Rocks	198?	6.00	15.00
		("What In The World's Come Over You," "Cool Water," Laugh And The World Laughs With You," "Oh, Little One," and "Step 1 And 2," are in stereo.)			
Avant PA-1001	(M)	If Only	198?	6.00	15.00
Rocket '88' RLP-5103	(M)	Great Scott!! It's Jack (2 LPs)	198?	6.00	15.00
SCOTT, LINDA					
Canad. Am. CALP-1005	(M)	Starlight, Starbright	1961	40.00	100.00
Canad. Am. SCALP-1005	(S)	Starlight, Starbright	1961	60.00	150.00
Canad. Am. CALP-1007	(M)	Great Scott!! Her Greatest Hits	1962	40.00	100.00
Canad. Am. SCALP-1007	(S)	Great Scott!! Her Greatest Hits	1962	60.00	150.00
Congress 3001	(M)	Linda	1962	14.00	35.00
Congress S-3001	(S)	Linda	1962	20.00	50.00
Kapp KL-1424	(M)	Hey, Look At Me Now	1965	14.00	35.00
Kapp KS-3424	(S)	Hey, Look At Me Now	1965	20.00	50.00
SCOTT, PEGGY, & JO JO BENSON					
SSS International 1	(S)	Soulshake	1969	10.00	25.00
SSS International 2	(S)	Lover's Heaven	1969	10.00	25.00
SCRAMBLERS, THE					
Diplomat D-2316	(M)	Motorcycle Scramble	1964	6.00	15.00
Diplomat DS-2316	(S)	Motorcycle Scramble	1964	8.00	20.00
Wyncote W-9048	(M)	Little Honda	1964	6.00	15.00
Wyncote WS-9048	(S)	Little Honda	1964	8.00	20.00

Freddie Scott, a contracted songwriter for Columbia in the early '60s, hit the big time in 1963 with his Top 10 hit, "Hey Girl." While he was never able to duplicate the commercial success of this first hit, he did wax a number of excellent sides for both Colpix and Shout in the '60s. His lone LP, Freddie Scott Sings And Sings And Sings, was initially issued by Colpix in mono and stereo with a gold label. Within months of its release, the album was in its second pressing, this time with the company's blue label, except that the stereo masters had slipped through a black hole and the later pressings are in rechanneled stereo!

Label & Catalog #		Title	Year	VG+	NM
Crown CLP-5384	(M)	Cycle Psychos	1964	6.00	15.00
Crown CST-384	(S)	Cycle Psychos	1964	8.00	20.00
		—Crown albums above have gray labels.—			
SEA DOG					
Buddah BDS-5104	(S)	Sea Dog	1972	4.00	10.00
SEALS & CROFTS					
T.A. 5001	(S)	Seals And Crofts	1969	4.00	10.00
T.A. 5004	(S)	Down Home	1970	4.00	10.00
Warner Bros. BS-2568	(S)	Year Of Sunday	1971	.80	4.00
Warner Bros. BS-2629	(S)	Summer Breeze	1972	.80	4.00
Warner Bros. BS4-2629	(Q)	Summer Breeze	1974	4.00	10.00
Warner Bros. BS-2699	(S)	Diamond Girl	1973	.80	4.00
Warner Bros. BS4-2699	(Q)	Diamond Girl	1973	4.00	10.00
Warner Bros. WS-2761	(S)	Unborn Child	1974	.80	4.00
Warner Bros. WS4-2761	(Q)	Unborn Child	1974	4.00	10.00
Warner Bros. 2WS-2809	(S)	Seals & Crofts 1 & 2 (2 LPs)	1974	1.00	5.00
		(W.B. 2809 reissues the two T.A. albums.)			
Warner Bros. BS-2848	(S)	I'll Play For You	1975	.80	4.00
Warner Bros. BS4-2848	(Q)	I'll Play For You	1975	4.00	10.00
Warner Bros. BS-2886	(S)	Greatest Hits	1975	.80	4.00
Warner Bros. BS-2907	(S)	Get Closer	1976	.80	4.00
Warner Bros. BS-2976	(S)	Sudan Village	1876	.80	4.00
Warner Bros. BSK-3109	(S)	Greatest Hits	1977	.80	4.00
Warner Bros. BSK-3163	(S)	Takin' It Easy	1978	.80	4.00
Warner Bros. BSK-3365	(S)	The Longest Road	1980	.80	4.00
SEARCHERS, THE					
Mercury MG-20914	(M)	Heart Heart	1964	20.00	50.00
Mercury SR-60914	(E)	Heart Heart	1964	16.00	40.00
		(Original covers make no mention of the Star Club on the front.)			
Mercury MG-20914	(M)	Heart Heart	1964	16.00	40.00
Mercury SR-60914	(E)	Heart Heart	1964	12.00	30.00
		(The cover has a sticker reading "Live From The Star Club.")			
Mercury MG-20914	(M)	Heart Heart	1964	12.00	30.00
Mercury SR-60914	(E)	Heart Heart	1964	10.00	25.00
		(Later covers have "Live From The Star Club" printed on the front.)			
Kapp KL-1363	(M)	Meet The Searchers	1964	16.00	40.00
Kapp KS-3363	(S)	Meet The Searchers	1964	20.00	50.00
		—Kapp albums above have black & blue labels.—			
Kapp KL-1363	(M)	Meet The Searchers	1964	10.00	25.00
Kapp KS-3363	(S)	Meet The Searchers	1964	12.00	30.00
Kapp KL-1409	(M)	This Is Us	1964	10.00	25.00
Kapp KS-3409	(S)	This Is Us	1964	12.00	30.00
Kapp KL-1412	(M)	The New Searchers LP	1965	12.00	30.00
Kapp KS-3412	(S)	The New Searchers LP	1965	16.00	40.00
		(Original covers list "Bumble Bee" on top. "What Have They Done To The Rain" is rechanneled.)			
Kapp KL-1412	(M)	The New Searchers LP	1965	8.00	20.00
Kapp KS-3412	(S)	The New Searchers LP	1965	10.00	25.00
Kapp KL-1449	(M)	The Searchers No. 4	1965	10.00	25.00
Kapp KS-3449	(S)	The Searchers No. 4	1965	12.00	30.00
Kapp KL-1477	(M)	Take Me For What I'm Worth	1966	10.00	25.00
Kapp KS-3477	(S)	Take Me For What I'm Worth	1966	12.00	30.00
Sire SRK-6082	(S)	The Searchers	1980	.80	4.00
Sire SRK-3523	(S)	Love's Melodies	1981	.80	4.00
Rhino RNLP-162	(S)	The Searchers' Greatest Hits	1984	.80	4.00
SEARCHERS, THE / THE RATTLES					
Mercury MG-20994	(M)	The Searchers Meet The Rattles	1965	30.00	75.00
Mercury SR-60994	(E)	The Searchers Meet The Rattles	1965	20.00	50.00
SEASTONES					
Seastones features Jerry Garcia, Mickey Hart and Phil Lesh of The Grateful Dead.					
Round RX-106	(S)	Seastones	1975	10.00	25.00
SEATRAIN					
Seatrain was formed by Roy Blumenfeld and Andy Kulberg of The Blues Project.					
A&M SP-4171	(S)	Seatrain	1969	6.00	15.00
Capitol SMAS-650	(S)	Seatrain	1971	6.00	15.00
Capitol SMAS-829	(S)	Marblehead Messenger	1972	6.00	15.00
		—Capitol albums above have green labels.—			
Warner Bros. BS-2692	(S)	Watch	1973	4.00	10.00
Capitol SN-16102	(S)	Seatrain	1980	.80	4.00
Capitol SN-16103	(S)	Marblehead Messenger	1980	.80	4.00

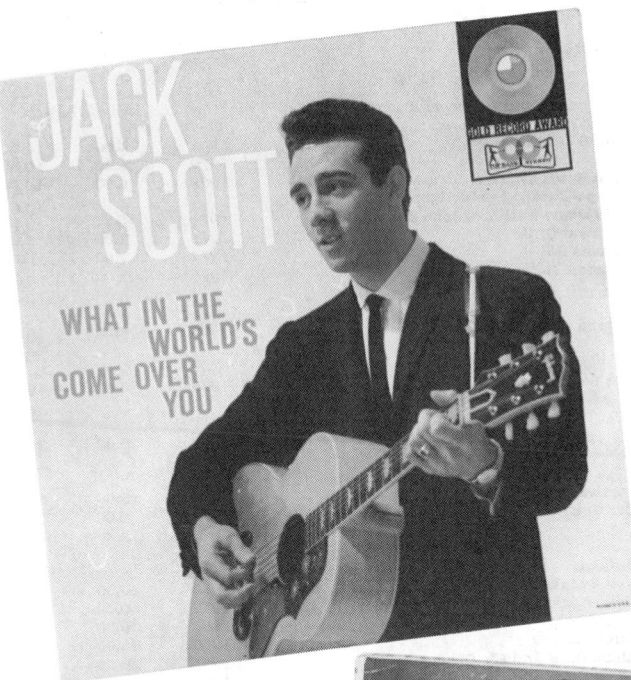

Singer and writer Jack Scalone Jr, known professionally as Jack Scott, placed nine sides on the Top 100 with Carlton, although neither of his albums, including his self-titled debut, fared well. Moving to Top Rank, he had seven more charters and three more long-players, including What In The World's Come Over You. He had three very minor hits with Capitol before fading from Top 40 popularity. None of his LPs fared well on the charts and each is a sought-after collectible today.

SEBASTIAN

MCA 7001	(S)	Rays Of Love	1970	4.00	10.00

SEBASTIAN, JOHN

*Mr. Sebastian is a folk-based guitar and harmonica player, singer and writer who was the heart and soul of The Lovin'
Spoonful. Refer to The Even Dozen Jug Band; Jesse Colin Young.*

MGM SE-4654	(S)	John B. Sebastian	1969	4.00	10.00
MGM SE-4720	(S)	John B. Sebastian Live	1970	4.00	10.00
Reprise RS-6379	(S)	John B. Sebastian (With insert)	1969	4.00	10.00
Reprise MS-2036	(S)	Cheapo-Cheapo Productions Presents Real Live John Sebastian	1971	3.20	8.00
Reprise MS-2041	(S)	The Four Of Us	1971	1.00	5.00
Reprise MS-2187	(S)	Tarzana Kid	1974	1.00	5.00
Reprise MS-2249	(S)	Welcome Back	1976	1.00	5.00

SECOND CITY

Mercury SR-61224	(S)	Second City Writhes Again	1969	4.00	10.00

SECOND COMING, THE

Mercury SR-61299	(S)	The Second Coming	1970	4.00	10.00

SECOND TIME, THE

Tower ST-5146	(S)	Listen To The Music	1968	8.00	20.00

SECRET OYSTER

Peters International 9003	(S)	Furtive Pearl	1973	12.00	30.00
Peters International 9009	(S)	Sea Son	1974	8.00	20.00

SEDAKA, NEIL

Refer to Paul Anka / Sam Cooke / Neil Sedaka.

RCA Victor LPM-2035	(M)	Neil Sedaka	1959	30.00	75.00
RCA Victor LSP-2035	(S)	Neil Sedaka	1959	40.00	100.00
RCA Victor LPM-2317	(M)	Circulate	1960	20.00	50.00
RCA Victor LSP-2317	(S)	Circulate	1960	30.00	75.00
RCA Victor LPM-2421	(M)	Little Devil And His Other Hits	1961	20.00	50.00
RCA Victor LSP-2421	(S)	Little Devil And His Other Hits	1961	30.00	75.00
RCA Victor LPM-2627	(M)	Neil Sedaka Sings His Greatest Hits	1962	14.00	35.00
RCA Victor LSP-2627	(S)	Neil Sedaka Sings His Greatest Hits	1962	20.00	50.00
		—RCA mono albums above have black "Long Play" or "Living Stereo" labels.—			
Camden ACL1-7006	(S)	Breaking Up Is Hard To Do	197?	.80	4.00
Kirshner KES-111	(S)	Emergence	1971	4.00	10.00
Kirshner KES-117	(S)	Solitaire (With backing by 10CC)	1972	4.00	10.00
Rocket 463	(S)	Sedaka's Back	1974	1.00	5.00
		(Rocket 463 is a compilation taken from Sedaka's previous UK LPs.)			
Rocket PIG-2157	(S)	The Hungry Years	1975	1.00	5.00
Rocket PIG-2195	(S)	Steppin' Out	1976	1.00	5.00
Rocket PIG-2297	(S)	Greatest Hits	1977	1.00	5.00
RCA Victor DPL2-0149	(S)	Original Hits (2 LPs)	1975	1.00	5.00
RCA Victor ANL1-0879	(S)	Oh Carol	1975	.80	4.00
RCA Victor ANL1-0928	(S)	Neil Sedaka Sings His Greatest Hits	1975	.80	4.00
RCA Victor ANL1-1314	(S)	Pure Gold	1976	.80	4.00
RCA Victor VPL1-1540	(S)	Live In Australia	1976	.80	4.00
RCA Victor APL1-1789	(S)	Emergence	1976	.80	4.00
RCA Victor APL1-1790	(S)	Solitaire	1976	.80	4.00
		(RCA 1789 and 1790 are reissues of Kirshner 111 and 117.)			
RCA Victor APL1-2254	(S)	Sedaka—The '50s & '60s	1977	.80	4.00
RCA Victor AFL1-2524	(S)	The Many Sides Of Neil Sedaka	1978	.80	4.00
RCA Victor ANL1-3465	(S)	Neil Sedaka Sings His Greatest Hits	1979	.80	4.00
Elektra 6E-102	(S)	A Song	1977	.80	4.00
Elektra 6E-161	(S)	All You Need Is Music	1978	.80	4.00
Elektra 6E-259	(S)	In The Pocket	1980	.80	4.00
Elektra 6E-348	(S)	Neil Sedaka	1981	.80	4.00
Accord SN-7152	(S)	Singer, Songwriter, Melody Maker	1981	.80	4.00

SEDAKA, NEIL, & THE TOKENS / THE COINS

Crown CLP-5366	(M)	Neil Sedaka & The Tokens & The Coins	1963	12.00	30.00
Crown CST-366	(E)	Neil Sedaka & The Tokens & The Coins	1963	8.00	20.00
		—Crown albums above have gray labels.—			
Vernon 518	(M)	Neil Sedaka With The Tokens	1963	8.00	20.00
Vernon 518	(E)	Neil Sedaka With The Tokens	1963	4.00	10.00

SEEDS, THE

The Seeds feature Sky Saxon. They can also be found on the Sidewalk soundtrack "Psych-Out."

Crescendo GNP-2023	(M)	The Seeds	1966	14.00	35.00
Crescendo GNPS-2023	(S)	The Seeds ("Pushin' Too Hard" is rechanneled)	1966	10.00	25.00
Crescendo GNP-2033	(M)	A Web Of Sound	1966	14.00	35.00
Crescendo GNPS-2033	(S)	A Web Of Sound	1966	10.00	25.00
Crescendo ST-91224	(S)	A Web Of Sound (Capitol Record Club)	1969	10.00	25.00

Label & Catalog #		Title	Year	VG+	NM
Crescendo GNP-2038	(M)	Future (With three inserts)	1967	16.00	40.00
Crescendo GNPS-2038	(S)	Future (With three inserts)	1967	14.00	35.00
Crescendo GNP-2038	(M)	Future (Without inserts)	1967	12.00	35.00
Crescendo GNPS-2038	(S)	Future (Without inserts)	1967	10.00	25.00
Crescendo GNP-2040	(M)	Full Spoon of Seedy Blues	1967	14.00	35.00
Crescendo GNPS-2040	(S)	Full Spoon of Seedy Blues	1967	10.00	25.00
Crescendo GNP-2043	(M)	Raw And Alive	1967	14.00	35.00
Crescendo GNPS-2043	(S)	Raw And Alive	1967	10.00	25.00
		—GNP albums above have red labels.—			

SEEKERS, THE
The Australian Seekers—Judy Durham, Athol Guy, Keith Potger and Bruce Woodley—are a folk-based vocal and instrumental pop group. After the breakup of the group, Potger formed The New Seekers.

Label & Catalog #		Title	Year	VG+	NM
Marvel 2060	(M)	The Seekers	1965	4.00	10.00
Marvel 3060	(E)	The Seekers	1965	4.00	10.00
		(Marvel 2060 contains earlier Australian recordings.)			
Capitol T-2319	(M)	The New Seekers	1965	5.00	12.00
Capitol ST-2319	(S)	The New Seekers	1965	6.00	15.00
Capitol T-2369	(M)	A World Of Our Own	1965	5.00	12.00
Capitol DT-2369	(E)	A World Of Our Own	1965	4.00	10.00
Capitol T-2431	(M)	Georgy Girl	1966	5.00	12.00
Capitol ST-2431	(S)	Georgy Girl	1966	6.00	15.00
		—Capitol albums above have black rainbow labels.—			
Capitol T-2746	(M)	The Best Of The Seekers	1967	4.00	10.00
Capitol ST-2746	(E)	The Best Of The Seekers	1967	5.00	12.00
		("Morningtown Ride," "Turn Turn Turn," and "We're Moving On" are in stereo on this and all subsequent pressings.)			
		—Capitol albums above have red & white Starline "bullseye" labels.—			
Capitol ST-2746	(E)	The Best Of The Seekers	1969	3.20	8.00
		—Capitol albums above have red & white Starline "star" labels.—			
Capitol SKAO-2821	(S)	Seekers Seen In Green	1968	6.00	15.00
Capitol ST-135	(S)	The Seekers Live	1969	4.00	10.00
		—Capitol albums above have black rainbow labels.—			
Capitol SM-2746	(E)	The Best Of The Seekers	197?	.80	4.00

SEEMON & MARIJKE
Label & Catalog #		Title	Year	VG+	NM
A&M SP-4309	(S)	Son Of America	1971	4.00	10.00

SEGALL, RICKY, & THE SEGALLS
Label & Catalog #		Title	Year	VG+	NM
Bell 1138	(S)	Ricky Segall & The Segalls	1973	6.00	15.00

SEGER, BOB
Albums below credit The Bob Seger System, which included drummer Pep Perrine (Capitol 172 through 731), Bob Seger, or Bob Seger & The Silver Bullet Band (1976 on).

Label & Catalog #		Title	Year	VG+	NM
Capitol ST-172	(S)	Ramblin' Gamblin' Man	1969	12.00	30.00
		—Capitol albums above have black rainbow labels.—			
Capitol ST-236	(S)	Noah	1969	12.00	30.00
Capitol SKAO-499	(S)	Mongrel (Gatefold cover)	1970	10.00	25.00
Capitol ST-731	(S)	Brand New Morning	1971	12.00	30.00
		—Capitol albums above have green labels.—			
Capitol SM-172	(S)	Ramblin' Gamblin' Man	1975	.80	4.00
Capitol SM-499	(S)	Mongrel	1975	.80	4.00
Palladium P-1006	(S)	Smokin' O.P.'s	1972	10.00	25.00
Reprise MS-2109	(S)	Smokin' O.P.'s	1972	6.00	15.00
Reprise MS-2126	(S)	Back In '72	1973	10.00	25.00
Reprise MS-2184	(S)	Seven/Contrasts	1974	6.00	15.00
Capitol ST-11378	(S)	Beautiful Loser	1975	1.00	5.00
Capitol SPRO-8433	(DJ)	"Live" Bullet (2 LPs)	1976	10.00	25.00
Capitol SKBB-11523	(S)	"Live" Bullet (2 LPs)	1976	1.20	6.00
Capitol ST-11557	(S)	Night Moves	1976	1.00	5.00
Capitol ST-11557	(S)	Night Moves (Picture disc)	1978	10.00	25.00
Capitol SW-11557	(S)	Night Moves	1980	.80	4.00
Capitol SW-11698	(S)	Stranger In Town	1978	1.00	5.00
Capitol ST-11746	(S)	Smokin' O.P.'s	1979	.80	4.00
Capitol ST-11748	(S)	Seven/Contrasts	1979	.80	4.00
Capitol SEAX-11904	(S)	Stranger In Town (Picture disc)	1979	10.00	25.00
Capitol SOO-12041	(S)	Against The Wind	1980	1.00	5.00
Capitol STBK-12182	(S)	Nine Tonight (2 LPs)	1981	1.20	6.00
Capitol STBK-12254	(S)	The Distance	1983	1.00	5.00
Capitol SN-16105	(S)	Ramblin' Gamblin' Man	1980	.80	4.00
Capitol SN-16106	(S)	Mongrel	1980	.80	4.00
Capitol SN-16107	(S)	Smokin' O.P.'s	1980	.80	4.00
Capitol SN-16108	(S)	Seven	1980	.80	4.00

SELLERS, BROTHER JOHN
Label & Catalog #		Title	Year	VG+	NM
Vanguard VRS-7022	(10")	Jack Of Diamonds (With Sonny Terry)	195?	40.00	100.00
Vanguard VRS-8005	(10")	Brother John Sellers	1954	40.00	100.00
Vanguard VRS-9036	(M)	Blues And Folk Songs	195?	40.00	100.00

Label & Catalog #		Title	Year	VG+	NM
SELLERS, BROTHER JOHN, & MICKEY BAKER					
Monitor MP-505	(M)	Big Beat Up The River	196?	60.00	150.00
Monitor MPS-6002	(M)	Big Beat Up The River	196?	80.00	200.00
SENOR SOUL					
Double Shot 5004	(S)	Funky Favorites	1968	6.00	15.00
Double Shot 5005	(S)	It's Your Thing	1969	6.00	15.00
SENSATIONS, THE					
The Sensations feature Yvonne Baker.					
Argo LP-4022	(M)	Let Me In/Music, Music, Music	1963	200.00	400.00
SENTINALS, THE					
Del-Fi DFLP-1232	(M)	Big Surf	1963	20.00	50.00
Del-Fi DFST-1232	(S)	Big Surf	1963	30.00	75.00
Del-Fi DFLP-1241	(M)	Surfer Girl	1963	20.00	50.00
Del-Fi DFST-1241	(S)	Surfer Girl	1963	30.00	75.00
Sutton SU-338	(M)	Vegas Go-Go	1964	14.00	35.00
Sutton SSU-338	(S)	Vegas Go-Go	1964	20.00	50.00
SERFS, THE					
Capitol SKAO-207	(S)	Earlybird Cafe	1969	6.00	15.00
SERPENT POWER					
Serpent Power features David and Tina Meltzer.					
Vanguard VRS-9252	(M)	Serpent Power	1967	12.00	30.00
Vanguard VSD-79252	(S)	Serpent Power	1967	16.00	40.00
SEVEN					
Thunderbird THS-9006	(S)	The Song is Song, The Album Is Album	197?	4.00	10.00
SEVENTH SONS, THE					
The Seventh Sons feature Buzzy Linhart.					
ESP-Disk' 1078	(S)	The Seventh Sons	1967	12.00	30.00
SEVENTH WAVE, THE					
Janus 7008	(S)	Things To Come	1974	8.00	20.00
Janus 7021	(S)	Psi Fi	1975	8.00	20.00
SEWARD, ALEC					
Bluesville BVLP-1076	(M)	Creepin' Blues	1963	30.00	75.00
—Bluesville albums above have bright blue labels with silver print.—					
Bluesville BVLP-1076	(M)	Creepin' Blues	1965	10.00	25.00
—Bluesville albums above have blue labels with a trident logo on the right side.—					
SEX PISTOLS, THE					
Warner Bros. BSK-3147	(S)	Never Mind The Bollocks, Here Come The Sex Pistols	1977	8.00	20.00
		(Original pressings of WB 3147 have custom label and inner sleeve. A sticker was affixed to the front cover and one that reads "Contains 'Sub Mission'" was affixed to the back cover.)			
Warner Bros. BSK-3147	(S)	Never Mind The Bollocks, Here Come The Sex Pistols	1977	12.00	30.00
		(Some stock copies were stamped "Not For Sale" and had a third sticker affixed to the cover that reads "This album may contain material unsuitable for airplay.")			
Warner Bros. BSK-3147	(S)	Never Mind The Bollocks, Here Come The Sex Pistols	1978	1.00	5.00
SHA NA NA					
Kama Sutra KLPS-2010	(S)	Rock & Roll Is Here To Stay!	1969	3.20	8.00
Kama Sutra KLPS-2034	(S)	Sha Na Na	1971	1.00	5.00
Kama Sutra KLPS-2050	(S)	The Night Is Still Young	1972	1.00	5.00
Kama Sutra KLPS-2073	(S)	The Golden Age Of Rock 'N' Roll (2 LPs)	1973	1.20	6.00
Kama Sutra KLPS-2075	(S)	From The Streets Of New York	1973	1.00	5.00
Kama Sutra KLPS-2077	(S)	Rock & Roll Is Here To Stay!	1973	1.00	5.00
Kama Sutra KSBS-2603	(S)	Hot Sox	1974	1.00	5.00
Kama Sutra KSBS-2605	(S)	Sha Na Now	1975	1.00	5.00
Kama Sutra KSBS-2609	(S)	The Best Of Sha Na Na	1976	1.00	5.00
Buddah BDS-5692	(S)	Rock & Roll Is Here To Stay!	1977	.80	4.00
Buddah BDS-5703	(S)	The Best Of Sha Na Na	1977	.80	4.00
Emus ES-12037	(S)	On Stage	1978	1.00	5.00
Nashville NR-12348-122	(S)	Rockin' In The '80s (2 LPs)	1980	1.00	5.00
K-Tel NV-9810	(S)	Silly Songs	1981	.80	4.00
Accord SN-7115	(S)	Remember Then	1981	.80	4.00
Accord SN-7146	(S)	Sh-Boom	1981	.80	4.00
Accord SN-7230	(S)	Just Hangin' Out	1983	.80	4.00

Label & Catalog #		Title	Year	VG+	NM

SHADES OF BLUE, THE

Label & Catalog #		Title	Year	VG+	NM
Impact IM-101	(M)	Happiness Is The Shades Of Blue	1966	12.00	30.00
Impact IM-1001	(S)	Happiness Is The Shades Of Blue	1966	16.00	40.00

SHADES OF JOY

Fontana SRF-67592	(S)	Shades Of Joy	1969	8.00	20.00

SHADOW MANN

Tomorrow's TPS-69001	(S)	Come Live With Me	1972	20.00	50.00

SHADOWS, THE

The original Shadows developed as Cliff Richard's backing group, first known as The Drifters. After changing their name in 1959, they enjoyed dual success on their own and as Richard's band. At the time of the name change, members were Hank Marvin, Bruce Welch, Jet Harris and Tony Meehan. Meehan left in 1961, replaced by Brian Bennett. Harris departed in '62, with Brian Locking joining, only to leave himself in 1963. He was replaced by John Rostill. The group disbanded after celebrating their tenth anniversary with Richard. Refer to Marvin, Welch & Farrar.

Atlantic 8089	(M)	Surfing With The Shadows	1963	60.00	150.00
Atlantic SD-8089	(S)	Surfing With The Shadows	1963	150.00	300.00
Atlantic 8097	(M)	The Shadows Know	1964	40.00	100.00
Atlantic SD-8097	(S)	The Shadows Know	1964	80.00	200.00

SHADOWS OF KNIGHT, THE

The original SOK were one of the pre-eminent punk bands of the '60s. But by the end of the decade they were the house band for the Buddah bubble gum groups. Refer to The Kasenetz-Katz Circus.

Dunwich 666	(M)	Gloria	1966	20.00	50.00
Dunwich S-666	(S)	Gloria	1966	30.00	75.00
Dunwich 667	(M)	Back Door Men	1966	20.00	50.00
Dunwich S-667	(S)	Back Door Men	1966	30.00	75.00
Super-K SKS-6002	(S)	The Shadows Of Knight	1969	20.00	50.00
Sundazed LP-5006	(M)	Raw And Live At The Cellar 1966	1992	4.00	10.00

SHAKERS, THE

Audio Fidelity AFLP-2155	(M)	The Shakers Break It All	1966	16.00	40.00
Audio Fidelity AFSD-6155	(S)	The Shakers Break It All	1966	24.00	60.00
		—Audio Fidelity albums above have silver labels.—			
Audio Fidelity AFSD-6155	(S)	The Shakers Break It All	197?	10.00	25.00
		—Audio Fidelity albums above have brown labels.—			

SHAKEY JAKE

Bluesville BVLP-1008	(M)	Good Times	1960	30.00	75.00
Bluesville BVLP-1027	(M)	Mouth Harp Blues	1961	30.00	75.00
		—Bluesville albums above have bright blue labels with silver print.—			
Bluesville BVLP-1008	(M)	Good Times	1964	10.00	25.00
Bluesville BVLP-1027	(M)	Mouth Harp Blues	1964	10.00	25.00
		—Bluesville albums above have blue labels with a trident logo on the right side.—			
World Pacific WPS-21886	(S)	Blues Makers	196?	6.00	15.00

SHAKEY LEGS

Paramount PAS-6022	(S)	Shakey Legs	1971	4.00	10.00

SHAKEY VICK

Janus JLS-3000	(S)	Little Woman, You're So Sweet	1970	8.00	20.00

SHALAMAR

Soul Train 2289	(S)	Uptown Festival	1977	1.00	5.00
Solar 2895	(S)	Disco Gardens	1978	1.00	5.00
Solar 3479	(S)	Big Fun	1979	1.00	5.00
Solar 3577	(S)	Three For Love	1981	1.00	5.00
Solar 3984	(S)	Friends	1982	1.00	5.00
Solar 60239	(S)	The Look	1983	1.00	5.00
Solar 60385	(S)	1984			

SHAM 69

Sire 6060	(S)	Tell Us The Truth	1978	4.00	10.00

SHANGO

A&M SP-4195	(S)	Shango	1969	6.00	15.00
Dunhill SD-50082	(S)	Trampin'	1970	6.00	15.00

SHANGRI-LAS, THE

The definitive white "girl group" were of two sets of sisters, Mary and Betty Weiss and Mary Ann and Margie Ganser.

Red Bird 20-101	(M)	Leader Of The Pack	1965	80.00	200.00
Red Bird 20-104	(M)	The Shangri-Las '65	1965	80.00	200.00
Red Bird 20-104	(M)	I Can Never Go Home Anymore	1966	40.00	100.00
		("I Can Never Go Home Anymore" is a repackage of "Shangri-Las '65" replacing "Sophisticated Boom Boom" with the title hit.)			
Mercury MG-21099	(M)	The Shangri-Las' Golden Hits	1966	16.00	40.00
Mercury SR-61099	(P)	The Shangri-Las' Golden Hits	1966	20.00	50.00

Label & Catalog #		Title	Year	VG+	NM
Post 4000	(S)	The Shangri-Las Sing	196?	10.00	25.00
Bac-Trac	(S)	The Best Of The Shangri-Las (Red vinyl)	1985	10.00	25.00
Bac-Trac	(S)	The Best Of The Shangri-Las	1985	1.00	5.00
		(The Post and Sea-Sac albums repackage Mercury material.)			
SHANKAR, ANANDA					
Ananda is Ravi's son.					
Reprise RS-6398	(S)	Ananda Shankar	1970	6.00	15.00
SHANKAR, L.					
Zappa SRZ-1-1602	(S)	Touch Me There (Produced by Frank Zappa)	1979	10.00	25.00
SHANNON, DEL					
Del Shannon is a pseudonym for Charles Westover.					
Big Top 12-1303	(M)	Runaway	1961	150.00	300.00
Big Top 12-1303	(S)	Runaway	1961	1,40.00	2,000.00
Big Top 12-1308	(M)	Little Town Flirt	1963	150.00	300.00
Big Top 12-1308	(S)	Little Town Flirt	1963	1,40.00	2,000.00
		(Stereo copies are not identified on the cover or label so they must be listened to, although an "S" may be etched in the trail-off vinyl.)			
Big Top 12-1308	(P)	Little Town Flirt	1963	500.00	1,000.00
		(Some stereo copies were erroneously pressed with one side in mono, the other in stereo.)			
Amy 8003	(M)	Handy Man	1964	20.00	50.00
Amy S-8003	(S)	Handy Man	1964	30.00	75.00
Amy 8004	(M)	Del Shannon Sings Hank Williams	1965	20.00	50.00
Amy S-8004	(S)	Del Shannon Sings Hank Williams	1965	30.00	75.00
Amy 8006	(M)	1,661 Seconds With Del Shannon	1965	20.00	50.00
Amy S-8006	(S)	1,661 Seconds With Del Shannon	1965	30.00	75.00
Liberty LRP-3453	(M)	This Is My Bag	1966	12.00	30.00
Liberty LST-7453	(S)	This Is My Bag	1966	16.00	40.00
Liberty LRP-3479	(M)	Total Commitment	1966	12.00	30.00
Liberty LST-7479	(S)	Total Commitment	1966	16.00	40.00
Liberty LRP-3539	(M)	Further Adventures Of Charles Westover	1968	20.00	50.00
Liberty LST-7539	(S)	Further Adventures Of Charles Westover	1968	30.00	75.00
Dot DLP-3824	(M)	The Best Of Del Shannon	1967	20.00	50.00
Dot DLP-25824	(E)	The Best Of Del Shannon	1967	16.00	40.00
Post 9000	(E)	Del Shannon Sings	196?	16.00	40.00
		(Post 9000 reissues Big Top material.)			
United Arts. LA151	(S)	Del Shannon Live In England	1973	10.00	25.00
Pickwick SPC-3595	(E)	The Best Of Del Shannon	197?	1.00	5.00
Sire SHAH-3708-2	(P)	The Vintage Years (2 LPs)	1975	10.00	25.00
		(Sire 3708 collects released and unreleased material.)			
Elektra 5E-568	(S)	Drop Down And Get Me	1981	1.00	5.00
		(Elektra 568 features Tom Petty & The Heartbreakers.)			
SHAPIRO, HELEN					
Epic LN-24075	(M)	A Teenager In Love	1963	14.00	35.00
Epic BN-26075	(S)	A Teenager In Love	1963	20.00	50.00
SHARP, DEE DEE					
Cameo C-1018	(M)	It's Mashed Potato Time	1962	16.00	40.00
Cameo C-1022	(M)	Songs Of Faith	1962	16.00	40.00
Cameo SC-1022	(S)	Songs Of Faith	1962	24.00	60.00
Cameo C-1027	(M)	All The Hits	1962	16.00	40.00
Cameo SC-1027	(S)	All The Hits	1962	20.00	50.00
Cameo C-1032	(M)	All The Hits, Vol. 2	1962	16.00	40.00
Cameo SC-1032	(S)	All The Hits, Vol. 2	1962	20.00	50.00
Cameo C-1050	(M)	Do The Bird	1963	16.00	40.00
Cameo SC-1050	(S)	Do The Bird	1963	20.00	50.00
Cameo C-1062	(M)	Biggest Hits	1963	16.00	40.00
Cameo C-1074	(M)	Down Memory Lane	1963	16.00	40.00
Cameo C-2002	(M)	18 Golden Hits	1964	16.00	40.00
Cameo SC-2002	(P)	18 Golden Hits	1964	20.00	50.00
Phila. Inter. PZ-33839	(S)	Happy 'Bout The Whole Thing	1976	1.00	5.00
Phila. Inter. PZ-34437	(S)	What Color Is Love	1977	1.00	5.00
Phila. Inter. JZ-36370	(S)	Dee Dee	1980	1.00	5.00
SHARP, DEE DEE, & CHUBBY CHECKER					
Cameo C-1029	(M)	Down To Earth	1962	16.00	40.00
Cameo SC-1029	(S)	Down To Earth	1962	20.00	50.00
SHAW, SANDI					
Reprise R-6166	(M)	Sandi Shaw	1965	16.00	40.00
Reprise RS-6166	(E)	Sandi Shaw	1965	12.00	30.00
Reprise R-6191	(M)	Me	1966	12.00	30.00
Reprise RS-6191	(S)	Me	1966	16.00	40.00

Del Shannon (known as Charles Westover to his parents) hit the top of every pop chart in the country in 1961 with "Runaway." He had fifteen charting sides through 1966 and then couldn't scare up air-play. This did not stop him from being idolized by the very musicians that had supplanted his popularity, named by one British act after another as an influence. While the most obvious example is Peter & Gordon's excellent version of Shannon's "I Go To Pieces," the fact that he was constantly touring England and that he recorded an album for Rolling Stones' manager and impresario Andrew Loog Oldham's Immediate label in 1966 was further proof for the pudding. His attempted comeback with United Artists led to the release of the truly under-rated Live In England album in 1973. Sire followed a couple of years later with The Vintage Years, a tasteful collection that covers Del's career and includes many rare and unreleased sides, including material from the aforementioned Immediate album. Both the U.A. and Sire packages were cut-out staples for years but the quantity dried up long ago. . .

Label & Catalog #		Title	Year	VG+	NM
SHAW, SERENA					
Rama LP-5001	(M)	Cry My Love	195?	300.00	500.00
SHEAR, JULES					
EMI 17092	(S)	Watch Dog	1983	4.00	10.00
SHELLS, THE					
Candlelite 1000	(M)	Acappela	197?	4.00	10.00
Johnson 1619	(M)	The Shells' Greatest Hits	197?	4.00	10.00
SHELTON, ROSCOE					
Excello LP-8002	(M)	Roscoe Shelton Sings	1961	300.00	600.00
Sound Stage-7 5000	(M)	Music In His Soul, Soul In His Music	1967	16.00	40.00
Sound Stage-7 15000	(S)	Music In His Soul, Soul In His Music	1967	20.00	50.00
SHEP & THE LIMELITES					

The Heartbeats are James "Shep" Sheppard of The Heartbeats with Clarence Bassett and Charles Baskerville. Refer to The Heartbeats / Shep & The Limelites.

Hull 1001	(M)	Our Anniversary	1962	500.00	1,000.00
Roulette R-25350	(M)	Our Anniversary	1967	30.00	75.00
Roulette RS-25350	(E)	Our Anniversary	1967	20.00	50.00
		(Roulette 25350 is a reissue of Hull 1991.)			
SHEPPARDS, THE					
Constellation C-4	(M)	Collectors Showcase: The Sheppards	1964	30.00	75.00
Constellation CS-4	(E)	Collectors Showcase: The Sheppards	1964	20.00	50.00
Solid Smoke SS-8004	(M)	The Sheppards	1980	4.00	10.00
Solid Smoke SS-8028	(M)	18 Dusty Diamonds	1984	4.00	10.00

SHERIDAN, TONY: *Refer to* THE BEATLES

SHERIDAN-PRICE

Rick Price of The Move and Dave Sheridan.

Gemini 1002	(S)	This Is To Certify That. . .	1970	6.00	15.00
SHERRYS, THE					
Guyden GLP-503	(M)	At The Hop With The Sherry's	1962	150.00	300.00
SHILOH					

Shiloh features Don Henley, later of The Eagles.

Amos AAS-7015	(S)	Shiloh	1969	30.00	75.00
SHINES, JOHNNY					
Advent 2803	(S)	Johnny Shines	1974	6.00	15.00
Blue Horizon BM-4607	(M)	Blues Masters	197?	6.00	15.00
Chess LP-411	(S)	Drop Down Mama	197?	6.00	15.00
Testament 2212	(S)	Master Of The Modern Blues	197?	4.00	10.00
Testament 2217	(S)	Johnny Shines With Big Walter Horton	197?	4.00	10.00
Blue Labor 110	(S)	Too Wet To Plow	1977	4.00	10.00
SHIP, THE					
Elektra EKS-75036	(S)	The Ship *(Produced by Gary Usher)*	1972	6.00	15.00
SHIRELLES, THE					
Scepter SRM-501	(M)	Tonight's The Night	1961	80.00	200.00
Scepter SRM-502	(M)	The Shirelles Sing To Trumpets & Strings	1961	80.00	200.00
—Scepter albums above have red labels with a black & silver scroll logo on top.—					
Scepter SRM-501	(M)	Tonight's The Night	1962	30.00	75.00
Scepter SPS-501	(S)	Tonight's The Night	1965	60.00	150.00
Scepter SRM-502	(M)	The Shirelles Sing To Trumpets & Strings	1962	30.00	75.00
Scepter SPS-502	(S)	The Shirelles Sing To Trumpets & Strings	1965	60.00	150.00
Scepter SRM-504	(M)	Baby It's You	1962	30.00	75.00
Scepter SPS-504	(S)	Baby It's You	1965	60.00	150.00
Scepter SRM-507	(M)	The Shirelles' Greatest Hits	1963	16.00	40.00
Scepter SPS-507	(P)	The Shirelles' Greatest Hits	1965	20.00	50.00
("Dedicated To The One I Love" is rechanneled on this album.)					
Scepter SRM-511	(M)	Foolish Little Girl	1963	20.00	50.00
Scepter SPS-511	(S)	Foolish Little Girl	1965	30.00	75.00
Scepter SRM-514	(M)	It's A Mad, Mad, Mad, Mad, World	1963	16.00	40.00
Scepter SPS-514	(S)	It's A Mad, Mad, Mad, Mad, World	1963	20.00	50.00
Scepter SRM-516	(M)	The Shirelles Sing The Golden Oldies	1964	16.00	40.00
Scepter SPS-516	(S)	The Shirelles Sing The Golden Oldies	1964	20.00	50.00
Scepter SRM-560	(M)	The Shirelles' Greatest Hits, Volume 2	1967	8.00	20.00
Scepter SPS-560	(S)	The Shirelles' Greatest Hits, Volume 2	1967	10.00	25.00
("Please Be My Boy Friend" is rechanneled on this album.)					
Scepter SRM-562	(M)	Spontaneous Combustion	1967	16.00	40.00
Scepter SPS-562	(S)	Spontaneous Combustion	1967	20.00	50.00
—Scepter albums above have orange labels with a black oval-like center.—					

After The Heartbeats hit with "A Thousand Miles Away," Shep & The Limelites "answered" with "Daddy's Home," a disc that topped pop charts around the country in 1961. Our Anniversary is the group's only long-playing collection. (Oh, the lead singer for The Heartbeats was one James Sheppard, known to friend and foe alike as "Shep.")

Label & Catalog #		Title	Year	VG+	NM
Coca-Cola TX-94	(DJ)	The Shirelles Swing The Jingle	1964	100.00	250.00
		(Both sides contain identical plugs for Coca-Cola.)			
Pricewise P-4001	(S)	Swing The Most	196?	10.00	25.00
Pricewise P-4002	(S)	Here And Now	196?	10.00	25.00
Scepter SPS-2-599	(P)	Remember When (2 LPs)	1972	6.00	15.00
RCA Victor LSP-4581	(S)	Happy And In Love	1971	6.00	15.00
RCA Victor LSP-4698	(S)	The Shirelles	1972	6.00	15.00
United Arts. LA-430E	(S)	The Very Best Of The Shirelles	1975	1.00	5.00
Everest 4102	(S)	The Shirelles	1981	1.00	5.00
Rhino RNDA-1101	(S)	Anthology (2 LPs)	1984	1.20	6.00

SHIRELLES, THE, & KING CURTIS

Scepter SRM-505	(M)	A Twist Party	1962	30.00	75.00
Scepter SPS-505	(S)	A Twist Party	1965	60.00	150.00
Scepter SRM-569	(M)	Eternally Soul	1967	8.00	20.00
Scepter SPS-569	(S)	Eternally Soul	1967	10.00	25.00

SHIRLEY & LEE
Shirley Goodman and Leonard Lee.

Aladdin 807	(M)	Let The Good Times Roll	1956	1,000.00	2,000.00
Score SLP-4023	(M)	Let The Good Times Roll	1957	400.00	800.00
		(Score 4023 is a reissue of Aladdin 807.)			
Warwick W-2028	(M)	Let The Good Times Roll	1961	60.00	150.00
Warwick W-2028ST	(S)	Let The Good Times Roll	1961	150.00	300.00
		(Warwick 2028 is new recordings with a rerecorded title tune.)			
Imperial LP-9179	(M)	Let The Good Times Roll	1962	150.00	300.00
		(Imperial 9179 is a reissue of Aladdin 807.)			

SHIVA'S HEADBAND

Armadillo	(S)	Coming To A Head	1969	100.00	250.00
Capitol ST-538	(S)	Take Me To The Mountains	1970	20.00	50.00
Ape 1001	(S)	Psychedelic Yesterday	1981	10.00	25.00

SHOCKING BLUE, THE

Colossus CS-1000	(S)	The Shocking Blue	1970	10.00	25.00
		("Venus" and "Send Me A Postcard" are rechanneled.)			

SHOES, THE
The Shoes released several albums privately.

PVC 7904	(S)	Black Vinyl Shoes	1978	4.00	10.00

SHONDELL, TROY

Everest LPBR-5206	(M)	The Many Sides Of Troy Shondell	1963	16.00	40.00
Everest SDBR-1206	(S)	The Many Sides Of Troy Shondell	1963	20.00	50.00
		(One track, "Na-Ne No," was produced by Phil Spector.)			
Sunset SUM-1174	(M)	This Time	1967	5.00	12.00
Sunset SUS-5174	(S)	This Time	1967	6.00	15.00

SHORTY
Shorty features Georgie Fame.

Epic BN-26563	(S)	Shorty	1970	4.00	10.00

SHOTGUN LTD.

Prophesy 6050	(S)	Shotgun Ltd.	1971	8.00	20.00

SIDE SHOW

Atlantic SD-8261	(S)	Side Show	1970	6.00	15.00

SIDEKICKS, THE

RCA Victor LPM-3712	(M)	Fifi The Flea	1966	8.00	20.00
RCA Victor LSP-3712	(S)	Fifi The Flea	1966	10.00	25.00

SIDEWINDERS, THE

RCA Victor LSP-4694	(S)	The Sidewinders	1972	8.00	20.00

SIEGEL-SCHWALL BAND, THE

Vanguard VRS-9235	(M)	The Siegel-Schwall Band	1966	6.00	15.00
Vanguard VSD-79235	(S)	The Siegel-Schwall Band	1966	6.00	15.00
Vanguard VSD-79249	(M)	Say Siegel-Schwall	1967	6.00	15.00
Vanguard VSD-79249	(S)	Say Siegel-Schwall	1967	6.00	15.00
Vanguard VSD-79289	(S)	Shake!	1968	6.00	15.00
Vanguard VSD-6562	(S)	Siegel-Schwall '70	1970	4.00	10.00
Wooden Nickel WNS-1002	(S)	The Siegel-Schwall Band	1972	1.00	5.00
Wooden Nickel WNS-1010	(S)	Sleepy Hollow	1972	1.00	5.00
Wooden Nickel BWL1-0121	(S)	953 West	1973	1.00	5.00
Wooden Nickel BWL1-0288	(S)	Last Summer-Live	1974	1.00	5.00
Wooden Nickel BWL1-0554	(S)	R.I.P.	1974	1.00	5.00

The Sherrys made the national pop charts twice with "Pop Pop Pop-Pie" in 1962 and "Slop Time" in '63. Needless to say, both were attempts to cash in on the dance craze that struck the nation in the wake of the twist. While neither was a particularly notable hit, Guyden followed with an album, something that few girl groups of the era were allowed. At The Hop With The Sherrys contained both of the aforementioned hits but , alas, was issued only monophonically.

Label & Catalog #		Title	Year	VG+	NM
SIEGLING & LARRABEE					
Look 11001	(S)	Siegling & Larrabee	1970	4.00	10.00
SIGLER, BUNNY					
Parkway P-50000	(M)	Let The Good Times Roll	1967	16.00	40.00
Parkway PS-50000	(S)	Let The Good Times Roll	1967	20.00	50.00
Phila. Inter. KZ-32859	(S)	That's How Long I'll Be Loving You	1974	1.00	5.00
Phila. Inter. KZ-33249	(S)	Keep Smilin'	1974	1.00	5.00
SILHOUETTES, THE					
Goodway GLP-100	(M)	The Silhouettes 1958-1968/Get A Job	1968	150.00	300.00
SILK					
ABC ABCS-694	(S)	Smooth As Raw Silk	1969	5.00	12.00
SILKIE, THE					
Fontana MGF-27548	(M)	You've Got To Hide Your Love Away	1965	20.00	50.00
Fontana SRF-67548	(E)	You've Got To Hide Your Love Away	1965	16.00	40.00
		(Original covers are in full-color.)			
Fontana MGF-27548	(M)	You've Got To Hide Your Love Away	1965	16.00	40.00
Fontana SRF-67548	(E)	You've Got To Hide Your Love Away	1965	12.00	30.00
		(Later covers are black & white cover with a violet tone.)			
SILLY SURFERS, THE / THE WEIRD-OHS					
Issued by the Hawk Model Co., The Surfers and The Weird-Ohs are Gary Usher & Co. projects. The tracks on this album were used by Gary to create individual albums by The Surfers (below) and The Weird-Ohs.					
Hairy 101	(DJ)	The Sounds Of The Silly Surfers / The Sounds Of The Weird-Ohs	1964	60.00	150.00
SILLY SURFERS, THE					
See note above.					
Mercury MG-20977	(M)	The Sounds Of The Silly Surfers	1965	40.00	100.00
Mercury SR-60977	(S)	The Sounds Of The Silly Surfers	1965	60.00	150.00
SILVER APPLES					
Kapp KS-3562	(S)	Silver Apples (With poster)	1968	16.00	40.00
Kapp KS-3562	(S)	Silver Apples (Without poster)	1968	12.00	30.00
Kapp KS-3584	(S)	Contact	1969	12.00	30.00
SILVER BEATLES, THE: *Refer to* **ELVIS PRESLEY / THE SILVER BEATLES**					
SILVER METRE					
National General NG-2000	(S)	Silver Metre	1970	6.00	15.00
SIMMONS, GENE					
Hi HL-2018	(M)	Jumpin' Gene Simmons	1964	20.00	50.00
Hi SHL-32018	(S)	Jumpin' Gene Simmons	1964	30.00	75.00
SIMMONS, GENE: *Refer to* **KISS**					
SIMMONS, JEFF					
Mr. Simmons was a member of The Easy Chair.					
Straight STS-1057	(S)	Lucille Has Messed Up My Mind	1969	30.00	75.00
Reprise STS-1057	(S)	Lucille Has Messed Up My Mind	1970	14.00	35.00
SIMMONS, JEFF, & RANDY STEIRLING					
Straight STS-1056	(S)	Naked Angels	1969	24.00	60.00
SIMON, CARLY					
Ms. Simon was half of The Simon Sisters. She can also be found on the Decca soundtrack "Taking Off."					
Elektra EKS-74082	(S)	Carly Simon	1971	1.00	5.00
Elektra EQ-4082	(Q)	Carly Simon	1971	6.00	15.00
Elektra EKS-75016	(S)	Anticipation	1974	1.00	5.00
Elektra EKS-75049	(S)	No Secrets	1972	1.00	5.00
Elektra EQ-5049	(Q)	No Secrets	1974	6.00	15.00
Elektra 7E-1002	(S)	Hotcakes	1974	1.00	5.00
Elektra EQ-1002	(Q)	Hotcakes	1974	6.00	15.00
Elektra 7E-1033	(S)	Playing Possum	1975	1.00	5.00
Elektra EQ-1033	(Q)	Playing Possum	1975	6.00	15.00
Elektra 7E-1048	(S)	The Best Of Carly Simon	1975	1.00	5.00
Elektra EQ-1048	(Q)	The Best Of Carly Simon	1975	6.00	15.00
Elektra 7E-1064	(S)	Another Passenger	1976	1.00	5.00
Elektra EQ-1064	(Q)	Another Passenger	1976	6.00	15.00
Elektra 6E-128	(S)	Boys In The Trees	1978	.80	4.00
Elektra 5E-506	(S)	Spy	1979	.80	4.00
Warner Bros. BSK-3443	(S)	Come Upstairs	1980	.80	4.00
Warner Bros. BSK-3592	(S)	Torch	1981	.80	4.00
Warner Bros. 23886	(S)	Hello Big Man	1983	.80	4.00

The Shirelles were Shirley Owens with Micki Harris, Doris Kenner and Beverly Lee. They were arguably the definitive "girl group" of the early '60s. They placed more than two-dozen sides, many of them genre classics, on the national charts before losing their audience to the British Invasion. The two LPs pictured here, their first and third, are the original mono versions. In attempting to cash in on the growing stereo market, Scepter reissued the group's first six albums in stereo in 1965. These stereo pressings are very rare and have started to receive attention from collectors in recent years.

Label & Catalog #		Title	Year	VG+	NM

SIMON, JOE

Sound Stage-7 SSM-5003	(M)	Pure Soul	1967	12.00	30.00
Sound Stage-7 SSS-15003	(S)	Pure Soul	1967	16.00	40.00
Sound Stage-7 SSS-15004	(S)	No Sad Songs	1968	16.00	40.00
Sound Stage-7 SSS-15005	(S)	Simon Sings	1969	16.00	40.00
Sound Stage-7 SSS-15006	(S)	The Chokin' Kind	1969	16.00	40.00
Sound Stage-7 SSS-15008	(S)	Joe Simon... Better Than Ever	1969	12.00	30.00
Buddah BDS-7512	(S)	Joe Simon	1969	10.00	25.00
Sound Stage-7 SSS-15009	(S)	The Best Of Joe Simon	1972	6.00	15.00
Sound Stage-7 KZ-31916	(S)	Greatest Hits	1972	4.00	10.00
Sound Stage-7 KZ-32536	(S)	The World Of Joe Simon (2 LPs)	1974	4.00	10.00
Sound Stage-7 BZ-33879	(S)	The Chokin' Kind / Joe Simon... Better Than Ever (2 LPs)	1975	4.00	10.00
Spring SPR-4701	(S)	The Sounds Of Simon	1971	10.00	25.00
Spring SPR-5702	(S)	Drowning In The Sea Of Love	1972	10.00	25.00
Spring SPR-5704	(S)	The Power Of Joe Simon	1973	10.00	25.00
Spring SPR-5705	(S)	Simon Country	1973	6.00	15.00
Spring SPR-6702	(S)	Mood, Heart And Soul	1974	6.00	15.00
Spring SPR-6706	(S)	Get Down	1975	6.00	15.00
Spring SPR-6710	(S)	Today	1975	6.00	15.00
Spring SPR-6713	(S)	Easy To Love	1977	6.00	15.00
Spring SPR-6716	(S)	Bad Case Of Love	1977	6.00	15.00
Spring SPR-6720	(S)	Love Vibrations	1978	6.00	15.00
Posse 10003	(S)	By Popular Demand	1982	1.00	5.00
Posse 10022	(S)	Glad You Came My Way	1981	1.00	5.00

SIMON, PAUL

Mr Simon is one-half of Simon & Garfunkel, below. . .

Crest EBM-7172	(DJ)	The Early Songs Of Paul Simon	1972	20.00	50.00
		(Collection of publishers demos from the pre-S&G period. Issued with a booklet and sheet music.)			
Columbia KC-30750	(S)	Paul Simon	1972	1.00	5.00
Columbia CQ-30750	(Q)	Paul Simon	1974	6.00	15.00
Columbia KC-32280	(S)	There Goes Rhymin' Simon	1973	.80	4.00
Columbia CQ-32280	(Q)	There Goes Rhymin' Simon	1974	6.00	15.00
Columbia PC-32855	(S)	Live Rhymin'	1974	.80	4.00
Columbia PC-33540	(S)	Still Crazy After All These Years	1975	.80	4.00
Columbia PCQ-33540	(Q)	Still Crazy After All These Years	1975	6.00	15.00
Columbia HC-43540	(S)	Still Crazy After All These Years (Half-speed)	1981	16.00	50.00
Columbia JC-35032	(S)	Greatest Hits, Etc.	1977	.80	4.00
Columbia HC-45032	(S)	Greatest Hits, Etc. (Half-speed master)	1981	16.00	50.00
Columbia C5X-37581	(S)	Collected Works (5 LP boxed set)	1981	10.00	25.00
MCP 9267	(S)	Paul Simon Plus	197?	6.00	15.00
Solo Music 166	(S)	Paul Simon	197?	6.00	15.00
Warner Bros. 3472	(S)	One-Trick Pony	1980	.80	4.00
Warner Bros. 23942	(S)	Hearts And Bones (Quiex II vinyl promo)	1983	6.00	15.00
Warner Bros. 23942	(S)	Hearts And Bones	1983	.80	4.00

SIMON & GARFUNKEL

Paul Simon and Art Garfunkel originally recorded "teen" music under the guise of Tom & Jerry; some of these sides are collected on the Pickwick and Sears albums. On their Columbia debut, they were non-electric folkies, forerunners of the singer/songwriters of the '70s. After producer Tom Wilson dubbed the electric backing onto the formerly acoustic "Sounds Of Silence," the duo was dragged into folk-rock. . . Refer to each artist's solo listings.

Pickwick SPC-3059	(E)	The Hit Sounds Of Simon & Garfunkel	1966	10.00	25.00
Sears SP-435	(E)	Simon & Garfunkel	1969	10.00	25.00
		(Sears 435 is a reissue of Pickwick 3059.)			
Columbia CL-2249	(M)	Wednesday Morning 3 A.M.	1964	5.00	12.00
Columbia CS-9049	(S)	Wednesday Morning 3 A.M.	1964	6.00	15.00
Columbia CL-2469	(M)	Sounds Of Silence	1965	5.00	12.00
Columbia CS-9269	(S)	Sounds Of Silence	1965	6.00	15.00
		(Original covers for 22/9049 have a picture on the back with Garfunkel holding a copy of "Tiger Beat" magazine.)			
Columbia CL-2469	(M)	Sounds Of Silence	1966	4.00	10.00
Columbia CS-9269	(S)	Sounds Of Silence	1966	5.00	12.00
		(Later covers have the magazine air-brushed out.)			
Columbia CL-2563	(M)	Parsley, Sage, Rosemary & Thyme	1966	4.00	10.00
Columbia CS-9363	(S)	Parsley, Sage, Rosemary & Thyme	1966	5.00	12.00
Columbia KCL-2729	(M)	Bookends (With poster)	1968	5.00	12.00
Columbia KCS-9529	(S)	Bookends (With poster)	1968	4.00	10.00
Columbia KCL-2729	(M)	Bookends (Without poster)	1968	3.20	8.00
Columbia KCS-9529	(S)	Bookends (Without poster)	1968	3.20	8.00
Columbia OS-3180	(S)	The Graduate	1968	3.20	8.00
Columbia KCS-9914	(S)	Bridge Over Troubled Water	1970	6.00	15.00

— Original Columbia albums above have "360 Sound" labels.—

Columbia PC-9049	(S)	Wednesday Morning 3 A.M.	197?	.80	4.00
Columbia PC-9269	(S)	Sounds Of Silence	197?	.80	4.00
Columbia PC-9363	(S)	Parsley, Sage, Rosemary & Thyme	197?	.80	4.00
Columbia PC-9529	(S)	Bookends	197?	.80	4.00

The Sounds Of The Silly Surfers / The Sounds Of The Weird-Ohs *was commissioned by the Hawk Model Company, manufacturer of plastic model kits, as a promotional one-shot. Vocals are credited to The Surfers and The Weird-ohs, both accompanied by Shary Richards, with production credit to Jimmie Haskell and Gary Usher. The illustrations above show the front and back cover of the album. Usher took the creations to Mercury where he released one complete album by each "group."*

Label & Catalog #		Title	Year	VG+	NM
Columbia OS-3180	(S)	The Graduate	197?	.80	4.00
Columbia PC-30995	(S)	Bridge Over Troubled Water	197?	.80	4.00
Columbia CQ-30995	(Q)	Bridge Over Troubled Water	197?	10.00	25.00
Columbia HC-49914	(S)	Bridge Over Troubled Water (Half-speed)	1982	10.00	25.00
Columbia KC-41350	(S)	Greatest Hits	1972	1.00	5.00
Columbia PC-41350	(S)	Greatest Hits	1978	.80	4.00
Columbia HC-41350	(S)	Greatest Hits (Half-speed master)	1982	10.00	25.00
Columbia TV-2002	(S)	The Complete Collection (5 LP box TV offer)	1974	12.00	30.00
Columbia C5X-37587	(S)	Collected Works (5 LP boxed set)	1981	10.00	25.00

SIMON SISTERS, THE
Carly and Lucy Simon are singers of folk-based pop music.

Kapp KL-1359	(M)	Winkin,' Blinkin' And Nod	1964	12.00	30.00
Kapp KS-3359	(S)	Winkin,' Blinkin' And Nod	1964	16.00	40.00
Kapp KL-1397	(M)	Cuddlebug	1964	16.00	40.00
Kapp KS-3397	(S)	Cuddlebug	1964	20.00	50.00
Columbia CC-24506	(S)	The Lobster Quadrille (With booklet)	1969	6.00	15.00
Columbia CR-21539	(S)	The Simon Sisters Sing For Children	1973	1.00	5.00
		(Columbia 21539 is a remixed repackage of 24506.)			

SIMS, FRANKIE LEE

Specialty SPS-2124	(M)	Lucy Mae Blues	1969	16.00	40.00

SIN SAY SHUNS, THE

Venett V-940	(M)	I'll Be There	196?	14.00	35.00
Venett VS-940	(S)	I'll Be There	196?	20.00	50.00

SINATRA, NANCY
Frank's delectable daughter can also be found on Elvis' "Speedway" and the U.A. soundtrack "You Only Live Twice."

Reprise R-6202	(M)	Boots	1966	10.00	25.00
Reprise RS-6202	(S)	Boots	1966	12.00	30.00
Reprise R-6207	(M)	How Does That Grab You?	1966	8.00	20.00
Reprise RS-6207	(S)	How Does That Grab You?	1966	10.00	25.00
Reprise R-6221	(M)	Nancy In London	1966	5.00	12.00
Reprise RS-6221	(S)	Nancy In London	1966	6.00	15.00
Reprise R-6239	(M)	Sugar	1966	5.00	12.00
Reprise RS-6239	(S)	Sugar	1966	6.00	15.00
Reprise R-6251	(M)	Country, My Way	1967	5.00	12.00
Reprise RS-6251	(S)	Country, My Way	1967	6.00	15.00
Reprise R-6277	(M)	Movin' With Nancy	1968	5.00	12.00
Reprise RS-6277	(S)	Movin' With Nancy	1968	5.00	12.00
Reprise RS-6333	(S)	Nancy	1969	8.00	20.00
Reprise RS-6409	(S)	Nancy's Greatest Hits	1970	10.00	25.00
RCA Victor VPS-6078	(S)	This Is Nancy Sinatra (2 LPs)	1972	20.00	50.00
RCA Victor LSP-4774	(S)	Woman	1972	10.00	25.00
Rhino RNLP-70227	(S)	Boots: Nancy Sinatra's All-Time Hits	1986	4.00	10.00

SINATRA, NANCY, & LEE HAZLEWOOD

Reprise R-6273	(M)	The Hits Of Nancy & Lee	1968	8.00	20.00
Reprise RS-6273	(S)	The Hits Of Nancy & Lee	1968	8.00	20.00
RCA Victor LSP-4645	(S)	Nancy And Lee Again	1972	12.00	30.00
Rhino R1-70166	(S)	Fairy Tales & Fantasies	1989	1.00	5.00

SING A SONG WITH THE BEATLES
While Tower 5000 features some gear photos of the Fab Four on the gatefold cover, the album contains anonymous "Instrumental Background Recreations of Their Big Hits."

Tower KAO-5000	(M)	Sing A Song With The Beatles	1965	60.00	150.00
Tower DKAO-5000	(E)	Sing A Song With The Beatles	1965	80.00	200.00

SIR DOUGLAS QUINTET, THE: Refer to DOUG SAHM

SIR LORD BALTIMORE

Mercury SR-61328	(S)	Kingdom Come	1970	10.00	25.00
Mercury SRM-1-613	(S)	Sir Lord Baltimore	1971	10.00	25.00

SIREN

Dandelion D9-104	(S)	Siren	1970	5.00	12.00
Elektra EKS-74087	(S)	Strange Locomotion	1971	5.00	12.00

6680 LEXINGTON

MGM SE-4783	(S)	6680 Lexington	1971	4.00	10.00

60,000,000 BUFFALO

Atco SD-36-384	(S)	Nevada Jukebox	1972	1.00	5.00

SKID ROW

Epic E-30404	(S)	Skid	1971	8.00	20.00
Epic E-30913	(S)	34 Hours	1971	12.00	30.00

Carly Simon began her career as half of the folk/pop duo with sister Lucy, making the charts briefly in 1964 with "Winkin', Blinkin' And Nod." Even with this utterly contrived photo, the Cuddlebug album makes evident the young lady's nascent sensuality. Years later she resurrected her career as a sort of yuppie-princess singer-songwriter. No Secrets, shown here in its rather rare quadraphonic incarnation, shows that there was no longer anything nascent about the allure of this woman.

Label & Catalog #		Title	Year	VG+	NM
SKIN ALLEY					
Stax STS-3013	(S)	**Two Quid Deal** *(With poster)*	1973	8.00	20.00
Stax STS-3013	(S)	**Two Quid Deal** *(Without poster)*	1973	5.00	12.00
Stax STS-3022	(S)	**Skin Tight**	1974	5.00	12.00
SKINNER, CORNELIA & OTIS					
Camden CAL-190	(M)	**Cornelia Skinner With Otis Skinner**	195?	14.00	35.00
		—Camden albums above have pink & purple labels.—			
SKYLINERS, THE					
Calico LP-3000	(M)	**The Skyliners**	1959	300.00	600.00
		—Calico albums above have yellow & blue labels.—			
Calico LP-3000	(M)	**The Skyliners**	196?	80.00	200.00
		—Calico albums above have blue labels.—			
Original Sound OS-8873	(M)	**Since I Don't Have You**	1963	20.00	50.00
Original Sound OSS-8873	(S)	**Since I Don't Have You**	1963	30.00	75.00
		("Since I Don't Have You," "One Night, One Night" and "This I Swear" are rechanneled.)			
Kama Sutra KSBS-2026	(S)	**Once Upon A Time**	1971	10.00	25.00
SLADE [AMBROSE SLADE]					
On their first album for Fontana, Ballzy, Slade was known as Ambrose Slade.					
Fontana SRF-67598	(S)	**Ballzy** *(White label promo)*	1969	20.00	50.00
Fontana SRF-67598	(S)	**Ballzy**	1969	30.00	75.00
Cotillion SD-9035	(S)	**Play It Loud**	1970	8.00	20.00
Polydor PD-5508	(S)	**Slade Alive!**	1972	6.00	15.00
Polydor PD-5524	(S)	**Slayed**	1973	6.00	15.00
Reprise MS-2173	(S)	**Sladest**	1973	3.20	8.00
Warner Bros. BS-2770	(S)	**Stomp Your Hands, Clap Your Feet**	1974	3.20	8.00
Warner Bros. BS-2865	(S)	**Slade In Flame**	1975	3.20	8.00
Warner Bros. BS-2936	(S)	**Nobody's Fools**	1976	3.20	8.00
SLANE, KEITH					
Aural Explorer 5011	(S)	**Star Captain**	1971	4.00	10.00
SLEDGE, H.Y.					
SSS International 22	(S)	**Bootleg Music**	1971	8.00	20.00
SLEDGE, PERCY					
Atlantic 8125	(M)	**When A Man Loves A Woman**	1966	20.00	50.00
Atlantic SD-8125	(E)	**When A Man Loves A Woman**	1966	14.00	35.00
Atlantic 8132	(M)	**Warm And Tender Soul**	1966	20.00	50.00
Atlantic SD-8132	(E)	**Warm And Tender Soul**	1966	14.00	35.00
Atlantic 8146	(M)	**The Percy Sledge Way**	1967	20.00	50.00
Atlantic SD-8146	(S)	**The Percy Sledge Way**	1967	24.00	60.00
Atlantic SC-8180	(S)	**Take Time To Know Her**	1968	24.00	60.00
		("I Love Everything About You" is rechanneled.)			
Atlantic SD-8210	(S)	**The Best Of Percy Sledge**	1969	20.00	50.00
		("When A Man Loves A Woman," "Warm And Tender Love," "Baby Help Me" and "It Tears Me Up" are rechanneled.)			
		—Atlantic stereo albums above have green & orange labels with 1841 Broadway" on the bottom.—			
Atlantic SD-8210	(S)	**The Best Of Percy Sledge**	1969	20.00	50.00
		—Atlantic stereo albums above have purple & brown labels.—			
Capricorn 0147	(S)	**I'll Be Your Everything**	1974	6.00	15.00
SLEEPY HOLLOW					
Family Prod. 2708	(S)	**Sleepy Hollow**	1973	6.00	15.00
SLICK, GRACE					
Ms Slick was a member of The Great Society, Jefferson Airplane, and Jefferson Starship. Refer to Paul Kantner & Grace Slick.					
Grunt DJL1-0347	(DJ)	**Manhole** *(Banded for air-play)*	1974	4.00	10.00
Grunt BFL1-0347	(S)	**Manhole**	1974	1.00	5.00
RCA Victor AFL1-3544	(S)	**Dreams**	1980	.80	4.00
RCA Victor DJL1-3601	(DJ)	**Through The Hoop With Grace Slick**	1980	4.00	10.00
RCA Victor AYL1-3736	(S)	**Manhole**	1980	.80	4.00
RCA Victor AQL1-3851	(DJ)	**Welcome To The Wrecking Ball**	1981	.80	4.00
RCA Victor DJL1-3922	(DJ)	**Welcome To The Wrecking Ball Interview**	1981	4.00	10.00
RCA Victor DJL1-3923	(DJ)	**RCA Special Radio Series** *(Interview)*	1981	4.00	10.00
SLIM HARPO					
Excello LP-8003	(M)	**Raining In My Heart**	1961	100.00	250.00
		(First pressings of Excello 8003 have a red & white drawing cover.)			
Excello LPS-8003	(M)	**Raining In My Heart**	1968	40.00	100.00
		(Later "Electronic Stereo" covers contain mono albums.)			
Excello LP-8005	(M)	**Baby, Scratch My Back**	1966	80.00	200.00
		(First pressings of Excello 8005 have a green & white drawing cover.)			

The first time I wrote a caption for this photo for a previous edition of this book I said "How Ms Sinatra's new label, RCA Victor, failed to title this two-LP collection Nancy's Back is be-yond me." I still think it's the wittiest caption I've written!

Label & Catalog #		Title	Year	VG+	NM
Excello LPS-8005	(M)	Baby, Scratch My Back	1968	40.00	100.00
		(Later "Electronic Stereo" covers contain mono albums.)			
Excello LPS-8008	(M)	Tip On In	1968	20.00	50.00
Excello LPS-8010	(M)	The Best Of Slim Harpo	1969	20.00	50.00
Excello LPS-8013	(M)	Slim Harpo Knew The Blues	1970	20.00	50.00
SLIM JIM					
Soma 1225	(M)	Slim Jim Sings	1958	20.00	50.00
		—Soma albums above have black labels.—			

SLOAN, P. F.
Phil Sloan was a writer, producer and singer. Along with his similarly talented partner, Steve Barri, they created and performed as The Fantastic Baggys, The Grass Roots, and The Rincon Surfside Band.

Dunhill D-50004	(M)	Songs Of Our Times	1965	12.00	30.00
Dunhill DS-50004	(S)	Songs Of Our Times	1965	16.00	40.00
Dunhill D-50007	(S)	Twelve More Times	1966	12.00	30.00
Dunhill DS-50007	(S)	Twelve More Times	1966	16.00	40.00
Atco SD-33-268	(S)	Measure Of Pleasure	1968	12.00	30.00
Mums KZ-31260	(S)	Raised On Records	1972	10.00	25.00

SLY & THE FAMILY STONE
Sly is Sylvester Stewart; The Family Stone features Larry Graham, later of Graham Central Station.

Epic LN-24324	(M)	A Whole New Thing	1967	8.00	20.00
Epic BN-26324	(S)	A Whole New Thing	1967	8.00	20.00
Epic BN-26371	(S)	Dance To The Music	1968	4.00	10.00
Epic BN-26397	(S)	Life	1968	4.00	10.00
Epic BN-26456	(S)	Stand!	1969	4.00	10.00
Epic KE-30325	(P)	Sly & The Family Stone's Greatest Hits	1970	4.00	10.00
		("Everybody Is A Star," "Hot Fun In The Summertime," and "Thank You" are rechanneled on this album.)			
Epic KE-30986	(S)	There's A Riot Goin' On	1971	4.00	10.00
		—Epic albums above have yellow labels.—			
Epic KE-30325	(P)	Sly & The Family Stone's Greatest Hits	1973	1.00	5.00
Epic EQ-30325	(Q)	Sly & The Family Stone's Greatest Hits	1973	40.00	100.00
		("Everybody Is A Star," "Hot Fun In The Summertime," and "Thank You" are remixed from the multi-tracks on this album.)			
Epic E-30333	(S)	Life	1973	1.00	5.00
Epic E-30334	(S)	Dance To The Music	1973	1.00	5.00
Epic E-30335	(S)	A Whole New Thing	1973	1.00	5.00
Epic KE-30986	(S)	There's A Riot Goin' On	1973	1.00	5.00
Epic KE-32134	(S)	Fresh	1973	3.20	8.00
Epic PE-32930	(S)	Small Talk	1974	3.20	8.00
Epic PEQ-32930	(Q)	Small Talk	1974	10.00	25.00
Epic PE-33462	(S)	High Energy *(2 LPs)*	1975	3.20	8.00
Epic PE-33835	(S)	High On You	1975	1.20	6.00
Epic PE-34348	(S)	Heard Ya Missed Me, Well I'm Back	1975	1.20	6.00
Epic AS-264	(DJ)	Everything You Always Wanted To Hear From Sly & The Family Stone But Were Afraid To Ask For	1976	10.00	25.00
		—Epic albums above have orange labels.—			
Epic KE-30325	(P)	Sly & The Family Stone's Greatest Hits	1978	.80	4.00
Epic E-30333	(S)	Life	1978	.80	4.00
Epic E-30334	(S)	Dance To The Music	1978	.80	4.00
Epic E-30335	(S)	A Whole New Thing	1978	.80	4.00
Epic KE-30986	(S)	There's A Riot Goin' On	1978	.80	4.00
Epic KE-32134	(S)	Fresh	1978	.80	4.00
Epic PE-33462	(S)	High Energy *(2 LPs)*	1975	1.20	6.00
Epic PEQ-33835	(Q)	High On You	1975	10.00	25.00
Epic PE-34348	(S)	Heard Ya Missed Me, Well I'm Back	1978	.80	4.00
Epic 35974	(S)	Ten Years Too Soon	1979	1.20	6.00
		—Epic albums above have black labels.—			
Warner Bros. 3303	(S)	Back On The Right Track	1979	1.20	6.00
Warner Bros. 23700	(S)	Ain't But The One Way	1982	1.20	6.00

SMALL, MILLIE

Smash MGS-27055	(M)	My Boy Lollipop	1964	20.00	50.00
Smash SRS-67055	(E)	My Boy Lollipop	1964	16.00	40.00

SMALL FACES, THE
The Small Faces were Steve Marriott, Ronnie Lane, Kenny Jones, and Ian McLagen. They disbanded in 1969. Within a year's time, the three remaining members were recording with Rod Stewart and Ron Wood as The Faces.

Immediate Z12-52002	(M)	There Are But Four Small Faces	1967	20.00	50.00
Immediate Z12-52002	(S)	There Are But Four Small Faces	1967	20.00	50.00
		(Original records have a color label in a full-color cover. Counterfeits have white labels with a green & white or black & white cover.)			
Immediate Z12-52008	(S)	Ogden's Nut Gone Flake *(Round cover)*	1968	20.00	50.00
Pride 0001	(E)	Early Faces	1972	6.00	15.00
		(Pride 0001 contains Decca sides recorded in 1965-66.)			
Pride 0014	(P)	The History Of The Small Faces	1973	4.00	10.00

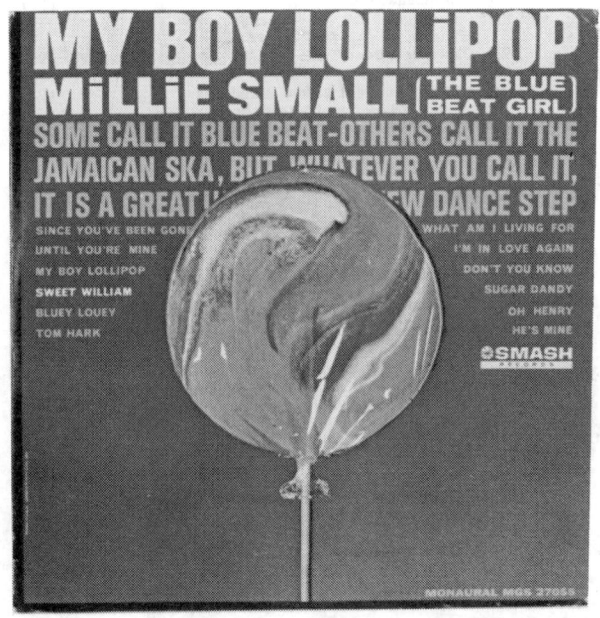

Millie Small was born Millicent Smith on Jamaica and was known as the "Blue Beat Girl." In 1964, "My Boy Lollipop" was the first major hit for a Jamaican artist using the unique rhythm then known as "ska." This was recorded in England under the auspices of record collector/dealer, producer, and future label owner (Island Records) Chris Blackwell and licensed worldwide. In the States, Smash followed with an album, My Boy Lollipop, which included the second single, "Sweet William," a modest hit. Eventually, ska evolved into "rock steady" and, by the time it had become known as "reggae," nobody seemed to remember Millicent.

Label & Catalog #		Title	Year	VG+	NM
Immediate 4225	(S)	Ogden's Nut Gone Flake *(Regular cover)*	1973	6.00	15.00
MGM M3F-4955	(S)	Archetypes	1974	4.00	10.00
Sire SASH-3709	(S)	The Immediate Story *(2 LPs)*	197?	4.00	10.00
Accord SN-7157	(S)	By Appointment	1982	.80	4.00
Compleat 2004	(S)	Big Music *(2 LPs)*	1985	1.00	5.00

SMILE

Pickwick SPC-3288	(S)	Smile	1973	12.00	30.00

SMITH
Smith features Gayle McCormack

Dunhill DS-50056	(S)	A Group Called Smith	1969	4.00	10.00
Dunhill DS-50081	(S)	Minus-Plus	1969	4.00	10.00

SMITH, AL

Bluesville BVLP-1001	(M)	Hear My Blues	1960	30.00	75.00
Bluesville BVLP-1013	(M)	Midnight Special	1961	30.00	75.00
		—Bluesville albums above have bright blue labels with silver print.—			
Bluesville BVLP-1001	(M)	Hear My Blues	1964	10.00	25.00
Bluesville BVLP-1013	(M)	Midnight Special	1964	10.00	25.00
Bluesville BVLP-1069	(M)	Blues Shout	1965	10.00	25.00
		(Bluesville 1069 is a reissue of 1001.)			

SMITH, BOB

Kent KST-551	(S)	The Visit *(2 LPs with poster)*	1969	40.00	100.00
Kent KST-551	(S)	The Visit *(2 LPs without poster)*	1969	30.00	75.00

SMITH, GEORGE "HARMONICA"

BluesWay BLS-6029	(S)	George Smith Of The Blues	1969	6.00	15.00
World Pacific ST-21887	(S)	Blues With A Feeling	196?	6.00	15.00
Deram DES-18059	(S)	Arkansas Trap	1971	6.00	15.00

SMITH, HUEY "PIANO"

Ace LP-1004	(M)	Having A Good Time	1959	200.00	400.00
Ace LP-1015	(M)	For Dancing	1961	150.00	300.00
Ace LP-1027	(M)	Twas The Night Before Christmas	1962	150.00	300.00
Grand Prix K-418	(M)	Huey "Piano" Smith (& Others)	196?	4.00	10.00
Grand Prix KS-418	(E)	Huey "Piano" Smith (& Others)	196?	1.00	5.00
Ace LP-2021	(M)	Rock 'N' Roll Revival	1971	12.00	30.00

SMITH, HURRICANE

Capitol ST-11139	(S)	Hurricane Smith	1972	8.00	20.00

SMITH, RAY
Refer to Ral Donner / Ray Smith / Bobby Dale.

Judd JLPA-701	(M)	Travelin' With Ray	1960	300.00	600.00
"T" 56062	(M)	The Best Of Ray Smith	196?	80.00	200.00
		("T" 56062 is a reissue of Judd 701.)			
Columbia CL-1937	(M)	Ray Smith's Greatest Hits	1963	10.00	25.00
Columbia CS-8737	(P)	Ray Smith's Greatest Hits	1963	12.00	30.00
		—Columbia albums above have "Guaranteed High Fidelity" or			
		"360 Sound Stereo" in black on the bottom label.—			
Wix 1000	(S)	I'm Gonna Rock Some More	197?	4.00	10.00

SMITH, RAY / PAT CUPP

Crown CLP-5364	(M)	Ray Smith And Pat Cupp	1963	12.00	30.00
Crown CST-364	(E)	Ray Smith And Pat Cupp	1963	6.00	15.00
		—Crown albums above have gray labels.—			

SMITH, ROBERT CURTIS

Bluesville BVLP-1064	(M)	Clarksdale Blues	1963	30.00	75.00
		—Bluesville albums above have bright blue labels with silver print.—			
Bluesville BVLP-1064	(M)	Clarksdale Blues	1964	10.00	25.00
		—Bluesville albums above have blue labels with a trident logo on the right side.—			

SMITH, TAB

United LP-001	(10")	Music Styled By Tab Smith	1955	80.00	200.00
United LP-003	(10")	Red, Hot And Cool Blues	1955	80.00	200.00
Checker LP-2971	(DJ)	Tab Smith *(Promo on multi-color vinyl)*	1960	300.00	600.00
Checker LP-2971	(M)	Tab Smith	1960	40.00	100.00
		—Checker albums above have black labels.—			

SMITHER, CHRIS

Poppy 5704	(S)	Don't It Drag On	1972	4.00	10.00

SMOKE, THE

Sidewalk ST-5912	(S)	The Smoke	1968	12.00	30.00
Tower ST-5912	(S)	The Smoke	1968	10.00	25.00

While The Sonics remain a legendary Northwest group, like too many regional wonders they were never able to place a hit on the national charts and gain wider recognition with the increased revenues that implies. Each of their albums, such as The Sonics Boom, is sought after both as a regional collectible and as fine examples of mid-'60s punk. Their label, Etiquette, issued the Merry Christmas album with tracks from their three biggest groups. It sold little and remains the label's rarest release.

Label & Catalog #		Title	Year	VG+	NM
SMOKE, THE					
Uni 73052	(S)	**The Smoke**	1969	8.00	20.00
Uni 73065	(S)	**At George's Coffee Shop**	1970	8.00	20.00
SMOKE RISE					
Paramount PAS-9000	(S)	**The Survival Of St. Joan** (2 LPs with book)	1971	6.00	15.00
SMOKESTACK LIGHTNIN'					
Bell 6026	(S)	**Off The Wall**	1969	6.00	15.00
SMOKEY & HIS SISTER					
Warner Bros. WS-1763	(S)	**Smokey And His Sister**	1968	4.00	10.00
SMOKEY BABE					
Bluesville BVLP-1063	(M)	**Hottest Brand Going**	1963	30.00	75.00
	— Bluesville albums above have bright blue labels with silver print.—				
Bluesville BVLP-1063	(M)	**Hottest Brand Going**	1964	10.00	25.00
	— Bluesville albums above have blue labels with a trident logo on the right side.—				
Folk-Lyric FL-108	(M)	**Smokey Babe**	196?	10.00	25.00
Arhoolie 2019	(M)	**Hot Blues**	196?	4.00	10.00
	(Arhoolie 2109 is a reissue of Folk-Lyric 108.)				
SMOTHERS, SMOKEY					
King 779	(M)	**The Backporch Blues**	1962	300.00	750.00
	—King albums above have crownless black labels.—				
SMUBBS, THE					
Monument SLP-8112	(S)	**This Is The End Of The Night**	1969	6.00	15.00
SNAKEFINGER					
Ralph SN-7909	(S)	**Chewing Hides The Sound**	1980	6.00	15.00
Ralph SN-8053	(S)	**Green Pastures**	1981	6.00	15.00
Ralph SN-8203	(S)	**Manual Of Errors**	1982	6.00	15.00
SNELL, TONY					
ESP-Disk' 3004	(S)	**Medieval And Latter Day Lays**	197?	8.00	20.00
SOCIETY OF SEVEN					
Silver Sword 7012	(S)	**How Has Your Love Life Been?**	1970	8.00	20.00
Uni 73095	(S)	**What Have We Got?**	1971	4.00	10.00
SOD					
Decca DL-75316	(S)	**Sod**	1971	5.00	12.00
Decca DL-75353	(S)	**Face The Music**	1972	6.00	15.00
SOFT MACHINE					
The Soft Machine features Robert Wyatt.					
Probe 4500	(S)	**The Soft Machine**	1968	16.00	40.00
	(The cover is a "machine" with movable parts.)				
Probe 4500	(S)	**The Soft Machine** (Standard cover)	1969	8.00	20.00
Probe 4505	(S)	**Soft Machine, Volume 2**	1969	8.00	20.00
Columbia G-30339	(S)	**Soft Machine Third** (2 LPs)	1970	6.00	15.00
Columbia KC-30754	(S)	**Soft Machine Fourth**	1971	4.00	10.00
Columbia KC-31604	(S)	**Soft Machine 5**	1972	4.00	10.00
Columbia KG-32260	(S)	**Soft Machine Six**	1973	4.00	10.00
Columbia KC-32716	(S)	**Soft Machine Seven**	1973	4.00	10.00
Command RS-964SD	(S)	**Soft Machine** (2 LPs)	1973	6.00	15.00
	(Command 964 is a reissue of Probe 4500 and 4505.)				
SONG					
MGM SE-4714	(S)	**The Song Album**	1970	6.00	15.00
SONICS, THE					
Etiquette ALB-024	(M)	**Here Are The Sonics!!!**	1965	100.00	300.00
Etiquette LPS-024	(S)	**Here Are The Sonics!!!**	1965	150.00	400.00
	—Etiquette albums above have red labels on non-flexible vinyl.—				
Etiquette LPS-024	(M)	**Here Are The Sonics!!!**	1966	70.00	200.00
Etiquette LPS-024	(S)	**Here Are The Sonics!!!**	1966	100.00	300.00
Etiquette ALB-027	(M)	**The Sonics Boom**	1966	100.00	300.00
Etiquette LPS-027	(E)	**The Sonics Boom**	1966	70.00	200.00
	—Etiquette albums above have purple labels on non-flexible vinyl.—				
Etiquette LPS-024	(S)	**Here Are The Sonics!!!**	197?	12.00	30.00
Etiquette LPS-027	(E)	**The Sonics Boom**	197?	12.00	30.00
	— Etiquette albums above have purple labels on flexible vinyl.—				
Jerden JRL-7007	(M)	**Introducing The Sonics** (White label promo)	1967	200.00	400.00
Jerden JRL-7007	(M)	**Introducing The Sonics**	1967	80.00	200.00
Jerden JRS-7007	(E)	**Introducing The Sonics**	1967	60.00	150.00
Buckshot BSR-001	(S)	**Explosives**	1974	20.00	50.00

Label & Catalog #		Title	Year	VG+	NM
First American FA-7715	(M)	Original Northwest Punk	1977	8.00	20.00
		(FA-7715 is a reissue of Jerden 7007.)			
Bomp 4011	(E)	The Sonics Boom	1980	4.00	10.00
First American FA-7719	(M	Unreleased	1980	8.00	20.00
First American FA-7779	(M)	Fire And Ice	1981	8.00	20.00

SONICS, THE / THE WAILERS / THE GALAXIES

Etiquette ALB-02	(M)	Merry Christmas	1965	250.00	500.00

SONNY
Sonny is Sonny Bono.

Atco 33-229	(M)	Inner Views	1967	4.00	10.00
Atco SD-33-229	(S)	Inner Views	1967	4.00	10.00

SONNY & CHER
Sonny Bono and Cher can also be found on the RCA soundtrack "Wild On The Beach."

Reprise R-6177	(M)	Baby Don't Go	1965	8.00	20.00
Reprise RS-6177	(S)	Baby Don't Go	1965	10.00	25.00
		(Reprise 6177 credits Sonny & Cher & Friends. It includes their single sides as Caesar & Cleo, along with tracks by The Blendells, The Lettermen, and Bill Medley. "Baby Don't Go," "La-La-La-La-La," "Walkin' The Quetzal," "When," and "Their Hearts Were Full Of Spring" are rechanneled.)			
Atco 33-177	(M)	Look At Us	1965	6.00	15.00
Atco SD-33-177	(S)	Look At Us	1965	8.00	20.00
Atco 33-183	(M)	The Wondrous World Of Sonny & Cher	1966	4.00	10.00
Atco SD-33-183	(S)	The Wondrous World Of Sonny & Cher	1966	5.00	12.00
Atco 33-203	(M)	In Case You're In Love	1967	4.00	10.00
Atco SD-33-203	(S)	In Case You're In Love	1967	5.00	12.00
Atco 33-214	(M)	Good Times	1967	4.00	10.00
Atco SD-33-214	(S)	Good Times	1967	5.00	12.00
Atco 33-219	(M)	The Best Of Sonny & Cher	1967	4.00	10.00
Atco SD-33-219	(S)	The Best Of Sonny & Cher	1967	5.00	12.00
		("What Now My Love," "A Beautiful Story," "But You're Mine" and "Laugh At Me" are rechanneled on this album.)			
Atco SD-2-804	(S)	The Two Of Us (2 LPs)	1972	1.00	5..00
		(Atco 804 repackages 177 and 203.)			
Kapp KS-3654	(S)	Sonny & Cher Live	1971	1.00	5.00
Kapp KS-3660	(S)	All I Ever Need Is You	1972	1.00	5.00
MCA 2009	(S)	Sonny & Cher Live	1973	.80	4.00
MCA 2021	(S)	All I Ever Need Is You	1973	.80	4.00
MCA 2101	(S)	Mama Was A Rock And Roll Singer— Papa Used To Write All Her Songs	1973	.80	4.00
MCA 8004	(S)	Live In Las Vegas, Vol. 2	1973	.80	4.00
MCA 2117	(S)	Greatest Hits	1974	.80	4.00

SONNY & THE DEMONS

United Arts. UAL-3316	(M)	Drag Kings	1964	20.00	50.00
United Arts. UAS-6316	(S)	Drag Kings	1964	30.00	75.00

SONS OF CHAMPLIN

Capitol SWBB-200	(S)	Loosen Up Naturally (2 LPs)	1969	20.00	50.00
		(Original covers had the English language's most oft-used four-letter word as part of the graffiti-like art. Capitol recalled the albums and had the offending expletive scratched off by hand!)			
Capitol SWBB-200	(S)	Loosen Up Naturally (2 LPs)	1969	6.00	15.00
		(The foul language scratched off of the cover.)			
Capitol SWBB-200	(S)	Loosen Up Naturally (2 LPs)	1969	6.00	15.00
		(Later pressings had the nasties airbrushed off of the cover.)			
		—Capitol albums above have black rainbow labels.—			
Capitol SKAO-322	(S)	The Sons	1969	4.00	10.00
Capitol ST-675	(S)	Follow Your Heart	1971	4.00	10.00
		—Capitol albums above have green labels.—			
Columbia KC-32341	(S)	Welcome To The Dance	1973	1.00	5.00
Ariola America ST-50002	(S)	The Sons Of Champlin	1975	1.00	5.00

SONS OF HEROES

MCA 39010	(S)	Sons Of Heroes (With Bill Wyman)	1983	8.00	20.00

SOPHOMORES, THE

Dawn DLP-1128	(M)	The Sophomores	1958	Unreleased?	
Dawn DSP-2001	(S)	The Sophomores	1958	Unreleased?	
		(Should the Dawn album exist, it would have a suggested NM value of $600-1,800.)			
Seeco CELP-451	(M)	The Sophomores	195?	150.00	300.00

SOPWITH CAMEL, THE

Kama Sutra KLP-8060	(M)	The Sopwith Camel	1967	12.00	30.00

Label & Catalog #		Title	Year	VG+	NM
Kama Sutra KLPS-8060	(S)	The Sopwith Camel	1967	16.00	40.00
Kama Sutra KSBS-2063	(S)	Hello, Hello	1973	8.00	20.00
		(Kama Sutra 2063 is a reissue of 8060.)			
Reprise MS-2108	(S)	The Miraculous Hump Returns	1973	10.00	25.00

SOUL

Musicor MS-3230	(S)	Can You Feel It?	1972	4.00	10.00

SOUL, JIMMY
Refer to Bobby Bland / Jimmy Soul.

S.P.Q.R. E-16001	(M)	If You Wanna Be Happy	1963	60.00	150.00

SOUL, JIMMY, & THE BELMONTS

Spin-O-Rama SP-123	(M)	Jimmy Soul And The Belmonts	1963	8.00	20.00
Spin-O-Rama SPS-123	(E)	Jimmy Soul And The Belmonts	1963	4.00	10.00

SOUL CHILDREN, THE

Stax STS-2018	(S)	Soul Children	1972	20.00	50.00
Stax ST-2043	(M)	The Best Of Two Worlds *(Promo)*	1972	20.00	50.00
Stax STS-2043	(S)	The Best Of Two Worlds	1972	20.00	50.00
Stax STS-3003	(S)	Genesis	1972	20.00	50.00
Stax STS-5507	(S)	Friction	1974	20.00	50.00

SOUL FINDERS, THE

Camden CAL-2239	(M)	An Explosive Album Of Soul	1968	12.00	30.00
Camden CAS-2239	(S)	An Explosive Album Of Soul	1968	12.00	30.00

SOUL GENERATION

Ebony Sound 2000	(S)	Beyond Body And Soul	1972	10.00	25.00

SOUL SEARCHERS

Sussex 7020	(S)	We The People	1973	4.00	10.00
Sussex 8030	(S)	Salt Of The Earth	1974	4.00	10.00

SOUL SET, THE

Johnson 1001	(S)	The Soul Set	196?	6.00	15.00

SOUL SISTERS, THE

Sue LP-1022	(M)	I Can't Stand It	1964	150.00	300.00
Sue STLP-1022	(S)	I Can't Stand It	1964	250.00	500.00
		— Sue albums above have orange labels. —			

SOUL SOCIETY, THE

Dot DLP-25842	(S)	Satisfaction	1969	10.00	25.00

SOUL SOUNDS, THE

SUS-5249	(S)	The Best of The Soul Hits	1969	4.00	10.00

SOUL SURVIVORS

Crimson LP-502	(M)	When The Whistle Blows Anything Goes	1967	10.00	25.00
Crimson LP-502	(S)	When The Whistle Blows Anything Goes	1967	12.00	30.00
		("Expressway To Your Heart" and "A Change Is Gonna Come" are rechanneled.)			
Atco SD-33-277	(S)	Take Another Look	1969	10.00	25.00

SOUND FOUNDATION

Smobro 9001	(S)	Sound Foundation	1971	10.00	25.00

SOUNDS OF MODIFICATIONS, THE

Jubilee JGS-8013	(S)	The Sounds Of Modification	197?	6.00	15.00

SOUNDS OF OUR TIME

Capitol T-2817	(M)	Music Of The Flower Children	1967	6.00	15.00
Capitol ST-2817	(S)	Music Of The Flower Children	1967	8.00	20.00

SOUP
Soup's first album was pressed privately.

Big Tree BTS-2007	(S)	The Soup Album	1971	8.00	20.00

SOUTH

A&M SP-4174	(S)	Hot Air Through A Straw From The South	1969	4.00	10.00

SOUTH, JOE

Capitol ST-108	(S)	Introspect	1968	6.00	15.00
		— Capitol albums above have black "rainbow" labels. —			
Capitol ST-108	(S)	Introspect	1969	3.20	8.00
Capitol ST-235	(S)	Games People Play	1969	3.20	8.00
Capitol ST-392	(S)	Don't It Make You Want To Go Home	1969	3.20	8.00

James McCleese, a.k.a. Jimmy Soul, hit the top of the charts in 1963 with "If You Wanna Be Happy." The single was in the vein of Gary U.S. Bonds' records, a happy dance beat that sounded like it was recorded live at a party. The lyrics were just slurred enough to allow all sorts of ridiculous sing-alongs. (Although we men laughed along with the advice "don't make a pretty woman your wife," few of us paid any heed). If You Wanna Be Happy was released on the tiny S.P.Q.R. label and is not known to exist in stereo.

Label & Catalog #		Title	Year	VG+	NM
Capitol ST-450	(S)	Joe South's Greatest Hits	1970	3.20	8.00
Capitol ST-637	(S)	So The Seeds Are Growing	1971	3.20	8.00
Capitol ST-845	(S)	Joe South	1972	3.20	8.00
		—Capitol albums above have green labels.—			
Capitol ST-1074	(S)	Look Inside	1972	3.20	8.00
Mine MSG-1100	(S)	Walkin' Shoes	1970	3.20	8.00
Island ILPS-9328	(S)	Midnight Rainbows	1975	3.20	8.00
Accord SN-7119	(S)	Party People	1981	.80	4.00

SOUTH CENTRAL AVENUE MUNICIPAL BLUES BAND

BluesWay BL-6018	(S)	The Soul Of Bonnie And Clyde	1968	10.00	25.00

SOUTH 40

Metrobeat MBS-1000	(S)	Live At The Someplace Else	1968	10.00	25.00

SOUTHERN COMFORT

Columbia CS-1011	(S)	Southern Comfort	1970	4.00	10.00
Capitol ST-800	(S)	Frog City	1971	4.00	10.00

SOUTHERN FRIED

Mercury SR-61338	(S)	A Little Taste Of Southern Fried	1971	1.00	5.00

SOUTHSIDE JOHNNY & THE ASBURY JUKES

Epic 34180	(S)	I Don't Want To Go Home	1976	1.00	5.00
Epic AS-275	(DJ)	Live At The Bottom Line	1976	10.00	25.00
Epic 34668	(S)	This Time It's For Real	1977	1.00	5.00
		(Epic 34688 features vocal backings by members of The Coasters, The Drifters and The Five Satins.)			
Epic AS-362	(DJ)	A Conversation With Southside Johnny & Ronnie Spector	1977	10.00	25.00
Epic 35488	(S)	Hearts Of Stone	1978	1.00	5.00
Mercury 3793	(S)	The Jukes	1979	1.00	5.00
Mercury 3836	(S)	Love Is A Sacrifice	1980	1.00	5.00
Mercury 8602	(S)	Live—Reach Up And Touch The Sky	1981	1.00	5.00
Mirage 90113	(S)	Trash It Up!	1983	1.00	5.00
Mirage 90186	(S)	In The Heat	1984	1.00	5.00

SOUTHWEST F.O.B.

Southwest F.O.B. feature England Dan and John Ford Coley.

Hip HIS-7001	(S)	Smell Of Incense	1969	12.00	30.00

SOUTHWIND

Venture VTS-4002	(S)	Southwind	1969	5.00	12.00
Blue Thumb BTS-13	(S)	Ready To Ride	1969	5.00	12.00
Blue Thumb BTS-26	(S)	What A Place To Land	1970	5.00	12.00

SPACE OPERA

Epic KE-32117	(S)	Space Opera	1973	5.00	12.00

SPACEMEN, THE

Roulette MG-25275	(M)	Rockin' In The 25th Century	1964	12.00	30.00
Roulette SR-25275	(S)	Rockin' In The 25th Century	1964	16.00	40.00
Roulette MG-25322	(M)	Music For Batman And Robin	1966	16.00	40.00
Roulette SR-25322	(S)	Music For Batman And Robin	1966	20.00	50.00

SPANDAU BALLET

Chrysalis 41403	(S)	True	1983	1.00	5.00
Chrysalis 41473	(S)	Parade	1984	1.00	5.00

SPANIELS, THE

Vee Jay LP-1002	(M)	Goodnite, It's Time To Go (Group cover)	1958	300.00	600.00
		—Vee Jay albums above have maroon labels.—			
Vee Jay LP-1002	(M)	Goodnite, It's Time To Go (Dogs cover)	1961	100.00	250.00
		(Counterfeits of this album exist with the dogs on the cover.)			
Vee Jay LP-1024	(M)	The Spaniels	1960	100.00	250.00
		—Vee Jay albums above have black rainbow labels.—			
Lost-Nite LP-137	(M)	The Spaniels	196?	20.00	50.00
Upfront UPF-131	(E)	The Hits Of The Spaniels	196?	4.00	10.00
Lost-Nite LLP-19	(10")	The Spaniels (Red vinyl)	1981	5.00	12.00
Solid Smoke 8028	(M)	Greatest Hits	1984	4.00	10.00

SPANKY & OUR GANG

Mercury MG-21124	(M)	Spanky And Our Gang	1967	4.00	10.00
Mercury SR-61124	(S)	Spanky And Our Gang	1967	4.00	10.00
Mercury SR-61161	(S)	Like To Get To Know You	1968	4.00	10.00
Mercury SR-61183	(S)	Without Rhyme Or Reason	1969	4.00	10.00
Mercury SR-61227	(S)	Spanky And Our Gang's Greatest Hits	1969	4.00	10.00
Mercury SR-61326	(S)	Live	1971	4.00	10.00

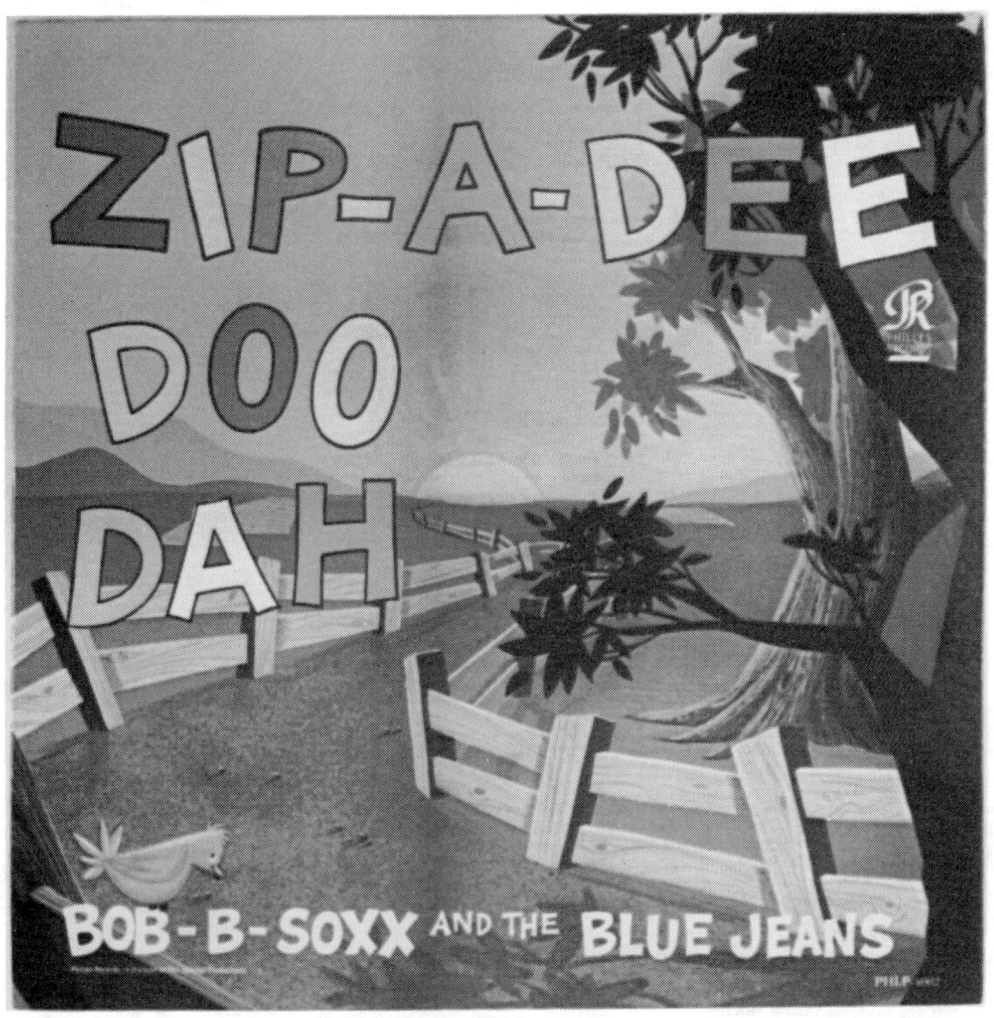

Phil Spector began his career as a singer and musician, hitting the big time as a member of The Teddy Bears, for whom he wrote "To Know Him Is To Love Him." Seeing that the fortunes of the recording industry went not to the recording artists but to just about everyone else, he created his own label, Philles (pronounced "Fill-Less" for the novice), where he would reap the rewards of writing, publishing, productions, etc. Of course, he was as stingy with sharing the profits with the artists as the very moguls he had left behind. Two of the LPs he released oh Philles were Bobb B. Soxx & The Blue Jeans' Zip-A-Dee Doo Dah and the Crystals' He's A Rebel. While Spector was elaborate achieving the musical goals he sought, he was very much a cost-cutter in other respects. His records were manufactured from the cheapest vinyl and plating available and decades later, collectors have a difficult time finding copies that play as good as they look.

Label & Catalog #		Title	Year	VG+	NM

SPANN, LUCILLE

| BluesWay BLS-6070 | (S) | Cry Before I Go | 1974 | 10.00 | 25.00 |

SPANN, OTIS

Otis Spann also recorded with Fleetwood Mac.

Candid CM-8001	(M)	Otis Spann Is The Blues	1960	60.00	150.00
Candid CS-9001	(S)	Otis Spann Is The Blues	1960	80.00	200.00
BluesWay BL-6003	(M)	The Blues Is Where It's At	1967	10.00	25.00
BluesWay BLS-6003	(S)	The Blues Is Where It's At	1967	12.00	30.00
BluesWay BLS-6013	(S)	The Bottom Of The Blues	1968	12.00	30.00
Archive Of Folk Music 217	(S)	Otis Spann	1968	4.00	10.00
London PS-543	(S)	Raw Blues	1968	12.00	30.00
London PS-551	(S)	Cracked Spanner Head	1969	12.00	30.00
Prestige PRST-7719	(S)	The Blues Will Never Die	1969	8.00	20.00
Vanguard VDS-6514	(S)	Cryin' Time	1970	8.00	20.00
Blues Time 9006	(S)	Sweet Giant Of The Blues	1970	8.00	20.00
Barnaby KZ-30246	(S)	Otis Spann Is The Blues	1970	8.00	20.00
Barnaby KZ-31290	(S)	Walking The Blues	1972	8.00	20.00
BluesWay BLS-6063	(S)	Heart Loaded With Trouble	1973	8.00	20.00

SPARK PLUGS, THE

| Sutton SU-322 | (M) | The Spark Plugs | 1963 | 10.00 | 25.00 |
| Sutton SSU-322 | (S) | The Spark Plugs | 1963 | 12.00 | 30.00 |

SPARKS

Sparks is brothers Ron and Russel Mael.

Bearsville BV-2048	(S)	Sparks	1971	4.00	10.00
		(Bearsville 2048 is a repackage of Halfnelson's eponymous LP.)			
Bearsville BR-2110	(S)	A Woofer In Tweeter's Clothing	1973	4.00	10.00
Island ILPS-9272	(S)	Kimono My House	1974	1.00	5.00
Island ILPS-9312	(S)	Propaganda	1975	1.00	5.00
Island ILPS-9345	(S)	Indiscreet	1975	1.00	5.00
Island ILPS-9493	(S)	The Best Of Sparks	1976	1.00	5.00
Columbia PC-34359	(S)	Big Beat	1977	1.00	5.00
Columbia PC-34901	(DJ)	Introducing Sparks (Red vinyl)	1977	4.00	10.00
Columbia PC-34901	(S)	Introducing Sparks	1977	1.00	5.00
Elektra 6E-186	(S)	Number One In Heaven	1979	1.00	5.00
RCA Victor AFL1-4091	(S)	Whomp That Sucker	1981	1.00	5.00
Atlantic SD-19347	(S)	Angst In My Pants	1982	1.00	5.00

SPARROW: *Refer to* JOHN KAY & SPARROW

SPARROW

| Spark 05 | (S) | Hatching Out | 1973 | 8.00 | 20.00 |

SPARROWS, THE

| Elkay 3009 | (M) | That Mersey Sound | 1964 | 16.00 | 40.00 |

SPATS

| ABC-Paramount ABC-502 | (M) | Cookin' With The Spats | 1965 | 8.00 | 20.00 |
| ABC-Paramount ABCS-502 | (S) | Cookin' With The Spats | 1965 | 12.00 | 30.00 |

SPECTOR, PHIL

After achieving a modicum of success with The Teddy Bears, Phil Spector noticed that the rewards of recording went to writers, publishers, producers and label executives. He became all of those with his Philles Records, rewriting the book on record production along the way. Compilations of his productions can be found in the Various Artists section under Philles, Apple, Warner Bros, Pavilion, Passport and Rhino. For individual artists or groups he worked with, refer to The Beatles; Bobb B. Soxx & The Bluejeans; Sonny Charles & The Checkmates Ltd; The Crystals; George Harrison; John Lennon; Ramones; The Righteous Brothers; The Ronettes; Troy Shondell; and Ike & Tina Turner.

SPECTOR, RONNIE

Ronnie was formerly a member of The Ronettes. Refer to Southside Johnny & Ronnie Spector.

| Polish PRG-808 | (S) | Siren | 1980 | 4.00 | 10.00 |

SPENCE, ALEXANDER "SKIP"

Mr Spence was an original member of Jefferson Airplane and Moby Grape.

| Columbia CS-9831 | (S) | Oar | 1969 | 24.00 | 60.00 |

SPENCER, JEREMY

Jeremy was a member of Fleetwood Mac.

| Columbia KC-31990 | (S) | Jeremy Spencer And The Children | 1971 | 6.00 | 15.00 |
| Atlantic SD-19236 | (S) | Flee | 1979 | 4.00 | 10.00 |

SPIDER-MAN

| Lifesong 6001 | (S) | Rock Reflections Of A Superhero | 1976 | 10.00 | 25.00 |

SPIDERS, THE

| Imperial LP-9140 | (M) | I Didn't Wanna Do It | 1961 | 500.00 | 1,000.00 |

Label & Catalog #		Title	Year	VG+	NM

SPIDERS FROM MARS, THE
The Spiders were formerly David Bowie's band.

Label & Catalog #		Title	Year	VG+	NM
Pye 12125	(S)	The Spiders From Mars	1976	6.00	15.00

SPINNERS, THE

| Time 52092 | (M) | Party-My Pad After Surfin' | 1963 | 14.00 | 35.00 |
| Time S-2092 | (S) | Party-My Pad After Surfin' | 1963 | 20.00 | 50.00 |

SPINNERS, THE

Motown M-639	(M)	The Original Spinners	1967	10.00	25.00
Motown MS-639	(S)	The Original Spinners	1967	12.00	30.00
		("That's What Girls Are Made For" is rechanneled on this album.)			
V.I.P. 405	(S)	2nd Time Around	1970	10.00	25.00
Motown M-769	(S)	The Best Of The Spinners	1973	4.00	10.00
Motown M5-109V	(S)	Superstar Series, Vol. 9	1980	.80	4.00
Motown M5-132V	(S)	The Original Spinners	1981	.80	4.00
Motown M5-199V	(S)	The Best Of The Spinners	1981	.80	4.00
Atlantic SD-7256	(S)	The Spinners	1973	1.00	5.00
Atlantic QD-7256	(Q)	The Spinners	1973	6.00	15.00
Atlantic SD-7296	(S)	Mighty Love	1974	1.00	5.00
Atlantic SD-18118	(S)	The New And Improved Spinners	1974	1.00	5.00
Atlantic QD-18118	(Q)	The New And Improved Spinners	1974	6.00	15.00
Atlantic SD-18141	(S)	Pick Of The Litter	1975	1.00	5.00
Atlantic SD-910	(S)	Spinners Live! (2 LPs)	1975	1.20	6.00
Atlantic SD-18181	(S)	Happiness Is Being With The Detroit Spinners	1976	1.00	5.00
Atlantic SD-19100	(S)	Yesterday, Today & Tomorrow	1977	1.00	5.00
Atlantic SD-19146	(S)	Spinners/8	1977	1.00	5.00
Atlantic SD-19179	(S)	The Best Of The Spinners	1978	1.00	5.00
Atlantic SD-19219	(S)	From Here To Eternally	1979	1.00	5.00
Atlantic SD-19256	(S)	Dancin' And Lovin'	1980	1.00	5.00
Atlantic SD-19270	(S)	Love Trippin'	1980	1.00	5.00
Atlantic SD-16032	(S)	Labor Of Love	1981	1.00	5.00
Atlantic SD-19318	(S)	Can't Shake This Feelin'	1982	1.00	5.00
Atlantic SD-80020	(S)	Grand Slam	1983	1.00	5.00

SPIRAL STARECASE, THE

| Columbia CS-9852 | (S) | More Today Than Yesterday | 1969 | 4.00 | 10.00 |
| | | *—Columbia albums above have "360 Sound" labels.—* | | | |

SPIRIT
Spirit was Randy California and his step-father, Ed Cassidy, with Mark Andes, Jay Ferguson, and John Locke. Cassidy, Ferguson and Andes quit in 1971, replaced by brothers Al and Chris Staehly for the group's final Epic album.

Ode Z12-44004	(S)	Spirit	1968	10.00	25.00
Ode Z12-44014	(S)	The Family That Plays Together	1968	10.00	25.00
Ode Z12-44016	(S)	Clear Spirit	1969	10.00	25.00
Epic KE-30267	(S)	Twelve Dreams Of Dr. Sardonicus	1970	8.00	20.00
Epic KE-31175	(S)	Feedback	1972	8.00	20.00
Epic KEG-31457	(S)	Spirit / Clear Spirit (2 LPs)	1972	6.00	15.00
		(Epic 31457 is a reissue of Ode 44004 and 44016.)			
Epic KE-31461	(S)	The Family That Plays Together	1972	4.00	10.00
		(Epic 31461 is a reissue of Ode 44014.)			
Epic KE-32271	(S)	Best Of Spirit	1973	4.00	10.00
		—Epic albums above have yellow labels.—			
Epic KE-30267	(S)	Twelve Dreams Of Dr. Sardonicus	197?	1.00	5.00
Epic KE-32271	(S)	Best Of Spirit	197?	1.00	5.00
		—Epic albums above have orange labels.—			
Mercury SRM-804	(S)	Spirit Of '76 (2 LPs)	1975	1.20	6.00
Mercury SRM-1053	(S)	Son Of Spirit	1976	1.00	5.00
Mercury SRM-1094	(S)	Farther Along	1976	1.00	5.00
Mercury SRM-1122	(S)	Future Games	1977	1.00	5.00
Potato PR-2001	(S)	Live	1978	1.00	5.00
Rhino RNSP-303	(S)	Potatoland	1981	1.00	5.00

SPIRIT & WORM

| A&M SP-4229 | (S) | Spirit And Worm | 1969 | 500.00 | 750.00 |

SPIRIT IN FLESH

| Metromedia 1041 | (S) | Spirit In Flesh | 1971 | 5.00 | 12.00 |

SPIRIT OF ATLANTA

| Buddah BDS-5135 | (S) | Burning Of Atlanta | 1973 | 1.00 | 5.00 |

SPIRIT OF US, THE

| Viva 36023 | (S) | Simple Songs Of Freedom | 1970 | 4.00 | 10.00 |

SPIRITUAL CONCEPT

| Phila. Inter. KZ-32404 | (S) | Spiritual Concept | 1973 | 1.00 | 5.00 |

Label & Catalog #		Title	Year	VG+	NM

SPIVEY, VICTORIA
Victoria Spivey is a piano player, singer and writer of blues music. Refer to Lonnie Johnson.

Spivey LP-1001	(M)	**Basket Of Blues**	1962	10.00	25.00
Spivey LP-1002	(M)	**Victoria And Her Blues**	1963	10.00	25.00
Spivey LP-1004	(M)	**Three Kings And A Queen**	1964	20.00	50.00
		(The three kings on both albums are Lonnie Johnson, Roosevelt Sykes and Big Joe Williams. Both feature Bob Dylan on harmonica on two tracks.)			
Spivey LP-1004	(M)	**Three Kings And A Queen**	1964	12.00	30.00
		(Later covers read "Historic Tracks/Bob Dylan appears with Big Joe Williams.")			
Spivey LP-1006	(M)	**The Queen And Her Knights**	1964	10.00	25.00
Spivey LP-1008	(M)	**The Bluesmen Of The Muddy Waters Band**	1964	10.00	25.00
Spivey LP-1009	(M)	**Encore For The Chicago Blues**	1964	10.00	25.00
Spivey LP-1010	(M)	**The Bluesmen Of The Muddy Waters Band, Volume Two**	1964	10.00	25.00
Spivey LP-1012	(M)	**Spivey's Blues Parade**	1964	10.00	25.00
Spivey LP-1014	(M)	**Three Kings And A Queen, Volume 2**	1964	12.00	30.00
Spivey LP-2001	(M)	**Victoria Spivey's Recorded Legacy Of The Blues**	196?	10.00	25.00
Spivey LP-1015	(M)	**Spivey's Blues Cavalcade**	196?	10.00	25.00
Spivey LP-1017	(M)	**Spivey's Blues Showcase**	196?	10.00	25.00

SPLINTER

Dark Horse SP-22001	(S)	**Place I Love**	1974	1.00	5.00
Dark Horse SP-22006	(S)	**Harder To Live**	1975	1.00	5.00
Dark Horse DH-3073	(S)	**Two Man Band**	1977	1.00	5.00

SPLIT LEVEL, THE

Dot DLP-25836	(S)	**The Split Level**	1968	6.00	15.00

SPOKESMEN, THE

Decca DL-4712	(M)	**Dawn Of Correction**	1965	10.00	25.00
Decca DL-74712	(S)	**Dawn Of Correction**	1965	12.00	30.00

SPONTANEOUS COMBUSTION

Capitol ST-11021	(S)	**Spontaneous Combustion**	1972	8.00	20.00
Harvest SW-11095	(S)	**Triad**	1972	8.00	20.00

SPOOKY TOOTH
Spooky Tooth features Mike Harrison, Mike Patto, and Gary Wright.

Bell 6019	(S)	**Spooky Tooth**	1968	10.00	25.00
A&M SP-4194	(S)	**Spooky Two**	1969	6.00	15.00
A&M SP-4225	(S)	**Ceremony**	1970	4.00	10.00
A&M SP-4266	(S)	**The Last Puff**	1970	4.00	10.00
A&M SP-4300	(S)	**Tobacco Road**	1971	4.00	10.00
A&M SP-4349	(S)	**Spooky Tooth**	1970	4.00	10.00
A&M SP-4385	(S)	**You Broke My Heart, So I Busted Your Jaw**	1973	4.00	10.00
		—A&M albums above have brown labels.—			
A&M SP-3528	(S)	**That Was Only Yesterday** (2 LPs)	1973	1.20	6.00
Island SW-9255	(S)	**Witness**	1973	1.00	5.00
Island SW-9292	(S)	**The Mirror**	1974	1.00	5.00
Accord SN-7168	(S)	**Hell Or High Water**	1982	.80	4.00

SPREADEAGLE

Charisma CAS1055	(S)	**Piece Of Paper**	1972	6.00	15.00

SPRING
Spring is Marilyn and Diane Rovell of The Honeys and features Brian Wilson as executive producer.

United Arts. UAS-5571	(S)	**Spring** (Promo)	1972	40.00	100.00
		(12" x 12" promo folder with LP, press kit and a packet of seeds.)			
United Arts. UAS-5571	(S)	**Spring** (With insert)	1972	10.00	25.00

SPRINGFIELD, DUSTY
Dusty can also be found on the soundtracks for Colgems' "Casino Royale," 20th Century-Fox's "The Sweet Ride," and U.A.'s "The Corrupt Ones." Refer to Led Zeppelin / Dusty Springfield; The Springfields.

Philips PHM-200-133	(M)	**Stay Awhile**	1964	12.00	30.00
Philips PHS-600-133	(P)	**Stay Awhile**	1964	16.00	40.00
Philips PHM-200-156	(M)	**Dusty**	1964	12.00	30.00
Philips PHS-600-156	(P)	**Dusty**	1964	16.00	40.00
Philips PHM-200-174	(M)	**Oooooo Weeee!!!**	1965	16.00	40.00
Philips PHS-600-174	(S)	**Oooooo Weeee!!!**	1965	20.00	50.00
Philips PHM-200-210	(M)	**You Don't Have To Say You Love Me**	1966	12.00	30.00
Philips PHS-600-210	(S)	**You Don't Have To Say You Love Me**	1966	16.00	40.00
Philips PHM-200-220	(M)	**Dusty Springfield's Golden Hits**	1966	10.00	25.00
Philips PHS-600-220	(P)	**Dusty Springfield's Golden Hits**	1966	14.00	35.00
		(Philips 220 was originally issued with "Goin' Back.")			
Philips PHM-200-220	(M)	**Dusty Springfield's Golden Hits**	1967	8.00	20.00
Philips PHS-600-220	(P)	**Dusty Springfield's Golden Hits**	1967	10.00	25.00
		(Later pressings were reissued without "Goin' Back.")			

After several years of pop hits with Philips, Dusty Springfield spent the better part of 1967 and '68 doing soundtrack work in relative obscurity. In 1969, Dusty traveled to Chips Moman's American Sound Studios in Memphis to record Dusty In Memphis. This was all but ignored until a glowing review appeared in Rolling Stone, which was apparently laughed at by the magazine's editors when first submitted. With the blessing of the then hip bible, the album found a wider, more appreciative audience and is now generally considered one of the finest white female pop albums of the '60s.

Label & Catalog #		Title	Year	VG+	NM
Philips PHM-200-256	(M)	The Look Of Love	1967	10.00	25.00
Philips PHS-600-256	(S)	The Look Of Love	1967	12.00	30.00
Philips PHM-200-303	(M)	Everything's Coming Up Dusty	1967	10.00	25.00
Philips PHS-600-303	(S)	Everything's Coming Up Dusty	1967	12.00	30.00
Atlantic SD-8214	(S)	Dusty In Memphis	1969	12.00	30.00
		—Atlantic albums above have purple & brown labels.—			
Atlantic SD-8214	(S)	Dusty In Memphis	1969	6.00	15.00
Atlantic SD-8249	(S)	A Brand New Me	1970	6.00	15.00
		—Atlantic albums above have green & orange labels with 1841 Broadway, NYC address.—			
Dunhill DSX-50128	(S)	Cameo	1973	6.00	15.00
Dunhill DSX-50186	(S)	Longings	1973	*Unreleased*	
United Arts. LA791	(S)	It Begins Again	1978	6.00	15.00
United Arts. LA936	(S)	Living Without Your Love	1979	6.00	15.00
Casablanca 7271	(S)	White Heat	1982	5.00	12.00

SPRINGFIELD REVIVAL, THE

MGM SE-4905	(S)	The Springfield Revival	1973	4.00	10.00

SPRINGFIELD RIFLE

Burdette ST-5159	(S)	Springfield Rifle	1968	10.00	25.00

SPRINGFIELDS, THE
Tom and Dusty Springfield.

Philips PHM-200-052	(M)	Silver Threads And Golden Needles	1962	12.00	30.00
Philips PHS-600-052	(S)	Silver Threads And Golden Needles	1962	16.00	40.00
Philips PHM-200-076	(M)	Folksongs From The Hills	1963	12.00	30.00
Philips PHS-600-076	(S)	Folksongs From The Hills	1963	16.00	40.00

SPRINGSTEEN, BRUCE [BRUCE SPRINGSTEEN & THE E STREET BAND]

Columbia KC-31903	(S)	Greetings From Asbury Park	1973	6.00	15.00
Columbia PC-31903	(S)	Greetings From Asbury Park	1975	.80	4.00
Columbia KC-32432	(S)	Wild, The Innocent & The E Street Shuffle	1973	6.00	15.00
		(The title on the cover is in yellow print.)			
Columbia PC-32432	(S)	Wild, The Innocent & The E Street Shuffle	1975	.80	4.00
Columbia PC-33795	(DJ)	Born To Run *(Test pressing)*	1975	800.00	1,200.00
		(Advance copy with the title in script print on the cover and issued in a special mailing envelope with a letter of introduction from CBS and an orange patch, which are included in the price. Should any of these be missing the price drops dramatically.)			
Columbia PC-33795	(DJ)	Born To Run *(White label promo)*	1975	40.00	100.00
Columbia PC-33795	(S)	Born To Run	1975	10.00	25.00
		(Jon Landau's name is misspelled as "John" on the back cover.)			
Columbia PC-33795	(S)	Born To Run	1975	6.00	15.00
		(A strip with Landau's name is added to the back cover.)			
Columbia PC-33795	(S)	Born To Run	1975	1.00	5.00
		(Landau's name is printed on the back cover.)			
Columbia JC-33795	(S)	Born To Run	1977	.80	4.00
Columbia HC-33795	(S)	Born To Run *(Half-speed master)*	1980	20.00	50.00
Columbia HC-43795	(S)	Born To Run *(Half-speed master)*	1981	13.00	40.00
Columbia PAL-35318	(DJ)	Darkness On The Edge Of Town *(Pic. disc)*	1978	30.00	75.00
Columbia JC-35318	(DJ)	Darkness On The Edge Of Town	1978	40.00	100.00
Columbia JC-35318	(S)	Darkness On The Edge Of Town	1978	1.00	5.00
Columbia HC-45318	(S)	Darkness On The Edge Of Town *(Half-speed)*	1981	13.00	40.00
Columbia AS-978	(DJ)	As Requested Around The World	1981	20.00	50.00
Columbia FC2-36854	(DJ)	The River *(2 LPs. White label with letter)*	1980	30.00	75.00
		(WLPs were issued with a photocopied letter from CBS.)			
Columbia FC2-36854	(DJ)	The River *(2 LPs. White label without letter)*	1980	14.00	35.00
Columbia FC2-36854	(S)	The River *(2 LPs)*	1980	3.20	8.00
Columbia QC-38358	(S)	Nebraska	1982	1.00	5.00
Columbia QC-38653	(S)	Born In The U.S.A.	1984	1.00	5.00
Columbia AS-1957	(DJ)	Born In The U.S.A. *(5 song mini-LP)*	1985	12.00	30.00
Columbia AS-1957	(DJ)	Born In The U.S.A. *(5 song mini-LP)*	1987	6.00	15.00
		(Second pressings note so on the label.)			

SQUEEZE

A&M SP-4687	(S)	Squeeze *(Red vinyl promo)*	1978	6.00	15.00
A&M SP-4687	(S)	Squeeze	1978	1.20	6.00
A&M SP-4659	(S)	Cool For Cats	1979	1.20	6.00
A&M SP-3719	(S)	Squeeze *(10" LP)*	1980	4.00	10.00
A&M SP-4802	(S)	Argybargy	1980	1.20	6.00
A&M SP-4854	(S)	East Side Story	1981	1.20	6.00
A&M SP-4899	(S)	Sweets From A Stranger	1982	1.20	6.00
A&M SP-4922	(S)	Singles—45's And Under	1983	1.20	6.00

SRC

Capitol ST-2991	(S)	SRC	1968	24.00	60.00
Capitol ST-134	(S)	Milestones	1969	16.00	40.00
Capitol SKAO-273	(S)	Travellers Tale	1970	16.00	40.00

Even Bruce's best, Born To Run *and* Darkness On The Edge Of Town, *could not make the CBS Mastersound Half-Speed Mastered series a success. Using relatively poor quality vinyl and plating and compromised masters, the discs simply did not live up to the levels of quality that market demanded. But as audiophile-oriented consumers would discover, they were a sonic treat when compared to the initial CDs that were palmed off onto the market by CBS!*

Label & Catalog #		Title	Year	VG+	NM

STACKRIDGE

Decca DL-75317	(DJ)	**Stackridge**	1971	20.00	50.00
		(Special promo package with bonus single as part of the cover.)			
Decca DL-75317	(S)	**Stackridge**	1971	10.00	25.00
MCA 308	(S)	**Friendliness**	1973	4.00	10.00
Sire SASD-7503	(S)	**Pinafore Days**	1974	4.00	10.00
Sire SASD-7508	(S)	**Extravaganza**	1975	4.00	10.00
Rocket 3	(S)	**Mr. Mick**	1976	4.00	10.00

STAFFORD, TERRY

Terry can also be found on the soundtracks for Tower's "Dr Goldfoot & The Girl Bombs" and RCA's "Wild Wheels."

Crusader CLP-1001	(M)	**Suspicion!**	1964	20.00	50.00
Crusader CLP-1001S	(P)	**Suspicion!**	1964	30.00	75.00
Atlantic SD-7282	(S)	**Hey, Has Anybody Seen My Sweet Gypsy Rose**	1973	1.00	5.00

STAINED GLASS

Capitol ST-154	(S)	**Crazy Horse Roads**	1969	12.00	30.00
Capitol ST-242	(S)	**Aurora**	1969	20.00	50.00

STAMPEDERS, THE

Bell 6068	(S)	**Sweet City Woman**	1971	4.00	10.00
Capitol ST-11288	(S)	**From The Fire**	1973	1.00	5.00
Capitol ST-11328	(S)	**New Day**	1974	1.00	5.00
Private Stock 1001	(S)	**Hit The Road**	1976	1.00	5.00

STANDELLS, THE

The Standells feature Dick Dodd. They can also be found on the Tower soundtrack "Riot On Sunset Strip."

Liberty LRP-3384	(M)	**The Standells In Person At P.J.'s**	1964	20.00	50.00
Liberty LST-7384	(S)	**The Standells In Person At P.J.'s**	1964	30.00	75.00
Sunset SUM-1136	(M)	**Live And Out Of Sight**	1966	10.00	25.00
Sunset SUS-5136	(S)	**Live And Out Of Sight**	1966	12.00	30.00
		(The Sunset album is a reissue of the Liberty album.)			
Tower T-5027	(M)	**Dirty Water**	1966	20.00	50.00
Tower ST-5027	(P)	**Dirty Water**	1966	24.00	60.00
Tower T-5044	(M)	**Why Pick On Me**	1966	20.00	50.00
Tower ST-5044	(S)	**Why Pick On Me**	1966	24.00	60.00
Tower T-5049	(M)	**Hot Ones**	1966	16.00	40.00
Tower ST-5049	(S)	**Hot Ones**	1966	20.00	50.00
Tower T-5098	(M)	**Try It**	1967	20.00	50.00
Tower ST-5098	(S)	**Try It**	1967	24.00	60.00
Rhino RNLP-107	(S)	**The Best Of The Standells**	1983	.80	4.00
Rhino RNLP-115	(S)	**Rarities**	1983	.80	4.00

STANLEY, PAUL: *Refer to* **KISS**

STANLEY STEAMER

Jolly Roger 5002	(S)	**Stanley Steamer**	1973	4.00	10.00

STAPLE SINGERS, THE [THE STAPLES]

The Staples are Roebuck "Pop" Staples with daughters Cleo, Mavis and Yvonne. They can be found on soundtracks for U.A.'s "The Landlord" and Atlantic's "Soul To Soul." Refer to Albert King & Steve Cropper & Pop Staples.

Vee Jay LP-5000	(M)	**Uncloudy Day**	1959	14.00	35.00
Vee Jay LPS-5000	(S)	**Uncloudy Day**	1959	20.00	50.00
Vee Jay LP-5008	(M)	**Will The Circle Be Unbroken**	196?	14.00	35.00
Vee Jay LPS-5008	(S)	**Will The Circle Be Unbroken**	196?	20.00	50.00
Vee Jay LP-5014	(M)	**Swing Low**	196?	14.00	35.00
Vee Jay LPS-5014	(S)	**Swing Low**	196?	20.00	50.00
Vee Jay LP-5019	(M)	**The Best Of The Staples**	196?	12.00	30.00
Vee Jay LPS-5019	(S)	**The Best Of The Staples**	196?	16.00	40.00
Vee Jay LP-5030	(M)	**Swing Low, Sweet Chariot**	196?	12.00	30.00
Vee Jay LPS-5030	(S)	**Swing Low, Sweet Chariot**	196?	16.00	40.00
Epic LN-24132	(M)	**Amen**	1966	12.00	30.00
Epic LN-26132	(S)	**Amen**	1966	16.00	40.00
Epic LN-24163	(M)	**Freedom Highway**	1966	12.00	30.00
Epic BN-26163	(S)	**Freedom Highway**	1966	16.00	40.00
Epic LN-24196	(M)	**Why**	1966	12.00	30.00
Epic LN-26196	(S)	**Why**	1966	16.00	40.00
Epic LN-24332	(M)	**For What It's Worth**	1967	10.00	25.00
Epic BN-26332	(S)	**For What It's Worth**	1967	12.00	30.00
Stax STS-2004	(S)	**Soul Folk In Action**	1968	12.00	30.00
Buddah BDS-2009	(S)	**The Best Of The Staple Singers**	1969	6.00	15.00
Buddah BDS-7508	(S)	**Will The Circle Be Unbroken**	1969	6.00	15.00
Epic EG-30635	(S)	**The Staple Singers Make You Happy** *(2 LPs)*	1971	6.00	15.00
Stax STS-2016	(S)	**We'll Get Over**	1971	8.00	20.00
Stax STS-2034	(S)	**The Staple Swingers**	1971	8.00	20.00
Stax STS-3002	(S)	**Beatitude: Respect Yourself**	1972	8.00	20.00
Stax STS-3015	(S)	**Be What You Are**	1973	8.00	20.00
Stax STS-5515	(S)	**City In The Sky**	1974	8.00	20.00

Label & Catalog #		Title	Year	VG+	NM
Stax STS-5523	(S)	The Best Of The Staple Singers	1974	6.00	15.00
Curtom 5005	(S)	Let's Do It Again	1975	4.00	10.00
Warner Bros 2945	(S)	Pass It On	1976	4.00	10.00

STAPLES, MAVIS
Mavis originally recorded with The Staple Singers above.

Volt VO-6007	(M)	Mavis Staples (White label promo)	1969	12.00	30.00
Volt VOS-6007	(S)	Mavis Staples	1969	8.00	20.00
Volt VO-6010	(M)	Only For The Lonely (White label promo)	1970	12.00	30.00
Volt VOS-6010	(S)	Only For The Lonely	1970	8.00	20.00

STARCASTLE

Epic PE-33914	(S)	Starcastle	1976	4.00	10.00
Epic PE-34375	(S)	Fountains Of Light	1977	4.00	10.00
Epic PE-34935	(S)	Citadel	1977	4.00	10.00
Epic PE-34935	(DJ)	Citadel (Picture disc)	1977	8.00	20.00
Epic PE-35???	(S)	Real To Reel	1978	4.00	10.00

STARDRIVE

Elektra EKS-75058	(S)	Intergalactic Trot	1973	3.20	8.00
Elektra EQ-5058	(Q)	Intergalactic Trot	1973	6.00	15.00
Columbia PC-33047	(S)	Stardrive	1974	3.20	8.00

STARK NAKED

RCA Victor LSP-4592	(S)	Stark Naked	1971	10.00	25.00

STARR, EDWIN

Gordy G-931	(M)	Soul Master (White label promo)	1968	12.00	30.00
Gordy GS-931	(S)	Soul Master	1968	8.00	20.00
		("Agent Double-O Soul" is rechanneled)			
Gordy GS-940	(S)	25 Miles	1969	8.00	20.00
Gordy GS-948	(S)	War And Peace	1970	8.00	20.00
Gordy GS-956	(S)	Involved	1971	8.00	20.00
Motown M-802	(S)	Hell Up In Harlem	1973	6.00	15.00
Motown M5-103V	(S)	Superstar Series, Vol. 3	1980	.80	4.00
Motown M5-170V	(S)	War And Peace	1981	.80	4.00
20th Cent.-Fox T-538	(S)	Edwin Starr	1977	1.00	5.00
20th Cent.-Fox T-559	(S)	Clean	1978	1.00	5.00
20th Cent.-Fox T-591	(S)	H.A.P.P.Y. Radio	1980	1.00	5.00
20th Cent.-Fox T-625	(S)	Ear Candy	1980	1.00	5.00
20th Cent.-Fox T-634	(S)	The Best Of Edwin Starr	1981	1.00	5.00

STARR, EDWIN, & BLINKY

Gordy GS-945	(S)	Just We Two	1969	8.00	20.00

STARR, RINGO
Richard Starkey, a.k.a. Ringo Starr, was the under-rated drummer with the greatest rock band the world will ever know. Refer to Badfinger; The Band; Leon Russell; Doris Troy.

Apple SW-3365	(S)	Sentimental Journey	1970	8.00	20.00
Apple SMAS-3368	(S)	Beaucoups Of Blues	1970	8.00	20.00
Apple SWAL-3413	(S)	Ringo	1973	200.00	400.00
		(First pressings of SWAL-3413 contain a longer, 5:26 version of "Six O' Clock." The record must be listened to for identification The cover incorrectly lists the second song as "Hold On.")			
Apple SWAL-3413	(S)	Ringo	1973	6.00	15.00
		(Second pressings contain a shorter version of "Six O' Clock." The cover incorrectly lists the second song as "Hold On.")			
Apple SWAL-3413	(S)	Ringo	197?	16.00	40.00
		(Later covers correctly list the song as "Have You Seen My Baby.")			
Apple SW-3417	(S)	Goodnight Vienna	1974	6.00	15.00
Apple SW-3422	(S)	Blast From Your Past	1975	6.00	15.00
Atlantic SD-18193	(S)	Ringo's Rotogravure (Promo)	1978	16.00	40.00
		(Promos for SD-18193 are standard copies of the album with "DJ only" etched in trail-off vinyl.)			
Atlantic SD-18193	(S)	Ringo's Rotogravure	1978	4.00	10.00
Atlantic SD-19108	(S)	Ringo The 4th (Promo)	1978	16.00	40.00
		(Promos for SD-19108 are standard copies of the album with "DJ only" etched in trail-off vinyl.)			
Atlantic SD-19108	(S)	Ringo The 4th	1978	4.00	10.00
Portrait JR-35378	(DJ)	Bad Boy	1978	40.00	100.00
		(White label with "Advance Promotion" issued in a plain white cover.)			
Portrait JR-35378	(DJ)	Bad Boy	1978	10.00	25.00
		(White label with "Demonstration" issued in regular cover.)			
Portrait JR-35378	(S)	Bad Boy	1978	3.20	8.00
Capitol SW-3365	(S)	Sentimental Journey	1978	16.00	40.00
Capitol SN-16114	(S)	Ringo	1978	8.00	20.00
Capitol SN-16218	(S)	Sentimental Journey	1978	10.00	25.00
Capitol SN-16219	(S)	Goodnight Vienna	1978	10.00	25.00

Label & Catalog #		Title	Year	VG+	NM
Capitol SN-16235	(S)	Beaucoups Of Blues	1978	10.00	25.00
Capitol SN-16236	(S)	Blast From Your Past	1978	6.00	15.00
		—Capitol albums above have green labels.—			
Boardwalk NB1-33246	(DJ)	Stop And Smell The Roses	1981	40.00	100.00
Boardwalk NB1-33246	(S)	Stop And Smell The Roses	1981	4.00	10.00
Rhino R11G-70199	(S)	Starr Struck (Ringo's Best 1976-1983)	1989	8.00	20.00
Rykodisc RALP-0190	(S)	Ringo & His All-Star Band (Clear vinyl)	1990	12.00	30.00
		(Limited edition sequentially numbered through #5000.)			

STARZ

Capitol ST-11539	(S)	Starz	1976	4.00	10.00
Capitol ST-11617	(DJ)	Violation (Yellow vinyl)	1977	8.00	20.00
Capitol ST-11617	(S)	Violation	1977	4.00	10.00
Capitol ST-11730	(S)	Attention Shoppers	1978	4.00	10.00
Capitol SPRO-8857/58	(DJ)	Live In Louisville	1978	12.00	30.00
Capitol ST-11861	(S)	Coliseum Rock	1978	4.00	10.00

STATUS CYMBAL

RCA Victor LSP-3993	(S)	In The Morning	1968	6.00	15.00

STATUS QUO, THE

Cadet Concept LPS-315	(E)	Messages From The Status Quo	1968	20.00	50.00
Janus JLS-3018	(S)	Ma Kelly's Greasy Spoon	1971	6.00	15.00
Pye 3301	(S)	Dog Of Two Heads	1972	6.00	15.00
A&M SP-3615	(S)	Hello!	1973	4.00	10.00
A&M SP-3649	(S)	Quo	1973	4.00	10.00
		—A&M albums above have brown labels.—			
A&M SP-4381	(S)	Piledriver	1974	1.00	5.00
A&M SP-4408	(S)	Hello!	1974	1.00	5.00
Capitol ST-11381	(S)	On The Level	1974	1.00	5.00
Capitol ST-11509	(S)	Status Quo	1976	1.00	5.00
Capitol STBB-11623	(S)	Status Quo "Live" (2 LPs)	1977	1.20	6.00
Capitol ST-11749	(S)	Rockin' All Over The World	1979	1.00	5.00
Riva 7402	(S)	Now Hear This	1981	1.00	5.00

STEALERS WHEEL

A&M SP-4377	(S)	Stealers Wheel	1973	1.00	5.00
A&M SP-4419	(S)	Ferguslie Park	1973	1.00	5.00
A&M SP-4517	(S)	Right Or Wrong	1974	1.00	5.00

STEAM

Mercury SR-61254	(S)	Steam	1969	4.00	10.00

STEAMHAMMER

Epic BN-26490	(S)	Reflection	1969	12.00	30.00
Epic BN-26552	(S)	Steamhammer	1970	10.00	25.00

STEAMPACKET

Steampacket features a pre-Jeff Beck Rod Stewart.

Springboard SPB-4063	(S)	Rod Stewart And Steampacket	1972	3.20	8.00

STEEL

Epic KE-30875	(S)	Steel	1971	10.00	25.00

STEEL RIVER

Evolution 2018	(S)	Weighin' Heavy	1970	5.00	12.00
Evolution 3006	(S)	A Better Road	1971	5.00	12.00

STEELEYE SPAN

Steeleye Span was formed by Ashley Hutchings, formerly of Fairport Convention. Refer to The Bunch.

Big Tree BTS-2004	(S)	Please To See The King	1971	12.00	30.00
		(Original copies of BTS-2004 have the matrix numbers stamped in the trail-off vinyl. Counterfeits have those numbers hand-etched.)			
Chrysalis CHR-1008	(S)	Below The Salt	1972	6.00	15.00
Chrysalis CHR-1046	(S)	Parcel Of Rogues	1973	6.00	15.00
Chrysalis CHR-1053	(S)	Now We Are Six	1974	6.00	15.00
Chrysalis CHR-1071	(S)	Commoners Crown	1975	6.00	15.00
Chrysalis CHR-1091	(S)	All Around My Hat	1975	6.00	15.00
Chrysalis CHR-1120	(S)	Hark The Village Wait	1976	6.00	15.00
Chrysalis CHR-1119	(S)	Please To See The King	1976	6.00	15.00
Chrysalis CHR-1121	(S)	Ten Man Mop	1976	6.00	15.00
Chrysalis CHR-1123	(S)	Rocket Cottage	1976	6.00	15.00
Chrysalis CHR-2-1136	(S)	The Steeleye Span Story (2 LPs)	1977	6.00	15.00
Chrysalis CHR-1151	(S)	Storm Force Ten	1978	5.00	12.00
Chrysalis CHR-1199	(S)	Live At Last	1978	5.00	12.00
Takoma 7097	(S)	Sails Of Silver	1981	4.00	10.00

Label & Catalog #		Title	Year	VG+	NM

STEELY DAN
Originally, Steely Dan was Walter Becker and Donald Fagen with Jeff Baxter, Denny Dias, and Jim Hodder. By 1975, the group was Becker and Fagen with hired studio assistance.

Label & Catalog #		Title	Year	VG+	NM
ABC X-758	(S)	**Can't Buy A Thrill**	1972	1.00	5.00
ABC X-779	(S)	**Countdown To Ecstasy**	1973	1.00	5.00
ABC D-808	(S)	**Pretzel Logic**	1974	1.00	5.00
ABC X-846	(S)	**Katy Lied**	1975	1.00	5.00
ABC D-931	(S)	**The Royal Scam**	1976	1.00	5.00
ABC AA-1006	(S)	**Aja**	1977	1.00	5.00
ABC AK-1107	(S)	**Greatest Hits** (2 LPs)	1978	1.00	5.00
Command QD-40009	(Q)	**Can't Buy A Thrill**	1974	6.00	15.00
Command QD-40010	(Q)	**Countdown To Ecstasy**	1974	6.00	15.00
Command QD-40015	(Q)	**Pretzel Logic**	1974	6.00	15.00
MCA 37040	(S)	**Can't Buy A Thrill**	1980	.80	4.00
MCA 37041	(S)	**Countdown To Ecstasy**	1980	.80	4.00
MCA 37042	(S)	**Pretzel Logic**	1980	.80	4.00
MCA 37043	(S)	**Katy Lied**	1980	.80	4.00
MCA 37044	(S)	**The Royal Scam**	1980	.80	4.00
MCA 1006	(S)	**Aja**	1980	.80	4.00
MCA 1107	(S)	**Greatest Hits** (2 LPs)	1980	.80	4.00
MCA 6102	(S)	**Gaucho**	1980	.80	4.00
MCA 16009	(S)	**Gaucho** (Half-speed master)	198?	12.00	36.00
MCA 5324	(S)	**Steely Dan Gold**	1982	.80	4.00
MCA 160??	(S)	**Steely Dan Gold** (Half-speed master)	198?	15.00	45.00

STEEPLECHASE

Polydor 24-4027	(S)	**Lady Bright**	1970	6.00	15.00

STEIN, MARK, & THE PIGEONS
Mark Stein is the former lead singer for Vanilla Fudge.

Wand WDS-687	(S)	**While The World Was Eating Vanilla Fudge**	1968	10.00	25.00

STEPHEN & THE FARM BAND: *Refer to* **THE FARM BAND**

STEPHENS, LEIGH
Leigh Stevens was a member of Blue Cheer.

Phillips PHS-600-294	(S)	**Red Weather**	1969	30.00	75.00

STEPPENWOLF
Steppenwolf was John Kay, Jerry Edmonton, Goldy McJohn, Michael Monarch, and Rushton Moreve, who had previously recorded as Sparrow. In 1967, Moreve was replaced by John Morgan, after which personnel changes were constant. They can also be found on the soundtracks to Dunhill's "Easy Rider" and ABC's "Candy."

Dunhill D-50029	(M)	**Steppenwolf**	1968	60.00	150.00
Dunhill DS-50029	(S)	**Steppenwolf**	1968	10.00	25.00
		—Dunhill albums above read "A Subsidiary of ABC Records" on the bottom of the label.—			
Dunhill DS-50029	(S)	**Steppenwolf**	1969	3.20	8.00
Dunhill D-50037	(M)	**The Second**	1968		*Released?*
Dunhill DS-50037	(S)	**The Second** (Chrome border cover)	1968	10.00	25.00
Dunhill DS-50037	(S)	**The Second** (White border cover)	196?	12.00	30.00
Dunhill DSX-50053	(S)	**At Your Birthday Party**	1969	3.20	8.00
Dunhill DSX-50060	(S)	**Early Steppenwolf**	1969	3.20	8.00
		("Early Steppenwolf" is actually a 1967 concert by Sparrow.)			
Dunhill DSX-50066	(S)	**Monster**	1969	3.20	8.00
Dunhill DSD-50075	(S)	**Steppenwolf Live** (2 LPs)	1970	4.00	10.00
Dunhill DSX-50090	(S)	**Steppenwolf 7**	1970	3.20	8.00
Dunhill DSX-50099	(S)	**Gold/Their Greatest Hits**	1970	3.20	8.00
Dunhill DSX-50110	(S)	**For Ladies Only**	1971	3.20	8.00
Dunhill DSX-50124	(S)	**Steppenwolf 1967-1972/Rest In Peace**	1972	3.20	8.00
Dunhill DSX-50135	(S)	**Sixteen Greatest Hits**	1973	3.20	8.00
		—Dunhill albums above have black labels with "Dunhill/ABC" on top and "Dunhill Records is a subsidiary" on the bottom.—			
ABC 30008	(S)	**The ABC Collection**	197?	1.00	5.00
ABC 4011	(S)	**16 Great Performances**	197?	1.00	5.00
ABC 5007	(S)	**Steppenwolf Live** (2 LPs)	197?	1.20	6.00
ABC 8613	(S)	**Gold/Their Greatest Hits**	197?	1.00	5.00
MCA 37045	(S)	**Steppenwolf**	197?	.80	4.00
MCA 37046	(S)	**The Second**	197?	.80	4.00
MCA 37047	(S)	**Steppenwolf 7**	197?	.80	4.00
MCA 37049	(S)	**Sixteen Greatest Hits**	197?	.80	4.00
Epic PE-33093	(S)	**Slow Flux**	1974	1.00	5.00
Epic PE-33583	(S)	**Hour Of The Wolf**	1975	1.00	5.00
Epic PE-34120	(S)	**Skullduggery**	1976	1.00	5.00
Epic PE-34382	(S)	**Reborn To Be Wild**	1977	1.00	5.00
Pickwick 3603	(S)	**Best Of Steppenwolf**	197?	1.00	5.00
Columbia P-14767	(S)	**Wild Gold** (Special Products)	197?	1.00	5.00

Label & Catalog #		Title	Year	VG+	NM

STEVENS, CAT

Deram DE-18005	(M)	Matthew And Son	1967	6.00	15.00
Deram DES-18005	(P)	Matthew And Son	1967	6.00	15.00
Deram DES-18010	(S)	New Masters	1968	6.00	15.00
Deram DES-18005/10	(P)	Matthew And Son/New Masters (2 LPs)	1971	1.20	6.00
Deram DES-18061	(E)	Very Young And Early Songs	1971	1.00	5.00
London LC-5000	(S)	Cat's Cradle	1977	1.00	5.00
A&M SP-4260	(S)	Mona Bone Jakon	1970	4.00	10.00
A&M SP-4280	(S)	Tea For The Tillerman	1971	4.00	10.00
A&M SP-4313	(S)	Teaser And The Firecat	1971	4.00	10.00
A&M SP-4365	(S)	Catch Bull At Four	1972	4.00	10.00
		—A&M albums above have brown labels.—			
A&M SP-4260	(S)	Mona Bone Jakon	197?	.80	4.00
A&M SP-4280	(S)	Tea For The Tillerman	197?	.80	4.00
A&M QU-54280	(Q)	Tea For The Tillerman	1974	6.00	15.00
A&M SP-4313	(S)	Teaser And The Firecat	197?	.80	4.00
A&M QU-54313	(Q)	Teaser And The Firecat	1974	6.00	15.00
A&M SP-4365	(S)	Catch Bull At Four	197?	.80	4.00
A&M QU-54365	(Q)	Catch Bull At Four	1974	6.00	15.00
A&M SP-4391	(S)	Foreigner	1973	.80	4.00
A&M QU-54391	(Q)	Foreigner	1974	6.00	15.00
A&M SP-3623	(S)	Buddha And The Chocolate Box	1974	.80	4.00
A&M QU-53623	(Q)	Buddha And The Chocolate Box	1974	6.00	15.00
A&M SP-4519	(S)	Greatest Hits	1975	.80	4.00
A&M QU-54519	(Q)	Greatest Hits	1975	4.00	10.00
A&M SP-4555	(S)	Numbers	1975	.80	4.00
A&M SP-4702	(S)	Izitso	1977	.80	4.00
A&M SP-4735	(S)	Back To Earth	1978	.80	4.00
A&M SP-3736	(S)	Footsteps In The Dark	1984	.80	4.00

STEWARD, ALEC

Bluesville BVLP-1076	(M)	Creepin' Blues	1963	30.00	75.00
		—Bluesville albums above have bright blue labels with silver print.—			
Bluesville BVLP-1076	(M)	Creepin' Blues	1964	10.00	25.00
		—Bluesville albums above have blue labels with a trident logo on the right side.—			

STEWART, AL

Epic BN-26564	(S)	Love Chronicles	1970	4.00	10.00
		—Epic albums above have yellow labels.—			
Janus 3063	(S)	Past, Present And Future	1974	1.00	5.00
Janus 7012	(S)	Modern Times	1975	1.00	5.00
Janus 7022	(S)	Year Of The Cat	1976	1.00	5.00
Janus 7026	(S)	The Early Years (2 LPs)	1977	1.00	5.00
Arista AL-4190	(S)	Time Passages	1978	.80	4.00
Arista AL-9520	(S)	24 Carrots	1980	.80	4.00
Arista AL-9523	(S)	Year Of The Cat	1980	.80	4.00
Arista AL-9524	(S)	Modern Times	1980	.80	4.00
Arista AL-9525	(S)	Past, Present And Future	1980	.80	4.00
Arista SP-40	(DJ)	The Live Radio Concert	1980	16.00	40.00
Arista A2L-8607	(S)	Live/Indian Summer (2 LPs)	1981	1.00	5.00

STEWART, BILLY

Chess LP-1496	(M)	I Do Love You	1965	40.00	100.00
Chess LPS-1496	(S)	I Do Love You	1965	60.00	150.00
		(Original covers for Chess 1496 are red with a black wheel design.)			
Chess LP-1496	(M)	I Do Love You	1965	20.00	50.00
Chess LPS-1496	(S)	I Do Love You	1965	30.00	75.00
		(Later pressings have a green cover with a woman at the bottom.)			
Chess LP-1499	(M)	Unbelievable	1965	20.00	50.00
Chess LPS-1499	(S)	Unbelievable	1965	30.00	75.00
Chess LP-1499	(M)	Summertime	1966	20.00	50.00
Chess LPS-1499	(S)	Summertime	1966	30.00	75.00
		("Summertime" is a retitled reissue of "Unbelievable.")			
Chess LP-1513	(M)	Billy Stewart Teaches Old Standards New Tricks	1967	16.00	40.00
Chess LPS-1513	(S)	Billy Stewart Teaches Old Standards New Tricks	1967	20.00	50.00
Chess LPS-1547	(S)	Billy Stewart Remembered	1968	12.00	30.00
		—Chess albums above have blue & white labels.—			

STEWART, JOHN

John Stewart is a guitar and banjo player, singer and writer of contemporary folk-based pop music and a former member of The Cumberland Three and The Kingston Trio.

Capitol T-2975	(M)	Signals Through The Glass	1968	12.00	30.00
Capitol ST-2975	(S)	Signals Through The Glass	1968	8.00	20.00
Capitol ST-203	(S)	California Bloodlines	1969	6.00	15.00
		—Capitol albums above have black "rainbow" labels.—			
Capitol ST-540	(S)	Willard	1970	6.00	15.00
		—Capitol albums above have green labels.—			
Capitol SM-2975	(S)	Signals Through The Glass	1975	.80	4.00

Label & Catalog #		Title	Year	VG+	NM
Capitol SM-203	(S)	California Bloodlines	1975	.80	4.00
Capitol SN-11987	(S)	California Bloodlines	1979	.80	4.00
Capitol SN-11988	(S)	Signals Through The Glass	1979	.80	4.00
Capitol SN-11989	(S)	Willard	1979	.80	4.00
Capitol SN-116150	(S)	California Bloodlines	1982	.80	4.00
Warner Bros. WS-1948	(S)	The Lonesome Picker Rides Again	1971	4.00	10.00
Warner Bros. BS-2611	(S)	Sunstorm	1972	4.00	10.00
RCA Victor LSP-4827	(S)	Cannons In Tne Rain	1973	3.20	8.00
RCA Victor CPL2-0265	(S)	The Phoenix Concerts-Live (2 LPs)	1974	4.00	10.00
RCA Victor APL1-0816	(S)	Wingless Angels	1975	1.00	5.00
RSO RS-3027	(S)	Fire In The Wind	1980	.80	4.00
RSO RS-3051	(S)	Bombs Away Dream Babies	1980	.80	4.00
RSO RS-3074	(S)	Dream Babies Go Hollywood	1980	.80	4.00
RCA Victor AFL1-3513	(S)	In Concert	1980	.80	4.00
		(RCA 3513 is a repackage of portions of 0265 with two outtakes from that project.)			
RCA Victor AYL1-3731	(S)	Cannons In Tne Rain	1981	.80	4.00
Camden ACL-7080	(S)	Wingless Angels	1980	.80	4.00
Allegiance AV-431	(S)	Blondes	1982	.80	4.00
Affordable Dreams AD-01	(S)	Trancas	1984	.80	4.00
Homecoming HC-00200	(S)	Centennial	1984	.80	4.00
Homecoming HC-00300	(S)	The Last Campaign	1985	.80	4.00

STEWART, JOHN, & NICK REYNOLDS

Takoma TAK-7106	(S)	Revenge Of The Budgie	1983	.80	4.00

STEWART, ROD

Refer to Steampacket; The Jeff Beck Group; The Faces.

Mercury SR-61237	(S)	The Rod Stewart Album	1969	10.00	25.00
		(Original covers for 61237 are yellow without a black border.)			
Mercury SR-61237	(S)	The Rod Stewart Album	197?	1.00	5.00
		(Later covers are yellow with a black border.)			
Mercury SR-61264	(S)	Gasoline Alley	1970	6.00	15.00
		(Original covers for 61264 are textured, especially on the pebbles.)			
Mercury SR-61264	(S)	Gasoline Alley	197?	1.00	5.00
		(Later covers are smooth without the textured pebbles.)			
Mercury SRM-1-609	(S)	Every Picture Tells A Story	1971	3.20	8.00
		(Original gatefold cover opens out into a tri-fold poster.)			
Mercury SRM-1-646	(S)	Never A Dull Moment (Gatefold cover)	1972	3.20	8.00
		—Mercury albums above have red labels with twelve logos around the perimeter.—			
Mercury SR-61237	(S)	The Rod Stewart Album	197?	.80	4.00
Mercury SR-61264	(S)	Gasoline Alley	197?	.80	4.00
Mercury SRM-1-609	(S)	Every Picture Tells A Story	197?	.80	4.00
Mercury SRM-1-646	(S)	Never A Dull Moment (Gatefold cover)	197?	.80	4.00
Mercury SRM-1-680	(S)	Sing It Again, Rod	1973	1.00	5.00
Mercury SRM-1-697	(S)	Rod Stewart/Faces Live: Coast To Coast Overture And Beginners	1974	1.00	5.00
Mercury SRM-1-1017	(S)	Smiler	1974	1.00	5.00
Mercury SRM-2-7507	(S)	Best Of Rod Stewart (2 LPs)	1976	1.00	5.00
Mercury SRM-2-7509	(S)	Best Of Rod Stewart, Volume 2 (2 LPs)	1977	1.00	5.00
		—Mercury albums above have red labels with seven logos around the perimeter.—			
Trip TOP-16-31	(S)	Looking Back/16 Early Hits	1974	1.00	5.00
Private Stock PS-2021	(S)	A Shot Of Rhythm & Blues	1976	3.20	8.00
Springboard SPB-4030	(S)	Rod Stewart And The Faces	197?	1.00	5.00
Warner Bros. BS-2875	(S)	Atlantic Crossing (Gatefold cover)	1975	.80	4.00
Warner Bros. BS-2938	(S)	A Night On The Town	1976	.80	4.00
Warner Bros. BSK-3092	(S)	Foot Loose & Fancy Free	1977	.80	4.00
Warner Bros. BSK-3108	(S)	Atlantic Crossing	1977	.80	4.00
Warner Bros. BSK-3116	(S)	A Night On The Town	1977	.80	4.00
Warner Bros. BSK-3261	(S)	Blondes Have More Fun	1978	.80	4.00
Warner Bros. BSP-3276	(S)	Blondes Have More Fun (Picture disc)	1979	4.00	10.00
Warner Bros. HS-3373	(S)	Rod Stewart's Greatest Hits	1979	.80	4.00
Warner Bros. HS-3485	(S)	Foolish Behavior	1980	.80	4.00
Warner Bros. BSK-3602	(S)	Tonight I'm Yours	1981	.80	4.00
Warner Bros. 1-23473	(S)	Absolutely Live	1982	.80	4.00
Warner Bros. 1-23473	(DJ)	Absolutely Live (2 LPs. Quiex II vinyl)	1982	10.00	25.00
Warner Bros. 1-23877	(S)	Body Wishes	1983	.80	4.00
Warner Bros. 1-25095	(S)	Camouflage	1984	.80	4.00
		(There are sixteen known back covers for 25095 that form a giant poster of Rod.)			
Warner Bros. 1-25446	(S)	Rod Stewart	1986	.80	4.00
Warner Bros. 1-25684	(S)	Out Of Order	1988	.80	4.00
Warner Bros. 1-25987	(S)	Storyteller	1989	.80	4.00
Warner Bros. 1-26158	(S)	Downtown Train	1990	.80	4.00
Warner Bros. 1-26300	(S)	Vagabond Heart	1991	.80	4.00
Accord SN-7142	(S)	Rod The Mod	1981	.80	4.00

Label & Catalog #		Title	Year	VG+	NM

STIDHAM, ARBEE

| Bluesville BVLP-1021 | (M) | Tired Of Wandering | 1961 | 40.00 | 100.00 |

—Bluesville albums above have bright blue labels with silver print.—

| Bluesville BVLP-1021 | (M) | Tired Of Wandering | 1964 | 12.00 | 30.00 |

—Bluesville albums above have blue labels with a trident logo on the right side.—

| Mainstream MRL-360 | (S) | Time For Blues | 1972 | 4.00 | 10.00 |

STILLROCK

| Enterprise ENS-1016 | (S) | Stillrock | 1971 | 6.00 | 15.00 |

STILLS, STEPHEN [STEPHEN STILLS & MANASSAS]

Mr Stills gained his initial fame as a member of Buffalo Springfield. Refer to The Au Go Go Singers; Mike Bloomfield, Al Kooper & Steve Stills; Crosby, Stills & Nash; Crosby, Stills, Nash & Young.

Atlantic SD-7202	(S)	Stephen Stills	1970	1.00	5.00
Atlantic SD-7206	(S)	Stephen Stills 2	1971	1.00	5.00
Atlantic SD-2-903	(S)	Manassas (2 LPs)	1972	1.20	6.00
Atlantic SD-7250	(S)	Down The Road (With Manassas)	1973	1.00	5.00

—Atlantic albums above have orange & green labels with an 1841 Broadway address.—

Atlantic SD-18156	(S)	Stephen Stills Live	1975	.80	4.00
Atlantic SD-18201	(S)	Still Stills—The Best Of Stephen Stills	1976	.80	4.00
Columbia PC-33575	(S)	Stills	1975	.80	4.00
Columbia PCQ-33575	(Q)	Stills	1975	4.00	10.00
Columbia PC-34148	(S)	Illegal Stills	1976	.80	4.00
Columbia JC-35380	(S)	Thoroughfare Gap	1978	.80	4.00
Atlantic 25343	(S)	Right By You	1984	.80	4.00
Gold Hill/Vision 3323	(S)	Stills Alone	1991	.80	4.00

STILLS-YOUNG BAND, THE

Stephen Stills and Neil Young.

| Reprise MS-2253 | (S) | Long May You Run | 1976 | .80 | 4.00 |

STINGERS, THE

| Crown CLP-5476 | (M) | Guitars A Go Go | 196? | 12.00 | 30.00 |
| Crown CST-476 | (S) | Guitars A Go Go | 196? | 16.00 | 40.00 |

STITES, GARY

| Carlton LP-120 | (M) | Lonely For You | 1960 | 30.00 | 75.00 |
| Carlton STLP-120 | (S) | Lonely For You | 1960 | 50.00 | 125.00 |

STOECKLEIN, VAL

Val Stoecklein originally recorded with The Blue Things.

| Dot DLP-????? | (S) | Grey Life | 1968 | 8.00 | 20.00 |

STOKES, SIMON

MGM SE04677	(S)	Simon Stokes & The Nighthawks	1970	4.00	10.00
Spindizzy KZ-32075	(S)	The Incredible Simon Stokes & The Black Whip Thrill Band	1973	4.00	10.00
United Arts. LA-769	(S)	The Buzzard Of Love	1977	4.00	10.00

STOMPERS, THE: *Refer to DICK DALE / THE STOMPERS*

STONE, ROLAND

| Ace LP-1018 | (M) | Just A Moment | 1961 | 60.00 | 150.00 |

STONE CIRCUS, THE

| Mainstream S-6119 | (S) | The Stone Circus | 1969 | 20.00 | 50.00 |

STONE COUNTRY

| RCA Victor LSP-3958 | (S) | Stone Country | 1968 | 6.00 | 15.00 |

STONE PILLOW

| London SP-44129 | (S) | Eleazar's Circus | 1969 | 5.00 | 12.00 |

STONE PONEYS, THE: *Refer to LINDA RONSTADT & THE STONE PONEYS*

STONE THE CROWS

Polydor 24-4019	(S)	Stone The Crows	1970	8.00	20.00
Polydor 24-5020	(S)	Teenage Licks	1972	6.00	15.00
Polydor 24-5037	(S)	Continuous Performance	1972	6.00	15.00

STONEGROUND

Stoneground features Sal Valentino. Refer to The Beau Brummels.

Warner Bros. WS-1895	(S)	Stoneground	1971	4.00	10.00
Warner Bros. 2ZS-1956	(S)	Family Album (2 LPs)	1971	6.00	15.00
Warner Bros. BS-2645	(S)	Stoneground 3	1972	6.00	15.00
Flat Out 101	(S)	Flat Out	1976	4.00	10.00

The quite psychedelic Strawberry Alarm Clock members were adamantly opposed to waxing the bubblegummy "Incense And Peppermints." The song finally made it onto tape with the lead vocals of a guest at the sessions! While the group then managed to gain control of its future, it never recaptured the success of the single that they didn't want to record.

Label & Catalog #		Title	Year	VG+	NM
STONEHILL, RANDY					
One Way JC-31252	(S)	**Born Twice**	1972	**20.00**	**50.00**
Solid Rock SRA-2002	(S)	**Welcome To Paradise**	1976	**4.00**	**10.00**
Solid Rock SRA-2005	(S)	**The Sky Is Falling**	1980	**6.00**	**15.00**
Myrrh MSB-6679	(S)	**Between The Glory And The Flame**	1981	**4.00**	**10.00**
STONEY & MEAT LOAF					
This Meat Loaf is the Meat Loaf.					
Rare Earth R-528	(S)	**Stoney And Meat Loaf**	1971	**6.00**	**15.00**
Prodigal 10	(S)	**Stoney And Meat Loaf**	1978	**1.00**	**5.00**
		(Prodigal 10 is a reissue of Rare Earth 5281.)			
STOOGES, THE					
The Stooges feature Iggy Pop.					
Elektra EKS-74051	(S)	**The Stooges** (White label promo)	1969	**60.00**	**150.00**
Elektra EKS-74051	(S)	**The Stooges**	1969	**20.00**	**50.00**
Elektra EKS-74101	(S)	**Fun House** (White label promo)	1970	**60.00**	**150.00**
Elektra EKS-74101	(S)	**Fun House**	1970	**20.00**	**50.00**
		—Elektra albums above have red labels.—			
Elektra EKS-74051	(S)	**The Stooges**	197?	**8.00**	**20.00**
Elektra EKS-74101	(S)	**Fun House**	197?	**8.00**	**20.00**
		—Elektra albums above have butterfly labels.—			
Columbia KC-32111	(S)	**Raw Power** (With inner sleeve)	1973	**20.00**	**50.00**
Import 1015	(S)	**Metallic K.O.**	1977	**4.00**	**10.00**
STORCH, JEREMY					
RCA Victor LSP-4541	(S)	**40 Miles Past Woodstock**	1971	**1.00**	**5.00**
STORIES					
The original group features Michael Brown. Refer to The Left Banke.					
Kama Sutra KSBS-2051	(S)	**Stories**	1972	**4.00**	**10.00**
Kama Sutra KSBS-2068	(DJ)	**About Us** (Gatefold cover)	1973	**8.00**	**20.00**
Kama Sutra KSBS-2068	(S)	**About Us** (Gatefold cover)	1973	**12.00**	**30.00**
Kama Sutra KSBS-2068	(S)	**About Us** (Standard cover)	1973	**4.00**	**10.00**
		(Only copies of 2068 with standard covers contain "Brother Louie.")			
Kama Sutra KSBS-2078	(S)	**Travelling Underground**	1974	**4.00**	**10.00**
STORM, BILLY					
Buena Vista BV-3315	(M)	**Billy Storm**	1963	**40.00**	**100.00**
Buena Vista STER-3315	(S)	**Billy Storm**	1963	**80.00**	**200.00**
		(Stereo copies of B.V. 3315 may be packaged in mono covers.)			
STORM, BILLY, & THE VALIANTS					
Famous F-504	(M)	**This Is The Night**	1969	**150.00**	**300.00**
		(Famous 504 contains Storm's early vocal group recordings.)			
STRANGELOVES, THE					
Bang BLP-211	(M)	**I Want Candy**	1965	**30.00**	**75.00**
Bang BLPS-211	(S)	**I Want Candy**	1965	**40.00**	**100.00**
STRAWBERRY ALARM CLOCK, THE					
The SAC can also be found on the soundtracks for Sidewalk's "Psych-Out" and 20th Century-Fox's "Beyond The Valley Of The Dolls." Refer to The Who / The Strawberry Alarm Clock.					
Uni 3014	(M)	**Incense And Peppermints**	1967	**20.00**	**50.00**
Uni 73014	(S)	**Incense And Peppermints**	1967	**16.00**	**40.00**
Uni 73025	(S)	**Wake Up It's Tomorrow**	1968	**16.00**	**40.00**
Uni 73035	(S)	**The World In A Sea Shell**	1968	**16.00**	**40.00**
Uni 73054	(S)	**Good Morning Starshine**	1969	**16.00**	**40.00**
Uni 73074	(S)	**The Best Of The Strawberry Alarm Clock**	1970	**16.00**	**40.00**
Vocalion VL-73915	(S)	**Changes**	1971	**20.00**	**50.00**
STRAWBERRY STREET SINGERS, THE					
RCA Victor LSP-4084	(S)	**Fresh Fruit**	1968	**4.00**	**10.00**
STRAWBS, THE					
A&M SP-4288	(S)	**Just A Collection Of Antiques And Curios**	1971	**1.00**	**5.00**
A&M SP-4304	(S)	**From The Witchwood**	1971	**1.00**	**5.00**
A&M SP-4344	(S)	**Grave New World**	1972	**1.00**	**5.00**
A&M SP-4383	(S)	**Bursting At The Seams**	1973	**1.00**	**5.00**
A&M SP-3607	(S)	**Hero And Heroine**	1974	**1.00**	**5.00**
A&M SP-4506	(S)	**Ghosts**	1975	**1.00**	**5.00**
A&M SP-5444	(S)	**Nomadness**	1975	**1.00**	**5.00**
Oyster OY-1603	(S)	**Deep Cuts**	1976	**1.00**	**5.00**
Oyster OY-1604	(S)	**Burning For You**	1977	**1.00**	**5.00**
Arista AB-4172	(S)	**Deadlines**	1978	**1.00**	**5.00**
A&M 6005	(S)	**Best Of The Strawbs** (2 LPs)	1978	**1.00**	**5.00**

Label & Catalog #		Title	Year	VG+	NM
STRAY					
Mercury SRM-1-611	(S)	Suicide	1971	6.00	15.00
Mercury SRM-1-624	(S)	Saturday Morning Pictures	1971	6.00	15.00
STREET					
Verve/Forecast FTS-3057	(S)	Street	1968	4.00	10.00
STREET NOISE					
Evolution 2010	(S)	Street Noise	1970	4.00	10.00
STRIDER					
Warner Bros. BS-2722	(S)	Exposed	1973	6.00	15.00
Warner Bros. BS-2???	(S)	Misunderstanding	1974	6.00	15.00
STRING CHEESE					
Wooden Nickel WNS-1001	(S)	String Cheese	1971	6.00	15.00
STRING DRIVEN THING					
Charisma CAS-1062	(S)	String Driven Thing	1972	4.00	10.00
Charisma CAS-1070	(S)	The Machine That Cried	1973	4.00	10.00
20th Cent.-Fox T-470	(S)	Please Mind Your Head	1974	4.00	10.00
20th Cent.-Fox T-503	(S)	Keep Yor 'And On It	1975	4.00	10.00
STRONG, NOLAN, & THE DIABLOS					
Fortune LP-8010	(M)	Fortune Of Hits	1961	80.00	200.00
Fortune LP-8012	(M)	Fortune Of Hits, Volume 2	1962	80.00	200.00
Fortune LP-8015	(M)	Mind Over Matter	1963	100.00	250.00
—Fortune albums above have purple labels on thick vinyl.—					
Fortune LP-8010	(M)	Fortune Of Hits	196?	20.00	50.00
Fortune LP-8012	(M)	Fortune Of Hits, Volume 2	196?	20.00	50.00
Fortune LP-8015	(M)	Mind Over Matter	196?	30.00	75.00
—Fortune albums above have yellow labels on thick vinyl.—					
Fortune LP-8010	(M)	Fortune Of Hits	198?	6.00	15.00
Fortune LP-8012	(M)	Fortune Of Hits, Volume 2	198?	6.00	15.00
Fortune LP-8015	(M)	Mind Over Matter	198?	8.00	20.00
—Fortune albums above have bluish purple labels on thin vinyl.—					
STRYPER					
Enigma E-1064	(S)	The Yellow And Black Attack (Yellow vinyl)	1984	16.00	40.00
Enigma 72077	(S)	Soldiers Under Command (White vinyl)	1985	5.00	12.00
Capitol SEAX-73277	(S)	To Hell With The Devil (Picture disc)	1986	6.00	15.00
Enigma PENVLP-501	(S)	In God We Trust (Picture disc)	1988	8.00	20.00
STUFFY & HIS FROZEN PARACHUTE BAND					
Stuffy & His Frozen Parachute Band issued their album privately before it was issued by Paramount.					
Paramount PAS-6070	(S)	Stuffy & His Frozen Parachute Band	1974	10.00	25.00
STURGES, JEFF					
MAM 1	(S)	Jeff Sturges & Universe	1971	6.00	15.00
STYLISTICS, THE					
Avco Embassy 33023	(S)	The Stylistics	1971	8.00	20.00
Avco Embassy 11006	(S)	Round 2	1972	8.00	20.00
Avco Embassy 11010	(S)	Rockin' Roll Baby	1973	8.00	20.00
Avco Embassy 69001	(S)	Let's Put It All Together	1974	8.00	20.00
Avco Embassy 69004	(S)	Heavy	1974	8.00	20.00
Avco Embassy 69008	(S)	Thank You Baby	1975	8.00	20.00
Avco Embassy 69010	(S)	You Are Beautiful	1975	8.00	20.00
H&L 69032	(S)	Wonder Woman	1976	4.00	10.00
Mercury SRM-3727	(S)	In Fashion	1978	4.00	10.00
TSOP FZ-36470	(S)	Hurry Up This Way Again	1980	1.00	5.00
TSOP FZ-37458	(S)	Closer Than Close	1981	1.00	5.00
TSOP FZ-37955	(S)	1928	1982	1.00	5.00
STYX					
Wooden Nickel WNS-1008	(S)	Styx	1972	4.00	10.00
Wooden Nickel WNS-1012	(S)	Styx II	1973	1.00	5.00
Wooden Nickel SWL-0287	(S)	The Serpent Is Rising	1974	1.00	5.00
Wooden Nickel BWL-0638	(S)	Man Of Miracles	1974	1.00	5.00
Wooden Nickel BWL-2250	(S)	The Best Of Styx	1977	.80	4.00
RCA Victor AFL1-3110	(S)	Styx	1980	.80	4.00
RCA Victor AFL1-3593	(S)	Styx II	1980	.80	4.00
RCA Victor AFL1-3594	(S)	Lady	1980	.80	4.00
RCA Victor AFL1-3595	(S)	The Serpent Is Rising	1980	.80	4.00
RCA Victor AFL1-3596	(S)	Man Of Miracles	1980	.80	4.00
RCA Victor AFL1-3597	(S)	The Best Of Styx	1980	.80	4.00
RCA Victor AYL1-4111	(S)	The Serpent Is Rising	1982	.80	4.00
RCA Victor AYL1-4233	(S)	Lady	1982	.80	4.00

Label & Catalog #		Title	Year	VG+	NM
A&M SP-4559	(S)	Equinox	1975	.80	4.00
A&M SP-4604	(S)	Crystal Ball	1976	.80	4.00
A&M SP-4637	(S)	The Grand Illusion	1977	.80	4.00
A&M SP-8431	(DJ)	The Styx Radio Special (2 LPs)	1977	10.00	25.00
A&M SP-17053	(DJ)	The Styx Radio Special (3 LP box)	1978	16.00	40.00
A&M SP-17222	(DJ)	The Styx Radio Sampler (2 LPs)	1978	10.00	25.00
A&M SP-4724	(S)	Pieces Of Eight	1978	.80	4.00
A&M SP-3711	(S)	Cornerstone (Silver vinyl)	1979	10.00	25.00
A&M SP-3711	(S)	Cornerstone	1979	.80	4.00
A&M SP-3719	(S)	Paradise Theater	1981	.80	4.00
A&M SP-3734	(S)	Kilroy Was Here	1983	.80	4.00
A&M SP-6514	(S)	Caught In The Act-Live (2 LPs)	1984	1.00	5.00

SUGAR BEARS, THE
The Bears feature Kim Carnes.

Big Tree BTS-2009	(S)	Introducing The Sugar Bears	1971	6.00	15.00

SUGAR CREEK
Sugar Creek features Jonathan Edwards.

Metromedia ???	(S)	Please Tell A Friend	197?	20.00	50.00

SUGARLOAF
Sugarloaf features Jerry Corbetta, later of The Four Seasons.

Liberty LST-7640	(S)	Sugarloaf	1970	10.00	25.00
Liberty LST-11010	(S)	Spaceship Earth (Promo box)	1971	30.00	75.00
		(Promo box with posters, a book, a button and other items.)			
Liberty LST-11010	(S)	Spaceship Earth	1971	10.00	25.00
Brut 6006	(S)	I Got A Song	1973	10.00	25.00
Claridge CL-1000	(S)	Don't Call Us	1975	10.00	25.00

SUMMER, DONNA

Oasis OCLP-5003	(S)	Love To Love You Baby (With poster)	1975	6.00	15.00
Oasis OCLP-5003	(S)	Love To Love You Baby (Without poster)	1975	3.20	8.00
Oasis OCLP-5004	(S)	A Love Trilogy	1976	3.20	8.00
Casablanca NBLP-7038	(S)	Four Seasons Of Love	1976	1.00	5.00
Casablanca NBLP-7056	(S)	I Remember Yesterday	1977	1.00	5.00
Casablanca NBLP-7078	(S)	Once Upon A Time... (2 LPs)	1977	3.20	8.00
Casablanca NBLP-7119	(S)	Best Of "Live & More" (Picture disc)	1979	4.00	10.00
Casablanca NBLP-7119	(S)	Live And More (2 LPs)	1978	3.20	8.00
Casablanca NBLP-7150	(S)	Bad Girls (2 LPs)	1979	3.20	8.00
Casablanca NBLP-7191	(S)	On The Radio—Greatest Hits I & II (2 LPs)	1979	3.20	8.00
Casablanca NBLP-7244	(S)	Walk Away—Collectors Edition (The Best Of 1977-1980)	1980	1.00	5.00
Geffen GHS-2000	(S)	The Wanderer	1980	1.00	5.00
Geffen GHS-2005	(S)	Donna Summer	1982	1.00	5.00
Mercury 812265	(S)	She Works Hard For The Money	1983	1.00	5.00
Geffen GHS-24040	(S)	Cats Without Claws (Quiex II vinyl promo)	1984	6.00	15.00
Geffen GHS-24040	(S)	Cats Without Claws	1984	1.00	5.00

SUMMERHILL

Tetragrammaton	(S)	Summerhill	1969	12.00	30.00

SUMMERS, ANDY, & ROBERT FRIPP
Mr. Summers was a member of The Police whilst Mr. Fripp recorded with King Crimson.

A&M SP-4913	(S)	I Advance Masked	1982	1.00	5.00
A&M SP9-5011	(S)	Bewitched	1984	1.00	5.00
A&M SP-17299	(DJ)	The Radio Interview	1984	6.00	15.00

SUNDANCE

Kapp KS-3659	(S)	Sundance	1971	6.00	15.00

SUNDAY FUNNIES, THE

Rare Earth RS-526	(S)	Sunday Funnies	1971	5.00	12.00
Rare Earth RS-538	(S)	Benediction	1972	5.00	12.00

SUNDAY'S CHILD

Reprise RS-6425	(S)	Sunday's Child	1970	4.00	10.00

SUNDOWNERS, THE

Decca DL-75036	(S)	Captain Nemo	1968	6.00	15.00

SUNGLOWS, THE
The Sunglows later recorded as Sunny & The Sunliners (below).

Sunglow SLP-101	(M)	Sonny Ozuna & The Sunglows	1963	40.00	100.00
Sunglow SLP-102	(M)	The Fabulous Sunglows	1964	40.00	100.00
Sunglow SLP-103	(M)	The Original Peanuts	1965	40.00	100.00
Sunglow SLP-103	(S)	The Original Peanuts	1965	60.00	150.00

After being fired by his sons as manager of The Beach Boys, the modestly talented Murray Wilson, under the delusion that he was the reason behind the group's success ("Yeah, Brian's got some talent, but you should hear my tunes!"), he found The Sunrays. Signing them to Capitol subsidiary Tower, he produced their two hits, "I Live For The Sun" and "Andrea." That they were both excellent pop/rock singles is undeniable; that they are blatant Beach Boy sound-alikes is equally true. When the originals' career came to an abrupt end, the desire to hear imitators dwindled. . . Their sole album attracts collectors of '60s pop, The Beach Boys and related efforts, and chart collectors seeking hits in stereo (both of the aforementioned charters are included).

Label & Catalog #		Title	Year	VG+	NM

SUNNY & THE SUNLINERS

Sunny Ozuna and his band also recorded as The Sunglows (above).

Tear Drop LPM-2000	(M)	Talk To Me/Rags To Riches	1963	40.00	100.00
Tear Drop LPM-2001	(M)	Las Vegas Welcomes Sunny & The Sunliners	1964	14.00	35.00
Tear Drop LPM-2008	(M)	Teardrop Presents Sunny & The Sunliners	196?	14.00	35.00
Key-Loc KL-3001	(M)	Smile Now, Cry Later	196?	10.00	25.00
Key-Loc KL-3002	(M)	No Te Chifles	196?	10.00	25.00
Key-Loc KL-3003	(M)	Sunny & The Sunliners Live In Hollywood	196?	10.00	25.00
Key-Loc KL-3004	(M)	Canta Sunny	196?	10.00	25.00
Key-Loc KL-3005	(M)	A Little Brown-Eyed Soul	196?	10.00	25.00
Key-Loc KL-3006	(M)	This Is My Band	196?	10.00	25.00
Key-Loc KL-3007	(M)	Versatile	196?	10.00	25.00
Key-Loc KL-3008	(M)	Adelante	196?	10.00	25.00
		(Key Loc 3002, 3004 and 3008 are Spanish language recordings.)			
Key-Loc KL-3009	(M)	Sky High	196?	10.00	25.00
Key-Loc KL-3010	(M)	The Missing Link	196?	10.00	25.00

SUNNYLAND SLIM

Bluesville BVLP-1016	(M)	Slim's Shout	1961	40.00	100.00
		—*Bluesville albums above have bright blue labels with silver print.*—			
Bluesville BVLP-1016	(M)	Slim's Shout	1964	12.00	30.00
		—*Bluesville albums above have blue labels with a trident logo on the right side.*—			
Prestige PRST-7723	(E)	Slim's Shout	1969	8.00	20.00
		(Prestige 7723 is a reissue of Bluesville 1016.)			
World Pacific WPS-21890	(S)	Slim's Got His Thing Goin' On	1969	8.00	20.00
Blue Horizon BM-4608	(M)	Blues Masters, Volume 8	197?	6.00	15.00
BluesWay BLS-6068	(S)	Ragtime Blues	1973	6.00	15.00
Jewel 5010	(S)	Sad And Lonesome	1973	4.00	10.00

SUNRAYS, THE

The Sunrays can also be found on the Sidewalk soundtrack "Psych-Out."

Tower T-5017	(M)	Andrea	1966	14.00	35.00
Tower ST-5017	(S)	Andrea	1966	20.00	50.00

SUNSET DRAGSTERS, THE

Palace M-775	(M)	Hot Rod Rally	196?	30.00	75.00
Palace PST-775	(S)	Hot Rod Rally	196?	40.00	100.00

SUNSETS, THE

Palace M-752	(M)	Surfing With The Sunsets	1963	16.00	40.00
Palace PST-752	(S)	Surfing With The Sunsets	1963	20.00	50.00

SUNSHINE

Back Beat 69	(S)	Here's Sunshine	1970	6.00	15.00

SUNSHINE COMPANY, THE

Imperial LP-9359	(M)	Happy Is The Sunshine Company	1967	6.00	15.00
Imperial LP-12359	(S)	Happy Is The Sunshine Company	1967	6.00	15.00
Imperial LP-9368	(DJ)	The Sunshine Company	1968	10.00	25.00
Imperial LP-12368	(S)	The Sunshine Company	1968	6.00	15.00
Imperial LP-12399	(S)	Sunshine And Shadows	1968	6.00	15.00

SUPER BLUES BAND, THE [THE SUPER SUPER BLUES BAND]

The SBB is Bo Diddley and Muddy Waters with Little Walter. The SSBB is Bo and Muddy with Howlin' Wolf.

Checker LP-3008	(M)	The Super Blues Band	1968	30.00	75.00
Checker LPS-3008	(S)	The Super Blues Band	1968	20.00	50.00
Checker LP-3010	(M)	The Super, Super Blues Band	1968	30.00	75.00
Checker LPS-3010	(S)	The Super, Super Blues Band	1968	20.00	50.00

SUPER STOCKS, THE

The Super Stocks are a creation of Gary Usher & Co.

Capitol T-1997	(M)	Hot Rod Rally	1963	20.00	50.00
Capitol ST-1997	(S)	Hot Rod Rally	1963	30.00	75.00
		(While this is actually a various artists compilation, half of the album consists of The Super Stocks' earliest recordings.)			
Capitol T-2060	(M)	Thunder Road (With poster)	1964	60.00	150.00
Capitol ST-2060	(S)	Thunder Road (With poster)	1964	80.00	200.00
		(Capitol 2060 was issued with a poster of a drawing of a hot rod.)			
Capitol T-2060	(M)	Thunder Road (Without poster)	1964	40.00	100.00
Capitol ST-2060	(S)	Thunder Road (Without poster)	1964	60.00	150.00
Capitol T-2113	(M)	Surf Route 101	1964	50.00	125.00
Capitol ST-2113	(S)	Surf Route 101	1964	60.00	150.00
		(Capitol 2113 was issued with a bonus single by Mr. Gasser & The Weirdos in a special "pocket" on the cover.)			
Capitol T-2113	(M)	Surf Route 101 (Without the single)	1964	40.00	100.00
Capitol ST-2113	(S)	Surf Route 101 (Without the single)	1964	50.00	125.00
Capitol T-2190	(M)	School Is A Drag	1964	50.00	125.00
Capitol ST-2190	(S)	School Is A Drag	1964	60.00	150.00

Label & Catalog #		Title	Year	VG+	NM
SUPERFINE DANDELION					
Mainstream 56102	(M)	Superfine Dandelion	1967	16.00	40.00
Mainstream S-6102	(S)	Superfine Dandelion	1967	20.00	50.00
SUPERSISTER					
Dwarf PDLP-2001	(S)	Supersister	197?	14.00	35.00
SUPERTRAMP					
A&M SP-4274	(S)	Supertramp	1970	1.20	6.00
A&M SP-4311	(S)	Indelibly Stamped	1971	1.20	6.00
		—A&M albums above have brown labels.—			
A&M SP-3647	(S)	Crime Of The Century	1974	.80	4.00
A&M SP-4560	(S)	Crisis? What Crisis?	1975	.80	4.00
A&M SP-4634	(S)	Even In The Quietest Moments...	1977	.80	4.00
A&M SP-4665	(S)	Supertramp	1978	.80	4.00
A&M SP-3708	(S)	Breakfast In America	1979	.80	4.00
A&M SP-6702	(S)	Paris (2 LPs)	1980	1.00	5.00
A&M SP-3129	(S)	Indelibly Stamped	1980	.80	4.00
A&M SP-3149	(S)	Supertramp	1980	.80	4.00
A&M SP-3730	(S)	Breakfast In America (Picture disc)	1980	200.00	400.00
		(This picdisc was pressed for in-house use with each disc featuring an A&M staffer with the model who appeared on the LP cover.)			
A&M SP-3732	(S)	...Famous Last Words...	1982	.80	4.00

SUPREMES, THE [DIANA ROSS & THE SUPREMES]
Original members include Florence Ballard, Diana Ross and Mary Wilson.

Label & Catalog #		Title	Year	VG+	NM
Motown M-606	(M)	Meet The Supremes	1963	300.00	600.00
		(Original covers of Motown 606 feature the group seated on stools.)			
Motown M-606	(M)	Meet The Supremes	1964	10.00	25.00
Motown MS-606	(S)	Meet The Supremes	1964	12.00	30.00
		(Later covers feature a close-up of the group.)			
Motown M-610	(M)	The Supremes Sing Ballads And Blues	1963	Unreleased	
Motown MS-610	(S)	The Supremes Sing Ballads And Blues	1963	Unreleased	
Motown M-621	(M)	Where Did Our Love Go	1964	10.00	25.00
Motown MS-621	(S)	Where Did Our Love Go	1964	12.00	30.00
Motown M-623	(M)	A Bit Of Liverpool	1964	16.00	40.00
Motown MS-623	(S)	A Bit Of Liverpool	1964	20.00	50.00
Motown M-625	(M)	The Supremes Sing Country, Western & Pop	1965	12.00	30.00
Motown MS-625	(S)	The Supremes Sing Country, Western & Pop	1965	16.00	40.00
Motown M-626	(M)	The Supremes Live! Live! Live!	1965	Unreleased	
Motown MS-626	(S)	The Supremes Live! Live! Live!	1965	Unreleased	
Motown M-627	(M)	More Hits By The Supremes	1965	10.00	25.00
Motown MS-627	(S)	More Hits By The Supremes	1965	12.00	30.00
Motown M-628	(M)	There's A Place For Us	1965	Unreleased	
Motown MS-628	(S)	There's A Place For Us	1965	Unreleased	
Motown M-629	(M)	We Remember Sam Cooke	1965	12.00	30.00
Motown MS-629	(S)	We Remember Sam Cooke	1965	16.00	40.00
Motown M-636	(M)	The Supremes At The Copa	1965	12.00	30.00
		(Original covers for M-636 have a b&w drawing of the group on the back.)			
Motown MS-636	(S)	The Supremes At The Copa	1965	12.00	30.00
		(Original covers for MS-636 do not have the drawing on the back.)			
Motown M-637	(M)	A Tribute To The Girls	1965	Unreleased	
Motown MS-637	(S)	A Tribute To The Girls	1965	Unreleased	
Motown M-638	(M)	Merry Christmas	1965	12.00	30.00
Motown MS-638	(S)	Merry Christmas	1965	16.00	40.00
Motown M-643	(M)	I Hear A Symphony	1966	10.00	25.00
Motown MS-643	(S)	I Hear A Symphony	1966	12.00	30.00
Motown M-648	(M)	Pure Gold	1966	Unreleased	
Motown MS-648	(S)	Pure Gold	1966	Unreleased	
Motown M-649	(M)	Supremes A' Go-Go	1966	10.00	25.00
Motown MS-649	(S)	Supremes A' Go-Go	1966	12.00	30.00
Motown M-650	(M)	The Supremes Sing Holland-Dozier-Holland	1967	12.00	30.00
Motown MS-650	(S)	The Supremes Sing Holland-Dozier-Holland	1967	12.00	30.00
Motown M-659	(M)	The Supremes Sing Rodgers And Hart	1967	12.00	30.00
		(The b&w photo on the back cover of M-659 has the girls in gowns.)			
Motown MS-659	(S)	The Supremes Sing Rodgers And Hart	1967	12.00	30.00
		(The b&w photo on the back cover of MS-659 has the girls in caped gowns.)			
Motown M-663	(M)	Greatest Hits (2 LPs with poster)	1967	10.00	25.00
Motown MS-663	(S)	Greatest Hits (2 LPs with poster)	1967	10.00	25.00
Motown M-663	(M)	Greatest Hits (2 LPs without poster)	1967	8.00	20.00
Motown MS-663	(S)	Greatest Hits (2 LPs without poster)	1967	8.00	20.00
Motown M-665	(M)	Reflections	1968	10.00	25.00
Motown MS-665	(S)	Reflections	1968	4.00	10.00
Motown MS-670	(S)	Love Child	1968	4.00	10.00
Motown M-672	(M)	Funny Girl	1968	10.00	25.00
Motown MS-672	(S)	Funny Girl	1968	4.00	10.00
Motown M-676	(M)	Live At London's Talk Of The Town (Promo)	1968	10.00	25.00
Motown MS-676	(S)	Live At London's Talk Of The Town	1968	4.00	10.00

Label & Catalog #		Title	Year	VG+	NM
Motown MS-682	(S)	TCB	1968	4.00	10.00
Motown MS-689	(S)	Let The Sunshine In	1969	4.00	10.00
Motown MS-694	(S)	Cream Of The Crop	1969	4.00	10.00
—Motown albums above have the company's Detroit, MI, address on the bottom of the label.—					
Motown MS-702	(S)	Greatest Hits, Volume 3	1970	3.20	8.00
Motown MS-708	(S)	Farewell (2 LPs)	1970	3.20	8.00
Motown MS-705	(S)	Right On	1970	3.20	8.00
Motown MS-720	(S)	New Ways But Love Stays	1970	3.20	8.00
Motown MS-737	(S)	Touch	1971	3.20	8.00
Doral	(S)	Doral Presents Diana Ross & The Supremes	1971	20.00	50.00
		(Promotional compilation of previously released material.)			
Motown PR-102	(DJ)	Touch Interview	1971	8.00	20.00
Motown MS-746	(S)	Promises Kept	1972	Unreleased	
Motown MS-751	(S)	Floy Joy	1972	4.00	10.00
Motown MS-756	(S)	The Supremes Produced And Arranged By Jimmy Webb	1972	4.00	10.00
Motown MS-794	(DJ)	Anthology 1962-1969 (3 LPs)	1974	16.00	40.00
Motown MS-794	(S)	Anthology 1962-1969 (3 LPs)	1974	4.00	10.00
Motown MS-828	(S)	The Supremes	1975	4.00	10.00
Motown MS-863	(S)	High Energy	1976	4.00	10.00
Motown MS-873	(S)	Mary, Scherrie And Susaye	1976	4.00	10.00
Motown M7-904	(S)	The Supremes At Their Best	1978	4.00	10.00
Natural Resources 49006	(S)	Where Did Our Love Go	1978	.80	4.00
Motown M5-101V	(S)	Superstar Series, Vol. 1	1980	.80	4.00
Motown M5-138V	(S)	The Supremes A' Go-Go	1982	.80	4.00
Motown M5-147V	(S)	I Hear A Symphony	1982	.80	4.00
Motown M5-158V	(S)	The Supremes Sing Country, Western & Pop	1982	.80	4.00
Motown M5-162V	(S)	Live At The Copa	1982	.80	4.00
Motown M5-182V	(S)	The Supremes Sing Holland-Dozier-Holland	1982	.80	4.00
Motown M5-203V	(S)	Greatest Hits, Vol. 3	1982	.80	4.00
Motown M5-223V	(S)	Meet The Supremes (Stool cover)	1982	.80	4.00
Motown M8-237V	(S)	The Supremes' Greatest Hits (2 LPs)	1982	.80	4.00

SUPREMES, THE, & THE FOUR TOPS

Motown MS-717	(S)	The Magnificent Seven	1970	3.20	8.00
Motown MS-736	(S)	The Return Of The Magnificent Seven	1971	3.20	8.00
Motown MS-745	(S)	Dynamite	1972	3.20	8.00
Motown M5-123	(S)	The Magnificent Seven	1982	.80	4.00

SUPREMES, THE, & THE TEMPTATIONS

Motown M-679	(M)	Diana Ross & The Supremes Join The Temptations	1968	10.00	25.00
Motown MS-679	(S)	Diana Ross & The Supremes Join The Temptations	1968	4.00	10.00
Motown MS-692	(S)	Together	1969	4.00	10.00
Motown MS-699	(S)	On Broadway	1969	4.00	10.00
Motown M5-139V	(S)	The Supremes Join The Temptations	1982	.80	4.00

SURF STOMPERS, THE

Del-Fi DFLP-1236	(M)	The Original Surfer Stomp	1963	30.00	75.00
Del-Fi DFST-1236	(S)	The Original Surfer Stomp	1963	40.00	100.00
		(Del-Fi 1236 is a reissue of 1228 credited to Bruce Johnston.)			

SURF TEENS, THE

Sutton SU-339	(M)	Surf Mania	196?	12.00	30.00
Sutton SSU-339	(S)	Surf Mania	196?	16.00	40.00

SURFARIS, THE: Refer to THE ORIGINAL SURFARIS

SURFARIS, THE
On the Dot album only "Wipe Out" and "Surfer Joe" are by The Surfaris; the other tracks were cut by The Challengers. The final two Decca albums are essentially Gary Usher & Co. with vocalist Ron Wilson. The group can also be found on the Decca soundtrack "The Lively Set." Refer to The Original Surfaris.

Dot DLP-3535	(M)	Wipe Out	1963	20.00	50.00
Dot DLP-25535	(P)	Wipe Out	1963	30.00	75.00
		(First pressings of Dot 3/25535 have a photo of the group with five members on the back cover.)			
Dot DLP-3535	(M)	Wipe Out	1963	16.00	40.00
Dot DLP-25535	(P)	Wipe Out	1963	20.00	50.00
		(Second pressings have a photo of the group with four members.)			
Dot DLP-3535	(M)	Wipe Out	1963	12.00	30.00
Dot DLP-25535	(P)	Wipe Out	1963	16.00	40.00
		(Later pressings delete the photo of the group on the back cover.)			
Decca DL-4470	(M)	The Surfaris Play Wipe Out	1963	10.00	25.00
Decca DL-74470	(S)	The Surfaris Play Wipe Out	1963	12.00	30.00
Decca DL-4487	(M)	Hit City '64	1964	20.00	50.00
Decca DL-74487	(S)	Hit City '64	1964	30.00	75.00

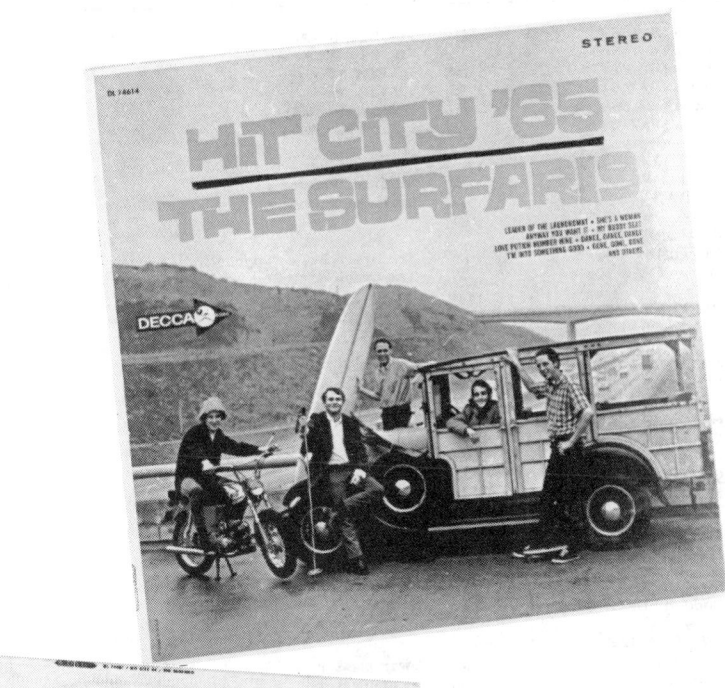

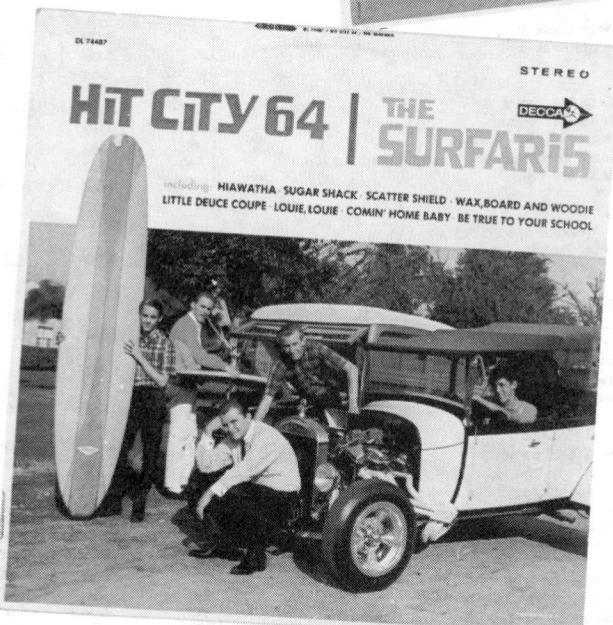

The original Surfaris consisted of Bob Berryhill, Pat Connolly, Jim Fuller, Jim Pash and Ron Wilson; their sides appear on the Dot album. After signing with Decca in 1963 and recording a few albums, only one of which saw the light of day on national charts, the group found themselves basically a touring band. The final brace of long-players credited to them were recorded by Gary Usher and crew, using Wilson as the lead vocalist. The covers of these two albums capture the mood of the period's West Coast [white] youth— rods, boards, woodies and bikes. (Hey, where are the honeys?)

Label & Catalog #		Title	Year	VG+	NM
Decca DL-4560	(M)	Fun City, U.S.A.	1964	16.00	40.00
Decca DL-74560	(S)	Fun City, U.S.A.	1964	20.00	50.00
Decca DL-4614	(M)	Hit City '65	1965	20.00	50.00
Decca DL-74614	(S)	Hit City '65	1965	30.00	75.00
Decca DL-4683	(M)	It Ain't Me, Babe	1965	12.00	30.00
Decca DL-74683	(S)	It Ain't Me, Babe	1965	16.00	40.00

SURFRIDERS, THE

| Vault LP-105 | (M) | Surfbeat, Volume 2 | 1963 | 12.00 | 30.00 |
| Vault VS-105 | (S) | Surfbeat, Volume 2 | 1963 | 16.00 | 40.00 |

SURFSIDERS, THE

| Design DLP-208 | (M) | The Beach Boy's Songbook | 1965 | 6.00 | 15.00 |
| Design DLPS-208 | (S) | The Beach Boy's Songbook | 1965 | 8.00 | 20.00 |

SURPRISE PACKAGE

| LHI S-12005 | (S) | Free Up | 1968 | 16.00 | 40.00 |

SWAGMEN, THE

| Parkway P-7015 | (M) | Meet The Swagmen | 1962 | 20.00 | 50.00 |

SWAMP DOGG

Canyon LP-7706	(S)	Total Destruction To Your Mind	1970	12.00	30.00
Elektra EKS-74089	(S)	Rat On	1971	8.00	20.00
Cream 9009	(S)	Cuffed, Collared And Tagged	1972	6.00	15.00
Musicor MUS-2504	(S)	Finally Caught Up With Myself	197?	6.00	15.00
Wizard 1306	(S)	Swamp Dogg	1978	4.00	10.00
Island ILPS-9299	(S)	Have You Heard This Story	1973	4.00	10.00
Takoma 7099	(S)	I'm Not Selling Out, I'm Buying In	1981	1.00	5.00

SWAMPGAS

| Buddah BDS-5102 | (S) | Swampgas | 1972 | 1.00 | 5.00 |

SWAMPWATER

| King 1122 | (S) | Swampwater | 1970 | 6.00 | 15.00 |
| RCA Victor LSP-4572 | (S) | Swampwater | 1971 | 5.00 | 12.00 |

SWANN, BETTYE

Money 1103	(M)	Make Me Yours	1967	8.00	20.00
Money S-1103	(S)	Make Me Yours	1967	10.00	25.00
Capitol ST-190	(S)	The Soul View Now	1969	6.00	15.00
Capitol ST-270	(S)	Don't You Ever Get Tired Of Hurting Me	1969	6.00	15.00
Abet 405	(S)	Make Me Yours	1972	4.00	10.00

SWEAT BAND
Sweat Band features William "Bootsy" Collins and Maceo Parker.

| Uncle Jam 36857 | (S) | Sweat Band | 1980 | 5.00 | 12.00 |

SWEET, THE

Bell 1124	(S)	The Sweet	1973	10.00	25.00
Kory 3009	(S)	The Sweet	1977	1.00	5.00
		(Kory 3009 is a reissue of Bell 1124.)			
Capitol ST-11395	(S)	Desolation Boulevard	1975	6.00	15.00
Capitol ST-11496	(S)	Give Us A Wink	1976	6.00	15.00
Capitol SPRO-8371/3	(DJ)	Sweet For A.O.R. Radio Only *(Sampler)*	1976	10.00	25.00
Capitol SKAO-11636	(S)	Off The Record	1977	6.00	15.00
Capitol SKAO-11744	(S)	Level Headed	1978	6.00	15.00
Capitol SPRO-8849	(DJ)	Short And Sweet	1978	12.00	30.00
Capitol PRO-11929	(DJ)	Cut Above The Rest	1979	20.00	50.00
		(Box contains LP, cassette, 8-track, photo and bio.)			
Capitol ST-11929	(S)	Cut Above The Rest	1979	4.00	10.00
Capitol ST-12106	(S)	Sweet VI	1980	4.00	10.00
Capitol SN-16115	(S)	Give Us A Wink	1980	.80	4.00
Capitol SN-16116	(S)	Off The Record	1980	.80	4.00
Capitol SN-16117	(S)	Level Headed	1980	.80	4.00
Capitol SN-16118	(S)	Cut Above The Rest	1980	.80	4.00
Capitol SN-16287	(S)	Desolation Boulevard	1980	.80	4.00

SWEET INSPIRATIONS, THE

Atlantic 8155	(M)	The Sweet Inspirations	1968	12.00	30.00
Atlantic SD-8155	(S)	The Sweet Inspirations	1968	10.00	25.00
Atlantic SD-8182	(S)	Songs Of Faith And Inspiration	1968	10.00	25.00
Atlantic SD-8201	(S)	What The World Needs Now Is Love	1969	10.00	25.00
Atlantic SD-8225	(S)	Sweets For My Sweet	1969	10.00	25.00
Atlantic SD-8253	(S)	Sweet, Sweet Soul	1970	10.00	25.00
Stax STS-3017	(S)	Estelle, Myrna And Sylvia	1973	10.00	25.00
RSO 1-3058	(S)	Hot Butterfly	1979	4.00	10.00

The Sweet Inspirations were Estelle Brown, Cissy Houston, Sylvia Shemwell, and Myrna Smith. After working with Aretha on her first sessions as backing vocalists, Jerry Wexler convinced them to form a group and record for Atlantic. The group toiled for several years, achieving one major pop hit in 1968 after which their sole album, Sweet Inspiration, was titled. While they never made it big as a star attraction, they backed Elvis Presley throughout the '70s on record and on stage, where he gave them their own portion of the bill as the opening act where they reached hundreds of thousands who might never have heard of them otherwise. (And, yes, Cissy is Whitney's mom.)

Label & Catalog #		Title	Year	VG+	NM
SWEET LIGHTNIN'					
RCA Victor LSP-4758	(S)	Sweet Lightnin'	1972	1.00	5.00
SWEET PAIN					
United Arts. LA-679	(S)	Sweet Pain	1971	6.00	15.00
SWEET SALVATION					
Elektra EKS-75045	(S)	Sweet Salvation	1972	4.00	10.00
SWEET STAVIN' CHAIN					
Cotillion SD-9021	(S)	Sweet Stavin' Chain	1970	4.00	10.00
SWEET THURSDAY					
Great Western 32039	(S)	Sweet Thursday	1969	6.00	15.00
Tetragrammaton T-112	(S)	Sweet Thursday	1969	4.00	10.00
SWEETWATER					
Reprise RS-6313	(S)	Sweetwater	1968	4.00	10.00
Reprise RS-6417	(S)	Just For You	1970	4.00	10.00
Reprise RS-6473	(S)	Melon	1971	4.00	10.00
SWIFT RAIN					
Hi SHL-32064	(S)	Coming Down	1971	10.00	25.00
SWINGIN' MEDALLIONS, THE					
Smash MGS-27083	(M)	Double Shot	1966	16.00	40.00
Smash SRS-67083	(S)	Double Shot	1966	20.00	50.00
		(Original pressings include an unedited version of "Double Shot.")			
Smash MGS-27083	(M)	Double Shot	1966	12.00	30.00
Smash SRS-67083	(S)	Double Shot	1966	16.00	40.00
		(Later pressings include the edited, single version of "Double Shot.")			
SWINGING BLUE JEANS, THE					
Imperial LP-9261	(M)	Hippy Hippy Shake	1964	40.00	100.00
Imperial LP-12261	(E)	Hippy Hippy Shake	1964	30.00	75.00
SWORDSMEN, THE					
RCA Victor LSP-4245	(S)	Swordsmen	1969	4.00	10.00
RCA Victor LSP-4544	(S)	What's It All About, World	1971	4.00	10.00
SYKES, KEITH					
Vanguard VSD-6548	(S)	Keith Sykes	1970	4.00	10.00
Vanguard VSD-6574	(S)	1-2-3	1971	4.00	10.00
SYKES, ROOSEVELT					
Refer to Memphis Slim & Roosevelt Sykes; Victoria Spivey.					
Bluesville BVLP-1006	(M)	The Return Of Roosevelt Sykes	1960	40.00	100.00
Bluesville BVLP-1014	(M)	The Honeydripper	1961	40.00	100.00
		—Bluesville albums above have bright blue labels with silver print.—			
Bluesville BVLP-1006	(M)	The Return Of Roosevelt Sykes	1964	12.00	30.00
Bluesville BVLP-1014	(M)	The Honeydripper	1964	12.00	30.00
		—Bluesville albums above have blue labels with a trident logo on the right side.—			
Crown CLP-5287	(M)	Roosevelt Sykes Sings The Blues	1962	20.00	50.00
Crown CST-287	(S)	Roosevelt Sykes Sings The Blues	1962	20.00	50.00
		—Crown albums above have gray labels.—			
Delmark DL-607	(S)	The Hard Driving Blues Of Roosevelt Sykes	1963	20.00	50.00
Delmark DL-616	(S)	Roosevelt Sykes In Europe	1969	10.00	25.00
United US-7792	(M)	Roosevelt Sykes Sings The Blues	1969	1.00	5.00
Prestige PRST-7722	(S)	The Blues Of Roosevelt Sykes	1969	6.00	15.00
		(Prestige 7722 is a reissue of Bluesville material.)			
Delmark DL-632	(S)	Feel Like Blowing My Horn	1973	8.00	20.00
BluesWay BLS-6077	(S)	Double Dirty Mother	1973	6.00	15.00
Fantasy 24717	(S)	Urban Blues (2 LPs)	1973	4.00	10.00
Jewel 5011	(S)	Meet Roosevelt Sykes	1973	4.00	10.00
Blind Pig 005	(S)	The Original Honeydripper	1978	1.00	5.00
SYLVESTER, TERRY					
Terry is a member of The Hollies.					
Epic KE-33076	(S)	Terry Sylvester	1974	4.00	10.00
SYNDICATE OF SOUND, THE					
Bell LP-6001	(M)	Little Girl	1966	14.00	35.00
Bell SLP-6001	(S)	Little Girl	1966	20.00	50.00

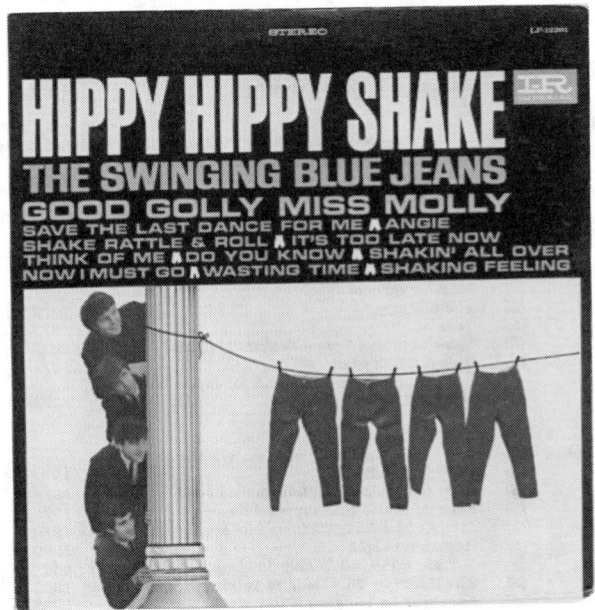

The Swinging Blue Jeans were brothers Ray and Ralph Ellis with Les Braid and Norman Kuhlke. They had three major hits on the UK charts in 1964: "Hippy Hippy Shake," "Good Golly Miss Mollie," and "You're No Good," all remakes of earlier hits. Only one, the first, had any real impact with US record buyers. Nonetheless, as part of the British Invasion, Imperial released an LP containing two of the aforementioned charters. As the multi-tracks were not available, Imperial electronically rechanneled the mono source tape (shown here). Like too many other groups of this era, they were far better than memory seems to serve fans and oldies stations. . . they really did swing!

T-BONES, THE

The T-Bones were a studio group under the direction of Joe Saraceno. Members included Dan Hamilton, Joe Frank Carollo, and Tommy Reynolds, who later recorded as Hamilton, Joe Frank & Reynolds.

Liberty LRP-3346	(M)	Boss Drag	1963	24.00	60.00
Liberty LST-7346	(S)	Boss Drag	1963	36.00	90.00
Liberty LRP-3363	(M)	Boss Drag At The Beach	1964	24.00	60.00
Liberty LST-7363	(S)	Boss Drag At The Beach	1964	36.00	90.00
Liberty LRP-3404	(M)	Doin' The Jerk	1965	14.00	35.00
Liberty LST-7404	(S)	Doin' The Jerk	1965	20.00	50.00
Liberty LRP-3439	(M)	No Matter What Shape	1966	8.00	20.00
Liberty LST-7439	(S)	No Matter What Shape	1966	10.00	25.00
Liberty LRP-3446	(M)	Sippin' And Chippin'	1966	10.00	25.00
Liberty LST-7446	(S)	Sippin' And Chippin'	1966	14.00	35.00
Liberty LRP-3471	(M)	Everyone's Gone To The Moon	1966	8.00	20.00
Liberty LST-7471	(S)	Everyone's Gone To The Moon	1966	10.00	25.00
Sunset SUM-1119	(M)	Shapin' Things Up	196?	4.00	10.00
Sunset SUS-5119	(S)	Shapin' Things Up	196?	5.00	12.00

T. I. M. E.

T.I.M.E. means Trust In Men Everywhere.

Liberty LST-7558	(S)	T. I. M. E.	1968	10.00	25.00
Liberty LST-7605	(S)	Smooth Ball (Die-cut cover)	1969	14.00	35.00

T-REX [TYRANNOSAURUS REX]

Tyrannosaurus Rex was the acoustic duo of Marc Bolan and Steve Peregrine Took, replaced by Mickey Finn in 1969. They add Steve Curry and Bill Legend in '70 and become the electric T-Rex.

Blue Thumb BTS-7	(S)	Unicorn	1969	8.00	20.00
Blue Thumb BTS-18	(S)	A Beard Of Stars (With bonus single)	1970	10.00	25.00
		(Issued with a promo single, "Ride A White Swan" / "Is It Love.")			
Blue Thumb BTS-18	(S)	A Beard Of Stars (Without bonus single)	1970·	8.00	20.00
Reprise PRO-511	(DJ)	An Interview With Marc Bolan	1971	40.00	100.00
Reprise RS-6440	(S)	T-Rex	1971	4.00	10.00
Reprise RS-6466	(S)	Electric Warrior	1971	4.00	10.00
Reprise MS-2095	(S)	The Slider	1972	4.00	10.00
Reprise MS-2132	(S)	Tanx	1973	4.00	10.00
A&M SP-3514	(S)	Tyrannosaurus Rex: A Beginning (2 LPs)	1972	4.00	10.00
MFP 5274	(S)	Ride A White Swan	1974	6.00	15.00
		(Manufactured by Capitol for export only.)			
Casablanca NBLP-9006	(S)	Light Of Love	1974	4.00	10.00

TALKING HEADS

Talking Heads is David Byrne, Chris Frantz, Jerry Harrison, and Tina Weymouth.

Sire 6036	(S)	Talking Heads: 77	1977	1.00	5.00
Sire 6058	(S)	More Songs About Buildings And Food	1978	1.00	5.00
Sire 6076	(S)	Fear Of Music (Die-stamped cover)	1979	1.00	5.00
Warner Bros. WBMS-104	(DJ)	Live At The Roxy (Counterfeits exist)	1979	20.00	50.00
Sire 6095	(S)	Remain In Light	1980	1.00	5.00
		(Sire 6058, 6076 and 6095 were produced by Eno.)			
Sire 3590	(S)	The Name Of This Band Is Talking Heads (2 LPs)	1982	3.20	8.00
Sire 23771	(S)	Speaking In Tongues (Clear vinyl)	1983	8.00	20.00
		(Issued in a clear plastic box with artwork by Robert Rauschenberg.)			
Sire 23883	(S)	Speaking In Tongues	1983	.80	4.00
Sire 25121	(S)	Stop Making Sense	1984	.80	4.00

TAMPA RED

Bluesville BVLP-1030	(M)	Don't Tampa With The Blues	1961	50.00	125.00
Bluesville BVLP-1043	(M)	Don't Jive Me	1962	50.00	125.00
		—Bluesville albums above have bright blue labels with silver print.—			
Bluesville BVLP-1030	(M)	Don't Tampa With The Blues	1964	14.00	35.00
Bluesville BVLP-1043	(M)	Don't Jive Me	1964	14.00	35.00
		—Bluesville albums above have blue labels with a trident logo on the right side.—			
Bluebird 2-5501	(S)	The Guitar Wizard (2 LPs)	1975	4.00	10.00
Yazoo 1039	(S)	Bottleneck Guitar	197?	1.20	6.00
Blues Classics 25	(S)	The Guitar Wizard	197?	3.20	8.00

Norma Tanega had a good-sized hit with the folk/bluesy "Walkin' My Cat Named Dog" for New Voice in 1966. The company followed the obvious course and issued an album titled after the hit. As was the norm, mono copies were pressed and distributed first. In the case of Ms. Tanega's album, apparently the sales were very slow and the stereo pressing (pictured here) was miniscule and has been a sought-after stereo collectible for years.

Label & Catalog #		Title	Year	VG+	NM
TAMS, THE					
ABC-Paramount 481	(M)	Presenting The Tams	1964	20.00	50.00
ABC-Paramount S-481	(E)	Presenting The Tams	1964	14.00	35.00
ABC-Paramount 499	(M)	Hey Girl, Don't Bother Me	1964	14.00	35.00
ABC-Paramount S-499	(S)	Hey Girl, Don't Bother Me	1964	20.00	50.00
ABC 596	(M)	Time For The Tams	1967	10.00	25.00
ABC S-596	(S)	Time For The Tams	1967	12.00	30.00
ABC S-627	(S)	A Little More Soul	1968	10.00	25.00
ABC S-673	(S)	A Portrait Of The Tams	1969	10.00	25.00
"1-2-3" 567	(S)	The Best Of The Tams	1970	8.00	20.00
Sounds South SO-16010	(S)	The Mighty, Mighty Tams	1977	6.00	15.00
Capitol SM-11839	(S)	The Best Of The Tams	1979	4.00	10.00
TANEGA, NORMA					
New Voice NV-2001	(M)	Walkin' My Cat Named Dog	1966	14.00	35.00
New Voice NVS-2001	(S)	Walkin' My Cat Named Dog	1966	30.00	75.00
TANGERINE DREAM					
Virgin 13-108	(S)	Phaedra	1974	4.00	10.00
Virgin V-2025	(S)	Rubycon	1975	4.00	10.00
Virgin V-2044	(S)	Ricochet	1975	4.00	10.00
Virgin PZ-34427	(S)	Stratosfear	1976	4.00	10.00
Virgin PZG-35014	(S)	Encore (2 LPs)	1977	5.00	12.00
MCA 2277	(S)	Sorcerer	1977	4.00	10.00
Virgin VI-211	(S)	Force Majeure	1978	4.00	10.00
Elektra 5E-521	(S)	Thief	1981	4.00	10.00
Elektra SE-557	(S)	Exit	1981	4.00	10.00
TANGERINE ZOO					
Mainstream S-6107	(S)	Tangerine Zoo	1968	20.00	50.00
Mainstream S-6116	(S)	Outside Looking In	1968	30.00	75.00
TAOS					
Mercury SR-61257	(S)	Taos	1970	4.00	10.00
TARANTULA					
A&M SP-4202	(S)	Tarantula	1969	8.00	20.00
TARTAGLIA					
Capitol ST-280	(S)	Good Morning Starshine	1969	3.20	8.00
TASAVALLAN PRESIDENT					
Janus 3065	(S)	Milky Way Moses	1974	5.00	12.00
TASTE					
Taste features Rory Gallagher.					
Atco SD-33-296	(S)	Taste	1969	12.00	30.00
Atco SD-33-322	(S)	On The Boards	1970	10.00	25.00
TATE, BABY					
Bluesville BVLP-1072	(M)	The What You Done	1963	30.00	75.00
		—Bluesville albums above have bright blue labels with silver print.—			
Bluesville BVLP-1072	(M)	The What You Done	1964	10.00	25.00
		—Bluesville albums above have blue labels with a trident logo on the right side.—			
TATE, ERIC					
Capricorn CP-0104	(S)	Drinking Man's Friend	1972	1.20	6.00
TAUPIN, BERNIE					
Bernie Taupin was Elton John's lyricist throughout John's '70's heyday.					
Elektra EKS-75020	(S)	Bernie Taupin	1972	4.00	10.00
Asylum 6E-263	(S)	He Who Rides The Tiger	1980	1.00	5.00
TAVENER, JOHN					
Apple SMAS-3369	(S)	The Whale	1972	8.00	20.00
TAX FREE					
Polydor 24-4053	(S)	Tax Free	1971	8.00	20.00
TAYLOR, BOBBY, & THE VANCOUVERS					
Gordy G-930	(M)	Bobby Taylor & The Vancouvers (White label)	1968	16.00	40.00
Gordy GS-930	(S)	Bobby Taylor & The Vancouvers	1968	10.00	25.00
Gordy GS-942	(S)	Taylor Made Soul	1968	10.00	25.00
TAYLOR, HOUND DOG					
Alligator 4701	(S)	Hound Dog Taylor	1971	10.00	25.00
Alligator 4704	(S)	Natural Boogie	1974	8.00	20.00
Alligator 4707	(S)	Beware Of The Dog (Thick cardboard cover)	1976	6.00	15.00

Label & Catalog #		Title	Year	VG+	NM
TAYLOR, JAMES					
Apple SKAO-3352	(S)	**James Taylor**	1969	10.00	25.00
		(Original covers for SKAO-3352 have the title in black print.)			
Apple SKAO-3352	(S)	**James Taylor**	1971	8.00	20.00
		(Later pressings have the title on the cover in orange print.)			
Warner Bros. WS-1843	(S)	**Sweet Baby James**	1970	1.00	5.00
Euphoria EST-2	(S)	**James Taylor & The Original Flying Machine 1967**	1971	1.00	5.00
		(Euphoria 2 contains work tapes by Danny Kortchmar and Taylor's group, The Flying Machine.)			
Warner Bros. BS-2561	(S)	**Mud Slide Slim**	1971	.80	4.00
Warner Bros. BS-2660	(S)	**One Man Dog**	1972	.80	4.00
Warner Bros. BS4-2660	(Q)	**One Man Dog**	1975	4.00	10.00
Warner Bros. BS-2794	(S)	**Walking Man**	1974	.80	4.00
Warner Bros. BS-2866	(S)	**Gorilla**	1975	.80	4.00
Warner Bros. BS4-2866	(Q)	**Gorilla**	1975	4.00	10.00
Warner Bros. BS-2912	(S)	**In The Pocket**	1976	.80	4.00
Warner Bros. BSK-3113	(S)	**Greatest Hits**	1976	.80	4.00
Trip TLP-9513	(S)	**Rainy Day Man**	197?	.80	4.00
		(Trip 9513 is a reissue of Euphoria 2.)			
Columbia JC-34811	(S)	**JT**	1977	.80	4.00
Columbia JC-36058	(S)	**Flag**	1979	.80	4.00
Columbia FC-37009	(S)	**Dad Loves His Work**	1981	.80	4.00
Columbia HC-47009	(S)	**Dad Loves His Work** *(Half-speed master)*	1983	13.00	40.00
TAYLOR, JOHNNIE					
Johnnie Taylor originally recorded with The Soul Stirrers.					
Stax ST-715	(M)	**Wanted: One Soul Singer**	1967	18.00	45.00
Stax STS-715	(M)	**Wanted: One Soul Singer**	1967	24.00	60.00
Stax STS-2005	(S)	**Who's Making Love?**	1968	20.00	50.00
Stax STS-2008	(S)	**Raw Blues**	1969	12.00	30.00
Stax STS-2012	(S)	**Rare Stamps**	1969	12.00	30.00
		("I Had A Dream" is rechanneled.)			
Stax STS-2023	(S)	**The Philosophy Continues**	1969	10.00	25.00
Stax STS-2030	(S)	**One Step Beyond**	1970	10.00	25.00
Stax STS-2032	(S)	**Johnnie Taylor's Greatest Hits**	1970	8.00	20.00
Stax STS-3014	(S)	**Taylored In Silk**	1973	8.00	20.00
Stax STS-5509	(S)	**Super Taylor**	1974	8.00	20.00
Stax STS-5522	(S)	**The Best Of Johnnie Taylor**	1975	8.00	20.00
Stax 88001	(S)	**Chronicle** *(2 LPs)*	1977	6.00	15.00
Columbia PC-33951	(S)	**Eargasm**	1976	1.00	5.00
Columbia PCQ-33951	(Q)	**Eargasm**	1976	8.00	20.00
Columbia PC-34401	(S)	**Rated Extraordinaire**	1977	1.00	5.00
Columbia PCQ-34401	(Q)	**Rated Extraordinaire**	1977	8.00	20.00
Columbia JC-35340	(S)	**Ever Ready**	1977	1.00	5.00
Columbia JC-36061	(S)	**She's Killing Me**	1979	1.00	5.00
Columbia JC-36548	(S)	**New Day**	1980	1.00	5.00
Columbia JC-37127	(S)	**The Best Of Johnnie Taylor**	1981	1.00	5.00
Beverly Glen 10001	(S)	**Just Ain't Good Enough**	1982	1.00	5.00
Stax 8520	(S)	**Super Hits**	1983	1.20	6.00
TAYLOR, KATE					
Cotillion SD-9045	(S)	**Sister Kate**	1971	5.00	12.00
TAYLOR, KINGSIZE, & THE DOMINOS					
Midnight HLP-2101	(M)	**Real Gonk Man**	1965	20.00	50.00
Midnight HST-2101	(S)	**Real Gonk Man**	1965	40.00	100.00
TAYLOR, KOKO					
Chess LPS-1532	(S)	**Koko Taylor**	1968	14.00	35.00
Chess CHS-50018	(S)	**Basic Soul**	1972	10.00	25.00
Alligator AL-4706	(S)	**I Got What It Takes**	1976	4.00	10.00
Alligator AL-4711	(S)	**The Earthshaker**	1978	4.00	10.00
Alligator AL-4724	(S)	**From The Heart Of A Woman**	1981	4.00	10.00
TAYLOR, LITTLE JOHNNY					
Galaxy 203	(M)	**Little Johnny Taylor**	1963	40.00	100.00
Galaxy 8203	(S)	**Little Johnny Taylor**	1963	60.00	150.00
Galaxy 207	(M)	**Little Johnny Taylor's Greatest Hits**	1964	40.00	100.00
Galaxy 8207	(S)	**Little Johnny Taylor's Greatest Hits**	1964	60.00	150.00
Ronn LPS-7530	(S)	**Everybody Knows About My Good Thing**	1972	10.00	25.00
Ronn LPS-7532	(S)	**Open House At My House**	1973	10.00	25.00
Ronn LPS-7535	(S)	**L.J.T.**	1979	8.00	20.00
TAYLOR, LITTLE JOHNNY, & TED TAYLOR					
Ronn LPS-7533	(S)	**The Super Taylors**	1973	6.00	15.00
TAYLOR, LIVINGSTON					
Capricorn 334	(S)	**Livingston Taylor**	1970	3.20	8.00

Label & Catalog #		Title	Year	VG+	NM
Capricorn 863	(S)	Liv	1971	1.20	6.00
Capricorn LP-0114	(S)	Over The Rainbow	1973	1.20	6.00

TAYLOR, MEL, & THE MAGICS

| Warner Bros. W-1624 | (M) | Mel Taylor In Action | 1966 | 14.00 | 35.00 |
| Warner Bros. WS-1624 | (S) | Mel Taylor In Action | 1966 | 20.00 | 50.00 |

TAYLOR, MICK
Mick Taylor was a member of John Mayall's Bluesbreakers and The Rolling Stones.

| Columbia JC-35076 | (S) | Mick Taylor | 1979 | 6.00 | 15.00 |

TAYLOR, R. DEAN

| Rare Earth 522 | (S) | I Think, Therefore I Am | 1970 | 4.00 | 10.00 |

TAYLOR, TED
Refer to Little Johnny Taylor & Ted Taylor.

OKeh OKM-12104	(M)	Be Ever Wonderful	1963	10.00	25.00
OKeh OKS-14104	(S)	Be Ever Wonderful	1963	14.00	35.00
OKeh OKM-12109	(M)	Blues And Soul	1965	10.00	25.00
OKeh OKS-14109	(S)	Blues And Soul	1965	14.00	35.00
OKeh OKM-12113	(M)	Ted Taylor's Greatest Hits	1966	8.00	20.00
OKeh OKS-14113	(S)	Ted Taylor's Greatest Hits	1966	10.00	25.00
Ronn LPS-7528	(S)	Shades Of Blue	1969	6.00	15.00
Ronn KPS-7529	(S)	You Can Dig It	1970	6.00	15.00
Ronn LPS-7531	(S)	Taylor Made	1972	6.00	15.00
MCA 3059	(S)	Keepin' My Head Above Water	1978	1.20	6.00

TEA COMPANY, THE

| Smash SRS-67105 | (S) | Come And Have Some Tea | 1968 | 20.00 | 50.00 |

TEARDROPS, THE

| 20th Century FXG-5011 | (S) | The Teardrops At Trinchi's | 197? | 4.00 | 10.00 |

TEDDY & THE PANDAS

| Tower ST-5125 | (S) | Basic Magnetism | 1968 | 10.00 | 25.00 |

TEDDY BEARS, THE
The TBs were Annette Kleinbard, who later recorded as Carol Connors, Marshall Leib, and Phil Spector.

| Imperial LP-9067 | (M) | The Teddy Bears Sing! | 1959 | 100.00 | 250.00 |
| Imperial LPS-12010 | (S) | The Teddy Bears Sing! | 1959 | 400.00 | 750.00 |

TEE SET, THE

| Colossus CCS-1001 | (S) | Ma Belle Amie | 1970 | 4.00 | 10.00 |

TEEGARDEN & VAN WINKLE

Atco SD-33-272	(S)	An Evening At Home	1968	6.00	15.00
Westbound 2003	(S)	But, Anyhow	1969	6.00	15.00
Westbound 2010	(S)	On Our Way	1972	6.00	15.00

TEEN QUEENS, THE

RPM LRP-3007	(M)	Eddie, My Love	1956	Unreleased	
Crown CLP-5022	(M)	Eddie, My Love	1956	150.00	400.00
		(Crown 5022 is a reissue of the unreleased RPM 3007.)			
		— Crown albums above have black labels with a silver "Crown" on top.—			
Crown CLP-5373	(M)	The Teen Queens	1963	20.00	50.00
Crown CST-373	(E)	The Teen Queens	1963	12.00	30.00
		—Crown albums above have gray labels.—			

TEENAGERS, THE
The Teenagers feature Frankie Lymon.

Gee GLP-701	(DJ)	The Teenagers Featuring Frankie Lymon	1957	750.00	1,500.00
		(White label promo on thick vinyl)			
Gee GLP-701	(M)	The Teenagers Featuring Frankie Lymon	1957	250.00	500.00
		— Gee albums above have red labels on non-flexible vinyl.—			
Gee GLP-701	(M)	The Teenagers Featuring Frankie Lymon	1961	60.00	150.00
Gee GLPS-701	(E)	The Teenagers Featuring Frankie Lymon	1961	80.00	200.00
		— Gee albums above have grey labels on non-flexible vinyl.—			
Gee GLP-701	(M)	The Teenagers Featuring Frankie Lymon	1978	4.00	10.00
		— Gee albums above have white labels on thin, flexible vinyl.—			

TELEVISION
Television features Tom Verlaine and Richard Lloyd, who later recorded as Richard Hell.

| Elektra 7E-1098 | (S) | Marquee Moon | 1977 | 6.00 | 15.00 |
| Elektra 6E-133 | (S) | Adventure | 1978 | 6.00 | 15.00 |

TEMPEST

| Warner Bros. BS-2682 | (S) | Tempest | 1973 | 12.00 | 30.00 |

The Teddy Bears Sing! *was one of the hottest early stereo LPs in the hobby for years. It peaked in value at the $1,000 range but has since slipped. While it is one of the earliest rock'n roll-based stereo albums, it is not a particularly "great" record and has suffered through word-of-mouth criticism. It remains an expensive collectible if only in that it features both Phil Spector and Annette Kleinbard, who later recorded as Carol Connors.*

Label & Catalog #		Title	Year	VG+	NM

TEMPESTS, THE

Label & Catalog #		Title	Year	VG+	NM
Smash MGS-27098	(M)	Would You Believe?	1966	10.00	25.00
Smash SRS-67098	(S)	Would You Believe?	1966	14.00	35.00

TEMPO, NINO

Liberty LRP-3023	(M)	Rock 'N Roll Beach Party	1958	60.00	150.00

TEMPO, NINO, & APRIL STEVENS

Atco 33-156	(M)	Deep Purple	1963	16.00	40.00
Atco SD-33-156	(S)	Deep Purple	1963	20.00	50.00
Atco 33-162	(M)	Nino Tempo & April Stevens Sing The Great Songs	1964	12.00	30.00
Atco SD-33-162	(S)	Nino Tempo & April Stevens Sing The Great Songs	1964	16.00	40.00
Atco 33-180	(M)	Hey Baby	1966	12.00	30.00
Atco SD-33-180	(S)	Hey Baby	1966	16.00	40.00
White Whale WW-113	(M)	All Strung Out	1967	8.00	20.00
White Whale WWS-7113	(S)	All Strung Out	1967	10.00	25.00

TEMPTATIONS, THE

The definitive male vocal group of the soulful '60s, the classic membership was Eddie Kendricks and David Ruffin with Melvin Franklin, Otis Williams and Paul Williams. Ruffin left in '68, replaced by Dennis Edwards. In '71, both Kendricks and Paul Williams quit. The new members were Damon Harris and Richard Street. Harris left in '75, replaced by Glenn Leonard. Edwards left in '78, replaced by Louis Price. Refer to The Supremes & The Temptations.

Gordy G-911	(M)	Meet The Temptations	1964	12.00	30.00
Gordy GS-911	(S)	Meet The Temptations	1964	16.00	40.00
Gordy G-912	(M)	The Temptations Sing Smokey	1965	12.00	30.00
Gordy GS-912	(S)	The Temptations Sing Smokey	1965	16.00	40.00
Gordy G-914	(M)	Temptin' Temptations	1965	10.00	25.00
Gordy GS-914	(S)	Temptin' Temptations	1965	12.00	30.00
		("Since I Lost My Baby" is rechanneled here and on 919 below.)			
Gordy G-918	(M)	Gettin' Ready	1966	10.00	25.00
Gordy GS-918	(S)	Gettin' Ready	1966	12.00	30.00
Gordy G-919	(M)	The Temptations' Greatest Hits	1966	10.00	25.00
Gordy GS-919	(S)	The Temptations' Greatest Hits	1966	10.00	25.00
Gordy G-921	(M)	The Temptations Live	1967	10.00	25.00
Gordy GS-921	(S)	The Temptations Live	1967	10.00	25.00
Gordy G-922	(M)	With A Lot O' Soul	1967	10.00	25.00
Gordy GS-922	(S)	With A Lot O' Soul	1967	10.00	25.00
		—Gordy albums above have "Gordy" in yellow script at the top of the label.—			
Gordy GS-911	(S)	Meet The Temptations	1967	6.00	15.00
Gordy GS-912	(S)	The Temptations Sing Smokey	1967	6.00	15.00
Gordy GS-914	(S)	Temptin' Temptations	1967	6.00	15.00
Gordy GS-918	(S)	Gettin' Ready	1967	6.00	15.00
Gordy GS-919	(S)	The Temptations' Greatest Hits	1967	6.00	15.00
Gordy GS-921	(S)	The Temptations Live	1967	6.00	15.00
Gordy GS-922	(S)	With A Lot O' Soul	1967	6.00	15.00
Gordy G-924	(M)	In A Mellow Mood	1967	10.00	25.00
Gordy GS-924	(S)	In A Mellow Mood	1967	10.00	25.00
Gordy G-927	(M)	The Temptations Wish It Would Rain *(White label)*	1968	16.00	40.00
Gordy GS-927	(S)	The Temptations Wish It Would Rain	1968	8.00	20.00
Gordy GS-933	(S)	The Temptations Show	1969	8.00	20.00
Gordy GS-938	(S)	Live At The Copa	1969	8.00	20.00
Gordy GS-939	(S)	Cloud Nine	1969	8.00	20.00
Gordy GS-947	(S)	Psychedelic Shack	1970	8.00	20.00
Gordy GS-949	(S)	Puzzle People	1969	8.00	20.00
Gordy GS-951	(S)	The Temptations' Christmas Card	1969	10.00	25.00
Gordy GS-953	(S)	Live At London's Talk Of The Town	1970	5.00	12.00
Gordy GS-954	(S)	The Temptations' Greatest Hits, Volume 2	1970	5.00	12.00
Gordy GS-957	(S)	Sky's The Limit	1971	5.00	12.00
Gordy GS-961	(S)	Solid Rock	1972	4.00	10.00
Gordy GS-962	(S)	All Directions	1972	4.00	10.00
Gordy GS-965	(S)	Masterpiece	1973	4.00	10.00
Gordy GS-966	(S)	1990	1973	3.20	8.00
Motown M-782	(S)	The Temptations/Anthology *(3 LPs)*	1973	8.00	20.00
Gordy GS-969	(S)	A Song For You	1976	3.20	8.00
Gordy GS-971	(S)	Wings Of Love	1976	3.20	8.00
Gordy GS-973	(S)	House Party	1975	3.20	8.00
Gordy GS-975	(S)	The Temptations Do The Temptations	1976	3.20	8.00
Kory 1009	(S)	Masterpiece	1977	1.00	5.00
Atlantic SD-19143	(S)	Hard To Tempt You	1977	1.00	5.00
Atlantic SD-19188	(S)	Bare Back	1978	1.00	5.00
Natural Resources 4005	(S)	In A Mellow Mood	1978	1.00	5.00
Gordy 994	(S)	Power	1980	1.00	5.00
Gordy 1006	(S)	The Temptations	1981	1.00	5.00
Motown M5-140V	(S)	Meet The Temptations	1981	.80	4.00
Motown M5-144V	(S)	Masterpiece	1982	.80	4.00
Motown M5-159V	(S)	Cloud Nine	1982	.80	4.00

The Teen Queens were sisters Betty and Rosie Collins, whose older brother, Aaron, was the lead singer for The Cadets/Jacks. Their sole hit on the national pop charts was "Eddie, My Love." An album was scheduled for release by RPM and then cancelled. The masters ended up with Crown, then a fledgling label wetting its feet with rhythm'n blues. Pictured here is the first album, Eddie, My Love, which sports an all too typical teen scene on the cover, although it is unlikely that many black teenagers would identify with the image. The second album, The Teen Queens, featuring a fabulous Fazzio cover, is an abridged (ten tracks versus twelve) reissue of the earlier title.

Label & Catalog #		Title	Year	VG+	NM
Motown M5-164V	(S)	Psychedelic Shack	1982	.80	4.00
Motown M5-172V	(S)	Puzzle People	1982	.80	4.00
Motown M5-205V	(S)	The Temptations Sing Smokey	1982	.80	4.00
Motown M5-212V	(S)	All The Million Sellers	1982	.80	4.00
Motown M5-235V	(S)	In A Mellow Mood	1982	.80	4.00
Motown 6008G	(S)	Reunion	1982	1.00	5.00
Motown 6032G	(S)	Surface Thrills	1983	1.00	5.00
Motown 6085G	(S)	Back To Basics	1983	1.00	5.00

TEMPTATIONS, THE / STEVIE WONDER

Gordy PR-101	(DJ)	The Sky's The Limit / Where I'm Coming From	1971	20.00	50.00

10CC

10CC was Lol Creme, Kevin Godley, Graham Gouldman, and Eric Stewart. Godley and Creme left in 1976 to work as a duo. Paul Burgess joined in '76 and Duncan Mackay in '78. This later quartet can also be found on the Arrival soundtrack "Sunburn." Refer to Godley & Creme; Graham Gouldman; Hotlegs; Neil Sedaka.

UK 53105	(S)	10CC	1973	3.20	8.00
UK 53107	(S)	Sheet Music	1974	3.20	8.00
UK 53110	(S)	100CC (The Greatest Hits)	1975	3.20	8.00
Mercury SRM-1-1029	(S)	The Original Soundtrack	1975	1.20	6.00
Mercury SRM-1-1061	(S)	How Dare You!	1976	1.20	6.00
Mercury SRM-1-3702	(S)	Deceptive Bends	1977	1.20	6.00
Mercury SRM-2-8600	(S)	Live And Let Live (2 LPs)	1977	3.20	8.00
Polydor PD1-6161	(S)	Bloody Tourists	1978	1.00	5.00
Polydor PD1-6186	(S)	The Things We Do For Love	1979	1.00	5.00
Polydor PD1-6244	(S)	Greatest Hits 1972-78	1979	1.00	5.00
Warner Bros. BSK-3442	(S)	Look Hear	1980	1.00	5.00

10,000 MANIACS

10,000 Maniacs issued two 12"-ers privately.

Elektra 60738-1	(S)	In My Tribe (Quiex II vinyl)	1987	6.00	15.00
Elektra 60738-1	(S)	In My Tribe	1987	1.00	5.00

TEN WHEEL DRIVE

Polydor 4008	(S)	Construction #1	1969	3.20	8.00
Polydor 4024	(S)	Brief Replies	1970	3.20	8.00
Polydor 4062	(S)	Peculiar Friends	1971	3.20	8.00
Capitol ST-11199	(S)	Ten Wheel Drive	1973	3.20	8.00

TEN YEARS AFTER

TYA features Alvin Lee.

Deram DES-18009	(S)	Ten Years After	1968	8.00	20.00
Deram DES-18016	(S)	Undead	1968	6.00	15.00
Deram DES-18021	(S)	Stonedhenge	1969	6.00	15.00
Deram DES-18029	(S)	Ssssh (Picture disc)	1969	See note below	

(London pressed up a small run of prototype picture discs to test the viability of a commercial release. Eight copies had the front cover of The Rolling Stones' "High Tide & Green Grass" on one side and "Sssh" on the other. Suggested NM value of $4,000-8,000.)

Deram DES-18038	(S)	Cricklewood Green	1970	4.00	10.00
Deram DES-18050	(S)	Watt	1970	4.00	10.00
Deram DES-18064	(S)	Alvin Lee And Company	1972	4.00	10.00

— Deram albums above have the "London" logo beneath Deram at the top of the label.—

Deram DES-18072	(S)	Goin' Home/Their Greatest Hits	1975	1.00	5.00
Columbia KC-30801	(S)	A Space In Time	1971	1.00	5.00
Columbia CQ-30801	(Q)	A Space In Time	1973	6.00	15.00
Columbia KC-31779	(S)	Rock And Roll Music To The World	1972	1.00	5.00
Columbia C2X-32288	(S)	Recorded Live (2 LPs)	1973	3.20	8.00
Columbia PC-32851	(S)	Positive Vibrations	1974	1.00	5.00
Columbia PC-34366	(S)	Classic Performances Of Ten Years After	1976	1.00	5.00
London LC-50008	(S)	London Collection-Greatest Hits	1977	1.00	5.00

TERMINAL BARBERSHOP

Atco SD-33-301	(S)	Hair Styles	1969	5.00	12.00

TERRELL, TAMMI

Refer to Marvin Gaye & Tammi Terrell; Chuck Jackson & Tammi Terrell.

Motown MS-652	(S)	Irresistible Tammi	1969	20.00	50.00
Motown M5-231V	(S)	Irresistible Tammi	1982	4.00	10.00

TERRENCE

Decca DL-75137	(S)	An Eye For An Ear	1969	6.00	15.00

TERRY, DEWEY

Refer to Don & Dewey.

Tumbleweed TWS-104	(S)	Chief	197?	6.00	15.00

Label & Catalog #		Title	Year	VG+	NM

TERRY, SONNY
Saunders Terrell aka Sonny Terry was a harmonica player and singer of traditional folk-based blues songs. Refer to Big Bill Broonzy; Woody Guthrie / Sonny Terry; Lightnin' Hopkins; Leadbelly / Josh White / Sonny Terry; Pete Seeger; Brother John Sellers & Sonny Terry.

Label & Catalog #		Title	Year	VG+	NM
Folkways FP-2006	(10")	Sonny Terry's Washboard Band (Red & white cover)	1950	60.00	150.00
Folkways FA-2006	(10")	Sonny Terry's Washboard Band (Black & white cover)	195?	40.00	100.00
Folkways FP-35	(10")	Harmonica And Vocal Solos	1952	40.00	100.00
Folkways FA-2035	(10")	Harmonica And Vocal Solos	1952	40.00	100.00
Stinson SLP-55	(10")	Sonny Terry And His Mouth Harp	1950	40.00	100.00
Elektra EKL-14	(10")	Folk Blues	1954	80.00	200.00
Elektra EKL-15	(10")	City Blues (With Alec Stewart)	1954	80.00	200.00
Riverside RLP-644	(M)	Sonny Terry And His Mouth Harp	195?	30.00	75.00
Bluesville BVLP-1025	(M)	Sonny's Story	1961	30.00	75.00
Bluesville BVLP-1059	(M)	Sonny Is King	1963	30.00	75.00
—Bluesville albums above have bright blue labels with silver print.—					
Bluesville BVLP-1025	(M)	Sonny's Story	1964	10.00	25.00
Bluesville BVLP-1059	(M)	Sonny Is King	1964	10.00	25.00
—Bluesville albums above have blue labels with a trident logo on the right side.—					
Prestige PRST-7802	(S)	Sonny Is King	1970	6.00	15.00
(Prestige 7802 is a reissue of Bluesville 1059.)					

TERRY, SONNY, & BROWNIE McGHEE
Sonny Terry and Brownie McGhee recorded together since 1939. The albums below may credit Sonny Terry or Brownie McGhee or both.. They can also be found on the Columbia soundtrak "Simply Heavenly" and Brut's "The Book Of Numbers."

Label & Catalog #		Title	Year	VG+	NM
Sharp 2003	(M)	Down Home Blues	195?	60.00	150.00
Topic T-29	(M)	Songs	1958	20.00	50.00
Roulette R-25074	(M)	The Folk Songs Of Sonny & Brownie	1959	20.00	50.00
Roulette SR-25074	(S)	The Folk Songs Of Sonny & Brownie	1959	30.00	75.00
World Pacific WP-1294	(M)	Blues Is A Story	1960	20.00	50.00
World Pacific ST-1294	(S)	Blues Is A Story	1960	30.00	75.00
World Pacific WP-1296	(M)	Down South Summit Meetin'	1960	20.00	50.00
World Pacific ST-1296	(S)	Down South Summit Meetin'	1960	30.00	75.00
Bluesville BVLP-1002	(M)	Down Home Blues	1960	30.00	75.00
Bluesville BVLP-1005	(M)	Blues And Folk	1960	30.00	75.00
Bluesville BVLP-1020	(M)	Blues All Around My Head	1961	30.00	75.00
Bluesville BVLP-1033	(M)	Blues In My Soul	1961	30.00	75.00
Bluesville BVLP-1058	(M)	Live At The Second Fret	1962	30.00	75.00
—Bluesville albums above have bright blue labels with silver print.—					
Bluesville BVLP-1002	(M)	Down Home Blues	1964	10.00	25.00
Bluesville BVLP-1005	(M)	Blues And Folk	1964	10.00	25.00
Bluesville BVLP-1020	(M)	Blues All Around My Head	1964	10.00	25.00
Bluesville BVLP-1033	(M)	Blues In My Soul	1964	10.00	25.00
Bluesville BVLP-1058	(M)	Live At The Second Fret	1964	10.00	25.00
—Bluesville albums above have blue labels with a trident logo on the right side.—					
Folkways FA-2327	(M)	Blues And Folksongs	1960	12.00	30.00
Folkways F-2421	(M)	Traditional Blues, Volume 1	1961	12.00	30.00
Folkways FS-2421	(S)	Traditional Blues, Volume 1	1961	16.00	40.00
Folkways F-2422	(M)	Traditional Blues, Volume 2	1961	12.00	30.00
Folkways FS-2422	(S)	Traditional Blues, Volume 2	1961	16.00	40.00
Verve MGV-3008	(M)	Blues Is My Companion	1961	30.00	75.00
Washington W-702	(M)	Talkin' 'Bout The Blues	1961	20.00	50.00
Fantasy F-3254	(M)	Sonny Terry & Brownie McGhee (Red vinyl)	1961	60.00	150.00
Fantasy F-3254	(M)	Sonny Terry & Brownie McGhee	1961	16.00	40.00
Fantasy F-3296	(M)	Just A Closer Walk With Thee (Red vinyl)	1962	60.00	150.00
Fantasy F-3296	(M)	Just A Closer Walk With Thee	1962	16.00	40.00
Fantasy F-3317	(M)	Blues & Shouts (Red vinyl)	1962	60.00	150.00
Fantasy F-3317	(M)	Blues & Shouts	1962	16.00	40.00
Fantasy F-3340	(M)	Sonny & Brownie At Sugar Hill (Red vinyl)	1962	60.00	150.00
Fantasy F-3340	(M)	Sonny & Brownie At Sugar Hill	196?	16.00	40.00
Fantasy FS-8091	(S)	Sonny & Brownie At Sugar Hill (Blue vinyl)	1962	60.00	150.00
Fantasy FS-8091	(S)	Sonny & Brownie At Sugar Hill	1962	20.00	50.00
—Fantasy albums above have maroon mono or blue stereo labels on non-flexible vinyl.—					
Kimberley 2017	(M)	Southern Meetin'	1963	8.00	20.00
Kimberley 11017	(S)	Southern Meetin'	1963	10.00	25.00
(Kimberley 2017 is a reissue of World Pacific 1296.)					
Folklore FRLP-14013	(M)	Down Home Blues	1964	16.00	40.00
Folklore FRST-14013	(S)	Down Home Blues	1964	20.00	50.00
(Folklore 14013 is a reissue of Bluesville 1002.)					
Verve/Folkways FV-9010	(M)	Get Together	1965	10.00	25.00
Verve/Folkways FVS-9010	(S)	Get Together	1965	12.00	30.00
Verve/Folkways FV-9019	(M)	Guitar Highway	1965	10.00	25.00
Verve/Folkways FVS-9019	(S)	Guitar Highway	1965	12.00	30.00
Smash MGS-27067	(M)	Brownie McGhee At The Bunkhouse	1965	12.00	30.00
Smash SRS-67067	(S)	Brownie McGhee At The Bunkhouse	1965	16.00	40.00

Label & Catalog #		Title	Year	VG+	NM
Mainstream MS-6049	(M)	Hometown Blues	1965	8.00	20.00
Mainstream MS-6049	(S)	Hometown Blues	1965	10.00	25.00
Everest 206	(S)	Sonny Terry	1968	10.00	25.00
Everest 242	(S)	Brownie McGhee & Sonny Terry	1969	10.00	25.00
Fontana SGF-67599	(S)	Where The Blues Begin	1969	10.00	25.00
Prestige PRLP-7715	(S)	Best Of Sonny Terry & Brownie McGhee	1969	6.00	15.00
Prestige PRLP-7802	(S)	Sonny Is King	1970	6.00	15.00
		(Prestige 7802 is a reissue of Bluesville 1059.)			
Prestige PRLP-7803	(S)	Live! At The 2nd Fret	1970	6.00	15.00
		(Prestige 7803 is a reissue of Bluesville 1058.)			
BluesWay BLS-6028	(S)	Long Way From Home	1969	6.00	15.00
BluesWay BLS-6059	(S)	Couldn't Believe My Eyes	1970	6.00	15.00
Olympic 7108	(S)	Hootin' & Hollerin'	1973	4.00	10.00
Savoy 12218	(S)	Down Home Blues	1973	4.00	10.00
A&M SP-34379	(S)	Sonny & Brownie	1973	5.00	12.00
Fantasy 24708	(S)	Back To New Orleans (2 LPs)	1972	6.00	15.00
Fantasy 24721	(S)	Midnight Special (2 LPs)	1977	4.00	10.00
Fantasy 24723	(S)	California Blues (2 LPs)	1981	4.00	10.00
TEX, JOE					
Checker LP-2993	(M)	Hold On	1964	60.00	150.00
King 935	(M)	The Best Of Joe Tex	1965	40.00	100.00
King KS-935	(E)	The Best Of Joe Tex	1965	30.00	75.00
		—King albums above have crownless black or blue labels.—			
Parrot PA-61002	(M)	The Best Of Joe Tex	1965	20.00	50.00
Parrot PAS-71002	(E)	The Best Of Joe Tex	1965	14.00	35.00
Atlantic 8106	(S)	Hold What You've Got	1965	20.00	50.00
Atlantic SD-8106	(S)	Hold What You've Got	1965	24.00	60.00
		("Hold What You've Got" is rechanneled on this album.)			
Atlantic 8115	(M)	The New Boss	1965	20.00	50.00
Atlantic SD-8115	(S)	The New Boss	1965	24.00	60.00
Atlantic 8124	(M)	The Love You Save	1966	20.00	50.00
Atlantic SD-8124	(S)	The Love You Save	1966	24.00	60.00
Atlantic 8133	(M)	I've Got To Do A Little Better	1966	20.00	50.00
Atlantic SD-8133	(S)	I've Got To Do A Little Better	1966	24.00	60.00
Atlantic 8144	(M)	The Best Of Joe Tex	1967	8.00	20.00
Atlantic SD-8144	(S)	The Best Of Joe Tex	1967	10.00	25.00
		("Hold On To What You've Got" is rechanneled on this album.)			
Atlantic SD-8156	(S)	Live And Lively	1968	8.00	20.00
Atlantic SD-8187	(S)	Soul Country	1968	8.00	20.00
Atlantic SD-8211	(S)	Happy Soul	1969	6.00	15.00
Atlantic SD-8231	(S)	Buying A Book	1969	6.00	15.00
Atlantic SD-8254	(S)	With Strings And Things	1970	6.00	15.00
Atlantic SD-8292	(S)	From The Roots Came The Rapper	1972	6.00	15.00
Dial DL-6002	(S)	I Gotcha	1972	6.00	15.00
Dial DL-6004	(S)	Spills The Beans	1973	6.00	15.00
Pride PRD-0020	(S)	The History Of Joe Tex	1973	1.20	6.00
Epic PE-34666	(S)	Bumps And Bruises	1977	1.00	5.00
Dial DL-6100	(S)	He Who Is Without Funk Cast The First Stone	1979	1.00	5.00
London 50017	(S)	London Collector-Super Soul	1979	1.00	5.00
Accord SN-7174	(S)	J.T.'s Funk	1982	1.00	5.00
TEXAS					
Bell 1128	(S)	Texas	1973	3.20	8.00
THAXTON, LLOYD					
Decca DL-4594	(M)	Lloyd Thaxton Presents	1964	8.00	20.00
Decca DL-74594	(S)	Lloyd Thaxton Presents	1964	10.00	25.00
THEE IMAGE					
Manticore MA6-50451	(S)	Thee Image	1975	4.00	10.00
Manticore MA6-50651	(S)	Inside The Triangle	1975	4.00	10.00
THEE PEDDLERS					
Epic BN-26458	(S)	Three In A Sell	1969	4.00	10.00
Epic BN-26529	(S)	Birthday	1970	4.00	10.00
THEE PROPHETS					
Kapp KS-3596	(S)	Playgirl	1969	4.00	10.00

THEM

For the group's first LP, the rhythm'n blues-based Them consisted of vocalist Van Morrison with Billy Harrison, Alan Henderson and brothers Jackie and Patrick McCauley, the latter four rarely being allowed the privilege of entering the studio to record the "group's" songs. By the time of the second album, Morrison was backed by Henderson with newcomers Jim Armstrong, Ray Elliott, and John Wilson. After which the singer left and the group disbanded. . .

Parrot PA-61005	(M)	Them Featuring "Here Comes The Night"	1965	30.00	75.00
Parrot PAS-71005	(E)	Them Featuring "Here Comes The Night"	1965	20.00	50.00

Label & Catalog #		Title	Year	VG+	NM
Parrot PA-61005	(M)	Them Featuring "Gloria"	1966	20.00	50.00
Parrot PAS-71005	(E)	Them Featuring "Gloria"	1966	16.00	40.00
		("Them" was issued twice with the cover promoting different singles.)			
Parrot PA-61008	(M)	Them Again	1966	30.00	75.00
Parrot PAS-71008	(E)	Them Again	1966	20.00	50.00
Parrot BP-71053	(E)	Them Featuring Van Morrison (2 LPs)	1972	4.00	10.00
		(71053 contains abridged versions of 71005 and 71008 except "Gloria," "Here Comes The Night," "One Two Brown Eyes," "If Only You And I Could Be As Two," and "One More Time" are in stereo.)			
London PS-639	(P)	Backtrackin'	1974	1.00	5.00
London LC-50001	(E)	The Story Of Them	1977	1.00	5.00

THEM
In 1967, Them reformed as a punk/psych band with former members Henderson, Armstrong and Elliott (above) joined by Dave Harvey and lead vocalist Ken McDowell.

Tower T-5104	(M)	Now And Them	1968	20.00	50.00
Tower ST-5104	(S)	Now And Them	1968	30.00	75.00
Tower T-5116	(M)	Time Out! Time In For Them	1968	30.00	75.00
Tower ST-5116	(S)	Time Out! Time In For Them	1968	40.00	100.00
Happy Tiger HT-1004	(S)	Them	1969	20.00	50.00
Happy Tiger HT-1012	(S)	Them In Reality	1971	50.00	125.00

THIN LIZZY
Thin Lizzy features Phil Lynott.

London PS-594	(S)	Thin Lizzy	1971	16.00	40.00
London PS-636	(S)	Vagabonds Of The Western World	1973	12.00	30.00
Vertigo 2002	(S)	Nightlife	1974	6.00	15.00
Vertigo 2005	(S)	Fighting	1975	6.00	15.00
Mercury SRM-1-1081	(S)	Jailbreak	1976	4.00	10.00
Mercury SRM-1-1107	(S)	Night Life	1976	4.00	10.00
Mercury SRM-1-1108	(S)	Fighting	1976	4.00	10.00
Mercury SRM-1-1119	(S)	Johnny The Fox	1976	4.00	10.00
Mercury SRM-1-1186	(S)	Bad Reputation	1977	4.00	10.00
London LC-50004	(S)	The Rocker 1971-1974	1977	4.00	10.00
Warner Bros. BS2-3213	(S)	Live And Dangerous (2 LPs)	1978	4.00	10.00
Warner Bros. BSK-3338	(S)	Black Rose/A Rock Legend	1979	4.00	10.00
Warner Bros. BSK-3496	(S)	Chinatown	1980	4.00	10.00
Warner Bros. BSK-3622	(S)	Renegade	1982	4.00	10.00
Warner Bros. 23831	(S)	Thunder And Lightning	1983	3.20	8.00
Warner Bros. 23986	(S)	Life/Live	1983	3.20	8.00
Grand Slamm SLAM-4	(S)	Lizzy Lives (1976-1984)	1989	3.20	8.00
Mercury 848-530	(S)	Dedication-The Very Best Of Thin Lizzy	1991	3.20	8.00

THINK

Laurie SLLP-2052	(S)	Encounter	1972	4.00	10.00

THIRD EAR BAND, THE

Harvest ST-376	(S)	Alchemy	1969	8.00	20.00

THIRD POWER, THE

Vanguard VSD-6554	(S)	The Third Power Believe	1970	16.00	40.00

THIRD RAIL, THE

Epic LN-24327	(M)	Id Music	1967	12.00	30.00
Epic BN-26327	(S)	Id Music	1967	16.00	40.00

13TH FLOOR ELEVATORS, THE
The Elevators feature Roky Erikson.

International Art. 1	(M)	Psychedelic Sounds (White label promo)	1967	300.00	600.00
International Art. 1	(M)	Psychedelic Sounds	1967	150.00	300.00
		—Original Int. Art. album above has green & yellow labels.—			
International Art. 1	(M)	Psychedelic Sounds	1968	60.00	150.00
International Art. 1	(S)	Psychedelic Sounds	1968	40.00	100.00
		("You're Gonna Miss Me" is rechanneled on this album.)			
International Art. 5	(M)	Easter Everywhere (White label promo)	1968	250.00	500.00
International Art. 5	(S)	Easter Everywhere (With inner sleeve)	1968	60.00	150.00
International Art. 5	(S)	Easter Everywhere (Without inner sleeve)	1968	40.00	100.00
International Art. 8	(S)	13th Floor Elevators Live (White label)	1968	80.00	200.00
International Art. 8	(S)	13th Floor Elevators Live	1968	30.00	75.00
International Art. 9	(S)	Bull Of The Woods (White label promo)	1968	80.00	200.00
International Art. 9	(S)	Bull Of The Woods	1968	30.00	75.00
		—Original Int. Art. albums above copies were pressed on thick vinyl—			
International Art. 1	(S)	Psychedelic Sounds	1979	12.00	30.00
International Art. 5	(S)	Easter Everywhere	1979	12.00	30.00
International Art. 8	(S)	13th Floor Elevators Live	1979	10.00	25.00
International Art. 9	(S)	Bull Of The Woods	1979	10.00	25.00
		—Int. Art. reissues above are on thinner vinyl with "Masterfonics" stamped in the trail-off vinyl.—			

Label & Catalog #		Title	Year	VG+	NM
THIRTY DAYS OUT					
Reprise MS-2085	(S)	**Miracle Lick**	1972	6.00	15.00
31 FLAVORS, THE					
Crown CST-592	(S)	**Hair**	1968	30.00	75.00
31ST OF FEBRUARY, THE					
The 31st Of February features Butch Trucks, later of The Allman Brothers.					
Vanguard VSD-6503	(S)	**The 31st Of February**	1969	16.00	40.00
THOMAS, ALLAN					
Sire 5901	(S)	**A Picture**	1971	1.20	6.00
THOMAS, B. J.					
Pacemaker PLP-3001	(M)	**B. J. Thomas & The Triumphs**	1965	80.00	200.00
Hickory LPM-133	(M)	**The Very Best Of B. J. Thomas**	1966	8.00	20.00
Hickory LPS-133	(S)	**The Very Best Of B. J. Thomas**	1966	10.00	25.00
Hickory T-90956	(M)	**The Very Best Of B. J. Thomas**	1966	10.00	25.00
Hickory ST-90956	(S)	**The Very Best Of B. J. Thomas** (Capitol Rec. Club)	1966	10.00	25.00
Scepter SRM-535	(M)	**I'm So Lonesome I Could Cry**	1966	8.00	20.00
Scepter SPS-535	(S)	**I'm So Lonesome I Could Cry**	1966	10.00	25.00
Scepter SRM-556	(M)	**Tomorrow Never Comes**	1966	6.00	15.00
Scepter SPS-556	(S)	**Tomorrow Never Comes**	1966	8.00	20.00
Scepter SRM-561	(M)	**For Lovers And Losers**	1967	6.00	15.00
Scepter SPS-561	(S)	**For Lovers And Losers**	1967	4.00	10.00
Scepter SPS-570	(S)	**On My Way**	1968	1.00	5.00
Scepter SPS-576	(S)	**Young And In Love**	1969	1.00	5.00
Scepter SPS-578	(S)	**B. J. Thomas' Greatest Hits**	1969	1.00	5.00
Scepter SPS-580	(S)	**Raindrops Keep Fallin' On My Head**	1969	1.00	5.00
Scepter SPS-582	(S)	**Everybody's Out Of Town**	1970	1.00	5.00
Scepter SPS-586	(S)	**Most Of All**	1970	1.00	5.00
Scepter SPS-597	(S)	**Greatest Hits, Volume Two**	1971	1.00	5.00
Scepter 5101	(S)	**Billy Joe Thomas**	1972	1.00	5.00
Doral	(S)	**Doral Presents B. J. Thomas**	1971	4.00	10.00
		(Promotional compilation of previously released material.)			
ABC D-858	(S)	**Reunion**	1975	1.00	5.00
MCA 2286	(S)	**B.J. Thomas**	1977	1.00	5.00
Cleveland Inter. 38561	(S)	**New Looks**	1983	1.00	5.00
THOMAS, CARLA					
Ms. Thomas also recorded with Otis Redding; Rufus Thomas.					
Atlantic 8057	(M)	**Gee Whiz**	1961	40.00	100.00
Atlantic SD-8057	(S)	**Gee Whiz**	1961	60.00	150.00
		—*Atlantic albums above have multi-color labels with a white "fan" logo on the right side.*—			
Atlantic 8057	(M)	**Gee Whiz**	196?	14.00	35.00
Atlantic SD-8057	(S)	**Gee Whiz**	196?	20.00	50.00
		—*Atlantic albums above have multi-color labels with a black "fan" logo on the right side.*—			
Atlantic SD-8232	(P)	**The Best Of Carla Thomas**	1969	10.00	25.00
Stax ST-706	(M)	**Comfort Me**	1966	14.00	35.00
Stax STS-706	(S)	**Comfort Me**	1966	20.00	50.00
		("Comfort Me" and "No Time To Lose" are rechanneled.)			
Stax ST-709	(M)	**Carla**	1966	14.00	35.00
Stax STS-709	(S)	**Carla**	1966	20.00	50.00
Stax ST-718	(M)	**The Queen Alone**	1967	14.00	35.00
Stax STS-718	(S)	**The Queen Alone**	1967	20.00	50.00
Stax STS-2019	(S)	**Memphis Queen**	1969	12.00	30.00
Stax STS-2044	(S)	**Love Means Carla Thomas**	1971	12.00	30.00
THOMAS, IAN					
Janus 3058	(S)	**Ian Thomas**	1973	1.20	6.00
Atlantic SD-19167	(S)	**Still Here**	1978	1.00	5.00
THOMAS, IRMA					
Imperial LP-9266	(M)	**Wish Someone Would Care**	1964	20.00	50.00
Imperial LP-12266	(S)	**Wish Someone Would Care**	1964	24.00	60.00
Imperial 9302	(M)	**Take A Look**	1966	20.00	50.00
Imperial LP-12302	(S)	**Take A Look**	1966	24.00	60.00
Fungus FB-25150	(S)	**In Between Tears**	1973	14.00	35.00
Bandy 700003	(S)	**Irma Thomas Sings**	197?	4.00	10.00
RCS 1004	(S)	**Safe With Me**	1980	1.20	6.00
THOMAS, JOE, & BILL ELLIOTT					
Sue SLP-1025	(S)	**Speak Your Piece**	1964	20.00	50.00
THOMAS, JON					
ABC-Paramount ABC-351	(M)	**Heartbreak**	1960	10.00	25.00
ABC-Paramount ABCS-351	(S)	**Heartbreak**	1960	14.00	35.00
		("Heartbreak" and "Buffalo Blues" are rechanneled.)			

Meet Sue Thompson (*the professional name of Ms Eva Sue McKee*) *introduced the market to the young singer who had two Top Tenners in 1961 with "Sad Movies (Make Me Cry)" and the deliriously loopy "Norman." Both are collected on this, her first Hickory album. After her popularity with the teen market waned, she gradually shifted towards a more comfortable niche in the country'n western world.*

Label & Catalog #		Title	Year	VG+	NM

THOMAS, RAY
Thomas is a member of The Moody Blues.

Threshold THS-016	(S)	From Mighty Oaks	1975	4.00	10.00
Threshold THSX-102	(DJ)	Ray Thomas Discusses The Recording Of His First Solo Album	1975	20.00	50.00
Threshold THS-017	(S)	Hopes, Wishes And Dreams	1976	4.00	10.00

THOMAS, RUFUS

Stax ST-704	(M)	Walking The Dog	1963	60.00	150.00
Stax STS-2028	(S)	Do The Funky Chicken	1970	10.00	25.00
Stax STS-2039	(S)	Doing The Push And Pull Live At P.J.'s	1971	10.00	25.00
Stax STS-3004	(S)	Did You Hear Me	1972	10.00	25.00
Stax STS-3008	(S)	Crown Prince Of Dance	1973	10.00	25.00
A.V.I. 6015	(S)	If There Were No Music	1977	6.00	15.00
A.V.I. 6046	(S)	I Ain't Gettin' Older, I'm Gettin' Better	1978	6.00	15.00
Gusto 0064	(S)	Thomas Rufus	1980	1.20	6.00

THOMAS, RUFUS & CARLA

| Stax 4124 | (S) | Chronicle | 1979 | 6.00 | 15.00 |

THOMAS, TIMMY

| Glades 33-6501 | (S) | Why Can't We Live Together | 1972 | 3.20 | 8.00 |
| Glades 33-7510 | (S) | The Magician | 1976 | 1.20 | 6.00 |

THOMPSON, DON

| Sunday KS-5101 | (S) | Jupiter | 197? | 3.20 | 8.00 |

THOMPSON, RICHARD [RICHARD & LINDA THOMPSON]
Mr Thompson was a member of Fairport Convention. While some albums credit him solely, Mrs Thompson appears on most, if not all, of them. Refer to The Bunch.

Reprise MS-2112	(S)	Henry The Human Fly	1972	8.00	20.00
Island ILPS-9241	(S)	Live! More Or Less (2 LPs)	1973	10.00	25.00
Island ILPS-9266	(S)	Hokey Pokey	1974	6.00	15.00
Island ILPS-9348	(S)	Pour Down Like Silver	1975	6.00	15.00
Chrysalis CHR-1177	(S)	First Light	1978	6.00	15.00
Hannibal HNBL-1303	(S)	Shoot Out The Lights	1982	3.20	8.00
Hannibal HNLP-1313	(S)	Hand Of Kindness	1983	3.20	8.00
Hannibal HNLP-1316	(S)	Small Town Romance	1984	3.20	8.00
Carthage CGLP-4403	(S)	Sunnyvista	1983	3.20	8.00
Carthage CGLP-4404	(S)	Pour Down Like Silver	1983	3.20	8.00
Carthage CGLP-4405	(S)	Henry The Human Fly	1983	3.20	8.00
Carthage CGLP-4407	(S)	I Want To See The Bright Lights Tonight	1983	3.20	8.00
Carthage CGLP-4408	(S)	Hokey Pokey	1983	3.20	8.00
Carthage CGLP-4409	(S)	Strict Tempo	1983	3.20	8.00
Carthage CGLP-4412	(S)	First Light	1984	3.20	8.00
Carthage CGLP-4413	(S)	Guitar, Vocal	1984	3.20	8.00
Polydor 825-421	(S)	Across A Crowded Room	1986	3.20	8.00
Polydor 829-728	(S)	Daring Adventures	1986	3.20	8.00
Capitol 48845	(S)	Amnesia	1988	3.20	8.00

THOMPSON, SONNY
For additional listings refer to Freddie King & Lula Reed & Sonny Thompson.

King 568	(M)	Moody Blues	1956	300.00	600.00
King 655	(M)	Mellow Blues For The Late Hours	1959	150.00	300.00
		—King albums above have crownless black labels.—			

THOMPSON, SUE

Hickory LPM-104	(M)	Meet Sue Thompson	1962	20.00	50.00
Hickory LPS-104	(S)	Meet Sue Thompson	1962	30.00	75.00
Hickory LPM-107	(M)	Two Of A Kind	1962	14.00	35.00
Hickory LPS-107	(S)	Two Of A Kind	1962	20.00	50.00
Hickory LPM-111	(M)	Sue Thompson's Golden Hits	1963	12.00	30.00
Hickory LPS-111	(S)	Sue Thompson's Golden Hits	1963	16.00	40.00
Wing MGW-12317	(M)	The Country Side Of Sue Thompson	1965	6.00	15.00
Wing SRW-16317	(S)	The Country Side Of Sue Thompson	1965	8.00	20.00
Hickory LPM-121	(M)	Paper Tiger	1965	12.00	30.00
Hickory LPS-121	(S)	Paper Tiger	1965	16.00	40.00
Hickory LPM-130	(M)	Sue Thompson With Strings Attached	1966	12.00	30.00
Hickory LPS-130	(S)	Sue Thompson With Strings Attached	1966	16.00	40.00
Hickory LPS-148	(S)	This Is Sue Thompson	1969	8.00	20.00
MGM/Hickory H3F-4511	(S)	Sweet Memories	1974	6.00	15.00
MGM/Hickory H3G-4515	(S)	...And Love Me	1974	6.00	15.00
MGM/Hickory H3G-4523	(S)	Big Mable Murphy	1975	6.00	15.00

THORINSHIELD

| Philips PHS-600-251 | (S) | Thorinshield | 1968 | 8.00 | 20.00 |

Who'da guessed that good ol' Three Dog Night— arguably the most successful group of their time with twelve charting albums for Dunhill and twelve Gold Records from the RIAA—would be the only group to have two albums recalled for objectionable cover art? It Ain't Easy was issued initially with the group posing in the buff! The original cover for Hard Labor featured a delivery scene with a monster of sorts presenting the world with a fluid-coated long-playing record. This was quickly amended by affixing a large band-aid over the jacket! Subsequent pressings had the band-aid printed into the art.

Label & Catalog #		Title	Year	VG+	NM
THORNTON, BIG MAMA					
Arhoolie F-1028	(M)	**Big Mama Thornton In Europe**	1966	12.00	30.00
Arhoolie F-1032	(M)	**The Queen At Monterey**	1967	12.00	30.00
Arhoolie F-1039	(M)	**Ball And Chain**	1967	12.00	30.00
Mercury SRM-1-61225	(S)	**Stronger Than Dirt**	1969	10.00	25.00
Mercury SRM-1-61249	(S)	**The Way It Is**	1970	10.00	25.00
Roulette SR-42050	(S)	**Maybe**	1970	10.00	25.00
Backbeat BLP-68	(E)	**She's Back**	1970	10.00	25.00
Pentagram PE-10,005	(S)	**Saved**	1971	6.00	15.00
Vanguard VSD-79351	(S)	**Jail**	1974	6.00	15.00
Vanguard VSD-79354	(S)	**Sassy Mama**	1975	6.00	15.00
THREE CHUCKLES, THE					
The Three Chuckles feature Teddy Randazzo.					
Vik LX-1067	(M)	**The Three Chuckles**	1956	150.00	300.00
THREE DEGREES, THE					
Roulette SR-42050	(S)	**Maybe**	1970	16.00	40.00
THREE DOG NIGHT					
Three Dog Night features Danny Hutton, Cory Wells and Chuck Negron.					
Dunhill DS-50048	(S)	**Three Dog Night**	1968	1.00	5.00
Dunhill DS-50058	(S)	**Suitable For Framing**	1969	1.00	5.00
Dunhill DS-50068	(S)	**Captured Live At The Forum**	1969	1.00	5.00
Dunhill DS-50078	(S)	**It Ain't Easy**	1970	40.00	100.00
		(Original covers for DS-50078 have the group posing in the nude.)			
Dunhill DS-50078	(S)	**It Ain't Easy** *(Gatefold cover)*	1970	1.00	5.00
Dunhill DSX-50088	(S)	**Naturally**	1970	1.00	5.00
Dunhill DSX-50098	(S)	**Golden Biscuits**	1971	1.00	5.00
Dunhill DSX-50108	(S)	**Harmony**	1971	1.00	5.00
Dunhill DSD-50118	(S)	**Seven Separate Fools**	1972	1.00	5.00
Dunhill DSY-50138	(S)	**Around The World With Three Dog Night** *(2 LPs)*	1973	1.20	6.00
Dunhill DSX-50158	(S)	**Cyan**	1973	1.00	5.00
Dunhill DSD-50168	(S)	**Hard Labor**	1974	12.00	30.00
		("First-state delivery cover." Original covers depict a hospital delivery with a female creature giving birth to a record album.)			
Dunhill DSD-50168	(S)	**Hard Labor**	1974	4.00	10.00
		("Second-state delivery cover." In a pique of embarrassment, Dunhill recalled the album and rather cleverly had a huge Band-Aid affixed to the jacket covering the "offending" scene.)			
Dunhill DSD-50168	(S)	**Hard Labor**	197?	1.00	5.00
		("Third-state delivery cover." Later covers have the Band-Aid printed on the cover as part of the artwork.)			
		—*Original Dunhill albums above have "A Subsidiary of ABC" on the bottom.*—			
Command QD-40014	(Q)	**Hard Labor**	1975	6.00	15.00
Dunhill DSD-50178	(S)	**Joy To The World: Their Greatest Hits**	1974	1.00	5.00
ABC X-888	(S)	**Coming Down Your Way**	1975	1.00	5.00
Command QD-40018	(Q)	**Coming Down Your Way**	1975	6.00	15.00
ABC D-928	(S)	**American Pastime**	1976	1.00	5.00
MCA Z-6018	(S)	**The Best Of Three Dog Night** *(2 LPs)*	1982	1.00	5.00
THREE FACES WEST					
Outpost 1000	(S)	**Three Faces West**	197?	8.00	20.00
THREE FLAMES, THE					
Mercury MG-20239	(M)	**At The Bon Soir**	1957	20.00	50.00
THREE GIRLS					
Phantom BPL1-0955	(S)	**The Deadly Nightshade**	1975	4.00	10.00
THREE MAN ARMY					
Three Man Army features brothers Adrian and Paul Gurvitz. Refer to The Baker-Gurvitz Army.					
Kama Sutra SKBS-2044	(S)	**A Third Of A Lifetime** *(Gatefold cover)*	1971	12.00	30.00
		—*Kama Sutra albums above have pink labels.*—			
Kama Sutra SKBS-2044	(S)	**A Third Of A Lifetime** *(Standard cover)*	1972	6.00	15.00
		—*Kama Sutra albums above have blue labels.*—			
Reprise MS-2150	(S)	**Three Man Army**	1973	10.00	25.00
Reprise MS-2182	(S)	**Three Man Army Two**	1974	10.00	25.00
THREE'S A CROWD					
Dunhill DS-50030	(S)	**Christopher's Movie Matinee**	1968	4.00	10.00
THRILLINGTON, PERCY "THRILLS"					
Thrills Thrillington is a pseudonym for Paul McCartney.					
Capitol ST-11642	(S)	**Thrillington**	1977	60.00	150.00

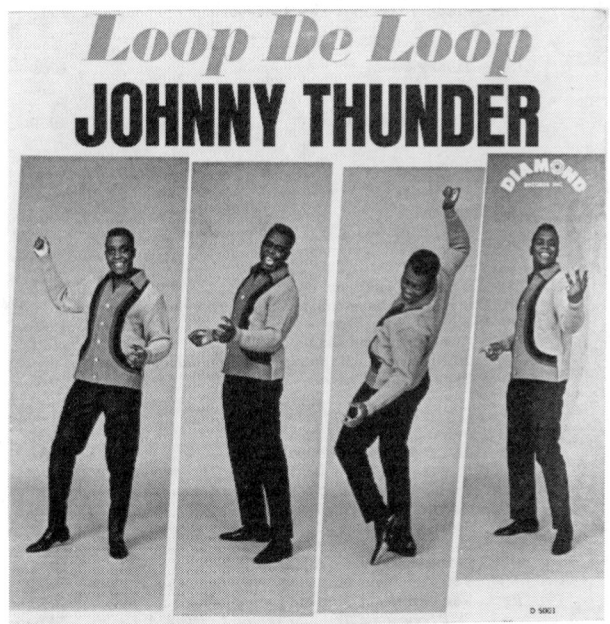

Johnny Thunder burst on the pop scene in the first weeks of 1963 with an uptempo version of the children's song "Loop De Loop." This inspired Diamond to release an LP with this stiltedly posed front cover that did little to convince the potential customer that the dance-oriented tracks contained within were other than lame.

Label & Catalog #		Title	Year	VG+	NM
THUNDER, JOHNNY					
Diamond D-5001	(M)	Loop De Loop	1963	40.00	100.00
Diamond SD-5001	(S)	Loop De Loop	1963	60.00	150.00
Real Records RR1	(S)	So Alone	196?	4.00	10.00
THUNDER					
Capitol ST-11279	(S)	Thunder	1974	1.20	6.00
THUNDER & ROSES					
United Artists UAS-6709	(S)	King Of The Black Sunrise	1969	12.00	30.00
THUNDERCLAP NEWMAN					
TN—Speedy Keen, Jimmy McCulloch, and Andy Newman—was produced by Pete Townshend.					
Track SD-8264	(S)	Hollywood Dream	1970	10.00	25.00
MCA/Track 354	(S)	Hollywood Dream	1973	3.20	8.00
THUNDERTREE					
Roulette SR-42038	(S)	Thundertree	1970	8.00	20.00
TIDBITS, THE					
Family Productions 2714	(S)	Greetings From Jamaica	1973	4.00	10.00
TIDES, THE					
Mercury MG-20714	(M)	Limbo Rock	1962	6.00	15.00
Mercury SR-60714	(S)	Limbo Rock	1962	8.00	20.00
Wing MGW-12248	(M)	The Best Of Bossa Nova	1963	5.00	12.00
Wing SRW-16248	(S)	The Best Of Bossa Nova	1963	6.00	15.00
Wing MGW-12265	(M)	Surf City And Other Surfin' Favorites	1963	10.00	25.00
Wing SRW-16265	(S)	Surf City And Other Surfin' Favorites	1963	12.00	30.00
TIEKIN, FREDDIE, & THE ROCKERS					
I.T. 2301	(M)	By Popular Demand	1957	20.00	50.00
I.T. 2304	(M)	Freddie Tiekin & The Rockers	1958	20.00	50.00
TIFFANY SHADE					
Mainstream S-6105	(S)	Tiffany Shade	1969	40.00	100.00
TIJUANA BEATLES, THE					
Alshire 5165	(S)	The Tijuana Beatles	1969	6.00	15.00
TIKIS, THE					
Minaret TLP-7001	(M)	The Tikis	1962	40.00	100.00
Philips PHM-200-043	(M)	The Tikis	1962	10.00	25.00
Philips PHS-600-043	(S)	The Tikis	1962	14.00	35.00
		(Philips 043 is a reissue of Minaret 7001.)			
TIL, SONNY, & THE ORIOLES					
RCA Victor LSP-4451	(S)	Sonny Til Returns	1970	8.00	20.00
		—RCA albums above have orange labels on non-flexible vinyl.—			
RCA Victor LSP-4451	(S)	Sonny Til Returns	1970	5.00	12.00
RCA Victor LSP-4538	(S)	Old Gold/New Gold	1971	6.00	15.00
		—RCA albums above have orange labels on flexible vinyl.—			
Dobre 1026	(S)	Back To The Chapel	1978	4.00	10.00
TILLOTSON, JOHNNY					
Cadence CLP-3052	(M)	Johnny Tillotson's Best	1961	14.00	35.00
Cadence CLP-25052	(S)	Johnny Tillotson's Best	1961	20.00	50.00
		("Dreamy Eyes," "True, True Happiness," "Without You" are rechanneled.)			
		—Cadence albums above have burgundy & silver labels.—			
Cadence CLP-3052	(M)	Johnny Tillotson's Best	1962	10.00	25.00
Cadence CLP-25052	(S)	Johnny Tillotson's Best	1962	12.00	30.00
Cadence CLP-3058	(M)	It Keeps Right On A-Hurtin'	1962	10.00	25.00
Cadence CLP-25058	(S)	It Keeps Right On A-Hurtin'	1962	12.00	30.00
Cadence CLP-3067	(M)	You Can Never Stop Me Loving You	1963	10.00	25.00
Cadence CLP-25067	(S)	You Can Never Stop Me Loving You	1963	12.00	30.00
		("Lonesome Town," "Donna," "I Got A Feelin'," "Where Is She?,"			
		"Venus" and "Come Softly To Me" are rechanneled.)			
		—Cadence albums above have red & black labels.—			
MGM E-4188	(M)	Talk Back Trembling Lips	1964	8.00	20.00
MGM SE-4188	(S)	Talk Back Trembling Lips	1964	10.00	25.00
MGM E-4224	(M)	The Tillotson Touch	1964	8.00	20.00
MGM SE-4224	(S)	The Tillotson Touch	1964	10.00	25.00
MGM E-4270	(M)	She Understands Me	1964	8.00	20.00
MGM SE-4270	(S)	She Understands Me	1964	10.00	25.00
MGM E-4302	(M)	That's My Style	1965	8.00	20.00
MGM SE-4302	(S)	That's My Style	1965	10.00	25.00
MGM E-4328	(M)	Our World	1965	8.00	20.00
MGM SE-4328	(S)	Our World	1965	10.00	25.00

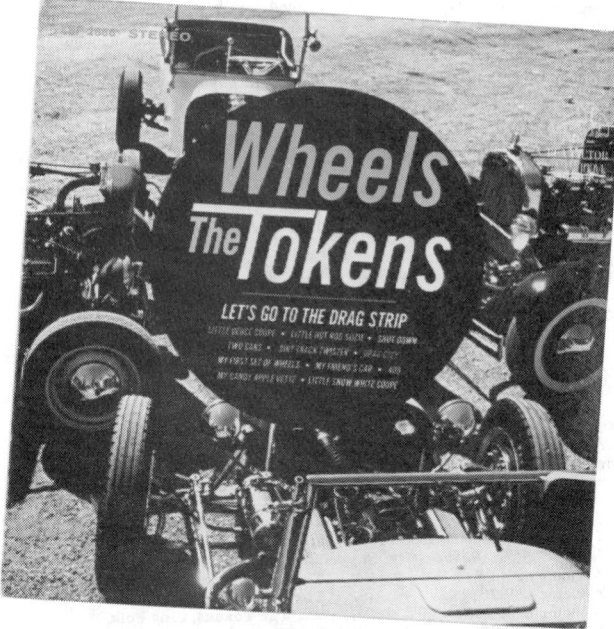

The original Tokens of the mid '50s were a white doo-wop group featuring Hank Medress and a pre-Julliard Neil Sedaka. By 1961 the group consisted of Medress with Jay Siegel and the Margo brothers, Mitch and Phil. "The Lion Sleeps Tonight" was a highly stylized pop arrangement of "Wimoweh," a traditional South African chant of apparent Zulu origin. This was the title of their first album, long the one most desired by collectors, But the continued growth in the demand for auto-oriented rock albums has placed the later, rarer Wheels on the same level of desirability (and value).

Label & Catalog #		Title	Year	VG+	NM
MGM E-4395	(M)	No Love At All	1966	8.00	20.00
MGM SE-4395	(S)	No Love At All	1966	10.00	25.00
MGM E-4402	(M)	The Christmas Touch	1966	8.00	20.00
MGM SE-4402	(S)	The Christmas Touch	1966	10.00	25.00
MGM E-4452	(M)	Here I Am	1967	8.00	20.00
MGM SE-4452	(S)	Here I Am	1967	10.00	25.00
		—MGM albums above have black labels.—			
MGM SE-4532	(S)	The Best Of Johnny Tillotson	1968	8.00	20.00
MGM SE-4814	(S)	The Very Best Of Johnny Tillotson	1971	4.00	10.00
Metro M-561	(M)	Johnny Tillotson Sings Tillotson	1967	4.00	10.00
Metro MS-561	(S)	Johnny Tillotson Sings Tillotson	1967	5.00	12.00
Amos 7006	(S)	Tears On My Pillow	1969	8.00	20.00
Buddah BDS-5112	(S)	Johnny Tillotson	1972	6.00	15.00
United Arts. LA-759G	(S)	Johnny Tillotson	1977	1.20	6.00
Everest 4113	(S)	Johnny Tillotson's Greatest Hits	1982	1.00	5.00
Accord SN-7194	(S)	Scrapbook	1982	1.00	5.00

TIMBER

Elektra EKS-74095	(S)	Bring America Home	1971	1.20	6.00

TIN HOUSE
Tin House features Rick Derringer.

Epic E-30511	(S)	Tin House	1971	8.00	20.00

TIN TIN

Atco SD-33-350	(P)	Tin Tin	1970	4.00	10.00
Atco SD-33-370	(S)	Astral Taxi	1971	4.00	10.00

TINGLING MOTHER'S CIRCUS

Musicor MS-3167	(S)	A Circus Of The Mind	1968	8.00	20.00

TINKER, BILL

Tower ST-5145	(S)	Inside Out	1969	4.00	10.00

TINY ALICE

Kama Sutra KLPS-2046	(S)	Tiny Alice	1972	1.20	6.00

TIR NA NOG

Chrysalis CHR-1006	(S)	A Tear And A Smile	1972	4.00	10.00
Chrysalis CHR-1047	(S)	Strong In The Sun	1973	4.00	10.00

TITANS, THE

MGM E-3992	(M)	Today's Teen Beat	1961	12.00	30.00
MGM SE-3992	(S)	Today's Teen Beat	1961	16.00	40.00

TITUS, LIBBY

Hot Biscuit ST-9101	(S)	Libby Titus	1968	4.00	10.00
Columbia PC-34152	(S)	Libby Titus	1977	1.00	5.00

TITUS GROAN

Janus JLS-3024	(S)	Titus Groan	1971	16.00	40.00

TOAD HALL

Liberty LST-7580	(S)	Toad Hall	1968	6.00	15.00

TOBIAS

MGM SE-5085	(S)	Dream No. 2	1972	3.20	8.00

TOE FAT

Rare Earth RS-511	(S)	Toe Fat	1970	10.00	25.00
Rare Earth RS-525	(S)	Toe Fat Two	1971	10.00	25.00

TOKENS, THE
The Tokens are brother Mitch and Phil Margo, Hank Medress, and Jay Siegel. After forming B.T. Puppy, they wrote and produced their own work along with that of others. Note: Medress and Siegel had recorded some sides in a group with Neil Sedaka. Refer to The Happenings; Neil Sedaka & The Tokens; The United States Double Quartet.

RCA Victor LPM-2514	(M)	The Lion Sleeps Tonight	1961	30.00	75.00
RCA Victor LSP-2514	(S)	The Lion Sleeps Tonight	1961	40.00	100.00
RCA Victor LPM-2631	(M)	We, The Tokens, Sing Folk	1962	16.00	40.00
RCA Victor LSP-2631	(S)	We, The Tokens, Sing Folk	1962	20.00	50.00
		—RCA mono albums above have black labels with "Long Play" or" Living Stereo" on the bottom.—			
RCA Victor LPM-2886	(M)	Wheels	1964	30.00	75.00
RCA Victor LST-2886	(S)	Wheels	1964	40.00	100.00
		—RCA mono albums above have black labels with "Mono" or" Living Stereo" on the bottom.—			
RCA Victor LPM-3685	(M)	The Tokens Again	1966	16.00	40.00
RCA Victor LSP-3685	(S)	The Tokens Again	1966	20.00	50.00
		—RCA mono albums above have black labels with "Monaural" or "Stereo" on the bottom.—			

Label & Catalog #		Title	Year	VG+	NM
Diplomat D-2308	(M)	Kings Of The Hot Rods	196?	10.00	25.00
Diplomat DS-2308	(S)	Kings Of The Hot Rods	196?	12.00	30.00
Warner Bros. W-1685	(M)	It's A Happening World	1967	6.00	25.00
Warner Bros. WS-1685	(S)	It's A Happening World	1967	8.00	20.00
B.T. Puppy BTP-1000	(M)	I Hear Trumpets Blow	1966	6.00	15.00
B.T. Puppy BTPS-1000	(P)	I Hear Trumpets Blow	1966	8.00	20.00
B.T. Puppy BTPS-1006	(S)	Tokens Of Gold	1969	10.00	25.00
B.T. Puppy BTPS-1012	(S)	Greatest Moments	1970	10.00	25.00
B.T. Puppy BTPS-1014	(S)	December 5th	1971	80.00	200.00
B.T. Puppy BTPS-1027	(S)	Intercourse	1971	250.00	500.00
Buddah BDS-5059	(S)	Both Sides Now	1971	6.00	15.00

TOKENS, THE / THE HAPPENINGS

B.T. Puppy BTP-1002	(M)	Back To Back	1967	6.00	15.00
B.T. Puppy BTPS-1002	(S)	Back To Back	1967	8.00	20.00

TOM & JERRY: *Refer to* **SIMON & GARFUNKEL**

TOM & JERRY
Tom & Jerry are Nashville pickers extraordinaire Charlie Tomlinson and Jerry Kennedy.

Mercury MG-20626	(M)	Guitar's Greatest Hits	1961	12.00	30.00
Mercury SR-60626	(S)	Guitar's Greatest Hits	1961	16.00	40.00
Mercury MG-20671	(M)	Guitars Play The Sound Of Ray Charles	1962	12.00	30.00
Mercury SR-60671	(S)	Guitars Play The Sound Of Ray Charles	1962	16.00	40.00
Mercury MG-20756	(M)	Guitar's Greatest Hits, Volume 2	1962	12.00	30.00
Mercury SR-60756	(S)	Guitar's Greatest Hits, Volume 2	1962	16.00	40.00
Mercury MG-20842	(M)	Surfin' Hootenanny	1963	14.00	35.00
Mercury SR-60842	(S)	Surfin' Hootenanny	1963	20.00	50.00

TOMMY & THE TWISTERS

Regent MG-6104	(M)	Let's All Do The Twist	1961	12.00	30.00

TOMORROW
Tomorrow features Steve Howe and Twink.

Sire SES-97912	(S)	Tomorrow	1968	30.00	75.00

("My White Bicycle" and "Revolution" are rechanneled.)

TONEY, OSCAR, JR.

Bell 6006	(M)	For Your Precious Love	1967	10.00	25.00
Bell S-6006	(S)	For Your Precious Love	1967	12.00	30.00

TONGUE & GROOVE (FEATURING LYNN HUGHES)

Fontana SRF-67593	(S)	Tongue & Groove	1968	8.00	20.00

TONTO'S EXPANDING HEAD BAND

Embryo SD-732	(S)	Zero Time	1971	8.00	20.00

TOPPER, GREG

Mad Dog 001	(S)	Breaking Out	197?	3.20	8.00

TOPSIDERS, THE

Josie J-4000	(M)	Rock Goes Folk	1963	8.00	20.00
Josie JS-4000	(S)	Rock Goes Folk	1963	10.00	25.00

TORNADOES, THE
This Tornadoes also recorded 45s as The Hollywood Tornadoes.

Josie J-4005	(M)	Bustin' Surfboards	1963	80.00	200.00
Josie JS-4005	(S)	Bustin' Surfboards	1963	150.00	300.00

TORNADOS, THE

London LL-3279	(M)	Telstar	1962	60.00	150.00
London LL-3293	(M)	The Sounds Of The Tornados	1963	80.00	200.00

(London 3293 is a repackage of 3279 with one track replaced, different sequencing, and a new cover.)

TORRANCE, RICHARD

Shelter 2112	(S)	Eureka	1974	1.20	6.00
Shelter 2134	(S)	Belle Of The Ball	1975	1.20	6.00

TORRES, GEORGE, & HIS TWISTERS

Seeco SCLP-9233	(M)	Let's Do The Twist	196?	80.00	200.00

TOTO

Columbia PC-35317	(S)	Toto	1978	.80	4.00
Columbia PJC-35317	(S)	Toto (Picture disc)	1979	6.00	15.00
Columbia PC-36229	(S)	Hydra	1979	.80	4.00
Columbia PC-36813	(S)	Turn Back	1981	.80	4.00
Columbia PD-36813	(DJ)	Turn Back (Picture disc)	1981	6.00	15.00

Label & Catalog #		Title	Year	VG+	NM
Columbia PC-37928	(S)	**Toto IV**	1982	.80	4.00
Columbia PJC-37928	(DJ)	**Toto IV** (Picture disc)	1982	6.00	15.00
Columbia HC-47928	(DJ)	**Toto IV** (Half-speed master)	1982	6.00	18.00
Columbia PC-39911	(S)	**Isolation**	1984	.80	4.00
Columbia 9C9-39911	(S)	**Isolation** (Picture disc)	1984	4.00	10.00
TOUCH, THE					
Coliseum DS-51004	(S)	**The Touch** (With poster)	1968	10.00	25.00
Coliseum DS-51004	(S)	**The Touch** (Without poster)	1968	8.00	20.00
TOUCH, THE					
Atco SD-38-123	(S)	**Touch**	1980	1.00	5.00
TOUCHSTONE					
Touchstone features Tom Constanten of The Grateful Dead.					
United Arts. UAS-5563	(S)	**Tarot**	1972	12.00	30.00
TOURISTS, THE					
The Tourists feature Annie Lennox and Dave Stewart, later The Eurythmics.					
Epic NJE-36386	(S)	**Reality Effect**	1979	4.00	10.00
Epic NJE-36757	(S)	**Luminous Basement**	1980	4.00	10.00
Epic PE-39318	(S)	**Should Have Been Greatest Hits**	1984	1.00	5.00
TOUSAN					
Tousan also recorded as Allen Toussaint.					
RCA Victor LPM-1767	(M)	**The Wild Sound Of New Orleans**	1958	150.00	300.00
		—RCA albums above have black "Long Play" labels.—			
TOUSSAINT, ALLEN					
Scepter 24003	(S)	**Toussaint**	1971	10.00	25.00
Reprise MS-2062	(S)	**Life, Love And Faith**	1972	10.00	25.00
Warner Bros. BSK-3142	(S)	**Motion**	1978	4.00	10.00
TOWER OF POWER					
San Francisco 204	(S)	**East Bay Grease**	1971	20.00	50.00
Warner Bros. BS-2616	(S)	**Bump City**	1972	3.20	8.00
Warner Bros. BS-2681	(S)	**Tower Of Power**	1973	3.20	8.00
Warner Bros. BS-2749	(S)	**Back To Oakland**	1974	1.20	6.00
Warner Bros. BS-2834	(S)	**Urban Renewal**	1975	1.20	6.00
Warner Bros. BS-2924	(S)	**Live And In Living Color**	1976	1.20	6.00
Columbia JC-34906	(S)	**We Came To Play**	1978	1.00	5.00
Columbia JC-35784	(S)	**Back On The Streets**	1979	1.00	5.00
TOWNSEND, HENRY					
Bluesville BVLP-1041	(M)	**Tired Bein' Mistreated**	1962	30.00	75.00
		—Bluesville albums above have bright blue labels with silver print.—			
Bluesville BVLP-1041	(M)	**Tired Bein' Mistreated**	1964	10.00	25.00
		—Bluesville albums above have blue labels with a trident logo on the right side.—			
Adelphi 1016	(S)	**Music Man**	1974	3.20	8.00
TOWNSHEND, PETE					
Townshend is a member of The Who. Refer to Thunderclap Newman.					
Track PR-A-160	DJ	**Pete Townshend Talks To & About**			
		Thunderclap Newman (One-sided)	1970	40.00	100.00
Track 79189	(S)	**Who Came First** (With poster)	1972	8.00	20.00
Track 79189	(S)	**Who Came First** (Without poster)	1972	6.00	15.00
Atco SD-32-100	(S)	**Empty Glass**	1980	1.00	5.00
Atco SD-38-149	(S)	**All The Best Cowboys Have Chinese Eyes**	1982	1.00	5.00
TOWNSHEND, PETE, & RONNIE LANE					
MCA 2295	(S)	**Rough Mix**	1977	6.00	15.00
TOYAH & ROBERT FRIPP					
Editions EG EGED-44	(S)	**The Lady Or The Tiger**	1986	1.20	6.00
TOYS, THE					
DynoVoice 9002	(M)	**A Lovers Concerto/Attack**	1966	16.00	40.00
DynoVoice 9002-S	(S)	**A Lovers Concerto/Attack**	1966	20.00	50.00
		("A Lover's Concerto," "Attack," "I Got A Man," and "This Night" are rechanneled.)			
TRACKS, THE					
Capitol ST-1188	(S)	**Even A Broken Clock Is Right Twice A Day**	1972	3.20	8.00
TRADER HORNE					
Janus 3012	(S)	**Morning Way**	1970	16.00	40.00

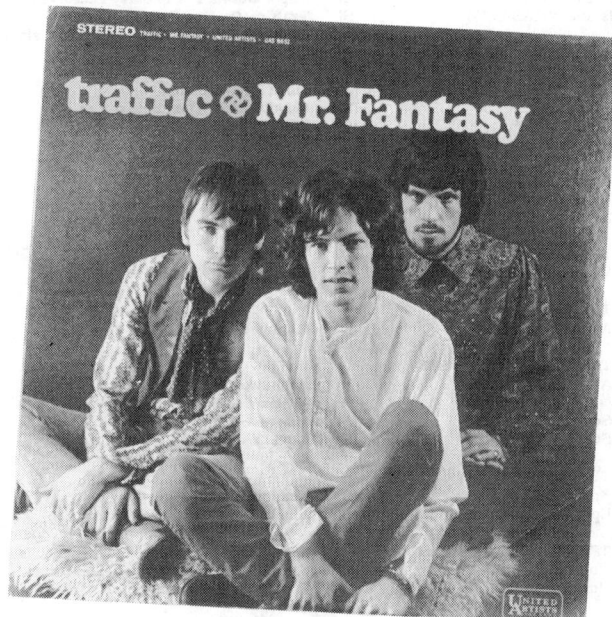

When originally released in the UK, Traffic's debut album was a wondrous display of the group's eclectic abilities, primarily those of the two singers and writers, Steve Winwood and Dave Mason. Dave left shortly thereafter and when the LP was issued in the US, titled Heaven Is In Your Mind, as was the British version, several of Mason's songs were replaced by new Winwood penned tracks. After the FM success of "Mr Fantasy," the album was reissued as Mr. Fantasy. While it never achieved best-seller status, it has aged well in both track line-ups and remains an under-rated classic of the psychedelic '60s.

			Title	Year	VG+	NM

THE

| | ⁷8 | (M) | The Tradewinds | 196? | 5.00 | 12.00 |
| | 278 | (S) | The Tradewinds | 196? | 6.00 | 15.00 |

TRADEWINDS, THE
The Tradewinds were Pete Anders and Vinnie Poncia.

| Kama Sutra KLP-8057 | (M) | Excursions | 1967 | 10.00 | 25.00 |
| Kama Sutra KLPS-8057 | (S) | Excursions | 1967 | 12.00 | 30.00 |

TRAFFIC
Traffic was Steve Winwood, Jim Capaldi, Dave Mason, and Chris Wood. Mason left after the first album, returned for the second, and then quit. The group disbanded in '69 but reformed during the recording of Winwood's first solo album in '70, which they released as the new Traffic album! New additions included Rick Grech in 1970 and Jim Gordon and Reebop Kawaku-Baah in '71. By the end of 1971, Grech, Gordon and Mason were gone. . .

United Arts. UAL-3651	(M)	Heaven Is In Your Mind	1967	30.00	75.00
United Arts. UAS-6651	(S)	Heaven Is In Your Mind	1967	20.00	50.00
United Arts. UAS-6651	(S)	Mr. Fantasy	1968	14.00	35.00
			("Mr. Fantasy" is a reissue of "Heaven Is In Your Mind." First pressing reissues have the original back covers with "Heaven Is In Your Mind" across the top.)			
United Arts. UAS-6651	(S)	Mr. Fantasy	1969	10.00	25.00
			(Second pressing reissues have a green strip across the top of the back cover listing the album's songs.)			
			— *United Arts. albums above have black labels.*—			
United Arts. UAS-6651	(S)	Mr. Fantasy	1969	4.00	10.00
United Arts. UAS-6676	(S)	Traffic	1968	4.00	10.00
United Arts. UAS-6702	(S)	Last Exit	1969	4.00	10.00
			— *United Arts. albums above have orange & purple labels.*—			
United Arts. UAS-5500	(S)	The Best Of Traffic	1970	3.20	8.00
United Arts. UAS-5504	(S)	John Barleycorn Must Die	1970	3.20	8.00
			— *United Arts. albums above have black & orange labels.*—			
United Arts. UAS-5550	(S)	Welcome To The Canteen	1971	1.20	6.00
Island SW-9306	(S)	The Low Spark Of High Heeled Boys	1971	1.20	6.00
Island SW-9323	(S)	Shoot Out At The Fantasy Factory	1973	1.20	6.00
Island SMAS-9336	(S)	Traffic—On The Road (2 LPs)	1973	3.20	8.00
			— *Island albums above have a sunrise label with "Island" on the bottom.*—			
Asylum 7E-1020	(S)	When The Eagle Flies	1974	1.00	5.00
United Artists LA421	(S)	Heavy Traffic	1975	.80	4.00
United Artists LA526	(S)	More Heavy Traffic	1975	.80	4.00
Island 90027	(S)	Shoot Out At The Fantasy Factory	1981	.80	4.00
Island 90055	(S)	When The Eagle Flies	1983	.80	4.00
Island 90056	(S)	Last Exit	1983	.80	4.00
Island 90057	(S)	The Best Of Traffic	1983	.80	4.00
Island 90058	(S)	John Barleycorn Must Die	1983	.80	4.00
Island 90059	(S)	Traffic	1983	.80	4.00
Island 90060	(S)	Mr. Fantasy	1983	.80	4.00

TRAIN, THE

| Vanguard VSD-6542 | (S) | Costumed Cuties | 1970 | 4.00 | 10.00 |

TRAMLINE

| A&M SP-4208 | (S) | Somewhere Down The Line | 197? | 10.00 | 25.00 |

TRAMMELL, BOBBY LEE

Atlanta 1503	(M)	Arkansas Twist	1962	500.00	1,000.00
			— *Atlanta albums above have black labels.*—			
Souncot SC-1102	(S)	I Dare America To Be Great	1971	4.00	10.00
Souncot SC-1141	(S)	Love Isn't Love Till You Give It Away	1972	4.00	10.00

TRANQUILITY

| Epic KE-31084 | (S) | Tranquility | 1972 | 4.00 | 12.00 |
| Epic KE-31989 | (S) | Silver | 1972 | 6.00 | 15.00 |

TRANSIENTS, THE

| Horizon T-1633 | (M) | Funky Twelve String | 1963 | 8.00 | 20.00 |
| Horizon ST-1633 | (S) | Funky Twelve String | 1963 | 10.00 | 25.00 |

TRAPEZE

Threshold THS-2	(S)	Trapeze	1970	6.00	15.00
Threshold THS-4	(S)	Medusa	1971	6.00	15.00
Threshold THS-8	(S)	You Are The Music, We're Just The Band	1972	6.00	15.00
Threshold THS-11	(S)	The Final Swing	1974	6.00	15.00
Warner Bros. BS-2828	(S)	Hot Wire	1974	1.00	5.00
Warner Bros. BS-2887	(S)	Trapeze	1975	1.00	5.00
Paid 2003	(S)	Hold On	1981	1.00	5.00

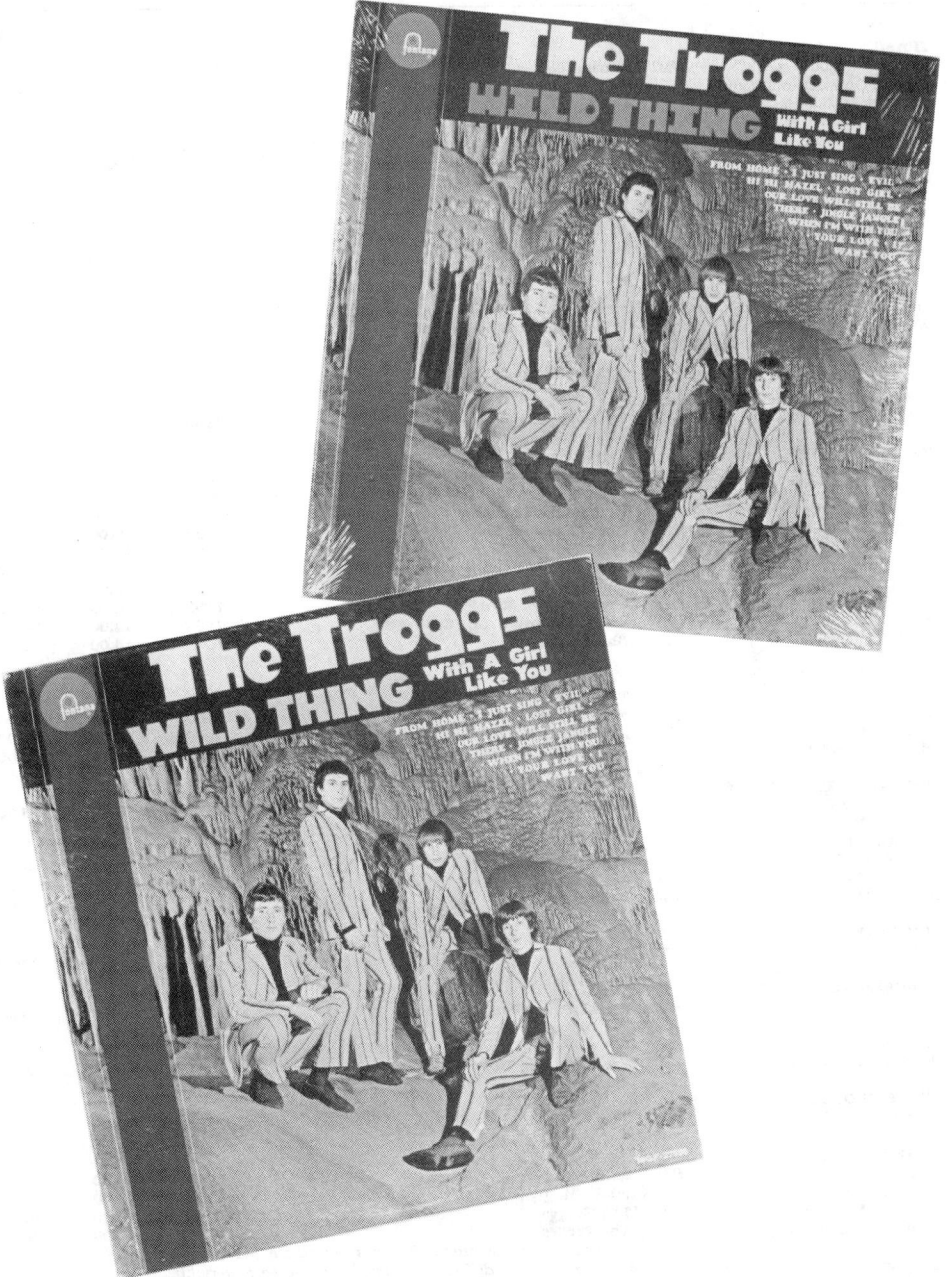

The Troggs' first album was the center of a contractual dispute that led to its being issued simultaneously by Fontana and Atco. The Fontana release shown here had two slight cover variations: Everything is the same except the type style used on the titles of the two hits, "Wild Thing" and "With A Girl Like You." While such a variance on a Beatles album would cause spasms in collectors, few pay attention to such things with lesser artists.

Label & Catalog #		Title	Year	VG+	NM
TRASHMEN, THE					
Garrett GA-200	(M)	**Surfin' Bird**	1964	80.00	200.00
Garrett GAS-200	(E)	**Surfin' Bird**	1964	150.00	300.00
TRAUM, HAPPY & ARTIE					
Happy and Artie Traum and a vocal and instrumental duo. Their folk LPs are not included here.					
Capitol ST-586	(S)	**Happy And Artie Traum**	1969	6.00	15.00
Capitol ST-799	(S)	**Doubleback**	1971	6.00	15.00
		—Capitol albums above have green labels.—			
TRAVEL AGENCY, THE					
Viva V-36017	(S)	**Viva**	1969	10.00	25.00
TRAVELING WILBURYS, THE					
The Wilburys are Bob Dylan, George Harrison, Jeff Lynne, Roy Orbison and Tom Petty.					
Wilbury 9-25796	(S)	**Traveling Wilburys, Vol. 1**	1988	4.00	10.00
Wilbury 9-26324	(S)	**Traveling Wilburys, Vol. 3**	1990	8.00	20.00
TREMBLERS, THE					
The Tremblers feature Peter Noone.					
Johnston JZ-36532	(S)	**Twice Nightly**	1980	1.00	5.00
TREMELOES, THE					
The Tremeloes originally functioned as Brian Poole's backing band. After splitting in late '65, the group—Alan Blakely,					
Dave Munden, Rick West, and new lead singer Len "Chip" Hawkes—recorded as a vocal group.					
Epic LN-24310	(M)	**Here Comes My Baby**	1967	12.00	30.00
Epic BN-26310	(E)	**Here Comes My Baby**	1967	8.00	20.00
Epic LN-24326	(M)	**Even The Bad Times Are Good**	1967	10.00	25.00
Epic BN-26326	(P)	**Even The Bad Times Are Good**	1967	12.00	30.00
Epic LN-24363	(M)	**Suddenly You Love Me**	1968	12.00	30.00
Epic BN-26363	(E)	**Suddenly You Love Me**	1968	8.00	20.00
Epic BN-26388	(S)	**World Explosion '58/'68**	1968	12.00	30.00
DJM 2	(S)	**Shiner**	1974	4.00	10.00
TRENIERS, THE					
Epic LG-3125	(M)	**The Treniers On TV**	1955	80.00	200.00
Dot DLP-3257	(M)	**Souvenir Album**	1960	60.00	150.00
Hermitage H-1002	(M)	**After Hours**	196?	30.00	75.00
Hermitage HS-1002	(S)	**After Hours**	196?	40.00	100.00
TRIALS & TRIBULATIONS					
Vanguard VSD-6565	(S)	**Trials And Tribulations**	1971	3.20	8.00
TRIBE, THE					
ABC X-807	(S)	**Ethnic Stew**	1973	3.20	8.00
ABC D-859	(S)	**Eat Tribe**	1974	3.20	8.00
Farr 1003	(S)	**Dedication**	1977	3.20	8.00
TRICYCLE					
ABC 674	(S)	**Tricycle**	1969	8.00	20.00
TRICKER, DAVID WHITE					
Bell 6062	(S)	**Pastel, Paint, Pencil And Ink**	1971	1.20	6.00
TRILOGY					
Mercury SR-61310	(S)	**I'm Beginning To Feel It**	1970	5.00	12.00
TRIPSICHORD MUSIC BOX, THE					
Janus JLS-3016	(S)	**The Tripsichord Music Box**	1971	100.00	250.00
TROGGS, THE					
Atco 33-193	(M)	**Wild Thing**	1966	20.00	50.00
Atco SD-33-193	(E)	**Wild Thing**	1966	16.00	40.00
Fontana MGF-27556	(M)	**The Troggs**	1966	16.00	40.00
Fontana SRF-67556	(E)	**The Troggs**	1966	12.00	30.00
		(The Atco and Fontana albums, released simultaneously due			
		to contractual differences, contain the same material.)			
Fontana SRF-67576	(E)	**Love Is All Around**	1968	12.00	30.00
Pye 12112	(S)	**The Troggs**	1975	4.00	10.00
Private Stock PS-2008	(S)	**The Trogg Tapes**	1976	4.00	10.00
Sire SASH-3714-2	(M)	**Vintage Years** *(2 LPs)*	1976	6.00	15.00
MKC 214	(S)	**Live At Max's, Kansas City**	1980	4.00	10.00
Rhino RNLP-800	(S)	**The Best Of The Troggs**	1984	1.00	5.00
TROLL					
Smash SRS-67114	(S)	**Animated Music**	1969	20.00	50.00

Label & Catalog #		Title	Year	VG+	NM

TROUT

MGM SE-4592	(S)	The Trout	1968	4.00	10.00

TROWER, ROBIN
Trower was a member of Procol Harum.

Chrysalis CHR-1039	(S)	Twice Removed From Yesterday	1973	4.00	10.00
Chrysalis CHR-1057	(S)	Bridge Of Sighs	1974	4.00	10.00
Chrysalis CHR-1073	(S)	For Earth Below	1975	4.00	10.00
Chrysalis CHR-1089	(S)	Live	1976	4.00	10.00
Chrysalis CHR-1148	(S)	In City Dreams	1977	4.00	10.00
Chrysalis CHR-1107	(S)	Long Misty Days	1976	4.00	10.00
Chrysalis CHR-1189	(S)	Caravan To Midnight	1978	4.00	10.00
Chrysalis CHR-1215	(S)	Victims Of Fury	1980	4.00	10.00
Chrysalis CHR-1324	(S)	B.L.T.	1981	4.00	10.00
Chrysalis CHR-1352	(S)	Truce	1982	4.00	10.00

TROY, BO: *Refer to* DICK DALE / BO TROY & HIS HOT RODS

TROY, DORIS

Atlantic 8088	(M)	Just One Look	1964	14.00	35.00
Atlantic SD-8088	(S)	Just One Look ("Just One Look" is rechanneled)	1964	20.00	50.00
Apple ST-3371	(S)	Doris Troy	1970	10.00	25.00
		(Features George Harrison on guitar and Ringo Starr on drums.)			

TROY, ROGER

RCA Victor AFL1-1910	(S)	Roger Troy	1976	1.20	6.00

TROYKA

Cotillion SD-9020	(S)	Troyka	1970	14.00	35.00

TRUE REFLECTION

Atco SD-36-7031	(S)	Where I'm Coming From	1973	1.20	6.00

TRUK

Columbia KC-30005	(S)	Truk Tracks	1970	6.00	15.00

T2

London PS-583	(S)	It'll All Work Out In Boomland	1971	30.00	75.00

TUBES, THE
Refer to Warren Richardson.

A&M SP-4334	(S)	The Tubes	1975	1.00	5.00
A&M SP-4580	(S)	Young And Rich	1976	1.00	5.00
A&M SP-4632	(S)	Now	1977	1.00	5.00
A&M SP-17012	(DJ)	The Tubes' First Clean Album (Sampler)	1978	4.00	10.00
A&M SP-6003	(S)	What Do You Want From Live (2 LPs)	1978	1.00	5.00
A&M SP-4751	(S)	Remote Control	1979	1.00	5.00
A&M SP-4870	(S)	T.R.A.S.H. (Tubes Rarities & Smash Hits)	1981	1.00	5.00
Capitol ST-12151	(S)	The Completion Backward Principle	1981	1.00	5.00
Capitol ST-12260	(S)	Outside Inside	1983	1.00	5.00
Capitol ST-12381	(S)	Love Bomb	1985	1.00	5.00

TUCKER, TOMMY

Checker LP-2990	(M)	Hi Heel Sneakers	1964	150.00	300.00
		—Checker albums above have black labels.—			
Checker LP-2990	(M)	Hi Heel Sneakers	196?	60.00	150.00
		—Checker albums above have blue checkers labels.—			

TUCKY BUZZARD

Capitol ST-787	(S)	Tucky Buzzard	1971	4.00	10.00
Capitol ST-864	(S)	Warm Slash	1971	4.00	10.00
Passport 97001	(S)	Alright In The Night	1973	4.00	10.00
Passport 98002	(S)	Tucky Buzzard	1974	4.00	10.00

TUFANO & GIAMMARESE
Dennis Tufano and Carl Giammarese are former members of The Buckinghams.

Ode 77017	(S)	Tufano And Giammarese	1973	4.00	10.00
Ode 77032	(S)	The Tufano And Giammarese Band	1974	4.00	10.00
Epic/Ode PE-34958	(S)	The Tufano And Giammarese Band	1976	1.00	5.00
		(Epic 34958 is a reissue of Ode 77032.)			
Epic/Ode PE-34969	(S)	Other Side	1977	1.00	5.00

TUNETOPPERS, THE

Amy A-1	(M)	At The Madison Dance Party	1960	14.00	35.00
Amy AS-1	(S)	At The Madison Dance Party	1960	20.00	50.00
		("The Madison" is rechanneled.)			

Label & Catalog #		Title	Year	VG+	NM

TURBANS, THE

Herald 5009	(M)	Presenting The Turbans	195?	See note below	
		(Herald 5009 by The Turbans is a bootleg worth $20-30.)			
Relic 5009	(M)	The Turbans' Greatest Hits	197?	4.00	10.00
Lost-Nite LLP-25	(10")	The Turbans (Red vinyl)	1981	4.00	10.00

TURNER, IKE

Crown CLP-5367	(M)	Ike Turner Rocks The Blues	1963	80.00	200.00
Crown CST-367	(E)	Ike Turner Rocks The Blues	1963	40.00	100.00
		—Crown albums above have gray labels.—			
Pompeii SD-6003	(S)	A Black Man's Soul	1969	6.00	15.00
United Artists UAS-5576	(S)	Blues Roots	1972	6.00	15.00
United Artists LA087	(S)	Bad Dreams	1973	6.00	15.00
Fantasy F-9597	(S)	The Edge	1980	4.00	10.00

TURNER, IKE & TINA

Mr and Mrs Turner can also be found on soundtracks for Atlantic's "Soul To Soul" and Decca's "Taking Off."

Sue LP-2001	(M)	The Soul Of Ike & Tina Turner	1961	200.00	500.00
Sue LP-2003	(M)	Ike & Tina Turner's Kings Of Rhythm Dance	1962	200.00	500.00
Sue LP-2004	(M)	Dynamite	1963	200.00	500.00
Sue LP-2005	(M)	Don't Play Me Cheap	1963	200.00	500.00
Sue LP-2007	(M)	It's Gonna Work Out Fine	1963	150.00	500.00
Sue LP-1038	(M)	Ike & Tina Turner's Greatest Hits	1965	80.00	350.00
Kent K-5014	(M)	The Ike & Tina Turner Revue Live	1964	12.00	30.00
Kent KST-514	(S)	The Ike & Tina Turner Revue Live	1964	16.00	40.00
Kent K-5019	(M)	The Soul Of Ike & Tina	1966	12.00	30.00
Kent KST-519	(S)	The Soul Of Ike & Tina	1966	16.00	40.00
Kent KST-538	(S)	Festival Of Live Performances	1969	12.00	30.00
Kent KST-550	(S)	Please Please Please	1971	12.00	30.00
Warner Bros. W-1579	(M)	The Ike & Tina Turner Show Live	1965	12.00	30.00
Warner Bros. WS-1579	(S)	The Ike & Tina Turner Show Live	1965	16.00	40.00
Warner Bros. WS-1810	(S)	Ike & Tina Turner's Greatest Hits	1969	10.00	25.00
Loma 5904	(M)	Live/The Ike & Tina Show	1966	12.00	30.00
Loma 5904	(S)	Live/The Ike & Tina Show	1966	16.00	40.00
Philles PHLP-4011	(M)	River Deep-Mountain High	1966	See note below	
		(Philles 4011, partially produced by Phil Spector, was pressed in minute quantities, most of which were destroyed at Spector's orders. No covers are known to exist. Suggested NM value for the record without the cover is $10,000-16,000.)			
Minit 24018	(S)	Ike & Tina Turner In Person	1968	10.00	25.00
Pompeii SD-6000	(S)	So Fine	1968	10.00	25.00
Pompeii SD-6004	(S)	Cussin,' Cryin' And Carryin' On	1969	10.00	25.00
Pompeii SD-6006	(S)	Get It Together	1969	10.00	25.00
A&M SP-4178	(S)	River Deep-Mountain High	1969	10.00	25.00
		—A&M albums above have brown labels.—			
A&M SP-4178	(S)	River Deep-Mountain High	197?	3.20	8.00
		(A&M 4178 is the official release of Philles 4011.)			
		—A&M albums above have silver labels.—			
A&M SP-3179	(S)	River Deep-Mountain High	1982	1.00	5.00
Sunset SUS-5265	(E)	The Fantastic Ike & Tina Turner	1969	6.00	15.00
Sunset SUS-5286	(E)	Ike & Tina Turner's Greatest Hits	1969	6.00	15.00
Harmony HS-11360	(S)	Ooh Poo Pah Doo	1969	6.00	15.00
Harmony HS-30567	(S)	Something's Got A Hold On Me	1971	6.00	15.00
Capitol ST-571	(E)	Her Man, His Woman	1969	6.00	15.00
Blue Thumb BTS-5	(S)	Outta Season	1969	6.00	15.00
Blue Thumb BTS-11	(S)	The Hunter	1969	6.00	15.00
Liberty LST-7637	(S)	Come Together	1970	6.00	15.00
Liberty LST-7650	(S)	Workin' Together	1970	6.00	15.00
ABC X-4014	(S)	16 Great Performances	1971	4.00	10.00
United Arts. UAS-9953	(S)	What You Hear Is What You Get (2 LPs)	1971	6.00	15.00
United Arts. UAS-5530	(S)	Nuff Said	1971	4.00	10.00
United Arts. UAS-5598	(S)	Feel Good	1972	4.00	10.00
United Arts. UAS-5660	(S)	Let Me Touch Your Mind	1972	4.00	10.00
United Arts. UAS-5667	(S)	Ike & Tina Turner's Greatest Hits	1973	4.00	10.00
United Arts. LA-064G	(S)	The World Of Ike & Tina Live (2 LPs)	1973	6.00	15.00
United Arts. LA-180F	(S)	Nutbush City Limits	1973	4.00	10.00
Blue Thumb BTS-49	(S)	The Best Of Ike & Tina Turner	1973	4.00	10.00
United Arts. LA-203G	(S)	The Gospel According To Ike & Tina Turner	1974	3.20	8.00
United Arts. LA-312G	(S)	Sweet Rhode Island Red	1974	1.00	5.00
United Arts. LA-592G	(S)	Greatest Hits	1976	1.00	5.00
United Arts. LA-707G	(S)	Delilah's Power	1977	1.00	5.00
United Arts. LA-917H	(S)	Airwaves	1978	1.00	5.00
Accord SN-7147	(S)	Hot And Sassy	1981	1.00	5.00

TURNER, "BIG" JOE

Joe Turner's jazz recordings are not included in this edition. Refer to Wynonie Harris / Joe Turner.

| Atlantic 1234 | (M) | The Boss Of The Blues | 1956 | 60.00 | 150.00 |
| Atlantic SD-1234 | (S) | The Boss Of The Blues | 1959 | 80.00 | 200.00 |

Ike Turner Rocks The Blues *on Crown is a collection of early RPM sides that features a cover painting by Fazzio. While Tina's long overdue solo success in the '80s brought the spotlight to focus on many of the less admirable aspects of Ike's personality (the interested are urged to see the excellent movie "What's Love Got To Do With It"), readers should be aware of the staggering importance he has played in the gestation and development of modern rhythm'n blues and rock'n roll as an artist, songwriter, producer and talent scout.*

Label & Catalog #		Title	Year	VG+	NM
Atlantic 8005	(M)	Joe Turner	1957	80.00	200.00
Atlantic 8023	(M)	Rockin' The Blues	1958	80.00	200.00
Atlantic 8033	(M)	Big Joe Is Here	1959	80.00	200.00
Atlantic 1332	(M)	Big Joe Rides Again	1959	60.00	150.00
Atlantic SD-1332	(M)	Big Joe Rides Again	1959	80.00	200.00
—Atlantic mono albums above have black labels; stereo albums have green labels.—					
Atlantic 1234	(M)	The Boss Of The Blues	1960	40.00	100.00
Atlantic SD-1234	(S)	The Boss Of The Blues	1960	60.00	150.00
Atlantic 8033	(M)	Big Joe Is Here	1960	60.00	150.00
—Atlantic mono albums above have white "bullseye" labels.—					
Atlantic 1234	(M)	The Boss Of The Blues	196?	16.00	40.00
Atlantic SD-1234	(S)	The Boss Of The Blues	196?	20.00	50.00
Atlantic 8005	(M)	Joe Turner	1960	16.00	40.00
Atlantic 8023	(M)	Rockin' The Blues	1960	16.00	40.00
Atlantic 8033	(M)	Big Joe Is Here	1960	16.00	40.00
Atlantic 1332	(M)	Big Joe Rides Again	1960	16.00	40.00
Atlantic SD-1332	(M)	Big Joe Rides Again	1960	20.00	50.00
—Atlantic albums above have multi-colored labels with a white "fan" logo.—					
Atlantic 1234	(M)	The Boss Of The Blues	196?	6.00	15.00
Atlantic SD-1234	(S)	The Boss Of The Blues	196?	8.00	20.00
Atlantic 8005	(M)	Joe Turner	196?	6.00	15.00
Atlantic 8023	(M)	Rockin' The Blues	196?	6.00	15.00
Atlantic 8033	(M)	Big Joe Is Here	196?	6.00	15.00
Atlantic 1332	(M)	Big Joe Rides Again	196?	6.00	15.00
Atlantic SD-1332	(M)	Big Joe Rides Again	196?	8.00	20.00
Atlantic 8081	(M)	The Best Of Joe Turner	1963	20.00	50.00
—Atlantic albums above have multi-colored labels with a black "fan" logo.—					
Atco SD-33-376	(P)	Joe Turner—His Greatest Recordings	1971	6.00	15.00

TURNER, SAMMY

Big Top 12-1301	(M)	Lavender Blue Mods	1962	150.00	300.00
Big Top S-12-1301	(S)	Lavender Blue Mods	1962	1,000.00	1,500.00

TURNER, SPYDER

MGM E-4450	(M)	Stand By Me	1967	10.00	25.00
MGM SE-4450	(S)	Stand By Me	1967	12.00	30.00
Whitfield K-3124	(S)	Music Web	1978	3.20	8.00
Whitfield K-3397	(S)	Only Love	1979	3.20	8.00

TURNER, TINA
Refer to Ike & Tina Turner.

United Arts. LA200	(S)	Turns The Country On	1972	6.00	15.00
United Arts. LA495	(S)	Acid Queen	1975	6.00	15.00
United Arts. LA919	(S)	Rough	1978	6.00	15.00
Springboard SPB-4033	(S)	The Queen	1972	1.20	6.00
Wagner 14108	(S)	Good Hearted Woman	1979	3.20	8.00

TURNER, TITUS

Jamie JLP-70-3018	(M)	Sound Off	1961	8.00	20.00
Jamie JLP-3018	(S)	Sound Off	1961	10.00	25.00

TURNER, VELVERT

Family Prod. FPS- 2704	(S)	Velvert Turner Group	1972	20.00	50.00

TURNQUIST REMEDY

Pentegram PE-10004	(S)	Turnquist Remedy	1970	10.00	25.00

TURTLES, THE
The Turtles feature Howard Kaylan and Mark Volman, who also recorded as Flo & Eddie.

White Whale WW-111	(M)	It Ain't Me Babe	1965	12.00	30.00
White Whale WWS-7111	(S)	It Ain't Me Babe	1965	16.00	40.00
White Whale WW-112	(M)	You Baby	1966	12.00	30.00
White Whale WWS-7112	(S)	You Baby	1966	16.00	40.00
White Whale WW-114	(M)	Happy Together	1967	8.00	20.00
White Whale WWS-7114	(S)	Happy Together	1967	10.00	25.00
White Whale WW-115	(M)	The Turtles' Golden Hits	1967	8.00	20.00
White Whale WWS-7115	(S)	The Turtles' Golden Hits	1967	8.00	20.00
White Whale WWS-7118	(S)	The Battle Of The Bands	1968	10.00	25.00
White Whale WWS-7124	(S)	Turtle Soup	1969	10.00	25.00
White Whale WWS-7127	(S)	More Golden Hits	1970	8.00	20.00
White Whale WWS-7133	(S)	Wooden Head	1971	8.00	20.00
Sire SASH-3703	(S)	Happy Together Again (2 LPs)	1974	8.00	20.00
Rhino RNLP-151	(S)	It Ain't Me Babe	1984	1.00	5.00
Rhino RNLP-152	(S)	Happy Together	1984	1.00	5.00
Rhino RNLP-153	(S)	You Baby	1984	1.00	5.00
Rhino RNLP-154	(S)	Wooden Head	1984	1.00	5.00
Rhino RNLP-160	(S)	The Turtles' Greatest Hits	1984	1.00	5.00

Label & Catalog #		Title	Year	VG+	NM
Rhino RNDP-901A	(S)	1968	1984	1.00	5.00
Rhino RNDP-901B	(S)	1968 (Picture disc)	1984	1.00	5.00
Rhino RNLP-280	(S)	Turtlesized	1984	1.00	5.00
TUTOR, TIM					
Playboy 122	(S)	Boppin' Through The Milky Way	1973	1.20	6.00
TUXEDOMOON					
Ralph TX-8004	(S)	Half Mute	1979	4.00	10.00
Ralph TX-8104	(S)	Desire	1980	4.00	10.00
TV & THE TRIBESMEN					
HBR HLP-9507	(S)	Barefootin'	1966	12.00	30.00
		(HBR 9507 is in compatible mono/stereo.)			
TWENTIETH CENTURY ZOO					
Vault LPS-122	(S)	Thunder On A Clear Day	1968	24.00	60.00
TWINK					
Refer to The Pretty Things; Tomorrow.					
Sire SES-97022	(S)	Think Pink	1970	50.00	125.00
TWINN CONNEXION					
Decca DL-75020	(S)	Twinn Connexion	1968	6.00	15.00
TWINS, THE					
RCA Victor LPM-1708	(M)	Teenagers Love The Twins	1958	20.00	50.00
TWISTERS, THE					
Treasure TLP-890	(M)	Doin' The Twist	1962	12.00	30.00
TWISTIN' KINGS, THE					
Motown MLP-601	(M)	Twistin' The World Around	1960	150.00	300.00

TWITTY, CONWAY
Conway Twitty is a pseudonym for Harold Jenkins. While his early recordings are rock'n roll with a noticeable Presley flavor, he later converted to his main love, country'n western. Those albums are not included in this edition.

			Year	VG+	NM
MGM E-3744	(M)	Conway Twitty Sings	1959	40.00	100.00
MGM SE-3744	(S)	Conway Twitty Sings	1959	60.00	150.00
		—MGM albums above have yellow labels—			
MGM E-3744	(M)	Conway Twitty Sings	196?	16.00	40.00
MGM SE-3744	(S)	Conway Twitty Sings	196?	20.00	50.00
MGM E-3744	(M)	Conway Twitty Sings (Orange cover)	196?	150.00	300.00
MGM SE-3744	(S)	Conway Twitty Sings (Orange cover)	196?	150.00	300.00
		(Some later pressings of MGM 3744 have an orange cover with a photo of a more clean-cut, countrified Conway.)			
MGM E-3786	(M)	Saturday Night With Conway Twitty	1959	30.00	75.00
MGM SE-3786	(S)	Saturday Night With Conway Twitty	1959	40.00	100.00
MGM E-3818	(M)	Lonely Blue Boy	1960	30.00	75.00
MGM SE-3818	(S)	Lonely Blue Boy	1960	40.00	100.00
MGM E-3849	(M)	Greatest Hits (With fold-open poster)	1960	26.00	65.00
MGM E-3849	(M)	Greatest Hits (Without the poster)	1960	16.00	40.00
MGM SE-3849	(P)	Greatest Hits (With fold-open poster)	1960	30.00	75.00
MGM SE-3849	(P)	Greatest Hits (Without the poster)	1960	20.00	50.00
MGM E-3907	(M)	The Rock And Roll Story	1961	20.00	50.00
MGM SE-3907	(S)	The Rock And Roll Story	1961	30.00	75.00
MGM E-3943	(M)	The Conway Twitty Touch	1961	20.00	50.00
MGM SE-3943	(S)	The Conway Twitty Touch	1961	30.00	75.00
MGM E-4019	(M)	Portrait Of A Fool And Others	1962	16.00	40.00
MGM SE-4019	(S)	Portrait Of A Fool And Others	1962	20.00	50.00
MGM E-4089	(M)	R&B '63	1963	16.00	40.00
MGM SE-4089	(S)	R&B '63	1963	20.00	50.00
MGM E-4217	(M)	Hit The Road	1964	10.00	25.00
MGM SE-4217	(S)	Hit The Road	1964	12.00	30.00
		—MGM albums above have black labels—			
Metro M-512	(M)	It's Only Make Believe	1965	6.00	15.00
Metro MS-512	(S)	It's Only Make Believe	1965	8.00	20.00
MGM GAS-110	(S)	Conway Twitty	1970	8.00	20.00
MGM SE-4799	(S)	Conway Twitty Hits	1971	5.00	12.00
MGM SE-4837	(S)	Conway Twitty Sings The Blues	1972	5.00	12.00
MGM SE-4884	(P)	Twenty Great Hits	1973	5.00	12.00
TYLER, ALVIN "RED," & THE GYROS					
Ace LP-1006	(M)	Rockin' And Rollin'	1960	60.00	150.00
Ace LP-1021	(M)	Twistin' With Mr. Sax	1961	60.00	150.00

Label & Catalog #		Title	Year	VG+	NM
TYLER, WILLIE & LESTER					
Tamla T-265	(M)	**Hello Dummy**	1965	80.00	200.00
Tamla TS-265	(S)	**Hello Dummy**	1965	80.00	200.00
TYMES, THE					
Parkway P-7032	(DJ)	**So Much In Love**	1963	40.00	100.00
		("Special edited version" for air-play)			
Parkway P-7032	(M)	**So Much In Love**	1963	20.00	50.00
		(Original covers have a photo of the group standing.)			
Parkway P-7032	(M)	**So Much In Love**	1963	80.00	200.00
		(Later covers have a head & shoulders photo of the group.)			
Parkway P-7038	(M)	**The Sound Of Wonderful Tymes**	1963	20.00	50.00
Parkway SP-7038	(S)	**The Sound Of Wonderful Tymes**	1963	30.00	75.00
Parkway P-7039	(M)	**Somewhere**	1964	20.00	50.00
Parkway P-7049	(M)	**18 Greatest Hits**	1964	20.00	50.00
Columbia CS-9778	(S)	**People**	1969	6.00	15.00
Abkco 4228	(S)	**The Best Of Tymes**	1974	4.00	10.00
RCA Victor APL1-0727	(S)	**Trustmaker**	1974	4.00	10.00
RCA Victor APL1-1835	(S)	**Turning Point**	1976	4.00	10.00
RCA Victor APL1-2406	(S)	**Diggin' Their Roots**	1977	4.00	10.00
TZUKE, JUDIE					
Rocket PIG-27001	(S)	**Stay With Me Till Dawn**	1979	3.20	8.00

U. F. O.

Rare Earth RS-524	(S)	UFO 1	1971	10.00	25.00
Chrysalis CHR-1059	(S)	Phenomenon	1974	3.20	8.00
Chrysalis CHR-1074	(S)	Force It	1975	3.20	8.00
Chrysalis CHR-1103	(S)	No Heavy Petting	1976	3.20	8.00
Chrysalis CHR-1127	(S)	Lights Out	1977	3.20	8.00
Chrysalis CHR-1182	(S)	Obsession	1978	1.20	6.00
Chrysalis CHR-1209	(S)	Strangers In The Night *(2 LPs)*	1979	3.20	8.00
Chrysalis CHR-1239	(S)	No Place To Run	1980	1.20	6.00
Chrysalis CHR-1307	(S)	The Wild, The Willing And The Innocent	1981	1.20	6.00
Chrysalis CHR-1360	(S)	Mechanix	1982	1.20	6.00

U.S. APPLE CORPS

SSS International	(S)	U.S. Apple Corps *(Blue vinyl)*	197?	8.00	20.00

ULTIMATE SPINACH

MGM E-4518	(M)	Ultimate Spinach	1968	8.00	20.00
MGM SE-4518	(S)	Ultimate Spinach	1968	10.00	25.00
MGM E-4570	(M)	Behold And See *(Yellow label promo)*	1968	20.00	50.00
MGM SE-4570	(S)	Behold And See	1968	10.00	25.00
MGM SE-4600	(S)	Ultimate Spinach	1969	10.00	25.00

UNCLE BILL

Dot DLP-25873	(S)	Uncle Bill Socks It To Ya	1968	4.00	10.00

UNCLE JIM'S MUSIC

Kapp KS-3661	(S)	Uncle Jim	1971	3.20	8.00
Kapp KS-3670	(S)	There's A Song In This	1972	3.20	8.00

UNDERGROUND, THE

Mercury MG-16337	(M)	Psychedelic Visions	1967	30.00	75.00
Mercury SR-16337	(S)	Psychedelic Visions	1967	40.00	100.00

UNDERGROUND SUNSHINE

Intrepid IT-74003	(S)	Let There Be Light	1969	12.00	30.00

UNDISPUTED TRUTH

Gordy G-955L	(S)	Undisputed Truth	1971	10.00	25.00
Gordy GS-959	(S)	Face To Face With The Truth	1971	6.00	15.00
Gordy GS-963	(S)	Law Of The Land	1973	6.00	15.00
Gordy GS-968	(S)	Down To Earth	1974	6.00	15.00
Gordy GS-970	(S)	Cosmic Truth	1975	6.00	15.00
Gordy GS-972	(S)	Higher Than High	1975	6.00	15.00
Whitfield K-2967	(S)	Method To The Madness	1977	3.20	8.00
Whitfield K-3202	(S)	Smokin'	1979	3.20	8.00

UNFOLDING, THE

Audio Fidelity AFLP-2184	(M)	How To Blow Your Mind And Have A Freakout Party	1967	30.00	75.00
Audio Fidelity AFSD-6184	(S)	How To Blow Your Mind And Have A Freakout Party	1967	40.00	100.00

UNICORN

Capitol ST-11334	(S)	Blue Pine Trees	1974	4.00	10.00
Capitol ST-11453	(S)	Unicorn 2	1976	4.00	10.00
Capitol ST-11692	(S)	One More Tomorrow	1977	4.00	10.00

UNIFICS, THE

Kapp KS-3582	(S)	Sittin' In At The Court Of Love	1968	10.00	25.00

UNION GAP, THE: *Refer to* GARY PUCKETT

UNIQUES, THE
The Uniques feature future country'n western star Joe Stampley.

Paula LP-2190	(M)	Uniquely Yours	1966	10.00	25.00
Paula LPS-2190	(P)	Uniquely Yours	1966	12.00	30.00

Label & Catalog #		Title	Year	VG+	NM
Paula LP-2194	(M)	Happening Now	1967	10.00	25.00
Paula LPS-2194	(S)	Happening Now	1967	12.00	30.00
Paula LP-2199	(M)	Playtime	1968	10.00	25.00
Paula LPS-2199	(S)	Playtime	1968	10.00	25.00
Paula LPS-2204	(S)	The Uniques	1969	10.00	25.00
Paula LPS-2208	(P)	Golden Hits	1970	10.00	25.00

UNIT 4 + 2

Label & Catalog #		Title	Year	VG+	NM
London LL-3427	(M)	Unit 4 + 2 #1	1965	16.00	40.00
London PS-427	(P)	Unit 4 + 2 #1	1965	20.00	50.00

(Half of this album is rechanneled including "Concrete And Clay.")

UNITED STATES DOUBLE QUARTET, THE
The U.S.D.Q. is The Tokens with The Kirby Stone Four.

Label & Catalog #		Title	Year	VG+	NM
B.T. Puppy BTS-1005	(S)	Life Is Groovy	1969	20.00	50.00

UNITED STATES OF AMERICA, THE

Label & Catalog #		Title	Year	VG+	NM
Columbia CL-2814	(M)	The United States Of America (White label promo)	1968	40.00	100.00
Columbia CS-9614	(S)	The United States Of America (Issued in a bag)	1968	30.00	75.00
Columbia CS-9614	(S)	The United States Of America (Without the bag)	1968	16.00	40.00

UNIVERSALS, THE

Label & Catalog #		Title	Year	VG+	NM
Relic 5006	(M)	Acapella Showcase	197?	4.00	10.00

UNSPOKEN WORD, THE

Label & Catalog #		Title	Year	VG+	NM
Ascot AS-16028	(S)	Tuesday, April 19th	1968	8.00	20.00
Atco SD-33-335	(S)	The Unspoken Word	1970	6.00	15.00

UNUSUAL WE

Label & Catalog #		Title	Year	VG+	NM
Pulsar 10608	(S)	Unusual We	1969	10.00	25.00

UPCHURCH, PHIL

Label & Catalog #		Title	Year	VG+	NM
Boyd B-398	(M)	You Can't Sit Down	1961	30.00	75.00
Boyd BS-398	(S)	You Can't Sit Down	1961	40.00	100.00
United Arts. UAL-3162	(M)	You Can't Sit Down, Part 2	1961	12.00	30.00
United Arts. UAS-6162	(S)	You Can't Sit Down, Part 2	1961	16.00	40.00
United Arts. UAL-3175	(M)	Big Hits Dances	1962	10.00	25.00
United Arts. UAS-6175	(S)	Big Hits Dances	1962	12.00	30.00
Milestone NSP-9010	(S)	Feeling Blue	1968	6.00	15.00
Cadet LPS-826	(S)	Phil Upchurch	1969	4.00	10.00
Blue Thumb BTS-59	(S)	Lovin' Feelin'	1973	3.20	8.00
Kudo 22	(S)	Phil Upchurch And Tennyson Stevens	1975	3.20	8.00

UPP

Label & Catalog #		Title	Year	VG+	NM
Epic PE-33439	(S)	Upp	1975	4.00	10.00
Epic PE-34177	(S)	This Way Upp	1975	4.00	10.00

URIAH HEEP

Label & Catalog #		Title	Year	VG+	NM
Mercury SR-61294	(S)	Uriah Heep	1970	1.00	5.00
Mercury SR-61319	(S)	Salisbury	1970	1.00	5.00
Mercury SRM-1-614	(S)	Look At Yourself	1971	1.00	5.00
Mercury SRM-1-630	(S)	Demons And Wizards	1972	1.00	5.00
Mercury SRM-1-652	(S)	The Magician's Birthday	1972	1.00	5.00
Mercury SRM-2-7503	(S)	Live (2 LPs)	1973	1.20	6.00
Warner Bros. BS-2724	(S)	Sweet Freedom	1973	.80	4.00
Warner Bros. BS-2800	(S)	Wonderworld	1974	.80	4.00
Warner Bros. BS-2869	(S)	Return To Fantasy	1975	.80	4.00
Mercury SRM-1-1070	(S)	The Best Of Uriah Heep	1975	.80	4.00
Warner Bros. BS-2949	(S)	High And Mighty	1976	.80	4.00
Warner Bros. BS-3013	(S)	Firefly	1977	.80	4.00
Warner Bros. BSK-3145	(S)	Innocent Victim	1978	.80	4.00
Chrysalis CHR-1204	(S)	Fallen Angel	1978	.80	4.00
Chrysalis CHR-1208	(S)	Sweet Freedom	1979	.80	4.00
Mercury SRM-1-4057	(S)	Abominog	1982	.80	4.00

URSA MAJOR

Label & Catalog #		Title	Year	VG+	NM
RCA Victor LSP-4777	(S)	Ursa Major	1972	6.00	15.00

USHER, GARY
Gary Usher was one of the most creative producers of the '60s. For his work as a producer refer to Keith Allison; The Beatles; Curt Boettcher; The Byrds; Chad & Jeremy; Danny Cox; Andy Goldmark; Bruce Johnston; Millenium; The Peanut Butter Conspiracy; Sagittarius; Ship; and Alan Watts. He also recorded and produced albums under a variety of pseudonyms. For these "Gary Usher Creations" refer to The Competitors; The Dragsters; The Ghouls; The Hondells; The Kickstands; The Knights; Mr. Gasser; The Revells; The Road Runners; The Silly Surfers; The Super Stocks; The Surfaris; and The Weird-Ohs.

USSERY

Label & Catalog #		Title	Year	VG+	NM
Mercury SRM-1-671	(S)	Ussery	1973	6.00	15.00

The cover for How To Blow Your Mind And Have A Freak-Out Party *reads "Mind Tripping Sound. Hallucinations. Journey Into Your Mind. Electric Buddhas. Love Supreme Deal. Play Your Game. Acid Rock. I've A Zebra. She Can Fly" and "Electric Mind Sound by Unfolding." Albums of this sort, exploiting the phenomenon of the late '60s and early '70s where people were using chemicals for other than recreational purposes, are far less common than the casual observer might think. But the recorded medium was as slow to recognize the potentials of the psychedelic era as the moving picture medium, which is even more bereft of anything resembling a serious consideration of the consciousness expansion movement. Neither medium would miss out on subsequent "fads," such as disco or new age-isms.*

Label & Catalog #		Title	Year	VG+	NM
U2					
Warner Bros. WBMS-117	(DJ)	Two Sides Live	1981	40.00	100.00
		(Originals are on black vinyl; counterfeits, on clear vinyl)			
Island 9646	(S)	Boy	1981	1.00	5.00
Island 9680	(S)	October	1981	1.00	5.00
Island 90067	(S)	War	1983	.80	4.00
Island 90127	(S)	Under A Blood Red Sky	1983	.80	4.00
Island 90231	(S)	The Unforgettable Fire	1984	.80	4.00

VALE, RICKY, & HIS SURFERS

Strand SL-1104	(M)	Everybody's Surfin'	1963	14.00	35.00
Strand SLS-1104	(S)	Everybody's Surfin'	1963	20.00	50.00

VALENS, RITCHIE

Del Fi DFLP-1201	(M)	Ritchie Valens	1959	200.00	400.00
		—Del Fi albums above have blue labels with a black border.—			
Del Fi DFLP-1201	(M)	Ritchie Valens	1959	80.00	200.00
Del Fi DFLP-1206	(M)	Ritchie	1959	80.00	200.00
Del Fi DFLP-1214	(M)	In Concert At Pacoima Jr. High	1960	150.00	300.00
Del Fi DFLP-1225	(M)	His Greatest Hits (Black cover)	1963	150.00	300.00
Del Fi DFLP-1225	(M)	His Greatest Hits (White cover)	1963	60.00	150.00
Del Fi DFLP-1247	(M)	His Greatest Hits, Volume 2	1965	60.00	150.00
		—Del Fi albums above have black labels with blue/gold diamonds around the perimeter—			
Guest Star GS-1469	(M)	The Original Ritchie Valens	1963	12.00	30.00
Guest Star GSS-1469	(E)	The Original Ritchie Valens	1963	8.00	20.00
Guest Star GS-1484	(M)	The Original La Bamba	1963	12.00	30.00
Guest Star GSS-1484	(E)	The Original La Bamba	1963	8.00	20.00
MGM GAS-117	(M)	Ritchie Valens	1970	12.00	30.00
Rhino RNDF-200	(M)	The Best Of Ritchie Valens	1981	.80	4.00
Rhino RNBC-2798	(M)	The History Of Ritchie Valens (3 LP box)	1981	6.00	15.00
Rhino	(M)	Ritchie Valens	1981	.80	4.00
Rhino	(M)	Ritchie	1981	.80	4.00
Rhino	(M)	In Concert At Pacoima Jr. High	1981	.80	4.00

VALENS, RITCHIE / JERRY KOLE
Jerry Kole is a pseudonym for Jerry Cole.

Crown CLP-5336	(M)	Ritchie Valens And Jerry Kole	1963	12.00	30.00
Crown CST-336	(E)	Ritchie Valens And Jerry Kole	1963	8.00	20.00
		—Crown albums above have gray labels.—			

VALENTI, DINO
Mr Valenti also recorded as a member of Quicksilver.

Epic LN-24335	(M)	Dino Valenti	1967	6.00	15.00
Epic BN-26335	(S)	Dino Valenti	1967	6.00	15.00

VALENTINE, HILTON
Valentine was a member of The Animals.

Capitol ST-330	(S)	All In Your Head	1969	12.00	30.00

VALENTINO, MARK

Swan LP-508	(M)	Mark Valentino	1963	20.00	50.00

VALHALLA

United Arts. UAS-6730	(S)	Valhalla	1969	10.00	25.00

VALIDS, THE

Amber 802	(M)	Accapella	196?	6.00	15.00

VALLEY, JIM
Valley was a member of Paul Revere's Raiders.

Panorama 104	(M)	Harpo	1968	16.00	40.00
Panorama 104-S	(S)	Harpo	1968	20.00	50.00
		(Panorama 104 features backing by Don & The Goodtimes.)			
Light LS-5564	(S)	Family	197?	6.00	15.00
First American 7710	(S)	Dance Inside Your Head	1977	6.00	15.00

VALLI, FRANKIE
Mr Valli was the lead singer for The Four Lovers and The Four Seasons.

Phillips PHM-200-247	(M)	Frankie Valli Solo	1967	8.00	20.00
Phillips PHS-600-247	(S)	Frankie Valli Solo	1967	10.00	25.00
Phillips PHS-600-274	(S)	Timeless	1968	10.00	25.00
Motown M6-852	(S)	Inside You	1975	6.00	15.00
Private Stock PS-2000	(S)	Close-up	1975	3.20	8.00
Private Stock PS-2001	(P)	Gold	1975	3.20	8.00
Private Stock PS-2006	(S)	Our Day Will Come	1975	3.20	8.00

Label & Catalog #		Title	Year	VG+	NM
Private Stock PS-2017	(S)	Valli	1976	3.20	8.00
Private Stock PS-7002	(S)	Lady Put The Light Out	1977	3.20	8.00
Private Stock PS-7012	(S)	Hits	1978	3.20	8.00
Warner Bros. BSK-3233	(S)	Is The Word	1978	1.00	5.00
MCA 5134	(S)	Heaven Above Me	1980	1.00	5.00
MCA 3198	(S)	The Very Best Of Frankie Valli	198?	1.00	5.00
Motown M5-104	(S)	Superstar Series, Vol. 1	1981	1.00	5.00

VAN DER GRAAF GENERATOR
VDGG features Peter Hammill.

Mercury SR-61238	(S)	The Aerosol Grey Machine	1969	40.00	100.00
Probe CLP-4515	(S)	The Least We Can Do Is Wave	1970	12.00	30.00
Dunhill DS-50097	(S)	H To He Who Am The Only One (Gatefold cover)	1970	6.00	15.00
Charisma CAS-1051	(S)	Pawn Hearts	1971	6.00	15.00
Mercury SRM-1-1069	(S)	Godbluff	1976	4.00	10.00
Mercury SRM-1-1096	(S)	Still Life	1976	4.00	10.00
Mercury SRM-1-1116	(S)	World Record	1976	4.00	10.00
PVC 9901	(S)	Vital (2 LPs)	1978	3.20	8.00

VAN DYKE, EARL

Motown M-631	(M)	The Motown Sound	1965	12.00	30.00
Motown MS-631	(S)	The Motown Sound	1965	16.00	40.00
Soul SS-715	(S)	The Earl Of Funk	1970	6.00	15.00

VAN DYKES, THE

Bell 6004	(M)	Tellin' It Like It Is	1967	20.00	50.00
Bell 6004	(S)	Tellin' It Like It Is	1967	30.00	75.00
Solid Smoke SS-8016	(S)	No Man Is An Island	1982	1.00	5.00

VAN EATON, LON & DEREK

Apple SMAS-3390	(S)	Brother (With insert)	1972	4.00	10.00
A&M SP-4507	(S)	Who Do You Out Do	1975	1.00	5.00

VAN HALEN
The original Van Halen featured Van Halen, guitar, and David Lee Roth, lead singer.

Warner Bros. 3075	(S)	Van Halen	1978	1.00	5.00
Warner Bros. PRO-705	(DJ)	Looney Tunes (EP on red vinyl)	1978	12.00	30.00
Warner Bros. 3312	(S)	Van Halen II	1979	1.00	5.00
Warner Bros. 3415	(S)	Women And Children First	1980	1.00	5.00
Warner Bros. 3540	(S)	Fair Warning	1981	1.00	5.00
Warner Bros. 3677	(S)	Diver Down	1982	1.00	5.00
Warner Bros. 23985	(S)	1984 (MCMLXXXIV) (Qulex II vinyl promo)	1984	10.00	25.00
Warner Bros. 23985	(S)	1984 (MCMLXXXIV)	1984	1.00	5.00

VAN PEEPLES, MELVIN

A&M SP-4161	(S)	Brer Soul	1968	4.00	10.00
A&M SP-4223	(S)	Ain't Supposed To Die A Natural Death	1970	1.20	6.00
A&M SP-4326	(S)	As Serious As A Heart Attack	1971	1.20	6.00
Stax STS-2-3006	(S)	Don't Play Us Cheap (2 LPs)	1971	3.20	8.00
Atlantic SD-7295	(S)	What The... You Mean I Can't Sing?	1973	1.20	6.00

VAN ZANDT, TOWNES

Poppy PYS-40001	(S)	For The Sake Of A Song	1968	10.00	25.00
Poppy PYS-40004	(S)	Our Mother, The Mountain	1969	6.00	15.00
Poppy PYS-40007	(S)	Townes Van Zandt	1969	6.00	15.00
Poppy PYS-40012	(S)	Delta Momma Blues	1970	6.00	15.00
Poppy PYS-5700	(S)	High, Low And In Between	1971	6.00	15.00
Poppy LA-004F	(S)	The Late Great Townes Van Zandt	1972	6.00	15.00
Tomato TOM-27001	(S)	Live At The Old Quarter, Houston, Texas	1977	3.20	8.00
Tomato TOM-7011	(S)	The Late Great Townes Van Zandt	1978	3.20	8.00
Tomato TOM-7012	(S)	High, Low And In Between	1978	3.20	8.00
Tomato TOM-7013	(S)	Delta Momma Blues	1978	3.20	8.00
Tomato TOM-7014	(S)	Townes Van Zandt	1978	3.20	8.00
Tomato TOM-7015	(S)	Our Mother, The Mountain	1978	3.20	8.00
Tomato TOM-7017	(S)	Flyin' Shoes	1978	3.20	8.00
		(Tomato 7011-7015 are reissues of the Poppy albums above.)			
Sugar Hill SH-1020	(S)	At My Window	1988	3.20	8.00
Sugar Hill SH-1026	(S)	Live & Obscure	1988	3.20	8.00

VANDROSS, LUTHER

Epic HE-37451	(S)	Never Too Much	1981	.80	4.00
Epic HE-47451	(S)	Never Too Much (Half-speed master)	1981	7.00	20.00

VANILLA FUDGE
VF was Carmine Appice, Tim Bogert, Vince Martell, and Mark Stein. Refer to Cactus; Cream / Vanilla Fudge.

Atco 33-224	(M)	Vanilla Fudge	1967	10.00	25.00
Atco SD-33-224	(S)	Vanilla Fudge	1967	8.00	20.00

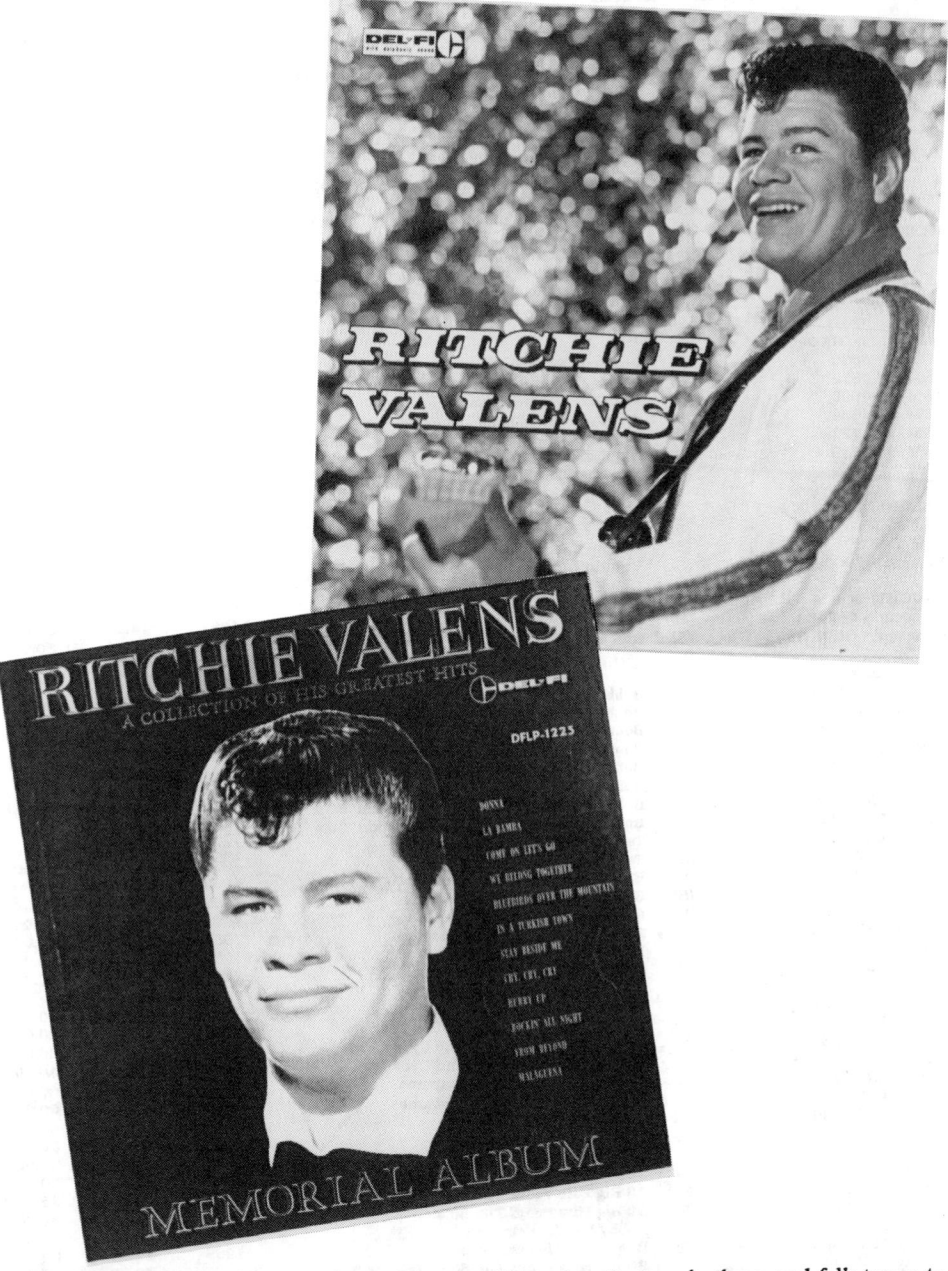

Ritchie Valens (born Richard Valenzuela) was able to fuse Latino rhythms and folk tunes to the rock'n roll beat and produce a pair of memorable hits, "La Bamba" being the most note-worthy. His emergence and acceptance on Top 40 radio was perceived by the Hispanic com-munities in the States as a cultural breakthrough. Unfortunately, Ritchie's career, and the potential it envisioned, were cut short when, along with Buddy Holly and the Big Bopper, he was killed in an airplane crash on February 3, 1959, immortalized on vinyl by Don McLean as "the day the music died."

Label & Catalog #		Title	Year	VG+	NM
Atco SD-33-237	(S)	The Beat Goes On	1968	8.00	20.00
Atco SD-33-244	(S)	Renaissance	1968	8.00	20.00
		—Atco stereo albums above have purple & brown labels.—			
Atco SD-33-224	(S)	Vanilla Fudge	1969	1.00	5.00
Atco SD-33-237	(S)	The Beat Goes On	1969	1.00	5.00
Atco SD-33-244	(S)	Renaissance	1969	1.00	5.00
Atco SD-33-278	(S)	Near The Beginning	1969	4.00	10.00
Atco SD-33-303	(S)	Rock 'N' Roll	1969	4.00	10.00
		—Atco albums above have yellow labels with "Atlantic Recording Co." on the bottom.—			
Atco 90006-1	(S)	The Best Of Vanilla Fudge	1982	1.00	5.00

VANITY FARE

Page One 2502	(S)	Early In The Morning	1970	30.00	75.00
		(Early pressings were mis-mastered with one side from the unreleased Sandy Coast album. These have fewer tracks than the label credits.)			
Page One 2502	(S)	Early In The Morning	1970	8.00	20.00

VANNELLI, GINO

A&M SP-3630	(S)	Powerful People	1974	1.00	5.00
A&M SP-4533	(S)	Storm At Sunup	1975	1.00	5.00
A&M SP-4596	(S)	The Gist Of The Gemini	1976	1.00	5.00
A&M SP-4664	(S)	A Pauper In Paradise	1977	1.00	5.00
A&M SP-4722	(S)	Brother To Brother	1978	.80	4.00
A&M SP-9539	(S)	Nightwalker	1981	.80	4.00
A&M SP-3729	(S)	The Best Of Gino Vanelli	1981	.80	4.00

VAUGHAN, STEVIE RAY

Epic E-38734	(S)	Texas Flood	1983	3.20	8.00
Epic E-39304	(S)	Couldn't Stand The Weather	1984	3.20	8.00
Epic 8E8-39609	(S)	Couldn't Stand The Weather (Picture disc)	1984	30.00	75.00

VAUGHT, BOB, & THE RENEGAIDS

Crescendo GNP-83	(M)	Surf Crazy	1963	14.00	35.00
Crescendo GNPS-83	(S)	Surf Crazy	1963	20.00	50.00

VEE, BOBBY

Liberty LRP-3165	(M)	Bobby Vee Sings Your Favorites	1960	20.00	50.00
Liberty LST-7165	(S)	Bobby Vee Sings Your Favorites	1960	30.00	75.00
Liberty LRP-3181	(M)	Bobby Vee	1961	14.00	35.00
Liberty LST-7181	(S)	Bobby Vee	1961	20.00	50.00
Liberty LRP-3186	(M)	Bobby Vee With Strings And Things	1961	14.00	35.00
Liberty LST-7186	(S)	Bobby Vee With Strings And Things	1961	20.00	50.00
Liberty LRP-3205	(M)	Bobby Vee Sings Hits Of The Rockin' 50's	1961	14.00	35.00
Liberty LST-7205	(S)	Bobby Vee Sings Hits Of The Rockin' 50's	1961	20.00	50.00
Liberty LRP-3211	(M)	Take Good Care Of My Baby	1961	14.00	35.00
Liberty LST-7211	(S)	Take Good Care Of My Baby	1961	20.00	50.00
Liberty LRP-3228	(M)	Bobby Vee Meets The Crickets	1962	14.00	35.00
Liberty LST-7228	(S)	Bobby Vee Meets The Crickets	1962	20.00	50.00
Liberty LRP-3232	(M)	A Bobby Vee Recording Session	1962	12.00	30.00
Liberty LST-7232	(S)	A Bobby Vee Recording Session	1962	16.00	40.00
Liberty LRP-3245	(M)	Bobby Vee's Golden Greats	1962	10.00	25.00
Liberty LST-7245	(S)	Bobby Vee's Golden Greats	1962	12.00	30.00
		("Suzie Baby" is rechanneled.)			
Liberty LRP-3267	(M)	Merry Christmas From Bobby Vee	1962	12.00	30.00
Liberty LST-7267	(S)	Merry Christmas From Bobby Vee	1962	16.00	40.00
Liberty LRP-3285	(M)	The Night Has A Thousand Eyes	1963	12.00	30.00
Liberty LST-7285	(S)	The Night Has A Thousand Eyes	1963	16.00	40.00
Liberty LRP-3289	(M)	Bobby Vee Meets The Ventures	1963	16.00	40.00
Liberty LST-7289	(S)	Bobby Vee Meets The Ventures	1963	20.00	50.00
Liberty LRP-3336	(M)	I Remember Buddy Holly	1963	16.00	40.00
Liberty LST-7336	(S)	I Remember Buddy Holly	1963	20.00	50.00
Liberty LRP-3352	(M)	The New Sound From England!	1964	10.00	25.00
Liberty LST-7352	(S)	The New Sound From England!	1964	12.00	30.00
Liberty LRP-3385	(M)	30 Big Hits From The 60's	1964	10.00	25.00
Liberty LST-7385	(S)	30 Big Hits From The 60's	1964	12.00	30.00
Liberty LRP-3393	(M)	Bobby Vee Live On Tour	1965	10.00	25.00
Liberty LST-7393	(S)	Bobby Vee Live On Tour	1965	12.00	30.00
Liberty LRP-3448	(M)	30 Big Hits From The 60's, Volume 2	1966	10.00	25.00
Liberty LST-7448	(S)	30 Big Hits From The 60's, Volume 2	1966	12.00	30.00
		—Liberty albums above have black labels with a gold logo on the left side.—			
Liberty LRP-3464	(M)	Bobby Vee's Golden Greats, Volume 2	1966	8.00	20.00
Liberty LST-7464	(S)	Bobby Vee's Golden Greats, Volume 2	1966	10.00	25.00
Liberty LRP-3480	(M)	Look At Me Girl	1966	8.00	20.00
Liberty LST-7480	(S)	Look At Me Girl	1966	10.00	25.00
Liberty LRP-3534	(M)	Come Back When You Grow Up	1967	8.00	20.00
Liberty LST-7534	(S)	Come Back When You Grow Up	1967	10.00	25.00
Liberty LST-7554	(S)	Just Today	1968	10.00	25.00
Liberty LST-7592	(S)	Do What You Gotta Do	1968	12.00	30.00

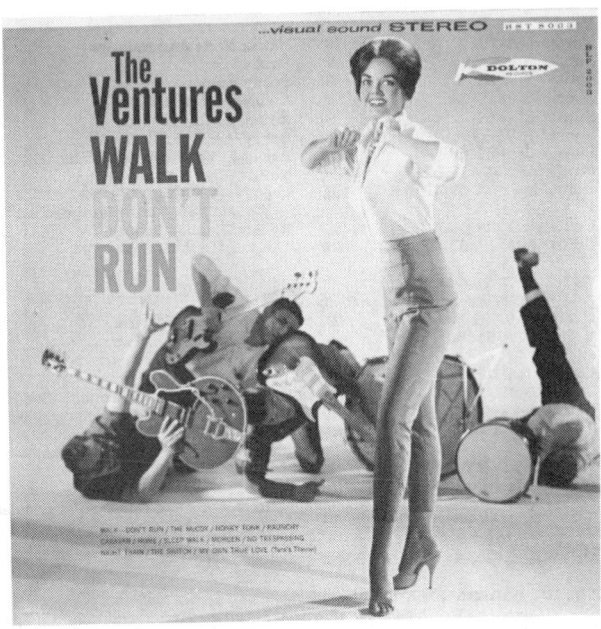

The Ventures were one of the biggest success stories to emerge from the dampened Pacific Northwest. They rank as the most successful white instrumental group of the rock'n roll era with over three dozen charting albums and three RIAA Gold Records. (And this pales in comparison with their deity-like status in Japan!) The original group was Bob Boyle, Nokie Edwards, Don Wilson and Howie Johnson, replaced by Mel Taylor in 1963. While their first album, Walk-Don't Run, holds the general collectors interest, (The) Ventures In Space also attracts automotive enthusiasts.

Label & Catalog #		Title	Year	VG+	NM
Liberty LST-7612	(S)	Gates, Grills And Railings	1969	12.00	30.00
Sunset SUM-1111	(M)	Bobby Vee	1966	4.00	10.00
Sunset SUS-5111	(S)	Bobby Vee	1966	4.00	10.00
Sunset SUM-1162	(M)	A Forever Kind Of Love	1967	4.00	10.00
Sunset SUS-5162	(S)	A Forever Kind Of Love	1967	4.00	10.00
Sunset SUM-1186	(M)	Bobby Vee's Christmas Album	1967	4.00	10.00
Sunset SUS-5186	(S)	Bobby Vee's Christmas Album	1967	4.00	10.00
United Arts. UAS-5656	(S)	Nothin' Like A Sunny Day	1972	4.00	10.00
United Arts. LA-025G	(S)	Legendary Masters (2 LPs)	1973	12.00	30.00
		("Suzie Baby" is rechanneled on this album.)			
United Arts. LA-085G	(S)	Robert Thomas Velline	1973	8.00	20.00
United Arts. LA-332E	(S)	The Very Best Of Bobby Vee	1975	.80	4.00

VEGAS, PAT & LOLLY
Pat and Lolly also recorded as Redbone.

Mercury MG-21059	(M)	At The Haunted House	1966	14.00	35.00
Mercury SR-61059	(S)	At The Haunted House	1966	20.00	50.00

VELEZ, MARTHA

Sire SES-97008	(S)	Fiends And Angels (Features Jimi Hendrix)	1969	12.00	30.00
Sire SES-7409	(S)	Matinee Weepers	1974	5.00	12.00
Polydor PD-5034	(S)	Hypnotized	197?	4.00	10.00

VELVET, JIMMY

United Arts. UAS-6653	(S)	A Touch Of Velvet	1968	6.00	15.00
		(U.A. 6653 is a reissue of a privately pressed album.)			

VELVET NIGHT

Metromedia 1026	(S)	Velvet Night	1970	12.00	30.00

VELVET UNDERGROUND, THE
The VU was Lou Reed, Sterling Morrison, Maureen Tucker and John Cale, replaced by Doug Yule in 1968.

Verve V-5008	(M)	The Velvet Underground & Nico	1967	150.00	300.00
Verve V6-5008	(S)	The Velvet Underground & Nico	1967	80.00	200.00
		(First pressings have a yellow, peel-off banana over the pink banana printed on the cover. The photo of the group on the back cover is framed by a male torso and face. The price here is for copies with the banana sticker completely intact on the cover.)			
Verve V-5008	(M)	The Velvet Underground & Nico	1967	60.00	150.00
Verve V6-5008	(S)	The Velvet Underground & Nico	1967	40.00	100.00
		(First pressings with the sticker removed from the cover.)			
Verve V-5008	(M)	The Velvet Underground & Nico	1967	150.00	300.00
Verve V6-5008	(S)	The Velvet Underground & Nico	1967	80.00	200.00
		(Second pressings have a yellow, peel-off banana over the pink banana printed on the cover. The photo of the group on the back is also covered with a sticker, hiding the torso and face. The price here is for copies with bot of the stickers completely intact on the cover.)			
Verve V-5008	(M)	The Velvet Underground & Nico	1967	60.00	150.00
Verve V6-5008	(S)	The Velvet Underground & Nico	1967	40.00	100.00
		(Second pressing with the sticker removed from the cover.)			
Verve V-5008	(M)	The Velvet Underground & Nico	1967	80.00	200.00
Verve V6-5008	(S)	The Velvet Underground & Nico	1967	60.00	150.00
		(Third pressings have a yellow, peel-off banana over the pink banana printed on the cover. The torso and face framing the photo of the group on the back cover has been airbrushed out. The price here is for copies with the banana sticker completely intact on the cover.)			
Verve V-5008	(M)	The Velvet Underground & Nico	1967	40.00	100.00
Verve V6-5008	(S)	The Velvet Underground & Nico	1967	30.00	75.00
		(Third pressing with the sticker removed from the cover.)			
Verve V6-5008	(S)	The Velvet Underground & Nico	1968	40.00	100.00
		(Later pressings have the un-peeled, yellow banana printed on the cover.)			
Verve V-5046	(M)	White Light/White Heat (White label promo)	1968	150.00	300.00
Verve V-5046	(M)	White Light/White Heat	1968	40.00	100.00
Verve V6-5046	(S)	White Light/White Heat (Yellow label promo)	1968	100.00	250.00
Verve V6-5046	(S)	White Light/White Heat	1968	20.00	50.00
		(Blue label. A black-on-black skull is visible in lower left corner of the front cover when viewed at an angle.)			
Verve V-5057	(M)	Velvet Underground	1968	Unreleased	
Verve V6-5057	(S)	Velvet Underground	1968	Unreleased	
MGM SE-4617	(S)	The Velvet Underground (Yellow label)	1969	100.00	250.00
MGM SE-4617	(S)	The Velvet Underground	1969	20.00	50.00
MGM GAS-131	(S)	The Velvet Underground	1970	10.00	25.00
Cotillion SD-9034	(S)	Loaded (White label promo)	1970	30.00	75.00
Cotillion SD-9034	(S)	Loaded (Light blue label)	1970	8.00	20.00
Cotillion SD-9500	(S)	Live At Max's Kansas City (White label)	1972	30.00	75.00
Cotillion SD-9500	(S)	Live At Max's Kansas City	1972	8.00	20.00
Mercury SRM-2-7504	(M)	Live 1969 (Gatefold cover. White label)	1972	20.00	50.00
Mercury SRM-2-7504	(M)	Live 1969 (Gatefold cover)	1972	6.00	15.00

Label & Catalog #		Title	Year	VG+	NM

VENTURAS, THE

Label & Catalog #		Title	Year	VG+	NM
Drum Boy DBM-1003	(M)	Here They Are	1964	80.00	200.00
Drum Boy DFS-1003	(S)	Here They Are	1964	150.00	300.00

VENTURES, THE

The Ventures were Nokie Edwards on lead guitar and Don Wilson, second guitar, with Bob Bogle and Howie Johnson. Johnson left in 1962 and was replaced by Mel Taylor. In '68, Edwards left with Jerry McGee taking over the lead spot. In '69, Johnny Durrill joins. In '72, McGee left and Edwards returned. They also recorded with Bobby Vee.

Label & Catalog #		Title	Year	VG+	NM
Dolton BLP-2003	(M)	Walk, Don't Run	1960	20.00	50.00
Dolton BST-8003	(S)	Walk, Don't Run	1960	24.00	60.00
		("Home" and "Walk, Don't Run" are rechanneled.)			
Dolton BLP-2004	(M)	The Ventures	1961	20.00	50.00
Dolton BST-8004	(S)	The Ventures	1961	24.00	60.00
Dolton BLP-2006	(M)	Another Smash!!!	1961	20.00	50.00
Dolton BST-8006	(S)	Another Smash!!!	1961	24.00	60.00
Dolton BLP-2008	(M)	The Colorful Ventures	1961	20.00	50.00
Dolton BST-8008	(S)	The Colorful Ventures	1961	24.00	60.00
Dolton BLP-2010	(M)	Twist With The Ventures	1962	20.00	50.00
Dolton BST-8010	(S)	Twist With The Ventures	1962	24.00	60.00
Dolton BLP-2014	(M)	The Ventures' Twist Party, Vol. 2	1962	20.00	50.00
Dolton BST-8014	(S)	The Ventures' Twist Party, Vol. 2	1962	24.00	60.00
		— Dolton albums above have light blue labels with the fish logo above the spindle hole. —			
Dolton BLP-2003	(M)	Walk-Don't Run	196?	10.00	25.00
Dolton BST-8003	(S)	Walk-Don't Run	196?	12.00	30.00
Dolton BLP-2004	(M)	The Ventures	196?	10.00	25.00
Dolton BST-8004	(S)	The Ventures	196?	12.00	30.00
Dolton BLP-2006	(M)	Another Smash!!!	196?	10.00	25.00
Dolton BST-8006	(S)	Another Smash!!!	196?	12.00	30.00
Dolton BLP-2008	(M)	The Colorful Ventures	196?	10.00	25.00
Dolton BST-8008	(S)	The Colorful Ventures	196?	12.00	30.00
Dolton BLP-2010	(M)	Dance!	196?	10.00	25.00
Dolton BST-8010	(S)	Dance!	196?	12.00	30.00
		("Dance!" is a repackage of "Twist With The Ventures.")			
Dolton BLP-2014	(M)	Dance With The Ventures	196?	10.00	25.00
Dolton BST-8014	(S)	Dance With The Ventures	196?	12.00	30.00
		("Dance With The Ventures" is a repackage of "Twist Party.")			
Dolton BLP-2016	(M)	Mashed Potatoes And Gravy	1962	12.00	30.00
Dolton BST-8016	(S)	Mashed Potatoes And Gravy	1962	16.00	40.00
Dolton BLP-2016	(M)	Beach Party	196?	10.00	25.00
Dolton BST-8016	(S)	Beach Party	196?	12.00	30.00
		("Beach Party" is a repackage of "Mashed Potatoes.")			
Dolton BLP-2017	(M)	Going To The Ventures' Dance Party!	1962	12.00	30.00
Dolton BST-8017	(S)	Going To The Ventures' Dance Party!	1962	16.00	40.00
		— Dolton albums above have dark green or light blue labels with a Sunset Blvd. address on the bottom. —			
Dolton BLP-2003	(M)	Walk-Don't Run	196?	6.00	15.00
Dolton BST-8003	(S)	Walk-Don't Run	196?	8.00	20.00
Dolton BLP-2004	(M)	The Ventures	196?	6.00	15.00
Dolton BST-8004	(S)	The Ventures	196?	8.00	20.00
Dolton BLP-2006	(M)	Another Smash!!!	196?	6.00	15.00
Dolton BST-8006	(S)	Another Smash!!!	196?	8.00	20.00
Dolton BLP-2008	(M)	The Colorful Ventures	196?	6.00	15.00
Dolton BST-8008	(S)	The Colorful Ventures	196?	8.00	20.00
Dolton BLP-2010	(M)	Dance!	196?	6.00	15.00
Dolton BST-8010	(S)	Dance!	196?	8.00	20.00
Dolton BLP-2014	(M)	Dance With The Ventures	196?	6.00	15.00
Dolton BST-8014	(S)	Dance With The Ventures	196?	8.00	20.00
Dolton BLP-2016	(M)	Beach Party	196?	6.00	15.00
Dolton BST-8016	(S)	Beach Party	196?	8.00	20.00
Dolton BLP-2017	(M)	Going To The Ventures' Dance Party!	196?	6.00	15.00
Dolton BST-8017	(S)	Going To The Ventures' Dance Party!	196?	8.00	20.00
Dolton BLP-2019	(M)	Telstar, The Lonely Bull	1963	12.00	30.00
Dolton BST-8019	(S)	Telstar, The Lonely Bull	1963	16.00	40.00
Dolton BLP-2022	(M)	Surfing	1963	12.00	30.00
Dolton BST-8022	(S)	Surfing	1963	16.00	40.00
Dolton BLP-2023	(M)	Ventures Play The Country Classics	1963	12.00	30.00
Dolton BST-8023	(S)	Ventures Play The Country Classics	1963	16.00	40.00
Dolton BLP-2024	(M)	Let's Go!	1963	12.00	30.00
Dolton BST-8024	(S)	Let's Go!	1963	16.00	40.00
Dolton BLP-2027	(M)	(The) Ventures In Space	1964	14.00	35.00
Dolton BST-8027	(S)	(The) Ventures In Space	1964	20.00	50.00
Dolton BLP-2029	(M)	The Fabulous Ventures	1964	12.00	30.00
Dolton BST-8029	(S)	The Fabulous Ventures	1964	16.00	40.00
Dolton BLP-2031	(M)	Walk, Don't Run, Volume 2	1964	12.00	30.00
Dolton BST-8031	(S)	Walk, Don't Run, Volume 2	1964	16.00	40.00
Dolton BLP-2033	(M)	The Ventures Knock Me Out!	1965	12.00	30.00
Dolton BST-8033	(S)	The Ventures Knock Me Out!	1965	16.00	40.00
Dolton BLP-2035	(M)	The Ventures On Stage	1965	12.00	30.00
Dolton BST-8035	(S)	The Ventures On Stage	1965	16.00	40.00

Label & Catalog #		Title	Year	VG+	NM
Dolton BLP-16501	(M)	Play Guitar With The Ventures	1965	10.00	25.00
Dolton BST-17501	(S)	Play Guitar With The Ventures	1965	12.00	30.00
Dolton BLP-16502	(M)	Play Guitar With The Ventures, Volume 2	1965	10.00	25.00
Dolton BST-17502	(S)	Play Guitar With The Ventures, Volume 2	1965	12.00	30.00
Dolton BLP-16503	(M)	Play Guitar With The Ventures, Volume 3	1965	10.00	25.00
Dolton BST-17503	(S)	Play Guitar With The Ventures, Volume 3	1965	12.00	30.00
Dolton BLP-16504	(M)	Play Guitar With The Ventures, Volume 4	1965	10.00	25.00
Dolton BST-17504	(S)	Play Guitar With The Ventures, Volume 4	1965	12.00	30.00
Dolton BLP-2037	(M)	The Ventures A Go-Go	1965	10.00	25.00
Dolton BST-8037	(S)	The Ventures A Go-Go	1965	12.00	30.00
Dolton BLP-2038	(M)	The Ventures' Christmas Album	1965	12.00	30.00
Dolton BST-8038	(S)	The Ventures' Christmas Album	1965	10.00	25.00
Dolton BLP-2040	(M)	Where The Action Is!	1966	10.00	25.00
Dolton BST-8040	(S)	Where The Action Is!	1966	12.00	30.00
Dolton BLP-2042	(M)	Batman Theme	1966	14.00	35.00
Dolton BST-8042	(S)	Batman Theme	1966	20.00	50.00
— Dolton albums above have dark blue/green labels with "A Division of Liberty." —					
Dolton BLP-2045	(M)	Go With The Ventures!	1966	10.00	25.00
Dolton BST-8045	(S)	Go With The Ventures!	1966	12.00	30.00
Dolton BLP-2047	(M)	Wild Things!	1966	10.00	25.00
Dolton BLP-8047	(S)	Wild Things!	1966	12.00	30.00
Dolton BLP-2050	(M)	Guitar Freakout	1967	10.00	25.00
Dolton BST-8050	(S)	Guitar Freakout	1967	12.00	30.00
— Dolton albums above have black labels with "A Division of Liberty." —					
Sunset SUM-1160	(M)	The Guitar Genius Of The Ventures	1967	5.00	12.00
Sunset SUS-5160	(S)	The Guitar Genius Of The Ventures	1967	5.00	12.00
Sunset SUS-5270	(S)	Super Group	1969	5.00	12.00
Liberty LST-8003	(S)	Walk-Don't Run	1969	5.00	12.00
		(Liberty 8003 is a reissue of Dolton 8003 with a new front cover with the new current members but the original Dolton back cover.)			
Liberty LST-8003	(S)	Walk-Don't Run	1970	8.00	20.00
		(Liberty 8003 is a reissue of Dolton 8003 with a new cover.)			
Liberty LST-8023	(S)	I Walk The Line & Other Giant Hits	1970	8.00	20.00
		(Liberty 8023 is a reissue of Dolton 8023.)			
Liberty LST-8031	(S)	Walk-Don't Run, Volume 2	1970	10.00	25.00
		(Liberty 8003 is a reissue of Dolton 8003 with a new cover.)			
Liberty LST-8050	(S)	Revolving Sounds	1970	14.00	35.00
		("Revolving Sounds" is a rare repackage of "Guitar Freakout.")			
Liberty LRP-2052	(M)	Super Psychedelics	1967	8.00	20.00
Liberty LST-8052	(S)	Super Psychedelics	1967	10.00	25.00
Liberty LST-8052	(S)	Changing Times	1970	16.00	40.00
		("Changing Times" is a rare repackage of "Super Psychedelics.")			
Liberty LRP-2053	(M)	Golden Greats By The Ventures	1967	6.00	15.00
Liberty LST-8053	(S)	Golden Greats By The Ventures	1967	6.00	15.00
Liberty LRP-2054	(M)	$1,000,000.00 Weekend	1967	6.00	15.00
Liberty LST-8054	(S)	$1,000,000.00 Weekend	1967	6.00	15.00
Liberty LRP-2055	(M)	Flights Of Fantasy	1968	6.00	15.00
Liberty LST-8055	(S)	Flights Of Fantasy	1968	6.00	15.00
Liberty LST-8057	(S)	The Horse	1968	6.00	15.00
Liberty LST-8057	(S)	On The Scene	1970	5.00	12.00
		("On The Scene" is a repackage of "The Horse.")			
Liberty LST-8059	(S)	Underground Fire	1969	6.00	15.00
Liberty LST-8060	(S)	More Golden Greats	1970	6.00	15.00
Liberty LST-8061	(S)	Hawaii Five-O	1969	6.00	15.00
Liberty LST-8062	(S)	Swamp Rock	1969	6.00	15.00
Liberty LST-35000	(S)	The Ventures' 10th Anniversary Album	1970	6.00	15.00
Liberty SCR-5	(S)	The Versatile Ventures (Record Club)	196?	5.00	12.00
Liberty BG-101	(DJ)	The Ventures (Compilation of 22 early tracks	196?	60.00	150.00
United Arts. UXS-80	(S)	The Ventures (2 LPs)	1971	5.00	12.00
United Arts. UAS-5547	(S)	Theme From Shaft	1972	4.00	10.00
United Arts. UAS-5575	(S)	Joy/The Ventures Play The Classics	1972	4.00	10.00
United Arts. UAS-5649	(S)	Rock And Roll Forever	1972	4.00	10.00
United Arts. UAS-6796	(S)	New Testament	1971	4.00	10.00
United Arts. LA147	(S)	Only Hits (2 LPs)	1973	5.00	12.00
United Arts. LA217	(S)	The Jim Croce Songbook	1974	4.00	10.00
United Arts. LA331	(S)	The Very Best Of The Ventures	1975	4.00	10.00
United Arts. LA586	(S)	Rocky Road	1976	4.00	10.00
United Arts. LA717	(S)	TV Themes	1977	10.00	25.00
Heritage Series HSRD-007	(S)	Movie Themes	1983	6.00	15.00
Heritage Series HSRD-010	(S)	Spotlight	1983	6.00	15.00

VERA, BILLY
Refer to Judy Clay & Billy Vera.

Atlantic SD-8197	(S)	With Pen In Hand	1968	10.00	25.00
Midsong Int. BKL1-2219	(S)	Out Of The Darkness	1977	3.20	8.00
ALFA 11012	(S)	Billy Vera	1982	1.20	6.00

Label & Catalog #		Title	Year	VG+	NM
VERITY BAND, JOHN					
Dunhill DSX-500170	(S)	The John Verity Band	1974	8.00	20.00
VERNE, LARRY					
Era 104	(M)	Mister Larry Verne	196?	30.00	75.00
VERSATONES, THE					
RCA Victor LPM-1538	(M)	The Versatones	1957	60.00	150.00
VETTES, THE					
The Vettes feature Bruce Johnston.					
MGM E-4193	(M)	Rev-Up	1963	40.00	100.00
MGM SE-4193	(S)	Rev-Up	1963	60.00	150.00
VIBRATIONS, THE					
Checker LP-2978	(M)	Watusi	1961	80.00	200.00
OKeh OKM-12111	(M)	Shout	1965	14.00	35.00
OKeh OKS-14111	(S)	Shout	1965	20.00	50.00
OKeh OKM-12112	(M)	Misty	1966	12.00	30.00
OKeh OKS-14112	(S)	Misty	1966	16.00	40.00
OKeh OKM-12114	(M)	New Vibrations	1967	12.00	30.00
OKeh OKS-14114	(S)	New Vibrations	1967	16.00	40.00
OKeh OKS-14129	(S)	The Vibrations' Greatest Hits	1969	12.00	30.00
Mandate 3006	(S)	Taking A New Step	1972	10.00	25.00
VICEROYS, THE					
Bolo BLP-8000	(M)	The Viceroys At Granny's Pad	1963	16.00	40.00
VICTORIA					
San Francisco 201	(S)	Secret Of The Bloom	1970	6.00	15.00
San Francisco 206	(S)	Victoria	1971	6.00	15.00
VIGRASS & OSBORNE					
Uni 73129	(S)	Queues	1971	4.00	10.00
Epic KE-33077	(S)	Steppin' Out	1975	4.00	10.00
VILLAGE PEOPLE, THE					
Casablanca NBLP-7064	(S)	Village People	1977	1.00	5.00
Casablanca NBLP-7064	(S)	Village People *(Picture disc)*	1978	6.00	15.00
Casablanca NBLP-7096	(S)	Macho Man	1978	1.00	5.00
Casablanca NBLP-7096	(S)	Macho Man *(Picture disc)*	1978	6.00	15.00
Casablanca NBLP-7118	(S)	Cruisin'	1978	1.00	5.00
Casablanca NBLP-7118	(S)	Cruisin' *(Picture disc)*	1978	6.00	15.00
Casablanca NBLP-7144	(S)	Go West	1979	1.00	5.00
Casablanca NBLP-7183	(S)	Live And Sleazy *(2 LPs)*	1979	1.20	6.00
Casablanca NBLP-7220	(S)	Can't Stop The Music	1980	1.00	5.00
RCA Victor 4105	(S)	Renaissance	1981	1.00	5.00
VINCENT, GENE					
Refer to Ferlin Husky / Sonny James / Tommy Sands / Gene Vincent.					
Capitol T-764	(DJ)	Bluejean Bop! *(Yellow label promo)*	1957	660.00	1,000.00
Capitol T-764	(DJ)	Bluejean Bop! *(Black label promo)*	1957	660.00	1,000.00
Capitol T-764	(M)	Bluejean Bop!	1957	200.00	400.00
Capitol T-811	(DJ)	Gene Vincent & The Blue Caps *(Yellow label)*	1957	660.00	1,000.00
Capitol T-811	(DJ)	Gene Vincent & The Blue Caps *(Black label)*	1957	660.00	1,000.00
Capitol T-811	(M)	Gene Vincent & The Blue Caps	1957	200.00	400.00
Capitol T-970	(DJ)	Gene Vincent Rocks! & The Blue Caps Roll *(Yellow label promo)*	1958	660.00	1,000.00
Capitol T-970	(DJ)	Gene Vincent Rocks! & The Blue Caps Roll *(Black label promo)*	1958	660.00	1,000.00
Capitol T-970	(M)	Gene Vincent Rocks! & The Blue Caps Roll	1958	200.00	400.00
Capitol T-1059	(DJ)	A Gene Vincent Record Date *(Yellow label)*	1958	660.00	1,000.00
Capitol T-1059	(DJ)	A Gene Vincent Record Date *(Black label)*	1958	660.00	1,000.00
Capitol T-1059	(M)	A Gene Vincent Record Date	1958	200.00	400.00
		—Capitol albums above have turquoise labels.—			
Capitol T-1207	(DJ)	Sounds Like Gene Vincent *(Black label)*	1959	500.00	750.00
Capitol T-1207	(M)	Sounds Like Gene Vincent	1959	150.00	300.00
Capitol T-1342	(DJ)	Crazy Times *(Black label promo)*	1960	500.00	750.00
Capitol T-1342	(M)	Crazy Times	1960	100.00	300.00
Capitol ST-1342	(S)	Crazy Times	1960	250.00	500.00
		—Capitol albums above have black rainbow labels with the logo on the left.—			
Capitol DKAO-380	(E)	Gene Vincent's Greatest	1969	20.00	50.00
		—Capitol albums above have green labels.—			
Dandelion 9-102	(S)	I'm Back And I'm Proud	1970	20.00	50.00
Kama Sutra 2019	(S)	Gene Vincent	1970	20.00	50.00
Kama Sutra 2027	(S)	The Day The World Turned Blue	1971	20.00	50.00
Capitol SM-11287	(M)	The Bop That Just Won't Stop	1974	6.00	15.00
		—Capitol albums above have red & gold labels.—			

Label & Catalog #		Title	Year	VG+	NM
Capitol SM-11287	(M)	The Bop That Just Won't Stop	1978	1.00	5.00
Capitol SM-380	(M)	Gene Vincent's Greatest	1978	1.00	5.00
Capitol SN-16208	(M)	Gene Vincent's Greatest	1981	.80	4.00
Capitol N-16209	(M)	The Bop That Just Won't Stop	1981	.80	4.00

VINEGAR JOE

Atco SD-36-7016	(S)	Rock 'N Roll Gypsies	1973	3.20	8.00

VINSON, EDDIE "CLEANHEAD"
Refer to Roy Brown; Jimmy Witherspoon.

Bethlehem BCP-5005	(M)	Cleanhead's Back In Town	1957	40.00	100.00
Aamco 312	(M)	Cleanhead's Back In Town	196?	16.00	40.00
		(Aamco 312 is a reissue of Bethlehem 5005.)			
Riverside RLP-502	(M)	Back Door Blues	1965	16.00	40.00
Riverside RLS-9502	(S)	Back Door Blues	1965	16.00	40.00
BluesWay BL-6007	(M)	Cherry Red	1967	8.00	20.00
BluesWay BLS-6007	(S)	Cherry Red	1967	10.00	25.00
King KS-1087	(M)	Cherry Red	1969	10.00	25.00
Bethlehem 6036	(S)	Back In Town	1978	6.00	15.00
Muse 5116	(S)	Clean Machine	1978	4.00	10.00
Delmark 631	(S)	Kidney Stew Is Fine	1980	3.20	8.00
Reggies 1000	(S)	Rollin' Over The Devil	1981	3.20	8.00

VIRTUES, THE [FRANK VIRTUOSO & THE VIRTUES]
The Virtues feature Frank Virtuoso, a.k.a. Frank Virtue.

Wynne WLP-111	(M)	Guitar Boogie Shuffle	1960	60.00	150.00
Wynne WLP-711	(S)	Guitar Boogie Shuffle	1960	80.00	200.00
Strand L-1061	(M)	Guitar Boogie Shuffle	1960	14.00	35.00
Strand SL-1061	(S)	Guitar Boogie Shuffle	1960	20.00	50.00
		(Strand 1061 is a reissue of Wynne 111.)			
CMI 122	(M)	Guitar Boogie Shuffle	196?	14.00	35.00
Fayette 1816	(M)	Frank Virtuoso & The Virtues *(Blue cover)*	196?	40.00	100.00
Fayette 1816	(M)	Frank Virtuoso & The Virtues *(White cover)*	196?	20.00	50.00

VISCOUNTS, THE

Madison 1001	(M)	The Viscounts	1960	100.00	250.00
Amy 8008	(M)	Harlem Nocturne	1965	14.00	35.00
Amy S-8008	(S)	Harlem Nocturne	1965	20.00	50.00
		("Harlem Nocturne" is rechanneled.)			

VISION OF SUNSHINE

Avco Embassy 33007	(S)	Vision Of Sunshine	1970	12.00	30.00

VOGUES, THE

Co&Ce LP-1229	(M)	Meet The Vogues	1965	20.00	50.00
Co&Ce LPS-1229	(S)	Meet The Vogues	1965	30.00	75.00
Co&Ce LP-1230	(M)	Five O' Clock World	1966	20.00	50.00
Co&Ce LPS-1230	(S)	Five O' Clock World	1966	30.00	75.00
Reprise RS-6314	(S)	Turn Around, Look At Me	1968	4.00	10.00
Reprise RS-6326	(S)	Till	1969	4.00	10.00
Reprise RS-6347	(S)	Memories	1969	4.00	10.00
Reprise RS-6371	(S)	Greatest Hits	1969	4.00	10.00
Reprise SW-93040	(S)	Greatest Hits *(Capitol Record Club)*	1969	4.00	10.00
Reprise RS-6395	(S)	The Vogues Sing The Good Old Songs	1970	4.00	10.00
		—*Reprise albums above have brown & orange labels with a steamboat on top.*—			
Pickwick SPC-3188	(S)	Five O' Clock World	1971	1.00	5.00
Pickwick SPC-3214	(S)	A Lover's Concerto	1971	1.00	5.00
SSS International 34	(S)	The Vogues' Greatest Hits	1977	1.00	5.00

VON RYAN'S EXPRESS

MGM SE-4752	(S)	Von Ryan's Express	1971	3.20	8.00

WACKERS, THE
Elektra EKS-74098	(S)	Wackering Heights	1971	3.20	8.00
Elektra EKS-75025	(S)	Hot Wacks	1972	3.20	8.00
Elektra EKS-75046	(S)	Shredder	1972	3.20	8.00

WADDLESWORTH
Martin MLM-38	(S)	The Trials Of Mary L.	1968	6.00	15.00

WADE, ADAM
Coed LPC-902	(M)	And Then Came Adam	1960	20.00	50.00
Coed LPCS-902	(S)	And Then Came Adam	1960	30.00	75.00
Coed LPC-903	(M)	Adam And Evening	1961	20.00	50.00
Coed LPCS-903	(S)	Adam And Evening	1961	30.00	75.00
Epic LN-24019	(M)	Adam Wade's Greatest Hits	1962	10.00	25.00
Epic BN-26019	(S)	Adam Wade's Greatest Hits	1962	14.00	35.00
Epic LN-24026	(M)	One Is A Lonely Number	1962	10.00	25.00
Epic BN-26026	(S)	One Is A Lonely Number	1962	14.00	35.00
Epic LN-24044	(M)	What Kind Of Fool Am I?	1963	10.00	25.00
Epic BN-26044	(S)	What Kind Of Fool Am I?	1963	14.00	35.00
Epic LN-24056	(M)	A Very Good Year For Girls	1963	10.00	25.00
Epic BN-26056	(S)	A Very Good Year For Girls	1963	14.00	35.00

— Epic albums above have yellow labels.—

WADSWORTH MANSION
Sussex SXBS-7008	(S)	Wadsworth Mansion	1971	4.00	10.00

WAILERS, THE
The Wailers were Mike Burk, Rick Dangel, John Greek, Mark Marush, and Kent Morrill. Refer to The Sonics / The Wailers / The Galaxies.
Golden Crest CR-3075	(M)	Fabulous Wailers (Full color cover photo)	1959	100.00	250.00
Golden Crest CR-3075	(M)	Fabulous Wailers (Black & white photo cover)	1962	40.00	100.00
Golden Crest CR-3075	(M)	Fabulous Wailers (Title cover)	196?	20.00	50.00
Etiquette ALB-01	(M)	Wailers At The Castle	1962	30.00	75.00
Etiquette ALB-022	(M)	Wailers & Company	1963	30.00	75.00
Imperial LP-9262	(M)	Tall Cool One	1964	20.00	50.00
Imperial LP-12262	(S)	Tall Cool One	1964	30.00	75.00
Etiquette ALB-023	(M)	Wailers, Wailers, Everywhere	1965	40.00	100.00
Etiquette ALB-026	(M)	Out Of Our Tree	1966	40.00	100.00
Etiquette ALBS-026	(E)	Out Of Our Tree	1966	30.00	75.00
United Arts. UAL-3557	(M)	Outburst!	1966	20.00	50.00
United Arts. UAS-6557	(S)	Outburst!	1966	30.00	75.00

("Out Of Our Tree" is rechanneled and "It's You Alone" is mono.)
Bell 6016	(M)	Walk Thru The People	1968	12.00	30.00

WAINWRIGHT, LOUDEN, III
Louden Wainwright is a guitar and piano player, singer and writer of folk-based pop songs.
Atlantic SD-8260	(S)	Album I	1970	3.20	8.00
Atlantic SD-8291	(S)	Album II	1971	3.20	8.00
Columbia KC-31462	(S)	Louden Wainwright III	1972	3.20	8.00
Columbia KC-32710	(S)	Attempted Mustache	1973	3.20	8.00
Columbia PC-33369	(S)	Unrequited	1975	3.20	8.00
Arista AL-4063	(S)	T-Shirt	1976	3.20	8.00
Arista AL-4173	(S)	Final Exam	1978	1.00	5.00
Rounder 3050	(S)	Live One	1980	1.00	5.00
Rounder 3076	(S)	Fame And Wealth	1983	1.00	5.00

WAKEFIELD SUN
MGM SE-4626	(S)	Wakefield Sun	1969	6.00	15.00

WAKEMAN, RICK
Wakeman was a member of Yes.
A&M SP-4361	(S)	The Six Wives Of Henry VIII	1973	1.00	5.00
A&M QU-54361	(Q)	The Six Wives Of Henry VIII	1973	10.00	25.00
A&M SP-3621	(S)	Journey To The Center Of The Earth	1974	1.00	5.00
A&M QU-53621	(Q)	Journey To The Center Of The Earth	1975	10.00	25.00

Label & Catalog #		Title	Year	VG+	NM
A&M SP-4515	(S)	Myths And Legends Of King Arthur	1975	1.00	5.00
A&M QU-54515	(Q)	Myths And Legends Of King Arthur	1975	10.00	25.00
A&M SP-4583	(S)	No Earthly Connection	1976	1.00	5.00
A&M SP-4614	(S)	White Rock	1977	1.00	5.00
A&M SP-4660	(S)	Criminal Record	1977	1.00	5.00
A&M SP2-6501	(S)	Rhapsodies (2 LPs)	1979	1.20	6.00

WALES, HOWARD

Coastal CST-1000	(S)	Rendezvous With The Sun	1976	5.00	12.00

WALES, HOWARD, & JERRY GARCIA

Douglas-5 KZ-30589	(S)	Hooteroll	1971	6.00	15.00

WALKER, JERRY JEFF
JJW is a guitar player, singer and writer of folk and country-based pop music. Refer to Circus Maximus.

Atco SD-33-259	(S)	Mr. Bojangles	1968	8.00	20.00
Atco SD-33-297	(S)	Five Years Gone	1969	12.00	30.00
Vanguard VSD-6521	(S)	Driftin' Way Of Life (Black label)	1969	8.00	20.00
Atco SD-33-336	(S)	Bein' Free	1970	8.00	20.00
Decca DL-75384	(S)	Jerry Jeff Walker	1972	6.00	15.00
MCA 382	(S)	Viva Terlingua	1973	3.20	8.00
MCA 450	(S)	Walker's Collectibles	1974	3.20	8.00
MCA 2202	(S)	It's A Good Night For Singin'	1976	3.20	8.00
MCA 50010	(S)	Jerry Jeff Walker	1977	1.20	6.00
MCA 2-6003	(S)	A Man Must Carry On (2 LPs)	1978	3.20	8.00
MCA 3041	(S)	Contrary To Ordinary	1978	1.20	6.00
MCA 5128	(S)	The Best Of Jerry Jeff Walker	1980	1.20	6.00
MCA 2156	(S)	Ridin' High	1980	1.20	6.00
Elektra 6E-163	(S)	Jerry Jeff	198?	1.00	5.00
Elektra 6E-239	(S)	Too Old To Change	198?	1.00	5.00

WALKER, JIMMY, & ERWIN HEFLER

Testament 2202	(S)	Rough And Ready	197?	4.00	10.00

WALKER, JOHNNY "BIG MOOSE"

BluesWay BLS-6036	(S)	Rambling Woman	1970	6.00	15.00

WALKER, JUNIOR, & THE ALL STARS

Soul 701	(M)	Shotgun	1965	30.00	75.00
Soul 702	(M)	Soul Session	1965	30.00	75.00
		—Soul albums above have purple & white labels.—			
Soul 701	(M)	Shotgun	1965	8.00	20.00
Soul SS-701	(S)	Shotgun	1965	12.00	30.00
Soul 702	(M)	Soul Session	1965	8.00	20.00
Soul SS-702	(S)	Soul Session	1965	12.00	30.00
Soul 703	(M)	Road Runner	1966	8.00	20.00
Soul SS-703	(S)	Road Runner	1966	12.00	30.00
Soul 705	(M)	Junior Walker & The All Stars Live	1967	8.00	20.00
Soul SS-705	(S)	Junior Walker & The All Stars Live	1967	12.00	30.00
Soul 710	(S)	Home Cookin'	1969	8.00	20.00
Soul SS-718	(S)	Greatest Hits	1969	8.00	20.00
Soul SS-721	(S)	Gotta Hold On To This Feeling	1969	8.00	20.00
Soul SS-721	(S)	What Does It Take To Win Your Love	1969	6.00	15.00
		(Repackage of "Gotta Hold On To This Feeling.")			
Soul SS-725	(S)	Junior Walker & The All Stars Live	1970	6.00	15.00
Soul SS-726	(S)	A Gasssss	1970	6.00	15.00
Soul SS-732	(S)	Rainbow Funk	1971	6.00	15.00
Soul SS-733	(S)	Moody Jr.	1971	6.00	15.00
Soul SS-738	(S)	Peace And Understanding Is Hard To Find	1973	6.00	15.00
Soul SS-742	(S)	Junior Walker & The All Stars	1973	Unreleased	
Soul S6-745	(S)	Hot Shot	1976	6.00	15.00
Soul S6-747	(S)	Sax Appeal	1976	6.00	15.00
Soul S6-748	(S)	Whopper Bopper Show Stopper	1976	6.00	15.00
Soul S7-750	(S)	Smooth	1978	6.00	15.00
Motown MS-786	(S)	Anthology (2 LPs)	1979	8.00	20.00
Whitfield K-3331	(S)	Back Street Boogie	1979	1.00	5.00
Motown M5-105V	(S)	Superstar Series, Volume 5	1980	.80	4.00
Motown M5-208V	(S)	Greatest Hits	1982	.80	4.00
Motown MS-5297	(S)	All The Great Hits	1983	.80	4.00

WALKER, LUCILLE

Checker LP-1428	(M)	The Best Of Lucille Walker	1957	Unreleased	

WALKER, SCOTT
Scott Walker is a pseudonym for Scott Engel. Refer to The Walker Brothers.

Smash SRS-67099	(S)	Aloner	1968	8.00	20.00
Smash SRS-67106	(S)	Scott, Volume 2	1968	8.00	20.00
Smash SRS-67121	(S)	Scott Walker 3	1969	8.00	20.00

After spending their salad days with the Northwest's Golden Crest and Etiquette labels, The Wailers signed with United Artists and issued this lone LP before parting ways. Long overlooked, the rarity of this piece is only now being recognized and its value rising accordingly.

Label & Catalog #		Title	Year	VG+	NM

WALKER, T-BONE

T-Bone Walker is a pseudonym for Aaron Walker.

Capitol H-370	(10")	Classics In Jazz	1953	250.00	500.00
Capitol T-370	(M)	Classics In Jazz	1953	200.00	400.00
Atlantic 8020	(M)	T-Bone Blues	1959	80.00	200.00
		—Atlantic albums above have black labels.—			
Atlantic 8020	(M)	T-Bone Blues	196?	30.00	75.00
		—Atlantic albums above have purple & orange labels.—			
Atlantic SD-8256	(S)	T-Bone Blues	1970	8.00	20.00
		(Atlantic 8256 is a reissue of 8020.)			
Imperial LP-9098	(M)	T-Bone Walker Sings The Blues	1959	200.00	400.00
Imperial LP-9116	(M)	Singing The Blues	1960	200.00	400.00
Imperial LP-9146	(M)	I Get So Weary	1961	250.00	500.00
Capitol T-1958	(M)	Great Blues Vocals And Guitar	1963	See note below	
		(The existence of T-1958 as an original with a black rainbow label remains unverified. Should one exist, it would carry a suggested Near Mint value of $1,000-5,000.)			
Capitol T-1958	(M)	Great Blues Vocals And Guitar	1963	60.00	150.00
		—Capitol albums above have black Starline labels.—			
Delmark D-633	(M)	I Want A Little Girl	1967	14.00	35.00
Delmark DS-633	(S)	I Want A Little Girl	1967	20.00	50.00
Wet Soul 1002	(M)	Stormy Monday Blues	1967	14.00	35.00
Wet Soul 1002	(S)	Stormy Monday Blues	1967	20.00	50.00
Brunswick BL-754126	(S)	The Truth	1968	14.00	35.00
Bluestime 29010	(S)	Blue Rocks	1968	14.00	35.00
BluesWay BLS-6008	(S)	Stormy Monday Blues	1968	14.00	35.00
BluesWay BLS-6014	(S)	Funky Town	1968	14.00	35.00
BluesWay BLS-6061	(S)	Blues Classics	1973	8.00	20.00
BluesWay BLS-6058	(S)	Dirty Mistreater	1973	8.00	20.00
Polydor PD-5521	(S)	Fly Walker Airlines	1973	6.00	15.00
Reprise 2XS-6483	(S)	Very Rare (2 LPs)	1973	8.00	20.00
Blue Note BNLA-533	(S)	T-Bone Walker	197?	6.00	15.00

WALKER BROTHERS, THE

The Walker Brothers feature Scott Engel, Gary Leeds and John Stewart as "brothers" Scott, Gary and John Walker. Refer to Scott Engel & John Stewart.

Smash MGS-27076	(M)	Introducing The Walker Brothers	1966	20.00	50.00
Smash SRS-67076	(E)	Introducing The Walker Brothers	1966	16.00	40.00
Smash MGS-27082	(M)	The Sun Ain't Gonna Shine Anymore	1967	16.00	40.00
Smash SRS-67082	(S)	The Sun Ain't Gonna Shine Anymore	1967	20.00	50.00
		("The Sun Ain't Gonna Shine (Anymore)" and "After The Lights Go Out" are rechanneled.)			

WALLACE BROTHERS, THE

Sims LP-128	(M)	Soul, Soul And More Soul	1965	40.00	100.00
Sims LPS-128	(S)	Soul, Soul And More Soul	1965	60.00	150.00

WALLACE CONNECTION

Capitol ST-350	(S)	Wallace Collection	1969	5.00	12.00

WALLER, GORDON

Gordon was one-half of Peter & Gordon.

ABC X-749	(S)	And Gordon	1972	4.00	10.00

WALLER, JIM, & THE DELTAS

Arvee A-432	(M)	Surfin' Wild	1963	30.00	75.00
Arvee AS-432	(S)	Surfin' Wild	1963	40.00	100.00

WALRUS

Janus 3051	(S)	Walrus	1973	4.00	10.00

WALSH, JOE

Walsh was a member of The James Gang; The Eagles.

Dunhill DS-50130	(S)	Barnstorm	1972	1.00	5.00
Dunhill DS-50140	(S)	The Smoker You Drink, The Player You Get	1973	1.00	5.00
Command QD-40016	(Q)	The Smoker You Drink, The Player You Get	1974	6.00	15.00
Dunhill DS-50171	(S)	So What	1974	1.00	5.00
Command QD-40017	(Q)	So What	1975	6.00	15.00
ABC D-932	(S)	You Can't Argue With A Sick Mind	1976	1.00	5.00
ABC A-1083	(S)	Best Of Joe Walsh	1978	1.00	5.00
Asylum 6E-141	(S)	But Seriously Folks	1978	1.00	5.00
Asylum 5E-523	(S)	There Goes The Neighborhood	1981	1.00	5.00
MCA 37053	(S)	Barnstorm	1979	.80	4.00
MCA 37054	(S)	The Smoker You Drink, The Player You Get	1979	.80	4.00
MCA 37055	(S)	So What	1979	.80	4.00
MCA 37112	(S)	Best Of Joe Walsh	1979	.80	4.00

The Wallace Brothers had a very minor Top 100 charter in 1964 with "Lover's Prayer." Sims issued an album collecting it and other less successful sides in 1965 to little fanfare or sales. A very rare soul album.

Label & Catalog #		Title	Year	VG+	NM

WALTON, MERCY DEE

Bluesville BVLP-1039	(M)	Pity And A Shame	1962	100.00	250.00
		—Bluesville albums above have bright blue labels with silver print.—			
Bluesville BVLP-1039	(M)	Pity And A Shame	1964	40.00	100.00
		—Bluesville albums above have blue labels with a trident logo on the right side.—			

WALTON, WADE

Bluesville BVLP-1060	(M)	Shake 'Em On Down	1963	80.00	200.00
		—Bluesville albums above have bright blue labels with silver print.—			
Bluesville BVLP-1060	(M)	Shake 'Em On Down	1964	30.00	75.00
		—Bluesville albums above have blue labels with a trident logo on the right side.—			

WAR

War originally recorded with Eric Burdon. They can also be found on the U.A. soundtrack "Youngblood."

United Arts. UAS-5508	(S)	War	1971	6.00	15.00
United Arts. UAS-5546	(S)	All Day Music	1971	6.00	15.00
United Arts. UAS-5652	(S)	The World Is A Ghetto	1972	6.00	15.00
United Arts. LA-128F	(S)	Deliver The Word	1973	6.00	15.00
United Arts. LA-193J	(S)	War Live	1974	6.00	15.00
United Arts. SP-103	(DJ)	Radio Free War (Blue vinyl)	1974	10.00	25.00
United Arts. LA-441G	(S)	Why Can't We Be Friends	1975	4.00	10.00
United Arts. LA-648G	(S)	Greatest Hits	1976	1.00	5.00
Blue Note LA-690G	(S)	Platinum Jazz (2 LPs)	1976	4.00	10.00
MCA 3030	(S)	Galaxy	1977	1.00	5.00
MCA 3085	(S)	Music Band	1979	1.00	5.00
MCA 3193	(S)	Music Band 2	1979	1.00	5.00
MCA 5156	(S)	Music Band Live	1980	1.00	5.00
MCA 5362	(S)	Best Of The Music Band	1982	1.00	5.00
RCA Victor AFL1-4208	(S)	Outlaw	1982	1.00	5.00

WARD, BILLY, & THE DOMINOES

Federal 295-94	(10")	Billy Ward & His Dominoes	1955	See note below	
		(Federal 94 has a suggested NM value of $15,000-25,000.)			
Federal 548	(M)	Billy Ward & His Dominoes	1958	See note below	
		(Federal 548 has a suggested NM value of $2,000-3,000.)			
Federal 559	(M)	Clyde McPhatter With Billy Ward & His Dominoes	1958	1,000.00	2,000.00
King 548	(M)	Billy Ward & His Dominoes	1958	Unreleased	
King 559	(M)	Clyde McPhatter With Billy Ward & His Dominoes (Yellow cover)	1958	500.00	750.00
King 559	(M)	Clyde McPhatter With Billy Ward & His Dominoes (Pink cover)	196?	250.00	500.00
King 733	(M)	Billy Ward & His Dominoes Featuring Clyde McPhatter And Jackie Wilson	1960	300.00	600.00
Decca DL-8621	(M)	Billy Ward & His Dominoes	1958	80.00	200.00
Liberty LRP-3056	(M)	Sea Of Glass	1957	16.00	40.00
Liberty LST-7056	(S)	Sea Of Glass	1957	20.00	50.00
Liberty LRP-3083	(M)	Yours Forever	1958	16.00	40.00
Liberty LST-7083	(S)	Yours Forever	1958	20.00	50.00
Liberty LRP-3113	(M)	Pagan Love Song	1959	16.00	40.00
Liberty LST-7113	(S)	Pagan Love Song	1959	20.00	50.00
King LP-952	(M)	Twenty Four Songs	1966	20.00	50.00
		—King albums above have crownless black labels.—			

WARD, ROBIN

| Dot DLP-3555 | (M) | Wonderful Summer | 1963 | 80.00 | 200.00 |
| Dot DLP-25555 | (S) | Wonderful Summer | 1963 | 150.00 | 300.00 |

WARLOCK

| Music Merchant 102 | (S) | Warlock | 1972 | 6.00 | 15.00 |

WARM DUST

| Uni 73109 | (S) | Peace For Our Time | 1971 | 5.00 | 12.00 |

WARWICK, DEE DEE

Mercury MG-21100	(M)	I Want To Be With You	1967	10.00	25.00
Mercury SR-61100	(S)	I Want To Be With You	1967	12.00	30.00
		("I Want To Be With You" is rechanneled.)			
Mercury SR-61221	(S)	Foolish Fool ("Alfie" is rechanneled)	1969	10.00	25.00
Atco SD-33-337	(S)	Turnin' Around	1970	10.00	25.00

WASHINGTON, BABY

Sue LP-1014	(M)	That's How Heartaches Are Made	1963	80.00	200.00
Sue LP-1042	(M)	Only Those In Love	1965	80.00	200.00
Sue LPS-1042	(S)	Only Those In Love	1965	150.00	300.00
Veep VPS-16528	(S)	With You In Mind	1968	10.00	25.00
Trip 8009	(S)	The One And Only Baby Washington	1971	6.00	15.00
A.V.I. 6038	(S)	I Wanna Dance	1978	4.00	10.00

After changing the face of popular rhythm'n blues music with his early groups, Billy Ward signed with Liberty and received decent national exposure on retail racks for the first time. Unfortunately, the music he was making was rather undistinguished, especially when compared to that he made with earlier groups fronted by Clyde McPhatter and Jackie Wilson. The Liberty albums did not capture either a large black or white audience nor have they set the hearts of collectors afire. Finally, the cover for Pagan Love Song is a kitsch classic and would not be out of place on any of the "exotic music" masters of the time.

Label & Catalog #		Title	Year	VG+	NM
WASHINGTON, ELLA					
Sound Stage-7 15007	(S)	**Ella Washington**	*1969*	**6.00**	**15.00**
WASHINGTON, GINO					
Atac AT-2743	(M)	**Gino Washington's Golden Hits**	*196?*	**12.00**	**30.00**
Kapp KL-1415	(M)	**Ram Jam Band**	*1965*	**8.00**	**20.00**
Kapp KS-3415	(S)	**Ram Jam Band**	*1965*	**10.00**	**25.00**
WASHRAG					
T.M.I. BTL1-1017	(S)	**Bang**	*1973*	**6.00**	**15.00**
WATCHPOCKET					
T.M.I. BTL1-1001	(S)	**Watchpocket**	*1972*	**6.00**	**15.00**
WATSON, JOHNNY "GUITAR"					
Refer to Bobby Bland / Jimmy Soul / Johnny Watson.					
King LP-857	(M)	**Johnny Guitar Watson**	*1963*	**250.00**	**500.00**
		—King albums above have crownless black labels.—			
Chess LP-1490	(M)	**Blues Soul**	*1965*	**30.00**	**75.00**
Chess LPS-1490	(S)	**Blues Soul**	*1965*	**40.00**	**100.00**
		—Chess albums above have blue & white labels.—			
OKeh OKM-12118	(M)	**Bad**	*1967*	**14.00**	**35.00**
OKeh OKS-14118	(S)	**Bad**	*1967*	**20.00**	**50.00**
OKeh OKM-12124	(M)	**In The Fats Bag**	*1967*	**14.00**	**35.00**
OKeh OKS-14124	(S)	**In The Fats Bag**	*1967*	**20.00**	**50.00**
Cadet LP-4056	(M)	**I Cried For You**	*1967*	**10.00**	**25.00**
Cadet LPS-4056	(S)	**I Cried For You**	*1967*	**12.00**	**30.00**
Fantasy F-9437	(S)	**Listen**	*1973*	**4.00**	**10.00**
Fantasy F-9484	(S)	**I Don't Want To Be Alone Stranger**	*1975*	**4.00**	**10.00**
DJM 3	(S)	**Ain't That A Bitch**	*1976*	**4.00**	**10.00**
DJM 7	(S)	**A Real Mother For You**	*1977*	**4.00**	**10.00**
DJM 19	(S)	**Giant**	*1978*	**4.00**	**10.00**
DJM 24	(S)	**What The Hell Is This?**	*1979*	**4.00**	**10.00**
DJM 31	(S)	**Love Jones**	*1980*	**4.00**	**10.00**
DJM 714	(S)	**Funk Beyond The Call Of Duty**	*1977*	**4.00**	**10.00**
DJM 501	(S)	**Johnny "Guitar" Watson & The Family Clone**	*1981*	**4.00**	**10.00**
Fantasy F-4503	(S)	**Greatest Hits**	*1981*	**1.20**	**6.00**
A&M SP-4880	(S)	**That's What Time It Is**	*1981*	**1.20**	**6.00**
MCA 5273	(S)	**The Very Best Of Johnny "Guitar" Watson**	*1981*	**1.20**	**6.00**
WATSON, JOHNNY "GUITAR", & LARRY WILLIAMS					
OKeh OKM-12122	(M)	**Two For The Price Of One**	*1967*	**20.00**	**50.00**
OKeh OKS-14122	(S)	**Two For The Price Of One**	*1967*	**30.00**	**75.00**
WAVECRESTS, THE					
Viking VKL-6606	(M)	**Surftime U.S.A.**	*1963*	**30.00**	**75.00**
Viking VKS-6606	(S)	**Surftime U.S.A.**	*1963*	**60.00**	**150.00**
WAVERLY CONSORT					
Vanguard VSD-71179	(S)	**Douce Dame**	*197?*	**3.20**	**8.00**
WAYNE, "WEE" WILLIE					
Imperial LP-9144	(M)	**Travelin' Mood**	*1961*	**250.00**	**500.00**
WAZOO					
Zig Zag 217	(S)	**Wazoo**	*197?*	**14.00**	**35.00**
WE FIVE, THE					
A&M LP-111	(M)	**You Were On My Mind**	*1965*	**5.00**	**12.00**
A&M SP-4111	(S)	**You Were On My Mind**	*1965*	**6.00**	**15.00**
		("You Were On My Mind" is rechanneled.)			
A&M LP-138	(M)	**Make Someone Happy**	*1967*	**5.00**	**12.00**
A&M SP-4138	(S)	**Make Someone Happy**	*1967*	**5.00**	**12.00**
A&M SP-4168	(S)	**The Return Of We Five**	*1969*	**5.00**	**12.00**
Vault 136	(S)	**Catch The Wind**	*1970*	**5.00**	**12.00**
A.V.I. 61016	(S)	**Take Each Day As It Comes**	*1977*	**4.00**	**10.00**
WEASELS, THE					
Wing MGW-12282	(M)	**The Liverpool Beat**	*1964*	**10.00**	**25.00**
Wing SRW-16282	(S)	**The Liverpool Beat**	*1964*	**12.00**	**30.00**
WEB, THE					
Deram DES-18018	(S)	**Fully Interlocking**	*1968*	**10.00**	**25.00**
WEDGES, THE					
Time T-2090	(M)	**Hang Ten (For Surfers Only)**	*1963*	**20.00**	**50.00**
Time ST-2090	(S)	**Hang Ten (For Surfers Only)**	*1963*	**30.00**	**75.00**

Just a teenager, Mary Wells was Motown's first big star: Under Smokey Robinson's direction she placed eight Top 40 hits on the pop charts before scoring the label's first #1 hit in early 1964 with "My Guy." Within a matter of months, her place at the pinnacle of Berry Gordy's fledgling empire was supplanted by the like-sounding Supremes. Her first two albums, Bye Bye Baby and The One Who Really Loves You, failed to make the pop charts and, while others did, only her greatest hits package had any real impact. By the time she was twenty-one and able to negotiate her contract, she split Motown for a better deal with 20th Century, where, unfortunately, her success was less than modest.

Label & Catalog #		Title	Year	VG+	NM

WEIDER, JOHN

| Anchor 2018 | (S) | John Weider | 1976 | 4.00 | 10.00 |

WEIGHT

| International 104 | (S) | Music Is The Message | 1970 | 8.00 | 20.00 |

WEINBERG METHOD, THE

| Anvil 1003 | (S) | Nonsynthetic Electronic Rock | 1970 | 6.00 | 15.00 |

WEIR, BOB [BOBBY & THE MIDNITES]
Mr Weir was a member of the late, great Grateful Dead. The Arista albums credit Bobby & The Midnites.

Warner Bros. BS-2627	(S)	Ace (Color photo on the back cover)	1972	16.00	40.00
Warner Bros. BS-2627	(S)	Ace (B&w photo on the back cover)	1972	12.00	30.00
Arista AL-4155	(S)	Heaven Help The Fool	1978	1.00	5.00
Arista AL-9568	(S)	Bobby & The Midnights	1981	1.00	5.00

WEIRD-OHS, THE
The Weird-Ohs are a creation of Gary Usher & Co. Refer to The Silly Surfers / The Weird-Ohs.

| Mercury MG-20976 | (M) | The Sounds Of The Weird-Ohs | 1964 | 60.00 | 150.00 |
| Mercury SR-60976 | (S) | The Sounds Of The Weird-Ohs | 1964 | 80.00 | 200.00 |

WELCH, BOB
Welch was a member of Fleetwood Mac.

Capitol ST-11663	(S)	French Kiss	1977	1.00	5.00
Capitol ST-11663	(DJ)	French Kiss (Picture disc)	1979	6.00	15.00
Capitol SO-11907	(S)	Three Hearts	1979	1.00	5.00
Capitol SW-12017	(S)	The Other One	1979	1.00	5.00
Capitol SOO-12107	(S)	Man Overboard	1980	1.00	5.00
RCA Victor AFL1-4107	(S)	Bob Welch	1981	1.00	5.00
Capitol SN-16125	(S)	French Kiss	1980	.80	4.00
Capitol SN-16126	(S)	Three Hearts	1980	.80	4.00
Capitol SN-16127	(S)	The Other One	1980	.80	4.00
Capitol SN-16269	(S)	Man Overboard	1982	.80	4.00

WELLS, CORY
Wells was a member of Three Dog Night.

| A&M SP-4673 | (S) | Touch Me | 1977 | 1.20 | 6.00 |
| A&M SP-4736 | (S) | Ahead Of The Storm | 1979 | 1.20 | 6.00 |

WELZ, JOEY

Palmer 13401	(S)	Vintage Ballads To Remember Her By	1970	6.00	15.00
Palmer 13402	(S)	Rock Revival	1970	6.00	15.00
Music City 5005	(S)	Kosmik City Blues And Mellow Dreams	1978	4.00	10.00

WELLS, JUNIOR

Delmark DL-612	(M)	Hoodoo Man Blues	1966	14.00	35.00
Delmark DS-612	(S)	Hoodoo Man Blues	1966	20.00	50.00
Vanguard VRS-9231	(M)	It's My Life Baby	1966	14.00	35.00
Vanguard VSD-79231	(S)	It's My Life Baby	1966	20.00	50.00
Delmark DLS-628	(S)	Southside Blues Jam	1967	12.00	30.00
Vanguard VSD-79262	(S)	Comin' At You	1968	12.00	30.00
Blue Rock 64002	(S)	You're Tuff Enough	1968	12.00	30.00
Blue Rock 64003	(S)	Live At The Golden Bear	1969	16.00	40.00
Delmark DLS-640	(S)	Blues Hit Big Town	1969	10.00	25.00
Blind Pig 1182	(S)	Drinkin' TNT 'N Smokin' Dynamite	1982	1.20	6.00

WELLS, MARY

Motown M-600	(M)	Bye, Bye Baby, I Don't Want To Take A Chance	1961	200.00	400.00
		—Motown albums above have white labels.—			
Motown M-600	(M)	Bye, Bye Baby, I Don't Want To Take A Chance	1962	80.00	200.00
Motown M-605	(M)	The One Who Really Loves You	1962	80.00	200.00
Motown M-607	(M)	Two Lovers	1963	80.00	200.00
Motown M-611	(M)	Recorded Live On Stage	1963	60.00	150.00
—Motown albums above have the company address above the spindle hole on the label.—					
Motown M-612	(M)	Second Time Around	1963	Unreleased	
Motown M-616	(M)	Mary Wells' Greatest Hits	1964	16.00	40.00
Motown MS-616	(S)	Mary Wells' Greatest Hits	1964	16.00	40.00
Motown M-617	(M)	My Guy	1964	20.00	50.00
Motown M-653	(M)	Vintage Stock	1966	16.00	40.00
Motown MS-653	(S)	Vintage Stock	1966	20.00	50.00
20th Century TFM-3171	(M)	Mary Wells	1965	20.00	50.00
20th Century TFS-4171	(S)	Mary Wells	1965	30.00	75.00
20th Century TFM-3178	(M)	Love Songs To The Beatles	1965	30.00	75.00
20th Century TFS-4178	(S)	Love Songs To The Beatles	1965	40.00	100.00
Movietone 71010	(M)	Ooh	1966	10.00	25.00
Movietone 72010	(S)	Ooh	1966	12.00	30.00
Atco 33-199	(M)	Two Sides Of Mary Wells	1966	10.00	25.00
Atco SD-33-199	(S)	Two Sides Of Mary Wells	1966	12.00	30.00

Label & Catalog #		Title	Year	VG+	NM
Jubilee JGS-8018	(S)	Servin' Up Some Soul	1968	10.00	25.00
EPK ARE-37540	(S)	In And Out Of Love	1981	6.00	15.00
Motown M5-161V	(M)	Bye Bye Baby	1982	1.00	5.00
Motown M5-167V	(S)	My Guy	1982	1.00	5.00
Motown M5-221V	(M)	Two Lovers	1982	1.00	5.00
Motown M5-233V	(M)	Greatest Hits	1982	1.00	5.00

WELLS, MARY, & MARVIN GAYE

Motown M-613	(M)	Together	1964	20.00	50.00

WENDY & BONNIE

Skye SK-1006D	(S)	Genesis	197?	20.00	50.00

WESLEY, FRED, & THE JB'S [FRED & THE NEW JB'S]
The JB's are James Brown's backing group and were produced by JB. Refer to The JB's.

People PE-5603	(S)	Doing It To Death	1973	8.00	20.00
People PE-6602	(S)	Damn Right I Am Somebody	1974	8.00	20.00
People PE-6604	(S)	Breakin' Bread	1974	8.00	20.00

WESLEY, FRED
Fred Wesley is a member of the Parliament/Funkadelic community.

Atlantic 18214	(S)	A Blow For Me, A Toot For You	1977	8.00	20.00

WEST

Epic BN-26380	(S)	West	1968	8.00	20.00
Epic BN-26433	(S)	Bridges	1969	8.00	20.00

WEST, LESLIE
West was a member of Mountain. Refer to West, Bruce & Laing.

Phantom BPL1-0954	(S)	The Great Fatsby	1975	4.00	10.00
Phantom BPL1-1258	(S)	The Leslie West Band	1976	4.00	10.00

WEST, TOMMY

Lifesong 6003	(S)	Home Town Frolics	197?	3.20	8.00

WEST, BRUCE & LAING
Leslie West, Jack Bruce and Corky Laing.

Columbia KC-31929	(S)	Why Dontcha'	1972	1.00	5.00
Columbia CQ-31929	(Q)	Why Dontcha'	1973	4.00	10.00
Columbia KC-32216	(S)	Whatever Turns You On	1973	1.00	5.00
Columbia CQ-32216	(Q)	Whatever Turns You On	1973	4.00	10.00
Columbia KC-32899	(S)	Live 'N Kickin'	1974	1.00	5.00

WEST COAST POP ART EXPERIMENTAL BAND
WCPAEB were Dan Harris, Shaun Harris and Bob Markley. They issued their first album privately.

Reprise R-6247	(M)	Part One	1967	20.00	50.00
Reprise RS-6247	(S)	Part One	1967	30.00	75.00
Reprise R-6270	(M)	Volume 2	1967	20.00	50.00
Reprise RS-6270	(S)	Volume 2	1967	30.00	75.00
Reprise RS-6298	(S)	A Child's Guide To Good And Evil	1968	40.00	100.00
Amos AAS-7004	(S)	Where's My Daddy	1969	20.00	50.00

WESTERMAN, FLOYD

Perception PLP-5	(S)	Custer Died For Your Sins	1970	4.00	10.00

WESTON, KIM
Ms. Weston also recorded with Marvin Gaye.

MGM E-4477	(M)	For The First Time	1967	14.00	35.00
MGM SE-4477	(S)	For The First Time	1967	20.00	50.00
MGM SE-4561	(S)	This Is America	1968	20.00	50.00
Volt VO-6014	(M)	Kim Kim Kim *(White label promo)*	1971	20.00	50.00
Volt VOS-6014	(S)	Kim Kim Kim	1971	10.00	25.00

WET WILLIE

Capricorn CP-861	(S)	Wet Willie	1971	1.20	6.00
Capricorn CP-0109	(S)	Wet Willie 2	1972	1.20	6.00
Capricorn CP-0113	(S)	Drippin' Wet Live	1973	1.00	5.00
Capricorn CP-0128	(S)	Keep On Smilin'	1974	1.00	5.00
Capricorn CP-0138	(S)	Wet Willie	1974	1.00	5.00
Capricorn CP-0149	(S)	Dixie Rock	1975	1.00	5.00
Capricorn CP-0166	(S)	The Wetter The Better	1977	1.00	5.00
Capricorn CP-0182	(S)	Left Coast Live	1977	1.00	5.00
Capricorn CP-0200	(S)	Greatest Hits	1977	1.00	5.00
Epic JE-34983	(S)	Manorisms	1978	1.00	5.00
Epic PRO-428	(DJ)	Live Concert Series	1978	10.00	25.00

WHEELS, THE

Montgomery Ward 10	(S)	Sounds Of The Hot Rods	196?	60.00	150.00

Label & Catalog #		Title	Year	VG+	NM
WHEELS, BURT, & THE SPEEDSTERS					
Coronet CX-216	(M)	Sounds Of The Big Racers	196?	10.00	25.00
Coronet CXS-216	(S)	Sounds Of The Big Racers	196?	14.00	35.00
WHISPERS, THE					
Soul Clock 22001	(S)	Planets Of Life	197?	40.00	100.00
Janus JLS-3041	(S)	The Whispers' Love Story	197?	20.00	50.00
WHITCOMB, IAN					
Tower T-5004	(M)	You Turn Me On	1965	10.00	25.00
Tower DT-5004	(E)	You Turn Me On	1965	8.00	20.00
Tower T-5042	(M)	Mod, Mod, Music Hall	1966	6.00	15.00
Tower ST-5042	(S)	Mod, Mod, Music Hall	1966	8.00	20.00
Tower T-5071	(M)	Yellow Underground	1967	6.00	15.00
Tower ST-5071	(S)	Yellow Underground	1967	8.00	20.00
Tower ST-5100	(S)	Sock Me Some Rock	1968	8.00	20.00
United Arts. LA021	(S)	Under The Ragtime Moon	1972	3.20	8.00
Sierra 8708	(S)	Pianomelt	1980	1.20	6.00
First American 7704	(S)	Crooner Tunes	1978	1.20	6.00
First American 7751	(S)	Instrumentals	1981	1.20	6.00
First American 7789	(S)	In Hollywood	1982	1.20	6.00
WHITE, BUKKA					
Arhoolie 1019	(M)	Sky Songs, Volume 1	1966	12.00	30.00
Arhoolie 1020	(M)	Sky Songs, Volume 2	1966	12.00	30.00
Takoma 1001	(M)	Mississippi Blues	1969	12.00	30.00
Herwin 201	(M)	Sic'em Dogs	1969	10.00	25.00
Blue Horizon 4604	(M)	Blues Masters, Volume 4: Bukka White	197?	10.00	25.00
WHITE, TONY JOE					
Monument SLP-18114	(S)	Black And White	1969	6.00	15.00
Monument SLP-18133	(S)	Tony Joe White Continued	1969	6.00	15.00
Monument SLP-18142	(S)	Tony Joe	1970	6.00	15.00
Warner Bros. BS-1900	(S)	Tony Joe White	1971	4.00	10.00
Warner Bros. BS-2580	(S)	The Train I'm On	1972	4.00	10.00
Warner Bros. BS-2708	(S)	Homemade Ice Cream	1973	4.00	10.00
20th Century 523	(S)	Eyes	1977	4.00	10.00
Casablanca 7233	(S)	Real Thang	1980	1.20	6.00
WHITE CHOCOLATE					
RCA Victor APL1-0349	(S)	White Chocolate	1973	3.20	8.00
WHITE CLOUD					
Good Medicine 3500	(S)	White Cloud	1972	5.00	12.00
WHITE DUCK					
Uni 73140	(S)	In Season	1972	6.00	15.00
Uni 73122	(S)	White Duck	1971	6.00	15.00
WHITE ELEPHANT					
Just Sunshine 3000	(S)	White Elephant	1973	6.00	15.00
WHITE LIGHTNIN'					
ABC 690	(S)	File Under Rock	1969	8.00	20.00
WHITE LIGHTNIN'					
Island 9325	(S)	White Lightnin'	1975	3.20	8.00
WHITE NOISE					
Island ST-9303	(S)	An Electrical Storm	1971	6.00	15.00
Antilles AN-7011	(S)	An Electrical Storm	197?	1.00	5.00
WHITE PLAINS					
Deram DES-18045	(S)	My Baby Loves Loving	1970	6.00	15.00
WHITE WATER					
RCA Victor APL1-0091	(S)	Out Of The Darkness	1973	1.20	6.00
WHITE WITCH					
Capricorn CPN-0107	(S)	White Witch	1973	10.00	25.00
Capricorn CPN-0129	(S)	A Spiritual Greeting	1974	10.00	25.00
WHITLOCK, BOBBY					
Dunhill DSX-50131	(S)	Raw Velvet	1972	1.20	6.00
Capricorn CP-0168	(S)	Rock Your Sox Off	1976	1.20	6.00

Label & Catalog #		Title	Year	VG+	NM

WHITNEY, MARVA

Label & Catalog #		Title	Year	VG+	NM
King KS-1053	(S)	I Sing Soul	1969	60.00	150.00
King KS-1062	(S)	It's My Thing	1969	60.00	150.00
King KS-1079	(S)	Live And Lowdown At The Apollo	1969	80.00	200.00
		(King 1053, 1062 and 1079 were produced by James Brown.)			

WHO, THE

The Who were Roger Daltrey, John Entwistle, Keith Moon, and Pete Townshend. Moon died in 1978 and was replaced by Kenny Jones, formerly of The Faces.

Label & Catalog #		Title	Year	VG+	NM
Decca DL-4664	(DJ)	The Who Sing My Generation *(White label promo)*	1966	150.00	300.00
Decca DL-4664	(M)	The Who Sing My Generation	1966	60.00	150.00
Decca DL-74664	(DJ)	The Who Sing My Generation *(White label promo)*	1966	80.00	200.00
Decca DL-74664	(E)	The Who Sing My Generation	1966	30.00	75.00
Life DL-74664	(E)	The Who Sing My Generation	1967	60.00	150.00
		(The Life album is a reissue on a little-known subsidiary of Decca.)			
Decca DL-4892	(DJ)	Happy Jack *(White label promo)*	1967	80.00	200.00
Decca DL-4892	(M)	Happy Jack	1967	30.00	75.00
Decca DL-74892	(DJ)	Happy Jack *(White label promo)*	1967	60.00	150.00
Decca DL-74892	(S)	Happy Jack	1967	20.00	50.00
		("Happy Jack" and "Don't Look Away" are rechanneled.)			
Decca DL-4950	(DJ)	The Who Sell Out *(White label promo)*	1967	150.00	300.00
Decca DL-74950	(DJ)	The Who Sell Out *(White label promo)*	1967	200.00	400.00
		(On some promos of DL-4950, side 1 is banded for air-play with a different song order and all of the "commercials" are on one side. The matrix number in the trail-off vinyl is "DL-34505".)			
Decca DL-4950	(DJ)	The Who Sell Out *(White label promo)*	1967	80.00	200.00
Decca DL-74950	(DJ)	The Who Sell Out *(White label promo)*	1967	100.00	250.00
		(The playing order is the same as the commercial version.)			
Decca DL-4950	(M)	The Who Sell Out	1967	40.00	100.00
Decca DL-74950	(S)	The Who Sell Out	1967	20.00	50.00
Decca DL-5064	(DJ)	Magic Bus/The Who On Tour *(White label promo)*	1968	80.00	200.00
Decca DL-75064	(DJ)	Magic Bus/The Who On Tour *(White label promo)*	1968	60.00	150.00
Decca DL-75064	(E)	Magic Bus/The Who On Tour	1968	20.00	50.00
		("Magic Bus," "I Can't Reach You" and "Tattoo" are in stereo.)			
Decca DXSW-7205	(DJ)	Tommy *(White label promo)*	1969	80.00	200.00
Decca DXSW-7205	(S)	Tommy *(2 LPs with booklet)*	1969	16.00	40.00
Decca DL-79175	(S)	Live At Leeds	1970	16.00	40.00
		(Important: All copies of DL-79175 look like some kind of important promo package, the gatefold jacket has two pockets on the inside one of which contains the record, which has a white label with sorta hand-written titles on it. The other pocket holds a variety of inserts and photos, including reproductions of old contracts.)			
Decca DL-79182	(S)	Who's Next	1971	10.00	25.00
Track 2408-102	(S)	Who's Next	1971	60.00	150.00
		(Black Track label reads "Made in USA" on the bottom. Manufactured for export and issued in a regular UK cover.)			
Decca DL-79184	(S)	Meaty Beaty Big & Bouncy *(With poster)*	1971	12.00	30.00
Decca DL-79184	(S)	Meaty Beaty Big & Bouncy *(Without poster)*	1971	8.00	20.00
		("I Can't Explain," "Anyway Anyhow Anywhere," "Substitute," "My Generation," "Pictures Of Lily," and "Magic Bus" are rechanneled.)			
Track 2126	(S)	Odds & Sods	1974	10.00	25.00
Track 2-4067	(P)	A Quick One/ The Who Sell Out *(2 LPs)*	1974	10.00	25.00
Track 2-4068	(P)	Magic Bus / My Generation *(2 LPs)*	1974	10.00	25.00
MCA 10004	(S)	Quadrophenia *(2 LPs)*	1973	6.00	15.00
MCA 10005	(S)	Tommy *(2 LPs)*	1973	4.00	10.00
MCA 2022	(S)	Live At Leeds	1973	1.00	5.00
MCA 2023	(S)	Who's Next	1973	1.00	5.00
MCA 2025	(S)	Meaty, Beaty, Big And Bouncy	1973	1.00	5.00
MCA 2044	(E)	The Who Sing My Generation	1974	20.00	50.00
MCA 2045	(P)	Happy Jack	1974	20.00	50.00
		(For some reason, MCA 2044 and 2045 are rather rare.)			
MCA 2161	(P)	The Who By Numbers	1975	3.20	8.00
MCA 3023	(S)	Live At Leeds	1977	1.00	5.00
MCA 3024	(S)	Who's Next	1977	1.00	5.00
MCA 3025	(S)	Meaty, Beaty, Big And Bouncy	1977	1.00	5.00
MCA 3026	(S)	The Who By Numbers	1978	1.00	5.00
MCA 3050	(DJ)	Who Are You *(White label promo)*	1978	10.00	25.00
		(Promos edit the line "Who the fuck are you?" in the title tune.)			
MCA 3050	(S)	Who Are You	1978	1.00	5.00
MCAP-14950	(S)	Who Are You *(Picture disc)*	1978	6.00	15.00
MCA 11005	(P)	The Kids Are Alright *(2 LPs)*	1979	4.00	10.00
MCA 5220	(S)	Who's Next	1979	.80	4.00
MCA 37001	(S)	Meaty, Beaty, Big And Bouncy	1979	.80	4.00
MCA 37002	(S)	The Who By Numbers	1979	.80	4.00
MCA 37003	(S)	Who Are You	1979	.80	4.00
Polydor 2-6235	(S)	Quadrophenia *(2 LPs)*	1979	1.20	6.00
Polydor CF-29502	(S)	Tommy *(2 LPs)*	1980	1.20	6.00
MCA 37169	(S)	Odds And Sods	1980	.80	4.00

Label & Catalog #		Title	Year	VG+	NM
MCA 2-6895	(S)	**Quadrophenia** *(2 LPs)*	1980	1.20	6.00
MCA 12001	(S)	**Hooligans** *(2 LPs)*	1981	1.20	6.00
MCA 5408	(S)	**Who's Greatest Hits**	1983	1.00	5.00
MCA 8018	(S)	**Who's Last** *(2 LPs)*	1984	1.20	6.00
Warner Bros. WBMS-116	(DJ)	**Filling In The Gaps** *(2 LP interview)*	1981	30.00	75.00
		(Original covers for WBMS-116 have a drawing.)			
Warner Bros. WBMS-116	(DJ)	**Filling In The Gaps** *(2 LP interview)*	1981	20.00	50.00
		(Later covers are a plain red WB omnibus cover.)			
Warner Bros. 3516	(S)	**Face Dances**	1981	1.00	5.00
Warner Bros. 23731	(S)	**It's Hard** *(Qutex II vinyl ptomo)*	1982	12.00	30.00
Warner Bros. 23731	(S)	**It's Hard**	1982	1.00	5.00

WHO, THE / THE STRAWBERRY ALARM CLOCK

Decca DL-734586	(S)	**The Who / The Strawberry Alarm Clock**	1969	40.00	100.00
		(Available briefly in 1969 through Philco Electronics stores.)			
Decca DL-734695	(S)	**The Who / The Strawberry Alarm Clock**	1970	20.00	50.00
		(Reissue from MCA Special Products.)			

WICHITA FALLS

Imperial LP-12417	(S)	**Life Is But A Dream**	1968	6.00	15.00

WICHITA TRAIN WHISTLE, THE
The Whistle features Michael Nesmith.

Dot DLP-25861	(S)	**The Wichita Train Whistle Sings**	1968	12.00	30.00
Pacific Arts 7-1??	(S)	**The Wichita Train Whistle Sings**	1978	4.00	10.00

WIGGY BITS

Polydor 1-6081	(S)	**Wiggy Bits**	1976	1.20	6.00

WIGWAM

Forecast FTS-3089	(S)	**Tombstone Valentine** *(2 LPs)*	1971	8.00	20.00

WILD BUTTER

United Arts. UAS-6766	(S)	**Wild Butter**	1970	10.00	25.00

WILD OATS

Alshire 5235	(S)	**Wild Oats**	1971	4.00	10.00

WILD ONES, THE

United Arts. UAL-3450	(M)	**The Arthur Sound**	1965	10.00	25.00
United Arts. UAS-6450	(S)	**The Arthur Sound**	1965	12.00	30.00

WILD TCHOUPITOULAS
Wild Tchoupitoulas is a pseudonym for The Neville Brothers.

Island ISLP-9360	(S)	**Wild Tchoupitoulas**	1976	4.00	10.00

WILD THING

Elektra EKS-74059	(S)	**Partyin'**	1969	6.00	15.00

WILD TURKEY

Reprise MS-2070	(S)	**Battle Hymn**	1972	5.00	12.00
Chrysalis CHR-1010	(S)	**Turkey**	1972	3.20	8.00
Chrysalis CHR-1045	(S)	**Battle Hymn**	1973	3.20	8.00

WILDCATS, THE

United Arts. UAL-3031	(M)	**Bandstand Record Hop**	1958	20.00	50.00
United Arts. UAS-6031	(S)	**Bandstand Record Hop**	1958	30.00	75.00

WILDE, MARTY

Epic LN-3686	(M)	**Bad Boy**	1960	30.00	75.00
Epic BN-5??	(S)	**Bad Boy**	1960	40.00	100.00
Epic LN-3711	(M)	**Wilde About Marty**	1960	30.00	75.00
Epic BN-575	(S)	**Wilde About Marty**	1960	40.00	100.00

WILDERNESS ROAD

Columbia C-31118	(S)	**Wilderness Road**	1972	4.00	10.00
Reprise MS-2125	(S)	**Sold For Prevention Of Disease Only**	1973	4.00	10.00

WILDWEEDS, THE
Wildweeds features Al Anderson, later of NRBQ.

Vanguard VSD-6552	(S)	**Wildweeds**	1970	10.00	25.00
Vanguard Q-40???	(Q)	**Wildweeds**	197?	16.00	40.00

WILKINSON TRI-CYCLE

Date TES-4016	(S)	**Wilkinson Tri-cycle**	1969	14.00	35.00

Maurice Williams had originally led The Gladiolas, but changed the group's name to The Zodiacs in 1959. He then replaced the original members with a new line-up and, billed as Maurice Williams & The Zodiacs, topped the pop charts during the 1960 Christmas season with "Stay." Pictured here is Stay on Herald, a rare record indeed. This was later reissued on Sphere Sound in both mono and electronically rechanneled stereo. All Through The Night (bottom) features the smooth rhythm'n blues-based vocalist Mel Williams backed by the redoubtable Johnny Otis and his orchestra.

Label & Catalog #		Title	Year	VG+	NM

WILLIAMS, DUKE, & THE EXTREMES

Label & Catalog #		Title	Year	VG+	NM
Capricorn CP-0119	(S)	A Monkey In A Silk Suit Is Still A Monkey	1973	1.20	6.00
Capricorn CP-0133	(S)	Fantastic Fedora	1974	1.20	6.00

WILLIAMS, "BIG" JOE
Joe Williams is a guitar player and singer of country blues. Refer to Victoria Spivey.

Folkways F-3820	(M)	Mississippi's Big Joe Williams	1962	14.00	35.00
Folkways FS-3820	(S)	Mississippi's Big Joe Williams	1962	20.00	50.00
Delmark DL-604	(M)	Blues On Highway 49	1962	20.00	50.00
Bluesville BVLP-1056	(M)	Blues For 9 Strings	1962	30.00	75.00
Bluesville BVLP-1067	(M)	Big Joe Williams At Folk City	1963	30.00	75.00
Bluesville BVLP-1083	(M)	Studio Blues	1964	30.00	75.00
— *Bluesville albums above have bright blue labels with silver print.* —					
Bluesville BVLP-1056	(M)	Blues For 9 Strings	1964	10.00	25.00
Bluesville BVLP-1067	(M)	Big Joe Williams At Folk City	1964	10.00	25.00
Bluesville BVLP-1083	(M)	Studio Blues	1964	10.00	25.00
— *Bluesville albums above have blue labels with a trident logo on the right side.* —					
Delmark DL-609	(M)	Starvin' Chain Blues	1966	10.00	25.00
Milestone 3001	(M)	Classic Delta Blues	1966	10.00	25.00
Folkways 31004	(M)	Hell Bound And Heaven Sent	1967	10.00	25.00
World Pacific WPS-21897	(S)	Big Joe Williams	1969	6.00	15.00

WILLIAMS, LARRY
Larry also recorded with Johnny Watson.

Specialty SP-2109	(M)	Here's Larry Williams	1959	200.00	400.00
— *Specialty albums above have black & gold labels on thick vinyl.*					
The labels and covers read "Stereo Natural Sound." —					
Chess LP-1457	(M)	Larry Williams	1961	80.00	200.00
— *Chess albums above have black labels.* —					
OKeh OKM-12123	(M)	Larry Williams' Greatest Hits	1967	12.00	30.00
OKeh OKS-14123	(S)	Larry Williams' Greatest Hits	1967	16.00	40.00

WILLIAMS, MAURICE, & THE ZODIACS

Herald HLP-1014	(M)	Stay	1961	250.00	500.00
Sphere Sound SR-7007	(M)	Stay	1965	60.00	150.00
Sphere Sound SSR-7007	(E)	Stay	1965	40.00	100.00
(Sphere Sound 7007 is a reissue of Herald 1014.)					
Snyder 5586	(M)	At The Beach	196?	40.00	100.00
Relic 5017	(M)	Greatest Hits	197?	8.00	20.00

WILLIAMS, MEL, & JOHNNY OTIS

Dig 103	(M)	All Through The Night	1955	300.00	600.00

WILLIAMS, OTIS, & THE CHARMS

Deluxe 570	(M)	Their All Time Hits	1957	1,000.00	1,500.00
King 570	(M)	Their All Time Hits	1957	500.00	750.00
King 614	(M)	This Is Otis Williams & The Charms	1959	300.00	500.00
— *King albums above have crownless black labels.* —					

WILLIAMS, OTIS, & THE MIDNIGHT COWBOYS

Stop STLP-1022	(S)	Otis Williams & The Midnight Cowboys	1971	10.00	25.00

WILLIAMS, PAT

Verve V6-5075	(S)	Heavy Vibrations	1969	4.00	10.00

WILLIAMS, ROBERT PETE

Folk/Lyric FL-109	(M)	Prison Blues	1960	40.00	100.00
Bluesville BVLP-1026	(M)	Free Again	1961	40.00	100.00
— *Bluesville albums above have bright blue labels with silver print.* —					
Bluesville BVLP-1026	(M)	Free Again	1964	12.00	30.00
— *Bluesville albums above have blue labels with a trident logo on the right side.* —					
Prestige PRST-7808	(E)	Free Again	1969	6.00	15.00
(Prestige 7808 is a reissue of Bluesville 1026.)					
Fantasy F-24716	(S)	Rural Blues (With Snooks Eaglin)	197?	4.00	10.00
Ahura Mazda 2002	(S)	Robert Pete Williams	197?	4.00	10.00
Takoma B-1001	(S)	Louisiana Blues	197?	4.00	10.00
Arhoolie 2015	(S)	Those Prison Blues	197?	4.00	10.00

WILLIAMS, TONY
Tony Williams was formerly the lead singer for The Platters.

Mercury MG-20454	(M)	A Girl Is A Girl Is A Girl	1959	14.00	35.00
Mercury SR-60138	(S)	A Girl Is A Girl Is A Girl	1959	20.00	50.00
Reprise R-6006	(M)	Tony Williams—His Greatest Hits	1961	10.00	25.00
Reprise R-96006	(S)	Tony Williams—His Greatest Hits	1961	12.00	30.00
Phillips PHM-200-051	(M)	Magic Touch Of Tony	1962	10.00	25.00
Phillips PHS-600-051	(S)	Magic Touch Of Tony	1962	12.00	30.00

Label & Catalog #		Title	Year	VG+	NM

WILLIAMSON, ROBIN
Robin was a member of The Incredible String Band.

Flying Fish 033	(S)	**Journey's End**	1977	1.20	6.00

WILLIAMSON, SONNY BOY
Sonny Boy Williamson #2 was later the pseudonym for Alec "Rice" Miller.

Checker LP-1437	(M)	**Down And Out Blues** *(White label promo)*	1959	750.00	1,500.00
Checker LP-1437	(M)	**Down And Out Blues**	1959	250.00	500.00
		—Checker albums above have black labels with silver print.—			
Chess LP-1437	(M)	**Down And Out Blues**	196?	*See note below*	
		(Chess 1437 was issued in a Checker jacket and is rare with a suggested NM value of $600-1,000.)			
		—Chess albums above have blue labels with silver print.—			
Chess LP-1503	(M)	**The Real Folk Blues** *(White label promo)*	1966	150.00	300.00
Chess LP-1503	(M)	**The Real Folk Blues**	1966	40.00	100.00
Chess LP-1509	(M)	**More Real Folk Blues** *(White label promo)*	1966	150.00	300.00
Chess LP-1509	(M)	**More Real Folk Blues**	1966	40.00	100.00
		—Chess albums above have black labels.—			
Chess LPS-1536	(S)	**Bummer Road**	1969	10.00	25.00
Chess 2CH-50027	(S)	**This Is My Story** *(2 LPs)*	1972	10.00	25.00
Chess LP-417	(S)	**One Way Out**	1976	6.00	15.00
Chess 2CH-206	(S)	**Sonny Boy Williamson** *(2 LPs)*	1976	6.00	15.00
Arhoolie 2020	(M)	**King Biscuit Time**	1976	1.20	6.00

WILLIAMSON, SONNY BOY, & MEMPHIS SLIM

Crescendo GNPS-10003	(S)	**In Paris**	1974	1.20	6.00

WILLIAMSON, SONNY BOY, & THE YARDBIRDS

Mercury MG-21071	(M)	**Sonny Boy Williamson & The Yardbirds**	1966	30.00	75.00
Mercury SR-61071	(E)	**Sonny Boy Williamson & The Yardbirds**	1966	20.00	50.00
		(Original covers have photos of Sonny Boy with The Yardbirds.)			
Mercury SR-61071	(E)	**Sonny Boy Williamson & The Yardbirds**	197?	10.00	25.00
		(Later covers have cartoon artwork.)			

WILLIE & THE MIGHTY MAGNIFICENTS

All Platinum 3008	(S)	**Very Soulful**	1972	4.00	10.00

WILLIE & THE RED RUBBER BAND

RCA Victor LSP-4074	(S)	**Willie And The Red Rubber Band**	1968	6.00	15.00
RCA Victor LSP-4193	(S)	**We're Comin' Up**	1969	6.00	15.00

WILLIS, CHUCK

Epic LN-3425	(M)	**Chuck Willis Wails The Blues**	1958	300.00	600.00
Epic LN-3728	(M)	**A Tribute To Chuck Willis**	1960	200.00	400.00
Atlantic 8018	(M)	**The King Of The Stroll**	1958	200.00	400.00
		—Atlantic albums above have black labels.—			
Atlantic 8018	(M)	**The King Of The Stroll**	1960	60.00	150.00
Atlantic 8079	(M)	**I Remember Chuck Willis**	1963	60.00	150.00
Atlantic SD-8079	(P)	**I Remember Chuck Willis**	1963	80.00	200.00
		—Atlantic albums above have orange & purple labels.—			

WILSON, AL

Soul City SCS-92006	(S)	**Searching For The Dolphins**	1969	10.00	25.00
Rocky Road RR-3601	(S)	**Show And Tell**	1973	6.00	15.00
Rocky Road 3600	(S)	**Weighing In**	1973	6.00	15.00
Rocky Road 3700	(S)	**La La Peace Song**	1974	6.00	15.00
Playboy 410	(S)	**I've Got A Feeling**	1976	6.00	15.00
Roadshow BXL1-3215	(S)	**Count The Days**	1979	1.20	6.00

WILSON, BRIAN
Brian Wilson was The Beach Boys. Refer to Spring.

Crawdaddy	(DJ)	**The Crawdaddy Brian Wilson Interview**	1977	60.00	150.00
Sire PRO-3248	(S)	**Words And Music** *(Promotional interview)*	1988	10.00	25.00
Sire 25669	(S)	**Brian Wilson**	1988	4.00	10.00

WILSON, CARL
Carl Wilson is a member of The Beach Boys.

Caribou JZ-37010	(S)	**Carl Wilson**	1981	4.00	10.00
Caribou ARZ-37970	(S)	**Youngblood**	1982	4.00	10.00

WILSON, DENNIS
Dennis Wilson was a member of The Beach Boys.

Caribou PZ-34354	(S)	**Pacific Ocean Blue** *(Special advance copy)*	1977	100.00	250.00
		(White label copies issued with a letter from DW printed on the cover and each copy signed in felt-tip pen by DW.)			
Caribou PZ-34354	(S)	**Pacific Ocean Blue**	1977	10.00	25.00

Label & Catalog #		Title	Year	VG+	NM

WILSON, J. FRANK, & THE CAVALIERS

Josie JM-4006	(M)	Last Kiss	1964	30.00	75.00
Josie JS-4006	(S)	Last Kiss	1964	40.00	100.00

WILSON, JACKIE
Mr. Wilson was formerly the lead singer for Billy Ward & The Dominoes.

Brunswick BL-54042	(M)	He's So Fine	1959	150.00	300.00
Brunswick BL-54045	(M)	Lonely Teardrops	1959	100.00	250.00
Brunswick BL-54050	(M)	So Much	1960	60.00	150.00
Brunswick BL-754050	(S)	So Much	1960	80.00	200.00
Brunswick BL-54055	(M)	Jackie Sings The Blues (Gatefold cover)	1960	60.00	150.00
Brunswick BL-754055	(S)	Jackie Sings The Blues (Gatefold cover)	1960	80.00	200.00
SeSac 160?	(M)	Jackie Wilson	1960	60.00	150.00
SeSac 160?	(S)	Jackie Wilson	1960	60.00	150.00
		(SeSac 160? is a reissue of Brunswick 54055).			
Brunswick BL-54058	(M)	My Golden Favorites	1960	20.00	50.00
Brunswick BL-54059	(M)	A Woman, A Lover, A Friend	1961	20.00	50.00
Brunswick BL-754059	(S)	A Woman, A Lover, A Friend	1961	30.00	75.00
Brunswick BL-54100	(M)	You Ain't Heard Nothin' Yet	1961	20.00	50.00
Brunswick BL-754100	(S)	You Ain't Heard Nothin' Yet	1961	30.00	75.00
Brunswick BL-54101	(M)	By Special Request	1961	20.00	50.00
Brunswick BL-754101	(S)	By Special Request	1961	30.00	75.00
Brunswick BL-54105	(M)	Body And Soul	1962	20.00	50.00
Brunswick BL-754105	(S)	Body And Soul	1962	30.00	75.00
Brunswick BL-54106	(M)	The World's Greatest Melodies	1962	20.00	50.00
Brunswick BL-754106	(S)	The World's Greatest Melodies	1962	30.00	75.00
Brunswick BL-54108	(M)	Jackie Wilson At The Copa	1962	20.00	50.00
Brunswick BL-754108	(S)	Jackie Wilson At The Copa	1962	30.00	75.00
Brunswick BL-54110	(M)	Baby Workout	1963	30.00	75.00
Brunswick BL-754110	(S)	Baby Workout	1963	40.00	100.00
		—Brunswick albums above have black & silver labels.—			
Brunswick BL-54058	(M)	My Golden Favorites	196?	10.00	25.00
Brunswick BL-54059	(M)	A Woman, A Lover, A Friend	196?	8.00	20.00
Brunswick BL-754059	(S)	A Woman, A Lover, A Friend	196?	10.00	25.00
Brunswick BL-54100	(M)	You Ain't Heard Nothin' Yet	196?	8.00	20.00
Brunswick BL-754100	(S)	You Ain't Heard Nothin' Yet	196?	10.00	25.00
Brunswick BL-54101	(M)	By Special Request	196?	8.00	20.00
Brunswick BL-754101	(S)	By Special Request	196?	10.00	25.00
Brunswick BL-54105	(M)	Body And Soul	196?	8.00	20.00
Brunswick BL-754105	(S)	Body And Soul	196?	10.00	25.00
Brunswick BL-54106	(M)	The World's Greatest Melodies	196?	8.00	20.00
Brunswick BL-754106	(S)	The World's Greatest Melodies	196?	10.00	25.00
Brunswick BL-54108	(M)	Jackie Wilson At The Copa	196?	8.00	20.00
Brunswick BL-754108	(S)	Jackie Wilson At The Copa	196?	10.00	25.00
Brunswick BL-54110	(M)	Baby Workout	1963	10.00	25.00
Brunswick BL-754110	(S)	Baby Workout	1963	12.00	30.00
Brunswick BL-54112	(M)	Merry Christmas From Jackie Wilson	1963	12.00	30.00
Brunswick BL-754112	(S)	Merry Christmas From Jackie Wilson	1963	16.00	40.00
Brunswick BL-54113	(M)	Shake A Hand (With Linda Hopkins)	1963	10.00	25.00
Brunswick BL-754113	(S)	Shake A Hand (With Linda Hopkins)	1963	12.00	30.00
Brunswick BL-54115	(M)	My Golden Favorites, Volume 2	1964	10.00	25.00
Brunswick BL-754115	(S)	My Golden Favorites, Volume 2	1964	12.00	30.00
Brunswick BL-54117	(M)	Somethin' Else	1964	10.00	25.00
Brunswick BL-754117	(S)	Somethin' Else	1964	12.00	30.00
Brunswick BL-54118	(M)	Soul Time	1965	10.00	25.00
Brunswick BL-754118	(S)	Soul Time	1965	12.00	30.00
Brunswick BL-54119	(M)	Spotlight On Jackie Wilson	1965	10.00	25.00
Brunswick BL-754119	(S)	Spotlight On Jackie Wilson	1965	12.00	30.00
Brunswick BL-54120	(M)	Soul Galore	1966	10.00	25.00
Brunswick BL-754120	(S)	Soul Galore	1966	12.00	30.00
Brunswick BL-54122	(M)	Whispers	1967	8.00	20.00
Brunswick BL-754122	(S)	Whispers	1967	10.00	25.00
Brunswick BL-54130	(M)	Higher And Higher	1967	8.00	20.00
Brunswick BL-754130	(S)	Higher And Higher	1967	10.00	25.00
Brunswick BL-754138	(S)	I Get The Sweetest Feeling	1968	8.00	20.00
Brunswick BL-754134	(S)	Manufacturers Of Soul (With Count Basie)	1968	8.00	20.00
		—Brunswick albums above have black labels with a "Division of Decca Records" on the left side.—			
Brunswick BL-754140	(S)	Jackie Wilson's Greatest Hits	1969	6.00	15.00
Brunswick BL-754154	(S)	Do Your Thing	1969	6.00	15.00
Brunswick BL-754158	(S)	It's All Part Of Love	1970	6.00	15.00
Brunswick BL-754167	(S)	This Love Is Real	1971	6.00	15.00
Brunswick BL-754172	(S)	You Got Me Walking	1971	6.00	15.00
Brunswick BL-754189	(S)	Beautiful Day	1973	4.00	10.00
Brunswick BL-754199	(S)	Nowstalgia	1974	4.00	10.00
Brunswick BL-754212	(S)	Nobody But You	1977	4.00	10.00

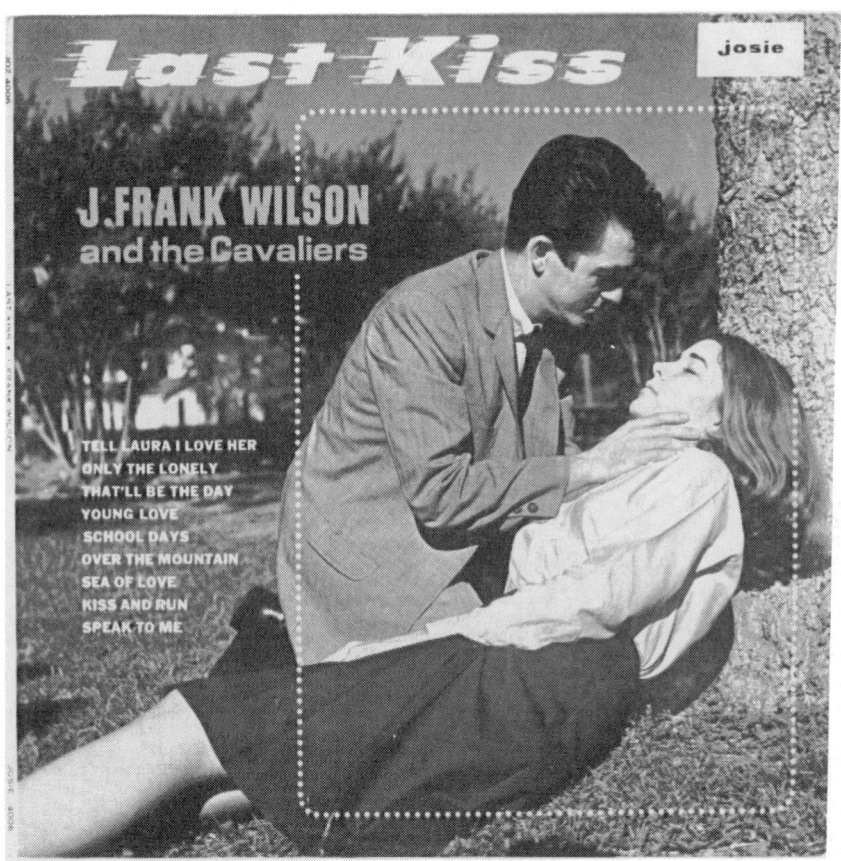

At the height of the British Invasion, J. Frank Wilson & The Cavaliers had a huge hit with "Last Kiss." Totally retro ("Where, oh where, can my baby be?/The good Lord took her away from me."), the song sounded like it had been around for years and suddenly discovered! The album shown here followed. With its hokey cover photo, it would have been more aptly titled "Sophomores In Love."

Label & Catalog #		Title	Year	VG+	NM

WILSON, MARY
Ms. Wilson was formerly a member of The Supremes.

Motown M7-927	(S)	Red Hot	1979	4.00	10.00

WINCHESTER, JESSE

Ampex A-10104	(S)	Jesse Winchester	1970	6.00	15.00
Bearsville BR-2045	(S)	Jesse Winchester	1971	1.20	6.00
Bearsville BR-2102	(S)	Third Down And 110 To Go	1972	1.20	6.00
Bearsville BR-6953	(S)	Learn To Love It	1974	1.20	6.00
Bearsville BR-6964	(S)	Let The Rough Side Drag	1976	1.20	6.00
Bearsville PRO-560	(DJ)	The Jesse Winchester Radio Show	1976	16.00	40.00
Bearsville BR-6968	(S)	Nothing But A Breeze	1977	1.20	6.00
Bearsville PRO-693	(DJ)	Live At The Bijou Cafe Plus A Live Interview At Media College In Montreal (2 LPs)	1977	12.00	30.00
Bearsville BRK-6984	(S)	A Touch On The Rainy Side	1978	1.20	6.00
Bearsville BRK-6889	(S)	Talk Memphis	1981	1.20	6.00

WIND

Life LLPS-2000	(S)	Make Believe	1969	4.00	10.00

WIND HARP

United Arts. UAS9963	(S)	Song From The Hill (2 LPs)	1972	8.00	20.00

WIND IN THE WILLOWS, THE
W.I.T.W. features Debbie Harry, later of Blondie.

Capitol SKAO-2956	(S)	The Wind In The Willows	1968	12.00	30.00

WINDSOR TUNNEL

Avco Embassy 33014	(S)	Windsor Tunnel	197?	4.00	10.00

WINGS

Dunhill DS-50046	(S)	Wings	1968	5.00	12.00

WINGS: *Refer to* **PAUL McCARTNEY**

WINNERS, THE

Crown CLP-5394	(M)	Checkered Flag	1963	10.00	25.00
Crown CST-394	(S)	Checkered Flag	1963	12.00	30.00
		—Crown albums above have gray labels.—			

WINSTONS, THE

Metromedia MD-1010	(S)	Color Him Father	1969	16.00	40.00

WINTER, EDGAR
Edgar Winter's band features Rick Derringer with Dan Hartman and Ronnie Montrose

Epic BN-26503	(S)	Entrance	1970	3.20	8.00
Epic KE-30512	(S)	Edger Winter's White Trash	1971	3.20	8.00
Epic KE-31249	(S)	Roadwork (2 LPs)	1972	4.00	10.00
Epic KE-31584	(S)	They Only Come Out At Night	1972	3.20	8.00
		—Epic albums above have yellow labels.—			
Epic BN-26503	(S)	Entrance	1970	1.00	5.00
Epic KE-30512	(S)	Edger Winter's White Trash	1971	1.00	5.00
Epic KE-31249	(S)	Roadwork (2 LPs)	1972	1.20	6.00
Epic KE-31584	(S)	They Only Come Out At Night	1972	1.00	5.00
Epic EQ-31584	(Q)	They Only Come Out At Night	1973	8.00	20.00
Epic PE-32461	(S)	Shock Treatment	1974	1.20	6.00
Epic PEQ-32461	(Q)	Shock Treatment	1974	8.00	20.00
Epic BG-33770	(S)	Entrance / White Trash (2 LPs)	1975	1.20	6.00
Blue Sky PZ-33483	(S)	Jasmine Nightdreams	1975	1.20	6.00
Blue Sky PZQ-33483	(Q)	Jasmine Nightdreams	1975	8.00	20.00
Blue Sky PZ-33798	(S)	Edger Winter Group With Rick Derringer	1975	1.20	6.00
Blue Sky PZQ-33798	(Q)	Edger Winter Group With Rick Derringer	1975	8.00	20.00
Blue Sky PZ-34858	(S)	Re-Cycled	1977	1.20	6.00
Blue Sky JZ-35989	(S)	The Edger Winter Album	1979	1.20	6.00
Blue Sky JZ-36494	(S)	Standing On Rock	1981	1.20	6.00

WINTER, EDGAR & JOHNNY
The Winter siblings, above and below.

Blue Sky ASZ-242	(DJ)	Johnny And Edger Discuss "Together"	1976	10.00	25.00
Blue Sky PZ-34033	(S)	Together	1976	1.20	6.00

WINTER, JOHNNY

Sonobeat RS-1002	(DJ)	Progressive Blues Experiment	1968	300.00	500.00
		(Issued in a plain cardboard jacket.)			
Imperial LP-12431	(S)	Progressive Blues Experiment	1969	20.00	50.00
		(Imperial 12431 is a reissue of Sonobeat 1002.)			
GRT 10010	(S)	The Johnny Winter Story	1969	6.00	15.00
Buddah BDS-7513	(S)	First Winter	1969	6.00	15.00

Label & Catalog #		Title	Year	VG+	NM
Columbia CS-9826	(S)	Johnny Winter	1969	8.00	20.00
Columbia CS-9947	(S)	Second Winter (2 LPs)	1969	10.00	25.00
Columbia KC-30221	(S)	Johnny Winter And	1970	8.00	20.00
	—Columbia albums above have "360 Sound Stereo" on the bottom of the label.—				
Columbia CS-9826	(S)	Johnny Winter	197?	1.00	5.00
Columbia CS-9947	(S)	Second Winter (2 LPs)	197?	3.20	8.00
Columbia KC-30221	(S)	Johnny Winter And	197?	1.00	5.00
Columbia KC-32188	(S)	Still Alive And Well	1973	3.20	8.00
Columbia CQ-32188	(Q)	Still Alive And Well	1973	8.00	20.00
Columbia KC-32715	(S)	Saints And Sinners	1974	3.20	8.00
Columbia CQ-32715	(Q)	Saints And Sinners	1974	8.00	20.00
Janus 3008	(S)	About Blues	1970	8.00	20.00
Janus 3023	(S)	Early Times	1970	10.00	25.00
Janus 3056	(S)	Before The Storm	1970	8.00	20.00
United Arts. LA139	(S)	Austin, Texas	1974	3.20	8.00
Blue Sky PZ-33292	(S)	John Dawson Winter III	1974	1.20	6.00
Blue Sky PZQ-33292	(Q)	John Dawson Winter III	1974	8.00	20.00
Crazy Cajun 1009	(S)	Early Winter	197?	5.00	12.00
Blue Sky PZ-33944	(S)	Captured Live!	1976	1.20	6.00
Blue Sky PZ-34033	(S)	Together	1976	1.20	6.00
Blue Sky PZ-34813	(S)	Nothin' But The Blues	1977	1.20	6.00
Blue Sky JZ-35475	(S)	White, Hot And Blue	1978	1.20	6.00
Blue Sky JZ-36343	(S)	Raisin' Cain	1980	1.20	6.00
Alligator 4735	(S)	Guitar Slinger	1984	1.00	5.00
Accord SN-7135	(S)	Saints And Sinners	197?	1.00	5.00

WINWOOD, STEVE
Mr Winwood achieved fame as the front man for The Spencer Davis Group. Refer to Traffic; Blind Faith.

United Arts. UAS-9950	(S)	Winwood (2 LPs with a bound-in booklet)	1971	8.00	20.00
United Arts. UAS-9950	(S)	Winwood (2 LPs without the booklet)	1971	4.00	10.00
Island ILPS-9494	(S)	Steve Winwood	1977	.80	4.00
Island ILPS-9576	(S)	Arc Of A Diver	1981	.80	4.00
Island ILPS-9777	(S)	Talking Back To The Night	1982	.80	4.00

WISHBONE ASH

Decca DL-75249	(S)	Wishbone Ash	1971	6.00	15.00
Decca DL-75295	(S)	Pilgrimage	1971	6.00	15.00
Decca DL-75437	(S)	Argus	1971	6.00	15.00
Decca DL-71919	(DJ)	An Evening Program With Wishbone Ash	1972	12.00	30.00
MCA 36	(S)	Pilgrimage	1973	.80	4.00
MCA 49	(S)	Argus	1973	.80	4.00
MCA 327	(S)	Wishbone Four	1973	.80	4.00
MCA 2-6006	(S)	Live Dates (2 LPs)	1973	1.00	5.00
MCA L33-1922	(DJ)	Live From Memphis	1974	20.00	50.00
MCA 464	(S)	There's The Rub	1974	.80	4.00
Atlantic SD-18164	(S)	Locked In	1976	.80	4.00
Atlantic SD-18200	(S)	New England	1976	.80	4.00
MCA 2311	(S)	Front Page News	1977	.80	4.00
MCA 3060	(S)	No Smoke Without Fire	1978	.80	4.00
MCA 2343	(S)	Wishbone Ash	1978	.80	4.00
MCA 2344	(S)	Argus	1978	.80	4.00
MCA 2348	(S)	Wishbone Four	1979	.80	4.00
MCA 3221	(S)	Just Testing	1980	.80	4.00
MCA 5200	(S)	Number The Brave	1981	.80	4.00
MCA 5283	(S)	Hot Ash	1982	.80	4.00

WISHFUL THINKING

Ampex A-10123	(S)	Hiroshima	1971	5.00	12.00

WITHERS, BILL
Mr Withers can also be found on the Sussex soundtrack "Man And Boy."

Sussex 7006	(S)	Just As I Am	1971	8.00	20.00
Sussex 7014	(S)	Still Bill	1972	8.00	20.00
Sussex 7025-2	(S)	Live At Carnegie Hall (2 LPs)	1973	8.00	20.00
Sussex 8032	(S)	Add'justments	1974	6.00	15.00
Sussex 8037	(S)	The Best Of Bill Withers	1975	6.00	15.00
Columbia PC-33704	(S)	Making Music	1975	1.20	6.00
Columbia PC-34903	(S)	Menagerie	1977	1.20	6.00
Columbia JC-35596	(S)	'Bout Love	1979	1.20	6.00

WITHERSPOON, JIMMY
Spoon's jazz albums are not listed below. Refer to Eric Burdon & Jimmy Witherspoon.

World Pacific WP-1267	(M)	Singin' The Blues	1959	40.00	100.00
World Pacific WP-1402	(M)	There's Good Rockin' Tonight	1961	24.00	60.00
		(W.P. 1402 is a reissue of 1267.)			
Crown CLP-5156	(M)	Jimmy Witherspoon	1959	30.00	75.00
Crown CLP-5192	(M)	Jimmy Witherspoon Sings The Blues	1960	30.00	75.00
	—Crown albums above have black labels with a silver "Crown" on top.—				

Label & Catalog #		Title	Year	VG+	NM
Crown CLP-5156	(M)	Jimmy Witherspoon	1961	10.00	25.00
Crown CLP-5192	(M)	Jimmy Witherspoon Sings The Blues	1961	10.00	25.00
Crown CST-215	(E)	Jimmy Witherspoon Sings The Blues (Red vinyl)	1961	30.00	75.00
Crown CST-215	(E)	Jimmy Witherspoon Sings The Blues	1961	8.00	20.00
		—Crown albums above have gray labels.—			
Reprise R-2008	(M)	Spoon	1961	20.00	50.00
Reprise R9-2008	(S)	Spoon	1961	30.00	75.00
Reprise R-6012	(M)	Hey, Mrs. Jones	1962	20.00	50.00
Reprise R9-6012	(S)	Hey, Mrs. Jones	1962	30.00	75.00
Reprise R-6059	(M)	Roots	1962	20.00	50.00
Reprise R9-6059	(S)	Roots	1962	30.00	75.00
Constellation CM-1422	(M)	Take This Hammer	1964	20.00	50.00
Constellation CMS1422	(E)	Take This Hammer	1964	12.00	30.00
ABC S-717	(S)	Handbags And Gladrags	1970	10.00	25.00
BluesWay BLS-6026	(S)	Blues Singer	1970	10.00	25.00
BluesWay BLS-6051	(S)	The Best Of Jimmy Witherspoon	1971	10.00	25.00
Fantasy F-24701	(S)	The Spoon Concerts (2 LPs)	1972	4.00	10.00
United US-7715	(E)	A Spoonful Of Blues	197?	1.00	5.00
Capitol ST-11360	(S)	Love Is A Five Letter Word	1974	1.00	5.00
Muse 5288	(E)	Jimmy Witherspoon Sings The Blues	1983	1.00	5.00

WITHERSPOON, JIMMY / EDDIE VINSON

King 634	(M)	Battle Of The Blues, Volume 3	1959	1,000.00	1,600.00

WIZARDS FROM KANSAS, THE

Mercury SR-61309	(S)	The Wizards From Kansas	1970	60.00	150.00

WOLF

London PS-644	(S)	Wolf	1974	3.20	8.00

WOLF MOON

Fungus 25149	(S)	Wolf Moon	1973	3.20	8.00

WOLFE

Rare Earth R-541	(S)	Wolfe	1972	3.00	15.00

WOLFMAN JACK

Bread BD-0170	(S)	Wolfman Jack And The Wolf Pack	197?	6.00	15.00
Wooden Nickel 1-1009	(S)	Wolfman Jack	1972	3.20	8.00
Wooden Nickel 1-0119	(S)	Through The Ages	1973	3.20	8.00
Columbia PC-33501	(S)	Fun 'N' Romance	1975	3.20	8.00

WOMACK, BOBBY

Minit LP-24014	(S)	Fly Me To The Moon	1968	14.00	35.00
Minit LP-24027	(S)	My Prescription	1969	14.00	35.00
Liberty LST-7646	(S)	Womack Live	1970	4.00	10.00
United Arts. UAS-5539	(S)	Communication	1971	1.20	6.00
United Arts. UAS-5225	(S)	Across 110th Street	1972	1.20	6.00
United Arts. UAS-5577	(S)	Understanding	1972	1.20	6.00
United Arts. LA043	(S)	The Facts Of Life	1973	1.20	6.00
United Arts. LA199	(S)	Lookin' For A Love Again	1973	1.20	6.00
United Arts. LA346	(S)	Greatest Hits	1974	1.20	6.00
United Arts. LA353	(S)	I Don't Know What The World Is Coming To	1975	1.20	6.00
United Arts. LA544	(S)	Safety Zone	1975	1.20	6.00
United Arts. LA638	(S)	Bobby Womack Goes C&W	1976	1.20	6.00
Columbia PC-34384	(S)	Home Is Where The Heart Is	1976	1.00	5.00
Columbia JC-35083	(S)	Pieces	1978	1.00	5.00
Arista 4222	(S)	Roads Of Life	1979	1.00	5.00
Beverly Glen 10000	(S)	The Poet	1981	1.00	5.00

WOMB

Dot DLP-25933	(S)	Womb	1969	8.00	20.00
Dot DLP-25959	(S)	Overdub	1969	8.00	20.00

WOMBLES, THE

Columbia KC-33140	(S)	Remember You're A Womble	1974	3.20	8.00

WONDER, STEVIE [LITTLE STEVIE WONDER]

For additional listings refer to The Temptations / Stevie Wonder.

Tamla T-232	(M)	A Tribute To Uncle Ray	1963	100.00	250.00
Tamla T-233	(M)	The Jazz Soul Of Stevie Wonder	1963	100.00	250.00
		—Tamla albums above have a disc overlapping a globe at the top of the label.—			
Tamla T-240	(M)	Recorded Live-The 12 Year Old Genius	1963	60.00	150.00
Tamla T-248	(M)	Workout Stevie, Workout	1963	Unreleased	
Tamla T-250	(M)	With A Song In My Heart	1963	30.00	75.00
Tamla T-255	(M)	Stevie At The Beach	1964	30.00	75.00
Tamla T-268	(M)	Up-Tight (Everything's Alright)	1966	10.00	25.00
Tamla TS-268	(S)	Up-Tight (Everything's Alright)	1966	12.00	30.00

Label & Catalog #		Title	Year	VG+	NM
Tamla T-272	(M)	Down To Earth	1966	8.00	20.00
Tamla TS-272	(S)	Down To Earth	1966	10.00	25.00
Tamla T-279	(M)	I Was Made To Love Her	1967	8.00	20.00
Tamla TS-279	(S)	I Was Made To Love Her	1967	10.00	25.00
		(Original pressings have the album title on two lines.)			
Tamla TS-279	(S)	I Was Made To Love Her	1968	8.00	20.00
		(Later pressings have the album title on three lines.)			
Tamla T-281	(M)	Someday At Christmas	1967	12.00	30.00
Tamla T-281	(S)	Someday At Christmas	1967	14.00	35.00
Tamla T-282	(M)	Stevie Wonder's Greatest Hits	1968	12.00	30.00
Tamla TS-282	(P)	Stevie Wonder's Greatest Hits	1968	6.00	15.00
Gordy GS-932	(S)	Eivets Rednow	1968	8.00	20.00
Tamla TS-291	(S)	For Once In My Life	1968	6.00	15.00
Tamla TS-296	(S)	My Cherie Amour	1969	6.00	15.00
Tamla TS-298	(S)	Stevie Wonder 'Live!'	1970	6.00	15.00
Tamla TS-304	(S)	Signed, Sealed And Delivered	1970	5.00	12.00
Tamla TS-308	(S)	Where I'm Coming From	1971	5.00	12.00
Tamla TO-313L	(S)	Stevie Wonder's Greatest Hits, Volume 2	1971	4.00	10.00
Tamla TS-314S1	(S)	Music Of My Mind	1972	4.00	10.00
Tamla TS-319	(S)	Talking Book (With braille note on cover)	1972	4.00	10.00
Tamla TS-319	(S)	Talking Book (Plain cover)	1972	1.20	6.00
Tamla TS-326	(S)	Innervisions (Textured cover)	1973	4.00	10.00
Tamla TS-332	(S)	Fulfillingness' First Finale	1974	1.20	6.00
Tamla TS-340	(S)	Songs In The Key Of Life (2 LPs)	1976	3.20	8.00
		(Issued with a bonus EP and booklet.)			
Tamla T8-373	(S)	Hotter Than July	1980	1.20	6.00
Tamla PR-61	(DJ)	Journey Through The Secret Life Of Plants	1979	6.00	15.00
Tamla T-13-371	(S)	Journey Through The Secret Life Of Plants (2 LPs)	1979	3.20	8.00
Motown PR-77	(DJ)	Hotter Than July	1980	10.00	25.00
Tamla 373	(S)	Hotter Than July	1980	1.20	6.00
Tamla 6002TL2	(S)	Original Musicquarium (2 LPs)	1982	3.20	8.00
Motown M9-804A3	(S)	Anthology (3 LPs)	1977	4.00	10.00
Motown M9-804LP3	(S)	Looking Back/Anthology (3 LPs)	1977	4.00	10.00
Motown M5-131V	(S)	Little Stevie Wonder The 12 Year Old Genius	1982	.80	4.00
Motown M5-150V	(S)	With A Song In My Heart	1982	.80	4.00
Motown M5-166V	(S)	Down To Earth	1982	.80	4.00
Motown M5-173V	(S)	A Tribute To Uncle Ray	1982	.80	4.00
Motown M5-176V	(S)	Signed, Sealed And Delivered	1982	.80	4.00
Motown M5-179V	(S)	My Cherie Amour	1982	.80	4.00
Motown M5-183V	(S)	Up-Tight	1982	.80	4.00
Motown M5-219V	(S)	The Jazz Soul Of Stevie Wonder	1982	.80	4.00
Motown M5-234V	(S)	For Once In My Life	1982	.80	4.00
Motown M5-298V	(S)	Alfie	1982	.80	4.00

WOOD, BRENTON

Brent 5100	(M)	Introducing Brenton Wood! Boogaloo	196?	14.00	35.00
Brent S-100	(S)	Introducing Brenton Wood! Boogaloo	196?	20.00	50.00
		(This is actually a various artists album with four tracks by Wood			
		and the rest by David Bryant, The Golden Boys, and Clarence Hill.)			
Double Shot 1002	(M)	Oogum Boogum	1967	10.00	25.00
Double Shot 5002	(S)	Oogum Boogum	1967	12.00	30.00
Double Shot 1003	(M)	Baby You Got It	1967	10.00	25.00
Double Shot 5003	(S)	Baby You Got It (Multi-color vinyl)	1967	80.00	200.00
Double Shot 5003	(S)	Baby You Got It	1967	12.00	30.00
Cream 1006	(S)	Come Softly	1977	6.00	15.00

WOOD, FRANK / DON COATS & THE PLAYBACKS

Round LPBP-1111	(M)	The Greatest Of The Latest	1965	40.00	100.00

WOOD, RON

Mr Wood was a member of The Jeff Beck Group, The Faces, and essential to the solo success of Rod Stewart. He is currently a Rolling Stone.

Warner Bros. BS-2819	(S)	I've Got My Own Album To Do	1974	4.00	10.00
Warner Bros. BS-2872	(S)	New Look (With Keith Richards)	1975	4.00	10.00
Atco SD-36126	(S)	Mahoney's Last Stand	1976	4.00	10.00
Columbia JC-35702	(S)	Gimme Some Neck	1979	4.00	10.00

WOOD, ROY

Mr Wood was the prime mover for The Move and ELO.

United Arts. LA042	(S)	Wizzard's Brew	1973	4.00	10.00
United Arts. LA168	(S)	Boulders	1973	4.00	10.00
United Arts. LA168	(S)	Boulder Folder	1973	16.00	40.00
		(Promo in a 13" x 13" folder with press kit and postcards.)			
United Arts. LA219	(S)	Introducing Eddie And The Falcons	1974	4.00	10.00
United Arts. LA575	(S)	Mustard	1974	4.00	10.00
Warner Bros. BSK-3247	(S)	On The Road Again	1979	3.20	8.00

Label & Catalog #		Title	Year	VG+	NM
WOODS, BILL					
Country Town CTR-24803	(M)	Bill Woods From Bakersfield	196?	40.00	100.00
WOODS, MACEO					
Volt VOS-6009	(S)	Hello Sunshine	1970	8.00	20.00
Volt VOS-6013	(S)	Step To Jesus	1971	8.00	20.00
WOODY'S TRUCK STOP					
Smash SRS-67111	(S)	Woody's Truck Stop	1969	10.00	25.00
WOOFERS, THE					
Wyncote W-9011	(M)	Dragsville	1964	16.00	40.00
Wyncote SW-9001	(S)	Dragsville	1964	20.00	50.00
WOOL					
ABC S-676	(S)	Wool	1969	6.00	15.00
WORLD OF OZ, THE					
Deram DES-18022	(S)	The World Of Oz	1969	16.00	40.00
WOULD					
Perception 24	(S)	Would	1972	12.00	30.00
WRAY, LINK [LINK WRAY & HIS WRAYMEN]					
Wray also recorded with Robert Gordon; Mordecai Jones; Vernon Wray.					
Epic LN-3661	(M)	Link Wray And The Wraymen	1960	150.00	300.00
Swan SLP-510	(M)	Jack The Ripper (White label promo)	1963	300.00	600.00
Swan SLP-510	(M)	Jack The Ripper	1963	100.00	250.00
Vermillion 1924	(M)	Great Guitar Hits	1963	60.00	150.00
Vermillion 1925	(M)	Link Wray Sings And Plays Guitar	1964	60.00	150.00
Record Factory 1929	(S)	Yesterday And Today	1969	40.00	100.00
Polydor PD-24-4064	(S)	Link Wray	1971	10.00	25.00
Polydor PD-5047	(S)	Be What You Want To	1973	10.00	25.00
Polydor PD-6025	(S)	The Link Wray Rumble	1974	10.00	25.00
Visa 7009	(S)	Bullshot	1979	1.20	6.00
Visa 7010	(S)	Live At The Paradiso	1980	1.20	6.00
WRAY, VERNON					
Vermillion 1972	(S)	Wasted (With Link Wray)	1972	60.00	150.00
WRIGHT, BETTY					
Atco SD-33-260	(S)	My First Time Around	1968	10.00	25.00
WRIGHT, CHARLES, & THE WATTS 103RD STREET RHYTHM BAND					
Warner Bros. WS-1741	(S)	The Watts 103rd St. Rhythm Band	1968	8.00	20.00
Warner Bros. WS-1761	(S)	Together	1968	8.00	20.00
Warner Bros. WS-1801	(S)	In The Jungle, Babe	1969	8.00	20.00
— Warner Bros. albums above have green "W7" labels.—					
Warner Bros. WS-1864	(S)	Express Yourself	1970	6.00	15.00
Warner Bros. WS-1904	(S)	You're So Beautiful	1971	6.00	15.00
Warner Bros. BS-2620	(S)	Rhythm And Poetry	1972	6.00	15.00
— Warner Bros. albums above have green "WB" labels.—					
Dunhill DS-30162	(S)	Doing What Comes Naturally (2 LPs)	1973	6.00	15.00
Dunhill DS-50187	(S)	Ninety Day Cycle People	1974	4.00	10.00
ABC ABCD-887	(S)	Lil' Encouragement	1975	4.00	10.00
WRIGHT, GARY					
Gary Wright was a member of Spooky Tooth.					
A&M SP-4277	(S)	Extraction	1970	3.20	8.00
A&M SP-4296	(S)	Footprint	1971	3.20	8.00
Warner Bros. BS-2868	(S)	Dream Weaver	1975	1.20	6.00
A&M SP-3528	(S)	That Was Only Yesterday (2 LPs)	1976	3.20	8.00
Warner Bros. WS-1904	(S)	Touch And Gone	1977	1.20	6.00
Warner Bros. BS-2951	(S)	Light Of Smiles	1977	1.20	6.00
WRIGHT, O. V.					
Back Beat 61	(M)	If It's Only For Tonight	1965	40.00	100.00
Back Beat 61	(S)	If It's Only For Tonight	1965	60.00	150.00
Back Beat 66	(S)	8 Men And 4 Women	1968	30.00	75.00
Back Beat 67	(S)	Nucleus Of Soul	1969	30.00	75.00
Back Beat 70	(S)	A Nickel And A Nail And Ace Of Spades	1972	24.00	60.00
Back Beat 72	(S)	Memphis Unlimited	1973	20.00	50.00
Hi SHL-6001	(S)	Into Something	1977	10.00	25.00
Hi SHL-6008	(S)	Bottom Line	1978	10.00	25.00
Hi SHL-6011	(S)	We're Still Together	1979	10.00	25.00

Label & Catalog #		Title	Year	VG+	NM

WRIGHT, RICK
Rick Wright is a member of Pink Floyd.

Columbia JC-35559	(S)	**Wet Dream** (White label promo)	1978	4.00	10.00
Columbia JC-35559	(S)	**Wet Dream**	1978	8.00	20.00

WRIGHT, STEVIE

Atco SD-36-109	(S)	**Hard Road**	1975	1.20	6.00

WYATT, ROBERT
Mr Wyatt was a member of The Soft Machine.

Virgin VR-13-112	(S)	**Rock Bottom**	197?	3.20	8.00

WYMAN, BILL
Mr. Wyman was a member of The Rolling Stones. Refer to The End; John Hammond; Sons Of Heroes. He can also be found on the Ripple soundtrack "Digital Dreams."

Roll. Stones COC-79100	(S)	**Monkey Grip**	1974	4.00	10.00
Roll. Stones QD-79100	(Q)	**Monkey Grip**	1974	8.00	20.00
Roll. Stones COC-79103	(S)	**Stone Alone**	1976	4.00	10.00
Roll. Stones QD-79103	(Q)	**Stone Alone**	1976	8.00	20.00

WYNDER K. FROG

United Arts. UAS-5740	(S)	**Into The Fire**	1970	4.00	10.00
United Arts. UAS-6695	(S)	**Out Of The Frying Pan**	1971	4.00	10.00

X

Slash 104	(S)	**Los Angeles**	1980	4.00	10.00
Slash 107	(S)	**Wild Gift**	1981	4.00	10.00
Elektra 60150	(S)	**Under The Big Black Sun**	1982	1.00	5.00
Elektra 60283	(S)	**More Fun In The New World**	1983	1.00	5.00

XIT
Xit originally recorded as Lincoln Street Exit.

Rare Earth R-536	(S)	**Plight Of The Redman**	1972	12.00	30.00
Rare Earth R-545	(S)	**Silent Warrior**	1973	10.00	25.00
Canyon 7121	(S)	**Relocation**	1977	10.00	25.00

XTC

Virgin VI-2095	(S)	**White Music**	1978	6.00	15.00
Virgin VI-2108	(S)	**Go 2** (With poster)	1978	8.00	20.00
Virgin VI-2108	(S)	**Go 2** (Without poster)	1978	6.00	15.00
Virgin VA-13134	(S)	**Drums And Wires**	1979	6.00	15.00
Virgin VR-13147	(S)	**Black Sea** (With green outer bag)	1980	8.00	20.00
Virgin VR-13147	(S)	**Black Sea** (Without the bag)	1980	6.00	15.00
Epic ARE-37???	(S)	**White Music**	198?	1.00	5.00
Epic ARE-37???	(S)	**Go 2** (With poster)	198?	1.00	5.00
Epic ARE-37???	(S)	**Drums And Wires**	198?	1.00	5.00
Epic ARE-37???	(S)	**Black Sea**	198?	1.00	5.00
Epic ARE-37943	(S)	**English Settlement**	1982	1.00	5.00
Geffen GHS-4027	(S)	**Mummer**	1983	1.00	5.00
Geffen GHS-4037	(S)	**Waxworks: Some Singles 1977-1982**	1983	1.00	5.00
Geffen GHS-24054	(S)	**The Big Express**	1984	1.00	5.00
Geffen GHS-24117	(S)	**Skylarking** (With "Mermaid Smiled")	1986	4.00	10.00
Geffen GHS-24117	(S)	**Skylarking** (With "Dear God")	1986	1.00	5.00

Y KANT TORI READ
YKTR features Tori and Kim Bullard, one of whom later recorded as Tori Amos.

Atlantic 81845-1	(S)	**Y Kant Tori Read**	1988	16.00	40.00
		(Promo issues are stock copies whose covers have a gold			
		embossed promo stamp and a cut-out mark.)			
Atlantic 81845-1	(S)	**Y Kant Tori Read**	1988	20.00	50.00

YAGER, LAURA

Ovation 1427	(S)	**Comin' Apart**	1972	3.20	8.00
Ovation QD-1427	(Q)	**Comin' Apart**	1972	6.00	15.00

YANKEE DOLLAR, THE

Dot DLP-25874	(S)	**The Yankee Dollar**	1968	60.00	150.00

YANOVSKY, ZALMAN
Zallie was a member of The Mugwumps and The Lovin' Spoonful.

Buddah BDS-5019	(S)	**Alive And Well In Argentina**	1968	16.00	40.00
Kama Sutra KSBS-2030	(S)	**Alive And Well In Argentina**	1971	8.00	20.00
		(Kama Sutra 2030 is a reissue of Buddah 5019.)			

YARDBIRDS, THE
Original recording members were Eric Clapton, Chris Dreja, Jim McCarty, Keith Relf, and Paul Samwell-Smith.
Clapton quit in 1965, replaced by Jeff Beck. Samwell-Smith left in '66, replaced by Jimmy Page. This group can also
be found on the MGM soundtrack "Blow Up." Refer to Armageddon; Philamore Lincoln; Renaissance; Sonny Boy
Williamson & The Yardbirds.

Epic LN-24167	(DJ)	**For Your Love** *(White label promo)*	1965	200.00	400.00
Epic LN-24167	(M)	**For Your Love**	1965	40.00	100.00
Epic BN-26167	(S)	**For Your Love**	1965	30.00	75.00
		("Sweet Music" is rechanneled. Poorly reproduced			
		counterfeits of BN-26167 exist.)			
Epic LN-24177	(DJ)	**Having A Rave Up**			
		With The Yardbirds *(White label promo)*	1965	200.00	400.00
Epic LN-24177	(M)	**Having A Rave Up With The Yardbirds**	1965	30.00	75.00
Epic BN-26177	(E)	**Having A Rave Up With The Yardbirds**	1965	20.00	50.00
		(Poorly reproduced counterfeits of BN-26177 exist.)			
Epic LN-24210	(DJ)	**Over Under Sideways Down** *(White label promo)*	1966	200.00	400.00
Epic LN-24210	(M)	**Over Under Sideways Down**	1966	24.00	60.00
Epic BN-26210	(S)	**Over Under Sideways Down**	1966	30.00	75.00
		("Over Under Sideways Down" is rechanneled.			
		Poorly reproduced counterfeits of BN-26210 exist.)			
Epic LN-24246	(DJ)	**The Yardbirds' Greatest Hits** *(White label promo)*	1966	150.00	300.00
Epic LN-24246	(M)	**The Yardbirds' Greatest Hits**	1966	20.00	50.00
Epic BN-26246	(P)	**The Yardbirds' Greatest Hits**	1966	12.00	30.00
Epic LN-24313	(DJ)	**Little Games** *(White label promo)*	1967	150.00	300.00
Epic LN-24313	(M)	**Little Games**	1967	30.00	75.00
Epic BN-26313	(S)	**Little Games**	1967	20.00	50.00
		(Poorly reproduced counterfeits of BN-26313 exist.)			
Epic EG-30135	(P)	**The Yardbirds Featuring Performances By Jeff Beck,**			
		Eric Clapton, Jimmy Page *(2 LPs)*	1970	14.00	35.00
Epic E-30615	(S)	**Live Yardbirds Featuring Jimmy Page**	1972	20.00	50.00
		(Originals have a full-color cover; counterfeits are black & white.)			
		—Epic albums above have yellow labels.—			
Epic BN-26177	(E)	**Having A Rave Up With The Yardbirds**	197?	12.00	30.00
		—Epic albums above have orange labels.—			
Epic PE-34490	(P)	**Yardbirds Favorites**	1977	4.00	10.00
Epic PE-34491	(P)	**Great Hits**	1977	4.00	10.00
Epic FE-38455	(M)	**Yardbirds**	1983	4.00	10.00
Epic HE-38455	(S)	**Yardbirds** *(Half-speed master)*	1983	30.00	90.00
		(Epic 33455 is a reissue of 26210 plus two extra tracks.)			
Columbia P-13311	(S)	**Live Yardbirds Featuring Jimmy Page**	197?	20.00	50.00
		(Columbia Special Products 13311 is a reissue of Epic 30615.)			
Springboard SPB-4036	(E)	**Eric Clapton & The Yardbirds**	1972	3.20	8.00
Springboard SPB-4039	(E)	**Shapes Of Things**	1972	3.20	8.00
Bomp 1045	(M)	**Shapes Of Things**	197?	1.00	5.00
Accord SN-7143	(S)	**For Your Love**	1981	1.00	5.00
Accord SN-7237	(E)	**Having A Rave Up With The Yardbirds**	1981	1.00	5.00

Label & Catalog #		Title	Year	VG+	NM
Rhino RNLP-2253	(M)	Afternoon Tea (Picture disc)	1982	1.00	5.00
Rhino RNLP-70128	(M)	The Yardbirds—Greatest Hits,			
		Volume One: 1964-1966	1986	1.00	5.00
Rhino RNLP-70189	(M)	Five Live Yardbirds	1986	1.00	5.00
		(Rhino 70189 is a reissue of the group's first UK LP from 1964.)			

YEAGER, ATLEE
Dunhill DS-50084	(S)	Atlee	1969	6.00	15.00
Chelsea BCL1-0366	(S)	Plant Me Now And Dig Me Later	197?	6.00	15.00

YELLO
Ralph YL-8059	(S)	Solid Pleasure	198?	6.00	15.00
Ralph YL-8159	(S)	Claro Que Se	198?	6.00	15.00

YELLOW BALLOON, THE
Canterbury CLPM-1502	(M)	The Yellow Balloon	1967	10.00	25.00
Canterbury CLPS-1502	(S)	The Yellow Balloon	1967	12.00	30.00

YELLOW HAND
Capitol ST-549	(S)	Yellow Hand	1970	6.00	15.00

YELLOW PAYGES, THE
Uni 73045	(S)	The Yellow Payges, Volume 1	1969	8.00	20.00

YES
Yes is Jon Anderson, Bill Bruford, Steve Howe, Tony Kaye, Chris Squire and Rick Wakeman.
Atlantic SD-8243	(S)	Yes	1969	4.00	10.00
Atlantic SD-8273	(S)	Time And A Word	1960	4.00	10.00
Atlantic SD-8283	(S)	The Yes Album	1971	4.00	10.00
Atlantic SD-7211	(S)	Fragile (Includes booklet)	1972	4.00	10.00
Atlantic SD-7244	(S)	Close To The Edge	1972	4.00	10.00
Atlantic 3-100	(S)	Yessongs (3 LPs)	1973	5.00	12.00
		—Atlantic albums above have green & orange labels with an 1841 Broadway address.—			
Atlantic 2-908	(DJ)	Tales From Topographic Oceans (2 LPs)	1974	10.00	25.00
		(Promo copies are banded for air play.)			
Atlantic 2-908	(S)	Tales From Topographic Oceans (2 LPs)	1974	1.20	6.00
Atlantic SD-18122	(DJ)	Relayer (Banded for air-play)	1974	6.00	15.00
Atlantic SD-18122	(S)	Relayer	1974	1.00	5.00
Atlantic PR-260	(DJ)	Yes Solos LP Sampler	1976	10.00	25.00
Atlantic PR-285	(DJ)	Yes Music: An Evening With Jon Anderson	1977	20.00	50.00
Atlantic SD-19106	(S)	Going For The One	1977	1.00	5.00
Atlantic SD-19131	(S)	The Yes Album	1980	1.00	5.00
Atlantic SD-19132	(S)	Fragile	1980	1.00	5.00
Atlantic SD-19133	(S)	Close To The Edge	1980	1.00	5.00
Atlantic SD-19134	(S)	Yesterdays	1975	1.00	5.00
Atlantic SD-19135	(S)	Relayer	1980	1.00	5.00
Atlantic SD-19202	(S)	Tormato	1978	1.00	5.00
Atlantic SD-16019	(S)	Drama	1980	1.00	5.00
Atlantic 2-510	(S)	Yesshows (2 LPs)	1980	1.20	6.00
Atlantic SD-19320	(S)	Classic Yes	1982	1.00	5.00

YESTERDAY'S CHILDREN
Map City 3012	(S)	Yesterday's Children	196?	30.00	75.00

YESTERDAY'S FOLK
Buddah BDS-5035	(S)	U. S. 69	1969	6.00	15.00

YOKOHAMA KNIGHTS
GRT 10002	(S)	Yokohama Knights	197?	6.00	15.00

YOST, DENNIS
Dennis Yost was the lead singer for The Classics IV.
Robox 7945	(S)	Going Through The Motions	1982	1.00	5.00

YOU KNOW WHO GROUP, THE
Inter. Allied 420	(M)	The You Know Who Group	1965	20.00	50.00

YOUNG, JESSE COLIN
Jesse Colin Young is a pseudonym for Perry Miller. He later formed The Youngbloods.
Capitol T-2070	(M)	Soul Of A City Boy	1964	20.00	50.00
Mercury MG-21005	(M)	Young Blood	1965	12.00	30.00
Mercury SR-61005	(S)	Young Blood	1965	16.00	40.00
Capitol T-2070	(M)	Jesse Colin Young & The Youngbloods	1967	12.00	30.00
Capitol ST-2070	(E)	Jesse Colin Young & The Youngbloods	1967	8.00	20.00
		("Jesse Colin Young & The Youngbloods" is a repackage of "Soul Of A City Boy" and does not feature The Youngbloods.)			

Label & Catalog #		Title	Year	VG+	NM
Mercury SR-61005	(S)	Jesse Colin Young & The Youngbloods	1969	8.00	20.00
		("Jesse Colin Young & The Youngbloods" is a repackage of "Young Blood" and does not feature The Youngbloods although it does feature John Sebastian's harmonica.)			
Warner/Raccoon BS-2588	(S)	Together	1972	1.00	5.00
Warner Bros. BS-2734	(S)	Song For Juli	1973	1.00	5.00
Warner Bros. BS-2790	(S)	Light Shine	1974	1.00	5.00
Warner Bros. BS-2845	(S)	Songbird	1975	1.00	5.00
Warner Bros. BS-3033	(S)	Love On The Wing	1977	1.00	5.00
Capitol ST-11267	(S)	Soul Of A City Boy	1974	1.00	5.00
Capitol N-16129	(S)	Soul Of A City Boy	1980	.80	4.00

YOUNG, JOHNNY

Label & Catalog #		Title	Year	VG+	NM
Arhoolie F-1029	(S)	Johnny Young And His Chicago Blues Band	1965	10.00	25.00
Arhoolie 1037	(S)	Chicago Blues (With Big Walter)	1966	10.00	25.00
Blue Horizon BM-4609	(S)	Blues Masters, Volume 9	1968	6.00	15.00
BluesWay BLS-6075	(S)	I Can't Keep My Foot From Jumping	1973	6.00	15.00

YOUNG, KATHY

Label & Catalog #		Title	Year	VG+	NM
Indigo LP-504	(M)	The Sound Of Kathy Young	1961	150.00	300.00
		(On Indigo 504, Ms Young is backed by The Innocents.)			
Mainstream S-6121	(S)	A Spoonful Of Kathy Young	1968	20.00	50.00

YOUNG, KENNY

Label & Catalog #		Title	Year	VG+	NM
Warner Bros. BS-2579	(S)	Clever Dogs Chase The Sun	1972	3.20	8.00
Warner Bros. BS-2676	(S)	Last Stage For Silverworld	1972	3.20	8.00

YOUNG, NEIL [NEIL YOUNG & CRAZY HORSE]

Neil Young's original claim to fame was as a member of Buffalo Springfield. Refer to Crazy Horse; Crosby, Stills, Nash & Young; The Stills-Young Band.

Label & Catalog #		Title	Year	VG+	NM
Reprise RS-6317	(S)	Neil Young	1968	60.00	150.00
		(Original covers for RS-6317 do not have "Neil Young" on the front.)			
Reprise RS-6317	(S)	Neil Young	1969	30.00	75.00
		(Second pressings in the original cover have four remixed tracks with "RE 1" etched in the trail-off vinyl)			
Reprise RS-6317	(S)	Neil Young	1969	20.00	50.00
		(Second "RE 1" pressings in the later cover which has "Neil Young" across the top on the front.)			
Reprise RS-6349	(DJ)	Everybody Knows This Is Nowhere (White label)	1969	30.00	75.00
Reprise RS-6349	(S)	Everybody Knows This Is Nowhere	1969	12.00	30.00
		— Reprise albums above have brown & orange labels.—			
Reprise RS-6317	(S)	Neil Young	1970	4.00	10.00
Reprise RS-6349	(S)	Everybody Knows This Is Nowhere	1970	4.00	10.00
Reprise RS-6383	(DJ)	After The Gold Rush (White label promo)	1970	24.00	60.00
Reprise RS-6383	(S)	After The Gold Rush	1970	16.00	40.00
		(Misprinted jacket with a photo of Marc Bolan on the inside cover.)			
Reprise RS-6383	(S)	After The Gold Rush	1970	14.00	35.00
		(Misprinted jacket with a photo of Neil printed upside down on the inside)			
Reprise RS-6383	(S)	After The Gold Rush	1970	6.00	15.00
Reprise RS-6383	(S)	After The Gold Rush	1978	16.00	40.00
		(Includes a remixed, extended version of "When You Dance I Can Really Love." Brown label with RE 2" etched in the trail-off vinyl. The title on the cover is in red print.)			
Reprise MS-2032	(S)	Harvest	1972	8.00	20.00
		(The jacket and the lyric sheet are printed on textured paper.)			
Reprise MS-2032	(S)	Harvest	1972	1.00	5.00
		(The jacket and the lyric sheet are printed on plain paper.)			
Reprise 2XS-6480	(DJ)	Journey Through The Past (2 LPs.)	1972	20.00	50.00
		(Promo with a sticker on the cover that reads "Album must be played prior to airing; this album may contain words offensive to the public.")			
Reprise 2XS-6480	(S)	Journey Through The Past (2 LPs)	1972	6.00	15.00
		(First pressing covers are die-cut with special inner sleeves.)			
Reprise 2XS-6480	(S)	Journey Through The Past (2 LPs)	1972	1.20	6.00
		(Later pressings have regular covers.)			
Reprise M-2151	(M)	Time Fades Away (White label promo)	1973	40.00	100.00
Reprise MS-2151	(S)	Time Fades Away (White label promo)	1973	14.00	35.00
Reprise MS-2151	(S)	Time Fades Away	1973	80.00	200.00
		(Originally issued with a cardboard inner sleeve that was withdrawn.)			
Reprise MS-2151	(S)	Time Fades Away	1973	1.00	5.00
Reprise MS-2180	(S)	On The Beach (Promo label)	1974	16.00	40.00
Reprise MS-2180	(S)	On The Beach	1974	1.00	5.00
Reprise MS-2221	(S)	Tonight's The Night (Promo label)	1975	16.00	40.00
Reprise MS-2221	(S)	Tonight's The Night	1975	1.00	5.00
Reprise MS-2242	(S)	Zuma (Promo label)	1975	12.00	30.00
Reprise MS-2242	(S)	Zuma	1975	1.00	5.00
Reprise MSK-2261	(S)	American Stars 'N' Bars	1977	1.00	5.00
Reprise 3RS-2257	(DJ)	Decade (3 LPs. Test pressing)	1976	250.00	500.00
		("Campaigner" contains a verse deleted from the official version.)			

After his solo career as a folk artist stalled, Jesse Colin Young formed The Youngbloods with Lyle "Banana" Levinger, Joe Bauer and Jerry Corbitt. Signing with RCA Victor as the label's second big rock act (Jefferson Airplane was first), they produced a marvelous first album. From it was lifted the seminal '60s classic, "Get Together," which was a minor hit in '67. It was re-released a year later, about the time their second album was released. Earth Music was upbeat folk-rock and led many fans and critics to assume great offings from the talented quartet. . . And then in 1969, "Get Together" became a major international hit in 1969 as the theme song for the National Council For Christians And Jews. At which point the first album was reissued with a new cover and a new title, Get Together— naturally.

Label & Catalog #		Title	Year	VG+	NM
Reprise 3RS-2257	(S)	Decade (3 LPs)	1977	4.00	10.00
Reprise MSK-2266	(DJ)	Give To The Wind	1978	See note below	
		(MSK-2266 was originally titled "Give To The Wind" and the initial test pressings have stock labels in plain jacket with inserts. Rare with a suggested NM value of $500-1,000.)			
Reprise MSK-2266	(S)	Comes A Time	1978	30.00	75.00
		(Original pressings of MSK-2266 play "Lotta Love" as the last song on the first side. The back cover lists "Lotta Love.")			
Reprise MSK-2266	(S)	Comes A Time	1978	1.00	5.00
		(Later pressings play "Peace Of Mind" as the last song on the first side. These second pressings may be found in original covers or second press covers that list "Peace Of Mind" on the back.)			
Reprise MSK-2277	(S)	Harvest	1978	.80	4.00
Reprise MSK-2282	(S)	Everybody Knows This Is Nowhere	1978	.80	4.00
Reprise MSK-2283	(S)	After The Gold Rush	1978	.80	4.00
Warner Bros. WBMS-107	(DJ)	A Conversation With Neil Young	1979	20.00	50.00
Reprise MSK-2295	(S)	Rust Never Sleeps	1979	1.00	5.00
Reprise 2AX-2296	(S)	Live Rust (2 LPs)	1979	1.20	5.00
Reprise HS-2297	(S)	Hawks And Doves	1980	1.00	5.00
Reprise HS-2304	(S)	Re-ac-tor	1982	1.00	5.00
Geffen GHS-2018	(S)	Trans (Quiex II vinyl promo)	1982	10.00	25.00
Geffen GHS-2018	(S)	Trans	1983	1.00	5.00
Geffen GHS-4013	(S)	Everybody's Rockin' (Quiex II vinyl promo)	1983	10.00	25.00
Geffen GHS-4013	(S)	Everybody's Rockin'	1983	1.00	5.00
Geffen GHS-24109	(S)	Landing On Water	1986	1.00	5.00
Geffen GHS-24154	(S)	Life	1987	1.00	5.00
Reprise 25899	(S)	Freedom	1989	6.00	15.00
Reprise 26315	(S)	Ragged Glory	1990	8.00	20.00

YOUNG, TOMMIE

Label & Catalog #		Title	Year	VG+	NM
Soul Power 3316	(S)	Do You Still Feel The Same Way	1973	6.00	15.00

YOUNG RASCALS, THE: Refer to THE RASCALS

YOUNGBLOOD, LONNIE

Label & Catalog #		Title	Year	VG+	NM
Turbo TU-7011	(S)	Sweet Sweet Tootie	1973	14.00	35.00
Turbo TU-7019	(S)	Lonnie Youngblood	1977	8.00	20.00

YOUNGBLOOD, TOMMY

Label & Catalog #		Title	Year	VG+	NM
United US-7758	(S)	The Soul Of Tommy Youngblood	196?	4.00	10.00

YOUNGBLOODS, THE
The Youngbloods were Jesse Colin Young with Joe Bauer, Jerry Corbitt, and Lowell "Banana" Levinger. Corbitt left in 1969 and Michael Kane joined in 1971. Refer to Banana & The Bunch.

Label & Catalog #		Title	Year	VG+	NM
RCA Victor LPM-3724	(M)	The Youngbloods	1967	16.00	40.00
RCA Victor LSP-3724	(S)	The Youngbloods	1967	10.00	25.00
RCA Victor LPM-3865	(M)	Earth Music	1968	20.00	50.00
RCA Victor LSP-3865	(S)	Earth Music	1968	10.00	25.00
		—RCA albums above have black labels with Nipper on top.—			
RCA Victor LSP-3724	(S)	Get Together	1969	4.00	10.00
		("Get Together" is a repackage of "The Youngbloods.")			
RCA Victor LSP-3865	(S)	Earth Music	1969	4.00	10.00
RCA Victor LSP-4150	(S)	Elephant Mountain	1969	8.00	20.00
RCA Victor LSP-4399	(S)	The Best Of The Youngbloods	1970	4.00	10.00
		—RCA albums above have orange labels on non-flexible vinyl.—			
RCA Victor LSP-3724	(S)	Get Together	197?	1.00	5.00
RCA Victor LSP-3865	(S)	Earth Music	197?	1.00	5.00
RCA Victor LSP-4399	(S)	The Best Of The Youngbloods	197?	1.00	5.00
RCA Victor LSP-4561	(S)	Sunlight	197?	1.00	5.00
RCA Victor VPS-6051	(S)	This Is The Youngbloods (2 LPs)	1972	3.20	8.00
		—RCA albums above have orange labels on flexible vinyl.—			
RCA Victor AYL1-3680	(S)	The Best Of The Youngbloods	1980	.80	4.00
RCA Victor AFL1-4150	(S)	Elephant Mountain	1981	.80	4.00
Mercury SR-61273	(S)	Two Trips (Gold bordered cover)	1970	10.00	25.00
Mercury SR-61273	(S)	Two Trips (Red bordered cover)	1971	8.00	20.00
		(Mercury 61273 contains group recordings from 1965 coupled with the best of Jesse Colin Young's "Young Blood" album.)			
Warner/Raccoon WS-1878	(S)	Rock Festival	1970	1.00	5.00
Warner/Raccoon BS-2563	(S)	Ride The Wind	1971	1.00	5.00
Warner/Raccoon BS-2566	(S)	Good And Dusty	1971	1.00	5.00
Warner/Raccoon BS-2653	(S)	High On A Ridgetop	1972	1.00	5.00

YUM YUM KIDS, THE

Label & Catalog #		Title	Year	VG+	NM
MGM E-4396	(M)	Yummy In Your Tummy	1966	6.00	15.00
MGM SE-4396	(S)	Yummy In Your Tummy	1966	8.00	20.00

ZAGER & EVANS

White Whale WW-7123	(S)	The Early Writings Of Zager And Evans	1969	4.00	10.00
RCA Victor LSP-4214	(S)	In The Year 2525	1969	4.00	10.00
RCA Victor LSP-4302	(S)	Zager And Evans	1970	4.00	10.00
Vanguard VSD-6568	(S)	Food For The Mind	1971	4.00	10.00
RCA Victor ANL1-1077	(S)	In The Year 2525	1975	.80	4.00

ZANIES, THE

Dore 321	(S)	The Zanies	1969	12.00	30.00
Dore 337	(S)	The Zanies (Dore 387 is a reissue of 321)	1979	6.00	15.00

ZAPPA, FRANK [THE MOTHERS OF INVENTION]

While Zappa was always in charge, early albums credit The Mothers Of Invention. Those released as "solo" albums by Zappa are marked with an asterisk. The original Mothers of 1964-69 were Zappa, Jimmy Carl Black, Ray Collins, Roy Estrada, and Elliott Ingber. The second group (1970-72) was Zappa, Underwood, George Duke, Aynsley Dunbar, Jim Pons, and Howard Kaylan and Mark Volman. After 1975, all albums were credited to Zappa solely. Refer to Captain Beefheart; Wild Man Fischer; Flo & Eddie; G.T.O.'s; Grand Funk; Sandy Hurvitz; John Lennon & Yoko Ono; Ruben & The Jets; L. Shankar; The Turtles. Also refer to the Various Artists section under Warner/Reprise.

Verve V-5005-2	(DJ)	Freak Out! (2 LPs. White label promo)	1966	200.00	400.00
Verve V-5005-2	(M)	Freak Out! (2 LPs)	1966	80.00	200.00
Verve V6-5005-2	(DJ)	Freak Out! (2 LPs. Yellow label promo)	1966	150.00	300.00
Verve V6-5005-2	(S)	Freak Out! (2 LPs)	1966	40.00	100.00
		(Original covers for Verve 5005 had a blurb on the inside advertising the availability of the mail-order map of "freak out hot spots" in L.A., which is priced separately below.)			
Verve 5005		Freak Out Spots In L.A. Map	1966	100.00	300.00
Verve V-5005-2	(M)	Freak Out! (2 LPs)	1967	60.00	150.00
Verve V6-5005-2	(S)	Freak Out! (2 LPs)	1967	30.00	75.00
		(Later covers for Verve 5005 delete the advertisement.)			
Verve V-5006	(M)	Freak Out!	1966	*Unreleased*	
Verve V6-5006	(S)	Freak Out!	1966	*Unreleased*	
		(Verve 5006 was issued as a single album in Europe.)			
Verve V6-5013	(DJ)	Absolutely Free (White label promo)	1967	150.00	300.00
Verve V-5013	(M)	Absolutely Free	1967	60.00	150.00
Verve V6-5013	(S)	Absolutely Free	1967	30.00	75.00
		(Covers for Verve 5013 featured a mail-order advertised for a libretto for the album's lyrics, priced separately below.)			
Verve 5013		Absolutely Free Libretto	1967	100.00	300.00
Verve V6-5045	(DJ)	We're Only In It For The Money (White label)	1968	150.00	300.00
Verve V-5045	(M)	We're Only In It For The Money	1968	60.00	150.00
Verve V6-5045	(S)	We're Only In It For The Money	1968	30.00	75.00
		(Original pressings have "V6 5045 MGS 1250-REV-F" scratched in the trail-off vinyl. Issued with a sheet of parodies of "Sgt Pepper" cut-outs.)			
Verve V6-5045	(S)	We're Only In It For The Money	1968	80.00	200.00
		(Later edited version: In the song "Who Needs The Peace Corps?" the line "I will love the police as they kick the shit out of me" has been deleted. Similarly, in the song "Let's Make The Water Turn Black" the line "And I still remember Mama with her apron and her pad feeding all the boys at Ed's Cafe" has also been erased. The trail off reads "V6 5045 MGS 1250-REV.")			
Verve V6-8741*	(DJ)	Lumpy Gravy (Yellow label promo)	1968	80.00	200.00
Verve V6-8741*	(S)	Lumpy Gravy	1968	20.00	50.00
Verve V6-5055	(DJ)	Cruising With Ruben & The Jets (Yellow label)	1968	80.00	200.00
Verve V6-5055	(S)	Cruising With Ruben & The Jets	1968	30.00	75.00
		(A set of three paper inserts may have been issued with this album. They include "The Story Of Ruben & The Jets," "How To Comb & Set A Jellyroll," and a guide on how to do the dance step, "bop." These may have been part of a mail-order or promotional package. Each of the items is rare with a suggested NM value of $100-200 apiece.)			
Verve V6-5068	(DJ)	Mothermania/ The Best Of The Mothers (Yellow label promo)	1969	60.00	150.00
Verve V6-5068	(S)	Mothermania/The Best Of The Mothers	1969	30.00	75.00

Label & Catalog #		Title	Year	VG+	NM
Verve V6-5074	(DJ)	The XXXX Of The Mothers Of Invention (Yellow label promo)	1969	60.00	150.00
Verve V6-5074	(S)	The XXXX Of The Mothers Of Invention	1969	20.00	50.00
MGM GAS-112	(DJ)	The Mothers Of Invention (Yellow label promo)	1970	40.00	100.00
MGM GAS-112	(S)	The Mothers Of Invention	1970	20.00	50.00
MGM SE-4754	(DJ)	The Worst Of The Mothers (Yellow label promo)	1971	60.00	150.00
MGM SE-4754	(S)	The Worst Of The Mothers	1971	20.00	50.00
Bizarre MS-2024	(DJ)	Uncle Meat (2 LPs with booklet. White label)	1969	30.00	75.00
Bizarre MS-2024	(S)	Uncle Meat (2 LPs with booklet)	1969	14.00	35.00
Bizarre RS-6356*	(DJ)	Hot Rats (White label promo)	1969	20.00	50.00
Bizarre RS-6356*	(S)	Hot Rats	1969	20.00	50.00
Bizarre RS-6370	(DJ)	Burnt Weenie Sandwich (White label promo)	1969	20.00	50.00
Bizarre RS-6370	(S)	Burnt Weenie Sandwich (With booklet)	1969	10.00	25.00
Bizarre MS-2028	(DJ)	Weasels Ripped My Flesh (White label promo)	1970	20.00	50.00
Bizarre MS-2028	(S)	Weasels Ripped My Flesh	1970	10.00	25.00
Bizarre MS-2030*	(DJ)	Chunga's Revenge (White label promo)	1970	20.00	50.00
Bizarre MS-2030*	(S)	Chunga's Revenge	1970	10.00	25.00
Bizarre MS-2042	(DJ)	The Mothers/Fillmore East—June 1971 (White label promo)	1971	20.00	50.00
Bizarre MS-2042	(S)	The Mothers/Fillmore East—June 1971	1971	10.00	25.00
United Arts. UAS-9956	(DJ)	Frank Zappa's 200 Motels (2 LPs. White label)	1971	30.00	75.00
United Arts. UAS-9956	(S)	Frank Zappa's 200 Motels (2 LPs)	1971	14.00	35.00
Bizarre MS-2075	(DJ)	Just Another Band From L.A. (White label promo)	1972	20.00	50.00
Bizarre MS-2075	(S)	Just Another Band From L.A.	1972	10.00	25.00
Bizarre MS-2093	(DJ)	The Grand Wazoo (White label promo)	1972	20.00	50.00
Bizarre MS-2093	(S)	The Grand Wazoo	1972	10.00	25.00
Bizarre MS-2094*	(DJ)	Waka/Jawaka—Hot Rats (White label promo)	1972	20.00	50.00
Bizarre MS-2094*	(S)	Waka/Jawaka—Hot Rats	1972	10.00	25.00
		—Bizarre albums above have blue Bizarre/Reprise labels.—			
Bizarre MS-2024	(S)	Uncle Meat (2 LPs)	1973	8.00	20.00
Bizarre RS-6356*	(S)	Hot Rats	1973	6.00	15.00
Bizarre RS-6370	(S)	Burnt Weenie Sandwich	1973	6.00	15.00
Bizarre MS-2028	(S)	Weasels Ripped My Flesh	1973	6.00	15.00
Bizarre MS-2030*	(S)	Chunga's Revenge	1973	6.00	15.00
Bizarre MS-2042	(S)	The Mothers/Fillmore East—June 1971	1973	6.00	15.00
Bizarre MS-2075	(S)	Just Another Band From L.A.	1973	6.00	15.00
Bizarre MS-2093	(S)	The Grand Wazoo	1973	6.00	15.00
Bizarre MS-2094*	(S)	Waka/Jawaka—Hot Rats	1973	6.00	15.00
		—Bizarre albums above have brown Reprise labels.—			
DiscReet MS-2149	(S)	Over-nite Sensation	1973	4.00	10.00
DiscReet MS4-2149	(Q)	Over-nite Sensation	1974	16.00	40.00
DiscReet DS-2175*	(DJ)	Apostrophe (White label promo)	1974	20.00	50.00
DiscReet DS-2175*	(S)	Apostrophe	1974	4.00	10.00
DiscReet DS4-2175	(Q)	Apostrophe	1974	16.00	40.00
DiscReet DSS-2202	(S)	Roxy And Elsewhere	1974	4.00	10.00
DiscReet DS-2216	(S)	One Size Fits All	1975	4.00	10.00
DiscReet DS-2234	(S)	Bongo Fury (With Captain Beefheart)	1975	4.00	10.00
Warner Bros. BS-2970	(S)	Zoot Allures	1976	4.00	10.00
DiscReet 2D-2290	(DJ)	Zappa In New York (2 LPs) (Test pressing with "Punky's Whips.")	1978	200.00	400.00
DiscReet 2D-2290	(S)	Zappa In New York (2 LPs) (Original covers erroneously list the deleted "Punky's Whips.")	1978	100.00	250.00
DiscReet 2D-2290	(S)	Zappa In New York (2 LPs) (Later covers delete the reference to "Punky's Whips.")	1978	4.00	10.00
DiscReet DSK-2291	(S)	Studio Tan	1978	4.00	10.00
DiscReet DSK-2292	(S)	Sleep Dirt	1979	4.00	10.00
DiscReet DSK-2294	(S)	Orchestral Favorites	1979	4.00	10.00
Zappa	(DJ)	Lather (4 LP test pressing)	197?	500.00	750.00
Zappa SRZ-2-1501	(S)	Sheik Yerbouti	1979	1.00	5.00
Zappa SRZ-1-1603	(S)	Joe's Garage, Act I	1979	1.00	5.00
Zappa SRZ-2-1502	(S)	Joe's Garage, Acts II & III (2 LPs)	1979	3.20	8.00
Barking Pumpkin AS-1???	(DJ)	Tinsel Town Rebellion (Promo sampler)	1981	12.00	30.00
Barking Pumpkin PW2-37336	(S)	Tinsel Town Rebellion (2 LPs)	1981	4.00	10.00
Barking Pumpkin AS-1???	(DJ)	You Are What You Is (Promo sampler)	1981	12.00	30.00
Barking Pumpkin PW2-37537	(S)	You Are What You Is (2 LPs)	1981	4.00	10.00
Barking Pumpkin BPR-1111	(S)	Shut Up'N Play Yer Guitar	1981	6.00	15.00
Barking Pumpkin BPR-1112	(S)	Shut Up'N Play Yer Guitar Some More	1981	6.00	15.00
Barking Pumpkin BPR-1113	(S)	Return Of Son Of Shut Up'N Play Yer Guitar	1981	6.00	15.00
Barking Pumpkin CS-66368	(S)	Shut Up'N Play Yer Guitar Box	1981	12.00	30.00
		(1111-1113 were mail-order only. 66368 is a boxed set of the three LPs.)			
Barking Pumpkin AS-1???	(DJ)	Ship Arriving Too Late To Save A Drowning Witch (Promo sampler)	1982	12.00	30.00
Barking Pumpkin FW-38066	(S)	Ship Arriving Too Late To Save A Drowning Witch	1982	4.00	10.00
Barking Pumpkin BPRP-1114	(S)	Zappa (Picture disc)	1982	6.00	15.00
Barking Pumpkin BPRP-1115	(S)	Baby Snakes (Picture disc)	1982	6.00	15.00
Barking Pumpkin AS-1594	(DJ)	The Man From Utopia (Promo sampler)	1983	12.00	30.00
Barking Pumpkin FW-38403	(S)	The Man From Utopia	1983	4.00	10.00
Barking Pumpkin 74203	(S)	Frank Zappa Meets The Mothers Of Prevention	1985	3.20	8.00

Should a hundred albums from the late '50s and early '60s with kitschy covers such as *The Zeniths'* Makin' The Scene *be locked in a time capsule and then, aeons from now, be discovered as the only artifacts of our age, no one would have a clue as to what was really going on during the '50s and '60s!*

Label & Catalog #		Title	Year	VG+	NM
ZAZU					
Wooden Nickel BWL1-0791	(S)	**Zazu**	1975	8.00	20.00
ZENITHS, THE					
Atlantic 8043	(M)	**Makin' The Scene**	1960	40.00	100.00
Atlantic SD-8043	(S)	**Makin' The Scene**	1960	60.00	150.00
		—*Atlantic albums above have black labels.—*			
ZEPHYR					
The first two Zephyr albums feature Tommy Bolin.					
Probe CPLP-4510	(S)	**Zephyr**	1969	16.00	40.00
Warner Bros. BS-1897	(S)	**Going Back To Colorado**	1971	12.00	30.00
Warner Bros. BS-2603	(S)	**Sunset Ride**	1972	6.00	15.00
ZEVON, WARREN					
Imperial LP-12456	(S)	**Wanted Dead Or Alive**	1970	8.00	20.00
Pickwick SPC-3715	(S)	**Wanted Dead Or Alive**	1975	1.00	5.00
		(*Pickwick 3715 is a reissue of Imperial 12456.)*			
Asylum 7E-1060	(S)	**Warren Zevon**	1976	1.00	5.00
Asylum 6E-118	(S)	**Excitable Boy**	1978	1.00	5.00
Asylum 5E-509	(S)	**Bad Luck Streak In Dancing School**	1980	1.00	5.00
Asylum 5E-519	(S)	**Stand In The Fire**	1980	1.00	5.00
Asylum E1-60159	(S)	**The Envoy**	1982	1.00	5.00
ZIG ZAG PEOPLE, THE					
Decca DL-75110	(S)	**The Zig Zag People Take Bubble Gum Music Underground**	1969	10.00	25.00
ZIP CODES					
Liberty LRP-3367	(M)	**Mustang**	1964	60.00	150.00
Liberty LST-7367	(S)	**Mustang**	1964	150.00	300.00
ZIPPERMAN, STAN					
Stanza ST-2-2001	(S)	**Everyhead: A Rock Opera**	197?	4.00	10.00

ZOMBIES

The Zombies were Colin Blunstone backed by Rod Argent, Paul Atkinson, Hugh Grundy, and Chris White. They can also be found on the RCA Victor soundtrack "Bunny Lake Is Missing."

Parrot PAR-61001	(M)	**The Zombies**	1965	24.00	60.00
Parrot PAS-71001	(E)	**The Zombies**	1965	18.00	45.00
Date TES-4013	(S)	**Odessey And Oracle**	1968	12.00	30.00
		(*First pressing covers make no mention of "Time Of The Season.")*			
Date TES-4013	(S)	**Odessey And Oracle**	1969	8.00	20.00
		(*Second pressing covers note the single "Time Of The Season." "This Will Be Our Year" is rechanneled both pressings.)*			
London PS-557	(S)	**Early Days** (*"Tell Her No" is rechanneled)*	1969	6.00	15.00
Epic KEG-32861	(S)	**Time Of The Zombies** (*2 LPs)*	1974	4.00	10.00
		(*All the tracks on side 1 are in mono.)*			
Rhino RNLP-120	(S)	**Live BBC Broadcasts, 1965-67**	1985	2.00	5.00
ZOO					
Sunburst 7500	(S)	**The Zoo Presents The Chocolate Mousse**	1968	20.00	50.00
ZOO					
Mercury SR-61300	(S)	**The Zoo**	1970	4.00	10.00

ZZ TOP

ZZ Top is Billy Gibbons, Dusty Hill, and Frank Beard. Refer to American Blues; Moving Sidewalks.

London PS-584	(S)	**First Album**	1971	1.20	6.00
London PS-612	(S)	**Rio Grande Mud**	1972	1.20	6.00
London XPS-631	(S)	**Tres Hombres**	1973	1.20	6.00
London PS-656	(S)	**Fandango**	1975	1.20	6.00
London PS-X-1001	(DJ)	**Takin' Texas to The People**	1976	20.00	50.00
London PS-680	(S)	**Tejas**	1977	1.20	6.00
London PS-706	(S)	**The Best Of ZZ Top**	1977	1.20	6.00
Warner Bros. BSK-3268	(S)	**First Album**	1979	1.00	5.00
Warner Bros. BSK-3269	(S)	**Rio Grande Mud**	1979	1.00	5.00
Warner Bros. BSK-3270	(S)	**Tres Hombres**	1979	1.00	5.00
Warner Bros. BSK-3271	(S)	**Fandango**	1979	1.00	5.00
Warner Bros. BSK-3272	(S)	**Tejas**	1979	1.00	5.00
Warner Bros. BSK-3273	(S)	**Best Of ZZ Top**	1979	1.00	5.00
Warner Bros. BSK-3361	(S)	**Deguello**	1979	1.00	5.00
Warner Bros. BSK-3593	(S)	**El Loco**	1981	1.00	5.00

Rockin' At The Movies

This section includes what are basically various artists compilations used as "soundtracks" for motion pictures. Since its inception as a part of everyday life, at least for AM radio listeners, rock'n roll has found its way onto the big screen. In fact, it was the exposure in 1955 via the film *Blackboard Jungle* that gave Bill Haley & The Comets worldwide air-play for "Rock Around The Clock," a single that had been released the year before to modest attention! The late '50s saw a spate of [generally insipid] movies with rocking themes and rocking sounds. While Elvis' trio of musically-based films (*Loving You, Jailhouse Rock* and *King Creole*) were the best and the biggest, there were others, usually forgettable to all but the devoted.

The early '60s saw teenagers flock to "beach" movies, usually starring Annette and Frankie, a genre only peripherally connected with rock'n roll (an assessment that can also be made of the Elvis movies of this decade). In 1964, The Beatles collaborated with director Richard Lester to realize a true rock'n roll movie, the brilliant *A Hard Day's Night*. While the actual number of films with a rock'n roll or rhythm'n blues basis of any real quality is slim, they *do* exist (Nicolas Roeg's *Performance* with commendable jobs from Mick Jagger and James Fox comes immediately to mind).

As for the records that often accompanied the movie, the most common rock'n roll soundtrack is basically a hits compilation: Previously released tracks were leased and assembled to the producer/director's needs. While this was done from the very beginning of the genre (including the legendary *Carnival*, which collects snippets of performances from more artists than should be found on a single long-player), it reached its zenith in 1973 with George Lucas' *American Graffiti*, four sides of "oldies" that captured the film's early '60s setting.

In some cases, songs were commissioned, written and recorded for the film. As these albums contain the first, and sometimes only, appearance of a song, they are more highly regarded than the aforementioned hits packages. Elvis' many movie related recordings are examples that can be found in Presley's own listings. For years, the soundtrack for *The Savage Seven* was the only place that fans of Cream could find "Anyone For Tennis" on an album. Another film in this genre deserves notice: *Saturday Night Fever* not only broke all sorts of sales records, it also broke disco as a national phenomenon and resurrected the flagging career of The Brothers Gibb.

With *Woodstock*'s phenomenal success (a triple-record set that topped the charts in 1970), the sense that live recordings from a documentary could fill a need was fully realized. Unfortunately, the demise of the big music festivals have made this type of package all but obsolete and there are few other examples of interest. (*Woodstock Two* and both volumes of *Wattstax* are examples from the same period.)

Finally, the collector should note that in the case of some soundtracks, particularly those of an obvious exploitational nature, what you see is *not* what you get. That is, the artists credited may not exist outside of the needs of the one project upon which they can be found. For instance, albums on Sidewalk and Tower often credits all sorts of "groups" with names, er, interesting enough to make some listeners want to hear more. However, for the most part, these were fictitious bands that featured the same studio musicians, all under the guidance of Mike Curb.

(No label)	(DJ)	**Carnival Rock** (*Red vinyl without a cover*) *Rare with a suggested NM value of $2,000-4,000.)*	1955	See note below	
(No label)	(DJ)	**Rock, Rock, Rock** (*Publisher's demo*) *A few copies of this demo were issued with covers. Rare with a suggested NM value of $3,000-5,000.)*	1955	See note below	
(No label)	(DJ)	**Rock, Rock, Rock** (*Publisher's demo*) *(Most copies were issued without a cover. Still rare with a suggested NM value of $2,000-3,000.)*	1955	See note below	
(No label)	(DJ)	**Go, Johnny, Go** *(Rare with a suggested NM value of $2,000-3,000.)*	1959	See note below	
A&M 6500	(S)	**American Hot Wax** (*2 LPs*)	1978	3.20	8.00
ABC S-OC-9	(S)	**Candy**	1968	6.00	15.00

Label & Catalog #		Title	Year	VG+	NM
ABC 2151	(DJ)	Zachariah: A Special One-Hour Open-End Radio Show (With script)	1970	20.00	50.00
ABC S-OC-13	(S)	Zachariah	1970	6.00	15.00
American Inter. ST-A-1033	(S)	The Cycle Savages	1970	20.00	50.00
American Int. ST-A-1042	(S)	Kidnapped	1972	10.00	25.00
Amos AAS-8002	(S)	Vanishing Point	1971	10.00	25.00
Ampex 50101	(S)	Jud	1971	6.00	15.00
Amsterdam AMS-12007	(S)	The Minx	1970	8.00	20.00
Apple SW-3377	(S)	Come Together	1971	10.00	25.00
Arista A-5000	(S)	Stardust (2 LPs)	1975	4.00	10.00
Arista A-8246	(S)	Ghostbusters	1984	.80	4.00
Asylum 9004	(S)	Heavy Metal (2 LPs)	1981	1.00	5.00
Atco 33-245	(M)	The Savage Seven (White label promo)	1968	20.00	50.00
Atco SD-33-245	(S)	The Savage Seven	1968	10.00	25.00
Atco SD-33-363	(S)	Melody	1971	6.00	15.00
Casablanca 7099	(S)	Thank God It's Friday (2 LPs)	1978	1.00	5.00
Casablanca 811492	(S)	Flashdance	1983	.80	4.00
Chess LP-1425	(M)	Rock, Rock, Rock	1958	150.00	300.00
Columbia OS-3240	(S)	You Are What You Eat	1968	4.00	10.00
—Original Columbia albums above have "360 Sound" on the bottom of the label.—					
Columbia OS-3540	(S)	Tell Me That You Love Me Junie Moon	1970	4.00	10.00
Columbia 36737	(S)	Caddyshack	1980	1.00	5.00
Cotillion SD-9037	(S)	Homer	1970	8.00	20.00
Cotillion CT3-500	(S)	Woodstock (3 LPs)	1970	10.00	25.00
Cotillion CT2-400	(S)	Woodstock, Volume 2 (2 LPs)	1971	10.00	25.00
—Original Cotillion albums above have grey labels with an 1841 Broadway address.—					
Decca DL-8349	(M)	The Wild One	1956	60.00	150.00
Decca DL-8429	(M)	Rock, Pretty Baby	1956	150.00	300.00
(Decca 8429 has three cover variations with the title on the cover in either blue, red or yellow print. At this time there is no difference in value between the three. A 10" promotional radio transcription of this soundtrack can be found listed under Universal International.)					
—Original Decca albums above have black labels with silver print.—					
Decca DL-9119	(M)	The Lively Set	1964	14.00	35.00
Decca DL-79119	(S)	The Lively Set	1964	20.00	50.00
Decca DL-4699	(M)	Wild, Wild Winter	1966	8.00	20.00
Decca DL-74699	(S)	Wild, Wild Winter	1966	12.00	30.00
Decca DL-4751	(M)	Out Of Sight	1966	12.00	30.00
Decca DL-74751	(S)	Out Of Sight	1966	16.00	40.00
Decca DL-75515	(S)	The Wild One (Reissue of 8349)	197?	4.00	10.00
Decca DL-79181	(S)	Taking Off	1971	16.00	40.00
Dunhill DS-50063	(S)	Easy Rider	1969	12.00	30.00
Fontana MGF-27569	(M)	To Sir With Love	1967	8.00	20.00
Fontana SRF-67569	(S)	To Sir With Love	1967	10.00	25.00
Full Moon 60158	(S)	Fast Times At Ridgemont High (2 LPs)	1982	3.20	8.00
HBR HLP-8500	(M)	A Swingin' Summer	1966	12.00	30.00
HBR HST-8500	(S)	A Swingin' Summer	1966	16.00	40.00
Inner City IC-4001	(S)	Betrayal	1977	3.20	8.00
Island 90017	(S)	Officer And A Gentleman	1982	.80	4.00
Liberty LRP-3430	(M)	C'mon Let's Live A Little	1966	6.00	15.00
Liberty LST-7430	(S)	C'mon Let's Live A Little	1966	8.00	20.00
MCA 8001	(S)	American Graffiti (2 LPs)	1973	3.20	8.00
MCA 2-12000	(S)	FM (2 LPs)	1978	3.20	8.00
MCA 11006	(S)	More American Graffiti (2 LPs)	1979	3.20	8.00
MCA	(DJ)	More American Graffiti (Picture disc)	1979	10.00	25.00
MCA 6127	(S)	Two Of A Kind	1983	.80	4.00
MCA 6492	(S)	Streets Of Fire	1984	1.00	5.00

Label & Catalog #		Title	Year	VG+	NM
Mercury MG-20293	(M)	Rock All Night	1958	100.00	250.00
MGM E-4273	(M)	Get Yourself A College Girl	1964	6.00	15.00
MGM SE-4273	(S)	Get Yourself A College Girl	1964	8.00	20.00
MGM E-4334	(M)	When The Boys Meet The Girls	1965	8.00	20.00
MGM SE-4334	(S)	When The Boys Meet The Girls	1965	10.00	25.00
MGM SE-4468	(S)	Zabriskie Point	1970	6.00	15.00
MGM SE-4506	(S)	What Am I Bid?	1971	8.00	20.00
MGM 1SE-11	(S)	Grand Prix	1971	6.00	15.00
MGM 2SE-14	(S)	The Strawberry Statement (2 LPs)	1971	8.00	20.00
		(Refer to "The Strawberry Statement" under Reprise.)			
MGM 1SE-21	(S)	Zigzag	1971	6.00	15.00
Mobile Fidelity MFSL-200	(S)	Woodstock (5 LP box)	198?	50.00	150.00
Motown 6062	(S)	The Big Chill	1983	1.00	5.00
Motown 6094	(S)	The Big Chill (More Songs From The Original Soundtrack)	1984	1.00	5.00
National General 1001	(S)	Grasshopper	1970	4.00	10.00
Ode SP-99001	(DJ)	Tommy (2 LP box)	1970	20.00	50.00
Ode SP-99001	(S)	Tommy (2 LP box)	1970	8.00	20.00
Ode SQ-99001	(Q)	Tommy (2 LP box)	1970	20.00	50.00
Paramount PAS-5005	(S)	Where's Jack	1969	16.00	40.00
Paramount PAS-6005	(S)	The Hard Ride	197?	6.00	15.00
Parkway P-7011	(M)	Don't Knock The Twist	1962	30.00	75.00
Pasha 3933	(S)	Up The Creek	1984	.80	4.00
Polydor PD-29502	(S)	Tommy (2 LPs)	1975	4.00	10.00
RCA Victor LPM-2314	(M)	High Time	1960	8.00	20.00
RCA Victor LSP-2314	(S)	High Time	1960	12.00	30.00
		—Original RCA albums above have black labels with "Long Play" or "Living Stereo" on the bottom.—			
RCA Victor LPM-3441	(M)	Wild On The Beach	1965	10.00	25.00
RCA Victor LSP-3441	(S)	Wild On The Beach	1965	16.00	40.00
		—Original RCA albums above have black labels with "Mono" or "Stereo" on the bottom.—			
Reprise 2MS-2031	(DJ)	The Strawberry Statement (2 LPs)	1970	24.00	60.00
		(Issued in a plain jacket with a "Rush release" sticker.)			
Roulette R-25168	(M)	Hey, Let's Twist	1962	12.00	30.00
Roulette SR-25168	(S)	Hey, Let's Twist	1962	16.00	40.00
RSO 4001	(S)	Saturday Night Fever (2 LPs)	1977	3.20	8.00
RSO 4100	(S)	Sgt. Pepper's Lonely Hearts Club Band (2 LPs)	1978	1.00	5.00
RSO 4203	(S)	Times Square (2 LPs)	1980	1.20	6.00
RSO 813269	(S)	Stayin' Alive	1983	.80	4.00
Sidewalk T-5902	(M)	Thunder Alley	1967	10.00	25.00
Sidewalk ST-5902	(S)	Thunder Alley	1967	12.00	30.00
Sidewalk T-5903	(M)	Teenage Rebellion	1967	12.00	30.00
Sidewalk DT-5903	(E)	Teenage Rebellion	1967	10.00	25.00
Sidewalk T-5908	(M)	The Trip	1967	14.00	35.00
Sidewalk ST-5908	(S)	The Trip	1967	20.00	50.00
Sidewalk T-5910	(M)	Glory Stompers	1967	14.00	35.00
Sidewalk DT-5910	(E)	Glory Stompers	1967	10.00	25.00
Sidewalk T-5911	(M)	Mary Jane	1968	20.00	50.00
Sidewalk DT-5911	(P)	Mary Jane	1968	12.00	30.00
Sidewalk ST-5913	(S)	Psych-Out	1968	20.00	50.00
Sidewalk ST-5914	(S)	Wild Racers	1968	16.00	40.00
Sidewalk ST-5918	(S)	Three In The Attic	1969	10.00	25.00
Sire 6070	(S)	Rock 'N' Roll High School	1979	3.20	8.00
Straight STS-1056	(S)	Naked Angels	1969	20.00	50.00
Tower T-5043	(M)	The Wild Angels	1966	12.00	30.00
Tower DT-5043	(E)	The Wild Angels	1966	10.00	25.00
Tower T-5056	(M)	The Wild Angels, Volume 2	1967	12.00	30.00
Tower DT-5056	(E)	The Wild Angels, Volume 2	1967	10.00	25.00
Tower T-5065	(M)	Riot On Sunset Strip	1967	16.00	40.00
Tower DT-5065	(E)	Riot On Sunset Strip	1967	12.00	30.00
Tower T-5074	(M)	Devil's Angels	1967	12.00	30.00
Tower DT-5074	(E)	Devil's Angels	1967	10.00	25.00

Label & Catalog #		Title	Year	VG+	NM
Tower T-5083	(M)	Mondo Hollywood	1968	20.00	50.00
Tower DT-5083	(E)	Mondo Hollywood	1968	12.00	30.00
Tower ST-5124	(E)	The Hellcats	1968	12.00	30.00
Tower ST-5128	(S)	Angels From Hell	1968	20.00	50.00
Tower ST-5141	(S)	Killers Three	1968	12.00	30.00
Tower ST-5148	(P)	Best Of The Soundtracks	1969	16.00	40.00
20th Century TFM-3131	(M)	Surf Party	1964	12.00	30.00
20th Century TFS-4131	(S)	Surf Party	1964	16.00	40.00
20th Century TFS-4211	(S)	Beyond The Valley Of The Dolls	1970	30.00	75.00
20th Century 522	(S)	All This And World War II (2 LP box)	1976	6.00	15.00
Uni 3005	(M)	Privilege	1967	8.00	20.00
Uni 73005	(S)	Privilege	1967	10.00	25.00
Uni 73091	(S)	Angels Die Hard	1970	10.00	25.00
United Arts. UAS-5175	(S)	Here We Go 'Round The Mulberry Bush	1968	6.00	15.00
United Arts. UAS-5185	(S)	Revolution	1968	6.00	15.00
United Arts. UAS-5195	(S)	Alice's Restaurant	1969	4.00	10.00
United Arts. UAS-5213	(S)	Ned Kelly	1970	6.00	15.00
United Arts. LA300G	(S)	Ned Kelly	1977	1.00	5.00
		("Wild Colonial Boy" is rechanneled on UAS-5213 and LA300G.)			
Universal Unlimited Pict.	(10")	Rock, Pretty Baby (Red vinyl)	1956	See note below	
		(Radio transcription for the film. Rare with a suggested NM value of $3,000-5,000. The soundtrack was issued commercially by Decca.)			
Viking 105	(S)	The Games	1970	80.00	200.00
Wand WDM-671	(M)	How To Stuff A Wild Bikini	1965	8.00	20.00
Wand WDS-671	(S)	How To Stuff A Wild Bikini	1965	12.00	30.00
Warner Bros. (No #)	(DJ)	Jamboree	1955	1,000.00	2,000.00
Warner Bros. BS-1846	(S)	Performance	1970	12.00	30.00
Warner Bros. BS-2554	(S)	Performance	1972	6.00	15.00
Warner Bros. BS-2565	(S)	Medicine Ball Caravan	1971	5.00	12.00
Warner Bros. BS-2662	(S)	Steel Yard Blues	1972	4.00	10.00
Warner Bros. 3441	(S)	Roadie (2 LPs)	1980	1.20	6.00
Warner/Reprise	(10")	Woodstock (Radio spots)	1970	200.00	400.00

Various Artists Compilations

Most of these albums have a nominal value, especially given their age and the fact that as a genre these albums didn't sell in overwhelming numbers. The presence of any collectible artist on an otherwise mediocre compilation will affect its value somewhat; a track by a major artist can dramatically increase a value. For instance, Clarion 609, *Discoteque In Astrosound*, an otherwise nondescript comp, is sought after by Beatles collectors because it contains one of the Tony Sheridan & The Beat Brothers sides. RCA Victor issued samplers to radio stations throughout the '50s and '60s, often containing an Elvis track; each of these fetches three-figures, even though the Elvis material is available elsewhere. To a lesser extent comps with tracks by The Beach Boys, Bowie, Dylan and The Stones also attract a premium from completists. It is simply not possible in this book to list each of the collectible artists who appear on the albums below, although a few special items have been singled out. Finally, several albums that are, in fact, various artists compilations have been listed under individual artists for technical reasons; a note refers the reader to the artist.

A-Bet LP-401	(M)	Records Galore	196?	12.00	30.00
A&M SP-8022	(DJ)	The A&M Bootleg Album (2 LPs with letter)	1973	10.00	25.00
A&M PR-4738	(DJ)	No Wave (Picture disc)	1978	6.00	15.00
A&M PR-4876	(DJ)	Propaganda (Picture disc)	1980	16.00	40.00
ABC-Paramount ABC-216	(M)	A Million Or More	1958	20.00	50.00
		(Original pressing covers and labels credit the last track as Tommy Roe's "Sheila" while the disc plays Paul Anka's "Diana.")			
ABC-Paramount ABC-504	(M)	Shindig!	1964	10.00	25.00
ABC-Paramount ABCS-504	(S)	Shindig!	1964	12.00	30.00
ABC 784	(S)	14 Golden Recordings From The Historic Vaults Of Duke-Peacock	1973	4.00	10.00
Ace 1012	(M)	Greatest 15 Hits	1960	40.00	100.00
Ace 1019	(M)	Let's Have A Dance Party	1961	40.00	100.00
Ace 1020	(M)	For Twisters Only	1962	40.00	100.00
Aladdin LP-710	(M)	Rock And Roll With Rhythm & Blues	195?	See note below	
		(Although this album carries Aladdin's 700 series number indicating a 10" album, this is a 12" album. Rare with a suggested NM value of $2,000-4,000.)			
Aladdin 812	(M)	Singing The Blues	1957	Unreleased	
Aladdin 813	(M)	Party After Hours	1957	Unreleased	
Allegro 1704	(M)	Let's Rock And Roll	1956	40.00	100.00
Almor A-103	(M)	Golden Souvenirs	1963	10.00	25.00
Almor AS-103	(S)	Golden Souvenirs	1963	10.00	25.00
Almor A-105	(M)	Teen Bandstand	1963	10.00	25.00
Almor AS-105	(S)	Teen Bandstand	1963	10.00	25.00
Almor A-108	(M)	The World Of Surfin'	1963	16.00	40.00
Almor AS-108	(S)	The World Of Surfin'	1963	20.00	50.00
Almor A-109	(M)	Hot Rod Drag Races	1963	20.00	50.00
Almor AS-109	(S)	Hot Rod Drag Races	1963	24.00	60.00
Amazon 1007	(M)	Greatest Rhythm & Blues Hits	195?	20.00	50.00
Amazon 1008	(M)	Greatest Rhythm & Blues Hits, Volume 2	195?	20.00	50.00
Apollo LP-477	(M)	Saxomaniac	1956	40.00	100.00
Apollo LP-490	(M)	Jackpot Of Hits	1957	60.00	150.00
Apple STCX-3385	(S)	The Concert For Bangla Desh: *Refer to* George Harrison & Friends			
Apple SW-3400	(M)	Phil Spector's Christmas Album	1972	12.00	30.00
		(SW-3400 is a reissue of Philles 4005.)			
Argo LP-649	(DJ)	Remember The Oldies (Multi-color vinyl)	1963	60.00	150.00
Argo LP-649	(M)	Remember The Oldies	1963	20.00	50.00
Argo LP-656	(M)	Fanfare Of Hits	1963	10.00	25.00
Argo LP-4026	(M)	The Blues, Volume 1	1963	10.00	25.00
Argo LPS-4026	(S)	The Blues, Volume 1	1963	10.00	25.00
Argo LP-4027	(M)	The Blues, Volume 2	1963	10.00	25.00
Argo LPS-4027	(S)	The Blues, Volume 2	1963	10.00	25.00
Argo LP-4031	(M)	Folk Festival Of The Blues	1964	20.00	50.00
Argo LPS-4031	(S)	Folk Festival Of The Blues	1964	20.00	50.00

Label & Catalog #		Title	Year	VG+	NM
Argo LP-4041	(M)	The Blues, Volume 3	1965	10.00	25.00
Argo LPS-4041	(S)	The Blues, Volume 3	1965	10.00	25.00
Argo LP-4042	(M)	The Blues, Volume 4	1965	10.00	25.00
Argo LPS-4042	(S)	The Blues, Volume 4	1965	10.00	25.00
Arrawak 100	(M)	A Night Train Of Oldies	195?	16.00	40.00
Arvee 433	(M)	Golden Echoes	1962	20.00	50.00
Ascot ALM-13007	(M)	All Girl Million Sellers	1964	14.00	35.00
Ascot ALS-16007	(P)	All Girl Million Sellers	1964	14.00	35.00
Astra 1001	(M)	Terry Lee Presents For Lovers Only	1964	20.00	50.00
Astra 1002	(M)	Pittsburgh's Golden Oldies, Vol. 1	1967	20.00	50.00
Atco 33-103	(M)	Rockin' Together	1958	50.00	125.00
Atco 33-118	(M)	The Good Old '50's	1960	30.00	75.00
Atco 33-143	(M)	The Great Group Goodies	1962	30.00	75.00
Atco 33-159	(M)	Apollo Saturday Night	1964	20.00	50.00
Atco SD-33-159	(S)	Apollo Saturday Night	1964	30.00	75.00
Atco 33-169		Ain't She Sweet: Refer to The Beatles			
Atco 33-171	(M)	Swinging The Bard	1964	5.00	12.00
Atco SD-33-171	(S)	Swinging The Bard	1964	6.00	15.00
Atco D-33-269	(S)	Soul Christmas	1968	10.00	25.00
Atco SD-33-279	(S)	The Super Groups	1969	6.00	15.00
Atco SD-33-281	(S)	Soul Clan	1969	6.00	15.00
Atco SD-33-314	(S)	Rock Begins, Volume 1	1970	6.00	15.00
Atco SD-33-315	(S)	Rock Begins, Volume 2	1970	6.00	15.00
Atlantic 1239	(M)	Rock & Roll Forever	1956	80.00	200.00
		—Original Atlantic albums above have black labels.—			
Atlantic 1348	(M)	Roots Of The Blues	1960	10.00	25.00
Atlantic SD-1348	(S)	Roots Of The Blues	1960	16.00	40.00
Atlantic 1352	(M)	The Blues Roll On	1960	10.00	25.00
Atlantic SD-1352	(S)	The Blues Roll On	1960	16.00	40.00
		—Atlantic albums above have multi-color labels with a white "fan" logo on the right side.—			
Atlantic 8001	(M)	The Greatest Rock & Roll	1956	60.00	150.00
Atlantic 8010	(M)	Rock & Roll Forever, Volume 1	1956	40.00	100.00
Atlantic 8013	(M)	Dance The Rock & Roll	1957	40.00	100.00
Atlantic 8021	(M)	Rock & Roll Forever, Volume 2	1957	40.00	100.00
Atlantic 8037	(M)	The Rockin' '50's	1959	40.00	100.00
		—Original Atlantic albums above have black labels.—			
Atlantic 8001	(M)	The Greatest Rock & Roll	196?	20.00	50.00
Atlantic 8010	(M)	Rock & Roll Forever, Volume 1	196?	20.00	50.00
Atlantic 8013	(M)	Dance The Rock & Roll	196?	20.00	50.00
Atlantic 8021	(M)	Rock & Roll Forever, Volume 2	196?	20.00	50.00
Atlantic 8037	(M)	The Rockin' '50's	196?	20.00	50.00
Atlantic 8058	(M)	The Greatest Twist Hits	1962	20.00	50.00
		—Atlantic albums above have multi-color labels with a white "fan" logo on the right side.—			
Atlantic 8001	(M)	The Greatest Rock & Roll	196?	10.00	25.00
Atlantic 8010	(M)	Rock & Roll Forever, Volume 1	196?	10.00	25.00
Atlantic 8013	(M)	Dance The Rock & Roll	196?	10.00	25.00
Atlantic 8021	(M)	Rock & Roll Forever, Volume 2	196?	10.00	25.00
Atlantic 8037	(M)	The Rockin' '50's	196?	10.00	25.00
Atlantic 8058	(M)	The Greatest Twist Hits	1962	10.00	25.00
Atlantic 8065	(M)	The Solid Gold Groups	1962	20.00	50.00
Atlantic 8068	(M)	Hound Dog's Old Gold	1962	20.00	50.00
Atlantic 8098	(M)	Jamaica Ska	1963	8.00	20.00
Atlantic SD-8098	(S)	Jamaica Ska	1963	10.00	25.00
Atlantic 8100	(M)	Porky's Golden Dusties	1964	16.00	40.00
Atlantic SD-8100	(S)	Porky's Golden Dusties	1964	20.00	50.00
Atlantic 8101	(M)	Saturday Night At The Uptown	1964	16.00	40.00
Atlantic SD-8101	(S)	Saturday Night At The Uptown	1964	20.00	50.00
Atlantic 8108	(M)	Killer Joe's International Disco	1965	8.00	20.00
Atlantic SD-8108	(S)	Killer Joe's International Disco	1965	12.00	30.00
Atlantic 8116	(M)	Solid Gold Soul	1965	6.00	15.00
Atlantic SD-8116	(S)	Solid Gold Soul	1965	8.00	20.00
Atlantic ALS-1	(S)	Atlantic/Atco All Star Showcase (Promo sampler)	1965	12.00	30.00
Atlantic 8140	(M)	Beach Beat	1967	8.00	20.00
Atlantic SD-8140	(S)	Beach Beat	1967	6.00	15.00
Atlantic SD-8161	(S)	The History Of Rhythm & Blues, Volume 1	1968	6.00	15.00
Atlantic SD-8162	(S)	The History Of Rhythm & Blues, Volume 2	1968	6.00	15.00
Atlantic SD-8163	(S)	The History Of Rhythm & Blues, Volume 3	1968	6.00	15.00
Atlantic SD-8164	(S)	The History Of Rhythm & Blues, Volume 4	1968	6.00	15.00
Atlantic SD-8167	(S)	Brazil's Super Hits	1968	6.00	15.00
Atlantic SD-8170	(S)	This Is Soul	1968	6.00	15.00
		—Atlantic albums above have multi-color labels with a black "fan" logo on the right side.—			

Label & Catalog #		Title	Year	VG+	NM
Atlantic SD-8191	(S)	Beach Beat, Volume 2	1968	6.00	15.00
Atlantic SD-501	(S)	The Super Hits	1968	6.00	15.00
Atlantic SD-8188	(S)	Super Hits, Volume 2	1968	6.00	15.00
Atlantic SD-8191	(S)	Beach Beat	1968	6.00	15.00
Atlantic SD-8193	(S)	The History Of Rhythm & Blues, Vol 5	1968	6.00	15.00
Atlantic SD-8194	(S)	The History Of Rhythm & Blues, Vol 6	1968	6.00	15.00
Atlantic SD-8203	(S)	Super Hits, Volume 3	1968	6.00	15.00
Atlantic SD-8208	(S)	The History Of Rhythm & Blues, Volume 7	1968	6.00	15.00
Atlantic SD-8209	(S)	The History Of Rhythm & Blues, Volume 8	1968	6.00	15.00
Atlantic SD-8224	(S)	Super Hits, Volume 4	1969	6.00	15.00
Atlantic SD-8274	(S)	Super Hits, Volume 5	1970	6.00	15.00
Atlantic SD-7226	(S)	Texas Guitar From Dallas To L.A.	1972	6.00	15.00
Atlantic SD-7227	(S)	Chicago Blues	1972	6.00	15.00
Audio Fidelity AFLP-2168	(M)	Where It's At (Live At The Cheetah)	1966	30.00	75.00
Audio Fidelity DF-7039	(M)	Discotheque Jet Set, Volume 1	196?	6.00	15.00
Audio Fidelity DFS-7039	(S)	Discotheque Jet Set, Volume 1	196?	6.00	15.00
Audio Fidelity DF-7040	(M)	Discotheque Jet Set, Volume 2	196?	6.00	15.00
Audio Fidelity DFS-7040	(S)	Discotheque Jet Set, Volume 2	196?	6.00	15.00
Audio Fidelity DFS-7777	(S)	Stereo Spectacular	196?	6.00	15.00
August 100	(M)	Money Music	1967	300.00	500.00
Authentic DTL-501	(M)	Rhythm & Blues Hit Vocal Groups	196?	150.00	300.00
		(Authentic 501 covers contain copies of the Dooto 501 disc.)			
Autumn 101	(M)	KYA's Memories Of The Cow Palace	1963	40.00	100.00
Bang LP-215	(M)	Golden Hits From The Gang At Bang	1966	8.00	20.00
Bang LPS-215	(P)	Golden Hits From The Gang At Bang	1966	10.00	25.00
Bang LP-220	(M)	Bang And Shout Super Hits	1967	6.00	15.00
Bang LPS-220	(S)	Bang And Shout Super Hits	1967	8.00	20.00
Bell 6009	(S)	More For Your Money	1968	8.00	20.00
Bell 6030	(S)	Dial A Hit	1969	10.00	25.00
Bell 6035	(S)	Summer Souvenirs	1969	10.00	25.00
Bell 1206	(S)	On Any Sunday	197?	6.00	15.00
Beta 1414S	(M)	Gathering At The Depot	196?	16.00	40.00
Blast 6803	(M)	Blasts From The Past With Clay Cole	196?	20.00	50.00
Blast 6805	(M)	16 Goodies: Blasts From The Past	196?	20.00	50.00
BluesWay BSL-6061	(M)	Classic Blues, Volume 1	196?	6.00	15.00
BluesWay BSL-6062	(M)	Classic Blues, Volume 2	196?	6.00	15.00
Bolo 8002	(M)	Bolo Bash	1964	20.00	50.00
Bonded 777	(M)	20 Original R&B Goodies	196?	20.00	50.00
Brooklyn 301	(M)	Murray The K's Greatest Holiday Show	196?	16.00	40.00
Brooklyn S-301	(S)	Murray The K's Greatest Holiday Show	196?	20.00	50.00
Brooklyn 302	(M)	Murray The K Presents	196?	16.00	40.00
Brooklyn S-302	(S)	Murray The K Presents	196?	20.00	50.00
Brunswick BL-744129	(S)	The Great Soul Hits Of...	1968	6.00	15.00
Bud Jet 311	(M)	Top Teen Bands (Volume 1)	1968	20.00	50.00
Bud Jet 312	(M)	Top Teen Bands (Volume 2)	1968	20.00	50.00
Bud Jet 313	(M)	Top Teen Bands (Volume 3)	1968	24.00	60.00
Buddah Vol. 1 No. 1	(P)	Current Audio Magazine	1972	10.00	25.00
Cadence CLP-3041	(M)	Rock-A-Ballads	1960	20.00	50.00
Cadence CLP-3042	(M)	Rock-A-Hits	1960	20.00	50.00
Cadence CLP-3043	(M)	Golden Encores	1960	20.00	50.00
Camay C-3012	(M)	Twelve Collector's Goodies	1963	12.00	30.00
Camden CAL-740	(M)	Original Rhythm & Blues Hits By Rhythm & Blues Stars	1963	20.00	50.00
Camden CAS-740	(E)	Original Rhythm & Blues Hits By Rhythm & Blues Stars	1963	10.00	25.00
Camden CAL-820	(M)	Special Delivery	1964	10.00	25.00
Camden CAS-820e	(E)	Special Delivery	1964	6.00	15.00

Label & Catalog #		Title	Year	VG+	NM
Capitol T-1009	(M)	Teenage Rock	1958	20.00	50.00
Capitol T-1025	(M)	Everybody Rocks	1958	20.00	50.00
Capitol T-1561	(M)	Golden Gassers	1961	10.00	25.00
Capitol ST-1561	(S)	Golden Gassers	1961	12.00	30.00
Capitol TBO-1572	(M)	Shake It And Break It (2 LPs)	1961	14.00	35.00
Capitol T-1837	(M)	Chartbusters	1963	8.00	20.00
Capitol DT-1837	(E)	Chartbusters	1963	6.00	15.00
Capitol T-1918	(M)	Shut Down	1963	12.00	30.00
Capitol ST-1918	(P)	Shut Down	1963	16.00	40.00
Capitol T-1939	(M)	My Son, The Surf Nut	1963	20.00	50.00
Capitol ST-1939	(S)	My Son, The Surf Nut	1963	30.00	75.00
Capitol T-1945	(M)	Chartbusters, Volume 2	1963	8.00	20.00
Capitol DT-1945	(E)	Chartbusters, Volume 2	1963	6.00	15.00
Capitol T-1995	(M)	Surfing's Greatest Hits	1963	8.00	20.00
Capitol ST-1995	(P)	Surfing's Greatest Hits	1963	12.00	30.00
Capitol T/ST-1997		Hot Rod Rally: Refer to The Super Stocks			
Capitol T-2006	(M)	Chartbusters, Volume 3	1963	10.00	25.00
Capitol DT-2006	(E)	Chartbusters, Volume 3	1963	8.00	20.00
Capitol T-2024	(M)	Big Hit Rod Hits	1963	20.00	50.00
Capitol ST-2024	(P)	Big Hit Rod Hits	1963	30.00	75.00
Capitol T-2094	(M)	Chartbusters, Volume 4	1964	20.00	50.00
Capitol ST-2094	(P)	Chartbusters, Volume 4	1964	30.00	75.00
Capitol T-2125	(M)	The Big Hits From England & U.S.A.	1964	16.00	40.00
Capitol DT-2125	(E)	The Big Hits From England & U.S.A.	1964	12.00	30.00
Capitol T-2565	(M)	Super Oldies, Volume 2	1966	6.00	15.00
Capitol ST-2565	(S)	Super Oldies, Volume 2	1966	8.00	20.00
Capitol T-2544	(M)	Liverpool Today	1966	8.00	20.00
Capitol ST-2544	(S)	Liverpool Today	1966	12.00	30.00
Capitol STBB-2???	(P)	Super Oldies (Vol. 1) (2 LPs)	1968	5.00	12.00
Capitol STBB-2???	(P)	Super Oldies (Vol. 2) (2 LPs)	1968	5.00	12.00
Capitol STBB-2910	(P)	Super Oldies (Vol. 3) (2 LPs)	1968	5.00	12.00
Capitol STBB-585	(P)	Peace On Earth	1970	6.00	15.00
Capitol SABB-12248	(S)	Concert For Bangla Desh: Refer to George Harrison & Friends			

—Special/Promotional Albums—

Capitol issued well over one hundred numbers of their "Silver Platter Service" series with hundreds of artists represented. Rather than list them all, the reader should be aware that this listing more or less suffices to cover the more desirable titles. An unlisted number with a major collectible name should increase the value somewhat. . .

Capitol PRO-2375/6	(M)	Balanced For Broadcast	1963	16.00	40.00
Capitol PRO-2377/8	(M)	Salesman's Demonstration Record	1963	20.00	50.00
Capitol PRO-239/66	(M)	Big Surfin' Sounds	1963	40.00	100.00
Capitol PRO-2463/4	(M)	Salesman's Demonstration Record	1963	20.00	50.00
Capitol PRO-2479/80	(M)	Hot Rod Music On Capitol	1963	100.00	250.00
Capitol PRO-2493/4	(M)	Salesman's Demonstration Record	1963	20.00	50.00
Capitol PRO-2537/8	(M)	Great New Releases From The Sound Capitol Of The World	1964	40.00	100.00
Capitol PRO-2556/7	(M)	Balanced For Broadcast	1964	40.00	100.00
Capitol PRO-2658/9	(M)	Big Surfin' Sounds	1964	100.00	250.00
Capitol PRO-2685/6	(M)	Balanced For Broadcast	1964	20.00	50.00
Capitol PRO-2744/5	(M)	Programming Aids From Capitol	1964	40.00	100.00
		(PRO-2744 contains The Beach Boys' "Auld Lang Syne" without voice-over.)			
Capitol PRO-3123/4	(M)	Silver Platter Service From Hollywood	1965	40.00	100.00
		(PRO-3123/4 features Brian Wilson introducing selections from The Hollyridge Strings' "Beach Boys Songbook.")			
Capitol PRO-3265/6	(M)	Silver Platter Service	1967	40.00	100.00
		(3265/6 features Brian Wilson briefly discussing "Smiley Smile.")			
Capitol PRO-4231/2	(M)	Your Introduction To The January 1967 Releases	1967	500.00	1,000.00
		(SPRO-4231/2 contains a commercial for The Beach Boys' "Smile" album.)			
Capitol PRO-4411/2	(M)	Capitol's 25th Anniversary Celebration	1967	12.00	30.00
Capitol SPRO-4673	(M)	Capitol Disc Jockey Album	1969	12.00	30.00
Capitol SPRO-4724	(M)	Capitol Hits Through The Years	1969	16.00	40.00
Capitol SPRO-5003	(M)	Listen In Good Health	1970	12.00	30.00
Capitol SPRO-8511	(M)	The Greatest Music Ever Sold	1976	12.00	30.00
Capitol SNP-6	(S)	The New Spirit Of Capitol	1968	2.40	6.00
Capitol L-6538	(M)	Groovy!	1966	5.00	12.00
Capitol SL-6538	(S)	Groovy!	1966	6.00	15.00
Capitol SL-6621	(S)	Wings	196?	2.40	6.00
Capitol SL-6696	(S)	Time To Get It Together	196?	2.40	6.00
Caribou CABPU	(DJ)	Caribou Fall Releases (Picture disc)	1977	6.00	15.00
Carlton 121	(M)	One Dozen Goldies	1958	20.00	50.00
CBS Songs	(DJ)	Radio's Million Performance Songs	1984	20.00	50.00
Celebrity 1000	(M)	World Famous Rhythm And Blues	195?	1,000.00	2,000.00

Label & Catalog #		Title	Year	VG+	NM
Century 23214	(M)	Milwaukee Sentinel— Young America Rock 'n' Roll Songs	1966	150.00	300.00
Chancellor CHL-5009	(M)	The Hit Makers	1961	10.00	25.00
Chancellor CHL-5017	(M)	Wild, Wild Twist Recorded Live!	1961	10.00	25.00
Chancellor CHLS-5017	(S)	Wild, Wild Twist Recorded Live!	1961	20.00	50.00
Chancellor CHL-5028	(M)	Dance On The Wild Side	1962	10.00	25.00
Checker LP-2973	(DJ)	Love Those Goodies (Multi-colored vinyl)	1959	400.00	750.00
Checker LP-2973	(M)	Love Those Goodies	1959	60.00	150.00
Checker LP-2975	(M)	Hits That Jumped	1959	60.00	150.00
Checker LP-2998	(M)	Sing A Song Of Soul	196?	40.00	100.00
Checker LPS-3014	(S)	In The Beginning...	1970	6.00	15.00
Chess LP-1439	(DJ)	Oldies In Hi Fi (Multi-colored vinyl)	1959	400.00	750.00
Chess LP-1439	(M)	Oldies In Hi Fi	1959	60.00	150.00
Chess LP-1441	(DJ)	Bunch Of Goodies (Multi-colored vinyl)	1960	400.00	750.00
Chess LP-1441	(M)	Bunch Of Goodies	1960	60.00	150.00
Chess LP-1446	(M)	Walking By Myself	1960	20.00	50.00
Chess LP-1458	(M)	Golden Gassers Across The U.S.A.	1960	60.00	150.00
		(Chess 1458 was given various titles for distribution to select regional markets across the States, although the contents remained the same.)			
Chess LP-1458	(M)	Murray The K's Golden Gassers	1961	60.00	150.00
		(This is the New York City, NY, version of Chess 1458.)			
Chess LP-1458	(M)	WAMO's Golden Gassers	1961	60.00	150.00
		(This is the Pittsburgh, PA, version of Chess 1458.)			
Chess LP-1458	(M)	KYA's Golden Gate Greats	1961	60.00	150.00
		(This is the Los Angeles, CA, version of Chess 1458.)			
Chess LP-1461	(M)	Murray The K's Blasts From The Past	1961	20.00	50.00
Chess LP-1470	(M)	Murray The K's Gassers For Submarine Race Watchers	1963	16.00	40.00
Chess LP-1474	(M)	Treasure Tunes From The Vault	1963	12.00	30.00
Chess LP-1476	(M)	Dance Tunes From The Vault	1964	12.00	30.00
Chess LP-1478	(M)	Group Of Goodies	1964	20.00	50.00
Chess LP-1491	(M)	Group Of Goodies, Vol. 2	1966	20.00	50.00
		— Original Chess albums above have black labels with silver print. —			
Chess LP-1520	(M)	Petal Pushers	1967	10.00	25.00
Chess LPS-1520	(S)	Petal Pushers	1967	10.00	25.00
Chess LP-1522	(M)	Heavy Heads	1967	10.00	25.00
Chess LPS-1522	(P)	Heavy Heads	1967	10.00	25.00
Chess LPS-1528	(P)	Heavy Heads, Voyage 2	1969	6.00	15.00
Chess LPS-1533	(P)	Blues From Big Bill's Copa Cabana	1969	12.00	30.00
Chess LPS-1544	(P)	Pop Origins	1969	10.00	25.00
Chess LPS-1546	(P)	Souled Out	1969	20.00	50.00
Chess 18635	(DJ)	Chess-Checker-Cadet LP Sampler	1970	4.00	10.00
Chess 2CH-50030	(M)	Golden Age Of Rhythm & Blues (2 LPs)	1972	12.00	30.00
Class 5004	(M)	Gone But Not Forgotten	1959	40.00	100.00
		(Class 5004 was reissued as Rendezvous 1314.)			
Collectables 1/2-2500	(P)	History Of Rock & Roll (2 LP picture disc)	1982	12.00	30.00
Collector's Edition 505	(P)	All-Time Christmas Favorites (5 LP box)	1978	80.00	200.00
Colpix CP-454	(M)	Bye Bye Birdie	1964	30.00	75.00
Colpix SCP-454	(S)	Bye Bye Birdie	1964	40.00	100.00
Colpix CP-466	(M)	Groovy Goodies	1964	30.00	75.00
Colpix SCP-466	(P)	Groovy Goodies	1964	40.00	100.00
Colpix 712	(S)	Mann & Weill: Solid Gold	196?	20.00	50.00
Colstar S-5001	(S)	San Francisco International Pop Festival, Volume 1	1968	40.00	100.00
Columbia CL-2172	(M)	The Exciting New Liverpool Sound	1964	6.00	15.00
Columbia CS-8972	(S)	The Exciting New Liverpool Sound	1964	8.00	20.00
Columbia CL-2539	(M)	Boss Oldies—Sounds From The Grooveyard	1966	4.00	10.00
Columbia CS-9339	(S)	Boss Oldies—Sounds From The Grooveyard	1966	6.00	15.00
Columbia CL-2574	(M)	Big Hits	1966	4.00	10.00
Columbia CS-9374	(S)	Big Hits	1966	6.00	15.00
Columbia CL-2600	(M)	Hall Of Fame	1967	4.00	10.00
Columbia CS-9400	(S)	Hall Of Fame	1967	4.00	10.00
Columbia CL-2667	(M)	18 King Size R&B Hits	1967	6.00	15.00
Columbia CS-9467	(E)	18 King Size R&B Hits	1967	4.00	10.00
Columbia CS-9660	(S)	Ballads And Breakdowns Of The Golden Era	1968	8.00	20.00
		— Original Columbia albums above have "360 Sound" on the bottom of the label. —			
Columbia P-14439	(P)	Surf And Drag	197?	10.00	25.00
Columbia KC-31171	(S)	A Tribute To Woody Guthrie, Part 1	1972	5.00	12.00
		(Part 2 was issued as Warner Bros. 46144.)			
Columbia P4S-5914	(S)	Rock's Greatest Hits (4 LP box)	1972	6.00	15.00

Label & Catalog #		Title	Year	VG+	NM
Columbia C2-38025	(P)	Psychedelic Dream (2 LPs)	198?	1.00	5.00
Columbia C-45018	(S)	Rock Classics Of The '60s	1989	4.00	10.00
		—Special/Promotional Albums—			
Columbia CLP-251	(M)	Power Train '66	1966	3.20	8.00
Columbia CSP-251	(S)	Power Train '66	1966	4.00	10.00
Columbia CLP-293	(M)	Teenscene	1966	3.20	8.00
Columbia CSP-293	(S)	Teenscene	1966	4.00	10.00
Columbia CLP-301	(M)	London Really Swings	1966	3.20	8.00
Columbia CSP-301	(S)	London Really Swings	1966	4.00	10.00
Columbia CLP-314	(M)	Sounds Of Mod Contact	1966	3.20	8.00
Columbia CSP-314	(P)	Sounds Of Mod Contact	1966	4.00	10.00
Columbia CLP-333	(M)	It's Happenin' Here	1966	3.20	8.00
Columbia CSP-333	(S)	It's Happenin' Here	1966	4.00	10.00
Columbia CSM-389	(M)	A Slice Of Lemon	1966	3.20	8.00
Columbia CSP-389	(S)	A Slice Of Lemon	1966	4.00	10.00
Columbia CSM-523	(M)	Zenith Salutes The Teen Sound	1966	3.20	8.00
Columbia CSS-523	(P)	Zenith Salutes The Teen Sound	1966	4.00	10.00
Columbia CSM-731	(M)	Groovy Sounds	1966	3.20	8.00
Columbia CSS-731	(P)	Groovy Sounds	1966	4.00	10.00
Columbia D-81	(M)	Disco Teen '65	1965	3.20	8.00
Columbia DS-81	(S)	Disco Teen '65	1965	4.00	10.00
Columbia D-127	(M)	Top Pop Song Hits, Volume 2	1966	3.20	8.00
Columbia DS-127	(S)	Top Pop Song Hits, Volume 2	1966	4.00	10.00
Columbia D-155	(M)	Disco Teen '66	1966	8.00	20.00
Columbia DS-155	(S)	Disco Teen '66	1966	20.00	50.00
		(DS-155 has an alternate stereo mix of Dylan's "Positively 4th Street.")			
Columbia TB-1	(M)	The Best Of '66	1966	3.20	8.00
Columbia TBS-1	(S)	The Best Of '66	1966	4.00	10.00
Columbia DS-486	(M)	The Columbia Sound	1968	3.20	8.00
Columbia A2S-174	(DJ)	The Heavyweights (2 LPs)	1975	16.00	40.00
Columbia A2S-890	(DJ)	Hitline '80 (2 LPs)	1980	12.00	30.00
Columbia AS-902	(S)	Highlights From CBS Mastersound (With booklet)	1981	20.00	50.00
Columbia AS-1522	(S)	New Music Seminar Sampler (2 LPs)	1982	3.20	8.00
Columbia CAS-2097	(S)	Wish It Were September	1985	3.20	8.00
Constellation C-1	(M)	Collectors Showcase, Volume 1	1962	30.00	75.00
Constellation CS-1	(E)	Collectors Showcase, Volume 1	1962	20.00	50.00
Constellation C-5	(M)	Collectors Showcase, Groups Three	1962	30.00	75.00
Constellation CS-5	(E)	Collectors Showcase, Groups Three	1962	20.00	50.00
Constellation C-7	(M)	Aces 3	1962	20.00	50.00
Constellation CS-7	(E)	Aces 3	1962	12.00	30.00
Coral CRL-57269	(M)	Hitsville	1959	30.00	75.00
Coral CRL-757269	(S)	Hitsville	1959	40.00	100.00
Coral CRL-57310	(M)	Million Airs	1959	12.00	30.00
Coral CRL-757310	(S)	Million Airs	1959	20.00	50.00
Coral CRL-57431	(M)	Teenage Goodies	1963	12.00	30.00
Coral CRL-757431	(S)	Teenage Goodies	1963	20.00	50.00
Cotillion SD-9032	(S)	Solid Gold Old Town - Vol. 1	1970	6.00	15.00
		(Cotillion 9032 is a reissue of Old Town 101.)			
		—Original Cotillion albums above have grey labels with an 1841 Broadway address.—			
Crescendo GNP-84	(M)	Original Surfin' Hits (With bonus photos)	1963	16.00	40.00
Crescendo GNPS-84	(P)	Original Surfin' Hits (With bonus photos)	1963	20.00	50.00
Crescendo GNP-84	(M)	Original Surfin' Hits (Without the photos)	1963	12.00	30.00
Crescendo GNPS-84	(P)	Original Surfin' Hits (Without the photos)	1963	16.00	40.00
Crescendo GNP-85	(M)	Winners Of The 18 Band Surf Battle	1963	10.00	25.00
Crescendo GNPS-85	(S)	Winners Of The 18 Band Surf Battle	1963	12.00	30.00
Crown CLP-5001	(M)	Rock & Roll Dance Party	1958	60.00	150.00
Crown CLP-5011	(M)	Hollywood Rock 'N Roll Record Hop	1958	60.00	150.00
Crown CLP-5013	(M)	Gigantic Stars Of Rock & Roll	1958	60.00	150.00
Crown CLP-5144	(M)	The Best Of Oldies And Goodies	1960	20.00	50.00
Crown CLP-5202	(M)	More Of The Oldies And Goodies	1961	20.00	50.00
Crown CLP-5238	(M)	Blues Oldies And Goodies	1961	20.00	50.00
Crown CLP-5241	(M)	Oldies And Goodies	1961	20.00	50.00
		—Crown albums above have black labels with a silver "Crown" on top.—			
Custom CM-2038	(M)	Come To A Shindig Dance Party	196?	4.00	10.00
Custom CS-2038	(S)	Come To A Shindig Dance Party	196?	4.00	10.00
Dawn DLP-1119	(M)	Rock And Roll Spectacular	195?	150.00	300.00
Decca DL-4036	(M)	Golden Oldies	1960	12.00	30.00
Decca DL-4045	(M)	Midnight Jamboree	1960	12.00	30.00
Decca DL-74045	(S)	Midnight Jamboree	1960	16.00	40.00

Label & Catalog #		Title	Year	VG+	NM
Decca DL-4434	(M)	Out Came The Blues	1964	16.00	40.00
Decca DL-74434	(E)	Out Came The Blues	1964	12.00	30.00
Decca DL-9157	(M)	Playback '66	1964	30.00	75.00
Decca DL-79157	(S)	Playback '66	1964	40.00	100.00
Decca DL-75181	(S)	Rock 'N' Roll Survival	1970	5.00	12.00
Del-Fi (No number)	(DJ)	Del-Fi Album Sampler (Green vinyl)	1959	200.00	400.00
Del-Fi DFLP-1210	(M)	Del-Fi Record Hop	1960	30.00	75.00
Del-Fi DFLP-1219	(M)	Barrel Of Oldies	1961	20.00	50.00
Del-Fi DFLP-1222	(M)	Twist To Radio KRLA	1962	12.00	30.00
Del-Fi DFST-1222	(S)	Twist To Radio KRLA	1962	20.00	50.00
Del-Fi DFLP-1227	(M)	Very Best Of The Oldies	1963	20.00	50.00
Del-Fi DFLP-1235	(M)	KYA's Battle Of The Surfing Bands	1964	20.00	50.00
Del-Fi DFST-1235	(S)	KYA's Battle Of The Surfing Bands	1964	30.00	75.00
Del-Fi DFLP-1235	(M)	KFWB's Battle Of The Surfing Bands	1964	20.00	50.00
Del-Fi DFST-1235	(S)	KFWB's Battle Of The Surfing Bands	1964	30.00	75.00
Del-Fi DFLP-1249	(M)	Big Surf Hits	1964	20.00	50.00
Del-Fi DFST-1249	(S)	Big Surf Hits	1964	30.00	75.00
Delmark DS-618	(M)	Sweet Home Chicago	1969	8.00	20.00
Design DLP-170	(M)	The Merseyside Sound	1964	6.00	15.00
Design DLPS-170	(S)	The Merseyside Sound	1964	6.00	15.00
Design DLP-178	(M)	The Young Lovers	1964	6.00	15.00
Design DLPS-178	(P)	The Young Lovers	1964	6.00	15.00
Design DLP-186	(M)	Swingin' Teen Sounds	196?	6.00	15.00
Design DLPS-186	(E)	Swingin' Teen Sounds	196?	4.00	10.00
Design DLP-187	(M)	Soundsville!	196?	8.00	20.00
Design SDLP-187	(S)	Soundsville!	196?	10.00	25.00
		(Design 187 includes tracks by The Beachnuts and The Roughnecks, both featuring Lou Reed.)			
Design DLP-190	(M)	Shindig!	196?	4.00	10.00
Design DLP-190	(S)	Shindig!	196?	5.00	12.00
Design DLP-210	(M)	Where The Action Is!	196?	4.00	10.00
Design DLP-210	(S)	Where The Action Is!	196?	5.00	12.00
Design DLP-211	(M)	Hullabaloo Au-Go-Go	196?	4.00	10.00
Design DLP-211	(S)	Hullabaloo Au-Go-Go	196?	5.00	12.00
Design DLP-252	(M)	The In Crowd	196?	4.00	10.00
Design DLP-252	(S)	The In Crowd	196?	5.00	12.00
Design DLP-256	(M)	Music For Longhairs	196?	5.00	12.00
Design DLP-256	(E)	Music For Longhairs	196?	4.00	10.00
Design DLP-263	(M)	A Happening!	196?	4.00	10.00
Design DLP-263	(S)	A Happening!	196?	5.00	12.00
Design DLP-269	(M)	Out Of Sight!	196?	6.00	15.00
Design DLP-269	(E)	Out Of Sight!	196?	5.00	12.00
		(Design 269 includes tracks by The Beachnuts featuring Lou Reed.)			
Design DLP-605	(M)	Original Country & Western Stars	1963	6.00	15.00
Design SDLP-605	(E)	Original Country & Western Stars	1963	4.00	10.00
Design DLP-611	(M)	Tennessee	1963	8.00	20.00
Design SDLP-611	(E)	Tennessee	1963	4.00	10.00
Design DLP-909	(M)	Three Of A Kind	196?	6.00	15.00
Design DLP-909	(S)	Three Of A Kind	196?	4.00	10.00
Diplomat D-2308	(M)	Kings Of The Hot Rods	1963	8.00	20.00
Diplomat DS-2308	(E)	Kings Of The Hot Rods	1963	4.00	10.00
Diplomat D-2311	(M)	Teen Dance Time	1963	8.00	20.00
Diplomat DS-2311	(E)	Teen Dance Time	1963	4.00	10.00
Diplomat D-2334	(M)	Discotheque Dance Party	1963	8.00	20.00
Diplomat DS-2334	(E)	Discotheque Dance Party	1963	4.00	10.00
Diplomat D-2397	(M)	Discotheque	1964	6.00	15.00
Diplomat DS-2397	(E)	Discotheque	1964	4.00	10.00
Diplomat S-2414	(M)	Teen Beat	1964	6.00	15.00
Diplomat DS-2414	(E)	Teen Beat	1964	4.00	10.00
Diplomat D-2430	(M)	The Four Seasons / Tommy Roe / Johnny Rivers / Tony Banon	1964	5.00	12.00
Diplomat DS-2430	(S)	The Four Seasons / Tommy Roe / Johnny Rivers / Tony Banon	1964	6.00	15.00
Do It Now LP-5000	(P)	First Vibration	1969	8.00	20.00
Domain 102	(M)	Rosko's Evergreens	1963	20.00	50.00
Dooto DTL-204	(M)	Best In Rhythm 'N Blues: Refer to The Penguins			
Dooto DTL-223	(M)	Rock & Roll Vs. Rhythm & Blues	195?	40.00	100.00
Dooto LP-224	(M)	Best Vocal Groups In Rhythm & Blues	195?	40.00	100.00
Dooto LP-855	(M)	Oldies	196?	6.00	15.00

Label & Catalog #		Title	Year	VG+	NM
Dot DLP-3049	(M)	Great Hits On Dot	1957	20.00	50.00
Dot DLP-3181	(M)	The Great Millions	1959	20.00	50.00
Dot DLP-3183	(M)	Young Love	1959	30.00	75.00
Dot DLP-3425	(M)	Million $ Music	1962	20.00	50.00
Dot DLP-25425	(S)	Million $ Music	1962	40.00	100.00
Dot DLP-3677	(M)	Great Hits On Dot	1965	5.00	12.00
Dot DLP-25677	(S)	Great Hits On Dot	1965	6.00	15.00
Duke DLP-73	(M)	Like 'Em Red Hot	1965	80.00	200.00
		— Duke albums above have yellow & purple labels. —			
Duke DLP-82	(M)	Blues That Gave America Soul	1966	8.00	20.00
Duke DLPS-82	(M)	Blues That Gave America Soul	1966	12.00	30.00
Dunhill DS-50057	(S)	A Treasury Of Great Contemporary Hits	1969	6.00	15.00
Dunhill DS-50070	(S)	The Original Hits Of Right Now	196?	6.00	15.00
Dunhill DS-50085	(S)	The Big Hits Now	1970	6.00	15.00
Dunhill DSX-50100	(S)	Monterey International Pop Festival	197?	6.00	15.00
Economic Consultants	(M)	A Journey Into Yesterday 1956*	1973	6.00	15.00
Economic Consultants	(M)	A Journey Into Yesterday 1957	1973	4.00	10.00
Economic Consultants	(M)	A Journey Into Yesterday 1958	1973	4.00	10.00
Economic Consultants	(M)	A Journey Into Yesterday 1959	1973	4.00	10.00
Economic Consultants	(M)	A Journey Into Yesterday 1960	1973	4.00	10.00
Economic Consultants	(M)	A Journey Into Yesterday 1961	1973	4.00	10.00
Economic Consultants	(M)	A Journey Into Yesterday 1962	1973	4.00	10.00
Economic Consultants	(M)	A Journey Into Yesterday 1963	1973	4.00	10.00
Economic Consultants	(M)	A Journey Into Yesterday 1964	1973	4.00	10.00
Economic Consultants	(M)	A Journey Into Yesterday 1965	1973	4.00	10.00
Economic Consultants	(M)	A Journey Into Yesterday 1966	1973	4.00	10.00
Economic Consultants	(M)	A Journey Into Yesterday 1967	1973	4.00	10.00
Economic Consultants	(M)	A Journey Into Yesterday 1968	1973	4.00	10.00
Economic Consultants	(M)	A Journey Into Yesterday 1969*	1973	6.00	15.00
Economic Consultants	(M)	Old & Heavy Gold 1956*	1973	6.00	15.00
Economic Consultants	(M)	Old & Heavy Gold 1957*	1973	6.00	15.00
Economic Consultants	(M)	Old & Heavy Gold 1958*	1973	6.00	15.00
Economic Consultants	(M)	Old & Heavy Gold 1959	1973	4.00	10.00
Economic Consultants	(M)	Old & Heavy Gold 1960*	1973	6.00	15.00
Economic Consultants	(M)	Old & Heavy Gold 1961*	1973	6.00	15.00
Economic Consultants	(M)	Old & Heavy Gold 1962*	1973	6.00	15.00
Economic Consultants	(M)	Old & Heavy Gold 1963	1973	4.00	10.00
Economic Consultants	(M)	Old & Heavy Gold 1964	1973	4.00	10.00
Economic Consultants	(M)	Old & Heavy Gold 1965	1973	4.00	10.00
Economic Consultants	(M)	Old & Heavy Gold 1966	1973	4.00	10.00
Economic Consultants	(M)	Old & Heavy Gold 1967	1973	4.00	10.00
Economic Consultants	(M)	Old & Heavy Gold 1968	1973	4.00	10.00
Economic Consultants	(M)	Old & Heavy Gold 1969	1973	4.00	10.00
		— Economic Consultants titles above marked with an asterisk contain at least one track by Elvis Presley. —			
Elektra EKL-264	(M)	The Blues Project	1964	8.00	20.00
Elektra EKLS-7264	(S)	The Blues Project	1964	12.00	30.00
Elektra EKL-299	(M)	Singer Songwriter Project	1965	8.00	20.00
Elektra EKS-7299	(S)	Singer Songwriter Project	1965	12.00	30.00
Elektra EKL-4002	(M)	What's Shakin' (With booklet)	1966	16.00	40.00
Elektra EKS-74002	(S)	What's Shakin' (With booklet)	1966	18.00	45.00
Elektra EKL-4002	(M)	What's Shakin' (Without booklet)	1966	10.00	25.00
Elektra EKS-74002	(S)	What's Shakin' (Without booklet)	1966	12.00	30.00
Elektra 7E-2006	(P)	Nuggets (2 LPs)	1972	12.00	30.00
Elektra S3-10	(S)	Garden Of Earthly Delights (3 LPs)	197?	6.00	15.00
Elektra 7559-60403	(P)	Electrock The Sixties (4 LP box)	198?	6.00	15.00
Ember 500	(M)	Carload O' Hits	1959	Unreleased?	
		(Reissued as Muse 500.)			
EMR Ent. RH-8	(DJ)	The Age Of Rock	1969	60.00	150.00
End LP-302	(M)	Having A Ball (Group cover)	1959	1,000.00	2,000.00
		— Original End albums above have black & silver labels. —			
End LP-302	(M)	Having A Ball (Group cover)	1960	400.00	750.00
End LP-302	(M)	Rock & Roll Jamboree (Puppet cover)	196?	80.00	200.00
		("Rock & Roll Jamboree" is a reissue of "Having A Ball.")			
End LP-305	(M)	Battle Of The Groups	1960	40.00	100.00
End LP-309	(M)	Battle Of The Groups, Volume 2	1960	40.00	100.00
End LP-310	(M)	12 + 3 + 15 Hits	1960	40.00	100.00
End LP-313	(M)	Alan Freed's Golden Picks	1961	30.00	75.00
End LP-314	(M)	Alan Freed's Top 15	1962	30.00	75.00
End LP-315	(M)	Alan Freed's Top 15	1962	30.00	75.00
		— Original End albums above have grey labels with dogs on top. —			

Label & Catalog #		Title	Year	VG+	NM
Epic XSB-139674	(S)	Epic Blockbuster Sampler Album	1968	6.00	15.00
Epic AS-537	(DJ)	Epic Records Sampler (Picture disc)	1978	6.00	15.00
Era ES Vol. 1	(P)	Golden Era Series, Volume 1	1966	10.00	25.00
Era ES Vol. 2	(P)	Golden Era Series, Volume 2	1966	10.00	25.00
Etiquette ETLB-028	(P)	The Northwest Collection (6 LP box)	197?	60.00	150.00
Evatone 106811	(M)	The Magic Cube	198?	30.00	75.00
		(10" flexidisc with cardboard "magic cube")			
Everlast 201	(M)	Our Best To You	196?	80.00	200.00
Excello LP-8001	(M)	Tunes To Be Remembered	1960	60.00	150.00
Excello LPS-8011	(M)	The Real Blues	1969	10.00	25.00
Excello LPS-8021	(M)	Blues Live In Baton Rouge	1971	10.00	25.00
Excello LPS-8025	(M)	The Excello Story (2 LPs)	1972	10.00	25.00
Famous 501	(M)	Rockin' Slumber Party	196?	12.00	30.00
Fanfare FM-101	(M)	Memories Of Garner State Park	196?	14.00	35.00
Felsted FAJ-7503	(M)	Night At The Boulevard	196?	40.00	100.00
Fillmore 31390	(S)	Last Days Of The Fillmore	1972	20.00	50.00
		(3 LP box with poster, booklet, bonus single and a ticket to the final show. Price is for the box with all of the inserts.)			
Fire FLP-100	(M)	Here Are The Hits	196?	250.00	500.00
		— Fire albums above have white & red labels.—			
Fire FLP-100	(M)	Memory Lane Hits By The Original Groups	196?	150.00	300.00
		— Fire albums above have red & black labels.—			
Flip 1001	(M)	Twelve Flip Hits	196?	150.00	350.00
Flip 1002	(M)	Original Recordings By The Artists Who Made Them Hits	196?	250.00	500.00
Fontana MGF-27570	(M)	England's Greatest Hits (With poster)	1967	20.00	50.00
Fontana MGF-27570	(M)	England's Greatest Hits (Without poster)	1967	14.00	35.00
Fontana SRF-67570	(E)	England's Greatest Hits (With poster)	1967	16.00	40.00
Fontana SRF-67570	(E)	England's Greatest Hits (Without poster)	1967	10.00	25.00
Fortune 8011	(M)	Treasure Chest Of Musty Dusties, Vol. 1	196?	30.00	75.00
Fortune 8016	(M)	From The Beginning To Now	196?	30.00	75.00
Fortune 8017	(M)	Treasure Chest Of Musty Dusties, Vol. 2	196?	30.00	75.00
		— Fortune albums above have blue labels on thick vinyl.—			
Forum F-9103	(M)	12 Million Sellers, Vol. 1	196?	4.00	10.00
Forum FS-9103	(M)	12 Million Sellers, Vol. 2	196?	4.00	10.00
Forum F-9111	(M)	Command Performance With The Greatest, Vol. 1	196?	4.00	10.00
Forum FS-9111	(M)	Command Performance With The Greatest, Vol. 2	196?	4.00	10.00
G.S.P. 6901	(M)	Beach Party	196?	40.00	100.00
Garrett 201	(M)	Big Hits Of Mid-America	1968	30.00	75.00
		(Garrett 201 is the same album as Soma 1245.)			
Gateway 9004	(M)	1964 In Review	1965	16.00	40.00
Gee GLP-702	(M)	Teenage Party	1958	80.00	200.00
		— Gee albums above have red labels.—			
Gee GLP-702	(M)	Teenage Party	196?	30.00	75.00
		— Gee albums above have gray labels.—			
Golden Era 123	(M)	Golden Era (3 LPs)	196?	20.00	50.00
Goodman Group PRO-1	(DJ)	Just Let Me Hear Some Of That Rock 'N' Roll Music	1979	16.00	40.00
Goodman Group PRO-?	(DJ)	Let It Rock (4 LPs)	1985	16.00	40.00
Gordy GS-935	(S)	Motown's Winner's Circle, Volume 1	1969	10.00	25.00
Gordy GS-936	(S)	Motown's Winner's Circle, Volume 2	1969	10.00	25.00
Gordy GS-943	(S)	Motown's Winner's Circle, Volume 3	1969	10.00	25.00
Gordy GS-946	(S)	Motown's Winner's Circle, Volume 4	1969	10.00	25.00
Gordy GS-950	(S)	Motown's Winner's Circle, Volume 5	1970	10.00	25.00
Grand Award 33-343	(M)	Rock & Roll	196?	8.00	20.00

Label & Catalog #		Title	Year	VG+	NM
Grand Prix K-431	(M)	The Greatest R&B Singing Groups	196?	10.00	25.00
Grand Prix KS-431	(E)	The Greatest R&B Singing Groups	196?	8.00	20.00
Grant GLP-3001	(M)	Original 13 Hits, Volume 1	196?	12.00	30.00
		(Grant 3001 is a collection of Dot material sold at W.T. Grant stores.)			
Guest Star 1GS-406	(M)	Rock & Roll Party	1964	8.00	20.00
Guest Star 1GS-406	(E)	Rock & Roll Party	1964	4.00	10.00
Guest Star GS-1432	(M)	Earth Angel	1964	8.00	20.00
Guest Star GS-1432	(E)	Earth Angel	1964	4.00	10.00
Guest Star GS- 1433	(M)	Surf Kings	1964	12.00	30.00
Guest Star GS- 1433	(E)	Surf Kings	1964	6.00	15.00
Guest Star GS-1474	(M)	Ten Million Sellers	1964	8.00	20.00
Guest Star GSS-1474	(E)	Ten Million Sellers	1964	4.00	10.00
Guest Star 1900	(M)	Rhythm & Blues	1965	8.00	20.00
Guest Star 1904	(M)	Shake A Hand	1965	6.00	15.00
Guest Star 1905	(M)	Let The Good Times Roll	1965	6.00	15.00
Guest Star 1906	(M)	Greatest Rhythm & Blues Stars	1965	6.00	15.00
Hammer 5007	(M)	Daddy 'O Presents Two Dozen Oldies	196?	30.00	75.00
Happy Tiger 1017	(P)	Early Chicago	1969	20.00	50.00
Harmony HS-30023	(S)	Chartbusters	1981	30.00	75.00
		(Includes both sides of Neil Diamond's first single, "Clown Town" and "I've Never Been The Same," in stereo.)			
Harvest SPRO-8795/6	(DJ)	Harvest Sampler	1978	4.00	10.00
Herald HLP-1010	(M)	Herald Of The Beat	1960	150.00	300.00
		—Herald albums above have black labels.—			
Herald HLP-1010	(M)	Herald Of The Beat	1960	60.00	150.00
Herald HLP-1015	(M)	Pot Of Golden Goodies	1960	60.00	150.00
		—Herald albums above have yellow labels.—			
Hi SHL-32049	(S)	The Greatest Hits From Memphis	1968	6.00	15.00
Hi SHLD-1	(DJ)	Hi Records Special DJ LP	1969	6.00	15.00
Hickory LP-154	(M)	Treasure Album	196?	10.00	25.00
Hickory LPS-154	(S)	Treasure Album	196?	20.00	50.00
		(LPS-154 contains several songs in stereo that are otherwise hard to find, including The Newbeats' "Bread And Butter.")			
Hitbound HR-1001	(S)	Rock 'N Roll City *(Promo only)*	1983	30.00	75.00
Hitbound HB-1003	(S)	Scrooges Rock & Roll Christmas	1983	6.00	15.00
Hitbound HB-1003	(S)	Scrooges Christmas Party	1983	6.00	15.00
Hitbound PL-1083	(S)	Rock 'N' Roll Again	1983	4.00	10.00
Hollywood 30	(M)	Rhythm & Blues In The Night	1957	400.00	750.00
Hollywood 31	(M)	18 Rock 'N' Roll Hits	1957	250.00	500.00
Hollywood 40	(M)	Red, Hot & Cool	1958	250.00	500.00
Hollywood 501	(M)	Merry Christmas, Baby	195?	200.00	400.00
Hollywood 503	(M)	R&B Hits	195?	150.00	300.00
Hot Wax 710	(S)	Hot Wax Greatest Hits	1972	6.00	15.00
Hull 1002	(M)	Your Favorite Singing Groups	195?	1,000.00	1,500.00
I.G.L. 103	(M)	Roof Garden Jamboree	1967	40.00	200.00
Impact LP-2	(M)	Shake, Shout And Soul	196?	40.00	200.00
Imperial LP-9084	(M)	Hitsville U.S.A., Volume 1	1960	16.00	40.00
Imperial LP-9099	(M)	Hitsville U.S.A., Volume 2	1960	16.00	40.00
Imperial LP-9230	(M)	Solid Gold Hits	1964	10.00	25.00
Imperial LP-9257	(M)	Best Of The Blues, Volume 1	1964	10.00	25.00
Imperial LP-12257	(E)	Best Of The Blues, Volume 1	1964	8.00	20.00
Imperial LP-9259	(M)	Best Of The Blues, Volume 2	1964	10.00	25.00
Imperial LP-12259	(E)	Best Of The Blues, Volume 2	1964	8.00	20.00
Imperial LP-9260	(M)	New Orleans, Our Home Town	1964	10.00	25.00
Imperial LP-12260	(E)	New Orleans, Our Home Town	1964	8.00	20.00
Imperial LP-9271	(M)	Giant Instrumental R&B Hits	1964	10.00	25.00
Imperial LP-12271	(E)	Giant Instrumental R&B Hits	1964	8.00	20.00
		—Original Imperial mono albums above have black labels with stars on top; stereo albums have black labels with silver print.—			
Imperial MM-423	(DJ)	Special Programmer Selection From 1965	1965	10.00	25.00
Imperial LM-94002	(M)	Blues Uptown	1968	6.00	15.00
Imperial LM-94003	(M)	The End Of An Era	1968	6.00	15.00

Label & Catalog #		Title	Year	VG+	NM
Imperial LM-94004	(M)	New Orleans Bounce	1968	6.00	15.00
Imperial LM-94005	(M)	Sweet And Greasy	1968	6.00	15.00
Imperial LM-94005	(M)	Rural Blues Down Home Stomp	1968	6.00	15.00
Increase LP-2000	(M)	Cruisin' 1955	1970	5.00	12.00
Increase LP-2001	(M)	Cruisin' 1956	1970	5.00	12.00
Increase LP-2002	(M)	Cruisin' 1957	1970	5.00	12.00
Increase LP-2003	(M)	Cruisin' 1958	1970	5.00	12.00
Increase LP-2004	(M)	Cruisin' 1959	1970	5.00	12.00
Increase LP-2005	(M)	Cruisin' 1960	1970	5.00	12.00
Increase LP-2006	(M)	Cruisin' 1961	1970	5.00	12.00
Increase LP-2007	(M)	Cruisin' 1962	1970	5.00	12.00
Increase LP-2008	(M)	Cruisin' 1963	1973	5.00	12.00
Increase LP-2009	(M)	Cruisin' 1964	1973	5.00	12.00
Increase LP-2010	(M)	Cruisin' 1965	1973	5.00	12.00
Increase LP-2011	(M)	Cruisin' 1966	1973	5.00	12.00
Increase LP-2012	(M)	Cruisin' 1967	1973	5.00	12.00
Increase	(DJ)	Cruisin' (Radio sampler)	1973	8.00	20.00

(Original pressings are copyrighted 1970 or 1973 on the back cover and each album was centered around the presentation of a popular disc jockey of the album's period; later reissues drop this format.)

Instant 71000	(M)	All These Things	196?	16.00	40.00
International Art. 13	(S)	Epitaph For A Legend (2 LPs)	1979	20.00	50.00
Island HELP-15	(S)	Soul Of Jamaica	1973	4.00	10.00
Island ILPS-9251	(S)	This Is Reggae Music, Vol. 1	1974	4.00	10.00
Island IXP-5	(S)	The Now Sound Reggae	1975	4.00	10.00
Island ILPS-7	(S)	Catch This Beat-The Rock Steady Years 66/68	1975	4.00	10.00
Island IRSP-1	(S)	One Big Happy Family	1980	3.20	8.00
Jamie JLPM-3017	(M)	The Sounds Of Success	1961	10.00	25.00
Jamie JLPS-3017	(S)	The Sounds Of Success	1961	12.00	30.00
Jamie JLPM-3031	(M)	Old 'N Golden	1964	10.00	25.00
Jamie JLPS-3031	(E)	Old 'N Golden	1964	8.00	20.00
JAS JAS-5001	(P)	San Francisco Roots (Photo cover)	1976	20.00	50.00
JAS JAS-5001	(P)	San Francisco Roots (Titles cover)	197?	10.00	25.00

(JAS 5001 is a reissue of Vault 119.)

Jerden JRL-7001	(M)	Original Great Northwest Hits, Volume 1	1965	20.00	50.00
Jerden JRL-7002	(M)	Original Great Northwest Hits, Volume 2	1965	20.00	50.00
Jerden JRL-7005	(M)	Hitmakers	1966	20.00	50.00
Jin 4002	(M)	Rockin' Date With The South Louisiana Stars	196?	16.00	40.00
Jin 4002	(M)	South Louisiana Juke Box Hits	196?	16.00	40.00
Jin 9001	(M)	Golden Dozen Hits	196?	16.00	40.00
Jobete PRO-1	(DJ)	The Top 10 Story In Sound	1972	16.00	40.00
Jobete PRO-2	(DJ)	The Songs Of Smokey Robinson (#1)	1972	16.00	40.00
Jobete PRO-2	(DJ)	The Songs Of Smokey Robinson (#2)	1972	16.00	40.00

(There are two different versions of PRO-2 with the same title.)

Jobete PRO-3	(DJ)	The Songs Of Ashford & Simpson	1974	16.00	40.00
Jobete PRO-4	(DJ)	The Songs Of Holland-Dozier-Holland	1974	16.00	40.00
Jobete PRO-5	(DJ)	The Songs Of Stevie Wonder	1974	16.00	40.00
Jobete PRO-6	(DJ)	The Songs Of Marvin Gaye	1974	16.00	40.00
Jobete PRO-7	(DJ)	The Songs Of Norman Whitfield	1976	16.00	40.00
Jobete PRO-8	(DJ)	The Songs Of Johnny Bristol / Frank Wilson / Mickey Stevenson / Freddie Perren	1977	16.00	40.00
Jobete PRO-9	(DJ)	Holland-Dozier-Holland: Yesterday, Today & Forever (3 LPs)	1977	20.00	50.00
Jobete PRO-10	(DJ)	Pure Magic: The Songs Of Pam Sawyer & Marilyn McLeod	1978	16.00	40.00
Josie JOZ-4002	(M)	Original Goldies From The Fabulous '50's, Vol. 1	1962	30.00	75.00
Josie JOZ-4003	(M)	Original Goldies From The Fabulous '50's, Vol. 2	1962	30.00	75.00
Josie JOZ-4009	(M)	Rumble	1963	60.00	150.00
Jubilee J-1014	(M)	The Best of Rhythm And Blues (Red vinyl)	1957	200.00	400.00
Jubilee J-1014	(M)	The Best of Rhythm And Blues	1957	80.00	200.00

—Jubilee albums above have blue labels.—

Jubilee J-1014	(M)	The Best of Rhythm And Blues	1957	60.00	150.00
Jubilee J-1107	(M)	Surprise Party (Vol. 1)	196?	60.00	150.00
Jubilee J-1114	(M)	Rumble	1960	60.00	150.00
Jubilee J-1118	(M)	Boppin'	1960	60.00	150.00
Jubilee J-1119	(M)	Whoppers	1960	60.00	150.00

—Jubilee albums above have black labels with a silver logo on top.—

Label & Catalog #		Title	Year	VG+	NM
Jubilee J-1014	(M)	The Best of Rhythm And Blues	196?	20.00	50.00
Jubilee J-1107	(M)	Surprise Party (Vol. 1)	196?	20.00	50.00
Jubilee J-1114	(M)	Rumble	196?	20.00	50.00
Jubilee J-1118	(M)	Boppin'	196?	20.00	50.00
Jubilee J-1119	(M)	Whoppers	196?	20.00	50.00
—Jubilee albums above have black labels with a multicolor logo on top.—					
Jubilee J-8019	(S)	Super Golden Hits	1968	60.00	150.00
Kama Sutra KLPS-2015	(S)	Rock 'N' Roll Revival	1970	6.00	15.00
KATS Karavan LP-100	(M)	Old Favorites	1960	40.00	100.00
Kent KST-9002	(M)	Memphis Blues	197?	6.00	15.00
Kent KST-9004	(M)	Blues From The Deep South	197?	6.00	15.00
KFM 1001	(M)	Live From The Brooklyn Fox	1962	20.00	50.00
King 513	(M)	All Star Rock And Roll Revue	1958	200.00	500.00
King 528	(M)	After Hours	1958	250.00	600.00
King 536	(M)	Rock & Roll Dance Party	1958	200.00	500.00
King 607	(M)	Battle Of The Blues Vol. 1: Refer to Roy Brown / Wynonie Harris			
King 627	(M)	Battle Of The Blues Vol. 2: Refer to Roy Brown / Wynonie Harris			
King 634	(M)	Battle Of The Blues Vol. 3: Refer to Jimmy Witherspoon / Eddie Vinson			
King 638	(M)	Rock & Roll Revue	1959	80.00	200.00
		(King 638 is a reissue of 513.)			
King 654	(M)	Rock & Roll Revue, Volume 2	1959	80.00	200.00
King 668	(M)	Battle Of The Blues, Vol. 4: Refer to Roy Brown / Wynonie Harris			
King 680	(M)	Merry Christmas	1959	80.00	200.00
King 725	(M)	25 Years Of Rhythm And Blues Hits	1960	40.00	100.00
King 737	(M)	Hit Makers And Record Breakers	1960	40.00	100.00
King 745	(M)	Solo Spotlights	1961	40.00	100.00
King 749	(M)	25 Years Of R&B Hits	1961	40.00	100.00
King 753	(M)	Bumper Crop Of All Stars	1961	40.00	100.00
King 792	(M)	Forgotten Million Sellers	1962	40.00	100.00
King 819	(M)	A Carnival Of Songs	1963	40.00	100.00
King 855	(M)	Surfin' On Wave Nine	1963	30.00	75.00
King 859	(M)	Turning Back The Clock Blue	1963	30.00	75.00
King 875	(M)	Everybody's Favorite Blues	1964	30.00	75.00
King 882	(M)	Look Who's Surfin' Now	1964	30.00	75.00
King 884	(M)	Top R&B Artists Sing Country	1964	60.00	150.00
King 893	(M)	14 Hit Flashbacks From The Group Era	1964	30.00	75.00
—King albums above have crownless black labels; stereo albums have crownless blue labels.—					
King K-1004	(M)	25 Years Of R&B Hits	1966	16.00	40.00
King KS-1026	(M)	18 All Time R&B Hits	1968	16.00	40.00
King KS-1050	(E)	Radar Blues	1969	12.00	30.00
—King albums above have black mono and blue stereo labels with a crown on top.—					
King KS-1133	(S)	Risky Blues	1971	6.00	15.00
King 16001	(E)	Old King Gold, Volume 1	1975	1.00	5.00
King 16002	(E)	Old King Gold, Volume 2	1975	1.00	5.00
King 16003	(E)	Old King Gold, Volume 3	1975	1.00	5.00
King 16004	(E)	Old King Gold, Volume 4	1975	1.00	5.00
King 16005	(E)	Old King Gold, Volume 5	1975	1.00	5.00
King 16006	(E)	Old King Gold, Volume 6	1975	1.00	5.00
King 16007	(E)	Old King Gold, Volume 7	1975	1.00	5.00
King 16008	(E)	Old King Gold, Volume 8	1975	1.00	5.00
King 16009	(E)	Old King Gold, Volume 9	1975	1.00	5.00
King 16010	(E)	Old King Gold, Volume 10	1975	1.00	5.00
King 5016	(M)	The King-Federal Rockabillys	197?	1.00	5.00
King 5017	(M)	The Starday-Dixie Rockabillys	197?	1.00	5.00
King 5018	(M)	Merry Christmas Baby	197?	1.00	5.00
King 5031	(M)	Starday-Dixie Rockabillys, Volume 2	197?	1.00	5.00
King 5032	(M)	Moanin' And Stompin'	197?	1.00	5.00
KRUX K-1360	(M)	Flashback	1963	40.00	100.00
Laurie LLP-2010	(M)	Great Groups Great Records	1961	10.00	25.00
Laurie LLP-2014	(M)	Greatest Golden Goodies	1963	10.00	25.00
Laurie LLP-2021	(M)	Pick Hits Of The Radio Good Guys	1963	10.00	25.00
Laurie SLP-2021	(E)	Pick Hits Of The Radio Good Guys	1963	10.00	25.00
Laurie LLP-2026	(M)	Pick Hits Of The Radio Good Guys, Vol. 2	1964	10.00	25.00
Laurie LLP-2028	(M)	Radio Smash Flashbacks/Drive Time	1965	10.00	25.00
Laurie LLP-2029	(M)	Radio Smash Flashbacks/Prime Time	1965	10.00	25.00
Laurie LLP-2041	(M)	Laurie Golden Goodies	1967	6.00	15.00
Laurie SLLP-2041	(P)	Laurie Golden Goodies	1967	10.00	25.00
Laurie LLP-2044	(M)	Rock & Roll: Evolution Or Revolution?	1968	6.00	15.00
Laurie LLP-2051	(M)	Collector's Records Of The '50's And '60's	1970	4.00	10.00
Laurie LES-4003	(S)	The Best Of Laurie	197?	1.00	5.00
Leader LEE-4057	(S)	Far Canadian Fields	1973	6.00	15.00

Label & Catalog #		Title	Year	VG+	NM
Liberty LRP-5503	(M)	Teensville	1962	16.00	40.00
Liberty LRP-5505	(M)	Golden Teen Hits	1962	16.00	40.00
Liberty MM-412	(DJ)	Explosive!	1962	20.00	50.00
Liberty MM-417	(DJ)	Spin Time With Liberty	1962	20.00	50.00
Liberty LRP-3048	(M)	Hot Rod Rumble	1957	14.00	35.00
Liberty LRP-3178	(M)	Original Hits, Volume 1	1961	8.00	20.00
Liberty LST-7178	(P)	Original Hits, Volume 1	1961	10.00	25.00
Liberty LRP-3180	(M)	Original Hits, Volume 2	1961	8.00	20.00
Liberty LST-7180	(P)	Original Hits, Volume 2	1961	10.00	25.00
Liberty LRP-3187	(M)	Original Hits, Volume 3	1961	8.00	20.00
Liberty LST-7187	(P)	Original Hits, Volume 3	1961	10.00	25.00
Liberty LRP-3200	(M)	Original Hits, Volume 4	1962	8.00	20.00
Liberty LST-7200	(P)	Original Hits, Volume 4	1962	10.00	25.00
Liberty LRP-3223	(M)	Fabulous Favorites Of Our Time	1962	5.00	12.00
Liberty LST-7223	(S)	Fabulous Favorites Of Our Time	1962	6.00	15.00
Liberty LRP-3235	(M)	Original Hits, Volume 5	1962	8.00	20.00
Liberty LST-7235	(P)	Original Hits, Volume 5	1962	10.00	25.00
Liberty LRP-3260	(M)	Original Hits, Volume 6	1962	6.00	15.00
Liberty LST-7260	(P)	Original Hits, Volume 6	1962	8.00	20.00
Liberty LRP-3274	(M)	Original Hits, Volume 7	1962	6.00	15.00
Liberty LST-7274	(P)	Original Hits, Volume 7	1962	8.00	20.00
Liberty LRP-3288	(M)	Original Hits, Volume 8	1963	6.00	15.00
Liberty LST-7288	(P)	Original Hits, Volume 8	1963	8.00	20.00
Liberty LRP-3325	(M)	Original Hits, Volume 9	1963	6.00	15.00
Liberty LST-7325	(P)	Original Hits, Volume 9	1963	8.00	20.00
Liberty LRP-3344	(M)	Original Hits, Volume 10	1964	6.00	15.00
Liberty LST-7344	(P)	Original Hits, Volume 10	1964	8.00	20.00
Liberty LRP-3366	(M)	Shut Downs And Hill Climbs	1964	16.00	40.00
Liberty LST-7366	(P)	Shut Downs And Hill Climbs	1964	20.00	50.00
Liberty LRP-3381	(M)	Original Rhythm & Blues Hits, Vol. 1	1964	8.00	20.00
Liberty LST-7381	(P)	Original Rhythm & Blues Hits, Vol. 1	1964	6.00	15.00
Liberty LRP-3418	(M)	#1 Hits, Volume 11	1964	6.00	15.00
Liberty LST-7418	(P)	#1 Hits, Volume 11	1964	8.00	20.00
Liberty LRP-3500	(M)	The Original Golden Greats	1967	6.00	15.00
Liberty LST-7500	(S)	The Original Golden Greats	1967	6.00	15.00
Liberty OKWB-63-1	(M)	KOWB Disc Coveries	1963	8.00	20.00
LJR 114	(M)	Sing A Song For A Souvenir	196?	60.00	150.00
London LL-3034	(M)	Music For Hand-Jiving	196?	6.00	15.00
London LL-3430	(M)	England's Greatest Hitmakers (White label promo)	1964	150.00	300.00
London LL-3430	(M)	England's Greatest Hitmakers	1964	40.00	100.00
London PS-430	(E)	England's Greatest Hitmakers	1964	40.00	100.00

— London albums above have maroon or dark blue labels with "Made in England by the Decca Record Co. Ltd"
at the very top with the "London/ffrr" logo beneath.—

London LL-3430	(M)	England's Greatest Hitmakers	1964	16.00	40.00
London PS-430	(E)	England's Greatest Hitmakers	1964	8.00	20.00

— London mono albums above have maroon labels with a silver "London" on top;
stereo albums above have deep blue labels with a silver "London" on top.—

Lost-Nite LP-10?	(M)	Jerry Blavat Presents For Lovers Only, Volume 1	1965	12.00	30.00
Lost-Nite LP-105	(M)	Jerry Blavat Presents For Teenagers Only	1965	12.00	30.00
Lost-Nite LP-107	(M)	Jerry Blavat Presents For Lovers Only, Volume 2	1965	12.00	30.00
Lost-Nite LP-114	(M)	Gary Stevens' 22 Good Guy Oldies	1965	12.00	30.00
Lost-Nite LP-119	(M)	Gary Stevens, Volume 2	1965	12.00	30.00
Lost-Nite LP-130	(M)	WIXY's Super Oldie Hits Of The Past, Volume 1	1965	12.00	30.00
Magna 71014	(M)	Northland Battle Of The Bands	1967	360.00	600.00
Mainstream 56100	(M)	A Pot Of Flowers	1967	30.00	75.00
Mainstream S-6100	(S)	A Pot Of Flowers	1967	40.00	100.00
Mercury MG-20493	(M)	14 Newies But Goodies	1960	10.00	25.00
Mercury SR-60172	(S)	14 Newies But Goodies	1960	12.00	30.00
Mercury MG-20511	(M)	Golden Goodies	1960	10.00	25.00
Mercury SR-60217	(S)	Golden Goodies	1960	12.00	30.00
Mercury MG-20581	(M)	14 More Newies But Goodies	1960	10.00	25.00
Mercury SR-60241	(S)	14 More Newies But Goodies	1960	14.00	35.00
Mercury MG-20583	(M)	More Golden Goodies	1960	10.00	25.00
Mercury SR-60249	(S)	More Golden Goodies	1960	14.00	35.00
Mercury MG-20651	(M)	Chart Winners	1962	10.00	25.00
Mercury SR-60651	(S)	Chart Winners	1962	14.00	35.00
Mercury MG-20687	(M)	Twist With The Stars	1962	10.00	25.00
Mercury SR-60687	(S)	Twist With The Stars	1962	12.00	30.00
Mercury MG-20809	(M)	Original Golden Hits Of The Great Groups	1963	12.00	30.00
Mercury SR-60809	(S)	Original Golden Hits Of The Great Groups	1963	12.00	30.00
Mercury MG-20826	(M)	The Great Blues Singers	1964	10.00	25.00
Mercury SR-60826	(S)	The Great Blues Singers	1964	12.00	30.00

Label & Catalog #		Title	Year	VG+	NM
Mercury MGH-25000	(M)	Original Golden Hits Of The Great Groups, Vol. II	1964	8.00	20.00
Mercury MGH-25001	(M)	Original Golden Instrumental Hits, Vol. I	1964	8.00	20.00
Mercury MGH-25002	(M)	Original Golden Hits Of The Great Blues Singers, Vol. II	1964	8.00	20.00
Mercury MGH-25003	(M)	Original Golden Hits Of The Great Blues Singers, Vol. III	1964	8.00	20.00
Mercury MGH-25004	(M)	Original Golden Teen Hits, Vol. I	1964	8.00	20.00
Mercury MGH-25005	(M)	Original Golden Hits, Vol. II	1964	8.00	20.00
Mercury MGH-25006	(M)	Original Golden Rhythm & Blues Hits, Vol. I	1964	8.00	20.00
Mercury MGH-25007	(M)	Original Golden Hits Of The Great Groups, Vol. III	1964	8.00	20.00
Mercury MGH-25009	(M)	Original Golden Teen Hits, Vol. III	1964	8.00	20.00
Mercury MGH-25010	(M)	Original Golden Hits Of The Great Groups, Vol. IV	1964	8.00	20.00
Mercury MGH-25011	(M)	Original Golden Hits Of The Great Blues Singers, Vol. IV	1964	8.00	20.00
Mercury SR-42041	(M)	Alan Freed's Memory Lane	197?	4.00	10.00
Mercury MK2-2-121	(DJ)	The Ultimate Radio Bootleg, Vol. 3	1976	10.00	25.00
Metro 563		This Is Where It Started: *Refer to* The Beatles			
Metro M-577	(M)	Mickie Most Presents English In-Groups	1965	5.00	12.00
Metro MS-577	(P)	Mickie Most Presents English In-Groups	1965	6.00	15.00
MGM E-3826	(M)	MGM Hits With A Beat	1963	8.00	20.00
MGM SE-3826	(P)	MGM Hits With A Beat	1963	10.00	25.00
MGM E-4306	(M)	Mickie Most Presents British Go-Go	1964	4.00	10.00
MGM SE-4306	(S)	Mickie Most Presents British Go-Go	1964	6.00	15.00
MGM E-4312	(M)	Solid Gold	1965	8.00	20.00
MGM SE-4312	(P)	Solid Gold	1965	8.00	20.00
MGM SNP-90569	(P)	Parade Of Stars *(Capitol Record Club)*	1965	8.00	20.00
MGM E-4352	(M)	Solid Gold	1966	6.00	15.00
MGM SE-4352	(S)	Solid Gold	1966	8.00	20.00
MGM SE-4669	(P)	The Core Of Rock	197?	5.00	12.00
MGM SE-4718	(P)	The Core Of Rock, Volume 2	197?	4.00	10.00
MGM ADV-1	(DJ)	MGM—Verve—Verve/Forecast Radio Commercials	1967	300.00	600.00
		(Promo with radio spots for The Mothers Of Invention, Tim Hardin, Nico, Sam The Sham and others issued without a cover.)			
Minit LP-0001	(M)	New Orleans: Home Of The Blues	1961	20.00	50.00
Minit LP-0003	(M)	We Sing The Blues	1962	20.00	50.00
Minit LP-0004	(M)	New Orleans: Home Of The Blues, Volume 2	1962	20.00	50.00
Modern 2001	(10")	Modern Records, Volume 1	1951	350.00	750.00
Modern 2002	(10")	Modern Records, Volume 2	1951	350.00	750.00
Modern 2003	(10")	Modern Records, Volume 3	1951	350.00	750.00
Modern LMP-1210	(M)	Rock & Roll Dance Party	195?	200.00	400.00
Modern LMP-1211	(M)	Rock & Roll Record Hop	195?	200.00	400.00
Modern Sound M-540	(M)	Discotheque A Go Go	196?	5.00	12.00
Modern Sound MS-540	(S)	Discotheque A Go Go	196?	6.00	15.00
Modern Sound M-1006	(M)	Tiger In My Tank	196?	5.00	12.00
Monument MLP-8010	(M)	Demand Performances	1963	10.00	25.00
Monument SLP-18010	(S)	Demand Performances	1963	12.00	30.00
Monument SLP-18096	(S)	Monumental Pop Hits	1968	10.00	25.00
Motown MLP-603	(M)	Motown Hits, Volume 1	1962	30.00	75.00
Motown MLP-609	(M)	Recorded Live At The Apollo: The Motortown Revue, Volume 1	1963	30.00	75.00
Motown MLP-614	(M)	A Package Of 16 Big Hits	1963	40.00	100.00
		(Original covers have a postal package motif.)			
Motown MLP-614	(M)	16 Original Big Hits, Volume 1	1967	8.00	20.00
Motown MS-614	(P)	16 Original Big Hits, Volume 1	1967	12.00	30.00
		(Later pressings have the standard "Big Hits" style cover.)			
Motown MLP-615	(M)	Recorded Live: The Motortown Revue, Vol. 2	1964	12.00	30.00
Motown MLP-624	(M)	16 Original Big Hits, Volume 3	1964	8.00	20.00
Motown MS-624	(S)	16 Original Big Hits, Volume 3	1964	10.00	25.00
Motown MLP-633	(M)	16 Original Big Hits, Volume 4	1965	8.00	20.00
Motown MS-633	(S)	16 Original Big Hits, Volume 4	1965	10.00	25.00
Motown M-642	(M)	In Loving Memory	1968	80.00	200.00
Motown MS-642	(S)	In Loving Memory	1968	80.00	200.00
		(Original pressings do not list the song titles on the cover.)			
Motown M-642	(M)	In Loving Memory	1968	60.00	150.00
Motown MS-642	(S)	In Loving Memory	1968	60.00	150.00
		(Second pressings list the song titles on the cover.)			
Motown M-642	(DJ)	In Loving Memory	1969	See note below	
		(This special edition has a custom label for the Loucye Gordy Wakefield Scholarship Fund with a silver gatefold cover. This was given to attendees of the October 4, 1969 Sterling Ball at Gordy Manor. Very rare with no transactions from which to suggest a value.)			

Label & Catalog #		Title	Year	VG+	NM
Motown M-651	(M)	16 Original Big Hits, Volume 5	1967	12.00	30.00
Motown MS-651	(S)	16 Original Big Hits, Volume 5	1967	6.00	15.00
Motown M-655	(M)	16 Original Big Hits, Volume 6	1967	12.00	30.00
Motown MS-655	(S)	16 Original Big Hits, Volume 6	1967	6.00	15.00
Motown M-661	(M)	16 Original Big Hits, Volume 7	1967	12.00	30.00
Motown MS-661	(S)	16 Original Big Hits, Volume 7	1967	6.00	15.00
Motown M-666	(M)	16 Original Big Hits, Volume 8	1967	12.00	30.00
Motown MS-666	(S)	16 Original Big Hits, Volume 8	1967	6.00	15.00
Motown M-668	(M)	16 Original Big Hits, Volume 9	1968	16.00	40.00
Motown MS-668	(S)	16 Original Big Hits, Volume 9	1968	6.00	15.00
Motown MS-681	(M)	Merry Christmas From Motown	1968	12.00	30.00
Motown MS-684	(S)	16 Original Big Hits, Volume 10	1969	6.00	15.00
Motown MS-688	(S)	The Motortown Revue Recorded Live!	1969	10.00	25.00
		— Original Motown albums above have a Detroit, MI, address on the label.—			
Motown MS-693	(S)	16 Original Big Hits, Volume 11	1969	4.00	10.00
Motown MS-701	(S)	Shades Of Gospel Soul	1970	4.00	10.00
Motown MS-703	(S)	Motown At The Hollywood Palace	1970	4.00	10.00
Motown MS-707	(S)	Motown Chartbusters, Volume 1	1970	4.00	10.00
Motown MS-715	(S)	Motown Chartbusters, Volume 2	1970	4.00	10.00
Motown MS-725	(S)	Christmas Gift Wrap (Re-issue of #681)	1970	4.00	10.00
Motown MS-5-726	(S)	The Motown Story (5 LPs)	1971	10.00	25.00
Motown MS-727	(S)	The Motown Story, Volume 1	1971	4.00	10.00
Motown MS-728	(S)	The Motown Story, Volume 2	1971	4.00	10.00
Motown MS-729	(S)	The Motown Story, Volume 3	1971	4.00	10.00
Motown MS-730	(S)	The Motown Story, Volume 4	1971	4.00	10.00
Motown MS-731	(S)	The Motown Story, Volume 5	1971	4.00	10.00
Motown MS-732	(S)	Motown Chartbusters, Volume 3	1971	4.00	10.00
Motown MS-734	(S)	Motown Chartbusters, Volume 4	1971	4.00	10.00
Motown M-739L	(DJ)	1971 Sterling Ball Benefit	1971	100.00	250.00
		(Issued in a custom silver gatefold cover with information on the Benefit.)			
Motown PR-121	(DJ)	The Motown Story (Boxed set)	1983	100.00	250.00
		(Motown 122 is a promotional boxed set of seven white label albums designated PR-121 A/B, C/D, E/F, G/H, I/J, K/L/ and M/N.)			
Motown PR-122	(DJ)	Moments Of Motown	1983	20.00	50.00
Moulty MLP-101	(M)	New England Teen Scene	198?	20.00	50.00
Moulty MLP-103	(M)	New England Teen Scene, Vol. 2	198?	8.00	20.00
Mt. Vernon MUM-109	(M)	Hitsville	196?	12.00	30.00
Muse 500	(M)	Carload Of Hits	196?	80.00	200.00
Musictone M-7001	(M)	Golden Memories Of The Past	196?	40.00	100.00
N.A.P.R.A.	(S)	Get Off	1973	6.00	15.00
N.A.P.R.A.	(S)	Get Off It (Get Off II)	1975	6.00	15.00
Northridge NM-101	(M)	Surf's Up! At Banzai Pipeline	1963	80.00	200.00
Old Town LP-101	(M)	Your Old Favorites On The Old Town	1962	80.00	200.00
		(Old Town 101 was reissued as Cotillion 9032.)			
Oldies-33 OL-8001	(M)	Oldies Dance Party, Volume 1	1963	8.00	20.00
Oldies-33 OL-8002	(M)	Oldies Dance Party, Volume 2	1964	8.00	20.00
Oldies-33 OL-8003	(M)	Oldies Dance Party, Volume 3	1964	10.00	25.00
Oldies-33 OL-8004	(M)	Great Boy Oldies	1964	10.00	25.00
Oldies-33 OL-8005	(M)	Soulful Oldies	1964	10.00	25.00
Oldies-33 OL-8007	(M)	D'oes Crazy Oldies	1964	10.00	25.00
Original Sound LPM-5001	(M)	Oldies But Goodies	1959	16.00	40.00
Original Sound LPM-5002	(M)	Oldies But Goodies, Volume 2	1960	16.00	40.00
Original Sound LPM-5003	(M)	Oldies But Goodies, Volume 3	196?	16.00	40.00
Original Sound LPM-5004	(M)	Oldies But Goodies, Volume 4	196?	16.00	40.00
Original Sound LPM-5005	(M)	Oldies But Goodies, Volume 5	196?	16.00	40.00
Original Sound LPM-5006	(M)	Oldies But Goodies, Volume 6	196?	16.00	40.00
Original Sound LPM-5007	(M)	Oldies But Goodies, Volume 7	196?	16.00	40.00
Original Sound LPM-5008	(M)	Oldies But Goodies, Volume 8	196?	16.00	40.00
Original Sound LPM-5009	(M)	Oldies But Goodies, Volume 9	196?	16.00	40.00
Original Sound LPM-5010	(M)	Oldies But Goodies, Volume 10	196?	16.00	40.00
		(Original pressings for the "Oldies But Goodies" series have advertisements on the back cover for preceding volumes and the next volume only.)			
Original Sound LPM-5001	(M)	Oldies But Goodies	196?	4.00	10.00
Original Sound LPS-5001	(E)	Oldies But Goodies	196?	1.00	5.00
Original Sound LPM-5002	(M)	Oldies But Goodies, Volume 2	196?	4.00	10.00
Original Sound LPS-5002	(E)	Oldies But Goodies, Volume 2	196?	1.00	5.00
Original Sound LPM-5003	(M)	Oldies But Goodies, Volume 3	196?	4.00	10.00
Original Sound LPS-5003	(E)	Oldies But Goodies, Volume 3	196?	1.00	5.00

Label & Catalog #		Title	Year	VG+	NM
Original Sound LPM-5004	(M)	Oldies But Goodies, Volume 4	196?	4.00	10.00
Original Sound LPS-5004	(E)	Oldies But Goodies, Volume 4	196?	1.00	5.00
Original Sound LPM-5005	(M)	Oldies But Goodies, Volume 5	196?	4.00	10.00
Original Sound LPS-5005	(E)	Oldies But Goodies, Volume 5	196?	1.00	5.00
Original Sound LPM-5006	(M)	Oldies But Goodies, Volume 6	196?	4.00	10.00
Original Sound LPS-5006	(E)	Oldies But Goodies, Volume 6	196?	1.00	5.00
Original Sound LPM-5007	(M)	Oldies But Goodies, Volume 7	196?	4.00	10.00
Original Sound LPS-5007	(E)	Oldies But Goodies, Volume 7	196?	1.00	5.00
Original Sound LPM-5008	(M)	Oldies But Goodies, Volume 8	196?	4.00	10.00
Original Sound LPS-5008	(E)	Oldies But Goodies, Volume 8	196?	1.00	5.00
Original Sound LPM-5009	(M)	Oldies But Goodies, Volume 9	196?	4.00	10.00
Original Sound LPS-5009	(E)	Oldies But Goodies, Volume 9	196?	1.00	5.00
Original Sound LPM-5010	(M)	Oldies But Goodies, Volume 10	196?	4.00	10.00
Original Sound LPS-5010	(E)	Oldies But Goodies, Volume 10	196?	1.00	5.00
		(Later pressings, and there are many, advertise the entire line of titles.)			
Original Sound OSR-11	(S)	Rock Rock Rock	1972	20.00	50.00
Original Sound OSR-11	(M)	All Star Rock, Volume 2	1972	16.00	40.00
		("All Star Rock" is a reissue of "Rock Rock Rock.")			
Panorama 103	(S)	Battle Of The Bands	1966	12.00	30.00
Panorama 108	(S)	Battle Of The Bands, Volume 2	1966	12.00	30.00
Parade 208	(M)	Top Tune Time	196?	6.00	15.00
Parkway P-7013	(M)	All The Hits By All The Stars	1962	12.00	30.00
Parkway P-7028	(M)	Million Seller Dance Hits	1963	12.00	30.00
Parkway P-7033	(M)	All The Stars-Biggest Hits	1963	12.00	30.00
Parkway P-7034	(M)	All The Stars-Biggest Hits, Volume 2	1963	20.00	50.00
		(Both Parkway 7033 and 7034 were issued with "Pull Off Pix" of the six artists on the album. The price is for the record and the jacket with the pix intact.)			
Parkway P-7035	(M)	Everybody's Goin' Surfin'	1963	20.00	50.00
Parkway P-7037	(M)	Oldies By The Dozen	1963	12.00	30.00
Parkway P-7041	(M)	Oldies By The Dozen, Vol. II	1963	12.00	30.00
Parrot PA-61010	(M)	The Greatest Hits From England	1964	8.00	20.00
Parrot PAS-71010	(P)	The Greatest Hits From England	1964	8.00	20.00
Parrot PA-61017	(M)	The Greatest Hits From England, Volume 2	1964	8.00	20.00
Parrot PAS-71017	(P)	The Greatest Hits From England, Volume 2	1964	8.00	20.00
Parrot PA-61023	(M)	All American Hits	1964	8.00	20.00
Parrot PAS-71023	(P)	All American Hits	1964	8.00	20.00
Passport PB-3604	(S)	Phil Spector's Christmas Album	1984	4.00	10.00
		(PB-3604 is a reissue of Philles 4005.)			
Pavillion PZ-37686	(S)	Phil Spector's Christmas Album	1981	6.00	15.00
		(PZ-37686 is a reissue of Philles 4005.)			
Paul Winley Prod. 1001	(M)	New York City's Greatest Oldies	196?	60.00	150.00
Peacock PLP-2000	(M)	Big Ones From Duke-Peacock Records	196?	6.00	15.00
Pepsi Cola PC-51668	(M)	Youth Market Radio (One-sided padio spots)	1968	30.00	75.00
		(Promo features Wilson Pickett, The Stone Poneys, and The Union Gap.)			
Philles PHLP-4004	(M)	Today's Hits (White label promo)	1963	600.00	1,200.00
Philles PHLP-4004	(M)	Today's Hits	1963	250.00	500.00
Philles PHLP-4005	(M)	A Christmas Gift For You (White label)	1963	600.00	1,200.00
Philles PHLP-4005	(M)	A Christmas Gift For You	1963	100.00	250.00
		—Philles albums above have blue labels.—			
Philles PHLP-4004	(M)	Today's Hits	1964	80.00	200.00
Philles PHLP-4005	(M)	A Christmas Gift For You	1964	30.00	75.00
		—Philles albums above have red & yellow labels.—			
Philles PHLP-100	(M)	The Phil Spector Spectacular	1966	See note below	
		(Promotional compilation of Spector's Philles hits. A miniscule press run for the record was done but no covers were manufactured. Most copies were subsequently destroyed with the few remaining handed out to friends and associates. Rare with a suggested NM value of $3,000-6,000.)			
Philo PH-1028	(S)	Good Time Music At The National	197?	3.20	8.00
Pickwick DLP-701	(M)	Golden Oldies Original Hits, Vol. 1	196?	6.00	15.00
Pickwick DLP-702	(M)	Golden Oldies Original Hits, Vol. 2	196?	6.00	15.00
Pickwick PTP-2060	(M)	Rockin' Originals	196?	6.00	15.00
Pickwick SPC-3280	(S)	Rock 'N' Roll Revival	1971	4.00	10.00
Pickwick CL-001	(S)	Moving Ahead With Music	197?	12.00	30.00
Prestige PR-7539	(S)	Take A Trip With Psychedelic Hits	196?	40.00	100.00

Label & Catalog #		Title	Year	VG+	NM
Pricewise 4004	(M)	Best Of The Girl Groups	196?	10.00	25.00
Prism 1966	(M)	WONE-The Dayton Scene	1966	150.00	300.00
Ralph 8205	(DJ)	10th Anniversary Radio Special (2 LPs)	1981	12.00	30.00
Ralph 8205D	(DJ)	10 Years In 20 Minutes (Clear vinyl. 75 pressed)	1981	20.00	50.00
Rampart LP-3303	(M)	East Side Revue (Gold vinyl)	196?	40.00	100.00
Rampart LP-3305	(M)	East Side Revue, Volume 2 (Colored vinyl)	196?	40.00	100.00
Rampart LP-3305	(M)	East Side Revue, Volume 2 Bonus Poster	1969	10.00	30.00
RCA Victor LPM-2740	(M)	Old 'n' Golden Goodies	1963	8.00	20.00
RCA Victor LSP-2740	(P)	Old 'n' Golden Goodies	1963	12.00	30.00
RCA Victor LPM-3632	(M)	The Best Of The Best Of	1966	8.00	20.00
RCA Victor LSP-3632	(P)	The Best Of The Best Of	1966	10.00	25.00
RCA Victor LPM-3641	(M)	Old 'n' Golden Goodies, Volume 2	1966	8.00	20.00
RCA Victor LSP-3641	(P)	Old 'n' Golden Goodies, Volume 2	1966	12.00	30.00
RCA Victor SP-33204	(M)	Buick Presents The Sound Of Tomorrow	196?	5.00	12.00
RCA Victor SPS-33204	(S)	Buick Presents The Sound Of Tomorrow	196?	6.00	15.00
		—Original RCA albums above have black labels.—			
Red Bird RB-20-102	(M)	Red Bird Goldies	1965	30.00	75.00
Regent MG-6015	(M)	Rock & Roll	195?	16.00	40.00
Regent MG-6042	(M)	Rock & Roll Party	195?	16.00	40.00
Ren-Vell 317	(M)	Battle Of The Bands, Volume 1	1967	150.00	300.00
Rendezvous M-1314	(M)	Gone But Not Forgotten	196?	10.00	25.00
		(Rendezvous 1314 is a reissue of Class 5004.)			
Reprise R-6094	(M)	Surf's Up At Banzai Pipeline	1963	40.00	100.00
Reprise RS-6094	(P)	Surf's Up At Banzai Pipeline	1963	60.00	150.00
Rhino RNDF-203	(M)	Phil Spector—The Early Years	1984	1.00	5.00
Rhino PRO-70170	(P)	The Golden Archives Series Sampler	198?	1.00	5.00
Rhino RNLP-025	(P)	Nuggets, Volume 1	198?	1.00	5.00
Rhino RNLP-026	(P)	Nuggets, Volume 2	198?	1.00	5.00
Rhino RNLP-027	(P)	Nuggets, Volume 3	198?	1.00	5.00
Rhino RNLP-028	(P)	Nuggets, Volume 4	198?	1.00	5.00
Rhino RNLP-029	(P)	Nuggets, Volume 5	198?	1.00	5.00
Rhino RNLP-030	(P)	Nuggets, Volume 6	198?	1.00	5.00
Rhino RNLP-031	(P)	Nuggets, Volume 7	198?	1.00	5.00
Rhino RNLP-70032	(P)	Nuggets, Volume 8	198?	1.00	5.00
Rhino RNLP-70033	(P)	Nuggets, Volume 9	198?	1.00	5.00
Rhino RNLP-70034	(P)	Nuggets, Volume 10	198?	1.00	5.00
Rhino RNLP-70035	(P)	Nuggets, Volume 11	198?	1.00	5.00
Rhino RNLP-70036	(P)	Nuggets, Volume 12	198?	1.00	5.00
Rhino RNLP-70136	(P)	Frat Rock!	198?	1.00	5.00
Riviera R-0052	(M)	Blues In My Heart	1959	80.00	200.00
Roadside RBF-20	(M)	Roots: Rhythm & Blues	196?	12.00	30.00
Ronco LP-1001	(P)	Do It Now!	1970	12.00	30.00
		—Ronco albums above have yellow labels.—			
Ronco LP-1001	(P)	Do It Now!	1970	6.00	15.00
		—Ronco albums above have green labels.—			
Roulette R-25021	(M)	Pajama Party	195?	16.00	40.00
		—Roulette albums above have black labels.—			
Roulette R-25059	(M)	Rock & Roll Record Hop	1959	12.00	30.00
Roulette R-25093	(M)	Rock & Roll Bandstand	1959	12.00	30.00
Roulette R-25106	(M)	Original Hit Records	1962	10.00	25.00
Roulette SR-25106	(S)	Original Hit Records	1962	12.00	30.00
Roulette R-25159	(M)	Murray The K's Sing Along With The Original Golden Gassers	1962	8.00	20.00
Roulette SR-25159	(S)	Murray The K's Sing Along With The Original Golden Gassers	1962	10.00	25.00
Roulette R-25176	(M)	The Most Of The Twist	1962	6.00	15.00
Roulette SR-25176	(S)	The Most Of The Twist	1962	8.00	20.00
Roulette R-25191	(M)	Murray & Jockey The K's Golden Gassers	1963	8.00	20.00
Roulette SR-25191	(S)	Murray & Jockey The K's Golden Gassers	1963	10.00	25.00
Roulette R-25192	(M)	Murray & Jockey The K's Golden Gassers For A Dance Party	1962	8.00	20.00
Roulette SR-25192	(S)	Murray & Jockey The K's Golden Gassers For A Dance Party	1962	10.00	25.00

Label & Catalog #		Title	Year	VG+	NM
Roulette R-25???	(M)	Instrumental Golden Goodies, Vol. 1	1963	6.00	15.00
Roulette SR-25???	(S)	Instrumental Golden Goodies, Vol. 1	1963	6.00	15.00
Roulette R-25???	(M)	Instrumental Golden Goodies, Vol. 2	1963	6.00	15.00
Roulette SR-25???	(S)	Instrumental Golden Goodies, Vol. 2	1963	6.00	15.00
Roulette R-25???	(M)	Instrumental Golden Goodies, Vol. 3	1963	6.00	15.00
Roulette SR-25???	(S)	Instrumental Golden Goodies, Vol. 3	1963	6.00	15.00
Roulette R-25???	(M)	Instrumental Golden Goodies, Vol. 4	1963	6.00	15.00
Roulette SR-25???	(S)	Instrumental Golden Goodies, Vol. 4	1963	6.00	15.00
Roulette R-25???	(M)	Instrumental Golden Goodies, Vol. 5	1963	6.00	15.00
Roulette SR-25???	(S)	Instrumental Golden Goodies, Vol. 5	1963	6.00	15.00
Roulette R-25???	(M)	Instrumental Golden Goodies, Vol. 6	1963	6.00	15.00
Roulette SR-25???	(S)	Instrumental Golden Goodies, Vol. 6	1963	6.00	15.00
Roulette R-25???	(M)	Instrumental Golden Goodies, Vol. 7	1963	6.00	15.00
Roulette SR-25???	(S)	Instrumental Golden Goodies, Vol. 7	1963	6.00	15.00
Roulette R-25???	(M)	Instrumental Golden Goodies, Vol. 8	1963	6.00	15.00
Roulette SR-25???	(S)	Instrumental Golden Goodies, Vol. 8	1963	6.00	15.00
Roulette R-25???	(M)	Instrumental Golden Goodies, Vol. 9	1963	6.00	15.00
Roulette SR-25???	(S)	Instrumental Golden Goodies, Vol. 9	1963	6.00	15.00
Roulette R-25???	(M)	Instrumental Golden Goodies, Vol. 10	1963	6.00	15.00
Roulette SR-25???	(S)	Instrumental Golden Goodies, Vol. 10	1963	6.00	15.00
Roulette R-25???	(M)	Instrumental Golden Goodies, Vol. 11	1963	6.00	15.00
Roulette SR-25???	(S)	Instrumental Golden Goodies, Vol. 11	1963	6.00	15.00
Roulette R-25???	(M)	Instrumental Golden Goodies, Vol. 12	1963	6.00	15.00
Roulette SR-25???	(S)	Instrumental Golden Goodies, Vol. 12	1963	6.00	15.00
Roulette R-25238	(S)	Instrumental Golden Goodies, Vol. 13	1963	8.00	20.00
Roulette SR-25238	(S)	Instrumental Golden Goodies, Vol. 13	1963	8.00	20.00
Roulette R-25249	(M)	20 Original Winners, Vol. 1	1963	6.00	15.00
Roulette SR-25249	(S)	20 Original Winners, Vol. 1	1963	8.00	20.00
Roulette R-25290	(M)	20 All Time No. 1 Hits, Vol. 1	1964	6.00	15.00
Roulette SR-25290	(S)	20 All Time No. 1 Hits, Vol. 1	1964	8.00	20.00
Roulette R-25293	(M)	20 Original Winners Of 1964	1964	6.00	15.00
Roulette SR-25293	(S)	20 Original Winners Of 1964	1964	8.00	20.00
Roulette R-25304	(M)	20 Big Boss Favorites	1964	6.00	15.00
Roulette SR-25304	(S)	20 Big Boss Favorites	1964	8.00	20.00
RPM 3001	(M)	Rock & Roll Dance Party	195?	250.00	500.00
San Francisco SD-158	(S)	San Francisco	196?	8.00	20.00
San Fran. Sound 11680	(S)	Fifth Pipe Dream (Black & white cover)	1968	60.00	150.00
San Fran. Sound 11680	(S)	Fifth Pipe Dream (Color cover)	1968	40.00	100.00
Santo Presents	(M)	Mexican Rock 'n Roll Rumble (Photocopied cover)	197?	8.00	20.00
Savoy MG-15008	(10")	Rhythm & Blues	1952	500.00	1,000.00
Scepter SP-510	(M)	Murray The K's 1962 Golden Gassers	1963	8.00	20.00
Scepter SPS-510	(P)	Murray The K's 1962 Golden Gassers	1963	10.00	25.00
Scepter SP-518	(M)	The Groups Are The Greatest	1963	8.00	20.00
Scepter SPS-518	(P)	The Groups Are The Greatest	1963	10.00	25.00
Scepter SP-524	(M)	The Fifth Beatle Gives You Their Golden Gassers	1964	8.00	20.00
Scepter SPS-524	(P)	The Fifth Beatle Gives You Their Golden Gassers	1964	10.00	25.00
Score LP-4002	(M)	I Dig Rock & Roll	1957	150.00	300.00
Score LP-4018	(M)	Rock & Roll Sock Hop	1958	150.00	300.00
Screen Gems/Colgems	(DJ)	212 Hits (2 LPs)	196?	10.00	25.00
Screen Gems/Colgems	(DJ)	More Solid Gold Programming (2 LPs)	196?	12.00	30.00
Screen Gems/Columbia	(DJ)	Solid Gold-Gerry Goffin & Carole King	196?	20.00	50.00
Shepherd 1300	(M)	Surf War	1963	30.00	75.00
Sidewalk T-5901	(M)	Freakout U.S.A.	1967	20.00	50.00
Sidewalk ST-5901	(E)	Freakout U.S.A.	1967	12.00	30.00
Sire SASH-3716	(P)	Nuggets (2 LP reissue of Elektra 2006)	1976	6.00	15.00
Smash MGS-27018	(M)	Smash Hits	1963	10.00	25.00
Smash SRS-67018	(P)	Smash Hits	1963	14.00	35.00
Smash MGS-27038	(M)	Group Oldies But Goodies	1964	16.00	40.00
Smash SRS-67038	(P)	Group Oldies But Goodies	1964	20.00	50.00
Smash MGS-27052	(M)	All Time Smash Hits	1964	10.00	25.00
Smash SRS-67052	(P)	All Time Smash Hits	1964	14.00	35.00
Soma MG-1245	(M)	Big Hits Of Mid America	1968	30.00	75.00
Soma MG-1246	(M)	Big Hits Of Mid America, Volume 2	1968	30.00	75.00
Somerset P-1300	(M)	Rock 'N' Roll Dance Party	1954	30.00	75.00

Label & Catalog #		Title	Year	VG+	NM
Soul SS-720	(S)	Switched On Blues	1969	60.00	150.00
Sounds Of Brooklin RLP-2	(P)	Roots Of S.O.B., Volume 2	198?	1.00	5.00
Sounds Of Hawaii 5014	(M)	Waikiki Surf Battle, Volume 1	1964	150.00	300.00
Sounds Of Hawaii 5014	(M)	Waikiki Surf Battle, Volume 2	1964	150.00	300.00
Specialty SP-2112	(M)	Our Significant Hits	1963	60.00	150.00
—Specialty albums above have black & gold labels on thick vinyl. The labels and covers read "Stereo Natural Sound."—					
Specialty SP-2114	(M)	Doo Wop	1970	10.00	25.00
Specialty SP-2115	(M)	Ain't That Good News	1970	10.00	25.00
Specialty SP-2117	(M)	This Is How It All Began, Volume 1	1970	10.00	25.00
Specialty SP-2118	(M)	This Is How It All Began, Volume 2	1970	10.00	25.00
Specialty SP-2129	(M)	Original Rock Oldies, Volume 1	1970	10.00	25.00
Specialty SP-2130	(M)	Original Rock Oldies, Volume 2	1970	10.00	25.00
Specialty SP-2149	(M)	Dark Muddy Bottom Blues	1971	10.00	25.00
Specialty SP-2151	(M)	In Loving Memory Of Brother Joe May	1971	10.00	25.00
—Specialty albums above have black & gold labels on thin vinyl. The labels and covers read "Natural Sound."—					
Spin-O-Rama M-190	(M)	Freakout!! The Great New Guitar Sounds	196?	6.00	15.00
Spin-O-Rama S-190	(S)	Freakout!! The Great New Guitar Sounds	196?	8.00	20.00
Spivey LP-1015	(M)	Spivey's Blue Cavalcade	196?	16.00	40.00
Star SRM-101	(M)	Battle Of The Bands	1964	60.00	150.00
Starla LPM-1960	(M)	Art Laboe's Memories Of El Monte	1960	30.00	75.00
Stax ST-702	(M)	Hits From The South	1962	40.00	100.00
Stax STS-702	(S)	Hits From The South	1962	40.00	100.00
(This album has the same catalog number as Gus Cannon's "Walk Right In.")					
Stax ST-703	(M)	Treasure Chest Goodies	1962	16.00	40.00
Stax STS-703	(S)	Treasure Chest Goodies	1962	16.00	40.00
(Stax 703 is a reissue of 702 above.)					
Stax ST-710	(M)	Memphis Gold	1966	10.00	25.00
Stax STS-710	(P)	Memphis Gold	1966	12.00	30.00
Stax/Volt 11	(DJ)	Stay In School, Don't Be A Dropout	1967	300.00	600.00
Stax ST-721	(M)	The Stax/Volt Revue: Live In London, Volume 1	1967	12.00	30.00
Stax STS-721	(S)	The Stax/Volt Revue: Live In London, Volume 1	1967	12.00	30.00
Stax ST-722	(M)	The Stax/Volt Revue: Live In London, Volume 2	1967	12.00	30.00
Stax STS-722	(S)	The Stax/Volt Revue: Live In London, Volume 2	1967	12.00	30.00
Stax ST-726	(M)	Memphis Gold, Volume 2	1967	12.00	30.00
Stax STS-726	(S)	Memphis Gold, Volume 2	1967	10.00	25.00
Stax ST-2-2007	(M)	Soul Explosion (2 LPs)	1969	10.00	25.00
Stax ST-2020	(M)	Jammed Together	1972	10.00	25.00
Stax STS-2-2024	(S)	Boy Meets Girl (2 LPs)	1972	8.00	20.00
Stax STS-2031	(S)	Gold Soul	1972	8.00	20.00
Stax STS-2-3010	(S)	Wattstax (2 LPs)	197?	6.00	15.00
Stax STS-2-3018	(S)	The Living Word—Wattstax (2 LPs)	197?	6.00	15.00
Stax STS-3021	(S)	Filet Of Soul	197?	6.00	15.00
Stax STS-3023	(S)	Memphis Millions	197?	6.00	15.00
Stax	(DJ)	Stax... Once You've Been There You Know You're Home (2 LPs)	197?	16.00	40.00
Stax SLE-0373	(DJ)	Dave Clark Thru '72	1972	20.00	50.00
(Stax 0373 consists of promo man Dave Clark reminiscing about the early days of the business.)					
Stax MPS-8519	(S)	It's Christmas Time Again	1982	4.00	10.00
Success SLP-1011	(M)	Only For Teenagers And Real Swinging Adults	196?	200.00	400.00
Sue LP-1021	(M)	The Sue Story (Black cover)	196?	80.00	200.00
Sue LP-1021	(M)	The Sue Story (Orange cover)	196?	40.00	100.00
Sue LP-1021	(M)	Old Goodies	196?	40.00	100.00
Sun LP-1250	(M)	Sun's Gold Hits	1961	150.00	300.00
Sutton SU-321	(M)	Jumpin'	1961	16.00	40.00
Sutton SSU-321	(S)	Jumpin'	1961	20.00	50.00
Sutton SU-323	(M)	Current Craze	1961	16.00	40.00
Sutton SSU-323	(S)	Current Craze	1961	20.00	50.00
Sutton SU-325	(M)	Great Popular Oldies, Volume 2	1961	16.00	40.00
Sutton SSU-325	(S)	Great Popular Oldies, Volume 2	1961	20.00	50.00
Swan LP-501	(M)	Treasure Chest Of Hits	1960	40.00	100.00
Swan LP-506	(M)	Twistin' All Night Long	1961	30.00	75.00
Swan LP-512	(M)	Hits I Forgot To Buy	1963	20.00	50.00

Label & Catalog #		Title	Year	VG+	NM
Tamla T-224	(M)	Tamla Special #1	1962	60.00	150.00
		—Tamla albums above have white labels.—			
Tamla T-224	(M)	Tamla Special #1	196?	30.00	75.00
		—Tamla albums above have yellow labels.—			
Tamla T-244	(M)	Recorded Live At The Regal	1963	Unreleased	
Tamla T-256	(M)	A Collection Of 16 Original Big Hits, Vol. 2	1964	8.00	20.00
Tamla TS-256	(S)	A Collection Of 16 Original Big Hits, Vol. 2	1967	16.00	40.00
Tamla T-264	(M)	Recorded Live The Motortown Revue In Paris	1965	10.00	25.00
Tamla TS-264	(S)	Recorded Live The Motortown Revue In Paris	1965	12.00	30.00
Teem 5002	(M)	Guaranteed To Please	196?	12.00	30.00
Teem 5003	(M)	Greatest Teenage Hits Of All Time	196?	14.00	35.00
Teem 5004	(M)	Approved By 10,000,000	196?	14.00	35.00
Teem 5005	(M)	Kings Sing The Blues	196?	12.00	30.00
Time T-10000	(M)	Goodies Old And New	1961	14.00	35.00
Time ST-70000	(S)	Goodies Old And New	1961	20.00	50.00
Time T-10006	(M)	Riot In Blues	1961	30.00	75.00
Time ST-70006	(S)	Riot In Blues	1961	40.00	100.00
Time 52082	(M)	Original Goodies	196?	14.00	35.00
Time S-2082	(S)	Original Goodies	196?	20.00	50.00
Together ST-1014	(S)	Early L.A.	1971	12.00	30.00
Tower T-5007	(M)	Three At The Top	1965	10.00	25.00
Tower DT-5007	(E)	Three At The Top	1965	8.00	20.00
Tower DT-5157	(E)	Instant Replay	1969	16.00	40.00
		(The Sunrays' "I Live For The Sun" and "Andrea" are stereo.)			
Tower ST-5168	(P)	Underground	1969	30.00	75.00
Tower PRO-4409/10	(M)	Tower September 1967 Album Releases	1967	80.00	200.00
		(Tower 4409/10 was issued with a 12" x 12" booklet of cover slicks, priced separately below.)			
Tower PRO-4409/10	(M)	Tower September 1967 Album Releases Booklet	1967	40.00	100.00
Trousdale Music Pub.	(S)	What's Going On Here? (Publishers Demo)	1966	60.00	150.00
		(Features unreleased Sloan & Barri material.)			
Unart M-20014	(M)	Unforgettable Oldies	1968	4.00	10.00
Unart S-21014	(S)	Unforgettable Oldies	1968	4.00	10.00
Unart M-20022	(M)	Soul Oldies, Volume I	1968	4.00	10.00
Unart S-21022	(S)	Soul Oldies, Volume I	1968	4.00	10.00
Unart M-20023	(M)	Soul Oldies, Volume II	1968	4.00	10.00
Unart S-21023	(S)	Soul Oldies, Volume II	1968	4.00	10.00
Unart M-20027	(M)	Unforgettable Oldies-Volume II	1968	4.00	10.00
Unart S-21027	(S)	Unforgettable Oldies-Volume II	1968	4.00	10.00
United US-770?	(S)	12 Original Artists Hits	196?	6.00	15.00
United US-7706	(S)	12 Original Artists Hits, Vol. 2	196?	6.00	15.00
United Arts. UAL-4027	(M)	Blues In The Mississippi Night	1959	14.00	35.00
United Arts. UAS-5027	(S)	Blues In The Mississippi Night	1959	20.00	50.00
United Arts. UAL-3196	(M)	Yesterday's Goodies	1961	8.00	20.00
United Arts. UAS-6196	(S)	Yesterday's Goodies	1961	10.00	25.00
United Arts. UAL-3314	(M)	Golden Treasure Chest	1963	8.00	20.00
United Arts. UAS-6314	(S)	Golden Treasure Chest	1963	10.00	25.00
United Arts. UAL-3317	(M)	Golden Souvenirs	1963	8.00	20.00
United Arts. UAS-6317	(S)	Golden Souvenirs	1963	10.00	25.00
United Arts. MX-22	(M)	Yesterday's Goodies	196?	4.00	10.00
United Arts. SX-72	(S)	Yesterday's Goodies	196?	6.00	15.00
United Arts. SP-70	(DJ)	N. A. P. R. A. 72 Vote	1972	16.00	40.00
USA LP-100	(M)	The KAAY Silver Dollar Special, Vol. 1	196?	20.00	50.00
Vanguard VRS-9145	(M)	Blues At Newport	1964	8.00	20.00
Vanguard VSD-79145	(S)	Blues At Newport	1964	10.00	25.00
Vanguard VRS-9216	(M)	Chicago/The Blues/Today! (Vol. 1)	1965	8.00	20.00
Vanguard VSD-79216	(S)	Chicago/The Blues/Today! (Vol. 1)	1965	10.00	25.00
Vanguard VRS-9217	(M)	Chicago/The Blues/Today! (Vol. 2)	1965	8.00	20.00
Vanguard VSD-79217	(S)	Chicago/The Blues/Today! (Vol. 2)	1965	10.00	25.00
Vanguard VRS-9218	(M)	Chicago/The Blues/Today! (Vol. 3)	1965	8.00	20.00
Vanguard VSD-79218	(S)	Chicago/The Blues/Today! (Vol. 3)	1965	10.00	25.00
Vanguard VSD-1/2	(S)	The Best Of Chicago Blues (2 LPs)	197?	6.00	15.00
Vault LP-103	(M)	Oldies, Goodies And Woodies	1964	16.00	40.00
Vault VS-103	(S)	Oldies, Goodies And Woodies	1964	20.00	50.00
Vault LP-104	(M)	Hot Rod City	1964	20.00	50.00
Vault VS-104	(S)	Hot Rod City	1964	30.00	75.00

Label & Catalog #		Title	Year	VG+	NM
Vault LP-113	(M)	West Coast Love-In	1967	12.00	30.00
Vault SLP-113	(S)	West Coast Love-In	1967	16.00	40.00
Vault VS-119	(P)	San Francisco Roots	1968	20.00	50.00
		(Vault 119 was reissued as JAS 5001.)			
Vee Jay LP-100	(M)	Kat's Karavan	1957	20.00	50.00
Vee Jay LP-1020	(M)	The Blues	1962	16.00	40.00
Vee Jay LP-1021	(M)	Teen Delights	1962	16.00	40.00
Vee Jay LP-1036	(M)	Teen Delights, Volume 2	1962	16.00	40.00
Vee Jay LP-1042	(M)	Tomorrow's Hits	1962	16.00	40.00
Vee Jay LP-1051	(M)	Unavailable	1962	16.00	40.00
Vee Jay LP-1074	(M)	Soul Meeting Saturday Night Hootenanny Style	1964	12.00	30.00
Vee Jay VJS-1074	(S)	Soul Meeting Saturday Night Hootenanny Style	1964	20.00	50.00
Vee Jay LP-1084	(M)	This Is Where It Is—The Original Nitty Gritty	1964	12.00	30.00
Vee Jay VJS-1084	(S)	This Is Where It Is—The Original Nitty Gritty	1964	20.00	50.00
Vee Jay LP-1112	(M)	Great Hits Of 1964	1964	12.00	30.00
Vee Jay SR-1112	(P)	Great Hits Of 1964	1964	20.00	50.00
Vee Jay LP-1136	(M)	More Great Hits Of 1964 & Other Golden Goodies	1965	12.00	30.00
Vee Jay SR-1136	(P)	More Great Hits Of 1964 & Other Golden Goodies	1965	20.00	50.00
Vernon V-521	(M)	Chartbusters!	196?	16.00	40.00
Verve V-2083	(M)	Teen Time: Refer to Rick Nelson			
Verve V6-653	(M)	24 Karat Gold From The Underground (2 LPs)	1968	10.00	25.00
Voxx VXS-200.063	(S)	The Dunwich Records Story	1990	6.00	15.00
Wand WDM-651	(M)	Rocket To The Stars	1961	20.00	50.00
Wand WDM-652	(M)	Show Stoppers	1961	16.00	40.00
Wand WDM-660	(M)	The Greatest Sing Their Soul Favorites	1964	12.00	30.00
Wand WDM-660	(M)	The Greatest Sing Their Soul Favorites	1964	16.00	40.00
Wand WDM-666	(M)	The Guys With Soul Are The Greatest	1965	12.00	30.00
Wand WDS-666	(S)	The Guys With Soul Are The Greatest	1965	16.00	40.00
Wand WDM-677	(M)	Greatest Hits From The Soul Of Texas	1966	12.00	30.00
Wand WDS-677	(S)	Greatest Hits From The Soul Of Texas	1966	16.00	40.00
Warner Bros. K-46144	(S)	A Tribute To Woody Guthrie, Part 2	1972	4.00	10.00
		(Part 1 was issued as Columbia 31171.)			
Warner Bros. PRO-289	(S)	Highlights From The			
		Tenth Anniversary Albums	1968	4.00	10.00
Warner Bros. PRO-290	(S)	Some Of Our Best Friends Are...	1968	4.00	10.00
Warner/Reprise PRO-351	(S)	October 10, 1969	1969	4.00	10.00
Warner/Reprise PRO-359	(S)	Schlagers (2 LPs)	1969	4.00	10.00
Warner/Reprise PRO-368	(S)	Zapped (Collage cover)	1969	12.00	30.00
Warner/Reprise PRO-368	(S)	Zapped (Photo cover)	1970	6.00	15.00
		(Various artists sampler for Frank Zappa's Bizarre and Straight labels. First pressing covers have a black & white collage of photos and art; second pressings have a black & white photo of Zappa.)			
Warner/Reprise PRO-450	(S)	Days Of Wine And Vinyl	1970	4.00	10.00
Warner/Reprise PRO-463	(S)	The Warner / Reprise Radio Show (2 LPs)	1971	4.00	10.00
Warner/Reprise PRO-509	(S)	KYA 1260 Great Ripoff Album	1971	4.00	10.00
Warner/Reprise PRO-525	(S)	Middle Of The Road (2 LPs)	1971	4.00	10.00
Warner/Reprise PRO-534	(S)	Voter Registration Spots	1972	20.00	50.00
Warner/Reprise PRO-578	(S)	Magnavox Presents	1973	4.00	10.00
Warner/Reprise PRO-604	(S)	Burbank's Finest—			
		100% All Meat (2 LPs. Brown vinyl)	1975	20.00	50.00
Warner/Reprise PRO-2896	(S)	Yulesville	1987	6.00	15.00
Warner/Reprise PRO-3328	(S)	Winter Warnerland (2 LPs on colored vinyl)	1988	10.00	25.00
Warner/Reprise 27607-2	(P)	Highs Of The Sixties	198?	1.00	5.00
Warner/Spector 9103	(S)	Phil Spector's Christmas Album	1975	8.00	20.00
		(W/S 9103 is a reissue of Philles 4005.)			
Warner/Spector 9104	(M)	Phil Spector's Greatest Hits (2 LPs)	1977	12.00	30.00
		("Spanish Harlem," "River Deep-Mountain High" and "He's Sure The Boy I Love" are in stereo.)			
Warwick W-2008	(M)	Gold Hits	1960	30.00	75.00
Warwick W-2025	(M)	Best Of The R&B Groups	1961	40.00	100.00
Warwick W-2026	(M)	Best Of Rhythm And Blues	1961	30.00	75.00
Warwick W-2044	(M)	More Gold Hits, Volume 2	1961	30.00	75.00
Warwick W-2048	(M)	Still More Gold Hits, Volume 3	1962	30.00	75.00
Welk Music W-3002	(M)	Blue Christmas	1984	20.00	50.00
Westchester 1005	(M)	Friday At The Cafe A Go Go	196?	50.00	125.00
White Whale WWS-7125	(S)	Footprints In Time	1970	10.00	25.00
White Whale WWS-7129	(S)	Super Groups From Holland	1970	10.00	25.00
White Whale WWS-7130	(S)	Dutch Explosion	1970	12.00	30.00

Label & Catalog #		Title	Year	VG+	NM
Winley 6001	(M)	Everybody Digs The Boss Record Hop	195?	200.00	400.00
Wing MGW-12371	(M)	Scrapbook Of Golden Hits	196?	6.00	15.00
Wing SRW-16371	(S)	Scrapbook Of Golden Hits	196?	6.00	15.00
Wyncote W-9012	(M)	Golden Hits	1965	1.20	6.00
Wyncote SW-9012	(S)	Golden Hits	1965	3.20	8.00
Wyncote W-9070	(M)	Shindig, Volume 2	1965	1.20	6.00
Wyncote W-9070	(S)	Shindig, Volume 2	1965	3.20	8.00
Wyncote W-9080	(M)	Hullabaloo With The Stars	1965	1.20	6.00
Wyncote SW-9080	(S)	Hullabaloo With The Stars	1965	3.20	8.00
Wyncote W-9111	(M)	Dance A Go Go With The Stars	1966	1.20	6.00
Wyncote SW-9111	(S)	Dance A Go Go With The Stars	1966	3.20	8.00
Wyncote W-9149	(M)	All Star 4	1966	1.20	6.00
Wyncote SW-9149	(S)	All Star 4	1966	3.20	8.00
Wyncote W-9187	(S)	The Stars Of Hitsville	1966	1.20	6.00
Wyncote W-9187	(S)	The Stars Of Hitsville	1966	3.20	8.00
Zephyr ZP-12010H	(M)	Premiere	195?	12.00	30.00

SELLING YOUR ALBUMS

By Perry Cox

[Perry Cox is one of the most well-known collectors and dealers in Beatles records in the world. He is also the author of The Beatles Price Guide For American Records, *from which this abridged article was taken. This article serves to show the similarity of opinion between Mr Cox and those expressed by myself in this edition's foreword. Differences do exist between us, as they should. − NU]*

Collectors and dealers all over the world keep a watchful eye on current market trends to see how their investments are doing, as well as what they can expect to pay for items that remain on their want lists. The burning questions, then, are: "How does one realistically go about selling their records? Sure, the guide says it's worth X dollar amount, but how do I market my item(s) anywhere near its value estimate?" There are several answers, all of which depend on the seller's situation and needs.

The "set-sale" method is probably the only way to achieve near, at, or above market value in a relatively short period of time. At the point you wish to market your item(s), the sale may take no longer than a phone call to complete. Of course, this method involves plenty of prior invested time and interaction with others. As a collector among collectors, it is ideal to socialize, share one's finds, interact for feedback and advice, and keep on the lookout for other collectors' wants. By acquiring a current list of items your friends and colleagues are looking for, you will be better able to determine what you can sell and for how much.

This is not only an ideal way to obtain maximum return from collectibles you have to sell, but this also allows you a keen advantage in terms of trading for items to fill your own collection. As well, many will appreciate your servicing their wants. The longer you are involved, the larger your customer/friendship base grows. This is, *if* you have kept the required high standards of dealing ethics which is absolutely essential in building a solid relationship with other collectors.

Ethics between buyer and seller *must* be given preference over all other factors. Your records and money mean little if your code of conduct allows for dissatisfaction with the other party, especially if you do not promptly remedy the problem to their satisfaction. Universal dealing principals equate to honestly and fairly grading the items. Since most prospective buyers are unable to personally inspect the items prior to the sale, it is good policy to institute a full "money back, satisfaction guarantee" coupled with a reasonable time limit for recourse (usually a couple of weeks is sufficient).

It is very important to formulate your selling prices *before* you contact prospective buyers. It is not wise to gauge your pricing on the customers level of desire or by pitting one customer against another. These tactics spawn little more than frustration and discontent for everyone. If you agree to a set price, do not raise that price if you later realize another party expresses interest in it. (As well, if you agree to buy an item for a certain price, nitpicking at minor flaws in hopes of getting a discount is not wise.)

In short, each must live by his own set of standards and always give great respect to another's valid concerns. Remember, if you get in the habit of making undesirable transaction, many will learn not to contact you the next time you have records to sell or trade.

Set Sale & Auctions In Trade Publications

The term "set sale" means to list your items at fixed prices; i.e., the items *are not* being auctioned. The advantage with this method is that your market potential is far greater due to the mass attention your items receive. The *actual* level of exposure depends on what publications you choose. If you have several "high ticket" items or a large amount of quality merchandise to sell, ads in several publications at once is certainly a viable option. This method is a bit more time consuming: ad preparation, distribution of the publication, and mail transactions involve time.

Preparing your ad needs special planning and considerations; you will need to figure the total number of lines each typewritten page gives you (normally between 50 and 60), the cost per ad, then the cost per line. Collectors tend to gravitate to the excellent condition items, so concentrate on listing in-demand items in quality shape. If you list thirty $10 items that take up half your full page ad space, you have only covered your ad cost, *if you sell them all.*

Keep in mind that a full page ad in these types of publications usually run about $300. Smaller space ads are considerably cheaper. The "Showcase" ad section in the back of *Goldmine* is very effective in presenting select items. The inexpensive rates include typesetting and placement among other eye appealing ads. This is often the first section viewed by readers.

When preparing your ad, by all means grade your items very conservatively (refer to the article on grading in this book.) Conservative, accurate grading provides a healthy, happy collecting environment for everyone. Also, you must be prepared to pack your items well with proper, snug packing and padding (2-3" of padding around the item is a good minimum). Always insure the items you are mailing; it is well worth the extra expense.

When dealing with mail-order, the buyers may notify you of their intent to reserve any particular item(s) they are interested in. Normally this is done by telephone (many buyers prefer to talk to the people they are dealing with, since it gives an added sense of security and provides an immediate response as to the availability of the item) or mail. The response you may receive from this type of advertising is an excellent way to broaden your list of other collectors.

If one has the time, this method has the potential of being the most rewarding in terms of highest yield plus it is a good way to learn just how much customers are willing to spend at any given time on any given item. With the mail-order auction, the seller sets a bid deadline; normally an auction runs for one month from the beginning of the issue's publication date. At the deadline all bids are evaluated and the highest bidders then notified.

In some cases, auctions have yielded sales substantially over the going set value; in other cases the results can be most disappointing. The factors involved in determining the final results are far too numerous to detail but the general spending mood of the public is probably the most important factor. When a given artist is focused on in the media, sales tend to surge accordingly. The death of a major star such as Elvis Presley or John Lennon is one example; the hoopla surrounding Madonna's or The Stones' big tours is another.

Reputable auction establishments such as Sothebys, Christies and Phillips are alternative auction methods. They can, however, take the longest time in that they only hold their auctions a few times a year. Exposure to collectors is also limited but the spending frenzy sometimes associated with these houses can often play a favorable role for the seller. One thing is certain: auctions do take the longest period of time on average to sell your items. From start to completion, a mail-order auction consumes an average of two months. This is not the way to go if one wishes to liquidate in a hurry.

Selling Your Items To A Dealer

The quickest manner to sell your items once you have exhausted retail sales to personal contacts is to sell them wholesale to a dealer. If you need cash and you need it right away, selling this way can be quite convenient. Your first responsibility is to contact a *reputable* dealer who is interested in mutual satisfaction between his interests and your own. One must keep in mind that a dealer is not in a position to pay top market dollar for your items. Like any commodity, the record dealer has to buy at a modest percentage of full value in order to make enough profit to stay in business.

As a rule, it is safe to say that the more significantly rare and valuable your item is, the more the dealer will be probably willing to pay, especially if they have a ready buyer. Although the dealer takes into consideration many factors when evaluating, the bottom line is usually this: "How long will one have to keep his money tied up before one actually sells the goods and recovers their money?" Some very rare and valuable items have been known to fetch as much as 60-65% of market retail. A good average for slow movers is about 30-40% of the dealer's opinion of the market value. If the period is lengthy or if the dealer has several copies of the item you are trying to sell, he'll be less generous in his offer or may not express any interest at all! If you intend to solicit offers from various dealers, please advise each dealer of this prior to negotiations to avoid hard feelings. This eliminates the impression the dealer may have in thinking he has an exclusive on your items.

Some dealers will agree to place items obtained from the owner on consignment. That is, he will not pay the owner until the item sells. Usually this method is not entertained unless the dealer feels the item is significant enough to yield a handsome return within a reasonable time. The retail value is mutually agreed upon, while the dealer assumes responsibility for the custody and sale of the item. The final say in retail value usually goes to the dealer who knows his area and market potential best. The average consignment fee is anywhere from 15% to 30% to the dealer, certainly better than the 40-50% usually obtained in a straight sale to the dealer. Compared with some of the others, this selling method can be quite time consuming without guaranteed sales, a factor that must be considered before locking your item(s) in a consignment agreement (which is, in effect, a contract).

ACETATES & TEST PRESSINGS

By Christopher Chatman

Many times I have been asked "What *are* acetates and test pressings?" followed closely by "Why do they cost so much?" Record collectors are continually in search of the "rarest records," the "best pressings." This has much to do with the demand for promotional records: they are usually much rarer than the stock copies and, because of their limited press runs, better sounding. However, promotional copies—and even test pressings—pale in comparison to acetates, both in terms of sound quality and particularly in rarity.

Acetates are the first step in the transfer of music from an electronic signal to the actual pressed record. They allow the musicians and producers to hear what the finished record will sound like without going through the time and expense of the plating and pressing. After all, they may decide that they don't like a particular version of a song and change it *or* not release it at all.

Acetates, also known as masters or reference discs, are usually black and 7" to 12" in diameter. While most records are made of vinyl, acetates are made out of aluminum coated with cellulose acetate. Thus, while they look like records, they weigh approximately five times as much. The cellulose acetate for these lacquers is made at a very high level of quality control. Acetates are very expensive to manufacture, therefore record companies normally make only five copies of any one record. Recently, with the sharp reduction of vinyl records, the number of acetates made has dropped dramatically.

After a recording has been taped, edited and equalized, an uncut acetate, or "blank," is sent to the mastering lab where it is placed on the turntable of an electronic lathe system. The master tape is played through a lathe system and electronically transmitted to the cutting needle so that the music literally cuts microscopic wiggles analogous to the sound waves that they represent directly into the acetate coating. Because of this direct cutting from the master tape and the high quality of the cellulose, the sound is substantially better than a record.

An acetate which has received approval is called a master lacquer. After a lacquer has been cut it is sent to a factory to be electroplated with nickel. A label from either the mastering lab or the record company is usually glued to the disc; reference discs *may* have no label at all and master lacquers rarely do. Although acetates are normally packaged in plain paper sleeves, in recent years many are shipped in special boxes with covers; this extra packaging tends to enhance the desirability of the acetate. After the music on a reference disc has been reviewed and the record pressed, the acetate is then discarded, having served its purpose.

Acetates should be treated even more carefully than records. Due to the brittleness of the cellulose, the action of playing an acetate with a phonograph needle is quite damaging to the disc's surface. After five plays, the needle begins to cut away at the finer microscopic grooves which produce the high frequencies. It is therefore advisable to play an acetate *once*, record it on tape, and then carefully store it away. Also, acetates chip easily; handle with care.

The nickel plating is then peeled away, which results in a negative metal print of the lacquer commonly referred to as a "mother." The first pressings to be run off the mother are test pressings; the final stop before the record is actually manufactured for mass consumption. Test pressings are vinyl facsimiles of the actual album; that is, they are 12" records pressed in extremely limited runs, usually at a plant that specializes in test pressings. It is not feasible for the large companies to turn on their enormous machines to print a handful of records.

These records allow the people involved to actually hear what the record will sound like as an LP. They may have special labels or they may be blank. Test pressings are checked for sound quality and technical defects; if they are satisfactory, then promotional copies are pressed, generally for distribution to radio stations. Finally, the commercial, or stock, copies are pressed for sale in your favorite endangered record store.

Since the value of an acetate depends primarily on the collectibility of the artist, they range in value from a few dollars to thousands of dollars. Acetates of released material are lowest on the value pyramid. Next are takes of released tracks prior to any sweetening being added, such as strings, horns, and background singers. Above that would be alternate takes of released material; unreleased live material would probably settle in between this level and the previous. The most valuable acetates are obviously those of unreleased material, regardless of the material's aesthetic qualities.

Acetates of albums by Elvis Presley and The Beatles have regularly sold for $500 and more; those by artists who are not quite as collectible have still sold for comparable prices. Hot new artists such as Depeche Mode and The Smiths are attracting serious bids when offered in auction. It is for this reason that some acetates have been bootlegged; be *sure* to check the reputation of the seller before spending heavy money on an acetate. It is important to note that the value increases dramatically when the material on the acetate is different from the released version of the record. However, whether or not the material is different, acetates are extremely rare and highly prized by collectors interested in owning the supposedly unattainable.

Test pressings are always worth several times the listed value of the stock copy. The most desirable are those of either unreleased albums such as Fats Domino's second album for Reprise, *Fats*, scheduled for release in 1971 and then withdrawn, or test pressings with different versions or mixes than the released album, such as the original version of Bob Dylan's *Blood On The Tracks*. Recorded with Eric Weisberg's group, Dylan pulled five of the tracks after hearing the test pressing and recorded them with another group of musicians to change the record's total mood. While the *Fats* album sells for three figures, *Blood On The Tracks* is one of the most valuable albums in the hobby.

A recent variation to the usual type of acetate is the direct metal master, or DMM. Instead of being made of aluminum coated with cellulose acetate, they are made of stainless steel coated with polished copper. The signal from the master tape is cut directly into the copper. This technology, designed to improve the sound quality of records, was designed just as the dominance of compact discs was forcing records into relative obscurity. This, combined with the fact that DMM is very expensive to convert has resulted in few mastering labs investing in this new method. Therefore, DMM acetates are very rare and, because of their beauty, highly prized by collectors.

COLLECTING GOLD & PLATINUM RECORD AWARDS

By Christopher Chatman

[Christopher Chatman is the proprietor of Beyond Records in Los Angeles, specializing in rare records and such music memorabilia as acetates, test pressings, RIAA Gold and Platinum Record Awards, original cover art and their four-color transparencies. This article originally appeared in Goldmine as part of an ad. It has been expanded, revised and is reprinted with his permission. — NU]

Collecting gold and platinum record awards has progressed and evolved into a specialized field of music memorabilia. Aside from the collectors, there are now investors, museums, and restaurants contributing to the rising popularity and escalating prices for key awards. Unfortunately, this increased interest and demand has also caused increased incidents of fraud *along* with a broad based abuse of the system by which the awards themselves are ordered. Still, gold and platinum awards *are* great investments if you spend your money on an artist who will maintain collectors' interest over the years. A wise purchase in the present has the potential to grow into a healthy investment for the future. Besides giving the reader a general introduction to this field, this article will include tips on avoiding bad purchases, which, needless to say, can be very expensive.

The *primary* purpose of this article is to give the reader a general acquaintance with the terms and descriptions commonly used and the different types, or formats, of the various awards. There are seven basic aspects that are crucial in determining the collectibility, or value, of a given award: the artist, the record's title, the organization recognizing the sales achievement, the award designation, the formatting of the award, the individual or group to whom the award was presented, and, finally, the condition of the award.

The Artist & The Title

The artist is probably the most important factor in determining the value of an award. A recent award for a Rolling Stones record would probably sell quicker and for a much higher value than a vintage award for a Isaac Hayes title, simply because they are so much more collectible. Current trends indicate even greater interest and emphasis is being placed on major artists. Nevertheless, since virtually all artists are collected to one extent or another, it is important to state that the tastes of the individual collector gauge desirability.

The title of the record greatly affects the desirability of an award. In recent years, an original RIAA Gold Record for *Sgt. Pepper's Lonely Hearts Club Band* presented to The Beatles sold for more than $20,000 at auction. Yet a few months later in an auction from the same house, an original RIAA Gold Record for *Rubber Soul* presented to The Beatles fetched under $10,000. While part of the reason for the staggering difference in the prices was condition (the *Pepper* award was graded higher), another was title, as *Sgt. Pepper* is one of *the* classic titles to own.

While different collectors will have differing opinions on what *is* "classic" and therefore desirable, certain constants do exist, such as an artist's first gold record, upon which most collectors place a certain premium. The individual's personal preference is a good thought to keep in mind as you read on, as this is a report on general trends, not absolute facts.

The Organization Recognizing The Sales Achievement

Most collectors in the United States prefer awards certified by the Record Industry Association of America, or RIAA, the membership of which includes most, but not all, of the major labels in the country. Formed in 1952 as a trade organization representing the interests of the country's major record manufacturers, the organization introduced its "official" Gold Record Award in January 1958 primarily to standardize the recognition of sales.

Record companies could, at their own expense, open their books to an independent auditor who would then verify the sales figures. The award would be presented afterward, often with some degree of formality, by the RIAA to the artist and the company. Of course, companies did not have to join nor open their books; subsequently, many major sellers have never been certified as gold records, notably the Motown hits of the '60s.

The RIAA has many other functions but the main one which concerns us here is that it acts as *an unbiased accounting firm to verify the actual number of units sold*. However, it is important to note that there are awards certified by the record company itself with outside certification by an umbrella organization. These are commonly referred to as "in-house" awards. These awards are produced by major record companies that belong to the RIAA *as well* as labels that do not. Major labels will often make in-house awards to avoid having to pay the RIAA their accounting and certification fee.

Or a label may choose an in-house award to create an award or plaque with design specifications that do not include the RIAA seal, making some in-house awards far more attractive than the regulation RIAA design. In-house awards are increasing in collectibility, the most obvious example being early awards from Berry Gordy's aforementioned Motown conglomeration. . .

Gold record awards from other countries are also collected, with those from the United Kingdom and Japan highly prized. The official organization certifying sales achievement in the U.K. is British Phonographics Industry, or BPI. Because of the blue, red and black felt backgrounds of these awards they are particularly nice to add to a collection. And, while awards from Japan tend to be in-house, they, too, are especially beautiful.

RIAA Award Designation

Qualification for RIAA awards have varied over the years, as the chart below illustrates. The original standards were based on one million as gold: 1,000,000 copies of a single and $1,000,000 at the manufacturer's wholesale price for an album, which generally meant *at least* 500,000 copies. Extended Play albums (EPs), which generally consisted of two tracks per side, required half of a single's sales, 500,000 units, to qualify. In 1970 the sales of tapes were included in the tallies for an album's certification. While the sales of reel-to-reels were negligible, the inclusion of the then popular eight-tracks had a noticeable affect on sales levels, similar to what would follow when the cassette was introduced as the industry standard years later.

By 1974 the increased cost of albums at the wholesale level had made it possible to qualify with approximately 450,000 sales. In 1975 the rules were altered so that an LP must sell both the $1,000,000 and the half-million units to qualify. This was followed in 1976 with the establishment of the RIAA Platinum Record Award: 2,000,000 for a single and 1,000,000 copies (i.e., $2,000,000) for an LP. The redundant (and self-explanatory) Multi-Platinum Award was introduced in 1984.

1958-1974

45	Gold Award	1,000,000 unit sales
EP	Gold Award	500,000 unit sales
LP	Gold Award	$1,000,000 wholesale net

1975-1988

45	Gold Award	1,000,000 unit sales
45	Platinum Award	2,000,000 unit sales
EP	Gold Award	500,000 unit sales
EP	Platinum Award	1,000,000 unit sales
LP	Gold Award	500,000 unit sales
LP	Platinum Award	1,000,000 unit sales

1989-1996

45	Gold Award	500,000 unit sales
45	Platinum Award	1,000,000 unit sales
EP	Gold Award	250,000 unit sales
EP	Platinum Award	500,000 unit sales
LP	Gold Award	500,000 unit sales
LP	Platinum Award	1,000,000 unit sales

The recent change in levels of unit sales in order to attain gold or platinum status reflect changing levels of difficulty in accruing these sales amounts. With the sales of vinyl dropping to all but non-existent and the industry's decision to phase out vinyl, Gold Record Awards to singles plummeted: in 1980 there were 42 Gold Awards for singles; by 1986 it was seven. The introduction of the cassette single (or cassingle) in 1987 didn't help much so the RIAA made a radical amendment to its standards: Beginning in 1989, the level of sales for qualification for a single would be halved from 1,000,000 and 500,000 to qualify for Gold and from 2,000,000 to 1,000,000 for Platinum. And, in a complete reversal of previous policies, the standards applied retroactively. . . opening a Pandora's box of possibilities—and complications.

Dates are worth knowing as the minimum requirement for RIAA certification. This is useful in spotting fakes. It is important to remember that platinum status was recognized by individual record companies years before "official" recognition by the RIAA. Therefore, platinum in-house awards prior to 1976 can be just as valid as an RIAA gold award presented at the same time.

Award Format

Over the years the RIAA has varied the formats, or style, in which the award is presented. Through 1989, the RIAA kept very strict control over the specifications that were used to construct each award. These standards are helpful in identifying the different formats as the rigid standards can make visual differences slight.

A. *White matte (1964-1975)*. Manufactured exclusively by New York Picture & Frame Company, the plaque was an off-white linen material in an unpainted, finished wood frame. This linen material will often turn a reddish-brown with age. The dedication on the plate was engraved with the RIAA seal usually etched in. In the case of LPs, the mini-cover was mounted separately from the plate. Because of their unique looks and the difficulty in counterfeiting them, white matte awards are the most desirable and collectible style (as recent sales trends and auction results bear out). Many collectors pursue this style alone.

B. *Floater (1975-1981)*. The award's background was dark, usually black, enclosed in a wood frame painted either gold or white. The disc and plate appear to be "floating" between the background and the Plexiglas. In the case of LPs, the mini-cover (also floating) was mounted separately from the plate.

C. *Strip-plate (1982-1984)*. The award's background was dark. Unlike previous awards, for LPs the plate containing the dedication and the mini-cover appeared on the same strip of metal. This was also the first format to include a gold or silver plated cassette, acknowledging the ever increasing contribution of the tapes to unit sales. These were located either directly beneath the album disc or resting atop the lower LP lip. However, not *all* Strip-plates included a cassette.

D. *Hologram (1984-1989)*. The award's background is dark. In the case of LPs, the dedication and the mini-cover appear on the same strip of metal. The RIAA logo on the plate is in a rainbow-like hologram to avoid unauthorized duplication. Most, if not all, of these awards have a gold or silver plated cassette's top shell beneath the album disc or resting atop the lower LP lip. Some include a gold or silver plated compact disc.

E. *'R'-Hologram (1990 to present)*. For this new format the traditional RIAA logo was replaced with a large 'R' in a hologram pattern. All size and style restrictions were relaxed, giving the record companies more freedom in choosing a design for a particular award. Thus one can see a multitude of styles during these years with only the 'R'-hologram logo remaining constant. (Both the hologram and the 'R'-hologram award can be found in a new "format," the compact disc award. These feature either a gold or silver plated compact disc with the dedication plate with or without the picture from the CD's jewel box.)

Award Recipient

Presentation has become increasingly important in the last few years. . . and with good reason. The more closely identifiable an award is with the artist, the more desirable the award. In descending order, the desirability of an award based on the recipient is 1) the artist who recorded the record, 2) the record company who released the record, 3) either an individual or organization closely connected with the production of the record, such as anyone listed on the album's credits, 4) the production company, 5) a radio station, or, finally, 6) a record company executive otherwise unknown in the collecting community.

Because of the increased popularity of collecting these awards, many recipients and record company executives have acquired extra awards to sell to the collectors market. These are either duplicates of presented awards or new awards signifying a higher level of sales achievement. For the past few years, a practice has run rampant across the country. Called "ordering," it occurs when a licensed manufacturer accepts orders from anyone other than a record company executive to have an RIAA certified award made. This has led to an explosion of hologram and 'R' hologram awards being produced that threaten the collectibility, value and, most importantly, the merit of these two formats.

This unfortunate turn of events has led to the gradual lessening of the prestige of owning awards in general with the latter two hologram styles taking the biggest fall in popularity. While many dealers defend ordering awards as a practice, it devalues the awards. I therefore recommend that, when purchasing an award, the prospective buyer should ask the seller if the award was ordered for the purpose of resale or was it obtained from a "legitimate" recipient. You should always deal with a seller who *will* tell you the truth as there is virtually no difference between the ordered awards and the presented awards *because they were made in the same place!*

The RIAA is presently taking steps to reduce illegitimate orders, including having all RIAA hologram awards carrying a serial number which will assist in keeping track of them in the future. In the meantime, they have assigned a representative to assist both sellers and buyers in determining whether or not a given award *was certified* at a certain level. Interested parties can write Angela Corio, Director of RIAA's Gold & Platinum Record Awards Program, at 1020 Nineteenth Street, Suite 200, Washington, D.C. 20036 or phone 202-775-0101. Keep in mind that she is only able to assist in verifying certification, *not authenticity.* For that you must turn to a knowledgeable, and trusted, expert. . .

Award Condition

The condition of the award is vital: *Everybody* wants *everything* Mint and award collectors are no exception. White matte collectors are particularly fussy, sometimes wanting only items that have never been repaired, even if the matte is yellowing. Personally, I would rather have an item that has been restored and looks beautiful than one that is original but looks terrible. (It is best *not* to attempt to repair an award unless you are qualified.)

When buying any award be sure the award is the original format (i.e., the style of the award offered for sale is consistent with the style of the period in which it was presented). The original format containing the original label of the record being certified will usually be the most collectible. Another point to remember is that record companies have been known to reframe awards in a style other than the prevailing format. This was often done to replace damaged frames or the requisite frame was unavailable at the time. Before 1989, when formats were still under strict control, this practice was not met with favor by the RIAA and generally discouraged.

From a collecting point of view it is better to buy an award in its original frame whenever possible. When white mattes are found with different frames the diligent collector will often replace the frame with an original from that period, especially if it is a highly desirable title. As a matter of fact, serious collectors have been known to use parts of a white matte of a less desirable artist to restore an award of an artist of greater value.

There *are* framed gold records that do not indicate any type of music organization recognizing the sales achievement. These are not awards produced by any framing store, trophy and plaque shop, or RIAA certified manufacturers. They are made by specialist establishments for one purpose, resale. The popularity of award collecting and the desire to own a trophy has caused the manufacture of these wall-hangings to escalate. These gold records are usually identifiable by the lack of any music industry seal on the plaque. The most widely distributed of these are the [admittedly beautiful] plaques produced by California Gold Records, now located in New Jersey. This company has produced a gold record for almost every title in The Beatles' catalog. However, as of this writing the company has discontinued all framed gold records of Beatles' records with the exception of a numbered "collectible" for John Lennon's "Imagine" single.

As the hobby develops, new and unusual awards are uncovered. Recently discovered was an award produced by a band and presented to the radio station disc jockey responsible for "breaking" their first certified gold single. Since this item is neither RIAA nor in-house, it represents a new classification where the "organization" recognizing the sales achievement is the artist itself!

Finally, when purchasing an award, compare prices which may vary widely. Consider all the factors mentioned above and be certain to consider the seller's reputation. A good price is a bad buy if you receive a bogus award (or, worse, no award at all). Remember, white mattes appear to be the best investment; while later awards can be enjoyable to own, because of the large amounts legitimately ordered and manufactured it is still uncertain as to the investment potential of awards since the strip plate format. My parting advice is to purchase the best awards you can afford but don't forget that collecting is *supposed* to be fun. Sometimes the best thing to own is simply the title you like the most. . .

Genuine, Pirate & Fake RIAA Awards— What Is Real And What Is A Fake

The proliferation of the sale of pirate and fake RIAA gold and platinum record "awards" has become epidemic in recent years. The combined number of pirate and fake RIAA awards offered for sale now probably equals or exceeds the number of genuine RIAA Awards available in the collectors' marketplace in any given month. Every RIAA format, including the coveted white matte format, has been either pirated or fraudulently manufactured. The business of dealing in pirate and fake RIAA awards has become a high profit industry, with the cost of manufacturing these frauds between $50 and $100 and then being offered for sale in the $300-500 range. A fake white matte may be offered for $600 to $2,000 or more! To further the distribution of accurate consumer information, the following guidelines and definitions are being offered in the hope of stemming the tide of these frauds as well as preserving the values of genuine RIAA Record Awards.

In order to truly understand what pirate and fake RIAA Awards are, let us first examine the process by which genuine RIAA Awards come into existence. The word "genuine" is described in *Webster's' New 20th Century Dictionary* as "really being what it is said to be; actually coming from the alleged source or origin; real; true; not counterfeit or artificial." A genuine RIAA Award is an award for a record or CD that has been certified by the RIAA, originates from a licensed RIAA Award manufacturer, *and has been distributed in accordance with the regulations specified in the license granted by the RIAA to the manufacturer.*

The first step a record company must take in order to have a record or CD certified by the RIAA is for the company to request that an audit be conducted by the RIAA of the company's sales records to determine that a record or CD has reached RIAA gold, platinum or multi-platinum status. Once the record company has received official RIAA status, the company then has the authorization to order an RIAA certified award from an RIAA licensed award manufacturer. One or more record executives at any given record company may be authorized to order RIAA Awards from an RIAA licensed award manufacturer. A licensing fee is paid by each RIAA licensed manufacturer on a yearly basis.

RIAA licensed award manufacturers are required to keep records of how many RIAA Awards they make. An additional fee is paid by the manufacturer for each award affixed with the [current] RIAA logo. The award is made according to the specifications spelled out by the record company with the presentation made out to whomever those specifications indicate. The finished award is then usually sent back to the record company, in care of the record company executive who ordered it, who may retain or delegate the responsibility of seeing to it that the award is delivered to whomever the award is presented.

As of September 1994, that is how *genuine* RIAA Awards are legitimately manufactured and distributed. Unless given specific permission to do otherwise by an authorized record company executive, *RIAA licensed award manufacturers may sell RIAA Awards only to the record companies who order them.* The record company is then the sole legal "distributor."

"Pirate" RIAA Record & CD Awards

Webster's defines the word "pirate" as a verb meaning "to publish or use in violation of a copyright or patent." A pirate award is one that has been manufactured or distributed in violation of the license agreement between the RIAA and the RIAA licensed manufacturer. Awards that have been sold by a licensed RIAA manufacturer "out the back door," to various individuals or organizations for resale to the marketplace are pirate awards.

The massive influx of pirate awards from licensed RIAA manufacturers into the collectors' market has adversely affected the value of genuine RIAA Awards. With the sudden, dramatic rise in popularity of award collecting in the late '80s, many collectors and dealers alike were frustrated by the scarcity of genuine RIAA Record Awards. The response of many dealers was to appeal to record company executives and have that executive order extra awards which the dealer would then purchase. In some cases, the executives actually contacted record dealers offering RIAA Awards for sale, probably an abuse of their position as record company executives. But these RIAA Awards at least went through the established channels as required by the RIAA license granted to the RIAA Award makers.

Unfortunately, other record dealers decided to go directly to the RIAA licensed award makers and seduce them into manufacturing pirate awards for whatever artists they wished. Some dealers have reported licensed RIAA manufacturers offering them *any* award they want and in *any* quantity for which they are willing to pay.

At first, licensed RIAA Award makers that succumbed to the lure of greatly increased sales would only pirate RIAA Awards presented to fictitious persons or radio stations. However, as the demand for better presentations increased, the RIAA Award manufacturers began to pirate RIAA awards made out to the record company and, eventually, to the artist. These pirates can be identical in every way to genuine RIAA Awards, *but most do not have the manufacturer's tag on the back* because the award maker will usually try to avoid having the pirate award traced back to his company. (This situation may have changed recently and pirate awards may indeed have the manufacturer's tag on the back.)

Since, in the case of Hologram and 'R'-Hologram format awards in particular there may be no physical difference between genuine and pirate awards, dealers selling pirate awards have asked me "What is the difference?" The difference between genuine and pirate awards is the difference between reality and illusion; between legitimacy and fraud; between owning a rare promotional treasure and owning something that purports to be promotional, but is actually just a wall hanging that anyone with money can buy.

Pirate awards are "ordered" and marketed to the public with the explanation that they are overruns of genuine awards, meaning that a licensed RIAA manufacturer made too many awards and sold the extras to the record dealer, who offers them for sale. According to the RIAA's Angela Corio, this method of disposing of extra awards is totally illegal. In the rare event that a licensed RIAA Award manufacturer does happen to make too many of a given award, the manufacturer is required to either sell the extras to the record company or to destroy them. The selling of these overruns to record dealers who then sell them to the public violates the distribution guidelines in the licensing agreement between the RIAA and manufacturers and makes overruns the same as a pirate award.

"Fake" RIAA Record & CD Awards

The word "fake" is defined in *Webster's* as "fraudulent; not genuine; sham; false." A fake RIAA record or CD award is exactly what the term implies; that is, a totally fraudulent imitation of an RIAA Award. It has become increasingly important to collectors and investors that RIAA Awards be in their original format. Also, with record prices being fetched for certain white matte awards, the demand for this format has skyrocketed.

Corrupt salespersons and award makers responded by the creation of fake RIAA awards, which are total fabrications of every format of genuine awards, including the white mattes. There are even reports that some of these fakes are being manufactured by licensed RIAA manufacturers, claiming that they have the right to reissue *(sic)* old formats of RIAA Awards. However, according to Ms. Corio, the RIAA has *never* licensed the use of the older RIAA trademarks in any recently constructed award, nor do they plan to in the future. Therefore, *any* old format awards recently constructed by anyone, *licensed or not,* are totally fraudulent! They are fakes being sold to soak unsuspecting consumers for large sums of money.

This current wave of fakes being dumped on the market are made of components that resemble those of genuine RIAA Awards enough so that they cannot be easily identified by studying a photograph of the item. and personal examination by an expert may be required. Fakes of older format RIAA Awards may be identified by the use of new construction materials. In other words, they look brand new. These fakes may be identified by the lack of a manufacturers' tag on the back. If there is a tag, it will also look brand new. In the case of white mattes, fakes can be rather obvious, since the last real white matte RIAA Award was presented twenty years ago. . .

Fakes of older format RIAA Awards may also have laser photocopies of the record labels. Laser photocopies weren't used until the mid to late '80s, so the use of them in a white matte, floater or strip-plate RIAA Award is a dead giveaway that the award has either recently undergone major reconstruction due to damage or is a fake.

This surge of new and improved fakes has had a deleterious effect on the market for all genuine RIAA Awards. Since museum quality photographs on quality paper of genuine RIAA Awards in each format have not yet been made available, the opportunity for fraud is great. Extreme caution in the purchase of older format fakes of awards is strongly recommended.

The large number of fake and pirate awards infesting the marketplace is both criminal and tragic. Unsuspecting and uninformed collectors and investors are being cheated because earnest people pay for something which they do not receive. Measures *are being taken* to alleviate this unfortunate state of affairs. In the meantime, each purchaser of a proposed RIAA Award should insist on a written guarantee from the seller that the award they are receiving is genuine and that it is not a pirate or a fake. This will provide additional documentation for legal recourse should the item they receive from *any* seller prove to be less than genuine.

GOLDEN YEARS & GOLDEN EARS: MONO, STEREO & AUDIOPHILES

By Neal Umphred

"I'm basically a one-mike mono man. . . I like natural sound. You know, stereo came in and set back the recording business twenty years, I think, with isolation and all that. . . The more mikes you have open and everything, the more distortion there is. [Tape] made it possible to make more dishonest records than there ever had been, through splicing." These quotes come from the legendary John Hammond from conversations with Ted Fox (from *In The Groove*, St. Martin's Press, 1986). Mr. Hammond's opinions are striking, powerful and, in many respects, correct although the "dishonest" records to which he is referring are almost exclusively heavily spliced classical recordings sold as "live" recitals. (Note that while the bulk of Hammond's work was in jazz, his opinions are applicable as a reflection of the technicians working in rock'n roll and rhythm'n blues.)

While this opinion may sound lunatically purist, if not damnably heretical, to the contemporary audiophile, Hammond is not alone in his beliefs. Phil Spector and Brian Wilson were firmly founded on the joys of single signal listening. And, of course, prime-mover and head Beatle John Lennon long maintained that "You haven't heard *Sgt. Pepper* if you haven't heard it in mono." Berry Gordy, whose creative role in the many accomplishments of his Motown empire should *never* be underestimated, is said to have assigned the mono mix-downs to his best engineers, allowing the novices the stereo mixing. That is why so many Motown stereo records sound anemic when A/B-ed with their mono counterparts. This is especially true when comparing *any* Motown single with its subsequent appearance on LP!

Of course, there *are* benefits to multi-track recording, *especially* if you are a fan of the many albums conceived and recorded in the mid-'60s. This was an era when, primarily due to budget consciousness, over-dubbing was still a "new" thing to countless engineers. What was particularly appealing to the Rock artists of the second half of the decade was that the tricks of the trade (including over-dubbing and tape loops, filtering and phasing, etc.) allowed them creative attempts at capturing on tape aspects of the ever lingering, often baffling, often profound effects of the "psychedelic experience."

Many of the recordings made today would be better off if they were cut "live" in an ambient environment with as few mikes as possible and a sensitive engineer at the board. . . That is not about to happen: For whatever reason, contemporary mainstream artists are immersed in technology. Certainly there is a move towards realism: There are artists and engineers who are returning to recording "live in the studio" on analog equipment and tape. Over-dubs are being held to a minimum and the final transfer is, of necessity, digital. Mind you, for the most part this is occurring with smaller, independent labels, but it is a positive sign for all concerned with "real" sounding music.

During the early years of stereo in the States, much of the best rock'n roll, rhythm'n blues and country'n western recordings were done under less than state-of-the-art conditions. Often the technicians involved were far more adept in mixing down to mono than creating a good stereo two-track master. Conversely, by the early 70s the ability, or sensibility, to mix multi-track recordings down to a single mono track had been "lost" by the majority of the engineers and producers of popular recordings.

Original two-channel stereo recordings went for effect, making no attempt at reality. (There is no "stereo" in everyday listening experience. Sound emanates from one source and is echoed off of countless objects, which adds depth and resonance, which is what stereo recording was attempting to add to the "flatter" sounds of mono.) It is known affectionately as "wide channel" stereo due to the distinct placement of the individual sounds in the two channels. This made for a more involving experience, essentially inviting the brain to participate in completing the mix-down from the widely disparate signals emanating from the two speakers.

Today's technicians have lost the means to mix contemporary multi-tracks (24, 48, 64, ad infinitum) down into the popular stereo of the '60s. Just as the means to duplicate the wondrous sound of Elvis in Sam Philips' Sun Studios was lost to '60s artists and technicians, so today is lost the bombast of Phil Spector's "wall of sound," or the "wild, mercurial sounds" of Dylan's mid-'60s "folk-rock." Consequently, when a CD version of a popular '50s or '60s multi-track recording is remixed, the listening experience for the older fan can be downright shocking! While the track *may* be cleaned up and the dynamics expanded, the new mix can be disconcertingly different from the original. The wide channel stereo sound is often gone, replaced by the more natural, less affecting mix (often referred to as "multi-channel mono") with which today's engineers are familiar.

Stereo: The Early Years

While two track recordings were made through the mid '50s, very few rock, blues or country records were cut that way. Early albums from these genres in true stereo are rare and, needless to say, desirable. The first rock'n roll LP to contain true stereo recordings appears to have been the 1958 release of Duane Eddy's *Have "Twangy" Guitar—Will Travel* on Jamie. Unfortunately, within a few years the stereo masters were lost! So, while Eddy's first album has been available in rechanneled stereo for thirty years, the early pressings are among the most sought-after stereo records of the '50s.

James Brown's first stereo outing was 1963's *Jump Around* while Chuck Berry didn't see a stereo release until 1964's *St. Louis To Liverpool*. This could at least be excused by the fact that they recorded for small, independent labels (King and Chess, respectively) that catered to a black market, those least likely to have replaced their hi-fi with a stereo. Even major labels balked at the expense involved of recording teen music on more than one track. *The Teddy Bears Sing!* on Imperial is a legendary stereo album from 1959, long commanding big bucks. Featuring neophyte Phil Spector, the clean, wide open sound makes this desirable as a rock'n roll rarity, as a stereo album and as a Spector artifact. *The Teddy Bears Sing!* has cooled off considerably in recent years, in response to a growing number of collectors who have decided that paying four figures for musically lame records, no matter how rare, might not make all that much sense. . .

While Elvis wasn't cut on two-track until *Elvis Is Back!*, recorded upon his release from the U.S. Army in 1960, the initial pressings used Victor's "Living Stereo" system on its "Miracle Surface" vinyl and remains one of Presley's, and rock'n roll's, best sounding records. Had his career not been impeded by military service it's *possible* RCA Victor might have seen fit to escort their bread and butter into one of their modern studios. The closest the biggest record seller in the world got to stereo prior to 1960 was during a session in January of 1957. Held at Radio Recorders in Hollywood, the studio's normal back-up recorder was on the blink so the new-fangled two-track recorder was used instead. These back-up recordings were eventually located and duly issued by RCA as *Stereo '57 (Essential Elvis, Vol. 2)* in 1988. While they are fun to hear, nobody is going to make any glowing claims for the stereophonic listening experience.

Other examples abound: Fats Domino's two lonely stereo releases for Imperial, *A Lot Of Dominos* and *Let The Four Winds Blow* are among Fats' rarest albums. Ricky Nelson, along with Fats, Imperial's biggest money-maker and as white a pop star as one could hope for, was not recorded in stereo by their companies until *More Songs By Ricky* in 1960.

Roy Orbison's first two for Monument, *Lonely And Blue* and *Crying*, are considered by many to be among the very finest pop/rock stereo records ever made. (Their continually escalating value as reflected in this book is an accurate reflection of their desirability.) In this case, the extraordinary sound was impeccably produced by Fred Foster and magically mixed by Bill Porter, the same engineer responsible for the *Elvis Is Back!* sessions. The sound and Roy's gorgeous performances more than justify the records' reps.

Del Shannon's first two albums on Big Top, *Runaway* and *Little Town Flirt*, were issued in stereo, apparently unknown to the artist. The albums were shipped in mono covers, sometimes stamped "Stereo," sometimes unmarked, saving the company the additional royalty payments to the artist the more expensive stereo discs required. *Little Town Flirt* even carries a mono label and must be played to ascertain whether or not it is mono or stereo! While these records are of modest artistic achievement and rudimentary stereo, they continue to escalate in value due not only to their rarity, which existed on the day of their release, but the fact that the stereo master tapes have long since vanished.

In some cases, everyday economics can affect a record's eventual rarity. Due to the incredible mix-up that the Chicago-based rhythm'n blues label Vee Jay went through in the '60s (a time when even having The Beatles *and* The Four Seasons on the label couldn't save them), many of their albums had miniscule stereo press runs. Gene Chandler's *Duke Of Earl* is virtually impossible to find in stereo. When boxes of supposedly stereo copies of *Duke Of Earl* found their way onto the market in the late '70s, the discs inside proved to be mono, leading many to believe they were reproductions.

Vee Jay's stereo problems didn't end with The Duke. Stereo copies of the label's biggest selling album, *Introducing The Beatles*, are so rare that any version of either the original 1963 pressing with "Love Me Do" and "P.S. I Love You" or the 1964 reissue with "Please Please Me" and "Ask Me Why" is a four figure record in any collectible condition. The same holds true for the stereo versions of *The Beatles Vs. The Four Seasons*, *The Beatles & Frank Ifield On Stage*, and *Songs, Pictures & Stories Of The Fabulous Beatles*.

When the British Invasion was in full swing, many of the tapes that were sent to the States were mono only. This "forced" engineers to rechannel them to meet the two-channel demands of the domestic market. Even when two-tracks were sent here, they were often dramatically altered: Because the British mixes were often simple two-track masters with no real attempt at producing an identifiable sound stage for the listener, the final results were deemed too "dry" for Stateside listeners. The American companies added over-generous echo and/or reverb to fill in the "hole" left by the "cleaner" British separation.

Thus, most U.S. fans grew up hearing a very different set of recordings than what their cross-Atlantic counterparts were listening to (or, for that matter, what the artists *intended* them to hear), at least as regards stereo LPs. This was so common that an attempt to list the tracks/albums affected would take up pages! When imports became common in the early '70s, listeners were often astounded at hearing the differences between the U.K. versions of albums such as *Aftermath* or *Revolver*, where the lack of echo made both Jagger's and Lennon's voices decidedly English, an effect softened by the American tinkering.

There are often non-annotated differences between mono and stereo versions of an album. While many of the studios began using two tracks as far back as 1956-57, most of them did so only for the increased latitude it allowed in mixing down to mono. When stereo became a viable commercial medium toward the end of the decade, some companies returned to the original multi-track tapes and mixed a few rock LPs for stereo release. Thus titles recorded with only mono in mind were issued to the new stereo enthusiasts. Many of these contain the most rudimentary form of stereo, with little or none of the stereophonic imaging that makes the enjoyment of stereo essential to most listeners.

Virtually every record collector enters a paroxysm of rage when electronically rechanneled stereo is brought up. [It should be noted that some rechanneled stereo albums are growing in value, mostly due to their rarity.] Every effort has been made to identify those records where the engineers took a mono signal and "created" a stereo effect with the use of boosted trebles/bass, echo, phase, etc. RCA Victor reissued all of Elvis' '50s albums in an "electronically rechanneled for stereo" format in the early '60s. This was acceptable *(sic)* as long as the mono versions of these records remained in print. But, by 1969 all a person could buy was the horrific fake stereo sound, leaving several generations of fans growing up with a very distorted concept of Elvis' sound.

Another extreme case is that of Brian Wilson and his Beach Boys. Brian was the first of the producer/artists who had complete control of the studio. But, as Mr. Wilson is deaf in one ear and can not hear stereophonically, all the group's early albums that appear in "full dimensional stereo" were mixed into two-tracks by Brian's engineer, Chuck Britz. While these are excellent wide channel separations, for the hard-core BW aficionado they are a step removed from the complete aural image intended by the artist. Unfortunately, this point was rendered moot in 1965 when the Beach Boys' albums were issued in "duophonic stereo," Capitol's trademarked fake stereo process that all but ruined the subtleties and nuances of Wilson's extraordinary mono productions.

As an aside, the British system of rechanneling is often noticeably superior to the American. Brian Wilson aficionados are advised to pick up a copy of World Records' boxed set, *The Beach Boys—The Capitol Years*. These six records in mono and stereo, programmed thematically, were the first to present listeners with a definitive overview *and* offer collectors hard-to-find tracks (a bonus seventh record contains all seventeen of BW's '60s productions for other Capitol artists). There are a number of reprocessed tracks, including almost the entirety of *Pet Sounds*, so neatly done that they have fooled more than a few listeners into believing they were hearing *Pet Sounds* in stereo for the first time!

Mono: The Final Years

While the major labels kept their mono stampers going through at least part of 1968, the press runs were miniscule. Just as stereo copies of Elvis' first few albums from 1960 are worth considerably more than the monos, the reverse is true for his albums from this period. The mono version of 1967's *Clambake* is currently worth nearly four times the original stereo version. But this pales in comparison to his 1968 albums: *Elvis' Gold Records, Volume 4* and *Speedway*, are worth 300 times the stereo originals! But this may not be true for smaller, independent labels, who, more wary of the bottom line, began deleting monos from their catalog as early as 1967. There may be considerably more mono titles from 1968 than remain undocumented.

Several West Coast bands have highly collectable mono records from this period: At one time or another, every member of Jefferson Airplane has expressed disgust with the distracting echo and distortion of the stereo *Surrealistic Pillow*. The mono mix is devoid of most of this echo and a more accurate reflection of the band's intentions (*and* a better listening experience). The Grateful Dead's self-titled debut is far more potent a mix than the readily available stereo version and essential for Deadheads.

The Doors is a must for Morrison aficionados. Seems that when Jim recorded the album's closer, "The End," he was still tingling from the previous night's acid experience (No, dear reader, there are no such things as "flashbacks") and was a bit more uninhibited than usual. At the song's climax, where he rants "Father, I want to kill you" and the band goes into its raga rave-up, there comes a point where Morrison can be heard chanting "Kill, kill, kill." He followed this with a muttered "Fuck, fuck, fuck," which was buried in the stereo mix but can be discerned on the up-front mono mix.

Sgt. Pepper's Lonely Heart's Club Band, while a cornerstone of multi-track recording and *still* a lot of fun to hear on head-phones, has its adherents as a monaural experience. The dub-downs from the multi-tracks to mono were supervised by producer and fifth Beatle George Martin, usually with the group, while the stereo mix-downs were left to the engineer. Unfortunately, by 1967, few of the group's legions of fans were interested in mono, making *Pepper* and *Magical Mystery Tour* among the rarest commercially issued Beatles albums on Capitol.

Some labels continued to release promotional albums in mono: *Electric Ladyland* is not only the most valuable mono promo, it is also the hottest and most sought-after of Jimi Hendrix's vinyl artifacts. Another collectible promo from this period is The Who's *Magic Bus*, which gathers some of its value due to the fact that several of the tracks on the stereo versions are messily rechanneled. Monomania is not restricted to "important" albums or "major" artists: While earlier records by The Monkees are garage-sale staples, *The Birds, The Bees & The Monkees* is the rarest commercially issued album by the post-fab four. Both *Steppenwolf* and *Steppenwolf The Second* are rare and sought after.

In many cases, when purchasing a late mono record all one is acquiring is a rarity. By the middle of 1967 many companies simply had their engineers take the two track stereo masters and dub them down into a single track instead of preparing a properly mixed mono master. Because of this, many of these albums are decidedly inferior to their stereo counterparts, producing an unbalanced, muddy sound. Considering the unlikelihood of the mono mixes of any of these LPs making it onto CD (although EMI/Capitol's issuing the Beatles complete catalog in mono *and* stereo is not only not out of the question, it is recommended), it becomes all the more desirable to own and hear the truly classic albums of the '60s the way the bands wanted you to hear them.

After the demise of mono, many of the majors appeared to rethink their position on the practise of "electronically rechanneling" mono masters into a horrid phony stereo. By the '70s archival material was surfacing in original mono for the first time in years. RCA again was notable with Elvis' *Sun Sessions* in 1975, compiling for the first time what many historians consider to be the most important body of rock'n roll music ever recorded.

Many important albums were issued in mono abroad after the American labels had discontinued the practice. These range from 1968's *The Beatles* and *Beggar's Banquet* (which is far more dynamic and powerful in mono) through 1969's *Let It Bleed*, *The Kinks Are The Village Green Preservation Society* and several prominent non-Beatles Apple titles. The collector interested in foreign pressings such as these is advised to expect a precarious but interesting pursuit.

Then there is the quadramania of the early '70s. Quadraphonic (a different signal emanating from four different channels and requiring separate electronic components to decode the signals) pressings are attractive for a variety of reasons, scarcity being the most obvious. But of far more interest is the fact that many quads have radically different, and sometimes superior, mixes to the original stereo. The best known instance is *Sly & The Family Stone's Greatest Hits*: The stereo record contains three singles— "Everybody Is A Star," "Hot Fun In The Summertime," and "Thank You (Falletinme Be Mice Elf Again)"— in fake stereo.

When their engineers mastered the quadraphonic record, they dug up the original multi-tracks and issued all of the tracks in four channel sound, the closest approximation of stereo that collectors have found of the aforementioned trio! Jefferson Airplane's *Volunteers* is also notable for including at least four tracks with alternate takes or mixes. These remained unavailable to the public until the release of the compact disc boxed set *Jefferson Airplane Loves You*.

Audiophilia: The Golden Ears

One interesting group of record collectors shuns the emulation of individual artists or styles in favor of the recording's overall sound. These collectors are concerned with an accurate recreation of the musical event as it originally occurred in its natural environment. Originally dubbed "golden ears," these hobbyists emerging from early hi-fi were not simply satisfied with whatever technology was available on a mass-produced basis for a reasonable price. They pursued a more perfect medium through the selection of the correct gear, the placement of speakers, the "tweaking" of each and every facet of their equipment and the environment in which it was enjoyed.

Often perceived as obsessed by the more relaxed majority, many of the innovations now taken for granted, both in the hardware (the playback equipment) and the software (the records), can be traced directly to the insights and perseverance of these pioneers. Many of these listeners place a primary emphasis on "sound field" recordings, those that, by use of the most appropriate equipment in the proper environment, with mikes properly placed and, most importantly, no post-recording manipulation of the signal, come closest to achieving the idealized sound presentation.

Needless to say, most of this is not applicable to popular music, where the very opposite is the case: Most pop recordings since the mid-'60s have been recorded in the sterile environment of the studio, often in bits and pieces, with the use of over-dubbing, compression, etc., grossly over-using the medium to manipulate the message. So, in record collecting, the term "audiophile" is generally applied to those who specialize in high-quality recordings on high-quality vinyl. While every LP *could have* been an audiophile pressing, few were and the standard of quality, especially in the amount of pressings done from each stamper to the quality of the vinyl used, dropped during the '70s. It was also quite normal for the major companies to finish up the making of an album—after the recording and post-production technical work is complete—by cutting a master lacquer disc in a matter of hours. From these are produced "mothers" and from them the "stampers" from which the records are actually pressed.

In a high volume business with a "name" star, the stampers can be used well past the point of their being able to reproduce the extremes in the highs and lows from the master. In fact, the industry's disregard for their customers and, of course, the apparent lack of discrimination *of* their customers, led to enormous quantities of noticeably inferior records flooding the American retail racks. Some sources claim that as much as 75% of the press run of Michael Jackson's *Thriller* were shipped defective. . . and the company knew and could not care less!

The vogue for half-speed mastered records was ushered in by Mobile Fidelity Sound Laboratories at the end of the '70s and lasted, more or less, through the early years of the "digital revolution" of the '80s. As the general level of quality of American manufactured records dropped like a proverbial SAT score, this enterprising company stepped in and leased master tapes from the original companies, manufacturing high quality records with a correspondingly high price. Eventually, several other companies followed suit and a mini-industry serving the perceived needs of a dedicated few blossomed.

Mobile Fidelity's "Original Master Recording" series utilized a mastering process whereby the master lacquer was cut at 16 2/3 RPM rather than the industry standard of 33 1/3 (hence, half-speed mastered). This allowed the cutting of the grooves twice as much time to capture each nuance of the analogue recording. The difference in the sound quality, even when it was not "astounding," was nonetheless evident to even the tinnest (sic) of ears.

Other steps—special mastering equipment including custom designed cutting heads, amplifiers, etc.—were taken to ensure accuracy but the most important to collectors was the shipping of the stampers to Japan where the records were pressed on JVC's trademarked "Super Vinyl". This not only ensured a more faithful reproduction of the sound but allowed the user to play the disc repeatedly with less fear of damaging the grooves. Each album was pressed with a maximum number of 5,000 copies from each of the four stampers taken from the "mother," at which point the stampers were destroyed. Thus each disc was a "limited edition" of such noticeably superior quality that left many a listener speechless upon first hearing.

Sheffield Lab, Wilson Audio and Reference Recordings, also specialized in audiophile pressings but their main output was jazz and classical and therefore outside the perimeters of this volume. The Nautilus label half-speed "SuperDiscs" were less successful on the market than MFSL and consequently their titles are a bit harder to find, although the demand is not as great from the collectors. Other collectible audiophile labels exist outside the boundaries of the increasingly xenophobic U.S., such as Cube (Germany), Vertigo (U.K.), CBS (Canada, Germany and Japan), Nimbus (U.K.) and A&M (Canada). These companies' products are often available domestically and sought out by audiophiles.

Among the major labels, CBS poured out a number of their Columbia and Epic catalog in this format, but these were done in relatively small printings, did not fare well on the retail racks and thus, the demand for certain titles is increasing. The actual pressings themselves, from inception through mastering and pressing, were qualitatively far behind the smaller companies, leaving a great deal to be desired. When the relative failure of this line was obvious, rather than simply delete the titles and make them available to cut-out bins nationwide, CBS simply recalled them and recycled the vinyl for future use, making many of the CBS titles difficult indeed to track down. Thus their value as collectibles outstrips their value as vehicles for a truly pleasing listening experience.

Finally, the concerns of the audiophile has spawned several nationally distributed publications, the best known being *Stereo Review* and *Audio*. The more arcane aspects of the hobby has also spawned at least two publications that deal at least peripherally with the concerns of the software (i.e., the recorded medium, either vinyl or CD). Both *The Absolute Sound* and *Stereophile* devote space to reviewing exceptionally well recorded and manufactured music and, while the emphasis is often on the more spectacular classical realms, they do pay some attention to other types of music. (All four of the aforementioned periodicals are available at any well-stocked magazine stand.)

The major complaint many have lodged against audiophiles in general is their eagerness to choose form over content. That the high muckety-mucks of the major labels were more willing to take the time and expense to properly record easy listening music (which was, after all, intended for "mature" tastes) is a given. This has placed many audiophiles to build collections of [non-classical] records that sound great to the ears but, well, don't sound all that rewarding to the gray matter between them.

That so many of the titles immortalized on these audiophile pressings were of utterly mediocre aesthetic quality was probably a prime factor in said companies failures in the marketplace. At one time MFSL auditioned several tapes of three of The Beach Boys early '70s albums on Reprise. Each was rejected for technical reasons, primarily excessive compression. For this listener, a sonically "good" Original Master Recording of a great album like *Sunflower* means far more than an aurally great half-speed of, well, let's say most of the titles that made the grade. . .

A BRIEF BIT O' BIO

Born to a modest family of registered Democrats in Wilkes-Barre General Hospital in 1951 (Virgo by birth, radically left by inclination), I can honestly count Marcel Duchamp and burning culm-banks as pivotal influences on my developing psyche. While my baby-book, long since lost in the Great Flood of '72, claimed my favorite song in my pre-literate years was "Sh-Boom," I remember "Hound Dog". . . Growing up, Wilkes-Barre seemed more a part of the past than the present: I can recall going to the movies on a Saturday afternoon for 15¢ with my brother Charles and good bud Donny Flynn, spending hours absorbing such seminal works of art as *Earth Vs The Flying Saucers* and *The Atomic Submarine*, *The Mask* and *Dementia 13*, *The Delicate Delinquent* and *Abbott & Costello Meet The Wolfman*, and the other staples of '50s and '60s matinees.

Way back then, comic books were 32 pages for a dime, 16 oz. RC Colas were 13¢, Tastycakes were, er, tasty, and I whiled many a day away readin' and sippin' in awe of The Fantastic Four, Batman, and especially Steve Ditko's Dr. Strange and Spiderman. By twelve I had passed through dinosaurs (a phase I joyfully find my seven-year old daughter, Ananda, locked in today—she wants to be a Tyrannosauus Rex for Halloween), the Civil War, military aircraft of the War To End All Wars (ho ho), and baseball cards. I was ready for something new. . .

I discovered the magic of the "elpee" in 1964 when I found that the big-record-with-the-little-hole played several songs before I had to get up and turn it over. Wow! My record collecting career began with the atrocious "electronically reprocessed stereo" reissues of *Elvis' Golden Records 1* and *2* and greatest hits collections of Chuck Berry, Little Richard, Fats Domino, Jerry Lee Lewis, and The Platters. As Northeastern Pennsylvania was a dumping grounds for cut-outs (all most of us could afford), I was able to pick up anything deleted, which is where my exposure to jazz came from.

Over the course of the next few years my nascent collection grew in rather odd directions: As both my brother, Charles, and my Aunt Judy were members of mail order record clubs, through cast-offs and trades I acquired such essentials as Gary Lewis & The Playboys' *Golden Grass* (still a favorite; Jerry's kid may not have had the world's greatest pipes but he had some of this planet's finest talents supporting him), The Dave Clark Five's *Coast To Coast* (which poses the burning question "Can an LP be less than twelve minutes per side and still be worth the money?" and leaves it unanswered) and Nancy "Yeah, Frank's m'dad but I love 'im anyway" Sinatra's *How Does That Grab You, Darlin'*?

I gradually learned to love an awfully broad spectrum of rock and pop music. (Although, as a pseudo-intellectual acne-ed white teenager I could not for the life of me figure out what alla those black people were moanin' n' groanin', wailin' n' railin', screechin' n' beseechin' about. Like *real* country music, that took a little maturation to make sense. . .) When the British Invasion hit I somehow managed to avoid the charm of The Beatles and The Stones. Don't ask me how; I was, how shall I put it, oh, headstrong? While my contemporaries were wearing the grooves out of The Beatles and The Stones—and, let's never forget Herman's Hermits—I stuck to the "old" stuff:

In 1965 The Byrds' "Mr. Tambourine Man" turned my entire perception of pop music inside out and I spent the next fifteen years or so listening exclusively to the Rock-With-A-Capital-R of the '60s: I became an avid reader of Paul Williams' *Crawdaddy*, which, more than anything else, helped shape my opinions on Rock-With-A-Capitol-R. I had discovered *Pet Sounds*, the album that has remained #1 in my heart for more than two decades, and such generally overlooked gems as the debut albums of Buffalo Springfield, the Byrds, Captain Beefheart, Dylan, Jefferson Airplane, Love, the Spoonful, Van Dyke Parks, and the Youngbloods remain favorites decades later. Still I religiously purchased each new [cheesy] Elvis soundtrack, but the necessity of taking home *Frankie And Johnnie* and *Spinout* in brown paper bags eventually woke up even this slow learner.

At a Christmas party in 1967 some noise blurted out of the speakers that had me entranced: "Why don't we sing this song all together, open our heads let the pictures come. . ." I figured it might be time for me to renege on my vow never to buy a record with Mick Jagger on it. Through the past two decades I have grown rather detached from the merchandising aspect of the biz, constantly reminding myself that it was to get away from alla the Mad Ave bullschidt that allowed rock 'n roll to occur. Still, albums such as *Born To Run, Armed Forces, Remain In Light, Dream Of Life* and *Skylarking* keep my hopes up.

Current non-musical obsessions include but are not limited to hiking the mountains of the Pacific Northwest; dreaming of pizza from Arcaro & Jenell's in Old Forge, PA; old movies with Fred Astaire, Jean Arthur, Carol Lombard and particularly Cary Grant; tall women who work out; books on mind-manifesting agents; rereading all of James Clavell's novels.

As for my origins as record collecting's "pricing guru," well. . . In 1983 I was drafted out of art classes for duty on the O' Sullivan Woodside line of record collectors price guides. This was caused by the departure of the former editor and the need for someone who knew the field in a broad sense; was capable of doing the necessary work; and, most importantly, was readily available! I authored the controversial and iconoclastic *1985-86 Rock Records Album Price Guide* and the *1985-86 Elvis Presley Record Price Guide* before that company's premature demise. In 1985 I inaugurated the *Goldmine* line of price guides for record collectors: *Goldmine's Price Guide To Collectible Record Album, Goldmine 45RPM Rock'n Roll Record Price Guide*, and this jazz book you are holding (with more in the future).

A Few Late Additions

GRATEFUL DEAD
Arista ADP-9630 (DJ) Grateful Dead Talk To Themselves *(Interview)* 1987 **10.00** **25.00**

KINKS, THE
Reprise (DJ) **Four More Respected Gentlemen** *(Test pressing)* 1968 *See note below*
(Test pressing for an unreleased studio album. Covers are not known
to exist. Rare with a suggested NM value of $400-800.)

Reprise (DJ) **God Save The Kinks** *(2 LPs. Test pressing)* 1969 *See note below*
(Test pressing for an unreleased compilation album. Covers are not known
to exist. Rare with a suggested NM value of $400-800.)

LED ZEPPELIN
Swan Song (DJ) **Robert Plant And John Paul Jones Talk**
About Led Zeppelin—Past, Present And Future 1979 *See note below*
(Unreleased promotional interview album. Only a handful of test pressings
with the cover exist with a suggested NM value of $2,000-4,000.
Test pressings without the cover, $1,000-2,000.)

REDDING, OTIS
For many, Otis Redding was, and always will be, the quintessential male soul singer. Following his overwhelming
success with the mostly white, perceived "hippy" audience at the Monterey Pop Festival in June '67, a chartered
airplane carrying him and his backing group, The Bar-Kays, crashed into Lake Monoma in Wisconsin in December.
There was only one survivor. . . Refer to Jimi Hendrix / Otis Redding. (And please, don't anyone ask me how I missed
Otis in the main entries.)

Atco 33-161	(M)	Pain In My Heart	1964	100.00	250.00
Atco SD-33-161	(E)	Pain In My Heart	1967	100.00	250.00
Volt 411	(M)	Soul Ballads	1965	50.00	125.00
Volt S-411	(E)	Soul Ballads	1967	50.00	125.00
Volt 412	(M)	Otis Blue/Otis Redding Sings Soul	1965	20.00	50.00
Volt S-412	(S)	Otis Blue/Otis Redding Sings Soul	1965	30.00	75.00
		("Respect" and "Old Man Trouble" were rerecorded in stereo.)			
Volt 413	(M)	The Soul Album	1966	20.00	50.00
Volt S-413	(P)	The Soul Album	1966	24.00	60.00
Volt 415	(M)	Dictionary Of Soul	1966	20.00	50.00
Volt S-415	(S)	Dictionary Of Soul	1966	24.00	60.00
Volt 416	(M)	Live In Europe	1967	16.00	40.00
Volt S-416	(S)	Live In Europe	1967	16.00	40.00
Volt 418	(M)	The History Of Otis Redding	1967	16.00	40.00
Volt S-418	(P)	The History Of Otis Redding	1967	16.00	40.00
Volt 419	(M)	The Dock Of The Bay	1968	20.00	50.00
Volt S-419	(P)	The Dock Of The Bay	1968	12.00	30.00
Atco SD-33-248	(E)	Soul Ballads	1968	12.00	30.00
		(Atco 248 is a reissue of Volt 411.)			
Atco SD-33-249	(S)	Dictionary Of Soul	1968	12.00	30.00
		(Atco 249 is a reissue of Volt 415)			
Atco 33-252	(M)	The Immortal Otis Redding *(White label promo)*	1968	20.00	50.00
Atco SD-33-252	(S)	The Immortal Otis Redding	1968	12.00	30.00
		—Atco albums above have purple & brown labels.—			
Atco SD-33-248	(E)	Soul Ballads	1969	6.00	15.00
Atco SD-33-249	(S)	Dictionary Of Soul	1969	6.00	15.00
Atco SD-33-252	(S)	The Immortal Otis Redding	1969	6.00	15.00
Atco SD-33-261	(P)	The History Of Otis Redding	1968	8.00	20.00
		(Atco 261 is a reissue of Volt 418.)			
Atco SD-33-265	(S)	In Person At The Whiskey A Go Go	1968	8.00	20.00
Atco SD-33-284	(S)	Otis Blue/Otis Redding Sings Soul	1969	8.00	20.00
		(Atco 284 is a reissue of Volt 412.)			
Atco SD-33-286	(S)	Live In Europe	1969	8.00	20.00
		(Atco 286 is a reissue of Volt 415.)			
Atco SD-33-288	(S)	The Dock Of The Bay	1969	8.00	20.00
		(Atco 288 is a reissue of Volt 419.)			
Atco SD-33-289	(S)	Love Man	1969	8.00	20.00
Atco SD-33-333	(S)	Tell The Truth	1970	8.00	20.00
Atco SD-2-801	(S)	The Best Of Otis Redding *(2 LPs)*	1972	8.00	20.00
		—Atco albums above have yellow labels with an 1841 Broadway address.—			
Atco SD-2-801	(S)	The Best Of Otis Redding *(2 LPs)*	197?	4.00	10.00
		—Atco albums above have yellow labels with a 75 Rockefeller Plaza address.—			
Atlantic 7 81762-2	(P)	The Otis Redding Story *(4 LPs)*	1987	6.00	15.00

REDDING, OTIS, & CARLA THOMAS
Refer to Carla Thomas.

Stax 716	(M)	King And Queen	1967	20.00	50.00
Stax S-716	(S)	King And Queen	1967	24.00	60.00

Fan Club Directory
from
Goldmine
The Collectors Record and Compact Disc Marketplace
Krause Publications

The following is a selected list of clubs and fanzines dedicated to recording artists. For more information about the clubs listed here, most require that you send them a self-addressed stamped envelope. For more information about fan clubs in general, including clubs formed in honor of actors, non-recording artists, sports figures, etc., we recommend that you contact the excellent National Association of Fan Clubs at 818-763-3280.

The information contained here comes, more or less, verbatim from the clubs, is not individually verified by *Goldmine*, and *Goldmine* cannot accept responsibility for any claims made by the clubs.

A

JOHN AGAR
The John Agar Fan Club
Attention: Scott Hughes, President
7901 Iroquois Ct.
Woodridge, IL 60517-3332
Hollywood's heartthrob since the 1940s and a favorite western and sci-fi film hero, John Agar has turned singer. For $3 annual dues, members receive an autographed snapshot and two newsletters telling the latest and best from and about John Agar. For a copy of the latest letter only, send $1.

LYNN ANDERSON
Lynn Anderson International Fan Club
Attention: Michael Dempsey
P.O. Box 90454
Charleston, SC 29410
Phone: 803-797-0802
Best time to call: Anytime
The Lynn Anderson fan club is the only official fan club for this legendary lady of country music. The club has been around since 1970 and offers its members an 8x10 autographed photo, biography, discography and quarterly newsletters.

ANTHRAX
NFC
Attention: Christine Vogel
P.O. Box 254
Kulpsville, PA 19443
Hotline: 215-721-6461
NFC is an official fan club and offers fans a bi-annual newsletter, fan club-only gigs, special merchandise, a signed band photo, a demo tape and Anthrax sticker.

B

BACHMAN TURNER OVERDRIVE
Canadian Friends of Mine
See Guess Who listing

SHIRLEY BASSEY
The Shirley Bassey Collectors Club
Attention: Arthur Rugg

35 Vasa Drive, R.D. #1
Hackettstown, NJ 07840
Phone: 201-691-1538
Best to call: Between 6 and 11:00 p.m.
This official club was formed in 1989 to honor Shirley Bassey's career. It offers two 30-page newsletters per year. Membership spans 11 countries and provides photos, videos, audios, CDs and LPs. Dues are $15 U.S. and $20 non-U.S.

the BEACH BOYS
Beach Boys Fan Club
Attention: President
P.O. Box 84282
Los Angeles, CA 90073
This club is an official Beach Boys fan club and has been in existence since 1976. The newsletter goes out five times a year. It is brief, contains the news only, but also has an extensive classified section. Send SASE for more information.

Endless Summer Quarterly
Attention: Lee Dempsey/David Beard
P.O. Box 470315
Charlotte, NC 28247
Published quarterly since 1987, the fanzine *Endless Summer Quarterly* features rare photos, exclusive interviews and articles, reviews of new CDs and videos (commercial and underground), and up to the minute recording and personal appearance information regarding Brian Wilson and the Beach Boys.

Recent scoops include exclusive interviews with Bruce Johnston, Van Dyke Parks, Andy Paley, David Leaf and Mark Linett.

Sample issues are $5, $6 non-U.S.

the BEATLES
Good Day Sunshine
Attention: Charles F. Rosenay!!!
Liverpool Productions
397 Edgewood Ave.
New Haven, CT 06511
203-865-8131
Best time to call: Anytime
This well-loved fanzine has been in publication since 1981. Every issue has 80 or more pages of Lennon/McCartney/Harrison/Starr news, reviews, collectors columns, exclusive photos, sales offers, ads and much more.

Write or call for more information.

Octopus's Garden
Attention: Beth Foster
21 Montclair Avenue,
Verona, NJ 07044
Phone: 201-239-7042
Best time to call: Evenings.
This Beatles fanzine is published quarterly. Each issue is completely different as members are constantly bringing in new ideas. It features short stories, poetry, games, cartoons, news, opinion articles, etc. It encourages everyone to participate and to give their input.

BEE GEES

Bee Gees Fan Club

Attention: Renee Schreiber
P.O. Box 2429
Miami Beach, FL 33140

Members of this club receive newletters with the latest info and current photos, contest with autographed prizes, membership card, color photos, black and white photos, a telephone hotline, bios, fact sheets, tour dates, television air-dates, listing of all clubs worldwide and, occasionally, tickets to shows.

BIG COUNTRY

All Of Us

Attention: James D. Birch
201 Gay Street, #4
Denton, MD 21629
Phone: 410-479-0777
Best time to call: 10:00 a.m. to 1:00 p.m.
EST, weekdays

After 18 months of productive growth, AOU is now the official Big Country fan club for North America. AOU is recognized by the band and their management.

The club publishes the Big Country fanzine which reprints articles about the band, features opinion pieces, fans' reviews, photos, interviews with the band and help in finding rare Big Country items. AOU is run by a dedicated fan who is committed to providing a quality publication.

THE BLASTERS AND DAVE ALVIN

American Music and the Blasters Newsletter

Attention: Billy Davis
80-16 64th Lane
Glendale, NY 11385-6819
Phone: 718-366-4163
Best time to call: 6-10:00 p.m.

This group provides a newsletter/fanzine that is normally seven or eight pages long, covering the Blasters, Dave Alvin and related members. All artists are extremely active in supporting and participating in the contents. Tour dates, album releases, stories, merchandise availability is published 4-6 times a year. The club also provides post card mailing updates when necessary.

BLIND MELON

Sleepy House

Attention: Christine Vogel
P.O. Box 290
Kulpsville, PA 19443

Sleepy House is an official fan club and offers signed photos, a newsletter, stickers and bios.

PAT BOONE

National Association of Pat Boone Fan Clubs

Attention: Ms. Chris Bujnovsky
1025 Park Road
Leesport, PA 19533

The NA is an official club and has been in existence since 1956. For $7 annually U.S. ($8 elsewhere), members receive three newsletters (*Pat's Pagette*), and one journal (*Pat's Pages*), per year. Members also receive a photo membership card and a photo of Boone upon joining.

JUNIOR BROWN

Junior Brown International Fan Club

P.O. Box 128203

Nashville, TN 37212

Join this official club and receive a membership kit which includes an 8x10 autographed photo of Brown, a biography, newsletter with concert schedule, official Junior Brown fan club member badge and special merchandise offerings.

The Eric Burdon Connection Newsletter

Info: P.O. BOX 700754
SASE TULSA, OK (74170) USA

ERIC BURDON

Eric Burdon Connection Newsletter

Attention: Ed Wincentsen
P.O. Box 700754
Tulsa, OK 74170

Eric Burdon, rock 'n' roll legend and Rock and Roll Hall of Fame inductee, contributes to the newsletter which prints his tour schedule, photos, articles, news on latest recordings, etc.

Send a self-addressed, stamped envelope for more information.

C

DAVID CASSIDY

Just David International David Cassidy Fan Club

Attention: Barbara Pazmino
979 East 42nd Street
Brooklyn, NY 11210

The Official David Cassidy fan club is celebrating its 22nd anniversary. Members get a tri-monthly newsletter containing interviews, photos, a raffle, ads and a pen pal section. Occasionally there's an actual photo print to take out and keep. Newsletters are printed in English and German, combined. Includes handwritten messages from Cassidy. Send SASE for more information.

The CASSIDYS, SHAUN, PATRICK, RYAN, DAVID and SHIRLEY JONES

Friends Of The Cassidys

Attention: Cheryl Corwin
2601 E. Ocean Blvd, #404
Long Beach, CA 90803-2503
Phone: 310-433-7448
Best time to call: After 5:00 p.m.

The Friends began in 1977 as Friends of Shaun Cassidy, but expanded in 1993 to include the rest of the family. It oversees a yearly collection for the Leukemia Society, provides its members with monthly newsletters and is supported by the family.

LOU CHRISTIE

Lou Christie International Fan Club

Attention: Harry Young
P.O. Box 748
Chicago, IL 60690-0748

The Lou Christie fan club was founded in 1977. The club publishes Lightning Strikes, a biannual 44-page fanzine packed with articles, news, reviews, photos and details, the inside story on all aspects of Lou Christie, past, present and future. Members also receive lists of upcoming concerts. The club has contributed to the making of the Rhino, Sequel and Varese Vintage Lou Christie reissues. Please send a SASE for information.

PETULA CLARK

The International Petula Clark Society

Attention: Bonnie O. Miller
50 Railroad Avenue
Madison, CT 06443

This is an international organization that features worldwide membership and publishes an in-depth quarterly newsletter. Petula and Company is the original and definitive organization and has been in existence for over 20 years. The publication features concert and CD reviews, interviews, print articles and nostalgia. It also offers opportunities to purchase current CD releases, photos or memorabilia for sale by the membership. Members receive information on concert dates, CD releases, etc.

BRUCE COCKBURN

Gavin's Woodpile

Attention: Daniel Keebler
7321 131st Avenue, S.E.
Snohomish, WA 98290
Phone: 360-568-9543
Best time to call: From 9:00 a.m. to 10:00 p.m.

Gavin's Woodpile is a non-profit newsletter designed to increase the awareness of the work and music of Bruce Cockburn, as well as to share interviews, concert dates, etc. Information is provided by Cockburn's management and record company.

An annual subscription is $10 U.S., $12 Canada, $15 elsewhere.

the COWSILLS

Cowsills Fan Club

Attention: Marsha Jordan
P.O. Box 83
Lexington, MS 39095

This is an official fan club that offers its members a quarterly newsletter. Annual dues are $10.

BURTON CUMMINGS

Canadian Friends Of Mine

See Guess Who listing.

D

OSCAR D'LEON

The International Oscar D'Leon Fan Club

Attention: Betsy Quillin, President
928 Myakka Ct., N.E.
St. Petersburg, FL 33702-2792
813-527-OSCAR

Oscar D'Leon is considered the "King Of Salsa." Send an SASE for more information.

NEIL DIAMOND

The Diamond Connection

Attention: June Allen
P.O. Box 2764
Witham, Essex CM8 2SF
England

The Diamond Connection is published bimonthly and includes articles, wants and swaps, memorabilia, photos and the latest information on Diamond. Cost of the 'zine is £2.50 for the U.K., $5 for the U.S. (a yearly subscription reduces the cost). For a sample copy please send a large self-addressed stamped envelope.

DION

Official Dion Fan Club

119 Hutton Street
Gaithersburg, MD 20877

Membership in this official club entitles one to an autographed photo, a quarterly newsletter with lots of information and an advance performance schedule and a membership card.

Dues are $10 U.S., annually ($15 elsewhere).

DOORS

The Doors Collectors Club

Attention Kerry Humpherys
P.O. Box 1441
Orem, UT 84059-1441
Phone: 801-224-7390
Fax: 801-224-5723
Best time to call: Anytime

The Doors Collectors Magazine is published four times a year. It includes a host of feature articles, including interviews with the surviving Doors members, Elektra's president, Jac Holzman, Morrison biographer Jerry Hopkins, as well as articles on collecting Doors memorabilia and more. Each issue contains the past quarter's Doors-at-auction report, bootleg reviews, letters to the editor, concert information for the surviving Doors members and tribute bands and much more.

Every summer the club sponsors a Los Angeles Feast Of Friends, which is a solid week of Doors-related activities usually culminating in a Doors member's performance.

Subscription also includes a membership card.

Rates are $20 a year U.S., $25 Canada and $30 elsewhere. Visa and Mastercard are accepted. For more information call toll free, 800-891-1736.

DURAN DURAN

Carnival: The Duran Duran trade magazine

Attention: Kimberly Blessing
930 Sassafras Circle
West Chester, PA 19382
E-mail: D2CARNIVAL@AOL.COM

Carnival is known to many fans as the Goldmine of the Duran realm. It maintains the largest and most complete Duran Duran discography, printed yearly, available on the Internet, and approved by Duran themselves. Quarterly issues include information on releases, interviews with band members, answers to questions on collecting, contests for valuable memorabilia, and ads from distributors and fans alike. Inquiries sent by mail must include a SASE for a response.

The Duranie Connection

Attention: Kapil Mathur
E-mail: http://www.chapman.edu/students/mather/duran.html

The Duranie Connection is a group of online Duran Duran fans who are affectionately called "Duranies." TDC's main focus is its World Wide Web page, which functions as an extended fanzine. However, it goes beyond a fanzine because it provides instant information. The Web page is updated almost daily so there is always new information to read or see.

It holds the most complete collection of lyrics to the music of DD and related groups. TDC also has a concert guide which lists all shows that Duran Duran has ever done as well as all upcoming shows. There are also articles written by fans, exclusive interviews with Duran Duran and relatives and links to every Duran Duran source on the Internet.

You can also find lists of magazines with feature articles dedicated to the group, as well as sources for Duran merchandise. Best of all, it is 100 percent free. All one needs is access to the World Wide Web.

UMF

Attention: Tina L. Lawson
P.O. Box 975
Dayton, OH 45409-0975
E-mail: lawsontl@udavxb.oca.udayton.edu (put UMF on the subject line)

UMF is a club for authors and artists inspired to create works after exposure to Duran Duran and its music. Anything submitted will be published in its quarterly fanzine without editing or censoring. The 200-plus-page issues cost $10 when new or $13.50 for back issues. Issue #5 is currently available. Any type of visual art, fiction or other types of prose will be accepted. Critiques are circulated from readers to creators in order to help members hone their craft. Send a SASE or IRC for information on membership or submissions.

ZTV

Attention: Liz Owens
132 St. Andrew's Court
Mt. Laurel, NJ 08054
Phone: 818-509-1731
Fax: 201-779-8434
E-mail: ZTVDD@aol.com

ZTV is a 30-minute public access show devoted to Duran Duran and its offshoot groups. The show covers live and media events, interviews and skits. It airs in several cities across the country as well as some foreign countries. Episodes are available; $15 each or three for $30.

ZTV also has concert footage of Duran Duran and Nuerotic Boy Outsiders. Concerts are $25 each or both for $40. Checks should be made payable to Katie Sandstrom. If you'd like to see ZTV air near you, contact Sandstrom for more information.

Privacy: The Warren Cuccurullo Fan Club

Attention: Cyndi Glass
P.O. Box 593
Vincennes, IN 47591
E-mail: cglass@vunet.vinu.edu

This is the official club for Warren Cuccurullo. Privacy covers Warren's career and music in and beyond Duran Duran (Zappa, Missing Persons, solo career, etc.). It offers a membership kit, mail forwarding, question and answer segments and a fanzine which is usually 20-25 pages and is published bimonthly. Send an SASE or International Reply Coupon for more information.

Dues are $10 a year, U.S., $15 non-U.S. (U.S. funds only please).

F

FISH

The Company North America

Attention: Eric D. Brooks
P.O. Box 207667
Castro Valley, CA 94546
E-mail: conapres@aol.com or http://www.livjm.ac.uk/fish/

This club is the official North American chapter of Fish's fan organization called "The Company." The fan club has been in existence since 1993. Membership includes four issues of both the Company North America fanzine (articles, reviews, photos, pen pals, other contacts, etc.), and the *FishNet Indie Review* (other indie progressive and celtic rock), a color membership card, extra mailings and more. For a free copy of the *FishNet Indie* send an addressed, stamped envelope.

The group also has an official live Fish/Marillion chat every Sunday at 8:00 p.m. EST on America Online in the Nightclub (keyword: Music chat).

TONY FORD

Tony Ford Fan Club

Attention: Billie Ford
945 Windy Hill Road, 2nd Floor, Suite 5
Smyrna, GA 30080
Phone: 770-434-3466, extension 18

Membership in this five-year-old club entitles one to at least three newsletters a year, tapes, t-shirts, posters, pictures etc., are offered for sale and a free autographed picture is sent to each new member immediately. Dues are $10 annually.

G

LESLEY GORE

Lesley Gore International Fan Club

Attention: Jack Natoli, President
141 Vernon Avenue
Paterson, NJ 07503
Phone/Fax: 201-523-9169
Best time to call: Evenings from 6-9:00 p.m. or on weekends.

This is the only authorized official fan club for Lesley Gore and was established 30 years ago by the same person who is currently the president, with the full support and cooperation of Lesley Gore. Membership include a fan club package of photos, record lists and quarterly newsletters. Dues are $6 and four current stamps.

GRATEFUL DEAD

Relix

P.O. Box 94
Brooklyn, NY 11229
718-258-0009

This magazine also features several like groups, including Hot Tuna, the Allman Brothers, and much more. Relix has been in publication for 22 years. Call or write for subscription information.

The GUESS WHO

Canadian Friends Of Mine

Attention: Kevin C. Beyer
8397 Birchwood Avenue
Jenison, MI 49428-8520
Phone: 616-667-1662
Fax: 616-667-1647
Best time to call: Anytime

CFOM is the only official Guess Who fan club and is 10 years old.

Members get four newsletters a year, personal contact with the band members, information about offshoot band Bachman Turner Overdrive and Burton Cummings. Current information and tour dates are provided as well and additional flyers are sent out that list rarities for sale. The club is international.

H

HALL & OATES

Rock And Soul International

Attention Diane Vaskas or Lori Allred
P.O. Box 450
Mansfield, MA 02048

This official club is eight years old and its newsletter includes reviews, updates on band members, pictures, ads and pen pals.

BETH HART

Beth Hart Fan Club

Attention: Jerry Hill
P.O. Box 48214
Minneapolis, MN 55448-0214

This club's members share information, ideas and enthusiasm about the work of Beth Hart. The club includes up-to-date information and special dispatches to its members. Please send a SASE when requesting information.

ANNIE HASLAM
The Annie Haslam Society
Attention: Joanne Shea
P.O. Box 12
Folsom, PA 19033

Organized in 1990, this group is official and recognized by the artist. The club offers a newsletter (about two a year), and postcard updates on concerts and career events. Haslam provides outstanding involvement-she receives all correspondence and responds personally when time permits.

There is no charge to join but stamps and IRC help greatly and are always appreciated. The introductory packet to new members needs a 10x13-inch mailer with $1.28 postage affixed.

JIMI HENDRIX
Straight Ahead-The International Jimi Hendrix Fanzine
Attention: Steven Roby
P.O. Box 965
Novato, CA 94948-0965
Phone: 415-898-4202
Best time to call: 3-7:00 p.m., PST

Established in 1989, this 'zine has recognition of the Hendrix family and former band members. Its main focus is interviews: Recent interviews were with Eric Burdon and Steve Winwood. A recent issue also included a special report on the 25th anniversary Hendrix tribute concert in Seattle.

HUEY LEWIS & THE NEWS
Newsline II
Attention: Debbie Parry
P.O. Box 99
Payson, UT 84651

Newsline II offers it smembers a quarterly newsletter and the cost to join is $10 per year U.S., $12.50 non-U.S.

ENGELBERT HUMPERDINCK
Engelbert's "Goils" Fan Club
Attention; Jeanne Friedl or Dot Gillberg
10880 Kader Drive
Cleveland, OH 44130

This is an official fan club that was formed in 1971. Its newsletter, Goil Talk, is bi-monthly and reports on record releases, news of Humperdinck's career, itinerary info and all things pertinent to his career. It is basically active in the Cleveland area, but has members worldwide and across the U.S. Its purpose is to support him in a dignified and responsible manner, always showing respect for his talent and person, wherever he appears.

Engel's Angels in Humperdinck Heaven
Attention: Jean Marshalek, President
3024 Fourth Avenue Carney
Baltimore, MD 21234-3208
Phone: 410-665-0744
Best time to call: From 10:30 a.m. - 10:00 p.m.

Founded in 1971, this non-profit group raises charity funds in Humperdinck's name, supports and promotes his career through meetings, video viewings, parties, attending concerts and purchasing all of his recordings and videos. Its award-winning newsletter, The Guardian Engle, is issued approximately seven times a year, as news is received from Humperdinck's office. Itineraries are mailed as soon as they come in.

Dues are $10, U.S., per year, "$5 husbands," and $15 non-U.S.

I

JULIO IGLESIAS
Friends Of Julio Eglesias
Attention: Isabel Butterfield, President
28 Farmington Avenue
Longmeadow, MA 01106
Phone: 413-567-0845
Best time to call: Evenings, before 8:00 or on weekends

This official fan club, honoring Julio Iglesias started in 1986. The club provides 3-4 newsletters a year, a tour schedule and regular updates as they become available, a photo and biography.

Dues are $18 U.S., $21 Canada, $24 Europe and $28 Asia.

IRON BUTTERFLY
Iron Butterfly Information Network
Attention: Rick Gagnon
9745 Sierra Avenue
Fontana, CA 92335

This official club was formed in 1985. Send a self-addressed stamped envelope for a membership certificate or to have specific questions answered.

J

JONI JAMES
Joni James International Fan Club
Attention Mr. Wayne Brasler
P.O. Box 7207
Westchester, IL 60154
Phone: 708-450-9024
Best time to call: Evenings, before 8:00

The official international fan club for Joni James, this club dates back to the dawn of her recording career in 1952. James has always been generously involved in the club. Membership is free.

Subscriptions to the club's newsletter, Joni, published four or more times a year, are available-write to the club for information about rates.

Joni includes news about James' latest activities, features about her career and abundant photos, many never before published. The club also accepts mail for Joni James and facilitates media contacts with her.

JAN & DEAN
Surfun
Attention: Lori Brown
328 Sumner Avenue
Summer, WA 98390

The official Jan & Dean fan club has been celebrating the accomplishments (past, present and future!) of the "The Laurel and Hardy of the Surf Crowd" since 1987.

Membership includes up-to-date concert information, quarterly newsletters, a photo, biography, discography and more. Send a SASE for more information. Membership fees are $7 U.S., $8 to Canada and Mexico, and $10 elsewhere.

ELTON JOHN
East End Lights
Attention: Tom Stanton
P.O. Box 760
New Baltimore, MI 48047
Phone: 810-949-7900
Best time to call: 9-5:00

East End Lights publishes an international Elton John magazine, featuring full-color covers, interviews with band members, tour dates and great insider information.

AL JOLSON

International Al Jolson Society

Attention: Mrs. Dolores Kontowicz, Secretary
11520 W. James Ave.
Franklin, WI 53132
Phone: 414-529-2868
Best time to call: Days

This club has been in existence since April of 1950. It was formed with Jolson's permission before he died.

The club publishes *The Jolson Journal* (and just recently published their 83rd volume) which contains stories on Jolson, many photos, articles by members, and an exchange column. It also issues four newsletters a year and has an annual convention that is held in different cities each time.

International Al Jolson Society

Attention: Otis R. Lowe, Director
2981 Westmoor Dr.
Columbus, OH 43204
Phone: 614-274-1507
Best time to call: Evenings, before 8:00

Serving Jolson admirers for seventeen years. Members receive six news bulletins a year with membership, plus the issuing of many color photos throughout the year. Offering audio and video tapes, sheet music, books, LPs, CDs, photos and many other Jolson items. Want lists are welcomed. Dedicated to perpetuating the memory of Al Jolson throughout the world.

SHIRLEY JONES

Shirley Jones Fan Club

Attention: Martina Schade
2295 Maple Road
York, PA 17404

Membership in this club entitles you to a beautiful 8x10 photo, two 4x6 photos, a bio/fact sheet and credit list, membership card, four copies of *Shirley's World*, the official newsletter, and Jones's personal appearance schedule, which is updated regularly.

Dues are $13 U.S., $16 Canada and $20 elsewhere.

K

DOUG KERSHAW

Doug Kershaw Fan Club

Attention: Gail Delmonico
P.O. Box 24762
San Jose, CA 95154

This club offers four newsletters, a biography and autographed 8x10.

KINGSTON TRIO

Kingston Korner

Attention: Allan Shaw
6 South, 230 Cohasset Road
Naperville, IL 60540-3535
Phone: 708-961-3559

This isn't an official fan club, and prefers to refer to itself as an information service. It circulates news of the group and makes itineraries and recordings available.

The KNACK

The Knack Fan Club

Attention: Ethen Barborka
P.O. Box 1022
Provo, UT 84603

The Knack fan club sends its members a quarterly newspaper in which the members celebrate the past, present and future of the Knack. Fans can also buy, sell or trade memorabilia in its Knick Knack department and it invites you to be a part of the Knack Knation.

L

FRANKIE LAINE

Frankie Laine Society of America

Attention: Helen Snow
P.O. Box 145
Lindenhurst, NY 11757-0145

The Frankie Laine Society has been in existence since 1949. It publishes three to five newsletters a year, offers members special discounts on videos, CDs, records and tapes and informs members of Laine's concerts and upcoming events.

ERNIE LANCASTER

Ernie Lancaster Fan Club

Attention: Vicki Newton, President
P.O. Box 629
Havre De Grace, MD 21078
Phone: 410-939-5864
Best time to call: From 7-10:00 p.m.

This is a start-up fan club for Ernie Lancaster, guitarist extraordinaire and writer of 99 percent of the music for Root Boy Slim and the Sex Change Band. It's new, hot and happenin'! Be there! It's free! *You can't quit this club!*

LEAD BELLY

Lead Belly Society

Attention: The Lead Belly Society fosters the appreciation and celebration of Lead Belly's music through the publication of the quarterly Lead Belly Letter, videos about Lead Belly and other projects. The society was established in 1990.

BRENDA LEE

The Brenda Lee International Fan Club

Attention: Ms. Pat O'Leary
P.O. Box 2700
Murfreesboro, TN 37133-2700

The Brenda Lee International Fan Club is an official club, authorized by Brenda Lee, and has been in existence since March 1994. It offers its members four newsletters a year, which contain an itinerary and news on Lee's career and personal life. Members receive U.S. and foreign discographies, and information about merchandise that's available: jackets, T-shirt sweatshirts, videos, pictures and more.

THE LETTERMEN

The Lettermen Fan Club

Attention: Sharon Stewart
P.O. Box 570727
Tarzana, Ca 91357-0727
Phone: 818-705-5326
Best time to call: Mondays, Wednesdays and Fridays, from 8:00 to 3:00 p.m.

Membership in this official, 17-year-old fan club includes biography information, discographys, touring schedules, and 8x10 autographed photo and quarterly eight page newsletter. Dues are $13 initial membership with annual $10 renewals.

LITTLE JIMMY & THE BAD BOYS

Little Jimmy & the Bad Boys

International Fan Club
Attention: Charlie Wolf
P.O. Box 111604
Nashville, TN 37222
    This is a brand new club, started in May, 1995, and has no dues at this time. It's in the process of compiling a mailing list. Dues will start as soon as the group's first CD is released (estimated date: February, 1996).

LORETTA LYNN
Loretta Lynn Swap Shop
Attention: Lenny Mattison/Andy Comer
R.R. 1, Box 63A
Parish, NY 13131
Phone: 315-298-6860
Best time to call: Anytime
    The club has been in existence since 1991. The membership kit includes four newsletters per year, etc. It offers members a way to swap, sell and buy Loretta Lynn memorabilia as well as reporting on past and present material regarding Loretta Lynn.

LOWEN & NAVARRO
International Lowen and Navarro Fan Club
Attention: Sue Dick or Margaret Allen
P.O. Box 19285
Alexandria, VA 22320
    Membership includes a subscription to the newsletter (L&N Wire), an autographed photo and member-only bumper sticker. Dues are $15 per year.

LYNYRD SKYNYRD
Lynyrd Skynyrd Fan Club
Attention: J. Howard/Administrator
P.O. Box 120855
Nashville, TN 37212
    Membership includes a specially designed club T-shirt, a band photo, biography and discography, current and vintage merchandise, an itinerary and four quarterly newsletters. The annual membership fee is $20 U.S., $25 non-U.S.

M

MADONNA
The Official Madonna Fan Club
Attn: Marcia Delvecchio/Coordinator
8491 Sunset Blvd., #485
West Hollywood, CA 90069
    This club, which is officially endorsed by Madonna, offers a quarterly magazine, *Icon*, membership kits and a mail-order catalog filled with over 400 Madonna collectibles. The club has been in existence for over five years.

BARRY MANILOW
Very Barry Kentuckiana Connection
Attention: Ann Harris
409 N. 28th Street
Louisville, KY 40212-1905
Phone: 502-772-0509
Best time to call: After 5:00 p.m.
    This official club has been in existence for over 10 years and is a member of the National Association of Fan Clubs. The group gets together to "celebrate their friend Barry!"

JIM MARLBORO
Jim Marlboro International Fan Club
Attention: David W Kelly

2011 State Ave. S.W
Decatur, AL 35601

JOHNNY MATHIS
Reflections On Mathis
Attention: Melanie Slavin
P.O. Box 182
Jacksonville, NC 28541
Phone: 910-346-4983
Best time to call: After 5:30 EST or leave message on machine.
    This club is an official chapter, eight years old. It provides a quarterly newsletter with special event updates and lots of surprises throughout the year.

MELANIE
Melanie Mania
Attention: Richard Dozier
32 Brookfield Lane
South Setauket, NY 11720
Phone: 516-696-7039
Best time to call: Noon to 3:00 p.m.
    Now in its seventh year, Melanie Mania provides the latest information on what this artist is doing in the studio and on the stage. Call or write with a SASE.

the MONKEES
Head Of The Monkees
Attention: Teresa Jones
262 Baltimore Avenue
Baltimore, MD 21222
    Head Of The Monkees is celebrating its 10th anniversary year. Membership includes four issues of *HTM News*, a folder, photo, fact sheets, club pencil, membership card and club certificate. Contests are held at least once a year.
    Membership is $10 a year with a 10 percent discount on renewals.

Monkeein' Around
Attention: Janet Marie Davis
41297 C.C. Road
Ponchatoula, LA 70454
    The newsletter of this club, started in 1988, contains a main news section, a "Fan Talk" section, articles from members, games, a pen pal directory, birthday section and occasional recipes.

MICHAEL MORIARTY
Michael Moriarty Official Fan Club
P.O. Box 68
Soddy Daisy, TN 37379
    Members of the Moriarty fan club receive a welcome letter, autographed photo, membership card and certificate, biography and newsletters.

ANNE MURRAY
Anne Murray Collectors Club
Attention: Rita Rose
1618 Park Ridge Way
Indianapolis, IN 46229
317-633-9269
    The Anne Murray Collectors Club specializes in locating Murray's recordings on vinyl, as well as sheet music, photos, tapes, tour books and other memorabilia.
    Its newsletter is issued four times a year.

N

MICHAEL NESMITH
Dedicated Friends
Attention: Donna Bailey
1807 Millstream Drive
Frederick, MD 21702
Phone: 301-694-8064

This club is recognized and approved by Michael Nesmith. Members receive four newsletters with color photos and current information on this very respected artist. Members are encouraged to be actively involved in this club's efforts to honor, support and express thanks to Michael Nesmith. One year membership is $12 U.S., $17 non-U.S.

NEW COLONY SIX
The New Colony Six Fan Club
Attention: Jerry Schollenberger
24435 Notre Dame
Dearborn, MI 48124

This official fan club, which provided the liner notes for both Rhino's and Sundazed's New Colony Six retrospectives, sends out show lists and is compiling a definitive international discography. Please send a SASE for more information.

OLIVIA NEWTON-JOHN
Hopelessly Devoted
Olivia Newton-John Fan Club
465 S. Poplar Street, #1110
Hazleton, PA 18201

The Hopelessly Devoted Olivia Newton-John fan club was founded in late 1991. The club has issued over 400 memberships and holds an annual convention. The 1996 convention will be in Pittsburgh, PA. Membership includes a biography on Olivia, color 8x10 photo, color photo membership card and four issues of the newsletter. U.S. membership is $20, Canada/Mexico $25, and elsewhere $30. (U.S. funds only, please.)

O

ROY ORBISON
In Dreams
Attention Bert Kaufman
484 Lake Park #80
Oakland, CA 94610
Phone 510-444-0805
Best time to call: early/late

More than just a fan club, In Dreams is a magazine/society supporting Orbison first and foremost, but also vintage rock n' roll (circa 1955-'64 primarily). Six years in existence and supported by Orbison Productions, it offers multi-media stuff, interviews, reviews and a pen pal section in its 90-100-page quarterly newsletter.

P

JOHN PATRICK
John Patrick Fan Club
Attention: Laurie Ewld
Cass City Road
Unionville, MI 48767

The John Patrick fan club has been in existence for nine years. It offers its members an 8x10 picture of Patrick and a newsletter three times a year.

PEARL JAM
Release
Attention Markus Wawzyniak
410 Gilbert Street, Apartment A.
Bryan, TX 77801-3407

Release is a fanzine for Pearl jam with readers all over the world. The zine is published twice a year with the fourth issue to be out by the end of 1995. Every issue (and back issues are still available) features show reviews, discography, collectible corner, articles on PJ side projects and tons of high quality photographs. *Release* is saddle stapled and printed on high quality paper.

PINK FLOYD
Brain Damage
Attention: Jeff Jensen or Steve Edwards
P.O. Box 109
Westmont, IL 60559

For nearly a decade, *Brain Damage* has been dedicated to the fans of Pink Floyd, Roger Waters, and Syd Barrett. Each issue is packed with timely, informative and entertaining articles along with rare full color pictures, book, video and CD reviews, Q&A's and much more. *Brain Damage* is great for casual fans, Floyd fanatics and serious collectors alike.

Subscribers receive a free mini-poster with each issue. $28 for U.S., Canada and Mexico (six issues), or $5 for sample issue. Elsewhere: $40 or $7 for sample.

GENE PITNEY
Gene Pitney International Fan Club
Attention: David P. McGrath
6201 39th Avenue
Kenosha, WI 53142

Gene Pitney's only fan club has been active for over 30 years. It currently has close to 2,000 members in 11 different countries. Pitney participates in all of the activities of the club.

It puts out three 16-page newsletters annually, which carry stories about Pitney, concert reviews, a regular letter from Pitney, merchandise for sale like videos, T-shirts, etc. It also holds a convention in the U.K. every two years.

ELVIS PRESLEY
Elvis Arkansas Style Fan Club
Attention: Beverly Rook
P.O. Box 898
Mabelvale, AR 72103
Phone: 501-455-1273
Best time to call: Before 10:00 p.m.

This official fan club makes Elvis information available to its members and works with the Make A Wish Foundation. Send a SASE for more information.

Elvis's Teddy Bear Fan Club
Attention: Mary Ann Parisi
744 Caliente Drive
Brandon, FL 33511
Phone: 813-684-6522
Best time to call: Weekends

This club, started in May, 1976, provides newsletters every three months and is recognized by Graceland.

The Elvis Beat
Attention: Troy Yeary
2716 Terry Drive
Richmond, VA 23228

The Elvis Beat offers a free quarterly newsletter to U.S. fans. Four 32-cent stamps are requested, but not required. Non-U.S. membership is $5. The unique newsletter features the latest Elvis news, reviews, and more. This club is registered at Graceland.

True Fans For Elvis Fan Club of Maine

Attention: Dot Gonyea, Chairperson
62 Lowell Street
South Portland, ME 04106

This club has been in existence since the spring of 1977 when Elvis was making his first appearance in Maine on May 24 at the Augusta Civic Center. The club was formed on the steps of the Civic Center while waiting in line for tickets for two days. It publishes four newsletters a year with information from the Elvis world and also all the activities taking place in Maine. It is a very social club and raises money year round in Elvis's memory: It supports several associations dedicated to medical research as well as Meals On Wheels, Elvis Presley Memorial Trauma Center, Camp Sunshine and many other worthwhile causes.

We Remember Elvis

Attention: Priscilla A. Parker, President
1215 Tennessee Ave.
Pittsburgh, PA 15216-2511

Members receive a membership kit with the most recent club newsletter, three 8x10 black and white photos of Elvis, stationery, a membership card, information booklet about the club and much more. It publishes six newsletters a year and works to keep the memory of Elvis alive through its works of charity.

Membership in this official Elvis fan club, established in 1982, costs $10 a year.

PRINCE

Uptown

Attention: Harold Lewis
P.O. Box 7071
Akron, OH 44306

Uptown, beginning its fifth year, is a quarterly fan magazine produced by some of the leading "Princeologists" in the world. Regular features include tour reports, color photos and exclusive interviews with Prince associates, past and present, plus all of the latest news.

PROCOL HARUM

Procol Harum Appreciation Society

Attention: Patrick Keating
8415 W. 89th Street
Overland Park, KS 66212

Since 1990, this club has kept members abreast of tour information, concert reports and new releases from the group. New members may join for $10 and receive everything to date that's been offered by the club.

R

EDDY RAVEN

Eddie Raven International Fan Club

Attention: Sheila Futch
P.O. Box 2476
Hendersonville, TN 37077

This official club is 10 years old. Members receive an 8x10 photo, button, membership card, quarterly newsletters, a biography, fact-sheet, discography, letters and the club makes tapes and t-shirts available.

LOU RAWLS

The Lou Rawls National Fan Club

Attention: Dottie Taylor, President
P.O. Box 8358
Langley Park, MD 20787

This club is official. Membership is $15. Write for more details.

HELEN REDDY

Helen Reddy Fan Club-East

Attention: Lorraine Breault
204 Thunder Circle
Bensalem, PA 19020
Phone: 215-702-1420
Best time to call: Anytime

This club is officially recognized by Reddy and is nine years old. New members receive an autographed photo of Reddy, news, letters and postcard updates.

MARTHA REEVES

Martha Reeves Exclusive Newsletter

P.O. Box 1987
Paramount, CA 90723
Phone: 310-634-4676
Best time to call: Evenings, after 5:00 p.m.

This is the official fan club for Martha Reeves, the "legendary diva of Motown." The club provides members with 12 newsletters a year with information about performfor Reeves's television, radio and live performances, exclusive photos and memorabilia.

R.E.M.

Country Feedback

Attention: Toni Sturtevant
RR1 North Road
Jefferson, NH 03583

This three-year-old fanzine includes original artwork, regular articles by the fans, contests, poetry, classic reprints and lots of photos, surprises and R.E.M. autographed items that are auctioned off for charity benefits.

REO SPEEDWAGON

REO Pals International

Attention: Jordan Taylor, President
P.O. Box 72423
Albany, GA 31708-2423
Phone: 912-432-7844
Best time to call: Evenings after 6:00 p.m., EST, and weekends.

This club is approved by REO Speedwagon and has been in existence since 1985. The club offers a detailed quarterly newsletter, including tour and studio updates, and offers an in-depth look at REO Speedwagon and its fans.

HAPPY RHODES

Rhodeways-The International Happy Rhodes Medium

Attention: Sharon Nichols
P.O. Box 1953
Kingston, NY 12401
Phone: 914-679-6291
Best time to call: Anytime

Rhodeways is the only official Happy Rhodes (recording artists similar to Kate Bush) club/'zine. A one-year (four-issue) subscription is $15 U.S. and $18 non-U.S.

The 'zine is 16 pages, professionally printed on glossy stock with halftones (screened photos).

Happy contributes artwork, articles and pictures to each issue.

CLIFF RICHARD

Cliff Richard Fan Club of America

Attention Mary Posner
8916 N. Skokie Blvd. #3
Skokie, IL 60077

This club is affiliated with the International Cliff Richard Movement, which oversees dozens of Cliff fan clubs around the world. In addition to distributing the ICRM's bimonthly newsletter, *Dynamite/International*, it also publishes its own U.S. newsletter, the Cliff Connection, six times a year. The club can be reached by mail or by e-mail at CRFCUSA@aol. com.

SMOKEY ROBINSON

SMOKEY ROBINSON and the MIRACLES

Smokey Robinson and the Miracles Fan Club

Attention: Marie Leighton
8 Hillside Road
Narragansett, RI 02882-2821
Phone: 401-789-8992
Best time to call: From 5-8 EST

This club is the officially authorized fan club of Smokey Robinson and the Miracles. It publishes a quarterly newsletter and frequent bulletins. It offers itineraries, contests, exclusive special offers and news of other Motown artists.

TOMMY ROE

Tommy Roe International Fan Club

Attention: Theresa Ehler
P.O. Box 813
Owatonna, MN 55060-0813

This is the only official Tommy Roe fan club, and it is six-years-old. It provides its members quarterly newsletters with an itinerary, current news, photos, etc. New members receive an 8x10 photo, fact-sheet, biography, discography, membership card and a special gift from Roe.

Dues are $12 U.S., $14 Canada and $17 elsewhere.

the ROLLING STONES

Beggar's Banquet

Attention: Bill German
P.O. Box 6152
New York, NY 10128

Formed in 1978, this club is recognized by the Stones and gets pretty good (better-than-average) input from the group.

Special features of the club include an attractive monthly fanzine, featuring exclusive news and photos of all of the Rolling Stones' latest activities, together or solo, personally or professionally. It also features exclusive interviews with the Stones, contests to win Stones autographs and offers for various Stones merchandise and collector's items. Cost is $20 per year (12 issues) U.S., $30 airmail overseas.

Gimme Shelter

Attention: David Conway
P.O. Box 163632
Austin, TX 78716-3632

Gimme Shelter is the only monthly Stones fanzine in the world. It started in October, 1992. It is unofficial but has interviewed Ron Wood, Mick Taylor, Bobby Wood and original Stones bass player, Dick Taylor.

Visual Radio

Attention: Joe Viglione
P.O. Box 2392
Woburn, MA 01888

ROOT BOY SLIM

Root Boy Slim Memorial Fan Club

Attention: Duane Straub, Director
3834 Sheffield Circle
Danville, CA 94506

Phone: 510-736-1480
Fax: 510-736-7844
Best time to call: From 6:00 p.m. to 6:00 a.m.

People loved this man-and a bizarre man he was. Many have a special story about Root Boy Slim, most have more than one. This club is devoted to tracking down episodes and tie-ins to a man with the strangest of messages, untangling the web, removing the cloak ... day by day, documenting and saluting the life and times of Root Boy Slim. Rare audios, videos, and much more. It's free. You can't quit this club!

RUSH

A Show Of Fans

Attention: Steve and Mandy Streeter
5411 E. State Street, #309
Rockford, IL 61108
Phone: 815-398-1250
Best time to call: Between 6-8 p.m.

This is a fanzine for and by Rush fans. In ASOF readers will find original photos and artwork, a wide open feedback section for fans to sound off and interact, tour hook-up section, announcements, free classifieds for subscribers, stories of "brushes with greatness," up-to-date listings of new Rush memorabilia and all the latest news.

S

SANTANA

Santana International Fan Club

Attention: Kitsaun King
P.O. Box 881630
San Francisco, CA 94188-1630

Lifetime membership in the Santana International fan club costs $25. Members receive the quarterly newsletter, advance notice of concerts when possible, a Santana merchandise catalog and other special goodies.

PAT SHEA

Pat Shea International Fan Club

Attention: Carol MacDonald
P.O. Box 905
Orchard Park, NY 14127
Phone: 716-941-5675
Best time to call: Evening

This official fan club was formed in 1989. Members receive a quarterly newsletter, membership card and certificate, a personally autographed photo, biography and merchandise offers.

FRANK SINATRA

International Sinatra Society

Attention: Gary Doctor
P.O. Box 7176
Lakeland, FL 33807
Phone: 941-646-7650
Best time to call: From 9-5, CST

This is the best Sinatra fan club and the only mailing list that you need to be on to keep up with all the latest Sinatra info and product. The club's newsletter includes discussion about all the latest CD releases, videos and laser discs. There's also an alternate takes column, a collectors column, many photos and more.

PHIL SEYMOUR AND DWIGHT TWILLEY

hearmore Seymour twilley

Attention: Karen Momme
P.O. Box 33151
Tulsa, OK 74153

This is the official fan club for Dwight Twilley and Phil Seymour, recognized by both artists, since 1987. It provides its members a newsletter, and merchandise when available. The fanzine is $4 per issue, U.S. and $6 overseas.

SIR DOUGLAS QUINTET, DOUG SAHM AND AUGIE MEYERS

Sir Douglas Quintet-Doug and Augie
Attention: K.P. Kosub
P.O. Box 3248
Corpus Christi, TX 78463-3248
Phone: 512-287-3945
Best time to call: Anytime

This club has been the official fan club for the Sir Douglas Quintet since 1980. It offers its members updates on the Quintet and the Texas Tornados. It offers rare records, memorabilia, videos and collectibles for fans worldwide and is approved by Doug and Augie. The fee for membership is $10 and members receive one CD and two 45s by Doug and Augie. Send an SASE for details.

the SMITHEREENS

The Smithereens Fan Club
Attention Faith McClintic/Karen Schell
P.O. Box 35226
Richmond, VA 23235
Hotline: 800-540-0018

This official club publishes a quarterly newsletter, 'Reen Thoughts, which includes articles written by the band members themselves. All members receive the newsletter for their $5 annual fee as well as other fan club benefits, including offers for merchandise, exclusive releases and contests.

SPACEMEN 3

Dreamweapon
Attention: Matt Hunter
P.O. Box 2813
New Orleans, LA 70176
504-486-7211
Best time to call: After 9:30 p.m. CST

Now in its second year, Dreamweapon has networked fans of Spacemen 3 and its side projects with tour information, merchandise offers and a resource for audio and video trades. While not an "official" club, band members are aware of the group and will probably be making contribution to the newsletter in 1996.

SPARKS

Sparks International Official Fan Club
Attention: Mary Martin, Secretary
Box 25038
Los Angeles, CA 90025

This fan club publishes six newsletters per year and also provides its members with a button badge and personally signed 8x10 glossy photo to new members. It is the only official club for Sparks and has been in existence since 1975.

RICK SPRINGFIELD

Rick's Loyal Supporters
Attention: Vivian Acinelli
4530 E. Four Ridge Road
Imperial, MO 63052
Fax: 314-942-9920
E-mail: 10256,1472@Compuserve.com
or VIV4RLS@aol.com

Established in 1989 and recognized by Rick Springfield, this club offers a fan club package including a club folder, photos, membership card, updates on Rick (between newsletters, if necessary), bio, discography and filmography. The Newsletter averages 30 pages, has a classified section, stories, poems, puzzles, raffles, photos and occasional updates from Springfield. Membership costs $15 U.S., $17 Canada, $20 elsewhere.

Write, fax or e-mail for more information.

Rick Springfield Quarterly
Attention: Robin Gregg
4611 S. University Drive, Suite #206
Davie, FL 33328
Send SASE to R.S.Q. for more information.

BRUCE SPRINGSTEEN, SOUTHSIDE JOHNNY, other Jersey Shore Artists

Backstreets
Attention Charles R. Cross
P.O. Box 51225
Seattle, WA 98115
Phone: 206-728-7603
Best time to call: 9:30-5:00, PST

Backstreets is a magazine and information service for fans of Bruce Springsteen and other Jersey Shore artists. (There is no official fan club-Backstreets is probably the closest thing to it.) The magazine has been around for 15 years, is published quarterly and is one of the largest and most respected fan organizations in the world. Subscriptions are $18 U.S., $25 non-U.S.

JIM STEINMAN

Rockman Philharmonic-The Jim Steinman Society for the Arts
Attention: Jacqueline Dillon
10 Cindy Lane
Wappingers Falls, NY 12590
Phone: 914-297-0731
Best time to call: Evenings, before 8:00

The Rockman Philharmonic is an official fan club. Membership is $20 U.S., $25 non-U.S. payable in U.S. funds to Jacqueline Dillon. It publishes a full-color magazine quarterly and sends special mailings as needed. The life and work of Jim Steinman (writer and producer of Meat Loaf, Bonnie Tyler, Sisters Of Mercy, Pandora's Box, Barbra Streisand, etc.), is explored at depth.

JOHN KAY and STEPPENWOLF

The Wolfpack Fan Club
Attention: Charlie Wolf, President
P.O. Box 1435
Franklin, TN 37065

Membership includes a welcome letter from John Kay, a biography, discography, Steppenwolf family tree, color photo (autographed), a window decal, a membership card and four quarterly issues of their newsletter, The Howl. The club is official and has been around for three years. Dues are $10 a year U.S., $15 non-U.S.

AR STEVENS & the RICOCHETTES

Ar Stevens & the Ricochettes Fan Club
Attention: Newell Shoup, Jr.
P.O. Box 18008
Fairground Annex
Des Moines, IA 50313

This is the official fan club, authorized by the band, and is starting its fourth year.

Membership is $8, renewals are $5. Members receive an 8x10 of the band and four newsletters per year.

ROD STEWART
Smiler
Attention: Kimberly Pingston
P.O. Box 766
Wayne, MI 48184

This quarterly fanzine is loaded with great pictures, interviews, upcoming tour information, etc. Yearly membership is $33 (make checks or money orders out to, Kim Pingston). Send a self-addressed stamped envelope for detailed fan club information. All inquiries are promptly answered.

T

THUNDER ROAD
Thunder Road Fan Club
Attention: Barbara Gentry
5926 Seminary Road
Smyrna, TN 37167

This is the only official fan club for Thunder Road. It offers a free cassette to new members, tour updates and contests. It also sends a newsletter six times a year to all members.

It has been in existence for three years and has 100 percent participation from the band.

TRAVIS TRITT
Travis Tritt's Country Club
Attention: Kim Walker
P.O. Box 440099
Kennesaw, GA 30144
Phone: 770-49909572
Best time to call: 9-5 EST
Write or call for more information.

TINA TURNER
Simply The Best Tina Turner Fan Club
Attention: Mark Lairmore
4566 S. Park Ave.
Springfield, MO 65810
Phone: 417-881-3746
Best time to call: After 6:00 p.m.

Tina Turner's fan club, organized six years ago, offers its members four quarterly newsletters and organizes an annual meeting in Nutbush, TN every August. Membership is $8 U.S., $12 non-U.S.

U

URGE OVERKILL
Secret Society Internationale
Attention: Christine Vogel
P.O. Box 354
Kulpsville, PA 19443
Hotline: 610-489-8810

This official club has been in existence for two years. Members receive *Bofonics*, a fanzine published twice a year, a fan club only single, Urge. Overkill sticker, correspondence from the band, tour itineraries and more.

V

BOBBY VINTON
Bobby Vinton Fan Club
Attention: Julia Walker, President
153 Washington Street
Mount Vernon, NY 10550-3541
914-664-6948
Best time to call: Anytime

New members of the club will receive a membership card and button, pictures of Vinton, including an autographed 8x10, a fact sheet, biography and letter from Bobby expressing his appreciation and welcome, participation in contests and much more.

Dues are $6 per year, plus seven current stamps, $11 for two years, plus 14 current stamps.

VOODOO MONKEY CHILD
V.M.C. / 1753
Attention Laurie Stansbury and Amy E. Allen
P.O. Box 2546
Glenview, IL 60025-2546
Phone: 312-283-2038
Best time to call: 7-11:00 p.m.

This official fan club of the rock band Voodoo Monkey Child, has been in existence approximately three years. It offers band promotional items, clothing, photos, stickers and even artwork. It also has exclusive interviews with band members and stage crew. A lifetime membership is $13.

W

JERRY JEFF WALKER
The Tried and True Warriors
Attention: Pam Stock
P.O. Box 39
Austin, TX 78767
Phone: 512-477-0036
Best time to call: 9-5:00 weekdays.

The Tried And True Warriors is a free fan club organized on behalf of singer/songwriter Jerry Jeff Walker. Benefits include a quarterly newsletter and preferential ticket selection to many of Walker's shows. The fan club also attends a weekend of concerts and events in Walker's hometown of Austin, Texas around the time of his birthday, each March.

WALKER BROTHERS/SCOTT WALKER
WalkerPeople
Attention: Lynne Goodall
71 Cheyne Court
Glengall Road
Woodford Green
Essex IG8 0DN

ROGER WATERS
Reg: The International Roger Waters Fan Club
Attention: Michael Simone
214 Lake Court
Aptos, CA 95003
Phone: 408-685-3950
Best time to call: Evenings, PST

The International Roger Waters Fan Club has members in Italy, Germany, France, Belgium, England, Scotland, Austria, the Netherlands, Malta, Spain, Portugal, Denmark, Sweden, Norway, Russia, the Ukraine, Japan, Australia, New Zealand, Canada, Argentina and all across the U.S.

Membership is $20 U.S. and Canada and $25 elsewhere. Membership fees pay for initiation fees, yearly club dues, subscription to the *REG* newsletter/magazine and club card fee. Send U.S. funds, international check or U.S. postal money order made payable to Michael Simone.

HANK WILLIAMS, JR.
Hank Williams Jr., Fan Club
Attention: Tracie Melton
P.O. Box 850
Paris, TX 38242
Phone: 800-FOR-HANK
Best time to call: 9-5 weekdays
    This club has been in existence for over 20 years. It offers T-shirts, a biography, newsletter, souvenir catalog, 8x10 photos and smaller souvenir items to all members.

DENNIS WILSON
Friends of Dennis Wilson
Attention: Chris Duffy
1381 Maria Way
San Jose, CA 95117
    FODW is an official fan/friend club, it's been in existence for over 12 years and it publishes a seasonal fanzine, *Dennymania*. FODW encourages member involvement.

WISHBONE ASH
USASH
Attention: Dr. John
2428 McKinney
Boise, ID 83704
Phone: 208-377-8742
Best time to call: 5-10:00 p.m. weekdays, Mountain time
    The Wishbone Ash fan club is an official club in its fifth year. Subscriptions are $14 per year for four issues. The club enjoys a lot of band participation, a World Wide Web page, fan club CDs and other merchandise.

TAMMY WYNETTE
Tammy Wynette International Fan Club
Attention: Cynthia King
P.O. Box 121926
Nashville, TN 37212
    Fan club membership includes an autographed color 8x10 photo, biography specially written for the club, a fact sheet that lists awards Wynette has received during her career, membership card, bumper sticker, and a quarterly newsletter including tour schedule. Dues are $10.

Y

DWIGHT YOAKAM
The Dwight Yoakam Express
Attention Andy Comer
P.O. Box 3013
Zanesville, OH 43702-3013
    The Express reports on past and present career moves of Yoakam. It offers a buy, sell and trade column in the fanzine that it publishes six times a year. The organization is over two years old and is an official fanzine.

Z

NORMA ZIMMER
Norma Zimmer National Fan Club
Attention: Frances L. Young, President
1604 E. Susquehanna St.
Allentown, PA 18103-4398
    Norma Zimmer is, of course, the lovely Champagne Lady on *The Lawrence Welk Show*. This is her official fan club and has been in existence for 35 years. Dues are $6 a year and members get a membership card, three bulletins a year, pictures of Norma, an eyeglass cleaner and lots more.